Literature Links to World History, K–12

Recent Titles in the
Children's and Young Adult Literature Reference Series

Catherine Barr, Series Editor

Beyond Picture Books: Subject Access to Best Books for Beginning Readers
Barbara Barstow, Judith Riggle, and Leslie Molnar

A to Zoo: Subject Access to Children's Picture Books. Supplement to the 7th Edition
Carolyn W. Lima and Rebecca L. Thomas

Gentle Reads: Great Books to Warm Hearts and Lift Spirits, Grades 5–9
Deanna J. McDaniel

Best New Media, K–12: A Guide to Movies, Subscription Web Sites, and Educational
Software and Games
Catherine Barr

Historical Fiction for Young Readers (Grades 4–8): An Introduction
John T. Gillespie

Twice Upon a Time: A Guide to Fractured, Altered, and Retold Folk and Fairy Tales
Catharine Bomhold and Terri E. Elder

Popular Series Fiction for K–6 Readers: A Reading and Selection Guide. 2nd Edition
Rebecca L. Thomas and Catherine Barr

Popular Series Fiction for Middle School and Teen Readers: A Reading and Selection Guide.
2nd Edition
Rebecca L. Thomas and Catherine Barr

Best Books for High School Readers, Grades 9–12. 2nd Edition
Catherine Barr and John T. Gillespie

Best Books for Middle School and Junior High Readers, Grades 6–9. 2nd Edition
Catherine Barr and John T. Gillespie

Green Reads: Best Environmental Resources for Youth, K–12
Lindsey Patrick Wesson

Best Books for Children: Preschool Through Grade 6. 9th Edition
Catherine Barr and John T. Gillespie

Literature Links to World History, K–12

Resources to Enhance and Entice

Lynda G. Adamson

Children's and Young Adult Literature Reference
Catherine Barr, Series Editor

LIBRARIES UNLIMITED

AN IMPRINT OF ABC-CLIO, LLC
Santa Barbara, California • Denver, Colorado • Oxford, England

Library of Congress Cataloging-in-Publication Data

Adamson, Lynda G.
  Literature links to world history, K–12 : resources to enhance and entice / Lynda G. Adamson.
      p. cm. — (Children's and young adult literature reference)
  Includes bibliographical references and index.
  ISBN 978-1-59158-470-4 (hardcover : acid-free paper) 1. World history—Juvenile literature—Bibliography. 2. Literature and history—Juvenile literature—Bibliography. 3. World history—CD-ROM catalogs. 4. World history—Juvenile films—Catalogs. 5. Children—Books and reading—Bibliography. I. Title.
  Z1037.A1A283   2010
  [PN50]
  028.1'62—dc22   2009046081

ISBN: 978-1-59158-470-4

14 13 12 11 10   1 2 3 4 5

This book is also available on the World Wide Web as an eBook.
Visit www.abc-clio.com for details.

Libraries Unlimited
An Imprint of ABC-CLIO, LLC

ABC-CLIO, LLC
130 Cremona Drive, P.O. Box 1911
Santa Barbara, California 93116-1911

This book is printed on acid-free paper ∞
Manufactured in the United States of America

For Frank

CONTENTS

PREFACE

STUDIES SHOW THAT PEOPLE REMEMBER THINGS TO WHICH THEY HAVE responded emotionally. As readers watch Liesel Meminger fall in love with words in her stolen *The Grave Digger's Handbook*, they will want to climb with her into the second-floor library belonging to the mayor of Molching, Germany. There they will wait for her to select another book to steal before she sneaks back down the ladder and runs back home. Then they will listen to her read the book to Max, the refugee hiding from the Nazis in her basement room (Markus Zusak's *The Book Thief*). Or, they will go with Tamar after her grandfather's unexpected suicide to search for the origins of the items in the box of World War II memorabilia that he left. They will shiver in the Dutch countryside during the "Hunger Winter" of 1944 with her namesake, Tamar, and Dart—members of the Dutch Resistance who live with the beautiful Marijke while intercepting Nazi code. They will ponder Tamar's discovery about that dangerous and cold winter (Mal Peet's *Tamar*). Readers' responses to these characters and the actions in which the characters participate may propel them toward other books, both fiction and nonfiction.

If a youthful reader becomes interested in a topic, a character, or a time period, and asks for books or multimedia about them, the adult consulted needs timely retrieval capabilities. I have attempted to fulfill that need. This resource connects historical fiction, historical fantasy, biography, history trade books, graphic novels, DVDs, and compact discs for individual grade levels within specific time periods or geographic areas. All entries have received at least one review. The annotations avoid being qualitative, but the best books in any category win awards. An annotation that contains awards shows that book's merits. All of the items are in print and available at press time.

The focus of this annotated bibliography is to link literature to history. Many good biographies and history trade books are now available. For that reason, I have listed biographies about the same person by several different authors. I have not made choices as to which are best, because each has a slightly different theme and tone. Authors of biography as literature try to make their subjects come alive, and the authors, for the most part, have achieved this goal. History trade books differ from history textbooks because trade authors, who also rely heavily on diaries, letters, documents, and other sources, often focus on the people who lived during the time. They tend to eschew inventories of incidents, passive voice, and litanies of dull dates. Thus, readers generally respond more favorably to trade books than to textbooks. Some of the history trade books included have more illustrations than text, but they can be valuable for enticing slow or unwilling readers to look for other books about the same topic. These information books bridge the distance between books without illustrations and DVDs. The relatively new genre of the "graphic novel," a term that also includes graphic histories and biographies, has evolved; graphic novels also attract many reluctant readers. The multimedia category contains DVDs and compact discs.

This reference includes as many good books and DVDs published since 2000 as possible, along with some highly regarded works from prior years. Adults will find the recommended books on library shelves, in bookstores, or online. The wide range of titles will give the researcher choices if the first title selected from the resource is not readily available.

My goal is for readers to have emotional responses to the people who have made history so that they, as future world citizens, can better understand themselves and the times in which they live.

I want to thank my husband who edited text and helped me find time to work. Additionally, Catherine Barr at Libraries Unlimited has offered advice and aid in an effort to make this resource available.

INTRODUCTION

THIS RESOURCE CONTAINS TITLES IN THE CATEGORIES OF HISTORICAL fiction and fantasy (time travel); history trade books; biography and collective biography; graphic novels, biographies, and histories; DVDs; and compact discs. Titles merit inclusion because they have received at least one mainstream review, and annotations accompanying them are descriptive rather than evaluative.

Chapter divisions are chronological time periods or areas of the world. A chapter titled "General" comes first and includes works spanning several different time periods, topics, or countries. Certain chapter divisions correspond as nearly as possible to major historical events in Europe and the British Isles, such as the era of the Roman Empire. Some entries appear in multiple chapters because their content is closely related to specific time periods. For example, Michelangelo, born in 1475, lived and worked in Italy until 1564. As his birth and youth fall in one time period, "Europe and the British Isles, 1290–1491" (the beginning of the Renaissance), books about him and their accompanying annotations will appear in that chapter. The rest of his career falls in the chapter, "Europe and the British Isles, 1492–1649" (the High Renaissance and the Age of Exploration). The author and title of works listed in multiple chapters appear in each chapter but reference the initial chapter of appearance for the annotation.

The chapters based on geographical areas loosely link countries within a particular part of the world. Identifying the specific geographical area a book covers may be difficult from the title alone; researchers will find more discrete information in the annotations. These chapters include "Afghanistan and the Indian Subcontinent," "Australasia and Antarctica," "Southeast Asia" (which includes Indonesia and the Philippines), and the "Middle East." Two companion volumes cover the American history.

In each chapter, I have listed works in the categories of historical fiction (including historical fantasy), history trade, biography (including collective biography), graphic novels (including graphic biographies and graphic histories), DVDs, and compact discs. Each entry appears alphabetically according to the author's last name. I have based grade-level choices on recommended grade levels in review sources or publisher catalogs. In some cases, when the grade levels based on reading and content seemed unusually low or high, I adjusted them after evaluating the text and the subject matter. Also included are books marketed for adults that reviewers thought would interest high school students. The bibliographic information includes author, title, illustrator, translator, narrator, series, publisher or imprint, ISBN, paper imprint, paper ISBN, number of pages, and grade levels.

For both DVDs and CDs, running time and names of narrators are given where known. The number of discs is also noted for CDs. Many DVDs are not assigned ISBNs.

GENERAL

Historical Fiction and Fantasy

1. **Bosworth, Beth.** *Tunneling.* Crown, 2003. 284pp. ISBN 978-0-609-61103-6; Three Rivers, 2004. paper ISBN 978-1-4000-5265-3. Grades YA.

Twelve years old in 1968, asthmatic and bookish Rachel Finch loves numbers, time travel, and Franz Kafka. Her secret life allows her to escape her illness and her dysfunctional family with S-Man, a superhero. Traveling through time, she visits Shakespeare and Elizabethan England to escape Teaneck, New Jersey. S-Man introduces her to Voltaire, Socrates, and Chinua Achebe.

2. **Brooks, Geraldine.** *People of the Book.* Viking, 2008. 372pp. ISBN 978-0-6700182-1-5. Grades YA.

Hanna Heath, an Australian rare-book expert, goes to Sarajevo to study a manuscript called the Sarajevo Haggadah. She discovers tiny imperfections in its binding that reveal its true origins. Among the clues are an insect's wings, white hair, and wine stains. Heath's investigations slowly reveal the origin of this amazing manuscript. The book moved around Europe beginning in 1480 until it arrived in Sarajevo in 1996, changing hands from anti-Nazi partisans to Viennese anti-Semites. And it may have been in Venice in 1609, when Grand Inquisitor Domenico Vistorini had a theological dispute with the rabbinical intellectual Judah Aryeh.

3. **Kimmel, Eric A.** *Brother Wolf, Sister Sparrow: Stories about Saints and Animals.* Holiday House, 2003. 64pp. ISBN 978-0-8234-1724-7. Grades 3–6.

A look at the lives of twelve saints and their interactions with animals. St. Francis loved animals, and bees clustered around St. Ambrose's mouth when he was a baby. St. Brigid milked her cow to feed a crowd. Bishop Hugh of England stopped a massacre of the Jews with swans. St. Hubert was associated with a stag, St. Hormisdas with camels, and St. Notburga with pigs. Charlemagne appears to St. Giles and a doe. Illustrations enhance the text. Note.

4. **Maalouf, Amin.** *Samarkand: A Novel.* Translated by Russell Harris. Interlink, 1997. 304pp. ISBN 978-1-56656-200-3; 1998. paper ISBN 978-1-56656-293-5. Grades YA.

The story begins in 11th-century Persia and ends when the *Titanic* sinks in 1912. The narrator, a 20th-century American, pursues the fate of *The Rubaiyat* of Omar

Khayyam. Khayyam was an astronomer, mathematician, and poet who did the best he could under the strictures of Muslim dogmatism. His poetry was not recognized during his lifetime, but Edward Fitzgerald later discovered and arranged it. *Samarkand,* with its exoticism, presents an intriguing story of politics and power in—as Khayyam said, a "chessboard of the world."

5. **Pears, Iain.** *The Dream of Scipio.* Riverhead, 2003. 398pp. Paper ISBN 978-1-57322-986-9. Grades YA.

Near the end of the Roman Empire, as barbarians are overrunning Gaul, Manlius Hippomanes writes an essay titled "The Dream of Scipio" to record the ideas of his teacher, the Neoplatonist Sophia. During the Black Death plague of the 14th century Oliver de Noyen finds the essay, and during World War II Julien Barneuve of Provence comes across it. They all must face their moral obligations as their societies fail around them. If you are civilized, how can you watch others massacre your neighbors?

6. **Prévost, Guillaume.** *The Book of Time.* Translated by William Rodarmor. Arthur A. Levine, 2007. 213pp. ISBN 978-0-439-88375-7. Grades 4–7.

When Sam Faulkner's father, who owns a bookshop, disappears, Sam searches in the shop and finds a stone and a secret room. In the room, Sam finds a book that tells him where his father has been. The stone sends Sam through time to the Middle Ages, to ancient Egypt, to the city of Bruges during the Renaissance, and to the French front during World War I. When Sam returns, he discovers that his father has sent him a message from Dracula's castle, where he has been imprisoned. Sam's aide in the search is his cousin, Lily, who helps him translate Latin through instant messaging and gives Sam her cellphone to take to Belgium.

7. **Rutherfurd, Edward.** *London: The Novel.* Ballantine, 2002. 829pp. Paper ISBN 978-0-345-45568-0. Grades YA.

The characters in this story experience the history of the city from Julius Caesar through the Industrial Revolution to the 20th century, know Chaucer, see Shakespeare perform in his plays, experience the plague, and flee from London's fires. The city grows and changes through the centuries within the novel's episodes.

8. **Rutherfurd, Edward.** *Russka: The Novel of Russia.* Ballantine, 2005. 760pp. Paper ISBN 978-0-345-47935-8. Grades YA.

Four families in a small Ukrainian village represent a microcosm of Russian history through the centuries, from 180 to the Russian Revolution in 1917. They cope with the Cossacks, the Tatars, and other interlopers as they attempt to survive as farmers on their bits of land.

9. **Rutherfurd, Edward.** *Sarum: The Novel of England.* Ballantine, 1997. 897pp. Paper ISBN 978-0-449-00072-4. Grades YA.

Five families living in the environs of Salisbury, England, represent the history of the area from the Ice Age through the 20th century. They experience the construction of Stonehenge and Salisbury cathedral. Then they fight in England's civil war, World War I, and World War II. Successive generations are connected through inheriting an amulet.

History

10.   Aaseng, Nathan. *Construction: Building the Impossible.*   Oliver, 1999. 144pp. ISBN 978-1-8815-0859-5. Grades 5–10.

This collective biography looks at eight builders throughout history and the ground-breaking projects they constructed. Included are Imhotep and his pyramid, Frank Crowe and the Hoover Dam, George W. Goethals and the Panama Canal, William Lamb and the Empire State Building, Alexandre Eiffel and the Eiffel Tower in Paris, Marc Isambard Brunel and the Thames River tunnel, and John and Washington Roebling with their Brooklyn Bridge. Photographs and drawings complement the text. Bibliography, Glossary, and Index.

11.   Aaseng, Nathan. *You Are the Explorer.*   Oliver, 1999. 160pp. ISBN 978-1-8815-0855-7. Grades 4–8.

The focus of this collective biography is on decisions that explorers have had to face. Those featured are Christopher Columbus, Vasco da Gama, Ferdinand Magellan, Hernán Cortés, Samuel de Champlain, Robert Scott, James Cook, and Meriwether Lewis. Each had to choose the best route to take in his travels based on what he wanted to achieve and what he knew. Some choices were disastrous while others worked. Readers may choose an option and see where it might have led. Photographs accompany the text. Bibliography, Notes, and Index.

12.   Aaseng, Nathan. *You Are the General.*   (Great Decisions) Oliver Press, 1995. 160pp. ISBN 978-1-881508-25-0. Grades 5 up.

Readers can decide what they would do if they found themselves in the same situations as several 20th-century generals. The dilemmas will help them understand those who had to make life-threatening decisions in the past. Included are generals from the Kaiser's army in August 1914, the German Reich in the summer of 1940, the Imperial Japanese Navy in June 1942, the Allied forces in June 1944, the United Nations forces in July 1950, the Vietnamese Communist forces in July 1967, and the coalition forces of Operation Desert Storm in February 1991. Source Notes, Bibliography, and Index.

13.   Aaseng, Nathan. *You Are the General II: 1800–1899.*   Oliver, 1995. 160pp. ISBN 978-1-8815-0825-0. Grades 5 up.

Battles involve carefully planned patterns of military strategy to gain territory, erode an enemy army's morale, and win a broader war. This book presents eight battles and the generals who fought them. The battles involve the British army at New Orleans in 1815, the Prussian army at Waterloo in 1815, the United States Army in Mexico in August 1847, the Allied armies in Crimea in September 1854, the Army of Northern Virginia at Chancellorsville in May 1863, the United States Army at Little Bighorn in June 1876, and the Boer army in Natal in December 1899. Source Notes, Bibliography, and Index.

14.   Adams, Simon. *The Kingfisher Atlas of Exploration and Empires.*   Kingfisher, 2007. 44pp. ISBN 978-0-7534-6033-7. Grades 4–7.

Among the illustrations contained in this history of conquest are seventeen hand-illustrated maps. Information about nations, empires, explorers, and expeditions between 1450 and 1800 offer an overview of the history of the world during that time. Index.

15. Adams, Simon. *The Kingfisher Atlas of the Modern World.* Kingfisher, 2007. 44pp. ISBN 978-0-7534-6034-4. Grades 4–7.

This atlas offers a synopsis of world history from 1800 to 2007. It includes double-page spreads with maps, texts, and illustrations that cover a variety of topics. It offers background on the two World Wars, events in Latin America, the Middle East, and Africa. Index.

16. Albala, Ken. *Cooking in Europe, 1250–1650.* (Daily Life Through History) Greenwood, 2006. 153pp. ISBN 978-0-313-33096-4. Grades 9 up.

Authentic recipes from Europe appear in their original form along with explanations of unfamiliar terms for ingredients and preparation. Recipes from three time periods are included: the Middle Ages from 1300 to 1450, the Renaissance, and the late Renaissance and Elizabethan Era. Bibliography, Glossary, Notes, and Index.

17. Ancona, George. *Murals: Walls That Sing.* Marshall Cavendish, 2003. 48pp. ISBN 978-0-7614-5131-0. Grades 5–8.

The forty murals featured in this book are "for the people" (*para el pueblo*), with themes of social justice, cultural diversity, and community. It begins with the cave paintings in Lascaux, France, and then looks at ancient Mexican frescoes and on through history to postrevolutionary Mexican murals. Photographs of murals in San Francisco, Philadelphia, Mexico, Boston, Albuquerque, Chicago, the South Bronx, and other places enhance the text.

18. Andryszewski, Tricia. *Walking the Earth: The History of Human Migration.* Lerner, 2006. 80pp. ISBN 978-0-7613-3458-3. Grades 5–9.

Humans have migrated across the earth in search of food, land, and peace for more than 150,000 years. This book is an examination of these migrations, some undertaken by choice or by force because of war and poverty. Hunter-gatherers left Africa more than 60,000 years ago and began populating Eurasia. Then they eventually came to the Americas and Australia. When the general migration ended 45,000 years ago, more than five million people had created diverse populations throughout the globe. They developed appropriate tools and clothing and established trade with one another. Sometimes they integrated or imposed old customs into their new cultures. Photographs and reproductions augment the text. Charts, Maps, Bibliography, Further Reading, Web Sites, and Index.

19. Aronson, Marc. *Race: A History Beyond Black and White.* Ginee Seo, 2007. 322pp. ISBN 978-0-689-86554-1. Grades 9 up.

In seven parts, this book examines the meaning of the term *race*. It looks at the concept of race or differences in skin color and culture before the term was defined in the ancient world and the Christian Era; its importance in the Americas; a time when race became tantamount to identity; racism after the Holocaust; and race in contemporary times. In essence, race is a relatively modern invention although hate is timeless. Aronson examines the laws that try to define race as it was in the past and as it is—and other issues of utmost importance in today's world are discussed. Photographs enlighten the text. Bibliography, Notes, and Index.

20. Ashenburg, Katherine. *The Dirt on Clean: An Unsanitized History.* North Point, 2007. 358pp. ISBN 978-0-86547-690-5. Grades YA.

People around the world have diverse attitudes about cleanliness, and this book looks at some of these beliefs throughout history. The aspect of being clean, or not, ties directly to history, spirituality, sexuality, warfare, and science. The ancient Romans bathed, but monks often did not. Some people brushed their teeth while others refused. Some used water in various kinds of baths; others avoided it. Ashenburg divides the text into time periods: the Greeks and the Romans, 200–1000, 1000–1550, 1550–1750, 1750–1815, 1815–1900 in both Europe and America, 1900–1950, and 1950 to the present. Notes and Index.

21. Ball, Philip. *Bright Earth: Art and the Invention of Color.* University of Chicago, 2003. Paper ISBN 978-0-226-03628-1. Grades YA.

A look at the evolution of color through its production for artistic and commercial uses and its effect on the growth of the modern chemical industry. Twenty-seven chapters discuss the history of the pigments used for paint, including color techniques in antiquity, attempts at alchemy, gold, light in paint, dyes, shades of black, problems with blue, reproducing color, and color as a form in modernism. Bibliography, Notes, and Index.

22. Ballard, Carol. *From Cowpox to Antibiotics: Discovering Vaccines and Medicines.* (Chain Reactions) Raintree, 2006. 64pp. ISBN 978-1-4034-8839-8. Grades 6–9.

The progress of vaccination and medicine, from ancient Egypt through Jenner's development of the smallpox vaccine and Fleming's discovery of penicillin. Contemporary research is also discussed. Photographs and reproductions highlight the text. Glossary, Chronology, Further Reading, Web Sites, and Index.

23. Ballard, Carol. *From Steam Engines to Nuclear Fusion: Discovering Energy.* (Chain Reaction) Raintree, 2007. ISBN 978-1-4034-9554-9. Grades 6–9.

This overview of the different kinds of energy sources from which humans can draw power includes steam, electricity, radioactivity, quantum theory, relativity, and nuclear power. After defining energy, the text looks at its sources, along with future energy theory, and profiles six significant scientists including Faraday and Fermi. Photographs and reproductions accompany the text. Glossary, Chronology, Further Reading, Web Sites, and Index.

24. Barnard, Bryn. *Outbreak! Plagues that Changed History.* Crown, 2005. 48pp. ISBN 978-0-375-82986-4. Grades 5–8.

A look at the effects of six diseases—bubonic plague, smallpox, yellow fever, cholera, tuberculosis, and influenza—on world history. Humans have tried to obliterate these diseases, but nature has often stymied the attempt with drug-resistant bacteria, new diseases, and changing ecologies. The author posits that poverty plays a large role in a disease's spread, but that once launched, a plague does not respect wealth or social status. Photographs and illustrations intensify the text. Bibliography, Further Reading, and Web Sites. *Voice of Youth Advocates Nonfiction Honor List.*

25. Bartlett, Wayne, and Flavia Idriceanu. *Legends of Blood: The Vampire in History and Myth.* Praeger, 2006. 205pp. ISBN 978-0-275-99292-7. Grades YA.

The authors trace the historical, literary, and religious origins of vampire legends that have been told through the centuries. Among the topics are vampire epidemics, magic, witches, and the undead. Among the motives are blood, eroticism, and nature, with supporting evidence from around the globe. Photographs highlight the text. Bibliography, Index.

26.   Beckett, Wendy. *The Story of Painting.*   DK, 2000. 400pp. ISBN 978-0-7894-6805-5. Grades YA.

An overview of Western painting from the Lascaux cave paintings to contemporary works, with an emphasis on the past 800 years. The material is chronological, with chapters grouped according to trends or movements. Each chapter features leading artists of the period, their most famous works, their lives, and the political, religious, and social influences on their work. Index.

27.   Beller, Susan Provost. *The History Puzzle: How We Know What We Know About the Past.*   Twenty First Century, 2006. 128pp. ISBN 978-0-7613-2877-3. Grades 5–8.

Beller provides answers to questions about how historical facts are discovered and become theory. Among the topics covered are the wreck of the *Edmund Fitzgerald* in 1975, the sister gunboats of Lake Champlain in 1776, Martin's Hundred, the Great Wall of China, Mesa Verde, Vikings at L'Anse aux Meadows, King Arthur, Italia as a Roman city, Herculaneum and Pompeii, Homer's Troy, the Egyptians, Noah's ark, the mysteries of the Stone Age, and cave drawings. Photographs and illustrations enliven the text. Further Reading, Web Sites, and Index.

28.   Bingham, Jane. *Science and Technology.*   (Through Artists' Eyes) Raintree, 2006. 56pp. ISBN 978-1-4109-2241-0. Grades 4–7.

Advances in technology and science fascinate not only engineers and scientists but also artists. Trains and steam engines appear in the work of Turner and Monet. Medicine fascinated Thomas Eakins. Other technologies discussed here include printing, engineering, time measurement, and communication. Photographs and reproductions augment the text. Further Reading, Time Line, Glossary, and Index.

29.   Blackburn, Ken, and Jeff R. Lammers. *Aviation Legends Paper Airplane Book.* Workman, 2001. 128pp. Paper ISBN 978-0-7611-2376-7. Grades YA.

This overview of aviation history beginning with Chinese kites includes directions to make paper models of twelve historically important planes. They include the *Spirit of St. Louis*, the P-51 *Mustang*, the Fokker Dr.I Triplane of Baron Manfred von Richthofen, the Wright Flyer, the F-117A Stealth Fighter, the 1935 DC-3 Douglas Sleeper Transport, the Rutan/Yeager *Voyager*, the Boeing F-15 *Eagle*, and the Bell X-1. Photographs and drawings show the airplanes.

30.   Blackwood, Gary L. *Legends or Lies.*   (Unsolved History) Benchmark, 2005. 72pp. ISBN 978-0-7614-1891-7. Grades 4–6.

Are the stories of Atlantis, the Amazons, King Arthur, Robin Hood, El Dorado, Welsh expeditions to America, and Pope Joan legends or lies? The author looks at the controversies surrounding each of these legends to discern if they were actual events, people, or places, and lets the reader examine all sides of the arguments. Photographs and reproductions highlight the text. Bibliography, Glossary, Notes, Further Reading, and Index.

31.   Blackwood, Gary L. *Perplexing People.*   (Unsolved History) Benchmark, 2005. 72pp. ISBN 978-0-7614-1890-0. Grades 4–6.

Some people have pretended to be long-lost famous persons who have reappeared. The text looks at several famous pretenders. They include individuals who claimed to be Joan of Arc, Anastasia, King Louis XVII, and Billy the Kid. Photographs and reproductions accompany the text. Bibliography, Glossary, Notes, Further Reading, and Index.

32. **Boorstin, Daniel J.** *The Creators: A History of Heroes of the Imagination.* Vintage, 1993. 811pp. Paper ISBN 978-0-679-74375-0. Grades YA.

This sequel to *The Discoverers* (1984) investigates people who have accomplished something new in the arts. Most of the chapters are essays within themselves, but their themes connect. Boorstin covers an enormous range of information across time and across countries as he examines the meaning of creativity. Annotated Chapter Bibliographies and Index.

33. **Boren, Mark Edelman.** *Student Resistance: A History of the Unruly Subject.* Routledge, 2001. 256pp. ISBN 978-0-415-92623-2; paper ISBN 978-0-415-92624-9. Grades YA.

Twelve chapters cover the history of student activism. The author looks at student unrest from the Renaissance through the 19th century; from 1900 to 1919; the 1920s and 1930s; the militancy of 1940–1959; student resistance in the 1960s; student power in 1968 and 1969; campus killings in the 1970s; revolution in the postmodern world of 1980–1989; and the beginning of the 21st century. Among the countries and regions included are China, Russia, India, the United States, Latin America, the Mideast, and Africa. Bibliography, Notes, and Index.

34. **Burleigh, Robert.** *Chocolate: Riches from the Rainforest.* Abrams, 2002. 40pp. ISBN 978-0-8109-5734-3. Grades 3–6.

The author traces the history of chocolate from its origin as an Olmec and Maya drink to its introduction to Europe and to the rest of the world. The book includes information about chocolate in all stages of production and discusses the fact that slave labor once underpinned the industry. Photographs highlight the text. Glossary. *Bluebonnet Award (Texas) nomination* and *Beehive Young Adult Book Award (Utah) nomination.*

35. **Capek, Michael.** *Artistic Trickery: The Tradition of Trompe l'Oeil Art.* (Art Beyond Borders) Lerner, 1995. 64pp. ISBN 978-0-8225-2064-1. Grades 5 up.

An enjoyable presentation of *trompe l'oeil* art—paintings that trick the eye into thinking it is seeing something that it really is not. The text looks at several contemporary artists who make *trompe l'oeil* paintings and discusses the subjects that have intrigued artists through the years. These themes include damaged goods, money and stamps, food, people, animals and insects, slates and letter racks, doors, landscapes, and murals. The earliest illustration comes from 1475, and other reproductions cover each century since. Glossary and Index. *IRA Children's Choices.*

36. **Chaikin, Miriam.** *Menorahs, Mezuzas, and Other Jewish Symbols.* Illustrated by Erika Weihs. Houghton Mifflin, 1990. 96pp. ISBN 978-0-89919-856-9; Clarion, 2003. paper ISBN 978-0-618-37835-7. Grades 5–7.

Chaikin traces Jewish symbols through history, starting with the rise of a new tribe in the Middle East around 1800 B.C.E. and Abraham and Sarah's belief in one God. Abraham's circumcision of himself and his followers was the first symbolic act of these Jews. Chaikin covers symbolic acts and ideas; symbolic garments and dress; symbols in

Jewish worship; symbols of the state of Israel; and symbols relating to numbers, holidays, and home. The information will be especially helpful to non-Jewish readers. Notes, Bibliography, and Index.

37.　Chapman, Caroline. *Battles and Weapons: Exploring History Through Art.* (Picture That!) Two-Can, 2007. 64pp. ISBN 978-1-58728-588-2. Grades 4 up.

Art is used to show the evolution of weapons and approaches to battles from ancient times to the 1950s. Murals, sculptures, artifacts, and paintings show how warfare has changed. Glossary, Further Reading, Chronology, and Index.

38.　Chrisp, Peter. *The Soldier Through History.* Illustrated by Tony Smith. Diane, 2000. 48pp. ISBN 978-0-7881-9447-4. Grades 4–7.

With emphasis on ground soldiers, military tactics, and weaponry, this text looks at Greek *hoplites* from 500 to 300 B.C.E., Roman soldiers, crusaders, Mongol horsemen, Aztecs, Prussians, and tank fighters in the Gulf War. Maps, illustrations, and sidebars complement the text. Further Reading, Glossary, and Index.

39.　Chrisp, Peter. *The Whalers.* (The Remarkable World) Thomson Learning, 1995. 48pp. ISBN 978-1-56847-421-2. Grades 4–6.

This book traces the history of whaling, beginning with the Inuits and the Basques. It describes the ships, men, and equipment—including the harpoon cannon (invented in 1868)—and the early attempts to curb whaling before its end in 1986. Photographs, drawings, and diagrams augment the text.

40.　Clements, Gillian. *The Picture History of Great Inventors.* Frances Lincoln, 2005. 77pp. Paper ISBN 978-1-845074-39-5. Grades 4–6.

Sixty major inventors are discussed, including Archimedes (287–212 B.C.E.), inventors in Alexandria during the 1st century, Gutenberg and da Vinci in the medieval period, and many in the 20th century. Illustrations of each inventor's contributions enhance the text. Glossary and Index.

41.　Cobb, Cathy. *Magick, Mayhem, and Mavericks.* Prometheus, 2002. 420pp. ISBN 978-1-57392-976-9. Grades YA.

A history of physical chemistry in six parts. It covers Aristotle and the ancients, the European scientific revolution, the first atomic wars, physics and chemistry, and the products of physical chemistry. Among the topics in each section are the beginnings of mathematics, physics, and chemistry; thermodynamics; electromagnetism from the sun; intermolecular forces; and nanotechnology. Anecdotes help to create a readable overview of this difficult subject. Bibliography, Notes, and Index.

42.　Cole, Alison. *Perspective.* DK, 2000. 64pp. ISBN 978-0-7894-5585-7. Grades 12 up.

In twenty-seven mini-chapters, Cole presents a guide to the theory and techniques of perspective, from its beginnings in the Renaissance in the 13th century to pop art and its flatness in the 20th. Chronology, Glossary, and Index.

43.　Coleman, Janet Wyman. *Secrets, Lies, Gizmos, and Spies: A History of Spies and Espionage.* Abrams, 2006. 113pp. ISBN 978-0-8109-5756-5. Grades 5–10.

This overview of espionage includes information on techniques and equipment, disguises, legendary male and female spies, and the future of spies and spying. More than

a history of espionage, this is a collection of anecdotes of both successful and failed spy missions along with information on fictional spies including Maxwell Smart and Austin Powers. Among the topics are codes, spy rings, double and triple agents, and traitors. Photographs embellish the text. Bibliography, Glossary, Chronology, Web Sites, and Index.

44. Colman, Penny. *Corpses, Coffins and Crypts: A History of Burial.* Holt, 1997. 212pp. ISBN 978-0-8050-5066-0. Grades YA.

Based on historical and anthropological research, intimate accounts, and interviews with people working in the funeral industry, this book looks at death and burial across centuries and cultures. Among the topics are how death is determined, how corpses are disposed of, burial practices, and burial containers. The subject needs serious social commentary, and this book offers it. Photographs augment the text. Bibliography, Glossary, Further Reading, and Index. *Garden State Teen Book Awards* (New Jersey), *Young Adult Book Award* (South Carolina) nomination, and *Tayshas High School Reading List* (Texas).

45. Colquhoun, Kate. *Taste: The Story of Britain Through Its Cooking.* Bloomsbury, 2007. 480pp. ISBN 978-1-59691-410-0. Grades YA.

A history of food in Britain—from prehistory to the present —in forty-six chapters. Neolithic farmers ate a tough grain called einkorn before the Romans introduced liquamen, a fermented fish condiment, to the country. Medieval cooks used pastry crusts. Silverware was brought to the table before the Elizabethan period. Georgians filled their food with melted butter. Colquhoun suggests that food influenced immigrants and invaders as well as class conflict. *School Library Journal Best Books for Young Adults.*

46. Crowe, David M. *A History of the Gypsies of Eastern Europe and Russia.* Palgrave Macmillion, 2007. 391pp. Paper ISBN 978-1-4039-8009-0. Grades YA.

Chapters discuss the Romish cultures in Bulgaria, Czechoslovakia, Hungary, Romania, Russia, and Yugoslavia. The history of the Roma in eastern Europe and Russia since 1994 is covered in one chapter. Bibliography, Notes, and Index.

47. Curlee, Lynn. *Skyscraper.* Atheneum, 2007. 44pp. ISBN 978-0-689-84489-8. Grades 4–8.

A history of the skyscraper, a purely American architectural invention. After the Chicago fire of 1871, the first skyscrapers were built in that city. The text looks at these, the tall buildings in New York, and other towers around the world. It notes the engineering advances that made them possible and how these buildings affect the ways people live and work. Acrylic paintings enhance the text.

48. Currie, Stephen. *Escapes from Natural Disasters.* (Great Escapes) Lucent, 2003. 112pp. ISBN 978-1-59018-278-9. Grades 5–8.

A look at some of the great escapes that people have made during five natural disasters. It covers how and why each happened, with stories of people who saved themselves and others. The five disasters included are the Johnstown flood on May 31, 1889; the Armenian earthquake on December 7, 1988; the fire at Storm King Mountain on July 3, 1994; the Frank landslide on April 29,1903; and the eruption of Mount St. Helens on May 18, 1980. Photographs and illustrations accompany the text. Bibliography, Notes, Further Reading, and Index.

49. Davis, Debra Lee. *When Smoke Ran Like Water: Tales of Environmental Deception and the Battle Against Pollution.* Basic, 2003. 336pp. Paper ISBN 978-0-465-01522-1. Grades YA.

Davis, an epidemiologist who researches the environmental causes of breast cancer and chronic diseases, thinks that pollution causes nearly 300,000 deaths each year. She grew up in Donora, Pennsylvania, where seventy people died from zinc factory smog in 1948. Four years later, thousands died in London from smog. Among the problems that the auto, oil, coal, and chemical industries cause are lung cancer, infertility, brain damage, and death. Notes and Index.

50. Davis, Lee. *Man-Made Catastrophes: From the Burning of Rome to the Lockerbie Crash.* Facts on File, 2002. 352pp. ISBN 978-0-8160-4418-4. Grades YA.

Two hundred and eighty-four incidents caused by humans, including railway disasters, space disasters, fires, explosions, air crashes, terrorism, riots, nuclear accidents, and maritime disasters. Bibliography and Index.

51. Deary, Terry. *The Wicked History of the World: History with the Nasty Bits Left In.* Illustrated by Martin Brown. Scholastic, 2006. 93pp. ISBN 978-0-439-87786-2. Grades 4–7.

Puns and illustrated facts introduce readers to history from prehistoric times through World War II. The "Rotten Rulers" section discusses China's Shang dynasty, the Roman emperor Claudius, Attila the Hun, Countess Elizabeth Bathory of Transylvania, and Josef Stalin. Other sections include "Beastly Barbarians" and "Vicious Villains."

52. Desnoettes, Caroline. *Look Closer: Art Masterpieces Through the Ages.* Walker, 2006. 64pp. ISBN 978-0-8027-9614-1. Grades 3–6.

Essays on eighteen art masterpieces created over seven centuries also discuss the artists. Among those included are Claude Monet, Leonardo da Vinci, Eugene Delacroix, Pablo Picasso, Georges de La Tour, Jean de Limbourg, Vincent van Gogh, and Marc Chagall. Flaps hide additional information about each artist and his work as well as questions for closer consideration. Index.

53. D'Harcourt, Claire. *Masterpieces Up Close.* Chronicle, 2006. 63pp. ISBN 978-0-8118-5403-0. Grades 3–8.

An examination of hundreds of details in twenty-one paintings. Among those included are the *Mona Lisa*, Michelangelo's *Creation of Adam*, Rembrandt's *Night Watch*, Andy Warhol's *Marilyn*, Giotto's frescoes, and Velasquez's *Las Meninas*. Background information about the paintings and biographical information about the artists are included.

54. Dickinson, Rachel. *Tools of Navigation: A Kid's Guide to the History and Science of Finding Your Way.* (Tools of Discovery) Nomad, 2006. 156pp. Paper ISBN 978-0-9749344-0-2. Grades 5–8.

This text looks at trade routes throughout the world and the navigational tools that people used when they took them. The topics covered include Ice Age navigators through the Bering Strait; ancient navigators who sailed without compasses; European explorers; land exploration through jungle, desert, and on mountains; and aeronautical navigation and the global positioning system. Some of the explorers presented are Livingstone, Stanley, Hillary, Scott, Amundsen, and Shackleton. Additionally, fifteen hands-on activities teach readers to use or make instruments such as an astrolabe, a clock, and a compass. Photographs, diagrams, and illustrations highlight the text. Bibliography, Glossary, Chronology, Notes, Further Reading, Web Sites, and Index.

55. Di Franco, J. Philip. *The Italian Americans.* (The Immigrant Experience) Chelsea House, 1995. 94pp. ISBN 978-0-7910-3353-1. Grades 5 up.

Although this book professes to discuss only Italian Americans, it recounts a brief history of Italy through its revolutions and the Italian unification movement. In the 19th century, the greed of the wealthy led to a difficult life for many southern Italians. The northern Italians emigrated first, with the southern Italians following them. The peak immigration years were 1900 to 1914, when more than 2 million Italians arrived in the United States. By 1980, 12 million Italians had settled in the United States. Famous Italian Americans include Fiorello La Guardia, Geraldine Ferraro, Mario Cuomo, Mother Cabrini (America's first saint), Joe DiMaggio, Mario Lanza, Frank Sinatra, Guglielmo Marconi, Enrico Fermi, Arturo Toscanini, Anne Bancroft, and Lee Iacocca. Selected References and Index.

56. Dillon, Douglas. *A Brief Political and Geographic History of Asia: Where Are Saigon, Kampuchea, and Burma?* (Places In Time) Mitchell Lane, 2008. 111pp. ISBN 978-1-58415-623-9. Grades 5–9.

The author discusses why some Asian places and peoples have disappeared from present-day geography. Among the countries discussed are Vietnam during the war, Cambodia under the Khmer, Burma's generals, Qin China, the Mughals, the Great Khans, Tibet, and the Japanese empire. Photographs, maps, and reproductions embellish the text. Bibliography, Glossary, Chronology, Notes, Further Reading, Web Sites, and Index.

57. Downing, David. *Democracy.* Raintree, 2007. 64pp. ISBN 978-1-4329-0233-9. Grades 5–8.

The various aspects of a democracy are discussed, including representative democracy, constitutions, economic theory, voting, and the nation-state. This book also looks at Greece and Rome and how events in France and England eventually led to democracy in America. Photographs and illustrations augment the text. Glossary, Chronology, Further Reading, Web Sites, and Index.

58. Dowswell, Paul. *Dictatorship.* (Systems of Government) World Almanac, 2006. 48pp. ISBN 978-0-8368-5884-6. Grades 4–6.

A history of dictatorships around the world with information on authoritarian, totalitarian, and cold war dictators. Among those included are Joseph Stalin and Fidel Castro. Photographs and illustrations highlight the text. Bibliography and Index.

59. Durschmied, Erik. *Blood of Revolution: From the Reign of Terror to the Rise of Khomeini.* Arcade, 2002. 336pp. ISBN 978-1-55970-607-0; 2003. paper ISBN 978-1-55970-656-8. Grades YA.

Durschmied allows readers to feel as if they are at the scene as he examines nine uprisings, from the French Revolution in 1792 to the demise of the Shah of Iran in 1979. The others are Tyrol against Napoleon on 13 August 1809, the Mexican Revolution on

18 November 1910, the fall of the Tzar on 7 November 1917, the German revolution on 9 January 1919, the rightist coup in Japan on 15 August 1945, and the death of Che Guevara on 8 October 1967. Photographs highlight the text. Bibliography and Index.

60. Fagan, Brian M. *Fish on Friday: Feasting, Fasting, and the Discovery of the New World.* Basic, 2006. 338pp. ISBN 978-0-465-02284-7; 2007. paper ISBN 978-0-465-02285-4. Grades YA.

An anthropologist, Fagan suggests that the Catholic tradition of eating fish on Fridays led to the discovery of North America. In religious communities such as Westminster Abbey, the men ate nearly 25,000 pounds of fish a year from 1495 to 1525. This demand led to the growth of a fishing industry in the North Atlantic and to the development of preserving fish by salting and smoking. Fagan shows that the "little Ice Age" moved fishing areas farther west and south, leading to the discovery of Nova Scotia. Photographs and illustrations complement the text. Bibliography, Chronology, and Index.

61. Farman, John. *The Short and Bloody History of Spies.* (Short and Bloody Histories) Lerner, 2002. 96pp. ISBN 978-0-8225-0845-8. Grades 5–8.

This history of espionage features anecdotes about spies from around the world. Spies were uncovered as long ago as 510 B.C.E. All types of people spy, including women and children. Some spies are deadly while others merely gather information. Also included is a look at gadgets and techniques. Cartoon illustrations highlight the text. Further Reading, Web Sites, and Index.

62. Finlay, Victoria. *Color: A Natural History of the Palette.* Random House, 2003. 448pp. Paper ISBN 978-0-8129-7142-2. Grades YA.

The author posits that color has influenced social, political, and cultural aspects of history. Art's first color, ochre, comes from Australia, so Finlay went there to ascertain its connection with the people and the place. Red comes from cochineal beetles, and yellow was once made in India from the urine of mango-leaf-eating cows. In Afghanistan the author toured an ancient lapis lazuli mine. Research on colors and pigments can produce stories of corruption, killing, and politics. Illustrations enhance the text. Bibliography, Notes, and Index.

63. Fleming, Thomas. *Socialism.* (Political Systems of the World) Benchmark, 2008. 144pp. ISBN 978-0-7614-2632-5. Grades 10 up.

This examination of socialism explains its goal of cradle-to-grave protection. It also includes the history of various socialist governments throughout the world. Photographs, maps, and illustrations enhance the text. Bibliography, Chronology, Notes, Further Reading, Web Sites, and Index.

64. Ford-Grabowsky, Mary. *Sacred Voices: Essential Women's Wisdom Through the Ages.* Harper San Francisco, 2002. 358pp. ISBN 978-0-06-251702-9. Grades YA.

A look at women's spiritual experiences throughout history, this book includes ancient and modern poetry, prayers, chants, writings, and meditations from more than one hundred and fifty female poets, sages, mystics, and saints. It begins around 2000 B.C.E. with Inanna, a goddess of Sumea, and ends in contemporary times with a look at spiritual women in Japan, Ghana, and the United States, including Louise Erdrich. Further Reading and Indexes of authors, sources, and titles.

65. Formichelli, Linda, and W. Eric Martin. *Tools of Timekeeping: A Kid's Guide to the History and Science of Telling Time.* (Tools of Discovery) Nomad, 2005. 137pp. Paper ISBN 978-0-9722026-7-1. Grades 5–8.

Readers will learn about the birth of time, how to tell time after twilight, what a clock actually is, escaping time traps of old, crystals as timekeepers, and measuring time without moving, Fifteen projects include shadow clocks, sextants, and sundials. Photographs, diagrams, and illustrations highlight the text. Bibliography, Glossary, Chronology, Notes, Further Reading, Web Sites, and Index.

66. Fradin, Dennis Brindell. *With a Little Luck: Surprising Stories of Amazing Discoveries.* Dutton, 2006. 184pp. ISBN 978-0-525-47196-7. Grades 6 up.

Many scientific discoveries happened unexpectedly. The unexpected breakthroughs included in this book are anesthesia, fossils, vulcanized rubber, penicillin, Pluto, bacteria, nuclear fission, cave paintings, pulsars and millisecond pulsars, and the Dead Sea Scrolls. Photographs and illustrations highlight the text. Bibliography.

67. Freedman, Estelle B. *No Turning Back: The History of Feminism and the Future of Women.* Ballantine, 2003. 446pp. Paper ISBN 978-0-345-45053-1. Grades YA.

The five parts of this history of feminism cover the beginnings and evolution of gender equality leading to western feminism. The sections discuss gender and power before feminism; the historical emergence of feminism; the politics of work, family, health, and sexuality; and the vision of feminism. This balanced view posits that feminism was already an international movement in 1900, but that after 1970 it came to the forefront of discussion and implementation. Among the topics covered are divorce, property ownership, wages, prostitution, rape, sexual harassment, wife and child abuse, and the politics of choice. Bibliography, Notes, and Index.

68. Freese, Barbara. *Coal: A Human History.* Basic, 2003. 308pp. ISBN 978-0-7382-0400-0; Penguin, 2004. paper ISBN 978-0-14-200098-4. Grades YA.

Freese became interested in coal while working on a legal case involving the global-warming effects of emissions from coal-burning power plants generating electricity. Her book traces coal use in Britain, the United States, and China and the tension between coal's creative and destructive abilities. Coal has played a huge role in the urbanization, centralization, industrialization, and mechanization of the world. This text offers anecdotes and scientific information to support the thesis that uncontrolled coal use will pollute the planet. Illustrations complement the text. Bibliography, Notes, and Index.

69. Fritz, Jean. *Around the World in a Hundred Years: From Henry the Navigator to Magellan.* Illustrated by Anthony Bacon Venti. Puffin, 1998. 128pp. Paper ISBN 978-0-698-11638-2. Grades 4–7.

In 1400 mapmakers named the space beyond the areas they had drawn "the Unknown." Later that century, explorers ventured into the Unknown searching for routes to the gold of China. The text discusses explorers beginning with Prince Henry the Navigator (1394–1460) and ending with Magellan (1480?–1521), whose ship continued around the world after he died in the Philippines. Other explorers include Bartholomew Diaz, Christopher Columbus, Vasco da Gama, Pedro Álvares Cabral, John Cabot, Amerigo Vespucci, Juan Ponce de León, and Vasco Núñez de Balboa. Notes, Bibliography, and Index.

70. George, Charles. *Pyramids.* (Mysterious and Unknown) Referencepoint, 2007. 104pp. ISBN 978-1-60152-027-2. Grades 5–9.

Why were the pyramids built? Who built them, and how? This book covers in detail the Egyptian and Central American pyramids, but it also includes lesser-known structures in South America, Asia, and Eastern Europe. If available, a scientific explanation about each pyramid is included, along with its historical significance, if known. Photographs and maps highlight the text. Notes, Further Reading, and Index.

71. Giblin, James Cross. *When Plague Strikes: The Black Death, Smallpox, AIDS.* Trophy, 1997. 212pp. Paper ISBN 978-0-06-446195-5. Grades 5–9.

Three major plagues have hit the world in the past thousand years: the Black Death, smallpox, and AIDS. They have killed millions and have created social, economic, and political havoc. Although each plague has helped to increase knowledge about the human body, each new one must be researched and tested for a cure. This book first tells of a plague that struck Athens in 430 B.C.E. Those who survived it had terrible scars or lost their eyesight or their memory. Today no one is sure what the disease might have been, although typhus, smallpox, and bubonic plague are candidates. The sure thing is that doctors did not know how to treat it. The author then discusses the three plagues that have ravaged the world since. Source Notes, Bibliography, and Index. *American Library Association Best Books for Young Adults, Notable Children's Trade Books in the Field of Social Studies,* and *American Library Association Notable Children's Books.*

72. Gordon, Matthew. *Islam.* Facts on File, 2006. 128pp. ISBN 978-0-8160-6612-4. Grades 7 up.

To understand Islam, knowledge of its origins and its history helps. This Facts on File publication looks first at the modern Islamic world before returning to the past. General topics covered are Muhammad and the founding of Islam; the spread of Islam; the Koran, Hadith, and law; the variety of Islamic religious life; and Muslim rituals. Glossary, Further Reading, and Index.

73. Grant, R. G. *Communism.* (Systems of Government) World Almanac, 2006. 48pp. ISBN 978-0-8368-5882-2. Grades 4–6.

An overview of communism as a system of government, including its beginnings, rise, and decline. Photographs and illustrations highlight the text, which discusses leaders such as Joseph Stalin, Fidel Castro, and Mao Tse-tung. Bibliography, Chronology, and Index.

74. Grant, R. G. *Flight: 100 Years of Aviation.* Kingfisher, 2002. 440pp. ISBN 978-0-7894-8910-4; 2007. paper ISBN 978-0-7566-1902-2. Grades YA.

The history of aviation from the first attempts during the medieval period to passenger flight and the space shuttle program. The future of flight—including light aircraft, pilotless planes, and space stations—is discussed. Four major sections cover winged flight through World War II. Two discuss postwar military aviation and space exploration, and a final section explores how flight "shrinks" the world. The thousands of color images drawn from resources at the Smithsonian Institution's National Air and Space Museum complement the text. Glossary and Index.

75. Greene, Janice. *Our Century: 1900–1910.* Gareth Stevens, 1993. 64pp. ISBN 978-0-8368-1032-5. Grades 3–10.

This book is written as if it were a newspaper; short articles give an overview of the decade. Included are statistics, information about daily life in America, and items about events around the world, including the Boxer Rebellion in China, the Boer War in South Africa, Russia's peasant revolt, McKinley's assassination and the San Francisco earthquake. Some of the people discussed are Henry Ford, Marie Curie, Albert Einstein, Sigmund Freud, Pablo Picasso, and Helen Keller. Glossary, Books for Further Reading, Places to Write or Visit, and Index.

76. Griffin, Justin E. *The Holy Grail: The Legend, the History, the Evidence.* McFarland, 2001. 157pp. Paper ISBN 978-0-7864-0999-0. Grades YA.

In a thorough examination of the Holy Grail, Griffin looks at the story behind it, the historical aspects that surround it, and the legitimacy of claims of ownership. Among the topics are the grail's biblical origins, holy war, heretics, relics, and Mary Magdalene and the alabastron. Bibliography and Index.

77. Gurstelle, William. *The Art of the Catapult: Build Greek Ballistae, Roman Onagers, English Trebuchets, and More Ancient Artillery.* Chicago Review, 2004. 172pp. Paper ISBN 978-1-55652-526-1. Grades 5 up.

This history of siege warfare covers devices used by Alexander the Great, Saladin, Richard the Lionheart, John Crabbe, and others. It includes a Viking catapult, a spring engine catapult, a Macedonian ballista, a Balearic hand sling, a Thracian staff sling, a traction-style catapult, and a cabulus. Illustrations complement the text. Bibliography, Glossary, and Index.

78. Halls, Kelly Milner. *Mysteries of the Mummy Kids.* Darby Creek, 2007. 72pp. ISBN 978-1-58196-059-4. Grades 4–8.

This book about the practices of mummification throughout the world focuses on the mummies of children and supposes the events that might have caused their deaths. Among those included are a seven-thousand-year-old mummy discovered near Chile's Camarones Valley and one from Washington, D.C., that was buried during the Civil War. Interviews with scientists and mummy hunters as well as a visit to a modern embalmer offer further information about the religious and medical reasons for mummification. Photographs, maps, and reproductions reinforce the text. Bibliography, Glossary, Further Reading, Web Sites, and Index.

79. Hamilton, John. *Castles and Dungeons.* (Fantasy and Folklore) ABDO, 2005. 32pp. ISBN 978-1-59679-335-4. Grades 4–6.

In looking at both the historical and legendary aspects of medieval life. Hamilton notes that not only the Byzantine and Muslim cultures had huge castles to protect their towns and their trade routes; the Japanese also built huge castles. References to dragons and to King Arthur and his sword, along with references to authors of fantasy works, offer insight into how fantasy writers have adapted both castles and dungeons in their work. Photographs augment the text. Glossary and Index.

80. Hamilton, Sue. *Lost Cities.* (Unsolved Mysteries) ABDO, 2008. 32pp. ISBN 978-1-59928-832-1. Grades 6–9.

Among the places discussed in this overview of lost cities are Shangri-La, El Dorado, Camelot, and Atlantis. Scientists, researchers, and historians discuss their knowledge of these cities. Reproductions and illustrations highlight the text. Glossary and Index

81. Harper, Charise Mericle. *Flush! The Scoop on Poop Throughout the Ages.* Little, Brown, 2007. 32pp. ISBN 978-0-316-01064-1. Grades 1–5.

The first toilet appeared more than ten thousand years ago, and the average person uses about 20,000 sheets of toilet paper a year. Other interesting information in this book includes some of the uses of urine and a description of some of the toilets of the world. It reveals that Elizabeth I rejected a mechanical toilet and that Louis XIV held meetings while sitting on a toilet shaped like a throne. Thirteen poems feature additional information about excrement disposal. Collage paintings highlight the text.

82. Harpur, James. *Warriors.* Atheneum, 2007. Unpaged. ISBN 978-1-416939-51-1. Grades 3 up.

Information about warriors throughout history including the Assyrians, Spartans, Macedonians, Romans, Vikings, samurai, medieval knights, Zulus, and Mongolians. *Warriors* provides details about training, tactics, customs, dress, organization, and more. Photographs, spreads, and pop-up pages augment the text. Chronology.

83. Harris, Nathaniel. *Monarchy.* (Systems of Government) World Almanac, 2006. 48pp. ISBN 978-0-8368-5885-3. Grades 4–6.

An overview of the monarchy as a system of government. Monarchs of the past and present are discussed, with an emphasis on their contributions to the world. Photographs and illustrations highlight the text. Bibliography and Index.

84. Haslam, Andrew. *Living History.* Two-Can, 2001. 256pp. ISBN 978-1-58728-381-9. Grades 3–6.

Each section features information about a civilization or era—the Stone Age, ancient Egypt, the Roman Empire, and the North American Indians. The topics discussed include housing, clothing, food, art, religion, class differences, and inventions. Instructions for making items such as an Egyptian game, Roman pottery, a Japanese shinto shrine, and a Sioux headdress also appear. Photographs of the items will help with readers' projects. Glossary and Index.

85. Haven, Kendall. *100 Greatest Science Discoveries of All Time.* Libraries Unlimited, 2007. 255pp. ISBN 978-1-59158-265-6. Grades 5–8.

This examination of one hundred discoveries that changed science identifies each discovery, how it was made, who made it, and why it was a breakthrough. It starts with levers and buoyancy around 2650 B.C.E. and covers discoveries such as the sun-centered universe, cells, atoms, electrochemical bonding, quasars and pulsars, and the human genome. Index.

86. Hayden, Deborah. *Pox: Genius, Madness, and the Mysteries of Syphilis.* Basic, 2003. 379pp. ISBN 978-0-465-02881-8; paper ISBN 978-0-465-02882-5. Grades YA.

A look at the disease and its influence on civilization. Some estimates suggest that about 15 percent of European men were infected during the 19th century. Not until penicillin was discovered in 1943 was the disease controlled. *Pox* covers the history, symptoms, and course of the disease. After initial symptoms disappear, victims have severe headaches, gastrointestinal pains, blindness, deafness, paralysis, insanity, and sometimes, amazing creativity. The impact of the disease on thirteen sufferers completes the information. People who might have had it include Oscar Wilde, Isak Dinesen, Adolf Hitler, Gustav Flaubert, Abraham Lincoln, and Vincent van Gogh. Index.

87.   Herbst, Judith. *The History of Transportation.* (Major Inventions Through History) Twenty-First Century, 2005. 56pp. ISBN 978-0-8225-2496-0. Grades 5–8.

     The wheel, the sail, the steam engine, the internal combustion engine, and the airplane are discussed. Readers will learn that the Romans created the first highway system of more than 50,000 miles of stone roads, that steam has been used to power a bicycle, and that automobile travel has fostered developments including motels, drive-ins, amusement parks, and parking meters. Photographs and illustrations highlight the text. Bibliography, Glossary, Chronology, Further Reading, Web Sites, and Index.

88.   Herbst, Judith. *The History of Weapons.* (Major Inventions Through History) Twenty-First Century, 2005. 56pp. ISBN 978-0-8225-3805-9. Grades 5–8.

     Included here are guns, dynamite and TNT, automatic weapons, and weapons of mass destruction. The Chinese first used gunpowder for firecrackers, and it came to be used in weapons of war. In the 1950s, the threat of the atomic bomb led people to build underground shelters. Photographs and illustrations highlight the text. Bibliography, Glossary, Chronology, Further Reading, Web Sites, and Index.

89.   Hinds, Kathryn. *Venice and Its Merchant Empire.* (Cultures from the Past) Benchmark, 2001. 80pp. ISBN 978-0-7614-0305-0. Grades 6–8.

     In five parts, the text looks at Venice's chronological and cultural history, beliefs, society, and legacy. Among the topics covered are its beginnings as a sea power during Roman times, its beauty, its churches and saints, its nobles and women, its pageantry, and its decline as a political power. Photographs and illustrations highlight the text. Bibliography, Glossary, Chronology, Further Reading, and Index.

90.   Hodgkins, Fran. *How People Learned to Fly.* Illustrated by True Kelley. (Let's-Read-and-Find-Out Science) Collins, 2007. 33pp. Paper ISBN 978-0-06-445221-2. Grades 1–3.

     An explanation of the scientific principles behind airplanes including gravity, thrust, and lift. Diagrams and illustrations make these complicated concepts easy to understand. Also included is an experiment with paper airplanes.

91.   Hooper, Meredith. *Gold Quest: A Treasure Trail Through History.* Illustrated by Stephen Biesty. Hodder & Stoughton, 2005. 48pp. Paper ISBN 978-0-340-78858-5. Grades 4–7.

     Follow a scrap of gold as it changes both forms and hands over thousands of years. It begins as part of a pharaoh's death mask, stolen by grave robbers. They quickly recast it as a chalice that ends up in a temple. There is information about historical figures who lived during the gold's journey, from Nero to chemist Robert Boyle. The gold travels the globe as a ring, a coin, part of an illuminated manuscript, a set of buttons, and a necklace. Illustrations complement the text.

92.   Hopkins, Lee Bennett. *America at War.* Illustrated by Stephen Alcorn. Margaret K. McElderry, 2008. 96pp. ISBN 978-1-4169-1832-5. Grades 5–8.

     Fifty-four poems address the major American wars. Not all were written specifically about the conflict to which the author has assigned them, but they address the universals inherent in war. The wars represented are the American Revolution; the Civil War; World Wars I and II; and the conflicts in Korea, Vietnam, the Persian Gulf, and Iraq. Among the poets included are Sir Walter Scott, Langston Hughes, Walt Whitman, Carl

Sandburg, Rebecca Kai Dotlich, e. e. cummings, Stephen Crane, and Eloise Greenfield. Index.

93. **Hourani, Albert.** *A History of the Arab Peoples.* Belnap, 2003. 551pp. ISBN 978-0-674-01017-8. Grades YA.

This look at Arab history and culture in the past twelve centuries attempts to show its complexities. Sections cover the beginnings of Islam in the 7th to 10th centuries, Arab Muslim societies in the 11th to 15th centuries, the Ottoman Age from the 16th to the 18th centuries, the age of European empires from 1800 to 1939, and the age of nation-states since 1939. Maps, Genealogies and Dynasties, Notes, Bibliography, and Index.

94. **Huff, Toby E.** *An Age of Science and Revolutions, 1600–1800.* (Medieval and Early Modern World) Oxford, 2005. 173pp. ISBN 978-0-19-517724-4. Grades 7 up.

This volume covers more than two hundred years of discovery and change—expanding trade, scientific advances, and political and religious reforms. The first part of the book looks at China, India, and the Middle East. Among the figures featured in the second part are Copernicus, Galileo, Descartes, and Newton. Maps, photographs, and illustrations complement the text. Bibliography, Chronology, Glossary, Notes, and Index.

95. **Hughes, Robert.** *Barcelona.* Vintage, 1993. 596pp. Paper ISBN 978-0-679-74383-5. Grades YA.

The story of Barcelona, Spain, the capital of Catalonia, from its founding in 230 B.C.E. during Roman times through the times of the Moors and Charlemagne to the 20th century. Hughes relates information on the arts, politics, personalities, religion, and business of this vibrant city, including both the ordinary and the exceptional. Extras such as local expressions, Catalan verse, and popular songs reveal Barcelona's cultural and societal norms and idiosyncrasies. Illustrations, Bibliography, and Index.

96. **Ikenson, Ben J.** *Patents: Ingenious Inventions, How They Work and How They Came to Be.* Black Dog & Leventha, 2004. 288pp. ISBN 978-1-57912-367-3. Grades YA.

Ingenious inventions have changed the lives of inventors and those who use their products. Thomas Jefferson received the first American patent in 1790 and since then more than six million patents have been filed. This book looks at many important patented inventions, the types of patents, the difference between patents and trademarks, and how to get a patent. Special chapters on topics such as Thomas Edison, Alessandra Volta, Levi Strauss, the computer age, and the atomic age are interspersed with chapters on specific inventions. The inventions include the artificial heart, DNA fingerprinting, dynamite, the helicopter, barbed wire, the bottle cap, bubble wrap, and many more. Photographs and illustrations augment the text. Further Reading, Bibliography, and Index.

97. **Jackson, Ellen.** *Turn of the Century.* Charlesbridge, 1998. Unpaged. ISBN 978-0-8810-6369-1; 2003. paper ISBN 978-0-8810-6370-7. Grades 3–5.

Readers will learn about the lives of children in the United States and Great Britain at the beginning of each century from 1000 to 2000. Each two-page spread tells about a child living in each century, starting in Great Britain in 1000 and in the United States in 1700. Readers look into children's homes and find out about aspects of childhood such as chores, prayer, and the home. Bibliography. *Bluegrass Awards* (Kentucky), *Bluebonnet Awards* (Texas), and *Children's Informational Book Awards* (Utah).

98. Jackson, Ellen. *The Winter Solstice.* Illustrated by Jan Davey Ellis. Millbrook, 1997. Unpaged. Paper ISBN 978-0-7613-0297-1. Grades 3–4.

The winter solstice was a time of ritual and tradition for the Celts, the Romans, and the Native Americans. Its magic has had an influence throughout history and is reflected in the present with the celebration of Halloween and All Souls' Day. A Cherokee legend is featured at the end of this book.

99. Janco-Cohen, Judith. *The History of Food.* (Major Inventions Through History) Twenty-First Century, 2005. 56pp. ISBN 978-0-8225-2485-7. Grades 5–8.

A look at the history of food, including canning, pasteurization, refrigeration, supermarkets, and genetically modified foods. Readers will learn that before food preserving was invented, sailors ate rotten food filled with worms when they took long journeys. In the 1800s children could die from drinking milk as no one knew that diseases could spread from cows to humans. Before refrigerators, large blocks of ice delivered to homes allowed people to keep their food chilled. Photographs and illustrations highlight the text. Bibliography, Glossary, Chronology, Further Reading, Web Sites, and Index.

100. Jedicke, Peter. *Great Inventions of the 20th Century.* (Scientific American) Chelsea House, 2007. 72pp. ISBN 978-0-7910-9048-0. Grades 5–8.

The inventions discussed in this volume are those that changed people's lives and that are continually being improved. For example, air conditioners once contained hazardous waste, but today the chemicals in them are much safer for the environment. Photographs and reproductions highlight the text. Bibliography, Glossary, Further Reading, and Web Sites.

101. Jerome, Kate Boehm. *Atomic Universe: The Quest to Discover Radioactivity.* (Science Quest) National Geographic, 2006. 59pp. ISBN 978-0-7922-5543-7. Grades 5–8.

Before Marie and Pierre Curie could discover radiation, other discoveries had to occur such as Wilhelm Roentgen's discovery of X-rays. Dimitri Mendeleyev's advancements in nuclear physics led him to create the periodic table of the elements. Without his work, nuclear reactors could not exist today. Readers will learn of these and other important aspects of the atomic universe. Photographs and illustrations highlight the text. Glossary, Web Sites, and Index.

102. Johmann, Carol A. *Skyscrapers! Super Structures to Design and Build.* Illustrated by Michael P. Kline. Williamson, 2001. 96pp. Paper ISBN 978-1-885593-50-4. Grades 3–6.

A look at the history, construction, environmental impact, and design of skyscrapers including the Empire State Building in New York, Petronas Towers in Kuala Lumpur, the Montauk Block in Chicago, the Millennium Tower in Tokyo, and others. The book also includes ideas for activities such as building a concrete floor with sand, cornstarch, and popsicle sticks; testing a toothpick-and-marshmallow building frame; and building an elevator. Photographs enhance the text.

103. Johnson, Rebecca L. *Genetics.* (Great Ideas in Science) Twenty-First Century, 2005. 80pp. ISBN 978-0-8225-2910-1. Grades 5–8.

Genetics, the science of heredity, can offer answers to many questions about characteristics that are passed down through families. The author explains how scientists discovered genetics and the code of life that revolutionized molecular biology. Also covered are the basic principles of genetics, Gregor Mendel's pea plant experiments, the discovery of DNA and its replication, how genes translate into cell proteins, and the mapping of the human genome. This book does not cover nonscientific controversies. Photographs and diagrams augment the text. Bibliography, Glossary, Chronology, Further Reading, Web Sites, and Index.

104. Kallen, Stuart A. *The History of Classical Music.* Lucent, 2002. 112pp. ISBN 978-1-59018-123-2. Grades 6–10.

An introduction to the history of classical music in six chapters—medieval times, the Renaissance, the Baroque Era, the Classical period, the Romantic Era, and the Modern Era. It includes primary information from articles, letters, and diaries, often in musicians' own words. It also gives overviews of musicians' lives, including their difficulties and their successes. Photographs and illustrations augment the text. Bibliography, Notes, Further Reading, and Index.

105. Kavin, Kim. *Tools of Native Americans: A Kid's Guide to the History and Culture of the First Americans.* (Tools of Discovery) Nomad, 2006. 122pp. Paper ISBN 978-0-9749344-8-8. Grades 5–8.

The reader will discover the inventiveness of Native Americans through their tools, technology, and cultural achievements. As the first Americans as early as 20,000 B.C.E., they built shelter, found food, created religions, invented games, and fashioned jewelry. The four sections of the text address the early indigenous Americans, the regions in which Native Americans lived, the recent history of Native Americans, and where to find more information. Among the groups covered are the Arctic tribes and their igloos, the Midwest tribes that discovered copper, and the Southwest tribes that grew maize and beans. Activities and illustrations augment the text. Maps, Appendix, Bibliography, Chronology, Glossary, Web Sites, and Index. *Social Studies Honor Book.*

106. Keegan, John. *A History of Warfare.* Vintage, 1994. 432pp. Paper ISBN 978-0-679-73082-8. Grades YA.

This survey of warfare starts at the beginning of history and ends with the dropping of the atomic bombs in Hiroshima and Nagasaki in 1945. Keegan believes that war is an extension not of politics, but of culture. He draws on history, anthropology, ethnology, and psychology to express his theory that today's threats to peace are countries that wage war as they did before government or politics were invented. Bibliography and Index.

107. Keenan, Sheila. *Animals in the House: A History of Pets and People.* Scholastic, 2007. 112pp. ISBN 978-0-439-69286-1. Grades 4–6.

This overview of pets includes the history of animals as household residents, famous pets and pet owners, and information on many animals including why they make good pets, what they are like in the wild, and how they became domesticated. It also looks at superstitions about pets. Birds, rodents, fish, cats, dogs, and reptiles are some of the featured animals. Photographs and illustrations highlight the text. Bibliography, Web Sites, and Index.

108. Khan, Aisha. *A Historical Atlas of Kyrgyzstan.* Rosen, 2004. 64pp. ISBN 978-0-8239-4499-6. Grades 7 up.

The text follows the history of Kyrgyzstan from the time of its first inhabitants, the nomads, until its 2003 referendum approving constitutional reforms. Chapters cover Russian imperialism and the Soviet period along with ancient and medieval conquerors. Illustrations and maps complement the text.

109. Konstam, Angus. *Historical Atlas of the Celtic World.* Mercury, 2004. 192pp. ISBN 978-1-904668-01-5. Grades YA.

This atlas reveals the importance of Celtic history as an aspect of the contemporary world. The thirteen chapters cover the origins of the Celtic people, Celtic art, Celtic beliefs, the Druids, Celts and Christianity, the Celtic legacy, and much more. Introduction, Color Illustrations, Maps, Chronology, Glossary and Genealogy Tables, and Index.

110. Kort, Michael. *Russia.* Facts on File, 2004. 228pp. ISBN 978-0-8160-5075-8. Grades 7 up.

A look at the history of Russia from its beginnings to the post-Soviet period. It discusses how government policies have affected ordinary citizens and carefully explains the difficulties Russia faced after the demise of the Soviet Union. Quotations from Russians living through this period give authenticity to the text. Among the chapter topics are politics, government, the new economy, and daily life. Photographs, Chronology, Further Reading, Notes, and Index.

111. Koscielniak, Bruce. *About Time: A First Look at Time and Clocks.* Houghton, 2004. Unpaged. ISBN 978-0-618-39668-9. Grades 3–5.

A look at concepts concerning time, such as days, months, years, and the Western calendar. This book also looks at devices that have been used throughout history to measure time—sundials, water clocks, hourglasses, mechanical clocks, and atomic clocks. It also discusses the theories of time put forth by the ancient Greeks, Saint Augustine, and Einstein. Illustrations enhance the text.

112. Koscielniak, Bruce. *Looking at Glass Through the Ages.* Houghton, 2006. 32pp. ISBN 978-0-618-50750-4. Grades 4–6.

An introduction to the art of glassmaking through history, from the stained-glass windows of medieval cathedrals to the lenses of modern telescopes. Egyptians were the first to use glass or faience around 2500 B.C.E. Among the materials important in glassmaking are silica sand and soda ash. Glassmakers can mold it, blow it as they have since around 30 B.C.E. in Syria, or use a float-glass process. The Romans produced luxury glass, the Venetians engraved it, and today glass tubes form neon lighting and optical fiber carries data. Illustrations. Maps.

113. Kurlansky, Mark. *Salt: A World History.* Penguin, 2003. 496pp. Paper ISBN 978-0-14-200161-5. Grades YA.

The only rock that humans eat is salt. This history of salt features twenty-six chapters in three parts—"A Discourse on Salt, Cadavers, and Pungent Sauces," "The Glow of Herring and the Scent of Conquest," and "Sodium's Perfect Marriage." It discusses salt as a preservation material, a food, and a necessary element for life itself. Salt has historical, culinary, political, commercial, and scientific importance. Bibliography and Index.

114. Kurlansky, Mark. *The Story of Salt.*   Illustrated by S. D. Schindler. Putnam, 2006. 48pp. ISBN 978-0-399-23998-4. Grades 4–6.

This history of salt is by the author of *Salt: A World History* (2003), which is for older readers. Since salt, the only rock that humans eat, is essential for human life, finding inexpensive ways to obtain it is important. Readers will learn many facts about salt, including that Gandhi led Indians on a "salt march" to protest being forced to buy salt only from the British. Illustrations complement the text. *Dorothy Canfield Fisher Children's Book Award* (Vermont) nomination.

115. Kyuchukov, Hristo, and Ian F. Hancock. *A History of the Romani People.*   Boyds Mills, 2005. 32pp. ISBN 978-1-56397-962-0. Grades 3–6.

This look at the Romani people (often called Gypsies) gives a brief introduction to their history, culture, and hardships. As Romani woodworkers, fortune-tellers, and bear-trainers have spread around the world, they have been misunderstood and mistreated. During the Holocaust, Hitler wanted all of them exterminated. Today, some societies impose curfews on them or force them to live in areas lacking running water or electricity. Photographs.

116. Landau, Elaine. *The History of Energy.*   (Major Inventions Through History) Twenty-First Century, 2005. 56pp. ISBN 978-0-8225-3806-6. Grades 5–8.

A history of the uses of fire, wind, and water; coal and steam; oil and gasoline; electricity; and nuclear energy. Supposedly the ancient Persians harnessed rivers to turn waterwheels that ground grain into flour, a practice that evolved into the giant hydroelectric plants that provide electricity today. In the 2nd century, the Romans burned coal, and in modern times, 90 percent of the coal produced by the United States is used to generate electricity. Not until 1859 was oil discovered in the United States, but fifty years later, nearly a half-million gasoline-powered cars rolled on the country's streets. Photographs and illustrations complement the text. Bibliography, Glossary, Chronology, Notes, Further Reading, Web Sites, and Index.

117. Landau, Elaine. *The History of Everyday Life.*   (Major Inventions Through History) Twenty-First Century, 2005. 56pp. ISBN 978-0-8225-3808-0. Grades 5–8.

This history looks at fireplaces and central heating, indoor plumbing, the washing machine, food and clothes production, and microwave opens. Before indoor plumbing and sewer systems, people tossed their waste into city streets, and the smell chased people to the country. Before washing machines, women boiled clothes and then scrubbed them by hand with a grainy soap. The military first used microwaves, but an engineer invented the oven when he discovered that radar equipment had melted his candy bar. Photographs and illustrations highlight the text. Bibliography, Glossary, Chronology, Notes, Further Reading, Web Sites, and Index.

118. Langley, Myrtle. *Eyewitness Religion.*   DK, 2005. 72pp. ISBN 978-0-7566-1087-6. Grades 4–7.

Different religions or facets of religions are presented on two-page spreads illustrated with photographs, drawings, and reproductions. Among the religions and beliefs introduced in this overview are the Egyptian, Greek, Primitive, Hindu, Buddhist, Confucian, Taoist, Jainist, Sikh, Zoroastrian, Judaic, Christian, and Islamic faiths. Index.

119. Lankford, Mary D. *Mazes Around the World.* Illustrated by Karen Dugan. Collins, 2008. 26pp. ISBN 978-0-688-16519-2. Grades 3–4.

A history of mazes beginning with the ancient Egyptian labyrinth that Herodotus recorded and the Minotaur's labyrinth on Crete. Others include the United Kingdom's turf mazes, the maize mazes in North America, South Africa's Soekershof maze and garden, and France's religious labyrinths. One side of each two-page spread features background about a type of maze, with an illustration or photograph on the facing page. Notes.

120. Lansford, Tom. *Democracy.* (Political Systems of the World) Benchmark, 2008. 144pp. ISBN 978-0-7614-2629-5. Grades 10 up.

This overview of democracy as a political system declares that it is the most common form of government in the world. It explains how presidential and parliamentary democracies differ from constitutional monarchies and gives the histories of democracies throughout the globe. Photographs, maps, and illustrations enhance the text. Bibliography, Chronology, Notes, Further Reading, Web Sites, and Index.

121. Lauber, Patricia. *What You Never Knew About Beds, Bedrooms, and Pajamas.* Illustrated by John Manders. (Around the House History) Simon & Schuster, 2006. Unpaged. ISBN 978-0-689-85211-4. Grades 2–5.

The history of sleeping habits, sleep attire, and bedrooms from the Stone Age to the present. In the Stone Age clans slept on the ground, as we do today on camping trips. Cartoon illustrations enliven the text.

122. Lee, Laura. *Blame It on the Rain: How the Weather Has Changed History and Shaped Culture.* HarperCollins, 2006. 314pp. Paper ISBN 978-0-06-083982-6. Grades YA.

This collection of essays discusses how weather conditions have affected some of history's major events. Arranged chronologically, examples start with the age of the dinosaurs and end with forecasts for the future. Lee posits that high temperatures led to the 1967 Detroit riots and that the "little Ice Age" from 1350 to 1850 led to witch hunts in Europe and may have had an influence on the wood that Stradivarius used in his violins. The bad weather on election day in 1948 may have contributed to Truman's election as president. A possible relationship exists between Edvard Munch's painting *The Scream"* and the 1883 volcanic eruption on Krakatoa.

123. Lewis, Bernard. *Islam in History: Ideas, People, and Events in the Middle East.* Open Court, 2001. 487pp. Paper ISBN 978-0-8126-9518-2. Grades YA.

Thirty-two essays present the author's assessment of topics such as the Salman Rushdie threat, Anwar Sadat's assassination, Khomeini's power in Iran, and the support for Saddam Hussein. Lewis has been researching the Middle East for many years, and his insights help Westerners to understand some of the complex attitudes in this part of the world. Bibliography, Index.

124. Lewis, Bernard. *Semites and Anti-Semites: An Inquiry into Conflict and Prejudice.* Norton, 1999. 283pp. Paper ISBN 978-0-393-31839-5. Grades YA.

A Jew, according to rabbinic law, is a person born to a Jewish mother or converted to the Jewish religion. To the Nazis, a Jew was a member of a specific race. Lewis investigates the origin of the hostilities in the Middle East between Arabs and Jews and sees that it stems from three kinds of prejudice. One is a conflict of peoples and nations over territory. Another is the disagreement between neighboring peoples who have different cultural traditions and backgrounds. The third, and the one most prevalent in the past decade, is a case of anti-Semitism in which Arabs see Jews or Israelis as the embodiment of evil. They have separated the concept of Zionism from that of Judaism. Additionally, in intellectual circles, anti-Semitism has been the accepted view, though scholars have met privately and personally to discuss their common interests. The views that Lewis discusses in detail give insight into the problems of the Middle East. Notes and Index.

125. Lewis, Bernard. *The World of Islam: Faith, People, Culture.* Norton, 1991. 360pp. Paper ISBN 978-0-500-27624-2. Grades YA.

When the prophet Muhammad died in 632, he had established a Muslim state in a large part of Arabia. The practice of Islam has continued since then. This book includes essays with accompanying color photographs on (among other topics) the Islamic faith; Islamic art, literature, and music; urban Islam; the Sufi tradition; Muslim contributions to science and warfare; Muslim India; and Islam today. Chronology, Select Bibliography, Index.

126. Liberman, Sherri. *A Historical Atlas of Azerbaijan.* Rosen, 2004. 64pp. ISBN 978-0-8239-4497-2. Grades 7 up.

Azerbaijan, a Soviet state, became a republic with the downfall of the Soviet Union in 1989. This atlas covers its earliest history and ends with its status in the early 20th century. It includes background on medieval conquerors, Russian imperialism, and the time of the Soviets.

127. Love, Ann, and Jane Drake. *Sweet! The Delicious Story of Candy.* Illustrated by Claudia Dávila. Tundra, 2007. 64pp. ISBN 978-0-88776-752-4. Grades 4–7.

This history of candy begins in 4000 B.C.E. with Papua New Guinea residents cutting sugarcane for its sweet sap. It ends in contemporary times with a trip to a candy store. In between, it discusses the ingredients—bee barf, mammal secretions, aphid poop, stem sap, root pulp, bean fat—that become marshmallows, fudge, gummy worms, and chocolate-chip cookies. Visits to a jelly-bean factory, a chocolatier, and a kitchen offer other insights. Cartoon illustrations enhance the text. Chronology.

128. Lowenherz, David H. *The 50 Greatest Love Letters of All Time.* Crown, 2002. 224pp. ISBN 978-0-8129-3277-5. Grades YA.

This collection of love letters, culled from many collections and several centuries, reveals the intelligence, wit, and passion of the writers. In sections called "Tender Love," "Crazy for You," "Painful Gyrations," "Passionate Prose," "Fire and Ice," and "Forbidden Love," readers will find letters by Wolfgang Amadeus Mozart, Harry Truman, Ernest Hemingway, Ronald Reagan, and many more.

129. Lucke, Deb. *The Book of Time-Outs: A Mostly True History of the World's Biggest Troublemakers.* Simon & Schuster, 2008. 32pp. ISBN 978-1-416-92829-4. Grades 3–6.

This collective biography features profiles of fourteen people in history who had to take "time-outs" for their behavior. They include Cleopatra, Napoleon, Susan B. Anthony, Babe Ruth, Louis Armstrong, Rosa Parks, and others. Illustrations complement the text.

130. Macaulay, David. *Ship.* Walter Lorraine, 1993. 80pp. ISBN 978-0-395-52439-8; 1995. paper ISBN 978-0-395-74518-2. Grades 5 up.

The "space shuttles" of the 15th century were small ships called caravels. No drawings remain to show what these ships looked like or how they were built. This book looks at a caravel that was recovered by archaeologists from Caribbean waters and recreates it piece by piece. Then it imagines in diary format the ship's last voyage from Seville and its sinking.

131. McClafferty, Carla Killough. *The Head Bone's Connected to the Neck Bone: The Weird, Wacky, and Wonderful X-Ray.* Farrar, 2001. 135pp. ISBN 978-0-374-32908-2. Grades 6–9.

In ten chapters, this is a look at the discovery of the X-ray, its uses, and its inherent dangers. Wilhelm Roentgen first amazed the world with his X-ray experiments showing that he could see inside the human body. Then X-rays were used not only for medical reasons but as part of novelty sideshows. Not for a long time did people discover the deadly effects of radiation. However, when used appropriately, X-rays are helpful in the fields of medicine, paleontology, art authentication, Egyptology, and astronomy. Photographs augment the text. Bibliography, Glossary, Further Reading, Web Sites, and Index.

132. Macy, Sue. *Swifter, Higher, Stronger: A Photographic History of the Summer Olympics.* National Geographic, 2008. 96pp. ISBN 978-1-4263-0290-9. Grades 5–9.

A look at the history of the Olympic Games since their rebirth during the late 1800s with anecdotes of some unusual moments during the games. This book also includes some of the controversies and attitudes toward sportsmanship. For instance, a contemporary marathon is 26 miles and 385 yards (rather than the Greek 26 miles) as established in 1908 because Queen Alexandra wanted a closer view . Some of the more famous Olympians are also featured. Notes, Further Resources, and Index.

133. Maestro, Betsy. *The Story of Money.* Illustrated by Giulio Maestro. Clarion, 1993. 48pp. ISBN 978-0-395-56242-0; Trophy, 1995. paper ISBN 978-0-688-13304-7. Grades 3–5.

Among the objects that have been used for money throughout history are tea leaves, shells, feathers, animal teeth, tobacco, blankets, barley, salt, feathers, and metal balls. When the Sumerians used metal bars of the same weight and stamped an amount on each bar, they invented the first known metal money. This book has other interesting information about money through the centuries and short chapters on American money, unusual money, and currencies of other countries. Illustrations complement the text.

134. Major, John S. *The Silk Route: 7000 Miles of History.* Illustrated by Stephen Fieser. Trophy, 1996. 32pp. Paper ISBN 978-0-06-443468-3. Grades 4–7.

Silk has long been a symbol of riches and luxury, and for centuries a 7,000-mile-long trade route flourished by which silk traveled from China throughout the East. The story begins in 700 with the Tang Dynasty. The trade journey began in the city of Chang'an, with traders stopping to pray at Dunhauang (a monastery), crossing the Taklamakan (a desert), stopping at Kashgar (an oasis), traveling over the Pamirs (mountains), stopping in Tashkent (a market), going through Transoxiana (a wild country with nomads), and visiting Herat (a Persian city), Baghdad (the greatest Islamic city), Damascus, Tyre, and Byzantium. *American Booksellers' Pick of the Lists.*

135. **Mark, Jan.** *The Museum Book: A Guide to Strange and Wonderful Collections.* Illustrated by Richard Holland. Candlewick, 2007. 52pp. ISBN 978-0-7636-3370-7. Grades 4–6.

This book looks at the word "museum" itself and at a number of famous museums throughout the world. It includes Alexandria, Egypt; the collections of Peter the Great; Oxford University's Ashmolean; Pitt River; museums with Middle Ages collections; and others. It also includes what one might find in a museum. Photographs and illustrations highlight the text. Glossary and Index.

136. **Mason, Antony.** *A History of Western Art: From Prehistory to the 20th Century.* Abrams, 2007. 128pp. ISBN 978-0-8109-9421-8. Grades 5 up.

An overview of Western art beginning with the Lascaux cave paintings and continuing to the present. Two-page spreads discuss different time periods or movements, contain representative work, and present aspects of the media used. Each section provides a showcase of the time period discussed. More than two hundred reproductions of sculpture, pottery, mosaics, paintings, etching, stained glass, and architecture complement the text. Index.

137. **Mayell, Hillary.** *Shipwrecks.* (Man-Made Disasters) Lucent, 2003. 112pp. ISBN 978-1-59018-058-7. Grades 5–8.

Many different kinds of vessels—including commercial fishing boats, ferries, luxury liners, and oil tankers—are lost at sea. Among the causes of shipwrecks are weather, design flaws, and crew errors. The text examines a number of shipwrecks and draws conclusions about why they happened. Illustrations, Photos, Bibliography, Further Reading, Glossary, Index, Notes, Web Sites.

138. **Mehling, Randi.** *Great Extinctions of the Past.* (Scientific American) Chelsea House, 2007. 72pp. ISBN 978-0-7910-9049-7. Grades 5–8.

An examination of mass extinctions in the history of the world, focusing mainly on the dinosaurs. One of the important goals of the future is to help the environment so that mass extinctions never again occur. Photographs and reproductions highlight the text. Bibliography, Glossary, Further Reading, and Web Sites.

139. **Mercer, Abbie.** *Happy St. Patrick's Day.* Powerkids, 2007. 24pp. ISBN 978-1-4042-3811-4. Grades 2–4.

Saint Patrick's Day is a time when the Irish honor Saint Patrick, the man who drove the snakes out of Ireland, with parades, dancing, and bagpipes. Photographs and illustrations highlight the text. Glossary, Web Sites, and Index.

140. **Middleton, Haydn.** *Great Olympic Moments.* (Olympics) Heinemann, 2007. 32pp. ISBN 978-1-4329-0264-3. Grades 4–8.

An overview of some of the great moments in the history of the Olympic Games. Among the sports that have generated high levels of excitement are gymnastics and soccer. Photographs accent each page. Glossary, Further Reading, Web Sites, and Index.

141. **Middleton, Haydn.** *Modern Olympic Games.* (Olympics) Heinemann, 2007. 32pp. ISBN 978-1-4329-0265-0. Grades 4–8.

The modern Olympic Games began in 1896 and have continued every four years since. This book features information about the competitions and Olympic history. The games in ancient Greece were similar to the modern games, but under Roman rule they became entertainment rather than competitions. Women were not allowed to participate until 1928. Photographs accent each page. Glossary, Further Reading, Web Sites, and Index.

142. Miles, Barry. *Peace: 50 Years of Protest.* Reader's Digest, 2008. 256pp. ISBN 978-0-7621-0893-0. Grades YA.

In preparing for a protest, a group wanted a symbol to represent their concerns. One of them combined the naval semaphores for the letters *N* and *D* (for nuclear disarmament) inside a circle. The group marched from London to Aldermaston, Britain's top-secret nuclear weapons factory, on April 8, 1958, using this symbol. Since then, it has become an internationally known sign for peace. The text also includes background on those who have staged peace protests throughout the world and have used this symbol. Index.

143. Mlodinow, Leonard. *Euclid's Window: The Story of Geometry from Parallel Lines to Hyperspace.* Free, 2002. Paper ISBN 978-0-684-86524-9. Grades YA.

The history of geometry in five parts, each one devoted to an important figure—Euclid, Descartes, Gauss, Einstein, and Witten. It stresses that Euclid's *Elements* is the greatest mathematics book of all time because of its description of three-dimensional space. Euclid codified an attitude essential for rational thinking: distrust of intuition and rejection of assumptions that cannot be justified. The text presents the theories of each man and how they have affected geometry. Notes and Index.

144. Morgan, Sally. *From Greek Atoms to Quarks: Discovering Atoms.* (Chain Reaction) Raintree, 2007. 64pp. ISBN 978-1-4034-9551-8. Grades 6–9.

This overview of atomic theory looks at the discovery of atoms, elements, chemicals, molecules, electrons, and neutrons. It then discusses atomic structure, antimatter, atomic bombs, and current atomic research. Photographs and reproductions highlight the text. Glossary, Chronology, Further Reading, Web Sites, and Index.

145. Morgan, Sally. *From Mendel's Peas to Genetic Fingerprinting: Discovering Inheritance.* (Chain Reaction) Heinemann, 2006. 64pp. ISBN 978-1-4034-8837-4. Grades 6–9.

One scientist's discovery often is built on the research of another. Then that discovery may lead another scientist to further breakthroughs. Gregor Mendel studied peas to understand dominant and recessive genes, and his work eventually led to the Human Genome Project and genetic fingerprinting. No scientist works in a vacuum, but draws on past knowledge for future discoveries. Photographs, diagrams, and illustrations highlight the text. Glossary, Chronology, Further Reading, Web Sites, and Index.

146. Morgan, Sally. *From Microscopes to Stem Cell Research: Discovering Regenerative Medicine.* (Chain Reaction) Heinemann, 2006. 64pp. ISBN 978-1-4034-8836-7. Grades 6–9.

One scientist's discovery often is built on the research of another. Then that discovery may lead another scientist to further breakthroughs. Robert Hooke discovered cells in the early 1660s, and since then, stem-cell research and regenerative medicine have caused both controversy and hope. No scientist works in a vacuum, but draws on past knowledge for future discoveries. Photographs, diagrams, and illustrations highlight the text. Glossary, Chronology, Further Reading, Web Sites, and Index.

147. Morgan, Sally. *From Sea Urchins to Dolly the Sheep: Discovering Cloning.* (Chain Reaction) Heinemann, 2006. 64pp. ISBN 978-1-4034-8838-1. Grades 6–9.

One scientist's discovery often is built on the research of another. Then that discovery may lead another scientist to further breakthroughs. In the 1890s, the possibility of cloning began with research on sea urchins. Finally in 2003, Dolly the sheep was completely cloned, an achievement that has led to ethical and medical questions. No scientist works in a vacuum, but draws on past knowledge for future discoveries. Photographs, diagrams, and illustrations highlight the text. Glossary, Chronology, Further Reading, Web Sites, and Index.

148. Morgan, Sally. *From Windmills to Hydrogen Fuel Cells: Discovering Alternative Energy.* (Chain Reaction) Raintree, 2007. 64pp. ISBN 978-1-4034-9555-6. Grades 6–9.

An introduction to alternative energy, including its history, current status, and future possibilities. Among the alternatives under consideration are wind power, solar power, nuclear power, and biopower. Photographs and reproductions highlight the text. Glossary, Chronology, Further Reading, Web Sites, and Index.

149. Murdoch, David H. *Cowboy.* Illustrated by Geoff Brightling. DK, 2000. 72pp. ISBN 978-0-7894-5854-4. Grades 3 up.

This overview of cowboys includes brief topics on dress such as hats, boots, chaps, and spurs. It also looks at *charros* and *vaqueros*, the best horses, saddles, life on the ranch, cattle and branding, ranges, trail drives, law and order, guns and gunslingers, the South American gauchos, the Camargue *Gardians* of France, cowgirls, cowboys in Australia, the rodeo, and the culture of the cowboy. Index.

150. Murray, Sarah. *Movable Feasts: From Ancient Rome to the 21st Century: The Incredible Journeys of the Food We Eat.* St. Martin's, 2007. 256pp. ISBN 978-0-312-35535-7. Grades YA.

In twelve chapters, Murray examines the ways in which food has been transported around the world. Among her topics are olive oil from Italy, Norwegian salmon that is de-boned in China, food preservation, the techniques behind the Berlin airlift from 1948 to 1952, the importance of refrigerated ships for transporting bananas, mobile biochemistry, oak barrels, tea, and strawberries that are transported by air. The trivia about food and its transportation through the centuries offer an unusual perspective about the dinner table. Bibliography and Index.

151. Owen, David. *Hidden Secrets.* Firefly, 2002. 224pp. Paper ISBN 978-1-55297-564-0. Grades YA.

Many anecdotes about espionage add interest to this five-section history of techniques, strategies, and equipment. Among the topics covered are spies in war and peace, codes and ciphers, electronic secrets on the ground, false intelligence, airborne and satellite intelligence, and spying on terrorists. Photographs and illustrations highlight the text. Glossary and Index.

152. Oxlade, Chris. *Airplanes: Uncovering Technology.* (Uncovering) Firefly, 2006. 52pp. ISBN 978-1-55407-134-0. Grades 4–8.

A historical overview of both civilian and military airplanes. Each spread features drawings and captioned photographs for a chronological presentation of airplanes and how they have made a difference in technology. Overlays show the inner workings of several airplanes. Index.

153. Oxlade, Chris. *Skyscrapers: Uncovering Technology.* (Uncovering) Firefly, 2006. 52pp. ISBN 978-1-55407-136-4. Grades 4–8.

A historical overview of skyscrapers. Each spread features drawings and captioned photographs for a chronological presentation of skyscrapers since the first one in New York in the 1880s. Among those included are the Tower of Babel, the Chrysler Building, the Petronas Tower in Kuala Lumpur, and the CCTV building planned for Beijing. Cross-section overlays reveal the inner aspects of three skyscrapers. Index.

154. Panchyk, Richard. *Archaeology for Kids.* Chicago Review, 2001. 160pp. Paper ISBN 978-1-55652-395-3. Grades 5–8.

Twenty-five activities suggest ways for readers to understand the science of archaeology. They include playing a survey game, dating coins, making footprints, measuring brain capacity, building a Paleolithic fireplace, making cave art, playing a seriation game, classifying pottery, and others. Each of the activities gives participants a chance to more closely observe their surroundings after they have reviewed the eight steps of archaeology, four of which are research, surveying, excavation, and preservation. Photographs and illustrations highlight the text. Bibliography, Glossary, Web Sites, and Index.

155. Parkyn, Neil. *The Seventy Wonders of the Modern World: 1500 Years of Extraordinary Feats of Engineering and Construction.* Thames & Hudson, 2002. 304pp. ISBN 978-0-500-51047-6. Grades YA.

Parkyn identifies seventy structures that he calls "wonders of the modern world." This book examines when and why each structure was built, the history and politics behind it, and its basic statistics. Parkyn groups the structures into seven categories: Churches, Mosques, Temples and Shrines; Palaces and Castles; Public and State Buildings; Towers and Skyscrapers; Bridges, Railways and Tunnels; Canals and Dams; and Colossal Statues. Among the structures included are the Statue of Liberty in New York, the Panama Canal, the Eiffel Tower in Paris, the Taj Mahal of India, the Forbidden City in Beijing, Frank Gehry's Guggenheim Museum in Bilbao, Spain; the Petronas Towers in Kuala Lumpur, Malaysia; the Channel Tunnel; and Mount Rushmore. Photographs, Diagrams, Drawings, Bibliography, and Index.

156. Pascoe, Elaine. *Fooled You! Fakes and Hoaxes Through the Years.* Holt, 2005. 96pp. ISBN 978-0-8050-7528-1. Grades 4–6.

Eleven notable hoaxes are covered. P. T. Barnum exhibited a mermaid in his circus during the 19th century. Edgar Allan Poe wrote a false newspaper article about a transatlantic balloon flight. In 1917, a "fairies in the garden" photograph fooled Sir Arthur Conan Doyle. Others include an "ether-driven" motor, the Piltdown Man fossil, film footage of Bigfoot, and crop circles in England. Cartoon illustrations highlight the text. Further Reading and Web Sites.

157. Peacock, Nancy. *Great Prosecutions.* (Crime, Justice, and Punishment) Chelsea House, 2001. 110pp. ISBN 978-0-7910-4292-2. Grades 6 up.

A look at five court cases involving heinous crimes: the Nuremberg genocide trials following World War II, and the trials of Byron De La Beck (for murdering civil rights activist Medgar Evers), serial rapist Tommy Lee Andrews, gangster Al Capone, and the

Manson family. Prosecutors in all of these cases paid extraordinary attention to presenting the details of the cases in order to obtain convictions, and each one established legal precedents. Photographs and illustrations enhance the text. Bibliography.

158. Perl, Lila. *Terrorism.* (Open for Debate) Benchmark, 2003. 142pp. ISBN 978-0-7614-1583-1. Grades 9 up.

Terrorism did not begin with the fall of the World Trade Center. Readers will learn of other terrorist groups such as the Ku Klux Klan, the Irish Republican Army, the Israelis and the Palestinians, the Symbionese Liberation Army, and the Baader-Meinhof Gang. Terrorist acts include taking hostages, hijackings, and bombings. Attack sites have also included the Pentagon and the USS *Cole*. Photographs, Bibliography, Further Reading, Notes, Web Sites, and Index.

159. Perl, Lila. *Theocracy.* (Political Systems of the World) Benchmark, 2008. 158pp. ISBN 978-0-7614-2631-8. Grades 9 up.

An introduction to theocracy as a political system, this book gives examples from countries such as Iran during the secular years under the Shah and, after the Islamic revolution, under the rule of the Ayatollah. This type of theocracy contrasts with that of the ancient Egyptians, the Incas, the Aztecs, and even Joseph Smith, who hoped to establish a theocracy in America under the aegis of the Church of Jesus Christ of Latter-Day Saints. Other theocracies also appear. Photographs, maps, and illustrations enhance the text. Bibliography, Chronology, Notes, Further Reading, Web Sites, and Index.

160. Perry, James M. *Arrogant Armies: Great Military Disasters and the Generals Behind Them.* Castle, 2006. 301pp. ISBN 978-0-7858-2023-9. Grades YA.

During two-and-a-half centuries of colonialism, many military expeditions have failed. Among those recounted here are General Edward Bradock's failure in the Ohio Valley, General Gordon's loss of Khartoum in the Sudan, General Baratieri's defeat in Ethiopia, and General Townshend's loss in the Mesopotamian campaign of World War I. The last segment concerns General Silvestre's Spanish troops in Morocco from 1921 to 1926. Loss of life and property was immeasurable in these displays of egotism. Bibliography and Index.

161. Pfeffer, Wendy. *The Shortest Day: Celebrating the Winter Solstice.* Illustrated by Jesse Reisch. Dutton, 2003. 40pp. ISBN 978-0-525-46968-1. Grades 2–5.

A look at how humans have reacted to the sun and how they have worshiped through the centuries. Ancient Egyptian, Chinese, Inca, and European astronomers measured the sun's movements in an attempt to understand why the days became shorter during the winter. Among the winter symbols that have endured through the centuries are evergreen wreaths and tree decorations. Illustrations highlight the text. Further Reading and Web Sites.

162. Phelan, Glen. *Double Helix: The Quest to Uncover the Structure of DNA.* (Science Quest) National Geographic, 2006. 59pp. ISBN 978-0-7922-5541-3. Grades 5–8.

Francis Crick and James Watson eventually determined the structure of DNA, but they could not have been successful without Gregor Mendel's experiments forming the basis of modern genetic research. Other scientists, especially Rosalind Franklin, helped Crick and Watson as well. Linus Pauling and Maurice Wilkins should also be acknowledged. Photographs and illustrations highlight the text. Glossary, Web Sites, and Index.

163. Piel, Gerald. *The Age of Science.* Basic, 2001. 400pp. ISBN 978-1-903985-07-6. Grades YA.

This overview of 20th-century science covers discoveries in natural history, cell and molecular biology, earth history, human evolution, cosmology, and the subatomic world. Perhaps the most important branch of science during this time is physics, and more than half of the book looks at its development during this period. Piel points out the irony of the fact that each field has become more specialized just as the sciences have become more interdisciplinary. Maps and diagrams augment the text. Notes and Index.

164. Pipes, Richard. *Communism: A History.* Modern Library, 2003. 144pp. Paper ISBN 978-0-8129-6864-4. Grades YA.

In forty-four short chapters, this volume covers the history of communism including the theory behind it, its development, and its inherent problems. Karl Marx wrote its tenets, based on Locke's concept of the human as a *tabula rasa.* In addition to looking at communism around the world, the text gives an in-depth analysis of Russia under Lenin and the Bolsheviks. Other leaders include Pol Pot, Castro, and Salvador Allende. Notes, Further Reading, and Index.

165. Porter, Roy. *London: A Social History.* Harvard University, 1998. 431pp. Paper ISBN 978-0-674-53839-9. Grades YA.

This history of London, from Roman times to Margaret Thatcher's days as prime minister, presents the city in its depths and at its heights. London has survived fires, wars, plagues, and rulers who would dismantle it. The fact that it is so old, and that it has come into the 20th century with modernization, is in itself amazing. It has had to clean its river, find supplies of pure drinking water, overcome class distinction to create universal education, try to keep its population civil, and create and update a public transportation system while expanding its commerce and industry. London has never been perfect, but the myriad facets of its history make it always exciting. Bibliography and Index.

166. Raum, Elizabeth. *The History of the Camera.* (Inventions That Changed the World) Raintree, 2007. 32pp. ISBN 978-1-4034-9647-8; paper ISBN 978-1-4034-9653-9. Grades 2–3.

Twelve chapters give a history of the camera from its invention to its digital reinvention. Raum explains how the camera has changed people's lives. She notes that paintings and drawings were the only source of pictures before cameras and that today, doctors can use tiny cameras inside human bodies. Illustrations augment the text. Chronology, Glossary, and Index.

167. Raum, Elizabeth. *The History of the Car.* (Inventions that Changed the World) Raintree, 2007. 32pp. ISBN 978-1-4034-9647-8; paper ISBN 978-1-4034-9654-6. Grades 2–3.

Twelve chapters give a history of the automobile beginning with life before cars, when people rode in horse-pulled buggies. The book goes on to look at steam cars, car seats and belts, and types of fuel. Raum discusses ways in which cars have influenced humans and their travel and work habits. Illustrations enhance the text. Chronology, Glossary, and Index.

168. Raum, Elizabeth. *The History of the Computer.* (Inventions that Changed the World) Raintree, 2007. 32pp. ISBN 978-1-4034-9649-2; paper ISBN 978-1-4034-9657-7. Grades 2–3.

Twelve chapters give a history of computers and discuss their influence on and necessity in daily life. Computers have changed the kinds of things people do and the ways in which they do them (for good and for ill) just as they have been reduced in size from huge to minuscule. Before computers, people copied complex mathematical problems by hand and solved problems with an abacus or a calculator. Illustrations highlight the text. Chronology, Glossary, and Index.

169. Raum, Elizabeth. *The History of the Telephone.* (Inventions that Changed the World) Raintree, 2007. 32pp. ISBN 978-1-4034-9650-8. Grades 2–3.

Twelve chapters give a history of the telephone and discuss its influence on and necessity in daily life. Bell was the first to test telephones and sell them. With telephones came services to automatically answer calls and books listing the numbers of those who owned telephones. After satellites started directing calls, cell phones evolved. Telephones have changed modern life. Illustrations highlight the text. Map, Chronology, Glossary, and Index.

170. Reynoldson, Fiona. *Conflict and Change.* (The Illustrated History of the World) Facts on File, 1993. 78pp. ISBN 978-0-8160-2790-3. Grades 4–7.

The reader will see the changes in European town and country life after 1650 and learn about absolute rulers, such as Peter the Great, and about the rise of science, industry, and the arts. It was an era of revolution in the American colonies and in France. In China, the Manchu ruled, and in Japan, the Tokugawa shogunate. The Moguls had power in Russia, and in Africa the slave trade was beginning. The Dutch entered South Africa; the aborigines were in Australia and the Maori in New Zealand. Illustrations highlight the text. Glossary, Further Reading, and Index.

171. Richardson, Tim. *Sweets: A History of Candy.* Bloomsbury, 2002. 392pp. ISBN 978-1-58234-229-0; 2003. paper ISBN 978-1-58234-307-5. Grades YA.

This history looks at candy from ancient times to the present including its composition, its position in folklore and myth, and its manufacturing. Among the specific candies discussed are Turkish delight, liquorice, Juicy Fruit, marzipan, baklava, marshmallows, and chewing gum. Ancient writings discuss how to keep bees for honey. The Turks first made caramel while the Janissaries carried trays of baklava through Istanbul's streets. Pastilles and gums were first important in medicine. Also included are overviews of cultural candy preferences, including the British preference for the smoothness of Cadbury chocolate rather than Hershey's graininess. Bibliography and Index.

172. Rinard, Judith E. *The Book of Flight: The Smithsonian National Air and Space Museum.* Firefly, 2007. 128pp. ISBN 978-1-55407-292-7; paper ISBN 978-1-55407-275-0. Grades 4–8.

This guide to flight documents most of the men and women who have been part of its history as well as the milestones of flight that have changed history. The topics covered include balloons, powered flights, and space flights. Illustrations and photographs augment the text. Chronology and Glossary.

173. Robb, Don. *Ox, House, Stick: The History of Our Alphabet.* Illustrated by Anne Smith. Charlesbridge, 2007. 48pp. ISBN 978-1-57091-609-0; paper ISBN 978-1-57091-610-6. Grades 4–7.

This history of writing examines each letter of the Roman alphabet. It follows the evolution from pictogram to written symbols standing for sounds and displays each letter in its Sinaitic, Phoenician, early Greek, classical Greek, and Roman forms. Additional information about punctuation, spacing conventions, alphabetical order, writing surfaces, and font styles is included. The author clarifies which information is fact and which is theory. Illustrations enhance the text. Chronology, Further Reading, and Web Sites.

174. Robinson, Francis. *The Cambridge Illustrated History of the Islamic World.* Cambridge University, 1999. 352pp. Paper ISBN 978-0-521-66993-1. Grades YA.

Thorough information about the religion of Islam. This book looks at the history and practice of its believers along with its economic, social, and intellectual aspects. Boxed text and inserts add more specific information about a variety of issues concerning this group of people. Bibliography, Glossary, and Index.

175. Robinson, James. *Inventions.* Kingfisher, 2006. 64pp. ISBN 978-0-7534-5973-7. Grades 3–7.

Brief overviews of various inventions that have served as a foundation for the modern age. Among them are surgical robots, cell phones, information technology, space travel photography, genetic engineering, medicine, and nanotechnology. The two-page summary of computers mentions the first computer of Charles Babbage (1792–1871), shifts to the British electronic digital computer in 1943, and suggests that quantum computers will be much faster than anything imaginable today. Illustrations highlight the text. Glossary, Web Sites, and Index.

176. Rosie, George. *Curious Scotland: Tales from a Hidden History.* Thomas Dunne, 2006. 244pp. ISBN 978-0-312-35416-9. Grades YA.

There is nothing plodding about this history book. It's full of unusual anecdotes about the country. For instance: some Scots always spit on a particular Edinburgh street, Daniel Defoe was a secret agent in Edinburgh before publishing *Robinson Crusoe,* and John Ross became the greatest Cherokee chieftain. This chronological presentation begins with stories during the time of King Arthur to the present. Chapters include "Operation Vegetarian," "The Blasphemer," and "The Glasgow Frankenstein." Other stories involve Bonnie Prince Charlie, the Scottish leadership of the Ku Klux Klan, and lesser-known groups and figures.

177. Ross, Stewart. *Conquerors and Explorers.* Stargazer, 2008. 48pp. ISBN 978-1-59604-195-0. Grades 4–6.

Many illustrations complement historical information about explorers and conquerors from the Greek period through the age of space exploration. Index.

178. Ross, Stewart. *Knights.* Stargazer, 2008. 48pp. ISBN 978-1-59604-197-4. Grades 4–6.

A look at knights throughout history. Among the knights included are ancient chariot riders, Hannibal, the Roman cavalry, Charlemagne, King Arthur, samurai warriors,

Mongols, and 20th-century "knights" such as World War I pilots and Canadian Mounties. Short chapters on chivalry, arms and armor, castles, and feudalism, along with brief profiles of famous and legendary knights, also appear. Diverse illustrations highlight the text. Chronology and Index.

179. Ross, Stewart. *The United Nations.* Heinemann/Raintree, 2002. 48pp. ISBN 978-1-4034-0152-6; 2003. paper ISBN 978-1-4034-4622-0. Grades 7 up.

The history of the United Nations from the days before the birth of the League of Nations to the present. The responsibilities of the United Nations are peacekeeping and safeguarding the rights and welfare of people around the globe. Black-and-white photographs supplement the text. Bibliography, Chronology, Glossary, Notes, and Index.

180. Rowland-Warne, L. *Costume.* DK, 2000. 63pp. ISBN 978-0-7894-5586-4. Grades 4–6.

All aspects of clothes—from shoes to hats. The illustrations and photographs give a good sense of dress in the 18th through the 20th centuries, although references to prehistory, Roman times, and the Viking era are included. Index.

181. Ruggiero, Adriane. *The Ottoman Empire.* (Cultures of the Past) Benchmark, 2002. 80pp. ISBN 978-0-7614-1494-0. Grades 6–10.

This history traces the earliest Turks from their nomadic beginnings to their dominance as Ottomans in the 13th century. The height of power occurred with Soleyman I in the 16th century, and the empire dissolved in 1922. Topics include Turkish culture; the five pillars of Islam; the society of Ottoman cities and towns with the Sultan at the center; and the legacy of the Ottomans, including calligraphy, ceramics, woven carpets, and miniature paintings. Photographs, maps, and reproductions highlight the text. Bibliography, Glossary, Chronology, Further Reading, and Index.

182. Russell, Sharman Apt. *Hunger: An Unnatural History.* Basic, 2006. 262pp. Paper ISBN 978-0-465-07165-4. Grades YA.

This book looks at the psychological and physical results of food deprivation and starvation. Among the topics are the process of hunger, the hunger strike, hunger diseases, the Minnesota experiment, anorexia nervosa, and hungry children. Our bodies tell us when to eat; if we do not eat, certain things happen to our bodies and minds. The text looks at malnourishment and hunger in parts of the Third World and discusses deliberate starvation. Bibliography and Notes.

183. Sawa, Maureen. *The Library Book: The Story of Libraries from Camels to Computers.* Illustrated by Bill Slavin. Tundra, 2006. 72pp. ISBN 978-0-88776-698-5. Grades 5–7.

This look at libraries throughout history emphasizes their global impact. Among the libraries and librarians discussed are the British Library's digital collections, a mobile library transported by camels in Kenya, and pack-horse librarians in Kentucky. Famous librarians in history include Gutenberg; Benjamin Franklin; Hypatia, the female librarian in Alexandria who was killed by a mob because she catalogued the works of Plato; and Vizier Abdul Kasem Ismail, who carried 117,000 books in alphabetical order on the backs of camels. Illustrations enhance the text. Bibliography and Index.

184. Sayre, Henry. *Cave Paintings to Picasso: The Inside Scoop on 50 Art Masterpeices.* Chronicle, 2004. 93pp. ISBN 978-0-8118-3767-5. Grades 5–20.

The text covers fifty works of art from the 24,000-year-old "Woman from Brassempouy" to Magritte's 1964 *Son of Man*. Among the other works covered are the Bayeux Tapestry, Michelangelo's *David*, a Mogul miniature, the Easter Island heads, a Moche pitcher, a Mandan hide robe, Chinese paintings, works by Picasso, and Andy Warhol's Campbell's soup can paintings. Photographs of each work are accompanied by background on the artist and social and historical context. Chronology and Index. *Capitol Choices Noteworthy Titles* (Washington, D.C.).

185. **Scandiffio, Laura.** *Escapes!* Illustrated by Stephen MacEachern. (True Stories from the Edge) Annick, 2003. ISBN 978-1-55037-823-8. Grades 5–9.

The stories of ten real-life escapes, ranging in time from 73 B.C.E. to 1979. Spartacus led slaves through mountains in 73 B.C.E. to escape death as gladiators. Winifred Maxwell smuggled her husband out of the Tower of London in 1716. In 1754, Henri Latude escaped from the Bastille in France. William and Ellen Craft pretended to be servant and mistress on a train trip escape from slavery in 1848. Hans Larive escaped a Dutch prison during World War II. In 1941, Douglas Bader escaped from the Luftwaffe by taking off his metal leg and parachuting into enemy territory. In 1979, six Americans with fictitious passports and disguised as Canadians escaped from Iran. Notes and Index.

186. **Scharfstein, Sol.** *Understanding Jewish History: From the Patriarchs to the Expulsion from Spain.* KTAV, 1996. 168pp. Paper ISBN 978-0-8812-5545-4. Grades 7 up.

Scharfstein gives a clear history of the Jews beginning in biblical times and continuing through the expulsion from Spain in 1492. Photographs, maps, and reproductions cover every page, keeping the historical account from being a litany of dates. Chronology and Index. A second volume is *Understanding Jewish History: From Renaissance to the 21st Century* (1997).

187. **Schimmel, Annemarie, and Franz Carl Endres.** *The Mystery of Numbers.* Oxford, 1994. 314pp. Paper ISBN 978-0-19-508919-6. Grades YA.

The author discusses numbers from 1 to 40 and various numbers from 42 to 10,000—including their "symbolism, religious connotation, and linguistic correlation." The reader will learn that many numbers have more than one meaning. Addressing mainly the Judaic, Christian, and Islamic heritages, Schimmel looks at the origin of Arabic numbers, the evolution of modern superstitions about numbers, number games, gnostic traditions, and mysticism. Some numbers are thought to be "lucky," "feminine," or "perfect." Reproductions and drawings complement the text. Bibliography and Index.

188. **Schroeder, Andreas.** *Thieves!* (True Stories from the Edge) Annick, 2005. 164pp. ISBN 978-1-55037-932-7; paper ISBN 978-1-55037-932-7. Grades 5–9.

A look at ten robberies, thefts, and failed heists. Dan Cooper parachuted from an airplane at night with $200,000 in extorted cash. A small group of Italians removed the *Mona Lisa* from the Louvre. The technique of Willie Sutton, a well-known American bank robber, attracted many copycats. Other thefts and thieves include the Great Train Robbery, the "Purolator Caper," and "the classiest thief in Manhattan." Illustrations highlight the text. Bibliography and Index.

189. **Shapiro, Stephen.** *Battle Stations! Fortifications Through the Ages.* Illustrated by Mei Tsao and Ken Nice. Annick, 2005. 32pp. ISBN 978-1-55037-889-4; paper ISBN 978-1-55037-888-7. Grades 5–8.

This book features a history of strongholds and forts that have been constructed to block invasions. It includes an ancient Egyptian fort, a fortified Gaulish town, the Great Wall of China, a 16th-century Japanese castle, an 18th-century European fortress, the Martello Tower built to fend off Napoleon in Britain, early 20th-century American port defenses, the fortresses along the Maginot Line in France and at Fort Drum in Manila Bay, and defenses during the cold war. Illustrations complement the text.

190. Shaskan, Kathy. *How Underwear Got Under There: A Brief History.* Illustrated by Regan Dunnick. Dutton, 2007. 48pp. ISBN 978-0-525-47178-3. Grades 5–8.

This history describes people's undergarments from ancient times to today. It discusses their shape, type, warmth, texture, and support as well as the body parts that certain garments attempt to protect. Since people do not tend to offer facts about their underwear, the text includes fewer references than might be desired. But it covers the available facts and suppositions in a humorous fashion.

191. Shephard, Sue. *Pickled, Potted, and Canned: How the Art and Science of Food Preserving Changed the World.* Simon & Schuster, 2006. 368pp. Paper ISBN 978-0-7432-5553-0. Grades YA.

Readers will learn how food has been preserved throughout history and how some preservation techniques changed the world. This book includes chemistry, cooks, legends, and innovation. Among the methods of preservation discussed are drying, salting, pickling in vinegar, smoking, canning, concentrating, dehydrating, refrigeration, freezing, and fermenting. Photographs enhance the text. Bibliography and Index.

192. Snyder, Paula. *The European Women's Almanac.* Colunbia University, 1992. 399pp. ISBN 978-0-231-08064-4. Grades YA.

This almanac discusses the status of women in Europe, their rights, and their advances in areas such as education, employment, and health care, arranged by country. First-person accounts, charts, tables, and diagrams make the text immediate and helpful. Bibliography.

193. Somervill, Barbara A. *The History of the Calendar.* (Our Changing World—The Timeline Library) Child's World, 2006. 32pp. ISBN 978-1-59296-436-9. Grades 3–7.

This history follows the development of the calendar by looking at its place in the world's civilizations including the Egyptians, the Chinese and their years of animals, and the Jews. Also examined are Pope Gregory's calendar and cesium clocks, which accurately record the passage of time. Different groups of people devised diverse ways to mark the passage of time into seconds, minutes, hours, days, weeks, months, and years. Photographs and illustrations illuminate the text. Bibliography, Chronology, Glossary, and Index.

194. Somervill, Barbara A. *The History of the Library.* (Our Changing World—The Timeline Library) Child's World, 2006. 32pp. ISBN 978-1-59296-438-3. Grades 3–7.

The history of the library from Ptolemy's library at Alexandria to Washington's Library of Congress to the World Wide Web. Around 3000 B.C.E. the ancient Egyptians used papyrus, but people later learned to make paper. The most important step in allowing libraries to flourish was Gutenberg's invention of the printing press. Photographs and illustrations illuminate the text. Bibliography, Chronology, Glossary, and Index.

195. Somervill, Barbara A. *The History of the Motion Picture.* (Our Changing World—The Timeline Library) Child's World, 2006. 32pp. ISBN 978-1-59296-440-6. Grades 3–7.

This book looks at the history of the motion picture by tracing the technological developments that have made it possible. In 1420, a "magic lantern" allowed light to cast unusual shadows. Puppets have long been popular, but not until the 20th century did motion pictures become truly advanced. Photographs and illustrations illuminate the text. Bibliography, Chronology, Glossary, and Index.

196. Steele, Philip. *Eyewitness: Vote.* DK, 2008. 72pp. ISBN 978-0-7566-3382-0. Grades 4–8.

This text examines the history of voting from ancient times to the present. The thirty two-page chapters discuss why people vote, voting's democratic beginnings, the first parliaments, revolution in North America, voting implements, France's revolution, slaves and their quest to become voting citizens, and votes for women. It continues with the "red revolution" in Russia, the fascists of China who wanted to vote, and modern struggles to vote. Other chapters describe American elections, polling days, what being voteless means, and other facts. Chronology, Glossary, and Index.

197. Steele, Philip. *Wonders of the World.* (Kingfisher Knowledge) Kingfisher, 2007. 64pp. ISBN 978-0-7534-5979-9. Grades 4–7.

Among the wonders that this book presents are the original seven wonders and others that have been acknowledged more recently. These include the Taj Mahal, the Hanging Gardens of Babylon, China's Three Gorges Dam, Venetian canals, the Great Wall of China, and modern buildings and bridges. The value of each structure or location is explained and other resources about the site are suggested. Further Reading, Glossary, Web Sites, and Index.

198. Steele, Philip. *The World of Pirates.* Kingfisher, 2004. 32pp. Paper ISBN 978-0-7534-5786-3. Grades 3–5.

Steele looks at the lives of pirates from Roman times through the 1990s. He tells about pirates in the Caribbean and in North America, China, the Middle East, Spain, and Britain. The illustrations decorating the capsule biographies of fifty rogues make his version especially attractive. Glossary and Index.

199. Stepan, Peter. *Photos That Changed the World: The 20th Century.* Prestel, 2006. 182pp. Paper ISBN 978-3-7913-3628-2. Grades YA.

This collection of approximately one hundred and fifty photographs from the 19th and 20th centuries includes images that have become a part of the American psyche. The compiler selected pictures that caused distress, disquiet, or sympathy in their viewers. Images that may be less familiar to the viewer show gold mine workers, Willy Brandt at the Warsaw Ghetto memorial, Pelé leading Brazil in the World Cup. Although mainly western, each picture represents an important moment in history. *School Library Journal Best Adult Books for Young Adults.*

200. *Street Smart! Cities of the Ancient World.* (Buried Worlds) Runestone, 1994. 80pp. ISBN 978-0-8225-3208-8. Grades 5–8.

Archaeologists designate their finds as "cities" only when at least several thousand people lived there and had control of an area outside the walls where they could grow food. Cities developed for economic reasons, for safety reasons, or for religious reasons.

The world's first city was probably Uruk in southern Mesopotamia, around 4000 B.C.E. Other Middle Eastern cities are Babylon (after 2000 B.C.E.), Zimbabwe (1000 B.C.E.), and Tell al-Amarna (1400 B.C.E.). Ancient cities of Asia along rivers include Mohenjo-Daro and Harappa (2400–1650 B.C.E.), Zhengzhou and An-Yang (1600–1400 B.C.E.), and Changan (207 B.C.E.). Ancient cities of the Mediterranean were Athens, Sparta, Knossos, Pompeii, and Rome. In the Americas, cities are still being discovered. The group that established the Olmec civilization's major city has not yet been identified. The Mayan Teotihuacán, destroyed in 750 C.E., was the first true urban center in the Americas. The largest Aztec city was Tenochtitln, lasting from 1325 until approximately 1521. Cuzco was a great Incan city, but thieves looted it in 1532. Pronunciation Guide, Glossary, and Index.

201. Sullivan, Robert. *Rats: Observations on the History and Habitat of the City's Most Unwanted Inhabitants.* Bloomsbury, 2004. 242pp. ISBN 978-1-58234-385-3; 2005. paper ISBN 978-1-58234-477-5. Grades YA.

Equipped with night-vision glasses, Sullivan spent time in an alley watching rats and noting their behavior. Here he describes their habits offers historical and anecdotal information about them. In the 1960s, a Harlem tenants' organizer named Jesse Ray fought against rats, as did Kit Burns in the 19th century. During the American Revolution Isaac Sears vowed to get rid of them. In the 1840s an Irish immigrant sponsored rat fights in his bar. The author notes that all large cities have rats—alley rats, sewer rats, and toilet rats—because they can live on garbage and quickly reproduce. *School Library Journal Best Adult Books for Young Adults* and *Alex Award*.

202. Swain, Ruth Freeman. *How Sweet It Is (and Was): The History of Candy.* Holiday House, 2003. 32pp. ISBN 978-0-8234-1712-4. Grades 2–5.

The author looks at popular candies and how they became connected to particular holidays—candy corn and Halloween, chocolate hearts for Valentine's Day. Swain covers Egyptian candy, Columbus's transportation of sugar cane seedlings to the Americas, Elizabethan sweetmeats, maple sugaring, South American chocolate production, and modern Denmark, where each Dane consumes 36 pounds of sweets a year (Americans typically eat 25 pounds). Recipes for sugar paste, Vassar fudge, and belly-guts taffy are included. Cross-hatched illustrations enhance the text. Bibliography and Chronology.

203. Tames, Richard. *Dictatorship.* Raintree, 2002. 64pp. ISBN 978-1-4034-0318-6. Grades 5–8.

A look at what makes a dictatorship, styles of dictatorship, fascism, and how a dictatorship ends. Short profiles of dictators including Mao, Sukarno, Pinochet, and Milosevic examine the actual behaviors of these leaders. Photographs and illustrations augment the text. Glossary, Chronology, Further Reading, Web Sites, and Index.

204. Tanaka, Shelley. *Mummies: The Newest, Coolest, and Creepiest from Around the World.* Abrams, 2005. 48pp. ISBN 978-0-8109-5797-8. Grades 4–7.

Readers will enjoy viewing full-color photographs of intact mummy faces of Tutankhamen, a seven-thousand-year-old child found in Chile, the Iceman of Europe, and contemporary Buddhist monks on display in Thailand. Mummy finds reveal the health, diet, cultural habits, and migration patterns of ancient societies. Chapters also cover how mummies are made and preserved as well as modern mummies of Vladimir Lenin and Mao Tse-tung. Photographs augment the text. Bibliography and Index. *Student Book Award* (Maine) nomination and *Voice of Youth Advocates Nonfiction Honor List*.

205. Taylor, Robert. *The History of Terrorism.* Lucent, 2002. 96pp. ISBN 978-1-59018-206-2. Grades 6 up.

This book examines individuals and groups throughout history who have used violent actions to create fear and advance their beliefs. The six chapters cover zealots; assassins; the Reign of Terror of the French Revolution; propaganda surrounding bombs; anti-colonial terrorism; terrorists of the left; separatist terrorism; and holy wars. It includes information on the terrorist mentality in a wide variety of settings, from presidential assassinations in the United States to the murder of Olympic athletes in Munich. Photographs and illustrations highlight the text. Bibliography, Notes, Further Reading, and Index.

206. Teresi, Dick. *Lost Discoveries: The Ancient Roots of Modern Science—From the Babylonians to the Maya.* Simon & Schuster, 2003. 453pp. Paper ISBN 978-0-7432-4379-7. Grades YA.

A look at the discoveries that ancient civilizations made in mathematics, astronomy, cosmology, physics, geology, chemistry, and technology. Among the civilizations presented are Sumerian, Babylonian, Mayan, Chinese, and other non-European groups. Sometimes discoveries by western groups such as the Greeks were replaced by better ideas developed elsewhere. The Sumerians discovered that the earth is round, the Arabs hypothesized that blood circulated, and the Indians used zero and negative numbers. Bibliography, Notes, and Index.

207. Thomas, Herbert. *Human Origins: The Search for Our Beginnings.* Translated by Paul G. Bahn. Abrams, 1995. 159pp. Paper ISBN 978-0-8109-2866-4. Grades YA.

The text covers various theories of early human life and who proposed them. As an introduction, it tells how the theories changed with new discoveries and increased scientific understanding. Photographs, maps, diagrams, and drawings augment the text. Bibliography, Chronology, Glossary, and Index.

208. Townsend, John. *Breakouts and Blunders.* (True Crime) Raintree, 2005. 48pp. Paper ISBN 978-1-4109-1433-0. Grades 5–9.

In a scrapbook format, a look at successful and unsuccessful prison escapes throughout history. Illustrations and photographs augment the text. Bibliography, Glossary, Further Reading, and Index.

209. Townsend, John. *Crime Through Time.* (Painful History of Crime) Raintree, 2005. 48pp. ISBN 978-1-4109-2051-5. Grades 6–9.

How people have broken laws, the types of crimes they have committed, what characteristics they tend to have, and how their crimes have been solved. Illustrations, photographs, and sidebars contain additional information. Glossary, Chronology, Further Reading, Web Sites, and Index.

210. Townsend, John. *Fakes and Forgeries.* (Painful History of Crime) Raintree, 2005. 48pp. ISBN 978-1-4109-1424-8; paper ISBN 978-1-4109-1430-9. Grades 6–9.

All about people who have engaged in swindling, money fraud, falsifying documents, and selling worthless "treasures." The scrapbook format features photographs and other illustrations to augment the text. Glossary, Further Reading, and Index.

211. Townsend, John. *Kidnappers and Assassins.* (True Crime) Raintree, 2005. 48pp. ISBN 978-1-4109-1426-2; paper ISBN 978-1-4109-1432-3. Grades 5–9.

Assassinations and kidnapping throughout history are discussed. Among the kidnapped are Patty Hearst, John Paul Getty III, and Elizabeth Smart. Those in the assassination section include Caesar, four U.S. presidents, Martin Luther King Jr., Malcolm X, and Robert F. Kennedy. Unsuccessful assassination attempts were made on Charles de Gaulle, Pope John Paul II, and President Reagan. Illustrations and photographs enhance the text. Bibliography, Glossary, Further Reading, and Index.

212. Townsend, John. *Prisons and Prisoners.* (Painful History of Crime) Raintree, 2005. 48pp. ISBN 978-1-4109-2053-9; paper ISBN 978-1-4109-2058-4. Grades 6–9.

The author examines prisons and prisoners throughout history from the days of the medieval castle dungeon to contemporary "supermax" prisons. He also considers prison reforms that have occurred through the years. Illustrations, photographs, and sidebars contain additional information. Glossary, Chronology, Further Reading, Web Sites, and Index.

213. Townsend, John. *Punishment and Pain.* (Painful History of Crime) Raintree, 2005. 48pp. ISBN 978-1-4109-2054-6; paper ISBN 978-1-4109-2059-1. Grades 6–9.

For criminals, torture and punishment are the norm. This book discusses methods of torture and death from the 1500s to the present. Illustrations, photographs, and sidebars contain additional information. Glossary, Chronology, Further Reading, Web Sites, and Index.

214. Walker, Richard. *Epidemics and Plagues.* (Kingfisher Knowledge) Kingfisher, 2006. 64pp. ISBN 978-0-7534-6035-1. Grades 6–9.

This history of epidemics and plagues covers the spread of infectious diseases and their impact on human populations beginning with the Black Death in medieval Europe. It includes a section on disease-causing pathogens and discusses contemporary plagues such as AIDS and SARS. Recent medical and scientific advances such as surveillance, prevention, and treatment have helped control some of these diseases, although much needs to be accomplished to stop them. Photographs, diagrams, and illustrations intensify the text. Glossary, Further Reading, Web Sites, and Index.

215. Whiting, Jim. *Bubonic Plague.* (Natural Disasters) Mitchell Lane, 2007. 32pp. ISBN 978-1-58415-494-5. Grades 4–6.

In Europe during the 1300s, a disease of unknown origin hit that killed people within hours or days. The text explains how this disease, labeled a natural disaster, spread through a population and discusses whether it could occur again. Photographs and illustrations augment the text. Chronology, Glossary, Further Reading, Web Sites, and Index.

216. Wilkinson, Philip. *Building.* Illustrated by Dave King and Geoff Dann. DK, 2000. 61pp. ISBN 978-0-7894-6026-4. Grades 4 up.

Photographs and drawings give clear pictures of the various aspects of construction. Topics covered in two-page spreads are structural engineering, house construction, and building materials. Readers will learn about wood, earth, bricks, stone, timber frames, roofs, thatching, columns and arches, vaults, staircases, fireplaces and chimneys, doors and doorways, windows, stained glass, balconies, and building on unusual topography. Index.

217. Winner, Cherie. *Circulating Life: Blood Transfusion from Ancient Superstition to Modern Medicine.* Twenty First Century, 2007. 112pp. ISBN 978-0-8225-6606-9. Grades 5–9.

This book discusses blood transfusions and blood itself. Early medical practitioners advocated bleeding and scarification and tried to transfer blood from person to person. When circulation became known, other aspects of blood became important. Researchers began blood typing, type matching, and fractionation with Charles Drew's work with plasma during World War II. Other advancements include the discovery of Rh factors, overcoming AIDS and other blood-transmitted viral diseases, the possibility of bionic blood, and the manufacture of artificial red blood cells. Photographs and illustrations highlight the text. Bibliography, Glossary, Further Reading, Web Sites, and Index.

218. Woods, Michael. *The History of Communications.* (Major Inventions Through History) Twenty-First Century, 2005. 56pp. ISBN 978-0-8225-3807-3. Grades 5–8.

The history of communications includes inventions such as the printing press, telephone, radio, television, and the Internet. These have influenced how people talk to one another and how information is conveyed between individuals and among groups. Before the printing press, all books were copied by hand. Radio waves were discovered in the 1800s, and today cellular telephones and wireless Internet connections continue to use them. Photographs and illustrations highlight the text. Bibliography, Glossary, Chronology, Notes, Further Reading, Web Sites, and Index.

219. Woods, Michael, and Mary B. Woods. *The History of Medicine.* (Major Inventions Through History) Twenty-First Century, 2005. 56pp. ISBN 978-0-8225-2636-0. Grades 5–8.

A look at the history of medicine through the topics of hand washing, vaccines, antibiotics, anesthetics, X-rays, and artificial limbs. Before physicians were aware of germs, people blamed their illnesses on witches and magic. Vaccines were introduced in 1796 and are still considered among the most important health inventions. Not until the mid-1880s did doctors begin to use anesthesia for operations. Before then, bones were set, teeth were pulled, and surgeries were performed without painkillers. Photographs and illustrations highlight the text. Bibliography, Glossary, Chronology, Further Reading, Web Sites, and Index.

220. Woolf, Alex. *Democracy.* (Systems of Government) World Almanac, 2006. 48pp. ISBN 978-0-8368-5883-9. Grades 4–6.

This history of democracy details what it is, how it works, and its problems and challenges. Photographs and illustrations highlight the text. Bibliography and Index.

221. Worth, Richard. *Gunpowder.* (Transforming Power of Technology) Chelsea, 2003. 112pp. ISBN 978-0-7910-7448-0. Grades 7–10.

A history of gunpowder and its impact on events. Gunpowder changed warfare and precipitated ethical issues associated with repeating rifles. Along with a study of weapons and warfare, this text looks at black powder and smokeless powder, two developments in this area. Illustrations highlight the text. Bibliography, Chronology, Further Reading, Web Sites, and Index.

222. Zimmerman, Karl. *Steam Boats: The Story of Lakers, Ferries, and Majestic Paddle-Wheelers.* Boyds Mills, 2007. 48pp. ISBN 978-1-5907-8434-1. Grades 4–8.

Readers will learn about the history and mechanics of steam-powered boats. Topics covered include the "age of steam," Mississippi River boating, and types of steamboats. These include paddle boats for leisure, "workhorse" ferries, and bulk carriers. Steamships also crossed the Atlantic, and the text includes details about these ships. Boxed sections include biographical profiles and extraneous information. Photographs enhance the text. Glossary, Web Sites, and Index.

223. Zoellner, Tom. *The Heartless Stone: A Journey Through the World of Diamonds, Deceit and Desire.* St. Martins, 2006. 293pp. ISBN 978-0-312-33969-2; Picador paper ISBN 978-0-312-33970-8. Grades YA.

This overview of diamonds and their history covers the world. Zoellner went to places where diamonds have been mined and focuses on them in each of his ten chapters. Diamonds were first discovered in India; since then, deposits have been discovered in locations including South Africa, Brazil, Canada, Angola, and Arkansas. All of the stages in diamond production—mining, manufacturing, trading, smuggling, marketing, and purchasing—involve some aspect of exploitation and deceit. New natural deposits and competition from synthetic diamond makers have finally helped loosen the De Beers cartel's grip on everything that has to do with this stone. Notes. *School Library Journal Best Adult Books for Young Adults.*

Biography and Collective Biography

224. Aaseng, Nathan. *Business Builders in Fashion.* Oliver, 2003. 160pp. ISBN 978-1-8815-0880-9. Grades 5–8.

This collective biography includes not only profiles of those who have made their names in fashion in Europe and America but also historical highlights of clothing since medieval times. Profiles include Charles Frederick Worth, Levi Strauss, Coco Chanel, Christian Dior, Mary Quant, Ralph Lauren, and Vera Wang. Photographs and illustrations highlight the text. Bibliography, Glossary, Chronology, Notes, and Index.

225. Aaseng, Nathan. *Business Builders in Toys and Games.* Oliver, 2003. 160pp. ISBN 978-1-8815-0881-6. Grades 5–8.

People need ways to spend their leisure time other than watching television. Some companies developed games before the advent of TV, and others have flourished in recent decades. This book looks at the history of games and then gives profiles of those who have successfully created, marketed, and sold them. Those included are Milton Bradley and his board games, Hiroshi Yamauchi and Nintendo, Albert Spaulding's sporting goods, Joshua Lionel Cowen and Lionel trains, Ruth Handler's Barbie doll and Mattel Corporation, Ole Kirk Christiansen's Legos, and Gary Gygax's Dungeons and Dragons. Photographs and illustrations highlight the text. Bibliography, Glossary, Chronology, Notes, and Index.

226. Armstrong, Mable. *Women Astronomers: Reaching for the Stars.* Stone Pine, 2008. 288pp. ISBN 978-0-9728929-5-7. Grades 5–7.

This collective biography introduces significant women in astronomy in chronological order, beginning with Enheduanna, the chief astronomer priestess who lived around 2350 B.C.E. Other women are Hypatia of Alexandria, Hildegard of Bingen, Caroline Herschel, Maria Mitchell, Williamina Stevens Fleming, Annie Jump Cannon, Henrietta Swan Leavitt, Antonia Caetano Maury, Cecilia Payne Gaposchkin, Helen Sawyer Hogg, Margaret Burbidge, Nancy Roman, Vera Rubin, Beatrice Tinsley, Jocelyn Bell Burwell, Margaret Geller, Carolyn Shoemaker, Sally Ride, Jill Tartar, and Wendy Freedman. They had to overcome much just to earn their degrees, get decent jobs, and make their discoveries. They are role models for younger women. Photographs highlight the text. Bibliography, Glossary, and Index.

227. Atkins, Jeannine. *How High Can We Climb? The Story of Women Explorers.* Farrar, 2005. 209pp. ISBN 978-0-374-33503-8. Grades 5–8.

This collective biography looks at women explorers who have overcome hardships to reach their goals. Those included are Jeanne Baret (who sailed around the world disguised as a boy), Florence Baker (who searched for the source of the Nile), Annie Smith Peck (a mountain climber), Josephine Peary (who explored the dangerous territory of the North Pole), Arnarulunguaq (who traced ancient Inuit stories), Elisabeth Casteret (a spelunker), Nicole Maxwell (who explored the rain forest), Sylvia Earle (who made a record deep-sea dive), Junko Tabei (who climbed Mount Everest), Kay Cotter (who made a nonstop solo voyage around the world in a 37-foot sloop), Sue Hendrickson (who discovered a *Tyrannosaurus Rex* skeleton), and Ann Bancroft (an Arctic explorer). Photographs and illustrations highlight the text. Bibliography, Chronology, Notes, and Index.

228. Ball, Heather. *Astonishing Women Artists.* (Women's Hall of Fame) Second Story, 2007. 120pp. Paper ISBN 978-1-897187-23-4. Grades 4–8.

This collective biography examines the artistic achievements of ten women who used their understanding of art in new ways for their times. Those included are Artemisia Gentileschi (Italy, 1593–1651/1653), Elisabeth Louise Vigée Le Brun (France, 1755–1842), Emily Carr (Canada, 1871–1945), Georgia O'Keeffe (United States, 1887–1986), Louise Nevelson (Russia and United States, 1899–1988), Frida Kahlo (Mexico, 1907–1954), Elizabeth Catlett (United States, 1915–), Kenojuak Ashevak (Canadian Inuit, 1927–), Faith Ringgold (United States, 1930–), and Mary Pratt (Canada, 1935–). Bibliography. *Voice of Youth Advocates Nonfiction Honor List.*

229. Ball, Heather. *Magnificent Women in Music.* (Women's Hall of Fame) Second Story, 2005. 108pp. Paper ISBN 978-1-897187-02-9. Grades 4–8.

This collective biography presents ten women who have made important contributions in music: Maria Anna "Nannerl" Mozart, Clara Schumann, Ethel Smyth, Marian Anderson, Ella Fitzgerald, Buffy Sainte-Marie, Joni Mitchell, k.d. lang, Chantal Kreviazuk, and Measha Brueggergosman. Anecdotes provide information about their lives and their accomplishments as well as the obstacles they faced and overcame in their attempts to make music. Photographs complement the text.

230. Bell-Scott, Patricia. *Life Notes: Personal Writings of Contemporary Black Women.* Norton, 1995. 429pp. Paper ISBN 978-0-393-31206-5. Grades YA.

This collective "biography" presents journal entries of fifty black women written as prose, poetry, letters, or meditations. The women are divorced, married, single mothers, disabled, educators, artists, lesbians, students, activists, and unemployed. They come from America, Africa, and Europe. They write about childhood, abuse, love, work, self identity, racial prejudice, politics, and creating one's place in society. Three common threads are that they are women, that they are black, and that they are honest. What they have to say gives insight into the human condition. Index.

231. Berliner, Don. *Aviation: Reaching for the Sky.* Oliver, 1996. 144pp. ISBN 978-1-881508-33-5. Grades 7 up.

People have been trying to fly for centuries. Berliner traces the accomplishments of men who, since the 18th century, built devices that actually stayed aloft. They include the Montgolfier brothers and the hot-air balloon (1783); Henri Giffard and the dirigible (1852); Otto Lilienthal and the glider (1891); Samuel Pierpont Langley and the *Aerodrome* (1896); the Wright brothers and their airplane (1903); Glenn Curtiss and the seaplane (1908); and Igor Sikorsky and the helicopter (1911). Photographs highlight the text. Important Events in Aviation History, Bibliography, and Index.

232. Blackwood, Gary L. *Highwaymen.* (Unsolved History) Benchmark, 2005. 72pp. ISBN 978-0-7614-1017-1. Grades 4–8.

The highwayman (or highwaywoman) has been around for a long time. This text looks at eight of them in Europe and the United States during the 18th century. They include Claude Duval, Mary Frith ("Moll Cutpurse"), William Nevison (the "Yorkshire Rogue"), Dick Turpin (the "Butcher Highwayman"), and John Thompson Hare. Photographs and reproductions highlight the text. Bibliography, Glossary, Notes, Further Reading, Web Sites, and Index.

233. Blackwood, Gary L. *Swindlers.* (Unsolved History) Benchmark, 2001. 72pp. ISBN 978-0-7614-1031-7. Grades 4–8.

Swindlers seem to have always been a part of society. This book looks at seven in Europe and the United States during the 19th century: Soapy Smith (a con artist of the American West), Joseph "Yellow Kid" Weil, Al Capone, Billy the Kid, William Henry Ireland (a forger of Shakespeare plays), Ellen Peck, and Fred Demara. Photographs and reproductions highlight the text. Bibliography, Glossary, Notes, Further Reading, Web Sites, and Index.

234. Bradley, Michael J. *The Birth of Mathematics: Ancient Times to 1300.* Chelsea House, 2006. 148pp. ISBN 978-0-8160-5423-7. Grades 6 up.

An introduction to nine men and one woman who made important contributions to mathematics from ancient times to 1300. It includes information about their discoveries, lives, and contributions, as well as further reading about each. Thales of Miletus (ca. 625–ca. 547 B.C.E.) made the earliest proofs of geometrical theorems. Pythagoras of Samos (ca. 560–ca. 480 B.C.E.) proved the theorem about right triangles, Euclid of Alexandria (ca. 325–ca. 270 B.C.E.) was a geometer who organized mathematics. Archimedes of Syracuse (ca. 287–12 B.C.E.) experimented with and developed techniques in geometry. Hypatia of Alexandria (ca. 370–415) was the first woman of mathematics. Aryabhata I (476–550) extrapolated the rotation of the earth from alphabetical numbers. Brahmagupta (598–668) became known as the father of numerical analysis. Abu Ja'far Muhammad ibn Musa al-Khwarizmi (ca. 800–ca. 847) is known as the father of algebra. Omar Khayyam (ca. 1048–ca. 1131) was not only a mathematician and astronomer but also a philosopher and poet. And finally, Leonardo Fibonacci (ca. 1175–ca. 1250) worked with Hindu-Arabic numerals in Europe and developed the Fibonacci series. Glossary, Further Reading, and Index.

235. Brill, Marlene Targ. *Extraordinary Young People.* Childrens, 1996. 212pp. Paper ISBN 978-0-51626-044-0. Grades 7 up.

Not all people wait until adulthood to show their talents. This book looks at more than fifty children and adolescents who have accomplished something during their young lives. Some of those included are Genghis Khan, Joan of Arc, John Stuart Mill, Phillis Wheatley, Wolfgang Amadeus Mozart, Rachel Carson, Maria Callas, S. E. Hinton, Wayne Gretzky, Pelé, and Maria Tallchief. More recent figures profiled include Wang Yani, Savion Glover, Tiger Woods, Midori, Nawrose Nur, and Ryan White. Additional essays cover engaging groups of young people who also made a mark on society. Photographs and reproductions highlight the text. Further Reading, Glossary, and Index.

236. Burns, Kevin. *Eastern Philosophy: The Greatest Thinkers and Sages from Ancient to Modern Times.* Enchanted Lion, 2006. 208pp. ISBN 978-1-59270-053-0. Grades 9 up.

Analysis of the work of nearly sixty of history's most influential Eastern thinkers. They include Indian, Islamic, Chinese, Korean, and Japanese philosophers. The philosophers are Charvaka, Vardhamana, Gautama, Kanada, Kapila, Patanjali, Jaimini, Badarayana, the Three Gunas, Nagarjuna, Vasubandhu, Gaudapada, Shankara, Ramanuja, Madhva Vivekananda, Mohandas Gandhi, Zoroaster (Zarathustra), Rabi'ah al'Adawiyah, Al-Kindi, Al-Hallaj, Al-Farabi, Al-Ash'ari, Avicenna (Ibn Sina), Al-Ghazali, Averroes (Ibn Rushd), Rumi, Ibn Khaldun, Confucius (Kongfuzi, K'ung Fu-Tzu), Mozi (Mo Tzu), Laozi (Lao Tzu), Zhuangzi (Chuang Tzu), Mencius (Mengzi, Menge K'e), Xunzi (Hsun Tzu), Hanfeizi (Han Fei Tzu), Huineng, Fazang (Fa Tsang), Zhang Zai, Zhuxi (Chu Hsi), Wang Yangming, Dai Zhen (Tai Chen), Mao Zedong (Mao Tse-tung), Honen, Shinran, Eisai, Dogen, Nichiren, and Nishida Kitaro. Bibliography, Notes, Glossary, Web Sites, and Index.

237. Cawthorne, Nigel J. *Military Commanders: The 100 Greatest Throughout History.* Enchanted Lion, 2004. 208pp. ISBN 978-1-59270-029-5. Grades 7 up.

Divided into eras, this book covers important figures in military history. Each entry includes a summary of the person's achievements and a chronology of major events of the time. Military leaders from the ancient world are Leonidas of Sparta, Sun Tzu, Alexander the Great, Hannibal, Scipio Africanus, Gaius Marius, Pompey, Julius Caesar, Marcus Agrippa, Augustus Octavian, Arminius, Claudius, Trajan, Constantine I, Alaric I, Flavius Aetius, Attila the Hun, and Belisarius. Important leaders of the Anglo-Saxons and the Vikings include Alfred the Great, Athelstan, Cnut, and Harold II. Listed as Middle Ages leaders are Charles Martel, Charlemagne, El Cid, Saladin, Richard the Lionheart, Genghis Khan, Alexander III of Scotland, Edward I, Edward III, Edward the Black Prince, Tamerlane, Henry V, and Gustavus II of Sweden. English Civil War leaders include Oliver Cromwell; Sir Thomas Fairfax; Prince Rupert; William of Orange; John Churchill; the Duke of Marlborough; and Charles XII. Leaders during the Restoration are John Campbell, Duke of Argyll; Charles Stuart; and William Augustus, Duke of Cumberland. During the Napoleonic Era, Lord Horatio Nelson; Sir John Moore; Arthur Wellesley, Duke of Wellington; Napoleon Bonaparte; and Michel Ney led their causes. The British Empire commanders include Lord Howard of Effingham, Sir Francis Drake, James Wolfe, Shaka Zulu, Sir Colin Campbell, and Charles Gordon. During the American War of Independence and the Civil War, George Washington, Andrew Jackson, Robert E. Lee, William T. Sherman, Ulysses S. Grant, and Thomas "Stonewall" Jackson led armies. Of the Native Americans, Cochise, Red Cloud, and Crazy Horse are included. From Prussia, the leaders are Frederick the Great, Graf Helmuth von Moltke, Prince Otto von Bismarck, and Alfred von Tirpitz. During the First World War, leaders of various groups include Paul von Hindenburg, John Joseph Pershing, Douglas Haig, Viscount Edmund Allenby, Sir Henry Rawlinson, Erich Ludendorff, Paul von Lettow-Vorbeck, and Kemal Ataturk. The Second World War leaders include Carl Gustav Mannerheim, Gerd von Rundstedt, Douglas MacArthur, Archibald Wavell, Viscount Alanbrooke, Yamamoto Isoroku, George S. Patton, Erich von Manstein, Bernard Law Montgomery, Heinz Guderian, Dwight D. Eisenhower, Erwin Rommel, Harold Alexander, Mao Tse-tung, William Slim, Omar Bradley, Georgy Zhukov, Ivan Konev, Vasily Chuikov, Orde Wingate, and Sir David Stirling. Military figures in the modern age are Vo Nguyen Giap, Moshe Dayan, and Colin Powell. Index.

238. **Chin-Lee, Cynthia.** *Akira to Zoltan: Twenty-Six Men Who Changed the World.*
Illustrated by Megan Halsey and Sean Addy. Charlesbridge, 2006. 32pp. ISBN 978-1-57091-579-6. Grades 3–7.

This book covers men in art, science, sports, and politics from around the world. Some of those included are Mohandas Gandhi, Walt Disney, Akira Kurosawa, Pelé, Ellison Shoji Ouizuka, Nelson Mandela, Langston Hughes, Diego Rivera, Greg Louganis, Octavio Paz, and Vine Deloria. Illustrations augment the text. Bibliography.

239. **Cropper, William H.** *Great Physicists: The Life and Times of Leading Physicists from Galileo to Hawking.* Oxford, 2004. 480pp. Paper ISBN 978-0-19-517324-6. Grades YA.

This collective biography presents thirty scientists and their contributions to society. The nine segments of the text feature brief biographies and descriptions of their work. Galileo Galilei and Isaac Newton represent mechanics. In the field of thermodynamics are Sadi Carnot, Robert Mayer, James Joule, Hermann Helmholtz, William Thomson, Rudolf Claudius, Willard Gibbs, and Walther Ernst. Michael Faraday and James Clerk Maxwell researched electromagnetism. Ludwig Boltzmann made discoveries in statistical mechanics while Albert Einstein understood relativity. In quantum mechanics, figures include Max Planck, Niels Bohr, Wolfgang Pauli, Werner Heisenberg, Erwin Schrodinger, and Louis de Broglie. Famous nuclear physicists include Marie Curie, Ernest Rutherford, Lise Meitner, and Enrico Fermi. Paul Dirca, Richard Feynman, and Murray Gell-Mann helped decipher particle physics. Edwin Hubble, Subrahmanyan Chandraskehar, and Stephen Hawking are known for astronomy, astrophysics, and cosmology. Chronology, Glossary, Further Reading, and Index.

240. **Ghezzi, Bert.** *Mystics and Miracles: True Stories of Lives Touched by God.* Loyola, 2004. 187pp. Paper ISBN 978-0-8294-2041-8. Grades YA.

This collective biography in six parts discusses different types of miracles and those who performed them. In "Miracles of Love" are St. Martin De Porres (1579–1639), St. Theresa Margaret (1747–1770), St. Elizabeth of Hungary (1207–1231), and Venerable Solanus Casey (1870–1957). The "Miraculous Prayer" section includes St. Catherine of Siena (1347–1380), St. Anthony of Egypt (ca. 251–356), St. Lutgarde of Aywieres (1182–1246), and St. Clare of Assisi (ca. 1193–1253). "Dreams, Visions, and Other Wonders" presents St. Perpetua (ca. 181–203), St. Gertrude the Great (1256–1302), and Blessed Padre Pio of Pietrelcina (1887–1968). "Miracles of Conversion" includes St. Dominic (1170–1221), St. Sabas and St. Apphian (the 4th century), St. Anthony of Padua (1195–1231), and St. Vincent Ferrer (ca. 1350–1419). "Miracles to Awaken" includes St. Francis of Assisi (1181–1226), St. Teresa of Avila (1515–1582), St. Francis of Paola (1416–1507), and St. John Bosco (1815–1888). Finally, in "Miracles that Changed History" are St. Joan of Arc (ca. 1412–1431), St. Patrick (ca. 389–ca. 461), St. Ignatius of Loyola (1491–1556), and St. Francis Xavier (1506–1552). Bibliography and Glossary.

241. Gifford, Clive. *Ten Explorers Who Changed the World.* Illustrated by David Cousens. Kingfisher, 2008. 63pp. ISBN 978-0-7534-6103-7. Grades 5–7.

This collective biography presents the journeys of ten explorers and examines their motivations, their routes, and their discoveries that changed history. Those included are Marco Polo (1254–1324), Christopher Columbus (1451–1506), Ferdinand Magellan (1480–1521), Samuel de Champlain (1567–1635), James Cook (1728–1799), Alexander von Humboldt (1769–1859), Meriwether Lewis (1774–1809), Richard Burton (1821–1890), Roald Amundsen (1872–1928), and Jacques Yves Cousteau (1910–1997). Photographs, maps, and illustrations highlight the text. Glossary and Index.

242. Gifford, Clive. *Ten Leaders Who Changed the World.* Illustrated by David Cousens. Kingfisher, 2008. 63pp. ISBN 978-0-7534-6104-4. Grades 5–7.

This collective biography focuses on ten leaders whose guidance changed the course of the 20th century, whether for good or for ill. The leaders included are Mohandas Gandhi (1869–1948), Winston Churchill (1874–1965), Charles de Gaulle (1890–1970), Franklin Delano Roosevelt (1882–1945), Mao Tse-tung (1893–1976), Joseph Stalin (1878–1953), Adolf Hitler (1889–1945), Mikhail Gorbachev (1931–) , Fidel Castro (1926–), and Nelson Mandela (1918–). Gifford provides information about their lives, their actions, and their decisions. Maps and illustrations highlight the text. Glossary and Index.

243. Harris, Bruce. *Wild About Flying: The Dreamers, Doers, and Daredevils of Aviation.* Illustrated by David Marshall. Firefly, 2003. 240pp. ISBN 978-1-55297-849-8. Grades YA.

Since 1903 when the Wright brothers first flew, aviation has changed drastically. More than 50 noteworthy pioneers, inventors, aviators, designers, engineers, navigators, test pilots, and visionaries from Great Britain, France, the Netherlands, Germany, Russia, and America have contributed to these changes. Some considered the airplane a weapon while others saw the commercial value of this machine. The book features short biographies in three sections: "The Dreamers," "The Doers," and "The Daredevils." With color paintings, archival photographs, and timelines.

244. Hatt, Christine. *Scientists and Their Discoveries.* Watts, 2001. 64pp. ISBN 978-0-531-14614-9. Grades 6–9.

Chemists, geologists, biologists, astronomers, and physicists are included in this collective biography. Primary and secondary sources such as diary entries, government documents, and newspaper accounts present background information. The two-page spreads contain maps, charts, and photographs. Illustrations also highlight the text. Index.

245. Hazell, Rebecca. *Heroines: Great Women Through the Ages.* Abbeville, 1996. 79pp. ISBN 978-0-7892-0210-9. Grades 5–8.

This book covers twelve women in history—from ancient Greece to contemporary times. In addition to information about each woman, Hazell provides background on the culture and times in which she lived. Included are Lady Murasaki Shikibu (973?–1025?), Sacagawea (1786?–1812), Agnodice of ancient Greece, Anna Akhmatova (1888–1966), Madame Sun Yat-Sen (1893–1931), Frida Kahlo (1907–1954), Eleanor of Aquitaine (1122–1202), Joan of Arc (ca. 1412–1431), Queen Elizabeth I (1533–1603), Harriet Tubman (1820?–1913), Marie Curie (1867–1934), and Amelia Earhart (1897–1937). Further Reading.

246. Herron, Carolivia. *Always an Olivia: A Remarkable Family History.* Illustrated by Jeremy Tugeau. Kar-Ben, 2007. 32pp. ISBN 978-0-8225-7049-3. Grades 1–4.

In 1957 Great-Grandma Olivia tells young Carol Olivia about their ancestors, Jews forced from Spain during the Inquisition of the 1400s. They went first to Portugal and then to Venice without revealing their religion. Many years later, pirates kidnapped a woman named Sarah, and she was rescued by James, also a captive. They escaped with the help of Jews from Tripoli in Libya and went to the Georgia Sea Islands near the United States in 1805. They married and assimilated among the Geechees, the free descendants of West African slaves, with Sarah taking the name Sarah Olivia. They forgot about being Jewish although they still lit Shabbat candles. Each generation remembered Sarah by giving one child the name Olivia, meaning "peace," since Sarah's Hebrew name, Shulamit, also means "peace." Paintings recreate the various moods that fill the story. Bibliography.

247. Hunter, Jason. *Communist Leaders.* (Profiles in History) Greenhaven, 2005. 240pp. ISBN 978-0-7377-2136-2. Grades 10 up.

This collective biography looks at the major figures who were part of the Communist movement and includes as primary sources some of their writings. Those featured are Marx, Engels, Lenin, Stalin, Fidel Castro, Ho Chi Minh, Mao Zedong, and Pol Pot. Bibliography, Further Reading, and Index.

248. Krull, Kathleen. *Lives of Extraordinary Women: Rulers, Rebels (and What the Neighbors Thought).* Illustrated by Kathryn Hewitt. Harcourt, 2000. 95pp. ISBN 978-0-15-200807-9. Grades 5–8.

Twenty of the most influential women in history appear in this collective biography that discusses their accomplishments and the quirks that made them individuals. Those included are Cleopatra, Eleanor of Aquitaine, Joan of Arc, Isabella I, Elizabeth I, Nzingha, Catherine the Great, Marie Antoinette, Victoria, Harriet Tubman, Tz'u-Hsi, Gertrude Bell, Jeanette Rankin, Eleanor Roosevelt, Golda Meir, Indira Gandhi, Eva Péron, Wilma Mankiller, Aung San Suu Kyi, and Rigoberta Manchu. Illustrations enhance the text. Further Reading.

249. Krull, Kathleen. *Lives of the Artists: Masterpieces, Messes (and What the Neighbors Thought).* Illustrated by Kathryn Hewitt. Harcourt, 1995. 96pp. ISBN 978-0-15-200103-2. Grades 4–8.

Chronologically arranged vignettes give interesting insights into artists' lives and sometimes their relationships to one another. The artists are Leonardo da Vinci (Italy, 1452–1519), Michelangelo Buonarroti (Italy, 1475–1564), Pieter Bruegel (Netherlands, 1525–1569), Sofonisba Anguissola—who served King Philip II of Spain although Italian (1532–1625), Rembrandt van Rijn (Holland, 1606–1669), Katsushika Hokusai (Japan, 1760–1849), Mary Cassatt (United States and France, 1845–1926), Vincent van Gogh (Holland, 1853–1890), Käthe Kollwitz (Germany, 1867–1945), Henri Matisse (France, 1869–1954), Pablo Picasso (Spain 1881–1973), Marc Chagall (Russia, 1887–1985), Marcel Duchamp (France, 1887–1968), Georgia O'Keeffe (United States, 1887–1986), William H. Johnson (United States, 1901–1970), Salvador Dali (Spain, 1904–1989), Isamu Noguchi (United States, 1904–1988), Diego Rivera (Mexico, 1886–1957), Frida Kahlo (Mexico, 1907–1954), and Andy Warhol (United States, 1928–1987). Artistic Terms, Index of Artists, and For Further Reading and Looking. *IRA Teachers' Choices, American Bookseller Pick of the Lists*, and *New York Public Library's Books for the Teen Age*.

250. Krull, Kathleen. *Lives of the Athletes: Thrills, Spills (and What the Neighbors Thought)*. Illustrated by Kathryn Hewitt. Harcourt, 1997. 96pp. ISBN 978-0-15-200806-2. Grades 4–8.

In capsule biographies, Krull tells a little about the lives of some international athletes away from their sports. She includes commentary on Jim Thorpe (1888–1953), Duke Kahanamoku (1890–1968), Babe Ruth (1895–1948), Red Grange (1903–1991), Johnny Weissmuller (1903–1984), Gertrude Ederle (1906–2003), Babe Didrikson Zaharias (1911–1956), Sonja Henie (1912–1969), Jesse Owens (1913–1980), Jackie Robinson (1919–1972), Sir Edmund Hillary (1919–2008), Maurice Richard (1921–), Maureen Connolly (1934–1969), Roberto Clemente (1934–1972), Wilma Rudolph (1940–1994), Arthur Ashe (1943–1993), Pete Maravich (1947–1988), Bruce Lee (1940–1973), Pelé (1940–), and Flo Hyman (1954–1986). Selected Bibliography.

251. Krull, Kathleen. *Lives of the Musicians: Good Times, Bad Times (and What the Neighbors Thought)*. Illustrated by Kathryn Hewitt. Harcourt, 1993. 96pp. ISBN 978-0-15-248010-3; 2002. paper ISBN 978-0-15-216436-2. Grades 4–8.

Vignettes on musicians, arranged chronologically, give interesting insights into their lives and sometimes their relationships to one another. The musicians included are Antonio Vivaldi (Italy, 1876–1741), Johann Sebastian Bach (Germany, 1685–1750), Wolfgang Amadeus Mozart (Austria, 1756–1791), Ludwig van Beethoven (Germany, 1770–1827), Frédéric Chopin (Poland, 1810–1849), Giuseppe Verdi (Italy, 1813–1901), Clara Schumann (Germany, 1819–1896), Stephen Foster (United States, 1826–1864), Johannes Brahms (Germany, 1833–1897), Peter Ilich Tchaikovsky (Russia, 1840–1893), William Gilbert (England, 1836–1911) and Arthur Sullivan (England, 1842–1900), Erik Satie (France, 1866–1925), Scott Joplin (United States, 1868–1917), Charles Ives (United States, 1874–1954), Igor Stravinsky (Russia, 1882–1971), Nadia Boulanger (France, 1887–1979), Sergei Prokofiev (Ukraine, 1891–1953), George Gershwin (United States, 1898–1937), and Woody Guthrie (United States, 1912–1967). Musical Terms, Index of Composers, and For Further Reading and Listening. *Boston Globe-Horn Book Honor*, *American Library Association Notable Children's Books*, *Notable Children's Trade Books in the Field of Social Studies*, *PEN Center USA West Literary Award*, *IRA Teachers' Choices*, *New York Public Library's Books for the Teen Age*, and *Golden Kite Honor*.

252. Krull, Kathleen. *Lives of the Writers: Comedies, Tragedies (and What the Neighbors Thought)*. Illustrated by Kathryn Hewitt. Harcourt, 1994. 96pp. ISBN 978-0-15-248009-7. Grades 4–8.

Vignettes on writers, arranged chronologically, give interesting insights into their lives and sometimes their relationships to one another. Writers covered are Murasaki Shikibu (Japan, 973?–1025?), Miguel de Cervantes (Spain, 1547–1616), William Shakespeare (England, 1564–1616), Jane Austen (England, 1775–1817), Hans Christian Andersen (Denmark, 1805–1875), Edgar Allan Poe (United States, 1809–1849), Charles Dickens (England, 1812–1870), Charlotte Brontë (England, 1816–1855) and Emily Brontë (England, 1818–1848), Emily Dickinson (United States, 1830–1886), Louisa May Alcott (United States, 1832–1888), Mark Twain (United States, 1835–1910), Frances Hodgson Burnett (England, 1849–1924), Robert Louis Stevenson (Scotland, 1850–1894), Jack London (United States, 1876–1916), Carl Sandburg (United States, 1878–1967), E. B. White (United States, 1899–1985), Zora Neale Hurston (United States, 1901?–1960), Langston Hughes (United States, 1902–1967), and Isaac Bashevis Singer (Poland and United States, 1904–1991). Literary Terms, Index of Writers, and For Further Reading and Writing. *American Bookseller Pick of the Lists*, *National Council of Teachers of English*

Notable Children's Trade Books in the Language Arts, and *International Reading Association Teachers' Choices*.

253. Landrum, Gene N. *Profiles of Female Genius: Thirteen Creative Women Who Changed the World.* Prometheus, 1994. 437pp. ISBN 978-0-8797-5892-9. Grades YA.

In looking at female genius, Landrum examines self-esteem, birth order, childhood transience, role models, education, intelligence, crisis, personality traits, and temperament. With strict criteria for selection, he presents profiles of thirteen women who helped make significant changes in their fields. The women are Mary Kay Ash in cosmetics (1917–), Maria Callas in opera (1923–1977), Liz Claiborne in women's clothes (1929–), Jane Fonda in video and movies (1937–), Estée Lauder in cosmetics (1908–), Madonna in entertainment (1958–), Golda Meir in politics (1898–1978), Ayn Rand in philosophical literature (1905–1982), Gloria Steinem in women's issues (1934–), Margaret Thatcher in politics (1925–), Lillian Vernon in catalog sales (1928–), Linda Wachner in lingerie (1946–), and Oprah Winfrey in television talk (1954–). References and Index.

254. Landrum, Gene N. *Profiles of Genius: Thirteen Creative Men Who Changed the World.* Prometheus, 1993. 236pp. ISBN 978-0-8797-5832-5. Grades YA.

By examining innovation, change, and personality, Landrum suggests ten reasons why traditional managers are not innovative. Using strict criteria for selection, he chooses thirteen innovators and discusses their characteristics. He presents Steven Jobs (1955–) and Apple Computers, Fred Smith (1944–) and Federal Express, Tom Monaghan (1937–) and Domino's Pizza, Nolan Bushnell (1943–) and Atari and Pizza Time Theater, William Gates III (1955–) and Microsoft, Marcel Bich (1914–) and Bic Pens, Solomon Price (1916–) and Price Club, Howard Head (1914–1991) and Head Ski and Prince Tennis, William Lear (1902–1978) and Learjet, Soichiro Honda (1906–1991) and Honda Motors, Akio Morita (1921–) and Sony, Arthur Jones (1923–) and Nautilus, and Ted Turner (1938–) and Turner Broadcasting. Bibliography and Index.

255. Laver, Sarah, and Rachel Hutchings. *1000 Years of Famous People.* Kingfisher, 2002. 256pp. ISBN 978-0-7534-5540-1. Grades 4 up.

This collective biography profiles more than a thousand people who achieved something during the last millennium. The ten sections look at world leaders, explorers, scientists, engineers and inventors, writers and reformers, stars of stage and screen, artists and architects, musicians and dancers, sports stars, and movers and shakers. Web Sites and Index.

256. McCullough, David. *Brave Companions: Portraits in History.* Touchstone, 1992. 240pp. Paper ISBN 978-0-671-79276-3. Grades YA.

The seventeen essays and speeches in this book sketch portraits of people important to the history of the United States, such as Alexander von Humboldt and his South American explorations, Louis Agassiz and his impact on American families and their education, Teddy Roosevelt and his conservationism, Miriam Rothschild and her work in zoology, and Harriet Beecher Stowe and her writing. Other figures come from the professions of social work, architecture, literature, etymology, and history. They include the Marquis de Morès, Frederick Remington, W. A. Roebling, Beryl Markham, Conrad Richter, Harry Caudill, David Plowden, and Simon Willard. Index.

257. McCutcheon, Marc. *The Kid Who Named Pluto: And the Stories of Other Extraordinary Young People in Science.* Illustrated by John Cannell. Chronicle, 2004. 85pp. ISBN 978-0-8118-3770-5; 2008. paper ISBN 978-0-8118-5451-1. Grades 3–6.

Young people have long made impacts on scientific research and discovery. This book profiles some of them, with information about their lives and their contributions. Philo T. Farnsworth first thought about the television at age 14. Mary Anning found an *ichthyosaur* specimen when she was 12. Others who blossomed early include rocketeer Robert Goddard, astronomer Truman Stafford, educator Louis Braille, and polymath Isaac Asimov. Illustrations enhance the text. Further Reading.

258. Meltzer, Milton. *Ten Kings: And the Worlds They Ruled.* Scholastic, 2002. 144pp. Paper ISBN 978-0-439-31293-6. Grades 4–8.

An examination of the lives and laws made by ten kings gives insight into their power and their understanding of their subjects. The kings included are Hammurabi, David, Peter the Great, Mansa Musa of the Mali, Atahualpa of the Inca, Alexander the Great, Attila the Hun, Kublai Khan, Charlemagne, and Louis XIV. In each chapter, Meltzer presents a map of the area over which the king ruled along with personal stories, information about the civilization and the time period in which he lived, and statistics about his reign. Illustrations, Notes, Bibliography, and Index. *Parents' Choice Gold Award.*

259. Raczka, Bob. *Here's Looking at Me: How Artists See Themselves.* Millbrook, 2006. 32pp. ISBN 978-0-7613-3404-0; paper ISBN 978-0-8225-7305-0. Grades 4–7.

Self-portraits of fourteen artists are accompanied by brief accounts of their lives and their works. Commentary on each artist faces a full-page portrait. Among the artists depicted are Albrech Durer, Francisco Goya, Marc Chagall, Norman Rockwell, Cindy Sherman, Artemisia Gentileschi, Jan Vermeer, and Chuck Close.

260. Rappoport, Ken. *Profiles in Sports Courage.* Peachtree, 2006. 151pp. ISBN 978-1-56145-368-9. Grades 4–8.

This book profiles twelve outstanding athletes of the 20th century. They include Jackie Robinson, Janet Guthrie, Gail Devers, Curt Flood, Junko Tabei (the first woman to climb Mount Everest), Jim Abbott, Muhammad Ali, Lance Armstrong, and Kerri Strug. The profiles concentrate on the athletes' specific challenges and how they overcame them to succeed. Photographs illustrate the text. Bibliography. *Voice of Youth Advocates Nonfiction Honor List.*

261. Sanderson, Ruth. *More Saints: Lives and Illuminations.* Eerdmans, 2007. ISBN 978-0-8028-5272-4. Grades 4–7.

This collective biography of saints from the second millennium profiles 36 men and women. They include Dominic, Clare, Thomas Aquinas, Joan of Arc, Francis, Padre Pio, Teresa, Rita of Cascia, Francis Xavier, and Elizabeth Anne Seton. Each saint's cause is included; their deaths are not described. Pencil-and-oil portraits highlight the text. Glossary, Further Reading, Web Sites, and Index.

262. Sanderson, Ruth. *Saints: Lives and Illuminations.* Eerdmans, 2003. 40pp. ISBN 978-0-8028-5220-5; 2007. paper ISBN 978-0-8028-5332-5. Grades 2–6.

This collective biography includes profiles of forty Roman Catholic and Orthodox saints from the first millennium. Among those included are Cecilia, Barbara, Christopher,

Patrick, Nicholas, Benedict, Scholastica, Augustine, Monica, Constantine, Helen, Maud, Theodora, Catherine, Stephen, and Dorothy. Although their deaths are not described, each patron saint's cause is included. Pencil and oil portraits highlight the text.

263. Scandiffio, Laura. *Evil Masters: The Frightening World of Tyrants.* Annick, 2005. 230pp. ISBN 978-1-55037-895-5; paper ISBN 978-1-55037-894-8. Grades 7–10.

This collective biography examines the lives of seven tyrannical rulers during the past 3,000 years. To gain and maintain control of their governments, they created fear and pitted people against each other. Those featured include Joseph Stalin, Adolf Hitler, Saddam Hussein, Robespierre, Ivan the Terrible, Nero, and Chinese emperor Qin Shi Huangdi. Others briefly mentioned are Francois Duvalier, Augusto Pinochet, Pol Pot, Idi Amin, and Kim Jong Il. Reproductions, maps, and photographs augment the text. Bibliography, Glossary, Chronology, Notes, Further Reading, Web Sites, and Index.

264. Scheller, William. *Amazing Archaeologists and Their Finds.* Oliver, 1994. 160pp. ISBN 978-1-881508-17-5. Grades 6 up.

Through the ceaseless work of people intrigued by the past, many secrets of history have been unlocked. The individuals and their finds discussed in this book are: Austen Henry Layard (1817–1884) and Hormuzd Rassam (1826–1910), who found Assyria; Henri Mouhot (1826–1861), discoverer of the Temple of Angkor in present-day Cambodia; Heinrich Schliemann (1822–1890), who uncovered Troy; Sir Arthur Evans (1851–1941), Knossos; Edward Thompson (1840–1935), the sacred well at Chichén Itzá; Hiram Bingham (1875–1956), the Inca hideaway at Machu Picchu; Howard Carter (1874–1939), the tomb of Tutankhamen in Egypt; and Kathleen Kenyon (1906–1978), the biblical city of Jericho. Time Line of Ancient Civilizations, Bibliography, and Index.

265. Turner, Pamela S. *A Life in the Wild: George Schaller's Struggle to Save the Last Great Beasts.* Melanie Kroupa, 2008. 103pp. ISBN 978-0-374-34578-5. Grades 4–8.

Conservationist George B. Schaller (1933–) has studied wildlife around the world by counting animals, observing them, and photographing them in their habitats. He has seen Central Africa's mountain gorillas and Tibet's snow leopards. This biography looks examines six of his studies in detail—gorillas in the Belgian Congo (1959–1960), a tiger clan in central India (1963–1965), lions in Tanzania (1966–1969), the snow leopard in the Himalayas of Pakistan and Nepal (1969–1975), pandas in central China (1980–1985), and asses and antelopes on the Tibetan Plateau of western China (1985 to the present). Photographs and illustrations intensify the text. Bibliography, Further Reading, Web Sites, and Index. *Notable Trade Books in the Field of Social Studies*

266. Vare, Ethlie Ann, and Greg Ptacek. *Patently Female: From AZT to TV Dinners, Stories of Women Inventors and Their Breakthrough Ideas.* John Wiley, 2001. 220pp. ISBN 978-0-471-02334-0. Grades YA.

This collective biography looks at women whose inventions affected almost everyone's life. The inventions are grouped into ten chapters, including "Practicalities" (Catherine Littlefield Greene's cotton gin, Mary Anderson's windshield wipers, and single mother Bessie Nesmith's Liquid Paper), "Woman's Work" (Hannah Slater's cotton sewing thread in 1793, Melitta Benz's drip coffee maker, Lucille Florence Taylor's fabric softener, TV dinners), "Computer Liberation" (Grace Murray Hopper's computer language), and "Fun and Games" (Ruth Handler's Barbie doll and Gertrude and Francis Rogallo's hang glider). Women invented the jockstrap, cordless telephone, voting machine, and Mars rover. They also discovered the pulsar and immunosuppressants as well as many other items and ideas. Chronology and Index.

267. Venables, Stephen. *Voices from the Mountains: 40 True-Life Stories of Unforgettable Adventure, Drama and Human Endurance.* Reader's Digest, 2006. 192pp. ISBN 978-0-7621-0810-7. Grades YA.

A history of attempts to conquer the earth's highest peaks from 1889 to recent years. Among the climbers included are Norway, Hillary, Messner, Martin Ekroll, and Bell. Some of the peaks are Mount Everest, Lhotse Middle, Mount Erebus, and El Capitan. The author presents statistics about each mountain's height, location, and first ascent before cataloging the mountain's successful climbers. Photographs enhance the text.

268. Williams, Marcia. *Hooray for Inventors!* Candlewick, 2005. 40pp. ISBN 978-0-7636-2760-7. Grades 2–5.

This collective biography profiles more than one hundred of the world's most influential inventors. Additional sidebars focus on particular inventions such as eyeglasses (1280), the toothpaste tube (1892), the ballpoint pen (1938), the chocolate bar (1819), and the personal computer (1977). Among the inventors are James Watt, Johannes Gutenberg, Guglielmo Marconi, John Logie Baird, Earle Dickson, Clarence Birdseye, and Antonio Meucci. Illustrations highlight the text. Index.

269. Wills, Garry. *Certain Trumpets: The Call of Leaders.* Touchstone, 1995. 336pp. Paper ISBN 978-0-684-80138-4. Grades YA.

To examine leadership, Wills looks at Cesare Borgia (1476?–1507), Dorothy Day (1897–1980), King David (?–961 B.C.E.), Mary Baker Eddy (1821–1910), Martha Graham (1893–1991), Martin Luther King, Jr. (1929–1968), Napoleon (1769–1821), Ross Perot (1930–), Franklin D. Roosevelt (1882–1945), Eleanor Roosevelt (1884–1962), Socrates (ca. 470–399 BC), Carl Stotz (1910?–1992), Harriet Tubman (ca. 1820–1913), Andrew Young (1932–), and George Washington (1732–1799). He analyzes what these people did, assesses their qualities to find what one should expect of a leader, and decides that good leaders concern themselves with the best situation for all, the "common good." Bibliography and Index.

270. Yolen, Jane. *Sea Queens: Women Pirates Around the World.* Illustrated by Christine Joy Pratt. Charlesbridge, 2008. ISBN 978-1-58089-131-8. Grades 4–6.

This collective biography of women who became pirates out of necessity, desperation, or greed covers the following: Artemisia, Admiral-Queen, Persia (500–480 B.C.E.); Queen Teuta, Illyria, (ca. 230 B.C.E.); Alfhild, Denmark (ca. 800); Jeanne de Belleville, Brittany (ca. 1350); Grania O'Malley, Ireland (ca. 1550); Lady Killigrew, England (ca.1590); Pretty Peg and the Dutch Privateer, Holland (ca. 1600); Charlotte de Berry, England (ca. 1650); Anne Bonney and Mary Read, American colonies (ca. 1725); Rachel Wall, United States (ca. 1789); Mary Anne Talbot, England (ca. 1790); and Madame Ching, China (ca. 1800). Madame Ching wins the tile of the "most successful pirate in the world." Both facts and legends swirl around these women, and the text tries to distinguish between them. Alfhild of Denmark kept a pet viper to deter men. Jeanne the Lioness of Brittany sold her land, bought ships, and attacked the French to avenge the murder of her husband. And Wall was the last woman hanged on Boston Common in

1789. Illustrations accompany the text. Bibliography, Web Sites, and Index. *Notable Trade Books in the Field of Social Studies.*

271. Zalben, Jane Breskin. ***Paths to Peace: People Who Changed the World.*** Dutton, 2006. 46pp. ISBN 978-0-525-47734-1. Grades 4–8.

This collective biography features sixteen peacemakers from around the world. They include Mahatma Gandhi, César Chavez, Anwar El-Sadat, Princess Diana, Ralph Waldo Emerson, Martin Luther King Jr., Daw Aung San Suu Kyi, Anne Frank, John F. Kennedy, Eleanor Roosevelt, Elie Wiesel, and Wangari Maathai. Illustrations enhance the text. Bibliography, Glossary, Notes, Further Reading, Web Sites, and Index.

Graphic Novels, Biographies, and Histories

272. Gonick, Larry. ***The Cartoon History of the Modern World, Part 1: From Columbus to the U. S. Constitution.*** Collins, 2007. 272pp. Paper ISBN 978-0-06-076004-5. Grades 9 up.

Beginning with a brief discussion of pre-Columbian America, the author presents topics relating to the modern world of the Americas from the Spanish conquest of South and Central America, especially Mexico, Peru, and the Caribbean. Portuguese trade and the United Provinces of the Netherlands are also included. The conquests of explorers Magellan and Vasco da Gama, along with the influences of Henry VIII, Machiavelli, the Protestant Reformation, Shakespeare, Hobbes, and Locke on the New World are topics delivered with humor and "political incorrectness." The cartoon graphics underscore the ironic and anecdotal presentation. Index.*School Library Journal Best Books for Young Adults.*

273. Gonick, Larry. ***The Cartoon History of the Universe III: From the Rise of Arabia to the Renaissance.*** Norton, 2002. 272pp. Paper ISBN 978-0-393-32403-7. Grades 9 up.

The text begins in 395 when Europe's pagan temples were closed, continues through the founding of Islam in the early 600s, and ends when Columbus departs from Spain in 1492. It covers Charlemagne, the Battle of Hastings, the Crusades, and Joan of Arc while discussing such topics as the Byzantine Empire, China, Turco-Mongol tribes, sub-Saharan Africa, and India. Cartoon graphics highlight the ironic and anecdotal nature of the text. Bibliography. The preceding volumes were *The Cartoon History of the Universe I: From the Big Bang to Alexander the Great, Vols. 1–7* and *The Cartoon History of the Universe II: From the Springtime of China to the Fall of Rome, Vols. 8–13.*

274. Rall, Ted. ***Silk Road to Ruin: Is Central Asia the New Middle East?*** Nantier Beall Minoustchine, 2006. 303pp. ISBN 978-1-56163-454-5. Grades YA.

Tajikistan, Kazakhstan, Turkmenistan, Kyrgyzstan, and Uzbekistan are former Soviet bloc countries that form the area of the world known as the "Silk Road." At present, they are places of discord and problems. The author traveled through them from 1997 to 2002, seeing their beauty and their bazaars. He relates his experiences along with the histories of these countries. Photographs and illustrations augment the text. *School Library Journal Best Adult Books for Young Adults.*

DVDs

275. *Discoveries . . . Spain: Castles, Cathedrals and Roman Ruins.* Bennett-Watt, 2003. 60 min. ISBN 978-1-932068-47-4. Grades 5 up.

This video traces the history of Spain through structures built by the Celts, Visigoths, Romans, Moors, and Christians. Today, Roman bridges, highways, and aqueducts still function, and Moorish tiles and carvings display eloquent beauty. Specific structures shown include Sevilla's Arabian palace; the castle in Segovia; Medellin's old Roman bridge; Trujillo's Moorish castle; and cathedrals at Astorga, Avila, Toledo, Segovia, and Sevilla.

276. *Einstein's Big Idea.* (NOVA) WGBH, 2005. 112 min. ISBN 978-1-59375-317-7. Grades YA.

Among those whose work preceded Einstein's discovery of E = mc? were Michael Faraday (a poor blacksmith's son), Antoine Lavoisier (punished with the guillotine), and Lise Meitner (a victim of Nazi persecution). This DVD presents biographical and historical information showing what the scientists prior to Einstein thought and how he questioned their theories. He needed their work in order to succeed in his own. Reenactments help to explain Einstein's ideas about light, atoms, and the theory of relativity.

277. *Famous Paintings.* Chip Taylor Communications, 2002. 20 min. Grades 7 up.

Clever clay animation creates narratives that evolve into famous paintings so that the viewer gains a completely different concept of the work. In Level 1, Koopman presents Breugel's *Tower of Babel*; van Gogh's *Bedroom at Arles*; Dali's *The Persistence of Memory*; Monet's *Nympheus*; Mondrian's *Broadway Boogie Woogie*; Vermeer's *Girl with a Pearl Earring*; Van Der Goes's *The Fall of Man*; Arcimboldo's *The Summer*; Cézanne's *Still Life with Apples and Mug*; and Magritte's *La Grande Guerre*, *Ceci N'est Pas une Pomme*, and *La Durée Poignardée*. Level 2 adds Ensor's *Squellettes se disputant un Pendu*; Goya's *Maja Desnuda*; Bosch's *Prodigal Son* and Rembrandt's *Jewish Bride*. *Special Jury Prize-Cannes Film Festival.*

278. *Fighting 20th-Century Tyranny.* Discovery Channel School, 2004. 52 min. ISBN 978-1-58738-968-9. Grades 6–12.

Graphics, archival video, and recreations discuss people who work to help their families and their countries. Among the countries covered are India, Pakistan, Uzbekistan, and others in their vicinity. Includes stories of escapes, educational reforms, and other victories.

279. *Forced to Flee: Famine and Plague.* Discovery Channel School, 2004. 55 min. ISBN 978-1-58738-970-2. Grades 7 –9.

This documentary looks at the effects of the Black Death and the potato famine on European history. The Black Death during the Middle Ages killed without mercy, and archaeologists and scientists now know how it started and how it spread. Viewers will discover that the bubonic plague has not been totally destroyed. In Ireland, the potato was cheap and nourishing, but when a bacteria destroyed the crop in the mid-19th century, people either starved or immigrated. Reenactments, archival photographs, and interviews accompany the information.

280. *French Impressionism at the Musée d'Orsay.* (Art and Splendor) VIEW, 2006. 40 min. ISBN 978-0-8030-2022-1. Grades 7 up.

One of Paris's most beautiful museums, the Musée d'Orsay, sits next to the Seine and once functioned as a train station. This DVD presents the Impressionist art collection now housed in this lovely space, especially the works of Manet, Renoir, Monet, van Gogh, Morisot, Degas, Cassat, Toulouse-Lautrec, Seurat, Caillibaut, and Cézanne.

281. *George Marshall and the American Century—Seapower to Superpower: The Story of Global Supremacy.* Janson, 2006. 88 min. ISBN 978-1-56839-229-5. Grades YA.

In the six chronological segments of this DVD, the idea that military power leads to military power comes to the fore. The segments discuss the political and military ascendancy of England after the defeat of the Spanish armada; the struggle between France and England in the 18th century; the Pax Britannica, when England's navy fostered worldwide colonization; the change when the United States became the primary naval power and Japan's failed challenge; and the space race, which signaled that power was shifting from the oceans to the skies to space. Features include re-creations, computer simulations, artwork, and interviews with historians. *Emmy Award CINE Golden Eagle, Silver Apple from the National Educational Film and Video Festival* (Oakland, California), Silver Award from *Worldfest* (Houston, Texas), Red Ribbon from the *American Film and Video Association* (Chicago, Illinois), and the Chris Statuette from the *Film Council of Greater Columbus.*

282. *Global Concerns.* (Global Human Rights) Disney Educational, 2006. 18 min. ISBN 978-1-59753-082-8. Grades 6 up.

This video looks at human rights abuses throughout the world using archival news footage. It focuses on the ethnic, religious, and political conflicts in Northern Ireland, Rwanda, and East Timor.

283. *Great Museums for Art.* Films Media, 2005. 4 DVDs. ISBN 978-1-4213-2952-9. Grades 7 up.

These DVDs present American art museums and a history of American art. The program includes photography of museums, the people who work in them, and their artwork to examine the concept of "art." Among the museums are the Metropolitan Museum in New York, the George Eastman House in Rochester, New York, the Pennsylvania Academy of Fine Arts in Philadelphia, and the National Museum of Women in the Arts in Washington, D.C.

284. *Greatest Speeches of the 20th Century: Voices in Time.* (Voices in Time) Library Video, 2006. 13 DVDs; 23 min. ea. ISBN 978-1-4171-0759-9. Grades 9 up.

This series of DVDs includes the greatest speeches of the 20th century. They are available as single DVDs. Visuals include both still and video images of the speakers along with their own voices as they delivered their most important speeches. Also included are brief biographical profiles and analysis of how the speeches affected their audiences. The speakers included are Winston Churchill, David Lloyd George, Adolf Hitler, Ho Chi Minh, John F. Kennedy, Nelson Mandela, Jawaharlal Nehru, Richard Nixon, Emmeline Pankhurst, Ronald Reagan, Franklin D. Roosevelt, Margaret Thatcher, and Woodrow Wilson.

285. *Gunpowder and the Explosion of World War.*   Discovery, 2004. 55 min. ISBN 978-1-58738-507-0. Grades 6 up.

This examination of war looks at key battles and developments from the 14th to the 17th centuries and suggests that guns are the one weapon that gave Europeans power during this time. Among the battles discussed are the Battle at Crecy in 1346 and the Ottoman Empire's Mehmet II's defeat of Constantinople's Christians in 1453. The Spanish destroyed the Aztecs with guns. Eventually the gun became the cannon.

286. *A History of Terrorism.*   (Terrorism in Our World) Library Video, 2003. 23 min. Grades 7 up.

Throughout history, some groups have used terrorism to control people and intimidate governments. In the 20th century, terrorism has again emerged as a serious threat to civilized people. Among the places where terrorism has flourished are Northern Ireland and the Middle East. Groups discussed here include anarchists of the early 20th century through Islamic terrorists in the early 21st century. Videos and still photographs accompany the commentary.

287. *Horsepower: Harnessed for War.*   Discovery, 2004. 55 min. ISBN 978-1-58738-506-3. Grades 6–12.

The horse as a weapon changed battle strategy, beginning with Attila the Hun's defeat of the Roman legions. The Arabs came to Spain and Portugal with horses and brought their Islamic culture. William the Conqueror on his horse won the Battle of Hastings.

288. *I Can Fly, Part III: Kids, Painting and Modern Art.*   L & S Video, Inc., . 28 min. Grades 4 up.

A teenager hosts this video featuring examples of modern artists and their styles. Seurat worked with pointillism, Matisse with fauvism, Man Ray in dadaism, Picasso with cubism, Jackson Pollack with abstract impressionism, and Escher in op art and pop art, while Chuck Close used photo-realism. Also featured are acclaimed contemporary theatrical troupes.

289. *Ireland: A Tribute.*   Questar, 2002. 61 min. ISBN 978-1-59464-076-6. Grades 7 up.

Interviews and contemporary footage cover the history and legend of Ireland, discussing the Celts, the Anglo-Normans, the British, partition, the potato famine, immigration, and "the troubles" of the Catholic-Protestant conflict. Footage of the island creates a lovely presentation.

290. *Islam: History, Society, and Civilization.*   Discovery Channel School, 2004. 52 min. ISBN 978-1-58738-974-0. Grades 6–12.

Segments recount the history and teachings of Islam; the conflict between the Muslims and Christians during the Crusades; Suleiman; and the contemporary history of Afghanistan. Additional questions and "did you know?" suggestions encourage reflection about the Muslim world.

291. *Jerusalem: The City Touched by God/To Live a Dream: The Story of Teddy Kollek.*   Sisu Home Entertainment, 2002. 110 min. ISBN 978-1-56086-169-0. Grades 9 up.

Liv Ullman narrates this documentary of the 3,000-year-old city of Jerusalem with the aid of art, artifacts, and film archives. The city has been and remains a faith center for Jews, Muslims, and Christians. The second part of the program features Jerusalem's mayor for many years, Teddy Kollek.

292. *The Ottomans and Their Capital, Istanbul.* (The Glories of Islamic Art:) Landmark Media, 2007. 45 min. Grades 11 up.

The last great Islamic dynasty had its capital in Istanbul. The Ottomans borrowed from the Byzantines with the creation of their Blue Mosque and Hagia Sophia, a converted Christian cathedral. The powerful and wealthy Suleiman the Magnificent became the patron for Sinan, an architect who constructed buildings throughout the empire. He designed the harem inside the Topkapi Palace with its beautiful Iznik tilework. Also covered in the DVD is Sufism, a branch of Islam focusing on meditation and inner strength, known for its whirling dervishes.

293. *Religion and Culture.* Discovery Channel, 2002. 26-51 min. ISBN 978-1-60288-515-8. Grades 7 up.

In three different programs, "Jesus and the Rise of Christianity," "Islam," and "Buddhism and the Dalai Lama," professors, archaeologists, and theologians examine several topics, including the role of women within each religion. Contemporary footage and reenactments add interest. The first part of the video on Jesus and Christianity covers Jesus' life and philosophy, ancient Jewish society, and significant stories about Jesus that appeared during his lifetime. The second part notes the reasons why he threatened the temple priests and includes reenactments of several of his parables. In Buddhism, blurry footage of the uprising between Tibetans and Chinese shows why His Holiness Tenzin Gyatso, the fourteenth Dalai Lama, has had to live in exile in India since 1959. In the video on Islam, information about Mohammed, Muslim beliefs, and the practices of the faithful appear against a backdrop of four cities strongly affected by Islam—Cairo, Fes, Marrakech, and Granada.

294. *The Shaman's Apprentice.* Bullfrog Films, 2001. 54 min. ISBN 978-1-59458-110-6. Grades 10 up.

The shamans of the rain forests have knowledge about the healing aspects of the plants that grow there. Since the beginning of the 20th century, ninety of Brazil's rain forest tribes have become extinct, and Dr. Mark Plotkin, an ethnobotanist, thinks that these shamans need preservation as much as the other species in the forests do. No one will know the value of many rain forest plants after they are gone, since the shamans are mostly preliterate, and with them will die the oral traditions of their trade. Dr. Plotkin believes that secrets to curing illnesses such as AIDS and diabetes may be known to the shamans and that Western medicine needs to listen to them.

295. *Slavery, Society and Apartheid.* Discovery Channel, 2004. 52 min. ISBN 978-1-58738-972-6. Grades 8–12.

Four segments discuss the effects of slavery and apartheid. The longest section (28 minutes) covers slave revolts including the 1733 revolt on the island of St. John. Two Akwamu chieftains led a revolt in an attempt to establish a kingdom, but the Danish and French colonists repressed them. Each of the other segments is 5 minutes. "Atlantic Slave Trade" covers slave vessels and the *Amistad* case. "Apartheid Takes Hold" discusses the South African government's policy and the attempt of the African National Congress to fight it. "End of Apartheid" describes the international and local protests against apartheid with Nelson Mandela's rise to the presidency. With reenactments, photographs, and film clips.

296. ***Turmoil in 20th Century Europe.*** Discovery Channel School, 2004. 52 min. ISBN 978-1-58738-956-6. Grades 6–12.

Graphics, archival video, and recreations present catastrophes that have changed lives in Europe and America. When the *Titanic* sank, many felt the disaster's effects in their own lives. In 1986, a nuclear accident affected those in the Ukraine. When the Berlin Wall fell, it changed the lives of many in both East Berlin and West Berlin. After the conflict with Serbia, a mine-clearing team had to sweep Kosovo.

297. ***Understanding Terrorism.*** (Terrorism in Our World) Library Video, 2003. 23 min. ISBN 978-1-4171-0721-6. Grades 7 up.

Modern terrorist groups have motivations and targets that the population at large often misunderstands. The video asks what terrorism is and why it happens. Historical examples of terrorism help to answer these questions by exploring strikes and targets. Experts explain the value of developing "profiles" of terrorists as a way to combat their threats.

298. ***What Is Buddhism?*** (Understanding World Religions) Library Video, 2006. 20 min. ISBN 978-1-4171-0578-6. Grades 4–7.

This video examines the history, traditions, beliefs, spiritual sites, sacred writings, and places of worship important to Buddhism. A male host and a group of middle-school students, along with live-action scenes of places and people, clarify some of the abstract ideas of the religion.

299. ***What Is Christianity?*** (Understanding World Religions) Library Video, 2003. 20 min. ISBN 978-1-4171-0579-3. Grades 4–7.

This video examines the history, traditions, beliefs, spiritual sites, sacred writings, and places of worship important to Christianity. A male host and a group of middle-school students, along with live-action scenes of places and people, clarify some of the abstract ideas of the religion.

300. ***What Is Hinduism?*** (Understanding World Religions) Library Video, 2006. 20 min. ISBN 978-1-4171-0580-9. Grades 4–7.

This video examines the history, traditions, beliefs, spiritual sites, sacred writings, and places of worship important to Hinduism. A male host and a group of middle-school students, along with live-action scenes of places and people, clarify some of the abstract ideas of the religion.

301. ***What Is Islam?*** (Understanding World Religions) Library Video, 2006. 20 min. Grades 4–7.

This video examines the history, traditions, beliefs, spiritual sites, sacred writings, and places of worship important to Islam. A male host and a group of middle-school students, along with live-action scenes of places and people, clarify some of the abstract ideas of the religion.

302. ***What Is Judaism?*** (Understanding World Religions) Library Video, 2006. 20 min. Grades 4–7.

This video examines the history, traditions, beliefs, spiritual sites, sacred writings, and places of worship important to Judaism. A male host and a group of middle-school students, along with live-action scenes of places and people, clarify some of the abstract ideas of the religion.

303. *What Is Religion?* (Understanding World Religions) Library Video, 2003. 20 min. ISBN 978-1-4171-0583-0. Grades 4–7.

This video examines the history, traditions, beliefs, spiritual sites, sacred writings, and places of worship important to various religions. A male host and a group of middle-school students, along with live-action scenes of places and people, clarify some of the abstract ideas of world religions.

304. *When Civilizations End.* Discover Channel School, 2004. 52 min. Grades 6–12.

The four segments of this program discuss great civilizations throughout the world and how they ended. They look at China's last dynasty; Peru's Chiribaya civilization; the disappeared civilization of Zimbabwe, once a major center of African culture; and the loss of African culture after the arrival of Europeans.

305. *The Women's Movement: Women and the World.* Disney Educational, 2006. 18 min. ISBN 978-1-59753-131-3. Grades 6–12.

The video offers a historial view of the women's movement with personal interviews, news footage, and archival photographs. Among the more recent issues facing the world's women include the post-Taliban situation in Afghanistan, where women must attend schools without furniture or supplies. In Japan, women have decided to delay marriage so that they can be independent longer. In 1995, a United Nations Conference on Women in Beijing discussed concerns and revealed that balances between tradition and contemporary values are often difficult to maintain.

306. *World History.* Discovery, 2004. 5 DVDs, varying. ISBN 978-1-58738-985-6. Grades 6 up.

The five DVDs of this set present topics in world history using live-action video on location, reenactments, news footage, photographs of period art and artifacts, and comments of historians and archaeologists. "Prehistory" includes the Iceman, the Nile, the Great Wall of China, and the lost city of Shang. "Ancient Civilization" covers Greece, ancient Rome, Alexander the Great, and Zimbabwe as "the lost city of Africa." "The Medieval Era" discusses life in the Middle Ages, the Black Death, Byzantium, and conquerors such as Suleyman the Magnificent; "The Modern Era" looks at Galileo's telescope, the Forbidden City, Peter the Great, and the French Revolution. "Contemporary History" adds the end of apartheid, Normandy and D-Day, the escape from Berlin, and the Taliban in Afghanistan.

Compact Discs

307. Brooks, Geraldine. *People of the Book.* Narrated by Edwina Ween. Penguin, 2008. 12 CDs; 14 hrs. ISBN 978-0-14-314298-0. Grades YA.

See entry 2.

308. Freese, Barbara. *Coal: A Human History.* Tantor Media, 2005. 7 CDs; 7 hrs. 37 min. ISBN 978-1-400-13087-0. Grades YA.

> See entry 68.

309. Krull, Kathleen. *Lives of Extraordinary Women: Rulers, Rebels (and What the Neighbors Thought).* Illustrated by Kathryn Hewitt. Narrated by John C. Brown and Melissa Hughes. Audio Bookshelf, 2001. 2 CDs; 2 hrs. ISBN 978-1-8833-3273-0. Grades 5–8.

> See entry 248.

310. Krull, Kathleen. *Lives of the Artists: Masterpieces, Messes (and What the Neighbors Thought).* Illustrated by Kathryn Hewitt. Narrated by John C. Brown and Melissa Hughes. Audio Bookshelf, 2001. 2 CDs; 3 hrs. ISBN 978-1-883332-63-1. Grades 4–8.

> See entry 249.

311. Krull, Kathleen. *Lives of the Musicians: Good Times, Bad Times (and What the Neighbors Thought).* Illustrated by Kathryn Hewitt. Narrated by John C. Brown and Melissa Hughes. Audio Bookshelf, 1996. 2 CDs; 2 hrs. ISBN 978-1-883332-23-5. Grades 4–8.

> See entry 251.

312. Krull, Kathleen. *Lives of the Writers: Comedies, Tragedies (and What the Neighbors Thought).* Illustrated by Kathryn Hewitt. Narrated by John C. Brown and Melissa Hughes. Audio Bookshelf, 1996. 96pp. 3 CDs; 3 hrs. ISBN 978-1-883332-24-2. Grades 4–8.

> See entry 252.

313. Prévost, Guillaume. *The Book of Time.* Narrated by Holter Graham. Translated by William Rodarmor. Arthur A. Levine, 2007. 213pp. 5 CDs; 6:36 hrs. ISBN 978-0-545-02467-9. Grades 4–7.

> See entry 6.

314. Rutherfurd, Edward. *Sarum: The Novel of England.* Narrated by Nadia May. Blackstone Audio, 2008. 18 CDs; 23 hrs. ISBN 978-1-4332-5470-3. Grades YA.

> See entry 9.

PREHISTORY AND THE ANCIENT WORLD TO 54 B.C.E.

Historical Fiction and Fantasy

315. Aubin, Henry Trocme. *Rise of the Golden Cobra.* Illustrated by Stephen Taylor. Annick, 2007. 255pp. ISBN 978-1-55451-060-3; paper ISBN 978-1-55451-059-7. Grades 6–10.

In Egypt in 728 B.C.E., Nebi, age 14, sees Count Nimlot murder his master and goes to warn the pharaoh by telling his sister, Princess Amonirdis. She rewards Nebi's bravery by allowing him to join the medical corps traveling north with the army to fight against the Assyrians. He meets Prince Shebitku, with whom he becomes friends, and when the pharaoh wins, Nebi sees him offer forgiveness to rebels.

316. Auel, Jean. *The Shelters of Stone.* (Earth's Children) Crown, 2002. 720pp. ISBN 978-0-609-61059-6; Bantam, 2003. paper ISBN 978-0-553-28942-8. Grades YA.

In the fifth volume of the Earth's Children series, Ayla and Jondalar try to cross Ice Age Europe to reach Jondalar's people in Zelandonii, a settlement of limestone cliff caves in what is now France. They bring their horses, Whinny and Racer, as well as Ayla's tame wolf, three animals that shock the people. A pregnant Ayla strives to give Jondalar support as they try to fit in with his people. Alya's abilities to look after animals and to heal lead the people to soon accept her as one of their own.

317. Baccalario, Pierdomenico. *The Long-Lost Map.* (Ulysses Moore) Scholastic, 2006. 272pp. ISBN 978-0-439-77439-0; paper ISBN 978-0-439-77673-8. Grades 4–6.

Eleven-year-old twins Jason and Julia and their friend Rick are transported through the Door to Time to ancient Egypt and are accidentally separated. Julia returns to Argo Manor in Cornwall, unable to get back to Egypt. Jason and Rick have to find the map of Kilmore Cove hidden in the past with Oblivia Newton trying to trace them. At Argo Manor, Julia and the caretaker, Nestor, have to fend off Oblivia's servant Manfred. In Egypt, Maruk, the high priest's daughter, and Mammon (Lucifer), the owner of the Shop of Long-Lost Maps, help Jason and Rick try to find the Room That Isn't There. At the end of the adventure, the boys themselves have not explained the map's importance. The second volume in the series.

318. Banks, Lynne Reid. *Tiger, Tiger.* Random House, 2005. 195pp. ISBN 978-0-385-90264-9. Grades 5–8.

Two foreign tiger cubs are taken to late-3rd-century Rome. One is sent to fight the Christians and slaves in the Colosseum; the other is given to Princess Aurelia, Caesar's daughter. Aurelia names her tiger Boots, and she and its keeper, the slave Julius, become interested in each other from afar. Aurelia's intended, Marcus, coerces her to play a trick on Julius, and as a result, Julius and Boots have to fight Brute in the Colosseum. *Maine Student Book Award Nomination, Publisher's Weekly Best Children's Books.*

319. Barrett, Tracy. *On Etruscan Time.* Holt, 2005. 176pp. ISBN 978-0-8050-7569-4. Grades 5–8.

Although preferring to remain in Tennessee with his friends, Hector, 11, spends the summer with his mother near Florence, Italy, on an archaeological dig. When he unearths a strange eye-shaped stone, it gives him nightmares about Arath, an Etruscan boy, who needs Hector's help to stop his uncle's plan to make him a human sacrifice. The stone transports each of them in and out of times two thousand years apart while Hector tries to figure out how to help his new friend.

320. Bradshaw, Gillian. *The Sand-Reckoner.* Forge, 2001. 351pp. Paper ISBN 978-0-312-87581-7. Grades YA.

As a young man, Archimedes (287?–212 B.C.E.) studies in Alexandria at Ptolemy's museum. When his father becomes ill, he returns to Syracuse to be with him. There he becomes a royal engineer to King Herion, creating a catapult that will defend the city against the Romans during the first Punic War, although he prefers to study geometry and pure mathematics. He falls in love with the king's half sister, Delia, after playing music with her. A subplot considers his relationship with his slave, Marcus, after he discovers that Marcus's brother is a Roman soldier. However, Archimedes must choose whether to return to Alexandria, stay with Delia, continue working for the king, or retire to the pleasure of geometry's puzzles. *Alex Award.*

321. Brennan, J. H. *Shiva Accused: An Adventure of the Ice Age.* Harper Trophy, 1993. 288pp. Paper ISBN 978-0-06-440431-0. Grades 5 up.

The orphan Shiva finds a saber-toothed tiger skull that her Shingu clan presents at the Star Jamboree meeting as a candidate for the Star Totem. The Barradik clan of thugs has held the prestige of owning the Star Totem for many years and in response to this Shingu challenge murders Hag, the crone-priestess who presides over the choice of the Star Totem. Then the Barradik clan manages to get Shiva accused of the murder. Shiva's friends, the ogres, help engineer a mammoth stampede that saves her from death by stoning. That Shiva has an ability to "see" helps her tribe.

322. Bunting, Eve. *I Am the Mummy Heb-Nefert.* Illustrated by David Christiana. Harcourt, 1997. 32pp. ISBN 978-0-15-200479-8; 2000. paper ISBN 978-0-15-202464-2. Grades 3–6.

Heb-Nefert lives a leisurely life with her royal husband on the banks of the Nile. Bunting imagines Heb-Nefert recalling these pleasant days as she lies as a mummy encased in museum glass. Her story tells of ancient Egypt and its customs.

323. Colum, Padraic. *The Children's Homer: Odysseus and the Tale of Troy.* Illustrated by Willy Pogany. Aladdin, 2004. 256pp. Paper ISBN 978-0-689-86883-2. Grades 4–8.

Odysseus leaves his home, his wife Penelope, and his son Telemachus to help his friend Menelaus retrieve his wife, who has run away with Paris to Troy. Odysseus is gone for ten years and during this time encounters fanciful creatures and people, but stays focused on his final goal: returning home to his people on the island of Ithaca.

324. Cooney, Caroline B. *For All Time.* Laurel-Leaf, 2003. 263pp. Paper ISBN 978-0-440-22931-5. Grades 6–10.

In 1999, Annie tries to return to her beloved boyfriend, Strat, who is in 1899 Egypt, but she ends up in 2500 B.C.E. Egypt. There she sees a tomb being built that Strat has just discovered in 1899, and becomes a pawn in a grave robber's plot. Fortunately, Strat finds her as she is being lowered into a tomb for a living death. Also see *Both Sides of Time*, *Out of Time*, and *Prisoner of Time*.

325. Cooney, Caroline B. *Goddess of Yesterday.* Laurel Leaf, 2003. Paper ISBN 978-0-440-22930-8. Grades 6–9.

King Nicander takes Anaxandra, 6, to become a companion for his crippled daugher, Princess Callisto, on the island of Siphnos. Six years later, pirates kill everyone living in the palace but Anaxandra; she was not inside. When Menelaus comes from Sparta and finds the massacre, he takes Anaxandra home with him because she claims to be Callisto. Helen suspects that she is not Callisto, but soon Helen leaves with Paris for Troy. Unfortunately, they take Helen's son, Pleisthenes, and Anaxandra with them, mistaking her for Helen's daughter, Hermione. Knowing that Helen's action will cause a war, Anaxandra pleads to her goddess, Medusa, to help her find safety, and then she saves Pleisthenes from Paris's sword. *Beehive Young Adults' Book Award* (Utah) nomination, *Sequoyah Book Award* (Oklahoma) nomination, *SCASL Book Award* (South Carolina) nomination, *Capitol Choices Noteworthy Titles* (Washington, D.C.), *Nutmeg Award* (Connecticut) nomination, *American Library Association Notable Children's Books*, and *Lone Star Reading List* (Texas).

326. Cowley, Marjorie. *Dar and the Spear-Thrower.* Clarion, 1996. 118pp. Paper ISBN 978-0-395-79725-9. Grades 4–7.

Around fifteen thousand years ago in France, during the Cro-Magnon period, Dar, 13, undergoes his clan's initiation into manhood. He hears about a spear-thrower, a device that will enable him to throw with greater power and be the warrior his tribe expects, and he goes on a dangerous journey in search of the item. What he finds is much more than he could have imagined.

327. Cowley, Marjorie. *The Golden Bull.* Charlesbridge, 2008. 206pp. ISBN 978-1-58089-181-3. Grades 5–8.

During a severe drought in Mesopotamia in 2600 B.C.E., Jomar, 14, and Zefa, his younger sister who plays the lyre competently, are sent to Ur by their parents so that Jomar can work for a goldsmith. On the way, temple official Malak spots them and makes them work on the crew patrolling the irrigation system. They run away to the goldsmith, Sidah, but his wife, Nari, does not want Zefa and accuses her of stealing. Zefa leaves and after meeting with a high priestess, Jomar finally clears Zefa's name and gets her a position playing the honored temple lyre.

328. Denenberg, Barry. *Pandora of Athens, 399 B.C.* (Life and Times) Scholastic, 2004. 166pp. ISBN 978-0-439-64982-7. Grades 5–9.

Unhappy about her restricted social life in Athens and her betrothal to someone twice her age, 13-year-old Pandora meets Socrates when she goes to get water at the well. She cuts off her hair to sneak out and hear Socrates talk at a meeting. While he is imprisoned, she talks with him and learns much from his wisdom before running away with a 17-year-old.

329. Doherty, P. C. *The Godless Man: A Mystery of Alexander the Great.* Carroll & Graf, 2002. 288pp. ISBN 978-0-7867-0995-3. Grades YA.

In 334 B.C.E., Alexander the Great defeats Darius III at the Battle of Granicus, and to control the citizens of his prized Ephesus, Alexander starts killing his enemies in the city. At the same time, savage murders of his own people—including his tutor, Leonidas—lead him to ask his physician, Telamon, to investigate. He suspects Darius's master spy, Lord Mithra, but the murderer is known only as the Centaur. Along with Cassandra, Telamon and Master of Secrets Aristander look for the culprit while trying to keep Alexander's anger from erupting.

330. Fletcher, Susan. *Alphabet of Dreams.* Simon & Schuster, 2006. 294pp. ISBN 978-0-689-85042-4; Simon Pulse, 2008. paper ISBN 978-0-689-85152-0. Grades 5–8.

Although they were born to royalty, Mitra, 14, and her brother Babak, 5, must live as beggars in the ancient Persian city of Rhagae because of their father's plot to overthrow the king. They wander through the City of the Dead with Mitra disguised as a boy and discover that Babak can tell the future through his dreams. When he sleeps with an item belonging to another person, he knows that person's dreams. Their lives begin to change as they use this gift to find their family.

331. Ford, Michael. *Birth of a Warrior.* (Spartan Quest) Walker, 2008. ISBN 978-0-8027-9794-0. Grades 5–9.

In the sequel to *The Fire of Ares*, 13-year-old Lysander, half-Helot and half-Spartan, must go to the mountains with his archenemy, Demaratos, to test his ability before he can become a warrior. A third companion, an older boy, seems happy to let them die. While Lysander survives, he must decide with whom his loyalties lie: the Spartans or the Helot slaves with whom he has lived most of his life.

332. Ford, Michael. *The Fire of Ares.* (Spartan Quest) Walker, 2008. 245pp. ISBN 978-0-8027-9744-5. Grades 6–10.

Lysander, a Helot of 12, works twice as hard in the fields so that his ill mother will be able to rest. When an older Spartan nobleman sees Lysander's hidden amulet, called the Fire of Ares, under Lysander's shirt, he realizes that the boy is his grandson. His grandfather places him in school to train as a warrior, but Lysander faces the derision of the other students because he is a *mythokes* or "half-breed." He gains some respect when he beats the other boys in the annual games.

333. Friesner, Esther. *Nobody's Princess.* Random House, 2008. 305pp. ISBN 978-0-375-87528-1; paper ISBN 978-0-375-87529-8. Grades 6–9.

Helen, later to become Helen of Sparta and Helen of Troy, grows up with boys and learns to fight, hunt, and ride horses. She wants more than the life of a typical female in ancient Greece. When her sister, Clytemnestra, goes to Mykenae for her marriage to Tantalus, Helen wants to go, and while there, she disguises herself to accompany her brothers, Castor and Polydeuces, on their hunt of the Caledonian boar. On the hunt she meets Atalanta, the princess who has chosen to be a hunter. On their way home they stop at Delphi, where Helen meets the oracle before joining Jason on his quest for the golden fleece.

334. Friesner, Esther. *Nobody's Prize.*   Random House, 2008. 320pp. ISBN 978-0-375-87531-1. Grades 6–9.

Still in the male disguise she donned in *Nobody's Princess*, Princess Helen of Sparta travels to Athens with the help of her friend Milo. She meets the crazy Herakles, the frightening Medea, and the Athenian king, Theseus, from whom she escaped earlier. She falls in love with a man who prefers boys, and her true sex is discovered, but not her identity, as she pretends to be Atalanta.

335. Gemmell, David. *Fall of Kings.*   (Troy) Ballantine, 2007. 447pp. ISBN 978-0-345-47703-3; 2009. paper ISBN 978-0-345-47704-0. Grades YA.

In this final book in the trilogy, Hector and Achilles kill each other in a duel. Then Agamemnon seeks to overwhelm Priam (for his hoard of treasure rather than to abduct the plain and plump Helen). The Trojan Horse, revised here, helps the Greeks win.

336. Gemmell, David. *Lord of the Silver Bow.*   (Troy) Del Ray, 2005. 512pp. ISBN 978-0-345-49457-3; Ballantine, 2006. paper ISBN 978-0-345-49457-3. Grades YA.

Andromache leaves her island of Thera and travels to Troy to become Hector's wife. But after her arrival and before she meets Hector, she becomes involved in the politics of the house of Priam, Hector's father. She meets and falls in love with Helikaon/Aeneas, Hector's good friend and the lord of the silver bow. Since Aeneas is a friend of Odysseus and an enemy of Agamemnon, he is disturbed when the relationship between Troy and Mycenae starts to deteriorate. He will have to choose which side to support. Agamemnon, however, believes the prophecy that Aeneas will have to die, and tasks his men with fulfilling it.

337. Gemmell, David. *Shield of Thunder.*   (Troy) Del Ray, 2007. 512pp. ISBN 978-0-345-47701-9; Ballantine paper ISBN 978-0-345-47702-6. Grades YA.

In the sequel to *Lord of the Silver Bow*, Agamemnon tightens his control over Troy through Achilles, the godlike warrior. Odysseus has had to swear allegiance to Agamemnon even though he foresees disaster. King Priam thinks that his city will have a future after his son Hector marries Princess Andromache because she supposedly will bear the eagle child, a king who can never be defeated and whose city will be eternal. But Priam wants to sleep with Andromache, and she agrees after Hector has been made impotent by battle. She makes Priam think that the child born later is his when it actually is the son of her lover, Aeneas. When Andromache learns that Hekabe, Priam's wife, has killed her own sister, Andromache kills her so that she will not poison Odysseus.

338. George, Margaret. *The Memoirs of Cleopatra: A Novel.*   Griffin, 1998. 964pp. Paper ISBN 978-0-312-18745-3. Grades YA.

Cleopatra is an intelligent and compassionate woman who knows that she must play politics to stay alive. She saw her mother die when she was three and decided that she would prepare for her demise with her own hands. Her life and her loves are inextricably tied to Rome, although her home is in North Africa.

339. Geras, Adele. *Cleopatra.* Illustrated by M. P. Robertson. Kingfisher, 2007. 64pp. ISBN 978-0-7534-6025-2. Grades K–4.

Nefret, Cleopatra's 10-year-old handmaid, watches the intrigues between Cleopatra and the men in her life—her brother and husband Ptolemy, Julius Caesar, and Marc Antony. Nefret records the happenings in the palace and the marketplace of Alexandria, and discusses cultural details such as the value of cats. Illustrations intensify the text.

340. Geras, Adele. *Ithaka.* Harcourt, 2006. 368pp. ISBN 978-0-15-205603-2; 2007. paper ISBN 978-0-15-206104-3. Grades 9 up.

Klymene serves Penelope while Penelope faithfully waits for her husband, King Odysseus, to return from the war in Troy. Penelope must withstand the unwelcome attentions of unsuitable and unscrupulous suitors. Klymene falls in love with Telemachus, Penelope's son. But Telemachus loves Melanthro, a maid whom Klymene's twin, Ikarios, also loves. Melanthro manipulates Telemachus and sleeps with the suitors. Eventually Odysseus returns and Penelope tests his identity by asking about their marriage bed. Then Odysseus and Telemachus together murder the suitors.

341. Geras, Adèle. *Troy.* Harcourt, 2002. 376pp. Paper ISBN 978-0-15-204570-8. Grades 9 up.

The orphan Xanthe, maidservant to Andromache, and Xanthe's sister Marpessa, a seer and maid to Helen of Troy, both fall in love with wounded soldier Alastor. Because Eros and Aphrophite have become bored with the ten-year battle against the Greeks that has pushed Hector, Paris, and Achilles into the forefront, they decide to entertain themselves with the sisters. The two become jealous of each other, especially when Xanthe heals Alastor but he chooses Marpessa. The gods Athena, Poseidon, Aphrodite, Hermes, Ares, Eros, and Zeus influence them all, male and female, in this terrible time. *Garden State Teen Book Award* (New Jersey) nomination, *Horn Book Fanfare, American Library Association Best Books for Young Adults* nomination, *Boston Globe/Horn Book Award Honor*, and *Tayshas Reading List* (Texas).

342. Gregory, Kristiana. *Cleopatra VII: Daughter of the Nile, Egypt, 57 B.C.* (Royal Diaries) Scholastic, 1999. 224pp. Paper ISBN 978-0-590-81975-6. Grades 4–8.

When Cleopatra was 12, she was trying to survive and become queen in an Egyptian court full of spies and assassins. She and her father, Ptolemy XII, traveled to Rome in an attempt to establish alliances with the leaders against their common enemies and her own sisters, who wanted to take the throne from her. Her father had already survived being bitten by an adder and poisoned by wine. In Rome Cleopatra met Caesar, Cicero, and Marc Antony. In a series of journal entries, she describes her life in Egypt and her reactions to the meetings in Rome, where she had the challenge of learning diplomacy and using foreign languages. Additionally, she creates a sense of the time as she describes the smells, tastes, sights, sounds, and other aspects of Rome. *Children's Book Award* (Georgia) nomination and *Children's Book Award* (Colorado) nomination.

343. Halter, Marek. *Sarah: A Novel.* (The Canaan Trilogy) Three Rivers, 2005. 294pp. Paper ISBN 978-1-4000-5278-3. Grades YA.

Sarai, a daughter of a lord of Ur in Sumeria, becomes frightened by her first menstrual blood and runs away from an arranged marriage only to meet a nomad named Abram. She leaves him after only one night, but still fearful of marriage, she buys herbs that make her infertile and becomes a priestess of Ishtar. Not until years later do Abram and Sarai meet again and marry. Then begins the story of Abraham and Sarah as she follows him to the valleys of Canaan. The first volume in the trilogy.

344. Harvey, Gill. *Orphan of the Sun.* Bloomsbury, 2007. 310pp. ISBN 978-1-58234-685-4. Grades 5–8.

Orphan Meryt-Re, 13, lives in the village of Set Maat, where the builders of the king's tomb live. Her uncle Senmut blames her for causing the family trouble and wants to marry her to a stonecutter. Villagers believe that she might be under the power of the goddess of pestilence and destruction, Sekhmet. When Baki, Senmut's son and Meryt's cousin, becomes ill after his ritual circumcision, Senmut blames Meryt and banishes her. Meryt asks the village "rekhet," Teti, for help, and Teti teaches Meryt how to use her dreams constructively. Her gift for predicting the future helps uncover the secrets plaguing her village and bring healing to her family.

345. Hawes, Louise. *Muti's Necklace: The Oldest Story in the World.* Illustrated by Rebecca Guay. Houghton, 2006. 32pp. ISBN 978-0-618-53583-5. Grades 2–4.

Muti's father gives her a beautiful necklace that she loses while rowing the pharoah's barge. She risks death by stopping the barge to retrieve her necklace, and her courage leads King Snefru to ask her to marry him. She declines because she wants to reunite with her family. Paintings complement the text.

346. Henty, G.A. *The Young Carthaginian: A Story of the Times of Hannibal.* Kessinger, 2004. 430pp. Paper ISBN 978-1-4192-8911-8. Grades YA up.

After Rome had viciously mistreated the people of Carthage, Carthaginian general Hannibal crossed the Alps with cannons and elephants to battle at Trebia, Lake Trasimenus, and Cannae, and almost capture Rome. In this story, a relative of Hannibal, young Malchus, joins him on the journey. Malchus cleverly escapes from lions and wolves and can adeptly maneuver a raft. Although Hannibal is eventually defeated, his army's efforts are surprising.

347. Howard, Annabelle. *The Great Wonder: The Building of the Great Pyramid.* Illustrated by Stephen Wells. Narrated by Garard Green. (Smithsonian Odyssey) Soundprints, 1996. 32pp. Paper ISBN 978-1-56899-351-5. Grades 2–5.

While viewing a film at the Smithsonian's National Museum of Natural History, Kevin finds himself in King Khufu's burial chamber while workers are building it — nearly 4,000 years in the past. He discovers that he was sent there to save Elidor and its treasures. Then Malebron sends him back to the modern world to keep the treasures safe.

348. Hunt, Jonathan. *Leif's Saga: A Viking Tale.* Macmillan, 1995. 32pp. ISBN 978-0-02-745780-3. Grades 2–4.

Sigrid's father, Asgrim, tells her as he builds his *knörr* that he got the oak wood for the boat from Leif Eiriksson, another man from Greenland who sailed farther than anyone else and brought back the logs. Eiriksson reached Helluland, Markland, and Vinland. Information about Eiriksson and the Norsemen appears in the endnote.

349. Jacq, Christian. *Nefer the Silent.* (Stone of Light) Atria, 2000. 400pp. Paper ISBN 978-0-7434-0346-7. Grades 7–12.

After Ardent, 16, saves Silent's life in Upper Egypt, Silent allows Ardent to fulfill his dream of entering the Place of Truth near West Thebes. Since Ardent is the son of a farmer, he has not been able to enter this hidden village for artists. Silent, who was born there, was wandering through Egypt searching for his identity. After his life is saved, Silent meets and elopes with Ubekhet, who later becomes the Wise Woman, a priestess. At the same time, Mehy, a man who nefariously gains power in Thebes, desires to destroy the Place of Truth. He tries to murder Ramses but fails when Ardent warns Ramses's allies. Mehy and his ambitious wife, Serketa, continue to collect spies and information to increase their power. Throughout, Sobek, the security commander for the Place of Truth, protects it and its residents—the artists, builders, and designers of the beautiful tombs in the Valley of the Kings and the Valley of the Queens. This is the first book in the Stone of Light series.

350. Jacq, Christian. *Paneb the Ardent.* (Stone of Light) Atria, 2001. 400pp. Paper ISBN 978-0-7434-0348-1. Grades 7–12.

Nefert, the master of the Place of Truth, initiates Paneb into the brotherhood and shares its mysteries with him. Paneb becomes a master himself and head of one of the two crews of workers. But one member of the community has become an ally of Mehy and, with Mehy, plots to steal the Stone of Light—which turns things into gold or makes matter translucent—and to destroy the village. Since Seth II and his son Amenmessu are both claiming to be the pharaoh, the resultant chaos seems a good time for Mehy and his ally to achieve their goal. Paneb must thwart the plan. The third book in the series.

351. Jacq, Christian. *The Place of Truth.* (Stone of Light) Atria, 2001. 384pp. Paper ISBN 978-0-7434-0349-8. Grades 7–12.

In this fourth book in the series, the artisans are mourning Nefert, the revered master of the Place of Truth who was assassinated by Mehy. But they continue their work under the new master, Paneb the Ardent. Not only must Paneb protect the village and its secrets, but he must also protect his wife, Uabet the Pure, and other members of his family. Finally Paneb's honor and loyalty help the village survive.

352. Jacq, Christian. *Wise Woman.* (Stone of Light) Atria, 2000. 432pp. Paper ISBN 978-0-7434-0347-4. Grades 7–12.

While Ramses lived, he fully supported the Place of Truth, the hidden village where the artists of the great pyramids and tombs create their work and where the Stone of Light is protected. Only the best artists are accepted into this work area. Nefer the Silent, a respected master builder and husband of Wise Woman, oversees the work on the Great Pharaoh's tomb after Ramses the Great has died and his son, Meneptah, has come to the throne. Mehy, a powerful man under Meneptah, resents being refused when he wants to work in the Place of Truth. Mehy begins gathering information about the Place of Truth, and as his power grows, the future of the village begins to darken. The second book in the series.

353. Jules, Jacqueline. *Abraham's Search for God.* Illustrated by Natascia Ugliano. Kar-Ben, 2007. 32pp. ISBN 978-1-58013-243-5. Grades K–3.

The story of Abraham, based on a *midrash* (a legend from biblical text), suggests that Abraham began worshiping one God when he was young. He might have viewed idol worshipers and wondered what advantage they had until he realized that one great power controlled the sun, moon, and clouds. Illustrations enhance the text.

354. Jules, Jacqueline. *Sarah Laughs.* Illustrated by Natascia Ugliano. Kar-Ben, 2008. 32pp. ISBN 978-0-8225-7216-9; paper ISBN 978-0-8225-9934-0. Grades K–3.

After Abraham becomes wealthy and content with his wife, Sarah, they welcome guests to their tent. Sarah encourages Abraham to father a son, Ishmael, with the servant Hagar since she cannot have children. Later, Sarah has her own son, Isaac, and brings laughter to their tent. Illustrations complement the text.

355. Kindl, Patrice. *Lost in the Labyrinth: A Novel.* Houghton, 2002. 194pp. ISBN 978-0-618-16684-8; Graphia, 2005. paper ISBN 978-0-618-39402-9. Grades 6–10.

Princess Xenodice, 14, generally tries to hide from the intrigue of the court at Knossos in Crete and responds to her sister Ariadne's expectations. Her two favorite pastimes are visiting with Icarus in his father's workshop and with her younger half brother, Asterius, who is half boy and half bull. When a ship of Athenian slaves arrives, one of them, Theseus, is determined to kill Asterius. Theseus has the help of Icarus, his father Daedalus, and Xenodice's own sister, Ariadne.

356. Kitamura, Satoshi. *Stone Age Boy.* Candlewick, 2007. 37pp. ISBN 978-0-7636-3474-2. Grades 1–4.

When a boy awakens after a fall, he finds himself in a Stone Age family's cave. He and a girl named Om communicate without language as she shows him how to make tools, to make a fire without matches, and to hunt reindeer. He sees art inside the cave—lifelike animal paintings. While evading a cave bear, the boy falls into a hole and back into the modern world. But when he grows up, he becomes an archaeologist in search of Om's cave. Cartoon illustrations complement the text. Chronology and Index.

357. Koralek, Jenny. *The Coat of Many Colors.* Illustrated by Pauline Baynes. Eerdman's, 2004. Unpaged. ISBN 978-0-8028-5277-9. Grades K–3.

Joseph's brothers become annoyed by the favoritism that their father Jacob shows to Joseph, especially when Jacob gives Joseph a coat of many colors. They decide to sell Joseph into slavery. Joseph ends up in Egypt, where the pharaoh asks him to interpret his dreams. Joseph advises the pharaoh to buy extra corn for a coming famine. The pharaoh takes his advice, and during the famine, Joseph's brothers come looking for food. Joseph has a powerful government position because of his intuitive abilities, and he helps his brothers.

358. Krebs, Laurie. *We're Sailing Down the Nile: A Journey Through Egypt.* Illustrated by Anne Wilson. Barefoot, 2007. Unpaged. ISBN 978-1-84686-040-9; 2008. paper ISBN 978-1-846861-94-9. Grades K–3.

When contemporary Egyptian children take a boat down the Nile, they visit seven ancient sites including the pyramids at Giza, the Valley of the Kings, the Al-Faiyum Oasis, Cairo, the temple at Abu Simbel, and others. The book includes facts about the areas and information about ancient Egypt. Illustrations reinforce the text. Map.

359. Le Guin, Ursula K. *Lavinia.* Harcourt, 2008. 288pp. ISBN 978-0-15-101424-8. Grades YA.

Eighteen-year-old Lavinia, daughter of King Latinus and Queen Amata—rulers of Latinum before the founding of Rome—expects to become engaged to Turnus, the handsome king of nearby Bulli. But she keeps delaying the final commitment. Then a fleet of ships sails up the Tiber from Troy under the command of Aeneas. Lavinia meets

Aeneas and discovers the love of her life. She chooses her own husband in this alternate view of *The Aeneid*.

360. Lester, Julius. *Pharaoh's Daughter: A Novel of Ancient Egypt.* Harper Trophy, 2002. 192pp. Paper ISBN 978-0-06-440969-8. Grades 7–12.

Mosis and his sister Almah alternate points of view to tell their story. The Egyptian princess Meryetamun sees the Habiru child Mosis with his sister Almah and takes him to the palace to raise as her son. Almah knows the Egyptian language of Khemetain and its customs so Meryetamun readily accepts her. Soon the pharaoh displaces his daughter with Almah because Almah reminds him of his dead wife, Nefertari. Simultaneously, Meryetamun finds herself enjoying the Habiru people more than the Khemetains. Almah becomes a priestess of Eset and dances at the festivals naked. In the second half of the book, Mosis, now 15, remains unsure of his allegiances until those from whom he wants approval reject him. He decides that he must defend the Habiru, who have toiled as slaves for Rameses. *Publishers Weekly Best Children's Books* and *Dorothy Canfield Fisher Children's Book Award* (Vermont) nomination.

361. Logan, Claudia. *The 5,000-Year-Old Puzzle: Solving a Mystery of Ancient Egypt.* Farrar, 2002. 41pp. ISBN 978-0-374-32335-6. Grades 3–5.

In 1924 Dr. George Reisner discovered a tomb in Giza, Egypt. Will Hunt goes with his family and Reisner to do research on the tomb, called Giza 7000 X. Among the illustrations are postcards, a hieroglyphic puzzle, sidebars, and paintings of different sizes that show the work that Will, Reisner, and the Qufti helpers do and how they finally reach the tomb in February of 1925. Photographs and illustrations enhance the text.

362. Lorenz, Albert. *The Trojan Horse.* Illustrated by Joy Schleh. Abrams, 2006. Unpaged. ISBN 978-0-8109-5986-6. Grades 2–6.

Along with background about Greek warships, the causes of the Trojan war, and the city of Troy, the text presents the Trojan Horse, the contraption in which Greek soldiers hid themselves in order to surprise their Trojan enemy. Illustrations blur the line between graphic novel and picture book.

363. Lottridge, Celia Barker. *Stories from Adam and Eve to Ezekiel.* Narrated by Gary Clement. Groundwood, 2004. 192pp. ISBN 978-0-8889-9490-5. Grades 4–8.

These thirty-two stories from the Bible's Old Testament include background about the incidents' time and place. Among the figures presented are Adam and Eve, Abraham, Moses, Daniel, Esther, Jonah, Daniel, Miriam, Ruth, David, Jacob, Leah, and Rachel. Illustrations complement the text.

364. McDonnell, Vincent. *Children of Stone.* Collins, 2006. 206pp. ISBN 978-1-903464-88-5. Grades 4–7.

While their father is away in Sarnay asking the lord of the area for protection and food for his Stone Age village, 12-year-old Bolan and his younger siblings are taken hostage. Their captor is a villager who wants to take power from their father, who is the village leader. The three escape and face wolves, bears, and wanderers in the forest while desperately trying to find their father and warn him of the danger at home.

365. McGraw, Eloise Jarvis. *The Golden Goblet.* Puffin, 1990. 248pp. Paper ISBN 978-0-14-030335-3. Grades 5–9.

Twelve-year-old Ranofer determines that his older half brother is stealing gold from his employer in this story set in ancient Egypt. Gebu not only takes Ranofer's inheritance and refuses to buy Ranofer an apprenticeship, but he also steals from a queen's tomb. When Ranofer realizes what is happening, he reports it to the palace, and the guards finally believe him when he identifies the objects. As a result of his loyalty, he becomes a goldsmith's apprentice. *Newbery Honor Book.*

366. McGraw, Eloise Jarvis. *Mara, Daughter of the Nile.* Puffin, 1985. 288pp. Paper ISBN 978-0-14-031929-3. Grades 4–7.

Mara, 17, has blue eyes, an unusual characteristic in Egypt during 1550 B.C.E. Although she is a slave, she speaks and reads Babylonian. This ability enables her to translate for the wife of Hatshepsut's brother, Thutmose, and to become a spy for evil brothers who are trying to destroy Thutmose. Then she begins to spy on the brothers for Thutmose's brother, Sheftu. After proving her loyalty to Sheftu, she marries him when the evil brothers are apprehended.

367. McLaren, Clemence. *Aphrodite's Blessings: Love Stories from the Greek Myths.* Atheneum, 2002. 202pp. ISBN 978-0-689-84377-8; Aladdin, 2008. paper ISBN 978-1-4169-7860-2. Grades 7 up.

In this story of three marriages, each woman must either sacrifice or make a promise to help her beloved. Atalanta loves running and defying the expectations for women in boring Arcadia. But she hears that the young men who lose to her in races will be killed, and she decides that she will let Milanion of Thrace win when he throws charmed golden apples in her path. Andromeda, sacrificed to a sea monster because of her mother's vanity, is rescued by Perseus, the hero she has seen in her dreams. Psyche's sisters poison her and tempt her to betray the trust of Eros, her love. She looks at Eros in the light and loses him, but she regains him and even wins the approval of his mother, Aphrodite.

368. McLaren, Clemence. *Inside the Walls of Troy: A Novel of the Women Who Lived the Trojan War.* Illustrated by Joel Peter Johnson. Simon & Schuster, 2004. 184pp. Paper ISBN 978-0-689-87397-3. Grades 7 up.

Helen of Troy relates the story of her elopement with Paris during the 14th or 15th century B.C.E. from a perspective that is very different from Homer's *Iliad*. She feels that beauty burdens her. Cassandra, Paris's sister, continues the story as she discusses the men in combat outside Troy's walls and the women struggling within. The women must comfort and nurse the men, supervise their homes, and gather food for their families during this terrible war. *SCASL Book Award* (South Carolina) nomination.

369. Manning, Mick. *Greek Hero.* Illustrated by Brita Granstrom. (Fly on the Wall) Frances Lincoln, 2008. 40pp. ISBN 978-1-8450-7683-2. Grades 3–5.

In 479 B.C.E. a Greek hoplite soldier, Argathon, listens to campfire stories while sleeping on the battlefield. He returns from battle on the merchant Lykon's boat. At home, he marries Lykon's daughter and decides to compete in the Olympic Games with Lykon's encouragement. Cartoon illustrations highlight the text.

370. Manning, Mick. *Pharaoh's Egypt.* Illustrated by Brita Granström. Frances Lincoln, 2006. 37pp. ISBN 978-1-845071-00-4. Grades 2–4.

Huya, a scribe in ancient Egypt, describes life in his country during the reign of Rameses the Great. Presented in an eye-catching layout, topics include the role of a scribe, the gods, the temple, priests, mummy-makers, the Nile, and other information about ancient Egyptian culture. Realistic details include Huya feeling sick when he visits the embalmer and a stonemason dropping a mallet on his foot.

371. Mitchell, Jack. *The Roman Conspiracy.* Tundra, 2005. Paper ISBN 978-0-88776-713-5. Grades 5–8.

In 63 B.C.E. Roman warrior Manlius takes Aulus Lucinus Spurinna's homeland of Etruria. His uncle then dies mysteriously, and Spurinna inherits his uncle's land (all of Etruria) while soldiers continue to pillage. Although Spurinna has always wanted to see Rome, he regrets having to go to there to ask for help from Cicero, his family's protector. Spurinna travels to Rome with his faithful and educated servant Homer, and in Rome, he meets Cicero's daughter, Tullia, who helps him reveal a complex conspiracy with the potential to overthrow the Roman Empire.

372. Montgomery, Claire, and Monte Montgomery. *Hubert Invents the Wheel.* Illustrated by Jeff Shelly. Walker, 2005. 192pp. ISBN 978-0-8027-8990-7. Grades 4–7.

Hubert, a 15-year-old ancient Sumerian, devises many inventions that do not work well. His father suggests that Hubert and his small horse help him haul items for their business. Hubert invents a wheel for the task and proves its value when he wins a race. Cartoon illustrations complement the text. *Bluebonnet Book Award* (Texas) nomination.

373. Morgan, Anna. *Daughters of the Ark.* Second Story, 2005. 230pp. Paper ISBN 978-1-8967-6492-4. Grades 7–9.

In a three-part look at Ethiopian Jews, Aleesha and her family leave Jerusalem in 939 B.C.E. with King Solomon's son to take the sacred ark and the Ten Commandments to Ethiopia to be safe. In 1984, 14-year-old Debritu lives in an Ethiopian community of African Jewish families, Beta Israel. They cross Ethiopia's mountains and Sudan's desert during famine and oppression to reach Khartoum and an airlift to Israel. Although Aleesha is fictional, Debritu is not, but the long exodus ends with her. Photographs and Maps.

374. Napoli, Donna Jo. *Sirena.* Scholastic, 2000. Paper ISBN 978-0-590-38389-9. Grades 7 up.

Sirena and her mermaid sisters often lure men to them with their songs, and one day Sirena discovers that these men lose their lives. She decides to live alone, without singing, on the island of Lemnos. But Philoctetes appears after being bitten by a snake and abandoned by his shipmates, and Sirena rescues him from the sea. Fearful that he, too, will lose his life, she hesitates to form a friendship. The Greek gods give Sirena the gift of immortality after Philoctetes's rescue since he is a friend of Hercules. But Philoctetes has to defend Greece in the Trojan War, and since he is not immortal, the two are separated when he dies. *Garden State Teen Book Awards* (New Jersey) nomination, *Young Readers Choice Awards Master List* (Pennsylvania), and *Tayshas High School Reading List* (Texas).

375. Platt, Richard. *Egyptian Diary: The Journal of Nakht.* Candlewick, 2005. 64pp. ISBN 978-0-7636-2756-0. Grades 4 up.

Around 1500 B.C.E., 9-year-old Nakht moves from the small Egyptian town of Esna to the city of Memphis where he studies to be a scribe like his father. He records his experiences in his diary, and among the sights he and his sister enjoy are youths drinking beer, bricks being made by hand, and crocodiles and hippos on the river Nile. He describes the hunting, home remodeling, feasting, farming, and funerals that he sees. Soon he and his sister discover a plot to rob nearby tombs. When they catch the mastermind, a high-ranking official, in their own home, King Hatshepsut invites them to the royal palace in Thebes. They are shocked to discover that the king is a woman. Time Line and Glossary.

376. Renault, Mary. *The Bull from the Sea.* Vintage, 2001. 343pp. Paper ISBN 978-0-375-72680-4. Grades YA.

Theseus returns to Athens but forgets to raise the white sail that will tell his father he is safe and his father kills himself in grief. Theseus tries to atone for his mistake by cleaning up the kingdom and adding Crete to his conquests. He agrees to marry Phaedra, daughter of the dead king Minos, when he comes of age. However, he meets Hippolyta, queen of the Amazons. and falls in love with her. She has his child, named Hippolytos, although they cannot marry. After Theseus marries Phaedra, Hippolyta sacrifices herself in battle, and Phaedra and his heir come to live with Theseus in Athens. Phaedra lusts after Hippolytos and tries to seduce him, but he refuses, and she accuses him of rape. Theseus condemns Hippolytos without asking what happened, and lives remorsefully because a tidal wave drowns Hippolytos just after Theseus curses him.

377. Renault, Mary. *Fire from Heaven.* Vintage, 2002. 374pp. Paper ISBN 978-0-375-72682-8. Grades YA.

Alexander shows political and military abilities at age 6, unnerves Demosthenes at age 10, and leads troops in combat at Thrace at age 15. When he serves as his father's regent, he founds a city and becomes a general at the age of 17. He astonishes various Persian ambassadors with his accomplishments from 352 until 336 B.C.E., when he becomes king after Philip's assassination. Alexander loves competition in athletics, in battle, and in politics. Although he is married, he also has a loving relationship with his military companion, Hephaiston.

378. Renault, Mary. *The King Must Die.* Vintage, 1988. 352pp. Paper ISBN 978-0-394-75104-7. Grades YA.

Theseus comes to Athens when he is 17 years old, but he soon has to leave for Crete as one of the seven youths sent as yearly tribute to King Minos of Crete. He falls in love with Minos's daughter Ariadne, who gives him the string that helps him free himself from the labyrinth and certain death in the ritual bull dance. Then he sees Ariadne and other women tear apart the local king as a ritual sacrifice to ensure fertility during the following year. He leaves the island in disgust. In Athens, he shifts to belief in a masculine religion rather than the traditional feminine beliefs as he unites Eleusis, Troizen, and Athens.

379. Renault, Mary. *The Last of the Wine.* Vintage, 2001. 389pp. Paper ISBN 978-0-375-72681-1. Grades YA.

Along with his schoolmate and male lover, Alexias becomes a soldier, athlete, citizen, and pupil of Socrates in Athens. As he tries to understand the ethical and philosophical truths that Socrates teaches, he cannot reconcile the insolence of the men who condemn Socrates in their quest for power and money.

380. Renault, Mary. *The Mask of Apollo.* Vintage, 1988. 384pp. Paper ISBN 978-0-394-75105-4. Grades YA.

Nikeratos, age 19, has studied acting with his father, and he understands the power of an actor over an audience. When his father dies, he joins a small troupe in which he gains enough experience to produce his own plays. When he plays Achilles for Alexander in Pella, he becomes for Alexander the definitive Achilles, the man of moderation who refused to kill Agamemnon near the beginning of the Trojan War and who later sees Hector kill his best friend, Patrokolus.

381. Renault, Mary. *The Persian Boy.* Vintage, 1988. 432pp. Paper ISBN 978-0-394-75101-6. Grades YA.

When Alexander the Great is 26 years old, he meets a Persian slave boy, Bagoas, who becomes his companion and lover. Bagoas once belonged to the Persian king Darius, and he understands Alexander's need for affection and his sympathy for his Persian subjects. Bagoas stays with Alexander until he dies from a fever.

382. Roberts, Katherine. *I Am the Great Horse.* Chicken House, 2006. 401pp. ISBN 978-0-439-82163-6. Grades 7 up.

Bucephalus, the horse of Alexander the Great, keeps his position as the leader of the pack as he tells about his master and those they conquer. The female groom, Charm, describes things that Bucephalus cannot observe but that they communicate to each other. His Alexander is a driven man who focuses on his plans and executes them appropriately. The three live and fight together throughout Greece, Persia, and India around 330 B.C.E.

383. Robinson, Lynda S. *Eater of Souls: A Lord Meren Mystery.* Ballantine, 1998. 229pp. Paper ISBN 978-0-345-39533-7. Grades YA.

After Tutankhamen has ruled for five years, Lord Meren and his adopted son Kysen, 18, must find the identity of a serial killer who dismembers his victims and then eats their hearts.

384. Robinson, Lynda S. *Murder at the Feast of Rejoicing: A Lord Meren Mystery.* Ballantine, 1995. 229pp. Paper ISBN 978-0-345-48292-1. Grades YA.

Lord Meren wants a vacation to get away from everyone after solving a problem for Tutankhamen, but when he returns to his village, he discovers that his sister has invited family and friends to greet him. Then his cousin Sennefer's shrewish wife, Anhai, turns up dead, and Lord Meren has another mystery to solve. When the pharaoh arrives and Meren's daughter, Bener, wants to help, discovering the murderer becomes more difficult.

385. Rockwell, Anne. *Romulus and Remus.* Aladdin, 1997. 40pp. Paper ISBN 978-0-689-81290-3. Grades 1–2.

A female wolf raises the twins Romulus and Remus. Remus especially enjoys hunting expeditions with the wolves. Romulus builds a city called Rome on seven hills and becomes its king.

386. Ross, Stewart. *Athens Is Saved! The First Marathon.* Illustrated by Susan Shields. (Coming Alive) Evans Brothers, 2007. 62pp. Paper ISBN 978-0-237-53152-2. Grades 3–5.

Cimon, the young athlete who supposedly ran to Athens with the news of the Greeks' victory over the Persians in the Battle of Marathon, inspired people around the world to compete in footraces. This story, based on the legend of the runner Pheidippides, recounts Cimon's military training and his selection as the messenger to announce the victory despite his stutter.

387. Ross, Stewart. *Curse of the Crocodile God.* Inklink, 2007. 48pp. ISBN 978-0-7566-2564-1; paper ISBN 978-0-7566-2563-4. Grades 3–6.

In ancient Egypt, Methen and Madja, both 13, discover that someone has robbed a tomb. They try to find the villain and solve the crime. However, the pharaoh threatens to execute them. Illustrations highlight the text, and "Did You Know" facts appear at the bottom of each page to tell more about Egyptian culture.

388. Ross, Stewart. *The Price of Victory.* Inklink, 2007. 48pp. ISBN 978-0-7566-2568-9; paper ISBN 978-0-7566-2567-2. Grades 3–6.

In ancient Greece, Kinesias plans to compete in the Olympic Games. But he and his brother Pylades are being pursued by someone who almost kills him by pushing over statues and sinking his boat. Illustrations highlight the text, and "Did You Know" facts appear at the bottom of each page to tell more about Egyptian culture.

389. Sabuda, Robert. *Tutankhamen's Gift.* Atheneum, 1994. Unpaged. ISBN 978-0-689-31818-4; Aladdin, 1997. paper ISBN 978-0-689-81730-4. Grades 3–5.

Pictures painted on papyrus authenticate this fictionalized account of Tutankhamen, the youngest son of an Egyptian queen and Amenhotep III. Tutankhamen came to the throne as a frail ten-year-old upon his brother Amenhotep IV's death. Notes on the text elaborate upon the story of the king who died young and without heirs, but who was fondly remembered by his subjects.

390. Saylor, Steven. *Arms of Nemesis: A Novel of Ancient Rome.* Minotaur, 2008. 336pp. Paper ISBN 978-0-312-38323-7. Grades YA.

Gordianus the Finder is called to Baiae on the Bay of Naples during the Spartacus slave revolt in 72 B.C.E. Two slaves are accused of murdering Lucius Licinius, and Gordianus has been requested to absolve them by finding the true murderer. He has only three days for his investigation before Crassus, Licinius's cousin, will kill all the slaves on his estate in retribution.

391. Saylor, Steven. *Catilina's Riddle: A Novel of Ancient Rome.* Minotaur, 2008. 448pp. Paper ISBN 978-0-312-38529-3. Grades YA.

In 63 B.C.E., Gordianus inherits an Etruscan farm from his benefactor, Lucius Claudius, but must fend off relatives and neighbors who want the land. His patron, Cicero, defends his claim and seeks payment. He asks Gordianus to watch his political rival, the senator Catilina. Soon headless bodies appear on the farm, and Gordianus begins to wonder about the qualities of both Catilina and Cicero.

392. Scieszka, Jon. *Tut, Tut.* Illustrated by Lane Smith and Adam McCauley. (Time Warp Trio, # 6) Penguin, 1996. 80pp. ISBN 978-0-670-84832-4; Puffin, 2004. paper ISBN 978-0-14-240047-0. Grades 3–6.

Joe's little sister Anna accidently opens a magical book, and Joe and his friends Sam and Fred end up in ancient Egypt. They must search for Anna, who has become lost with the cat, Cleo, and the book. To succeed, they must stop a pharaoh's evil priest, escape from a mummy-making chamber, and keep crocodiles from swallowing them. *Children's Book Award* (Massachusetts) and *Sasquatch Reading Award* (Washington).

393. Scott, Manda. ***Boudica: Dreaming the Bull.*** (Boudica) Dell, 2008. 384pp. Paper ISBN 978-0-440-24109-6. Grades YA.

In *Dreaming the Eagle*, Breaca loses her brother, Bán, when he is captured by the Romans in battle. She goes to the sacred isle of Mona to raise her children and to prepare to meet the Romans again. In Rome, Bán learns about Roman ways and rises in the Roman army as Julius Valerius. He becomes the leader of a group of soldiers returning to Britannia. Breaca and her husband, Caradoc, continue to battle the Romans, and their son, Cunomar, anticipates the day when he will kill his first Roman.

394. Scott, Manda. ***Boudica: Dreaming the Eagle.*** (Boudica) Dell, 2008. 465pp. Paper ISBN 978-0-440-24109-6. Grades YA.

Breaca nic Graine, the Celtic warrior queen known as Boudica, wants to be a dreamer when she grows up. In her society, dreamers advise the tribal leaders and the community depends on their perceptions. Her brother, Bán, foresees her as part of the terrible future when she must take the responsiblity of defending the tribe against strong enemies. Therefore, she is not a dreamer; she is a warrior, and she travels to Mona where she learns the art of war. There she meets Caradoc, saved by her people after a shipwreck, and he shows himself her equal in intelligence and courage.

395. Scott, Manda. ***Boudica: Dreaming the Hound.*** (Boudica) Delacorte, 2006. 415pp. ISBN 978-0-385-33672-7; Delta, 2007. paper ISBN 978-0-385-33775-5. Grades YA.

In the summer of 60 C.E., Breaca (now Boudica) must provide guidance to the Eceni if they are to rid their land of the enemy. The Eceni leadership has decided to accept the Romans and do their bidding. Boudica wants to fight the Roman legions since they have exiled her husband, Carodoc. Bán/Valerius must reconcile the Eceni and Roman sides of his life and his two destinies as warrior and dreamer after betraying the Eceni to the Romans. He saves Boudica from being crucified by the emperor after her daughter, Graine, is repeatedly raped. But Boudica still must face the Romans in a last battle.

396. Scott, Manda. ***Boudica: Dreaming the Serpent Spear.*** (Boudica) Delta, 2007. 445pp. Paper ISBN 978-0-385-33835-6. Grades YA.

In 60 C.E., an attempt to distract the Roman legions, the Eceni stage a sacrifice of their sacred citadel of Mona. Boudica must lead her people one last time even though she suffers physically from a severe beating and psychologically from the gang rape of her daughter, Graine. Her brother, Valerius, helps her. The war party of 5,000 gathers, and they destroy the two legions that come to Mona before burning Camulodunum, Rome's capital in Britannia. In the end, Boudica can fight no more, but she has almost stopped the invading Romans.

397. Sedgwick, Marcus. ***The Dark Horse.*** Laurel-Leaf, 2004. 160pp. Paper ISBN 978-0-440-41908-2. Grades 5–8.

Sigurd, 16, has become chief of his people, the Storn, as they prepare to face the invading Dark Horse people in ancient Britain. A blond-haired, black-palmed stranger arrives, wanting to know about a lost magic box and bringing death with him. He also knows the identify of Mouse, the waif rescued by Sigurd five years before who can communicate with animals. The intersection of events causes Mouse to unexpectedly betray Sigurd as the people cope with change. *Great Lakes Children's Book Award* (Michigan) nomination and *Tayshas High School Reading List* (Texas).

398. Service, Pamela F. *The Reluctant God.* Juniper, 1997. 211pp. Paper ISBN 978-0-449-70339-7. Grades 6–9.

Lorna, in England, wants to be back in Egypt with her widowed father at his archaeological dig. After Lorna returns to Egypt, she meets Ameni in a tomb where he is searching for Eternity as he trains to be a priest in 2000 B.C.E. Elsewhere his twin brother prepares to become the Pharaoh Senusert III. Lorna takes Ameni back to England with her to find a relic that he needs to fulfill his destiny. *Golden Kite Award.*

399. Shecter, Vicky Alvear. *Alexander the Great Rocks the World.* Illustrated by Terry Naughton. Darby Creek, 2006. 128pp. ISBN 978-1-58196-045-7. Grades 5–8.

Alexander the Great of Macedonia and his famous horse, Bucephalus, conquered his known world in the 4th century B.C.E. and established one language and one currency within Alexander's realm, mostly before he turned 30. He was not only a great leader, but he was also a courageous man who respected women and different cultures. The flippant, comic tone of this book shows an unusual side of Alexander and his importance to the generations that succeeded him. Illustrations complement the text. Notes and Bibliography. *Voice of Youth Advocates Nonfiction Honor List.*

400. Sutcliff, Rosemary. *Warrior Scarlet.* Sunburst, 1994. 207pp. Paper ISBN 978-0-374-48244-2. Grades 4–7.

In this story set in the Bronze Age, Drem looks forward to wearing the scarlet cloak that will identify him as a tribal warrior. But he must first kill a wolf. Because he has only one good arm, he fails and is cast out of the tribe. Later he kills three wolves while trying to protect another outcast, and tribal leaders reconsider their law. They recognize that Drem has more than earned the right to wear a scarlet cloak. First published in 1958. *International Board of Books for Young People* and *Carnegie Commendation.*

401. Taylor, Cora. *The Deadly Dance.* Coteau, 2003. 160pp. Paper ISBN 978-1-55050-272-5. Grades 7 up.

While visiting Crete with her parents, Penny, a 15-year-old gymnast, sees a Minoan painting on the wall in the Palace of Knossos and finds herself transported to the time of Theseus as a bull dancer. As a bull charges at her, she and other members of her troop perform stunts to stay alive in a "deadly dance." Although she begins to fall in love with one of the dancers, she escapes when an earthquake destroys the palace and returns to her own time better able to understand her difficult relationship with her brother and to resolve her eating disorder.

402. Tomlinson, Theresa. *The Moon Riders.* Eos, 2006. 400pp. ISBN 978-0-06-084736-4. Grades 7 up.

Myrina, a member of the Mazagardi tribe, joins the Moon Riders, a group of warrior women known as Amazons, when she is 13 years old. She has to serve with the group, who worship Earth Mother Maa, for seven years. Then she meets Odysseus and Achilles and becomes involved in the life of the princess Cassandra and the ten-year-long Trojan War. Myrina tries to help her before the city falls to the Greeks.

403. Uderzo, Albert. *Asterix and the Actress.* Translated by Anthea Bell and Derek Hockridge. Orion, 2001. 48pp. ISBN 978-0-7528-4657-6; paper ISBN 978-0-7528-4658-3. Grades 4–7.

In 50 B.C.E., Pompey hires the actress Latraviata to portray Panacea so he can reclaim his sword and helmet from Asterix and Obelix, who are visiting their Gaulish village to celebrate their joint birthdays. After thwarting Pompey, Asterix and Obelix must rescue their fathers from a Roman prison. Cartoon illustrations enhance the funny text.

404. Unsworth, Barry. *The Songs of the Kings.* Double Talk, 2003. 338pp. ISBN 978-0-385-50114-9; Norton, 2004. paper ISBN 978-0-393-32283-5. Grades YA.

When unfavorable winds keep King Agamemnon from sailing toward Troy to defeat Paris and return Helen to Menelaus, he must sacrifice his daughter Iphigenia to the gods of the wind. To lure Iphigenia to Aulis from Mycenae, she is told that she has been promised in marriage to Achilles. She arrives with her mother Clytemnestra to discover that the planned event is not a wedding.

405. Williams, Maiya. *The Hour of the Cobra.* Harry N. Abrams, 2006. 312pp. ISBN 978-0-8109-5970-5; 2007 paper ISBN 978-0-8109-9362-4. Grades 4–9.

In this sequel to *The Golden Hour*, 14-year-old African American twins Xanthe and Xavier carry out a mission with Rowan Poplewell, 13, and his younger sister, Nina, to save manuscripts from Alexandria's library. To participate in the Twilight Tourist Time-Travel Program, one must do nothing to change the course of history. But Xanthe forgets and befriends the young Cleopatra when Cleopatra thinks she is Isis and asks for her help. Xanthe's advice changes history; therefore all four must put history back in place before they return home. Rowan and Nina's Aunt Agatha is arrested, and the four must escape from being trapped inside the Great Pyramid to free her. Rowan and Xavier also battle gladiators before they can end the experience.

406. Would, Nick. *The Scarab's Secret.* Illustrated by Christina Balit. Walker, 2006. 32pp. ISBN 978-0-8027-9561-8. Grades K–3.

Khepri, the scarab beetle whose name means "rising sun" and who is a sacred extension of the Egyptian sun god Ra, meets a prince on the banks of the Nile. The prince tells him that the two will meet again. They do meet when the beetle wanders into a tomb that the prince is inspecting. There the beetle finds a trapdoor that the prince's enemies have designed that kills anyone who falls through it. Khepri is able to lead the prince away from the impending danger to which three workmen have led him.

History

407. Adams, Simon. *Ancient Egypt.* (Voyages) Kingfisher, 2006. 54pp. ISBN 978-0-7534-6027-6. Grades 4–6.

Egyptologist Kent Weeks looks at three areas of ancient Egypt—the Nile Delta, the Nile Valley, and Upper Egypt and beyond. Weeks explains the engineering of the pyramids and the practice of embalming. He also notes that some things remain unknown, such as how the ancient Egyptians raised an obelisk. In addition to sidebars, charts, and maps, the layout includes foldout pages and transparent overlays. Glossary, Chronology, and Index.

408. Adkins, Lesley, and Roy A. Adkins. *Handbook to Life in Ancient Greece.* Facts on File, 2005. 514pp. ISBN 978-0-8160-5659-0. Grades YA.

The authors examine life in ancient Greece by looking at its history of city-states and empires, its rulers and leaders, military affairs, geography, economy and trade, transport, and towns and countryside. They give an overview of ancient Greek religion, art, science, and philosophy as revealed in extant writing by the Greeks themselves. Additionally, readers will find what life was like every day for people of different classes. Bibliography and Index.

409. Aliki. *Mummies Made in Egypt.* Harper Trophy, 1985. 32pp. Paper ISBN 978-0-06-446011-8. Grades 2–6.

This book describes various rituals of Egyptian life, the preparation of the dead, the belief in the afterlife, and the gods and goddesses of the dead. *Notable Trade Books in the Field of Social Studies, IRA Children's Choices,* and *Garden State Children's Book Awards* (New Jersey).

410. Arnold, Caroline. *Stone Age Farmers Beside the Sea: Scotland's Prehistoric Village of Skara Brae.* Photos by Arthur P. Arnold. Houghton Mifflin, 1997. 48pp. ISBN 978-0-395-77601-8. Grades 4 up.

Skara Brae, in northern Scotland's Orkney Islands, predates the Egyptian pyramids, having been inhabited from 3100 to 2500 B.C.E. and buried under sand until 150 years ago. Arnold describes the construction of the stone houses there, the daily life of the people who lived there, and how archaeologists have uncovered the site. Glossary and Index. *Best Books for Children.*

411. Barter, James. *The Ancient Persians.* (Lost Civilizations) Lucent, 2005. 112pp. ISBN 978-1-59018-621-3. Grades 3–6.

An overview of the daily lives of the ancient Persians including their culture, society, art, and religion. Among their important contributions to civilization are the Hammurabi code of law, a monetary system, and a communication system. Although diplomatic, they conquered the Babylonians in 540 B.C.E. By 333 B.C.E., the civilization had begun to decline. Illustrations augment the text. Bibliography, Maps, and Index.

412. Benduhn, Tea. *Ancient Greece.* (Life Long Ago) Weekly Reader, 2006. 24pp. ISBN 978-0-8368-7782-3; 2007. paper ISBN 978-0-8368-8038-0. Grades 1–3.

This brief but clear introduction to ancient Greece includes background on the gods and goddesses along with information on the people's lives, travels, and entertainment. Illustrations highlight the text.

413. Bingham, Jane. *The Ancient World.* (History of Costume and Fashion) Facts on File, 2005. 64pp. ISBN 978-0-8160-5944-7. Grades 5–8.

A discussion of jewelry, textile production, hair care, grooming, hygiene, battle dress, and clothing for men and women in different classes, along with the impact of climate, geography, leaders, and significant historical events on modes of dress in the ancient world. As tools become more sophisticated, so do materials. Photographs and illustrations highlight the text. Bibliography, Glossary, Chronology, Notes, Further Reading, Web Sites, and Index.

414. Broida, Marian. *Projects About Ancient Greece.* (Hands-on History) Benchmark, 2006. 47pp. ISBN 978-0-7614-2259-4. Grades 3–5.

Information about ancient Greece is accompanied by projects that help readers to understand its people and society. The projects include a Minoan bull-dancer painting, Mycenaean writing, black-figure pottery, an Athenian ostrakon, a Spartan shield, and knucklebones. Photographs and illustrations augment the text. Glossary, Further Reading, Web Sites, and Index.

415. Buller, Laura. *Ancient Egyptians.* Illustrated by Rich Cando. (History Dudes) DK, 2007. 64pp. ISBN 978-0-7566-2941-0. Grades 4 up.

The text covers the religion, society, government, culture, and daily lives of the Egyptians. It also features brief biographies of important figures including Rameses the Great and figures of legend and myth. The cartoon format, filled with puns and slang, also discusses the hieroglyphic writing system of the Egyptians. Chronology and Index.

416. Cahill, Thomas. *Sailing the Wine-Dark Sea: Why the Greeks Matter.* Doubleday, 2003. 320pp. ISBN 978-0-385-49553-0; Anchor, 2004. paper ISBN 978-0-385-49554-7. Grades YA.

The Greeks have given the West a varied legacy. Cahill begins with Homer's *Iliad* and *Odyssey* as a background to the history of Greece. Then he discusses the Greek alphabet, drama and poetry (Sophocles, Aeschylus, Euripides, Sappho), political system (Solon), philosophers (pre-Socratics, Plato, Aristotle), and artists (Praxiteles). The Greeks contributed to our vocabulary, our logic, and our system of categorization and developed the basis for understanding philosophy, mathematics, physics, and medicine. But they also created militarism by idealizing the warrior and they repressed women by refusing to allow them to become citizens. Additionally, they socially segregated the sexes. In the final chapter, Cahill analyzes the effects of the Judeo-Christian and the Greco-Roman worlds on each other and notes that Greek, not Hebrew, became the language of Christianity.

417. Charman, Andrew. *Life and Times in Ancient Rome.* Kingfisher, 2007. 32pp. Paper ISBN 978-0-7534-6151-8. Grades 1–5.

The simple text examines the life in Rome. Two-page spreads cover the topics of transportation, clothing, food and drink, shopping, homes, baths, theater, the *circus maximus*, the Colosseum, temples and worship, the countryside, and life in the city. Illustrations complement the text.

418. Chrisp, Peter. *Pyramid.* Dorling Kindersley, 2006. 67pp. ISBN 978-0-7566-1410-2. Grades 4–8.

With storyboard text on full-color illustrations, *Pyramid* shows the steps for building the Great Pyramid of Giza. It also features information about settlement on the Nile, tools used in construction, the tombs and their secrets, and other pertinent information.

419. Clare, John D. *Ancient Greece.* Gareth Stevens, 2004. 64pp. ISBN 978-0-8368-4198-5. Grades 6–9.

Complemented by posed photographs, this book looks at life in Greece from about 800 B.C.E. until 146 B.C.E. Short discussions present the Greek world, farming in Attica, Sparta, gods and goddesses, heroes, the Olympic Games, Greek colonies, Marathon, Thermopylae and Salamis, Athenian democracy and empire, art and architecture, theater, knowledge and philosophy, doctors and medicine, rituals, craftspeople and traders, the agora, old age and death, plague and war, Philip and Alexander, Alexandria, the rise of Rome, and women's roles. A concluding essay explores the ways in which people today benefit from knowing about this ancient civilization. Index. *Notable Children's Trade Books in the Field of Social Studies.*

420. Cline, Eric H., and Jill Rubalcaba. *The Ancient Egyptian World.* (World in Ancient Times) Oxford, 2005. 190pp. ISBN 978-0-19-517391-8. Grades 6–10.

Chronological chapters present the history of ancient Egypt, its people, its culture, and its contribution to Western society. Among the topics are geography, religion, medicine, fashion, arts, magic, and rulers. Also included are portraits of Pepi II (a boy of six who commanded Egyptian armies), Hatshepsut (Egypt's only female pharaoh), Tutankhamen, Rameses II (conqueror of the Hittites), and Cleopatra. Information comes from scarabs, papyri, tomb inscriptions, mummies, and other primary sources. Illustrations and maps augment the text. Index.

421. Connolly, Peter. *Pompeii.* Oxford, 1994. 77pp. Paper ISBN 978-0-19-917158-3. Grades 6–8.

The author looks at the eruption of Vesuvius, the volcano that destroyed Pompeii in 79, by examining the excavation finds at the site. Connolly includes detailed drawings recreating the scenes that might have been caught in the lava that day. Maps, Glossary, and Index.

422. Connolly, Peter, and Hazel Dodge. *The Ancient City: Life in Classical Athens and Rome.* Oxford, 2000. 256pp. Paper ISBN 978-0-19-521582-3. Grades 9 up.

A look at life in the two ancient cities. Readers will learn about daily life in Athens, the cradle of democracy in Greece, as well as the Greeks' work, houses, temples, festivals, and theater. The section on Rome covers its site, government, food and water, houses and apartments, daily life, shops, restaurants, gods, races, theater, baths, and Colosseum, as well as the age of Apollodorus and its late antiquity. Photographs and illustrations highlight the text. Bibliography, Glossary, and Index.

423. Connolly, Peter, and Andrew Solway. *Ancient Greece.* Oxford, 2001. 64pp. ISBN 978-0-19-910810-7. Grades 3–6.

The authors examine the daily lives of ancient Greeks in Athens, Sparta, and Persia. The topics include houses, religion, government, work, social life, sports and games, and the theater. Illustrations intensify the text. Glossary and Index.

424. Curlee, Lynn. *Parthenon.* Atheneum, 2004. 34pp. ISBN 978-0-689-84490-4. Grades 3–8.

This history of the Parthenon includes how it was constructed and later restored. Terms for the building's parts are included, and the information covers its purpose, proportions, and construction. The author also discusses the removal of the so-called Elgin Marbles to London's British Museum in 1812. A map and floor plan add to the reader's understanding of this amazing edifice. Acrylic illustrations complement the text. Bibliography. *Parents Choice Award.*

425. Curlee, Lynn. *The Seven Wonders of the Ancient World.* Simon & Schuster, 2002. 40pp. ISBN 978-0-689-83182-9. Grades 3–7.

This book examines the structures determined to be the seven wonders of the ancient world and asks what purposes these structures had and how people had the means to construct them. The seven structures are the Hanging Gardens of Babylon, the Colossus of Rhodes, the Great Pyramid at Giza, the Mausoleum at Halicarnassus, the Statue of Zeus at Olympia, the Temple of Artemis at Ephesus, and the Lighthouse of Alexandria. Curlee examines each wonder in a four-page spread, examining its design and scope. Maps and Illustrations. *Emphasis on Reading* (Alabama) nomination.

426. Dargie, Richard. *Ancient Greece: Health and Disease.* Illustrated by Adam Hook. Narrated by Hook. (Changing Times) Compass Point, 2007. 32pp. ISBN 978-0-7565-2087-8. Grades 5–7.

After some background about the ancient Greeks, twelve two-page chapters cover their beliefs about medicine and sickness. Along with gods that healed, the Greeks had doctors who gave diagnoses. They used herbs and drugs for pregnancy and childbirth, epidemics, wounds, operations, and mental illness. Photographs, maps, and reproductions illuminate the text. Glossary, Chronology, Further Reading, and Index.

427. Dargie, Richard. *Ancient Greece : Crime and Punishment.* Illustrated by Adam Hook. Narrated by Hook. (Changing Times) Compass Point, 2007. 32pp. ISBN 978-0-7565-2084-7. Grades 5–7.

After some background about the ancient Greeks, twelve two-page chapters cover the kinds of crimes Greeks were likely to commit and their penalties. For theft, assault, impiety, and murder, Greeks received different punishments—including exile and execution. Photographs, maps and reproductions illuminate the text. Glossary, Chronology, Further Reading, and Index.

428. Davis, Kenneth C. *Don't Know Much About Mythology.* HarperCollins, 2005. 545pp. ISBN 978-0-06-019460-4; 2006. paper ISBN 978-0-06-093257-2. Grades YA.

In a question-and-answer format, Davis covers mythology throughout the world—Egypt, Mesopotamia (Gilgamesh), Greece, Rome, India, China, Japan, sub-Saharan Africa, the Americas, the Pacific Islands, and the Celts (Finn McCool) and the Norse (Sigurd). For each culture, he includes important events and characters and explains origins, symbolism, and cultural importance. In the initial chapter, he gives an overview of mythology's history. He also discusses the influence of mythology on contemporary culture in movies, art, music, and literature.

429. Deem, James M. *Bodies from the Bog.* Houghton Mifflin, 2005. 43pp. ISBN 978-0-618-47308-3; Houghton, 2003. paper ISBN 978-0-618-35402-3. Grades 4–8.

In 1952 Danish workmen found the body of a dead Iron Age man hidden in peat. Since neither written records nor artifacts from the Iron Age remain, bodies buried in peat can offer information. Among the information gleaned from these bodies are that some died sacrificial deaths; others were buried with jewelry, a wagon, a cauldron, and unusual clues. Still others had been stabbed or hanged. Scientists assess that these bodies were buried between 4500 B.C.E. and 1500 C.E. Photographs enliven the text. Bibliography and Index. *Young Readers Choice Awards* (Pennsylvania), *Capitol Choices Noteworthy Titles* (Washington, D.C.) and *Young Reader Book Awards* (Virginia).

430. Deem, James M. *Bodies from the Ice: Melting Glaciers and the Recovery of the Past.* Houghton, 2008. 58pp. ISBN 978-0-618-80045-2. Grades 5–10.

Retreating glaciers are revealing the past. This account includes the story of Ötzi, a body discovered in the Alps in 1991 that has proven to be more than five thousand years old. The bodies of Inca children have been identified on peaks in the Andes. The body of George Mallory, a climber who died on Mount Everest in 1924, has reappeared. And in northern British Columbia, a man who died between 1670 and 1850 was found to have DNA connected to Canadian First Nations. Such finds give humans a chance to better understand those who preceded them. Photographs augment the text. Bibliography, Further Resources, Web Sites, and Index. *Capitol Choices Noteworthy Titles* (Washington, D.C.), *Notable Trade Books in the Field of Social Studies.*

431. De Medeiros, James. *Parthenon.* (Structural Wonders) Weigl, 2007. 32pp. ISBN 978-1-59036-727-8; paper ISBN 978-1-59036-728-5. Grades 6–9.

The author examines the structure of the Parthenon in Athens, Greece, giving its cultural history and current status along with information about its architecture and the science behind it. This book also covers its construction and who the workers who built it were. To present a perfect balance in the building, the architects decided that optical illusions would work best, and they incorporated them into the design. Photographs, maps, and illustrations highlight the text. Glossary and Web Sites.

432. Dickinson, Rachel. *Tools of the Ancient Romans: A Kid's Guide to the History and Science of Life in Ancient Rome.* (Tools of Discovery) Nomad, 2006. 139pp. Paper ISBN 978-0-9749344-5-7. Grades 5–8.

This history of Rome emphasizes its scientific innovations, weapons, government, religion, and sports, which all continue to be influential in contemporary society. Craft activities scattered throughout the text include making an abacus, a laurel wreath, and a mosaic. Photographs, diagrams, and illustrations highlight the text. Bibliography, Glossary, Chronology, Notes, Further Reading, Web Sites, and Index.

433. Facchini, Fiorenzo. *A Day with Homo Habilis: Life 2,000,000 Years Ago.* Illustrated by Alessandro Baldanzi. (Early Humans) Twenty-First Century, 2003. 48pp. ISBN 978-0-7613-2765-3. Grades 5–9.

Two chapters based on archaeological discoveries create the possible daily life of the *Homo habilis* by placing them into families. Watu, his wife, and children live in a village with huts where Watu works with the tools available to him. Illustrations augment the text. Maps, Glossary, and Index.

434. Filer, Joyce. *Pyramids.* Oxford, 2006. 48pp. ISBN 978-0-19-530521-0. Grades 3–8.

The author examines eight pyramid complexes in ancient Egypt, including their earliest beginnings and their temples and walls. It includes background on the kings for whom they were built and the builders who built them. Each pyramid complex required different construction methods. Among those included are the Step Pyramid of King Djoser, the pyramids of the fourth dynasty, the nearly collapsed pyramid of Ahmose in the eighteenth dynasty, and the Great Pyramid of Giza. Photographs, maps, and illustrations accompany the text. Further Reading and Index.

435. Fleischman, Paul. *Dateline: Troy.* Illustrated by Gwen Frankfeldt and Glenn Morrow. Candlewick, 2006. 80pp. ISBN 978-0-7636-3083-6; paper ISBN 978-0-7636-3084-3. Grades 7 up.

Fleischman compares contemporary news to the events surrounding the Battle of Troy and shows the similarities between the Troy of 3,000 years ago and the culture of today. Using modern newspaper clippings, he compares such topics as people's beliefs, concepts of beauty, and ideals of war. He reveals that neither things nor people have changed much over the centuries. *Booklist Best Books for Young Adults.*

436. Gaff, Jackie Bunn. *Ancient Olympics.* Heinemann, 2003. 32pp. ISBN 978-1-40344-676-3. Grades 3–6.

Two-page spreads introduce the ancient Greeks and the various people, rules, politics, and organization of the original Olympic Games. Photographs augment the text. Chronology, Glossary, and Bibliography.

437. Ganeri, Anita. *Ancient Greeks.* Illustrated by Terry Riley. (Ancient Civilizations) Compass Point, 2006. 32pp. ISBN 978-0-7565-1646-8; paper ISBN 978-0-7565-1757-1. Grades 3–5.

All about the society, laws, drama, language, commerce, and religion during the time of the Greeks, with sidebars offering clarification. Illustrations and maps enrich the text.

438. Gay, Kathlyn. *Science in Ancient Greece.* Franklin Watts, 1999. 95pp. Paper ISBN 978-0-53115-929-3. Grades 4–6.

An introduction to ancient Greece and its science precedes chapters on different developments by scientists from this culture. They include mathematicians and geometers, stargazers, geographers, physicians and anatomists, biologists and botanists, "purists" and practical scientists, and engineers and builders. Also discussed are the Greeks' explanations of the universe and modern society's debt to Greek culture for its discoveries. Photographs and drawings enhance the text. Glossary, Further Reading, and Index.

439. Getz, David. *Frozen Man.* Holt, 1996. 68pp. Paper ISBN 978-0-8050-4645-8. Grades 4–7.

A body found in the Alps between Austria and Italy seemed unexceptional until an archaeologist examined it and discovered that the man had died more than five thousand years ago. By examining his body, archaeologists have learned what life in Europe might have been like during that time, including what clothing was worn, what type of food was eaten, and what the people looked like. Glossary, Bibliography, and Index.

440. Gibbons, Gail. *Mummies, Pyramids, and Pharaohs: A Book About Ancient Egypt.* Little, Brown, 2004. 32pp. ISBN 978-0-316-30928-8. Grades K–3.

Two-page spreads with ink-and-watercolor illustrations present background about Egypt. The topics include society, clothing, farming, homes, crafts, pharaohs, pyramids, mummies, and burial practices.

441. Giblin, James Cross. *The Riddle of the Rosetta Stone: Key to Ancient Egypt.* Trophy, 1993. 85pp. Paper ISBN 978-0-06-446137-5. Grades 5–9.

In 1799 Napoleon's soldiers found a black stone in an old fort north of Alexandria, Egypt, and sent it to Cairo to be examined by scholars accompanying Napoleon on his campaign. They could not decipher the three languages inscribed on the stone before the British routed Napoleon and claimed the stone for the British Museum. Several other scholars who worked on the problem discovered that the three languages on the stone were Greek (Alexander ruled during its creation), Demotic (of the people), and hieroglyphic (sacred). A few years later, a poor young French student, Champollion, met some of the men who had been with Napoleon. He dedicated himself to finding the connection among the languages. In 1824 his book showed that the hieroglyphs were both sound and symbol and he correlated the three segments of the stone. Afterword about the Demotic translation, Bibliography, and Index. *Notable Trade Books in the Field of Social Studies* and *American Library Association Notable Books for Children*.

442. Giblin, James Cross. *Secrets of the Sphinx.* Illustrated by Bagram Ibatoulline. Scholastic, 2004. 47pp. ISBN 978-0-590-09847-2. Grades 7 up.

The facts behind the Great Sphinx of Egypt are that it is 4,500 years old, as long as a city block, and as tall as a six-story building. But no one knows for certain what it is. It could be a pharaoh's portrait or have another significance. Giblin gives a sense of the scholarship surrounding this figure and its history while also addressing the difficulties of its restoration and preservation. Full-bleed watercolors enhance the text. Bibliography and Index. *Children's Book Award* (Rhode Island) nomination and *Orbis Pictus Honor*.

443. Granström, Brita, and Mick Manning. *Fly on the Wall: Pharaoh's Egypt.* Frances Lincoln, 2006. 36pp. ISBN 978-1-8450-7100-4. Grades 2–4.

A look at Egyptian life during the rule of Rameses II. It covers the tombs, temples, activities, palace scribes, and customs of the people. Illustrations add to the text. Glossary and Index.

444. Green, Jen. *Ancient Celts: Archaeology Unlocks the Secrets of the Celts' Past.* (National Geographic Investigates) National Geographic, 2007. 64pp. ISBN 978-1-4263-0225-1. Grades 5–8.

The Celtic culture existed in Europe from approximately 800 B.C.E. through 500 C.E. This book introduces the Celts and connects them to customs that continue today. Among the issues discussed are human sacrifices, what happened to the "bog people," and the importance of Stonehenge. Information about how archaeologists have studied the Celts adds interest. Photographs highlight the text. Bibliography, Glossary, Chronology, Further Reading, Web Sites, and Index. *Notable Trade Books in the Field of Social Studies*.

445. Green, Jen. *Tutankhamen's Tomb.* Illustrated by Gary Slater. (Discoverology) Barron's, 2007. 30pp. ISBN 978-0-7641-5999-2. Grades 2–6.

Pop-ups, flaps, and slides reveal different aspects of items inside King Tutankhamen's tomb. Readers will learn about Howard Carter's discovery of the tomb, the contents of it, and the new insights into Egyptian civilization that the find offered.

446. Harris, Geraldine. *Ancient Egypt.* (Cutural Atlas for Young People) Chelsea House, 2007. 96pp. ISBN 978-0-8160-6823-4. Grades 6–9.

This oversized book groups its topics into two segments: Egypt before the pharaohs and a trip down the Nile. Illustrations augment the history with cartouches of pharaoh's names, human forms of Egyptian deities, maps, and photographs. The text concentrates on archaeological information gleaned from ancient Egyptian sites in Karnak and Abu

Simbel. It discusses mummy preparation, the construction of the pyramids, and many other topics that reveal the lives of the ancient Egyptians. Chronology, Glossary, Gazetteer, and Index.

447. Harris, Nathaniel. *Everyday Life in Ancient Egypt.* Illustrated by Keith Maddison. Creative, 2005. 32pp. ISBN 978-1-932889-78-9. Grades 3–5.

Two-page spreads cover topics such as food, clothing, housing, education, religion, and architecture. Illustrations of artifacts such as pottery and jewelry complement and clarify the text as it presents the social life and customs of ancient Egyptians. Index.

448. Hart, George. *Ancient Egypt.* Illustrated by Stephen Biesty. DK, 2008. 72pp. ISBN 978-0-756637-65-1. Grades 4–7.

Although the layout is busy, with from two to ten carefully labeled photographs on each page and some general text, Hart's book covers many topics. The contents include Egypt before the pharaohs, practices in life and the afterlife, gods and godesses, religion, writing, war, the Nile, various trades, daily habits, leisure activities, and a brief look at Egypt after the pharaohs. Index.

449. Hawass, Zahi. *Curse of the Pharaohs: My Adventures with Mummies.* National Geographic, 2004. 144pp. ISBN 978-0-7922-6665-5. Grades 4–8.

After the opening of King Tut's tomb, several people involved died, and the idea of a "pharaoh's curse" lingers in Hollywood and the media. This book, written by the head of Egypt's Supreme Council of Antiquities, Zahi Hawass, supplies "natural explanations" for the deaths and states that some were merely coincidental. It also describes many of the sites around Egypt. Photographs illuminate the text. Bibliography, Glossary, Chronology, Web Sites, and Index. *Bulletin Blue Ribbon Book.*

450. Hibbert, Clare. *Rich and Poor in Ancient Egypt.* Creative, 2005. 32pp. ISBN 978-1-58340-720-2. Grades 3–6.

This history of ancient Egypt covers the food, homes, religious practices, transportation, work, sports, clothing, and burial customs of different classes of people. Among the photographs and illustrations are artifacts, statues, and other art. Glossary, Chronology, Glossary, Web Sites, and Index.

451. Hinds, Kathryn. *The City.* (Life in Ancient Egypt) Benchmark, 2006. 72pp. ISBN 978-0-7614-2184-9. Grades 6–9.

All about daily life in the cities of ancient Egypt from approximately 1550 B.C.E. to 1070 B.C.E., this book focuses on the roles of various people and what being a child during this era would have been like. Includes quotations from Egyptians and in-depth articles on a variety of topics. Further Reading, Notes, Bibliography, Glossary, Web Sites, and Index.

452. Hinds, Kathryn. *The City.* (Life in Elizabethan England) Marshall Cavendish, 2007. 80pp. ISBN 978-0-7614-2544-1. Grades 6–9.

During Elizabethan times, the period from 1558 to 1603 in England, cities held all levels of society—and all kinds of diseases spread by the lack of sanitation. Hinds uses quotations, primary source documents, and photographs of items and paintings to discuss people's lives during this time. They attended the theater, sang, explored the world, and worked to survive. Sidebars feature interesting bits of poetry, plays, and recipes as well as other pertinent information. Bibliography, Further Reading, Glossary, Web Sites, and Index.

453. Hinds, Kathryn. *The Countryside.* (Life in Ancient Egypt) Benchmark, 2006. 70pp. ISBN 978-0-7614-2185-6. Grades 6–9.

This look at daily country life in ancient Egypt from approximately 1550 B.C.E. to 1070 B.C.E. focuses on ordinary people and on childhood during that era. Includes quotations from Egyptians and in-depth articles on a variety of topics. Further Reading, Notes, Bibliography, Glossary, Web Sites, and Index.

454. Hinds, Kathryn. *The Pharaoh's Court.* (Life in Ancient Egypt) Benchmark, 2006. 72pp. ISBN 978-0-7614-2183-2. Grades 6–9.

All about what life was like for the upper classes in the New Kingdom period of ancient Egypt—from approximately 1550 B.C.E. to 1070 B.C.E. The focus is on the adults and children who surrounded the pharaoh. Also featured are quotations from Egyptians and in-depth articles on a variety of topics. Further Reading, Notes, Bibliography, Glossary, Web Sites, and Index.

455. Hinds, Kathryn. *Religion.* (Life in Ancient Egypt) Benchmark, 2006. 72pp. ISBN 978-0-7614-2186-3. Grades 6–9.

Hinds discusses religion during the New Kingdom period, 1550 B.C.E. to 1070 B.C.E., presenting the diverse gods and goddesses, creation myths, and priests. The gods were so much a part of life that no word to describe religion as a concept existed. Quotes from a variety of Egyptians — from women and children to workers and peasants — reveal much about the practices of the times.

456. Hinshaw, Kelly Campbell. *Art of Ancient Egypt.* (Art Across the Ages) Chronicle, 2007. 32pp. ISBN 978-0-8118-5668-3; paper ISBN 978-0-8118-5669-0. Grades 1–3.

This book asks questions of young readers and points out details in photographs and reproductions that will help them understand ancient Egypt's art. Readers learn the importance of the Nile as a source of life and as a place along which tombs were carved.

457. Hooper, Meredith. *Who Built the Pyramid?* Illustrated by Robin Heighway-Bury. Candlewick, 2006. 40pp. Paper ISBN 978-0-7636-3046-1. Grades 3–5.

Who built the pyramid more than four thousand years ago? Ten different men say, "I did!" Those questioned are Wah, the water carrier; Senwosret, the king of Egypt; the high priest; the laborer; the quarry master; the gang foreman; the stonemason; Montuhotep, the king's son; the architect; and Inyoref, the capstone sculptor. The one who does not care who built it is the tomb robber; he only wants to know how to break into it. Two-page spreads enhance the text.

458. Kaplan, Sarah Pitt. *The Great Pyramid at Giza: Tomb of Wonders.* (Digging up the Past) Childrens, 2005. 48pp. ISBN 978-0-51625-131-3; paper ISBN 978-0-51625-095-3. Grades 5–8.

A presentation of the history of the Great Pyramid at Giza's construction, this book describes the civilization that spent twenty years building it during the fourth dynasty for King Khufu ("Cheops" in Greek). It includes the process of removing a deceased person's organs during mummification. Photographs complement the text. Glossary and Further Reading.

459. Kennett, David. *Pharaoh: Life and Afterlife of a God.* Walker, 2008. 48pp. ISBN 978-0-8027-9567-0. Grades 3–6.

When Seti I died during the New Kingdom period of Egyptian history (1550–1070 B.C.E.), he was succeed by his son, Rameses II. This book looks at Seti's burial, the funeral preparations, his journey through the afterlife, and the rise of his son. The author also examines the role of a pharaoh in public life through religion, war, trade, and the Nile's floods. Acrylic paintings of many different things—including jewelry, statues, motifs, tools, figures, and faces—add interest. Maps and Glossary.

460. Konstam, Angus. *Historical Atlas of Ancient Greece.* Mercury, 2006. 192pp. ISBN 978-1-904668-16-9. Grades YA.

This atlas traces the cultural, historical, and political aspects of Greek culture from the Myceneans until the end of the empire. The Greeks created the first democratic society and at one point ruled the known world under Alexander the Great. Writers, poets, politicians, philosophers, and architects established the Greek cultural and political legacy important to contemporary western society. The fifteen chapters are "Greek Dawn," "Greek Mythology and Religion," "The Age of Heroes: Mycenaean Greece," "The Thinking Process," "The Rise of the City-States," "Politics and the People," "War with Persia," "Society and Everyday Life," "Athens and the Classical Greek Age," "Recreation and Religious Festivals," "The Peloponnesian War," "The Greek Art of War," "Alexander the Great," "Art and Architecture," and "The World of Hellas." Introduction, Color Illustrations, Maps, Chronology, Glossary and Genealogy Tables, and Index.

461. Kramer, Ann. *Egyptian Myth: A Treasury of Legends, Art, and History.* (World of Mythology) Sharpe Focus, 2007. 96pp. ISBN 978-0-7656-8105-8. Grades 5–8.

This treasury begins with the Egyptian creation story and includes other tales important to and about this civilization. Among topics covered are music, culture, religions, gods and their roles, and the afterlife. Photographs enhance the text. Chronology, Further Reading, Glossary, Web Sites, and Index.

462. Lace, William W. *The Curse of King Tut.* (Mysterious and Unknown) Referencepoint, 2007. 104pp. ISBN 978-1-60152-024-1. Grades 5–9.

Some believe King Tut's tomb was cursed because a number of tragedies have been associated with its excavation. Accounts of the discovery of the tomb and its opening in 1922 along with its relation to ancient Egyptian history and burial practices in general debunk this idea. Photographs and maps highlight the text. Notes, Further Reading, and Index.

463. Leech, Bonnie Coulter. *Mesopotamia: Creating and Solving Word Problems.* (Math for the Real World) Rosen, 2007. 32pp. ISBN 978-1-4042-3357-7; 2005. paper ISBN 978-1-4042-6067-2. Grades 4–8.

The text begins with the earliest days of civilization between the Tigris and the Euphrates rivers, when nomadic people decided to settle and become farmers of the fertile soil. As a group, they established a government. The mathematical aspects of this story include multiplication, division, percentages, and determining area and volume. The text also compares the Sumerian and Babylonian number systems of cuneiform and base ten. Charts and Chronology.

464. MacDonald, Fiona. *I Wonder Why Greeks Built Temples: And Other Questions About Ancient Greece.* Kingfisher, 2006. 32pp. Paper ISBN 978-0-7534-5961-4. Grades 2–4.

On two-page spreads, the story of the Greeks unfolds through questions and answers. Among the sections are everyday life, customs, religion, government, famous people, and military life. Index.

465. McGee, Marni. *Ancient Greece: Archaeology Unlocks the Secrets of Greece's Past.* (National Geographic Investigates) National Geographic, 2006. 64pp. ISBN 978-0-7922-7826-9. Grades 3–7.

This overview of important archaeological finds from Greek civilization includes an interview with Faith Hentschel, an underwater archaeologist, about some of the amazing discoveries under the sea. Additional information about the process archaeologists use to study the ancient Greeks aids in understanding. Photographs highlight the text. Bibliography, Glossary, Chronology, Further Reading, Web Sites, and Index.

466. Malam, John. *Ancient Greece.* (Picturing the Past) Enchanted Lion, 2004. 32pp. ISBN 978-1-59270-022-6. Grades 3–6.

Two-page chapters cover the geography, government, history, home life, religion, sports, and arts of ancient Greece. Each topic includes a picture or photograph of an item such as a piece of pottery, a ruin, or a statue. Glossary, Chronology, Further Reading, Web Sites, and Index.

467. Mann, Elizabeth. *The Great Pyramid: The Story of the Farmers, the God-King and the Most Astounding Structure Ever Built.* Illustrated by Laura Lo Turco. (Wonders of the World Book) Mikaya, 1996. 48pp. ISBN 978-0-965049-31-3; 2006. paper ISBN 978-1-931414-11-1. Grades 4–6.

Mann looks at the Great Pyramid in Giza through the eyes of the farmers and the Pharaoh Khufu who would have been living at the time it was constructed. Complementing the text are photographs, archival reproductions, and paintings. A four-page foldout helps give a sense of the size of this fifty-story structure. Index.

468. Mann, Elizabeth. *The Parthenon: The Height of Greek Civilization.* (Wonders of the World Book) Mikaya, 2006. 48pp. ISBN 978-1-931414-15-9. Grades 4–6.

This book features information about the engineering feats involved in the building of the ancient Greek temple the Parthenon. Under construction for fifteen years, it was completed in 432 B.C.E. and honored Athena. It also held symbolism for the civilization, people, rulers, religion, and democracy of Athens. Photographs, maps, and illustrations enhance the text. Bibliography and Glossary.

469. Marston, Elsa. *The Ancient Egyptians.* Benchmark, 1996. 80pp. ISBN 978-0-7614-0073-8. Grades 5–8.

The author looks at the artifacts, monuments, domestic scenes, and historical aspects of ancient Egypt while telling about the evolution of the Egyptian dynasties. A competent explanation of complex Egyptian religious beliefs is also presented. Photographs, Drawings, Bibliography, Chronology, Further Reading, Glossary, and Index.

470. Matthews, Sheelagh. *Pyramids of Giza.* (Structural Wonders) Weigl, 2007. 32pp. ISBN 978-1-59036-725-4; paper ISBN 978-1-59036-726-1. Grades 6–9.

This look at the structure of the Pyramids at Giza gives their cultural history and current status along with information about their architecture. It also discusses their construction, who the workers were, and the actual science of the design. Photographs, maps, and illustrations highlight the text. Glossary and Web Sites.

471. Mellor, Ronald J., and Marni McGee. *The Ancient Roman World.* (World in Ancient Times) Oxford, 2004. 192pp. ISBN 978-0-19-515380-4. Grades YA.

In a thorough treatment of the ancient Roman world, the authors cover the founding of Rome, the Etruscans, the republic, class conflict, religion, the battle to control the Mediterranean, the influence of Greek culture and Cato, slavery, the Gracchi, Cicero, Julius Caesar, Cleopatra and Egypt, Augustus and his successors, women and children, Pompeii, Roman houses, Trajan and his army, gladiators, business and trade, Hadrian, the empire, Jews, Christianity, barbarians, and Rome's fall. Each subject begins with a primary source from antiquity such as a quotation, a coin, or a piece of pottery. Maps, Photos, Reproductions, Chronology, Further Reading, Web Sites, and Index.

472. Millard, Anne, and Steve Noon. *Story of the Nile: A Journey Through Time Along the World's Longest River.* Dorling Kindersley, 2003. 32pp. ISBN 978-0-7894-9871-7. Grades 3–6.

The Nile extends from the Mediterranean Sea to Uganda and Ripon Falls, more than four thousand miles. Two-page spreads reveal key locations in geographical sequence and present the historical importance of this river for the past 4,500 years. Among the places highlighted are Meroe around 50 C.E., the Sudd swampland in 62 C.E., Khartoum in 1840 C.E., and Abu Simbel, King Khufu's tomb in Giza, around 2500 B.C.E.

473. Nardo, Don. *Ancient Greece.* Greenhaven, 2006. 381pp. ISBN 978-0-7377-3388-4. Grades 9 up.

A book of definitions and descriptions of terms, people, and events important to the history of ancient Greece—from "Academy" to "Zeus." It starts approximately four thousand years ago and ends with the Roman conquest. Photographs, maps, and illustrations highlight the text. Chronology, Further Reading, and Index.

474. Nardo, Don. *Ancient Greece.* Lucent, 2000. 112pp. ISBN 978-1-59018-651-0. Grades 7 up.

This history of ancient Greece uses sources written during the period, the research of recognized scholars, and recent archaeological evidence in its clear and concise overview of the time. The text begins with the Minoans (2200–1450 B.C.E.) and their advanced culture on Crete, where women and men were equal and the people revered a "Great Mother" and worshiped bulls. The Minoans contrast in temperament with the more militaristic Myceneans on the mainland, who eventually invaded Troy around 1200 B.C.E. The civilization disappeared between 1600 and 1450 B.C.E., when the volcanic island of Thera exploded in an eruption that affected the entire Mediterranean. (Thera's demise is probably the Atlantis that Plato discusses.) After the Dorians arrived in 1100 B.C.E. and were overcome, the city-states such as Athens and Sparta began to rise, and the recognition of the worth of individuals (except women, foreigners, and slaves) led to the creation of democracy. In 776 B.C.E., the Olympic Games began, and Homer wrote the *Iliad* and the *Odyssey.* The Greek and Persian wars followed. When the Greeks won, Athens began its golden age and, according to one historian, made Europe itself possible. But the city-states could not coexist; the Peloponnesian wars between

Sparta and Athens began and lasted for twenty-seven years. The paucity of funds and men allowed the Macedonians under Philip II and Alexander to invade and spread Greek culture throughout the known world. With Greek decline in the Hellenistic age, the cities of Alexandria and Antioch became the most prestigious in the ancient world. Notes, For Further Reading, Works Consulted, and Index.

475. Nardo, Don. *Atlantis.* (Mystery Library) Gale, 2003. 112pp. ISBN 978-1-59018-287-1. Grades 6–9.

Plato wrote about a lost continent in 399 B.C.E., describing its land, people, cities, and government. Although some believe that Plato imagined this place, some, including the Roman historian Ammianus Marcellinus and the Greek philosopher Proclus, thought he was describing an actual place. No one, however, knows exactly where it might have been although some of the candidate locales include the Atlantic ocean, Morocco, Tunisia, Europe, Malta, Iran, and Arabia. Modern researchers such as Ignatius Donnelly have their own interpretations of this mysterious civilization. Maps, Photographs, Bibliography, Further reading, Notes, Web Sites, and Index.

476. Nardo, Don. *Living in Ancient Egypt.* (Exploring Cultural History) Gale, 2004. 159pp. ISBN 978-0-7377-1452-4. Grades 9 up.

One of the earliest civilizations known to humans is ancient Egypt. This book discusses how the ancient Egyptians lived—their families, food, attitudes toward women, religious beliefs, art, traditions, celebrations, education, and medical knowledge. The importance of the Nile to every aspect of their lives is highlighted. The practice of mummification and their structured belief in an afterlife are also discussed. Much of the information here comes from contemporary scholars who have studied and excavated within Egypt's borders. Maps, Photographs, Bibliography, Further reading, Notes, Web Sites, and Index.

477. Nardo, Don. *Living in Ancient Greece.* (Exploring Cultural History) Gale, 2004. 144pp. ISBN 978-0-7377-1455-5. Grades 9 up.

Ancient Greece was an important civilization that remains influential on contemporary Western life. Its citizens' sense of responsibility and approval of government still resonate today. The text discusses the way in which people lived in ancient Greece— their families, food, attitudes toward women, religious beliefs, art, traditions, celebrations, education, and medical knowledge. The Greeks celebrated the Olympics, a competition still important throughout the world. Much of the information here comes from contemporary scholars who have studied and excavated within Greece's borders. Maps, Photographs, Bibliography, Further Reading, Notes, Web Sites, and Index.

478. Nardo, Don. *Mesopotamia.* (World History) Lucent, 2004. 112pp. ISBN 978-1-59018-292-5. Grades 6–9.

The Sumerians, Assyrians, Babylonians, and Persians rose in power and developed a culture in ancient Mesopotamia, the "land between two rivers." The first cities, empires, large engineering projects, and written literature appeared in this area. This book includes information about these cultures as well as the influence of the Persians Cyrus II and Darius I, the invasions of Alexander the Great and the Greeks, and the rise of Arab influence. Nardo uses primary and secondary sources from both ancient and contemporary historians. Maps, Photographs, Bibliography, Further Reading, Notes, Web Sites, and Index.

479. Nardo, Don. *Ramesses II: Ruler of Ancient Egypt.* (Rulers of the Ancient World) Enslow, 2006. 160pp. ISBN 978-0-7660-2562-2. Grades 6–9.

One of Egypt's greatest pharaohs, Rameses II (1279–1213 B.C.E.), lived during the nineteenth dynasty. Among his consorts was Nefertari, his first and most beloved. The bust he had sculpted of her still survives. He is also believed to have been Ozymandias (from the John Keats poem) and the pharaoh of the exodus. Among the memorials he left are Abu Simbel, Luxor, and Karnak. Photographs and illustrations augment the text. Glossary, Chronology, Notes, Further Reading, Web Sites, and Index.

480. Pearson, Anne. *Ancient Greece.* DK, 2004. 72pp. ISBN 978-0-7566-0648-0. Grades 6–9.

To give an understanding of Greek art, architecture, and artifacts, illustrations accompany the text. Topics covered on two-page spreads include Minoan and Mycenaean civilization, Athenian politics, mythology, religion, women's lives, childhood, games, food and drink, theater, hygiene, clothing, sports, art, agriculture, trade, crafts, warfare, science and medicine, philosophy, death and the afterlife, Alexander the Great, and Hellenism. Index.

481. Pearson, Anne. *Everyday Life in Ancient Greece.* Creative, 2005. 72pp. ISBN 978-1-932889-77-2. Grades 3–6.

Two-page spreads featuring photographs and drawings discuss various facets of Greek life. Some of the topics covered are farming and fishing, homes, women's rooms, clothes and jewelry, school, childhood, craftsmen, markets, sports and games, theater, the army, religion, death, and burial. Index.

482. Pemberton, Delia. *Atlas of Ancient Egypt.* Abrams, 2005. 96pp. ISBN 978-0-8109-5796-1. Grades 5 up.

This atlas is divided into four sections—an introduction to ancient Egypt through its history and geography; how Egypt was formed and the environment's influence on the people; places, customs, and beliefs; and recent history. It contains much information about the people and the land. Photographs, maps, and illustrations highlight the text. Bibliography, Glossary, and Index. *Voice of Youth Advocates Nonfiction Honor List.*

483. Powell, Anton. *Ancient Greece.* Chelsea House, 2007. 96pp. ISBN 978-0-8160-6821-0. Grades 6–9.

As much as possible about ancient Greece appears in this book, complemented by full-color illustrations. Topics that help readers to understand the life of the ancient Greeks include the Minoan, Cretan, and Mycenaen civilizations of the 15th and 14th centuries B.C.E.; the Trojan War, of which Homer wrote; Homer's primitive Greece; Athens and its dramatists, historians, and philosophers; the growth of Athens; the Olympic Games, and much more. Chronology, Glossary, Gazetteer, and Index.

484. Powell, Anton, and Philip Steele. *The Greek News.* (History News) Candlewick, 2009. 32pp. Paper ISBN 978-0-7636-4197-9. Grades 5 up.

This newspaper-style presentation of the ancient Greeks highlights fashion, sports, trade, food, and the military. Each page has headlines, sometimes with classified advertising items such as instruments. Highly readable and slightly sensational (with headlines such as "Olympic Games Spoiled"), this format seems much more accessible than a textbook. Maps and Index.

485. Putnam, James. *The Ancient Egypt Pop-Up Book.* Universe, 5-8. 7pp. ISBN 978-0-7893-0985-3. Grades 5–8.

This pop-up book features items of interest about civilization in Egypt as it grew around the banks of the Nile. Readers will learn that mummification took seventy days and that the Egyptians practiced dentistry. They used hieroglyphic symbols to communicate in writing and had specific rituals to worship their gods. The seven spreads include pop-ups of boats, pyramids, temples and gods, pharaohs, and fine arts and crafts. There are also flaps to open and small pop-ups. Photographs of artifacts in the British Museum's Egyptian antiquities collection highlight the text.

486. Putnam, James. *Mummy.* Illustrated by Peter Hayman. DK, 2009. 72pp. ISBN 978-0-7566-4541-0. Grades 4 up.

Two-page spreads on mummies include a large Egyptian section that covers Egyptian mummies, how to wrap mummies, mummy masks, Egyptian mythology, Tutankhamen's treasures, and the mummy's curse. Other mummies discussed are those of Greeks, Romans, Sicilians, people in the Andes, the "Iceman," the "Bog Man," and those of animals. Archaeologists have located still other mummies in several additional places. Photographs and Index.

487. Reece, Katherine. *The Egyptians: Builders of the Pyramids.* (Ancient Civilizations) Rourke, 2006. 48pp. ISBN 978-1-59515-505-4. Grades 4–6.

This introduction to the civilization of ancient Egypt includes its location, the people who lived there, what the people ate and wore, what they traded, their commerce, their beliefs and gods, their arts and architecture, and their legacy. Photographs and illustrations augment the text. Glossary, Chronology, Further Reading, Web Sites, and Index.

488. Reece, Katherine. *The Greeks: Leaders in Democracy.* (Ancient Civilizations) Rourke, 2006. 48pp. ISBN 978-1-59515-506-1. Grades 4–6.

This introduction to the the civilization of ancient Greece includes its location, the people who lived there, what the people ate and wore, what they traded, their commerce, their beliefs and gods, their arts and architecture, and their legacy. Photographs and illustrations augment the text. Glossary, Chronology, Further Reading, Web Sites, and Index.

489. Rees, Rosemary. *The Ancient Egyptians.* Heinemann/Raintree, 2006. 64pp. ISBN 978-1-4034-8746-9; paper ISBN 978-1-4034-8752-0. Grades 3–4.

Each topic fills a two-page spread of color photographs, maps, museum artifacts, and drawings. Among the subjects covered are the Egyptians' social life, economics, political arena, cultural life, and religion, along with the pharaohs and pyramids. Chronology, Glossary, and Index.

490. Rees, Rosemary. *The Ancient Greeks.* Heinemann/Raintree, 2006. 64pp. ISBN 978-1-4034-8747-6; paper ISBN 978-1-4034-8753-7. Grades 3–4.

Information about the social and cultural life, the economics, the political system, and the religion of the Greeks fills two-page spreads of color photographs, maps, museum artifacts, and drawings. Special topics concern the Olympics and the theater. Chronology, Glossary, and Index.

491. Reynolds, Susan. *The First Marathon: The Legend of Pheidippides.* Illustrated by Daniel Minter. Albert Whitman, 2006. Unpaged. ISBN 978-0-8075-0867-1. Grades 2–4.

Facing the Persian army on the plain of Marathon 2,500 years ago, a small band of Greeks needed help. Pheidippides ran 140 miles to neighboring Sparta to ask for assistance. Then he returned to report that help was on the way. Illustrations complement the text. Notes.

492. Roberts, Jennifer, and Tracy Barrett. *The Ancient Greek World.* (World in Ancient Times) Oxford, 2004. 192pp. ISBN 978-0-19-515696-6. Grades 7–10.

In a thorough treatment of the ancient Greek world, the authors cover the history of Greece from the Minoans to the death of Alexander the Great. Among the topics covered are defining a Greek, the Greek religion's gods and priests, the earliest Greeks, the Mycenaeans, the Trojan War, the early poets, colonies and city-states, the rise of Athens, slavery, the life of a Greek citizen beginning with childhood, women in ancient Greece, life in Sparta, the war with the Persian Empire, democracy in Athens, the Peloponnesian War, science and medicine, the Olympic Games, the visual arts, drama, education, philosophy, leaders, and the legacy of the Greeks. Each subject opens with an item from antiquity such as a quotation, a coin, or a piece of pottery. Maps, Photos, Reproductions, Chronology, Further Reading, Web Sites, and Index.

493. Ross, Stewart. *Ancient Greece Daily Life.* Illustrated by Adam. Narrated by Hook. (Changing Times) Compass Point, 2007. 32pp. ISBN 978-0-7565-2085-4. Grades 5–7.

After an introduction to the ancient Greeks, twelve two-page chapters cover the daily life of the Greeks. Topics covered are marriage, games, education, clothing, food and drink, warfare, slavery, children, jobs, religion, and funerals. Photographs, maps and reproductions illuminate the text. Glossary, Chronology, Further Reading, and Index.

494. Ross, Stewart. *Ancient Greece Entertainment.* Illustrated by Adam. Narrated by Hook. (Changing Times) Compass Point, 2007. 32pp. ISBN 978-0-7565-2086-1. Grades 5–7.

After an introduction to the ancient Greeks, twelve two-page chapters cover the entertainment that Greeks enjoyed. Some of the pastimes presented are hunting, fishing, parties, art, music, festivals, dance, poetry, drama, storytelling, and the Olympic Games. Photographs, maps and reproductions illuminate the text. Glossary, Chronology, Further Reading, and Index.

495. Ross, Stewart. *Egypt: In Spectacular Cross-Section.* Illustrated by Stephen Biesty. Scholastic, 2005. 32pp. ISBN 978-0-439-74537-6. Grades 3–7.

The young Dedia takes a trip down the Nile with his merchant father in 1230 B.C.E. Along the way, they see ten important sites including Amun-Ra's temple at Karnak, the great palace at Piramesse, and the Valley of the Kings. The cross-section illustrations show plants, buildings, artifacts, and rooms, revealing aspects of the everyday life, culture, and religion of ancient Egyptians. Glossary and Index.

496. Rubalcaba, Jill. *Ancient Egypt: Archaeology Unlocks the Secrets of Egypt's Past.* (National Geographic Investigates) National Geographic, 2006. 64pp. ISBN 978-0-7922-7784-2. Grades 3–7.

This book gives background on archaeological discoveries, especially Egypt's tombs, which are revealing new information about ancient Egypt. Additional information about how archaeologists work aids understanding. Photographs highlight the text. Bibliography, Glossary, Chronology, Further Reading, Web Sites, and Index.

497. Sands, Emily. *The Egyptology Handbook.* Candlewick, 2005. 80pp. ISBN 978-0-7636-2932-8. Grades 5–7.

Flaps, foldouts, and other paraphernalia guide the viewer through ancient Egypt by reviewing its culture, history, and archaeological finds.

498. Scarre, Christopher, and Rebecca Stefoff. *The Palace of Minos at Knossos.* Oxford, 2003. 48pp. ISBN 978-0-19-514272-3. Grades 5–8.

A discussion of the ancient Minoan civilization of Knossos, on the island of Crete, that probably existed in the 13th or 14th century B.C.E. Sir Arthur Evans excavated there beginning in 1900 after discovering the site. Evans imagined what the structures might have looked like from what he and others learned about the Minoans. Modern archaeology adds more information. Illustrations of Evans and his work, diagrams, and photographs of artifacts highlight the text. Bibliography and Index.

499. Schomp, Virginia. *The Ancient Greeks.* Benchmark, 2007. 79pp. ISBN 978-0-7614-2547-2. Grades 5–8.

The author presents the artifacts, monuments, domestic habits, and historical aspects of ancient Greece as it examines the everyday life of the people. It covers the chronological and cultural history; the Greek belief system, defined by the twelve Olympian gods and goddesses; the societal mores; and the Greek legacy. To the Greeks, gods and goddesses were an important part of daily life, and the text develops this idea. Photographs, Drawings, Bibliography, Chronology, Further Reading, Glossary, and Index.

500. Sloan, Christopher E. *Bury the Dead: Tombs, Corpses, Mummies, Skeletons, and Rituals.* Illustrated by Bruno Frohlich. National Geographic, 2002. 64pp. ISBN 978-0-7922-7192-5. Grades 6–10.

People throughout history have been interested in burial customs. This book discusses how different cultural groups have buried their dead by examining excavations, artifacts, and burial sites. It presents Neanderthals, ancient Egyptian mummies, the caparisoned grave of the Moche Lord of Sipan, the golden graves of the Scytho-Siberians, the terra-cotta soldiers of the Chinese Qin dynasty, Russian tombs of ancient Amazon women, and the Yanomami practice of pulverizing and eating their dead. It also explores the meaning of the rituals to those still living. A final chapter looks at modern rituals surrounding death including sugar skulls for the Day of the Dead. Photographs of tombs, mummies, skeletons, and other archaeological finds re-create the times in which these people were buried. Photographs, Maps, Diagrams, Illustrations, and Index. *School Library Journal Best Books of the Year*, *Booklist Editor's Choice*, and *Garden State Children's Book Award* (New Jersey) nomination.

501. Spirn, Michele Sobel. *Mysterious People: A Chapter Book.* (True Tales) Children's, 2005. 48pp. ISBN 978-0-51625-181-3. Grades 3–6.

This book looks at four people who died mysteriously: Egypt's Queen Nefertiti, a teenage German boy named Caspar Hauser, Ishi (the last survivor of his Yahi tribe), and Otzi, found frozen in the Alps and presumed to have died more than 5,000 years ago. Photographs and reproductions highlight the text. Glossary, Further Reading, Web Sites, and Index.

502. Steedman, Scott. *The Egyptian News.* (History News) Candlewick, 2009. 32pp. Paper ISBN 978-0-7636-4198-6. Grades 5 up.

This approach to the Egyptians in the style of a newspaper highlights fashion, sports, trade, food, and the military. Each page has headlines, sometimes with classifieds advertising items such as used papyrus. Highly readable and slightly sensational (with information under headlines such as "Boy-King Murdered?"), this format seems much more accessible than a textbook. Maps and Index.

503. Steele, Philip. *I Wonder Why Pyramids Were Built: And Other Questions About Ancient Egypt.* Kingfisher, 1995. 32pp. ISBN 978-1-856975-50-6; 2006. paper ISBN 978-0-7534-5963-8. Grades 4–6.

With questions and answers, the text and illustrations look at ancient Egypt using a humorous tone. Diagrams and Maps. Index.

504. Stewart, David. *You Wouldn't Want to Be Tutankhamen! A Mummy Who Really Got Meddled With.* (You Wouldn't Want To . . .) Franklin Watts, 2007. 32pp. ISBN 978-0-531-18725-8; paper ISBN 978-0-531-18924-5. Grades 3–6.

Tutankhamen, known as the boy king, was an Egyptian pharaoh whose power was envied by many. Although plots against him have been discovered, he died of illness. Illustrations, cartoons, creative dialogue, and "hints" highlight the story. Glossary, Maps, and Index.

505. Strachan, Bruce. *Ancient Egypt: A First Look at People of the Nile.* Holt, 2008. 32pp. ISBN 978-0-8050-7432-1. Grades 2–4.

A look at ancient Egypt complemented with photographs of 3-D clay-and-wood tableaux. Among the topics covered are the Nile; pharaohs; pyramids and how they were built; the blessing, preparation, and preservation of mummies; the Sphinx at Giza; Queen Hatshepsut; Rameses the Great; and King Tutankhamen's tomb. Bibliography.

506. Strom, Laura Layton. *The Egyptian Science Gazette.* (Shockwave) Children's, 2008. 36pp. ISBN 978-0-531-17582-8. Grades 4–7.

Facsimile newspaper articles, each written by a different "reporter," describe science in Egypt. Information about mummification, building the pyramids, and current techniques in science help readers discover the lives of the ancient Egyptians. Photographs and illustrations augment the text. Glossary, Chronology, Notes, Further Reading, Web Sites, and Index.

507. Strom, Laura Layton. *Tombs and Treasure: Ancient Egypt.* (Shockwave) Children's, 2008. 36pp. ISBN 978-0-531-17787-7. Grades 4–7.

A discussion of Egyptian hieroglyphics, beliefs, and the tombs of the pharaohs in Egypt. Sidebars feature additional information. Photographs and illustrations augment the text. Glossary, Chronology, Notes, Further Reading, Web Sites, and Index.

508. Trumble, Kelly. *The Library of Alexandria.* Illustrated by Robina MacIntyre Marshall. Houghton Mifflin, 2003. 80pp. ISBN 978-0-395-75832-8. Grades 5–9.

The library built by Ptolemy I Soter and his adviser Demetrius in Alexandria, Egypt, became the most famous in the ancient world. Scholars used it for major research, especially in astronomy, geography, mathematics, and medicine. Among the scholars and rulers associated with its greatness were Euclid, Archimedes, Erastosthenes (who calculated the circumference of the earth), Herophilus (who used dissection to acquire information about the human body), Alexander the Great, Caesar, and Cleopatra. This book examines methods of research — including Herophilus's vivisections of the human anatomy — and the use of parchment and papyrus. No one today knows exactly what the library looked like. Its vast collections rivaled the Pergamum library in Asia Minor. Watercolor and gouache paintings highlight the text. Maps, Genealogy, Glossary, Further Reading, Bibliography, and Index. *Voice of Youth Advocates Nonfiction Honor List.*

509. Tyldesley, Joyce. *Egypt.* (Insiders) Simon & Schuster, 2007. 64pp. ISBN 978-1-416-93858-3. Grades 5–8.

This view of Egypt's ancient civilization gives background on the Great Pyramids, mummification, and King Tut's tomb. It also offers a look at the religion, the various lifestyles, and the activities of the people. Three-dimensional illustrations augment the text. Glossary and Index.

510. Van Vleet, Carmella. *Great Ancient Egypt Projects You Can Build Yourself.* Nomad, 2006. 122pp. Paper ISBN 978-0-977129-45-4. Grades 4–6.

This interactive book has hands-on projects related to the daily lives of ancient Egyptians—including building papyrus boats, making berry ink, and cooking flatbread. The text covers food, housing, games, farming, medicine, clothing, religion, and jewelry. Photographs and illustrations augment the text. Maps, Bibliography, Glossary, Chronology, Further Reading, Web Sites, and Index.

511. Walker, Susan, and Peter Higgs. *Cleopatra of Egypt: From History to Myth.* Princeton, 384p. 364pp. ISBN 978-0-691-08835-8. Grades YA.

The authors present Cleopatra (d. 30 B.C.E.) as an offspring of the Ptolemies in Alexandria and examine her role in two lands and her myth in Egypt. This book contains a catalog of more than six hundred images—first collected by the British Museum in London—of paintings, sculptures, ceramics, pottery, jewelry, and coins that feature Cleopatra and her family. Bibliography, Glossary, Chronology, Concordance of Objects, and Index.

512. Weatherill, Sue, and Steve Weatherill. *Egyptian Activity Book.* Barron's Educational, 2006. 24pp. ISBN 978-0-7641-3414-2. Grades 2–4.

Readers can try ten activities and crafts related to ancient Egypt. Additional trivia and information, along with a chronology, tell how each activity relates to the Egyptians. Illustrations complement the text. Chronology and Time Line.

513. Winters, Kay. *Voices of Ancient Egypt.* Illustrated by Barry Moser. National Geographic, 2003. 32pp. ISBN 978-0-7922-7560-2; 2009. paper ISBN 978-1-4263-0400-2. Grades 3–6.

In this collection of poetry, workers in ancient Egypt discuss their jobs as goldsmiths, dancers, pyramid builders, clothes washers, and more. Each two-page spread introduces the profession and offers information about it. Illustrations highlight the text. Bibliography and Notes. *Booklist Editor's Choice* and *Prairie Pasque Book Award* (South Dakota) nomination.

514. Woods, Geraldine. *Science in Ancient Egypt.* Franklin Watts, 1998. 92pp. Paper ISBN 978-0-531-15915-6. Grades 5–8.

An introduction to Egypt and its science precedes chapters on different developments from this culture. These include the pyramids, mathematics, astronomy and timekeeping, medicine, writing and agriculture, and crafts and technology. The author discusses the contemporary debt to the Egyptians for their discoveries. Photographs and drawings enhance the text. Glossary, Further Reading, and Index.

515. Wright, Anne. *Art and Architecture.* (Inside Ancient Greece) Sharpe Focus, 2007. 80pp. ISBN 978-0-7656-8130-0. Grades 6–10.

A look at the art and architecture of ancient Greece, this book contains information about the arts of vase painting, sculpture, frescoes, mosaics, jewelry, and coins. It also looks at the architecture of homes, public buildings, amphitheaters, tombs, and temples. Explanations of artists' techniques cover the lost-wax technique for casting statues. Photographs and illustrations highlight the text. Glossary, Further Reading, and Index.

516. Wright, Anne. *City States.* (Inside Ancient Greece) Sharpe Focus, 2007. 80pp. ISBN 978-0-7656-8129-4. Grades 6–10.

A look at the city-states of ancient Greece, this book reviews commerce, government, sports, medicine, childhood, education, women, domestic life, food, clothing, and slavery. It also details the different city-states and their attributes. Photographs, maps, and illustrations highlight the text. Glossary, Further Reading, and Index.

517. Wright, Anne. *Mythology.* (Inside Ancient Greece) Sharpe Focus, 2007. 80pp. ISBN 978-0-7656-8132-4. Grades 6–10.

This introduction to Greek mythology covers the major gods and goddesses and their places in the Greek pantheon. It relates the stories of the Trojan War, Odysseus, Heracles, and the great quests. Photographs, maps, and illustrations highlight the text. Glossary, Further Reading, and Index.

518. Zoehfeld, Kathleen Weidner. *The Curse of King Tut's Mummy.* Illustrated by Jim Nelson. (Stepping Stone) Random House, 2007. 99pp. ISBN 978-0-375-93862-7; paper ISBN 978-0-375-83862-0. Grades 2–4.

Howard Carter, the Chief Inspector of Antiquities in Upper Egypt, and the financier Lord Carnarvon wanted to find King Tutankhamen's tomb. Carter had visited Egypt as a young man, worked with archaeologists, and became convinced that at least one more tomb was undiscovered in the Valley of the Kings. After he met Lord Carnarvon, the two began searching. In 1922, they successfully located this tomb filled with incredible gold. Illustrations accompany the text.

Biography and Collective Biography

519. Anderson, Margaret J. *Aristotle: Philosopher and Scientist.* (Great Minds of Science) Enslow, 2004. 112pp. ISBN 978-0-7660-2096-2. Grades 5–8.

As a student of Plato who had studied under Socrates, Aristotle in turn tutored Alexander and founded the Lyceum. He wrote about physics, metaphysics, botany, chemistry, and biology before any of these fields had been named. He understood that animals needed to be classified as an aspect of zoology. He had no modern tools such as a telescope or microscope, but his ideas served as a basis for modern science. He also wrote about art, literature, ethics, and theology with special attention to the field of logic. Aristotle's contributions to history cannot be overestimated. Photographs, Reproductions, Chronology, Further Reading, Glossary, Notes, Web Sites, and Index.

520. Baker, Rosalie F., and Charles F. Baker, III. *Ancient Greeks: Creating the Classical Tradition.* Oxford, 1997. 254pp. ISBN 978-0-19-509940-9. Grades 7 up.

Five sections in chronological order feature biographies about several Greeks of the time period and information about their professions and backgrounds, revealing details about Greek culture as well. Subjects include politicians, philosophers, mathematicians, dramatists, authors, and soldiers. Commentary shows both disagreement and accord from scholars who have written about the subjects. Chronology, Further Reading, Glossary, and Index.

521. Behnke, Alison. *The Conquests of Alexander the Great.* (Pivotal Moments in History) Twenty First Century, 2007. 160pp. ISBN 978-0-8225-5920-7. Grades 6 up.

Alexander the Great (356–323 B.C.E.) took power when he was twenty after his father, King Philip, was assassinated. The text examines his life, his successes and failures as a commander, and many of his battles. He was an excellent battle strategist and knew to assimilate new cultures into his empire. Additional information about the world in which he lived gives context for his achievements. Photographs and illustrations highlight the text. Bibliography, Glossary, Chronology, Notes, Further Reading, Web Sites, and Index.

522. Beneduce, Ann Keay. *Moses: The Long Road to Freedom.* Illustrated by Gennady Spirin. Orchard, 2004. 32pp. ISBN 978-0-439-35225-3. Grades 2–5.

This story of Moses draws from the Torah, the King James Bible, and modern commentary. Born as the son of a slave and adopted by the pharaoh's daughter, Moses grew up to lead the Hebrew slaves out of Egypt. Exquisite illustrations enhance the text. Note.

523. Bruns, Roger. *Julius Caesar.* (World Leaders Past and Present) Facts on File, 1987. ISBN 978-0-87754-514-9. Grades 5 up.

Julius Caesar (b. 100 B.C.E.) spent his life working toward the highest position in Rome, first as an emerging politician who appealed directly to the people and later as part of a governing triumvirate with Pompey and Crassus. With the Gauls, from 58 to 51 B.C.E., he used brutality to gain what he wanted. In 49 B.C.E., he declared war on an elite group of conservative senators and wrested power from them. On the Ides of March, 44 B.C.E., he was stabbed to death at the Roman senate by men who thought he wanted too much power. Yet he brought glory to Rome, along with elaborate celebrations and many reforms. Photographs and reproductions enhance the text. Chronology, Further Reading, and Index.

524. Doherty, Paul C. *The Mysterious Death of Tutankhamun.* Basic, 2003. 260pp. Paper ISBN 978-0-7867-1245-8. Grades YA.

Many mysteries surround the death of 18-year-old King Tutankhamun (or Tutankhamen) in 1323 B.C.E. during the eighteenth dynasty. Copious research leads to the possibility that he was murdered. Clues that have led to this conclusion are his hasty embalming, the poor burial site for such an important person, swelling behind his left ear, his partially missing sternum and rib cage, and his missing brain. This book, however, suggests that he might have had a tumor from a hereditary disease from which he would eventually die. His adviser, Chancellor Ay, might have hastened Tutankhamun's demise with drugs so that he could wrest the throne from General Horemheb, who was away at war. This interpretation works as well as the others. Bibliography and Index.

525. Green, Robert. *Alexander the Great.* Franklin Watts, 1996. 63pp. Paper ISBN 978-0-531-15799-2. Grades 4–6.

Alexander (356–323 B.C.E.) conquered most of the known world before his death at 33. This book introduces his life and his achievements. Photographs, illustrations, and reproductions enhance the text. Index.

526. Green, Robert. *Tutankhamun.* Franklin Watts, 1996. 63pp. Paper ISBN 978-0-531-15802-9. Grades 5–7.

This book looks at Howard Carter's exciting discovery of King Tut's tomb in 1922 and gives a biography of this young pharaoh (reigned 1333–23 B.C.E.) culled from information about artifacts found in the tomb. It also includes a list of Internet sources with other information on the king. Chronology and Index.

527. Hasan, Heather. *Archimedes: The Father of Mathematics.* (The Library of Greek Philosophers) Rosen, 2006. 112pp. ISBN 978-1-4042-0774-5. Grades 6–10.

This overview of the life and achievements of Archimedes, a Greek, describes his early years, travels, and education within the context of his times. He was a gifted mathematician who was also a physicist, engineer, astronomer, and philosopher. He helped develop military weapons, a controversial endeavor, but he made other major contributions to the world's knowledge. Some of the discoveries attributed to him might have been the work of others. Illustrations highlight the text. Bibliography, Glossary, Chronology, Notes, Further Reading, Web Sites, and Index.

528. Hayhurst, Chris. *Euclid: The Great Geometer.* (The Library of Greek Philosophers) Rosen, 2006. 112pp. ISBN 978-1-4042-0497-3. Grades 6–10.

This overview of the life and achievements of Euclid, a Greek, describes his early years, travels, and education within the context of his times. He was a gifted mathematician known as the "father of geometry." His book on geometry has lasted more than two thousand years. Some of the discoveries attributed to him might have been the work of others. Illustrations highlight the text. Bibliography, Glossary, Chronology, Notes, Further Reading, Web Sites, and Index.

529. Hodges, Margaret. *Moses.* Illustrated by Barry Moser and Mike Wimmer. Harcourt, 2006. 32pp. ISBN 978-0-15-200946-5. Grades 2–5.

While the Hebrew slaves worked in Egypt, they longed to return home. Moses' mother hid him in the bulrushes, and the pharaoh's daughter found him. Then he ended up leading the Hebrews out of Egypt and almost reached the promised land before he died. Also in this retelling, Moses goes up to Mount Sinai and receives the Ten Commandments. Illustrations complement the text.

530. Hoffman, Mary. *Kings and Queens of the Bible.* Illustrated by Christina Balit. Holt, 2008. ISBN 978-0-8050-8837-3. Grades 2–5.

This collective biography looks at the lives of seven Old Testament kings and queens and how they affected their subjects. Those included are Moses, David, Solomon, Esther, Balkis, Jezebel, and Belshazzar. Among the themes these selections contain are the wisdom and power of the rulers, with some using violence or wealth to accomplish their goals. For example, dogs ate Queen Jezebel. Watercolor, ink, and pencil drawings enhance the text.

531. Holub, Joan. *Cleopatra and the King's Enemies: A True Story of Cleopatra in Egypt.* Illustrated by Nonna Aleshina. (Young Princesses Around the World) Simon & Schuster, 2007. 48pp. ISBN 978-0-689-87196-2; Aladdin paper ISBN 978-0-689-87194-8. Grades K–2.

While a young princess in Egypt, Cleopatra (d. 30 B.C.E.) must worry about her looks. But she uses her wits to help her father protect his throne when those around him, including his own daughters, plot to take it away from him. Chronology.

532. Karamanides, Dimitra. *Pythagoras: Pioneering Mathematician and Musical Theorist of Ancient Greece.* (The Library of Greek Philosophers) Rosen, 2006. 112pp. ISBN 978-1-4042-0500-0. Grades 6–10.

This overview of the life and achievements of Pythagoras, a Greek, describes his early years, travels, and education within the context of his times. As a gifted mathematician, he introduced the Pythagorean theorem and is known as "the father of numbers." However, he had a secret society of disciples that caused controversy during his time and through the years. Illustrations highlight the text. Bibliography, Glossary, Chronology, Notes, Further Reading, Web Sites, and Index.

533. Lasky, Kathryn. *The Librarian Who Measured the Earth.* Illustrated by Kevin Hawkes. Little Brown, 1994. 48pp. ISBN 978-0-316-51526-9. Grades 2–5.

More than two thousand years ago, the Greek Eratosthenes, from Cyrene on the coast of Africa, measured the earth. Though he used only camels, plumb lines, and angles of shadows, his calculation differed by just two hundred miles from recent measurements made with highly technical instruments. He studied in Athens and wrote a comedy, a history, and a book on the constellations. Then he went to Alexandria to serve as tutor to Ptolemy III's son, Philopator. Soon after he arrived, Eratosthenes became the head librarian of the greatest library in the world. Bibliography.

534. León, Vicki. *Uppity Women of Ancient Times.* Conari, 1995. 260pp. Paper ISBN 978-1-57324-010-9. Grades YA.

This anecdotal collective biography presents approximately two hundred women who lived in ancient times. They were gladiators, public servants, scientists, murderers, rulers, and homemakers. Some of their names were Berenice, Eudoxia, Musa, and Sabina. The chapters are "Uppity B.C.E. Defined and Discovered," "Singers, Sexual Stand-Ins & a Sassy Slave or Two" (Babylon & Mesopotamia), "Pharaohs, Physicians, Fat Cats & Filly-Fanciers" (Egypt & North Africa), "Track Stars, Tricky Queens, Trollops & True-Blue Martyrs" (Asia Minor & the Holy Land), "Pirates, Politicians, Porn Artists & Pure Maidens" (Greece & the Islands), and "Poisoners, Poets, Power Brokers & Paragons of Virtue" (Rome & the Western Provinces). Illustrations augment the text. Bibliography, Notes, and Index.

535. McGowen, Tom. *Alexander the Great: Conqueror of the Ancient World.* (Rulers of the Ancient World) Enslow, 2006. 160pp. ISBN 978-0-7660-2560-8. Grades 6 up.

Alexander the Great (359–323 B.C.E.) fought his first battle as a warrior-king at the age of 16. His innovations helped him first conquer India and then continue in his quest to unite all peoples in the known world. He had a reputation as an extremely strong and handsome man. Illustrations enhance the text. Bibliography, Chronology, Notes, Maps, Glossary, Further Reading, Web Sites, and Index.

536. Nardo, Don. *Cleopatra: Egypt's Last Pharoah.* Lucent, 2005. 112pp. ISBN 978-1-59018-660-2. Grades 7 up.

Cleopatra (69–30 BC.) became queen in 51 B.C.E., but her brother Ptolemy XIII drove her from Alexandria in 49 B.C.E. Caesar helped her regain the throne the following year. After Caesar was assassinated in 44 B.C.E., Cleopatra and Antony began their relationship, but Antony left to marry Octavian's sister Octavia. He returned to Cleopatra in 37 B.C.E. Antony's campaign against Carthia ended in failure in 36 B.C.E., but he proclaimed Cleopatra "Queen of Kings" in 34 B.C.E. The two prepared for war against Rome, but Octavian defeated them at Actium in Greece. They then committed suicide. Included are chapters on Egypt and Rome as the world of Cleopatra's childhood, her quest for power by joining Caesar, and the concept of Cleopatra as the new Isis. Among the facts and the fictions discussed in this book is the Romans' hatred for Cleopatra because she was a foreigner and a woman and had, according to them, corrupted both Caesar and Antony. Reproductions and photographs augment the text. For Further Reading, Works Consulted, and Index.

537. Navia, Luis E. *Socrates: A Life Examined.* Prometheus, 2007. 290pp. ISBN 978-1-59102-501-6. Grades YA.

This study of the life and worldviews of Socrates concludes that Socrates thought reason was the only thing that could make human life meaningful and happy. His tenet was "know thyself." Chapters look at the Socratic enigma, Socrates on the comic stage, Xenophon's recollections, Plato's recordings of his ideas, Socrates in Aristotle, the search for the soul, and the Socratic faith. The material that modern society has about Socrates comes from four works: Aristophanes' comedy *Clouds*, Xenophon's dialogues, Plato's dialogues, and Aristotle's tracts. They all say that Socrates resembled an ugly gnome. Aristophanes disliked him, while Xenophon and Plato admired him. Those who accused Socrates of worshiping gods not recognized by the state (*asebia*) eventually got rid of him through trial and execution.

538. Sapet, Kerrily. *Cleopatra: Ruler of Egypt.* Morgan Reynolds, 2007. 176pp. ISBN 978-1-59935-035-6. Grades 8 up.

This biography of Cleopatra, the queen of Egypt (d. 30 B.C.E.), offers a balanced account of her life while clearly stating that most of what is known about her comes from writings by the Romans, who hated her. It includes background about her education and what life would have been like in her world. It also discusses Egyptian culture and religion, the role of women in her society, and life in the Nile Valley. Maps, photographs, and reproductions enhance the text. Bibliography, Chronology, Notes, Web Sites, and Index.

539. Usher, M. D. *Wise Guy: The Life and Philosophy of Socrates.* Farrar, 2005. 40pp. ISBN 978-0-374-31249-7. Grades 3–6.

This biography of Socrates gives background about his life and philosophy and about the world of ancient Greece in which he lived. He believed that one could obtain wisdom only through questioning ideas and values—not by accepting that which someone else had decided. He was not only seeking the truth but also enjoyed other people and parties. However he was tried and convicted for unsubstantiated charges made by jealous citizens and executed; he was made to drink hemlock. Bibliography.

540. Whiting, Jim. *The Life and Times of Aristotle.* (Biography from Ancient Civilizations) Mitchell Lane, 2006. 48pp. ISBN 978-1-58415-508-9. Grades 6–9.

This biography gives background about the life of Greek philosopher and scientist Aristotle. He created a system of Western philosophy that included morality and aesthetics, politics and metaphysics, and logic and science—views that extended into the Renaissance although modern physics replaced them. Some of his biological observations were not confirmed until the 19th century. He had a huge influence on philosophical and theological thinking in the Islamic and Jewish traditions as well as Christian theology. He is still studied today although most of his writings have been lost. Photographs and illustrations highlight the text. Bibliography, Chronology, Notes, Glossary, For Further Reading, Web Sites, and Index.

541. Whiting, Jim. *The Life and Times of Herodotus.* (Biography from Ancient Civilizations) Mitchell Lane, 2006. 48pp. ISBN 978-1-58415-509-6. Grades 6–9.

This biography of Herodotus (ca. 484–ca. 425 B.C.E.), an ancient Greek writer and historian, includes background about the Greek institutions of politics, economics, science, and sports. Today, people regard Herodotus as "the father of history." He was the first to collect his material systematically and to try to test its accuracy. His histories are the best-known of his works, and in them he included an account of the Greco-Persian Wars (490 B.C.E. and 480–479 B.C.E.) based on others' reports. Photographs and illustrations highlight the text. Bibliography, Chronology, Notes, Glossary, For Further Reading, Web Sites, and Index.

542. Whiting, Jim. *The Life and Times of Plato.* (Biography from Ancient Civilizations) Mitchell Lane, 2006. 48pp. ISBN 978-1-58415-507-2. Grades 6–9.

Plato, a classical Greek scholar, helped his mentor, Socrates, and his student, Aristotle, lay the groundwork for Western philosophy. The teachings of Socrates—along with the way he died—influenced Plato enormously. He was a mathematician and writer who founded the Academy in Athens, the Western world's first institution of higher learning. His dialogues have been used in teaching a variety of subjects including rhetoric, mathematics, philosophy, and logic. Photographs and illustrations highlight the text. Bibliography, Chronology, Notes, Glossary, For Further Reading, Web Sites, and Index.

Graphic Novels, Biographies, and Histories

543. Burgan, Michael. *The Curse of King Tut's Tomb.* Illustrated by Barbara Schulz. Graphic Library, 2005. 32pp. ISBN 978-0-7368-3833-7; paper ISBN 978-0-7368-5244-9. Grades 3–5.

When the tomb of Tutankhamen was opened in 1922, several mysterious deaths occurred. First, financier Lord Carnarvon was bitten by a mosquito. He later slashed the bite with a razor, it became infected, and he died of blood poisoning. Eight others died of various causes within twelve years, but fifty lived long lives. Illustrations help readers to visualize the text. Bibliography, Glossary, Further Reading, and Index.

544. Demolay, Jack. *Atlantis: The Mystery of the Lost City.* (Jr. Graphic Mysteries) PowerKids, 2006. 24pp. ISBN 978-1-4042-3407-9. Grades 3–5.

This graphic history looks first at the mystery behind the lost city of Atlantis. Then it covers some of the questions that surround the legend of the city. Much of the book discusses where the city could have been located and offers several suggestions, including the Azores, Crete, and Cuba. Glossary, Web Site, and Index.

545. Hynson, Colin. *The Building of the Great Pyramid.* (Stories from History) School Speciality, 2006. 48pp. ISBN 978-0-7696-4708-1; paper ISBN 978-0-7696-4692-3. Grades 5–8.

More than five thousand years ago, thousands of workers took more than twenty years to construct the Great Pyramid in Egypt for Pharaoh Khufu. They dragged the stones into the proper positions and hand-cut them to fit perfectly. This book presents the lives of a farmer and a pharaoh in their connections to the pyramid's construction. Full-color illustrations enhance the text. Chronology, Notes, Further Reading, Glossary, and Index.

546. Ross, Stewart. *Ancient Greece.* Illustrated by Richard Bonson. Dorling Kindersley, 2004. 31pp. ISBN 978-0-7566-0554-4. Grades 3–7.

As the Olympic Games are about to begin in 416 B.C.E., Lykourgos, Sparta's leading athlete, wants to beat Kinesias, the top athlete in Athens. Lykourgos decides to use supernatural warnings and sabotage. If they do not work, he will use other methods. As he considers his procedure, he must deal with aspects and expectations of Grecian life—gods and goddesses, the theater, the harbor at Athens, and others. Index.

547. Ross, Stewart. *Tales of the Dead: Ancient Egypt.* Dorling Kindersley, 2003. 32pp. ISBN 978-0-7894-9857-1. Grades 3–7.

In 1795 B.C.E., Methen, a scribe in the temple of Sobek the crocodile god, is with a servant when they see the chief embalmer raid a pyramid tomb. The embalmer tries to kill them when he discovers that they are trying to amass evidence against him. Eventually he is discovered and killed while trying to escape. Included in the story are facts about the pyramids and other aspects of ancient Egyptian society.

548. Saunders, Nicholas. *The Life of Alexander the Great.* (Stories from History) School Speciality, 2006. 48pp. ISBN 978-0-7696-4713-5; paper ISBN 978-0-7696-4694-7. Grades 5–8.

Alexander III, called Alexander the Great (356–323 B.C.E.), earned his name by being undefeated in battle and one of the most successful military commanders of all time. He conquered most of the world known to the ancient Greeks. In seven chapters, this book describes Alexander as a young leader, his role as king upon the death of Philip II (who may have been the victim of a conspiracy), the Battle of Issus, the Battle of Gaugamela, Alexander's experience in India, and his final years. Also included is background on Alexander's personal life including his horse Bucephalus and his long friendship with Hephaestion. Illustrations enhance the text. Map, Chronology, Glossary, Further Reading, and Index.

549. Saunders, Nicholas. *The Life of Julius Caesar.* (Stories from History) School Speciality, 2006. 48pp. Paper ISBN 978-0-7696-4697-8. Grades 5–8.

Julius Caesar (100?–44 B.C.E.) was a ruthless Roman leader. While in power he increased Rome's control of the existing world with his military prowess and his ability to defeat foreign enemies and keep control in Rome. Political intrigues, marriages for wealth, and friendships helped his ambition. As he gained more power, he became dictator for life. He was assassinated in 44 B.C.E., but he helped to create one of the great empires of history. Illustrations enhance the text. Map, Chronology, Glossary, Further Reading, and Index.

550. Shanower, Eric. *Betrayal.* (Age of Bronze) Image Comics, 2007. 72pp. ISBN 978-1-58240-845-3; paper ISBN 978-1-58240-755-5. Grades YA.

When High King Agamemnon desires to conquer wealthy Troy while retrieving Queen Helen of Sparta, Achilles leads the attack on the island of Tenedos, just off the coast of Troy, where he slays the royal family. Paris attempts to assassinate his rival for Helen, her husband Menelaus. The Trojans prepare for the attack by gathering their allies. Agamemnon offers a peace embassy to King Priam, but only a few (including Hector) believe him. Helen continues to beautify herself throughout all the turmoil, seemingly ignoring all that is happening. The third volume in the series.

551. Shanower, Eric. *Sacrifice: Age of Bronze.* (Age of Bronze) Image Comics, 2005. 72pp. Paper ISBN 978-1-58240-399-1. Grades YA.

Paris comes to Achaea to recover his father Priam's imprisoned sister Hesione. Instead he takes Helen, wife of the Spartan ruler Menelaus, back with him to Troy. Priam tries to refuse her entry when his daughter Kassandra foretells that Troy will be cursed. But Helen is pregnant with Paris's child, the ruling bloodline of Troy. After the Achaean fleet mistakenly attacks Mysia while trying to reach Troy, High King Agamemnon must fulfill a promise made to Artemis fourteen years before. He must sacrifice his eldest daughter, Iphigenia, for the fleet to sail again. Black-and-white graphics highlight this second volume in the series.

552. Shanower, Eric. *A Thousand Ships.* (Age of Bronze) Image Comics, 2001. 72pp. Paper ISBN 978-1-58240-200-0. Grades YA.

The Trojan War begins when Helen, queen of Sparta, willingly accompanies Paris of Troy to his home. Her husband, King Menelaus, decides to get her back regardless of the cost. Therefore, all of the kings of Greece who have pledged to support one another must join the Mycenaean high king, Agamemnon, on this journey to Troy. Achilles and Odysseus unwillingly leave to fight against Paris, his father Priam, and his friend Hector. This graphic representation (the first in a series) brings history alive. Bibliography, Genealogy, Glossary, Variant Spellings. *Will Eisner Comics Industry Award for Best Writer/Artist* and *Young Reader's Choice Award* (Pennsylvania) nomination.

DVDs

553. *Ancient Egypt: 3000 B.C.–300 B.C.: Back in Time.* (Hands-On Crafts for Kids Series 6) Chip Taylor Communications, 2003. 30 min. Grades 4–6.

This production begins with a narrator reading the list of materials appearing on the screen. Teachers construct objects from Egyptian times—a cobra pen topper, hieroglyphics (with more than seven hundred letters but no vowels), a collar and cuffs, a potpourri mummy, and a papyrus fan. Each item helps explain an important aspect of Egyptian culture.

554. *Ancient Greece: 2000 B.C. to 400 A.D.: Back in Time.* (Hands-On Crafts for Kids Series 6) Chip Taylor Communications, 2003. 30 min. Grades 4–6.

This production begins with a narrator reading the list of materials appearing on the screen. Teachers construct objects from ancient Greece including an olive wreath to symbolize the crown at the Olympics, mathematical solids (shapes), pots, a tragedy/comedy mask, and a column chalkboard. Each item helps explain an important aspect of Greek culture.

555. *Ancient History.* Centre, 2007. 6 DVDs; 30 min. ea. Grades 7 up.

This series of DVDs presents the ancient societies of the mound builders in America, the builders of Stonehenge and Celtic Iron Age hill forts in Britain, the Anasazi, the Greeks and their accomplishments such as the city-state and democracy, and the Incas. Each segment examines the social, economic, and cultural achievements of each group rather than the wars it fought. The program also tries to trace the roots, development, zenith, and decline of each group.

556. *The Cave Painter of Lascaux.* Crystal, 2007. 7:52 min. ISBN 978-1-56290-542-2. Grades 1–3.

Anna is uninterested in visiting Lascaux, France. However, once her class arrives, she wanders away from the group and discovers a man dressed as a caveman who starts describing the pictures on the walls inside the caves. Then an actual caveman joins them and tells about life during the Stone Age. He gives Anna a necklace before she runs off to catch her departing bus.

557. *Culture and Math: The Egyptians.* Discovery School, 2006. 15 min. ISBN 978-1-59380-543-2. Grades 10 up.

A presentation of the ancient Egyptians and their use of technology, numerical systems, geometry, multiplication, and fractions. The people in the Nile Valley of 3100 B.C.E. developed bucket-based irrigation technology, while papyrus boats led to trading. Astronomy and mathematical calculations helped build the pyramids. Mathematics helped Egyptians apportion land and bread. The program includes photography of the area.

558. *Democracy in the Ancient World.* (Democracy in World History, 1) Hawkhill, 2006. 26 min. ISBN 978-1-55979-170-0. Grades 7 up.

This look at democracy in the ancient world covers political structures from the times of tribal societies to just before the Renaissance. Still photography, live action, and graphics help summarize the development of democracy. Cultures other than western ones give the approach a depth not often available.

559. *Egypt: Secrets of the Sand.* (Middle East Studies) Chip Taylor Communications, . 20 min. Grades 7 up.

The Egyptologist who is considered to be the authority on the pyramids at Giza is Dr. Zahi Hawass, an archaeologist who has spent many years studying these structures. He says that much is still to be learned and hopes that all who excavate will publish their findings to help those who come after them. Images from space indicate that the Sahara was once irrigated and, most likely, the site of an important civilization that probably moved to the Nile delta when the land became too arid. The movement of these people suggests that slaves did not build the pyramids, as many have thought.

560. *The Egypt Detectives.* Films Media, 2006. 6 DVDs; 25 min ea. ISBN 978-1-4213-5107-0. Grades 9 up.

This DVD features an archaeologist and an Egyptologist who explore the mysteries of ancient Egypt. They try to solve historical puzzles including who the Egyptians were ("The First Egyptians"), how the workers moved a three-ton stone five hundred miles ("The Pharaoh's Stone"), why pyramid builders changed locations ("The Pyramids"), why Akhenaten decided that polytheism was not desirable ("The Rebel Pharaoh"), why animals were made into mummies ("The Animal Mummies"), and what the treasures left in Tutankhamen's tomb meant ("Tutankhamun's Treasures").

561. *Egyptian: New Kingdom to Modern Day.* (Timelines of Ancient Civilizations) Film Ideas, 2003. 16 min. Grades 7 up.

The New Kingdom in Egypt began around 1550 B.C.E. and included the pharaohs Thutmose I, Hatshepsut, Amenhotep III, Akhenaten, and Tutankhamen. This DVD continues to the end of modern times, a period of more than three thousand years. It presents dynasties and their importance, many of the "firsts" of these times, the position of women, enemies, and other information. Graphics, photographs, maps, aerial views of ruins, and documentary footage contribute to the overall effect.

562. *Egyptian: Stone Age to Middle Kingdom.* (Timelines of Ancient Civilizations) Film Ideas, 2003. 16 min. Grades 7 up.

The Stone Age in Egypt, called the Predynastic period, was prior to 3100 B.C.E. This video continues to the end of the Middle Kingdom, approximately 1640 B.C.E., a period of more than 1500 years. It presents dynasties and their significance, many of the "firsts" of these times, the position of women, enemies, and other information. Graphics, photographs, maps, aerial views of ruins, and documentary footage contribute to the overall effect.

563. *The Egyptian Empire.* (The Fall of Great Empires) Schlessinger, 2004. 35 min. ISBN 978-1-57225-951-5. Grades 9 up.

The video shows how the Egyptian Empire began and grew, the problems resulting from its decline and fall, and its contributions to Western culture. Other topics include dealing with empire outposts, changes in populations, religious upheaval and external threats. Not until the 19th century, when explorers began to search for archaeological treasures in Egypt, did the importance of ancient traditions begin to unfold. The Egyptian Empire survived external and internal threats for over three thousand years, until the rule of Cleopatra. Its significance remains today. The video includes live-action footage, ancient art, recreations of important events, and computer simulations.

564. *Egyptian Monumental Structures.* (Technology & Architecture in Ancient Civilizations) New Dimension Media, 2006. 30 min. ISBN 978-1-59522-566-5. Grades 8 up.

This DVD features dramatizations of workers constructing ancient Egypt's monuments and computer simulations suggesting the shapes of the original structures. Also included are comments from experts about the monuments and their possible functions. It offers historical detail on several pharaohs as well.

565. *Greek Designs of Beauty.* (Technology & Architecture in Ancient Civilizations) New Dimension Media, 2006. 30 min. ISBN 978-1-59522-568-9. Grades 8 up.

This DVD features dramatizations of workers constructing ancient Greece's monuments, computer simulations of what the original structures looked like, and comments from experts. It includes a segment on the temple of the Delphi oracle, located on a fault line where noxious gases seeped up from below the earth as the oracle pronounced prophecies. Another segment presents the first Olympics.

566. *The Hidden History of Egypt.* Discovery Communications, 2002. 26 min. ISBN 978-0-7365-6757-2. Grades 5–9.

An Egyptologist accompanies a narrator to Egypt and compares modern-day practices to those of ancient Egypt. Life has changed little, since contemporary Egyptians often sleep on the roof where it is cooler and drink beer and eat bread as did Egyptians more than three thousand years ago. Additionally, contemporary homes have the same center columns that excavations revealed in ancient homes. The Coptic church keeps the ancient language alive, and the Nile still brings needed silt to fertilize crops during floods.

567. *Infinite Secrets: The Genius of Archimedes.* (Nova) WGBH, 2003. 60 min. ISBN 978-1-59375-106-7. Grades 7 up.

Archimedes (ca. 287–ca. 212 B.C.E.) understood mathematics and designed war machines that his army in Syracuse used against the Romans. Much of his work disappeared during the Middle Ages. The scientists of the Renaissance were unable to build upon his advanced ideas. In 1991, some of Archimedes' original writings were discovered underneath a religious text in a small Medieval prayer book. Scholars have found how wonderful his concepts and theories, work known as "the Method," actually were. He was the Einstein of his time—more than two thousand years ago.

568. *Mummies and Pyramids: Egypt and Beyond.* Choices, 2003. 200. ISBN 978-1-930545-90-8. Grades 6 up.

Archaeologists reveal their knowledge of mummies and pyramids against a background of ruins and excavations. Mummies have been found all over the world, from the heat of Peru and Egypt to the cold of Antarctica. In this video, experts in the anthropological, medical, and scientific communities on location at digs discuss how mummies came into being. Information about history, geography, and technology explains about pyramids' origins. Among those discussed are the Pyramid of the Moon in Peru, which has become known as the "pyramid of doom" because of the rituals performed by the people who lived near it, and a pyramid in the Atacama Desert in Chile.

569. *The Mummy Who Would Be King: Nova.* WGBH, 2006. 56 min. ISBN 978-1-59375-179-1. Grades 7 up.

In the 1800s when the Egyptians had more mummies than they wanted, a Canadian museum in Niagara Falls bought several to add to its collection. During the 1960s a German investigator visited the museum and determined that one of the mummies was the pharaoh Ramses I because his arms were crossed high on his chest and his bone structure resembled others the man had seen. He obtained permission to examine the mummy and used X-rays of the skull, radiocarbon dating, and DNA testing with modern medical equipment to convince experts at Emory University that this mummy was the famous pharaoh. The museum returned the mummy to the Archaeological Museum in Cairo. The DVD includes brief historical background as well as the process of the investigation itself.

570. *Parthenon: Design and Architecture.*   Discovery Channel, 2002. 52 min. ISBN 978-1-58738-273-4. Grades 6 up.

    The first part of this production presents the construction of the Parthenon while the second part asks why Pericles created it in 447 B.C.E. The tilted and tapered columns of the building create an optical illusion, and the marble blocks (some more than 14 feet long and weighing 5 to 10 tons) fit so tightly that a human hair cannot be inserted between them. Archaeologists first thought the building was a temple, but its inscriptions and writings from the time period indicate that it may have housed Athenian treasure. On-site footage of the restoration and interviews with experts reveal many unexpected facts.

571. *Toward Civilization.*   Discovery, 2004. 52 min. ISBN 978-1-58738-491-2. Grades 6–12.

    The four segments of this DVD looks at the development of human civilization. The first, "Before We Ruled the Earth," examines life before humans existed. The second, "Out of Africa" discusses archaeological finds relating to the first humans on the continent of Africa. In the third, "Secrets of the Iceman," viewers will learn of the discovery of a frozen body in Switzerland in 1991 and how it has helped scientists discover traits of humans and their possible lifestyle 3,500 years ago. The final segment moves back to Africa with "The Nile: Where Egypt Began," and the Nile's reputation as a source of life.

Compact Discs

572. Baccalario, Pierdomenico. *The Long-Lost Map.*   Narrated by Michael Page. (Ulysses Moore, No. 2) Brillance Audio, 2006. 4 CDs; 5 hrs. ISBN 978-1-4233-1327-4. Grades 4–6.

    See entry 317.

573. Banks, Lynne Reid. *Tiger, Tiger.*   Narrated by Jan Francis. Random House, 2005. 195pp. 4 CDs; 4.8 hrs. ISBN 978-0-307-24340-9. Grades 5–8.

    See entry 318.

574. Cahill, Thomas. *Sailing the Wine-Dark Sea: Why the Greeks Matter.*   Narrated by Olympia Dukakis. Random House Audio, 2003. 6 CDs. ISBN 978-0-7366-9572-5. Grades YA.

    See entry 416.

575. Cooney, Caroline B. *Goddess of Yesterday.* Narrated by Christina Moore. Recorded Books, 2003. 8 CDs; 9 hrs. ISBN 978-1-4025-6603-5. Grades 6–9.

See entry 325.

576. Davis, Kenneth C. *Don't Know Much About Mythology.* Narrated by John Lee. Random House, 2005. 14 CDs. ISBN 978-0-7393-1747-1. Grades YA.

See entry 428.

577. Fletcher, Susan. *Alphabet of Dreams.* Narrated by Meera Simhan. Listening Library, 2006. 8 CDs; 9 hrs. 20 min. ISBN 978-0-7393-3549-9. Grades 5–8.

See entry 330.

578. Gregory, Kristiana. *Cleopatra VII: Daughter of the Nile, Egypt, 57 B.C.* Narrated by Josephine Bailey. (Royal Diaries) Tantor Media, 2006. 3 CDs; 4.75 hrs. ISBN 978-1-4001-0243-3. Grades 4–8.

See entry 342.

579. Halter, Marek. *Sarah: A Novel.* Narrated by Kate Burton. (The Canaan Trilogy) Random House, 2004. 8 CDs. ISBN 978-1-4159-0017-8. Grades YA.

See entry 343.

580. Henty, G.A. *The Young Carthaginian: A Story of the Times of Hannibal.* Narrated by William Sutherland. Blackstone Audio, 2002. 7 CDs; 9 hrs. 13 min. ISBN 978-0-7861-9538-1. Grades YA up.

See entry 346.

581. Howard, Annabelle. *The Great Wonder: The Building of the Great Pyramid.* Illustrated by Stephen Wells. Narrated by Garard Green. (Smithsonian Odyssey) Soundprints, 1996. ISBN 978-1-56899-355-3. Grades 2–5.

See entry 347.

ROMAN EMPIRE, 54 B.C.E. TO 476 C.E.

Historical Fiction and Fantasy

582. Balit, Christina. *Escape from Pompeii.* Holt, 2003. 32pp. ISBN 978-0-8050-7324-9. Grades 5–9.

A Roman boy, Tranio, and his friend Livia seek shelter on a Greek fishing boat when Vesuvius erupts in 79 and destroys Pompeii. When the two are old, they travel from Greece to visit the site and to place flowers on their buried city. Illustrations highlight the text.

583. Bradley, Marion Zimmer. *The Forest House.* Roc, 2007. 416pp. Paper ISBN 978-0-451-46153-7. Grades YA.

In Roman Britain, Eilan, a Druid, falls in love with Gaius, a Roman whose mother was a Druid and whose father is an important officer in the Roman legions. The inevitable clash between the two cultures occurs with Eilan's belief in the cult of the goddess, in which the priestess has the power, and Gaius's belief in a patriarchal society. Their son offers hope of unification.

584. Browne, N. M. *Warriors of Alavna.* Bloomsbury, 2002. 312pp. ISBN 978-1-58234-775-2; 2004. paper ISBN 978-1-58234-916-9. Grades 5–10.

In this historical fantasy, contemporary students Ursula—overweight and 6 feet tall—and Dan—popular and athletic—disappear in a yellow fog at the battlefield of Hastings as the Romans begin to conquer it in 75. The Combrogi princess Rhonwen has summoned them to Britain to help her brother battle the invading Ravens. Ursula becomes a warrior and Dan a "berserker." With her newfound power, Ursula enlists a Roman legion to help the Combrogis and then tries to get herself and Dan back to their origins. However, both of them wonder who is worse: the Combrogis who collect severed heads for trophies or the Ravens who fight in legions but slaughter entire villages.

585. Browne, N. M. *Warriors of Camlann.* Bloomsbury, 2003. 400pp. ISBN 978-1-58234-817-9. Grades 6–9.

Dan and Ursula, a magician and warrior, want to return to their own time through the Veil, but they instead find themselves in the 5th century serving Sartorius Ursus, War Duke of Britain, as the Saxons try to conquer the Romans and the Celtics. They witness Arthur and the knights of the Round Table engaging in exploits that will become the stuff of legend.

586. **Davis, Lindsey.** *Shadows in Bronze.* (Marcus Didius Falco Mysteries) Minotaur, 2007. 343pp. Paper ISBN 978-0-312-35776-4. Grades YA.

In 70 Marcus Didius Falco works for the Roman emperor Vespasian as a detective. He hears that Barnabus has instigated a plot to overthrow Vespasian and kill Marcus. In disguise he trails Barnabus and finds that the path also leads him to his only love.

587. **Davis, Lindsey.** *The Silver Pigs.* (Marcus Didius Falco Mysteries) Minotaur, 2006. 343pp. Paper ISBN 978-0-312-35777-1. Grades YA.

In 70 Marcus Didius Falco helps to uncover a Roman plot against Nero's successor, Emperor Vespasian. Falco must find the men chasing a senator's daughter because she knows where traitors have hidden the "silver pigs" (lead ingots with silver inside) that they smuggled into the capital as part of their plot against the emperor.

588. **De Carvalho, Mario.** *A God Strolling in the Cool of the Evening: A Novel.* Translated by Gregory Rabassa. Grove, 2001. 265pp. Paper ISBN 978-0-8021-3774-6. Grades YA.

In Portugal, Lucius Valerius Quintius rules the small city of Tarcisis. His hero is Marcus Aurelius, and all he wants to do is make just decisions for his people. Problems become dilemmas, however, which he must solve to the best of his ability. *Pegasus Prize.*

589. **Denenberg, Barry.** *Atticus of Rome, 30 B.C.* (Life and Times) Scholastic, 2004. 166pp. ISBN 978-0-439-52453-7. Grades 5–9.

After Roman soldiers capture 12-year-old Atticus and sell him into slavery, his owner, Lucius Opimius, needs someone to spy for him. Atticus uncovers a plot to murder the emperor and reunites with his own father, a gladiator. Then his master wills his wealth to him after giving him his freedom.

590. **Gormley, Beatrice.** *Salome.* Knopf, 2007. 274pp. ISBN 978-0-375-83908-5. Grades 7 up.

As a descendant of Herod the Great, the Jewish Salome grows up in Rome, where she wants to be a priestess in Diana's temple. Her mother, however, who divorced her father and married Herod Antipas, the ruler of the Jews in Tiberias, takes her far away from the city to a new home. Salome begins noticing political nuances, but her egotistical and insecure mother and her lecherous stepfather force her into asking for John the Baptist's head after she performs the dance of the seven veils.

591. **Gray, Kes.** *Vesuvius Poovius.* Illustrated by Chris Mould. Trafalgar, 2005. 32pp. Paper ISBN 978-0-340-87336-6. Grades 1–4.

This book discusses one of Rome's big problems—getting rid of human waste. In this story, Vesuvius Poovius invents plumbing, calling it the Vesuvius Poovius Loovius, or the "loo." Also presented are the foods that Romans enjoyed eating before they needed to use this appliance.

592. **Harris, Robert.** *Imperium: A Novel of Ancient Rome.* Pocket, 2007. 305pp. Paper ISBN 978-0-7434-9866-1. Grades YA.

Tiro, the confidential secretary and manservant of the senator Marcus Cicero in ancient Rome, relates the story of Cicero's rise from a nobody in the years 79 to 64 B.C.E. As a lawyer of 27, Cicero arrived in Rome and intellectually challenged Pompey, Caesar, and Crassus. When he discovered Julius Caesar's and Marcus Crassus's plot to rig elections, he achieved his great goal of having supreme power. Evidence indicates that Tiro actually wrote a biography of Cicero that disappeared during the Middle Ages.

called the Patron may be responsible. On his trail, they end up in the caves of Sorrento, where they meet hostile pirates and vicious slave traders. The 3rd volume in the series.

603. Lawrence, Caroline. *The Secrets of Vesuvius.* (The Roman Mysteries) Puffin, 2004. 192pp. Paper ISBN 978-0-14-240118-7. Grades 6–9.

In 79 Flavia, Jonathan, Nubia, and Lupus rescue an admiral after a boating accident. He gives them a riddle to solve that may lead to a treasure if they can find the blacksmith on whose wall it was printed. Afterward, they go to spend the summer with Flavia's uncle in Pompeii, where they find Vulcan, the blacksmith of the riddle. An orphan, he wants to know what happened to his parents. But as they begin to work on the solution, Vesuvius erupts and they must flee the city. The 2nd volume in this mystery series.

604. Lawrence, Caroline. *The Sirens of Surrentum.* (The Roman Mysteries) Roaring Brook, 2007. 176pp. ISBN 978-1-59643-084-6. Grades 6–9.

In June of 80 Flavia, Jonathan, Lupus, and Nubia are invited to visit Pulchra at the Villa Limona. There they discover that one of the other house guests is trying to poison Pulchra's mother, and although Flavia's betrothed is scheduled to arrive almost immediately, they must take time to find the evildoer. The 11th volume in the series.

605. Lawrence, Caroline. *The Thieves of Ostia.* (The Roman Mysteries) Puffin, 2004. 160pp. Paper ISBN 978-0-14-240147-7. Grades 4–6.

Flavia Gemina, a Roman sea captain's daughter, is 12 and living in the port of Ostia in 79 during the tenth year of Emperor Vespasian's reign. She and her secretly Christian neighbors, Jonathan and Miriam—along with an African slave, Nubia (whom Flavia has purchased with birthday money in order to free), and a tongueless beggar boy, Lupus— attempt to find who beheaded Jonathan's watchdog. Among the adversaries in their hunt are evil slave dealers, wild dogs, and an unhappy sailor. Eventually their suspect commits suicide by jumping from a lighthouse. The 1st volume in the series.

606. Lawrence, Caroline. *The Twelve Tasks of Flavia Gemina.* (The Roman Mysteries) Roaring Brook, 2004. 176pp. ISBN 978-1-59643-012-9. Grades 6–9.

Miriam, the sister of Flavia's friend Jonathan, is betrothed to Flavia's uncle, and Flavia's father meets and falls in love with a new woman in Ostia. He decides that he must find a husband for Flavia. However, Flavia thinks that Cartilia must have bewitched her father for him to become concerned about such a subject. When Flavia dreams of Hercules, she knows that she must investigate Cartilia's past. Then Flavia falls in love with an older man as she solves the mystery of the twelve labors associated with Hercules. Set in 80, this is the 6th volume in the series.

607. Llywelyn, Morgan. *Druids.* Ivy, 1993. 456pp. Paper ISBN 978-0-8041-0844-7. Grades YA.

Ainvar becomes a druid after being fascinated by the Order of the Wise as a child. His belief in the immortal soul interests Vercingetorix of Gaul, and Ainvar becomes his servant. They try to unite the tribes of Gaul to ready them for fighting the approaching Roman troops, but Caesar invades and wins by 58 B.C.E. After watching Vercingetorix maintain his dignity as a defeated king even when spit upon by the Romans, Ainvar escapes to continue his druidic life.

608. Llywelyn, Morgan. *The Greener Shore: A Novel of the Druids of Hibernia.* Del Ray, 2007. 301pp. Paper ISBN 978-0-345-47767-5. Grades YA.

The great druid Ainvar, his three wives, and his clan flee Celtic Gaul when Julius Caesar and his army invade. They take their ancient knowledge with them to the strange world of Hibernia (Ireland), home of the Gael. There they find other Celts, and Ainvar and his wife Briga, a powerful druid herself, set out to rebuild their lives in this sequel to *Druids*.

609. McCullough, Colleen. *Caesar's Women.* (Masters of Rome) Avon, 2008. 696pp. Paper ISBN 978-0-06-158242-4. Grades YA.

McCullough explores Julius Caesar's relationships with women — in particular, his mother, his second wife, and his daughter Julia — and how he balances his personal and political priorities in this fourth book in the series.

610. McCullough, Colleen. *The First Man in Rome.* (Masters of Rome) Avon, 2008. 896pp. Paper ISBN 978-0-06-158241-7. Grades YA.

In Rome in 110 B.C.E. Gaius Marius is a man full of ambition and prepared to use all his political skills to attain his goal by controlling not only slaves but also free citizens. The first volume in the series.

611. McCullough, Colleen. *Fortune's Favorites.* (Masters of Rome) Avon, 2008. 696pp. Paper ISBN 978-0-06-158240-0. Grades YA.

After returning from exile, Sulla becomes dictator but suddenly retires. Pompey designates himself as "Magnus" ("The Great") and begins his climb upward. His rival, however, is Julius Caesar, who rises to power in the 1st century B.C.E. in this sequel to *The First Man in Rome* and *The Grass Crown*.

612. McCullough, Colleen. *The Grass Crown.* (Masters of Rome) Avon, 2008. 696pp. Paper ISBN 978-0-06-158239-4. Grades YA.

The focus in McCullough's second book about Rome in the 1st century B.C.E. (after *The First Man in Rome*) is Lucius Cornelius Sulla. He protects his position of leadership as well as he can given the opposition and intrigue surrounding him.

613. Moss, Marissa. *Galen: My Life in Imperial Rome.* (Ancient World Journals) Harcourt, 2002. 48pp. ISBN 978-0-15-216535-2. Grades 3–7.

Galen, 12, is one of Emperor Augustus's slaves in Rome in 2 B.C.E. As the son of an educated mural painter, he paints when he can, helps his father decorate Livia's new house, enjoys doing things with his friend Micio, and never suffers corporal punishment. His worst problem is Agrippa, Augustus's grandson. When Galen uncovers a plot to assassinate Augustus, he gains his freedom. Maps and Supplementary Information.

614. Napoli, Donna Jo. *Song of the Magdalene.* Simon Pulse, 2004. 240pp. Paper ISBN 978-0-689-87396-6. Grades YA.

Miriam loves to run alone into the fields from her home during the early years of the 1st century C.E. One day, as she enjoys the beauty of nature, she suffers an epileptic fit. Fearful that she has devils within her, she tells no one. Not until she has a second seizure in front of her physically disabled friend Abraham, and he assures her that neither of them have sinned enough to earn these afflictions, does she begin to accept herself. She discovers that she loves Abraham, a highly intelligent man who teaches her to read the

Torah. After she becomes pregnant with his child, he dies, and a hostile villager rapes her. She leaves the village to go to other relatives. Because she is traveling alone she is called a prostitute. On this journey she hears about a man named Joshua. After she has another fit at a well near him, he declares that she has no devils in her. *American Library Association Notable Books for Young Adults* and *Booklist Best Books for Young Adults*.

615. Osborne, Mary Pope. *Vacation Under the Volcano.* Illustrated by Sal Murdocca. (Magic Tree House) Random House, 1998. 80pp. ISBN 978-0-679-99050-5; paper ISBN 978-0-679-89050-8. Grades K–3.

Master librarians Jack and Annie go to Pompeii to retrieve an endangered story. Although they do not know it, it is the myth of Hercules. Before they can find it, the volcano overlooking the town erupts and Hercules helps them escape.

616. Pipe, Jim. *You Wouldn't Want to Be Cleopatra! An Egyptian Ruler You'd Rather Not Be.* (You Wouldn't Want To . . .) Franklin Watts, 2007. 32pp. ISBN 978-0-531-18726-5; paper ISBN 978-0-531-18923-8. Grades 3–6.

During her life as a queen, Cleopatra was the target of many who would usurp her power. The text examines the plots against her along with the customs of the times. Cartoon illustrations, entertaining dialogue, and "hints" are part of a creative layout. Glossary, Maps, and Index.

617. Roberts, Katherine. *The Cleopatra Curse.* (Seven Fabulous Wonders) HarperCollins, 2006. 288pp. Paper ISBN 978-0-00-711284-5. Grades 3–6.

Zeuxis, a lighthouse boy who collects fuel for Alexandria's Pharos lighthouse in Egypt, wants to become a charioteer. Queen Cleopatra and her nefarious brother, Prince Ptolemy, turn down his request. However, Julius Caesar's envoys allow him to race. What Zeuxis does not know is that Caesar needs an inexperienced charioteer to help him complete his plans to invade Queen Cleopatra's palace in 48 B.C.E.

618. Rubalcaba, Jill. *The Wadjet Eye.* Houghton Mifflin, 2000. 160pp. ISBN 978-0-395-68942-4; Clarion, 2006. paper ISBN 978-0-618-68927-9. Grades 4–6.

In 45 B.C.E., after mummifying his deceased mother who may have had the plague, medically trained 17-year-old Damon travels from Alexandria to Spain to bring the news of her death to his father, who is fighting with Caesar. When Damon and his best friend, Artemas, are shipwrecked and attacked by sharks, Cleopatra rescues them and sends them to spy on Cicero, Caesar's enemy. Eventually, Damon sees his father for the first time in six years as he lies in a hospital close to the battlefield. There, as Damon helps surgeons amputate and repair, he and his father are reconciled. Glossary and Bibliography.

619. Saylor, Steven. *A Murder on the Appian Way: A Novel of Ancient Rome.* Minotaur, 2009. 448pp. Paper ISBN 978-0-312-53968-9. Grades YA.

Caesar and Pompey try to control the Roman Empire in 52 B.C.E. while Titus Milo competes with Publius Clodius for control of Rome itself. But Clodius is murdered on the Appian Way, and the city becomes chaotic. To stop the rioting, Pompey and Clodius's widow, Fulvia, implore Gordianus the Finder to investigate, but only after Cicero's oration at the trial does a cover-up surface.

620. Saylor, Steven. *Roman Blood: A Novel of Ancient Rome.* Minotaur, 2008. 363pp. Paper ISBN 978-0-312-38324-4. Grades YA.

In the 1st century B.C.E. Cicero hires Gordianus to gather evidence for his defense of Sextus Roscious, a farmer accused of patricide. As Gordianus investigates, he finds conspiracy and lies.

621. Saylor, Steven. *The Venus Throw.* Minotaur, 2008. 308pp. Paper ISBN 978-0-312-53967-2. Grades YA.

When an Egyptian ambassador comes to Rome, he fears that the Egyptian king is trying to have him killed. When he is murdered after he leaves the home of his friend Gordianus the Finder, Gordianus helps his sister Clodia Pulcher (later the Lesbia made famous by Catullus) accuse his neighbor Marcus Caelius. Caelius's defender, however, is Marcus Tullius Cicero, the great orator.

622. Scarrow, Simon. *Under the Eagle: A Tale of Military Adventure and Reckless Heroism with the Roman Legions.* Thomas Dunne, 2002. 256pp. Paper ISBN 978-0-312-30424-9. Grades YA.

Lucius Cornelius Macro, an experienced centurion, fights with Quintus Licinius Cato, an imperial slave who was forced to enlist, and Cato's fighting earns him freedom. The two head for Britain as part of the invading army in 42 C.E. and find themselves trying to foil a political plot. Throughout, Macro tries to hide his illiteracy. Before they finish the campaign, Cato has taught him to read and write.

623. Scieszka, Jon. *See You Later, Gladiator.* Illustrated by Adam McCauley. (Time Warp Trio) Penguin, 2000. 96pp. ISBN 978-0-670-89340-9; Puffin, 2004. paper ISBN 978-0-14-240117-0. Grades 3–6.

When Joe, Fred, and Sam find themselves in Rome, they confront dangers including crocodiles and an emperor intent on poisoning them. They attend Dorkius's gladiator school because they must fight in the Colosseum. There they reveal favorite wrestling moves such as the "Time Warp Trio Blind Ninja Smackdown." After they win their fights, they have to reclaim The Book from a Vestal Virgin so they can return to the present. The 9th volume in the series. *Garden State Children's Book Awards* (New Jersey) nomination and *ABC Children's Booksellers Choices Awards.*

624. Speare, Elizabeth George. *The Bronze Bow.* Houghton Mifflin, 1997. 256pp. ISBN 978-0-395-13719-2. Grades 7 up.

Eighteen-year-old Daniel detests the Roman soldiers in Palestine. They crucified his father and uncle for unpaid taxes and sold him to a contemptible blacksmith. He joins an outlaw hiding in the mountains, but then he hears about a man named Jesus who preaches nonviolence. Daniel's new employer leaves Daniel in charge of the forge as he follows Jesus, and Daniel thinks that the man Jesus may be able to help his sister, still in mourning for their family. *Newbery Medal* and *International Board of Books for Young People.*

625. Sutcliff, Rosemary. *The Eagle of the Ninth.* Sunburst, 1993. 264pp. Paper ISBN 978-0-374-41930-1. Grades YA.

Marcus wounds his leg and has to resign from his post as a Roman soldier serving in Britain. He visits his uncle and when they go to the Saturnalia games Marcus decides to offer a defeated gladiator a post as his servant. They become friends and travel north to look for information about Marcus's father, lost with the Ninth Legion. When they see the Epidaii tribe flaunting the eagle insignia of the Ninth, they steal it and return home with it. They know the fate of the legion's men, and can only mourn their loss. First published in 1954. *Carnegie Commendation*.

626. Sutcliff, Rosemary. *Frontier Wolf.* Front Street, 2008. 196pp. Paper ISBN 978-1-59078-594-2. Grades YA.

In the 4th century, Alexios takes charge of a Roman outpost known for renegade British soldiers. Although the men suspect that Alexios may not have the strength to lead them, he learns that he must work with the local leaders, and he is successful. First published in 1980.

627. Sutcliff, Rosemary. *The Lantern Bearers.* Sunburst, 1994. 248pp. Paper ISBN 978-0-374-44302-3. Grades YA.

The Romans leave Britain, but Aquila deserts the army in 410 because he has never lived in Rome and wants to remain in Britain. Saxons capture him and take him as a slave to their homeland but bring him back when they return to Britain to fight. Aquila escapes them and joins Ambrosius's forces against the Saxon king Vortigern. In a battle, Aquila recognizes his nephew as one of the wounded, and he returns to help the boy— even though he is an enemy—after the battle ends. He sends his sister, married to a Saxon, a ring so that she can return it after his nephew arrives home safely. First published in 1959. *Carnegie Medal.*

628. Sutcliff, Rosemary. *The Mark of the Horse Lord.* Front Street, 2008. 276pp. Paper ISBN 978-1-932425-62-8. Grades YA.

In Britain in the first century C.E., slave gladiator Phaedrus wins his freedom but royal officials ask him to impersonate Midir, the blind king of the Dalraidian [Dál Riata] tribe in Scotland, in order to keep control of his kingdom. The people believe that any disability in the king reflects weakness in the kingdom, and they will kill a blind man. First published in 1965. *Phoenix Award.*

629. Sutcliff, Rosemary. *Outcast.* Sunburst, 1995. 229pp. Paper ISBN 978-0-374-45673-3. Grades YA.

Beric, a Roman orphan raised in a British tribe and cast out during a famine, boards a ship sailing for Rome and is sold into slavery by the crew. He escapes, but authorities accuse him of a crime he did not commit and he serves his sentence as a galley slave. A fight on board causes the overseer to toss Beric into the sea, and he swims ashore to Britain. There he sees people whom he has known before and finds a better life. First published in 1955.

630. Sutcliff, Rosemary. *The Silver Branch.* Peter Smith, 1994. 231pp. ISBN 978-0-8446-6780-5; Farrar, 1993. paper ISBN 978-0-374-46648-0. Grades YA.

After arriving in Britain around 300 C.E., timid Justin discovers that the legion's finance minister, Allectus, is betraying the Romans, and Allectus tries to kill him and the others who know. When Justin tries to leave Britain, some of the men who are planning to kill Allectus convince Justin to stay and help. When they then destroy the evil man, Justin gains confidence in his own decisions. First published in 1957. *Carnegie Commendation.*

631. Tarr, Judith, and Harry Turtledove. *Household Gods.* Tom Doherty, 1999. 672pp. ISBN 978-0-312-86487-3; 2000. paper ISBN 978-0-8125-6466-2. Grades 9 up.

Nicole Gunther-Perrin, a divorced mother of two preschoolers, dislikes her job in a Los Angeles law firm and the mundane life of childcare. After an especially difficult day she prays to Roman gods of freedom Liber and Libera and awakens as Umma, a widowed tavernkeeper in 170 in the town of Carnuntum on the Roman frontier. Although she is initially delighted with the change, she soon discovers that life is still complicated. She contends with dirt, pain, and violence while dealing with drunks and those who think watching gladiators kill humans is entertaining. Nicole worries about her children "back" in the 20th century and copes with her present. She falls in love with Titus Calidius Severus, a decent man, but he dies of the plague. Then the Germans invade, and Nicole is raped by a Roman soldier. The best news to her is that Emperor Marcus Aurelius is an honest man. When she returns to the present, she accepts it with new understanding.

632. Trease, Geoffrey. *Word to Caesar.* Hillside, 2005. ISBN 978-0-9766386-2-9. Grades 5–8.

Exiled Roman poet Lucius Fabius Severus rescues Paul from the Caledonians at Ravenglass after his arm is severely wounded and his Roman soldier father dies. Severus takes him to his friend Veranius's villa in Bath, where Severus tells Paul that the emperor Trajan banished him because of his verses. The wealthy Calvus, a blackmailer who "bought" the services of all classes of men, including Severus's trusted copier, was told of Severus's satiric verses about him. Calvus made the copier replace them with poorly written words satirizing Trajan. Soon Paul hears news of Trajan's death and of the new emperor, Hadrian. Paul travels to Rome, not without hardship and peril, to tell Hadrian of the crime against Severus. Hadrian tells Paul he must have evidence of the crime, and with great difficulty, Paul gets it. Hadrian allows Severus to return to Rome and then assures Paul's security by hiring him.

633. Wallace, Lew. *Ben-Hur: A Tale of Christ.* Wildside, 2002. 558pp. ISBN 978-1-58715-539-0; paper ISBN 978-1-58715-538-3. Grades 7 up.

Jewish prince Judah Ben-Hur lives in Judea when a man named Jesus is becoming known for his radical teachings and opinions. When Ben-Hur's friend from childhood, Messala, now an ambitious Roman tribune, asks Ben-Hur to help him arrest those who are speaking against the emperor, Ben-Hur refuses, and Messala plans to punish him for his disobedience. He has Ben-Hur tried for attempting to kill the provincial governor, and Ben-Hur is convicted and placed on a Roman galley. His mother and sister are also imprisoned. In a battle at sea, Ben-Hur saves his commander, Quintus Arrius, and Quintus adopts him. Quintus gives him control of a stable of horses, and Ben-Hur begins his search for his mother and sister. During this time, he keeps coming across Jesus, each time feeling more interested in the man's beliefs. In a chariot race for his life, Ben-Hur exacts justice.

634. Williams, Mark London. *Ancient Fire.* (Danger Boy, No. 1) Candlewick, 2004. 224pp. ISBN 978-0-7636-2152-0; 2006 paper ISBN 978-0-7636-3092-8. Grades 4–8.

Twelve-year-old Eli Sands becomes involved with his parents' time-travel experiments in 2019. He and his father, Sandusky, moved to California from New Jersey after Eli's mother disappeared in an explosion while working on a spacetime sphere experiment. Sandusky's boss finds him and demands that he continue his experiments for the government. As a result of another lab accident, Eli enters another dimension and ends up in Alexandria, Egypt, 415 C.E. There he meets Thea, the 13-year-old daughter of Alexandria's last librarian, and Clyne, an intelligent dinosaur from another planet. When

All about the daily lives of ancient Romans. The topics include houses, street life, food, shopping, work, the theater, the races, the amphitheater, the baths, eating out, the Roman forum, and the Romans' many gods. Illustrations intensify the text. Glossary and Index.

646. Corbishley, Mike. *Everyday Life in Roman Times.* Creative, 2005. 96pp. ISBN 978-1-932889-79-6. Grades 6–9.

A description of life in all areas of the Roman Empire: Rome itself, other areas of Italy, Africa, Spain, Gaul, Greece, Britain, and Asia Minor. Sidebars and beautiful color illustrations reveal the Rome of the Caesars, the Greek influence on poets and dramatists, and aspects of daily life during Roman times. Bibliography, Chronology, Glossary, Gazetteer, and Index.

647. Dargie, Richard. *Rich and Poor in Ancient Rome.* (Rich and Poor) Creative, 2005. 32pp. ISBN 978-1-58340-722-6. Grades 3–6.

A look at daily life for people of all social classes in ancient Rome. It includes information about homes, family life, clothing, sports, food, health, medicine, work, religion, death, and burial. Among the photographs and illustrations are artifacts, statues, and other art. Glossary, Chronology, Glossary, Web Sites, and Index.

648. Deckker, Zilah. *Ancient Rome: Archaeology Unlocks the Secrets of Ancient Rome.* National Geographic, 2007. 64pp. ISBN 978-1-4263-0128-5. Grades 5–9.

This book begins, as Rome did, with the legend of Romulus and Remus, the twin sons of the war god Mars. Among the topics discussed in this view of Rome are its layers of history, its people—including the Latin farmers and the Sabines of the 10th century B.C.E., and Italy's unification in 1871. Archaeologists' discoveries give insight into the everyday lives of ordinary Romans as well as those of the upper class. Illustrations and photographs highlight the text. Maps, Chronology, Glossary, Bibliography, and Index.

649. Deem, James M. *Bodies from the Ash.* Houghton, 2005. 48pp. ISBN 978-0-618-47308-3. Grades 4–8.

When Vesuvius erupted on August 24, 79, the residents of Pompeii, Italy, were covered in ash. Not until the 18th century did excavations begin to uncover the dead. As the bodies of the victims decayed, holes were formed in the ash. Giuseppe Fiorelli realized that these holes could be filled with plaster and these casts showed the facial expressions, body positions, clothing, and possessions of the residents of Pompeii at the moment the ash covered them. Researchers have used these molds and other evidence to determine the lifestyles and final moments of some of the victims. *Young Readers Choice Awards* (Louisiana) nomination, *Prairie Pasque Award* (South Dakota) nomination, *Beehive Young Adult Book Award* (Utah) nomination, *School Library Journal Best Children's Books, Voice of Youth Advocates Nonfiction Honor List,* and *Dorothy Canfield Fisher Children's Book Award* (Vermont) nomination.

650. Faas, Patrick. *Around the Roman Table.* University of Chicago, 2005. 371pp. Paper ISBN 978-0-226-23347-5. Grades YA.

A look at what Romans ate during the Age of Kings (753–509 B.C.E.), the republic (506–507 B.C.E.), and the empire (7 B.C.E.–476 C.E.). This book covers menus, ingredients, beverages, fish and fowl, cooks and the flavors they used, what the Romans took from the land, and where they got their meat. Slaves grew long hair to wipe their masters' hands after eating. The Romans loved exotic items but used no forks. Photographs enhance the text. Bibliography, Glossary, and Index.

651. Ganeri, Anita. *The Ancient Romans.* (Ancient Civilizations) Compass Point, 2006. 32pp. ISBN 978-0-7565-1644-4; paper ISBN 978-0-7565-1759-5. Grades 3–5.

All about the daily life of the people living in ancient Rome, this book offers background on their culture and history, focusing on Roman contributions to contemporary society along with their food, entertainment, work, and government. Sidebars provide clarification. Illustrations and maps enrich the text.

652. Gilman, Benedicte. *Ashen Sky: The Letters of Pliny the Younger on the Eruption of Vesuvius.* Illustrated by Barry Moser. Translated by Benedicte Gilman. Getty Museum, 2007. 32pp. ISBN 978-0-89236-900-3. Grades 4 up.

Pliny the Younger's firsthand account of the eruption of Vesuvius in 79 details the event. Illustrations help to recreate the scene of panic and frustration. Further Reading.

653. Hanel, Rachael. *Gladiators.* (Fearsome Fighters) Creative Education, 2007. 48pp. ISBN 978-1-58341-535-1. Grades 5–8.

A look at the Roman spectator sport in which men fought to the death. Gladiators had to be brutal and crafty to save their lives when faced with opponents with the same goal. This book covers fighting techniques, the weapons that gladiators used, and the history of the sport. It also looks at the types of people who either volunteered or were forced into the amphitheaters to fight. Illustrations augment the text. Bibliography, Glossary and Index.

654. Harris, Jacqueline L. *Science in Ancient Rome.* Franklin Watts, 1998. 72pp. Paper ISBN 978-0-531-15916-3. Grades 5–8.

An introduction to ancient Rome and its science precedes chapters on different developments from this culture. Subjects include the building of arches and houses; the mining of brass and gold; physicians; sewers and aqueducts and their importance to public health; the Roman calendar; and contemporary debt to the Romans for their discoveries. Photographs supplement the text. Glossary, Further Reading, and Index.

655. Hinds, Kathryn. *The Ancient Romans.* Benchmark, 1996. 80pp. ISBN 978-0-7614-0090-5. Grades 7 up.

Among the topics presented are the Romans' practicality, their ability to construct aqueducts and buildings, their entertainment (such as gladiatorial games and chariot races), and their religious views. Color photographs and reproductions highlight the text. Chronology, Further Reading, Glossary, and Index.

656. James, Simon. *Ancient Rome.* DK, 2008. 72pp. ISBN 978-0-7566-3766-8. Grades 4–6.

A look at the Augustan Age at the height of the early Roman Empire. Four cross-sections show the insides of various places. The two-page spreads cover topics including family life, food and festivals, houses, government, work, public life, science and philosophy, and sports and games. Chronology, Glossary, and Index.

657. Konstam, Angus. *Atlas of Ancient Rome.* Mercury, 2003. 192pp. ISBN 978-1-904668-40-4. Grades YA.

The Romans rose from a small Iron Age tribe living on the banks of the Tiber river to one of the most dominant civilizations in history. This atlas traces the historical, political, and cultural developments that allowed this rise to occur. Rome's legionaries protected Roman rule throughout the Western world while her philosophers, poets, architects, and politicians established a cultural legacy. Introduction, Color Illustrations, Maps, Chronology, Glossary and Genealogy Tables, and Index.

658. Langley, Andrew, and Philip De Souza. *The Roman News.* (History News) Candlewick, 2009. 32pp. Paper ISBN 978-0-7636-4199-3. Grades 5 up.

This newspaper-style presentation of the Romans highlights fashion, sports, trade, food, and the military. Each page has headlines, sometimes with classifieds advertising items such as resusable wax tablets. Highly readable and slightly sensational (with information under headlines such as "Caesar Stabbed"), this format seems much more accessible than a textbook. Maps and Index.

659. Mulvihill, Margaret. *Roman Forts.* Illustrated by Gerald Wood. (Hallmarks of History) Stargazer, 2007. 32pp. ISBN 978-1-59604-121-9. Grades 4–6.

This book examines the structure and defenses of ancient Roman forts as well as military life and how the army influenced both the growth and the decline of the Roman Empire. The military helped to establish outposts and built roads to reach them after the Romans gained control of an area. Color illustrations and photographs enhance the text. Chronology, Glossary, and Index.

660. Murrell, Deborah. *The Best Book of Ancient Rome.* Kingfisher, 2004. 31pp. ISBN 978-0-7534-1103-2. Grades 3–6.

The text covers many topics concerning ancient Rome including the historical founding of the city (but not Romulus and Remus). It contains information on daily life, the home, leisure, slaves, scribes, rulers, buildings, acquisitions of the empire, the Vandal conquest, and Rome's legacy. Two-page chapters include full-page paintings and sidebars. Glossary and Index.

661. Nardo, Don. *From Founding to Fall: A History of Rome.* (Lucent Library of Historical Eras) Lucent, 2003. 112pp. ISBN 978-1-59018-254-3. Grades 8 up.

Supposedly founded by Romulus in 753 B.C.E., Rome lasted until about 456. This text examines primary sources and other materials that give information about the lives of Rome's citizens in chapters on different aspects of their culture. It covers the republic, the conquest and control of the Mediterranean world, the fall of the republic, the empire under Augustus, the Pax Romana, anarchy, the later empire, the rise of Christianity, and the invasions of the barbarians, which led to Rome's fall. Illustrations complement the text. Bibliography, Maps, and Index.

662. Nardo, Don. *Life of the Ancient Romans: Arts, Leisure, and Entertainment.* (Lucent Library of Historical Eras) Lucent, 2003. 128pp. ISBN 978-1-59018-317-5. Grades 8 up.

Although most primary sources tell about the powerful, this book gives good information about slaves and lower-class inhabitants of Rome. Among the aspects of Roman culture discussed here are communal bathing, gladiatorial games, chariot races, and the theater's plays, mimes, and concerts. Romans enjoyed dining and entertaining. They played board games, hunted and fished, and exercised outside. Bibliography, Illustrations, and Index.

663. Nardo, Don. *Living in Ancient Rome.* (Exploring Cultural History) Gale, 2004. 143pp. ISBN 978-0-7377-1456-5. Grades 9 up.

The Romans once controlled the entire Mediterranean region. This book discusses the way people lived during that time—their families, food, attitudes toward women, religious beliefs, art, traditions, celebrations, education, slaves, marriage, roads and travel, chariot races, and more. The information comes from both ancient and contemporary scholars and writers who have studied Rome. Maps, Photographs, Bibliography, Further Reading, Notes, Web Sites, and Index.

664. Nardo, Don. *Roman Amphitheaters.* Franklin Watts, 2002. 63pp. ISBN 978-0-53112-036-1; paper ISBN 978-0-53116-224-8. Grades 4–6.

In five chapters, this text looks at Roman amphitheaters and places them in the context of their societies. Topics include the early wooden arenas, the first stone amphitheaters, construction of amphitheaters, the combat that occurred in them, and the fate of the amphitheaters. Photographs and illustrations highlight the text. Glossary, Chronology, Notes, Further Reading, and Index.

665. Nardo, Don. *The Roman Army: Instrument of Power.* (Lucent Library of Historical Eras) Lucent, 2003. ISBN 978-1-5901-8316-8. Grades 6–10.

The reader will learn of the rise and fall of the Roman army from 350 B.C.E. to 476. The book tells about the army's subjugation of other Italian states, its Punic Wars against Carthage, its control of Greek city-states, and its conquest of both Gaul and Britain. The army's weapons, armor, tactics, and formations were ever-evolving, allowing its success. A detailed discussion of a legion reveals why it was better than a Greek phalanx. Illustrations and diagrams of many battles highlight the text. Bibliography, Illustrations, and Index.

666. Nardo, Don. *The Roman Empire.* Lucent, 2005. 112pp. ISBN 978-1-59018-657-2. Grades 7 up.

In 79 a volcanic eruption destroyed Pompeii and Herculaneum. In a way this disaster was a gift to modern people because the volcanic ash preserved a view of life in the Roman Empire (30 B.C.E.–476 C.E.) for archaeologists to discover. The Romans believed that their system, beginning with the democratic Roman Republic, was the most logical devised on Earth, and they imposed it on everyone they ruled. This book discusses the rulers of the empire—including Octavian, the Caesars, Nero, Nerva, Trajan, Hadrian, Antonius Pius, and Marcus Aurelius—and the effects their actions had on the people they ruled. Over the centuries Rome slowly disintegrated, with the final defeat of the western half occurring in 476 when the German general Odoacer removed Augustus from the throne. The eastern half did not fall until 1453, when the Turks took Constantinople. The Romans left a legacy of farming, public works, language, laws, and transmission of Greek culture and ideas. Notes, Further Reading, Works Consulted, and Index.

667. Nardo, Don. *The Roman Republic.* Lucent, 2005. 112pp. ISBN 978-1-59018-658-9. Grades 7 up.

The official date of Rome's founding on the Tiber river is 753 B.C.E., although towns dotted the area before then; the official legend is that the Roman people descended from Aeneas, prince of Troy, through Romulus and Remus. With the unification of Italy, the Etruscan kings were expelled, and the Roman Republic (510 B.C.E.–30 B.C.E.)

gave the people a voice when power became divided among several leaders. After winning the Punic Wars against Carthage in 201 B.C.E., Rome began its expansion, and the Mediterranean became a "Roman lake." Julius Caesar's ambition, ruthlessness, and dishonesty followed, and after he returned from Egypt and Cleopatra's seduction, senators murdered him in 44 B.C.E. Three men—Mark Antony, Octavian, and Marcus Lepidus—then vied for leadership. Octavian was the victor and assumed the status of Augustus, "the exalted one." Notes, For Further Reading, Works Consulted, and Index.

668. Nardo, Don. *Words of the Ancient Romans: Primary Sources.* (Lucent Library of Historical Eras) Thomson Gale, 2003. 128pp. ISBN 978-1-59018-318-2. Grades 7 up.

The Roman world was home to many writers. Primary materials included here cover the topics of Rome's founding and expansion, Julius Caesar's triumphs, the Augustan Age, family life, slaves, religious beliefs and worship, and festivals and celebrations. Among the writers whose works describe the Roman world are Plutarch, Livy, Suetonius, Juvenal, Ovid, and Caesar. Bbliography, Illustrations, and Index.

669. Osborne, Mary Pope. *Pompeii: Lost and Found.* Illustrated by Bonnie Christensen. Knopf, 2006. 40pp. ISBN 978-0-375-82889-8. Grades 1–5.

The text, complemented with contemporary frescoes resembling the art buried in the eruption of Vesuvius over Pompeii in 79, reveals the daily lives of the ancient citizens of this city. Topics include food, baths, homes, soldiers' uniforms, shops, leisure activities, and everyday items. *Bluebonnet Award* (Texas) nomination.

670. Parker, Vic. *Pompeii AD 79: A City Buried by a Volcanic Eruption.* (When Disaster Struck) Raintree, 2006. 56pp. ISBN 978-1-4109-2276-2. Grades 4–7.

An examination of the eruption of Vesuvius in 79 that destroyed Pompeii. The author describes the city itself and presents scientific background on Vesuvius and its condition when it spewed forth the lava that covered the city and most of its citizens. Parker also discusses the excavation of Pompeii and the information it provided about the daily lives of the people. He ends with a discussion of what would cause Vesuvius to erupt again. Maps, Photographs, Reproductions, Bibliography, Chronology, Further Reading, Notes, Web Sites, and Index.

671. Platt, Richard. *Through Time: Pompeii.* Illustrated by Manuela Cappon. Kingfisher, 2007. 48pp. ISBN 978-0-7534-6044-3. Grades 3–6.

To create a continuum of history, Platt begins his story in 750 B.C.E. with one man building a hut on a street that becomes part of the city of Pompeii. Changes occur, including advances in building techniques and a rise in the number of soldiers, until the city seems to peak in 60. Then in 79, Vesuvius erupts and covers all that created in the preceding centuries. Included here are people's daily habits, social structure, home life, fashions, and other pertinent information about Pompeii. Cutaway views highlight the text. Maps, Chronology, Glossary, and Index.

672. Reece, Katherine. *The Romans: Builders of an Empire.* (Ancient Civilizations) Rourke, 2006. 48pp. ISBN 978-1-59515-507-8. Grades 4–6.

This background on the civilization of ancient Rome includes the city's location, who lived there, what the people ate and wore, what they traded, their type of commerce, their beliefs and gods, their arts and architecture, and their contributions to the modern world. Photographs and illustrations augment the text. Glossary, Chronology, Further Reading, Web Sites, and Index.

673. Riley, Peter, and Thorsten Opper. *The Pompeii Pop-Up.* Illustrated by David Hawcock. Universe, 2007. 2007pp. ISBN 978-0-7893-1569-4. Grades 3–6.

This pop-up book allows readers to look inside extant buildings while it gives background information about the eruption of Vesuvius in 79. It provides background about life in the city such as its commerce, religion, entertainment, people, homes, and activities. A 3-D view of a volcano is especially interesting. Photographs and maps.

674. Solway, Andrew. *Rome: In Spectacular Cross Section.* Illustrated by Stephen Biesty. Scholastic, 2003. 29pp. ISBN 978-0-439-45546-6. Grades 4–7.

Titus Cotta Maximus, a wealthy Roman boy, visits the Colosseum, a festival, the docks, chariot races, and his home during a typical day. This book includes information about—and some cross-sections of—each location with details about people and places such the Colosseum's underground passages, the public restrooms, the baths of Trojan, and the temple of Jupiter.

675. Sonneborn, Liz. *Pompeii.* (Unearthing Ancient Worlds) Twenty First Century, 2008. 80pp. ISBN 978-0-8225-7505-4. Grades 5–9.

In the 1700s Colonel Roque Joachim de Alcubierre and Karl Jakob Weber made many discoveries in the area of Pompeii, including Herculaneum. Among their finds were mosaics, frescoes, and statues. They had a rather haphazard approach to the site and did not take contemporary precautions to preserve and organize. Later excavations have been much more deliberate and helpful. Photographs, maps, diagrams, and illustrations highlight the text. Bibliography, Glossary, Chronology, Notes, Further Reading, Web Sites, and Index.

676. Stewart, David. *You Wouldn't Want to Be a Roman Soldier! Barbarians You'd Rather Not Meet.* Illustrated by David Antram and David Salariya. (You Woudn't Want To . . .) Franklin Watts, 2006. 32pp. ISBN 978-0-531-12423-9; 2007. paper ISBN 978-0-531-12448-2. Grades 3–6.

A Roman soldier in 98 thinks he wants to escape his dull life and see the world. What he discovers is that being a soldier involves much unpleasantness—from cold nights and stiff clothing to long marches and scary battles. Illustrations and sidebars highlight the text.

677. Watkins, Richard. *Gladiator.* Houghton, 2000. 87pp. Paper ISBN 978-0-618-07032-9. Grades 5–8.

Gladiators served as entertainment for all levels of Roman society. This book examines their history and the training that gladiators had to undergo before they traded the shame of slavery for the confidence of combat. Illustrations show the cruelty of these games and the bloodthirsty spectators who demanded them.

678. Weatherill, Sue, and Steve Weatherill. *Roman Activity Book.* Barron's Educational, 2006. 24pp. ISBN 978-0-7641-3415-9. Grades 2–4.

Readers will enjoy ten activities and crafts related to Rome. Among them are an abacus, a toga, a tabula, and a water clock. Additional triva and information along with a chronology explain how each activity relates to the Romans. Illustrations complement the text. Chronology and Time Line.

Biography and Collective Biography

679. Demi. *Mary.* Margaret K. McElderry, 2006. 48pp. ISBN 978-0-689-87692-9. Grades 3–6.

Drawing from the New Testament and sources outside the biblical canon such as the Book of Mary and the Pseudo-Melito, Demi tells the story of the mother of Jesus from her childhood to her assumption and coronation in heaven. The illustrations are even more ornate and gilded than those in Demi's other books.

680. DePaola, Tomi. *Patrick: Patron Saint of Ireland.* Holiday House, 1992. Unpaged. ISBN 978-0-8234-0924-2; 1994. paper ISBN 978-0-8234-1077-4. Grades K–3.

Although Patrick (d. 461) was born into a noble British family, bandits captured him, took him to Ireland, and sold him as a slave. He worked for six years as a shepherd until he heard a voice telling him to return to "his own country." He left, but then heard other voices, and went back to establish the first church in Ireland. He converted thousands to the Christian faith, risking his life many times in the process. This book includes the story of the saint's life and some of the legends that have developed around Patrick's deeds.

681. Everitt, Anthony. *Cicero: The Life and Times of Rome's Greatest Politician.* Random House, 2003. 359pp. Paper ISBN 978-0-375-75895-9. Grades YA.

Marcus Tullius Cicero (ca. 103–43 B.C.E.) wrote his friend Atticus many letters, and this book relies on these letters to create a portrait of Cicero as the politician and statesman who helped to shape the final days of the Roman Republic. Cicero battled Julius Caesar and Mark Antony as he followed the traditional route to power through political offices to become a consul in 63 B.C.E. He defended citizens who were out of favor and stopped the Catalina conspiracy. Eventually a tribune that he had not supported testified against him and he was banished from Rome. Index.

682. Freeman, Philip. *St. Patrick of Ireland: A Biography.* Simon & Shuster, 2005. 216pp. Paper ISBN 978-0-7432-5634-6. Grades YA.

In this biography, Freeman examines the manuscripts, artifacts, and monuments of the era of Saint Patrick (373?–463?). Extant letters that Saint Patrick wrote tell of his childhood in Britain, his kidnapping and enslavement by Irish pirates, and his relationship to his God. The book also gives insight into the Celtic world of Patrick's time. Photographs of archaeological sites and artifacts highlight the text. Bibliography, Chronology, and Index.

683. Galford, Ellen. *Julius Caesar: The Boy Who Conquered an Empire.* (World History Biography) National Geographic, 2007. 64pp. ISBN 978-1-4263-0064-6. Grades 5–8.

Using a scrapbook format, this book looks at Julius Caesar's childhood. Four main sections set the historical context of his life and the everyday lives of people during his time. Side material covers related topics such as the Roman army and religion. Photographs enhance the text. Bibliography, Glossary, Web Sites, Maps, and Index.

684. Kent, Zachary. *Hannibal: Great General of the Ancient World.* (Rulers of the Ancient World) Enslow, 2006. 160pp. ISBN 978-0-7660-2564-6. Grades 6 up.

Known for crossing the Alps with elephants, Hannibal Barca was a brave military officer who felt compelled to attack the Romans after they had encroached on Carthage. He fought the second Punic War from 218 to 201 B.C.E. and became known for his military strategies. The author gives a history of Hannibal's time and his land. Illustrations highlight the text. Bibliography, Chronology, Notes, Maps, Glossary, Further Reading, Web Sites, and Index.

685. Kent, Zachary. *Julius Caesar: Ruler of the Roman World.* (Rulers of the Ancient World) Enslow, 2006. 160pp. ISBN 978-0-7660-2563-9. Grades 6 up.

Eleven chapters discuss the childhood of Julius Caesar, his service as a senator and consul, his role as a provincial governor, his relationship with Cleopatra, and his military victories. Finally, his friends assassinated him after he crossed the Rubicon river and started a civil war. Many have considered him Rome's greatest leader. After his death, his adopted son, Octavian, rose to power. Illustrations enhance the text. Chronology, Notes, Further Reading, Glossary, Web Sites, and Index.

686. León, Vicki. *Uppity Women of Ancient Times.* Conari, 1995. 260pp. Paper ISBN 978-1-57324-010-9. Grades YA.

See entry 534.

687. Lottridge, Celia Barker. *Stories from the Life of Jesus.* Narrated by Linda Wolfsgruber. Groundwood, 2007. 168pp. ISBN 978-0-8889-9840-8. Grades 4–8.

These stories from the Bible's four gospels include thirty-five incidents set in their time and place. They form a chronological look at Jesus' life, death, and resurrection. Illustrations complement the text.

688. Love, D. Anne. *Of Numbers and Stars: The Story of Hypatia.* Illustrated by Pam Paparone. Holiday House, 2006. Unpaged. ISBN 978-0-8234-1621-9. Grades 2–5.

Hypatia (d. 415), daughter of the mathematician Theon, became one of the greatest philosophers of her day. Her father determined that she would be educated (unlike most girls of her time), and she mastered many outdoor skills. She studied literature, writing, and natural science before realizing that her true love was mathematics. She learned arithmetic, geometry, astronomy, and then studied philosophy and oration. Her fame spread because of her writing and teaching. Illustrations highlight the text. Bibliography.

689. Tracy, Kathleen. *The Life and Times of Cicero.* (Biography from Ancient Civilizations) Mitchell Lane, 2006. 48pp. ISBN 978-1-58415-510-2. Grades 6–9.

This biography of Cicero, an ancient Roman orator, is a chronological look at his life. Cicero adapted the chief schools of Greek philosophy to a Latin philosophical approach and became a distinguished linguist, translator, and philosopher. He is known for his humanism and political writings along with his correspondence, most addressed to his friend Atticus. He criticized the political climate of his day, to his detriment. Photographs and illustrations highlight the text. Bibliography, Chronology, Notes, Glossary, Further Reading, Web Sites, and Index.

690. Worth, Richard. *Cleopatra: Queen of Ancient Egypt.* Enslow, 2006. 160pp. ISBN 978-0-7660-2559-2. Grades 6–9.

This biography of Cleopatra (d. 30 B.C.E.) covers the time in her life when she entertained Roman lovers as the queen of Egypt. It includes much about her times and her lands. Photographs and illustrations highlight the text. Glossary, Chronology, Notes, Further Reading, Web Sites, and Index.

Graphic Novels, Biographies, and Histories

691. Ross, Stewart. *Ancient Rome.* Illustrated by Richard Bonson. Dorling Kindersley, 2005. 31pp. ISBN 978-0-7566-1147-7. Grades 3–7.

When a brother and sister living in North Africa around 145 are separated from their father, Romans capture them and make them slaves. They go to Rome and observe and describe everyday life there before being reunited with their father.

692. Ross, Stewart. *The Terror Trail.* (Graphic Readers) DK, 2007. 48pp. ISBN 978-0-7566-2570-2; paper ISBN 978-0-7566-2569-6. Grades 3–6.

In Rome, Publius and Sabina are enslaved when someone kidnaps them from their injured father. They escape but are recaptured and sold as arena slaves for Rome's Colosseum. As the story continues, they must save their father. Illustrations add interest and "Did You Know" facts appear at the bottom of each page to tell more about the culture.

DVDs

693. *Ancient Refuge in the Holy Land.* WGBH, 2005. 60 min. ISBN 978-1-59375-203-3. Grades 7 up.

In the 2nd century, Bar-Kokhba and other Jews seeking refuge from the Romans hid in caves along the Dead Sea. This program reveals the location of these caves. Researchers looking for clues about this historical time and for a relic of Jerusalem's Great Temple found many artifacts. In 1960, an Israeli archaeologist found a bag of letters that Bar-Kokhba had written in 132. Since then, other historians and scientists have tried to add to the knowledge about this area and its people.

694. *The Legacy of the Roman Empire.* Discovery Channel School, 2004. 52 min. ISBN 978-1-58738-973-3. Grades 6–12.

This program covers the rise of ancient Rome, the governance of the empire's lands outside Rome, the empire's decline, and the rise of Byzantium. Among the specific topics are the Roman Republic's growth, with Julius Caesar as dictator, his assassination, and the resulting peace. In the British Isles, Rome controlled the garrison Vidolanda. Artifacts and surviving Roman writings reveal aspects of Roman life in the British Isles. Also included are segments on the battle at Mons Graupius and the building of Hadrian's Wall. Luxury contrasted with poverty and led to the empire's division when the Germanic tribes successfully invaded. When the Byzantine Empire rose, it combined the cultures of the East and West and influenced Russia before its own decline.

695. *Pompeii: A City Rediscovered.* (Secrets of Archaeology) Film Ideas, 2003. 25 min. ISBN 978-1-57557-254-3. Grades 7 up.

When Pompeii's ruins were discovered in the 18th century, they revealed secrets of life in a community destroyed by the eruption of Vesuvius in 79. This program recreates the town and the volcano that killed so many. Archaeologists know from the ruins that the people were farmers and that they used herbs and plants for healing and perfume. Many of the citizens were educated and ran businesses that were important to the community. The video presents these facts and other aspects of life in Pompeii before it was destroyed.

696. *The Roman Empire.* (The Fall of Great Empires) Schlessinger, 2004. 30 min. ISBN 978-1-4171-0663-9. Grades 9 up.

This video shows how the Roman Empire began and grew, the problems resulting from its decline and fall, and its contributions to Western culture. Other topics include dealing with empire outposts, changes in populations, religious upheval, and external threats. It includes live-action footage, ancient art, recreations of important events, and computer simulations. Western civilization would not be the same without Rome. Its citizens had organized agriculture and transportation that allowed trade to flourish and the military to move. When migatory tribes arrived at its borders, Rome could not cope, and it lost its power by 476.

697. *Roman Feats of Engineering.* (Technology & Architecture in Ancient Civilizations) New Dimension Media, 2006. 30 min. ISBN 978-1-59522-570-2. Grades 8 up.

This DVD features dramatizations of workers constructing ancient Roman buildings and engineering marvels, computer simulations of the original structures, and comments from experts. It includes a segment on the Colosseum and what happened there (including the practice of giving the worst of the 80,000 seats to women; male slaves got better seats). It also presents a segment on the aqueduct system, one of Rome's major contributions to civilization.

Compact Discs

698. Freeman, Philip. *St. Patrick of Ireland: A Biography.* Narrated by Alan Sklar. Tantor Media, 2005. 5 CDs. ISBN 978-1-4001-3111-2. Grades YA.

See entry 682.

699. Harris, Robert. *Imperium: A Novel of Ancient Rome.* Narrated by Oliver Ford Davies. Simon & Schuster, 2009. 12 CDs; 13.5 hrs. ISBN 978-0-7435-7649-9. Grades YA.

See entry 592.

700. Harris, Robert. *Pompeii: A Novel.* Narrated by Michael Cumpsty. Random House Audio, 2006. 5 CDs. ISBN 978-0-7393-4177-3. Grades YA.

See entry 593.

701. Lawrence, Caroline. *The Thieves of Ostia.* (The Roman Mysteries) Random House, 2004. 3 hrs. 56 min. ISBN 978-0-8072-2341-3. Grades 4–6.

See entry 605.

702. Llywelyn, Morgan. *The Greener Shore: A Novel of the Druids of Hibernia.* Narrated by Simon Vance. Tantor, 2006. 10 CDs; 10.5 hrs. ISBN 978-1-4001-0253-2. Grades YA.

See entry 608.

703. Speare, Elizabeth George. *The Bronze Bow.* Narrated by Mary Woods. Blackstone Audio, 2005. 6 CDs; 7 hrs. ISBN 978-0-7861-9714-9. Grades 7 up.

See entry 624.

704. Sutcliff, Rosemary. *The Eagle of the Ninth.* Narrated by Charlie Simpson. Naxos Audio, 2006. 4 CDs. ISBN 978-962-634-423-1. Grades YA.

See entry 625.

705. Sutcliff, Rosemary. *The Lantern Bearers.* Narrated by Johanna Ward. Blackstone Audio, 2003. 8 CDs. ISBN 978-0-7861-9733-0. Grades YA.

See entry 627.

706. Sutcliff, Rosemary. *Outcast.* Narrated by Johanna Ward. Blackstone Audio, 2003. 7 CDs. ISBN 978-0-7861-9759-0. Grades YA.

See entry 629.

707. Sutcliff, Rosemary. *The Silver Branch.* Narrated by Johanna Ward. Blackstone Audio, 2003. 7 CDs. ISBN 978-0-7861-9749-1. Grades YA.

See entry 630.

EUROPE AND THE BRITISH ISLES, 476–1289 C.E.

Historical Fiction and Fantasy

708. Alder, Elizabeth. *The King's Shadow.* Laurel Leaf, 1997. 272pp. Paper ISBN 978-0-440-22011-4. Grades 7–12.

Evyn, a young Welsh serf, wants to be a traveling storyteller. But ruffians destroy his dream by killing his parents and cutting out his tongue. Then his uncle sells him into slavery. Although he cannot speak to the people with whom he works, he learns to read and write, and eventually he begins to serve Harold Godwinson, the charismatic man who becomes the king of England. Evyn loves Harold as a father and stays by him until his death at the Battle of Hastings in 1066, when William the Conqueror defeats Harold and becomes king. Harold's widow takes Evyn home and nurses him back to health so that Evyn can write about his former master, the king, whose shadow he had been. *American Library Association Best Books for Young Adults, Young Reader's Award* (Arizona) nomination, and *Great Stone Face Children's Book Award* (New Hampshire) nomination.

709. Barrett, Tracy. *Anna of Byzantium.* Laurel-Leaf, 2000. 209pp. Paper ISBN 978-0-440-41536-7. Grades 6–9.

From 1083 to 1118, Alexius I Comnenus ruled Byzantine. He raised his daughter, Anna Comnena (1083–1153), to succeed him, but after his death, her younger brother John seized power. In this story, Anna recalls her battle for control of the throne in a convent, where she has been exiled because she schemed to assassinate John to regain her rightful position as monarch. In the convent, she continues *The Alexiad*, an eleven-volume epic of her father's life. *Lonestar Reading List* (Texas).

710. Bennett, Holly. *The Warrior's Daughter.* Orca, 2007. 224pp. Paper ISBN 978-1-55143-607-4. Grades 7–10.

Daughter of the renowned Irish warrior Cuchulainn, educated young Luaine knows kings, queens, and druids. But she has to leave home with her mother while her father fights Queen Maeve's army. After both her parents die, Luaine has to marry old King Conchobor. Then a poet curses her, and she must hide until the curse is lifted.

711. Bradley, Marion Zimmer. *Lady of Avalon.* Roc, 2007. 456pp. Paper ISBN 978-0-45146-181-0. Grades 7 up.

This prequel to *The Mists of Avalon* tells the story of three powerful priestesses who over the centuries have a strong influence on their kingdom. In the first century C.E. Gawen, the son of Eilan and Gaius, is raised by his grandmother, High Priestess Caillean. Designated the Sacred King, he fathers a child with Sianna, a daughter of the Faerie Queen, who survives him. Then High Priestess Dierna marries her daughter Taleri to Carausius, who becomes the emperor of Britannia at the end of the 3rd century and whom she recognizes as a reincarnation of Gawen. Carausius dies in battle, and returns as Vortimer in a second reincarnation in the mid-5th century, when he marries Viviane. But Viviane raises her mother Lady Ana's child Igraine, who incorporates the blood lines in Avalon.

712. Bradshaw, Gillian. *The Wolf Hunt.* Tor, 2002. 384pp. Paper ISBN 978-0-312-87595-4. Grades YA.

A Norman abducted from a convent and taken to the court of Brittany, Marie Penthiáevre of Chalendrey falls in love with Tiarnâan of Talensac. But he marries another woman, and after his mysterious disappearance, his "widow" seizes his land. Marie is drawn to a lone wolf that appears at the court in Rennes, and she deduces the wolf's identity. She risks all to save him from his fate.

713. Buechner, Ferderick. *Godric.* Harper, 1983. 178pp. Paper ISBN 978-0-06-061162-0. Grades YA.

Godric travels to Rome and Jerusalem, beginning in 1065, before becoming a hermit. He experiences the life of the Middle Ages as the Normans take over England. After consummating his love with the one woman he adores, both feel guilty for a variety of reasons and separate immediately. As a hermit, Godric (later to be voted a saint) realizes that the important things in life are those that money cannot buy, including his friendships with two snakes that stay by his fire.

714. Bulla, Clyde Robert. *The Sword in the Tree.* Illustrated by Paul Galdone. (Trophy Chapter Books) Harper Trophy. 112pp. Paper ISBN 978-0-06-442132-4. Grades 4–6.

Shan's Uncle Lionel reappears at Weldon Castle after many years and disposes of Shan's father so that he may take the family inheritance. Shan and his mother escape and search for King Arthur at Camelot with the help of herdsmen. When they return to the castle with Sir Gareth, he challenges Lionel to a fight for the castle and wins. When they discover Shan's father alive in the dungeon, they realize that Shan's courage has reunited the family.

715. Burnham, Sophy. *The Treasure of Montségur.* Harper San Francisco, 2003. 276pp. Paper ISBN 978-0-06-000080-6. Grades YA.

In 1209 Jeanne is orphaned in the Beziers massacre. Lady Esclarmonde of the Cathar religious sect takes her into her home but finds Jeanne's spirit incompatible with the sect's strict rules on chastity, prayer, and poverty. Jeanne becomes the guardian of a Bible that belongs to the Cathars, and she hides it at Montségur, her new home after she upsets Lady Esclarmonde. As an adult, Jeanne returns there, but is a target of the Inquisition, which is against a Bible that allows its readers to actually understand religion.

716. Cadnum, Michael. *The Book of the Lion.* Puffin, 2001. 204pp. Paper ISBN 978-0-14-230034-3. Grades 6–10.

After his master—who made coins for the king—has his arm hacked off as a punishment for alleged cheating, 17-year-old Edmund goes to the Holy Land. He serves as a squire to the knight crusader Sir Nigel, who expects to meet Richard Lionheart and his men. Edmund ends up fighting in the Battle of Arsuf and learns about the horrors of war. He then returns to England with Nigel after Nigel's arms are crushed.

717. Cadnum, Michael. *The Dragon Throne.* Viking, 2005. 224pp. ISBN 978-0-670-03631-8. Grades 6–10.

In this final book of the trilogy begun in *The Book of the Lion* and *The Leopard Sword* (2002), new knights Edmund and Herbert want to return home to England from the Crusades. But Eleanor of Aquitaine wants them to escort Ester de Laci to Rome. As they trek through the Alps, Prince John sends pursuers. Ester's ability to use a crossbow helps them overcome the bandits, and they eventually reach their destination.

718. Cadnum, Michael. *Forbidden Forest: The Story of Little John and Robin Hood.* Scholastic, 2002. 224pp. ISBN 978-0-439-31774-0. Grades 7 up.

In 12th-century England John Tannerson, a son of a tanner, works for a dishonest ferryman who fights with a knight and kills him. John is blamed for the murder, and the disreputable nobleman Red Roger protects him and trains him in the ways of outlaws. Little John eventually escapes into the forest where he meets Robin Hood and his men, who treat him with respect when he proves his worth. Margaret Lea, a Nottingham tradesman's daughter, married at 16, but her nobleman husband was murdered on their wedding night. The sheriff's greedy deputy attempts blackmail and blames Lady Margaret for the murder. She escapes to Sherwood with her maid Bridgit, and Little John rescues her. Respect grows between the two, and Little John devises a way to clear Margaret's name and free himself from Red Roger's control. The realities of medieval sordidness are revealed. *Georgia Children's Book Award* nomination.

719. Cadnum, Michael. *In a Dark Wood: A Novel.* Puffin, 1999. 246pp. Paper ISBN 978-0-14-130638-4. Grades 9 up.

Geoffrey, the sheriff of Nottingham, and his young squire, Hugh, tell the story of Robin Hood, the one highwayman who has ever outwitted them and who they have yet to bring to the king. Geoffrey has a number of other problems overwhelming him, including his affair with an abbess, his wife's disdain, his unexpected feelings for Hugh, his anger at the fool who apes him, and his seeming weakness in front of his subjects. The medieval period is presented realistically, including sexual aspects, the lure of the hunt, and graphic torture scenes. *Capitol Choices Noteworthy Titles* (Washington, D.C.).

720. Cadnum, Michael. *The King's Arrow.* Viking, 2008. 176pp. ISBN 978-0-670-06331-4. Grades 6–10.

In England in 1100, 18-year-old Simon joins Walter Tirel on a deer hunt and sees Tirel shoot King William II of England (William Rufus), son of William the Conqueror, with an arrow. Did Tirel deliberately shoot William? Or was it indeed an accident? The two must flee for their lives in this novel that reveals many medieval customs and beliefs.

721. Cadnum, Michael. *Raven of the Waves.* Orchard, 2001. 224pp. Paper ISBN 978-0-531-30334-4. Grades 9 up.

Seventeen-year-old Lidsmod sails on the *Raven* from Spjothof, Norway, in 794 for his first Viking raid. After he plunders English villages, he is given the responsibility of guarding Wiglaf, a captured 13-year-old boy with a withered arm. Wiglaf has learned how to heal as an apprentice to the old Abbot Aethelwulf. But Wiglaf cannot stop the brutal Viking destruction and the belief that war is a way to honor the gods. Wiglaf's father reveals his own brutal streak and Aethelwulf proves himself militarily adept. Lidsmod eventually helps Wiglaf escape after Wiglaf saves the life of one of his captors, but Lidsmod keeps the holy relics his people have stolen from the abbey. Cadnum's graphic descriptions present the realities of medieval times.

722. Chabon, Michael. *Gentlemen of the Road: A Tale of Adventure.*   Illustrated by Gary Gianni. Del Rey, 2007. 204pp. ISBN 978-0-345-50174-5. Grades YA.

Frankish physician Zelikman and the giant African Abram, swords for hire and "gentlemen of the road," help Filaq, the kidnapped young heir to the Khazar kingdom, because they smell money. Filaq wants to regain his kingdom from Buljan, a usurper who has murdered its rulers. Filaq does not trust the two swordsmen and steals Zelikman's dearest possession—his horse, Hillel. The two men follow Filaq through the country, which is infiltrated by unrest. Finally, Filaq gathers an army, including the two swordsmen, to fight for his birthright and defeats Buljan. Illustrations augment the story.

723. Clement-Davies, David, and Rand Huebsch. *The Telling Pool.*   Amulet, 2006. 360pp. ISBN 978-0-8109-5758-9; HNA, 2007. paper ISBN 978-0-8109-9257-3. Grades 6 up.

Rhodri Falcon learns from an old blind blacksmith that a quest, a sword, and a mysterious pool lie in his future. The son of Owen—a Welsh falconer serving a Norman lord in the third Crusade with Richard the Lionheart—Rhodri does not know that he is a descendant of Guinevere, King Arthur's wife. As Rhodri looks after the family manor while his father is on the crusade, Tantallon teaches him to look for answers in a magical pool deep in the forest. When Rhodri's father Owen returns, clearly dazed by the horror of the crusade, the evil Homeira lures him to her and Rhodri must find the strength to save his father.

724. Coldsmith, Don. *Runestone.*   Bantam, 1995. 489pp. Paper ISBN 978-0-553-57280-3. Grades YA.

In this fictional work, Coldsmith speculates on who might have been the ancestors of the blond, blue-eyed Native Americans who live in Oklahoma today. The protagonist, Nils Thorsson, a Viking shipmaster, lands in Newfoundland, Canada, and begins exploring the continent. He and his friend have problems that they cannot solve without the help of Odin, a Native American. The two Vikings become assimilated into Odin's tribe and father children. Their exciting story may or may not answer the original question.

725. Cole, Joanna. *Ms. Frizzle's Adventures: Medieval Castles.*   Illustrated by Bruce Degen. Scholastic, 2003. 48pp. ISBN 978-0-590-10820-1. Grades 1–5.

Ms. Frizzle and her student Arnold take an underground passage below Craig's Castle Shop, and Ms. Frizzle's watch leads them to the middle of a castle siege in the 12th century. Afterward, the women control the castle while Arnold smuggles out a letter to Lord Robert, asking for his help. Cartoon illustrations complement the text.

726. Cooney, Caroline B. *Enter Three Witches: A Story of Macbeth.*   Scholastic, 2007. 281pp. ISBN 978-0-439-71156-2. Grades 6 up.

Lady Mary, 14, daughter of the Thane of Cawdor, goes to stay with Lady Macbeth to learn domestic arts. Her father is declared a traitor to the king and hanged. After her fiancé dies, Lady Mary is unwillingly betrothed to the despicable Seyton, Macbeth's supporter. At the same time, Banquo must decide if he supports Macbeth after men kill his father. The kitchen manager Swin seems to be cold-hearted but he helps Mary and others behind the scenes while Lady and Lord Macbeth crush anyone in their way as they climb to power. *Taysha's Reading List* nomination.

727. Cornwell, Bernard. *Enemy of God: A Novel of Arthur.* Griffin, 1998. 416pp. Paper ISBN 978-0-312-18714-9. Grades YA.

Derfel tells about Arthur, one of his closest friends, in the sequel to *The Winter King.* Arthur tries to unite the Britons against the Saxons, who want their land and Christianity, while Merlin's followers want to preserve the Celtic Druid ways.

728. Cornwell, Bernard. *The Last Kingdom.* (The Saxon Chronicles) HarperCollins, 2006. 333pp. Paper ISBN 978-0-06-088718-6. Grades YA.

After the Danes invade Northumbria and capture Uhtred, the 10-year-old rightful heir of the earldom of Bebbanburg, he is raised by Ragnar the Terrible, a kind surrogate father. Uhtred fights as a Dane but remembers that he has claims elsewhere. When Kjartan, a fellow Dane, betrays and kills Ragnar, Uhtred joins Alfred of Wessex (849–899) and awaits his chance to defeat Kjartan and regain his earldom from his lying uncle.

729. Cornwell, Bernard. *Lords of the North.* (The Saxon Chronicles) HarperCollins, 2007. 336pp. ISBN 978-0-06-088862-6; 2008. paper ISBN 978-0-06-114904-7. Grades YA.

Uhtred of Bebbanburg, 21, returns home in 878 after helping Alfred of Wessex defeat the Danes. On the way he meets Guthred, the self-proclaimed king of Northumbria. He joins Guthred to teach him warfare and political strategy. But Guthred sells Uhtred into slavery to seal a deal (probably directed by Alfred), and when Uhtred returns after two years at sea, he plots to reclaim his land and to avenge the deaths of his family members. Then Uhtred's Danish foster brother, Ragnar, joins him to fight Kjartan the Cruel.

730. Cornwell, Bernard. *The Pale Horseman.* (The Saxon Chronicles) HarperCollins, 2007. 349pp. Paper ISBN 978-0-06-114483-7. Grades YA.

In 877 Uhtred, a dispossessed English nobleman, finds his life changed by Iseult, a powerful sorceress, as he rediscovers his deep loyalty to his native country and joins King Alfred to fight against the Danes. He realizes that he has more power as a Saxon landowner. The second volume in the series.

731. Cornwell, Bernard. *The Winter King: A Novel of Arthur.* St. Martins, 1997. 431pp. Paper ISBN 978-0-312-15696-1. Grades YA.

Derfel Cadarn, one of Merlin's foundlings in the 6th century, tells the story of fighting with Arthur, his hero. Since Arthur is illegitimate, he has no political clout that he does not earn, and he works hard to rid the country of the invading Saxons. Unfortunately, he chooses to marry the scheming Guinevere instead of his intended, Ceinwyn, and he must deal with her as well as the cowardly Lancelot.

732. Coulter, Catherine. *Lord of Falcon Ridge.* (Viking Trilogy) Jove, 1995. 365pp. Paper ISBN 978-0-515-11584-0. Grades YA.

In the third novel of the Viking trilogy, after *Lord of Raven's Peak* and *Lord of Hawk-fell Island*, Cleve goes to Chessa, the queen of Ireland, to arrange Chessa's marriage to William of Normandy. Chessa is interested in neither William nor Ragnor of York—she wants to marry Cleve himself. In a dream, Cleve realizes that he has land in Scotland and wants to claim it. Chessa and Cleve fall in love, and Cleve uses his father's magic to save her from Ragnor and others.

733. Coulter, Catherine. *Lord of Hawkfell Island.* (Viking Trilogy) Jove, 1996. 365pp. Paper ISBN 978-0-515-11230-6. Grades YA.

In 915 Viking Rorik Haraldsson seeks revenge on the Irish warrior Einar for the murder of Rorik's wife and children. Rorik kidnaps Einar's half sister, an independent woman who was orphaned at 12 and learned how to defend herself. She and Rorik fall in love before Einar's men kidnap her and return her to his home. She must then wait for Rorik to rescue her.

734. Coulter, Catherine. *Lord of Raven's Peak.* (Viking Trilogy) Jove, 1996. 365pp. Paper ISBN 978-0-515-11351-8. Grades YA.

Rorik (of *Lord of Hawfell Island*) has a younger brother, Merrik Haraldsson. In a Kiev slave market, Merrik buys Taby and his older brother. But this older brother is actually Taby's sister Lauren. The two are nobles who were kidnapped. The beautiful Lauren, also a *skald* (a poet), discovers why Merrick's vicious brother Erik was murdered in this novel set in Norway in 916.

735. Coulter, Catherine. *The Penwyth Curse.* Jove, 2003. 345pp. Paper ISBN 978-0-515-13436-0. Grades YA.

In 1278 Sir Bishop of Lythe saves King Edward I's daughter and receives Penwyth Castle as a gift—along with Merryn de Gay as his wife. Merryn is the target of a curse and anyone who marries her will die—although she is only 18, she already has four deceased husbands. When Bishop arrives at the castle, he tells the residents that the king has sent him as a wizard to end the curse. When Bishop takes Merryn on a trip, supposedly to quell the curse, he starts to have dreams of a powerful wizard and a witch—dreams that could be mirroring their own relationship.

736. Cross, Donna Woolfolk. *Pope Joan: A Novel.* Ballantine, 1997. Paper ISBN 978-0-345-41626-1. Grades YA.

In the 9th century a female pope named Joan of Ingelheim (b. 814) may have risen from being the daughter of a village canon to the highest church office. Several men betray her, including her father, who refuses to let her study even though her brothers have taught her to read and write. She dresses as a man after her family dies in a Viking raid and enters the Benedictine monastery at Fulda. She works there for many years, recovers from the plague, goes to Rome, and uses her healing skills to save Pope Sergius. She encounters a man with whom she had fallen in love before entering the monastery, and they work together after the people, who think she is male, elect her as pope. As plotters try to kill her, she learns that she is pregnant, and eventually dies in childbirth. *School Library Journal Best Adult Books for Young Adults.*

737. Crossley-Holland, Kevin. *At the Crossing Places.* (Arthur Trilogy) Arthur A. Levine, 2002. 394pp. ISBN 978-0-439-26598-0; Scholastic, 2004. paper ISBN 978-0-439-26599-7. Grades 5–8.

The sequel to *The Seeing Stone* starts in January of 1200. Arthur, 13, moves from Caldicot Manor to Holt Castle, where he will be a squire. Since he now knows his father's identity as the murderer Sir William, he wants to find out about his mother and is sorry he cannot marry Grace because she is his half sister. He becomes interested in 10-year-old Winnie de Verdon as a possibility instead. Then he and the kindly Lord Stephen, whom he serves, travel to Champagne and swear allegiance to Count Thibaud and his Holy Land crusade. Throughout, Arthur looks into a "seeing stone" and finds a parallel life to the King Arthur of yore.

738. Crossley-Holland, Kevin. *Crossing to Paradise.* Arthur A. Levine, 2008. 400pp. ISBN 978-0-545-05866-7. Grades 5–9.

Gatty, a 15-year-old field hand with a beautiful voice, joins a group that Lady Gwyneth has chosen to accompany her on a pilgrimage from Wales to Jerusalem in 1203. The others in the group are a choirmaster, a merchant, a chamber servant, a cook, a stableman, a wise woman, and a priest. Gatty serves as the second chamber servant. On the journey, which includes London and Venice, Gatty takes part exuberantly in several incidents, both good and bad, including saving someone's life. The group encounters assassins, potential rapists, a human body-parts dealer, and robbers. Glossary and Note.

739. Crossley-Holland, Kevin. *The Seeing Stone.* Illustrated by David Kline. (Arthur Trilogy) Arthur A. Levine, 2002. 340pp. Paper ISBN 978-0-439-26327-6. Grades 4–8.

In the late 12th century during the reign of Richard the Lionhearted, 13-year-old Arthur wants to become a squire rather than a "schoolman"—his abilities with sword and lance are better than his talents with quill and ink. He remembers how his friend Merlin gave him a magical stone with images of the legendary King Arthur, whose life was much like his. His father grants him permission to be a squire and go on the fourth Crusade to Jerusalem with his stone. *Horn Book Fanfare.*

740. Cushman, Karen. *Matilda Bone.* Clarion, 2000. 167pp. ISBN 978-0-395-88156-9; Yearling, 2002. paper ISBN 978-0-440-41822-1. Grades 4–8.

Matilda, 14, is apprenticed to Red Peg the Bonesetter after living with Father Leufredus in an English manor house and learning Latin from him. In her job with Red Peg, she learns about bloodlettings, bone settings, surgeries, and remedies. She also learns that fine clothing does not symbolize goodness in the people who wear it. *Young Reader's Award* (Arizona) nomination, *School Library Journal Best Books of the Year, American Library Association Best Books for Young Adults, Student Book Award* (Maine) nomination, *Young Readers Choice Awards* (Pennsylvania) Master List, and *Volunteer State Book Awards* (Tennessee).

741. Cushman, Karen. *The Midwife's Apprentice.* Clarion, 1995. 122pp. ISBN 978-0-395-69229-5; Trophy, 1996. paper ISBN 978-0-06-440630-7. Grades 5–9.

After a midwife finds Brat, aged 12 or 13, hiding in a dungheap, she calls the girl Beetle and gives her a job as midwife's assistant. As Beetle becomes more confident and more articulate, she renames herself Alyce, and soon realizes that midwifery is the profession for her. She works to become more proficient as she copes with those around her in this novel set in the 12th century. *American Library Association Notable Books for Children, American Library Association Notable Books for Young Adults, Booklist Books for Youth Editors' Choices, American Booksellers' Pick of the Lists, Horn Book Fanfare Honor List, School Library Journal Best Book*, and *Newbery Medal.*

742. Egielski, Richard. *Saint Francis and the Wolf.* Laura Geringer, 2005. 40pp. ISBN 978-0-06-623870-8. Grades 1–3.

When a wolf terrorizes the town of Gubbio, Italy, knights and armies with war machines try to stop it. But only Saint Francis can speak the wolf's language. He talks to the wolf and makes a compromise: the town will feed the wolf, and it will not bother the people. Illustrations enhance the text.

743. Eisner, Michael Alexander. *The Crusader: A Novel.* Anchor, 2003. 288pp. Paper ISBN 978-0-385-72141-7. Grades YA.

In 1275 Francisco Montcada, an aristocrat just returned from the Crusades, asks Brother Lucas—an ambitious monk whom he befriended eleven years before—to drive the demons from him. Francisco tells Lucas about the horrors of the battlefield; the tension between their commander and the king's illegitimate son, the evil torturer Don Fernando; and his love for his cousin Isabel. Lucas finally has to choose between his own ambition and his loyalty to Francisco.

744. French, Jackie. *Rover.* HarperCollins, 2007. 304pp. ISBN 978-0-06-085078-4. Grades 6–9.

Hekja, 12, is captured by the Vikings who rape and kill her mother in their Scottish fishing village. They take her to Freydis, daughter of Eric the Red, and Freydis takes her as a slave. Hekja's dog, Rover, can locate icebergs, and Hekja is strong and helpful so Freydis takes her on her journey to Vinland in the New World. There Freydis must battle both the natives and her countrymen, who do not want a woman as leader. Eventaully, Hekja marries a Norwegian.

745. Funke, Cornelia. *Igraine the Brave.* Narrated by Xanthe Elbrick. Translated by Anthea Bell. Chicken House, 2007. 212pp. ISBN 978-0-439-90379-0. Grades 3–5.

Igraine the Brave, 12, does not want to be a magician like her parents and brother in medieval Germany. She wants to be a knight and have adventures and win tournaments. Osmund the Greedy arrives at the family castle, and Igraine proves her worth with her suit of magical armor. Her parents, however, mistakenly turn themselves into pigs, and Igraine has to find a giant to give her hair. During her search, she has a number of adventures and helps others. Ink drawings enhance the story.

746. Furlong, Monica. *Wise Child.* Random House, 1989. 228pp. Paper ISBN 978-0-394-82598-4. Grades 6–8.

Juniper, an outcast, looks after 9-year-old Wise Child after Wise Child's mother deserts her and her father does not return from sea. In early Christian times, the Scottish village mistrusts Juniper's powers of healing, and the villagers need a scapegoat to blame for an outbreak of smallpox. Wise Child sees that Juniper's magic is nothing more than her close attention to detail, which helps her observe illnesses and remember the appropriate cures.

747. Gallico, Paul. *The Small Miracle.* Illustrated by Carolyn Croll. Translated by Reteller Robert Barton. Amereon, 1976. 32pp. ISBN 978-0-8488-0494-7. Grades K–2.

When Pepino was a small orphan in Assisi, he shared his stable home with the donkey Violetta. When Violetta becomes ill, Pepino thinks that the only way he can cure her is to get her to the crypt of Saint Francis, a lover of animals.

748. Garwood, Julie. *Saving Grace.* Pocket, 1996. 407pp. Paper ISBN 978-0-671-87011-9. Grades YA.

Although inconsistencies in Scottish customs may appear in the details, this book nevertheless spins a worthy tale. Lady Johanna, widowed by the age of 16, marries a Scot instead of the cruel baron whom King John of England has chosen for her. The Scottish lord delights in the land she brings into the marriage, but Johanna has to gain respect from his people while she adjusts to a different way of life.

749. Garwood, Julie. *The Secret.* Pocket, 1992. 379pp. Paper ISBN 978-0-671-74421-2. Grades YA.

In 1200 Judith travels from her home in England to the wild highlands of Scotland. She unexpectedly falls in love, decides to marry and stay in the village, and finds the father whom she has never known. She asserts her rights and surprises the village.

750. Gibfried, Diane Friemoth J. *Brother Juniper.* Illustrated by Meilo So. Houghton Mifflin, 2006. 32pp. ISBN 978-0-618-54361-8. Grades 3–7.

In 13th-century Italy Brother Juniper is left in charge of the church while the seven other friars and Father Francis go off to preach. This worries the brothers, since they know that Brother Juniper is so generous that he will give away anything—including the shirt off his back. When they return from preaching one day, he stands naked in what remains of the chapel. But what they gain because of Brother Juniper's kindness is a new beautiful church.

751. Grant, K. M. *Blaze of Silver.* (De Granville Trilogy, # 3) Walker, 2007. 261pp. ISBN 978-0-8027-9625-7; 2008. paper ISBN 978-0-8027-9737-7. Grades 6–9.

In the sequel to *Blood Red Horse* (2005) and *Green Jasper* (2006) of the de Granville trilogy, William has to deliver his share of the treasure to ransom King Richard, who is being held in Germany. However, the evil Old Man of the Mountain has other plans for the money, including revenge. His messenger, Amal, with a silver Arabian horse, convinces Kamil to lead Will and Ellie into a trap, and the ransom is stolen. Then Kamil repents and wants their forgiveness. Will rushes to save the king, and only when Richard reads Amal's diary can he trust Will and spare his life.

752. Grant, K. M. *Blood Red Horse.* (De Granville Trilogy) Walker, 2005. 277pp. ISBN 978-0-8027-8960-0; 2006. paper ISBN 978-0-8027-7734-8. Grades 6–9.

Thirteen-year-old Will and his brother, Gavin de Granville, must join King Richard for a crusade to fight with the Knights of England in 1185. People laugh when Will chooses Hosanna, a puny but charismatic red stallion, for his warhorse. But after recovering from a grave injury, Hosanna earns respect from those on the journey. Back in England is Ellie, a young woman who is betrothed to Gavin but prefers Will. And in Jerusalem is Kamil, Saladin's ward, who wants Hosanna when he sees the horse. However, Will is able to return with her to England in 1193. The first volume in the trilogy.

753. Grant, K. M. *Blue Flame.* (Perfect Fire) Walker, 2008. 246pp. ISBN 978-0-8027-9694-3. Grades 6 up.

As a young boy, Parsifal found himself the protector of the legendary Blue Flame, a treasure that was supposedly lit when Christ died and that will be returned to the Occitan to keep the area free. In 1242, forty years after receiving the flame, Parsifal becomes friends with two young lovers—Raimon, the son of a Cathar weaver, and Yolanda, daughter of the Catholic Count Berenger. Berenger has permitted the Cathars and Catholics to live peacefully, but this is no longer true. The Blue Flame reappears and chooses Raimon to help Parsifal reunite the people. However, the French want the area, and Yolanda's uncle, Girald, makes her home his headquarters as he purges the area of the heretic Cathars during his Inquisition. Raimon balks at Girald's bullying, and Girald condemns him to die at the stake. However, Raimon initially escapes the pyre as he and Yolanda try to save their love. The first volume in a trilogy.

754. Grant, K. M. *Green Jasper.* (De Granville Trilogy) Walker, 2006. 249pp. ISBN 978-0-8027-8073-7; 2007. paper ISBN 978-0-8027-9627-1. Grades 5–9.

Brothers Will and Gavin de Granville return to England after the Crusades and discover that the political climate is unstable. King Richard I is supposedly dead and King John has taken the throne. During Gavin and Ellie's wedding ceremony, Constable de Scabious kidnaps Ellie, planning to marry her himself. The brothers disagree on how to rescue her; Gavin wants to proceed cautiously and Will wants to storm the castle. While waiting, Ellie continues to hold on to the green jasper necklace Gavin has given her. Will and Gavin reunite and use their red warhorse, Hosanna, in the rescue, but Gavin ultimately sacrifices himself in this sequel to *Blood Red Horse. Capitol Choices Noteworthy Titles* (Washington, D.C.).

755. Gregory, Kristiana. *Eleanor: Crown Jewel of Aquitaine.*   Scholastic, 2002. 187pp. ISBN 978-0-439-16484-9. Grades 3–6.

Eleanor (1122?–1204), the oldest daughter of the Duke of Aquitaine, keeps a diary from 1136 to 1137, when she marries Louis VII and becomes the queen of France at age 15. She tells about the parasites and other conditions around the castle. She also discusses her relationships with her grandmother, her younger sister Petronitia, and her troubled father, with whom she lives at Poitiers, in France, until his death. Photographs augment the text. Glossary of Characters, Note.

756. Grove, Vicki. *Rhiannon.*   Putnam, 2007. 347pp. ISBN 978-0-399-23633-4. Grades 6–9.

In Wales in 1120, 14-year-old Rhiannon lives on Clodaghcombe Bluff with her mother, Aigneis, and her grandmother, far from the village below. They use herbal remedies to heal village outcasts. When one of their patients is convicted of a stabbing, Rhia has to leave the bluff to interact with the townspeople in an effort to save him. Her investigations culminate on Beltane Eve when the real murderer is revealed.

757. Hendry, Frances Mary. *Quest for a Maid.*   Sunburst, 1992. 273pp. Paper ISBN 978-0-374-46155-3. Grades 5 up.

Meg, age 9, thinks her sister used witchcraft to kill King Alexander of Scotland to help a woman who wanted to claim the throne for her son. As a helper in the home of Sir Patrick Spens in the 13th century, Meg gets to accompany Sir Spens to Norway to return with Margaret, the rightful heir to the throne. Meg discovers that her sister should not be accused of the king's murder because she did not commit it. *Bulletin Blue Ribbon Book* and *American Library Association Notable Books for Children.*

758. Jinks, Catherine. *Babylonne.* (Pagan's Chronicles, Book 5) Candlewick, 2008. 384pp. ISBN 978-0-7636-3650-0. Grades 6 up.

Pagan Kidrouk, a Christian Arab, has become the Archdeacon of Carcassonne in this sequel to *Pagan's Scribe* set in 1227. Babylonne, Kidrouk's 16-year-old out-of-wedlock daughter, runs away from her grandmother, who wants to marry her off to an old man. As she runs away, a Roman Catholic priest, Father Isidore, seems to be following her. But he is a protector, rather than the sinister man she envisions. Then Babylonne becomes part of Languedoc's horrible Siege of La Becede.

759. Jinks, Catherine. *Pagan in Exile.* (Pagan Chronicles, Book 2) Candlewick, 2004. 326pp. ISBN 978-0-7636-2020-2; 2005. paper ISBN 978-0-7636-2691-4. Grades 6–10.

As Knight Templar Sir Roland Roucy de Bram's squire, Pagan Kidrouk returns to Roland's castle in the Languedoc region of France after fighting the Crusades in 1188. The de Bram family has become involved in a violent feud with a monastery, and the derelicts in the castle contrast vividly with the pious community of the Cathars. Sir Roland and Pagan cannot protect the others, and they decide to enter the monastery to escape the violence of the world. Glossary. *Bulletin Blue Ribbon.*

760. Jinks, Catherine. *Pagan's Crusade.* (Pagan Chronicles, Book 1) Candlewick, 2003. 256pp. ISBN 978-0-7636-2019-6; 2004. paper ISBN 978-0-7636-2584-9. Grades 6–10.

When the orphaned Pagan Kidrouk is 16, the Knights Templar assign him to work for Lord Roland Roucy de Bram as Saladin's armies close in on Jerusalem in 1187. Pagan calls Lord Roland "Saint George" and slowly grows to respect him. When Lord Roland prepares for death at Saladin's hand, Pagan devises a desperate ploy to get them on the road to Tyre—and perhaps to France. Maps. *Voice of Youth Advocates Perfect Ten List.*

761. Jinks, Catherine. *Pagan's Scribe.* (Pagan Chronicles, Book 4) Candlewick, 2005. 368pp. ISBN 978-0-7636-2022-6; 2006. paper ISBN 978-0-7636-2973-1. Grades YA.

In 1209, 20 years after *Pagan's Vows*, Pagan, now an archdeacon, hires Isidore, an orphaned 15-year-old epileptic, to be his new scribe. Pagan has to go on a mission to bring the heretic Cathars back to the Church, but northern armies invade with instructions from the Pope to route out evil as quickly as possible. In his work, Isidore is as impetuous as Pagan was as a boy, and he gains the friendship of Lord Roland, Pagan's beloved mentor. As they adjust to their charge, they must try to survive the siege of Carcassonne. *Bulletin Blue Ribbon.*

762. Jinks, Catherine. *Pagan's Vows.* (Pagan Chronicles, Book 3) Candlewick, 2004. 330pp. ISBN 978-0-7636-2021-9; 2005. paper ISBN 978-0-7636-2754-6. Grades 6–10.

In 1188 Pagan and Lord Roland enter the Abbey of St. Martin and dedicate their lives to God. Pagan must learn Latin, rhetoric, and other scholarly subjects while adjusting to the asceticism of the community. But deceit is also found at the monastery. Pagan sets out to discover who is committing the immoral acts of theft and pederasty. He must question his loyalty when he thinks the unhappy Lord Roland may be one of the guilty.

763. King, Susan Fraser. *Lady Macbeth.* Crown, 2008. 352pp. ISBN 978-0-307-34174-7. Grades YA.

Lady Gruadh, the last female descendant of Scottish royalty, is wed in an arranged marriage to a northern warrior and lord. Then Macbeth appears, murders her husband, and forces her to marry him. Macbeth and Lady Gruadh subsequently unite in battle against others as they strive to protect their land—and Gruadh's son, Lulach—from Vikings, Saxons, and Lord Malcolm. Lady Gruadh knows how to be a pawn, a wife, a widow, a mother, and then a very good queen in this story set in the 11th century.

764. Klein, Lisa M. *Ophelia.* Bloomsbury, 2006. 336pp. ISBN 978-1-58234-801-8; 2007. paper ISBN 978-1-59990-228-9. Grades 8 up.

Ophelia reveals much about herself and Hamlet in this first-person narrative about their relationship. She loves him, and they marry secretly before Hamlet rejects her for his single-minded pursuit of his father's killer. She realizes that a woman has no rights, but she does have influence over Hamlet's actions for most of their time together.

765. Konigsburg, E. L. *A Proud Taste for Scarlet and Miniver.* Atheneum, 1973. 202pp. ISBN 978-0-689-30111-7; Aladdin, 2001. paper ISBN 978-0-689-84624-3. Grades 6 up.

As she waits for Henry II to arrive in heaven, Eleanor of Aquitaine (ca. 1122–1204) and her companions remember her life. They recall incidents in France and England. Eleanor was the mother of two kings—King Richard the Lionheart and King John—and the wife of two kings, Henry II of England and Louis VII of France. *Phoenix Honor Book.*

766. Koons, Jon. *Arthur and Guen: An Original Tale of Young Camelot.* Illustrated by Igor Oleynikov. Dutton, 2008. 40pp. ISBN 978-0-525-47934-5. Grades K–3.

After leaving a tournament when Sir Kay taunts him, young Arthur wanders into the woods and meets Guen. They play until an unruly band of men shows up. Miraculously, a sword appears from the nearby water and Arthur fends off the men. Watching from the trees, Merlin declares that Arthur and Guenevere have met too soon and erases their memories of the event. Illustrations complement the text.

767. Kurland, Lynn. *From This Moment On.* Berkley, 2002. 418pp. Paper ISBN 978-0-425-18685-5. Grades YA.

After fleeing from her stepmother and an unwanted marriage to Colin of Berkhamshire, known as "The Butcher," Aliénore of Solonge disguises herself as a knight and gets a position attending Lady Sybil of Maignelay. When Lady Sybil becomes engaged, Aliénore, known as Henri, must escort her to her betrothed, who happens to be Colin. After their arrival, Colin condemns Aliénore for her unmanly ways as a knight and decides he will teach her how to be a knight in this 13th-century romance.

768. Langrish, Katherine. *Troll Blood.* Illustrated by Tim Stevens and David Wyatt. Eos, 2008. 340pp. ISBN 978-0-06-111674-2. Grades 5–8.

In the sequel to *Troll Mill*, Peer and Hilde join Gunnar and his quarrelsome son, Harald, on a Viking longship to Vinland. When the Mi'kmaq Indians see one of the crew murder a man, they know things will be difficult. However, they are able to overcome the supernatural when they discover secrets of Gunnar's past. Bibliography.

769. Langrish, Katherine. *Troll Mill.* Eos, 2006. 261pp. ISBN 978-0-06-058307-1; 2008. paper ISBN 978-0-06-058309-5. Grades 5–8.

Orphan Peer Ulfsson, 15, lives with Hilde's family in the land of the Norse. After Kirsten, a neighbor, disappears into the sea, the family helps her husband, Bjorn, by adopting her half-selkie baby with webbed fingers, infuriating the other nonhuman troll neighbors. The same night, the abandoned mill that Peer's treacherous uncles once owned begins working after dark. Then the sheep disappear from the mountains. These problems all fall into Peer's life at the same time he falls in love with Hilde.

770. Langton, Jane. *Saint Francis and the Wolf.* Narrated by Ilse Plume. Godine, 2007. Unpaged. ISBN 978-1-56792-320-9. Grades K–2.

Saint Francis of Assisi (1182–1226) helps the people of Gubbio when they are imprisoned inside their town walls while a wolf lurks outside. Saint Francis talks to the wolf and then tells the people that all the wolf wants is food. If they will feed it, it will no longer bother their livestock or their crops. Illustrations enliven the text.

771. Lawhead, Steve. *The Black Rood.* (The Celtic Crusades) Eos, 2001. 437pp. Paper ISBN 978-0-06-105110-4. Grades YA.

After his wife dies, Duncan Ranulfson decides to go to the Holy Land in 1132 to recover the Black Rood, a piece of Christ's cross. He traces his father Murdo's steps through Byzantium on his quest. Accompanying him on the trip are Padraig, a priest of the Celtic Cele De; and in France, Prince Roupen of Armenia. Among the many opposed to his journey are the Byzants, the Saracens, and the Knights Templar.

772. Leeds, Constance. *The Silver Cup.* Viking, 2007. 224pp. ISBN 978-0-670-06157-0. Grades 7 up.

In 1095 Anna, 16, and Gunter, her merchant father, live in Germany just as the first Crusade is beginning. Her father takes Anna to Worms, where she meets Leah, daughter of the spice merchant. When soldiers on the way to the Crusades storm through her Jewish neighborhood, they kill all of Leah's family and eight hundred others. All Leah has left is her father's silver cup for blessing the wine on the Sabbath and at holidays. Anna shuns convention and takes Leah home with her. Eventually, Leah makes connections in another Jewish community.

773. Love, D. Anne. *The Puppeteer's Apprentice.* Margaret K. McElderry, 2003. 192pp. ISBN 978-0-689-84424-9; Aladdin, 2004. paper ISBN 978-0-689-84425-6. Grades 3–7.

Mouse, a 12-year-old orphaned scullery maid, runs away to be a puppeteer's apprentice in this story set in the Middle Ages. Although she makes mistakes, she devotes herself to learning the craft. Ordin, a shadowy figure, lurks around the traveling puppeteers, and he makes Mouse feel uncomfortable. Eventually, she discovers that the puppeteer is a woman, and although their traveling together has been wonderful, they must separate. Mouse has learned independence and a trade. Bibliography and Notes.

774. Low, Robert. *The Whale Road.* Thomas Dunne, 2007. 352pp. ISBN 978-0-312-36194-5. Grades YA.

When his mother dies, Orm Rurikson goes to live with his uncle. At age 15 in 965, he is conscripted to sail on his father's ship. After he seemingly kills a polar bear by himself, the men on board think he is charmed and make him an Oathsworn. These men, committed to each other and the captain, take the "whale road" from Norway to Russia as mercenaries while seeking Attila the Hun's lost treasure. They must fight Bluetooth—the king of the Danes who wants the same reward—and a Catholic monk looking for the "Spear of Destiny," the sword used to pierce Christ's side that is supposedly with the silver treasure. What the other men do not know is that the bear died when it fell while chasing Orm, who was running away from it.

775. McCaffrey, Anne. *Black Horses for the King.* Magic Carpet, 2008. 223pp. Paper ISBN 978-0-15-206378-8. Grades 7 up.

After Galwyn's father loses his money and dies during the time of the Saxon raids, Galwyn must work on his uncle's ship, although he prefers to work with the horses that he loved on his father's land. His ability to learn languages quickly makes him valuable to one of the ship's passengers, King Arthur. Galwyn translates for Arthur when the king buys horses strong enough to breed good stock for his army to challenge the raiding Saxons. Galwyn's knowledge of horses also helps Arthur after his return. Galwyn learns how to put the new iron sandals on the horses' hooves and is ready to go with the armies to war as a blacksmith. Simultaneously, Galwyn must protect the horses from a vindictive young man who was dismissed from service. *Capitol Choices Noteworthy Titles* (Washington, D.C.).

776. **McDonnell, Kathleen.** *1212: Year of the Journey.*   Second Story, 2007. Paper ISBN 978-1-8971-8711-1. Grades 7–9.

A poor shepherd boy from Cloyes, France, Etienne has a vision telling him to lead a peaceful crusade of children to free the Holy Land from the infidels. Abel, a Jewish boy studying in Paris, and Blanche, a member of the Good Christians who do not follow Rome, go with him. In 1212, they gather children to make the journey from Paris to Marseilles, where they board ships for Palestine. They do not survive.

777. **McKenzie, Nancy.** *Guinevere's Gift.*   (The Chrysalis Queen Quartet) Knopf, 2008. 327pp. ISBN 978-0-375-84345-7. Grades 6–10.

Guinevere is a 12-year-old orphan living with her uncle, King Pellinore of Gwynedd, and aunt, Queen Alyse. She has difficulty believing the prophecy made at her birth— that she will marry a great king. She must offer companionship to her awful cousin, Elaine, while waiting for something to happen. When King Pellinore is away fighting with Arthur, Alyse has to defend her castle and Guinevere has to rescue Elaine from abductors. Then she is recognized for her courage and horsewomanship.

778. **McNaughton, Janet.** *An Earthly Knight.*   HarperCollins, 2004. 272pp. ISBN 978-0-06-008992-4; Trophy, 2005. paper ISBN 978-0-06-008994-8. Grades 7 up.

In 1162 Jenny Avenel's father promises her to the king's boorish brother after her sister embarrasses the family by running away with her father's knight and then killing him. But Lady Jeanette falls in love with Tam Lin, a man under the fairy queen's enchantment. She has to help him escape his fate of haunting her family home—and save herself.

779. **Malone, Patricia.** *Lady Ilena: Way of the Warrior.*   Laurel-Leaf, 2007. 232pp. Paper ISBN 978-0-440-23901-7. Grades 6–9.

As chief of Dun Alyn, 15-year-old Ilena (introduced in *The Legend of Lady Ilena*) has to defend the land from tribes who have allied with the Saxons to seize it. She refuses to marry Faolan, the warrior from Dun Struan, so she knows that war is pending and that she must prepare herself and her people for the days ahead. Her fiance, Durant, has been summoned to return to Arthur's legendary table, and Ilena does not succeed in the battle. Under Druid law, she must die, but her people allow her to leave the tribe and prove her worthiness to lead elsewhere. She succeeds admirably in all the tests and proves herself to be a born leader, especially when she rescues the kidnapped Arthur. She returns to her rightful place as chief with faith in herself.

780. **Malone, Patricia.** *The Legend of Lady Ilena.*   Laurel-Leaf, 2003. 232pp. Paper ISBN 978-0-440-22909-4. Grades 6–9.

In 6th-century Britain (now Scotland), Ilena, 15, has learned the ways of warriors from her father, but after she is orphaned, she leaves her village to fulfill her father's last request. He told her, "Go to Dun Alyn. Find Ryamen." On her way, she encounters blue-painted barbarians and slave raiders, but also kindness and refuge. When she gets to Dun Alyn and finds Ryamen, he tells her secrets of her lineage. She becomes the center of a power struggle between the Christian chieftain Belert and his rival, the Druid Ogern, who wants to sacrifice humans to the gods. She then rescues a man who follows King Arthur and guides her to discover that she is heir to the throne.

781. Matthews, John. *The Barefoot Book of Knights.* Illustrated by Giovanni Manna. Barefoot, 2006. 80pp. ISBN 978-1-84686-034-8. Grades 4–7.

Tom of Warwick, age 10, becomes a page for Sir Brian des Isles and finds the castle quite unfriendly. Then he becomes friends with Master William, the armorer, and feels inspired to work hard enough to one day become a real knight. The tales included in the text come from medieval stories about how to be a knight. Illustrations augment the text.

782. Medeiros, Teresa. *Fairest of Them All.* Bantam, 2008. 371pp. Paper ISBN 978-0-553-59227-6. Grades YA.

When Holly de Chaste, the most beautiful woman in England, discovers that her father has offered her as a prize in a tournament of knights, she decides to disguise her beauty. Then she meets one of the knights, a handsome Welshman, and has to reassess her decision.

783. Miles, Rosalind. *Child of the Holy Grail.* (The Guenevere Novels) Three Rivers, 2002. 448pp. Paper ISBN 978-0-609-60624-7. Grades YA.

In the last book of the Guenevere trilogy, the evil Mordred attempts to take his seat at the round table and is accepted as Arthur's heir. Sir Galahad, a handsome young knight, arrives and announces that he is Lancelot's son from Lancelot's one night with Elaine. He convinces the knights that they need to go to Jerusalem to find the Holy Grail. The kingdom and Guenevere, left unprotected, suffer when Guenevere is found with Lancelot and sentenced to burn at the stake. She survives, but Camelot dies.

784. Miles, Rosalind. *Guenevere: Queen of the Summer Country.* (The Guenevere Novels) Crown, 2001. 424pp. Paper ISBN 978-0-609-80650-0. Grades YA.

The beautiful Queen Guenevere shows her courage in the matriarchal society of Camelot. She can love whomever she wishes, but after her mother dies, her uncle Malgaunt tries to take power from her. When she has almost acquiesced and taken Malgaunt as her husband, Arthur appears and saves her.

785. Miles, Rosalind. *Isolde: Queen of the Western Isle.* (Tristan and Isolde Novels) Three Rivers, 2003. 349pp. Paper ISBN 978-1-400-04786-4. Grades YA.

In the first volume of a trilogy, Isolde, a healer and princess, nurses a wounded knight, Tristan, and heals him. Simultaneously, she falls in love with him although his uncle, King Mark of Cornwall, is her Irish queen mother's enemy. Then her mother reconciles with King Mark by offering Isolde to Mark as a bride. Unhappy Tristan must accompany Isolde to Cornwall to meet and marry Mark. During the voyage, the two unwittingly drink a potion that binds them together in love forever.

786. Miles, Rosalind. *The Knight of the Sacred Lake.* (The Guenevere Novels) Crown, 2001. 417pp. Paper ISBN 978-0-609-80802-3. Grades YA.

In the sequel to *Guenevere: Queen of the Summer Country*, Morgan le Fay, King Arthur's half sister, along with Mordred, her bastard son by Arthur, threaten Camelot. Morgan plans to avenge her youth as a starved convent resident. Also, Guenevere has begun an affair with the knight Lancelot, and she must choose between him and her duty to her husband and her subjects. Not until the end of the story does Merlin discover Mordred after spending years looking for him.

787. Miles, Rosalind. *The Lady of the Sea.* (Tristan and Isolde Novels) Three Rivers, 2005. 356pp. Paper ISBN 978-0-307-20985-6. Grades YA.

Invading Picts from the North threaten Queen Isolde as her marriage to King Mark of Cornwall disintegrates and members of their court scheme against them in the third volume of this medieval trilogy. Throughout, Isolde misses her champion, Tristan of Lyonesse, and in desperation she turns to the mystical Lady of the Sea for help. She returns to Ireland and helps resolve the muddle while her husband remains ineffectual.

788. Miles, Rosalind. *The Maid of the White Hands.* (Tristan and Isolde Novels) Three Rivers, 2005. 320pp. Paper ISBN 978-1-400-08154-7. Grades YA.

In Cornwall, Isolde is unhappily married to King Mark when her mother, the Irish queen, dies, and Isolde becomes the queen of Ireland. Mark banishes Tristan from the court and sends him to France. There Tristan succumbs to battle wounds in the second volume of the trilogy.

789. Moodie, Craig. *The Sea Singer.* Roaring Brook, 2005. 176pp. ISBN 978-1-59643-050-1. Grades 5–8.

Twelve-year-old Finn stows away on Leif Ericsson's ship and sails to North America trying to find his father and brothers, who failed to return from a prior voyage to the West. When Finn is discovered he has to coil line, haul the sail, cook, care for the animals, stand lookout, and perform as a *skald*, reciting poems for the crew. They follow the route of Finn's father, Olaf Farseeker, but encounter dangerous weather that could cause the ship to lose its way. In essence, Finn proves himself a Viking, and the ship arrives in North America. He finds his family but not before he has seen bloodshed with the Native Americans.

790. Mora, Pat. *The Song of Francis and the Animals.* Illustrated by David Frampton. William B. Eerdmans, 2005. 32pp. ISBN 978-0-8028-5253-3. Grades K–3.

Saint Francis of Assisi loved animals, and in this playful book he interacts with cicadas, nightingales, chickens, earthworms, a wolf threatening the citizens of Gubbio, and others. Saint Francis also recreates a manger scene with the help of some of the animals. Woodcuts complement the text. *Catholic Press Association Awards* nomination.

791. Morris, Gerald. *The Lioness and Her Knight.* (The Squire's Tales) Houghton, 2005. 353pp. ISBN 978-0-618-50772-6. Grades 6–9.

Luneta, 16, is delighted when her mother lets her leave home to live with her mother's friend Laudine in Camelot. Ywain, her cousin, serves as her escort on the journey, and on the way, they encounter the handsome Rhience, who has to be a fool for one year. After their arrival in Camelot, Ywain falls in love with Laudine, and Luneta's great-aunt, Morgan le Fay, declares her an enchantress. Their adventures lead Luneta to discover that she has more in common with her mother than she could have imagined.

792. Morris, Gerald. *The Princess, the Crone, and the Dung-Cart Knight.* (The Squire's Tales) Houghton, 2004. 310pp. ISBN 978-0-618-37823-4; 2006. paper ISBN 978-0-618-73748-2. Grades 5–9.

Princess Sarah, 13, sees Sir Meliagant kidnap Queen Guinevere and Sir Kai, renewing her determination to avenge her mother's murder. She searches for the knight responsible for the deaths of her mother and a Jewish peddler. Soon after she finds herself going to search for the queen with Sir Gawain and Squire Terence. On their way, they encounter an old woman, a magical sword, a faery, a monk who wants to build Sir Lancelot's tomb, and a knight in a dung cart. *Dorothy Canfield Fisher* nomination (Vermont).

793. Morris, Gerald. *The Quest of the Fair Unknown.* (The Squire's Tales) Houghton, 2006. 264pp. ISBN 978-0-618-63152-0. Grades 5 up.

After his mother dies, 17-year-old Beaufils leaves his isolated forest for Camelot to find his father. Along the way he encounters evil in various guises and unwittingly overcomes it. He has never seen a human other than his mother so does not expect duplicity. Once he arrives in Camelot, he joins Sir Gawain and Sir Galahad as they visit hermits and travel into the fairy world, seeing everything through innocent eyes.

794. Morris, Gerald. *The Savage Damsel and the Dwarf.* (The Squire's Tales) Houghton, 2000. 213pp. ISBN 978-0-395-97126-0; 2004. paper ISBN 978-0-618-19681-4. Grades 5–8.

With a clever dwarf and a kitchen knave, Lynet, 16, journeys to King Arthur's court expecting to find a knight to rescue her older and shallower sister, Lyonesse, from the Red Knight, a suitor who slaughters his rivals. On her journey, she meets several knights and realizes that they are not what they seem—nor is anyone else, including herself. Eventually she meets one that she likes. *Dorothy Canfield Fisher Children's Book Award* (Vermont) nomination, *Junior Book Award* (South Carolina) nomination, and *Student Book Award* (Maine) nomination.

795. Napoli, Donna Jo. *Hush: An Irish Princess' Tale.* Atheneum, 2007. 308pp. ISBN 978-0-689-86176-5; Simon Pulse, 2008. paper ISBN 978-0-689-86179-6. Grades 8 up.

In 10th-century Ireland Melkora's father plans to avenge a brutal Norse attack. To protect Melkora and his second daughter, he dresses them as boys and sends them away. But Russian slave traders capture them and put them on their ship. Melkora initially refuses to speak to them because she disdains slaves, but soon she realizes that her muteness gives her power. Simultaneously, she notices that slaves are not the awful beings that she had imagined. Even after she becomes the concubine of a wealthy Norseman, she will not speak because silence gains her much more than speech.

796. Newman, Sharan. *The Devil's Door.* (Catherine LeVendeur Mystery) Forge, 2004. 384pp. Paper ISBN 978-0-7653-1034-7. Grades YA.

As a novice in Hëloïse's convent of the Paraclete in France during 1140, Catherine LeVendeur wants to find the attacker of a wealthy countess who dies after being brought to the convent for help. Catherine suspects the countess's husband of beating her, but when Catherine's betrothed, Edgar, arrives to take her home, she feels torn between finding the attacker and her impending marriage. Hëloïse requests that Catherine go on an important journey for her, so Catherine and Edgar go to Abelard and his son Astrolabe while they wait for the heresy trial against Abelard. After the worst occurs, Catherine and Edgar realize that they must go where they are needed.

808. Penman, Sharon Kay. *When Christ and His Saints Slept.* Ballantine, 1996. 746pp. Paper ISBN 978-0-345-39668-6. Grades YA.

As Henry I, the youngest son of William the Conqueror, nears the end of his life and his reign, he names Maude as his heir. Maude's battles with King Stephen of England disturb the 12th-century countryside for too many years.

809. Peters, Ellis. *An Excellent Mystery.* (Brother Cadfael) Grand Central, 1997. 190pp. Paper ISBN 978-0-446-40532-4. Grades YA.

When King Stephen and Empress Maud draw Henry of Blois, the Bishop of Winchester, into their struggle for the crown, fire destroys Winchester. Two of the brothers from that priory seek refuge at Shrewsbury. When a visitor arrives talking about a girl's disappearance, Brother Cadfael has another murder to solve.

810. Peters, Ellis. *The Heretic's Apprentice.* (Brother Cadfael) Mysterious, 1990. 186pp. ISBN 978-0-8929-6381-2. Grades YA.

When Elave brings his master to Shrewsbury for burial on the abbey grounds in 1143, another visitor accuses Elave of heresy when he says that everyone will find salvation. The trial leads to a murder that requires Brother Cadfael's talents of investigation.

811. Peters, Ellis. *Monk's Hood.* (Brother Cadfael) Mysterious, 1992. 224pp. Paper ISBN 978-0-446-40300-9. Grades YA.

Monk's hood, a medicine that is poisonous if ingested, seems to be what has caused a guest at the abbey to become deathly ill. Brother Cadfael's investigation shows that the guest's stepson did not try to poison the man, although he had many reasons to do so.

812. Peters, Ellis. *A Morbid Taste for Bones.* (Brother Cadfael) Mysterious, 1994. 208pp. Paper ISBN 978-0-446-40015-2. Grades YA.

When Brother Cadfael and Prior Robert go to a small town in Wales to retrieve the bones of Saint Winifred, a murder occurs. Brother Cadfael helps to solve the murder, but the fact that the Gwytherin parish enjoys more renown because of the murder annoys Prior Robert in this mystery set in the 12th century.

813. Peters, Ellis. *The Summer of the Danes.* (Brother Cadfael) Mysterious, 1991. 251pp. ISBN 978-0-8929-6448-2. Grades YA.

During a time of peace between King Stephen and Empress Maud in 1144, Brother Cadfael grabs a chance to go to Wales with Brother Mark. In Wales, Danish mercenaries fighting for Cadwaladr capture Brother Cadfael and a woman. While he waits to be released, he solves the murder of one of Owain's prisoners, Cadwaladr's brother.

814. Peters, Ellis. *The Virgin in the Ice.* (Brother Cadfael) Mysterious, 1995. 220pp. Paper ISBN 978-0-446-40439-0. Grades YA.

In 1139, during the civil war between King Stephen and Empress Maud, two orphans and their chaperone become lost in the winter woods. Their nearest kinsman supports Empress Maud, so he cannot come to look for them without jeopardizing his life. Brother Cadfael becomes involved while on his way to the priory of Bromfield. He investigates a murder and finds information about his own son.

815. Pyle, Howard. *Otto of the Silver Hand.* IndyPublish, 2002. 173pp. ISBN 978-1-4043-2304-9; Kessinger, 2004. paper ISBN 978-1-4191-3940-6. Grades 5–9.

In medieval Germany, Otto's mother has died and his father is a robber baron. Since the household constantly fights, he is raised in a monastery. When he returns to his father's home at the age of 12, he becomes involved in a blood feud between his father and the house of Trutz-Drachen. The rival family captures him and mutilates him, but their daughter Pauline helps him escape. When Otto returns safely, the monks place him under the emperor's protection. He receives a silver hand as a replacement for the one he lost and eventually marries Pauline.

816. Quick, Amanda. *Mystique.* Bantam, 1996. 357pp. Paper ISBN 978-0-553-57159-2. Grades YA.

Alice decides that she will marry Hugh the Relentless, a knight who needs a housekeeper, to escape her controlling uncle and create a better life for her brother. After she settles into the new life, she has to rescue her neighbor, Lady Emma, the wife of Hugh's main enemy. Later Hugh is poisoned (but not killed) and no one is sure who could have done it. Alice and Hugh learn to appreciate each other in this romance set in England.

817. Reeve, Philip. *Here Lies Arthur.* Scholastic, 2008. 339pp. ISBN 978-0-545-09334-7. Grades 6 up.

When Myrddin sees Gwyna swimming away from her burning home after Arthur and his men have destroyed it he decides to disguise her as a boy and make her his accomplice. He wants to groom Arthur to take leadership of England and keep the Saxons out in this story set in the 5th century. He asks Gwyna to pretend to be the Lady of the Lake and to allow Arthur to take a sword from her so that Arthur will think he has been mystically chosen for Myrddin's job. After Arthur takes the sword, Myrddin places Gwyna in his service. When she gets too old for disguise, she becomes a handmaiden to Arthur's new wife, Gwenhwyfar, whom he does not love. Then Gwenhwyfar and Bedwyr have an affair and Arthur's nephew, Medrawt, defeats Arthur. Gwyna buries Myrddin in a tree trunk and begins to tell her own stories. She realizes how politics works and what one must do to get one's wishes accomplished. *Kirkus Best Young Adult Books.*

818. Roberts, Judson. *Dragons from the Sea.* (Strongbow Saga) HarperTeen, 2007. 346pp. ISBN 978-0-06-081300-0. Grades 9 up.

Halfdan Hroriksson hopes to join the crew of the *Gull*, a longship in one of Jutland's coastal towns, even though he can only shoot a bow. His honesty and skill with the longbow get him the job, and he hopes not only to gain wealth but also to defeat the murderer of his half-brother and thief of his inheritance. When the boat reaches France, Hroriksson must make unexpected decisions so that he will not compromise his ethics, and he finds himself isolated from a crew that does not share his convictions. The second volume in the series set in 845.

819. Roberts, Judson. *Viking Warrior.* (Strongbow Saga) HarperCollins, 2007. 260pp. ISBN 978-0-06-079996-0; HarperTeen paper ISBN 978-0-06-079999-1. Grades 9 up.

In Denmark in 845 Halfdan, although he is the son of a chieftain and a princess, serves as a *thrall*—a slave. His mother, Derdriu, sacrifices her life to free him. He trains as a warrior, and his half brother, Harald, helps him. Their stepbrother, Toke, hates both of them. After Toke's actions lead to Harald's death, Halfdan determines that he will prove Toke's guilt. The opening volume in the series.

820. Roth, Susan L., and Angelo Mafucci. *Do Re Me: If You Can Read Music, Thank Guido d'Arezzo.* Houghton, 2007. 40pp. ISBN 978-0-618-46572-9. Grades 2–5.

Guido d'Arezzo (991?–1033?) was a singer in a boy choir who thought that singing would be easier if the notes were written down, making memorization unnecessary. He created a system of symbols on lines to indicate the notes, but other monks discouraged his attempts. Then he went to Pomposa, where a Brother Michael encouraged him. Back in Arezzo, Bishop Teodaldo asked him to direct the children's choir. Guido tried his idea with them, and they successfully learned the new approach. The pope then wanted him to come to Rome, but Guido refused. He has the title "Father of Music" for his invention of the musical staff. Illustrations highlight the text. Bibliography and Glossary.

821. Sandell, Lisa Ann. *Song of the Sparrow.* Scholastic, 2007. 394pp. ISBN 978-0-439-91848-0. Grades 7 up.

Elaine, 17, moves from her destroyed home on the island of Shalott to live with her father and brothers in Arthur's army's encampment in 5th-century Britain. She meets Gwynivere, a new girl, and wonders whether she will be a friend or a competitor for Lancelot's love. Elaine soon realizes that Gwynivere is a rival and that she is haughty and flirtatious. When invading Saxons kidnap them and hold them hostage, they must relate to each other. As Elaine matures she realizes that Lancelot loves Gwynivere and that Tristan is more desirable. *Taysha's Reading List* nomination.

822. Sauerwein, Leigh. *Song for Eloise.* Front Street, 2003. 136pp. ISBN 978-1-8869-1090-4. Grades YA.

In medieval France, the sixth Crusade has ended, and Lady Eloise's Uncle John has chosen a husband for her, the older and devoted Robert of Rochefort. Only 15, she unexpectedly encounters an old friend, Thomas, a troubadour who comes to sing at the castle. She still loves him, but she cannot act on her feelings without damaging three lives.

823. Schlitz, Laura Amy. *Good Masters! Sweet Ladies! Voices from a Medieval Village.* Illustrated by Robert Byrd. Candlewick, 2007. 85pp. ISBN 978-0-7636-1578-9. Grades 4–8.

In nineteen short overviews of life in 1255, this book presents people of different levels of society and different backgrounds. Some items resemble skits for two people, some are poetic, and others are prose. Sidebars define words appropriate for medieval times but no longer in the lexicon. Among the people presented are a lord's daughter, a half-wit, a doctor's son, a female blacksmith, and an eel-catcher. Watercolor illustrations enhance the text. *Newbery Medal, Booklist Editor's Choice, American Library Association Notable Children's Books, School Library Journal Best Books for Children, Bulletin Blue Ribbon, Kirkus Reviews Critics Choice, Capitol Choices Noteworthy Titles* (Washington, D.C.), and *Parents Choice Award.*

824. Scieszka, Jon. *Viking It and Liking It.* Illustrated by Adam McCauley. (Time Warp Trio) Penguin, 2002. 80pp. ISBN 978-0-670-89918-0; Puffin, 2004. paper ISBN 978-0-14-240002-9. Grades 2–4.

When Joe, Sam, and Fred say "Thursday" too many times next to the magic book, they are transported to the year 1000 because Thursday refers to the Viking god Thor. It is Thor's Day. They eat walrus and whale blubber, sail with Leif Erickson and his vicious Vikings, and listen to poets (*skalds*) Fulluvit and Bullshik. They also encounter Grim Snake-in-the-Grass, who is feuding with Erickson, and use football "trash talk" as they fight with words and weapons. They are searching for the Book to return to the present, and after runes and references to the Valkyries and Valhalla, they find themselves back in Brooklyn. The 12th volume in the series. *Garden State Children's Book Awards* (New Jersey) nomination.

825. **Sensel, Joni.** *The Humming of Numbers.* Holt, 2008. 256pp. ISBN 978-0-8050-8327-9. Grades 6 up.

In 10th-century Ireland, novice monk Aiden, 17, looks forward to taking his vows because he wants to illuminate manuscripts and copy scriptures. He also has the secret ability to hum numbers and to judge people based on the numbers surrounding them. Lara, the illegitimate daughter of the local all-powerful lord, comes to the monastery for punishment. Aiden, put in charge of her care as a test to see if he is ready for induction, discovers that she hums the number eleven, the largest number of any human he has met. Her secret is that she is a wood witch, and she and Aiden are thrown together when the Vikings arrive and start plundering and burning the village. The two use their talents to defeat the invaders and save residents.

826. **Shinn, Sharon.** *The Safe-Keeper's Daughter.* Viking, 2004. 222pp. ISBN 978-0-670-05910-2; Firebird, 2005. paper ISBN 978-0-14-240357-0. Grades 6–9.

In 11th-century England, Fiona, a Safe-Keeper in the village of Tambleham, hears secrets that neighbors and strangers will not tell anyone else. On the night Fiona was born, the king's messenger brought a baby to her mother, Damiana, and asked her to keep the child. Fiona grows up with Reed and without a father, but when Damiana becomes ill, the two discover all kinds of secrets about their families.

827. **Shulevitz, Uri.** *The Travels of Benjamin of Tudela: Through Three Continents in the Twelfth Century.* Farrar, 2005. 48pp. ISBN 978-0-374-37754-0. Grades 3–7.

In 1159 Benjamin of Tudela starts out on a fourteen-year journey that takes him to holy places in Italy, Greece, Palestine, Persia, China, Egypt, and Sicily. On his interesting trip, he encounters illness, thieves, hunger, and assassins. The text comes from Benjamin's own diary. Illustrations complement the text. Bibliography. *School Library Journal Best Children's Books.*

828. **Skurzynski, Gloria.** *The Minstrel in the Tower.* Illustrated by Julek Heller. Random House, 1988. 60pp. Paper ISBN 978-0-394-89598-7. Grades 2–4.

In 1195, when their mother is sick, 8-year-old Alice and 11-year-old Roger go to find an uncle of whom they have just become aware. Scoundrels kidnap them, but Alice escapes and finds her uncle. He tells her that her father has died in the Crusades at Acre, and then he goes with the two to help their mother.

829. **Spradlin, Michael.** *The Youngest Templar.* (Keeper of the Grail) Putnam, 2008. 248pp. ISBN 978-0-399-24763-7. Grades 4–8.

During the third Crusade in 1191, 15-year-old Tristan, who was orphaned as a baby and raised in an English abbey, becomes Sir Thomas's squire of the Knights Templar. Tristan is quickly on his way to Acre in pursuit of the Holy Grail. When he meets Sir Hugh and King Richard the Lionheart they are hostile to him. But Tristan gets the Grail and flees with it, outwitting attacking bandits and Saracens. Robard Hode, an unhappy king's archer, and Maryam, a Saracen assassin, assist him in his attempt to reach England.

830. **Springer, Nancy.** *I Am Mordred: A Tale from Camelot.* Firebird, 2002. 184pp. Paper ISBN 978-0-698-11841-6. Grades 7 up.

Merlin prophesies that Mordred, bastard son of King Arthur and his half sister Morgause, will kill his father, the beloved king. Mordred struggles with this knowledge, hating the king who tried to kill him as a baby but idolizing him when he gets to know him at Camelot. At Merlin's request, Arthur put baby Mordred on a boat and sent it to sea, but he survived, with a fisherman and his wife raising him until the sorceress Nyneve took him to be trained in nobility at the court of King Lothe and Queen Morgause. *Student Book Award* (Maine) nomination, *Garden State Teen Book Award* (New Jersey), *Young Adult Book Award* (South Carolina) nomination, *Lonestar Reading List* (Texas), *Capitol Choices Noteworthy Titles* (Washington, D.C.), and *Dorothy Canfield Fisher Children's Book Awards* (Vermont).

831. Springer, Nancy. *Rowan Hood: Outlaw Girl of Sherwood Forest.* (Tales of Rowan Hood) Putnam, 2002. 192pp. Paper ISBN 978-0-698-11972-7. Grades 5–7.

Rosemary, 13, disguises herself as a boy and goes into hiding in Sherwood Forest after the local gentry immolate her mother, the woodwife (healer) Celandine. She has met neither her father, Robin Hood, nor her mother's people, the aelfe ("old ones"). In hiding, she meets the nasty outlaw Guy of Gisborn, who dislikes her. She finds Robin Hood and saves him from death before she tells him her identity. She collects her own outlaw band with her wolf-dog Tykell: Etty, a princess escaping from an arranged marriage, and Lionel, a dimwitted but kind minstrel boy. *Young Reader's Choice Award* (Pennsylvania) nomination.

832. Springer, Nancy. *Rowan Hood Returns: The Final Chapter.* (Tales of Rowan Hood) Philomel, 2005. 169pp. ISBN 978-0-399-24206-9; Puffin, 2006. paper ISBN 978-0-14-240685-4. Grades 4–7.

Rowan, daughter of woodwife Celandine and Robin Hood, vows to kill the four knights who burned her home with her inside and killed her mother. She discovers that she no longer has the power to hear the trees and stones—or her distant father. But she is determined, and she and her friends Ettarde, Beau, and the minstrel Lionel return to the site of her home. There she discovers Jasper, the third knight, who has gone mad. Rowan heals him and recovers her abilities in this final segment of the series.

833. Springer, Nancy. *Wild Boy: A Tale of Rowan Hood.* (Rowan Hood) Penguin, 2004. 128pp. ISBN 978-0-399-24015-7; Puffin, 2005. paper ISBN 978-0-14-240395-2. Grades 5–8.

The orphaned Rook feels almost like a wolf surviving in the forest and wants to avenge the sheriff of Nottingham's murder in a "man trap" of his swineherd father. When Robin Hood captures the sheriff's son, Tod, in the same kind of trap, Rook almost leaves him in the trap to suffer. However, Rook's humanity returns to him, and he asks Rowan to heal Tod's broken leg. He discovers that while he is grieving, Tod has had to live with his abusive father. *Garden State Children's Book Awards* (New Jersey) nomination.

834. Sutcliff, Rosemary. *Knight's Fee.* Illustrated by Charles Keeping. Front Street, 2008. 264pp. Paper ISBN 978-1-59078-640-6. Grades YA.

In the 10th century, Randal, a 10-year-old dog keeper, grows to be a 21-year-old knight. During that time, he helps foil a plot against the lord of his manor. He also goes to Normandy to fight beside the son of the manor lord. When the son dies, Randal returns, is knighted, and becomes heir to the land. First published in 1960.

835. Sutcliff, Rosemary. *The Shield Ring.* Illustrated by C. Walter Hodges. Front Street, 2007. 251pp. Paper ISBN 978-1-59078-522-5. Grades YA.

A spy, Bjorn fears that he will reveal Saxon secrets if the Normans capture and torture him. But as a harper, he is the only one who can infiltrate the enemy strongholds and learn their plans. The Normans do capture and torture him, and he finds out that he is stronger than he had imagined. First published in 1956. *Carnegie Commendation.*

836. Sutcliff, Rosemary. *The Shining Company.* Sunburst, 1992. 304pp. Paper ISBN 978-0-374-46616-9. Grades 6–10.

Around 600, 12-year-old Prosper dreams of becoming Prince Gorthyn's shield bearer; two years later, near Edinburgh, he succeeds. Gorthyn is one of King Mynyddog's 300 men training for battle. In the Saxon battle near York, only Prosper and one other survive. To escape their loneliness, they travel to Constantinople, the source of a merchant's tales. *American Library Association Notable Books for Children.*

837. Tingle, Rebecca. *The Edge on the Sword.* Speak, 2003. 277pp. Paper ISBN 978-0-14-250058-3. Grades 7 up.

Aethelflaed, 15, daughter of King Alfred the Great of West Saxony, lives in Britain during the 9th century. Her father arranges for her to be married to Ethelred of Mercia in order to form an alliance against the Danes. The four sections of the story, "Late Winter," "Spring," "Summer," and "Summer's End," tell of Flaed learning to defend herself like a man by fighting with weapons on horseback and on foot; studying; and trying to escape her Mercian bodyguard, Red. When the Danes try to capture her, she fights, wins, and saves her people. *Black-Eyed Susan Book Award* (Maryland) nomination, *Junior Book Award* (South Carolina) nomination, and *Lonestar Reading List* (Texas).

838. Tingle, Rebecca. *Far Traveler.* Putnam, 2005. 240pp. ISBN 978-0-399-23890-1. Grades 7 up.

Seventeen-year-old Aelfwyn has to choose between a convent and marriage after the death of her mother, Aethelflaed of Mercia, in 919. She decides to disguise herself as a *scop* (a traveling bard) and escape both alternatives. Wilfrid, the king of Northumbria, offers her protection during the Norse invasions, but a threat to England forces Aelfwyn to choose whether to stay with her Wessex people or with Wilfrid. The sequel to *The Edge on the Sword.*

839. Treece, Henry. *Road to Miklagard.* Illustrated by Christine Price. S. G. Phillips, 1957. 254pp. ISBN 978-0-87599-118-4. Grades 6–10.

Harald, the Viking hero of *Viking's Dawn* (1956), wants more excitement, so he joins Prince Arkil of Denmark and they sail to Ireland to take the treasure guarded by the giant Grummoch. They enslave the giant in 785, but Turkish slavers capture them and sell them to Abu Mazur of Spain. Arkil dies, but Harald rescues Abu Mazur from a traitorous gardener, and Abu Mazur asks Harald to take his daughter to Miklagard (Istanbul). In Miklagard, Marriba and Irene, Constantine's mother, disagree, and Harald sends Marriba back to Spain while he and Grummoch return home.

840. Vining, Elizabeth Gray. *Adam of the Road.* Illustrated by Robert Lawson. Puffin, 2006. 320pp. Paper ISBN 978-0-14-240659-5. Grades 4–8.

After Adam's minstrel father, Roger, returns from France, the two walk from place to place in England and are separated at a large fair in Winchester. Adam falls off a wall and knocks himself unconscious; while he slowly recovers, his father does not know where Adam is. When he is well enough, Adam goes to London to search for Roger. He does not find him until the following spring when they both return to St. Alban's. *Newbery Medal.*

841. Wright, Randall. *Hunchback.* Holt, 2004. 256pp. ISBN 978-0-8050-7232-7. Grades 6–9.

Hodge, 14, is a hunchback orphan in Castle Marlby, where the royal family used to vacation but no longer visits. Hodge wants to serve a prince, but he mainly cleans privies. Then Prince Leo—who is either a captive or in hiding—appears, befriends Hodge, and teaches him to play chess. The attention so pleases Hodge that Hodge fights his own brother Fleet when Fleet warns him that Prince Leo is a traitor to King Alfred. Hodge then helps Prince Leo escape, and after seeing the awful battles, realizes that Prince Leo has only used him for his own needs. When Hodge returns to the castle, Fleet has left to find him, and on his journey to find Fleet, Hodge helps save the kingdom.

History

842. Adkins, Jan. *What If You Met a Knight? An Historical Voyage of Yeomanly Speculation.* Roaring Brook, 2006. 32pp. ISBN 978-1-59643-148-5. Grades 4–8.

This book covers knighthood's myths and realities. It shows knights supervising and protecting their peasants, tithing, settling disputes, administering justice, managing their fields, and providing food and fuel for the winter. Illustrations enhance the text.

843. Aliki. *A Medieval Feast.* Trophy, 1986. Paper ISBN 978-0-06-446050-7. Grades 1–5.

When the king decides to visit Camdenton Manor with his retinue, the manor folk must prepare food. Readers will learn about the types of food that were served and the customs for serving it. *Notable Trade Books in the Field of Social Studies, Booklist Children's Editor's Choices,* and *School Library Journal Best Book.*

844. Berger, Melvin, and Gilda Berger. *The Real Vikings: Craftsmen, Traders, and Fearsome Raiders.* National Geographic, 2003. 64pp. ISBN 978-0-7922-5132-3. Grades 4–6.

Although history remembers the fierceness of Vikings in their raids, there were other aspects to Viking life. This book shows that the Vikings were skilled craftsmen, good farmers, successful merchants, and believers in independence and democracy. They built beautiful sailing ships that allowed them to rule the seas for more than three hundred years and to travel to Russia, North America, and the Middle East. Unfortunately, they left few written records. Illustrations and photographs highlight the text. Maps, Further Reading, Time Line, Web Sites, Bibliography, and Index.

845. Bhote, Tehmina. *Medieval Feasts and Banquets: Food, Drink, and Celebration in the Middle Ages.* (Library of the Middle Ages) Rosen, 2003. 64pp. ISBN 978-0-8239-3993-0. Grades 5–8.

The class system of the Middle Ages dictated the lives of all. This book looks at the production and distribution of food, cooking procedures, famine, types of food, how people ate and drank, and how they celebrated with ceremonies and entertainment.

Everyone, regardless of class, could enjoy feasts and banquets. Illustrations highlight the text. Glossary, Bibliography, Further Reading, Web Sites, and Index.

846. Binns, Tristan Boyer. *The Vikings.* Illustrated by Ross Watton. (Ancient Civilizations) Compass Point, 2006. 32pp. ISBN 978-0-7565-1678-9; paper ISBN 978-0-7565-1760-1. Grades 4–6.

An introduction to the history of the Vikings—those who explored the seas and invaded other lands as well as those who stayed at home. It includes background on their beliefs, traditions, explorations, legends, and culture. Maps and illustrations complement the text.

847. Bloch, R. Howard. *A Needle in the Right Hand of God: The Norman Conquest of 1066 and the Making and Meaning of the Bayeux Tapestry.* Random House, 2006. 230pp. ISBN 978-1-4000-6549-3. Grades YA.

All about the creation and history of the Bayeux Tapestry, which depicts the Norman Conquest of Britain in 1066. This famous piece of embroidery—230 feet long and about 20 inches high—has much mystery behind it. No one is certain who made it or why or even when it was made although speculation places it around 1080. Its images reflect medieval life and blend French, Anglo-Saxon, and Scandinavian cultures before William conquered Harold of England at the Battle of Hastings. Bloch suggests that the piece notes the history of nationalism in Europe. Notes and Index.

848. Buller, Laura. *Vikings.* Illustrated by Rich Cando. (History Dudes) DK, 2007. 64pp. ISBN 978-0-7566-2940-3. Grades 4 up.

Brief biographies of important Vikings include figures such as Lief Erickson as well as those known through legend or myth (such as Bjorn the Beserk). In cartoon format, filled with puns and slang, the book also discusses the runic writing system that the Vikings used. Chronology and Index.

849. Cahill, Thomas. *How the Irish Saved Civilization: The Untold Story of Ireland's Heroic Role from the Fall of Rome to the Rise of Medieval Europe.* Doubleday, 1995. 246pp. 8 CDs. ISBN 978-0-385-41848-5; Anchor, 1996. paper ISBN 978-0-385-41849-2. Grades YA.

Saint Patrick, Columcille, and other monks kept the scholarship of the Greeks and Romans alive by copying manuscripts they found in Europe. Their work ensured that civilization continued past the Dark Ages. Columbanus established more than sixty monasteries in which men worked during the 7th through 9th centuries. They made Ireland a place of leadership in the world, a position that Ireland held until the Vikings invaded in the 11th century. Bibliography, Chronology, and Index.

850. Cahill, Thomas. *Mysteries of the Middle Ages: The Rise of Feminism, Science and Art from the Cults of Catholic Europe.* Anchor, 2008. ISBN 978-0-385-49556-1. Grades YA.

This examination of the Middle Ages contains nine chapters covering the transformation of the Romans into Italians; the value of religion and women with Hildegarde von Bingen; Aquitaine and Saint Francis of Assisi; and the importance of Paris, Padua, Florence, and Ravenna. It covers the rebirth of scholarship, art, literature, philosophy, and science. Illustrations enhance the text. Bibliography, Notes, and Index.

851. Charman, Andrew. *Life and Times in the Viking World.* Kingfisher, 2007. 32pp. Paper ISBN 978-0-7534-6152-5. Grades 1–5.

Simple text examines life in the Viking world. Two-page spreads cover transportation, clothing, cooking, food and drink, trading, homes, and daily living. Illustrations complement the text.

852. Corbishley, Mike. *The Middle Ages.* Chelsea House, 2007. 96pp. ISBN 978-0-8160-6825-8. Grades 6–9.

Beginning with an overview of medieval Europe, this book then covers the barbarians, the Crusades, and empires of the time. Sidebars feature information on topics such as stained glass design and the Bayeux Tapestry, which illustrates William's landing in England in 1066. The second section covers the history of each region of Europe, including Scandinavia and Russia. Informative color illustrations augment the text. Bibliography, Chronology, Glossary, Gazetteer, and Index.

853. Crompton, Samuel Willard. *The Third Crusade: Richard the Lionhearted vs. Saladin.* (Great Battles Through the Ages) Chelsea, 2004. 112pp. ISBN 978-0-7910-7437-4. Grades 6 up.

During the third Crusade, 1189–1192, Richard I of England (called the Lionhearted) fought Saladin, the great Muslim leader. The author briefly discusses the course of the first two Crusades and indicates that the Christians slaughtered many people when they went into Jerusalem in 1099. When Saladin retook the city in 1187, the majority of the Christian population was ransomed. Richard took Acre and slaughtered more than three thousand civilian prisoners. A contrast in the approaches and personalities of these two men reveals that Richard did not have the gentlemanly qualities that Saladin exhibited. Photographs augment the text. Chronology, Bibliography, and Index.

854. Currie, Stephen. *Miracles, Saints, and Pagan Superstition: The Medieval Mind.* (Lucent Library of Historical Eras) Lucent, 2006. 104pp. ISBN 978-1-59018-861-3. Grades 7 up.

Using primary and secondary sources, the author examines the cultural, political, and social events of the medieval period. He discusses medieval thinking that allowed the growth of Christianity and the belief in miracles, prayers, and relics. The same mindset also accepted magic and superstition. Such aspects reveal why the Crusades might have taken place. Illustrations augment the text. Bibliography and Index.

855. Galloway, Priscilla. *Archers, Alchemists, and 98 Other Medieval Jobs You Might Have Loved or Loathed.* Illustrated by Martha Newbigging. Annick, 2003. ISBN 978-1-55037-811-5; paper ISBN 978-1-55037-810-8. Grades 4–6.

The author presents one hundred medieval careers and additional information about medieval life for nobles, clergy, specialists, peasants, and women between 1000 and 1500. The book also describes how one would have chosen a career. The categories include "bread-and-butter" trade jobs, religious jobs, castle jobs such as falconer and archer, "wonder workers" such as stonemasons and goldsmiths, "life-and-death" jobs including surgeon and apothecary, "sit-down" jobs such as alchemist and philosopher, artistic jobs including painter and poet, dirty jobs such as bathhouse attendant and witch hunter, law-and-order jobs such as bandit and hangman, and traveling jobs including minstrel and explorer. Further Reading, Web Sites, and Index. *Voice of Youth Advocates Nonfiction Honor List.*

856. Gibbons, Gail. *Knights in Shining Armor.*   Little Brown, 1998. Unpaged. Paper ISBN 978-0-316-30038-4. Grades K–3.

Called *ritters* in Germany, *chevaliers* in France, and *caballeros* in Spain, knights fought in Europe during the Middle Ages from 500 to 1500. Men trained for many years before they could reach the rank of knight, using specific tactics and weapons that are illustrated in the text. Brief comments about King Arthur and his favorite knights are included, as well as brief retellings of three different dragon legends.

857. Gravett, Christopher. *Knight.*   Illustrated by Geoff Dann. DK, 2004. 72pp. ISBN 978-0-7566-0695-4. Grades 4–8.

Text and photographs give detailed information about the history of knights, their training, their armor, and the rituals of knighthood. Two-page spreads include topics such as the first knights, the Normans, armor, arms, horses, castles at war and under siege, battle, castles in peace, lords and ladies of the manor, chivalry, tournaments and jousts, foot combat, heraldry, hunting and hawking, faith and pilgrimage, the Crusades, the Knights of Christ, the Knights of the Rising Sun, professional knights, and the decline of chivalry by the 17th century. Index.

858. Gravett, Christopher. *Knight: Noble Warrior of England 1200–1600.*   Osprey, 2008. 288pp. ISBN 978-1-846033-42-1. Grades 5 up.

A look at the life of the medieval knight during times of war and times of peace, with details of clothing and armor, weapons, castles, hunting, tournaments, chivalry, and so forth.

859. Gravett, Christopher. *Real Knights: Over 20 True Stories of Chivalrous Deeds.* Enchanted Lion, 2005. 48pp. ISBN 978-1-59270-034-9. Grades 4–6.

Five sections cover the topics of medieval knights, the Crusades, chivalry, the Hundred Years War, and other aspects of knighthood. Among those famous names identified with knights are El Cid, Braveheart, Richard the Lionheart, and Joan of Arc. Some that are not so famous are Sir John Chandos, who had a lance thrust in his eye, William Marshal with his helmet hammered from his head, and Henry of Monmouth, who had surgery to have an arrow removed from his cheekbone. A section on tournaments, including information on food and logistics for all those attending, affords an unusual approach to knighthood. Glossary and Index.

860. Hamilton, Janice. *The Norman Conquest of England.*   (Pivotal Moments in History) Twenty First Century, 2007. 160pp. ISBN 978-0-8225-5902-3. Grades 7–9.

A valuable overview of the Norman conquest of England. It includes background about the events that led to the Norman conquest under William, Duke of Normandy, in 1066 and his defeat of Harold at the Battle of Hastings. England's rulers became French-speaking, and the country was allied more with the continent than with Scandinavia. It also began a rivalry with France that continued for more than eight centuries. Photographs, sidebars, maps, and illustrations highlight the text. Bibliography, Glossary, Chronology, Further Reading, Web Sites, and Index.

861. Hamilton, John. *Knights and Heroes.*   (Fantasy and Folklore) ABDO, 2005. 32pp. ISBN 978-1-59679-336-1. Grades 4–6.

The author examines the historical and legendary aspects of medieval life. This book in the Fantasy and Folklore series covers knights and heroes of the time. References to

King Arthur are both historical and legendary. The book includes background on authors of fantasy works as well. Photographs augment the text. Glossary and Index.

862. Hamilton, John. *Weapons of Fantasy and Folklore.* (Fantasy and Folklore) ABDO, 2005. 32pp. ISBN 978-1-59679-340-8. Grades 4–6.

All about the historical and legendary aspects of weapons, this book discusses legends such as King Arthur and his famous sword and Saint George fighting the dragon. Photographs augment the text. Glossary and Index.

863. Hanawalt, Barbara A. *Growing Up in Medieval London: The Experience of Childhood in History.* Oxford, 1995. 300pp. Paper ISBN 978-0-19-509384-1. Grades YA.

Using sources such as court documents, wills, advice manuals, and literary works, Hanawalt argues that childhood and adolescence in 13th- and 14th-century London were recognized as distinct stages in the lives of young people. She looks at birth, the establishment of social and family connections, social and educational activities during early childhood, the broader range of connections in later childhood, and adolescence as the last stage before adulthood. She includes London orphans and their situations, apprentices and their relationships to their masters, children as servants, and the upper class. Bibliography and Index.

864. Hanel, Rachael. *Knights.* (Fearsome Fighters) Creative Education, 2007. 48pp. ISBN 978-1-58341-536-8. Grades 5–8.

Hanel looks at knights as warriors and details their weapons, armor, and fighting techniques and includes background on the concept of chivalry and the use of armies during the medieval period. Archival reproductions augment the text. Bibliography, Glossary, and Index.

865. Hilliam, David. *Castles and Cathedrals.* (Library of the Middle Ages) Rosen, 2003. 64pp. ISBN 978-0-8239-3990-9. Grades 5–8.

Many castles were built in Europe after 1000 and the invasion of William the Conqueror. This book examines the designs of castles, the roles of castles in peace and war, famous castles throughout history, the role of cathedrals in the lives of the people, and the great cathedrals in European history. Illustrations highlight the text. Glossary, Bibliography, Further Reading, Web Sites, and Index.

866. Hilliam, David. *Richard the Lionheart and the Third Crusade: The English King Confronts Saladin in A.D. 1191.* (Library of the Middle Ages) Rosen, 2003. 64pp. ISBN 978-0-8239-4213-8. Grades 5–8.

Richard the Lionheart and King Philip of France led a crusade in 1191 to the Holy Land. They quarreled, leaving Jerusalem in Saladin's control. Richard made a truce with Saladin and left, but while Richard traveled home, the Duke of Austria captured and imprisoned him. This book examines the first crusades, Richard's crusade, the armies of his crusade in Jerusalem, and his departure from the Holy Land. Illustrations highlight the text. Glossary, Bibliography, Further Reading, Web Sites, and Index.

867. Hoggard, Brian. *Crusader Castles: Christian Fortresses in the Middle East.* (Library of the Middle Ages) Rosen, 2003. 64pp. ISBN 978-0-8239-4212-1. Grades 5–8.

The author notes that the three groups responsible for building the crusader castles were the new kings in Jerusalem, the knights and lords who participated in the crusades, and the warrior-monks of the military orders known as the Knights Templar and the Knights Hospitaller. These groups built castles for different reasons, but life in the different castles was similar. The castles served as protection during war, and some survive (although many in ruins) today, with the Krak des Chevaliers probably being the most impressive. Persons discussed include the king of Jerusalem, Baldwin I; Godfrey de Bouillon; Sultan Qala'un, and Pope Urban III. Illustrations highlight the text. Glossary, Bibliography, Further Reading, Web Sites, and Index.

868. Hopkins, Andrea. *Damsels Not in Distress: The True Story of Women in Medieval Times.* (Library of the Middle Ages) Rosen, 2003. 64pp. ISBN 978-0-8239-3992-3. Grades 5–8.

This book about roles of women in the Middle Ages covers the topics of women in the home, women and power, women in the church, and women in business. Some were doctors, writers, poets, and businesspersons who worked equally with their husbands rather than as lesser partners. Ancillary topics include marriage, motherhood, nobility, wealth, education, and literacy. Some of the women noted are Eleanor of Aquitaine, Jacoba Felicia, Hilda of Whitby, Hildegard of Bingen, and Saint Clara. Illustrations highlight the text. Glossary, Bibliography, Further Reading, Web Sites, and Index.

869. Hopkins, Andrea. *Tournaments and Jousts: Training for War in Medieval Times.* (Library of the Middle Ages) Rosen, 2003. 64pp. ISBN 978-0-8239-3994-7. Grades 5–8.

The author stresses the importance of tournaments and jousts to people in the Middle Ages. The tournament started as a way for men to gather and display their talents. To stage a tournament—with places for the knights and their attendants to stay and eat as well as groom and feed their horses—was a huge organizational effort and required money from various sources. When men were not needed to protect their lords, they entered tournaments for social reasons. Dress, customs, armor, participants, and other topics complete the discussion. Illustrations highlight the text. Glossary, Bibliography, Further Reading, Web Sites, and Index.

870. Jovinelly, Joann, and Jason Netelkos. *The Crafts and Culture of a Medieval Monastery.* (Crafts of the Middle Ages) Rosen, 2006. 2006pp. ISBN 978-1-4042-0759-2. Grades 4–8.

Following a discussion of the culture in a medieval monastery, the text describes various aspects of a monk's life such as his diet and his work, typically in a scriptorium or a garden. Crafts include a hornbook, prayer beads, and an illuminated manuscript. Photographs highlight the text. Glossary, Chronology, Further Reading, Web Sites, and Index.

871. Jovinelly, Joann, and Jason Netelkos. *The Crafts and Culture of a Medieval Town.* (Crafts of the Middle Ages) Rosen, 2006. 2006pp. ISBN 978-1-4042-0761-5. Grades 4–8.

Following a discussion of the culture in a medieval town, the text describes various aspects of a peasant's life, including diet, living conditions, and health. Crafts to make include pretzels and a plague mask. Photographs embellish the text. Glossary, Chronology, Further Reading, Web Sites, and Index.

872. Koestler-Grack, Rachel A. *Eleanor of Aquitaine: Heroine of the Middle Ages.* (Makers of the Middle Ages and Renaissance) Chelsea, 2005. 158pp. ISBN 978-0-7910-8633-9. Grades 6 up.

Eleanor of Aquitaine (1122?–1204) married two kings, France's King Louis VII and England's Henry II, and had two sons who became kings: Richard the Lionheart and

King John. This book examines her childhood, her numerous struggles and conquests, and the political aspects of her times. She was a strong woman who went on a crusade, helped free her son Richard when the enemy captured and imprisoned him, and survived when her husband had her imprisoned. Photographs and illustrations highlight the text. Bibliography, Glossary, Chronology, Web Sites, and Index.

873. Konstam, Angus. *Historical Atlas of the Crusades.* Mecury, 2004. 192pp. ISBN 978-1-904668-00-8. Grades YA.

In November 1095 Pope Urban II decided that Christian rulers and knights in Europe should drive all Muslims from the Holy Land, and that any crusader who died in the cause would be rewarded in heaven. This atlas considers the causes, developments, and people of the conflict that lasted three centuries, ending finally in 1291. During the Crusades, the unsophisticated Frankish states in Western Europe met the somewhat civilized Muslim world, resulting in more interest in the spoils of war than religious belief. Although primarily an atlas, the text covers the history of the six separate Crusades by examining events leading to the crusade, those involved, and the outcome. The nine chapters are "Jerusalem the Holy," "All the Powers of Christendom: The Crusader's World," "God Wills It: The First Crusade," "Outremer: Holy Kingdom," "Jihad: The Islamic Response," "Richard and Saladin: The Third Crusade," "The Sword and the Scimitar: Crusading Warfare," "The Fourth Crusade," and "The Last Crusaders." Introduction, Color illustrations, Maps, Chronology, Glossary and Genealogy Tables, and Index.

874. Konstam, Angus. *Historical Atlas of the Viking World.* Mercury, 2004. 192pp. ISBN 978-1-904668-12-1. Grades YA.

When the longships first appeared on the North Sea coast of England around 800, they brought fierce warriors who conquered the people and established settlements. The Vikings based their raids from Orkney, Ireland, and the Isle of Man as they prepared to create Scandinavian colonies in Normandy, England, and Ireland. Some went to America; others to Africa and Russia. This atlas, arranged thematically, uses archaeological evidence along with Norse saga and mythology to present the achievements and developments of Viking culture. The ten chapters are "The Scandinavian Homeland," "Viking Religious Belief," "Viking Ships," "The Sea Raiders," "Viking Art and Literature," "Exploring the Northern Seas," "Viking Warriors," "A Scandinavian Empire," "Rivers to the East," and "Last of the Vikings." Introduction, Color illustrations, Maps, Chronology, Glossary and Genealogy Tables, and Index.

875. Lace, William W. *The Unholy Crusade: The Ransacking of Medieval Constantinople.* (Lucent Library of Historical Eras) Lucent, 2006. ISBN 978-1-59018-846-0. Grades 7 up.

The author examines the planning of the fourth Crusade, its execution from 1202 to 1204, and Constantinople's ultimate destruction. Primary sources offer valuable insight into this process. Leaders expected to leave Venice and conquer Muslim Jerusalem by invading via Egypt. Instead, the crusaders went to the Eastern Orthodox (Christian) city of Constantinople because many were not particularly concerned about these plans. They first attacked Zara and then went to Constantinople, where they demanded that Isaac II be restored to the throne. The citizens were uninterested in their requests so the crusaders ransacked the city. Illustrations highlight the text. Bibliography, Illustrations, and Index.

876. Langley, Andrew. *Medieval Life.* Illustrated by Geoff Dann and Geoff Brightling. DK, 2004. 72pp. ISBN 978-0-7566-0705-0. Grades 5–8.

The profuse illustrations augmenting the text give an overview of medieval life. Topics covered in the two-page spreads include the structure of society, daily life in different societal levels, the role and influence of religion, health and disease, jobs, and culture and the arts. Index.

877. Levy, Debbie. *The Signing of the Magna Carta.* (Pivotal Moments in History) Twenty First Century, 2007. 160pp. ISBN 978-0-8225-5917-7. Grades 7–9.

A valuable overview of the events that led to the 1215 signing of the treaty that became the Magna Carta. Money and property were central to the document, since the king's power was limited, an idea threatening to both the church and secular institutions. The Magna Carta also established rights of the individual, a concept that was adopted by those who wrote the Constitution of the United States. Photographs, sidebars, maps, and illustrations highlight the text. Bibliography, Glossary, Chronology, Further Reading, Web Sites, and Index.

878. Macaulay, David. *Castle.* Walter Lorraine, 1977. 80pp. ISBN 978-0-395-25784-5; 1982. paper ISBN 978-0-395-32920-7. Grades 5 up.

The castle that Macaulay portrays is imaginary but is based on the concept, construction process, and physical appearance of several castles built to help the English conquer Wales between 1277 and 1305. These castles, and the towns around them, were the culmination of more than two centuries of development in Europe and the Holy Land of the castle as a way to keep military forces together. Illustrations and Glossary. *Caldecott Honor Book.*

879. Macaulay, David. *Cathedral: The Story of Its Construction.* Walter Lorraine, 1973. 77pp. ISBN 978-0-395-17513-2; 1981. paper ISBN 978-0-395-31668-9. Grades 3 up.

Macaulay builds an imaginary cathedral based on the French cathedral at Reims. He discusses the people's reasons for wanting a cathedral, how they got the money to build it, and how long it took them to complete such a huge building in the 12th century. Illustrations and diagrams reveal what an enormous accomplishment building a cathedral was—and also the prestige that a cathedral brought to the village in which it was constructed.

880. MacDonald, Fiona. *The World in the Time of Charlemagne: AD 700–900.* (The World in the Time of) Facts on File, 2000. 48pp. ISBN 978-0-7910-6030-8. Grades 6–9.

A discussion of the reign and life of Charlemagne (742–814) and the world around him. This book includes background material about his achievements along with important developments in science, religion, education, and the arts during the two hundred years in which his influence was greatest. Photographs, Reproductions, and Index.

881. Margeson, Susan M. *Viking.* Illustrated by Peter Anderson. (Eyewitness Books) DK, 2005. 63pp. ISBN 978-0-7566-1095-1. Grades 4–6.

Two-page spreads, illustrated with photographs and drawings, cover who the Vikings were; their warships, warriors, and weapons; how they terrorized both West and East; their forts; their kings, freemen, women, and children; their games; their gods, legends, and burials; Viking runes; and the Jelling memorial stone. Index.

882. Marston, Elsa. *The Byzantine Empire.* (Cultures of the Past) Benchmark, 2002. 80pp. ISBN 978-0-7614-1495-7. Grades YA.

The Byzantine Empire rose out of the demise of the Roman Empire and from Constantinople; it ruled from 330 to 1453, when the Ottoman Turks took power. This book discusses the culture, religion, history, and influences of this empire. Illustrations, Time Line, Web Sites, Bibliography, Glossary, and Index.

883. Mulvihill, Margaret. *Viking Longboats.* Illustrated by Tony Smith. (Hallmarks of History) Stargazer, 2007. 32pp. ISBN 978-1-59604-120-2. Grades 4–6.

Background on the construction and use of Viking longboats. A chart lists comparative dates of events in Africa, Asia, America, and Europe. Photographs and illustrations highlight the text. Chronology and Index.

884. Orme, Nicholas. *Medieval Children.* Yale, 2003. 400pp. Paper ISBN 978-0-300-09754-2. Grades YA.

This scholarly text looks at the lives of children in medieval England from birth to adolescence. Among the topics covered are family life, danger, death, songs and rhymes, play, church, reading, and maturing. After defining the period of childhood during this time period, Orme covers the lives of children in different social and economic classes. Children during this time had to marry earlier, and untimely deaths from war, plague, and other diseases and disasters were common. Illustrations enhance the text. Bibliography, Notes, and Index.

885. Platt, Richard. *Castle.* Illustrated by Stephen Biesty. DK, 2007. 65pp. ISBN 978-0-7566-2838-3. Grades 5–10.

Platt shows what happened both inside and outside a castle by examining it layer by layer and including intriguing bits of information. For example, lords needed to get licenses to crenellate (fortify) their castles. Subjects covered here are defense and siege, garrison and prisoners, building a castle, trades and skills, lifestyles of the lords, food and feasting, entertainment, livestock and produce, weapons, and punishments. Glossary and Index.

886. Rubenstein, Richard E. *Aristotle's Children: How Christians, Muslims, and Jews Rediscovered Ancient Wisdom and Illuminated the Middle Ages.* Harvest, 2004. 384pp. Paper ISBN 978-0-15-603009-0. Grades YA.

In 1136 Arab, Jewish, and Christian scholars gathered in Toledo, Spain, to translate and study the recently rediscovered works of Aristotle, including *De Anima* (*On the Soul*). Aristotle's ideas offered a scientific view of the world and the soul of man that interested all. The horrified Catholic Church denounced his position, and students rioted in Paris and Oxford. Rubenstein contends that Aristotle's ideas contribute to the huge contemporary dichotomy between reason and religion. He also answers the question of why works from the Greeks and Romans were lost and how they were found at the beginning of the Renaissance. Among the figures discussed are Abelard, Aquinas, Innocent II, Siger de Brambant, and Augustine. Notes, Select Bibliography, and Index.

887. Steele, Philip. *Castles.* Kingfisher, 1995. 63pp. ISBN 978-1-856975-47-6. Grades 3–7.

This presentation of castles includes fold-out cross-sections of a castle's interior. The chapters include information on the age during which castles were built, the towns surrounding a castle, castle defenses, all aspects of castle life (food, kitchens, fashions, hunting and hawking, jousting, heraldry), and what happened when a castle was besieged. Castles in History, Glossary, and Index.

888. Steele, Philip. *I Wonder Why Castles Had Moats: And Other Questions About Long Ago.* Illustrated by Tony Kenyon. Kingfisher, 2004. 32pp. Paper ISBN 978-0-7534-5809-9. Grades 4–6.

With questions and answers, the text and illustrations look at the Middle Ages using a humorous tone. Diagrams and Maps. Index.

889. Steer, Dugald. *Knight: A Noble Guide for Young Squires.* Illustrated by Milivoj Ceran and Neil Chapman. Candlewick, 2006. Unpaged. ISBN 978-0-7636-3062-1. Grades 2–6.

While being held captive by a French knight, Sir Geoffrey de Lance writes a letter to his son Hector telling him how to be a knight. He discusses weapons, horses, heraldry, jousting, castles, sieges, feasting, storytelling, and the knight's noble destiny. He hopes that one day Hector will come to free him. Flaps, pull-tabs, and pop-up illustrations enhance the text.

Biography and Collective Biography

890. Ashby, Ruth. *Caedmon's Song.* Illustrated by Bill Slavin. Eerdmans, 2006. 32pp. ISBN 978-0-8028-5241-0. Grades 2–3.

Caedmon, a cowherd on the grounds of Yorkshire Abbey in the 7th century, could never recite poems or stories by heart and thought he had no stories to tell. Then one night he had a dream and composed a hymn titled "Caedmon's Hymn." The import of the event led Caedmon to join the monastery and compose songs for the rest of his life. Acrylic illustrations complement the text.

891. Brooks, Polly Schoyer. *Queen Eleanor: Independent Spirit of the Medieval World.* Houghton, 1999. 176pp. Paper ISBN 978-0-395-98139-9. Grades 8 up.

Born in 1122, Eleanor inherited the Duchy of Aquitaine in 1137 and married Louis, who became the king of France. She dedicated the abbey church of St. Denis, the first Gothic building, in 1144; the next year, she had the first of her ten children. In 1147, she joined Louis on the Second Crusade. Four years later, she met Duke Henry of Normandy, whom she married the next year after divorcing Louis. In 1153, she bore the first of Henry's five sons, William. In 1154, Henry and Eleanor became king and queen of England, ruling from the borders of Scotland to the borders of Spain. In 1166, as a result of Henry's affair with "Fair Rosamond," Eleanor returned to France and established the court of love in Poitiers. Eleanor's sons, with her support, rebelled against Henry in 1173, and he imprisoned her. In 1189, Henry died, and Richard, as crowned king of England, freed his mother. In 1194, after Germans captured Richard, Eleanor traveled across the Alps to ransom him. In 1199, Richard died and John became king. Eleanor died in 1204 before the English made John sign the Magna Carta. *American Library Association Notable Book, School Library Journal Best Book, Notable Children's Trade Books in the Field of Social Studies,* and *Boston Globe–Horn Book Honor Book.*

892. Brown, Don. *Across a Dark and Wild Sea.* Roaring Brook, 2002. 32pp. ISBN 978-0-7613-2415-7. Grades K–3.

In the 6th century Columba or Columcille (521–597) was a prince in an Irish clan. He learned to read and write, which was unusual for the time. Then he became a monk. In love with a rare book of Bible psalms, he decided to make a copy. But the king declared that the copy also belonged to the owner of the original. A battle ensued, and Columba left Ireland for the island of Iona, where he and twelve others established a monastery. They continued to make copies of manuscripts. Eventually he became Saint Columba. Illustrations enhance the text. Bibliography.

893. Davenport, John C. *Dante: Poet, Author, and Proud Florentine.* (Makers of the Middle Ages and Renaissance) Chelsea, 2005. 158pp. ISBN 978-0-7910-8634-6. Grades 6 up.

This biography of Dante Alighieri (1265–1321) reveals the influence of his life and times on his religious thought and political understanding. Since his surroundings tended to be filled with untrustworthy people, his *Divine Comedy* shows a dark view of life with a lack of tolerance for immorality and a propensity to judge. The work covers his childhood and background along with his writing. Photographs and illustrations highlight the text. Bibliography, Glossary, Chronology, Notes, Further Reading, Web Sites, and Index.

894. Demi. *Marco Polo.* Marshall Cavendish, 2008. Unpaged. ISBN 978-0-7614-5433-5. Grades 3–7.

This biography of Marco Polo (1254–1323?) features brief text complemented with beautiful illustrations incorporating designs from the many places that Polo visited. From the age of 17, he traveled more than 33,000 miles from Venice to Kublai Kahn and China over a period of twenty-four years and recorded his experiences in his journal. In 1298 he dictated his memoirs while imprisoned for defending his city during a war with Genoa. Questions remain as to what is true and what Polo embellished. Notes and Map.

895. Freedman, Russell. *The Adventures of Marco Polo.* Illustrated by Bagram Ibatoulline. Arthur A. Levine, 2006. 63pp. ISBN 978-0-439-52394-3. Grades 5–9.

This biography takes readers on Polo's journey, beginning at his deathbed, where his family is asking him to confess his exaggerations. Some do not believe that Polo actually went to China or that he traveled all of the 24-year journey of 6,500 miles that included a stay at the court of Kublai Khan. Freedman traces the journey as Polo recorded it and offers varied views from scholarship about the veracity of Polo's claims. The illustrations recreate the art of both the East and the West, as appropriate to Polo's locale. Notes and Index. *Dorothy Canfield Fisher* (Vermont) nomination, *School Library Journal Best Children's Books,* and *Booklist Editor's Choice.*

896. Harkins, Susan Sales, and William H. Harkins. *The Life and Times of King Arthur: The Evolution of a Legend.* (Biography from Ancient Civilizations) Mitchell Lane, 2006. 48pp. ISBN 978-1-58415-513-3.

The authors cover the historical record of King Arthur and separate it from the legends that have surrounded his name. History suggests that Arthur was the son of a Roman soldier who stayed in Britain after the Romans left. As a warrior, Arthur was successful in defending the Britons against invaders, leading to Britain's Golden Age. Photographs and illustrations highlight the text. Bibliography, Chronology, Notes, Glossary, For Further Reading, Web Sites, and Index.

897. Kennedy, Robert F., Jr. *Saint Francis of Assisi: A Life of Joy.* Illustrated by Dennis Nolan. Hyperion, 2005. 31pp. ISBN 978-0-7868-1875-4. Grades 2–5.

The story of Saint Francis of Assisi (1182–1226), a man who rejected his wealth to serve the poor. He worked with animals and the environment and tried to console lepers. Realistic paintings complement the text.

898. McGowen, Tom. *William the Conqueror: Last Invader of England.* (Rulers of the Ancient World) Enslow, 2007. 160pp. ISBN 978-0-7660-2713-8. Grades 7–9.

The accomplishments of William the Conqueror when he crossed the channel into France and won the battle of Hastings in 1066. Photographs enhance the text. Chronology, Further Reading, Glossary, Notes, Web Sites, and Index.

899. Pandell, Karen. *Saint Francis Sings to Brother Sun: A Celebration of His Kinship with Nature.* Illustrated by Bijou Le Tord. Candlewick, 2005. 64pp. ISBN 978-0-7636-1563-5. Grades 3–7.

This biography of Saint Francis of Assisi (1182–1226) incorporates stanzas from "Canticle of Brother Sun" into background on his life and work. As the patron saint of ecology, Francis loved flora and fauna. The canticle and the facts support this conclusion. Illustrations enhance the text. Bibliography and Notes.

900. Sapet, Kerrily. *Eleanor of Aquitaine: Medieval Queen.* (European Queens) Morgan Reynolds, 2006. 192pp. ISBN 978-1-931798-90-7. Grades 6 up.

Eleanor of Aquitaine (1122?–1204) was trained to be the queen of France as wife of Louis VII, but she also became a queen of England when she married Henry II. When she rebelled against Henry II, he imprisoned her, but she outlived eight of her ten children before she died at the age of 82. Her sons Richard and John became kings of England after their father's death. She also participated in the second Crusade to Jerusalem. Illustrations augment the text. Bibliography, Notes, Chronology, Web Sites, Maps, and Index.

901. Spoto, Donald. *Reluctant Saint: The Life of Francis of Assisi.* Penguin, 2003. 256pp. Paper ISBN 978-0-14-219625-0. Grades YA.

In his biography of Saint Francis of Assisi (1182–1226), Spoto points out several similarities between Francis and Jesus. Both were probably born into wealthy families (carpenters were respected in Jesus' time), abandoned the world, fasted, and avoided comfort. Francis served the sick, unconcerned about his own health.

902. Streissguth, Thomas. *Richard the Lionheart: Crusader King of England.* (Rulers of the Ancient World) Enslow, 2007. 160pp. ISBN 978-0-7660-2714-5. Grades 7–9.

As the son of Henry II of England and Eleanor of Aquitaine, Richard the Lionheart won a reputation as a great leader because he led a crusade to the Holy Land. Photographs enhance the text. Chronology, Further Reading, Glossary, Notes, Web Sites, and Index.

903. Visconti, Guido. *Clare and Francis.* Illustrated by Bimba Landmann. Eerdmans, 2004. 40pp. ISBN 978-0-8028-5269-4. Grades 2–3.

Both Francis of Assisi (1182–1226) and Clare of Assisi (1194–1253) were wealthy and renounced their lives to found religious orders espousing peace, poverty, and humility. Growing up, however, they had problems—like other children—with family disagreements, wanting material pleasures, and longing to find their true selves. Clare nursed Francis through his final illness. Gilt illustrations complement the text. Chronology.

904. Whiting, Jim. *The Life and Times of Charlemagne.* (Biography from Ancient Civilizations) Mitchell Lane, 2005. 48pp. ISBN 978-1-58415-346-7. Grades 6–8.

Emperor Charlemagne (742–814), one of the world's great military leaders, became the ruler of the Franks in 768. Then he expanded his territory to most of western Europe and Pope Leo III crowned him emperor in 800. He had a keen interest in education for all and assembled Europe's brightest scholars at his capital, Aachen, Germany, where they contributed to the Carolinian Renaissance. Innovations in learning, architecture, and manuscript preservation occurred during this period of his reign. Photographs and illustrations highlight the text. Bibliography, Chronology, Notes, Glossary, For Further Reading, Web Sites, and Index.

905. Wildsmith, Brian. *Saint Francis.* Eerdmans, 1996. 34pp. ISBN 978-0-8028-5123-9. Grades 1–4.

As a young man at the beginning of the 13th century, Francis of Assisi was wealthy and thoughtless, but he gave up his social class and privileges to help others. This book looks at his love of nature and the legends that have evolved about his contributions. *American Bookseller's Pick of the Lists.*

906. Wilson, Derek Hinshaw. *Charlemagne.* Doubleday, 2006. 226pp. ISBN 978-0-385-51670-9; Vintage, 2007. paper ISBN 978-0-307-27480-9. Grades YA.

Charlemagne, son of King Pippin the Short and Bertrada of Laon, had the foresight to understand the value of education in improving a civilization. He led the Holy Roman Empire in uniting the nations of Europe. Pope Leo III crowned him emperor on December 25, 800, to revive this empire. Although he was ruthless when necessary, he was also wise, an excellent politician, and a devout Christian believer. However, he thought himself above Church rules in his sexual conquests and his cold-blooded murders. He began a revival of culture in western Europe. Bibliography and Index.

907. Winter, Jonah. *The Secret World of Hildegard.* Illustrated by Jeanette Winter. Arthur A. Levine, 2007. Unpaged. ISBN 978-0-439-50739-4. Grades 1–4.

Saint Hildegard von Bingen (1098–1179) went to live with holy women when her parents gave her to the Church. She lived in a room with one nun who taught her to sing, read, and pray. Later, she became the mistress of the abbey in which she lived. As a child she had headaches accompanied by visions. God directed her to share her visions, and she wrote about music, medical treatments, and religious ideas. She also had her nuns singing complex musical works that she composed. Her work influenced both a pope and a king. Bibliography.

Graphic Novels, Biographies, and Histories

908. Lassieur, Allison. *Lords of the Sea: The Vikings Explore the North Atlantic.* Illustrated by Charles Barnett, III and Ron Frenz. Graphic Library, 2005. 32pp. ISBN 978-0-7368-4974-6; paper ISBN 978-0-7368-9688-7. Grades 3–5.

The author looks at Viking exploration of the North Atlantic during the 10th and 11th centuries. Illustrations extend the text. Bibliography, Glossary, Further Reading, and Index.

909. Manning, Mick, and Brita Granström. *Viking Longship.* (Fly on the Wall) Frances Lincoln, 2007. 40pp. ISBN 978-1-8450-7465-4. Grades 2–4.

Ninth-century Vikings go raiding on a longship. When they return from Ireland with a group of prisoners, Viking men prepare the ship for another voyage. They train for battle while others farm. This book includes background on the Norse gods, the role of women, foods, feasting, and rituals for the burial of a brave warrior. Cartoon illustrations highlight the text.

910. Smalley, Roger. *The Adventures of Marco Polo.* Illustrated by Brian Bascle. Graphic Library, 2005. 32pp. ISBN 978-0-7368-3830-6; paper ISBN 978-0-7368-5240-1. Grades 3–5.

This introduction to the life of Italian explorer Marco Polo (1254–1323?) focuses on his trip to the court of Kublai Khan in China and his journey on the Silk Road. Illustrations extend the text. Glossary.

DVDs

911. *The Byzantine Empire.* (The Fall of Great Empires) Schlessinger, 2004. 30 min. ISBN 978-1-57225-950-8. Grades 9 up.

Upon the fall of the Roman Empire, a new empire rose in the East. From Constantinople—the "new Rome"—the Byzantine Empire's political and economic power extended from Spain across Mesopotamia and Asia to Egypt. A rift in the Roman Catholic Church in 1054 led to the establishment of the Eastern Christian Church. Although the Byzantine Empire lasted a thousand years, crusader attacks weakened Constantinople and it eventually fell to Ottoman armies.

912. *The Holy Roman Empire.* (The Fall of Great Empires) Schlessinger, 2004. 30 min. ISBN 978-1-4171-0662-2. Grades 9 up.

All about how the Holy Roman Empire began and grew, the problems resulting from its decline and fall, and its contributions to Western culture. Other topics include dealing with empire outposts, changes in populations, religious upheaval, and external threats. This program includes live-action footage, ancient art, recreations of important events, and computer simulations. The Holy Roman Empire once extended from Sicily to the North Sea. Among its rulers were Charlemagne and Napoleon and it lasted for more than one thousand years. The discovery of the New World, the Protestant Reformation, and the French Revolution in 1789 contributed to its final decline.

913. *The Middle Ages, Europe 1100–1450 A.D.: Back in Time.* (Hands-On Crafts for Kids Series 6) Chip Taylor Communications, 2003. 30 min. Grades 4–6.

This production begins with a narrator reading the list of materials appearing on the screen. Teachers construct objects from the Middle Ages—a windmill, a shield, a tournament flag, a shop sign, and a faux marble heraldry journal. Pre-made samples allow the film to flow. Among the materials used are wood plaques, precut wooden shapes, dowels, adhesive-backed foam, and screw eyes.

914. *Vikings and Explorers 800–1200 A.D.: Back in Time.* (Hands-On Crafts for Kids Series 6) Chip Taylor Communications, 2003. 30 min. Grades 4–6.

This production begins with a narrator reading the list of materials appearing on the screen. Teachers construct objects from the time of the Vikings. They include a coin, a weathervane, a longboat, a helmet, and a runic bracelet. Each item helps explain an important aspect of Viking culture.

Compact Discs

915. Cahill, Thomas. *How the Irish Saved Civilization: The Untold Story of Ireland's Heroic Role from the Fall of Rome to the Rise of Medieval Europe.* Narrated by Donal Donnelly. Random House Audio, 2003. 8 CDs. ISBN 978-0-7393-0965-0. Grades YA.

See entry 849.

916. Cahill, Thomas. *Mysteries of the Middle Ages: The Rise of Feminism, Science and Art from the Cults of Catholic Europe.* Narrated by John Lee. Random House Audio, 2006. 8 CDs. ISBN 978-0-7393-3431-7. Grades YA.

See entry 850.

917. Cooney, Caroline B. *Enter Three Witches: A Story of Macbeth.* Recorded Books, . 7 CDs; 7:30 hrs. ISBN 978-1-4281-6336-2. Grades 6 up.

See entry 726.

918. Cornwell, Bernard. *The Last Kingdom.* Narrated by Jamie Glover. (The Saxon Chronicles) HarperAudio, 2006. 5 CDs. ISBN 978-0-06-112657-4. Grades YA.

See entry 728.

919. Cornwell, Bernard. *Lords of the North.* (The Saxon Chronicles) HarperCollins, 2007. 5 CDs; 6 hrs. ISBN 978-0-06-115578-9. Grades YA.

See entry 729.

920. Cornwell, Bernard. *The Pale Horseman.* (The Saxon Chronicles) HarperAudio, 2006. 5 CDs; 6 hrs. ISBN 978-0-06-078748-6. Grades YA.

See entry 730.

921. Funke, Cornelia. *Igraine the Brave.* Narrated by Xanthe Elbrick. Translated by Anthea Bell. Listening Library, . 4 CDs; 5.35 hrs. ISBN 978-0-7393-5618-0. Grades 3–5.

See entry 745.

922. Grant, K. M. *Blood Red Horse.* Narrated by Maggie Mash. (De Granville Trilogy) Recorded Books, 2005. 9 CDs; 9.75 hrs. ISBN 978-1-4193-5606-3. Grades 6–9.

See entry 752.

923. Grant, K. M. *Green Jasper.* Narrated by Maggie Mash. (De Granville Trilogy) Recorded Books, 2006. 8 CDs; 8 hrs. ISBN 978-1-4193-9470-6. Grades 5–9.

See entry 754.

924. King, Susan Fraser. *Lady Macbeth.* Narrated by Wanda McCaddon. Tantor, 2008. 9 CDs; 11.5 hrs. ISBN 978-1-4001-0615-8. Grades YA.

See entry 763.

925. Peters, Ellis. *An Excellent Mystery.* Narrated by Vanessa Benjamin. (Brother Cadfael) Blackstone Audio, 2001. 7 CDs; ca. 7 hrs. ISBN 978-0-7861-9780-4. Grades YA.

See entry 809.

926. Peters, Ellis. *The Pilgrim of Hate.* Narrated by Vanessa Benjamin. (Brother Cadfael) Blackstone Audio, 2000. 7 CDs. ISBN 978-0-7861-9834-4. Grades YA.

To honor the bones of Saint Winifred in 1141, four years after the bones arrived at Shrewsbury, pilgrims come to the abbey. Two of them seem to have a connection with a knight at Winchester who supports Empress Maud. Brother Cadfael solves the mystery and realizes that one of the men is the husband of the empress.

927. Pyle, Howard. *Otto of the Silver Hand.* Narrated by Geoffrey Howard. Blackstone Audio, 2007. 2 CDs; 2.5 hrs. ISBN 978-0-7861-6061-7. Grades 5–9.

See entry 815.

928. Schlitz, Laura Amy. *Good Masters! Sweet Ladies! Voices from a Medieval Village.* Illustrated by Robert Byrd. Narrated by Various. Recorded Books, 2008. 2 CDs; 1.5 hrs. ISBN 978-1-4361-1963-4. Grades 4–8.

See entry 823.

929. Springer, Nancy. *Rowan Hood: Outlaw Girl of Sherwood Forest.* Narrated by Emily Gray. (Tales of Rowan Hood) Recorded Books, 2002. 4 CDs; 4 hrs. ISBN 978-1-4025-3407-2. Grades 5–7.

See entry 831.

930. Springer, Nancy. *Rowan Hood Returns: The Final Chapter.* Narrated by Emily Gray. (Tales of Rowan Hood) Recorded Books, 2005. 4 CDs; 4 hrs. ISBN 978-1-4193-4986-7. Grades 4–7.

See entry 832.

931. Sutcliff, Rosemary. *The Shining Company.*　Narrated by Johanna Ward. Blackstone Audio, 2001. 7 CDs. ISBN 978-0-7861-9726-2. Grades 6–10.

> See entry 836.

932. Yolen, Jane. *Sword of the Rightful King: A Novel of King Arthur.*　Narrated by Steven Crossley. Recorded Books, 2003. 7 CDs; 8 hrs. ISBN 978-1-4193-0189-6. Grades 5–8.

> Although Arthur has been king for four years in post-Roman Britain, many small fiefdoms question his authority—especially because Arthur's father, Uther Pendragon, usurped the throne. More importantly, his older half sister, North Witch Morgause, wants to unseat him because she believes that her own son Gawaine, 17, has as much right as Arthur to rule. At the same time, Gawaine is Arthur's friend and wants to remain so. To quell the questions, Merlinnus decides that Arthur should retrieve a sword from a stone to prove his right. Young Gawen, at Arthur's castle to train as a knight, makes himself indispensable to Merlinnus, only to eventually reveal himself as Guinevere, unhappy that Gawaine supposedly rejected her sister in marriage, and the rightful retriever of the sword from the stone. *Capitol Choices Noteworthy Titles* (Washington, D.C.).

EUROPE AND THE BRITISH ISLES, 1290–1491

Historical Fiction and Fantasy

933. Abalos, Rafael. *Grimpow: The Invisible Road.* Delacorte, 2007. 493pp. ISBN 978-0-385-73374-8. Grades 6–9.

In 14th-century Europe, Grimpow leaves his isolated forest home and discovers a stone in the pocket of a dead knight. He takes the stone and finds that he can read foreign languages and has wise insights about unusual topics. Pope Clement VI and King Philip IV of France want the mysterious treasure for themselves. And since they have hunted down many of the Knights Templar heretics and burned them at the stake, they are interested in Grimpow's fate.

934. Arrigan, Mary. *Mario's Angels: A Story About the Artist Giotto.* Frances Lincoln, 2006. 26pp. ISBN 978-1-84507-404-3. Grades K–2.

When Mario visits Giotto during the 14th century while Giotto is painting his *Nativity* in Padua, Mario offers to help. Giotto refuses but answers questions about his work and his style. He does admit to not knowing how to fill the sky behind Mary in the painting. During the night, Mario dreams about the picture, and he thinks of a way to help Giotto complete the fresco. He remembers his father playing with his sister, Bianca, and suggests that Giotto put angels there. Giotto uses Mario for his model. Illustrations enhance the text.

935. Avi. *Crispin: At the Edge of the World.* Hyperion, 2006. 234pp. ISBN 978-0-7868-5152-2; 2008. paper ISBN 978-1-4231-0305-9. Grades 5–9.

After Crispin discovers his identity in *Crispin: The Cross of Lead*, he and Bear search for freedom in 14th-century England. The Brotherhood hunts Bear and shoots him with an arrow. The only help Crispin can find is an old healer, Aude, who protects Troth, a young girl shunned by her village because she has a cleft lip. Aude heals Bear as well as she can before the village turns against her. Bear, Crispin, and Troth flee together across the choppy English Channel. There the British army makes them assist in an unwelcome battle. But they stay together, wanting to be free to do as they wish.

936. Avi. *Crispin: The Cross of Lead.* Hyperion, 2002. 262pp. ISBN 978-0-7868-0828-1; 2004. paper ISBN 978-0-7868-1658-3. Grades 3–7.

In 1377, Crispin, a serf known only as "Asta's Son," receives a lead cross from the village priest after his mother dies. The priest is murdered before he can tell the illiterate Crispin the words written on the cross. The late Lord Furnival's steward, Aycliffe, declares that Crispin is the murderer and condemns him as a "wolf's head"—someone who can be killed on sight. Crispin escapes and meets Bear, an entertainer who trains him to play the recorder and join his act as they travel around, just ahead of the searching steward. Eventually Crispin discovers that his father is Lord Furnival and that Aycliffe is trying to kill him so that Crispin cannot claim his rightful inheritance. *Children's Book Award, Rhode Island* nomination, *Nene Award* (Hawaii) nomination, *Land of Enchantment Book Award* (New Mexico) nomination, *Young Reader's Choice Award* (Pennsylvania) nomination, *Blue Spruce Young Adult Book Award* (Colorado) nomination, *Dorothy Canfield Fisher Children's Book Award* (Vermont) nomination, *William Allen White Children's Book Award* (Kansas) nomination, *Mark Twain Award* (Missouri) nomination, *Children's Book Award* (Massachusetts) nomination, *Great Stone Face Children's Book Award* (New Hampshire) nomination, *Children's Book Award* (North Carolina) nomination, *Pacific Northwest Young Reader's Award* nomination, *Bluegrass Award* (Kentucky) nomination, and *Newbery Medal*.

937. Banks, Lynne Reid. *The Dungeon.* HarperCollins, 2002. 288pp. ISBN 978-0-06-623782-4. Grades 7 up.

When Laird Archibald MacInnes kidnaps and kills Laird Bruce MacLennan's wife and children, MacLennan vows to get revenge and has a castle built with a dungeon in which to imprison a captured MacInnes. During construction, MacLennan decides to follow the route of Marco Polo and ends up as a mercenary soldier in China. After he meets the young slave Mudan (Peony), he buys her so that she can serve him tea. They eventually return to Scotland, and when MacLennan fails to defeat MacInnes, he proclaims that Peony is a witch and encloses her in the dungeon without food or water. Peony's friend, the stable boy Fin, finds her too late and trades her body for MacLennan's own imprisonment.

938. Beaufrand, Mary Jane. *Primavera.* Little, Brown, 2008. 260pp. ISBN 978-0-316-01644-5. Grades 6–9.

At birth, Flora Pazzi, now 14, was almost drowned for ugliness, and only her grandmother has cared for her in their Florentine household. Her classically beautiful older sister, Domenica, has been promised to the Medici son, Guiliano, and the family gives the Medici a Botticelli portrait of Domenica in honor of the union. Guiliano, however, has decided to enter the priesthood. Infuriated, Flora's father tries to assassinate him. He fails and is killed himself. Flora starts working in a goldsmith's shop without revealing her identity. And although she has taken flawed diamonds from her father and hidden them for her future escape, she and her friend, Emilio, have to use swordplay instead. Eventually artist Sandra Botticelli sees Flora's beauty and she becomes his model for his painting *Primavera*.

939. Bell, Hilari. *The Last Knight.* (Knight and Rogue) Eos, 2007. 368pp. ISBN 978-0-06-082503-4; 2008. paper ISBN 978-0-06-082505-8. Grades 7–9.

Sir Michael Sevenson, 18, decides that his calling in life is to be a knight errant, even though no knights have existed for more than two hundred years. His trusty squire, Fisk, 17, is as crafty as Sir Michael is courageous. They decide to rescue Lady Ceceil, a damsel in distress. After they free her, Sir Michael's father, Baron Seven Oaks, is furious. Lady Ceceil was being held for poisoning her husband. The two knights then have to find her, but she captures Sir Michael first. Fisk's job is to rescue Sir Michael, and Fisk does not believe in violence.

940. Bellairs, John. *The Trolley to Yesterday.* Illustrated by Edward Gorcy. (Johnny Dixon) Turtleback, 1989. 192pp. ISBN 978-0-606-04556-7. Grades 4–6.

In this historical fantasy, 13-year-old Johnny and his friend join Professor Childermass on a trolley to Egypt in 14 B.C.E. and to Constantinople, arriving in 1453. In Turkey, they try to save people during the invasion, but are unsuccessful. When they return to the 1950s, they are relieved to be alive.

941. Branford, Henrietta. *Fire, Bed and Bone.* Illustrated by Bryan Leister. Candlewick, 2006. 128pp. Paper ISBN 978-0-7636-2992-2. Grades 5–9.

An aging hound appreciates the humble family that gave her "fire, bed, and bone"— Rufus, his wife Comfort, and their children. The dog objectively tells the story of her masters during the Peasants' Revolt of 1381. When her owners are arrested for participating in the rebellion, the dog helps the children find another home, takes the baby's hat to the couple as they walk toward prison so they will know the child is safe, and views Rufus's unjust execution and the greedy miller's unlawful taking of Rufus's property. *Carnegie Medal* nomination, *Guardian Children's Fiction Prize*, *Nestlé Children's Book Prize* nomination, *Student Book Award* (Maine) nomination, *Capitol Choices Noteworthy Titles* (Washington, D.C.), and *Young Reader's Award* (Arizona) nomination.

942. Chandler, Pauline. *Warrior Girl: A Novel of Joan of Arc.* HarperCollins, 2006. 368pp. ISBN 978-0-06-084102-7. Grades 6 up.

Mariane de Courcey, a young mute who lives with her cousin Jehanne d'Arc (Joan of Arc) during the 15th century, fights beside her to liberate the French from the English. At first only a few people think that Jehanne is mad, and they believe she has faith. Mariane can barely communicate with Jehanne since Jehanne is illiterate and Mariane has not spoken since the English murdered her mother. Mariane's uncle, Sir Gaston de Louvier, hides from her the fact that she has inherited a manor, and eventually Mariane discovers that her uncle was involved in her mother's death. She searches for her deceased father's seal and takes it to the family estate to claim her right. When Jehanne is burned at the stake, her angel restores Mariane's voice.

943. Chevalier, Tracy. *The Lady and the Unicorn.* Penguin, 2003. 250pp. ISBN 978-0-00-714090-9; Plume, 2004. paper ISBN 978-0-452-28545-3. Grades YA.

In Paris in 1490 nobleman Jean Le Viste commissions Nicolas des Innocents to design six tapestries to celebrate Le Viste's status at court. Des Innocents focuses on the unicorn, a symbol of mystery and male virility. While the artist lives in the household of the nobleman, he creates chaos among the women—the mother, Geneviève; the daughter, Claude, who is determined that des Innocents will deflower her; a servant; and a lady-in-waiting. When he takes his designs north to Brussels to be woven, the Flemish master weaver Georges de la Chapelle uses the finest materials and stops everything to finish the intricate tapestries so they can reach their client in time. Des Innocents becomes involved with the weaver's blind daughter, Alienor, doomed to marry a wool dyer. Although the unicorn tapestries on display in the Cluny Museum in Paris seem to depict the seduction of a unicorn, the story of Nicolas des Innocents hides behind them. *School Library Journal Best Adult Books for Young Adults.*

944. Cornwell, Bernard. *The Archer's Tale.* (The Grail Quest) HarperCollins, 2005. 368pp. Paper ISBN 978-0-06-093576-4. Grades YA.

Archer Thomas of Hookton, bastard son of a priest, hears as his father lies dying that he has an aristocratic heritage. He joins King Edward III's army in 1343 as it prepares to attack France, Then Thomas rescues a woman known as Blackbird from Sir Simon Jekyll, who nearly rapes her during one of the raids into France. Jekyll, furious, becomes Thomas's rival as he continues to pursue her. Thomas has to leave the unit when he fails to kill Jekyll in an assassination attempt. He recovers, joins Blackbird, and returns to France before Blackbird leaves him for the Prince of Wales. At Crécy, they all meet, and Thomas must face his family's legacy and go on a quest for the Holy Grail.

945. Cupp, Bob. *The Edict: A Novel from the Beginnings of Golf.* Knopf, 2007. 225pp. ISBN 978-0-307-26645-3. Grades YA.

When King James II of Scotland declared on March 6, 1457, that Scots could no longer play either golf or football, he disrupted important activities. He wanted the men to spend more time on their archery skills so that they could defeat England. Caeril Paterstone, a young shepherd, wants to become the champion golfer, and he must compete against established winners. What comes to light is that his opponent needs the prize money to pay a bad wager and has convinced the king to declare the game illegal.

946. Cushman, Karen. *Catherine, Called Birdy.* Clarion, 1994. 174pp. ISBN 978-0-395-68186-2; Trophy, 1995. paper ISBN 978-0-06-440584-3. Grades 7–10.

At the suggestion of her favorite brother, 13-year-old Catherine writes in a diary about her life in 1290. Meanwhile, her father is trying to marry her to the man offering the most money for her hand. Each entry in Catherine's diary starts with the name of the saint celebrated on that day and the reason the person is a saint. Catherine thinks that all the women are saints because they kept their chastity and did things of which men approved. She hates women's work. One of her brothers loves drawing and the idea of fighting in the Crusades. Catherine's diary clearly shows the role of women in the Middle Ages. *American Library Association Best Books for Young Adults, Carl Sandburg Award for Literary Excellence, American Library Association Notable Children's Books, YASD Best Books for Young Adults, Booklist Children's Editors' Choice, Parenting Magazine Ten Best, School Library Journal Best Books, Golden Kite Award*, and *Newbery Honor Book.*

947. De Angeli, Marguerite. *The Door in the Wall: A Story of Medieval London.* Laurel-Leaf, 1998. Paper ISBN 978-0-440-22779-3. Grades 3–7.

In 1325 Robin becomes ill after his parents leave to serve King Edward III and his queen. A monk takes him to a hospice for his long recovery, patiently teaching him to carve, write, read, play music, and swim to strengthen his arms. They travel to meet Robin's parents, but soon after they arrive at the castle the Welsh attack it. Robin's ability to swim allows him to go for reinforcements, and ultimately the castle defenders defeat the Welsh soldiers. When his parents and King Edward III return, Edward knights Robin for his bravery. Robin has learned from the monk that one must do one's best with what one has. *Newbery Medal.*

948. Edwards, Julie Andrews, and Emma Walton Hamilton. *Simeon's Gift.* Illustrated by Gennady Spirin. HarperCollins, 2003. 40pp. ISBN 978-0-06-008914-6; Trophy, 2006. paper ISBN 978-0-06-008916-0. Grades K–4.

Simeon, a modest Renaissance musician, tries to find the perfect gift for Sorrel, the woman he loves. But on his quest, he hears many different rhythms and harmonies. So he returns home to let his inspiration come from within himself. Exquisite illustrations enhance the text.

949. Ellis, Deborah. *A Company of Fools.* Fitzhenry & Whiteside, 2004. 191pp. Paper ISBN 978-1-55041-721-0. Grades 5–8.

In 1348 Henri, a choir student at France's Abbey of St. Luc, remembers the year before, when the Black Death arrived in the country and Micah came to the abbey with Brother Bartholomew. Although unruly, Micah sings beautifully. To cheer up the people after the plague, Henri and Micah form the Company of Fools so they can sing music other than funeral dirges. The abbey prior decides to claim that Micah's singing can even cure the plague, and Micah believes him. But Henri gently shows him that other things are more important than Micah's singing. *Children's Book Award* (West Virginia) nomination.

950. Heuston, Kimberley. *Dante's Daughter.* Front Street, 2003. 307pp. ISBN 978-1-886910-97-3. Grades YA.

Antonia, or Bice, the daughter of Dante Alighieri (1265–1321), wants a stable place to live with her mother during her father's numerous political exiles. She tells the story of her life beginning in Florence in 1301 and ending in Ravenna in 1350. Among other talents, she prepares vellum and illuminates it while living with artistic relatives. After the Black Plague, she becomes a nun.

951. Hoffman, Mary. *The Falconer's Knot: A Story of Friars, Flirtation and Foul Play.* Bloomsbury, 2007. 297pp. ISBN 978-1-59990-056-8. Grades 7–10.

In Umbria in 1316, Silvano, 16, is attracted to a local merchant's wife, Angelica, and when her husband is murdered, he becomes a suspect. He hides in a Franciscan friary and begins making pigments for Simone Martini, a painter working in Assisi. Helping Silvano is a young novice at the adjoining abbey, Chiara. Chiara's brother has left her there because he has no money for her dowry. When two friars die and two other women become widows, the suspicion around Silvano increases. Silvano must find the criminal and an image in Simone's painting provides the necessary clue. *Booklist Editor's Choice.*

952. Karr, Kathleen. *Fortune's Fool.* Knopf, 2008. 224pp. ISBN 978-0-375-84816-2. Grades 6–9.

In Germany during the 14th century, court jester Conrad, 15, decides to escape from his employer, Otto the Witless. He takes with him a servant girl, Christa the Fair (disguised as a boy), and Grock, a "natural" fool. They also have Conrad's horse, Blackspur. As they travel through the countryside looking for steady work, Conrad uses his intelligence to keep them from leering monks and other travelers who would harm them.

953. Katz, Welwyn W. *Out of the Dark.* Groundwood, 2001. 192pp. Paper ISBN 978-0-88899-262-8. Grades 6–9.

Ben Elliot and his younger brother, Keith, have to move to their father's boyhood home in a tiny Newfoundland village after their mother dies. Ben hates leaving all his friends, and the children in the new town resent his attitude toward them. As he spends time in a nearby Viking settlement, Ben imagines that he is Tor, a Viking shipbuilder. His imaginings become reality in this historical fantasy when Ben finds himself inside the Viking world. *CLA Young Adult Book Award* nomination and *Mr. Christie's Book Awards* nomination.

954. Kelly, Eric. *The Trumpeter of Krakow.* Illustrated by Janina Domanska. Scholastic, 1968. 224pp. ISBN 978-0-02-750140-7; Aladdin, 1992. paper ISBN 978-0-689-71571-6. Grades 7 up.

In 1461 when Joseph is 15 years old his family's Ukrainian farm is burned down. He and his parents leave for Krakow, Poland. They begin their new lives with the help of people they meet, but the alchemists in their neighborhood almost destroy the family in their repeated attempts to make gold. Joseph's forefathers made a promise to the Polish king hundreds of years earlier, and his father wants to fulfill this promise to Casimir IV. He needs to do it before whoever destroyed their home finds them and the treasure they keep. *Newbery Medal.*

955. Konigsburg, E. L. *The Second Mrs. Gioconda.* Simon Pulse, 2005. 160pp. Paper ISBN 978-1-4169-0342-0. Grades 5–9.

Salai, a young thief of 13, is apprenticed to Leonardo da Vinci in Milan. He exhibits little talent except the ability to make Leonardo laugh. The two live with the merchant Duke Il Moro and his wife, Beatrice de Este. Because of Beatrice's kindness, both men come to greatly appreciate her character. Leonardo decides to paint her as the Mona Lisa rather than respond to others throughout Europe who want to commission him for their own portraits.

956. Little, Melanie. *The Apprentice's Masterpiece: A Story of Medieval Spain.* Annick, 2008. 310pp. ISBN 978-1-55451-117-4. Grades YA.

Ramon Benveniste, 15, belongs to a family of *conversos* (Jews who have had to convert to Christianity to save themselves) in Spain during the 15th-century Inquisition. Ramon is annoyed when his father treats their Muslim slave Amir like a family member. Amir's most treasured possession, Hafiz's poetry from the Koran, shows the beauty of illumination work and he shares his appreciation of it with Ramon's father. Ramon develops a relationship with a Christian girl that jeopardizes the family's safety. The choices the two teens make affect all their lives. *Capitol Choices Noteworthy Titles* (Washington, D.C.).

957. Paton Walsh, Jill. *The Emperor's Winding Sheet.* Front Street, 2004. 288pp. Paper ISBN 978-1-886910-88-1. Grades 7 up.

When Piers is shipwrecked off the coast of Constantinople, he ends up at the court of Emperor Constantine XI just before the Turks defeat him and end the Eastern Roman Empire in 1453. Because Piers comes to admire Constantine, he stays with the former emperor after the defeat, even though Constantine has given him his freedom.

958. Penman, Sharon Kay. *The Sunne in Splendour.* Griffin, 2008. 936pp. Paper ISBN 978-0-312-37593-5. Grades YA.

After 1483, Richard III's two nephews never again appeared in public, and people accused Richard of having them murdered in the Tower of London. Tudor historians also report that Richard was deformed, although the claim has never been substantiated. Richard seems to have loved and respected his older brother Edward IV and his wife, Anne, as well. This story covers medieval England and its wars from 1459 to 1483 between the houses of Lancaster and York.

959. Pyle, Howard. *Men of Iron.* Kessinger, 2004. 220pp. ISBN 978-1-4326-1764-6; paper ISBN 978-1-4179-3977-0. Grades YA.

In 1400, Henry IV is declared king of England when the evil Richard II is dethroned. Knights successful during Richard's reign plotted to kill Henry IV but failed. When Myles Falworth is 8 years old, his father is blinded at a joust. Lord Falworth had been a faithful counselor to Richard but has no influence on Henry, although he has never deceived him. Myles and his family survive, and when Myles is a young man he defends his family's and his father's honor.

960. Rees, Elizabeth M. *The Wedding: An Encounter with Jan van Eyck.* (Art Encounters) Watson-Guptill, 2005. 144pp. ISBN 978-0-8230-0407-2. Grades 8 up.

In 1433 Giovanna Cenami, 14, falls in love with Angelo, a stranger employed by Jan van Eyck as a troubador. Her father has arranged a marriage for her with a wealthy family friend, Giovanni Arnolfini. Because her father faces financial ruin, he moves the wedding date closer. Giovanna runs away with Angelo and jeopardizes the family's name and finances. The couple in van Eyck's famous painting on display at London's National Gallery, *The Arnolfini Portrait*, might be Giovanna and her unwanted husband, Giovanni.

961. Resnick, Mike. *Lady with an Alien: An Encounter with Leonardo da Vinci.* (Art Encounters) Watson-Guptill, 2005. 176pp. ISBN 978-0-8230-0323-5. Grades 6–9.

Mario Ravelli is guardian to a blue creature from 2523 that meets Leonardo da Vinci. Mario travels for a vacation to the time of Leonardo, and the two become friends. Leonardo's painting *Lady with an Ermine* has been considered his most beautiful, but viewers may wonder if the ermine is exactly what the title says. Possibly Leonardo acknowledged his friendship with Mario—and their talks about technology, art, and philosophy—in this painting.

962. Riley, Judith Merkle. *In Pursuit of the Green Lion: A Margaret of Ashbury Novel.* Three Rivers, 2006. 440pp. Paper ISBN 978-0-307-23788-0. Grades YA.

After Margaret becomes a widow in 1356, Brother Gregory's father kidnaps her and makes her marry Brother Gregory, whose secular name is Gilbert de Vilers. Margaret shocks Gilbert's family with her opinions, and when Gilbert's father expects him to beat Margaret and keep her quiet, Gilbert refuses. After Gilbert has to go to France to fight in the Hundred Years' War, Margaret goes to retrieve him, bargains for him with loaded dice, and brings him home.

963. Riley, Judith Merkle. *A Vision of Light: A Margaret of Ashbury Novel.* Three Rivers, 2006. 442pp. Paper ISBN 978-0-307-23787-3. Grades YA.

In 1355, when Margaret of Ashbury decides to write a book, she shocks Gregory, the friar whom she asks to be her chronicler. Since he needs food, he compromises his ethical beliefs and works with her. Margaret's incredible experiences include surviving the plague and inventing forceps to extract children during the birth process. She also has had many positive relationships with other people. After she becomes a wealthy widow, Gregory's practical father demands that she marry Gregory's brother, and Gregory finally realizes that he must marry her instead.

964. Russell, Christopher. *Dogboy.* Greenwillow, 2006. 259pp. ISBN 978-0-06-084116-4. Grades 5 up.

Orphaned kennel boy Brind, 12, goes to France with his master Sir Edmund and the hunting dogs he has raised at the beginning of the Hundred Years' War. He becomes separated from Sir Edmund and his dogs at the battle of Crécy and searches desperately for them, especially his best friend, Glaive, the pack's alpha male. During Brind's search, he meets 10-year-old Aurélie, who accompanies Brind in the forest. Adults along the way either thwart his search or exploit his abilities. *Great Stone Face Book Award* (New Hampshire) nomination.

965. Russell, Christopher. *Hunted.* Greenwillow, 2007. 254pp. ISBN 978-0-06-084119-5. Grades 5–9.

In this sequel to *Dogboy*, Brother Rohan blames Brind, the 14-year-old dogboy at Dowe Manor, and the maid Aurélie for the death of Sir Edmund's wife and banishes them. They discover that the plague killed her as it is killing many others. Just as they are to be killed themselves, an outlaw named Chanterelle comes into town and saves them. But she has her own reasons for rescuing them and they must escape from her too.

966. Scieszka, Jon. *Da Wild, Da Crazy, Da Vinci.* Illustrated by Adam McCauley. (Time Warp Trio) Penguin, 2004. 96pp. ISBN 978-0-670-05926-3; 2006. paper ISBN 978-0-14-240465-2. Grades 3-6.

Joe, with his friends Fred and Sam, wants to discover who made the Book that has allowed them to travel through time. Their search leads from Brooklyn to 16th-century Italy, where they meet Leonardo da Vinci, foil Machiavelli, and learn about Thomas Crapper. Da Vinci likes to pull practical jokes, and he entertains him with his wit. The 14th volume in the series.

967. Skelton, Matthew. *Endymion Spring.* Delacorte, 2006. 392pp. ISBN 978-0-385-73380-9; 2008. paper ISBN 978-0-385-73456-1. Grades 4–7.

Blake Winter, 12, reluctantly goes to Oxford with his academic mother and his bothersome sister. In the Bodleian Library, he happens to touch a book brought to England in 1453 by Johann Gutenberg's mute apprentice. The book contains the secrets of eternal wisdom and continually rewrites itself. Called *Endymion Spring*, it is written on a mythical leafdragon and is supposedly indestructible. Blake becomes involved in the mystery surrounding the evil Johann Fust in Gutenberg's shop and the contemporary "Person in Shadow," both closely intertwined with the book. *Soaring Eagle Book Award* (Wyoming) nomination.

968. Slatton, Traci L. *Immortal.* Delta, 2008. 515pp. Paper ISBN 978-0-385-33974-2. Grades YA.

In the 14th century, 9-year-old Luca Bastardy becomes the property of Silvanos, a cruel brothel owner who abducts him from the streets. After being held captive for many years, Luca kills the man. When the plague arrives in the city, he discovers that he has healing talents, longevity, and psychic abilities. Although the descendants of Silvanos pursue him, he meets many of Florence's major figures including Cosimo de' Medici, his grandson Lorenzo, Grotto, Leonardo da Vinci, Botticelli, alchemists, physicians, and philosophers. Finally he encounters the fanatic Savonarola.

969. Stevenson, Robert Louis. *The Black Arrow.* Amereon, 2003. 356pp. ISBN 978-0-8488-1182-2; 1st World Publishing, 2004. paper ISBN 978-1-59540-511-1. Grades 7 up.

Richard Shelton faces many obstacles as he tries to rescue his love, Joanna Sedley, during the War of the Roses in England during the 15th century. He once told her he was uninterested in marriage, but his attitude has changed. At the same time, he wants to find the murderer of his father, Sir Harry Shelton. As he continues to battle for Joanna, Dick comes to the conclusion that his own guardian, Sir Daniel Brackley, had his father killed. Because Dick suspects Brackley, Brackley turns against him, and Dick has no choice but to become a member of Ellis Duckworth's outlaw group in Tunstall Forest. Duckworth's weapon is a black arrow, and once Shelton joins the group, he is able to fulfill his desires.

970. Temple, Frances. *The Ramsay Scallop.* Trophy, 1995. 310pp. Paper ISBN 978-0-06-440601-7. Grades YA.

In 1299 in England, Elenor is 14 and waiting with trepidation for the return of her betrothed, Thomas, from the Crusade. When he arrives, Thomas is also unsure about marriage. The village priest sends them on a pilgrimage to Santiago de Compostela in Spain and the journey gives them time to get to know each other better. *Booklist Editor's Choice, Booklinks,* and *American Library Association Best Books for Young Adults.*

971. Yolen, Jane, and Robert J. Harris. *Girl in a Cage.* Speak, 2004. 234pp. Paper ISBN 978-0-14-240132-3. Grades 6–10.

In 1306 the king of England, Edward Longshanks, has Marjorie, 11, captured and placed in a cage in the town square after her father, Robert the Bruce, declares himself king of Scotland. Marjorie has to remember that she is a princess and try to survive the public humiliation. *Libraries' Blue Hen Award* (Delaware) nomination, *Read-Aloud Book Award* (Indiana) nomination, *Black Eyed Susan Book Award* (Maryland) nomination, *The Land of Enchantments Children's Book Award* (New Mexico) nomination, *Young Reader Award* (Nevada) nomination, *Young Readers Choice Book Award* (Pennsylvania) nomination, *Young Adult Reading Program* (South Dakota) nomination, *School Library Journal Best Books for Children,* and *Beehive Young Adult Book Award* (Utah) nomination.

History

972. Anderson, Dale. *Churches and Religion in the Middle Ages.* (World Almanac Library of the Middle Ages) World Almanac Library, 2006. 48pp. ISBN 978-0-8368-5892-1. Grades 5–8.

Some of the most beautiful churches in the western world were built in the Middle Ages. This volume examines the rise of cathedrals, the role of the people in their construction, traditions of worship, and religious beliefs. Illustrations highlight the text. Chronology, Time Line, Glossary, Further Reading, and Index.

973. Anderson, Dale. *Monks and Monasteries in the Middle Ages.* (World Almanac Library of the Middle Ages) World Almanac Library, 2005. 48pp. ISBN 978-0-8368-5897-6. Grades 5–8.

Monasticism developed during the Middle Ages. Concerned that the Church needed reform, both men and women entered cloistered life to become closer to God. This book examines the monastic life for priests and nuns, military orders with laws of celibacy, and the simple but busy life of the monastery. Illustrations highlight the text. Chronology, Time Line, Glossary, Further Reading, and Index.

974. Anderson, Mercedes Padrino. *Cities and Towns in the Middle Ages.* (World Almanac Library of the Middle Ages) World Almanac Library, 2006. 48pp. ISBN 978-0-8368-5893-8. Grades 5–8.

Readers will learn about life in the Middle Ages, the urban environment, social classes and social roles, town government, working life, and education. The author also discusses the daily life of the people, their entertainment, and the role of women in all levels of society. Illustrations highlight the text. Chronology, Time Line, Glossary, Further Reading, and Index.

975. Banfield, Susan. *Joan of Arc.* (World Leaders Past & Present) Chelsea House, 1985. 120pp. ISBN 978-1-59155-556-9. Grades 5 up.

With little formal education, Joan of Arc (ca. 1412–1431) helped the French overcome the English occupation. She heard voices from Saint Michael, Saint Catherine, and Saint Margaret, convincing her that she had to help France. She persuaded the Dauphin Charles to give her an army and in 1429 she led the French to victory at Orléans. She was eventually captured, imprisoned, tried, and executed. The Catholic Church declared her a saint in 1920, and her bravery is still legend. Photographs and reproductions enhance the text. Chronology, Further Reading, and Index.

976. Byrne, Joseph P. *Daily Life During the Black Death.* (Greenwood Press Daily Life Through History) Greenwood, 2006. 326pp. ISBN 978-0-313-33297-5. Grades YA.

This book about the Black Death (or the second pandemic of bubonic plague) from 1348 to 1722 includes twelve chapters about the medical school, the doctor's office, homes, churches, the bishop's palace, the monastery, the pest house, city hall, streets, booksellers, and the theater. People restricted their diets, took medicines, were quarantined, and took other measures to avoid and stop the plague. By looking at these areas of daily life, the reader begins to understand the religious, political, and economic aspects of the plague. The last major plague in Europe occurred in Marseille, France, from 1720 to 1722. Illustrations augment the text. Notes, Bibliography, Chronology, and Index.

977. Claybourne, Anna. *The Renaissance.* (Time Travel Guides) Raintree, 2007. 64pp. ISBN 978-1-4109-2910-5; paper ISBN 978-1-4109-2916-7. Grades 5–9.

Written as a travel guide to the Renaissance, this book relates the cultural and historical details of this time period. Using the concept of time travel, Claybourne imparts facts about key locations, relics and artifacts, and other salient aspects. Photographs, maps, and reproductions enhance the text. Glossary, Chronology, Further Reading, and Index.

978. Corrick, James A. *The Byzantine Empire.* (World History) Lucent, 2006. 109pp. ISBN 978-1-59018-837-8. Grades 7–10.

This book, with visual accents and boxed excerpts from primary and secondary sources, tells the interesting story of the Byzantines, who came to power after the fall of the Roman Empire. Bibliography, Chronology, Further Reading, and Index.

979. Crompton, Samuel Willard. *The Printing Press.* (Transforming Power of Technology) Chelsea House, 2004. 112pp. ISBN 978-0-7910-7451-0. Grades 7–10.

The author examines the changes that occurred after Johannes Gutenberg invented the printing press nearly seven hundred years ago. This innovation had an immediate impact on religion, government, and personal life, and was one of the most important inventions in history. Photographs augment the text. Chronology, Bibliography, and Index.

980. Feldman, Ruth Tenzer. *The Fall of Constantinople.* (Pivotal Moments in History) Twenty-First Century, 2008. 160pp. ISBN 978-0-8225-5918-4. Grades 7–9.

A number of factors led to the decline of the Byzantine Empire, according to the seven chapters of this book. Much discord and destruction in Constantinople and the area around it allowed the Ottomans to rise. Then in 1453, the Ottoman Turks seiged Constantinople and named the city Istanbul. Using primary sources, Feldman closely examines the economic, social, political, religious, and military factors in place for the final downfall. The text also examines why this city has been so important to so many empires through its history. Photographs and illustrations highlight the text. Bibliography, Chronology, Notes, Further Reading, Glossary, Web Sites, and Index.

981. Fritz, Jean. *Around the World in a Hundred Years: From Henry the Navigator to Magellan.* Illustrated by Anthony Bacon Venti. Puffin, 1998. 128pp. Paper ISBN 978-0-698-11638-2. Grades 4–7.

See entry 69.

982. Haywood, John. *Medieval Europe.* (Time Travel Guides) Raintree, 2007. 64pp. ISBN 978-1-4109-2909-9; paper ISBN 978-1-4109-2915-0. Grades 5–9.

Written as a travel guide to medieval Europe, this book provides cultural and historical details about this time period. Using the concept of time travel, Haywood imparts facts about the culture, locations, relics and artifacts, and other salient information. Photographs, maps, and reproductions enhance the text. Glossary, Chronology, Further Reading, and Index.

983. Konstam, Angus. *Historical Atlas of Medieval Europe.* Mercury, 2007. 192pp. ISBN 978-1-904668-10-7. Grades YA.

Beginning with the Dark Ages and continuing through the spread of religion, the Norman Conquest, the Crusades, the development of towns, and the Renaissance, this atlas looks at centuries and themes. Discussions of battlegrounds, trade centers and routes, and empire territories underscore the military, political, and cultural aspects of the times. The ten chapters are "The Recovery of Europe," "The Norman Achievement," "Popes and Emperors—The Crisis of Church and State," "God Wills It—The Crusades," "The Flowering of Europe," "Feudal Europe in the 13th Century," "The Calamitous 14th Century," "Europe Comes of Age," "Ottomans and Slavs," and "The Birth of Renaissance Europe." Introduction, Color Illustrations, Maps, Chronology, Glossary and Genealogy Tables, and Index.

984. Koscielniak, Bruce. *Johann Gutenberg and the Amazing Printing Press.* Houghton Mifflin, 2003. ISBN 978-0-618-26351-6. Grades 2–5.

Although the Chinese invented paper in 105, books were not printed until Johann Gutenberg invented movable type in Mainz, Germany, around 1450. The author examines the history of paper and ink and how they are made. He also discusses how scribes made copies of books before the printing press was invented. Line drawings with watercolor complement the text.

985. Langley, Andrew. *Medieval Life.* Illustrated by Geoff Dann and Geoff Brightling. DK, 2004. 72pp. ISBN 978-0-7566-0705-0. Grades 5–8.

See entry 876.

986. MacDonald, Fiona. *Knights, Castles, and Warfare in the Middle Ages.* (World Almanac Library of the Middle Ages) World Almanac Library, 2006. 48pp. ISBN 978-0-8368-5895-2. Grades 5–8.

During the Middle Ages, knights supposedly defended their lords and the people. The author examines knights and who they were, what they wore, what weapons they fought with, and how the development of weapons for use during warfare changed the role of the knight. Illustrations highlight the text. Chronology, Time Line, Glossary, Further Reading, and Index.

987. MacDonald, Fiona. *Monarchs in the Middle Ages.* (World Almanac Library of the Middle Ages) World Almanac Library, 2005. 48pp. ISBN 978-0-8368-5896-9. Grades 5–8.

During the Middle Ages, monarchs had royal responsibilities. They built kingdoms throughout Europe and beyond as people migrated. They fought one another in attempts to increase their wealth. Eventually, they redrew the boundaries of Europe and clashed over the role of church and state. Illustrations highlight the text. Chronology, Time Line, Glossary, Further Reading, and Index.

988. MacDonald, Fiona. *The Plague and Medicine in the Middle Ages.* (World Almanac Library of the Middle Ages) World Almanac Library, 2005. 48pp. ISBN 978-0-8368-5898-3. Grades 5–8.

In the Middle Ages, the plague ravaged cities and towns, and people did not know what caused it. This book discusses the people's faith, their attempts to heal those stricken with the plague, the medical profession at the time, the diagnosis and treatment of diseases, the lack of cleanliness, and other aspects that caused the spread of the plague. Illustrations highlight the text. Chronology, Time Line, Glossary, Further Reading, and Index.

989. MacDonald, Fiona. *Travel and Trade in the Middle Ages.* (World Almanac Library of the Middle Ages) World Almanac Library, 2006. 48pp. ISBN 978-0-8368-5899-0. Grades 5–8.

During the Middle Ages, people traveled across Europe and beyond. This book examines the types of travel, the technology of travel, why people traveled, the role of markets and traveling merchants, and how all this movement affected the population. Illustrations highlight the text. Chronology, Time Line, Glossary, Further Reading, and Index.

990. Olmon, Kyle. *Castle: Medieval Days and Knights.* Illustrated by Tracy Sabin. (Sabuda & Reinhart Present) Orchard, 2006. 6pp. ISBN 978-0-439-54324-8. Grades 2–5.

This pop-up book displays medieval castles with detailed interiors. It includes two-page spreads that open to reveal walls, courtyards, drawbridges, towers, chapels, weaponry, feasts, and other aspects of a medieval castle. The text discusses how castles were constructed, who lived inside, and the times.

991. Orme, Nicholas. *Medieval Children.* Yale, 2003. 400pp. Paper ISBN 978-0-300-09754-2. Grades YA.

    See entry 884.

992. Padrino, Mercedes. *Feudalism and Village Life in the Middle Ages.* (World Almanac Library of the Middle Ages) World Almanac Library, 2006. 48pp. ISBN 978-0-8368-5894-5. Grades 5–8.

    During the Middle Ages, people were bound to their economic and social classes. The author discusses feudalism and manorialism, life in the village, the lord's household, the peasant's household, culture and relationships, dress, food and drink, and entertainment. Illustrations highlight the text. Chronology, Time Line, Glossary, Further Reading, and Index.

993. Paris, Erna. *The End of Days: A Story of Tolerance, Tyranny, and the Expulsion of the Jews from Spain.* Prometheus, 1995. 327pp. ISBN 978-1-57392-017-9. Grades 7 up.

    In the 15th century Spain degenerated from a place where Christians, Jews, and Moors could live together into a country where the Spanish Inquisition ruled. Paris traces two hundred years of Spanish history to show the changes that occurred before the plague, which killed 30 percent of Europe's population and for which Spanish citizens began to blame non-Christians. Paris also discusses the motives of the inquisitors, their actions, and the fates of the accused, along with the actual expulsion of the Jews in 1492. Bibliography and Index.

994. Scott, Margaret. *Medieval Clothing and Costumes: Displaying Wealth and Class in Medieval Times.* (Library of the Middle Ages) Rosen, 2003. 64pp. ISBN 978-0-8239-3991-6. Grades 5–8.

    The author discusses the importance of dress in medieval life. She covers the beginning of fashion, unusual or foolish fashions (such as talking clothes), and the clothes of the wealthy—especially brides, princes, and the d'Este sisters in Italy. At this time, the most expensive clothes were made of a wool known as scarlet, created with an expensive dye called kermes. In addition to red, scarlet cloth could be in other colors including green and blue. Laws controlled who could wear scarlet. Illustrations highlight the text. Glossary, Bibliography, Further Reading, Web Sites, and Index.

995. Senker, Cath. *The Black Death 1347–1350: The Plague Spreads Across Europe.* (When Disaster Struck) Raintree, 2006. 56pp. ISBN 978-1-4109-2278-6. Grades 4–7.

    A history of the plague from its beginnings in central Asia to its spread through Europe, where one-third of the population died. Despite the fact that certain symptoms were recognized, a lack of sanitation allowed the disease to spread. Jews and others were persecuted in a mistaken effort to arrest the epidemic. This book also discusses the pandemics of the 20th century (such as influenza) and the possibility of more in the future. Photographs augment the text. Maps, Chronology, Further Reading, Glossary, Web Sites, and Index.

996. Sider, Sandra. *Handbook to Life in Renaissance Europe.* (Handbook to Life) Facts on File, 2005. 382pp. ISBN 978-0-8160-5618-7; Oxford, 2007. paper ISBN 978-0-19-533084-7. Grades 10 up.

A look at European culture and history during the Renaissance, a term first used by Italian painter and architect Giorgio Vasari. The Renaissance began in the late 1300s and continued through the 17th century. The author discusses history, government, society, economy, religion, art, travel, performing arts, daily life, environment, population, literature, music, warfare, commerce, science, and education. Photographs and illustrations augment the text. Bibliography and Index.

997. Singman, Jeffrey L., and Will McLean. *Daily Life in Chaucer's England.* (Daily Life Through History) Greenwood, 1995. 252pp. ISBN 978-0-313-29375-7. Grades 7 up.

The book's eight chapters look at life, time, environment, clothing, arms and armor, food and drink, and leisure in Chaucer's England. Also included is historical background on the time, with descriptions of the feudal system during the 1300s, the medieval calendar, and other aspects of life. Bibliography, Glossary, Notes, and Index.

998. Solway, Andrew. *Castle Under Siege! Simple Machines.* Raintree, 2005. 32pp. Paper ISBN 978-1-4109-1949-6. Grades 4–7.

Information about the principles behind levers, wheels and axles, pulleys, inclined planes, wedges, and screws help readers understand the mechanical aspects of castles. Photographs and diagrams offer clear examples of these concepts. Further Reading, Glossary, and Index.

999. Steele, Philip. *Castles.* Kingfisher, 1995. 63pp. ISBN 978-1-856975-47-6. Grades 3–7.

See entry 887.

1000. Steele, Philip. *The Medieval World.* (History of Costume and Fashion) Facts on File, 2005. 64pp. ISBN 978-0-8160-5945-4. Grades 5–8.

The author discusses jewelry, textile production, hair care, grooming, hygiene, battle dress, and clothing for men and women in different classes, along with the impacts of climate, geography, leaders, and significant historical events on modes of dress in the medieval world. As tools became more sophisticated, so did materials. Photographs and illustrations highlight the text. Bibliography, Glossary,

1001. Weir, Alison. *The Wars of the Roses.* Ballantine, 1995. 287pp. Paper ISBN 978-0-345-40433-6. Grades YA.

Beginning with a short history of the house of Plantaganet and the rule of Richard II, this account continues to the Battle of Tewkesbury and the murder of King Henry VI, covering the years 1399 to 1500. It looks at the family rivalries and personalities that made this period so complex and so interesting. Bibliography and Index.

1002. Wiesner-Hanks, Merry E. *An Age of Voyages, 1350–1600.* Oxford, 2005. 189pp. ISBN 978-0-19-517672-8. Grades 7 up.

A look at the cultural life of Italian city-states during this time. They profited from new trading alliances and contact with other areas of the world. But at the same time this contact led to diseases and religious power struggles. Quotations from leaders, philosophers, voyagers, and merchants reveal the tenor of the times. Maps, photographs, and illustrations complement the text. Bibliography, Chronology, Glossary, Notes, and Index.

1003. Wroe, Ann. *A Fool and His Money: Life in a Partitioned Town in 14th-century France.* Hill & Wang, 1996. Paper ISBN 978-0-8090-1592-4. Grades YA.

When Wroe wanted to understand how a medieval town worked, she researched Rodez, a town in southern France caught in the Hundred Years War beginning around 1337. Rodez was divided into two parts: the city section ruled by a bishop, and the bourg section ruled by a count. The English conquered the town in 1360, but the French reclaimed it in 1369. In court registers, the author found information about Peyre Marques, an old man who hid gold coins (probably to escape the high taxes levied by both the count and the bishop to pay for the war) but later could not remember where he put them. His story, combined with the town's, offers insight about ordinary lives in this period. Bibliography and Index.

Biography and Collective Biography

1004. Alper, Ann Fitzpatrick. *Forgotten Voyager: The Story of Amerigo Vespucci.* (Trailblazer Biographies) Lerner, 1991. 112pp. ISBN 978-0-87614-442-8. Grades 4–9.

This biography of Amerigo Vespucci (1451–1512) discusses his discoveries and explorations for Spain. In 1499 he sailed to the West Indies and discovered the mouth of the Amazon. Later (in 1501) he sailed along the northern coast of South America and proved that the land was one continent. Bibliography and Index.

1005. Brooks, Polly Schoyer. *Beyond the Myth: The Story of Joan of Arc.* Houghton, 1999. 176pp. Paper ISBN 978-0-395-98138-2. Grades 8 up.

Beginning with a discussion about the disarray of the 15th century, Brooks shows how people could believe in a young girl who thought she could rid France of the British and set the rightful heir on the French throne. Born in Domremy in 1412, Joan heard voices that convinced her that she should save France. She persuaded others, including Charles, the heir apparent, to give her an army. She defeated the British at Orléans, but after she accomplished what she had promised, she was tried and burned at the stake in 1431. The book gives extensive background on this unusual young woman. Bibliography and Index. *Bulletin Blue Ribbon Book.*

1006. Burch, Joann Johansen. *Fine Print: A Story About Johann Gutenberg.* Illustrated by Kent Alan Aldrich. (Creative Minds) Carolrhoda, 1991. 64pp. ISBN 978-0-87614-682-8; 1992. paper ISBN 978-0-87614-565-4. Grades 3–6.

Because information about Gutenberg's (1397?–1468) life is very limited, this book discusses the times during which he lived in Mainz, based on chronicles and the status of books before his invention of moveable type. His family was very wealthy; his father owned three homes and several books, very expensive items before his son's invention. Gutenberg was a stonecutter and polisher, but he experimented with metal letters to see if he could make them print. When his invention was ready he spent several years trying to print the Bible, but would reject a page if just one letter was blurred. One of his investors sued him, and Gutenberg had to give the creditor all his printing equipment to pay back the loan. He received no credit during his time for the first printing of the Bible, but history has called that book the Gutenberg Bible. His invention changed the world. Sources and For Further Reading.

1007. Byrd, Robert. *Leonardo, the Beautiful Dreamer.* Penguin, 2003. 40pp. ISBN 978-0-525-47033-5. Grades 3–8.

Leonardo da Vinci was a prankster, painter, philosopher, musician, writer, sculptor, engineer, and scientist. The author includes excerpts from Leonardo's notebooks and twenty ink-and-watercolor renditions of his drawings (some in a cartoon style) that examine themes from Leonardo's life. Notes, Time Line, Bibliography, Sources, and Web Sites. *Golden Kite Award, Student Book Award* (Maine) nomination, *School Library Journal Best Books for Children, Publisher's Weekly Best Children's Books*, and *National Council Teachers of English Orbis Pictus Honor.*

1008. Davenport, John C. *Dante: Poet, Author, and Proud Florentine.* (Makers of the Middle Ages and Renaissance) Chelsea, 2005. 158pp. ISBN 978-0-7910-8634-6. Grades 6 up.

See entry 893.

1009. Freedman, Russell. *The Adventures of Marco Polo.* Illustrated by Bagram Ibatoulline. Arthur A. Levine, 2006. 63pp. ISBN 978-0-439-52394-3. Grades 5–9.

See entry 895.

1010. Fritz, Jean. *Leonardo's Horse.* Illustrated by Hudson Talbott. Penguin, 2001. 48pp. ISBN 978-0-399-23576-4. Grades 3–6.

In 1482 the duke of Milan commissioned Leonardo da Vinci (1452–1519) to create a huge bronze horse in honor of his father. Leonardo began by making a 24-foot clay model. However, it could not be cast before the French and the rain destroyed it in 1499 and the duke used the bronze for arms. It is said that Leonardo mourned the destruction of his horse for the remainder of his life. Then retired pilot Charles Dent decided to enlist the help of sculptor Nina Akamu to recreate the horse five hundred years later. They used Leonardo's original ideas to make the horse, which was presented to Italy after Dent died in 1994. *American Library Association Notable Books for Children, Beehive Informational Children's Book Award* (Utah) nomination, *National Council Teachers of English Orbis Pictus Award Honor, Great Stone Face Book Award* (New Hampshire) nomination, *Great Lakes' Great Books Award* (Michigan) nomination, *Bluegrass Award* (Kentucky) nomination, *Children's Book Award* (Rhode Island) nomination, *Children's Book Award* (North Carolina) nomination, *ABC Children's Booksellers Choices Awards, Children's Book Award* (Maryland) nomination, *Bluebonnet Award* (Texas) nomination, *Sequoyah Book Award* (Florida) nomination, *Young Hoosier Book Award* (Indiana) nomination, *Young Readers' Choice Award* (Louisiana) nomination, *SCASL Book Award* (South Carolina) nomination, and *Prairie Pasque Award* (South Dakota) nomination.

1011. Goldberg, Enid A., and Norman Itzkowitz. *Tomas de Torquemada: Architect of Torture During the Spanish Inquisition.* (Wicked History) Watts, 2007. 128pp. ISBN 978-0-531-12598-4. Grades 6–8.

Tomas de Torquemada (1420–1498), the first Grand Inquisitor in Spain, believed that he was doing God's work. He approved of torture, but he was also very devout. He thought that torment would help save souls. The authors examine his motives by asking the reader questions to answer after learning the history of the situation. Photographs highlight the text. Chronology, Further Reading, Glossary, Web Sites, and Index.

1012. Goldberg, Enid A., and Norman Itzkowitz. *Vlad the Impaler: The Real Count Dracula.* (Wicked History) Watts, 2007. 128pp. ISBN 978-0-531-12599-1. Grades 6–8.

Vlad the Impaler (1430?–1476) was the product of a violent childhood and repeated betrayal. For many years, the Turks had him imprisoned. His murders were most likely retaliation for the cruelty to his family while he was a child. He could also have been trying to scare the gigantic Ottoman Empire. The authors examine his motives by asking the reader questions to answer after learning the history of the situation. Photographs highlight the text. Chronology, Further Reading, Glossary, Web Sites, and Index.

1013. Hubbard-Brown, Janet. *Chaucer: Celebrated Poet and Author.* (Makers of the Middle Ages and Renaissance) Chelsea, 2005. 158pp. ISBN 978-0-7910-8635-3. Grades 6 up.

This biography of Geoffrey Chaucer (d. 1400) reveals the influence of his life and times on his religious thought and political understanding. Since his readers were mostly nonjudgmental and open to entertainment, his *Canterbury Tales* is humorous and filled with satire. The author covers his childhood and background along with his writing. Photographs and illustrations highlight the text. Bibliography, Glossary, Chronology, Notes, Further Reading, Web Sites, and Index.

1014. Krull, Kathleen. *Leonardo da Vinci.* Illustrated by Boris Kulikov. (Giants of Science) Viking, 2005. 124pp. ISBN 978-0-670-05920-1; Puffin, 2008. paper ISBN 978-0-14-240821-6. Grades 5–8.

This biography of Leonardo da Vinci (1452–1519) examines his life as an apprentice in Milan and his scientific studies leading to an investigation of the human body. His notebooks are the main sources for the biography, and Krull suggests that their publication during his lifetime would have changed the course of science. As a lonely, illegitimate child, Leonardo developed a relationship with his scientist-farmer uncle. Then his father arranged an apprenticeship with Florence's leading painter and sculptor, Andrea del Verrocchio. He learned that an artist must ask about everything and, in his notebooks, he describes natural phenomena by using scientific observation. As a scientist, he tried to understand and explain all the processes of the human body. One chapter presents the thoughts of various historians about Leonardo's sexual orientation. Ink drawings illustrate the text. Bibliography, Web Sites, and Index. *Kirkus Reviews Editor's Choice.*

1015. León, Vicki. *Uppity Women of the Renaissance.* Conari, 1999. 260pp. Paper ISBN 978-1-57324-127-4. Grades YA.

This collective anecdotal biography presents approximately two hundred women— poets, courtesans, artists, authors, and others—who lived during the Renaissance and managed to surface from its oppressive patriarchy. The groups are "Crafty Women and Artful Iron Maidens," "Disorderly Dames, Ardent Altruists and Law-and-Order Ladies," "Brilliant Blue Collars, Soulful Femmes and Yuppies of Yore," "Rolling Stones and Gender-Adventurous Gals," "Slick Talkers and Awesome Networkers," "Career Virgins, Saintly Souls and Wa-a-ayward Women," "The Mrs., Misses and Near Misses of King Henry VIII," and "Better Halves, Daring Daughters and Significant Others of the Rich and Famous." Illustrations augment the text. Bibliography, Notes, and Index.

1016. Mason, Antony. *Leonardo da Vinci.* (Lives of the Artists) Gareth Stevens, 2004. 48pp. ISBN 978-0-8368-5599-9; paper ISBN 978-0-8368-5604-0. Grades 5–8.

Leonardo da Vinci (1452–1519) was a sculptor, painter, scientist, and engineer. This text discusses his life and gives much detail about the social and historical aspects of the times in which he lived. Included are photographs of his works. Reproductions, Glossary, Maps, Photographs, Time Line, and Index.

1017. Pinguilly, Yves. *Da Vinci: The Painter Who Spoke with Birds.* Translated by John Goodman. Chelsea House, 1994. 62pp. ISBN 978-0-7910-2808-7. Grades 3–6.

Letters between an uncle and niece introduce the life and work of Leonardo da Vinci in Italy during the Renaissance. Reproductions and drawings highlight the text. Chronology and Glossary.

1018. Poole, Josephine. *Joan of Arc.* Illustrated by Angela Barrett. Knopf, 1998. Unpaged. ISBN 978-0-679-89041-6. Grades 2–5.

Saint Joan of Arc (ca. 1412–1431) heard "voices from heaven" that led her to offer her services to Charles, her king, to defeat the English. The French could not accept her spiritual claims and burned her at the stake. Illustrations and maps enhance the text. Chronology. *American Library Association Notable Children's Book* and *Capitol Choices Noteworthy Titles* (Washington, D.C.).

1019. Rabb, Theodore K. *Renaissance Lives: Portraits of an Age.* Basic, 2000. 262pp. Paper ISBN 978-0-465-06800-5. Grades YA.

The fifteen people presented in this collective biography exemplify, according to the author, the new way of thinking that came about in the Renaissance. The book's subjects are categorized as dissenters, rulers, artists, warriors, and explorers. Among the individuals included are Titian, Artemesia Gentileschi, John Milton, Teresa of Avila, John Hus, Catherine de' Medici, Galileo, Walter Raleigh, and Gluckel of Hameln (a businesswoman, mother, and defender of her Jewish faith). A companion to the public television series. Index.

1020. Stanley, Diane. *Joan of Arc.* Trophy, 2002. Unpaged. Paper ISBN 978-0-06-443748-6. Grades 4–8.

This picture book of Saint Joan of Arc (ca. 1412–1431) contains text based on Joan's own words before the Inquisition and on the one hundred and fifteen eyewitness accounts recorded in the Trial of Rehabilitation after her martyrdom. It is complemented with gilded artwork similar to medieval illuminated manuscripts. Also included is reference to the political situation in France and England that led to Joan's vision and decision to join Charles VII in the battle against the English. *Student Book Award* (Maine) nomination, *Garden State Children's Book Awards* (New Jersey), *Capitol Choices Noteworthy Titles* (Washington, D.C.), *Bulletin Blue Ribbon*, and *Children's Book Award* (South Carolina) nomination.

1021. Stanley, Diane. *Leonardo da Vinci.* Morrow, 1996. 48pp. ISBN 978-0-688-10437-5; Trophy, 2000. paper ISBN 978-0-688-16155-2. Grades 4–7.

In addition to presenting the known facts about Leonardo da Vinci (1452–1519), Stanley also recreates the time in Florence during which he lived. She describes the preliminary steps for painting and sculpting and the problems da Vinci had in getting materials and investigating his ideas. She uses da Vinci's own writing to show his intelligence and inquisitiveness. Bibliography. *Bulletin Blue Ribbon Book, American Library Association Notable Books for Children; Orbis Pictus Award for Outstanding Nonfiction for Children, School Library Journal Best Book, Boston Globe/Horn Book Award Honor,* and *Capitol Choices Noteworthy Titles* (Washington, D.C.).

1022. Sutcliffe, Jane. *Juan Ponce de León.* (History Maker Bios) Lerner, 2005. 48pp. ISBN 978-0-8225-2944-6. Grades 3–5.

Juan Ponce de León (1460?–1521) first sailed with Christopher Columbus on one of his journeys. He later returned to Puerto Rico, where he found gold. The Spanish king then sent him back there and he was appointed governor of the island. Ponce de León has become known for what he did not find: the fountain of youth. However, he did discover Florida. Illustrations highlight the text. Bibliography, Further Reading, Glossary, Maps, Time Line, Web Sites, and Index.

1023. Tello, Antonio. *My Name Is Leonardo da Vinci.* Illustrated by Johanna A. Boccardo. (My Name Is . . .) Barron's, 2006. 63pp. Paper ISBN 978-0-7641-3392-3. Grades 4–6.

This biography of the artist starts with his birth in Vinci and discusses his reputation in Florence and his inventions. Although he is best known today for painting the *Mona Lisa,* he invented weapons used by the Florentine military and he studied human anatomy. Photographs and illustrations highlight the text.

1024. Thompson, Paul B. *Joan of Arc: Warrior Saint of France.* (Rulers of the Middle Ages) Enslow, 2007. 160pp. ISBN 978-0-7660-2716-9. Grades 7–9.

This biography of Joan of Arc (ca. 1412–1431) features background on her life and her achievements. Chronology, Glossary, Further Reading, Web Sites, and Index.

1025. Thomson, Andy. *Morning Star of the Reformation.* Bob Jones University, 1988. 134pp. Paper ISBN 978-0-8908-4453-3. Grades YA.

Around 1345 in medieval England, during a time of plague, John Wycliffe attended Oxford University and developed his intellectual pursuits. He refused to accept the Catholic Church's abuses of the clergy as well as its beliefs in transubstantiation and papal supremacy, and he was branded a heretic. He initiated the English translation of the Bible, and his followers, the Lollards, took the Bible to people in the countryside and urged them to read it for themselves. Among his friends were luminaries such as John Aston, John Purvey, and Nicholas Hereford, but Wycliffe is called the "Morning Star of the Reformation." The 16th-century schism of the Church rested on his work.

1026. Tompert, Ann. *Joan of Arc: Heroine of France.* Boyds Mills, 2003. 32pp. ISBN 978-1-59078-009-1. Grades 2–5.

This biography focuses on the trial of Joan of Arc (ca. 1412–1431) and features letters and testimony that were used to accuse her of heresy and condemn her to death at the stake. Charles drove the English from France, saying he felt "filled with her winning spirit," and, after burning her, others realized they had murdered someone holy. Illustrations enhance the text.

1027. Venezia, Mike. *Botticelli.* (Getting to Know the World's Greatest Artists) Children's Press, 1991. 32pp. ISBN 978-0-516-02291-8; paper ISBN 978-0-516-42291-6. Grades K–5.

Sandro Botticelli (1444?–1510) was an important Italian painter during the Renaissance. His *Birth of Venus* is one of many paintings that show his love of mythological subjects. Illustrations enhance the text.

1028. Venezia, Mike. *Da Vinci.* (Getting to Know the World's Greatest Artists) Children's Press, 1989. 32pp. ISBN 978-0-516-02275-8; paper ISBN 978-0-516-42275-6. Grades K–5.

Leonardo da Vinci (1452–1519) was one of the greatest artists in history. *The Mona Lisa* and *The Last Supper* are two of his few paintings. He was also greatly interested in why things happen, and he filled his notebooks with investigative drawings. Illustrations highlight the text.

1029. Venezia, Mike. *Giotto.* (Getting to Know the World's Greatest Artists) Children's Press, 2000. 32pp. ISBN 978-0-516-21592-1; paper ISBN 978-0-516-27040-1. Grades K–5.

Giotto di Bondone (1267–1337) traveled from his birthplace near Florence to the city of Florence around 1280. He signed only three works: the Arena Chapel frescoes in Padua, the Bardi and Peruzzi Chapel frescoes in Florence's Santa Croce, and the Ognissanti Madonna in the Church of All Saints. Experts disagree about other works said to have been painted by him. He remains one of the most important artists in history because he was one of the first to use perspective—to see that figures could be represented on a flat surface as three-dimensional. Illustrations enhance the text.

1030. Wagner, Heather Lehr. *The Medicis: A Ruling Dynasty.* (Makers of the Middle Ages and Renaissance) Chelsea, 2005. 156pp. ISBN 978-0-7910-8630-8. Grades 6 up.

This book examines the role of the Medici family in shaping Florence, Italy, during the 15th century. The six chapters discuss their rise to power, their role as bankers to the republic, the position of the pope, and two important figures: Lorenzo the Magnificent and Catherine de' Medici. There is also discussion of the family's decline as a major power in the Renaissance. Photographs and illustrations highlight the text. Bibliography, Glossary, Chronology, Web Sites, and Index.

1031. Whiting, Jim. *The Life and Times of Joan of Arc.* (Biography from Ancient Civilizations) Mitchell Lane, 2005. 48pp. ISBN 978-1-58415-345-0. Grades 5–8.

This biography of Joan of Arc (ca. 1412–1431) examines her life from historical and contemporary perspectives. It looks at the French political situation in the years before her aid, her ability to call for military action on behalf of Charles, her work to help him become king, her arrest, and her execution by the English. Although condemned for "hearing voices," Joan was actually being true to her times, when such situations were acceptable. Photographs and illustrations highlight the text. Bibliography, Chronology, Notes, Glossary, For Further Reading, Web Sites, and Index.

1032. Wilkinson, Philip. *Joan of Arc: The Teenager Who Saved Her Nation.* (World History Biography) National Geographic, 2007. 64pp. ISBN 978-1-4263-0116-2; 2009. paper ISBN 978-1-4263-0415-6. Grades 4–7.

Throughout this biography of Joan of Arc (ca. 1412–1431) are two-page spreads that cover topics including medieval warfare, the Church, and the Hundred Years War. The four sections discuss subjects including her major achievements, her trial, and her legacy. Illustrations highlight the text. Bibliography, Glossary, Chronology, and Index.

Graphic Novels, Biographies, and Histories

1033. Decker, Timothy. *Run Far, Run Fast.* Front Street, 2007. Unpaged. ISBN 978-1-59078-469-3. Grades 4 up.

In 1384, a carpenter's wife tells her 10-year-old daughter to flee their plague-ridden village. The girl departs and encounters outside the gates of her town a troubled world that is depopulated, fearful, and dangerous. But she does find people who help her and realizes that hope remains even in a seemingly hopeless situation.

DVDs

1034. *Everyday Life in the Renaissance.* (Renaissance for Students) Library Video, 2003. 23 min. ISBN 978-1-57225-696-5. Grades 5–9.

In the Renaissance, the improved economy and increased trade in Europe gave many people more money to improve their lifestyles. They purchased new items for their homes, sampled new foods from exotic places, and wore extravagant clothes. Their work, education, religion, entertainment, and art changed during the three centuries now called the Renaissance. This DVD examines typical homes, foods, and clothing of the times with footage on location, maps, photographs of artworks, and reenactments.

1035. *A History of the Renaissance.* (Renaissance for Students) Library Video, 2003. 23 min. ISBN 978-1-57225-695-8. Grades 5–9.

This DVD answers the questions of how the Renaissance began and why. The humanist Petrarch rediscovered ancient Greek and Roman culture and ideas, civilizations that were forgotten during the Middle Ages. As monarchs and religious figures tried to strengthen their power during this era, others including Martin Luther questioned their power. Reenactments show these events and photographs display Renaissance art and architecture.

1036. *The Middle Ages, Europe 1100–1450 A.D.: Back in Time.* (Hands-On Crafts for Kids Series 6) Chip Taylor Communications, 2003. 30 min. Grades 4–6.

See entry 913.

1037. *The Reluctant Saint: Francis of Assisi.* Narrated by Liev Schreiber. Vision Video, 2003. 1 hr. ISBN 978-1-56364-726-0. Grades 10 up.

Based on Donald Spoto's biography of Saint Francis of Assisi, this video was filmed on location in Italy. It reveals Francis's concern that his friends not make a saint of him even though he changed so dramatically during his life. He was a wealthy playboy, businessman, and soldier before he became a defender of the poor and a mystic who revered nature. Saint Francis has become an inspiration to many during the hundreds of years since his death.

1038. *The Renaissance: 1450–1700 A.D.: Back in Time.* (Hands-On Crafts for Kids Series 6) Chip Taylor Communications, 2003. 30 min. Grades 4–6.

The production begins with a narrator reading the list of materials appearing on the screen. Teachers construct objects from the Renaissance era. They include Milano keys, Venetian glass, a bookmark, a landscape painting, and a millefiori design. Each item helps explain an important aspect of the Renaissance era.

1039. *Renaissance Art, Music and Literature.* (Renaissance for Students) Library Video, 2003. 23 min. ISBN 978-1-57225-697-2. Grades 5–9.

During the Renaissance, artists, writers, and musicians flourished. New musical instruments were invented and musical style changed. Among the creators presented in this DVD are writers Machiavelli and Shakespeare and artist Leonardo da Vinci. Reenactments, footage on location in Europe, and photographs augment the information.

1040. *Renaissance Science and Invention.* (Renaissance for Students) Library Video, 2003. 23 min. ISBN 978-1-57225-698-9. Grades 5–9.

During the Renaissance, scientists began studying and challenging existing beliefs. They performed laboratory and hands-on experiments to prove their theories. Scientific breakthroughs occurred in areas including physics, anatomy, astronomy, and mathematics. New concepts of engineering allowed architects to design and create the dome of the Florence cathedral. However, not all theories were acceptable to those in power, and some caused great controversy. Among the figures presented in this DVD are Kepler, Galileo, and Brunelleschi. Reenactments, footage on location in Europe, and photographs augment the information.

1041. *Renaissance Travel, Trade, and Exploration.* (Renaissance for Students) Library Video, 2003. 23 min. ISBN 978-1-57225-699-6. Grades 5–9.

During the Renaissance, navigational tools such as the lateen sail and the astrolabe as well as improved shipbuilding allowed men to sail into uncharted lands. The wealth retrieved from newly discovered lands by explorers such as Columbus, Magellan, and da Gama created a wealthy merchant class and increased trade around the world. Reenactments, footage on location in Europe, and photographs augment the information in this DVD.

1042. Venezia, Mike. *Da Vinci.* (Getting to Know the World's Greatest Artists) Getting to Know, 2006. 24 min. Grades K–8.

See entry 1028.

Compact Discs

1043. Abalos, Rafael. *Grimpow: The Invisible Road.* Narrated by Richard McGonagle. Listening Library, 2007. 11 CDs; 13 hrs. 20 m. ISBN 978-0-7393-5963-1. Grades 6–9.

See entry 933.

1044. Avi. *Crispin: At the Edge of the World.* Narrated by Ron Keith. Recorded Books, 2006. 5 CDs; 6 hrs. ISBN 978-1-4281-1797-6. Grades 5–9.

See entry 935.

1045. Avi. *Crispin: The Cross of Lead.* Narrated by Ron Keith. Recorded Books, 2003. 6 CDs; 6.25 hrs. ISBN 978-1-4025-4553-5. Grades 3–7.

See entry 936.

1046. Branford, Henrietta. *Fire, Bed and Bone.* Illustrated by Bryan Leister. Narrated by Eve Karpf. BBC Audiobooks, 2002. 2 CDs; 2 hrs. 40 min. ISBN 978-0-7540-6504-3. Grades 5–9.

See entry 941.

1047. Dana, Barbara. *Young Joan: A Novel.* Narrated by Susan O'Malley. Blackstone Audio Books, 2001. 7 CDs. ISBN 978-0-7861-9691-3. Grades 5–9.

Joan of Arc (ca. 1412–1431) supposedly heard her name being spoken aloud in a garden where no other human was present. After a time, she allowed herself to think that she might be the maid of whom Merlin had spoken, the one who would help France. This book looks at Joan of Arc's early life, seeing her as a mystic rather than someone who was either hysterical or a feminist. Joan's favorite activity was praying, and although she enjoyed her family and her pets, God was the center of her life. With this focus, she convinced the Dauphin that she could save France—and she did. Bibliography and Index. *Bulletin Blue Ribbon.*

1048. Scott, Michael. *The Alchemyst: The Secrets of the Immortal Nicholas Flamel.* Narrated by Denis O'Hare. Listening Library, 2007. 8 CDs; 10:02 hrs. ISBN 978-0-385-73600-8. Grades 6–9.

Fifteen-year-old twins Josh and Sophie Newman become unwittingly involved in a plot to steal the Codex from Nick Fleming, Josh's boss, who is really Nicholas Flamel, a medieval alchemist. Flamel has kept the book containing the secret for eternal youth for many centuries in order to stop the "Elder Race" from dominating the world. John Dee, the Elders' representative, uses the twins to help him gain possession of the Codex in modern-day California.

1049. Skelton, Matthew. *Endymion Spring.* Narrated by Richard Easton. Listening Library, 2006. 8 CDs; 10 hrs. 9 min. ISBN 978-0-7393-3644-1. Grades 4–7.

See entry 967.

EUROPE AND THE BRITISH ISLES, 1492–1649

Historical Fiction and Fantasy

1050. Alphin, Elaine Marie. *Tournament of Time.* Bluegrass, 1994. 125pp. Paper ISBN 978-0-9643683-0-9. Grades 4–6.

Disappointed in her British classmates' reaction to her, Jess becomes homesick for America while living in York, where her father is teaching at the university for a year. But she discovers that the spirits of two princes who were murdered during the 15th century speak to her from York Cathedral's stained-glass windows. Along with newfound friends, she and her brothers solve the mystery.

1051. Anholt, Laurence. *Leonardo and the Flying Boy: A Story About Leonardo da Vinci.* Barron's Educational, 2000. 32pp. ISBN 978-0-7641-5225-2. Grades 2–4.

During the Renaissance, Zoro's teacher Leonardo da Vinci works on a strange machine, one that the teacher plans to fly. Salai, a street urchin who also studies with Leonardo, convinces the honest and diligent Zoro to steal the machine, take it to the top of a hill, and try to fly on it. The boys discover that the machine is not yet ready for human flight. Included are snippets of information about Leonardo's interests and his artistic works.

1052. Armstrong, Alan. *Raleigh's Page.* Illustrated by Tim Jessell. Random House, 2007. 328pp. ISBN 978-0-375-83319-9. Grades 4–7.

In 1584 Andrew Saintleger, 11, leaves his Devon home to become Walter Raleigh's page. Within two years, he visits France as a spy where he steals an important map and then travels to Virginia where he befriends a Native American boy. Then he becomes the secretary to Thomas Harriot, the mathematician and astronomer who manages Raleigh's accounts, and there he enjoys adventures and discoveries. Black-and-white illustrations highlight the text.

1053. Blackwood, Gary L. *The Shakespeare Stealer.* Puffin, 2000. 208pp. Paper ISBN 978-0-14-130595-0. Grades 4–8.

Widge, an orphan of 14 in 1601, has an order from his employer, Simon Bass, to steal Shakespeare's play *Hamlet* by copying it using his talent at "charactery" (shorthand). Bass wants to present the play without paying royalties. Widge infiltrates Lord Chamberlain's Men at the Globe Theatre but discovers that he likes the actors and wants to work with them. *School Library Journal Best Books of the Year*; *Mark Twain Award* nomination; *Dorothy Canfield Fisher Children's Book Award* (Vermont) nomination; *William Allen White Children's Book Award* (Kansas) nomination; *Young Hoosier Book Award* (Indiana) nomination; *Nutmeg Children's Book Award* (Connecticut); *Volunteer State Book Award* (Tennessee) nomination; *Young Reader's Award* (Arizona) nomination; *Young Reader's Choice Award* (Pennsylvania) nomination; *Land of Enchantment Book Award* (New Mexico) nomination; and *Children's Book Award* (Massachusetts) nomination.

1054. Blackwood, Gary L. *Shakespeare's Scribe.* Penguin, 2000. 224pp. ISBN 978-0-525-46444-0; 2002. paper ISBN 978-0-14-230066-4. Grades 5–8.

An outbreak of the Black Plague closes the Globe Theatre in Elizabethan England, and the Lord Chamberlain's Men troupe—with its playwright William Shakespeare—begins a tour of the small towns in the countryside. Widge, an orphan who has become an actor in the troupe, is good at "swift writing" and is able to decipher Shakespeare's scribbles. When ex-soldier Jamie Redshaw appears, claiming to be Widge's father, he jeopardizes Widge's future with the company in this sequel to *The Shakespeare Stealer* (1998) until Widge can prove that Redshaw is a con man. *SCASL Book Award* (South Carolina) nomination and *American Library Association Best Books for Young Adults*.

1055. Blackwood, Gary L. *Shakespeare's Spy.* Penguin, 2003. 281pp. ISBN 978-0-525-47145-5; Puffin, 2005. paper ISBN 978-0-14-240311-2. Grades 5–8.

As Queen Elizabeth I's health fails in late 1602, Widge writes a play that he hopes will attract Judith, Shakespeare's daughter, to him. In this sequel to *The Shakespeare Stealer* (1998) and *Shakespeare's Scribe* (2000), Widge's acting has improved and his "swift writing" allows him to crack a code and help uncover a spy from the Admiral's Men who is stealing scripts from the Lord Chamberlain's Men.

1056. Brittney, Lynn. *Dangerous Times.* 283pp. ISBN 978-0-312-36962-0. Grades 6–9.

In 1587, 13-year-old Nathan Fox agrees to forsake his career as an actor and serve Sir Francis Walsingham, England's spymaster. His ability to disguise himself will be helpful on his mission to Venice with the spy's agent, John Pearce. Also in attendance is his sister Marie, who is a spy pretending to be a gypsy healer. As Nathan is leaving the theater, his friend Will Shakespeare, whom Nathan discovers is also a spy, requests that Nathan tell him about his experiences. In Venice, Nathan becomes involved in the jealousy and intrigue surrounding General Othello and his wife, Desdemona. After he witnesses the results of their misunderstanding he returns to tell Shakespeare.

1057. Buckley, Fiona. *To Shield the Queen: An Ursula Blanchard Mystery at Queen Elizabeth I's Court.* Pocket, 2006. 278pp. Paper ISBN 978-0-7434-8907-2. Grades YA.

Ursula Blanchard is the lady-in-waiting to Queen Elizabeth in 1600. She goes to visit Robin Dudley's wife, who is ill and whom people suspect is slowly being poisoned so that Lord Dudley can marry Elizabeth. But while Ursula is with her, Lady Dudley dies of a broken neck, and expectations change rapidly.

1058. Cadnum, Michael. *Ship of Fire.* Penguin, 2003. 208pp. ISBN 978-0-670-89907-4. Grades 9 up.

Thomas Spyre, 17, sets sail for Spain in 1587 on Sir Francis Drake's ship *Elizabeth Bonaventure* as a surgeon's apprentice after his master loses money gambling on bear-baiting. Thomas is surprised to discover that one of his duties is to spy on Drake because the crown thinks he is not reporting all the spoils taken during battle. When his master dies during the voyage, Thomas suddenly becomes the ship's surgeon because he removed a splinter from Drake's thumb. Sir Robert Garr, an educated philosopher and writer, helps him through the test of performing his first amputation. Then Drake needs Thomas's help as a fighter during a raid on the port of Cadiz. The vivid battles, descriptions of medical supplies and practices, and details of ship life show the realities of the 16th century.

1059. Casanova, Mary. *A Curse of the Winter Moon.* Hyperion, 2000. 144pp. ISBN 978-0-7868-2475-5; 2002. paper ISBN 978-0-7868-1602-6. Grades 3–7.

Marius, who is 12 in 1559, looks after his 6-year-old brother Jean-Pierre, whom the French villagers think will become a *loup garou* (a werewolf), because he was born on Christmas Eve and because their mother, who died in childbirth, said, "Tell Marius to take good care of his brother." Their blacksmith father does little to temper the town's hostility toward Jean-Pierre. Their father has become a Huguenot and has been damned as a heretic by the Catholic Church since he can read. When the Church burns his father at the stake and takes his brother, Marius promises an abbot that he will serve the Church if Jean-Pierre is kept safe. When Jean-Pierre dies, Marius rescues his body only to discover that he is not dead after all. An uncle helps the two boys escape from the horrors that superstition and repression can foster. *Minnesota Book Award.*

1060. Cavendish, Grace. *Conspiracy.* (The Lady Grace Mysteries) Random House, 2005. 208pp. ISBN 978-0-385-73153-9. Grades 3–7.

While the court is traveling during the summer, Lady Grace Cavendish, 13-year-old maid of honor to Elizabeth I, writes in her diary about her attempts to discover who is counterfeiting the new English coin. She collects several suspects when the queen gets into a series of minor accidents. The third volume in the series.

1061. Cavendish, Grace. *Exile.* (The Lady Grace Mysteries) Dell, 2006. 208pp. ISBN 978-0-385-73322-9. Grades 4–7.

When the princess of Sharakand arrives at the court of Queen Elizabeth I in January of 1570, maid of honor Lady Grace Cavendish, 13, tries to identify who has stolen the princess's magical Heart of Kings ruby. Although everyone thinks that Grace's friend Ellie, the laundry maid, took the jewel, Grace knows otherwise. Grace writes her thoughts and feelings in her new pink vellum-covered daybook, a New Year's gift from the Queen. The fifth volume in the series.

1062. Cheaney, J. B. *The Playmaker.* Yearling, 2002. 307pp. Paper ISBN 978-0-440-41710-1. Grades 5–9.

When Richard Malory is 14 in 1597, his mother dies and he goes to London to find his father. His only clue is the name of an attorney who once sent the family money after his father disappeared. What he finds is a Catholic plot to overthrow Queen Elizabeth I. He also meets Henry Condell through a young housemaid who gives him a job with Lord Chamberlain's Men, a group performing the works of playwright Will Shakespeare. Richard feels guilty at first because his Puritan mother had taught him that acting was the work of the devil, but he discovers that he has talent. Richard finds his father, witnesses the beheading of the traitors to the queen, and learns the secrets of an actor's life.

1063. Cheaney, J. B. *The True Prince.* Yearling, 2004. 352pp. Paper ISBN 978-0-440-41940-2. Grades 5–9.

As London's finest young actor, Kit Glover plays women's roles with aplomb. Off-stage, his actions change so rapidly that his rival in the company, Richard Malory, wonders if Kit and his friends are involved in the crimes being perpetrated against other actors, gentlemen, and rivals of the Duke of Essex in Elizabeth's court. The troupe's patron has lost part of his fortune, and as a result the troupe has lost its status as the Admiral's Men and become Lord Hunsdon's Men. During Richard's quest, the beauty of the theater and the language of Shakespeare's plays—especially the two concerning King Henry IV—become apparent, along with the customs of the Elizabethan era.

1064. Chevalier, Tracy. *The Lady and the Unicorn.* Penguin, 2003. 250pp. ISBN 978-0-00-714090-9; Plume, 2004. paper ISBN 978-0-452-28545-3. Grades YA.

See entry 943.

1065. Chisholm, P. F. *A Famine of Horses.* (Sir Robert Carey Mysteries) Poisoned Pen, 1999. 270pp. Paper ISBN 978-1-890208-27-1. Grades YA.

In 1592 Sir Robert Carey becomes Queen Elizabeth's deputy warden of the West March, on the border with Scotland. Almost immediately he has to worry about civil war because of the difference between English and Scottish laws. He also has to discover who murdered Sweetmilk Graham before the clans fight around him. Meanwhile Sir Richard Lowther is furious that he did not get Carey's job. Carey dresses as a peddler to get inside a nearby enemy's tower headquarters and solves the murder with the help of his sister, Philadelphia, and her friend, Elizabeth Widdrington.

1066. Chisholm, P. F. *A Season of Knives.* (Sir Robert Carey Mysteries) Poisoned Pen, 1999. 231pp. Paper ISBN 978-1-890208-32-5. Grades YA.

In Carlisle, near the Scottish border, Sir Robert Carey hears that the Graham clan plans to kidnap Lady Elizabeth Widdrington for a ransom. She is married unhappily to Sir Henry Widdrington, and Carey suspects her husband. After Carey returns from a chase, he discovers that his enemy Sir Richard Lowther has accused Carey's loyal servant, Barnabas, of murdering Jemmy Atkinson and has cast him into prison. Among those suspected are Atkinson's wife, her lover Andy Nixon, and others.

1067. Chute, Marchette G. *The Wonderful Winter.* Green Mansion, 2002. 256pp. ISBN 978-0-9714612-1-5. Grades 5–8.

In 1596 Sir Robert Wakefield ("Robin") decides he must escape from the three aunts who control his life. He visits several places with his dog Ruff and finds that he must go to London for a job because men in small towns do not hire outsiders. In London, when a man tries to steal Ruff, Robin runs inside the Globe Theatre. His new life begins in the properties room, where John Heminges discovers him asleep. He takes Robin home, and Robin begins working for his loving family. When Robin saves Heminges's daughter Seena from drowning, Heminges allows Robin to work in the theater. Robin's first role is in *Romeo and Juliet*, a new play by Shakespeare. Robin loves the theater and wants to stay, but when the season is over, Heminges tells him that the players expect to lose the building. He offers to find him an apprentice job at another theater, but Robin reveals his background and the fact that his love of animals and nature calls him back to his native Suffolk. At home, his aunts welcome him and accept him as the new master of the house.

1068. Conrad, Pam. *Pedro's Journal: A Voyage with Christopher Columbus August 3, 1492–February 14, 1493.* Illustrated by Peter Koeppen. Boyds Mills, 1991. 81pp. ISBN 978-1-878093-17-2; Scholastic, 1992. paper ISBN 978-0-590-46206-8. Grades 3–7.

Pedro accompanies Christopher Columbus on the *Santa Maria* in 1492 because he can read and write. Pedro records the crew's frustration, Columbus's responses to events, encounters with natives, and the fierceness of the storms on their return to Spain.

1069. Cooper, Susan. *King of Shadows.* Illustrated by John Clapp. Simon & Schuster, 1999. 192pp. ISBN 978-0-689-82817-1; Aladdin, 2005. paper ISBN 978-1-4169-0532-5. Grades 5–8.

In London with an American drama troupe to play Puck in *A Midsummer Night's Dream* in the new Globe Theatre replica, modern-day orphan Nat Field goes to bed ill (with symptoms of the plague) and wakes up in 1599. There he is also cast as Puck in a new play and adores his director. This man, William Shakespeare, fulfills Nat's need for a father just as Nat helps him adjust to the death of his own son. Shakespeare also helps Nat overcome his sorrow at his mother's death and his father's suicide. Additionally, Nat adjusts to the costumes, stage effects, makeup, and other practices of 16th-century theater. *Publishers Weekly Best Books of the Year, Carnegie Medal* nomination, *Dorothy Canfield Fisher Children's Book Award* (Vermont) nomination, *Guardian Children's Fiction Prize* nomination, *Boston Globe-Horn Book Awards* nomination, *Bluegrass Award* (Kentucky) nomination, *Children's Book Award* (Maryland) nomination, *Great Stone Face Children's Book Award* (New Hampshire) nomination, *Black-Eyed Susan Book Award* (Maryland) nomination, *Nene Award* (Hawaii) nomination, *Eliot Rosewater Award* (Indiana) nomination; *Sequoyah Book Award* (Oklahoma) nomination, *Land of Enchantment Book Award* (New Mexico) nomination, and *ABC Children's Booksellers Choices Award.*

1070. Curry, Jane Louise. *The Black Canary.* Margaret K. McElderry, 2005. 288pp. ISBN 978-0-689-86478-0. Grades 5–9.

Although he is the child of two musicians, biracial James Parrett, 12, does not like music until he discovers a portal in his uncle's London basement that leads to Elizabethan England. He becomes a recruit into the Children of the Chapel Royal, obtains a part in Benjamin Jonson's new play *Cynthia's Revels*, and prepares a solo for the queen's Twelfth Night celebration. Only after these experiences does he realize how much singing means to him, and he returns to the present with this newly found knowledge.

1071. Deary, Terry. *Top Ten Shakespeare Stories.* (Top Ten) Scholastic, 1999. 192pp. Paper ISBN 978-0-439-08387-4. Grades 6 up.

Ten of Shakespeare's plays, ranked from tenth to first, are discussed. Each chapter also addresses Shakespeare's life and work. The plays are *A Midsummer Night's Dream, King Lear, Twelfth Night, The Tempest, The Merchant of Venice, Romeo and Juliet, Julius Caesar, The Taming of the Shrew, Macbeth,* and *Hamlet.* Topics include the ten ages of Shakespeare, ten actors' tales, a Shakespeare time line, the playwright's use of wordplay, the authorship of the plays, and their audiences. An epilogue completes the discussion.

1072. Duble, Kathleen Benner. *Quest.* Margaret K. McElderry, 2008. 256pp. ISBN 978-1-416-93386-1. Grades 5–8.

The story of the final voyage of Henry Hudson (d. 1611) in 1602 on the *Discovery* as he tries to find a northwest passage to the Orient is told from four different points of view. Those who relate the story are Hudson's son, John, 17; his younger son, Richard, who stays in England with his mother; a stowaway aboard the ship; and a young noble-woman, Isabella Digges, who is a British spy trying to find secret maps from the Dutch East Indies Company in the Netherlands. Letters, diary entries, and personal narratives relate the tale.

1073. Faulkner, Matt. *The Pirate Meets the Queen.* Philomel, 2005. 32pp. ISBN 978-0-399-24038-6. Grades 3–5.

The English capture Toby, the son of Irish pirate queen Granny O'Malley, and Granny tries to meet with Queen Elizabeth I (or "Red Liz," as Granny calls her) to obtain his freedom. Red Liz recognizes Granny as "a woman of consequence," and although Granny promises never to raid Red Liz's ships, she does not quite keep her promise.

1074. Feather, Jane. *Kissed by Shadows.* Bantam, 2003. 469pp. Paper ISBN 978-0-553-58308-3. Grades YA.

When Lady Philippa Nielson, a young bride, meets the handsome Lionel Ashton, she thinks they may have met before. What she does not know is that her husband, Lord Nielson, a favorite of Queen Mary, has involved her in a plot to help King Philip and the Catholic succession. Philip is blackmailing her husband and making him drug her at night so that Philip can try to have a child by her. She has seen Ashton while she was drugged. He is the only person who can help her.

1075. Fiedler, Lisa. *Romeo's Ex: Rosaline's Story.* Holt, 2006. 246pp. ISBN 978-0-8050-7500-7. Grades 7 up.

In Verona in 1595 Rosaline, who is 16 and studying to be a healer, becomes involved with the Montague family just as her cousin, Juliet Capulet, decides to secretly marry Romeo. Romeo had first loved Rosaline, but she has decided to remain chaste. However, Benvolio, Romeo's cousin, saves Rosaline from death during a Capulet-Montague fight, and the two (who have both sworn never to love) fall for each other. Then Rosaline must decide between a career as a healer and marriage.

1076. Francis, Pauline. *Sam Stars at Shakespeare's Globe.* Illustrated by Jane Tattersfield. Frances Lincoln, 2006. 32pp. ISBN 978-1-8450-7406-7. Grades 1–3.

When Sam arrives in London with his mother, they live on London Bridge. He needs work immediately and dresses up to visit the Globe Theatre. He gets a job acting in small parts, but he wants to play Juliet more than anything. When the voice of the boy playing Juliet begins to crack, Sam quickly learns the role and delights the audience with his performance.

1077. Gardner, Sally. *I, Coriander.* Dial, 2005. 280pp. ISBN 978-0-8037-3099-1; Puffin, 2007. paper ISBN 978-0-14-240763-9. Grades 3–7.

Coriander Hobie has inherited magic from her mother. After her Royalist father flees his political enemies in 1643, she must stay with the awful stepmother her father married to save his land. But after her stepmother and a Puritan minister punish her harshly, Coriander wakes up in another world. She learns that her mother was a fairy princess and that the evil stepmother controls people in her real world. She must use the items that her mother left her to help herself and someone in her mother's fairy world. *Great Stone Face Book Award* (New Hampshire) nomination, *School Library Journal Best Books for Children*, and *Publishers Weekly Best Children's Books*.

1078. Garfield, Henry. *The Lost Voyage of John Cabot.* Simon Pulse, 2007. 320pp. Paper ISBN 978-1-416-95460-6. Grades YA.

In 1498 John Cabot went to the New World with two of his sons. His third son, Sebastian, 15, remained in England, annoyed at being left behind. Letters to Sebastian from his brother, Sancio, 14, tell of shipwreck, clashes with the Native Americans, and the arrival of another European fleet. However, Sancio never sent his letters. The oldest brother, Ludovico, is third in command on the *Matthew*, another ship in the fleet. When Sebastian does not hear from them, he goes to the New World to search for them in 1529 and discovers what might have happened. Maps and Glossary.

1079. Gavin, Jamila. *The Blood Stone.* Farrar, 2005. 352pp. ISBN 978-0-374-30846-9. Grades 7 up.

In the 17th century Filippo, 12, and his family face threats from his guardian and brother-in-law Bernardo Pagliarin, who plans to usurp their wealth. Filippo's father, Geronimo, has been gone for the full twelve years of his life, but the family, apart from Bernardo, still believes him to be alive. Filippo departs on a journey to ransom his father with a huge diamond hidden in his skull. He travels to the Hindustan courts with the diamond and the Third Eye of vision that it gives him, allowing him to see both what is happening at home and the futures of the many people he meets. He finally arrives in the Hindu Kush to rescue his father from an Afghan warlord, after selling the jewel to the Shah Jahan.

1080. Gleiter, Jan, and Kathleen Thompson. *Christopher Columbus.* Illustrated by Rick Whipple. Steck-Vaughn, 1995. 32pp. Paper ISBN 978-0-8114-9351-2. Grades 4–7.

In this fictional biography, 13-year-old Ferdinand tells about his father, Christopher Columbus, on his fourth voyage to the New World. As he recounts the other voyages, the son tries to protect his father from the men who want to go ashore against his father's orders. Key Dates.

1081. Greene, Jacqueline Dembar. *One Foot Ashore.* Iuniverse, 2006. 196pp. Paper ISBN 978-0-595-39627-6. Grades 5–8.

Maria Ben Lazar is 10 in 1648 when, during the Portuguese Inquisition, she and her sister Isobel (age 6) are taken from their Jewish parents to Brazil, where they are made to work as slaves and learn the Catholic religion. Maria escapes in 1654 and stows away on a ship to Amsterdam in search of her parents and her sister, from whom she has been separated. In Amsterdam, the Dutch painter Rembrandt, who lives in the Jewish quarter, keeps her in his house until she has the unexpected happiness of being reunited with her parents and later finding that her sister is in New Amsterdam. Isobel's story appears in *Out of Many Waters* (1988). *One Foot Ashore* was first published in 1994.

1082. Grey, Christopher. *Leonardo's Shadow: Or, My Astonishing Life as Leonardo da Vinci's Servant.* Atheneum, 2006. 394pp. ISBN 978-1-416-90543-1; Simon Pulse, 2008. paper ISBN 978-1-416-90544-8. Grades 6–9.

In 1497 Giacomo, 15, becomes Leonardo da Vinci's servant and helps him overcome procrastination to finish *The Last Supper* and avoid his creditors. Giacomo has his own dreams of being an artist and finding who his parents are. He thinks da Vinci might be his father, but as he becomes more mature, he begins to worry about the political intrigue that might affect their livelihood. *IRA Children's Book Award.*

1083. Harding, Georgina. *The Solitude of Thomas Cave.* Bloomsbury, 2007. 240pp. ISBN 978-1-59691-272-4. Grades YA.

In 1616 experienced sailor and whaler Thomas Cave accepts a shipmate's bet to live at a Greenland whaling station through the winter. He hunts and dries reindeer and collects grasses to prepare for the winter. He has a fiddle, but he refuses to play, fearful he will remember his wife Johanne and their baby, who both died five days after the baby's birth. During the winter he remembers other things about his life and comes to understand that the only demons are within his mind, not without. The crew finds him slimmer and quieter when they return.

1084. Harrison, Cora. *My Lady Judge: A Mystery of Medieval Ireland.* Minotaur, 2007. 320pp. ISBN 978-0-312-36836-4; 2008. paper ISBN 978-0-312-38611-5. Grades YA.

In the 16th century, after her appointment as a *brehon*, or judge, Mara goes to Burrens, a western Irish kingdom where the people still live according to their Celtic ancestors' laws. There she must investigate the death of her assistant during a traditional May Day festival. She identifies the criminal using her powers of observation.

1085. Hassinger, Peter W. *Shakespeare's Daughter.* HarperCollins, 2004. 320pp. ISBN 978-0-06-028467-1. Grades 5 up.

Susanna Shakespeare, 14, thinks that London would be much more exciting than Stratford-upon-Avon and that there she would be allowed to sing on stage. After her brother Hamnet suddenly dies, she leaves for London and narrowly escapes a rape. Her rescuer is Emilia—clearly the Dark Lady of Shakespeare's sonnets—who still loves Shakespeare. When Susanna finally arrives in London, she finds that things are not what she expected. She falls in love with Thomas Cole, a Catholic chorister; she discovers family secrets; and she must decide if she can be friends with Emilia without betraying her mother. Eventually Tom and Susanna travel to Italy where he can practice Catholicism and she can sing as a chorister.

1086. Hearn, Julie. *The Minister's Daughter.* Simon Pulse, 2006. 272pp. Paper ISBN 978-0-689-87691-2. Grades YA.

Grace, 15, and her younger sister Patience, the daughters of a Puritan minister, accuse a healer and her granddaughter, Nell, of witchcraft in 1645 when the healer refuses to give Grace an abortion. Grace's tryst occurred on May Day, and the healer says that babies conceived at such times are "merrybegot" and should live. Grace and Patience stage sickroom theatrics, and the villagers dunk the old healer and condemn Nell to hang. They act as scapegoats as Grace grows monthly. The chapters alternate between 1645 and the testimony that Patience gives in Salem, Massachusetts, in 1692. *Horn Book Fanfare*, *Kirkus Reviews Editor's Choice*, and *Capitol Choices Noteworthy Titles* (Washington, D.C.).

1087. Hoffman, Alice. *Incantation.* Little, Brown, 2006. 166pp. ISBN 978-0-316-01019-1; 2007. paper ISBN 978-0-316-15428-4. Grades 8 up.

Estrella, 16, believes she is a Catholic—her family has lived in their Spanish village of Encaleflora for 500 years. During the Inquisition, however, she discovers that she is a Marrano and that her family is underground Jewish. Her best friend, Catalina, betrays their secret when Catalina's boyfriend Andres appears to fall in love with Estrella, and the family suffers torture and murder. *Tayshas Reading List* (Texas), *Sydney Taylor Honor*

Book, Quill Awards nomination, *Teen Book Award* (Rhode Island) nomination, *Publisher's Weekly Best Children's Books* and *Book Award* (Massachusetts).

1088. Hoffman, Mary. ***Stravaganza: City of Flowers.*** (Stravaganza) Bloomsbury, 2005. 496pp. ISBN 978-1-58234-887-2; 2006 paper ISBN 978-1-58234-749-3. Grades 6 up.

Sky Meadow, 17, joins Georgia and the other Stravaganti when he leaves London for Giulia, a city in Talia, during the 16th century. His talisman, an antique perfume bottle, relieves him from the care of his invalid mother for a while. He pretends to be a novice friar as he tries to negotiate between warring Giulia [Florence] families. The di Chimici [Medici] make plans for weddings to unite and strengthen their power while the evil Duke Niccolo plans to involve the young Duchess of Bellezza [Venice]. The complications of the plot and the people allow Sky to survive and succeed. The third volume in the series.

1089. Hoffman, Mary. ***Stravaganza: City of Masks.*** (Stravaganza) Bloomsbury, 2004. 344pp. Paper ISBN 978-1-58234-917-6. Grades 6 up.

Lucien, 15, is at home in England, sick in bed with cancer and coping with chemotherapy, but he makes a journey to a place very much like Venice, Italy, in the parallel world of Bellezza, where he is caught in political intrigue between the Duchess and the di Chimici [Medici]. He uses a "stravagation," a talisman, to travel between his two worlds and gains with it the protection of a powerful noble and a friendship with Adrianna, who wants to be a mandolier. Women cannot follow this career in the 16th century, and when Lucien is given a place in the Schola Mandoliera, Adrianna is furious. As the book ends, Lucien dies in the present but continues to live in the past. This is the first volume in the series. *Booklist Editor's Choice, Pacific Northwest Young Reader's Choice Book Award* nomination, *Capitol Choices Noteworthy Titles* (Washington, D.C.), and *Junior Book Award* (South Carolina) nomination.

1090. Hoffman, Mary. ***Stravaganza: City of Stars.*** (Stravaganza) Bloomsbury, 2005. 452pp. Paper ISBN 978-1-58234-982-4. Grades 6 up.

Georgia, 15, loves horses and hates her older stepbrother. When she buys a winged-horse figurine, she finds she can be transported from London into the 16th century to the city of Remora in Talia [Sienna, Italy]. As a Stravaganta (time traveler between London and Talia), she finds friends and a chance to ride in the Stellata, the annual horse race in the city. She also becomes involved with Cesar, the son of a horsemaster, who has just observed the birth of a real winged horse. Falco, the young son of the di Chimici family, has recently been crippled, and when he learns of Georgia's time travel he asks her to take him into the future to see if a modern treatment can help him. The second volume in the series.

1091. Hofmeyr, Dianne. ***The Faraway Island.*** Illustrated by Jude Daly. Frances Lincoln, 2008. 32pp. ISBN 978-1-8450-7644-3. Grades 1–3.

In the 16th century a Portuguese sailor jumps ship to live on the island of St. Helena by himself. Through the years, other sailors stop and leave seeds, trees, and animals. He plants them and grows a verdant, beautiful garden. The queen of Portugal summons him to her court, and he declares himself a monster before hurrying back to his island. The court seamstress follows, refusing to listen to his protests, and gardens silently beside him until both are content. Illustrations complement the story.

1092. Horowitz, Anthony. *The Devil and His Boy.* Puffin, 2007. 182pp. Paper ISBN 978-0-14-240797-4. Grades 5–8.

In 1593 Tom, 13, hates working at the Pig's Head Inn with the horrible Sebastian and Henrietta Slope. A gentleman takes him from the inn to London, and then the high-wayman Ratsey murders the man. Moll Cutpurse, a pickpocket, befriends Tom, and he decides to become an actor. Will Shakespeare has no parts for him in his new play at the Rose Theater, so Tom agrees to work for Dr. Mobius in *The Devil and His Boy*, a play to be presented before Queen Elizabeth. An actor warns Tom that Ratsey is looking for him, and during the play, as Tom tries to save the queen's life, he ends up in her lap. Throughout this picaresque novel, Tom remains innocent and acted upon rather than understanding much about what he affects. *Voice of Youth Advocates Perfect Ten List.*

1093. Jacobson, Rick. *The Master's Apprentice.* Illustrated by Laura Fernandez. Tundra, 2008. Unpaged. ISBN 978-0-88776-783-8. Grades 3–8.

In 1503 Marco is apprenticed to Michelangelo Buonarroti (1475–1564) and the senior apprentice, Ridolfo, becomes jealous of him. Marco mixes a beautiful emerald green paint that pleases Michelangelo, who wants to know its formula. Since the formula belongs to his chemist father, Marco must decide if he will please his master or his father. Because he chooses his father, Michelangelo chooses Marco instead of Ridolfo to accompany him to Rome to complete his Sistine Chapel commission. Illustrations augment the story.

1094. Jacques, Brian. *The Angel's Command.* Illustrated by David Elliot. (Castaways of the Flying Dutchman) Penguin, 2003. 384pp. ISBN 978-0-399-23999-1; Puffin, 2005. paper ISBN 978-0-14-240285-6. Grades 5 up.

Ben and his black Labrador Ned meet French buccaneer Captain Thuron in 1628 as he gambles with another captain in a Caribbean tavern. Ben tells Captain Thuron that his opponent is cheating. As a reward the captain takes Ben and Ned aboard his ship, *La Petite Marie.* During their voyage, an English privateer and a Spanish buccaneer pursue them. After Thuron dies and the ship has sunk, Ben and Ned go to their next mission in France to help Father Mattieu, Thuron's brother, and to rescue Comte Vicente Bregon. They travel to the Spanish Pyrenees and get the help of Karayna, a gypsy girl who sings and picks pockets, and the artist known as the Facemaker of Sabada. The second volume in the series.

1095. Jacques, Brian. *Castaways of the Flying Dutchman.* Illustrated by Ian Schoenherr. Penguin, 2001. 336pp. ISBN 978-0-399-23601-3; Puffin, 2003. paper ISBN 978-0-14-250118-4. Grades 5 up.

Neb, a mute boy of 13, and his dog Denmark wash overboard in 1620 when they are castaways on the ghost ship *The Flying Dutchman*, which an angel has cursed to sail throughout eternity without rest. The angel that doomed the ship makes Neb and Den immortal and restores Neb's voice. The dog and boy are able to read each other's thoughts; however, they must endlessly roam the earth helping people in trouble until they hear a bell ringing. Then they must help someone else. In 1896 the pair (now known as Ben and Ned) end up in the small English village of Chapelvale, which will be destroyed to create a limestone quarry unless they can prove that a Mrs. Winifred Winn owns the land. The first in a series.

1096. Kolosov, Jacqueline. *The Red Queen's Daughter.* Hyperion, 2007. 399pp. ISBN 978-1-4231-0797-2. Grades 9 up.

After her father, Thomas Seymour, and her mother, Catherine Parr, die, the orphaned Lady Mary Seymour's guardian, the fey Lady Strange, decides that she is a white magician and must protect Elizabeth I. She learns about potions, the power in jewels, and England's history. When called to Elizabeth's presence, Lady Mary's ability to tell a person's character through their auras and jewels disintegrates when she meets her cousin Edmund Seymour. She falls in love with him and becomes his prey in a plot against Elizabeth I.

1097. Lasky, Kathryn. *Blood Secret.* HarperCollins, 2004. 256pp. ISBN 978-0-06-000066-0; Harper Trophy, 2006. paper ISBN 978-0-06-000063-9. Grades 7 up.

Jerry Luna, 14, has been selectively mute in the years since her mother's disappearance from a campground. After living in different Catholic Charities homes, she goes to live with her great-great-aunt Constanza in New Mexico and discovers a trunk with mementos—a silver medal, lace, a publication—that take her into the world of her ancestors. Miriam speaks from Seville in 1391 where she watched her relatives burn to death and converted to Christianity to save herself. The survivors of Jerry's Jewish family fled to Mexico. Jerry also finds that Aunt Constanza still lights Sabbath candles and follows other rituals unknown to Jerry, who was raised a Catholic. Slowly, as Jerry identifies herself and her past, she begins to speak again. *Garden State Teen Book Award* (New Jersey) nomination.

1098. Lasky, Kathryn. *Mary, Queen of Scots: Queen Without a Country.* Scholastic, 2002. 202pp. ISBN 978-0-439-19404-4. Grades 5–8.

Mary, the 11-year-old Scottish queen, receives a diary from her mother and records her experiences while living in the French court of King Henry II while she awaits her marriage to Henry's son, Francis. Mary knows her position yet wants love and friendship. She likes pretty clothes and dances but wants to be respected and treated as an adult. She misses her mother and Scotland terribly, but must stay where she is since it is safer than Scotland. Note.

1099. Lawlor, Laurie. *The Two Loves of Will Shakespeare.* Holiday House, 2006. 256pp. ISBN 978-0-8234-1901-2. Grades 12 up.

Although Will Shakespeare, 18, serves as an apprentice in his father's glove-making business, he prefers to bed the barmaid Mops, carouse with his drunken Uncle Hal, or dream about the theater. His friend Richard asks him to write some sonnets for him to give to his girlfriend, Anne Whateley, and Will borrows some lines from his literate sister. But Will falls in love with Anne Whateley as well and applies for a license to marry her. But when the older Anne Hathaway (who is 26) seduces him, he willingly acquiesces. His second marriage license is to her, and the result is their daughter Susanna.

1100. Libby, Alisa M. *The Blood Confession.* Dutton, 2006. 389pp. ISBN 978-0-525-47732-7. Grades YA.

In Hungary during the 16th century Countess Erzebet Bizeca (based on the real Countess Bathory) recounts her story as she awaits execution for murdering many of her servant girls. After Erzebet's mother went insane, Erzebet began bathing in blood to retain her youth and beauty. She soon convinced herself that she could achieve immortality through committing murder. As she considered peasants expendable, she continued to drink the blood of her servants as she dissolved into her own insanity.

1101. Llorente, Pilar Molina. *The Apprentice.* Illustrated by Juan Ramon Alonso. Translated by Robin Longshaw. Sunburst, 1994. 101pp. Paper ISBN 978-0-374-40432-1. Grades 6–9.

Arduino wants to become a painter's apprentice in Florence, Italy, during the Renaissance. He gets his chance, but finds that his dream of painting frescoes does not match the reality of cleaning and mixing pigments. He also finds that the Maestro is keeping the previous apprentice chained in the attic because his talent promised to be greater than the Maestro's. When the Maestro becomes ill, Arduino convinces him to free Donato from the attic and let him complete an important commission. He does, and Donato and Arduino save the Maestro's reputation. A serving woman, also annoyed by various situations, and a duchess show the female point of view and demonstrate that women never had a chance to be apprentices in the Renaissance. *Mildred L. Batchelder Award.*

1102. Llywelyn, Morgan. *The Last Prince of Ireland: A Novel.* Tor, 2001. 445pp. Paper ISBN 978-0-8125-7913-0. Grades YA.

Donal Cam O'Sullivan decides that he will defend Ireland against the British after he finds his sons murdered. He and his clan flee their wet and cold countryside in 1602 after the Battle of Kinsale to find protection inland at the stronghold of Brian O'Rourke. There they wait for a better opportunity to defeat the British.

1103. Maguire, Gregory. *Mirror Mirror.* ReganBooks, 2004. 304pp. Paper ISBN 978-0-06-098865-4. Grades YA.

In 1502, 7-year-old Bianca de Navada lives on her father Don Vicente's farm in Montefiore, Italy. One day Casare Borgia and his sister Lucrezia appear at the farm, and Lucrezia sends Don Vicente on a quest to find a branch from the biblical Tree of Knowledge. Lucrezia looks after Bianca, but when Cesare becomes attracted to Bianca four years later, Lucrezia orders a hunter to murder her in the forest. Seven dwarfs find and save her. After seventeen years, Vicente returns home with the branch and discovers his daughter is missing and most likely dead. Lucrezia pursues her with a poisoned apple after her grandson Ranucchio reveals Bianca's location to Vicente. But Bianca survives and Lucrezia suffers in this retelling of the Snow White tale.

1104. Mallory, Tess. *Highland Fling.* Love Spell, 2003. 320pp. Paper ISBN 978-0-505-52526-0. Grades YA.

On a trip to Scotland, Texas scientist and wallflower Chelsea Brown meets Griffin Campbell when he is transported to the 21st century from 1605. Then the two of them end up in the Wild West. Griffin cannot become the Clan Campbell's chieftain until he marries, but he hates his betrothed and vomits every time he tries to get romantic with any woman. He and Chelsea, however, immediately fall in love while anguishing that they can never be together. Chelsea saves Griffin from a dishonest sheriff and they solve some of their problems.

1105. Marston, Edward. *The Laughing Hangman.* (Missing Mysteries) Poisoned Pen, 2002. 248pp. Paper ISBN 978-1-59058-023-3. Grades YA.

When Lord Westfield's men decide to present Jonas Applegarth's irreverent play *The Misfortunes of Marriage*, they disturb their rivals, the Blackfriars, and attract Applegarth's many enemies. After his murder, they understand the play in a different way, and perform it stunningly. Nick Bracewell must keep the troupe together throughout the affair while watching for the murderer.

1106. Marston, Edward. *The Mad Courtesan.* (Missing Mysteries) Poisoned Pen, 2002. 248pp. Paper ISBN 978-1-890208-83-7. Grades YA.

Nicholas Bracewell, stage manager for Lord Westfield's Men in London, has several problems. The leading man of Nick's troupe has fallen in love with a beauty; the health of Elizabeth I, Good Queen Bess, is in decline; a rival company begins to do well; and someone murders the gentleman player Sebastian Carrick. Bracewell wonders why he feels as if a shadow has fallen over him and the times.

1107. Marston, Edward. *The Merry Devils.* (Missing Mysteries) Poisoned Pen, 2001. 237pp. Paper ISBN 978-1-890208-55-4. Grades YA.

Lord Westfield's Men, an actors' troupe, loses one of its devils in the second performance of *The Merry Devils*. The leader, Nicholas Bracewell, has to investigate the mystery. He is able to put the pieces together when the troupe goes to Parkbrook to perform the play for Francis Jordan. He finds out that Jordan has tried to get rid of the estate's real heir but failed.

1108. Marston, Edward. *The Nine Giants.* (Missing Mysteries) Poisoned Pen, 2001. 236pp. Paper ISBN 978-1-890208-68-4. Grades YA.

Nicholas Bracewell, the stage manager for Lord Westfield's Men, an acting troupe in Elizabethan England, must look after the company's logistics as well as the men. In this book, the company's star has an affair, someone assaults an apprentice, Bracewell and the local waterman find a body in the Thames, and the troupe faces possible expulsion from the theater if its ownership changes hands. The problems come to a head at the Lord Mayor's Show, when people line the streets and the Thames for parade and pomp.

1109. Marston, Edward. *The Queen's Head.* (Missing Mysteries) Poisoned Pen, 2000. 237pp. Paper ISBN 978-1-890208-45-5. Grades YA.

In 1588, Nicholas Bracewell, stage manager of Lord Westfield's Men in London, has to find a replacement for the company's leading actor and keep his promise to a dying man that he will find the murderer. Accidents, robberies, and other misfortunes occur, but the company receives an invitation to appear at the court of Queen Elizabeth. At the court performance, Bracewell identifies the murderer.

1110. Marston, Edward. *The Roaring Boy.* (Missing Mysteries) Poisoned Pen, 2002. 237pp. Paper ISBN 978-1-59058-001-1. Grades YA.

Nicholas Bracewell, the Elizabethan stage manager, helps to create a new kind of play based on a murder case. When Lord Westfield's Men stage it, Bracewell has to deal with the result. *Edgar Nomination.*

1111. Marston, Edward. *The Silent Woman.* (Missing Mysteries) Poisoned Pen, 2002. 237pp. Paper ISBN 978-1-59058-000-4. Grades YA.

When fire destroys the London home of Lord Westfield's Men, the troupe has to go on tour to make money. Before they leave, a woman trying to deliver a message to

Nicholas Bracewell, the troupe's stage manager, is killed before she reaches him. Bracewell realizes that he must return to his childhood home to solve the murder, and there he meets his past.

1112. Marston, Edward. *The Trip to Jerusalem.* (Missing Mysteries) Poisoned Pen, 2001. 223pp. Paper ISBN 978-1-59058-860-8. Grades YA.

Nicholas Bracewell and the acting troupe Lord Westfield's Men plan to leave London during the Black Plague to tour the North. But one of their members dies before they are able to leave, and after they depart they discover that Banbury's Men, a rival troupe, has been stealing their best plays. While they present a play in York the threads of a murderous plot come together.

1113. Matas, Carol. *The Burning Time.* Orca, 1996. 113pp. Paper ISBN 978-1-55143-624-1. Grades 6–10.

Rose Rives, aged 15 in 1600, helps her mother with herbs and midwifery in France. When her father falls off a horse and dies, her life changes. Rose's mother saves the life of the wife and child of their chateau owner, but the doctor says that her mother must be evil to be able to do things he cannot. This attitude extends into the village, and Rose's mother and other women are accused of witchcraft. Rose sees her mother scalded in torture, and she gives her herbs in secret to save her from further suffering before escaping herself. Not for five years are the innocent women cleared, but by then, almost all of them have been burned.

1114. Maxwell, Robin. *The Secret Diary of Anne Boleyn.* Arcade, 1997. 288pp. ISBN 978-1-55970-375-8; Touchstone, 1998. paper ISBN 978-0-684-84969-0. Grades YA.

In her secret diary, Anne Boleyn keeps a log of her life and warns her daughter to never let a man control her the way she let Henry finally have control over her. In her childhood, Elizabeth hears only that her mother was an adulterer and a traitor. When Elizabeth receives her mother's diary from an old friend of her mother's after she becomes queen, she learns about the real woman Anne Boleyn was.

1115. Melnikoff, Pamela. *Prisoner in Time: A Child of the Holocaust.* Jewish Publication Society, 2001. 144pp. ISBN 978-0-8276-0735-4. Grades 6–10.

In 1942, 12-year-old Jan leaves the Prague attic in which he is hiding and visits an old cemetery. He picks up an amulet that takes him back to Prague in the 16th century. There he meets Rabbi Judah Loew ben Bezalel (ca. 1525–1609), and the two create the monster Golem to scare those in the area who are accusing Jews of killing Christian children. Back in 1942, the Nazis transport Jan to Terezin concentration camp and he sees the guards fixing up the camp for a scheduled Red Cross inspection. But, like the other 15,000 children in Terezin, Jan later goes to a death camp.

1116. Meyer, Carolyn. *Beware, Princess Elizabeth.* (Young Royals) Gulliver, 2002. 224pp. Paper ISBN 978-0-15-204556-2. Grades 5–8.

Elizabeth, 13, endures the political intrigues that befall her 9-year-old half brother, Edward, and her half sister, Mary, after the death of their father, King Henry VIII, in 1547. To survive all of the plots and cope with those adults who broke faith with her after she trusted them, Elizabeth becomes ruthless and self-absorbed. After eleven years, she becomes the queen of England herself and rules with intelligence.

1117. Meyer, Carolyn. *Doomed Queen Anne.* (Young Royals) Gulliver, 2004. 230pp. Paper ISBN 978-0-15-205086-3. Grades 5–9.

When Anne Boleyn (1507–1536) was 6 years old, she went to court in the Netherlands and when she was 7, to the French court. She was the sister of King Henry VIII's mistress, and at 13 she decided that she wanted the king's attention. He acknowledged her and she began to subtly seduce him by withholding her sexual gifts. He eventually married her and she became queen. During her attempt to marry him, she made many enemies in the court and did not get much sympathy when he imprisoned her in the Tower of London on false charges and had her beheaded. During their marriage, she bore the king a daughter who would become Queen Elizabeth I.

1118. Meyer, Carolyn. *Duchessina: A Novel of Catherine de' Medici.* (Young Royals) Harcourt, 2007. 261pp. ISBN 978-0-15-205588-2. Grades 9 up.

Catherine de' Medici, although the sole heiress to the Medici wealth, spent her childhood in a cold convent. In 1533, when she was 14, her uncle, Pope Clement VII, decided she would marry Prince Henri of France, in line to be king. Catherine, then in her uncle's household, must adjust to this position and learn how to become one of France's most powerful queens.

1119. Meyer, Carolyn. *Loving Will Shakespeare.* Harcourt, 2006. 272pp. ISBN 978-0-15-205451-9. Grades 8–12.

Agnes (Anne) Hathaway, living with an unloving stepmother and her farmer father, thinks about the much younger Will Shakespeare, 18, all the time, and when he kisses her, she decides to marry him. Although this allows her to leave her childhood home, she cannot escape many of the societal expectations for women. She must stay in her own home and raise her children while Will continues to enjoy himself. Eventually he even leaves her to move to London to follow his love of the theater.

1120. Meyer, Carolyn. *Patience, Princess Catherine.* (Young Royals) Harcourt, 2004. 208pp. ISBN 978-0-15-216544-4; Gulliver, 2005. paper ISBN 978-0-15-205447-2. Grades YA.

Spanish princess Catharine of Aragon, 15, arrives in England in 1501 to marry Arthur, King Henry VII's oldest son. He unexpectedly dies six months later. The marriage was unconsummated and Catherine's future seems unresolved. However, she decides that she will one day be England's queen, hoping to marry Arthur's brother Henry. And indeed, when Prince Henry becomes king, they marry. In 1533, she remembers these days as she refuses to release Henry VIII from their marriage after the birth of their daughter Mary so that he can make Anne Boleyn his queen.

1121. Napoli, Donna Jo. *Daughter of Venice.* Laurel-Leaf, 2003. 275pp. Paper ISBN 978-0-440-22928-5. Grades 6–10.

In 1529 Donata, 14, has difficulty living under the strict rules of her Venetian family. She cannot leave the palazzo for an education so she disguises herself as a boy and sneaks out to see life in the streets. During her wanderings, she meets Noe, a Jewish copyist, and falls in love with him. At the same time, she begs her father to let her sit with her brothers during their tutoring sessions so she can get an education. Donata wants to live within the conventions of her family and somehow she succeeds without sacrificing her own happiness.

1122. Orgad, Dorit. *The Boy from Seville.* Illustrated by Avi Katz. Translated by Sondra Silverston. Kar-Ben, 2007. 200pp. ISBN 978-1-58013-253-4. Grades 5–7.

Manuel, 11, has to keep his Jewish identity completely secret in Seville, Spain, during the 17th century after his family moves from Portugal. In fact, his family has become *conversos*: Jews nominally converted to Christianity. His father, a revered physician, has saved many during the Black Death, but this will do nothing to save the family if servants or others spy on them and report any celebration of the Sabbath or high holidays. His grandparents were burned at the stake by the Inquisition, and the rest of his family could also suffer this fate. When he meets Violanti, also a *converso*, he is happy to be able to share his difficulties, but the family flees to Amsterdam.

1123. Ortiz, Michael J. *Swan Town: The Secret Journal of Susanna Shakespeare.* HarperCollins, 2006. 208pp. ISBN 978-0-06-058126-8. Grades 6–10.

In 1597 William Shakespeare's daughter Susanna, 13, angry at not being allowed to practice Catholicism or to see a Puritan medical student, writes in a journal and composes a play. She lives in Stratford, a place she calls Swan Town, but she wants to travel to London to act in plays as her father does. Unfortunately, women are prohibited from acting. Her brother Hamnet dies of the plague, she sees a Catholic chapel being destroyed, and her parents are sent to prison on charges of religious treason. Then Susanna gets to visit London, where she persuades the clown at the Globe Theatre to let her and her sister Judith present her play as a prologue to her father's premier performance of *Hamlet*. At the same time, her relationship with Dr. John Hall develops. Susanna records these events in her diary and infuses phrases from her father's plays into her musings about life.

1124. Osborne, Mary Pope. *Monday with a Mad Genius.* Illustrated by Sal Murdocca. (Magic Tree House) Random House, 2007. 110pp. ISBN 978-0-375-83729-6. Grades K–3.

Jack and Annie end up in Florence, Italy, where they help Leonardo da Vinci (1452–1519) in hope of finding another secret to happiness. They sit for the *Mona Lisa* and try to use the artist's flying machine. The 38th volume in this long-running series.

1125. Otto, Whitney. *The Passion Dream Book.* HarperCollins, 1998. 276pp. Paper ISBN 978-0-06-109623-5. Grades YA.

To be an artist in Renaissance Florence, Giulietta Marcel must dress herself as a man and spy on Michelangelo for the man who wants to write Michelangelo's biography. She learns about art from him and wonders how to become an artist herself. In Los Angeles in 1918, Romy March, Giulietta's descendent, wants to be an artist, and she teams with the African American photographer Augustine Marks. They move to Harlem, where the dark-skinned Romy passes as black. They open a studio and begin to document another renaissance in Harlem. However, Romy cannot succeed until she moves to Paris and becomes part of a third renaissance.

1126. Pope, Elizabeth Marie. *The Perilous Gard.* Illustrated by Richard Cuffari. Houghton, 2001. 272pp. ISBN 978-0-618-17736-3; paper ISBN 978-0-618-15073-1. Grades 6 up.

In 1558 Queen Mary sends Kate from Hatfield House to Sir Geoffrey's Elvenwood Hall in Derbyshire, the place known as the "perilous gard." The people there are fearful of fairy folk who live in the caves and think that Kate is one of them. She shows that she is not by saving a boy during a flash flood. But when Sir Geoffrey's young daughter disappears, Kate realizes that the fairy folk have kidnapped her for their All Hallows' Eve sacrifice. She follows them and tells her friend Christopher where to go to trade places with Kate. Because she learns their rules, Kate claims Christopher before the sacrifice, and the fairy folk must free him. *Newbery Honor Book.*

1127. Richardson, V. A. *The House of Windjammer.*   Bloomsbury, 2003. 300pp. ISBN 978-1-58234-811-7; paper ISBN 978-1-58234-984-8. Grades 6–9.

In 1636, the year that tulip fever overtook Amsterdam, the Windjammer family lost its entire trading fleet. Adam, 14, has to reestablish the family's reputation and business after his father dies. His most formidable enemy, banker Hugo van Helsen, wants his money, and his daughter Jade and Abner Heems, an evil preacher, have a hand in the Windjammer ruin. Adam almost finds the rare Black Pearl tulip that will help him meet his creditor's deadline, but other creditors help him finish his vessel, *Draco,* so that he can sail to America.

1128. Richardson, V. A. *The Moneylender's Daughter.*   Bloomsbury, 2006. 382pp. ISBN 978-1-58234-885-8. Grades 7–10.

In 1637 young Adam Windjammer decides to sail to America after his family loses all its money. He hopes to find his uncle's shipwreck and some of the goods that would restore the family's name. But on his journey, he continues to think of Jade van Helsen, the daughter of the moneylender who stripped the family of its wealth. Jade still desires her ruthless father's approval and tries to save him from a huge financial error by marrying a wealthy and elderly English gentleman in this sequel to *The House of Windjammer.*

1129. Rinaldi, Ann. *Nine Days a Queen: The Short Life and Reign of Lady Jane Grey.* HarperCollins, 2005. 192pp. ISBN 978-0-06-054923-7; Trophy, 2006. paper ISBN 978-0-06-054925-1. Grades 7 up.

Lady Jane Grey (1537–1554), forced to become the queen of England by marriage to keep the Catholic Mary off the throne, finds herself suffering for her parents' political aspirations when nine days later she is beheaded. She speaks from the grave to tell the story of her youth; her friendships with cousins Edward, Mary, and Elizabeth; and her happiest days, which were spent away from her scheming parents.

1130. Rinaldi, Ann. *The Redheaded Princess.*   HarperCollins, 2008. 224pp. ISBN 978-0-06-073374-2. Grades 5–8.

By the time Elizabeth is 9 years old in 16th-century England, she has learned not to trust anyone. She is intelligent and knows how to survive. During her ascension to the throne to become Elizabeth I after the death of her half sister Mary, she sees her father, Henry VIII, rid himself of wives who do not give him a male heir. She becomes enamored with Robin Dudley although he is married to someone else and enjoys Sir Thomas Seymour's flattery—but enjoys wise counsel from those who support her.

1131. Rogers, Gregory. *The Boy, the Bear, the Baron, the Bard.*   Roaring Brook, 2004. 32pp. ISBN 978-1-59643-009-9; 2007. paper ISBN 978-1-59643-267-3. Grades K–2.

When a young boy kicks his soccer ball through the window of an old theater, he goes inside to retrieve it and discovers himself in Elizabethan London on the stage of the Globe Theatre. Shakespeare, angry with his interruption, chases him away, but the boy becomes friends with a bear. The watercolor pictures of this wordless picture book reveal a brief encounter with Elizabeth I and with a condemned prisoner in the Tower of London. *New York Times Best Illustrated Books, Kirkus Reviews Editor's Choice, Publisher's Weekly Best Children's Books, School Library Journal Best Books for Children,* and *American Library Association Notable Children's Books.*

1132. Sabuda, Robert. *Uh-Oh, Leonardo! The Adventures of Providence Traveler.* Simon & Schuster, 2003. 48pp. ISBN 978-0-689-81160-9. Grades 2–4.

Providence Traveler, a mouse, admires Leonardo da Vinci since she loves to make things. She discovers a mechanical mouse with a key in its back in one of the books about his inventions and has finished making it when her brother and the McMuzzin twins rush in and turn the key in the mouse. Suddenly they find themselves in Florence, Italy, in 1503, when Leonardo is working there. After meeting a number of mice with unusual occupations, Providence has the opportunity to meet her hero. To get back to their homes, the four mice must find the key to the mechanical mouse that has come with them.

1133. Selfors, Suzanne. *Saving Juliet.* Walker, 2008. 256pp. ISBN 978-0-8027-9740-7. Grades 8 up.

Mimi Wallingford, 17, who has performed on stage since the age of 3, often hears from her mother about their family's reputation and how she must keep it intact. With intense stage fright, Mimi wants to go to medical school instead. However, she finds herself cast as Juliet opposite a teen idol's Romeo, and is transported to Verona to meet the real Juliet after inhaling the smoke of a burned Shakespearean quill. Realizing that they share mothers forcing them to do something unwanted, Mimi decides that she will save Juliet. This takes more than one attempt as Mimi also tries to return to Manhattan and her parents' failing Shakespeare theater.

1134. Silbert, Leslie. *The Intelligencer.* Simon & Schuster, 2005. 368pp. Paper ISBN 978-0-7434-3293-1. Grades YA.

Detective Kate Morgan has to investigate an attempted murder connected to a Tudor spy's scrapbook that shows up in modern London. The information about murders during the Renaissance—including that in 1593 of playwright Christopher Marlowe, who served as a spy for Queen Elizabeth I's secret service—is written in ciphers that must be decoded. As the setting shifts between modern-day and Elizabethan England, Kate's firm wants to take her off the case because a descendant of those murderers is threatening her U.S. senator father. Kate's knowledge of Renaissance history and her ability as a private eye twist the plot. *Dilys Award* nomination.

1135. Singleton, Sarah. *Out of the Shadows.* Clarion, 2008. 252pp. ISBN 978-0-618-92722-7. Grades 6–10.

In 1586 Elizabeth Dyer's Catholic family hides a priest from Protestant reformers. Elizabeth also befriends Isabella, a shy girl with greenish skin who appeared near a stream. She discovers that Isabella's mother, Ruth, was accused of and executed for witchcraft in 1241. Before her death, she arranged for the Crow people to protect Isabella and gave them Isabella's half-faerie brother, John. As Elizabeth's family comes closer to torture and prosecution, Isabella helps her create a pact with the faeries to save Elizabeth's family. Note.

1136. Thomas, Jane Resh. *The Counterfeit Princess.* Clarion, 2005. 208pp. ISBN 978-0-395-93870-6. Grades 6–10.

In 1553 the Duke of Northumberland executes Iris's parents and takes over their estate. Iris, 15, begins training as a spy for Elizabeth. With her red-gold hair and stubborn ways, Iris resembles the Princess Elizabeth so much that she acts as her double when trying to escape Northumberland's men before Queen Mary's Catholic supporters overthrow him. Elizabeth and Iris have the pleasure of confirming that he is confined in the Tower. Iris continues enjoying the independence that she has gained by serving Elizabeth.

1137. Thomson, Sarah L. *The Secret of the Rose.* Greenwillow, 2006. 296pp. ISBN 978-0-06-087250-2. Grades 6–9.

In 1592, after her father has died while imprisoned for being Catholic, 14-year-old Rosalind and her brother must hide their beliefs. They also must get jobs, and Rosalind disguises herself as a boy so that they both can get jobs at London's Rose Theatre. Rosalind becomes a servant to playwright Christopher Marlow. He has his own secrets that endanger her and lead to his murder. Through it all, Rosalind finds a place for herself and a promising life.

1138. Townley, Roderick. *The Red Thread: A Novel in Three Incarnations.* Atheneum, 2007. 294pp. ISBN 978-1-416-90894-4. Grades 7 up.

Sixteen-year-old Dana becomes bothered with insomnia, nightmares, and claustrophobia and sees Dr. Sprague, a therapist who hypnotizes her into remembering her past lives. She finds herself in 18th-century London as the niece of a cruel aunt, and as a small boy named William in 1583 who is murdered for his inheritance. In her present life, she visits England with her wheelchair-bound brother and her boyfriend, Chase, to take a portrait of the young William Breen to the Breen family castle. During the journey, she realizes that facing her past might help her find her place in the present.

1139. Treviño, Elizabeth Borton de. *I, Juan de Pareja.* Farrar, 1965. 192pp. ISBN 978-0-374-33531-1; Sunburst, 1987. paper ISBN 978-0-374-43525-7. Grades 6–9.

In the 17th century Juan is artist Diego Velasquez's slave while Velasquez serves King Philip IV in Spain. Juan loves to watch the painter at work, and although slaves are banned by law from painting, Juan secretly does so. He sees Peter Paul Rubens during a court visit in 1628 and hears that he uses nudes as models. Juan goes with Velasquez to Italy in 1649 to paint nobles and to collect artworks for the king. At the age of 40, Juan tells Velasquez and the king that he has been painting, and Velasquez frees him immediately so that he will not suffer punishment of any kind. Juan learns the value of truth in life and in painting according to Velasquez. *Newbery Medal.*

1140. Turnbull, Ann. *No Shame, No Fear.* Candlewick, 2004. 293pp. ISBN 978-0-7636-2505-4; 2006. paper ISBN 978-0-7636-3190-1. Grades 7–12.

In 1662 Susanna Thorn, 15, falls in love with William Heywood, who is 17. She is Quaker, and he is a wealthy Anglican. Since the law has declared Quaker observance illegal, they are both compromised when Will decides to change his religion. Susanna's parents are imprisoned and persecuted, and Susanna is also condemned when she continues to meet with Quaker children while the adults serve time in jail. *Capitol Choices Noteworthy Titles* (Washington, D.C.).

1141. Vreeland, Susan. *The Passion of Artemisia.* Penguin, 2003. 288pp. Paper ISBN 978-0-14-200182-0. Grades YA.

Artemisia Gentileschi (1593–1652), a superb painter, found herself compromised as a young woman in Rome when her father's painting partner, Agostino Tassi, raped her. Although he was convicted, he was released after eight months in jail, and Artemisia asks her father to get her a husband. She marries Pietro Stiatessi, a painter living in Florence, and they have a daughter, Palmira. Artemisia, however, is a better artist than her husband, and he becomes jealous of her talent. The Medicis offer her patronage, and she is the first woman elected to the Academia dell'Arte. She leaves to paint in Venice and Naples but sends money home to support her daughter. She eventually accepts patronage in Genoa. Near the end of her father's life, she reconciles with him as well as her daughter.

1142. Weir, Alison. *Innocent Traitor: A Novel of Lady Jane Grey.* Ballantine, 2007. 402pp. ISBN 978-0-345-49485-6; paper ISBN 978-0-345-49534-1. Grades YA.

As the great-niece of King Henry VIII of England, Lady Jane Grey became a political pawn. When Edward VI died, her parents tried to get her on the throne in place of the legal heiress, Mary. After Mary ascended to the throne, she beheaded Lady Jane. As Jane tells her story, she shows that she is intelligent but that she cannot control those around her.

1143. Weir, Alison. *The Lady Elizabeth.* Ballantine, 2008. 480pp. ISBN 978-0-345-49535-8. Grades YA.

Declared a bastard after Henry VIII has her mother, Anne Boleyn, beheaded, Lady Elizabeth finds herself third in line to the throne. She has to protect herself from dangers all around. Her stepfather, Thomas Seymour, tries to molest her. Her fanatical Catholic sister, Queen Mary I, tries to kill her, seeing her as a Protestant threat. And she has to decide what opinions she will have as an adult toward power, women, religion, and politics. Among her decisions is never to marry after a painful experience with romance when she is 14. Notes.

1144. Wooderson, Philip. *The Plague: Rachel's Story / Robert's Story.* Kingfisher, 2006. 96pp. Paper ISBN 978-0-7534-5990-4. Grades 5–8.

In London in 1665, Rachel and her family try to maintain a normal life even though the plague surrounds them. Friends and servants die, and then Rachel's cousin Robert, who is also her father's clerk, disappears. The family finally flees to Saxton, where Robert's family lives, and Rachel's mother brings her Versailles fabric imported by her husband's business rival, Gilles Pethbridge. They find Robert. He tells them that he was press-ganged into warfare but was able to desert and return to Saxton to hide. He sees the fabric and realizes that Pethbridge and his crony, the Earl of Styx, had received concealed messages from France inside the fabric folds during a conspiracy to restore Catholicism in England. He also thinks that the fabric may have transmitted the plague but has no way to prove his theory. Robert's story appears on one side of the book and Rachel's on the other.

1145. Yolen, Jane, and Robert J. Harris. *Queen's Own Fool: A Novel of Mary Queen of Scots.* Puffin, 2001. 390pp. Paper ISBN 978-0-698-11918-5. Grades YA.

Twelve-year-old Nicola Ambruzzi leaves Troupe Brufort to serve as the fool for Mary Queen of Scots (1542–1567). In this position, she is close to political and religious unrest in both France and Scotland. Her job is to tell the queen truths and entertain her; she does so in ways that do not insult the queen but make her laugh as she observes her pompous advisers, her lords, and her womanizing husband. *School Librarians Battle of the Books* (Alaska) nomination, *Student Book Award* (Maine) nomination, *American Library Association Association Notable Books for Children, Young Adult Reading Program* (South Dakota), and *Capitol Choices Noteworthy Titles* (Washington, D.C.).

History

1146. Aronson, Marc, and John W. Glenn. *The World Made New: Why the Age of Exploration Happened and How It Changed the World.* National Geographic, 2007. 64pp. ISBN 978-0-7922-6454-5. Grades 4–6.

Three general sections introduce the civilizations living in the Americas and in Europe before Columbus arrived, the impact of explorers between 1492 and 1586, and the idea that the arrival of explorers in 1492 was equal to the surprise of space travel in the modern era. The explorers presented are Cortes, Pizarro, Cartier, De Soto, and Drake. The consequences of their exploration included new plants and animals, the introduction of disease, changes in populations, migration, and the spread of different ideas. Illustrations enhance the text. Chronology, Further Reading, Glossary, Maps, Bibliography, Web Sites, and Index.

1147. Berleth, Richard. *The Twilight Lords: Elizabeth I and the Plunder of Ireland.* Roberts Rinehart, 2002. 340pp. Paper ISBN 978-1-57098-376-4. Grades YA.

Sixteenth-century Ireland was a place of clans and chieftains, feudal relationships and tribes, and regional and hereditary conflicts. The English, under Queen Elizabeth, thought the Irish were an inferior race and they decided to take Irish land for themselves between 1579 and 1599. The feudal barons of Ireland (Gerald Fitzgerald, Earl of Desmond; James Fitzmaurice, Captain of Desmond; and Hugh O'Neill, Earl of Tyrone) tried to defend themselves against Peter Carew, Warham St. Leger, Edmund Spenser, Walter Raleigh, Francis Walsingham, and others. The queen's men won after they decimated the population of southern Ireland. They destroyed anyone standing in their way to wealth and control. Genealogies, Select Chapter Bibliographies, and Index.

1148. Bernhard, Brendan. *Pizarro, Orellana, and the Exploration of the Amazon.* (World Explorers) Facts on File, 1991. 120pp. ISBN 978-0-7910-1305-2. Grades 4 up.

Francisco de Orellana (d. 1546?) and Francisco Pizarro (ca. 1475–1541) journeyed through the Amazon Basin in the early 16th century. This book also discusses the Inca and the Spanish conquest of South America. Bibliography and Index.

1149. Elgin, Kathy. *Elizabethan England.* (History of Costume and Fashion) Facts on File, 2005. 64pp. ISBN 978-0-8160-5946-1. Grades 5–8.

A discussion of jewelry, textile production, hair care, grooming, hygiene, battle dress, and clothing for men and women in different classes as well as the impact of climate, geography, leaders, and significant historical events on modes of dress in Elizabethan England. As tools became more sophisticated, so did materials. Photographs and illustrations highlight the text. Bibliography, Glossary, Chronology, Notes, Further Reading, Web Sites, and Index.

1150. Forward, Toby. *Shakespeare's Globe: An Interactive Pop-Up Book.* Illustrated by Juan Wijngaard. Candlewick, 2005. 14pp. ISBN 978-0-7636-2694-5. Grades 8 up.

A pop-up of Shakspeare's Globe Theatre in 1612 gives a 3-D aspect to the tour led by actor Richard Burbage. Readers will see the pit below the stage and the ceiling painted to resemble the sky. Twenty press-out figures give the book more life, along with facts about the theater's history, its design, and its performers. Two enclosed booklets contain scenes from plays including *A Midsummer Night's Dream, Romeo and Juliet, Twelfth Night,* and *As You Like It.*

1151. Fritz, Jean. *Around the World in a Hundred Years: From Henry the Navigator to Magellan.* Illustrated by Anthony Bacon Venti. Puffin, 1998. 128pp. Paper ISBN 978-0-698-11638-2. Grades 4–7.

See entry 69.

1152. Hinds, Kathryn. *The Church.* (Life in Elizabethan England) Marshall Cavendish, 2007. 80pp. ISBN 978-0-7614-2545-8. Grades 6–8.

To describe the Church during Elizabethan times (the period from 1558 to 1603 in England) Hinds uses quotations, primary source documents, and contemporary photographs of items and paintings. She discusses the rituals and the expectations for all classes when Protestantism came to the fore after Henry VIII banned Catholicism. Sidebars contain interesting bits of poetry, plays, recipes, and other pertinent information. Bibliography, Further Reading, Glossary, Web Sites, and Index.

1153. Hinds, Kathryn. *The Countryside.* (Life in Elizabethan England) Marshall Cavendish, 2007. 80pp. ISBN 978-0-7614-2543-4. Grades 6–8.

See entry 453.

1154. Hinds, Kathryn. *Elizabeth and Her Court.* (Life in Elizabethan England) Marshall Cavendish, 2007. 80pp. ISBN 978-0-7614-2542-7. Grades 6–8.

During her reign from 1558 to 1603 Elizabeth and her court presided over England's change from a backwoods country to a thriving world leader. This volume discusses both Elizabeth's ardent supporters and her greatest enemies as well as her responses to them—sometimes with anger, other times with cunning. Her rule left a lasting mark on the nation. Sidebars contain interesting bits of poetry, plays, recipes, and other pertinent information. Bibliography, Further Reading, Glossary, Web Sites, and Index.

1155. Kermode, Frank. *The Age of Shakespeare.* (Chronicles) Random House, 2005. 240pp. Paper ISBN 978-0-8129-7433-1. Grades YA.

The author explains the history and culture of Elizabeth I's age to reveal information about William Shakespeare's life, his poetry, and his plays. Kermode examines each play in the context of the events of the year in which it was written. Additionally, he discusses the theater companies of the time, the actors appearing with them, their facilities, and their financing. He also offers new insight into some of the themes and characters in the plays. The conciseness of this critical history adds to its value. Bibliography and Index. *School Library Journal Best Adult Books for Young Adults.*

1156. Konstam, Angus. *Historical Atlas of Exploration: 1492–1600.* Mercury, 2007. 192pp. ISBN 978-1-904668-08-4. Grades YA.

Beginning in the 15th century, European powers became rivals outside their borders as they tried to discover and claim the richest lands as their own. Among explorers chronicled here are Prince Henry the Navigator, Vasco da Gama, Pedro Alvarez Cabral, Diebo Lopes de Sequeira, John Cabot, Juan Ponce de León, Giovanni de Verrazzano, Amerigo Vespucci, Francisco Pizarro, Pedro de Alvarado, and Jacques Cartier. The thirteen chapters are "Europe in the 15th Century," "An African Prelude," "Wind and Current," "Across the Ocean Sea," "Sea Routes to the Indies," "The Coastline of North America," "The Discovery of South America," "The Conquest of Central America," "The Pacific and Around the Globe," "The Northwest Passage," "Island Quests," "Mapping the Discoveries," and "The Prize and Legacy of Discovery." Introduction, Color illustrations, Maps, Chronology, Glossary and Genealogy Tables, and Index.

1157. Lace, William W. *Elizabethan England.* (World History) Lucent, 2005. 112pp. ISBN 978-1-59018-655-8. Grades 8 up.

This biography of Elizabeth I (1558–1603) discusses the English court, the queen's contemporaries, the role of the Church of England and the Catholics, and exploration in the New World. Also included is information about city and country life and persons such as William Shakespeare and Mary Queen of Scots. During her reign, Elizabeth I clearly brought stability and new wealth to the country. Photographs and reproductions highlight the text. Bibliography, Chronology, Notes, Glossary, Further Reading, Web Sites, and Index.

1158. Pelta, Kathy. *Discovering Christopher Columbus: How History Is Invented.* Lerner, 1991. 112pp. ISBN 978-0-8225-4899-7. Grades 6–9.

Following a look at the life of Christopher Columbus and his voyages from 1492 to 1506, the author examines the historical response to his discovery in the subsequent centuries. A closing chapter titled "You, the Historian" shows how incorrect information can be disseminated when historians copy what other historians have written instead of turning to original sources. Sometimes even primary sources are unreliable. Pelta comments on a letter from Columbus that washed ashore in a barrel. It would have been interesting, except that it was written in modern English, a language that was not even spoken during Columbus's lifetime. Sources and Information. *Outstanding Social Studies Trade Book for Children* and *American Library Association Notable Children's Book.*

1159. Sider, Sandra. *Handbook to Life in Renaissance Europe.* (Handbook to Life) Facts on File, 2005. 382pp. ISBN 978-0-8160-5618-7; Oxford, 2007. paper ISBN 978-0-19-533084-7. Grades 10 up.

See entry 996.

1160. Singman, Jeffrey L. *Daily Life in Elizabethan England.* (Daily Life Through History) Greenwood, 1995. 227pp. ISBN 978-0-313-29335-1. Grades 7 up.

A brief overview and chronology of Elizabethan England. The chapters cover health, housing, living environments, clothing, food and drink, and entertainment. Other topics include popular songs and fabric patterns, as well as a guide to the costs of items in terms that correspond to contemporary rates. Diagrams and drawings complement the text. Appendix, Bibliography, Chronology, Glossary, Notes, and Index.

Biography and Collective Biography

1161. Adams, Simon. *Elizabeth I: The Outcast Who Became England's Queen.* (World History Biographies) National Geographic, 2005. 64pp. ISBN 978-0-7922-3649-8. Grades 3–6.

For Elizabeth I (1558–1603) to become queen of England, others in line to succeed to the throne had to die. The daughter of Anne Boleyn, Elizabeth been declared illegitimate. But her early childhood and her associations prepared her for facing the challenge of ruling Britain wisely and well. Photographs enhance the text. Bibliography, Glossary, Web Sites, Maps, and Index.

1162. Adler, David A. *A Picture Book of Christopher Columbus.* Illustrated by John and Alexandra Wallner. (Picture Book Of) Holiday House, 1991. 32pp. ISBN 978-0-8234-0949-5; 1992 paper ISBN 978-0-8234-0949-5. Grades K–3.

Born into a wool weaver's family in the city-state of Genoa (before Italy was founded) in 1451, Columbus (1451–1506) read of Marco Polo's travels across Asia and decided that he wanted to find China. In 1484 Columbus first attempted to get provisions for a journey to Japan, which he thought was 2,400 miles away (it is actually four times farther). Adler describes the types of people Columbus hired for the voyage and notes that the date of departure—August 3, 1492—was one day after Ferdinand and Isabella's proclamation that all unconverted Jews had to leave Spain. The pen-and-ink sketches show scenes as they might have been. The text recounts the tragedy that Columbus's arrival was for the people in the New World, who caught new diseases or were enslaved by the Spaniards, as well as the tribulations Columbus faced on his subsequent voyages. Index.

1163. Aliki. *William Shakespeare and the Globe.* Illustrated by author. HarperCollins, 2000. 48pp. Paper ISBN 978-0-06-443722-6. Grades 4–7.

Using quotations from William Shakespeare's plays, this biography presents what is known and what is suggested about his life and work. Framing this story is that of Sam Wanamaker (1919–1993), the man who wanted to restore the Globe Theatre, where Shakespeare's plays were first performed. Readers will learn of the people who raised funds, researched, and constructed the Globe replica. Detailed illustrations enhance the text. *Boston-Globe/Horn Book Award*, *Bluegrass Awards* (Kentucky), *Children's Book Award* (South Carolina) nomination, *Bluebonnet Awards* (Texas), *School Library Journal Best Books for Children*, and *Children's Informational Book Awards* (Utah).

1164. Aller, Susan Bivin. *Christopher Columbus.* (History Makers Bios) Lerner, 2003. 48pp. ISBN 978-0-8225-0398-9. Grades 3–5.

Italian explorer Christopher Columbus (1451–1506) is best known for his discovery of America. Thus his love for the sea and sailing changed the history of the continent. Illustrations highlight the text. Bibliography, Further Reading, Glossary, Maps, Time Line, Web Sites, and Index.

1165. Anderson, Maxine. *Amazing Leonardo da Vinci: Inventions You Can Build Yourself.* Nomad, 2006. 122pp. Paper ISBN 978-0-9749344-2-6. Grades 5–8.

Nineteen hands-on projects resemble Leonardo da Vinci's inventions. Among them are a perspectograph, a hydrometer, a safety bridge, walk-on-water shoes, and a camera obscura. Detailed instructions complement the information on how and why Leonardo wanted to invent each object, as detailed in his notebooks. Photographs and illustrations augment the text. Maps, Bibliography, Glossary, Chronology, Further Reading, Web Sites, and Index. *Voice of Youth Advocates Nonfiction Honor List.*

1166. Aronson, Marc. *John Winthrop, Oliver Cromwell, and the Land of Promise.* Clarion, 2004. 224pp. ISBN 978-0-618-18177-3. Grades 7 up.

This look at Britain and America in the 17th century focuses on John Winthrop, the first governor of Massachusetts Bay Colony, and the Puritan Oliver Cromwell. It details the reality of their religious faiths and the clash of beliefs with the concepts of democracy and equality. A comparison between that time and today's religious right, terrorism, and theocracy make this an especially interesting study. Photographs and illustrations highlight the text. Bibliography, Chronology, Notes, and Index.

1167. Aronson, Marc. *Sir Walter Ralegh and the Quest for El Dorado.* Clarion, 2000. 222pp. ISBN 978-0-395-84827-2. Grades 7 up.

This biography of Sir Walter Raleigh (1552?–1618) details his life from his position as Elizabeth's courtier to his quests in the New World and his search for El Dorado. An intelligent and ambitious man, Raleigh (who often spelled his name Ralegh) liked risk and was a soldier, sailor, writer, schemer, and explorer. He was imprisoned in the Tower of London three times. He was released the first two times to go on explorations for gold, but the third time, he was beheaded. Illustrations, maps, and prints complement the text. Bibliography, Glossary, Chronology, Notes, and Index. *Dorothy Canfield Fisher Children's Book Awards* (Vermont), *Capitol Choices Noteworthy Titles* (Washington, D.C.), *Boston Globe/Horn Book Award, School Library Journal Best Books for Children, Robert F. Sibert Honor Book, Bulletin Blue Ribbon*, and *Student Book Award* (Maine) nomination.

1168. Bastable, Tony. *John Cabot.* World Almanac Library, 2003. 48pp. ISBN 978-0-8368-5012-3; 2004 paper ISBN 978-0-8368-5172-4. Grades 5 up.

Giovanni Caboto, known as John Cabot (1450–1498), was an Italian who claimed land in the New World for England in 1497. He wanted to go to Asia but found North America, Newfoundland, and the Grand Banks instead. Sidebars, photographs, and graphics augment the text. Bibliography, Glossary, Maps, and Index.

1169. Blassingame, Wyatt. *Ponce de León.* (Junior World Explorers) Chelsea House, 1991. 80pp. ISBN 978-0-7910-1493-6. Grades 3–7.

Juan Ponce de León (1474–1521) learned to be a soldier as a boy so that he could fight the Moors in Spain. He decided to join Columbus's second voyage, and he and his family spent the rest of his life in the New World. He is still credited with discovering Florida, although John Cabot might have been there 15 years previously, and the Norsemen 500 years before.

1170. Byrd, Robert. *Leonardo, the Beautiful Dreamer.* Penguin, 2003. 40pp. ISBN 978-0-525-47033-5. Grades 3–8.

See entry 1007.

1171. Castor, Helen. *Blood and Roses: One Family's Struggle and Triumph During the Tumultuous Wars of the Roses.* Harper Perennial, 2007. 426pp. Paper ISBN 978-0-00-716222-2. Grades YA.

The Paston family struggles during the English Civil War to rise from peasant farmers to landed gentry. This book, based on more than a thousand letters found in an old home, shows how the family changed in four generations. Much of their effort was directed toward acquiring land and keeping it out of the hands of neighbors competing for it. This biography reveals a nation in which the Wars of the Roses changed the status quo so much that its inhabitants had to reconsider their identity.

1172. Connolly, Sean. *Michelangelo.* (Lives of the Artists) Gareth Stevens, 2004. 48pp. ISBN 978-0-8368-5600-2; paper ISBN 978-0-8368-5605-7. Grades 5–8.

Michelangelo Buonarroti (1475–1564) was one of the world's greatest artists. In addition to being a painter (although he preferred to be known as a sculptor), Michelangelo was a poet and an architect. This book covers his youth, his interest in stone, his masterpieces including the Sistine Chapel, his architectural prowess, *The Last Judgment*, his unhappy old age, and his legacy. Reproductions highlight the text. Glossary, Time Lines, and Index.

1173. Crompton, Samuel Willard. *Ferdinand Magellan and the Quest to Circle the Globe.* (Explorers of New Lands) Chelsea House, 2005. 144pp. ISBN 978-0-7910-8608-7. Grades 4–8.

Ferdinand Magellan (1480–1521), a Portuguese explorer, set out to find the Spice Islands of the Far East and went around the world instead. He went to sea for the first time in 1505. He eventually obtained five ships for an expedition and left southern Spain in 1519. He could not find a way around South America by sea until 1520, when he reached a strait (now called the Strait of Magellan) through which he could sail. After thirty-eight days he arrived in the Pacific Ocean. Finally in March of 1521 he arrived in Guam. Then in the Philippines, he died after being shot in the foot with a poisoned arrow. Only one of his ships returned to Spain, and only 18 of his 250 men survived. Photographs and illustrations enhance the text. Bibliography, Chronology, Further Reading, Web Sites, and Index.

1174. Crompton, Samuel Willard. *Francis Drake and the Oceans of the World.* (Explorers of New Lands) Chelsea House, 2005. 138pp. ISBN 978-0-7910-8615-5. Grades 5–8.

Sir Frances Drake (1540?–1596), a British explorer, traveled around the globe from 1577 to 1580 while Elizabeth I sat on the English throne. Included in this book is information about the dangers of life at sea, the difficulty of sailing unfamiliar waters, the encounters with native people, and the demands of the royals who financed the expeditions. The Spanish though Drake merely a pirate while the English treated him as a hero. To others, he was a slaver, navigator, and a politician. He served as second-in-command during the defeat of the Spanish armada in 1588. Photographs and illustrations enhance the text. Bibliography, Chronology, Further Reading, Web Sites, and Index.

1175. Dunn, Jane. *Elizabeth and Mary: Cousins, Rivals, Queens.* Knopf, 2004. 480pp. ISBN 978-0-375-40898-4; Vintage paper ISBN 978-0-375-70820-6. Grades YA.

Elizabeth I of England (1533–1603), Protestant daughter of King Henry VIII and Anne Boleyn, and Mary Queen of Scots (1542–1587), Catholic daughter of King James V of Scotland and his French wife, Mary of Guise, were cousins. Very different, both sought the power offered by sitting on a throne. Elizabeth had no expectations that she would rule, but Mary was always convinced that she would, even as she matured in France as the future bride of the dauphin. The two women wrote to each other and questioned anyone who knew the other, but they never met. Elizabeth chose not to marry, and Mary married poorly. When Mary's Catholicism became a threat to Eliza-beth, she had Mary imprisoned in the Tower of London and beheaded twenty years later. This biography tells their intertwined stories and reveals the intrigues in Great Britain at the time. Bibliography and Index.

1176. Erickson, Carolly. *The First Elizabeth.* St. Martins, 1997. 447pp. Paper ISBN 978-0-312-16842-1. Grades YA.

Queen Elizabeth (1533–1603) learned as a child to be careful about her words and ac-tions, because others always had ulterior motives in their relationships with her. She ruled England for forty years, refusing to marry. She was a diplomat who improved the lives of her subjects as the Renaissance came north from Italy, and she kept Spain out of the country in 1588. Bibliography and Index.

1177. Erickson, Carolly. *Mistress Anne: The Exceptional Life of Anne Boleyn.* Griffin, 1998. 288pp. Paper ISBN 978-0-312-18747-7. Grades YA.

Anne Boleyn (1507–1536), the second of Henry VIII's six wives, courted Henry for six years before she secretly married him. After their marriage and Henry's divorce from Catherine, Anne was crowned queen. She encouraged the split with the Church of Rome, and her child, a girl, became Elizabeth I, queen of England. After Anne had a mis-carriage she was accused of incest and adultery, tried, and condemned to death. Her head was displayed on London Bridge as an example of the consequences of unac-ceptable morals. Through the years, her reputation has been tarnished because of the unreliable sources upon which biographical material has been based. Bibliography and Index.

1178. Fritz, Jean. *Where Do You Think You're Going, Christopher Columbus?* Illustrated by Margot Tomes. Putnam, 1980. 128pp. ISBN 978-0-399-20723-5; Puffin, 1997. paper ISBN 978-0-698-11580-4. Grades 3–6.

Red-headed Christopher Columbus (1451–1506) nearly drowned off the coast of Por-tugal when he was 25; after living through that experience, he seemed to think that he was blessed by God in whatever he did. He read Marco Polo's book about his travels and a book by Dr. Toscanelli that claimed that Japan was 3,000 nautical miles to the west. He wanted to follow this route to the riches that Marco Polo had been able to carry away before the Turks blocked his travel. Eventually Columbus convinced Isabelle of Castile that he would convert the people he met to Christianity, so she gave him money for the thirty-seven-day voyage from the Canary Islands to San Salvador. Although some of his friends, and certainly his enemies, believed that Columbus lacked leadership ability, he undertook more trips, still insisting that the island of Cuba was actually the mainland. After him, Amerigo Vespucci, John Cabot, and Vasco da Gama found the true mainland, but not Japan, which was actually 10,000 miles away. Notes and Index.

1179. Gingerich, Owen. *The Book Nobody Read: Chasing the Revolutions of Nicolaus Copernicus.* Walker, 2004. 256pp. ISBN 978-0-8027-1415-2. Grades YA.

Nicolaus Copernicus published *On the Revolutions of the Heavenly Spheres* (*De Revolu-tionibus*) in 1543 while he was a Catholic canon at the cathedral in Frauenburg, Poland. His conclusion was that Earth revolves around the sun (heliocentrism). Gingerich de-fies the pronouncement that no one read this difficult book by finding all the extant copies (around six hundred) of the first and second editions and documenting every-thing that he could find in travels through Europe, the Soviet Union, Egypt, Australia, and China. He shows that the work had a huge influence on early astronomers. He assesses marginalia to see how many people had owned extant copies, tracks the books as they progress across Europe, and checks the watermarks and glue to see if the books have been altered. The story tells about Copernicus, his community, and the printing and distribution of his book. Notes, Bibliography, Maps, and Index.

1180. Gingerich, Owen, and James MacLachlan. *Nicolaus Copernicus: Making the Earth a Planet.* (Oxford Portraits in Science) Oxford, 2003. 144pp. ISBN 978-0-19-512049-3. Grades YA.

Nicolaus Copernicus (1473–1543) determined that the earth orbited the sun, a revolutionary idea in 1543 when his book *On the Revolutions of the Heavenly Spheres* was published. This biography details his life as a doctor, lawyer, church official, and amateur astronomer and provides information about his experiments. Illustrations highlight the text. Chronology, Further Reading, Web Sites, and Index.

1181. Goodman, Joan Elizabeth. *A Long and Uncertain Journey: The 27,000 Mile Voyage of Vasco da Gama.* Illustrated by Tom McNeely. (Great Explorers Books) Mikaya, 2001. 48pp. ISBN 978-0-9650493-7-5. Grades 3–6.

Vasco da Gama (1469–1524) sailed around Africa to the Orient in 1497. The journal of one of his crew records an account of the trip with thoughts about da Gama's disregard for the natives of Africa and the Near East—despite his bravery and persistence. His journey, funded by African slave trading, yielded little treasure, but he proved that the route was possible. The text, in addition to the illustrations, offers background on Portuguese exploration and the role of Henry the Navigator. Maps, Time Line, and Index.

1182. Heinrichs, Ann. *Gerardus Mercator: Father of Modern Mapmaking.* (Signature Lives) Compass Point, 2007. 112pp. ISBN 978-0-7565-3312-0. Grades 6–9.

Gerardus Mercator (1512–1594), known as the father of modern mapmaking, met resistance from religious authorities for his innovation. This book looks at his life and at his most important legacy: his 1569 map called the Mercator projection. He solved the problem of how to portray a round Earth on a flat surface. He also coined the term "atlas" to refer to a collection of maps. Photographs and illustrations highlight the text. Bibliography, Chronology, Glossary, Notes, Further Reading, Web Sites, and Index.

1183. Hibbert, Christopher. *The Virgin Queen: Elizabeth I, Genius of the Golden Age.* Da Capo, 1992. 287pp. Paper ISBN 978-0-201-60817-5. Grades YA.

The author of this biography of Queen Elizabeth I (1533–1603) tries to reveal Elizabeth the person rather than Elizabeth the queen. Hibbert details Elizabeth's whims and interests, although it is difficult to ascertain what is personal and what is political when he discusses her attitudes toward men, marriage, and religion. Almost murdered when a child and always in the public eye as queen, she must have known that she could never be completely honest. Index.

1184. Holub, Joan. *Elizabeth and the Royal Pony: A True Story of Elizabeth I of England.* Illustrated by Nonna Aleshina. (Young Princesses Around the World) Simon & Schuster, 2007. 48pp. ISBN 978-0-689-87193-1; Aladdin paper ISBN 978-0-689-87191-7. Grades K–2.

In this story, Elizabeth (1533–1603) is 9, and she loves to ride her pony. But the pony refuses to jump over a stone wall. Fortunately, Elizabeth's father, Henry VIII, gives her advice, and she succeeds. Chronology.

1185. Koestler-Grack, Rachel A. *Vasco da Gama and the Sea Route to India.* (Explorers of New Lands) Chelsea House, 2005. 146pp. ISBN 978-0-7910-8611-7. Grades 6–8.

Vasco da Gama (1469–1524) wanted to find a sea route to the East Indies from Europe and took a 27,000-mile voyage. This book chronicles the dangers of being at sea, the difficulties of navigating unfamiliar waters, and the demands of rulers who financed the explorations. Sidebars, maps, and illustrations augment the text. Bibliography, Chronology, Further Reading, Web Sites, and Index.

1186. Krull, Kathleen. *Leonardo da Vinci.* Illustrated by Boris Kulikov. Viking, 2005. 124pp. ISBN 978-0-670-05920-1; Puffin, 2008. paper ISBN 978-0-14-240821-6. Grades 5–8.

See entry 1014.

1187. Kurtz, Jane. *What Columbus Found: It Was Orange, It Was Round.* Illustrated by Paige Billin-Frye. Simon & Schuster, 2007. Unpaged. ISBN 978-0-689-86763-7; Aladdin paper ISBN 978-0-689-86762-0. Grades K–2.

This brief rhyming biography of Columbus tells of his unexpected discovery of the New World. Cartoon illustrations complement the text.

1188. Landau, Elaine. *Ferdinand Magellan.* (History Makers Bios) Lerner, 2005. 48pp. ISBN 978-0-8225-2942-2. Grades 3–5.

The first man to sail around the world, Ferdinand Magellan was born around 1480 and grew up in Portugal. After several years in the Portuguese navy, Magellan left for Spain, Portugal's greatest rival, in an attempt to further his career. He set sail in search of a strait through South America to reach the Spice Islands, and he became the first explorer to cross the Pacific Ocean and circumnavigate the globe. Illustrations highlight the text. Bibliography, Further Reading, Glossary, Maps, Time Line, Web Sites, and Index.

1189. León, Vicki. *Uppity Women of the Renaissance.* Conari, 1999. 260pp. Paper ISBN 978-1-57324-127-4. Grades YA.

See entry 1015.

1190. Levinson, Nancy Smiler. *Magellan and the First Voyage Around the World.* Clarion, 2001. 144pp. ISBN 978-0-395-98773-5. Grades 5–8.

In 1519 the superb Portuguese seaman Ferdinand Magellan left Spain with the patronage of King Charles I to search for a new route to the Spice Islands. His journey—filled with intrigue, mutiny, violent weather, and hunger—led him to his death. But he was able to name the Pacific Ocean and the Strait of Magellan and he observed the galaxies that we now call the Magellanic Clouds. Some of his crew made the full journey round the world. Photographs, maps, and illustrations enhance this book. Bibliography, Chronology, Notes, and Index.

1191. Lewis, J. Patrick. *Michelangelo's World.* Creative Editions, 2007. 40pp. ISBN 978-1-56846-167-0. Grades 7 up.

This unusual biography of Michelangelo Buonarroti (1475–1564) contains photographs of his main works, each with an explanation of when and why he created it and a poem about it, recreating the life and time of the artist. Bibliography.

1192. McPherson, Stephanie Sammartino. *Sir Walter Raleigh.* (History Makers Bios) Lerner, 2005. 48pp. ISBN 978-0-8225-2945-3. Grades 3–5.

Born in England in the 1550s, Walter Raleigh was a soldier, a poet, an author, a member of Parliament, an explorer, a pirate, and above all, a loyal attendant to Queen Elizabeth I. The Queen was so fond of him that she limited his explorations so she would not have to be without his company for extended periods of time. After her death, the new king did not share this fondness for Raleigh and arrested him for treason. Raleigh was forced to live in the Tower of London for thirteen years before being executed. Illustrations highlight the text. Bibliography, Further Reading, Glossary, Maps, Time Line, Web Sites, and Index.

1193. Mason, Antony. *Leonardo da Vinci.* (Lives of the Artists) Gareth Stevens, 2004. 48pp. ISBN 978-0-8368-5599-9; paper ISBN 978-0-8368-5604-0. Grades 5–8.

See entry 1016.

1194. Mis, Melody S. *Rembrandt.* (Meet the Artists) PowerKids, 2007. 24pp. ISBN 978-1-4042-3840-4. Grades 2–4.

This biography of Rembrandt (1606–1669) contains many reproductions of his work that enhance the narrative. The first chapter covers his life and childhood. Subsequent chapters cover the developments of his life and his art. Glossary, Further Reading, Web Sites, and Index.

1195. Moore, Christopher. *Champlain.* Illustrated by Francis Back. Tundra, 2004. 55pp. ISBN 978-0-8877-6657-2. Grades 4–6.

Samuel de Champlain (1567–1635) explored eastern Canada, mapped the area, and established a settlement at Quebec in 1608. This biography recounts what is known of his life. It also provides information about beaver skins, Native Americans including the Huron and the Iroquois, and other First Nations people. Photographs, maps, and illustrations highlight the text. Bibliography and Index.

1196. Nardo, Don. *Ivan the Terrible.* (History's Villains) Blackbirch, 2005. 112pp. ISBN 978-1-56711-900-8. Grades 5–7.

Ivan IV Vasilyevich (1530–1584) ruled Russia with such cruelty that he earned the nickname "Terrible." Initially, Ivan served as a reformer who increased the Russian empire's size with military conquests. But he refused to lose any political battles, freely murdering anyone in his way. The author includes observations made by foreigners and comments made by Ivan that reveal the harshness of his deeds against his people. Illustrations augment the text. Bibliography, Maps, and Index.

1197. Nardo, Don. *Tycho Brahe: Pioneer of Astronomy.* (Signature Lives) Compass Point, 2007. 112pp. ISBN 978-0-7565-3309-0. Grades 6–9.

Tycho Brahe (1546–1601), a Danish nobleman, worked to combine the geometrical benefits of the Copernican system (that Earth and other planets revolve around the sun) with the philosophical benefits of the Ptolemaic system (that Earth is the universe's center) into his own model of the universe, the Tychonic system. For the last year of

Tycho's life, Johannes Kepler assisted him, and he later used Tycho's information to develop his own ideas. Tycho was the most accurate astronomical observer of his time and had successes despite that the lack of mathematical tools that were invented after his lifetime. He cataloged the movement of the planets carefully enough to realize that the Copernican system made more sense in describing the universe. Photographs and illustrations highlight the text. Bibliography, Chronology, Glossary, Notes, Further Reading, Web Sites, and Index.

1198. Pescio, Claudio. ***Rembrandt.*** Illustrated by Sergio. (Art Masters) Oliver, 2008. 64pp. ISBN 978-1-934545-02-7. Grades 7 up.

A look at Rembrandt's life (1606–1669) in terms of the times in which he lived. This volume also includes small reproductions of 112 of his paintings, with a thorough analysis of five of them (including *The Anatomy Lesson of Dr. Nicolaes Tulp* and *The Night Watch*). Extra information appears about landscape painting and other aspects of 17th-century Dutch artwork. Bibliography, Chronology, and Index.

1199. Pinguilly, Yves. ***Da Vinci: The Painter Who Spoke with Birds.*** Translated by John Goodman. Chelsea House, 1994. 62pp. ISBN 978-0-7910-2808-7. Grades 3–6.

See entry 1017.

1200. Rabb, Theodore K. ***Renaissance Lives: Portraits of an Age.*** Basic, 2000. 262pp. Paper ISBN 978-0-465-06800-5. Grades YA.

See entry 1019.

1201. Roberts, Russell. ***The Life and Times of Nostradamus.*** (Biography from Ancient Civilizations) Mitchell Lane, 2008. 48pp. ISBN 978-1-58415-544-7. Grades 6–8.

Nostradamus (1503–1566), an astrologist, physician, herbalist, and author, made a number of predictions about the future that have caused much controversy. He lived an interesting life while he espoused his theories. Photographs and illustrations highlight the text. Bibliography, Glossary, and Chronology.

1202. Rosen, Michael. ***Shakespeare: His Work and His World.*** Illustrated by Robert R. Ingpen. Candlewick, 2006. 96pp. Paper ISBN 978-0-7636-3201-4. Grades 4–8.

During the time since William Shakespeare (1564–1616), critics and scholars have often questioned his ability to write such wonderful plays. No information exists about his life between the ages of 18 and 28, and all wonder why he left all of his possessions except his second-best bed to his daughter, Susanna. The text examines British history during Shakespeare's life and how it might have affected him. It also introduces four of the plays: *A Midsummer Night's Dream*, *Macbeth*, *King Lear*, and *The Tempest*. Illustrations enliven the book and include a cross-section of the Globe Theatre. Bibliography. *School Library Journal Best Books for Children.*

1203. Schwartz, Gary. ***Rembrandt.*** Abrams, 1992. 92pp. ISBN 978-0-8109-3760-4. Grades YA.

The author looks at the Dutch artist's life (1606–1669) and work. He shows the various periods of Rembrandt's career and his difficulties in later life as members of his family died and he lost his money. His paintings revealed people the way they actually appeared, with honest expressions, rather than unnaturally attractive. He tried to portray their souls. Color Reproductions and Index.

1204. Shackelford, Jole. *William Harvey and the Mechanics of the Heart.* (Oxford Portraits in Science) Oxford, 2003. 144pp. ISBN 978-0-19-512049-3. Grades YA.

William Harvey (1578–1657) determined how blood circulates in the heart, along with the importance of the arteries and veins in the circulation of the blood. He was not the first to do so, but the manuscripts of Michael Servetus were destroyed, and no one knew about his research until Harvey's discovery of it in Italy. Harvey wanted to use the methods of the early Greeks in his scientific experiments, and he saw the value of dissection and vivisection. Reproductions augment the text. Further Reading, Chronology, and Index.

1205. Sís, Peter. *Starry Messenger: Galileo Galilei.* Farrar, Straus and Giroux , 1996. Unpaged. Starburst, 2000 Paper ISBN 978-0-374-47027-2. Grades 1–5.

When Galileo Galilei (1564–1642) said that the earth is not the fixed center of the universe, he was basing his statement on discoveries he made when using his telescope to map the heavens. Galileo was a scientist, mathematician, astronomer, philosopher, and physicist. When his ideas became too popular, Catholic Church leaders decided that these concepts conflicted with the Bible, and they imprisoned him in his home. A simplified text accompanies writings in Galileo's own hand and illustrations about Galileo's life and discoveries. *Caldecott Honor Book.*

1206. Somervill, Barbara A. *Catherine de Medici: The Power Behind the French Throne.* (Reformation Era) Compass Point, 2005. 112pp. ISBN 978-0-7565-1581-2. Grades 5–8.

Catherine de' Medici (1519–1589), daughter of Lorenzo de' Medici (Lorenzo the Magnificent) and Madeleine de la Tour d'Auvergne, became the wife of King Henry II. She had an enormous influence on the French court as the mother of the last three Valois kings. She married her daughter Elizabeth to the king of Spain and another daughter, Margaret, to King Henry of Navarre, who became Henry IV. She was also an instigator during the Catholic-Huguenot wars and helped plan the St. Bartholomew's Day Massacre in 1572, when more than 50,000 Huguenots were killed. Illustrations enhance the text. Bibliography, Notes, Maps, Glossary, and Index.

1207. Stanley, Diane. *Michelangelo.* HarperCollins, 2000. ISBN 978-0-688-15085-3; Trophy, 2003. paper ISBN 978-0-06-052113-4. Grades 5–8.

This biography of Michelangelo Buonarroti (1475–1564) presents him as Renaissance sculptor, painter, architect, and poet. Although his father wanted him to learn a trade, Michelangelo defied him to pursue his art and leave behind masterpieces for the world. The author places Michelangelo within the culture, history, politics, and expectations of his time. Mixed-media illustrations enhance the text. Bibliography. *Student Book Award* (Maine) nomination, *School Library Journal Best Books of the Year*, and *Capitol Choices Noteworthy Titles* (Washington, D.C.).

1208. Steele, Philip. *Galileo: The Genius Who Faced the Inquisition.* (World History Biographies) National Geographic, 2005. 64pp. ISBN 978-0-7922-3656-6. Grades 3–6.

When Galileo (1564–1642) discovered that the earth revolved around the sun, he had to face the Inquisition for his heresy. This book discusses his childhood, youth, and family, along with providing a view of everyday life during Galileo's time. Photographs enhance the text. Bibliography, Chronology, Notes, Maps, Glossary, Further Reading, Web Sites, and Index.

1209. Sundel, Al. ***Christopher Columbus and the Age of Exploration.*** (In World History) Enslow, 2002. 128pp. ISBN 978-0-7660-1820-4. Grades 7 up.

This examination of the voyages and life of Christopher Columbus focuses on the explorer's less-heroic aspects. He had many failures, and he condoned massacre and torture of the Native Americans. After his first Caribbean landfall, his men committed a number of crimes against the natives. The author also compares the Columbus voyages to those of other Euoprean explorers. Archival prints augment the text. Chronology, Notes, Further Reading, Web Sites, and Index.

1210. Sutcliffe, Jane. ***Juan Ponce de León.*** (History Makers Bios) Lerner, 2005. 48pp. ISBN 978-0-8225-2944-6. Grades 3–5.

See entry 1022.

1211. Tello, Antonio. ***My Name Is Leonardo da Vinci.*** Illustrated by Johanna A. Boccardo. (My Name Is . . .) Barron's, 2006. 63pp. Paper ISBN 978-0-7641-3392-3. Grades 4–6.

See entry 1023.

1212. Venezia, Mike. ***Botticelli.*** (Getting to Know the World's Greatest Artists) Children's Press, 1991. 32pp. ISBN 978-0-516-02291-8; paper ISBN 978-0-516-42291-6. Grades K–5.

See entry 1027.

1213. Venezia, Mike. ***Da Vinci.*** (Getting to Know the World's Greatest Artists) Children's Press, 1989. 32pp. ISBN 978-0-516-02275-8; paper ISBN 978-0-516-42275-6. Grades K–8.

See entry 1028.

1214. Venezia, Mike. ***Diego Velazquez.*** (Getting to Know the World's Greatest Artists) Children's Press, 2004. 32pp. ISBN 978-0-516-22580-7; paper ISBN 978-0-516-26980-1. Grades K–5.

Diego Velazquez (1599–1660) was famous for his portraits of royalty, especially those of Philip IV. As court painter, Velazquez was the only artist allowed to paint Philip. Velazquez tried to emphasize the wealth and power of his subjects with lavish clothing and glittering jewels, obviously aspects of the paintings that his subjects enjoyed. He also painted religious subjects and *bodegons*—tavern scenes displaying people enjoying food and drink. His famous paintings include *Christ in the House of Martha and Mary*; *Philip IV in Armour*; *Infanta Maria, Later Queen of Hungary*; *Prince Baltasar Carlos with a Dwarf*; *Infanta Margarita*; and his most famous, *Las Meninas* (*The Handmaidens*). Illustrations enhance the text.

1215. Venezia, Mike. ***El Greco.*** (Getting to Know the World's Greatest Artists) Children's Press, 1997. 32pp. ISBN 978-0-516-20586-1; 1998 paper ISBN 978-0-516-26243-7. Grades K–5.

Known as El Greco in Spain, the Greek Domenicos Theotocopoulous (1541?–1614) was born in Crete and studied with Titian in Venice before settling in Toledo, Spain. His best-known works include *The View of Toledo* and *The Burial of Count Orgaz*. Illustrations highlight the text.

1216. Venezia, Mike. *Michelangelo.* (Getting to Know the World's Greatest Artists) Children's Press, 1991. 32pp. ISBN 978-0-516-02293-2; paper ISBN 978-0-516-42293-0. Grades k–5.

    Michelangelo Buonarroti (1475–1564) was one of the world's greatest artists. He is known for his painting of the Sistine Chapel in the Vatican and his sculptures such as *David*, now located in Florence, Italy. Illustrations highlight the text.

1217. Venezia, Mike. *Pieter Bruegel.* (Getting to Know the World's Greatest Artists) Children's Press, 1992. 32pp. ISBN 978-0-516-02279-6; 1993 paper ISBN 978-0-516-42279-4. Grades K–5.

    Pieter Bruegel (ca. 1525–1569) was a Flemish painter known for his scenes of everyday life. This book describes the times he lived in and shows illustrations of his art.

1218. Venezia, Mike. *Raphael.* (Getting to Know the World's Greatest Artists) Children's Press, 2001. 32pp. ISBN 978-0-516-22028-4; 1998 paper ISBN 978-0-516-27285-6. Grades K–5.

    Raphael (1483–1520) was born Raffaello Sanzio in Umbria, Italy. He was the last great painter of the Renaissance and knew Michelangelo and Leonardo da Vinci. He worked for Pope Julius at St. Peter's in Rome. Illustrations highlight the text.

1219. Venezia, Mike. *Rembrandt.* (Getting to Know the World's Greatest Artists) Children's Press, 1988. ISBN 978-0-516-02272-7. Grades K–5.

    Considered one of the greatest painters of all time, Rembrandt Harmenszoon van Rijn (1606–1669) lived in Holland. His paintings, often dark because brightly colored paints were more expensive, have their own brilliance. *The Night Watch*, a huge painting with faces of many people Rembrandt knew, is perhaps his most famous. Illustrations enhance the text.

1220. Venezia, Mike. *Titian.* (Getting to Know the World's Greatest Artists) Children's Press, 2003. 32pp. ISBN 978-0-516-22575-3; paper ISBN 978-0-516-26975-7. Grades K–5.

    Titian (1477–1576) went to Venice when he was 10 to learn to be a painter. He painted more than six hundred works and is recognized as one of the greatest painters who ever lived. Illustrations highlight the text.

1221. Weatherly, Myra. *Elizabeth I: Queen of Tudor England.* (Signature Lives) Compass Point, 2005. 112pp. ISBN 978-0-7565-0988-0; paper ISBN 978-0-7565-1861-5. Grades 6–9.

    This biography of Elizabeth I (1533–1603) covers her forty-five years as queen of England, focusing more on her political and social liaisons than her achievements. During her time, religious conflicts erupted between Catholics and Protestants, the Spanish armada was defeated, and the English established colonies in North America. Photographs and illustrations highlight the text. Bibliography, Further Reading, Web Sites, and Index.

1222. Weir, Alison. *The Princes in the Tower.* Fawcett, 1995. 287pp. Paper ISBN 978-0-345-39178-0. Grades YA.

    The two sons of Edward IV—12-year-old Edward V and his 10-year-old brother disappeared in the Tower of London. In the 1520s Thomas More accused Richard III of being a murderer, but many contemporary historians think the Tudors maligned Richard. Weir makes assessments based on primary accounts of More's informants. She argues that Richard most likely was directly involved in the young princes' demise. Bibliography and Index.

1223. Weisberg, Barbara. *Coronado's Golden Quest.* Illustrated by Mike Eagle. Steck-Vaughn, 1992. 79pp. Paper ISBN 978-0-8114-8072-7. Grades 5–9.

Viceroy Mendoza of Spain spent his personal fortune to send Coronado (1510–1554) and an army to find the seven cities of gold that they had heard so much about. They left in 1540, but after more than a year of searching and treachery, they realized that gold was not to be found in the American Southwest. Coronado was wounded when he fell from a horse, and other incidents doomed the journey. A slave named Turk convinced the party that Quivera, his home, had gold and that he would lead them from Cicuye to their rewards. They discovered that he was lying to escape his captors. Epilogue, Afterword, and Notes.

1224. Whiting, Jim. *Michelangelo.* Mitchell Lane, 2007. 48pp. ISBN 978-1-58415-562-1. Grades 4–7.

According to reports, the mother of Michelangelo (1475–1564) fell off her horse while going to Caprese, his birthplace, while she was pregnant with him. The short chapters in this biography reveal his difficulties as an artist, his works, his family, and his life, placing him within the context of his times. Photographs and illustrations highlight the text. Bibliography, Glossary, Chronology, and Index.

1225. Yount, Lisa. *William Harvey: Discoverer of How Blood Circulates.* (Great Minds of Science) Enslow, 2008. 128pp. ISBN 978-0-7660-3010-7. Grades 4–8.

William Harvey (1578–1657) was the first of seven sons born to his Folkestone, England, family. After attending Cambridge, he went to Padua, Italy, for advanced medical training. He heard Fabricius, his anatomy teacher, talk about little flaps or doors on blood vessels, and he remembered this later as he tried to understand how blood moved through the body. In 1628 he published a book on the movement of the heart and the blood. He was a supporter of King Charles; when Cromwell defeated the king, Harvey lost everything but kept working on his ideas. Afterword: A New Kind of Science, Activities, Chronology, Notes, Glossary, and Index.

Graphic Novels, Biographies, and Histories

1226. Hynson, Colin. *Elizabeth I and the Spanish Armada.* (Stories from History) School Speciality, 2006. 48pp. ISBN 978-0-7696-4703-6; paper ISBN 978-0-7696-4629-9. Grades 5–8.

Elizabeth I of England (1533–1603) sent her navy to defeat the Spanish Armada. This graphic novel presentation in 39 short chapters covers her childhood, her half-sister Mary's death, her relationship with Sir Francis Drake, her relationship with the pope, the execution of Mary Queen of Scotland, the preparations for confronting the Armada, and her speech at Tilbury when the threat was over. Maps show the routes the ships took during the Spanish conflict and where the battles happened. Although this book does not fully examine Elizabeth's life, it gives the reader a sense of her accomplishments. Maps, Chronology, Glossary, and Index.

1227. Wade, Mary Dodson. *Christopher Columbus: Famous Explorer.* (Graphic Biographies) Graphic Library, 2007. 32pp. ISBN 978-0-7368-6853-2; paper ISBN 978-0-7368-7905-7. Grades 3–5.

This short graphic biography of Christopher Columbus (1451–1506), who loved the sea and sailing as a boy, relates the story of his voyages to the New World and his discovery of America. A yellow background sets direct quotations from Columbus apart from the fictional aspects of the story. Web Sites.

DVDs

1228. *Hernando de Soto.* (Famous Explorers) Film Ideas, 2003. 22 min. ISBN 978-1-57557-366-3. Grades 5–8.

Hernando de Soto (1496/1497–1542), the first European to discover the Mississippi River, also participated in Pizarro's conquest of the Inca empire. De Soto sailed Florida's west coast to Tampa Bay and explored the inland north to Alabama. Focused only on finding gold, he cruelly subjugated any natives he met and missed an opportunity to gain real wealth for Spain by establishing Spanish rule in this New World. He left a mixed legacy as illustrated through contemporary footage on location, maps, and period art.

1229. *The Renaissance: 1450–1700 A.D.: Back in Time.* (Hands-On Crafts For Kids Series 6) Chip Taylor Communications, 2003. 30 min. Grades 4–6.

See entry 1038.

1230. *Renaissance Art and Music.* Clearvue/EAV, 2002. 54 min. Grades 7 up.

Renaissance artists and musicians evolved from a new emphasis on humanistic philosophy. Under the patronage of the wealthy, they developed new techniques of oil painting including perspective, shading, three-dimensional views, and portraiture. Musicians created new sounds with four-part polyphony. Artists include Botticelli, Brunelleschi, Ghiberti, Giotto, Leonardo, Michelangelo, and Tintoretto. Musicians such as des Prez, Dufay, and Dunstable evoked emotional aspects of the High Renaissance, and their compositions form a background for the artists' works presented in the film.

1231. *Renaissance, Reformation and Enlightenment.* (Democracy in World History) Hawkhill, 2006. 31 min. ISBN 978-1-55979-172-4. Grades YA.

From the 15th through the 17th centuries, the Renaissance and Reformation changed Europe and led the way to the Enlightenment. The DVD presents these changes and how the concern with the individual led to the desire for self-government and the ensuing revolutions that brought it. During the Enlightenment, scientific, philosophical, and religious beliefs expanded. The DVD includes background and information about these periods as well as the personages involved. Live-action footage along with art and illustration enhance the production.

1232. *Torchlighters: The William Tyndale Story.*   (Heroes of the Faith) Vision Video, 2005. 30 min.

The church and government of England under King Henry VIII made it illegal to read, write, or even speak of the Bible in the vernacular (English) rather than Latin. In 1535 William Tyndale (1494–1536) disagreed and published a translation in English of the Old and New Testaments. He had to move from town to town to avoid capture by Henry's bounty hunters. Tyndale's translation was the first into English from the Greek and Hebrew texts, and he was able to take advantage of the newly invented printing press to widely distribute it. Much of his work eventually became part of the King James version, published in 1611.

1233. Venezia, Mike. *Da Vinci.*   (Getting to Know the World's Greatest Artists) Getting to Know, 2006. 24 min. Grades K–8.

See entry 1028.

1234. Venezia, Mike. *Michelangelo.*   (Getting to Know the World's Greatest Artists) Getting to Know, 2006. 24 min. Grades K–8.

See entry 1216.

1235. Venezia, Mike. *Rembrandt.*   (Getting to Know the World's Greatest Artists) Getting to Know, 2002. 24 min. Grades K–8.

See entry 1219.

Compact Discs

1236. Blackwood, Gary L. *The Shakespeare Stealer.*   Narrated by Ron Keith. Recorded Books, 2001. 5 CDs. ISBN 978-1-4025-1970-3. Grades 4–8.

See entry 1053.

1237. Dunn, Jane. *Elizabeth and Mary: Cousins, Rivals, Queens.*   Narrated by Isla Blair. Random House, 2004. 6 CDs; 6.5 hrs. ISBN 978-0-739-30982-7. Grades YA.

See entry 1175.

1238. Gardner, Sally. *I, Coriander.*   Narrated by Juliet Stevenson. Listening Library, 2006. 6 CDs; 7.5 hrs. ISBN 978-0-3072-8419-8. Grades 3–7.

See entry 1077.

1239. Harding, Georgina. *The Solitude of Thomas Cave.*   Illustrated by John Lee. Narrated by Gareth Armstrong. Blackstone, 2007. 5 CDs; 5.5 hrs. ISBN 978-1-4332-0761-7. Grades YA.

See entry 1083.

1240. Hoffman, Alice. *Incantation.*   Narrated by Jenna Lamia. Brilliance, 2006. 3 CDs; 3 hrs. ISBN 978-1-4233-2360-0. Grades 8 up.

See entry 1087.

1241. Jacques, Brian. *The Angel's Command.*   Narrated by Brian Jacques. (Castaways of the Flying Dutchman) Recorded Books, 2004. 384pp. 8 CDs; 11 hrs. ISBN 978-1-4025-8067-3. Grades 5 up.

See entry 1094.

1242. Jacques, Brian. *Castaways of the Flying Dutchman.*   Narrated by Brian Jacques. (Castaways of the Flying Dutchman) Recorded Books, 2004. 7 CDs; 8.25 hrs. ISBN 978-1-4025-0521-8. Grades 5 up.

See entry 1095.

1243. *Masters of the Renaissance: Michelangelo, Leonardo da Vinci, and More.*   Narrated by Jim Weiss. Greathall, 2006. 78 min. ISBN 978-1-882513-88-8. Grades 5 up.

This CD offers an overview of the Renaissance and artists who made it a time of culture and innovation. Among the artists featured are Felippo Brunelleschi, Donatello, Lorenzo Ghiberti, Leonardo da Vinci, and Michelangelo.

1244. Meyer, Carolyn. *Loving Will Shakespeare.*   Narrated by Katherine Kellgren. Recorded Books, 2006. 272pp. 6 CDs; 6.5 hrs. ISBN 978-1-4281-4503-0. Grades 8–12.

See entry 1119.

1245. Ortiz, Michael J. *Swan Town: The Secret Journal of Susanna Shakespeare.*   Narrated by Bianca Amato. Recorded Books, 2006. 5 CDs; 6 hrs. ISBN 978-1-4281-1143-1. Grades 6–10.

See entry 1123.

1246. Osborne, Mary Pope. *Monday with a Mad Genius.*   Illustrated by Sal Murdocca. Narrated by Mary Pope Osborne. (Magic Tree House) Listening Library, 2007. 1 CD; 1 hr. 18 min. ISBN 978-0-7393-5646-3. Grades K–3.

See entry 1124.

1247. Treviño, Elizabeth Borton de. *I, Juan de Pareja.*   Narrated by Johanna Ward. Blackstone Audiobook, 2006. 4 CDs; 5 hrs. ISBN 978-0-7861-6640-4. Grades 6–9.

See entry 1139.

EUROPE AND THE BRITISH ISLES, 1650–1788

Historical Fiction and Fantasy

1248. Alexander, Bruce. *Blind Justice.* (Sir John Fielding) Berkley, 1995. 254pp. Paper ISBN 978-0-425-15007-8. Grades YA.

In this first volume of a series, Sir John Fielding helps to create London's first police force even though he is blind. This mystery involves Fielding's investigation of a murder in 18th-century London with the help of Jeremy Proctor.

1249. Alexander, Bruce. *Murder in Grub Street.* (Sir John Fielding) Berkley, 1996. 276pp. Paper ISBN 978-0-425-15550-9. Grades YA.

Jeremy Proctor, age 13, teams up with Sir John Fielding, the blind magistrate and creator of London's first police force. They investigate the murder of the printer Ezekiel Crabb, his family, and two employees on the day before Jeremy was to become apprenticed to him. As Sir John's eyes, Jeremy eventually earns a place in the household. In the course of their investigations, the pair go throughout 18th-century London, from Covent Garden to the Bedlam madhouse, as they search for answers.

1250. Anholt, Laurence. *Leonardo and the Flying Boy: A Story About Leonardo da Vinci.* Barron's Educational, 2000. 32pp. ISBN 978-0-7641-5225-2. Grades 2–4.

See entry 1051.

1251. Bradley, Kimberly Brubaker. *The Lacemaker and the Princess.* Margaret K. McElderry, 2007. 199pp. ISBN 978-1-416-91920-9. Grades 5–7.

In 1788 Isabelle, 11, lives near Versailles Palace with her lace maker grandmother and mother. She becomes a companion to Marie Antoinette's daughter, Princess Thérèse, and sees her in the afternoon after making lace at home in the morning. But they have problems with their friendship because of their class difference and the swirling political unrest. Isabelle observes a court with few sanitary facilities, crowds of vagrants overrunning the palace, and Louis XVI vacillating when dealing with the National Guard. Isabelle tries to explain to Thérèse how people live outside the palace, but Thérèse refuses to believe her or to understand.

1252. Brooks, Geraldine. *Year of Wonders: A Novel of the Plague.* Penguin, 2002. 308pp. Paper ISBN 978-0-14-200143-1. Grades YA.

In 1666 the vicar's 18-year-old maid, Anna Firth, lives in Eyam, a remote English village, with her two young boys after the death of her husband in a mining accident. The plague arrives in Eyam on a piece of cloth that the tailor has requested. He is the first to die in a village that decides on the advice of the vicar to voluntarily quarantine itself for a year. It eventually, however, loses one-third of its population. During this entire time, Anna becomes close to the vicar's young wife and helps all those in need around her. *Alex Award.*

1253. Buckley-Archer, Linda. *Gideon the Cutpurse: Being the First Part of the Gideon Trilogy.* (Gideon Trilogy) Simon & Schuster, 2006. 406pp. ISBN 978-1-4169-1525-6; Aladdin, 2007. paper ISBN 978-1-4169-1526-3. Grades 5 up.

After being sent to Derbyshire for the weekend, Peter Schock, 12, and his friend Kate Dyer experiment with an antigravity machine at a science lab and find themselves in England during 1763 where they meet the reformed cutpurse Gideon Seymour hiding from the Tar Man. The Tar Man absconds with their machine, and they have no way to return to the 21st century. They have to rapidly adjust to the time of King George III, with its bugs and diseases, on a long road trip to London. At the same time, their parents and NASA officials are desperately trying to locate them. *Lone Star Reading List* (Texas).

1254. Byrd, Max. *Jefferson: A Novel.* Anchor, 1998. 424pp. Paper ISBN 978-0-553-37937-2. Grades YA.

In 1784 Thomas Jefferson's young secretary in Paris tries to figure out his employer. Jefferson and his enigmatic ways baffle the man as he observes Jefferson dealing with the French, debating with his American colleagues, and becoming friends with married women. The secretary does his best to understand Jefferson, but all he can do is report what he sees.

1255. Celenza, Anna Harwell. *Bach's Goldberg Variations.* Illustrated by JoAnn E. Kitchel. Charlesbridge, 2004. 32pp. ISBN 978-1-57091-510-9. Grades K–3.

An orphan, Johann Gottlieb Goldberg, works in the household of Count Keyserlingk in Gdansk, Poland, in 1737. Johann Sebastian Bach (1685–1750) brings the count to his church to hear the boy play the harpsichord. Since Goldberg cannot play during work hours, he plays at night. The count hears him and wants him to play something different. Bach gives him new music, and each week Goldberg plays one of these variations. Supposedly, Bach composed his *Goldberg Variations* for this reason. Regardless, the real Goldberg became the court harpsichordist. Illustrations complement the text.

1256. Celenza, Anna Harwell. *The Farewell Symphony.* Illustrated by JoAnn E. Kitchel. Charlesbridge, 2000. 32pp. ISBN 978-1-57091-406-5; 2005. paper ISBN 978-1-57091-407-2. Grades 2–4.

When Prince Nicholas goes to his summer palace of Esterhaza in Hungary during 1772, he refuses to let his musicians' families come with them. The musicians become homesick as the Prince extends his stay into the fall. Joseph Haydn writes his Symphony No. 45 in F-sharp minor to show the anger, sadness, and frustration of the musicians. The musicians play the piece and then stand up one by one, snuff their candles, and leave the hall—their actions naming this The Farewell Symphony. When Nicholas hears it, he finally decides to return home.

1257. Chevalier, Tracy. *Girl with a Pearl Earring.* Plume, 2005. 233pp. Paper ISBN 978-0-452-28702-0. Grades YA.

Griet, 16, takes a job as a maid for the painter Johannes Vermeer (1632–1675) in 1664 after her father loses his eyesight in an accident. Vermeer enjoys her easy manner and he eventually asks her to mix colors, clean his studio, and be a model when one of his does not appear. One of Vermeer's patrons demands a painting of Griet wearing his wife's pearl earring. When his wife, Catharina, sees the picture, she is furious, and Griet must decide what to do. *Alex Award.*

1258. Costanza, Stephen. *Mozart Finds a Melody.* Illustrated by author. Henry Holt, 2004. 40pp. ISBN 978-0-8050-6627-2. Grades K–3.

As a young man, Mozart has composer's block, and to combat it he stands on his head and sings or throws darts at pages of music. However, he only has five days to compose a concerto. His inspiration comes from the seventeen-note song of his pet starling, whom he calls Miss Bimms. She flies away, and Mozart rushes out to find her in Vienna. When he hears all of the city's sounds, he incorporates them in his piece and delights his 18th-century audience.

1259. Cowling, Douglas. *Hallelujah Handel.* Illustrated by Jason Walker. Scholastic, 2003. 48pp. ISBN 978-0-439-05850-6. Grades 3–6.

George Frideric Handel (1685–1759) befriends Thomas, a young orphan, who sings beautifully but is unable to speak. The wicked Keeper hires him out to sing for the wealthy. When Thomas disappears, friends ask Handel to help find him. They find the boy backstage at an opera house where he is singing like an "angel." Handel takes the children to live at the Foundling Hospital, where Thomas finds a place for his voice with the chapel singers. This story connects to Handel's gift to this hospital of the score of the *Messiah.* Illustrations enhance the text. Notes.

1260. Cullen, Lynn. *I Am Rembrandt's Daughter.* Bloomsbury, 2007. 307pp. ISBN 978-1-59990-046-9. Grades 7–10.

After her mother dies of the plague and her beloved half-brother Titus marries a wealthy woman and leaves home, 14-year-old Cornelia van Rijn becomes her father's servant. The half-mad elderly Rembrandt's work is out of favor in Amsterdam because he believes that God tells him what to paint, not the patron. Cornelia becomes isolated from society as others shun her. Two young men, however, continue to visit her: Neel, her father's remaining student, and Carel, a shipping magnate's son.

1261. Cullen, Lynn. *Moi and Marie Antoinette.* Illustrated by Amy Young. Bloomsbury, 2006. 32pp. ISBN 978-1-58234-958-9. Grades K–3.

The dog of Marie Antoinette, Sebastien, tells of Marie, 14, leaving Austria to come to the court in France to marry the king's grandson. Since she is so busy with the life in the court, he is unhappy until she has a daughter. When Thérèse is 6, she starts playing with Sebastien, and his life is again happy. The illustrations contain much historical information about the court prior to 1789.

1262. Dick, Lois Hoadley. *False Coin, True Coin.* Bob Jones University, 1993. 172pp. Paper ISBN 978-0-8908-4664-3. Grades 6–10.

Cissy Nidd's father, in addition to being the Bedford jailer in Stuart-era England, deals in counterfeit coins. Cissy meets John Bunyan, a dissenter against the monarchy's state religion, who has been jailed. He helps her to see that life offers more than drudgery and deceit. She suffers, but because she has been kind to others, they in turn try to help her through her trials.

1263. Dines, Carol. *The Queen's Soprano.* Harcourt, 2006. 336pp. ISBN 978-0-15-205477-9; 2007. paper ISBN 978-0-15-206102-9. Grades 9 up.

Seventeen-year-old Angelica Voglia (ca. 1670) wants to sing and to marry the low-born artist she loves in 17th-century Rome. People stand under her shutters to hear her practice. When she is ordered to marry a nobleman, and because Pope Innocent IX has declared that women cannot sing in public, she flees to the court of Queen Christina, an expatriate Swede turned Catholic who rules one-quarter of Rome, wanting to become the queen's soprano and to live her own life. When Queen Christina nears death, Angelica's social-climbing mother threatens her happiness.

1264. Follett, Ken. *A Place Called Freedom.* Crest, 1996. 407pp. Paper ISBN 978-0-449-22515-8. Grades YA.

Mack lives in Scotland in the 1770s and mines coal to survive. He wants freedom from this drudgery, and the only choice he has is to leave. He travels to America via London and arrives in Virginia. There he begins to work in tobacco fields owned by the Jamisson family, who also own the Scottish mine where he worked previously. The interchange between Mack, the spoiled Jamisson son Jay, and Jay's more compassionate fiancée Lizzie, give a sense of place and social status.

1265. Forsyth, Kate. *The Gypsy Crown.* (Chain of Charms) Hyperion, 2008. 400pp. ISBN 978-1-4231-0494-0. Grades 6–9.

Although her baba, Maggie Finch, has told her family not to go into a local town to entertain, Emilia Finch, 13, accompanies her Rom (gypsy) family because they need to make some money at the local fair. It is the mid-17th century, and Oliver Cromwell's heartless agent Coldham confronts the "infidels" and jails them. Emilia and her cousin Luka are the only two who escape, and during the next twenty days they rush around England to gather five charms from five gypsy families. Their dog, horse, bear, and monkey accompany them as they stay ahead of Coldham in their quest to keep the government from hanging their family.

1266. Gavin, Jamila. *Coram Boy.* Farrar, 2005. 336pp. Paper ISBN 978-0-374-41374-3. Grades 6–9.

In 1741 a peddler offers to take unwanted children from mothers, promising to deliver them to Coram, a foundling home. However, he sells the older ones and buries the babies, sometimes alive. The specters of the babies haunt his simpleton son, Meshak, and Meshak can only escape by looking at the beauty of Gloucester Cathedral's stained glass windows. One night Meshak saves Melissa's ill-fated baby Aaron and takes him to Coram. The baby's father, Alexander Ashbrook, a man disinherited because he loves music, does not know the baby exists. At the age of 8, Aaron leaves the orphanage, is apprenticed to a musician, and reveals talents like those of his father. *Whitbread Prize* and *Capitol Choices Noteworthy Titles* (Washington, D.C.).

1267. Grant, K. M. *How the Hangman Lost His Heart.* Walker, 2007. 244pp. ISBN 978-0-8027-9672-1. Grades 5–8.

In 1746 Alice sees her favorite uncle, Frank, executed for treason against King George II for his support of the Stuart Bonnie Prince Charlie. His severed head is placed over London's Temple Bar, and she wants it to be buried with his body. She elicits the help of his executioner, Dan Skinslicer, who feels sorry for her; Captain Hew French becomes involved; and both fall in love with Alice. All three are charged as traitors, and as they speed through the countryside, Major Slavering chases them.

1268. Gregory, Kristiana. *Catherine: The Great Journey.* (The Royal Diaries) Scholastic, 2006. 169pp. ISBN 978-0-439-25385-7. Grades 4–7.

Princess Sophie Augusta Fredericka of Anhalt-Zerbst keeps a diary from 1743 to 1745 before she marries her second cousin, Peter, Grand Duke of Russia, when she is 15, and takes the name Catherine. Sophie discusses her life at home and her difficult travel to Russia for Peter's mother, the Empress Elizabeth, to vet her. She also recounts some of the difficulties in Russia at the time. Maps.

1269. Griffin, Margot. *Dancing for Danger.* Illustrated by P. John Burden. (Meggy Tales) Stoddart, 2001. 112pp. Paper ISBN 978-0-7737-6136-0. Grades 4–6.

Meggy and her brother Dan study their Irish culture along with other Irish Catholic friends in a secret school during the 1700s under their wonderful teacher, Master Cleary. The Penal Code of Ireland forbids them to study Irish culture, and after English soldiers destroy their first school they find another. Master Cleary nearly dies in a raid but Meggy protects him by dancing to keep him hidden until help arrives. Illustrations augment the text.

1270. Hawes, Charles Boardman. *The Dark Frigate.* Kessinger, 2005. 264pp. ISBN 978-1-4326-0971-9; paper ISBN 978-1-4179-3209-2. Grades 7 up.

Philip Marsham, an orphan in 17th-century England, has to flee London after an accident for which he is blamed. He signs up to sail on the *Rose of Devon*, a frigate leaving for Newfoundland. The ship rescues a group of men from a shipwreck, but they make the crew accompany them on their pirate expeditions. Philip becomes an outlaw and knows that he will face a hangman when he returns to England. *Newbery Medal.*

1271. Hearn, Julie. *Sign of the Raven.* Ginee Seo, 2005. 336pp. ISBN 978-0-689-85734-8; Simon Pulse, 2008. paper ISBN 978-0-689-85735-5. Grades 6–9.

When Tom's mother has a mastectomy, she takes Tom, 12, to London with her to stay at her estranged mother's home. Tom finds a time portal in the basement that takes him to 1717 and to some deformed people who need to be freed from working as sideshow attractions at Bartholomew's Fair. A young changeling child, Astra, is forced into prostitution, and another, the Giant, wants to be saved from grave robbers—unethical surgeons who want unusual specimens to dissect. While helping them, Tom realizes that his grandfather is the villain in both worlds, and that he deserves to die alone. He sold his family in the 18th century and deserted his contemporary family.

1272. Holmes, Victoria. *Rider in the Dark: An Epic Horse Story.* HarperCollins, 2004. 320pp. ISBN 978-0-06-052025-0; 2006 paper ISBN 978-0-06-052027-4. Grades 6 up.

In England in 1740, Lady Helena, the 15-year-old daughter of magistrate Lord Roseby, enjoys life on the family estate where her best friend Jamie, the stable boy, arranges for her to ride her father's powerful horses bareback. Her father wins a new stallion, Oriel, after betting that he cannot be tamed, but Helena disagrees and rides him at midnight. On the ride, she discovers that estate staff, including Jamie, are smuggling in order to avoid paying the king's taxes on imports, but she does not want to betray him. However, when wreckers deliberately mislead seamen in order to plunder their cargo, she risks her life by riding Oriel to relight a beacon to guide the sailors. She also discovers on that ride that her father is involved in the smuggling, just as he discovers who has been training Oriel.

1273. Hooper, Mary. *Newes from the Dead.* Roaring Brook, 2008. 256pp. ISBN 978-1-59643-355-7. Grades 8 up.

Robert, a medical student in 1650, prepares himself to endure the dissection of Anne Green, a housemaid of 22, executed for murdering her child. In alternating chapters, Anne recalls her life as she lies on the dissection table while Robert reveals his own inadequacies and amazement at the proceedings before him. In reality, Anne's child was stillborn, and Robert's realization that Anne is still breathing saves her from death even though those under Cromwell want her dead as an example to the populace. Christopher Wren enters the story when one of the attending surgeon's disdains his poetry. Based on a true story. *Capitol Choices Noteworthy Titles* (Washington, D.C.).

1274. Hooper, Mary. *Petals in the Ashes.* Bloomsbury, 2004. 200pp. ISBN 978-1-58234-936-7; 2006. paper ISBN 978-1-58234-720-2. Grades 6–10.

In 1666 Hannah and her older sister Sarah escape London during the plague in this sequel to *At the Sign of the Sugared Plum.* Unwelcome at the home of their Aunt Lady Jane outside the city, they are quarantined in a pestilence house for forty days. Before returning to London, they stop at their family home in Chertsey. Sarah decides to stay, but Hannah and her younger sister, Anne, 14, go to London to manage the family's sweetmeats shop, and Hannah discovers that her boyfriend Tom is well and working with a magician. When fires spread around the city, the two sisters have to leave again to survive. After the Great Fire is contained, they find their shop ruined and Tom beaten after a mob blames his employer, Count de'Ath, for starting the fire.

1275. Hooper, Mary. *The Remarkable Life and Times of Eliza Rose.* Bloomsbury, 2006. 334pp. ISBN 978-1-58234-854-4. Grades 7 up.

At the age of 15, in 1670, when her stepmother makes her leave the family home, Eliza Rose goes to London to find her father. She steals food and is incarcerated in Clink Prison, where Ma Gwyn likes her black hair and green eyes and frees her to become one of the prostitutes in her establishment. But Ma Gwyn's daughter Nell saves Eliza, who becomes Nell's companion before Nell is officially recognized as the mistress of Charles II of England. The prologue relates the story of a girl baby being swapped for a boy to please the father, and then Eliza Rose's story begins fifteen years later.

1276. Kirkpatrick, Katherine. *Escape Across the Wide Sea.* Holiday House, 2004. 210pp. ISBN 978-0-8234-1854-1. Grades 5–8.

In 1686 Daniel Bonnet, 9, and his Huguenot family escape France on a ship they believe to be bound for England. Instead they end up in Africa to pick up slaves, go to Guadeloupe, and then finally reach New York. On board, Daniel, although wounded by a dragoon's bayonet at home, performs chores that take him to the ship's hold. There he meets Seynabou and learns about the slaves' conditions. Then Daniel's family becomes part of a group that establishes the community of New Rochelle, where Daniel's father is able to take up his weaving trade again. Bibliography, Glossary, and Note.

1277. Laker, Rosalind. *The Golden Tulip.*   Three Rivers, 2007. 585pp. Paper ISBN 978-0-307-35257-6. Grades YA.

Francesca, the daughter of a temperamental but talented painter in Amsterdam during the 1660s, likes to visit Rembrandt's studio. Later she goes to Delft to become Vermeer's apprentice. When her mother dies, Francesca's father's debts lead him to arrange a marriage between her and an older wealthy man. Her intended husband is also disagreeable, and she loves someone else. When the French invade Holland, her fiancé is revealed as a traitor, and he dies before she has to marry him.

1278. Laker, Rosalind. *The Venetian Mask.*   Three Rivers, 2008. 585pp. Paper ISBN 978-0-307-35256-9. Grades YA.

After Marietta's mother, a Venetian carnival mask maker, dies in 1775, Marietta goes to live in the orphan housing for children with musical talent. She trains there, makes friends, and grows up. She and her two close friends become involved in a feud between two noble families. Before they have happier lives, they are further separated from loved ones by both death and imprisonment.

1279. Malterre, Elona. *The Last Wolf of Ireland.*   Clarion, 1990. 127pp. ISBN 978-0-395-54381-8. Grades 5–7.

Around 1786 in Ireland, Devin and his friend Katey see the Squire kill a mother wolf, and they save the litter. They feed them until a village boy informs others what they are doing. Devin saves one male, but the society hates wolves, and when the wolf is grown, someone mortally wounds it. Because Devin has cared for it, the wolf returns to him before dying.

1280. Meyer, Carolyn. *In Mozart's Shadow.*   Harcourt, 2008. 368pp. ISBN 978-0-15-205594-3. Grades 6 up.

Maria Anna "Nannerl" Mozart, 13, has an 8-year-old brother, Wolfgang, with whom she performs music in public. But as she matures and looks less like a child and as Wolfgang's musical talents become even more evident, her father begins excluding her from the performances. Then he starts taking Wolfgang abroad for solo performances, leaving Nannerl at home. He also refuses to allow Nannerl to marry the man she loves, to study abroad, or to pursue a position as a court musician. Everything in the Mozart family becomes focused on Wolfgang's success. Note.

1281. Morgan, Nicola. *The Highwayman's Footsteps.*   Candlewick, 2007. 354pp. ISBN 978-0-7636-3472-8. Grades 6–9.

In 1761 William de Lacy, 14, flees his home with his politician father's purse after refusing to join the king's army. In this suspenseful novel based on Alfred Noyes's poem, he meets Bess, the 14-year-old love-child of the dead highwayman and the landlord's daughter. Young Bess, who is following in her father's footsteps, steals William's money. Instead of reporting her to the authorities, William decides to join her. She hates all Redcoats and is determined to help the poor. Together they face soldiers, private militia, superstitious villagers, and share family secrets.

1282. Morrow, James. *The Last Witchfinder.* Harper Perennial, 2007. 526pp. Paper ISBN 978-0-06-082180-7. Grades YA.

In 1688 the father of 11-year-old Jennet Stearne, Walter, condemns his own sister-in-law, the wealthy Isobel Mowbray and Jennet's beloved aunt, to burn at the stake. Jennet decides she will work to abolish the Parliamentary Witchcraft Act of 1604. She consults Isaac Newton before she goes to the colonies with her father who has been exiled to Massachusetts, but she continues to read Newton's writings of scientific inquiry. In the New World, she witnesses some of the Salem trials, is kidnapped by Algonquins, and eventually reaches Philadelphia after a marriage. There she takes Ben Franklin as a lover, works with him, and eventually wins her desire.

1283. O'Brien, Patrick. *The Mutiny on the Bounty.* Walker, 2007. 40pp. ISBN 978-0-8027-9587-8. Grades 3–6.

In 1787 William Bligh (1754–1817) and his second-in-command, Fletcher Christian, sailed from England for Tahiti. During the voyage, there was much discontent and the crew became mutinous. Christian took command of the ship, forcing Bligh and his supporters into a small boat. Bligh and his men survived and returned to England. Some of the mutineers returned to Tahiti, and others went to Pitcairn Island. Watercolor and gouache illustrations highlight the events. Bibliography.

1284. Paton Walsh, Jill. *A Parcel of Patterns.* Farrar, 1992. 139pp. Paper ISBN 978-0-374-45743-3. Grades YA.

Mall, age 16, watches helplessly in 1665 as people in her small Derbyshire village of Eyam die after the plague arrives from London in a damp package of dress patterns. She tries to save her family and friends—and her fiancé, by having someone tell him that she has died, so that he will not come to town and contract the disease. Her plan fails when he comes anyway, despondent over her supposed death. He gets sick and dies, the very thing that Mall tried to avoid.

1285. Pietri, Annie, and Catherine Temerson. *The Orange Trees of Versailles.* Yearling, 2005. 144pp. Paper ISBN 978-0-440-41948-8. Grades 7 up.

In 1674 France, Marion Dutilleul, 14, begins service to the Marquise de Montespan, Louis XIV's mistress. Marion has an unusual ability to smell that helps her mix lovely perfumes. But she can also smell that which is not so pleasant. Her "nose" senses a poison that the Marquise creates to kill Queen Marie-Therese.

1286. Putney, Mary Jo. *A Kiss of Fate.* Ivy, 2005. 352pp. Paper ISBN 978-0-345-44917-7. Grades YA.

Lord Ballister, Duncan Macrae of Scotland, hates the continued difficulties between England and Scotland in 1745 in this historical fantasy. He has the secret powers of a "Guardian"—mystical abilities to control natural forces and see into the heart of another. When he meets beautiful English widow Gwynne Owens, a librarian and a scholar of Guardian history, he falls in love with her. Gwynne's father was a Guardian, but she does not believe she has inherited his power. When the Guardian council asks her to marry Duncan, she accepts him. Her power becomes apparent after her first sexual experience with him (her first marriage had been platonic). Their backgrounds continue to conflict as Duncan is called upon to help Bonnie Prince Charlie and Gwynne must betray her husband to the British.

1287. Quick, Barbara. *Vivaldi's Virgins.* HarperCollins, 2007. 284pp. ISBN 978-0-06-089052-0; 2008. paper ISBN 978-0-06-089053-7. Grades YA.

Antonio Vivaldi was maestro at Venice's Ospedale della Pietà between 1703 and 1740. One of his foundling musicians, Anna Maria "dal Violin," is one of the *figlie de coro* and the star violinist. Although she knows nothing about her parents, a nun encourages her to write letters to her mother. These letters alternate with Anna Maria's adult recollections of her life in the orphanage. She remembers Vivaldi encouraging the girls to sneak out and slide on a frozen canal, to attend the opera, and to crash a masked ball honoring Vivaldi's patron, King Frederick of Denmark. There they hear the handsome Scarlatti compete with Handel on the piano. And Annina meets Franz, the man with whom she falls in love. Annina then risks everything to sneak into the Jewish quarter in hopes of finding her parents.

1288. Rees, Celia. *Pirates!* Bloomsbury, 2003. 340pp. ISBN 978-1-58234-816-2. Grades 7 up.

Nancy Kington, a 16-year-old English heiress, and her mulatto maid, Minerva Sharpe, join the crew of a pirate ship plundering the West Indies in 1722 to escape Nancy's arranged marriage and Minerva's life as a Jamaican plantation worker. Nancy's brothers have planned her marriage to a wealthy plantation owner in order to retrieve the family's fortunes lost upon the death of her father, a sugar merchant and slave trader. During Nancy and Minerva's adventure at sea, they encounter slave dealers, British authorities, and mutinous mates. However, Nancy's most difficult task is facing her childhood true love, a British naval officer, in her new role as an outlaw. Minerva, however, falls in love for the first time with another mulatto, Vincent Crosby. They eventually discover that Minerva is actually Nancy's half-sister. *Capitol Choices Noteworthy Titles* (Washington, D.C.), *American Library Association Best Books for Young Adults, Bluegrass Award* (Kentucky) nomination, *Thumbs Up Award* (Michigan) nomination, *Eliot Rosewater Award* (Indiana) nomination, *Young Readers' Award* (Nevada) nomination, *Tayshas Reading List* (Texas), *Flume Award* (New Hampshire) nomination, *Young Reader's Award* (Arizona) nomination, *Junior Book Award* (South Carolina) nomination, and *High School Book Award* (Iowa) nomination.

1289. Schmidt, Gary D. *Anson's Way.* Clarion, 1999. 213pp. ISBN 978-0-395-91529-5. Grades 5–9.

Anson Granville Stapleton serves as a British Fencible drummer on a peace mission in Ireland in the 18th century. When he arrives in Dublin, the first thing he sees is the brutal whipping of a "hedge master" whose only crime is teaching Irish children their forbidden language, history, and culture. He finds himself in conflict with King George II's laws and does not want to use violence to maintain peace. As the son of a long line of Fencibles, he has wanted to serve all his life, the reality of the situation makes him question his commitment.

1290. Sturtevant, Katherine. *At the Sign of the Star.* Sunburst, 2002. 144pp. Paper ISBN 978-0-374-40458-1. Grades 4–7.

In London in 1677, 12-year-old Meg Moore must adjust to her widowed bookseller father's sudden decision to remarry and to his chosen wife, the young Susannah Beckwith. Meg has always wanted to be independent and own the bookstore called the Sign of the Star, but she understands that Susannah might have children with her father and jeopardize Meg's future. In the store, Meg has had the opportunity to read almanacs, sermons, plays, and poetry while meeting such writers as John Dryden and Aphra Behn. Meg is hostile to Susannah and is anguished when Susannah tries to teach her how to act like a woman. When a son is born, Meg realizes that he will inherit the shop, but Mr. Winter encourages Meg to look to her future with all of its wonderful possibilities. Meg learns to accept her new position as she forges ahead to write plays like Aphra Behn. *Capitol Choices Noteworthy Titles* (Washington, D.C.) and *Book Awards* (California) nomination.

1291. Sturtevant, Katherine. *A True and Faithful Narrative.* Farrar, 2006. 250pp. ISBN 978-0-374-37809-7. Grades 7 up.

In the sequel to *At the Sign of the Star*, Meg, 16, has to decide which of two suitors to marry in Restoration London in 1681. She flippantly tells Edward, who is leaving on a sea voyage, to get captured in North Africa and bring back a good story for her father's bookstore. He does get captured, and she has to collect money in order to free him with the help of her second suitor, her father's apprentice Will. Edward returns and tells his story only to show his new interest in Muslims in appreciation of the kind treatment he received during his captivity in Algiers. At the same time, Meg wants to be independent and write herself. *American Library Association Best Books for Young Adults, School Library Journal Best Books for Children*, and *Capitol Choices Noteworthy Titles* (Washington, D.C.).

1292. Sutcliff, Rosemary. *Bonnie Dundee.* Peter Smith, 1991. 204pp. ISBN 978-0-8446-6363-0. Grades YA.

In the late 1680s Colonel John Graham of Claverhouse fights against William of Orange in support of King James. As an old man in exile in Holland, Hugh Herriot tells his grandson the story of his youth as an orphan stable boy who met and followed the kind and faithful "Bloody Claver'se," who died in a Jacobite battle. Herriot also remembers the importance of the mysterious gypsy "tinkers" who appeared when needed and helped to save his life as well as others. First published in 1983.

1293. Taylor, G. P. *Shadowmancer.* Penguin, 2004. 304pp. ISBN 978-0-399-24256-4; Puffin, 2005. paper ISBN 978-0-14-240341-9. Grades t yo.

In Whitby, England, in the 18th century, Vicar Obadiah Demurral wants to gain control of the universe's highest power, but two children, Kate and Thomas, and their odd friend Raphah, a shipwrecked sailor who has come from Africa to reclaim the icon that Demurral stole from him, stand in his way. Demurral thinks that control of both the icon and of Raphah is all he needs for success, but a fallen angel thinks otherwise. *Galaxy British Book Awards* nomination.

1294. Treviño, Elizabeth Borton de. *I, Juan de Pareja.* Farrar, 1965. 192pp. ISBN 978-0-374-33531-1; Square Fish, 2008. paper ISBN 978-0-312-38005-2. Grades 7 up.

See entry 1139.

1295. Turnbull, Ann. *Forged in the Fire.* Candlewick, 2007. 312pp. ISBN 978-0-7636-3144-4. Grades 7 up.

Will and Susanna, in the sequel to *No Shame, No Fear*, face further difficulties. Will's father has disowned him for becoming Quaker, and Will plans to go to London. Susanna, 18, has been separated from Will for three years, and looks forward to his arrival so they can be married. What they do not realize is that the summer of 1665 will bring with it the plague and increased surveillance of Quakers, and will be followed by a huge fire in 1666. Even with all this, the two survive and have hope for the future.

1296. Vreeland, Susan. *The Girl in Hyacinth Blue.* Penguin, 2003. 242pp. Paper ISBN 978-0-14-029628-0. Grades YA.

After the Dutch master Vermeer paints *The Girl in Hyacinth Blue*, it disappears. A mathematician, Cornelius Engelbrecht, finds the painting in a basement. He inherited it from his father, a Nazi who stole paintings from the Jews in 1940. The Jews got the painting from a Dutch merchant whose ownership of the picture threatened his marriage because he had taken the picture from his mistress, wife of the French counsel. It came to her from a flooded Dutch farmhouse in 1717, and the owners of the house got it from Vermeer. Vermeer painted it to free himself from debt and feed his eleven children.

1297. Woodruff, Elvira. *Fearless.* Scholastic, 2008. 208pp. ISBN 978-0-439-67703-5. Grades 5–8.

Digory, 11, and his brother, Cubby, 9, head to Plymouth to see if their father has survived a shipwreck. He has not, but they meet Henry Winstanley (1644–1703), an architect who thinks his most marvelous achievement is a lighthouse erected on the Eddystone Reef to warn ships. He hires Digory as an apprentice, and when Digory has to take candles to him while he repairs the lighthouse, the "Storm of the Century" begins, and Digory has to overcome his fear of the sea. *Notable Trade Books in the Field of Social Studies.*

1298. Woodruff, Elvira. *The Ravenmaster's Secret: Escape from the Tower of London.* Scholastic, 2003. 240pp. ISBN 978-0-439-28133-1; 2005. paper ISBN 978-0-439-28134-8. Grades 4–8.

In 1735 Forrest, 11, son of the Tower of London's Ravenmaster, makes friends with Maddy, daughter of a Scottish spy being held prisoner, when he brings her food. He begins to admire and respect her, soon realizing that if he does not help her escape she will be executed along with her father and uncle. Action like this would mean defying his father, but he knows that saving her is right. A chimney sweep's "climber," Ned, and a rat catcher's apprentice known as "Rat" become his allies as Forrest frees both Rat and Maddy. Maps, Bibliography, Notes, and Glossary.

History

1299. Dash, Joan. *The Longitude Prize.* Illustrated by Dusan Petricic. Frances Foster, 2000. 200pp. ISBN 978-0-374-34636-2. Grades 6 up.

As a British inventor of watches and clocks, John Harrison (1693–1776) spent 40 years working on a machine that would determine longitude at sea, so that sailors could pinpoint their location. His instruments provided a way for a ship to measure east to west. However, he had many failures before he identified the correct technique. Ink drawings enhance the text. Bibliography, Glossary, Chronology, and Index. *Boston Globe/Horn Book Award, Robert F. Sibert Honor Book* and *Capitol Choices Noteworthy Titles* (Washington, D.C.).

1300. Frader, Laura Levine. *The Industrial Revolution: A History in Documents.* (Pages from History) Oxford, 2004. 157pp. ISBN 978-0-19-512817-8. Grades 10 up.

During the Industrial Revolution, social, economic, and cultural changes occurred. This account uses primary documents including newspaper clippings, letters, diaries, posters, prenuptial agreements, land deeds, and laws to describe these changes. Illustrations enhance the text. Further Reading, Chronology, and Index.

1301. Hibbert, Christopher. *Redcoats and Rebels: The American Revolution Through British Eyes.* Norton, 2002. 375pp. Paper ISBN 978-0-393-32293-4. Grades YA.

Hibbert looks at the American Revolution from the British point of view, discussing the blunders and decisions that the British could have changed to win the war. He also shows that the colonists were as hostile toward the Loyalist or Tory neighbors as the British had been toward the Scots. The biographical sketches here are not those of American military figures, but of British leaders such as Thomas Gage, Francis Smith, Hugh Percy, William Howe, John Burgoyne, Nathaniel Green, and Charles Cornwallis. Bibliography and Index.

1302. Holmes, Mary Tavener. *My Travels with Clara.* Illustrated by Jon Cannell. Getty Museum, 2007. 32pp. ISBN 978-0-89236-880-8. Grades 2–4.

In the 1740s Clara, a 5,000-pound rhinoceros, was famous in Europe. Her owner, Dutchman Douwe Van der Meer, toured with her from Rome to Berlin by ship, horse-drawn cart, and raft. Her life-size portrait became the centerpiece for the J. Paul Getty Museum's exhibition *Oudry's Painted Menagerie.* Illustrations enhance the text.

1303. Sharp, S. Pearl, and Virginia Schomp. *The Slave Trade and the Middle Passage.* (Drama of African-American History) Benchmark, 2006. 70pp. ISBN 978-0-7614-2176-4. Grades 5–8.

During the slave trading days, slavers traveled a triangle from Africa to the American colonies and then to Europe in any order necessary to collect money for their cargo. In six chapters, the authors discuss the African complicity in the slave trade, the ships, and the effects of the trade on the three continents. Chapters contain complementary photographs, illustrations, documents, and maps. Glossary, Bibliography, Further Reading, and Index.

1304. Whitaker, Robert J. *The Mapmaker's Wife: A True Tale of Love, Murder, and Survival in the Amazon.* Basic, 2004. 368pp. ISBN 978-0-7382-0808-4; Delta paper ISBN 978-0-385-33720-5. Grades YA.

In 1735 French mapmakers went with Charles-Marie de La Condamine to the New World in hopes of adding to the knowledge about the size and the shape of the earth. The youngest expedition member, Jean Godin, fell in love with 13-year-old Peruvian Isabel Grameson and they married in 1741. When the expedition neared its end toward 1745, Godin was concerned that the trip back across the Andes would be too dangerous for his pregnant wife. He went ahead alone. When he reached French Guiana, disaster occurred, and he and Isabel were separated by 3,000 miles. In 1769 Isabel crossed the Andes and floated down the Amazon to rejoin her husband. Her party ran aground on the Bobonaza River, and she managed to survive alone in the rainforest. She was finally reunited with her husband after 20 years apart. Maps, Bibliography, Notes, and Index.

Biography and Collective Biography

1305. Aliki. ***The King's Day: Louis XIV of France.***   Illustrated by author. Harper Trophy, 1991. 32pp. Paper ISBN 978-0-06-443268-9. Grades 2–6.

The ritual of Louis XIV's day—*lever, petit couvert*, exercise, *apartement*, and *coucher*—must have exhausted his servants and courtiers. Because he became king at age 5 in 1643, he likely saw himself as the most important man alive. Aliki's illustrations and brief text reveal the king's vanity, appetite, and control over his subjects. Chronology and Definitions.

1306. Aller, Susan Bivin. ***Musical Genius: A Story About Wolfgang Amadeus Mozart.*** Illustrated by Jane Hamlin. (Creative Minds) Lerner, 2004. 64pp. ISBN 978-1-57505-604-3; Darby Creek paper ISBN 978-1-57505-637-1. Grades 3–5.

Wolfgang Amadeus Mozart (1756–1791) was a prodigy who could write music before he could write words, and became the Emperor Joseph's Imperial Court composer. When he was a young adult, he was the most important composer of his time. However, Mozart faced a number of hardships and died relatively young with little money. Black-and-white illustrations highlight the text. Bibliography and Index.

1307. Anderson, M. T. ***Handel: Who Knew What He Liked.***   Illustrated by Kevin Hawkes. Candlewick, 2001. 48pp. ISBN 978-0-7636-1046-3; 2004. paper ISBN 978-0-7636-2562-7. Grades 3–6.

George Frideric Handel (1685–1759) had to disobey his father to become a musician. As a child, he smuggled a clavichord into his attic. Then he traveled throughout Italy as a young man listening to all kinds of music, studying it, and then composing. In England, he became a composer for the court. Acrylic illustrations complement the text. Chronology, Discography, and Further Reading. *American Library Association Notable Children's Books, Garden State Nonfiction Book Award* (New Jersey) nomination, *Children's Book Award* (South Carolina) nomination, and *Horn Book/Boston Globe Book Award.*

1308. Anderson, Margaret J. ***Carl Linnaeus: Father of Classification.***   (Great Minds of Science) Enslow, 1997. 128pp. ISBN 978-0-89490-786-9; 2001. paper ISBN 978-0-7660-1867-9. Grades 4–10.

Carl Linnaeus (1707–1778), a Swedish botanist, invented the binomial nomenclature for classifying plants and animals. Photographs of places where he lived and worked illustrate the text, which includes much about him and his scientific expeditions. Chronology, Further Reading, Glossary, and Index.

1309. Anderson, Margaret J. ***Isaac Newton: The Greatest Scientist of All Time.***   (Great Minds of Science) Enslow, 1996. 128pp. ISBN 978-0-89490-681-7; 2001. paper ISBN 978-0-7660-1872-3. Grades 5–8.

Isaac Newton (1642–1727) made enormous scientific advances, but they did not keep him from skipping meals or holding grudges against his colleagues. Anderson places Newton within the context of his times and shows the relationship between his life and his work. Photographs, Reproductions, Further Reading, Glossary, Notes, and Index.

1310. Aykroyd, Clarissa. ***Savage Satire: The Story of Jonathan Swift.***   (World Writers) Morgan Reynolds, 2006. 160pp. ISBN 978-1-59935-027-1. Grades 7–10.

Jonathan Swift (1667–1745), born in Ireland of English parents, became a clergyman unhappy with his advancement. He traveled often between the two countries, eventually settling in Dublin as the dean of St. Patrick's Cathedral in 1713. He spent most of his life writing satires of the government and political decisions of the day. In one of his works, *A Modest Proposal,* he suggested that Ireland would have less poverty if parents cannibalized their many children. *Gulliver's Travels* remains his best-known work and is included on many high school syllabi. Reproductions and illustrations highlight the text. Bibliography and Index.

1311. Baxter, Roberta. *Skeptical Chemist: The Story of Robert Boyle.* (Profiles in Science) Morgan Reynolds, 2006. 128pp. ISBN 978-1-59935-025-7. Grades 6 up.

Robert Boyle (1627–1691) grew up wealthy and privileged in both Ireland and England where he investigated alchemy and natural philosophy as a dilettante scientist, refusing to accept the conclusions of earlier scientists including Aristotle. He set the standards for scientific methods by creating experiments that could be successfully replicated. His Boyle's Law stated that pressure and volume are inversely proportional in a fixed amount of gas at a fixed temperature: if volume increases, pressure decreases, and vice versa. Portraits, paintings, and engravings illustrate the text. Time Line, Notes, Bibliography, Web Sites, and Index.

1312. Bingham, Jane. *Captain Cook's Pacific Explorations.* (Great Journeys Across Earth) Raintree, 2007. 48pp. ISBN 978-1-4034-9756-7; paper ISBN 978-1-4034-9764-2. Grades 4–6.

An account of the explorations of Captain James Cook (1728–1779) as he traveled to Tahiti, New Zealand, Australia, Antarctica, and the Hawaiian Islands. However, Hawaiian natives murdered him so he never returned to England. Illustrations augment the text. Chronology, Glossary, Further Reading, and Index.

1313. Boerst, William J. *Isaac Newton: Organizing the Universe.* (Renaissance Scientists) Morgan Reynolds, 2004. 144pp. ISBN 978-1-931798-01-3. Grades 8 up.

Isaac Newton (1642–1727) took the discoveries of scientists before him and decided that all the physical laws that governed the universe also governed Earth. He discovered new paths in mathematics and science including laws of motion and centripetal force. Newton's own childhood was difficult, but he became the master of the Mint, a politician, and a Unitarian. His writings include *Principia Mathematica* and *Defending Calculus.* Reproductions enhance the text. Time Line, Notes, Bibliography, Web Sites, and Index.

1314. Borden, Louise. *Sea Clocks: The Story of Longitude.* Illustrated by Erik Blegvad. Simon & Schuster, 2004. 48pp. ISBN 978-0-689-84216-0. Grades 2–4.

Because sailors could not measure longitude, many were lost at sea. In 1714 the English government offered a prize of £20,000 (today's equivalent of several million dollars) for the creation of a clock that could keep time accurately at sea regardless of weather or water conditions. John Harrison (1693–1776), a village clock maker without scientific training, invented the chronometer and spent forty years trying to perfect it. His achievement was a "sea clock" that accurately helped captains ascertain their longitude and stay on course. Parliament recognized his accomplishment in 1773, ten years after he finished. Crosshatched pen-and-ink illustrations with watercolors enhance the text. *Bluebonnet Award* (Texas) nomination.

1315. Brewster, Hugh. *The Other Mozart: The Life of the Famous Chevalier de Saint-George.* Illustrated by Eric Velasquez. Abrams, 2007. 48pp. ISBN 978-0-8109-5720-6. Grades 6–9.

Joseph Bologne, Chevalier de Saint-George (1745–1799), was the son of a black slave and a white plantation owner in Guadeloupe. Bologne became a noted French court favorite because of his talents as a fencer, soldier, and musician. In France he was schooled in fencing and music, and Marie Antoinette even asked him to play violin while she played piano. The French would not allow mulattos to conduct the opera, but Bologne became conductor of the Paris Orchestra for which Haydn wrote six symphonies. He also composed music and was known in France as "Le Mozart Noir." Illustrations illuminate the text. Bibliography, Note, Glossary, and Discography.

1316. Broderick, Enid. *Captain James Cook.* (Great Explorers) World Almanac, 2003. 48pp. ISBN 978-0-8368-5014-7; 2004. paper ISBN 978-0-8368-5174-8. Grades 5 up.

Captain James Cook (1728–1779), an English explorer and cartographer, searched for a Northwest passage. Then he took three voyages to the Pacific Ocean. On the first, from 1768 to 1771, he mapped the New Zealand coastline. Then he sailed toward Australia and became the first European to record contact with southeastern Australia. On his second voyage, from 1772 to 1775, he unsuccessfully searched for a larger land mass to the south of New Zealand. He almost reached Antarctica but turned back to resupply his ship. Although he retired, he decided to take a third voyage. He traveled from 1776 to 1779 and became the first European to travel in the Hawaiian Islands. After leaving there and then returning, tribal members killed him because of unrest to which he may have unwittingly contributed. Readers will learn about the life on board his ships, his reasons for travel, the people and places he saw, and his legacy. Glossary, Further Reading, and Index.

1317. Christianson, Gale E. *Isaac Newton and the Scientific Revolution.* Oxford, 2005. 155pp. ISBN 978-0-19-530070-3. Grades 8 up.

This biography of Isaac Newton (1642–1727) covers his life, emphasizing that he spent much of it in retribution for his treatment as a child. After his father died, Newton's mother remarried a rich man and insisted that Newton receive a trust. In return, Newton lived with his grandparents. Newton felt spurned and he carried his grudge throughout his life. He attended Cambridge, arriving in 1661, and by the time he was 24, he was the most advanced mathematician the world had known. But after that, he defied Robert Hooke, astronomer John Flamsteed, fellow mathematician Gottfried Leibniz, and the philosopher John Locke. He craved a government position and finally received an appointment as the head of the Royal Mint. Notes, Further Reading, and Index.

1318. Conley, Kate A. *Joseph Priestley and the Discovery of Oxygen.* (Uncharted, Unexplored, and Unexplained Scientific Advancements) Mitchell Lane, 2005. 48pp. ISBN 978-1-58415-367-2. Grades 6–8.

Joseph Priestley (1733–1804) grew up in Fieldhead, England, and became a theologian. He was also a dissenter, natural philosopher, educator, and political theorist who published more than 150 works. Usually credited with discovering oxygen, he actually isolated it in its gaseous state. He also invented soda water and wrote about electricity. Reproductions accompany the text. Glossary, Chronology, Further Reading, Web Sites, and Index.

1319. Ekker, Ernst A. *Wolfgang Amadeus Mozart: A Musical Picture Book.* Illustrated by Doris Eisenburger. North-South, 2006. Unpaged. ISBN 978-0-7358-2056-2. Grades 3–6.

Wolfgang Amadeus Mozart (1756–1791) was a child prodigy who became a renowned composer. He spent his life at court in the 18th century and has a reputation of being intolerant and arrogant in his brilliance. Illustrations complement the text. Chronology.

1320. Erickson, Carolly. *Great Catherine.* St. Martins, 1995. 392pp. Paper ISBN 978-0-312-13503-4. Grades YA.

Catherine II (1729–1796), Empress of Russia, wrote memoirs on which Erickson draws for this account. Catherine wanted to be a Western-style ruler but her subjects saw her as an enlightened despot. Catherine drafted laws, reformed her government, and improved conditions for her people. She also had a reputation for forming liaisons with the men in her court. The narrative reveals much about this complex and powerful woman. Index.

1321. Erickson, Carolly. *To the Scaffold: The Life of Marie Antoinette.* Griffin, 2004. 384pp. Paper ISBN 978-0-312-32205-2. Grades YA.

In this biography, Erickson presents Marie Antoinette (1755–1793), the queen-consort of Louis XVI of France from 1774 to 1792, as a person who was too naive to appropriately assess the events occurring around her. A beautiful woman with average intelligence, she was disinterested in developing qualities that would make her a better queen. This account looks closely at her daily activities and gives a special view of this woman whose name is often associated with the reasons why the French peasants revolted in 1789.

1322. Fox, Mary Virginia. *Scheduling the Heavens: The Story of Edmond Halley.* (Profiles in Science) Morgan Reynolds, 2007. 128pp. ISBN 978-1-59935-021-9. Grades 5–7.

This biography of Edmond Halley (1656–1742) reveals that he was much more than the discoverer of a comet, first called the Great Comet of 1682, for which he accurately calculated the orbit and predicted its return on a regular schedule. He also studied demographics, navigation, physics, mathematics, and more. He published the first meteorological chart, cataloged unmapped Southern Hemisphere stars, designed and tested a diving bell, and sailed around the globe to measure variations in magnetic field. This volume describes his tools and his techniques as well as his encouragement of other scientists and their research. Bibliography, Chronology, Web Sites, and Index.

1323. Fritz, Jean. *Can't You Make Them Behave, King George?* Illustrated by Tomie DePaola. Coward McCann, 1977. 48pp. ISBN 978-0-399-23304-3; Puffin, 1996. paper ISBN 978-0-698-11402-9. Grades 3–6.

At the age of 22, in 1760, George III (1738–1820) was crowned King of England. Before his coronation, he chose a bride from Germany whom he had not seen but who sounded as if she would make a good queen. He and Princess Charlotte of Mecklenburg raised a family, and George was as careful in his private life as he was in his public life. He decided to tax the American colonists and was surprised that they did not want to pay. He expected them to be dutiful children. He did not want to fight, but their refusal left him no choice. When his government was ready for peace, he did not want to surrender, but he had to do what the Parliament decreed. Notes from the Author.

1324. Getzinger, Donna, and Daniel Felsenfeld. *Antonio Vivaldi and the Baroque Tradition.* Morgan Reynolds, 2004. 144pp. ISBN 978-1-931798-20-4. Grades 6 up.

In eight chapters, this book introduces Antonio Vivaldi (1678–1741), who played music in his father's barbershop before becoming a priest in Venice. Each month he wrote two concerti using complex techniques. For a time he also composed four operas a year that thrilled those who heard them. He was troubled by rumors that he had an affair with one of his students. He carefully cultivated favor among Italian and German nobility, but eventually his proud demeanor and his music became unfashionable; he died a poor man. In the early 20th century, his music was rediscovered. The text also explains some of his music, especially *The Four Seasons*. Reproductions highlight the text. Bibliography, Time Line, Glossary, Notes, Web Sites, and Index.

1325. Getzinger, Donna, and Daniel Felsenfeld. *George Frideric Handel and Music for Voices.* (Masters of Music) Morgan Reynolds, 2004. 144pp. ISBN 978-1-931798-23-5. Grades 6–10.

The life of George Frideric Handel (1685–1759) and his importance to music becomes clear in this biography. Although his father believed music to be an unacceptable profession, Handel managed to pursue it. After he left Hamburg, he went to Italy and then on to England where he spent much of his adult life at the royal court. Among his compositions were operas and oratorios, especially the *Messiah*. Period portraits and reproductions highlight the text. Bibliography, Glossary, Chronology, Notes, Web Sites, and Index.

1326. Getzinger, Donna, and Daniel Felsenfeld. *Johann Sebastian Bach and the Art of Baroque Music.* Morgan Reynolds, 2004. 144pp. ISBN 978-1-931798-22-8. Grades 6 up.

An introduction to the life of Johann Sebastian Bach (1685–1750). Nine chapters cover his education, his organ music, his difficulty finding consistent employment, his devotion to church music, his associations with dukes, his friends, his classes and his cantatas, his final years, and a revival of his work. Bach began studying music, his family's trade, by playing the violin, but he soon became interested in the organ and other keyboard instruments. He wanted to create a complex music, and by doing so, he became the center of classical music. His German environment greatly influenced the choices that he could make for himself. Reproductions enhance the text. Bibliography, Chronology, Glossary, Notes, Web Sites, and Index.

1327. Gibson, Karen Bush. *The Life and Times of Catherine the Great.* (Biography from Ancient Civilizations) Mitchell Lane, 2005. 48pp. ISBN 978-1-58415-347-4. Grades 6–8.

Catherine II (1729–1796), a German princess, became Russia's empress and ruled for 34 years. Her reforms included widespread education, more medical care, the introduction of art and culture, and improvements in the legal system. She read extensively and got many of her insights from the Enlightenment in Europe. Her leadership laid the groundwork for Russia to become a world power in the 20th century. Photographs and illustrations highlight the text. Bibliography, Chronology, Notes, Glossary, Further Reading, Web Sites, and Index.

1328. Gow, Mary. *Robert Hooke: Creative Genius, Scientist, Inventor.* (Great Minds of Science) Enslow, 2007. 128pp. ISBN 978-0-7660-2547-9. Grades 5–9.

Robert Hooke (1635–1703), known as the "father of microscopy," coined the term "cell" to describe the basic unit of life. He was an architect and a chief London surveyor after the Great Fire. He also built some of the earliest Gregorian telescopes. He believed in evolution and investigated refraction. But his principal claim to fame was the law of elasticity (Hooke's Law). Photographs of places where he lived and worked illustrate the text, which includes much about him and his scientific explorations. Chronology, Further Reading, Glossary, and Index.

1329. Kraske, Robert. *Marooned: The Strange But True Adventures of Alexander Selkirk, the Real Robinson Crusoe.* Illustrated by Robert Andrew Parker. Clarion, 2005. 128pp. ISBN 978-0-618-56843-7. Grades 5–8.

Abandoned on the uninhabited Pacific island of Juan Fernandez after arguing with a ship's captain, Alexander Selkirk (1676–1721) lived there for four years before a British privateer found him in 1709. He survived by hunting seals, making primitive tools, wearing goatskin clothing, and reading his Bible. After he was found, he served as second mate on two ships before capturing a Spanish treasure ship and returning to England a wealthy man. Living in civilization no longer appealed to him, however, and he joined the Royal Navy before dying of a tropical disease at the age of 41. He was the inspiration for Daniel Defoe's *Robinson Crusoe*. Illustrations highlight the text. Bibliography, Glossary, and Note.

1330. Krull, Kathleen. *Isaac Newton.* Illustrated by Boris Kulikov. (Giants of Science) Viking, 2006. 126pp. ISBN 978-0-670-05921-8. Grades 5–9.

Sir Isaac Newton (1642–1727) developed the scientific method of research, invented calculus, built the first reflecting telescope, and identified many laws of physics such as gravity and optics. As a child he was lonely, and as an adult he was secretive and obsessive and often insulted other scientists. Krull speculates that Newton may have had either Asperger's or mercury poisoning. He lived during the time of the plague and the Great Fire of London. Illustrations augment the text. Bibliography, Web Sites, and Index. *School Library Journal Best Children's Books* and *Bulletin Blue Ribbon*.

1331. Lasky, Kathryn. *The Man Who Made Time Travel.* Illustrated by Kevin Hawkes. Farrar, Straus and Giroux, 2003. 48pp. ISBN 978-0-374-34788-8. Grades 4–6.

When John Harrison (1693–1776) was 21, he heard about the problem of measuring longitude when the British Parliament offered a Longitude Prize—£20,000 (approximately $12 million in today's currency). Latitude, the distance north or south of the equator, could be measured, but not the position east or west of a particular point. Although Harrison was a clock maker rather than a sailor, he imagined a seafaring clock and created it over the next forty years. He had to understand such aspects as the Lunar Distance Method and a gridiron pendulum. Harrison created five prototypes before he perfected his chronometer, and finally, ten years after his achievement, Parliament acknowledged his achievement but never gave him the prize money. Full-page color paintings enhance the text. Bibliography and Notes. *School Library Journal Best Books of the Year, American Library Association Notable Books for Children, Booklist Editors' Choice,* and *National Council of Teachers of English Orbis Pictus Honor.*

1332. Lee, Lavinia. *Handel's World.* (Music Throughout History) Rosen, 2007. 64pp. ISBN 978-1-4042-0726-4. Grades 5–8.

George Frideric Handel (1685–1759) was a German who spent much of his adult life working for the British monarchy composing operas, oratorios, and *concerti grossi*. Perhaps his most famous work is the *Messiah*. But other well-known compositions are "Water Music" and "Music for the Royal Fireworks." This biography presents excerpts from letters from or about the composer and includes photographs of places he lived and reproductions of people he knew. The six chapters discuss his early life, his family, his social status, his personality, his best-known music, and the importance of his work. Illustrations augment the text. Bibliography, Glossary, Chronology, Further Reading, Web Sites, and Index.

1333. Mis, Melody S. *Rembrandt.* (Meet the Artist) PowerKids, 2007. 24pp. ISBN 978-1-4042-3840-4. Grades 2–4.

See entry 1194.

1334. Norton, James R. *Haydn's World.* (Music Throughout History) Rosen, 2007. 64pp. ISBN 978-1-4042-0727-1. Grades 5–8.

This biography of Franz Joseph Haydn (1732–1809) relies on primary sources such as excerpts from letters. Haydn has been called the "Father of the Symphony" and "Father of the String Quartet." He spent his life in Austria, much of it as the court musician for a wealthy Hungarian family, the Esterházys. With photographs of places where he lived and reproductions of people he knew, the six chapters discuss his early life, family, social status, personality, best-known music, and the importance of his work. Illustrations augment the text. Bibliography, Glossary, Chronology, Further Reading, Web Sites, and Index.

1335. Rice, Earle, Jr. *Canaletto.* (Art Profiles for Kids) Mitchell Lane, 2007. 48pp. ISBN 978-1-58415-561-4. Grades 7 up.

This biography of Canaletto (1697–1768) covers his childhood, artistic training, travel, influences in his life, and his place in history. It shows his styles and the subjects that he chose to paint as well as the critical reaction to his work. Many of his paintings offer "photographic" views of Venice and its canals. Reproductions enhance the text. Glossary, Chronology, Notes, Further Reading, Web Sites, and Index.

1336. Schanzer, Rosalyn. *George vs. George: The American Revolution as Seen from Both Sides.* Illustrated by author. National Geographic, 2004. 60pp. ISBN 978-0-7922-7349-3; 2007. paper ISBN 978-1-4263-0042-4. Grades 4–7.

This collective biography looks at George Washington and King George III of England, the two main adversaries in the American Revolution. Two-page spreads examine the men themselves, their beliefs about government and taxation, their armies, and the battles of the Revolution. Watercolor illustrations complement the text. Bibliography and Index. *Capitol Choices Noteworthy Titles* (Washington, D.C.), *Young Hoosier Book Award* (Indiana) nomination, *Kirkus Starred Reviews*, *Student Book Award* (Maine) nomination, *School Library Journal Best Books of the Year*, and *Beehive Children's Book Award* (Utah) nomination.

1337. Schwartz, Gary. *Rembrandt.* Abrams, 1992. 92pp. ISBN 978-0-8109-3760-4. Grades YA.

See entry 1203.

1338. Shefelman, Janice. *I, Vivaldi.* Illustrated by Tom Shefelman. Eerdmans, 2008. 32pp. ISBN 978-0-8028-5318-9. Grades 2–5.

Vivaldi begins this narration of his life with his birth in Venice, Italy, in 1678 during an earthquake. Born a weakly infant, his mother promised him to the priesthood if he lived. His violinist father taught him to play the violin, and Vivaldi loved the music. He became a priest, known as the "Red Priest" because of his hair. When he kept rushing away from mass to write down music, the Cardinal recognized his talent and commanded him to teach the violin to orphaned girls. It was then that he composed one of his famous pieces, *The Four Seasons*, for his students. Ink and watercolor illustrations enhance the text.

1339. Siepmann, Jeremy. *Mozart: His Life and Music.* Sourcebooks, 2006. 256pp. ISBN 978-1-4022-0752-5. Grades 9 up.

Wolfgang Amadeus Mozart (1756–1791), a composer and performer, was one of the world's greatest musicians and child prodigies. This book and accompanying compact discs are valuable for those with little, if any, musical background. The music provided includes symphonies, concertos, his "Minuet in G," piano sonatas, the "Mass in C Minor," operas, the "Requiem," and "Serenade in B-flat for 13 Wind Instruments." In addition to information based on primary sources—including quotations, letters, and journals about Mozart's childhood under his father's tutelage, his marriage, his compositions, and the times in which he lived—Siepmann discusses the different genres of the music and Mozart's innovations. Reproductions augment the text. Bibliography, Glossary, Web Sites, and Index.

1340. Sís, Peter. *Play, Mozart, Play!* Illustrated by author. Greenwillow, 2006. Unpaged. ISBN 978-0-06-112181-4. Grades K–2.

This picture-book biography presents a brief view of the childhood of Wolfgang Amadeus Mozart (1756–1791). He performed all over Europe playing his and others' compositions on the piano. His father determined early that Mozart was gifted, and pushed his son to keep playing even when the boy was uninterested. Illustrations complement the text. *School Library Journal Best Books for Children.*

1341. Sobel, Dava. *Longitude: The True Story of a Lone Genius Who Solved the Greatest Scientific Problem of His Time.* Walker, 2007. 184pp. Paper ISBN 978-0-8027-1529-6. Grades YA.

Being off course poses many dangers to sailors, and over the centuries various efforts were made to find a way to measure longitude. Some seamen used lunar tables, and inventors worked on clocks that would be accurate regardless of bad weather and ocean swells. The perseverance of John Harrison (1693–1776), despite delays caused by pettiness and politics, eventually solved the problem. This narrative also includes interesting anecdotal information, such as the fact that sauerkraut (rather than limes) was the original cure for scurvy. Bibliography and Index.

1342. Steele, Philip. *Isaac Newton: The Scientist Who Changed Everything.* (World History Biography) National Geographic, 2007. 64pp. ISBN 978-1-4263-0114-8. Grades 4–7.

This biography of Isaac Newton (1642–1727) offers an overview of the scientist's life. As a teenager, he showed himself to be an inept farmer, leading his family to agree to his pursuing university studies. Topics covered include his major achievements, difficulties such as his irritable personality, and his legacy. Illustrations highlight the text. Bibliography, Glossary, Chronology, and Index.

1343. Venezia, Mike. *George Handel.* Illustrated by author. (Getting to Know the World's Greatest Composers) Children's Press, 1999. 32pp. ISBN 978-0-516-04539-9; 2000 paper ISBN 978-0-516-26534-6. Grades K–5.

George Frideric Handel (1685–1759) was a well-known composer during his lifetime, and he traveled in Europe, especially Germany and Italy, to learn more about music. He finally moved to London, England, in 1712 and stayed there. When he was young, his father did not want him to study music, but his talent impressed a duke who heard him and encouraged his father to change his mind. Because of this decision, Handel's wonderful oratorios and symphonic works can still be heard. Illustrations augment the text.

1344. Venezia, Mike. *Johann Sebastian Bach.* Illustrated by author. (Getting to Know the World's Greatest Composers) Children's Press, 1998. 32pp. ISBN 978-0-516-20760-5; paper ISBN 978-0-516-26352-6. Grades K–5.

The people who knew Johann Sebastian Bach (1685–1750) thought of him more as an organist or a harpsichord player than a composer because they heard him play at the royal court or in the local church. His compositions did not become famous until long after his death, and today they are very important. Illustrations enhance the text.

1345. Venezia, Mike. *Johannes Vermeer.* Illustrated by author. (Getting to Know the World's Greatest Artists) Children's Press, 2002. 32pp. ISBN 978-0-516-22282-0; paper ISBN 978-0-516-26999-3. Grades K–5.

Johannes Vermeer (1632–1675) lived in Delft, Holland, all of his life and is considered the finest genre painter of his century. His subjects are usually single females doing simple tasks such as reading, pouring milk, or making lace. Illustrations highlight the text.

1346. Venezia, Mike. *Rembrandt.* Illustrated by author. (Getting to Know the World's Greatest Artists) Children's Press, 1988. 32pp. ISBN 978-0-516-02272-7; paper ISBN 978-0-516-42272-5. Grades K–5.

See entry 1219.

1347. Venezia, Mike. *Wolfgang Amadeus Mozart.* Illustrated by author. (Getting to Know the World's Greatest Composers) Children's Press, 1995. 32pp. ISBN 978-0-516-04541-2; 2003 paper ISBN 978-0-516-44541-0. Grades K–5.

Wolfgang Amadeus Mozart (1756–1791) learned to play the violin when he was only 4 years old and wrote his first concerto when he was 6. The author portrays Mozart as a child managed by his father. Illustrations enhance the text.

1348. Vernon, Roland. *Introducing Bach.* Chelsea House, 2000. 32pp. ISBN 978-0-7910-6037-7. Grades 5–7.

Johann Sebastian Bach (1685–1750) wrote music to the glory of God, but people in his own time knew him best as an organist. Tradition, important to Bach, became his way of expressing himself, because he took the styles of the past to new heights. This account places Bach in the context of his family and his times, as an organ virtuoso, in the Weimar court, in Cöthen, as cantor of Leipzig, and as a church musician. Stunning color photographs and reproductions augment the text. Chronology, Glossary, and Index.

1349. Vernon, Roland. *Introducing Mozart.* Chelsea House, 2000. 32pp. ISBN 978-0-7910-6041-4. Grades 3–6.

This brief overview of Wolfgang Amadeus Mozart (1756–1791) includes full-color drawings, photographs, and engravings as well as sidebar information on events, artistic movements, and people in the late 18th century. Although short, the text is sophisticated, and places Mozart in his times. Glossary and Index.

1350. Weeks, Marcus. *Mozart: The Boy Who Changed the World with His Music.* (World History Biography) National Geographic, 2007. 64pp. ISBN 978-1-4263-0002-8. Grades 5–8.

This text looks at the young Wolfgang Amadeus Mozart (1756–1791) using a scrapbook layout. The four main sections of the text cover the historical context of his life, the daily lives of people during his time, and offer side material on related topics such as the Age of Enlightenment. Photographs enhance the text. Bibliography, Glossary, Web Sites, Maps, and Index.

1351. Whiting, Jim. *James Watt and the Steam Engine.* (Uncharted, Unexplored, and Unexplained) Mitchell Lane, 2005. 48pp. ISBN 978-1-58415-371-9. Grades 5–8.

James Watt (1736–1819) invented the steam engine. This biography looks at his childhood, his education, and other achievements resulting from his research and experimentation. Illustrations enhance the text. Glossary, Chronology, and Further Reading.

1352. Yount, Lisa. *Antoni Van Leeuwenhoek: First to See Microscopic Life.* (Great Minds of Science) Enslow, 2008. 128pp. ISBN 978-0-7660-3012-1. Grades 4–8.

Antoni Van Leeuwenhoek (1632–1723) lacked formal scientific training, but his interest in a variety of subjects led him from his profession as a cloth merchant to making his own microscopes. When he first saw the lice living on his leg magnified by microscope, he was rather disturbed. Other aspects of his life are covered in the text, which includes diagrams and illustrations. Photographs, Further Reading, Glossary, Notes, and Index.

Graphic Novels, Biographies, and Histories

1353. Blain, Christophe. *Isaac the Pirate: To Exotic Lands.* Translated by Joe Johnson. ComicsLit, 2003. 96pp. Paper ISBN 978-1-56163-366-1. Grades YA.

In the late 1700s before the French Revolution, unemployed artist Isaac accepts an offer from a rich captain to sail with him and paint the scenes in the New World to which they are delivering supplies. Isaac wants to make quick money and return to marry his wonderful love, Alice. On the seas, Isaac discovers that the sea captain, known as Captain John the Pillager, plans to go to the South Pole and find so much money that he will be a pirate legend. Thus the adventure, filled with dark turns and complexity, becomes much longer than Isaac expected, while back home, Alice is struggling to make enough money to pay the rent. When she obtains a good job at the home of an aristocrat, Philip, her employer, begins wooing her. The text is a translation of Blain's two graphic novels about Isaac—*Les Ameriques* and *Les Glaces. Angoulème Festival Prize.*

DVDs

1354. *Glory to God Alone: The Life of J. S. Bach.* Vision Video, 2003. 89 min. ISBN 978-1-56364-703-1. Grades 9 up.

Johann Sebastian Bach (1685–1750) composed his music solely for the glory of God. When he died he was not famous, but now musicians play and sing his works throughout the world. This DVD examines his life by visiting places in Germany that helped to shape his beliefs and where he was a musician. Scholars discuss his achievements, and musicians, including guitarist Christopher Parkening, offer examples.

1355. *The Industrial Revolution: 1700–1900: Back in Time.* (Hands-On Crafts for Kids Series 6) Chip Taylor Communications, 2003. 30 min. Grades 4–6.

This production begins with a narrator reading the list of materials appearing on the screen. Teachers demonstrate crafts relating to the Industrial Revolution: a zoetrope, Morse code, Wedgwood, cotton bags, and pointillism. Each item helps explain an important achievement during the Industrial Revolution.

1356. *Newton's Dark Secrets.* (NOVA) WGBH Boston, 2006. 56 min. ISBN 978-1-59375-323-8. Grades 7 up.

While he was working with optics, physics, and calculus, Isaac Newton (1642–1727) also wanted to know what hidden information the Bible contained and how to create gold using alchemy. Newton believed that God created material existence, and during his life, alchemy was outlawed. This DVD carefully describes Newton's three laws of motion and his Universal Law of Gravitation, as well as others.

1357. Venezia, Mike. *Rembrandt.* (Getting to Know the World's Greatest Artists) Getting to Know, 2002. 32pp. 24 min. ISBN 978-0-5160-2272-7. Grades K–8.

See entry 1219.

Compact Discs

1358. Buckley-Archer, Linda. *Gideon the Cutpurse: Being the First Part of the Gideon Trilogy.* Narrated by Gerard Doyle. (Gideon Trilogy) Simon & Schuster, 2006. 10 CDs; 11.5 hrs. ISBN 978-0-7435-5558-6. Grades 5 up.

See entry 1253.

1359. Rees, Celia. *Pirates!* Narrated by Jennifer Wiltsie. Random House, 2007. 8 CDs; 9 hrs. ISBN 978-1-4000-8622-1. Grades 7 up.

See entry 1288.

1360. Sturtevant, Katherine. *At the Sign of the Star.* Narrated by Emily Gray. Recorded Books, 2002. 4 CDs; 4 hrs. ISBN 978-1-4025-3302-0. Grades 4–7.

See entry 1290.

1361. Treviño, Elizabeth Borton de. *I, Juan de Pareja.* Narrated by Johanna Ward. Blackstone Audio, 2006. 4 CDs; 5 hrs. ISBN 978-0-7861-6640-4. Grades 7 up.

See entry 1139.

EUROPE AND THE BRITISH ISLES, 1789–1859

Historical Fiction and Fantasy

1362. Aiken, Joan. *Bridle the Wind.* Harcourt, 2007. 242pp. Paper ISBN 978-0-15-206058-9. Grades 7 up.

In the early 1800s Felix, age 13, wakes up in a monastery near the coast on the border of France and Spain; he has been ill for three months following a shipwreck. He has to escape into Spain when he realizes that the monastery's abbot is trying to detain him. Various persons pursue him at the behest of the abbot, and he barely escapes. Felix is especially surprised to discover that the boy with whom he escaped is actually a girl.

1363. Aiken, Joan. *The Teeth of the Gale.* Harcourt, 2007. 307pp. Paper ISBN 978-0-15-206070-1. Grades 7 up.

In the 1820s Felix, a college student in Salamanca, Spain, gets a letter from his grandfather requesting that he return home to help Dona Conchita find her three children, kidnapped by her felon husband. He rushes home so that he will also have a chance to see his friend Juana, whom he met in *Bridle the Wind* (1983), who is preparing to take her religious vows. During his search for the children, villains pursue Felix for the money they think he has hidden but realize that he is honest in his denials. He succeeds in his quest. This novel was first published in 1988.

1364. Avi. *The Escape from Home.* (Beyond the Western Sea) Harper Trophy, 1997. 336pp. Paper ISBN 978-0-380-72875-3. Grades 5–9.

Patrick and his sister Maura have to escape from Ireland in 1851 after their landlord destroys their hovel. Also trying to catch the *Robert Peel* from Liverpool, England, on January 24 is 11-year-old Laurence, the son of an English lord; Laurence is running away from abuse and his own guilt. The three face various obstacles in getting to the ship. The novel spans the five days before they finally get on board and start their trip. *Booklist Starred Review, Bulletin Blue Ribbon, American Library Association Best Books for Young Adults*, and *Capitol Choices Noteworthy Titles* (Washington, D.C.).

1365. Avi. *Lord Kirkle's Money.* (Beyond the Western Sea) Scholastic, 1996. 336pp. ISBN 978-0-531-08870-8; Harper Trophy, 1998. paper ISBN 978-0-380-72876-3. Grades 5–9.

Patrick O'Connell and his sister Maura, along with their friends Mr. Horatio Drabble and Laurence Kirkle, sail on the *Robert Peel* from England to Boston in 1851. After arriving they all go to Lowell, Massachusetts, where the O'Connells find out that the their father has died. The characters endure prejudice and hardship but eventually overcome the evil forces that would ruin their lives. The second installment in the series. *Capitol Choices Noteworthy Titles* (Washington, D.C.).

1366. Avi. *The Traitor's Gate.* Illustrated by Karina Raude. Richard Jackson, 2007. 353pp. ISBN 978-0-689-85335-7. Grades 5–9.

In 1849 John Huffman, 14, has to find money to support his family after his Aunt Euphemia refuses to pay his father's gambling debt and his father is sent to London's debtor's prison. John realizes that many spies surround the family, and he must try to find out what secret his father is hiding and who these people might be. His father's boss at the Royal Navy suspects that his father is trying to sell a secret about new weapons. In a Dickensian plot, John becomes friends with an orphaned housemaid, Sary the Sneak, who, like the other characters, is not what she seems. *Dorothy Canfield Fisher Children's Book Award* (Vermont) nomination and *Land of Enchantment Book Award* (New Mexico) nomination.

1367. Barron, Stephanie. *Jane and His Lordship's Legacy: Being the Eighth Jane Austen Mystery.* (Jane Austen) Bantam, 2005. 292pp. ISBN 978-0-553-80225-2; paper ISBN 978-0-553-58407-3. Grades YA.

After Jane's love, the Lord Harold Trowbridge, dies in 1809, Jane receives his bequest of a box containing his personal papers. She and her mother have just arrived at a new home, Chawton Cottage, belonging to Jane's brother Edward. The villagers are angry that Widow Seward has been removed from the premises, and relatives are annoyed about Jane's gift. Jane must also find out who murdered Shafto French, whose body was found lying in the Chawton basement. When Jack Hinton is accused of killing French, Jane must find the real murderer while she protects her property.

1368. Barron, Stephanie. *Jane and the Barque of Frailty: Being the Ninth Jane Austen Mystery.* (Jane Austen) Bantam, 2006. 297pp. ISBN 978-0-553-80226-9; 2007 paper ISBN 978-0-553-58408-0. Grades YA.

In 1811 Jane goes to London to stay with her brother Henry and his wife Eliza while awaiting the publication of *Sense and Sensibility.* When a Russian princess, Evgenia Tscholikova, is found dead on a former Tory minister's doorstep, Jane and Eliza end up in possession of the princess's jewels, trying to sell them for the impoverished Comtesse d'Entraigues. The women have one week to prove that they did not commit the murder, and Jane thinks that the Tory minister's enemies may be trying to manipulate his arrest. She investigates.

1369. Barron, Stephanie. *Jane and the Genius of the Place: Being the Fourth Jane Austen Mystery.* (Jane Austen) Bantam, 2000. 290pp. Paper ISBN 978-0-553-57839-3. Grades YA.

While staying with her brother Neddie and his wife Lizzy in Kent, Jane Austen attends the Canterbury Races. She sees the French-born Françoise Grey strike a man with her whip, and after the race, Mrs. Grey's body is found behind the race grounds in Denys Collingforth's chaise. People in Kent want Neddie to arrest Collingforth, but Jane suspects more. Among those who possibly murdered Mrs. Grey are her husband, Valentine Grey, who denies her infidelities; Mrs. Grey's relative and perhaps lover, the

Comte de Penfleur; and the Austen family governess, Anne Sharpe, who is overly distressed by the event. Jane investigates.

1370. Barron, Stephanie. *Jane and the Ghosts of Netley: Being the Seventh Jane Austen Mystery.* (Jane Austen) Bantam, 2004. 291pp. Paper ISBN 978-0-553-58406-6. Grades YA.

While visiting Netley Abbey ruins on the Southampton coast in the fall of 1808, Jane Austen receives a message from Lord Harold Trowbridge. He asks that she befriend Sophia Challoner, a widow living at nearby Netley Lodge, whom he suspects of spying for the French. Jane cannot believe that the widow could be involved but soon an enemy sets fire to a frigate in Southampton Water and murders its shipwright. Jane must reconsider her impressions.

1371. Barron, Stephanie. *Jane and the Man of the Cloth: Being the Second Jane Austen Mystery.* (Jane Austen) Bantam, 1997. 274pp. Paper ISBN 978-0-553-57489-0. Grades YA.

Jane, her sister, Cassandra, and their parents travel from Bath to Lyme in a coach that overturns in the rain, injuring Cassandra. When Jane goes to a nearby house for help, she meets Geoffrey Sidmouth. Cassandra returns to London, and Jane learns about events that seem to point to Sidmouth as a smuggler of luxury items from France. After two murders, Jane begins to investigate.

1372. Barron, Stephanie. *Jane and the Prisoner of Wool House: Being the Sixth Jane Austen Mystery.* (Jane Austen) Crime Line, 2002. 291pp. Paper ISBN 978-0-553-57840-9. Grades YA.

Jane Austen goes to visit her brother Frank, a Royal Navy post captain, in Southampton in 1807. Frank's friend Captain Tom Seagrave has been accused of killing a French officer. Frank does not believe his friend is guilty, but Tom's wife Louisa is furious with her husband; Navy Board member Sir Francis Farnham wants to get rid of him; a French prisoner at Wool House, Étienne LaForge, also asserts guilt; and Phoebe Carruthers, mother of a child who died in Seagrave's charge, wants Seagrave dead. Jane investigates.

1373. Barron, Stephanie. *Jane and the Stillroom Maid: Being the Fifth Jane Austen Mystery.* (Jane Austen) Bantam, 2001. 277pp. Paper ISBN 978-0-553-57837-9. Grades YA.

While Jane Austen visits her rector cousin, Mr. Edward Cooper, in Staffordshire in 1806, she goes for a walk in the hills of nearby Derbyshire and discovers the mutilated body of Tess Arnold, a servant on a local estate with skills as a herbalist. Arnold's body indicates that she might have been mistaken for a local apothecary believed to be a witch or murdered by a Mason who considers her a traitor. Jane's friend Lord Harold Trowbridge shows up at a neighboring estate to mourn a late friend, and alerts Jane to Arnold's connection to this powerful Whig family. Jane's own escort on her walk, Mr. Hemming, disappears before the inquest.

1374. Barron, Stephanie. *Jane and the Unpleasantness at Scargrave Manor: Being the First Jane Austen Mystery.* (Jane Austen) Bantam, 2008. 289pp. Paper ISBN 978-0-553-38561-8. Grades YA.

Jane Austen visits her friend Isobel, Countess of Scargrave, when she and her older husband return from their honeymoon in the early 1800s. At a ball, Isobel's husband is found dead from poisoning, and when Isobel and her husband's handsome nephew are accused of the murder, Jane knows she must investigate and clear them of the unwarranted charges.

1375. Bell, Ted. *Nick of Time.* Griffin, 2008. 432pp. ISBN 978-0-312-38068-7. Grades 6–9.

In 1939 Nick McIver, 12, discovers a sea chest that has washed up on shore near his house on Graybeard Island in the English Channel. Inside is a time machine with a plea from a Nick McIver living in 1805, asking for help because his ship is about to be destroyed in the Napoleonic Wars. A pirate tries to get both Nicks while Nazis patrol off the English shore in 1939. Eventually, everyone gets sorted out, but the pirate remains alive.

1376. Bennett, Veronica. *Cassandra's Sister: Growing Up Jane Austen.* Candlewick, 2007. 227pp. ISBN 978-0-7636-3464-3. Grades 8 up.

In the late 1700s Cass Austen and her younger sister Jenny (Jane), 19, share all of their secrets. Engaged to Thomas Fowle, Cass waits for him to have enough money for them to marry. Jenny meets someone at a ball, but he proposes to another young woman. Instead of complaining, she writes stories in which she incorporates her experiences. Among her compositions are *Elinor and Marianne* and *First Impressions.* They discuss marriage and children and grieve over the death of Cass's fiancé. Some aspects of the text come from Jane Austen's letters.

1377. Bennett, William J. *Angelmonster.* Candlewick, 2006. 234pp. ISBN 978-0-7636-2994-6; 2007. paper ISBN 978-0-7636-3407-0. Grades 9 up.

Mary Godwin (Wollstonecraft Shelley), 16, elopes with the married Percy Bysshe Shelley to have his child. Instead of a happy love story, she becomes enmeshed in a scandal that eventually leads to her creation of *Frankenstein.* When she and Percy first go from England to Europe, Mary's stepsister accompanies them and begins an affair with Shelley. During this chaotic time, friends commit suicide, others have affairs, Mary suffers depression, and three of her four children die. This novel does not reveal whether Mary retrieved Percy's heart from his funeral pyre before it completely burned.

1378. Bredsdorff, Bodil. *The Crow-Girl: The Children of Crow Cove.* Farrar, 2004. 160pp. ISBN 978-0-374-31247-3; 2006. paper ISBN 978-0-374-40003-3. Grades 4–7.

After her grandmother dies, a young orphaned peasant girl whom strangers begin to call Crow-Girl, leaves her seaside home in Denmark where she has eaten mussels and sand snails and built driftwood fires. She leaves her first protector who has evil intentions and meets others along the way who have endured terrible losses. She bonds with them, remembering her grandmother's belief that one always gets what one wished for even if not in the form one expected. Since Crow-Girl's wish that her grandmother would not die could not be granted in a real world, Crow-Girl discovers that she has taken her grandmother's strength. The group of individuals she meets need each other, and they reassemble at the home where Crow-Girl lived with her grandmother to create their own family. *Mildred L. Batchelder Honor Book, Booklist Editors' Choice, Parents Choice Award Silver,* and *School Library Journal Best Children's Books.*

1379. Brighton, Catherine. *My Napoleon.* Illustrated by author. Diane, 2005. 26pp. ISBN 978-0-7567-8931-2. Grades K–4.

Betsy Balcombe was a child when Napoleon (1769–1821) lived in her home during his exile on St. Helena. She wrote about him in a journal, and Brighton uses this journal as her source for the story. Betsy seems to have a rapport with Napoleon after she overcomes her fear of him and his status as "V.I.P.N." or "Very Important Prisoner, Napoleon." He takes her for carriage rides and gives her enough candy to make her sick. When her family leaves for England, Betsy regrets parting from him.

1380. Buckley-Archer, Linda. *The Time Thief.* (Gideon Trilogy) Simon & Schuster, 2007. 491pp. ISBN 978-1-4169152-7-0; 2008. paper ISBN 978-1-4169152-8-7. Grades 5–8.

After Kate Dyer returns to the present, she wants to go back to 1763 to rescue her fellow time traveler Peter Schock. He, however, has resigned himself to living in that century since he has had to remain there for 29 years. Kate and her father return to 1792 in an unsuccessful rescue attempt, and Peter does not identify himself because he hopes they can still get their time machine to work in 1763 and get him back home. At the same time, the Tar Man, a thief from the 18th century who has come in Peter's place to the 21st century, is enjoying the mayhem he can create even though the modern gadgets confuse him. Peter decides to keep waiting to be saved, preferably at the age of 12 rather than 41, and will probably have success in installment three of the series that started with *Gideon the Cutpurse* (2006).

1381. Cameron, Eleanor. *The Court of the Stone Children.* Puffin, 1990. 208pp. Paper ISBN 978-0-14-034289-5. Grades 4–7.

Nina wants to become a museum curator because she finds solace in San Francisco's French Museum, a place where Chagall's painting *Time Is a River Without Banks* greets her. In this historical fantasy, Nina meets Dominique, a figure in an early 19th-century painting. Dominique says she dreamed about Nina as a girl and wants Nina to help her find out what happened to her father. Nina solves the puzzle by guessing about a painting and shows Dominique that her father was innocent of charges made against him by Napoleon's army. *American Book Award, National Book Awards,* and *Mark Twain Award* nomination.

1382. Celenza, Anna Harwell. *The Heroic Symphony.* Illustrated by JoAnn E. Kitchel. Charlesbridge, 2004. 32pp. ISBN 978-1-57091-509-3. Grades 2–4.

When he discovers he is going deaf, Ludwig van Beethoven (1770–1827) decides to write a symphony in honor of Napoleon's heroic accomplishments and composes his Symphony No. 3. Soon after, he hears that Napoleon has declared himself Emperor of France, and Beethoven rips up the copy of the score he had intended to give to Napoleon. A friend stops Beethoven from destroying other copies of the work. Later, Beethoven renames the symphony the "Eroica." Illustrations complement the text.

1383. Cole, Shelia. *The Dragon in the Cliff: A Novel Based on the Life of Mary Anning.* Illustrated by T. C. Farrow. Backinprint.Com, 2005. 211pp. Paper ISBN 978-0-595-35074-2. Grades 5–7.

Mary Anning, age 7, climbs the cliffs surrounding the beaches of Lyme Regis, England, to find fossils that her father can clean and sell to tourists. In 1810 her father dies and Mary works to support her family. In 1812 she discovers a fossil ichthyosaurus, or "crocodile," as she called it, that measures 17 feet. She makes other discoveries, but because women of that time were not paleontologists and never wrote scientific papers, no one mentions her work. Although poor and uneducated, she is very intelligent and teaches herself about her discoveries.

1384. Cornwell, Bernard. *Sharpe's Prey: Richard Sharpe and the Expedition to Copenhagen, 1807.* Perennial, 2003. 272pp. Paper ISBN 978-0-06-008453-0. Grades YA.

In 1807 Richard Sharpe has returned home from India and is unhappy with his post, especially since his wife Grace has died. Then he asked to become the bodyguard of Captain John Lavisser, the Duke of York's aide, while he delivers a bribe on a sensitive diplomatic mission to Copenhagen, Denmark. Sharpe finds out that Lavisser is a French double agent trying to get the Danes to help the French, and the British must bomb Copenhagen to foil Lavisser's plan.

1385. Crosbie, Duncan. *Life on a Famine Ship: A Journal of the Irish Famine 1845–1850.* Barron's, 2006. 25pp. ISBN 978-0-7641-6004-2. Grades 4–6.

In the 1840s the famine ship *Dunbrody* carries Irish immigrants to America. One of the passengers, 9-year-old Michael, writes journal entries describing his family's experiences such as the failure of crops and the long sea journey. Forty years later, he finishes his journal and refers to the Molly Maguires. Pop-up illustrations of home interiors, a sailing ship, and other details augment the text.

1386. D'Alessandro, Jacquie H. *The Bride Thief.* Dell, 2002. 384pp. Paper ISBN 978-0-440-23712-9. Grades YA.

In 1820, 26-year-old Samantha Briggeham knows she has little time left to marry successfully but she refuses to marry a man she does not love. As Sammie likes books and conducts scientific experiments with her brother Hubert, 16, she thinks she will never meet someone suitable. Her father offers her in an unwelcome marriage to an old family friend who spent years in the army, but just before the wedding, a masked man rescues her on horseback. He has dedicated himself to rescuing unfortunate women and sending them to America, but Sammie wants to remain with her family. He acquiesces. Sammie has no idea who this Bride Thief might be, but when she meets Eric Landsdowne, the Earl of Wesley, she is intrigued. She decides to become involved with him and when their liaison is discovered, the earl proposes. Sammie hesitates about losing her independence, but Hubert soon discovers that the Earl of Wesley and the Bride Thief are the same man.

1387. Dietrich, William. *Napoleon's Pyramids.* (Ethan Gage) HarperCollins, 2007. 374pp. ISBN 978-0-06-084832-3; 2008. paper ISBN 978-0-06-084833-0. Grades YA.

Expatriate American Ethan Gage wins a medallion with seemingly indecipherable writing on it in a Parisian card game in 1798. Masons who want the amulet frame Gage for two murders. Then Napoleon takes Gage to Egypt, thinking the medallion might reveal the Great Pyramid's secrets. The result brings forth more puzzles and mysteries for Gage to consider. The first in a series.

1388. Dietrich, William. *The Rosetta Key.* (Ethan Gage) HarperCollins, 2008. 352pp. ISBN 978-0-06-123955-7; Harperluxe paper ISBN 978-0-06-146881-0. Grades YA.

After becoming Napoleon's enemy, Ethan Gage goes to Egypt in 1798 in search of his love, Astiza, who may have been kidnapped by Napoleon's lackey Alessandro Milano. Astiza was last seen falling from a hot-air balloon into the Nile. Gage also searches for an ancient Egyptian scroll, the Book of Thoth, hoping to secure it for the British. Moses had originally stolen it from the Great Pyramid and taken it to Israel. Gage uses knowledge of electricity gained from Benjamin Franklin, his gambling skills, and his wit to keep him alive during his searches. The second volume in the series.

1389. Dowswell, Paul. *Powder Monkey: The Adventures of Sam Witchall.* Bloomsbury, 2005. 300pp. ISBN 978-1-58234-675-5; 2007. paper ISBN 978-1-58234-748-6. Grades 6 up.

Although he wants to go to sea and secures a post on a merchant ship, 13-year-old Sam Witchall is pressed into service aboard the *H.M.S. Miranda* before the ship wrecks. During sea battles, he must run gun powder from below deck to his cannon crew. Other troubles, however, also befall him including vicious storms, punishment, and mutiny.

1390. Dowswell, Paul. *Prison Ship: Adventures of a Young Sailor.* Bloomsbury, 2006. 313pp. ISBN 978-1-58234-676-2; 2007. paper ISBN 978-1-59990-156-5. Grades 6 up.

In a sequel to *Powder Monkey*, 13-year-old Sam Witchall and his friend Richard must go to Australia after someone frames them for being cowards in the Battle of Copenhagen under Admiral Nelson in March of 1801. After traveling 15,000 miles in eight months, Sam reaches the penal colony and then escapes into the Australian bush. There a cannibal tries to kill him before two other fugitives rescue Sam and Richard so that they may return to civilization.

1391. Doyle, Marissa. *Bewitching Season.* Holt, 2008. 352pp. ISBN 978-0-8050-8251-7. Grades 7–10.

Persy (Persephone) Leland, 17, wants only to read her books and practice magic, rather than prepare for a London debut into society in 1837. But Lochivar Seton, a childhood friend, reappears and Persy finds herself interested. When someone kidnaps the governess who has taught Persy magic, Persy uses her knowledge of creating spells, a practice that does not belong in her society. She and her twin have a lot of problems they must overcome with their boyfriends and the sinister situation behind the governess's disappearance.

1392. Flanagan, Thomas. *The Year of the French.* (New York Review Books Classics) New York Review of Books, 2004. 516pp. Paper ISBN 978-1-59017-108-0. Grades YA.

In August and September 1798 French soldiers come to Vinegar Hill in Ireland to help the Irish with their rebellion against the English. Five narrators—a Protestant clergyman, a solicitor, a wife, a schoolmaster, and a soldier—tell about the event from their individual perspectives. A poet named Owen also becomes involved in the rebellion because he feels an affinity with his Irish past and is *fey*. The rebellion, planned by people with personal motives, fails.

1393. Foley, Gaelen. *Lord of Fire.* Ivy, 2002. 432pp. Paper ISBN 978-0-449-00637-5. Grades YA.

When innocent Alice Montague comes looking for her sister at Lord Lucien Knight's Regency country estate, Revell Court, Lord Knight is unsure how to handle her. He has only socialized with "loose" women who have attended his lavish parties. But he is actually a spy who uses the gatherings for intelligence, so he decides to keep Alice with him for a week to protect her. They soon fall for each other, although a few unexpected twists initially thwart their relationship.

1394. Frost, Helen. *The Braid.* Frances Foster, 2006. 95pp. ISBN 978-0-374-30962-6. Grades 8 up.

In 1850 teenagers Jeannie and Sarah and their family are evicted from their Western Isles home in Scotland as a result of the Clearings. Jeannie goes with her family and younger siblings to Cape Breton, Canada. Sarah stays with their old grandmother. Before they part, the sisters braid their hair together, and they cut off the braid, each taking half of it, saying they will always be sisters together through their hair. Their alternate narrative poems reveal that Jeannie's father and younger siblings die during the rough ocean crossing. Sarah feels lonely, falls in love, and has an illegitimate child. Between each poem is an ode praising an idea in the previous narrative. They both want love, a family, and to be together. *School Library Journal Best Books for Children* and *American Library Association Best Books for Young Adults*.

1395. Gardner, Sally. *The Red Necklace: A Story of the French Revolution.* Dial, 2008. 384pp. ISBN 978-0-8037-3100-4. Grades 7–10.

In the late 1780s gypsy orphan voice-thrower and mind-reader Yann Margosa, 14, encounters shy Sido, 12, daughter of a marquis, when he returns from being spirited to London after Count Kallovski murders his employer, a stage magician. Yann has returned to find the dwarf named Têtu who raised him, and to help Sido escape marrying Count Kallovski.

1396. Giff, Patricia Reilly. *Maggie's Door.* Yearling, 2005. 160pp. Paper ISBN 978-0-440-41581-7. Grades 5–9.

In the sequel to *Nory Ryan's Song*, Nory leaves Ireland to escape the potato famine several days after the departure of her friend, Sean Red Mallon, his mother, and her 4-year-old brother Patch, during the 1840s. The two relate their stories in alternating chapters as they try to reach Nory's sister Maggie's house in Brooklyn. They face cruelty, starvation, and filth on the way over in "coffin" ships, but they focus on the future and meeting at 416 Smith Street.

1397. Giff, Patricia Reilly. *Nory Ryan's Song.* Yearling, 2002. 148pp. Paper ISBN 978-0-440-41829-0. Grades 5–8.

Nory Ryan, 12, lives in Maiden Bay, Ireland, in 1845 with her grandmother, two sisters, and brother. When the potatoes begin rotting, she has to scavenge for food for her younger brother by scaling cliff walls for bird eggs and making herbal broth with Anna, the local herbalist. Eventually, Nory's father sends them tickets to America so they can find a new life. *School Library Journal Best Books for Children, Children's Book Award* (Colorado) nomination, *Dorothy Canfield Fisher Children's Book Award* (Vermont) nomination, *Rebecca Caudill Award* (Illinois) nomination, *Student Book Award* (Maine) nomination, *Mark Twain Award* (Missouri) nomination, *Land of Enchantment Book Award* (New Mexico) nomination, *Young Reader's Choice Award* (Pennsylvania) nomination, *Bluebonnet Award* (Texas) nomination, *Battle of the Books Award* (Wisconsin) nomination, and *Children's Book Award* (West Virginia) nomination.

1398. Golding, Julia. *Cat Among the Pigeons.* (A Cat Royal Adventure) Roaring Brook, 2008. 368pp. ISBN 978-1-59643-352-6. Grades 5–9.

In the 1790s Cat Royal lives in London's Theater Royal on Drury Lane. She needs to protect Pedro Hawkins, a former slave whose ex-master, the awful Kingston Hawkins, wants him back. Pedro, an excellent actor, as he has proven in the role of Ariel in *The Tempest*, needs not only her protection but that of the whole troupe. But Cat gets into trouble herself and has to hide at her friend Lord Francis's Westminster School disguised as a boy. Simultaneously, Billy Boil appears and extracts a promise from Cat that she does not want to keep in this sequel to *The Diamond of Drury Lane*.

1399. Golding, Julia. *The Diamond of Drury Lane.* (A Cat Royal Adventure) Roaring Brook, 2008. 432pp. ISBN 978-1-59643-351-9. Grades 5–9.

In 1790s London Catherine "Cat" Royal still lives in the Drury Lane Theater where she was left as a baby. One of her tasks is to protect the diamond that Mr. Sheridan, the theater owner, has hidden inside. When she tries to find it, those around her become involved—revolutionary cartoonist and theater prompter Johnny; roughneck Billy, who loves her; freed slave Pedro, a virtuoso violinist; and the royal Lord Francis and Lady Elizabeth. *Smarties Prize.*

1400. Hart, J. V. *Capt. Hook: The Adventures of a Notorious Youth.* Illustrated by Brett Helquist. Laura Geringer, 2005. 352pp. ISBN 978-0-06-000220-6; Trophy, 2007. paper ISBN 978-0-06-000222-0. Grades 7–10.

In the 19th century 15-year-old James Matthew, the illegitimate son of an aristocrat whom he has barely seen and a mother he does not know, attends Eton College in England. The head of his house, Arthur Darling, leads the other boys against him, and he takes revenge. After he is expelled, his father sentences him to seven years on the *Sea Witch*, an old ship with a nasty captain. It happens to be a slave ship, and James sides with the slaves to earn his name, "Hook." He eventually earns his own ship and becomes the Captain Hook who threatens Peter Pan.

1401. Hausman, Gerald, and Loretta Hausman. *Napoleon and Josephine: The Sword and the Hummingbird.* Scholastic, 2004. 288pp. ISBN 978-0-439-56890-6. Grades 7 up.

Rose Tascher de la Pagerie, called the "Hummingbird," grows up in Martinique but dreams of moving to Paris, and an arranged marriage to a French nobleman takes her there. She soon divorces and has a difficult time during the French Revolution. When she holds a party, General Napoleon attends and he renames her "Josephine." They become lovers. Very little is revealed about the other affairs of either of them.

1402. Heneghan, James. *The Grave.* Groundwood, 2003. 238pp. Paper ISBN 978-0-88899-499-8. Grades 7–10.

At the age of 13, Tom Mullen has spent his life in foster homes in Liverpool, England, since his parents abandoned him in a department store as a toddler. When he visits a mass grave that construction workers recently discovered in a local cemetery in 1974, he falls through a hole into 1847 Ireland. There the Monaghan family of Tully, Hannah, and the mentally disabled Brendan, lovingly accepts him after he uses CPR to save the life of the drowning Tully. As Tom tries to help them survive the famine, he has difficulty avoiding explanations of such things as the zipper holding his jacket together. After the family travels to Liverpool, hoping to take a ship to America, he understands that many of the Irish of the time are those in the mass grave. He eventually realizes that Tully is his great-grandfather, and he returns to 1974 with a better understanding of the challenges of his disabled foster brother Brian and ready to reunite realistically with his own parents.

1403. Hess, Donna L. *In Search of Honor.* (Light Line) Bob Jones University, 1991. 153pp. Paper ISBN 978-0-8908-4595-0. Grades YA.

When Jacques Chenier's father wants to give his wife a gift in 1787, he poaches a pigeon outside Paris. Jacques watches the warden murder his father for the deed. Trained by his father to sculpt in both stone and wax, Jacques continues the business until authorities arrest him for helping a friend collect money that is rightfully the friend's. In the Bastille, Jacques meets its oldest prisoner, Pierre-Joseph, who helps him begin to understand that bitterness has no place in life. After Jacques escapes from the Bastille, he takes part in the French Revolution with Danton and Robespierre. He frees Pierre-Joseph who comes to live with him while offering Jacques advice not to trust those whom he has joined in the Revolution.

1404. Hill, Laban Carrick. *A Brush with Napoleon: An Encounter with Jacques-Louis David.* (Art Encounters) Watson-Guptill, 2007. 161pp. ISBN 978-0-8230-0417-1. Grades 6 up.

When Jean Martin, 17, serves Napoleon's army in Egypt, he stays in the rear with Napoleon's artists and discovers that he has both a talent and a passion for drawing. He wants to be a soldier like his father, however, so he continues to fight until he is severely injured in battle against the Austrians at Marengo. His friend Alain convinces him to study art, and he luckily gets a commission to study under Jacques-Louis David. After struggling with class distinctions and politics, Jean earns his right to be an apprentice.

1405. Holeman, Linda. *Search of the Moon King's Daughter: A Novel.* Tundra, 2003. 309pp. Paper ISBN 978-0-8877-6609-1. Grades 8–11.

In the 1830s, after their illiterate mother becomes an addict and their educated father dies of cholera, 15-year-old Emmaline Roke goes to London to find her brother Tommy, sold into servitude as a chimney sweep by their mother. She gets a job and reads Wordsworth to her elderly employer, locates Tommy, and gains wealth when her employer bequeaths her two valuable books. Eventually she falls in love with young Thomas, who also has a commitment to books.

1406. Holub, Josef. *An Innocent Soldier.* Translated by Michael Hofmann. Arthur A. Levine, 2005. 240pp. ISBN 978-0-439-62771-9; Scholastic, 2007. paper ISBN 978-0-439-62772-6. Grades 8 up.

Adam Feuchter, a 16-year-old orphan, must enter Napoleon's Grand Armée when his farmer employer substitutes him for his drafted son under the name of Georg Bayh. At first Adam is pleased to be part of the plan to conquer Moscow, but he quickly becomes disillusioned with the drudgery and horror of war under a terrible sergeant. However, the noble Lieutenant Konrad Klara chooses Adam as a personal servant and his life improves. They see the soldiers treat the locals with disdain, endure starvation and cholera, and ward off Cossack attacks. When they lose in Moscow, the two survive, and as they slowly retreat, their bond of friendship forms across class lines. *Horn Book Fanfare, Mildred L. Batchelder Award* and *Battle of the Books Award* (Wisconsin) nomination.

1407. Jackson, Dave, and Neta Jackson. *The Drummer Boy's Battle: Florence Nightingale.* Illustrated by Julian Jackson and Catherine R. McLaughlin. (Trailblazer) Bethany House, 2001. 144pp. Paper ISBN 978-1-55661-740-9. Grades 3–7.

In 1854, 12-year-old Robbie Robinson serves as a drummer boy during the Crimean War in Russia to earn money for his family after his father dies. Robbie's older brother dies in the Charge of the Light Brigade, and Robbie is wounded. He is sent to Barracks Hospital in Scutari, Turkey, where a thoughtless doctor amputates his left hand, and Florence Nightingale becomes his nurse. She cares for him, trying some of her new techniques for improving the medical care of soldiers. As Robbie becomes her "right-hand man," he runs errands for her and reports hospital conditions while hearing that the doctors at the site dislike Nightingale's improvements.

1408. Lawrence, Iain. *The Buccaneers.* (High Seas Trilogy) Yearling, 2003. 256pp. Paper ISBN 978-0-440-41671-5. Grades 5–9.

At the age of 16 in 1801 John Spencer sails from England to the West Indies on his father's trading ship, the *Dragon*, under Captain Butterfield. The schooner rescues a sailor named Mr. Horn from a lifeboat in the open sea, and the crew wonders if he is a *Dragon*, as the ship's one-eyed gunner thinks, or good luck. Among the difficulties the ship encounters are storms, pirates, disease, and betrayal. When the *Dragon* comes out of a fog, it is heading toward the Tombstones, the same rocks that wrecked the *Isle of Skye* in the first book in the series. This is the third volume. *Manitoba Literary Awards—Young Readers Choice* nomination.

1409. Lawrence, Iain. *The Cannibals.* (The Curse of the Jolly Stone Trilogy) Laurel-Leaf, 2007. 230pp. Paper ISBN 978-0-440-41933-4. Grades 5–9.

In the 1820s Tom Tin, 14, and his blind friend Midgely, along with other juvenile criminals, escape from the ship taking them to Australia and head for a Pacific Island. Tom has been convicted of a murder he did not commit. Even though Tom's father has warned them about headhunters, cannibals, and pirates, Midgely wants Tom to return to England and recover a jewel that he has buried. They do reach an island, and they encounter all that Tom's father warned about and much more in this sequel to *The Convicts*.

1410. Lawrence, Iain. *The Castaways.* (The Curse of the Jolly Stone Trilogy) Delacorte, 2007. 234pp. ISBN 978-0-385-73090-7. Grades 5–9.

Tom Tin and the blind Midgely board an abandoned ship in the South Seas, but two stranded sailors take over their ship and give them to slave traders. Tom's knowledge helps save them and they eventually get back to London where Tom can retrieve the Jolly Stone, the huge diamond nearly the size of a doorknob, and seek revenge against Mr. Goodfellow, the man who had him transported to Australia initially.

1411. Lawrence, Iain. *The Convicts.* (The Curse of the Jolly Stone Trilogy) Delacorte, 2005. ISBN 978-0-385-73087-7; Laurel-Leaf, 2007. paper ISBN 978-0-440-41932-7. Grades 5–10.

After Tom Tin's unemployed ship captain father has to go to debtor's prison, Tom, 14, must survive in 19th-century London. After he tries to take revenge on his father's nemesis, Mr. Goodfellow, he finds a diamond, joins a street gang, and helps steal a corpse. During the grave robbery he loses the diamond. Arrested as a thief and convicted of murder, he ends up on a prison ship bound for Van Diemen's Land (Australia). On the ship, Tom meets the blind Midgely, and the two make plans to escape. They do, but in the ensuing adventures, Tom discovers that his own father is the captain of the ship. *Kirkus Reviews Editor's Choice*.

1412. Lawrence, Iain. *The Smugglers.* (High Seas Trilogy) Yearling, 2000. 192pp. Paper ISBN 978-0-440-41596-1. Grades 5–9.

In 1801 John Spencer, 16, sails as second in command on his father's new schooner, the *Dragon*. Someone warned John's father that the *Dragon* had been a smuggler's vessel sailing between England and France, but he purchases the ship anyway, planning to transport wool. Once out at sea off the Cornish coast, the shifty Captain Crowe changes course because he and the crew are indeed smugglers. John has to use his wits and the help of a stowaway unsympathetic to the captain to overcome his enemies and return the *Dragon* safely to port. The second volume in the trilogy. *American Library Association Best Books for Young Adults, Bulletin Blue Ribbon,* and *Garden State Teen Book Award* (New Jersey) nomination.

1413. Lawrence, Iain. *The Wreckers.* (High Seas Trilogy) Yearling, 1999. 224pp. Paper ISBN 978-0-440-41545-9. Grades 5–9.

In 1799, when wreckers lure John Spencer, 14, and his father's boat, the *Isle of Skye*, to the coast of Cornwall with a false beacon, he watches scavengers murder his shipmates. John escapes up a cliff to Pendennis where Simon Mawgan, who has first rights to shipwrecked goods, protects him. Mawgan does not know that the wreckers are deliberately luring ships; however, he is much more eager to know whether the ship carries gold, contraband, or liquor than to help John. Mawgan's rival has chained John's father in a cellar where he will drown when high tides flood in, but Mawgan's niece Mary helps John rescue his father and stop another wrecking attempt. The first volume in a trilogy. *Rebecca Caudill Young Readers' Book Award* (Illinois) nomination, *Manitoba Literary Awards, Young Readers Choice Award* (Louisiana) nomination, *Geoffrey Bilson Award for Historical Fiction for Young People, School Library Journal Best Books of the Year, Young Reader's Choice Award* (California) nomination, *William Allen White Children's Book Award* (Kansas) nomination, *Student Book Award* (Maine) nomination, *Great Stone Face Children's Book Award* (New Hampshire) nomination, *Young Reader's Choice Award* (Pennsylvania) nomination, *SCASL Book Award* (South Carolina) nomination, *Evergreen Young Adult Book Award* (Washington), *Bulletin Blue Ribbon*, and *Capitol Choices Noteworthy Titles* (Washington, D.C.).

1414. Marcellino, Fred. *I, Crocodile.* Illustrated by author. HarperCollins, 1999. 32pp. ISBN 978-0-06-205168-4; HarperTrophy, 2002. paper ISBN 978-0-06-008859-0. Grades K–3.

On August 17, 1799, in Egypt, Napoleon decides that, in addition to mummies, a sphinx, an obelisk, and palm trees, he will bring a crocodile back to France. In Paris, all are interested in this creature with a huge appetite. Although pleased with the attention from the Parisians, the animal is missing his easy life on the banks of the Nile. However, the crocodile eventually loses favor, and before a chef can chop him up for Napoleon's dinner, he dives into a sewer. Not able to find food, he solves his problem by reappearing and grabbing an upper-class delectable lady. *American Library Association Notable Books for Children, Publishers Weekly Best Books of the Year, Children's Picture StoryBook Award* (Georgia) nomination, and *Red Clover Award* (Vermont) nomination.

1415. Meyer, L. A. *Bloody Jack: Being an Account of the Misadventures of Mary "Jacky" Faber, Ship's Boy.* (Bloody Jack Adventures) Harcourt, 2002. 278pp. ISBN 978-0-15-216731-8; 2004 paper ISBN 978-0-15-205085-6. Grades 6–9.

Orphaned by the pestilence when she was 8, Mary, now 12 in 1801, sleeps under Blackfriars Bridge in London with other unfortunates, stealing and begging to survive. When her friend Charlie is murdered, she puts on his clothes, calls herself Jacky Faber, and signs up to be a ship's boy on the Royal Navy's *HMS Dolphin*. When she falls in love with Jaimy, also a ship's boy, she tells him her secret. When "Jacky" kills a man, she becomes known as "Bloody Jack." *Booklist Editors' Choice, Dorothy Canfield Fisher Children's Book Award* (Vermont), *American Library Association Best Books for Young Adults, Bulletin Blue Ribbon*, and *Peach Award* (Georgia) nomination.

1416. Meyer, L. A. *My Bonny Light Horseman: Being an Account of the Further Waterborne Adventures of Jacky Faber.* (Bloody Jack Adventures) Harcourt, 2008. 436pp. ISBN 978-0-15-206187-6. Grades 8 up.

After an English warship captures Jacky Faber, 15, she agrees to act as an American dancer in France. After a time in France's *demimonde*, she wrangles military secrets from a French general. Then she disguises herself as a boy and serves Napoleon while continually trying to free her friends, especially her love, Jaimy, from prison. Because of her wit, she never has to succumb to any truly distasteful behavior.

1417. Michaels, Kasey. *The Kissing Game.* Forever, 2003. 334pp. Paper ISBN 978-0-446-61085-8. Grades YA.

Lady Allegra Nesbitt goes to London with her father, Oxie Nesbitt, to find a husband, but London society shuns them. Five years earlier, after her father had assumed the title of earl, he and her mother had entered society, but London had not appreciated her mother's country manners and her father's jokes. To stop his joking, Allegra joins forces with her handsome neighbor, Armand Gauthier, and the two find they have quite a lot in common in this Regency novel.

1418. Molloy, Michael. *Peter Raven Under Fire.* Scholastic, 2005. 502pp. ISBN 978-0-439-72454-8; paper ISBN 978-0-439-72457-9. Grades 6–9.

In Portsmouth, England, in 1800, Peter Raven, 13, becomes a midshipman on the *Torren*. Sadistic pirates murder everyone on his ship except Peter and Matthew Book. Peter is apprenticed to a British spy, Commodore Beaumont. He goes with him to Paris where General Ancre, the head of France's secret service, becomes Napoleon's envoy to meet with the wealthy but insane Count Vallon on his Caribbean Island. In return for his aid in helping Napoleon conquer America, Vallon expects to become the King of America. Simultaneously, Lucy Cosgrove, a young American planning to attend Princeton, discovers that her parents are sending her to Paris. When Vallon transports coins to France for Napoleon, Peter helps Beaumont intercept the money and stop Napoleon. While in Paris, Lucy entertains the Bonapartes, and all thwart Napoleon's plan.

1419. Morgan, Jude. *Passion.* Griffin, 2006. 536pp. Paper ISBN 978-0-312-34369-9. Grades YA.

Lady Caroline Lamb, lover of Lord Byron, relates the experiences of her close circle of literary and political revolutionaries. Other narrators are Mary Shelley, Percy Shelley's lover and then wife; Fanny Brawne, lover of John Keats; Augusta Leigh, Byron's half-sister and lover; and Claire Clairemont, Mary Shelley's half-sister and also Byron's lover. Incest, infidelity, bastard children, tragedy, and scandal permeate their lives as the characters interact with each other. The men write poetry, and Mary Shelley creates *Frankenstein* as they wander from place to place. Eventually, Keats expires of tuberculosis in Rome, Shelley drowns in Italy, and Byron dies in Greece.

1420. Morgan, Nicola. *Fleshmarket.* Trafalgar, 2006. 272pp. Paper ISBN 978-0-340-85557-7. Grades 8 up.

In 1822 Scotland when Robbie Anderson is 8, his mother has a mastectomy and dies five days later. Robbie's father starts drinking, loses his money, and leaves Robbie to look after his younger sister Essie. To support her, Robbie gets a job with two men who deliver "fresh bodies" to a doctor for pay. By the time he is 14, Robbie realizes that this man is the same Dr. Knox who operated on his mother. Dismayed and distressed, Robbie also starts drinking, but eventually a doctor who knows Robbie's potential turns him away from his despair. *American Library Association Best Books For Young Adults* and *Abraham Lincoln High School Book Award* (Illinois) nomination.

1421. Moser, Nancy. *Just Jane: A Novel of Jane Austen's Life.* Bethany, 2007. 367pp. Paper ISBN 978-0-7642-0356-5. Grades 9 up.

Jane Austen (1775–1817) keeps a journal in which she records her daily thoughts while attempting to write *First Impressions* (later retitled *Pride and Prejudice*) through her publication of *Emma*. She details her disappointment over her romance with Tom Lefroy when she was 20, resents her parents and the loss of the family home at Stevenson when her father moved to Bath, and thinks about her relationship with God. The story uses quotes from her letters to speculate what she might have said during this time of her life until her late thirties.

1422. O'Brian, Patrick. *The Commodore.*   (Aubrey-Maturin) Norton, 1995. 281pp. ISBN 978-0-393-03760-9; 1006. paper ISBN 978-0-393-31459-5. Grades YA.

In this early 19th-century episode, Captain Jack Aubrey and his surgeon/spy friend Stephen Maturin spend more time on land than sea as they try to find the roots of family secrets. Aubrey's wife begins to assert her independence, while Maturin sees his young daughter for the first time. He discovers that she is autistic and that his wife has left him. Aubrey is promoted to commodore and given a fleet of ships, ostensibly to stop slavers out of Africa, although his real mission is to keep the French from Ireland.

1423. O'Brian, Patrick. *Desolation Island.*   (Aubrey-Maturin) Norton, 1994. 325pp. ISBN 978-0-393-03705-0; 1991. paper ISBN 978-0-393-30812-9. Grades YA.

Captain Jack Aubrey and his friend Stephen Maturin, a surgeon and a spy, sail on the *Leopold* for Australia during the days of Lord Nelson in the early 19th century. In the hold are convicts; above is a beautiful woman who also happens to be a spy.

1424. O'Brian, Patrick. *The Far Side of the World.*   (Aubrey-Maturin) Norton, 1992. 281pp. Paper ISBN 978-0-393-30862-4. Grades YA.

Captain Jack Aubrey and his friend, Stephen Maturin, a surgeon and a spy, set sail for the Great South Sea and the rounding of Cape Horn in the early 19th century. Their enemy awaits them.

1425. O'Brian, Patrick. *The Fortune of War.*   (Aubrey-Maturin) Norton, 1994. 329pp. ISBN 978-0-393-03706-7; 1991. paper ISBN 978-0-393-30813-6. Grades YA.

At the outbreak of the War of 1812 Captain Jack Aubrey and his friend Stephen Maturin, a surgeon and a spy, rush from the Dutch East Indies to England. From there, they go to meet their enemy.

1426. O'Brian, Patrick. *The Golden Ocean.*   Norton, 1994. 285pp. ISBN 978-0-393-03630-5; 1996. paper ISBN 978-0-393-31537-0. Grades YA.

In this adventure, Peter Palafox faces the perils of the sea in the early 19th century.

1427. O'Brian, Patrick. *H.M.S. Surprise.*   (Aubrey-Maturin) Norton, 1994. 379pp. ISBN 978-0-393-03703-6; 1991. paper ISBN 978-0-393-30761-0. Grades YA.

Captain Jack Aubrey and his friend Stephen Maturin, a surgeon and a spy, sail on the Indian Ocean during the days of Lord Nelson in the early 19th century. There they must save themselves from a local pirate almost as cunning as them. First published in 1973.

1428. O'Brian, Patrick. *The Ionian Mission.*   (Aubrey-Maturin) Norton, 1994. 367pp. ISBN 978-0-393-03708-1; 1991. paper ISBN 978-0-393-30821-1. Grades YA.

Aubrey and Maturin head for the Greek islands on a serious mission for the British Navy and find their assignment quite hazardous. First published in 1981.

1429. O'Brian, Patrick. *The Letter of Marque.*   (Aubrey-Maturin) Norton, 1994. 367pp. ISBN 978-0-393-02874-4; 1991. paper ISBN 978-0-393-30905-8. Grades YA.

In this volume, Aubrey and Maturin sail on a mission against the French in hope of redeeming Aubrey from disgrace. First published in 1988.

1430. O'Brian, Patrick. *Master and Commander.* (Aubrey-Maturin) Norton, 2003. 459pp. Paper ISBN 978-0-393-32517-1. Grades YA.

After being ashore on half-pay, Captain Jack Aubrey gladly joins his friend Stephen Maturin, a surgeon and a spy, to go on a frigate to the Cape of Good Hope. There they plan to help take the islands of Mauritius and La Réunion from Napoleon in this first episode of their exploits, first published in 1970.

1431. O'Brian, Patrick. *The Mauritius Command.* (Aubrey-Maturin) Norton, 1994. 348pp. ISBN 978-0-393-03704-3; 1991. paper ISBN 978-0-393-30762-7. Grades YA.

Captain Jack Aubrey of the British Navy and his friend, Stephen Maturin, a surgeon and a spy, go to the Indian Ocean to capture the islands of Reunion and Mauritius from the French. There they face unexpected difficulties in the early 19th century. First published in 1977.

1432. O'Brian, Patrick. *The Nutmeg of Consolation.* (Aubrey-Maturin) Norton, 1991. 315pp. ISBN 978-0-393-03032-7; 1993. paper ISBN 978-0-393-30906-5. Grades YA.

Shipwrecked on a remote island, Aubrey and Maturin have only their wrecked schooner from which to fashion a seaworthy vessel on which to escape.

1433. O'Brian, Patrick. *Post Captain.* (Aubrey-Maturin) Norton, 1994. 496pp. ISBN 978-0-393-03702-9; 1990. paper ISBN 978-0-393-33076-1. Grades YA.

After Captain Jack Aubrey escapes from debtors' prison in France, he and his friend Stephen Maturin avoid a mutiny as they pursue their enemies into a harbor held by the French.

1434. O'Brian, Patrick. *The Reverse of the Medal.* (Aubrey-Maturin) Norton, 1994. 287pp. ISBN 978-0-393-03711-1; 1992. paper ISBN 978-0-393-30960-7. Grades YA.

Aubrey needs the help of his friend Stephen Maturin to escape from the London criminal underground while involved in British government espionage.

1435. O'Brian, Patrick. *The Surgeon's Mate.* (Aubrey-Maturin) Norton, 1994. 382pp. ISBN 978-0-393-03707-4; 1992. paper ISBN 978-0-393-30820-4. Grades YA.

Our heroes Aubrey and Maturin find themselves chased through the Grand Banks by two privateers. The fog and the shallow water make their flight especially dangerous.

1436. O'Brian, Patrick. *The Truelove.* (Aubrey-Maturin) Norton, 1992. 256pp. ISBN 978-0-393-03109-6; 1993. paper ISBN 978-0-393-31016-0. Grades YA.

Aubrey and Maturin rush on the *Surprise* to recapture a British whaler that the French have taken in the Sandwich Islands. Their journey poses many problems.

1437. O'Brian, Patrick. *The Unknown Shore.* Norton, 1995. 313pp. ISBN 978-0-393-03859-0; 1996. paper ISBN 978-0-393-31538-7. Grades YA.

On board the *Wager* are the midshipman Jack Byron and his friend Tobias Barrow. Barrow is so naive that he is unaware of the deep problems they face. This novel details sea life during the early 19th century.

1438. O'Brian, Patrick. *The Wine-Dark Sea.* (Aubrey-Maturin) Norton, 1993. 261pp. ISBN 978-0-393-03558-2; 1994. paper ISBN 978-0-393-31244-7. Grades YA.

Captain Jack Aubrey and his friend Stephen Maturin sail across the Great South Sea in pursuit of a valuable prize. But first they face storms and icebergs.

1439. Perrine, Jane Myers. *The Mad Herringtons.* Avalon, 2002. 201pp. ISBN 978-0-8034-9536-4. Grades YA.

In this Regency novel, Aphrodite Myrabella Herrington refuses to submit to passion, although her sisters have run wild. When Frederick Horne invites her to a house party with her sisters she discovers that Viscount Thomas Warwick, with whom she once had a flirtation, is also a guest. Although Frederick is dependable and likes her, she decides that passion might be better with Warwick.

1440. Perry, Anne. *Defend and Betray.* (William Monk) Ivy, 1993. 385pp. Paper ISBN 978-0-8041-1188-1. Grades YA.

The protagonist of this novel set in 1857 London is Hester Latterly, who served in the Crimean War with Florence Nightingale. Hester suspects that a wife who confessed to the murder of her husband did not do it, and that she is protecting someone else. Detective William Monk investigates the crime. The author illuminates the treatment of women and their limited rights during the Victorian period, as well as other hypocritical aspects of that era's social attitudes.

1441. Perry, Anne. *The Hyde Park Headsman.* (Thomas and Charlotte Pitt) Crest, 1995. 392pp. Paper ISBN 978-0-449-22350-5. Grades YA.

At first one, then two, and unfortunately, three headless corpses are found in Hyde Park. The first belongs to Oakey Winthrop, a naval captain in a titled family, and Nigel Utley, the candidate for a Parliamentary by-election and a member of the secret society of the Inner Circle, condemns the police, especially Thomas Pitt, for not immediately finding the murderer. Pitt's wife Charlotte and her sister, Emily Radley, begin to gather information with their gossipy set to find the secret of the killings.

1442. Perry, Anne. *Pentecost Alley.* (Thomas and Charlotte Pitt) Gold Medal, 1997. 405pp. Paper ISBN 978-0-449-22566-0. Grades YA.

After the reign of Jack the Ripper ends, more terror hits Whitechapel with the murder of a prostitute. Thomas Pitt, head of the Bow Street command, has to find the killer. Pitt is relieved that a gentleman is cleared of the deed, but after someone else has been executed for the crime, an identical murder occurs. Pitt hates the indifference of the upper economic class toward the lower class, but has to face it in his search for the killer.

1443. Perry, Anne. *The Sins of the Wolf.* (William Monk) Ivy, 1995. 374pp. Paper ISBN 978-0-8041-1383-0. Grades YA.

In a mystery set in Victorian London which reveals attitudes and expectations of the mid-19th century, Hester Latterly, a nurse, and the private detective William Monk investigate the murder of a wealthy woman traveling with her nurse. The murdered woman's family accuses the nurse, but Hester defends her, as does Florence Nightingale in a surprise courtroom visit.

1444. Perry, Anne. *A Sudden, Fearful Death.* (William Monk) Ivy, 1994. 338pp. Paper ISBN 978-0-8041-1283-3. Grades YA.

After the detective William Monk goes to see a woman in Victorian London to discuss an attack on her sister in their back yard, he becomes involved in another case involving the murder of a nurse in a nearby hospital. Connections between the two crimes appear as the novel develops, and the courtroom revelations at the Old Bailey contain surprises. Additionally, Perry gives insight into the social expectations of the mid-19th century.

1445. Pullman, Philip. *Spring-Heeled Jack: A Story of Bravery and Evil.* Illustrated by David Mostyn. Knopf, 2002. 112pp. ISBN 978-0-375-81601-7; Wendy Lamb, 2004. paper ISBN 978-0-440-41881-8. Grades 4–8.

With their mother dead and their father having disappeared at sea, three orphans run away, intending to sail to America. Mack the Knife, however, grabs them. Spring-Heel Jack, with springs in his shoes and clothes like the devil, comes to rescue them. One of the stories is presented in cartoons, while the other is in regular text in this historical fantasy set in the 19th century. In the end, their father reappears on the ship sailing to America. *School Library Journal Best Book.*

1446. Rabin, Staton. *Betsy and the Emperor.* Simon Pulse, 2006. 304pp. Paper ISBN 978-1-4169-1336-8. Grades 7 up.

Betsy Balcome, 14, and her family entertain Napoleon Bonaparte in their home in 1815. The former emperor of France, he is now a British captive confined to the island of St. Helena in Betsy's house with more than 2,000 British troops guarding him. Betsy returns from boarding school in London and, unimpressed with Napoleon's former power over 82 million people, becomes the only friend that "Boney" has. He helps her realize that she can follow, if not fulfill, her dreams, and she enables him to face his own dark future. Eventually, Betsy creates a plan to free him, a plan that risks both their lives. *Volunteer State Book Award* (Tennessee) nomination.

1447. Ramsay, Eileen. *Lace for a Lady.* Severn House, 2002. 224pp. ISBN 978-0-7278-5846-7. Grades YA.

Tired of being poor, Liddy Carpenter takes on the persona of Euan Pate, smuggler. Also wanting to be a smuggler is Keir Galloway, Lord Pittenmuir, because he wants to trap the traitor who is selling British secrets to the French during Napoleon's reign. They meet on Scotland's rugged coast, and their concealed identities double the intrigue.

1448. Rees, Celia. *Sovay.* Bloomsbury, 2008. 404pp. ISBN 978-1-59990-203-6. Grades 9 up.

In 1794 the beautiful Sovay Middleton, 17, becomes bored waiting for her father at his estate. She disguises herself as a highwayman and holds up her cheating fiancé's coach. He fails her test of faithfulness, but she loves the experience and continues to be "Captain Blaze." After stealing the papers of a passenger during her forays that could lead to her father's arrest for treason, she teams up with other highwaymen, Captain Greenwood and Virgil Barrett, and goes to France with them in the midst of the Revolution to rescue her father.

1449. Robards, Karen. *Irresistible.* Pocket, 2002. 402pp. Paper ISBN 978-0-7434-1060-1. Grades YA.

Lady Claire Banning has decided she will adjust to her new aristocratic husband's wastrel ways, but then Hugh Battancourt rescues her from an almost fatal accident. He happens to be waiting on shore to grab a female traitor when he sees Claire and believes she is the spy. After a lot of convincing, she and he decide otherwise in this Regency romance.

1450. Tanner, Janet. *Morwennan House.* Severn House, 2002. 320pp. ISBN 978-0-7278-7347-7. Grades YA.

Foundling Charity Palfrey is reminded of her childhood with the rector and his wife while working as a governess for lovely little Charlotte at Morwennan House around 1800. At the same time, she becomes infatuated with Tom Stanton, a business associate of her employer, Mr. Trevelyan. She thinks Tom is a wrecker, a smuggler who lures unsuspecting ships onto shore. She cannot decide whether to contact the authorities even though danger continues to threaten all.

1451. Tennant, Emma. *Pemberley: Or, Pride and Prejudice Continued.* St. Martin's, 1993. 184pp. ISBN 978-0-312-10793-2; paper ISBN 978-0-312-36179-2. Grades YA.

Elizabeth Bennet Darcy, in this "tribute" to *Pride and Prejudice,* waits apprehensively for her recently widowed mother, sisters, Wickham, and Lady Catherine de Bourgh to come to Pemberley for one of her first Christmases after marrying Darcy. She is distressed not to have borne an heir; her sister Jane is already expecting her second child. Crudity and suspicion mar the gathering.

1452. Tetzner, Lisa. *The Black Brothers: A Novel in Pictures.* Illustrated by Hannes Binder. Front Street, 2004. 144pp. ISBN 978-1-932425-04-8. Grades 4–7.

In the middle of the 19th century, Giorgio, like many young men, is sent to Milan to work as a slave, and although his life is extremely difficult, he is able to survive because of the friendship and solidarity he experiences with a secret band known as "the black brothers."

1453. Thornton, Elizabeth. *Almost a Princess.* Bantam, 2002. 367pp. Paper ISBN 978-0-553-58489-9. Grades YA.

When Case Devere, Earl of Castleton, helps track a vicious killer, he sees the killer's signal, a pebble, and knows that it is "La Roca," his sadistic enemy. Then he meets Jane Mayberry, a spinster dedicated to the Ladies' Library. But she is not what she seems in this Regency romance. Ladies' Library is a cover for women fighting for their rights and provides shelter for abuse victims. She also has secrets, one that makes her a murder target, and Case falls for her.

1454. Thornton, Elizabeth. *The Perfect Princess.* Bantam, 2001. 342pp. Paper ISBN 978-0-55358-123-2. Grades YA.

In the late 18th century Richard Maitland, a convicted murderer and former chief of the British Secret Service, takes Lady Rosamund Devere as his hostage when she is visiting Newgate Prison. During their escape, Maitland's behavior convinces Rosamund that he has been unjustly charged. She becomes a willing accomplice in helping him clear his name.

1455. Weaver, Anne H. *The Voyage of the Beetle: Journey Around the World with Charles Darwin and the Search for the Solution to the Mystery of Mysteries, as Narrated by Rosie, an Articulate Beetle.* Illustrated by George Lawrence. University of New Mexico, 2007. 80;pp. ISBN 978-0-8263-4304-8. Grades 5–8.

While Charles Darwin is trying to understand how so many different species can live on earth, each fitted to its environment, he goes on a voyage around the world on the *H.M.S. Beagle* from 1831 to 1835. With him is a beetle, Rosie, who helps him solve the "mystery of mysteries." She explains how she gives him guidance, with clues and hints that help him understand what he is seeing and lead him to create his theory of natural selection.

1456. Welsh, T. K. *Resurrection Men.* Dutton, 2007. 214pp. ISBN 978-0-525-47699-3. Grades 9 up.

Tyrolean soldiers kill Victor's parents, and Victor, 12, leaves Modena, Italy, on a merchant ship. When Victor breaks his leg, a crew member throws him overboard, and Victor washes up in England. An elderly gentleman nurses him to health and teaches him English before selling him to Tipple and Boggs, two "Resurrection Men" working in London in 1830. They dig up recently buried bodies and sell them to doctors who need them for research and dissection. He only makes two friends in the beggars' den where he lives, Rebecca and Nico, before Dr. Quigley becomes interested in him and takes him on as an apprentice. Later, as he watches Dr. Crumm dissect a body, he realizes that the victim is Nico. He understands then that Dr. Quigley has deliberately infected street children with cholera so that they will die and doctors can study the disease through their dissections.

1457. Williams, Jeanne. *Daughter of the Storm.* Backinprint.Com, 2000. 311pp. Paper ISBN 978-0-595-00448-5. Grades YA.

The orphan Christy always feels unwelcome, because she took the place of her foster mother Mairi's daughter, dead at birth in 19th-century Scotland. But she has the love of others in the home—Mairi's grandmother and Mairi's son David. Joy and much pain fill their lives as they try to protect their Scottish lands from owners who take their grazing land and rent it to rich American hunters. Eventually David, crippled at the age of 12 by falling down a cliff, becomes a lawyer and helps the crofters, a group of honest and hard-working but much maligned people. Christy earns her place in the islands by teaching and playing the invaluable harp given to her by one of the natives. After many of the islanders are wounded in a hostile encounter with landowners at Greenyards, Mairi begins to accept Christy's gifts, in this sequel to *The Island Harp.*

1458. Williams, Jeanne. *The Island Harp.* Backinprint.Com, 2000. 338pp. Paper ISBN 978-0-595-09582-7. Grades YA.

Mairi MacLeod, age 17, becomes the de facto head of her Scottish clan when her grandfather dies of burns after the landowner's agents torch her family's homes in 1844. She also inherits his harp, Cridhe. When a member of the gentry, Iain MacDonald, leases part of the estate and lets them live there, she is surprised. She eventually falls in love with him, but refuses to acknowledge the other landowners. After the birth of their illegitimate son, she hears news of Iain's death in Afghanistan. However, he returns and still wants to marry her, even after he hears her song about the landowners deceiving the Celtic clans.

1459. Williams, Maiya. *The Golden Hour.* Harry N. Abrams, 2006. 288pp. Paper ISBN 978-0-8109-9216-0. Grades 5–8.

The father of Rowan Popplewell, 13, and Nina, 11, sends them to spend the summer with their great-aunts Agatha and Gertrude, in Owatannauk, Maine, after a drunk driver kills their mother. They meet twins Xavier and Xanthe who show them the town's old hotel, a place that their great-aunt warns them not to enter because it is a "portal." They ignore the warning and enter one of the two times a day the hotel is open—"the golden hour," or the hour just before sunset. They see an "alleviator," a device that will take them anywhere in time for seven days. Nina goes missing, and Rowan figures out that she will be in Paris during 1789 just before the French Revolution. Searching for her, Rowan and the twins encounter the entire gamut of French society—from Marie Antoinette to peasants on the street. Rowan pretends to be a courtier and Xanthe and Xavier, African Americans, pretend to be an artist and a freed slave. They check all of the prisons for Nina, and during their search, Rowan realizes that he is grieving for his mother. Eventually, when Rowan realizes that Nina is probably in Brooklyn at a time when their mother was still alive, they reunite. *Young Reader's Choice Award* (Pennsylvania) nomination and *International Reading Association Children's Book Awards*.

1460. Woodruff, Elvira. *Small Beauties: The Journey of Darcy Heart O'Hara.* Illustrated by Adam Rex. Knopf, 2006. Unpaged. ISBN 978-0-375-82686-3. Grades 1–5.

In the 1840s the young Irish girl Darcy Heart O'Hara has a gift of noticing small things. She collects flower petals, butterfly wings, a bead from Granny's rosary, dried blossoms of heather and buttercup, and small pebbles, and takes them home in the hem of her ragged dress. Soon the potato famine ravishes the country and her family has to leave for America. While they are trying to adjust to their new home, Darcy's small wonders keep them reminded of the love in their old one. Illustrations enhance the text.

1461. Wrede, Patricia C., and Caroline Stevermer. *The Grand Tour.* Harcourt, 2004. 469pp. ISBN 978-0-15-204616-3; Magic Carpet, 2006. paper ISBN 978-0-15-205556-1. Grades 8 up.

In 1817 cousins Kate and Cecy go with their new husbands, Thomas and James, on a "Grand Tour of the Continent" for their honeymoons, along with Lady Sylvia. They discover a plot to create a new, magical Emperor Napoleon of Europe. The three women wizards try to thwart the evildoers, but during the intrigues, they worry more about their clothes and decorum than the danger of their situation.

1462. Wrede, Patricia C., and Caroline Stevermer. *The Mislaid Magician or Ten Years After: Being the Private Correspondence Between Two Prominent Families Regarding a Scandal Touching the Highest Levels of Government and the Security of the Realm.* Harcourt, 2006. 336pp. ISBN 978-0-15-205548-6; Magic Carpet, 2009. paper ISBN 978-0-15-206209-5. Grades 8 up.

In the third installment of letters between cousins Cecelia and Kate, the two women and their husbands, Thomas and James, search for a missing German railway engineer who happens to be a magician in 1828 at the Duke of Wellington's request. James and Cecy, using the wizardry skills that help them understand ancient underground magic, discover a plot that threatens England's unity. Meanwhile, Kate looks after their six children. The two other books in the series are *Sorcery and Cecelia* and *The Grand Tour*.

1463. Wrede, Patricia C., and Caroline Stevermer. *Sorcery and Cecelia: Or the Enchanted Chocolate Pot.* Harcourt, 2003. 320pp. ISBN 978-0-15-204615-6; Magic Carpet, 2004. paper ISBN 978-0-15-205300-0. Grades YA.

Two cousins, Kate in London and Cecelia in the country, write each other in 1817 to inform each other of their daily lives. Kate soon becomes involved with the sorceress Miranda, who is trying to steal power from Thomas, Marquis of Schofield. While the two cousins try to stop Miranda's success, Cecy encounters the infuriating James Tarleton. The wizard Sir Hilary tangles the plot, but the two cousins prevail. *Capitol Choices Noteworthy Titles* (Washington, D.C.) and *Voice of Youth Advocates Perfect Ten List*.

1464. Yolen, Jane, and Robert J. Harris. *The Rogues.* Philomel, 2007. 277pp. ISBN 978-0-399-23898-7. Grades 7 up.

Wealthy lords "clear" their estates in Scotland during the 18th century, and Roddy Macallan's family is one of those who have to leave, heading for Glasgow or American cities. Roddy returns to the cottage before its destruction to search for a jewel that his mother said was there before she died. He finds it, but he must deal with the lord of the land's lackey, Willie Rood, and the rogue Alan Dunbar, who also seems to have designs on the stone. But Dunbar helps him escape with the brooch, and they eventually reach a settlement in North Carolina.

History

1465. Bartoletti, Susan Campbell. *Black Potatoes: The Story of the Great Irish Famine, 1845–1850.* Sandpiper, 2005. 184pp. Paper ISBN 978-0-618-54883-5.

From 1845 to 1850 the Great Irish Famine killed 1 million Irish and caused 2 million more to emigrate. Primary sources—eyewitness accounts and memories—reveal that the famine could have been avoided, and that the Irish have maintained a bitter resentment of British landowners who exported food that the Irish needed. The social structure of the country was nearly destroyed, and the situation brought about the advent of workhouses, soup kitchens, evictions, a shortage of medical care, and quarantined homes burned. Laissez-faire economics and religious and ethnic prejudices kept the British from helping even though the prime minister, Sir Robert Peel, was determined that government aid would be forthcoming. Maps, Bibliography, Chronology, Notes, and Index. *Robert F. Sibert Award.*

1466. Egendorf, Laura K. *The French Revolution.* (Opposing Viewpoints) Greenhaven, 2004. ISBN 978-0-7377-1815-7. Grades 9–12.

Readers will learn about the French Revolution that began in 1789 and changed French society after its end in 1799. Primary and secondary documents arranged according to pro and con arguments on a particular topic examine the problems of the people and how they resolved them. Bibliography, Glossary, Maps, and Index.

1467. Fleisher, Paul. *Evolution.* (Great Ideas of Science) Twenty-First Century, 2005. 80pp. ISBN 978-0-8225-2134-1. Grades 5–8.

This account presents the background behind Charles Darwin's formulation of his evolution theory when he was traveling on the *Beagle* around South America. His journey led to his publication *The Origin of Species* (1859). The book also mentions Alfred Russel Wallace, the British researcher who was discovering basically the same theory in his work at home at the same time. It also includes how evolution works and research about genetics and other scientific fields that support Darwin's findings. Fleisher has no doubt that evolution supports the development of life on Earth; he notes that creationism and intelligent design are religious teachings rather than scientific theories. Photographs, diagrams, and illustrations complement the text. Bibliography, Glossary, Chronology, Further Reading, Web Sites, and Index.

1478. Woodworth, Bradley D., and Constance E. Richards. *St. Petersburg.* Chelsea House, 2005. 137pp. ISBN 978-0-7910-7837-2. Grades 11 up.

Created from a swamp, the city of St. Petersburg became the setting for literary works by Dostoevsky, Gogol, and Pushkin. It attracted and supported many authors and artists, and was known for its salons, tenements, teas, and freezing garrets. Photographs accompany the text. Bibliography, Glossary, Notes, Further Reading, Web Sites, and Index.

Biography and Collective Biography

1479. Adler, David A. *A Picture Book of Florence Nightingale.* Illustrated by Alexandra and John Wallner. Holiday House, 1992. 32pp. ISBN 978-0-8234-0965-5; paper ISBN 978-0-8234-1284-6. Grades K–3.

Florence Nightingale (1820–1910) was a 19th-century upper-class English woman who followed her calling to work in hospitals and improve the conditions for treating the sick.

1480. Adler, David A. *A Picture Book of Louis Braille.* Illustrated by John and Alexandra Wallner. (Picture Book of) Holiday House, 1997. 34pp. ISBN 978-0-8234-1291-4; paper ISBN 978-0-8234-1413-0. Grades K–3.

Louis Braille (1809–1852) developed the system for reading that the blind now use. This illustrated biography looks at his life as a young student and teacher and his contributions to the blind community. Important Dates.

1481. Aller, Susan Bivin. *Florence Nightingale.* Illustrated by Tad Butler. (History Maker Bios) Lerner, 2007. 48pp. ISBN 978-0-8225-7609-9. Grades 3–5.

After her birth in Florence, Italy, Florence Nightingale (1820–1910) returned with her family to England. She claimed that God spoke to her in 1837, telling her to serve. She eventually realized that she wanted to be a nurse. While helping soldiers during the Crimean War, she was responsible for several important improvements in care for the wounded. Illustrations highlight the text. Bibliography, Further Reading, Glossary, Maps, Chronology, Web Sites, and Index.

1482. Allman, Barbara. *Her Piano Sang: A Story About Clara Schumann.* Illustrated by Shelly O. Haas. (Creative Minds) Lerner, 1996. 64pp. ISBN 978-1-57505-012-6; 2003. paper ISBN 978-1-57505-151-2. Grades 3–7.

Clara Schumann (1819–1896) made her professional debut as a pianist when she was only 9 years old. Her father demanded much of her, and when she married Robert Schumann after a long courtship it was against her father's wishes. She raised her family as Robert developed mental illness, but she continued to compose and perform. She pursued a career that had been open only to men, and succeeded. Illustrations highlight the text. Index.

1483. Anderson, Margaret J. *Charles Darwin: Naturalist.* (Great Minds of Science) Enslow, 1994. 128pp. ISBN 978-0-89490-476-9; 2001. paper ISBN 978-0-7660-1868-6. Grades 4–10.

Charles Darwin (1809–1882) shared his birthdate with Abraham Lincoln, but rather than trying to stop a civil war, he almost caused one when he published *The Origin of Species* in 1859. His book claimed that, over time, small differences among similar plants and animals can cause new species to evolve. He did much of his research on a five-year trip around the world on the *H.M.S. Beagle.* His three main ideas were that plants and animals have more offspring than needed; that, overall, numbers of each kind of plant and animal remain stable; and that all offspring are not alike. The offspring survive based on natural selection. People who believed that all species had been created and "fixed" by God were horrified by this theory. Notes, Chronology, Glossary, Further Reading, and Index.

1484. Andronik, Catherine M. *Wildly Romantic: The English Romantic Poets: The Mad, the Bad, and the Dangerous.* Holt, 2007. 262pp. ISBN 978-0-8050-7783-4. Grades 9 up.

A subversive group of poets during the early 19th century were the English romantics. They believed that poetry should use ordinary language to express emotions. The poets included in this account are Lord Byron (1788–1824), Percy Bysshe Shelley (1792–1822), Samuel Taylor Coleridge (1782–1834), William Wordsworth (1770–1850), and John Keats (1795–1821). Each segment offers a biographical profile, a selection of poems, and reasons why the poems were important as a statement of society at the time. Among the anecdotes Andronik includes are that Byron had sex with boys and mistresses; the youthful revolutionary Wordsworth became ultraconservative as an older man, and that several were drug addicts. Bibliography, Notes, Further Reading, and Index.

1485. Anholt, Laurence. *Stone Girl, Bone Girl: The Story of Mary Anning.* Illustrated by Sheila Moxley. Frances Lincoln, 2007. Unpaged. Paper ISBN 978-1-8450-7700-6. Grades 1–4.

Mary Anning (1799–1847), 12, was walking along the shore cliffs near her home and came upon a giant fossilized skeleton. It turned out to be an ichthyosaur skeleton, more than 165 million years old. Mary's father had already shown her some of the "curiosities" around their home in Dorset's Lyme Regis before his death, and she had sold some to support the family. Later, a scientist, Annie Philpot, explained what fossils were to Mary, and she understood what she had been seeing and their value. *Readers Choice Awards* (Michigan).

1486. Armentrout, David, and Patricia Armentrout. *Florence Nightingale.* (Discover the Life of Someone Who Made a Difference) Rourke, 2007. 24pp. Paper ISBN 978-1-58952-799-7. Grades 2–4.

Florence Nightingale (1820–1910), born into luxury, studied nursing books secretly and gave herself to work with the wounded in the Crimean War, earning the name "The Lady with the Lamp." Her work changed the concept of hospitals from a place to die to a place to heal. This biography in eight chapters traces her life and work to the founding of modern nursing. Photographs highlight the text. Bibliography, Glossary, Chronology, Web Sites, and Index.

1487. Bedard, Michael. *William Blake: The Gates of Paradise.* Tundra, 2006. 192pp. ISBN 978-0-8877-6763-0. Grades 9 up.

William Blake (1757–1827), a romantic poet, was also a dreamer, artist, genius, and visionary. He learned engraving and took advantage of the new techniques offered by the

Industrial Revolution to illustrate his poems with dreamlike watercolors. Photographs and reproductions enhance the text. Further Reading, Notes, Bibliography, and Index.

1488. Blackburn, Julia. *Old Man Goya.* Vintage, 2003. 239pp. Paper ISBN 978-0-375-70579-3. Grades YA.

Francisco Goya (1746–1828) was an important painter who became deaf at the age of 47. This profile, which focuses on the second half of Goya's life, presents some of his personal correspondence and includes information about Madrid, the court of Charles IV, the horrors of famine and war, Goya's long marriage and liaison with a much younger woman after his wife's death, and his work itself. Index.

1489. Blake, William, and John Maynard. *William Blake.* Illustrated by Alessandra Cimatoribus. (Poetry for Young People) Sterling, 2007. 48pp. ISBN 978-0-8069-3647-5. Grades 5–9.

Some of the poems of William Blake (1757–1827) are presented, with introductory remarks and rich illustrations in blues, greens, and golds. Blake had an unusually individual worldview with visions of the natural and supernatural realms. Among the poems are the well-known "The Tyger" and "The Lamb." Other selections come mainly from *Songs of Innocence* and *Songs of Experience.* Index.

1490. Bradley, Michael J. *The Foundations of Mathematics: 1800 to 1900.* (Pioneers in Mathematics) Chelsea House, 2006. 148pp. ISBN 978-0-8160-5425-1. Grades 6 up.

Ten men and women helped establish the structure of mathematics in the 19th century. This volume includes their discoveries, pertinent information, a conclusion about their contributions, and further reading about each. Marie-Sophie Germain (1776–1831) discovered prime numbers and elasticity. Carl Friedrich Gauss (1777–1855) has the title of the "Prince" of mathematics. Mary Fairfax Somerville (1780–1872) has become known as the "Queen" of 19th-century science. Niels Henrik Abel (1802–1829) worked with elliptic functions. Evariste Galois (1811–1832) was the revolutionary founder of group theory. Augusta Ada Lovelace (1815–1852) developed the first computer program. Florence Nightingale (1820–1910) based much of her health care on statistics. Georg Cantor (1845–1918) was the father of set theory. Sonya Kovalevsky (1850–1891) was a pioneering female mathematician. And Henri Poincare (1854–1912) became known as a universal mathematician. Glossary, Further Reading, and Index.

1491. Brewster, Hugh. *The Other Mozart: The Life of the Famous Chevalier de Saint-George.* Illustrated by Eric Velasquez. Abrams, 2007. 48pp. ISBN 978-0-8109-5720-6. Grades 6–9.

See entry 1315.

1492. Brombert, Beth Archer. *Edouard Manet: Rebel in a Frock Coat.* University of Chicago, 1997. 505pp. Paper ISBN 978-0-226-07544-0. Grades YA.

Edouard Manet (1832–1883) exhibited his painting *Le Dejeuner sur l'Herbe* in the 1863 Salon des Refuses. Then he exhibited a nude, *Olympia*, at the Salon of 1865, starting a scandal among Parisian critics. He refused to join the Impressionists when they exhibited in the 1870s separately from the Salons. Brombert says Manet was neither radical nor revolutionary; he simply wanted to go "through the main door" of the Salon. After inheriting money from his father, Manet brought his mistress and their son into the house he shared with his mother, and they lived as a bourgeois family from that point on. Brombert uses diaries, letters, documents, and memoirs to give a sense of the political and social timbre of the day, including the influence of mistresses on composers' and artists' creative work. Bibliography and Index.

1493. Burleigh, Robert. *Napoleon: The Story of the Little Corporal.* Abrams, 2007. 48pp. ISBN 978-0-8109-1378-3. Grades 1–4.

This biography examines the life of Napoleon I, Emperor of the French (1769–1821) and asks questions that have remained unanswered since his death. Did Napoleon protect the ideals espoused during the French Revolution or was he merely ambitious? Was he a military genius or just lucky? Regardless, he was a poor Corsican scholarship student snubbed by the wealthy boys in his school, but he became the most important man in the country and was responsible for battles that killed hundreds of thousands of people. Maps and illustrations enhance the text. Bibliography and Notes.

1494. Collins, David R. *Tales for Hard Times: A Story About Charles Dickens.* Illustrated by David Mataya. Carolrhoda, 1990. 64pp. ISBN 978-0-8761-4433-6. Grades 4–8.

Writing about life in the 19th century, Charles Dickens (1812–1870) drew on his own poverty-stricken past and delighted his audiences around the world. Drawings complement the text. Bibliography.

1495. Conley, Kate A. *Joseph Priestley and the Discovery of Oxygen.* (Uncharted, Unexplored, and Unexplained Scientific Advancements) Mitchell Lane, 2005. 48pp. ISBN 978-1-58415-367-2. Grades 6–8.

See entry 1318.

1496. Davidson, Margaret. *Louis Braille.* Illustrated by Janet Compere. Scholastic, 1991. 80pp. Paper ISBN 978-0-590-44350-0. Grades 2–5.

Louis Braille (1809–1853) lost his sight at the age of 3. He was a musician and educator, but most importantly, he invented a system of writing for visually impaired people in 1829, called the Braille system. Although initially blocked by people who thought they knew more than he did about teaching the blind to read, his system became accepted and is still in use.

1497. DiConsiglio, John. *Robespierre: Master of the Guillotine.* (Wicked History) Watts, 2008. 128pp. ISBN 978-0-531-18554-4; paper ISBN 978-0-531-20503-7. Grades 6–9.

This look at Robespierre (1758–1794) gives an overview of his life and his place in the aftermath of the French Revolution. He was considered to be "The Incorruptible" as a member of the Committee of Public Safety. After the Revolution, he played a part in identifying the enemy within Paris, and extended the list of enemies to include the moderates and "false revolutionaries." In 1794 he was arrested, accused, and executed for his role in the Reign of Terror. Maps and reproductions augment the text. Bibliography, Glossary, Chronology, Further Reading, Web Sites, and Index.

1498. Donaldson, Madeline. *Louis Braille.* (History Makers Bios) Lerner, 2007. 48pp. ISBN 978-0-8225-7608-2. Grades 3–5.

This volume in five chapters relates the life of French-born Louis Braille (1809–1852). He was always curious, and when he attended school, he became an excellent student. He was accepted at the Royal Institution where he became disappointed in the treatment of the blind. He created a way for the blind to read and developed the raised dot system now known as Braille, the system that is still in use today. Bibliography, Further Reading, Glossary, Maps, Time Line, Web Sites, and Index.

1499. Erickson, Carolly. *Great Catherine.*   St. Martin's, 1995. 392pp. Paper ISBN 978-0-312-13503-4. Grades YA.

See entry 1320.

1500. Erickson, Carolly. *Her Little Majesty: The Life of Queen Victoria.*   Simon & Schuster, 1997. 288pp. Paper ISBN 978-0-7432-3657-7. Grades YA.

Victoria (1819–1901) became queen at the age of 18 after a lonely childhood in the care of a dictatorial mother. She fell in love with her cousin Albert, and together they raised children and ruled England until his death. Afterward, she had to adjust to his absence with the help of advisers and family. During her reign, England and the world changed dramatically.

1501. Erickson, Carolly. *To the Scaffold: The Life of Marie Antoinette.*   Griffin, 2004. 384pp. Paper ISBN 978-0-312-32205-2. Grades YA.

See entry 1321.

1502. Freedman, Russell. *Out of Darkness: The Story of Louis Braille.*   Illustrated by Kate Kiesler. Clarion, 1997. 81pp. ISBN 978-0-395-77516-5; 1999. paper ISBN 978-0-395-96888-8. Grades 3–6.

Louis Braille (1809–1852) struggled to communicate after he became blind, and he developed his alphabet. Freedman's rendering is lively, and informative about the difficulties that Braille faced. Index.

1503. Getzinger, Donna, and Daniel Felsenfeld. *Richard Wagner and German Opera.* (Masters of Music) Morgan Reynolds, 2004. 144pp. ISBN 978-1-931798-24-2. Grades 6–10.

The life of Richard Wagner (1813–1883) and his importance in the opera world become clear in this biography. He was convinced of his own genius at a young age and struggled to get the establishment to accept his radical ideas about opera. His legacy includes majestic music as well as infidelity and racism. Period portraits and reproductions highlight the text. Bibliography, Glossary, Chronology, Notes, Web Sites, and Index.

1504. Gordon, Lyndall. *Charlotte Brontë: A Passionate Life.*   Norton, 1996. 416pp. Paper ISBN 978-0-393-31448-9. Grades YA.

According to Gordon, Charlotte Brontë (1816–1855), the author of *Jane Eyre* and *Villette*, was a very resourceful woman committed to her writing. She survived during a time inhospitable to women and incorporated autobiographical elements in her novels. Gordon also explores the relationship between Brontë and the publisher George Smith. Chronology, Bibliography, and Index.

1505. Hannah, Julie, and Joan Holub. *The Man Who Named the Clouds.*   Illustrated by Paige Billin-Frye. Albert Whitman, 2006. 40pp. ISBN 978-0-8075-4974-2. Grades 3–5.

Howard Luke (1772–1864) began keeping a weather journal when he was 10 years old. Although he became a chemist, he maintained an interest in the weather and the clouds. In 1802 he suggested a classification of clouds into seven types using the Latin words *cirrus*, *cumulus*, and *stratus*. His terms are still used today. In the form of a weather journal, this book gives information about the formation of rain and snow, the make-up of fog, and using clouds to predict weather. Illustrations complement the text. Bibliography.

1506. Hebron, Stephen. *John Keats.* (British Library Writers' Lives) Oxford, 2002. 128pp. ISBN 978-0-19-521787-2. Grades 9 up.

John Keats (1795–1821) wrote only three volumes of poetry in his short life, but he remains one of the most beloved British romantic poets. Keats was dedicated to his family. Between the years of 1811 and 1816 he held a medical apprenticeship that became an apprenticeship of poetry after which he published *Endymion* in 1817. The next year he traveled north before publishing *Hyperion* and returning to London's Wentworth Place. In 1819 he went to the Isle of Wight and Winchester, returning to London in 1820. Afterward, he traveled to Italy where he died from tuberculosis at the young age of 25. Photographs and paintings highlight the text. Bibliography, Chronology, Further Reading, and Index.

1507. Hesse, Karen. *The Young Hans Christian Andersen.* Illustrated by Erik Blegvad. Scholastic, 2005. ISBN 978-0-439-67990-9. Grades 2–4.

Among the incidents in Hans Christian Andersen's own life (1805–1875) that translated into his writing were that his father was a steadfast Napoleonic soldier, he himself was an ugly duckling, and as a boy he had a lovely soprano voice like a nightingale. Hesse presents nineteen vignettes from his titles that she links with Andersen's life. Illustrations enhance the text. Bibliography and Note.

1508. Ingram, Scott. *King George III.* (Triangle History of the American Revolution) Blackbirch, 2003. 104pp. ISBN 978-1-56711-779-0. Grades 6–9.

The seven chapters of this biography of George III (1738–1820) trace his childhood, early reign, protests against him at home and abroad, his actions that led the American colonies to rebel, his defeat in the American Revolution, and his final years, along with his role in history. The author posits that he was not all-powerful and that his unscrupulous advisers led him to make decisions that were inappropriate. Photographs and reproductions augment the text. Glossary, Further Reading, and Index.

1509. Johnson, Paul. *Napoleon.* Viking, 2002. 190pp. ISBN 978-0-670-03078-1. Grades YA.

This biography examines the life and career of Napoleon I (1769–1821), Emperor of the French. Johnson sees Napoleon as an opportunist who took advantage of events and situations that allowed him to wrest total control. He failed as a politician, which eventually led to him failing as a general. Index.

1510. Kenyon, Karen Smith. *The Brontë Family: Passionate Literary Geniuses.* Lerner, 2002. 128pp. ISBN 978-0-8225-0071-1. Grades 5–9.

This biography of Charlotte (1816–1855), Emily (1818–1848), Branwell (1817–1848), and Anne (1820–1849) Brontë reveals how the four siblings helped each other creatively and how their lives became details in the lives of characters in their fiction. Their mother and two sisters died from illness when the four were young, a major influence in their lives, and they all wrote tiny books in their youth. Branwell became an alcoholic. Among the classics the three sisters wrote were *Jane Eyre*, *Wuthering Heights*, and *Agnes Grey*. They also wrote under the male pseudonyms of Currer Bell (Charlotte), Acton Bell (Anne), and Ellis Bell (Emily) so that they could get published. Illustrations, Photographs, Bibliography, Web Sites, and Index.

1511. Landau, Elaine. *Napoleon Bonaparte.* Twenty-First Century, 2006. 112pp. ISBN 978-0-8225-3420-4. Grades 7–10.

This biography covers the life of Napoleon Bonaparte (1769–1821), the military strategist who crowned himself and established an empire. It includes his childhood and early influences as well as his faults and accomplishments. Photographs highlight the text. Bibliography, Chronology, Further Reading, Web Sites, and Index.

1512. Locke, Juliane. *England's Jane: The Story of Jane Austen.* Morgan Reynolds, 2006. 144pp. ISBN 978-1-931798-82-2. Grades 7 up.

This biography (1775–1817) draws on letters, biographical works, and archival reproductions to help readers understand Austen's life and her novels. Topics include Austen's family, childhood, social life, manners, customs, entertainment, career, and writing style. Bibliography, Chronology, Notes, Web Sites, and Index.

1513. Loumaye, Jacqueline. *Degas: The Painted Gesture.* Illustrated by Nadine Massart. Translated by John Goodman. Chelsea House, 1994. 57pp. ISBN 978-0-7910-2809-4. Grades 4–8.

Students observe and discuss the life and work of Edgar Degas (1834–1917). By examining his paintings almost as if they were characters themselves, the author reveals the man and his time. Chronology and Glossary.

1514. Malaspina, Ann. *Chopin's World.* (Music Throughout History) Rosen, 2007. 64pp. ISBN 978-1-4042-0723-3. Grades 5–8.

This biography of Frédéric Chopin (1810–1849) relies on primary sources to examine his life. He was an extraordinary pianist whose compositions demand much from the performer both technically and expressively. He made major innovations in forms that included the piano sonata, prélude, étude, nocturne, and waltz. This volume presents excerpts from letters and includes photographs of places he lived and reproductions of people he knew. The six chapters discuss his early life, family, social status, characteristics of his personality, his best-known music, and the importance of his particular work. Illustrations augment the text. Bibliography, Glossary, Chronology, Further Reading, Web Sites, and Index.

1515. Markham, J. David. *Napoleon for Dummies.* For Dummies, 2005. 364pp. Paper ISBN 978-0-7645-9798-5. Grades YA.

Markham discusses the military campaigns, relationships, power, and loss of power of Napoleon Bonaparte, known as Napoleon I, Emperor of the French (1769–1821). Divided into ten parts, each focusing on a specific theme, this biography presents some of his revolutionary reforms and ideas along with his impact elsewhere in Europe. The parts include building an empire and losing it, being a true revolutionary, influencing nations with diplomacy, why remember Napoleon, changes in France's institutions, influences in Europe, and Napoleon's legacy. Index.

1516. Markus, Julia. *Dared and Done: The Marriage of Elizabeth Barrett and Robert Browning.* Ohio University, 1998. 382pp. Paper ISBN 978-0-8214-1246-6. Grades YA.

Elizabeth Barrett (1806–1861) and Robert Browning (1812–1889) courted by letter after Browning first wrote to Barrett, an internationally known poet, as an enamored fan.

Barrett's father had forbidden all of his twelve children ever to marry, and she had been an invalid who relied on morphine most of her life. After twenty months of writing to each other, Barrett and Browning ran away to Italy and had a marriage in which they both thrived. Notes, Selected Bibliography, and Index.

1517. Marrin, Albert. *Dr. Jenner and the Speckled Monster: The Search for the Smallpox Vaccine.* Dutton, 2002. 120pp. ISBN 978-0-525-46922-3. Grades 4–8.

Edward Jenner (1749–1823), an English country surgeon, used his powers of observation and experimentation to develop a smallpox vaccine when he realized that milkmaids who contracted cowpox never got smallpox. This biography of Jenner and history of smallpox also includes background on the disease's destructive forces. It arrived in the Americas after Cortés invaded Mexico, spread to the Aztec Empire in 1521, and ravaged Europe at various times. A final chapter notes that smallpox can become a weapon of mass human destruction. Photographs enlighten the text. Bibliography, Web Sites, and Index. *Capitol Choices Noteworthy Titles* (Washington, D.C.).

1518. Mayer-Skumanz, Lene. *Ludwig van Beethoven.* Illustrated by Winfried Opgenoorth. Translated by Alexis L. Spry. (Musical Picture Book) NorthSouth, 2007. Unpaged. ISBN 978-0-7358-2123-1. Grades 4–6.

In this picture-book biography, facts about the life of Ludwig van Beethoven (1770–1827) pair with his compositions. It places Beethoven within his world with its problems and people, including Mozart, Napoleon, and Goethe. Color illustrations enhance the text. Chronology and Discography.

1519. Miller, Raymond H. *The Brothers Grimm.* Kidhaven, 2005. 48pp. ISBN 978-0-7377-3157-6. Grades 4–6.

This biography recounts the lives of Jacob (1785–1863) and Wilhelm (1786–1859) Grimm, beginning with their childhoods and continuing with later facts, including their lives within the historical context of the Napoleonic wars. Their extensive scholarly research led to the publication of their versions of folktales and fairy tales that they collected in the German countryside. They sometimes explained changes between the German and French versions.

1520. Morris, Edmund. *Beethoven: The Universal Composer.* (Eminent Lives) HarperCollins, 2005. 243pp. ISBN 978-0-06-075974-2. Grades YA.

The biography divides the career of Ludwig van Beethoven (1770–1827) into three stylistic periods: emulating the classicism of his mentor Haydn, his heroic style, and his own distinctive stylistic genius during which he wrote the *Missa Solemnis, Fidelis*, and the *Ninth Symphony*. He lived a lonely life, unable to connect with unmarried women, and had only a nephew whom he raised after his brother Casper died. As a child prodigy he had to practice constantly—either the violin or the piano—and was unhappy with this pressure. He started going deaf in his late twenties, and because he had been destitute while young, became quite extravagant when he had money. Illustrations highlight the text. Bibliography and Glossary.

1521. Muhlberger, Richard. *What Makes a Degas a Degas?* Viking, 2002. 48pp. ISBN 978-0-670-03571-7. Grades 5–9.

Hilaire-Germain-Edgar Degas (1834–1917) was born in Paris to parents who exposed him to music and art. After a rift with his father over becoming a painter, Degas pursued the traditional route of traveling to Italy to study the masters. He returned to Paris and joined the Impressionists, but he preferred to paint inside, plan his paintings, and base them on strong drawing, unlike his friends. He thus bridged the new and the old in the art of his time. In his work, he cut figures off at the edge of the canvas for a candid effect, tipped the stage upward as if viewed from above, painted patches of brilliant color to augment movement, and opened large spaces in the background to take the eye into the depths. Works reproduced and discussed are *The Bellelli Family, A Woman Seated Beside a Vase of Flowers, Carriage at the Races, The Orchestra at the Opéra, Race Horses at Longchamp, Portraits in an Office (New Orleans), The Dance Class, Miss La La at the Cirque Fernando, Woman Ironing, The Singer in Green, The Millinery Shop*, and *Dancers, Pink and Green*.

1522. Nardo, Don. ***Charles Darwin.*** Lucent, 2004. 112pp. ISBN 978-1-59018-339-7. Grades 7 up.

When he returned from his five-year voyage around the world, Charles Darwin began to formulate his theory of evolution. He waited 28 years before publishing it, to be sure that he could support it through his investigations of nature. The publication of *On the Origin of Species* infuriated many clergy, who felt that it undermined the teachings in the Bible; but many scientists saw that it made sense. This biography, with photographs and reproductions, looks at Darwin's life and work. Further Reading, Chronology, and Index.

1523. Norton, James R. ***Haydn's World.*** (Music Throughout History) Rosen, 2007. 64pp. ISBN 978-1-4042-0727-1. Grades 5–8.

See entry 1334.

1524. O'Connor, Barbara. ***The World at His Fingertips: A Story About Louis Braille.*** Carolrhoda, 1997. 64pp. ISBN 978-1-57505-052-2. Grades 3–6.

Louis Braille (1809–1852), blind from age 3 when he poked an awl in one eye and the ensuing infection spread to the other, helped other blind people to "see." When he attended school in Paris, he created the Braille alphabet, which made sense to him and to others who wanted to read more rapidly with their fingertips. Bibliography and Index.

1525. Parker, Steve. ***Louis Pasteur and Germs.*** Chelsea House, 1995. 32pp. ISBN 978-0-7910-3002-8. Grades 3–7.

Louis Pasteur (1822–1895) founded the science of microbiology, which is the study of living things, such as bacteria and viruses, that are visible only with the aid of a microscope. His research made advances possible in medicine, public health, and hygiene. He initiated vaccinations and invented the pasteurization of milk. Parker looks at Pasteur in terms of his times and his work. Glossary and Index.

1526. Redmond, Shirley Raye. ***The Dog That Dug for Dinosaurs: A True Story.*** Illustrated by Simon Sullivan. Aladdin, 2004. 32pp. Paper ISBN 978-0-689-85708-9. Grades 1–4.

In the early 1800s Mary Ann Anning, 12, owned a dog, Tray, who led her to dinosaur bones on the beach close to her home in Lyme Regis, England. Anning was the first to find a pterodactyl, and she also found an ichthyosaurus and a plesiosaur, all on display in London's Natural Museum of History. Illustrations complement the text.

1527. Reich, Susanna. ***Clara Schumann: Piano Virtuoso.*** Clarion, 1999. 118pp. ISBN 978-0-395-89119-3; 2005. paper ISBN 978-0-618-55160-6. Grades 5–8.

The seven chapters of this biography offer information about Clara Schumann (1819–1896) who made her professional piano debut at the age of 9 as Clara Wieck in Leipzig, Germany. Her father controlled her concert tours, and she had to sue him in order to get permission to marry Robert Schumann and to acquire some of the money she had earned. She had eight children and continued to play throughout her life, although Robert's depression led him to an asylum where he died. Among her friends were Brahms, Liszt, and Mendelssohn. She overcame many obstacles during a time when women had few rights and little prestige. Letters, paintings, and photographs highlight the text. Index. *School Library Journal Best Books for Children.*

1528. Roberts, Jason. *A Sense of the World: How a Blind Man Became History's Greatest Traveler.* HarperCollins, 2006. 382pp. ISBN 978-0-00-716106-5; Perennial, 2007. paper ISBN 978-0-00-716126-3. Grades YA.

James Holman (1786–1857), a Royal Navy lieutenant, went blind when he was 25. After he lost his sight, he decided to take his half-pension and become a world traveler and author, visiting West Africa, Ceylon, New Zealand, Brazil, the Levant, and Siberia. Although he has been largely forgotten, he had great fame during his lifetime for his adventures covering more than 250,000 miles. Illustrations highlight the text. Notes and Further Reading. *School Library Journal Best Adult Books for Young Adults.*

1529. Rosen, Michael. *Dickens: His Work and His World.* Illustrated by Robert R. Ingpen. Candlewick, 2005. 96pp. ISBN 978-0-7636-2752-2; 2008. paper ISBN 978-0-7636-3888-7. Grades 4–8.

This biography of Charles Dickens (1812–1870) covers his life, work, and legacy. It begins with Dickens's last stage performance and segues into his life, a twisted tale that seems almost fictional. He was part of the politics and social upheavals leading to progressivism that influenced London. He also took part in the publishing revolution that enabled his novels to be serialized and thus gain a huge reading public awaiting each installment. This biography also looks at four of his publications in detail: *A Christmas Carol, Oliver Twist, David Copperfield,* and *Great Expectations.* Illustrations enhance the text. Chronology and Index. *School Library Journal Best Children's Books.*

1530. Rumford, James. *Seeker of Knowledge: The Man Who Deciphered Egyptian Hieroglyphs.* Illustrated by author. Houghton, 2000. Unpaged. ISBN 978-0-395-97934-1; Sandpiper, 2003. paper ISBN 978-0-618-33345-5. Grades 2–5.

Jean-François Champollion (1790–1832) became fascinated with Egyptian hieroglyphs when he was only 11, and he vowed that he would be the first to decipher them. He became expert in all known ancient languages by age 16, and had studied Egyptology so that he could work on the Rosetta Stone. When he was about 30, he had an epiphany—the characters related to both meaning and sound. France was delighted with his work and sent him to Egypt to learn more, so he had a chance to explore the Nile. Watercolor illustrations complement the text. *Capitol Choices Noteworthy Titles* (Washington, D.C.).

1531. Schoell, William. *Giuseppe Verdi and Italian Opera.* Morgan Reynolds, 2007. 128pp. ISBN 978-1-59935-041-7. Grades 9 up.

This biography of Giuseppe Verdi (1813–1901) looks at his personal life and interests as well as providing brief information on each of his works. Photographs and reproductions augment the text. Bibliography, Chronology, Notes, and Index.

1532. Shichtman, Sandra, and Dorothy Indenbaum. *Gifted Sister: The Story of Fanny Mendelssohn.* (Classical Composers) Morgan Reynolds, 2007. 128pp. ISBN 978-1-59935-038-7. Grades 7–9.

Fanny Mendelssohn Hensel (1805–1847), sister of Felix Mendelssohn, was also a musical prodigy. When she was 15, her father encouraged her to compose music to be played at home while her brother wrote for the public. She could not follow a professional music career because society expected her to marry and have children, but she continued to compose, perform, and meet with musicians of the day including Bach and Mozart. After her parents died, she also published her music. Bibliography, Chronology, Notes, Web Sites, and Index.

1533. Siepmann, Jeremy. *Beethoven: His Life and Music.* Sourcebooks, 2006. 256pp. ISBN 978-1-4022-0751-8. Grades 9 up.

This narrative, along with two compact discs, describes the life of Ludwig van Beethoven (1770–1827) and his music. Siepmann also describes the times in which Beethoven lived using primary sources such as quotations, journals, and letters. Other chapters introduce short biographies of Beethoven's family and friends. Reproductions, Bibliography, Glossary, and Index.

1534. Sís, Peter. *Play, Mozart, Play!* Illustrated by author. Greenwillow, 2006. Unpaged. ISBN 978-0-06-112181-4. Grades K–2.

See entry 1340.

1535. Sís, Peter. *The Tree of Life: A Book Depicting the Life of Charles Darwin: Naturalist, Geologist and Thinker.* Illustrated by author. Frances Foster, 2003. 44pp. ISBN 978-0-374-45628-3. Grades 4–7.

This biography of Charles Darwin (1809–1882) contains information from his notebooks, diaries, correspondence, and published writings. It presents his discoveries in understandable text with accompanying illustrations and maps. The core of the work is his scientific study and voyage on the *Beagle,* from which he observed nature around the world, leading him to the theory he presented in *The Origin of Species. Horn Book Fanfare, School Library Journal Best Books for Children, Publishers Weekly Best Books for Children,* and *Capitol Choices Noteworthy Titles* (Washington, D.C.).

1536. Smiley, Jane. *Charles Dickens.* Viking, 2002. 212pp. ISBN 978-0-670-03077-4. Grades YA.

Charles Dickens (1812–1870) was a man of his times. He wrote about the life around him, beginning with his serialization of *The Pickwick Papers,* and became the first modern celebrity. This biography looks at his narrative techniques, his use of voice, themes in his work, and the interaction of his life and his work. He juggled writing, giving readings, and being a father and family man. Index.

1537. Smith, Denis Mark. *Garibaldi: A Great Life in Brief.* Greenwood, 1982. 215pp. ISBN 978-0-313-23618-1. Grades YA.

According to Smith, Garibaldi (1807–1882) was just over 50 years of age when he ceased to be merely a sailor, pirate, farmer, or radical revolutionary and became the national hero with a place in history textbooks. The text presents Garibaldi's life chronologically, mentioning the places where he fought (including the Rio Grande, Montevideo, Rome, Sicily, and Naples) before he tried to establish his own government in Sicily. Because Garibaldi believed in nationalism, he would have been surprised by

Italy's decision in World War II to become an aggressor nation rather than merely protecting its own lands from invasion. The text examines all of these concepts. Index.

1538. Sunstein, Emily W. *Mary Shelley: Romance and Reality.* Johns Hopkins University, 1991. 478pp. Paper ISBN 978-0-8018-4218-4. Grades YA.

Using letters and writings from Mary Shelley's (1797–1851) family—parents William Godwin and Mary Wollstonecraft, and husband Percy Bysshe Shelley—Sunstein pieces together Shelley's life. She challenges many of the views surrounding Shelley during the romantic period and shows that she deserves much more attention and a more positive attitude than she has previously received. Sunstein worked on this book for almost 15 years, and in the course of her research learned much about Shelley that other biographers had not uncovered. Bibliography and Index.

1539. Tieck, Sarah. *Florence Nightingale.* (First Biographies) Buddy, 2006. 32pp. ISBN 978-1-59679-786-4. Grades K–3.

"The Lady with a Lamp," Florence Nightingale (1820–1910), became a nurse during the Crimean War. When she returned to England, she continued to help those in need by changing hospitals into places of healing rather than death. Photographs and illustrations highlight the text. Glossary, Chronology, and Index.

1540. Turner, Barrie Carson. *Ludwig van Beethoven.* (Famous Childhoods) Chrysalis, 2003. 32pp. ISBN 978-1-59389-112-1. Grades 2–4.

This volume presents the early life of Ludwig van Beethoven (1770–1827) in twelve chapters. They include his birth, music lessons, first performances, problems in his family, a major influence in his life, and the end of his schooling. He becomes a published composer and visits the Netherlands before his career as a professional musician and an assistant organist. Eventually he meets Mozart. Illustrations of families and contemporaries augment the text. Glossary and Index.

1541. Varmer, Hjordis. *Hans Christian Andersen: His Fairy Tale Life.* Illustrated by Lilian Brogger. Translated by Tiina Nunnally. Groundwood, 2005. 112pp. ISBN 978-0-88899-690-9; 2007. paper ISBN 978-0-88899-798-2. Grades 5–8.

This biography of Hans Christian Andersen (1805–1875) shows him as a poor child whom a fortune teller predicted would be a great man. And Andersen endured many physical and emotional trials to do just that—become a great writer acclaimed around the globe. Andersen said he lived a fairy tale life, going from poor to wealthy. He was an extrovert and saw stories in everything that happened to him. Anecdotes about his self-absorption show that he intrigued his friends and delighted his patrons. He also created paper cutouts that reflected his stories, and some of them appear in the text. Bibliography.

1542. Venezia, Mike. *Camille Pissarro.* Illustrated by author. (Getting to Know the World's Greatest Artists) Children's Press, 2003. 32pp. ISBN 978-0-516-22577-7; 2004 paper ISBN 978-0-516-26977-1. Grades K–5.

Camille Pissarro (1830–1903), a renowned artist known as the "Father of Impressionism," was an important painter of the rural scenes around Paris. He loved nature and often painted roads leading into villages. He also liked markets and Parisian streets as subjects. Some of his paintings include *Hoarfrost, The Boulevard Montmartre on a Cloudy Morning, Boulevard Montmartre on a Sunny Afternoon*, and *The Red Roofs*. Illustrations complement the text.

1543. Venezia, Mike. *Eugene Delacroix.* Illustrated by author. (Getting to Know the World's Greatest Artists) Children's Press, 2003. 32pp. ISBN 978-0-516-22576-0; paper ISBN 978-0-516-26976-4. Grades K–5.

Eugene Delacroix (1798–1863) began his studies in Bordeaux as a musician, but in 1805 went to Paris and changed to art. His works appeared at the Paris Salon art shows, and he loved the Renaissance subjects of religious figures, musicians, and animals. He painted mainly with blues and greens, deep reds, and flesh tones that lit up his world. Illustrations highlight the text.

1544. Venezia, Mike. *Francisco Goya.* Illustrated by author. (Getting to Know the World's Greatest Artists) Children's Press, 1991. 32pp. ISBN 978-0-516-02292-5; paper ISBN 978-0-516-42292-3. Grades K–5.

Francisco Goya (1746–1828), a Spanish artist, was known for his work showing the political and social influences of his time. Illustrations enhance the text.

1545. Venezia, Mike. *Frederic Chopin.* Illustrated by author. (Getting to Know the World's Greatest Composers) Children's Press, 1999. 32pp. ISBN 978-0-516-21588-4; 2000 paper ISBN 978-0-516-26534-6. Grades K–5.

Frederic Chopin (1810–1849), from Zelazowa-Wola, Poland, composed beautiful and complicated music for the piano, basing some of his compositions on folk dances such as the mazurka. Student pianists always learn Chopin waltzes. Illustrations highlight the text.

1546. Venezia, Mike. *Ludwig van Beethoven.* Illustrated by author. (Getting to Know the World's Greatest Composers) Children's Press, 1995. 32pp. ISBN 978-0-516-04542-9; 2003 paper ISBN 978-0-516-20069-9. Grades K–5.

Ludwig van Beethoven (1770–1827) is recognized today as one of the greatest composers who ever lived. He had a somewhat tumultuous life and was deaf in his later years. Venezia details his life with facts and humorous cartoons.

1547. Venkatraman, Padma. *Double Stars: The Story of Caroline Herschel.* (Profiles in Science) Morgan Reynolds, 2007. 176pp. ISBN 978-1-59935-042-4. Grades 8 up.

Caroline Herschel (1750–1848), daughter in a working-class Hanover, Germany (Prussia) family, remained a slave to her mother although her father thought she should receive an education. Fortunately, her brother William took her to England with him. There, at first, she managed his estate and took voice lessons. After she became a renowned soprano, she decided to assist her brother in his work as an astronomer. She soon made her own discoveries and became an astronomer in her own right. Photographs augment the text. Bibliography, Chronology, Further Reading, Notes, Glossary, Web Sites, and Index.

1548. Viegas, Jennifer. *Beethoven's World.* (Music Throughout History) Rosen, 2007. 64pp. ISBN 978-1-4042-0724-0. Grades 5–8.

This biography of Ludwig van Beethoven (1770–1827) relies on primary sources. A German composer and pianist, he made the transition from the classical to the romantic period with his compositions and remains one of Western music's most influential composers. His symphonies are known and played worldwide. Viegas includes excerpts from letters from or about the composer, photographs of places where he lived, and reproductions of people he knew. The six chapters discuss his early life, family, social status, characteristics of his personality, his best-known music, his deafness, and the importance of his work. Illustrations augment the text. Bibliography, Glossary, Chronology, Further Reading, Web Sites, and Index.

1549. Wagner, Heather Lehr. *Jane Austen.* (Who Wrote That?) Chelsea House, 2003. 112pp. ISBN 978-0-7910-7623-1. Grades 4–7.

This biography of Jane Austen (1775–1817) describes her life and the novels in which she creates her vivid characters including *Pride and Prejudice, Emma*, and *Sense and Sensibility*. She wrote about marriage customs, English society, and family life with irony and humor. The text includes commentary about her family, her education, writing career, and other influences. Photographs and illustrations highlight the text.

1550. Waldron, Ann. *Claude Monet.* Abrams, 1991. 92pp. ISBN 978-0-8109-3620-1. Grades 8 up.

Claude Monet (1840–1926) was always fascinated with natural light. He experimented endlessly with its effects and pioneered the impressionist movement as a style emphasizing the points of light on a canvas. This volume includes reproductions and explanations of his technique of applying paint to a surface. He struggled to maintain his artistic integrity while painting during a period when art critics were hostile toward his work. List of Illustrations and Index.

1551. Winter, Jonah. *The 39 Apartments of Ludwig van Beethoven.* Illustrated by Barry Blitt. Schwartz & Wade, 2006. 32pp. ISBN 978-0-375-83602-2. Grades 2–5.

Each time Ludwig van Beethoven (1770–1827) moves to a new apartment in Vienna with his five legless pianos, his neighbors complain about the noise. In total, he moved 39 times. Among the reasons for moving, in addition to noise, might have been that he could not afford the rent or endure the smells in the neighborhood. But his movers must have had great difficulty transporting the pianos. Illustrations complement the text.

1552. Wooldridge, Connie Nordhielm. *Thank You Very Much, Captain Ericsson.* Illustrated by Andrew Glass. Holiday House, 2005. 32pp. ISBN 978-0-8234-1626-4. Grades 1–5.

Swedish-born John Ericsson (1803–1889) had ideas that others would not accept. The British rejected his invention of the steam locomotive and screw propeller, and he brought them to America. There he built the *Monitor*, using his invention, and helped the Union defeat the *Merrimac* during the Civil War. He later created a super-powered pump for fire trucks. Cartoon figures highlight the text. Bibliography and Chronology.

1553. Yolen, Jane. *The Perfect Wizard: Hans Christian Andersen.* Illustrated by Dennis Nolan. Dutton, 2005. 40pp. ISBN 978-0-525-46955-1. Grades 1–4.

The Danish fairy tale writer Hans Christian Andersen (1805–1875) continues to entertain children with his stories more than a century after his death. This picture-book account offers information about his youth, when he actually felt like an "ugly duckling." Lacking education, he was poor, unusual, and physically unattractive. But his illiterate mother told him stories and, with his own idiosyncratic talents, he was able to turn them into fairy tales that have enchanted children. Textured illustrations highlight the text. Bibliography and Notes.

Graphic Novels, Biographies, and Histories

1554. Geary, Rick. *The Case of Madeleine Smith.* (Treasury of Victorian Murder) NBM, 2006. ISBN 978-1-56163-467-5. Grades YA.

In 1855 Madeleine Smith, daughter of a prosperous Scottish architect, was accused of poisoning her lover so that she could marry a wealthy merchant. Evidence against her was circumstantial, and the verdict was "Not Proven." She moved to London, married a Pre-Raphaelite associate, bore two children, divorced, moved to New York and married again, and survived her husband in her continued life as a nonconformist.

1555. Robbins, Trina. *Florence Nightingale: Lady with the Lamp.* Illustrated by Anne Timmons. (Graphic Biographies) Graphic Library, 2005. 32pp. ISBN 978-0-7368-6850-1; paper ISBN 978-0-7368-7902-6. Grades 3–5.

This short graphic biography of Florence Nightingale (1820–1910) relates the story of the woman who left England to serve her country by nursing the wounded during the Crimean War. She has been named the "mother of nursing." Direct quotes from Nightingale are set apart from the fictional aspect of the narration. Web Sites.

DVDs

1556. *Charles Dickens.* (Great Authors) Naxos, 2003. 3 DVDs, 8:30 hrs. Grades 7 up.

Charles Dickens (1812–1870) endured many financial crises during his life as an author. He was 12 when his idyllic childhood ended because he was forced to work after his father was imprisoned as a debtor. Dickens went on to become one of the world's best-known writers. His works have never gone out of print. The three DVDs cover his life, his times, and his work. Reenactments and documentary footage show adaptations of *David Copperfield* and *A Christmas Carol* with such actors as Daniel Radcliffe, Ian McKellan, Dame Maggie Smith, and Bob Hoskins. An additional bonus covers the making of the DVD set.

1557. *Goya: Awakened in a Dream.* (Artists' Specials) Devine, 2000. 55 min. ISBN 978-1-894449-62-5. Grades 5–9.

When Francisco de Goya (1746–1828) meets Rosarita a a local church, he notices her artistic talent and agrees to hire her mother, Leocadia, as a housekeeper. At Goya's home in the country, he becomes ill, and Rosarita convinces him to keep fighting and to work. He begins "The Black Paintings." *Writers Guild of Canada Top Ten Award.*

1558. *The Industrial Revolution: 1700–1900: Back in Time.* (Hands-On Crafts for Kids Series 6) Chip Taylor Communications, 2003. 30 min. Grades 4–6.

See entry 1355.

1559. *Robber of the Cruel Streets: The Prayerful Life of George Muller.* Vision Video, 2006. 90 min. Grades 9 up.

George Müller (1805–1898), a German playboy, found Christianity and determined that his mission in life was to rescue orphans from street life in Bristol, England. He rescued, cared for, fed, and educated thousands of children. He did not ask for money, and the children never missed a meal. Dramatizations and documentary footage tell his story. *Adam Award*, Sabaoth Film Festival, Milan, Italy; *Platinum Winner*, Worldfest Houston International Film Festival.

Compact Discs

1560. Avi. *The Escape from Home.*   Narrated by Simon Prebble. (Beyond the Western Sea) Recorded Books, 1997. 9 CDs; 10.5 hrs. ISBN 978-1-4193-7431-9. Grades 5–9.

See entry 1364.

1561. Avi. *Lord Kirkle's Money.*   Narrated by Simon Prebble. (Beyond the Western Sea) Recorded Books, 1997. 11 CDs; 12.75 hrs. ISBN 978-1-4193-7435-7. Grades 5–9.

See entry 1365.

1562. Avi. *The Traitor's Gate.*   Narrated by John Keating. Recorded Books, 2007. 7 CDs; 8:15 hrs. ISBN 978-1-4281-6326-3. Grades 5–9.

See entry 1366.

1563. Bell, Ted. *Nick of Time.*   Narrated by John Shea. MacMillan Audio, 2008. 10 CDs; 11.5 hrs. ISBN 978-1-4272-0466-0. Grades 6–9.

See entry 1375.

1564. Buckley-Archer, Linda. *The Time Thief.*   Narrated by Gerald Doyle. (Gideon Trilogy) Simon & Schuster, 2007. 12 CDs; 13.5 hrs. ISBN 978-0-7435-6914-9. Grades 5–8.

See entry 1380.

1565. Dietrich, William. *The Rosetta Key.*   Narrated by Jeff Woodman. (Ethan Gage) HarperAudio, 2008. 11 CDs; 12.5 hrs. ISBN 978-0-06-146885-8. Grades YA.

See entry 1388.

1566. Giff, Patricia Reilly. *Nory Ryan's Song.*   Narrated by Susan Lynch. Listening Library, 2008. 3 CDs; 3 hrs. 31 min. ISBN 978-0-7393-6327-0. Grades 5–8.

See entry 1397.

1567. Hart, J. V. *Capt. Hook: The Adventures of a Notorious Youth.*   Narrated by John Keating. HarperCollins, 2005. 7 CDs; 8.5 hrs. ISBN 978-0-06-082075-6. Grades 7–10.

See entry 1400.

1568. Lawrence, Iain. *The Buccaneers.*   Narrated by Ron Keith. (High Seas Trilogy) Recorded Books, 2002. 6 cass., 7:30 hrs. ISBN 978-1-4025-3307-5. Grades 5–9.

See entry 1408.

1569. Lawrence, Iain. *The Convicts.* Narrated by John Keating. (The Curse of the Jolly Stone Trilogy) Recorded Books, 2005. 6 CDs; 6:45 hrs. ISBN 978-1-4193-6714-4. Grades 5–10.

See entry 1411.

1570. Lawrence, Iain. *The Smugglers.* Narrated by Ron Keith. (High Seas Trilogy) Recorded Books, 2000. 5 CDs; 5.50 hrs. ISBN 978-0-7887-4734-2. Grades 5–9.

See entry 1412.

1571. Meyer, Louis A. *Bloody Jack: Being an Account of the Misadventures of Mary "Jacky" Faber, Ship's Boy.* Narrated by Katherine Kellgren. (Bloody Jack Adventures) Listen & Live, 2007. 6 CDs; 8 hrs. ISBN 978-1-59316-094-4. Grades 6–9.

See entry 1415.

1572. O'Brian, Patrick. *The Commodore.* Narrated by Simon Vance. (Aubrey-Maturin) Blackstone Audio, 2006. 8 CDs. ISBN 978-0-7861-5991-8. Grades YA.

See entry 1422.

1573. O'Brian, Patrick. *Desolation Island.* Narrated by Simon Vance. (Aubrey-Maturin) Blackstone Audio, 2004. 9 CDs. ISBN 978-0-7861-8399-9. Grades YA.

See entry 1423.

1574. O'Brian, Patrick. *The Far Side of the World.* Narrated by Simon Vance. (Aubrey-Maturin) Blackstone Audio, 2006. 10 CDs. ISBN 978-0-7861-7282-5. Grades YA.

See entry 1424.

1575. O'Brian, Patrick. *The Fortune of War.* Narrated by Simon Vance. (Aubrey-Maturin) Blackstone Audio, 2005. 9 CDs. ISBN 978-0-7861-7994-7. Grades YA.

See entry 1425.

1576. O'Brian, Patrick. *H.M.S. Surprise.* Narrated by Simon Vance. (Aubrey-Maturin) Blackstone Audio, 2004. 10 CDs. ISBN 978-0-7861-8633-4. Grades YA.

See entry 1427.

1577. O'Brian, Patrick. *The Ionian Mission.* Narrated by Simon Vance. (Aubrey-Maturin) Blackstone Audio, 2005. 10 CDs. ISBN 978-0-7861-7783-7. Grades YA.

See entry 1428.

1578. O'Brian, Patrick. *The Letter of Marque.* Narrated by Simon Vance. (Aubrey-Maturin) Blackstone Audio, 2006. 8 CDs. ISBN 978-0-7861-6649-7. Grades YA.

See entry 1429.

1579. O'Brian, Patrick. *Master and Commander.* Narrated by Simon Vance. (Aubrey-Maturin) Blackstone Audio, 2004. 11 CDs. ISBN 978-0-7861-8629-7. Grades YA.

See entry 1430.

1580. O'Brian, Patrick. *The Nutmeg of Consolation.* Narrated by Simon Vance. (Aubrey-Maturin) Blackstone Audio, 2007. 9 CDs; 11 hrs. ISBN 978-0-7861-6048-8. Grades YA.

See entry 1432.

1581. O'Brian, Patrick. *Post Captain.* Narrated by Simon Vance. (Aubrey-Maturin) Blackstone Audio, 2004. 13 CDs. ISBN 978-0-7861-8628-0. Grades YA.

See entry 1433.

1582. O'Brian, Patrick. *The Reverse of the Medal.* Narrated by Simon Vance. (Aubrey-Maturin) Blackstone Audio, 2006. 9 CDs. ISBN 978-0-7861-4473-0. Grades YA.

See entry 1434.

1583. O'Brian, Patrick. *The Surgeon's Mate.* Narrated by Simon Vance. (Aubrey-Maturin) Blackstone Audio, 2005. 10 CDs; 12.5 hrs. ISBN 978-0-7861-7784-4. Grades YA.

See entry 1435.

1584. O'Brian, Patrick. *The Thirteen Gun Salute.* Narrated by Simon Vance. (Aubrey-Maturin) Blackstone Audio, 2006. 9 CDs; 11 hrs. ISBN 978-0-7861-6576-6. Grades YA.

Captain Jack Aubrey and Stephen Maturin, sailing on the *Diane*, undertake a British diplomatic mission to keep the sultan of Borneo from signing a treaty with the French during the Napoleonic wars.

1585. O'Brian, Patrick. *The Truelove.* Narrated by Simon Vance. (Aubrey-Maturin) Blackstone Audio, 2007. 8 CDs; 9 hrs. ISBN 978-0-7861-6049-5. Grades YA.

See entry 1436.

1586. O'Brian, Patrick. *The Wine-Dark Sea.* Narrated by Simon Vance. (Aubrey-Maturin) Blackstone Audio, 2006. 8 CDs; 10 hrs. ISBN 978-0-7861-5978-9. Grades YA.

See entry 1438.

EUROPE AND THE BRITISH ISLES, 1860–1918

Historical Fiction and Fantasy

1587. Akunin, Boris. *Murder on the Leviathan.* Translated by Andrew Bromfield. Random House, 2005. 240pp. Paper ISBN 978-0-8129-6879-8. Grades YA.

Someone murders Lord Littleby, seven servants, and two children inside his Parisian house in 1878. The police commissioner, "Papa" Gauche, only has a gold key shaped like a whale that allows him on a luxury liner, the *Leviathan*, to start his investigation. He boards the ship on its maiden voyage to India and meets Erast Fandorin, a former inspector with the Moscow Police Department. The two work together to find the murderer who is on board the ship.

1588. Alexander, Lloyd. *The Xanadu Adventure.* Dutton, 2005. 160pp. ISBN 978-0-525-47371-8; Puffin, 2007. paper ISBN 978-0-14-240786-8. Grades 5–8.

In 1876 Vesper Holly, her guardians Mary and Professor Brinton Garrett, boyfriend Tobias "The Weed" Pasavant, and twins Smiler and Slider go to Troy in search of a Rosetta stone. When they arrive at Xanadu, the villain, Dr. Desmond Helvitius captures Vesper's companions and imprisons them in the palace. Vesper has to create a plan to free them and to keep Dr. Helvitius from capturing all the oil that he thinks is the wealth and power of the future. She succeeds.

1589. Alexander, Robert. *The Kitchen Boy.* Penguin, 2004. 229pp. Paper ISBN 978-0-14-200381-7. Grades YA.

Leonka, 14, a young kitchen boy in the household of the Czar Nicholas II in 1918, sees the Bolsheviks arrest the family and take them away. As a grandfather many decades later, Misha remembers what he saw and has never told and records it on tape for his granddaughter. He saw Alexandra and Nicholas as loving but flawed, while the Bolsheviks were almost like comic book villains. He also has a thought about what might have happened to the two Romanov children, Alexei and Maria, who were not in the family grave when it was exhumed in 1991. He saw Alexei, after being shot, fall off the wagon that carried the family away, and Maria, who fell off, he tried to save.

1590. Anholt, Laurence. *The Magical Garden of Claude Monet.* Illustrated by author. (Anholt's Artists Books for Children) Barron's, 2003. 32pp. ISBN 978-0-7641-5574-1; 2007. paper ISBN 978-0-7641-3855-3. Grades K–3.

Julie's mother takes her from Paris to visit the lovely Giverny in France. She sees a beautiful garden and thinks the man working there is the gardener. Instead, he owns the garden. Julie befriends the painter Claude Monet who shows her the garden and takes her and her dog for a boat ride on his lake. The illustrations resemble some of Monet's paintings. Julie's mother happens to be Berthe Morisot, a painter and Monet's close friend.

1591. Augarde, Steve. *Celandine.* David Fickling, 2006. 486pp. ISBN 978-0-385-75048-6. Grades 7–10.

After Celandine's brother dies in World War I, and boarding school becomes un-bearable, Celandine runs away to her parents' farm in Somerset, England. There she uses her ability to reach the Various: winged warriors, travelers, foragers, and others who trust neither each other nor humans. She figures out how to become a part of their world and helps them when a tribal war erupts.

1592. Bagdasarian, Adam. *Forgotten Fire.* Laurel-Leaf, 2002. 272pp. Paper ISBN 978-0-440-22917-9. Grades 8 up.

Varan Kenderian, 12, lives in Turkey with his wealthy and influential Armenian fam-ily in 1915. Soon one and one-half million of his Armenian countrymen are dead from the Turkish genocide. Innocent Varan sees police lead his father away and kill family and friends in front of him. His sister poisons herself rather than be raped. His mother begs him and his brother to run away; they do and his brother dies. Varan worries that he has made the wrong decision. Eventually he accepts help from the Turkish governor and pretends to be a deaf mute in order to escape the country. *Teen Book Awards* (Iowa), *Rose-water High School Book Award* (Indiana) nomination, *State Reading Association Charlotte Book Award* (New York) nomination, *Young Adult Reading Program* (South Dakota), *Tayshas High School Reading List* (Texas), *Capitol Choices Noteworthy Titles* (Washington, D.C.), *Bulletin Blue Ribbon*, and *Evergreen Young Adult Award* (Washington) nomination.

1593. Bajoria, Paul. *The God of Mischief.* Illustrated by Bret Bertholf. Little, Brown, 2007. 389pp. ISBN 978-0-316-01091-7; paper ISBN 978-0-316-01628-5. Grades 6–9.

In the sequel to *The Printer's Devil*, orphans Mog (Imogen) and Nick are living at Kniveacres Hall in 1828 with their mother's last living relative, Sir Septimus Cloy. After he gives them freedom to roam the grounds, they ask Miss Thynne, their governess, to help them find their connection to Sir Septimus. They discover secret passages and a crypt while noticing that the villagers dislike the Hall. After Miss Thynne disappears, they realize that someone has killed her, and they need to find the killer. This research shows them that Cloy and his hostile servants, Hieronymous Bonefinger and Melibee, are part of the problem.

1594. Bajoria, Paul. *The Printer's Devil.* Illustrated by Bret Bertholf. Little, Brown, 2007. 377pp. Paper ISBN 978-0-316-10678-8. Grades 6–9.

In Victorian London, Mog, 12, works as an apprentice printer or printer's devil pro-ducing "Wanted" posters of criminal suspects. When the *Sun of Calcutta*, a mysterious ship, comes into port with an unknown cargo, he sees thieves from some of his "Wanted" posters on the dock. He investigates and meets Nick, a boy who seems to be his double in appearance. Mog's desire for adventure keeps getting him in trouble, and he becomes mixed up with Nick in a situation in which their pasts begin to come to light.

1595. Baker, Donna. *Fortune's Song.* Severn House, 2002. 256pp. ISBN 978-0-7278-7134-3. Grades YA.

In 1860 Megan Price, 18, lives in a Welsh mining town after her father dies, and her family starves. Her mother's only solution is to marry a man whom Megan detests, and when he tries to abuse Megan, Megan leaves for her grandmother's home in London. Shocked by the city, she suffers the theft of her money and her grandmother's address. Tom Bradley, a baker's son, befriends her and helps her during one of London's coldest winters on record. Although seemingly bleak, the atmosphere improves as the winter passes.

1596. Barnes, Julian. *Arthur and George.* Knopf, 2006. 385pp. ISBN 978-0-307-26310-0; Vintage, 2007. paper ISBN 978-1-4000-9703-6. Grades YA.

Sir Arthur Conan Doyle, the creator of Sherlock Holmes, was also a gentleman, spiritualist, athlete, and physician. George Edalji had a different background: he lived in Staffordshire with his Parsi vicar father and his Scots mother and became a solicitor. Throughout his life people bullied him and treated him poorly. When he was unjustly convicted in the early 1900s of the crime of mutilating a pony, Doyle became George's advocate, realizing that George's conviction rested on racial prejudice. Both men reason and fantasize as they attempt to free George from prison. This case led to the establishment of the Court of Appeals. *Man Booker Prize* nomination and *Dublin Literary Award* nomination.

1597. Barron, Stephanie. *A Flaw in the Blood.* Bantam, 2006. 289pp. ISBN 978-0-553-80524-6; 2008 paper ISBN 978-0-553-58444-4. Grades YA.

The lawyer, Patrick Fitzgerald, and his ward, Dr. Georgiana Armistead, go to France to visit Prince Albert and Queen Victoria's son, Prince Leo, in an effort to stop his hemophilia. When the two go to Windsor Castle, someone attacks their carriage, but they escape. After Prince Albert dies, they investigate their situation and the death of Fitzgerald's partner after their office is ransacked. They think that Wolfgang von Stühlen, a German count, might be behind the secrecy, and he might be fulfilling the requests of Queen Victoria who tries to hide her own secrets.

1598. Bjork, Cristina. *Linnea in Monet's Garden.* Illustrated by Lena Anderson. Translated by Joan Sandin. R & S, 1987. 56pp. ISBN 978-912-95831-4-4. Grades 4–7.

Linnea and her friend Mr. Bloom go from Sweden to Paris to visit the Marmottan Museum where many of Monet's paintings hang. Then they go to Giverny, his garden outside of Paris. There Linnea sees some of the lovely scenes Monet painted. The author also includes information about Monet's life as an impressionist painter (1840–1926).

1599. Blackwell, Lawana. *The Maiden of Mayfair.* Bethany, 2001. 432pp. Paper ISBN 978-0-7642-2258-0. Grades YA.

Dorothea Blake removes Sarah Matthews, 13, from the St. Matthew Methodist Foundling Home for Girls in Victorian London's Drury Lane. Startled, Sarah goes to live with her, but Dorothea does not let her know that she might be her granddaughter, the abandoned child of Dorothea's profligate son. While in the Blake home, Sarah earns the love and admiration of all for her gentle ways and becomes friends with the cook, Naomi. The question is whether she will choose to marry the man who wants her inheritance or Naomi's dear nephew, William.

1600. Bray, Libba. *A Great and Terrible Beauty.* (Gemma Doyle Trilogy) Random House, 2003. 416pp. ISBN 978-0-385-73028-0; 2005. paper ISBN 978-0-385-73231-4. Grades 9 up.

In 1895 Gemma, 16, returns to England from India after her mother's suicide, an event that Gemma foresaw in a dark vision. At Spence, a boarding school, Gemma is lonely but one day she spots, lurking around the school yard, the Indian man she saw in Bombay the day her mother died. Then she reads in the diary of former Spence girl Mary Dowd that the class of 1871 had a secret. Eventually, Gemma and three other girls—Felicity, Ann, and Pippa—encounter the secrets of The Realm, a cave on the school grounds where they find a world populated with goddess figures and Gemma's deceased mother. Gemma discovers that she has a mission connected to her mother and a secret that she must fulfill. *Original Voices Award* nomination, *American Library Association Best Books for Young Adults, Blue Spruce Award* (Colorado) nomination, *Young Reader's Choice Award* (Pennsylvania) nomination, *Tayshas Reading List* (Texas), *Garden State Teen Book Award* (New Jersey) nomination, *Lincoln Award* (Illinois) nomination, *High School Book Award* (Iowa) nomination, *Capitol Choices Noteworthy Titles* (Washington, D.C.), and *Flume Award* (New Hampshire) nomination.

1601. Bray, Libba. *Rebel Angels.* (Gemma Doyle Trilogy) Delacorte, 2005. 548pp. ISBN 978-0-385-73029-7; 2006. paper ISBN 978-0-385-73341-0. Grades 8 up.

In a sequel to *A Great and Terrible Beauty*, Gemma Doyle leaves Spence Academy in 1896 and takes her friends Felicity and Ann to London for the New Year. She has vivid visions of three girls dressed in white, and she must go to her realms to explain them and help her overcome the evil Circe and others who want her magic for themselves.

1602. Breslin, Theresa. *Remembrance.* Laurel Leaf, 2004. 304pp. Paper ISBN 978-0-440-23778-5. Grades 7 up.

In the summer of 1915, working class John Malcolm, 18, enlists in the army to fight World War I, leaving behind his love, upper-class Charlotte Armstrong-Barnes, 15, whom he will never be allowed to marry. He is killed, and his twin sister Maggie begins creating a new, more independent life for herself. At the same time, Francis, Charlotte's younger brother, feels pressure to enlist, and when he corresponds with Maggie from the French front, giving her vivid details of the war, the two slowly become aware of each other's best qualities. Alex, Maggie's younger brother, worries that the war will end before he can join; therefore, he lies about his age and enters Germany to become another casualty of the trenches. Charlotte gains experience helping in the local hospital, and she and Maggie go to France where Maggie's business skills learned in her father's shop gain her a position as an administrator, an opportunity she would not have had without the war. *ALA Best Books for Young Adults.*

1603. Brewster, Hugh. *Carnation, Lily, Lily, Rose: The Story of a Painting.* Illustrated by John Singer Sargent. Kids Can, 2007. 48pp. ISBN 978-1-55453-137-0. Grades 3–5.

Using a scrapbook format, Brewster presents Kate Millet, thrilled to be a model for John Singer Sargent while he stays with her family in England in 1885 and 1886. When he chooses two other girls to model, Kate goes to her room crying. But as she watches

news that the war has ended on November 11, 1918. Pen-and-ink illustrations complement the text with information not appearing in the words.

1615. Douglas, Carole Nelson. *Irene at Large.* Tor, 1993. 381pp. Paper ISBN 978-0-8125-
1702-6. Grades YA.

   Irene, her husband, and her friend Nell rescue Quentin in 1890 when he falls in front
of them on a Paris street. Thinking that he might have been poisoned, they proceed to
save him. Quentin had been on his way to warn Dr. Watson that someone was trying to
kill Watson because he had been kind to Quentin in India ten years before. After they
identify Dr. Watson's enemy, Quentin disappears.

1616. Dugain, Marc. *The Officer's Ward.* Translated by Howard Curtis. Soho, 2002. 135pp.
Paper ISBN 978-1-56947-307-8. Grades YA.

   During World War I Adrian Fournier, 24, starts his career as a civil engineer, but is
soon called for duty in the war. He scouts for locations for battle on the Meuse River.
His two colleagues are killed, and he receives a "maxillofacial" wound, an injury that destroys the center part of his face. He spends the rest of the war and longer—until April
1919—in a hospital where he has sixteen operations. None of them actually restores his
face, and he wonders if he can restore his life. *Prix des Libraries*.

1617. Emery, Joanna. *Brothers of the Falls.* Illustrated by David Erickson. (Adventures in
America) Silver Moon, 2004. 92pp. ISBN 978-1-893110-37-3. Grades 4–6.

   In 1847 Thomas and James Doyle decide to go to America because the potato famine
has decimated the food crops in Ireland. When the ship leaves early, older brother
Thomas has not boarded, and James, 13, must sail to America alone. He gets a job at the
Niagara Inn in Niagara Falls, New York, and tries to earn enough money to return to Ireland and reunite with his brother. He meets a Native American who shows him the impressive falls, and he experiences other excitements that help him cope with his
separation from Thomas.

1618. Fine, Anne. *Frozen Billy.* Illustrated by Georgina McBain. Farrar, 2006. 175pp. ISBN
978-0-374-32481-0. Grades 4–6.

   Clarrie and Will live with their negligent uncle in Edwardian England since their
mother has been wrongfully imprisoned in Ireland while their father is in Australia.
Uncle Len, a music hall ventriloquist, entertains with his dummy, Frozen Billy, but
spends his pay on alcohol and gambling. Will decides to become the second dummy so
they can make more money. Will, however, slowly deteriorates and Clarrie makes a plan
to get him away. Her efforts save them all. Line drawings augment the text.

1619. Geras, Adèle. *Voyage.* Harcourt, 2007. 194pp. Paper ISBN 978-0-15-206100-5. Grades
5–9.

   Mina, age 14, and her family leave Russia in the early 20th century for America, to escape the pogroms against Jews. On board the ship, Mina uses her energy to help those
who can barely survive from the seasickness, the hunger, and the filth that surrounds
them. The omniscient point of view exposes the diverse responses of the ship's passengers to this difficult experience.

1620. Granger, Ann. *A Mortal Curiosity.* (Lizzie Martin Mysteries) St. Martins, 2008.
320pp. ISBN 978-0-312-36352-9. Grades YA.

To escape her Aunt Parry, 30-year-old Lizzie accepts a temporary position at Shore House in Hampshire as companion to Lucy Craven, 17, who refuses to believe that her baby has died. When a rat catcher is found murdered on the property, Inspector Benjamin Ross, who has been courting Lizzie, arrives from London to help with the investigation. Lucy's mental instability makes her a suspect.

1621. **Grosjean, Didier, and Claudine Roland.** *Rousseau: Still Voyages.* Illustrated by John Goodman. Translated by Francine De Boeck. Chelsea House, 1994. 60pp. ISBN 978-0-7910-2816-2. Grades 3–7.

An 11-year-old boy becomes interested in pictures, supposedly painted by a customs officer, that show jungles and wild animals. He begins reading a boring book and finds out that Henri Rousseau (1844–1910), called "Le Douanier," was a "Sunday" painter who had a full-time job during the week. The boy goes with his parents to Paris to investigate some of the information he discovered in the book, and their explorations reveal many interesting facts about Rousseau, his life, and the influences on his paintings. Reproductions, Glossary, and Chronology.

1622. **Hamley, Dennis.** *Without Warning: Ellen's Story 1914–1918.* Candlewick, 2007. 326pp. ISBN 978-0-7636-3338-7. Grades 6–9.

Ellen Wilkins, 15, sees her brother Jack, 19, enlist in the army when recruiters come to her town during World War I. Her father is pleased and her mother disturbed. The entire community feels anti-German, and anyone who questions the country's war is automatically disloyal. Ellen remains at home to placate her mother, but her boyfriend dies. Then Jack returns depressed and without a leg. She makes a great effort to refocus his feelings of despair before she goes off to be a nurse in Abbeville, France. Thus, she fulfills her own dream of helping with the war effort both at home and abroad.

1623. **Hartnett, Sonya.** *The Silver Donkey.* Illustrated by Don Powers. Candlewick, 2006. 266pp. ISBN 978-0-7636-2937-3; 2007. paper ISBN 978-0-7636-3681-4. Grades 4–6.

During World War I in France, Coco, 8, and her sister Marcelle, 10, discover a blind British soldier who wants to cross the Channel and return home. They bring him blankets but realize they cannot help him further, so they enlist the help of their brother Pascal, 13, and of an adult, Fabrice. All are intrigued by the stories the soldier tells about his good luck charm, a silver donkey. Each story involves some aspect of courage, patience, humility, and forgiveness, all characteristics of the donkey. They eventually realize that the man has only blinded himself to the horrors of war, not to human kindness.

1624. **Havill, Juanita.** *Eyes Like Willy's.* HarperCollins, 2004. 135pp. ISBN 978-0-688-13672-7. Grades 4–7.

In the summer of 1906 when Guy and Sarah Masson travel from Paris to Lake Constance in Austria for their vacation, they meet Willy Schiller, 10. They have a delightful time swimming, racing their model sailboats, fighting duels, and playing chess. Each summer they renew and deepen their friendship until World War I breaks out in 1914. In 1915 when Guy joins the army, he knows that he might face Willy on the opposite side.

1625. **Hearn, Julie.** *Ivy.* Ginee Seo, 2008. 368pp. ISBN 978-1-416-92506-4. Grades 9 up.

In Victorian London Ivy finds herself mistreated and abused, but her lovely red hair attracts the attention of a pre-Raphaelite artist who hires her as a model. She goes to his apartment and returns to her own home where her relatives bully her and others. Then the artist's mother herself plots evil schemes. Throughout, Ivy has to try to overcome her worst problem: taking the prevalent drug laudanum.

1626. Heneghan, Judith. *The Magician's Apprentice.* Holiday House, 2008. 168pp. ISBN 978-0-8234-2150-3. Grades 6–8.

In Winchester, England, in 1874, Jago Stonecipher has to work as an assistant to his unscrupulous magician uncle. A beggar and unwilling thief, Jago overhears a conversation that leads him to a gold watch with a note inside. Then he finds a maid and her gentleman lover with a con man who has found a mark. He determines to stop the greedy fortune hunters, and he ends up on a ship to Brazil where his intelligence helps him succeed.

1627. Howard, Ellen. *The Gate in the Wall.* Aladdin, 2007. 148pp. Paper ISBN 978-1-4169-6796-5. Grades 5–7.

In 19th-century England, orphaned Emma, 10, works 10 hours a day at the silk-spinning factory to help support her sister, her sister's baby, and her sister's alcoholic husband. When her boss locks her out for being a minute late, she goes through a gate and finds a canal world where boats transport cargo along the water. Hungry, she steals a potato off one of them, and the owner, Mrs. Minshull catches her. She demands that Emma work for her on her boat, the *Cygnet*. Emma does, and during this time, she has food, clothing, and care for the first time since her parents died. She makes new friends and gains confidence in her own abilities. *Dorothy Canfield Fisher Children's Book Awards (Vermont).*

1628. Ibbotson, Eva. *A Countess Below Stairs.* Speak, 2007. 383pp. Paper ISBN 978-0-14-240865-0. Grades 8 up.

When the Russian Revolution destroys their way of life in 1917, Anna and her privileged family escape to London. Anna becomes a maid on a country estate. She has never worked before and the other servants are skeptical about her abilities, but she wins their respect. The estate's owner, Rupert, the Earl of Westerholme, announces his engagement to Muriel, whose senseless and thoughtless actions disturb everyone. A few days before the wedding, Rupert and Anna realize they are in love, and Rupert has to extricate himself from a loveless marriage.

1629. Ibbotson, Eva. *The Star of Kazan.* Illustrated by Kevin Hawkes. Puffin, 2006. 405pp. Paper ISBN 978-0-14-240582-6. Grades 4–8.

In the early 1900s two loving servants and three sibling professors raise the foundling Annika, 12, until Edeltraut von Tannenberg, a rich aristocratic woman appears, claiming to be her mother. She takes Annika to a remote castle in the north, where Annika begins to wonder about her family's secrets while missing her loving life in Vienna. Her Viennese family helps her expose these schemers. *Booklist Editors' Choice, Nene Award* (Hawaii) nomination, *Rebecca Caudill Award* (Illinois) nomination, *Children's Book Award* (Massachusetts) nomination, *Student Book Award* (Maine) nomination, *Great Stone Face Book Award* (New Hampshire) nomination, *Beehive Young Adult Book Award* (Utah) nomination, *Capitol Choices Noteworthy Titles* (Washington, D.C.), and *Pacific Northwest Young Reader's Choice Book Award* nomination.

1630. Kimmel, Eric A. *A Picture for Marc.* Illustrated by Matthew Trueman. Random House, 2007. 101pp. ISBN 978-0-375-83253-6; 2008. paper ISBN 978-0-375-85225-1. Grades 2–5.

Marc discovers his talent for drawing after a friend and art teacher encourage him. The story, based loosely on the childhood of Marc Chagall (1887–1985), shows a Russian boy in Vitebsk having to beg his parents to let him take art lessons. Illustrations augment the text. Bibliography.

1631. Knight, Joan. *Charlotte in Giverny.* Illustrated by Melissa Sweet. Chronicle, 2000. Unpaged. ISBN 978-0-8118-2383-8; 2007. paper ISBN 978-0-8118-5803-8. Grades 3–7.

In 1892 Charlotte Glidden travels with her family from Boston across the Atlantic through Paris on the way to Giverny to a house not far from Monet's home. She meets several painters over the next year at holidays, picnics, and other events. They include William Merritt Chase, Lilla Cabot Perry, and Monet himself. She keeps a journal-sketchbook about the year. Illustrations enhance the text.

1632. Knight, Joan. *Charlotte in London.* Illustrated by Melissa Sweet. Chronicle, 2008. Unpaged. ISBN 978-0-8118-5635-5. Grades 3–7.

Charlotte Glidden travels with her family from Boston to London so that she can have her portrait painted by John Singer Sargent. She meets other artists through social connections during the war and records her experiences in her journal-sketchbook. Illustrations enhance the text.

1633. Knight, Mary-Jane. *Vampyre: The Terrifying Lost Journal of Dr. Cornelius Van Helsing.* Illustrated by Gary Blythe, et al. HarperCollins, 2007. ISBN 978-0-06-124780-4. Grades 5–10.

Dr. Cornelius Van Helsing and his assistant Gustav have to leave Britain for Transylvania in 1907 because Abraham, Cornelius's brother who killed Dracula in Bram Stoker's story, has taken ill and thinks Dracula has returned to life. Numerous cards, messages, and newspaper clippings flap in the text, giving the sense of a scrapbook of the event. Photographs and maps enhance the text.

1634. Krull, Kathleen, and Paul Brewer. *Fartiste.* Illustrated by Boris Kulikov. Simon & Schuster, 2008. 40pp. ISBN 978-1-416-92828-7. Grades 3–5.

Joseph Pujol (1857–1945) learned when he was young that he could rhythmically control the gas noises of his bowels. In the army, he entertained his buddies by "squeezing" out songs or sounds of war. He became a baker, but to earn more money to support his many children, began entertaining with his unusual talent. He went to the Moulin Rouge where he became popular, and then he entertained royalty and other famous people. Illustrations complement the text.

1635. Lackey, Mercedes G. *The Gates of Sleep.* Penguin, 2002. ISBN 978-0-7564-0060-6; D A W, 2003. paper ISBN 978-0-7564-0101-6. Grades YA.

In Edwardian England Marina Saverson's parents practice Elemental Magic, and an evil prophecy has told her father that her own aunt will kill her before she becomes 18. Therefore, Marina's parents send her away from home to stay with family friends when she is young, where she enjoys water sprites and nymphs as friends, but she does not know why. When her parents die in an "accident" before her 18th birthday, her cold and controlling but beautiful Aunt Arachne makes her come to live with her. Marina senses that something is wrong, and when she has both physical and metaphysical revelations at her aunt's pottery factory, she takes heed of the warnings. The story gives a modern twist to the "Sleeping Beauty" fairy tale.

1636. LaFevers, R. L. *Theodosia and the Serpents of Chaos.* Illustrated by Yoko Tanaka. Houghton, 2007. 344pp. ISBN 978-0-618-75638-4. Grades 4–8.

Theo Throckmorton, 11, lives in London in 1906 with her parents and spends most of her time in the antiquities museum that her father administers. Inside are objects from her archaeologist mother's trips to Egypt. But Theo worries about these artifacts and their possibility of harm to her mother because they contain virulent ancient curses. Only she has the ability to detect and destroy them. Her mother returns with an amulet having enough power to destroy the world, and Theo herself becomes caught in its web of danger as German operatives wanting to gain control of England try to grab it. She finally confronts her enemies alone while she sleeps in a tomb inside the museum. There she makes other discoveries about herself as well.

1637. Lasky, Kathryn. *Broken Song.* Viking, 2005. 160pp. ISBN 978-0-670-05931-7; Puffin, 2007. paper ISBN 978-0-14-240741-7. Grades 5–8.

In 1897 Russia, Reuven Bloom, a talented violinist of 15, has to take his little sister Rachel with him on a dangerous journey after Cossacks murder their parents in a pogrom. They finally reach family in Poland where Reuven rejects his violin and decides to join an elite revolutionary group and become a demolition expert. He lets Rachel go to America with the family, but when he is close to achieving his revenge, he merely wants to retrieve his stolen violin and join Rachel.

1638. Lasky, Kathryn. *The Night Journey.* Illustrated by Trina Schart Hyman. Viking, 2005. 152pp. ISBN 978-0-670-05963-8; Puffin paper ISBN 978-0-14-240322-8. Grades 5–9.

Not until she is 13 does Rache hear the story of Jewish pogroms and her grandmother's escape from Russia with her family in 1900. Her grandmother hid under chicken crates, paraded as a Purim player, and crossed the border with her cookies. The cookies held the family's gold. *National Jewish Awards, American Library Association Notable Children's Book, Association of Jewish Libraries Award*, and *Sydney Taylor Book Award*.

1639. Lawrence, Iain. *Lord of the Nutcracker Men.* Laurel Leaf, 2003. 224pp. Paper ISBN 978-0-440-41812-2. Grades 5–8.

Johnny Briggs, 10, lives with his aunt in the small village of Cliffe in 1914 when exiled from London at the start of World War I. His father is fighting abroad and his mother works in a munitions factory. Johnny enjoys playing with his favorite possession, the toy "nutcracker men" that his father made for him, as a way to escape from his dislike of the town. His father's first letters describe the horrors of the war, but soon the subject changes to discussions of billiards and movies. But he continues to carve soldiers between battles and send them to Johnny from France. Unfortunately, the toys become more grotesque as the war progresses. Johnny thinks that having the French, English, and German soldiers fight each other fiercely will determine the outcome of the war and begins to worry that his games might actually harm his father. He even thinks he may have caused the death of his father's best friend. Johnny's teacher helps him cope, but the next-door neighbor, Murdoch, shoots himself in the leg to keep from returning to the front lines. *Publishers Weekly Best Children's Books* nomination, *School Library Journal Best Books of the Year, Student Book Award* (Maine) nomination, *Beehive Young Adults' Book Award* (Utah) nomination, and *Reader's Choice Awards* (Virginia) nomination.

1640. Lewis, J. Patrick. *The Stolen Smile.* Creative, 2004. 40pp. ISBN 978-1-56846-192-2. Grades 3–6.

In 1911 Italian Vincenzo Peruggia stole Leonardo da Vinci's *Mona Lisa* from the Louvre where he was an employee. In his own voice, he explains how he evaded the guards, transported the painting to his apartment, and kept it for two years while planning how to hang it in Florence's Uffizi Gallery where he thought it belonged. In this story based on fact, he is arrested before completing his goal. He states some of the questions readers will ask: "Am I, Vincenzo Peruggia, Italian patriot without peer, villain or victim? Victor or vanquished? Savior or scoundrel?"

1641. Llywelyn, Morgan. *1916: A Novel of the Irish Rebellion.* Tor, 1999. 447pp. Paper ISBN 978-0-8125-7492-0. Grades YA.

Ned Halloran from Ireland's countryside gets the opportunity to attend St. Enda's, an experimental private school founded by poet Patrick Pearse. There he hears ideas that shock him as he receives training as both a scholar and a soldier. He becomes an ardent supporter of establishing an Irish Republic and enlists in the Volunteers. During the 1916 Easter Rebellion that lasts for five days, he joins the battle for control of Dublin. The British, however, defeat them, and Pearse along with other leaders is executed.

1642. Lord, Michelle. *Little Sap and Monsieur Rodin.* Illustrated by Felicia Hoshino. Lee and Low, 2006. Unpaged. ISBN 978-1-58430-248-3. Grades 2–5.

In 1906 the king of Cambodia takes forty-two dancers to perform in France. The artist Auguste Rodin becomes captivated by them and asks to sketch three of them. One of them, Little Sap, is a poor country girl from Cambodia's rice fields who wanted to earn money as one of the dancers so that her family could have a better life. She dances so beautifully that Rodin gives her a special prize.

1643. McClintock, Barbara. *Adèle and Simon.* Illustrated by author. Frances Foster, 2006. 40pp. ISBN 978-0-374-38044-1. Grades K–3.

While Adèle and her brother Simon walk home from school in Paris past the market, the Jardin du Luxembourg, and the Louvre around 1900, Simon manages to lose his hat, gloves, scarf, coat, knapsack, books, crayons, and a drawing of a cat that he made at school. At the Louvre, Mary Cassatt and Edgar Degas help him locate his crayons. When they eventually reach home, people who have retrieved the other items meet them and return each one. Watercolors illuminate the text. *Capitol Choices Noteworthy Titles* (Washington, D.C.).

1644. McCourt, Frank. *Angela and the Baby Jesus.* Illustrated by Raúl Colón. Simon & Schuster, 2007. 32pp. ISBN 978-1-416-93789-0. Grades 1–5.

In 1912 when Angela, 6, goes inside St. Joseph's Church in Limerick, Ireland, she sees the Baby Jesus on the altar. The church is cold on that December night so she takes him home to get warm. She has difficulty getting over the garden wall while carrying him, but no one pays much attention to her until the priest discovers that Jesus is missing from his normal place. McCourt retells this story from one his mother, Angela (of *Angela's Ashes*), related to him about her own childhood.

1645. McCully, Emily Arnold. *Mirette on the High Wire.* Illustrated by author. Putnam, 1992. 32pp. ISBN 978-0-399-22130-9; Puffin, 1997. paper ISBN 978-0-698-11443-2. Grades K–4.

After Bellini comes to live at her mother's boardinghouse in Paris in the late 19th century, Mirette sees him walking on a high wire in the backyard. She wants to learn and

1656. Perry, Anne. *Belgrave Square.* Fawcett, 1993. 361pp. Paper ISBN 978-0-449-22227-0. Grades YA.

In London around 1890, Weems, a moneylender who blackmails people as a sideline, is murdered. After police identify the murderer they find an unexpected complication.

1657. Perry, Anne. *Death of a Stranger.* Fawcett, 2003. 337pp. Paper ISBN 978-0-345-44006-8. Grades YA.

During the reign of Victoria, after a railway tycoon dies in a brothel, William Monk, private detective, takes a job from a mysterious client who wants to know if her fiancé, a railway firm executive, is guilty of fraud. Monk's wife Hester runs Coldbath Square clinic, a place for prostitutes to get medical help, and in the aftermath of the death she sees many women whose pimps have battered them because the police have asked for their help in the situation. The case also stirs memories from Monk's past before his amnesia wiped it out.

1658. Perry, Anne. *The Face of a Stranger.* (William Monk) Ballantine, 2008. 328pp. Paper ISBN 978-0-345-51355-7. Grades YA.

In Perry's first book about William Monk, set in the 1890s, he is a police detective who has amnesia after an accident in London. He cannot verify what people say about his past. He continues to work on cases and tries to find out who murdered a Crimean War hero from the upper class. Although he eventually solves the crime, he is uncertain for much of the time as to whether he himself might be the criminal he is seeking.

1659. Peters, Elizabeth. *The Ape Who Guards the Balance.* (Amelia Peabody Mystery) Avon, 1999. 376pp. Paper ISBN 978-0-06-053811-8. Grades YA.

Ramses, Amelia Peabody's son; his friend David; and Amelia's ward Nefret Forth end up with a rare papyrus on a dig in Egypt. The killer Tour and the ancient gods pursue them.

1660. Peters, Elizabeth. *Crocodile on the Sandbank.* (Amelia Peabody Mystery) Mysterious, 1988. 273pp. Paper ISBN 978-0-445-40651-3. Grades YA.

After her father dies, 32-year-old Amelia Peabody rejects typical Victorian spinsterhood and travels to Egypt in pursuit of her love of archaeology. Intruders, other archaeologists, and a disappearing mummy challenge her. The first in a series.

1661. Peters, Elizabeth. *The Curse of the Pharaohs.* (Amelia Peabody Mystery) Mysterious, 1992. 357pp. Paper ISBN 978-0-445-40648-3. Grades YA.

Amelia Peabody and her new husband, Radcliffe Emerson, solve three murders in the Valley of the Kings while escaping from villains who would prefer them dead.

1662. Peters, Elizabeth. *The Deeds of the Disturber.* Narrated by Susan O'Malley. (Amelia Peabody Mystery) Twilight, 2000. 289pp. Paper ISBN 978-0-380-73195-4. Grades YA.

A priest at the British Museum says he has cursed someone for desecrating a mummy, but Amelia Peabody refuses to accept this. Her investigation of the priest uncovers a murderer.

1663. Peters, Elizabeth. *Falcon at the Portal.* (Amelia Peabody Mystery) Avon, 2000. 366pp. Paper ISBN 978-0-380-79857-5. Grades YA.

In 1911, after Amelia and her family arrive in Egypt for their archaeological dig, David, the husband of Amelia's niece, is accused of selling fake Egyptian artifacts. Other complications include immorality, drug dealing, and murder.

1664. Peters, Elizabeth. *The Golden One.* (Amelia Peabody Mystery) Avon, 2003. 448pp. Paper ISBN 978-0-380-81715-3. Grades YA.

In 1917 Amelia Peabody goes back to Egypt with her husband, Radcliffe Emerson; her son, Ramses; and Nefret, Ramses' wife. After arriving in Luxor she finds that the war has come to Egypt, but she also discovers a murdered body and becomes involved with double agents. Then Ramses has to go to Gaza for the British government, and the family follows him. When the Turkish secret service head, Sahin Pasha, captures Ramses, the family helps him escape before returning to solve the murder in Luxor.

1665. Peters, Elizabeth. *Guardian of the Horizon.* (Amelia Peabody Mystery) Avon, 2005. 399pp. Paper ISBN 978-0-06-103246-2. Grades YA.

After Amelia Peabody and her family are banished from the Valley of the Kings in 1907 and 1908, Prince Tarek from the Lost Oasis pleads for their help. Ramses, however, wants to pursue his courtship of his love, Nefret.

1666. Peters, Elizabeth. *He Shall Thunder in the Sky.* (Amelia Peabody Mystery) Avon, 2001. 728pp. Paper ISBN 978-0-380-79858-2. Grades YA.

While Amelia Peabody and her husband Emerson work on an archaeological dig in Egypt, a nationalist foments trouble in the town. Additionally, Amelia's enemy Sethos reappears.

1667. Peters, Elizabeth. *The Hippopotamus Pool.* (Amelia Peabody Mystery) Grand Central, 1997. 384pp. Paper ISBN 978-0-446-60398-0. Grades YA.

Amelia Peabody, the archaeologist, goes to Egypt in the 19th century looking for finds at the pyramids. On New Year's Eve in Cairo, a stranger hands her a scarab ring that he says came from the tomb of Queen Tetisheri. In her investigation of its authenticity, she confronts a mystery.

1668. Peters, Elizabeth. *The Last Camel Died at Noon.* (Amelia Peabody Mystery) Grand Central, 1994. 352pp. Paper ISBN 978-0-446-36338-9. Grades YA.

While in Egypt with her husband Radcliffe and her son Ramses, Amelia Peabody and Ramses search for an archaeologist in the Sudan who disappeared fourteen years before. The sixth volume in the series.

1669. Peters, Elizabeth. *Lord of the Silent.* (Amelia Peabody Mystery) Avon, 2002. 404pp. Paper ISBN 978-0-380-81741-6. Grades YA.

In Egypt in 1915, Amelia Peabody and her husband escape German submarines and the warring Senussi to continue their archaeological work. They find a recently dead corpse, however, and must find a live killer.

1670. Peters, Elizabeth. *The Mummy Case.* (Amelia Peabody Mystery) Avon, 2006. 313pp. Paper ISBN 978-0-06-087811-5. Grades YA.

Amelia Peabody, her husband, and their son Ramses go to Egypt to excavate. A dealer in stolen antiquities is murdered, and Amelia spends her time investigating the case instead. The third volume in the series.

1671. Peters, Elizabeth. *Seeing a Large Cat.*   (Amelia Peabody Mystery) Grand Central, 1998. 386pp. Paper ISBN 978-0-446-60557-1. Grades YA.

In 1903 Amelia Peabody and her husband, Emerson, receive a threat to keep them from going to the Valley of the Kings. They ignore the warning, and there they find an assassin trying to stop their work and a spiritualist who offers false information.

1672. Peters, Elizabeth. *The Snake, the Crocodile and the Dog.*   (Amelia Peabody Mystery) Aspect, 1992. 340pp. ISBN 978-0-446-51585-6; Grand Central, 1994. paper ISBN 978-0-446-36478-2. Grades YA.

When Amelia Peabody and her husband go to Egypt in the late 1800s without their son, they plan to enjoy each other's company romantically. But while they excavate a grave site, a criminal causes them much discomfort and ruins their plans.

1673. Pullman, Philip. *The Ruby in the Smoke.*   (Sally Lockhart Mystery) Peter Smith, 2002. 230pp. ISBN 978-0-8446-7230-4; Knopf, 2008. paper ISBN 978-0-375-84516-1. Grades 8 up.

Sally Lockhart, age 16, kills a man by merely mentioning words from her late father's cryptic note, found after his death in 1872. Sally becomes the subject of deceit and ill will at the hands of people who want her dead. Her final confrontation on London Bridge allows her to find out how her father provided for her well-being. *IRA Teachers' Choice, Children's Book of the Year* (Great Britain), *Capitol Choices Noteworthy Titles* (Washington, D.C.) and *School Library Journal Best Book.*

1674. Pullman, Philip. *The Shadow in the North.*   (Sally Lockhart Mystery) Peter Smith, 2006. 320pp. ISBN 978-0-8446-7289-2; Knopf, 2008. paper ISBN 978-0-375-84515-4. Grades 8 up.

Sally (of *The Ruby in the Smoke*) goes into business for herself as a financial consultant in London. In 1878 one of her clients loses money based on her advice, and Sally works to recover the loss. After finding the man responsible and knowing that he has caused several deaths, Sally agrees to marry him if he repays. But she destroys the factory housing his unscrupulous business, and he happens to be inside at the time. *American Library Association Best Book for Young Adults, IRA Teacher's Choice, Booklist Editors' Choice, Capitol Choices Noteworthy Titles* (Washington, D.C.), and *Edgar Allen Poe Award* nomination.

1675. Pullman, Philip. *The Tiger in the Well.*   (Sally Lockhart Mystery) Knopf, 2008. 407pp. Paper ISBN 978-0-375-84517-8. Grades 8 up.

Sally from *The Ruby in the Smoke* receives a court summons stating that her husband wants to divorce her and take custody of their daughter. Although Sally has never married, or even heard of the man named on the summons, her handwriting appears in the registry at the church. She has to find a way to prove there is a mistake. What she finds is a man accused of crimes because he is Jewish, and whom someone is attempting to extradite. As she falls in love with him, the puzzle pieces begin to fit. The person who is causing the trouble turns out to be Ay Ling, the man Sally thought she had killed in *The Ruby in the Smoke. Capitol Choices Noteworthy Titles* (Washington, D.C.).

1676. Pullman, Philip. *The Tin Princess.*   (Sally Lockhart Mystery) Knopf, 2008. 407pp. Paper ISBN 978-0-375-84514-7. Grades 8 up.

Adelaide (from *The Ruby in the Smoke*), Becky's language student, has married into the Razkavia royal family. Becky, age 16 in 1882, participates in this complex plot in which Sally, the heroine of other Pullman books, appears. Much political intrigue involves these characters, as well as others with Middle European backgrounds.

1677. Rabin, Staton. *The Curse of the Romanovs.* Margaret K. McElderry, 2007. 273pp. ISBN 978-1-4169-0208-9. Grades 6–8.

The Russian heir to the throne in 1916, Tsarevich Alexei, suffers from hemophilia, and his mother thinks that Father Grigory Rasputin is the only one who can help him. Alexei knows that Rasputin is a fraud, and when he tells a relative, the relative supposedly assassinates Rasputin. Although Rasputin rises from the river in which he has been tossed to chase Alexei, the boy realizes that his "blood-river" can move him back and forth through time so he escapes to 2010. Varda, 15, a future relative researching hemophilia, finds him nearly dead in the river. Rasputin, however, finds him and lurks as the janitor of Alexei's New York City high school. Finally, they return to Russia to the time of the Romanovs where Rasputin is properly killed and Alexei and Varda try to rescue Alexei's imprisoned family.

1678. Raphael, Marie. *Streets of Gold.* Persca, 2001. 224pp. Paper ISBN 978-0-89255-256-6. Grades 6–10.

Marisia, 15, and her family escape from Poland in 1901 on a ship headed for America. (Her oldest brother has already been conscripted into the czar's army, but her older brother Stefan refuses to serve and the family flees with him.) At Ellis Island, doctors discover that her little sister Katrina has tuberculosis. Marisia's parents must return to Germany with the two younger children while Marisia and Stefan stay in America to find housing and jobs so they can send money to their parents. Marisia works as a maid in the home of a young Polish girl living in New York. After Katrina's death, the family reunites in America.

1679. Rennison, Nick. *Sherlock Holmes: The Unauthorized Biography.* Atlantic Monthly, 2006. 280pp. ISBN 978-0-87113-947-4; Grove, 2007. paper ISBN 978-0-8021-4325-9. Grades YA.

This fictional biography of Sherlock Homes, detective, offers an overview of his lonely childhood, the years he was missing, his work for the British government, and the story behind his cocaine addition. He also befriended such figures as Sigmund Freud and Oscar Wilde. It also looks at his connections to the British criminal underworld, his criminal investigations, and his influence on the political situation of his time.

1680. Richards, Justin. *The Death Collector.* Bloomsbury, 2006. 320pp. ISBN 978-1-58234-721-9; 2007. paper ISBN 978-1-59990-148-0. Grades 7 up.

Fourteen-year-old pickpocket Eddie, 18-year-old clergyman's daughter Liz, and 19-year-old British Museum horologist George join forces to thwart an attempt by Mr. Lorimore to reanimate the dead. Their efforts lead them into danger, but Lorimore's intent becomes more apparent when Albert Wilkes comes home to tea four days after his death.

1681. Richler, Nancy. *Your Mouth Is Lovely: A Novel.* Ecco, 2003. 368pp. Paper ISBN 978-0-06-009678-6. Grades YA.

Miriam, a young Jewish woman, lives in Russia at the turn of the 20th century. As she sits in prison in 1911, she writes letters to the daughter she was forced to relinquish at birth. The daughter now lives with Miriam's Aunt Bayla in Canada. Miriam writes about her bitter but wise stepmother—Bayla's older sister Tsila— who raised Miriam after her mother's suicide and her father's abandonment. Tsila taught Miriam to speak by saying "your mouth is lovely"—she had to slice open Miriam's trachea when the girl had diphtheria as a child. Miriam left the shtetl for Kiev, where she became involved with revolutionaries and was imprisoned for murder during the Revolution of 1905. She now awaits either release or execution while writing her letter.

1682. Roiphe, Katie. *Still She Haunts Me: A Novel of Lewis Carroll and Alice Liddell.* Delta, 2002. 228pp. Paper ISBN 978-0-385-33530-0. Grades YA.

Lewis Carroll or Charles Dodgson (1832–1898), mathematician and photographer, had a friendship with Alice Liddell (1852–1934), daughter of a dean in his college. Their mutual admiration led Dodgson to write *Alice In Wonderland* for her. Roiphe examines Dodgson's photographs of Alice to interpret their possible relationship. Dodgson, a misfit, felt sexually attracted to Alice and he uses the surreal imagery of his story in which to create a fantastic place to live with Alice in this fictional account.

1683. Scott, Elaine. *Secrets of the Cirque Medrano.* Charlesbridge, 2008. 216pp. ISBN 978-1-57091-712-7. Grades 5–8.

After her mother dies, Brigitte Dubrinsky, 14, leaves Warsaw in 1904 to work with her aunt and uncle in their Parisian café. She hates the drudgery there and their assistant, Henri, but loves the performers at the Cirque Medrano. She and Picasso, who often eats at the café, join forces for their love of the cirque, and the situation lays the basis for Picasso's painting, "Family of Saltimbanques." As Bridgette becomes enamored with Montmartre, she discovers that Henri may be trying to sway Picasso to his revolutionary point of view as a member of the Russian Secret Police.

1684. Sedgwick, Marcus. *The Foreshadowing.* Wendy Lamb, 2006. 293pp. ISBN 978-0-385-74646-5; Laurel-Leaf, 2008. paper ISBN 978-0-553-48785-5. Grades 9 up.

Sasha, 15, wants to become a nurse during World War I, but her wealthy family has kept her sheltered. She then volunteers at the hospital, and she can foresee when someone is going to die. Her parents react uncomfortably to her confession, and they forget about it. Then when she gets a postcard from her brother Edgar who is serving in France, she hears his voice saying that he is dead. Later, she has a dream in which she sees another brother, Tom, being shot at Somme. She secretly travels to France to prevent his death. She meets Hoodoo Jack, who can also see the future, and he helps her find Tom.

1685. Simmons, Alex, and Bill McCay. *Buffalo Bill Wanted!* (Raven League) Razorbill, 2007. 202pp. ISBN 978-1-59514-073-9. Grades 4–6.

When Buffalo Bill Cody and a member of his troupe, a Sioux warrior, are touring in London, police blame them for attacking another policeman and scalping him. Buffalo Bill asks the Raven League for help in absolving them of the crime, as Sherlock Holmes is out of town.

1686. Simmons, Alex, and Bill McCay. *The Raven League: Sherlock Holmes Is Missing!* (Raven League) Sleuth RazorBill, 2006. 188pp. ISBN 978-1-59514-072-2. Grades 3–7.

The Baker Street Irregulars, the gang of urchins who assist Sherlock Holmes with his cases, kick Archie Wiggins out of the group. But almost immediately, Holmes goes missing. Archie makes three friends and forms the Raven League in order to help Holmes. While tracking the villains and attempting to convince Dr. Watson that Holmes is actually missing, they also uncover a plot to assassinate Queen Victoria on Jubilee Day. They are all able to save Holmes and Queen Victoria.

1687. Sole, Linda. *The Rose Arch.* Severn House, 2002. 224pp. ISBN 978-0-7278-7179-4. Grades YA.

In the late 19th century Jenny Heron must leave her life in France's Loire Valley for a convent in Paris when her mother discovers she has kissed someone. Her school friend runs away with a man, and then Jenny's mother dies. As the ward of Laurent de Array, she meets his son, Gerard, and falls in love.

1688. Sole, Linda. *A Rose in Winter.* Severn House, 2002. 256pp. ISBN 978-0-7278-7221-0. Grades YA.

During World War I, Julia, 17, falls in love with Charles Hamilton, a war hero amnesiac. They marry, but as Charles regains his memory, he has horrible mood swings. Julia discovers that he has been married before and that his wife died suspiciously. Then she finds out that someone, perhaps an inhabitant of the Hamilton's estate of Rondebush, is trying to kill her.

1689. Spillebeen, Geert. *Kipling's Choice.* Narrated by Terese Edelstein. Houghton, 2005. 160pp. ISBN 978-0-618-43124-3; Graphia, 2007. paper ISBN 978-0-618-80035-3. Grades 7 up.

Lt. John Kipling, 18, son of Rudyard Kipling, remembers his boyhood and events from his life while he lies dying during his only battle in Loos, France, in World War I. Because the British refused to accept him in the army due to his extreme nearsightedness, his overly zealous and patriotic father had made contacts with the Irish Guards so that John could prove himself. And most importantly, the narrative shows Rudyard Kipling wondering what he has done and if he has "written" other boys into their graves.

1690. Springer, Nancy. *The Case of the Bizarre Bouquets: An Enola Holmes Mystery.* (Enola Holmes Mystery) Philomel, 2008. 176pp. ISBN 978-0-399-24518-3. Grades 5–8.

Enola Holmes, 14, is still hiding in London's East End from her brothers, Mycroft and Sherlock. She has been using the alias "Ivy Meshle," but she decides to take a new identity when she thinks they have discovered her. She becomes "Viola Oversea." Her new case is finding Dr. Watson at the request of Mrs. Watson who has received a bizarre bouquet. Enola interprets the flowers as meaning that someone wants revenge, and she pursues the case in London during 1889.

1691. Springer, Nancy. *The Case of the Left-Handed Lady.* (Enola Holmes Mystery) Sleuth, 2007. 234pp. ISBN 978-0-399-24517-6; Puffin, 2008. paper ISBN 978-0-14-241190-2. Grades 5–9.

Enola Holmes, 14, does not want her brothers to send her to finishing school. She uses disguises as she sets up her own detective agency and then pretends to be the secretary so that she can solve the cases herself. When Sherlock Holmes's partner, Dr. Watson, asks her to find Lady Cecily, the missing teenage daughter of Sir Eustance Austair, she must keep a low profile as she moves around London seeking to solve the mystery.

1692. Springer, Nancy. *The Case of the Missing Marquess: An Enola Holmes Mystery.* (Enola Holmes Mystery) Philomel, 2006. 216pp. ISBN 978-0-399-24304-2; Puffin, 2007. paper ISBN 978-0-14-240933-6. Grades 4–8.

Enola Holmes, 14, calls her brothers, Sherlock and Mycroft, when her mother goes missing on Enola's birthday. The brothers arrive and assure Enola that they will find their mother, but that she has to return to boarding school. Enola travels to London in disguise where she thinks her mother may be. On the way, she becomes involved in the disappearance of a young marquess who seems to have been kidnapped. Enola uses her deductive powers to figure out his location, looks after herself, locates her mother, and establishes her business as "Perditorian," a person who will find things and other people. *Dorothy Canfield Fisher Children's Book Award* (Vermont) and *Great Stone Face Award* (New Hampshire) nomination.

1693. Springer, Nancy. *The Case of the Peculiar Pink Fan: An Enola Holmes Mystery.* (Enola Holmes Mystery) Philomel, 2008. 183pp. ISBN 978-0-399-24780-4. Grades 4–8.

Enola Holmes, 14, tries to save Lady Cecily Alistair, a hostage in a terrible orphanage, from an unwanted arranged marriage to her dandy cousin. Enola continues to evade her brothers and their determination that she receive a proper upbringing, by disguising herself as Ivy Meshle, secretary to a Dr. Leslie Ragostin. But when her brother Sherlock discovers her investigation, he helps; still, her other brother Mycroft tries to thwart her.

1694. Tal, Eve. *Double Crossing.* Cinco puntos, 2005. 216pp. ISBN 978-0-938317-94-4; 2007. paper ISBN 978-1-933693-15-6. Grades 5–9.

In 1905 Jewish Raizel, 11, and her father flee from Jibatov in the Ukraine to America, hoping to earn money and bring the rest of the family out of their restrictive life and danger from pogroms. Raizel thinks her brother should go on this journey, but he has to attend school and she does not. On the trip, her father is determined to keep kosher, and Raizel does not have enough to eat. To entertain them on the lengthy days aboard ship, she tells traditional stories to her father so that they can cope until they reach Ellis Island.

1695. Taylor, G. P. *Mariah Mundi: The Midas Box.* Putnam, 2008. 304pp. ISBN 978-0-399-24347-9. Grades 6–9.

In England during 1886, Mariah Mundi, 15, leaves London and starts working at the Prince Regent Hotel near the sea as a magician's assistant. He soon discovers that previous workers have disappeared, and he wants to find out the reason. Adults from the Bureau of Antiquities, a secret organization, help him since they are dedicated to keeping magic out of the hands of those who would abuse it.

1696. Todd, Charles. *A Fearsome Doubt: An Inspector Ian Rutledge Mystery.* (Inspector Ian Rutledge) Bantam, 2003. 304pp. Paper ISBN 978-0-55358-317-5. Grades YA.

In 1919, seven years after Ben Shaw is sent to the gallows for murdering elderly women, Shaw's widow tells Inspector Ian Rutledge that her husband was innocent. At the same time, Rutledge's sidekick, the ghost of the late Hamish MacLeod, whom Rutledge had executed during World War I, comments on the case. Rutledge fears that he may have sent the wrong man to the gallows when the widow offers new evidence that points to another serial killer. Rutledge investigates again and checks on the murder of two Kentish ex-soldiers.

1697. Toews, Mari. *Black and White Blanche.* Illustrated by Dianna Bonder. Fitzhenry & Whiteside, 2006. 32pp. ISBN 978-1-55005-132-2. Grades K–3.

Because Queen Victoria is mourning her husband and keeps herself draped in black, Blanche Weatherspoon's father requires that everyone in his household from siblings to servants should also wear black. Blanche, however, wants a pink dress. She tries to dye her petticoat pink with rose petals, and she visits Felicity, the local flower seller, attempting to add color to her life. Her father eventually realizes that color should be acceptable. Illustrations enhance the text.

1698. Trottier, Maxine. *The Long White Scarf.* Illustrated by David Craig. Fitzhenry & Whiteside, 2005. 32pp. ISBN 978-1-55005-147-6. Grades 1–4.

Queen Victoria's long white scarf blows away in the breeze. Among those who find it are first a Thames fisherman who gives it to his daughter. Then she gives it to her brother when he goes to war. When he is injured, the scarf becomes his sling and remains in the family when he returns. Later another breeze flies it to a shopkeeper who displays it. Then a little girl and her grandmother purchase it as a gift for the queen on her jubilee. A note adds that Queen Victoria crocheted eight scarves for soldiers herself. Illustrations enhance the text.

1699. Ungar, Richard. *Rachel's Library.* Illustrated by author. Tundra, 2004. 32pp. ISBN 978-0-8877-6678-7. Grades 2–4.

In the 19th century Rachel's shtetl of Chelm no longer wants to be considered foolish. She becomes a stowaway in a group of townspeople visiting Warsaw to decide what the town should do to improve its image. Rachel then goes to the Warsaw library and borrows a book. Afterward, she suggests that the town build a library. So to attract everyone, Chelm builds it around the village water pump. Illustrations complement the text.

1700. Updale, Eleanor. *Montmorency: Thief, Liar, Gentleman?* (Montmorency) Orchard, 2004. 240pp. ISBN 978-0-439-58035-9; Scholastic, 2005. paper ISBN 978-0-439-58036-6. Grades 6–10.

In 1875 Victorian London a young physician, Dr. Farcett, saves the life of a thief named Montmorency who fell through a glass roof while attempting to escape from the police. While in prison, Montmorency becomes the patient on display in a lecture showcasing Dr. Farcett's pioneering surgical skills, and overhears a description of the new 83-mile-long sewer system. Once released, he uses his knowledge about the sewer system, realizing it is a perfect escape route for any thief leaving an address in a wealthy neighborhood. He plans to use his new wealth to live as a gentleman in the elegant Marimion Hotel and snub any of the snobs who condescended to him when he was a medical exhibit. At the same time, he needs an alter ego, Scarper, who serves as Montmorency's sly thief and humble servant, slithering around back stairs and down sewers. Montmorency carefully prepares for each crime as he simultaneously hides his identity from his new society friends and from Dr. Farcett, who knows everything about his body. He eventually develops a conscience and decides to abandon crime for international intelligence work. The first volume in the series. *Nestlé Children's Book Prize* nomination, *Young Reader's Choice Award* nomination, *Beehive Young Adults' Book Award* (Utah) nomination, *Best Books for Children, American Library Association Best Books for Young Adults, Tayshas Reading List* (Texas), *Isinglass Award* (New Hampshire) nomination, *School Library Journal Best Children's Books,* and *Pacific Northwest Young Reader's Award* nomination.

1701. Updale, Eleanor. *Montmorency and the Assassins.* (Montmorency) Orchard, 2006. 404pp. ISBN 978-0-439-68343-2; Scholastic, 2007. paper ISBN 978-0-439-68344-9. Grades 6–10.

Montmorency has finally freed himself of his awful alter ego, Scarper, after being a gentleman for twenty years, but when a young friend needs his help after being caught in a political murder, Montmorency must resurrect Scarper. He and his friend Lord Fox-Selwyn go to Italy searching for rare specimens missing from Baron Astleman's natural history collection. There Fox-Selwyn's nephew Frank reveals knowledge of Italian anarchists with terrorist plans. The men then have to journey to America during these Victorian times to solve the problem.

1702. Updale, Eleanor. *Montmorency on the Rocks: Doctor, Aristocrat, Murderer.* (Montmorency) Orchard, 2005. 362pp. ISBN 978-0-439-60676-9; Scholastic, 2006. paper ISBN 978-0-439-60677-6. Grades 6–10.

Five years after Montmorency returns to society, he and Scarper, his alter ego, cooperate with Dr. Farcett to cure Montmorency's opium addiction. They go to Scotland where they must find out why Scottish children are being poisoned. Lord Fox-Selwyn works to rescue Montmorency from Scarper because threats to England's rail lines endanger all of them, and only Montmorency has the knowledge of the London underworld to identify the culprits. The second installment in the series.

1703. Updale, Eleanor. *Montmorency's Revenge.* (Montmorency) Orchard, 2007. 289pp. ISBN 978-0-439-81373-0. Grades 6–10.

While Queen Victoria lies dying, Montmorency and his friends try to help her family, in danger after anarchists have killed George Fox-Selwyn. Frank, George's nephew, and Montmorency want revenge while Dr. Farcett has become too depressed to function well. He remains in danger after his trips to four countries to find the killers when Frank assumes Montmorency's alter ego, Scarper. The fourth in the series.

1704. Uris, Leon. *Trinity.* Avon, 2006. 144pp. Paper ISBN 978-0-06-082788-5. Grades YA.

Seamus is 11 years old in 1885 when his friend Conor's grandfather, Kilty, dies. Kilty had survived the Irish potato famine and the unrest between the Irish Catholics and the ruling British Protestants. The same year, Seamus and Conor see Catholic homes and businesses destroyed, and they become part of the battle to win Ireland's freedom from England. Conor rises to leadership in the Irish Republican Army, and Seamus becomes a reporter. They tell the story of the hardships of the Irish in their fight for freedom.

1705. Vanneman, Alan. *Sherlock Holmes and the Giant Rat of Sumatra.* Carroll & Graf, 2003. 316pp. Paper ISBN 978-0-7867-1125-3. Grades YA.

After the death of a London rooming house resident, Sherlock Holmes and his sidekick Dr. Watson search for the murderer in Egypt, India, and Singapore. Among the enemies they encounter are the evil Harat and Lord Barrington, a dishonest blueblood. Surprisingly, Captain MacDougall and the beautiful widow Han help them find the culprit.

1706. Wallace, Karen. *The Unrivalled Spangles.* Atheneum, 2006. 240pp. ISBN 978-1-416-91503-4. Grades 6–10.

Ellen Spangle, 16, and her sister Lucy, 14, called the Amazing Scarletta Sisters, are the equestrienne stars of their father's circus in late 19th-century London's East End. But Ellen secretly wants to be a governess and has been earning money from homemade healing potions to pay a tutor to prepare her. A wealthy young man seems attracted to her, but he actually likes the act and her stage persona, Sapphire Scarletta. Then Lucy falls during a dangerous stunt and breaks her neck. Later, Ellen becomes enamored with a rival circus owner's son, Joe. All of this complicates her quest to be a governess. She must decide if she wants to help the family business or herself.

1707. Waters, Sarah. *Fingersmith.* Riverhead, 2002. 464pp. Paper ISBN 978-1-57322-972-2. Grades YA.

Sue Trinder, 17, an orphan raised in a loving family of thieves headed by Mrs. Sucksby, has to help the family steal more money. She becomes a maid to Maude Lilly, a wealthy girl who will be led to Richard Rivers (known as "Gentleman" to fingersmiths [thieves]) in Victorian London and presumably will marry him. He will take her money and then send her to the madhouse. But after Sue starts working she begins to like Maude and want to protect her. After an odd situation, Sue returns to the den where she discovers an unexpected relationship between her and Maude.

1708. Wax, Wendy. *Renoir and the Boy with the Long Hair: A Story About Pierre-Auguste Renoir.* Illustrated by Nancy Lane. Barron's, 2007. 28pp. ISBN 978-0-7641-6041-7. Grades 1–5.

When Renoir's son is an adult, standing in an art gallery, a bystander admires the girl in a Renoir painting. He corrects her, saying it is a boy and is in fact himself. Against all of his protests as a child, Renoir made him keep his hair long. Finally, when he is 7, another child was born, and the whole family goes to the barber to see his locks removed. He adds that Cézanne told him his father liked to see the light shining in his curls. Illustrations complement the text.

1709. Whelan, Gloria. *Angel on the Square.* HarperCollins, 2003. 304pp. Paper ISBN 978-0-06-440879-0. Grades 5–9.

In 1913 Russia 12-year-old Katya plays with Grand Duchess Anastasia while her widowed mother Irina performs her duties as lady-in-waiting to Empress Alexandra, wife of Tsar Nicholas II. Although aristocrats, Katya and her mother have difficulty supporting Tsar Nikolai's treatment of those less fortunate. Katya's friend Misha continues to talk of the poverty and hardships of child laborers. Katya sees Tsar Nikolai's love for his family and wonders at his behavior. When rioters begin the Russian Revolution and imprison the Romanovs in their home, Katya and Irina leave. They realize that the new regime will not allow them the life they once selfishly enjoyed, and they travel to their summer dacha. But it has been destroyed, so Katya herself builds her mother a home. After she completes it she takes control of her own life and, at 18, returns to St. Petersburg to join Misha. *Great Lakes Great Books Award* (Michigan) nomination and *Beehive Award* (Utah) nomination.

1710. Whelan, Gloria. *Parade of Shadows.* HarperCollins, 2007. 295pp. ISBN 978-0-06-089028-5. Grades 7 up.

In 1907 Julia Hamilton, 16, accompanies her diplomat father on a tour of the Ottoman cities of of Istanbul, Damascus, Palmyra, and Aleppo. Julia soon learns that the journey has unexpected dangers, and she notices political problems and corrupt officials. When she falls in love with Graham, a young man accompanying them who has his own agenda, she begins to weigh her father's view against that of the Young Turks who seek power.

1711. Whitehouse, Howard. *The Faceless Fiend: Being the Tale of a Criminal Mastermind, His Masked Minions and a Princess with a Butter Knife, Involving Explosives and a Certain Amount of Pushing and Shoving.* Illustrated by Bill Slavin. (Mad Misadventures of Emmaline and Rubberbones) Kids Can, 2007. 272pp. ISBN 978-1-55453-130-1; paper ISBN 978-1-55453-180-6. Grades 5–8.

In 1894 Emmaline, 14, and her friend Rubberbones escape along with Princess Purdah from St. Grimelda's School for Young Ladies and go to Yorkshire to live with Emmaline's batty Aunt Lucy Butterworth. The Faceless Fiend is trying to kidnap Princess Purdah and take over her country of Chilgrit on the border of India and Tibet, so they try to protect her and the butler, Lal Singh. To help them foil the criminals is Sherlock Holmes and his group of Irregulars. At the climax, Emmaline gets a chance to fly a glider.

1712. Whitehouse, Howard. *The Strictest School in the World: Being the Tale of a Clever Girl, a Rubber Boy and a Collection of Flying Machines, Mostly Broken.* Illustrated by Bill Slavin. (Mad Misadventures of Emmaline and Rubberbones) Kids Can, 2006. 252pp. ISBN 978-1-55337-882-2. Grades 5–8.

The parents of Emmaline Cayley, 14, send her back to England from India so she can learn to be a proper young lady and forget about designing flying machines. She must attend St. Grimelda's School for Young Ladies, a place that proves to be horrible, with an evil head mistress and two pterodactyls to keep girls from escaping. Eventually Emmaline's friend Robert Burns (known as Rubberbones because he can fall without getting hurt) and her mad Aunt Lucy help her to escape.

1713. Williams, Marcia. *Archie's War: My Scrapbook of the First World War.* Illustrated by author. Candlewick, 2007. 48pp. ISBN 978-0-7636-3532-9. Grades 3–6.

In 1914 Archie Albright, 10, lives in East London. His Uncle Colin sends him a scrapbook, and Archie begins placing photographs and other items that chronicle World War I. He shows the rise of patriotism among those he knows, including the shunning of those with German names and his father's refusal to allow his sister to join antiwar protests. His Uncle Teddy dies in battle, a friend's street is bombed, Archie's brother returns injured, and a neighbor is shell-shocked. He wants to hear from his father on the front and secretly admires the German pilot known as the Red Baron. As Archie concludes his scrapbook four years later, he hopes that this is the last war but realizes he can no longer trust adults. Glossary.

1714. Wilson, John. *And in the Morning.* Kids Can, 2003. 200pp. ISBN 978-1-55337-400-8; 2004. paper ISBN 978-1-55337-348-3. Grades 8 up.

Jim Hay, 15, faces the death of his father in World War I by entering the service himself after his mother has an emotional breakdown. He has to leave Scotland to fight in the trenches of France during the Battle of Somme in 1916, a situation that changes his attitude. He records his feelings in a diary and in letters to his girlfriend, Anne Cunningham. He admits to wanting someplace clean without the horror of war surrounding him. But his family has a secret, and in the end this secret is revealed. Note.

1715. Zangwill, Israel. *The Big Bow Mystery.* Illustrated by Justin Weber and Thien Tran. Dybbuk, 2007. 196pp. Paper ISBN 978-0-9766546-3-6. Grades YA.

Mrs. Drabdump's tenant, a labor leader, does not respond to her knock on the door. She calls Inspector Goodman who knocks down the door, and they find the tenant dead in his bedroom with his throat cut. Oddly, the door is locked from the inside. Among the Victorian characters in this first locked-door mystery first published more than one hundred years ago are the poet, Denzil Cantercot, who eschews humor, and Peter Crowl, the cobbler who thinks he can think, and other odd characters.

History

1716. Adams, Simon. *World War I.* Illustrated by Andy Crawford. Kingfisher, 2004. 64pp. ISBN 978-0-7566-0740-1. Grades 6 up.

The author looks at life in the trenches during World War I and the loss of life on both sides due to combat and non-combat causes. The two-page spreads cover topics including enlisting, communication, supplies, bombardment, women in the war, Zeppelin, Gallipoli, Verdun, the Eastern Front, espionage, and tank warfare. Illustrations enhance the text. Glossary and Index.

1717. Allan, Tony. *The Causes of World War I.* (20th Century Perspectives) Heinemann, 2002. 48pp. ISBN 978-1-4034-0148-9; 2003. paper ISBN 978-1-4034-4620-6. Grades 7 up.

Readers will learn about the reasons for World War I as well as the key issues and consequences of the Great War. Illustrations highlight the text. Bibliography, Further Reading, Glossary, and Index.

1718. Allan, Tony. *The Russian Revolution.* (20th Century Perspectives) Heinemann, 2002. 48pp. ISBN 978-1-4034-0151-9. Grades 4–8.

A look at the causes of the Russian Revolution, key issues and events, and the aftermath, with profiles of leaders and important figures. Bibliography, Further Reading, Glossary, Index.

1719. Baker, Julie. *The Great Whaleship Disaster of 1871.* Morgan Reynolds, 2007. 144pp. ISBN 978-1-59935-043-1. Grades 6 up.

In 1871 thirty-two ships trapped in Arctic ice carried 1,200 men, women, and children with limited supplies. The difficult decision was made to leave the ships and set out in small boats. Baker provides lots of background information on whaling and the related hazards. Archival photographs and illustrations highlight the text. Bibliography, Chronology, Web Sites, and Index.

1720. Beller, Susan Provost. *The Doughboys Over There: Soldiering in World War I.* (Soldiers on the Battlefront) Lerner, 2003. 112pp. ISBN 978-0-8225-6295-5. Grades 5–8.

The author examines the events leading up to the war, the principal battles, and the major leaders involved. She also notes the horrors that the Allied troops faced and the ensuing conflicts. Fact boxes offer extraneous but important information about such topics as poison gas used against the soldiers fighting in the trenches. Black-and-white photographs highlight the text. Bibliography, Chronology, Further Reading, Web Sites, and Index.

1721. Bingham, Mindy. *Berta Benz and the Motorwagen.* Illustrated by Itoko Maeno. Advocacy, 1992. 48pp. ISBN 978-0-911655-38-4. Grades K–5.

In 1888 a German housewife and her two sons steal away from home in one of the motorcars that Karl Benz has invented. A local law restricts the use of the invention, so Benz cannot prove how useful it can be. His wife purchases fuel at pharmacies, but the cross-country trip is successful in showing the value of the invention.

1722. Blackwood, Gary L. *The Great Race: The Amazing Round-the-World Auto Race of 1908.* Abrams, 2008. 144pp. ISBN 978-0-8109-9489-8. Grades 5–9.

In 1908 the *New York Times* and the French paper *Le Matin* sponsored a race around the world in which six cars took part, crossing America, Siberia, and then Europe before ending in Paris. Since cars were not yet dependable, the racers needed a crew that could display ingenuity in dealing with mechanical malfunctions. Cars had several gas tanks, got no more than 8 miles per gallon, and could go as fast as 50 miles per hour. Among the problems were broken crankshafts, twisted axles, and blown pistons, but someone finally won by driving on railroad tracks. Illustrations enhance the text. Bibliography, Notes, and Web Sites.

1723. Bosco, Peter I., and Antoinette Bosco. *World War I.* Facts on File, 2003. 162pp. ISBN 978-0-8160-4940-0. Grades YA.

Before World War I the United States had established a policy of isolationism. Bosco tells why America changed its policy to enter World War I and discusses military logistics, political maneuvering, and the terrors of battle. He focuses on several conflicts such as Belleau Wood and the Argonne. Bibliography and Index.

1724. Caper, William. *Nightmare on the Titanic.* (Code Red) Bearport, 2007. 32pp. ISBN 978-1-59716-362-0. Grades 3–6.

The author examines the sinking of the "unsinkable" *Titanic* in 1912 based on primary sources from those who witnessed it. Additional brief profiles of people who affected the situation also appear. Photographs, maps, and reproductions highlight the text. Glossary, Further Reading, Web Sites, and Index.

1725. Chambers, Paul. *Jumbo: This Being the True Story of the Greatest Elephant in the World.* Steerforth, 2008. 224pp. ISBN 978-1-58642-141-0. Grades YA.

Jumbo, the world's most famous elephant, was born in Africa in 1862 and captured by ivory hunters who killed his mother and the rest of his family. He traveled to zoos in Europe and eventually to America to join P. T. Barnum's Greatest Show on Earth. For twenty years, Matthew Scott was his keeper. Jumbo died when he was struck by a locomotive in 1885. Bibliography and Notes.

1726. Coetzee, Frans, and Marilyn Shevin-Coetzee. *World War I: A History in Documents.* (Pages from History) Oxford, 2002. 176pp. ISBN 978-0-19-513746-0. Grades 7 up.

World War I remains in memory based on how soldiers, politicians, artists, writers, and civilians have depicted it. In the United States the war led to technological improvements, experimentation in the arts, and furthered women's suffrage. This account includes excerpts from memoirs, diaries, poetry, fiction, posters, song lyrics, and government documents to create a concept of the effect of this war on the world. Reproductions highlight the text. Further Reading, Time Line, Maps, and Index.

1727. Curlee, Lynn. *Liberty.* Illustrated by author. Aladdin, 2003. 41pp. Paper ISBN 978-0-689-85683-9. Grades 3–8.

Curlee presents the details that enabled France's gift of the Statue of Liberty to be designed by Frédéric Auguste Bartholdi (1834–1904), sculpted, and shipped to the United States with funds raised mainly by Joseph Pulitzer. Curlee personifies the statue, Lady Liberty, and explains many of the difficulties behind her construction. Illustrations complement the text. Chronology. *Student Book Award* (Maine) nomination, *Capi-*

tol Choices Noteworthy Titles (Washington, D.C.), and *Children's Book Awards* (Rhode Island).

1728. Damon, Duane C. *Life in Victorian England.* (Way People Live) Lucent, 2005. 112pp. ISBN 978-1-56006-391-9. Grades 9 up.

Damon looks at life in England during Queen Victoria's reign, most of the 19th century. The book covers the quality of life for all classes, education reform, social life and courtship, leisure activities, and religion. Sidebars discuss slum diseases, getting married, funeral rituals, and other aspects of this time with primary source quotations. Photographs and illustrations highlight the text. Bibliography, Further Reading, Web Sites, and Index.

1729. Dando, William A. *Russia.* (Modern World Nations) Chelsea House, 2007. 141pp. ISBN 978-0-7910-9248-4. Grades 8 up.

Readers will learn about Russia's history from the tsarist period through the Soviet Union and the Russian Federation. Topics include population, economic developments, government, landscape, and culture. Illustrations highlight the text along with maps. Bibliography, Chronology, Further Reading, Glossary, Web Sites, and Index.

1730. Dowswell, Paul. *Weapons and Technology of World War I.* (20th Century Perspectives) Heinemann, 2002. 48pp. ISBN 978-1-58810-662-9. Grades 5–8.

In World War I a number of new weapons were developed. Among these were more effective machine guns; the "Big Bertha" howitzer; grenades containing chlorine, phosgene, or mustard gas; improved communication with radios and telephones; tanks known as "the Chariots of God"; and planes. The author discusses these technologies and their uses. Illustrations highlight the text. Bibliography, Further Reading, Glossary, Index.

1731. Finkelstein, Norman. *Captain of Innocence: France and the Dreyfus Affair.* Backinprint.Com, 2001. 160pp. Paper ISBN 978-0-595-15651-1. Grades YA.

Alfred Dreyfus, a quiet Jewish army captain, was "degraded" in January of 1895 after exemplary military service. The question remains as to whether he was guilty of his alleged crime or if he was a victim of anti-Semitism. Émile Zola, a well-known French writer, wrote an article about the "Dreyfus affair," titled *J'accuse*, which stunned the world. Zola noted various discrepancies in the evidence presented at the court martial. Finkelstein explores the events that led to Dreyfus's arrest, imprisonment, and subsequent trial. Time Line, Who's Who, Selected Bibliography, and Index.

1732. Granfield, Linda. *In Flanders Fields.* Illustrated by Janet Wilson. Fitzhenry & Whiteside, 2005. Unpaged. Paper ISBN 978-1-55005-144-5. Grades 4–6.

Using the poem "In Flanders Fields" as a base, Granfield discusses the poem, gives an overview of World War I, and briefly describes the life of the Canadian poet John McCrae. Sketches, photographs, and memorabilia add to the illustrations.

1733. Granfield, Linda. *Where Poppies Grow: A World War I Companion.* Stoddard, 2002. 48pp. ISBN 978-0-7737-3319-0; Fitzhenry & Whiteside, 2005. paper ISBN 978-1-55005-146-9. Grades 6–10.

This World War I scrapbook for older readers contains letters, cartoons, postcards, prints, newspaper clippings, photographs, and other memorabilia to give an overview of war in Europe, the United States, and Canada. Double-page spreads focus on aspects including the effects of the war, daily life, patriotism, and conditions in the trenches. Index.

1734. Grant, R. G. *Armistice 1918.* (World Wars) Raintree, 2001. 64pp. ISBN 978-0-7398-2753-6. Grades 5–9.

Primary source documents and firsthand accounts detail the negotiations for peace in World War I. Grant reviews the trench warfare that occurred, the main battles, and other aspects of the war before the terms of the Treaty of Versailles were reached and the League of Nations formed. However, the League failed, and the punishments imposed upon countries after the war as a result of the treaty led directly to World War II. Illustrations and photographs enhance the text. Maps, Chronology, Bibliography, and Glossary.

1735. Greene, Meg. *The Eiffel Tower.* (Building World Landmarks) Blackbirch, 2003. 48pp. ISBN 978-1-56711-315-0. Grades 5–8.

Gustav Eiffel designed his tower using inventive construction techniques, and he was determined to finish it ahead of schedule. Officials appreciated his timely completion of the ambitious project. Photographs enhance the text. Chronology, Glossary, Further Reading, and Index.

1736. Greenwood, Mark. *The Donkey of Gallipoli: A True Story of Courage in World War I.* Illustrated by Frane Lessac. Candlewick, 2008. 32pp. ISBN 978-0-7636-3913-6. Grades 5–7.

When Jack Simpson is a boy, he works with his friend Billy in northeast England in the summers at a beachfront donkey ride. After Jack emigrates to Australia when he is 17, he enlists in the army and goes to fight during World War I in Gallipoli against the Turks. As an ANZAC stretcher bearer, he sees a donkey cowering in a ditch, and he carefully soothes the frightened animal. Then the donkey helps him carry the wounded, even transporting the unrecognized and wounded Billy before he dies from a bullet like 300,000 of his peers. Gouache paintings enhance the text. Bibliography and Notes. *Kirkus Reviews Editor's Choice, Notable Trade Books in the Field of Social Studies.*

1737. Hamilton, John. *Aircraft of World War I.* (World War I) ABDO, 2003. 32pp. ISBN 978-1-57765-912-9. Grades 5–8.

The author examines the events that led to the outbreak of World War I in 1914 and how the fighting during that war changed modern warfare. Along with trench warfare and new weapons were aircraft. This account traces the beginning of airplanes as fighting machines and the advent of "Aces," men recognized as heroes. Photographs and illustrations highlight the text. Glossary, Chronology, and Index.

1738. Hamilton, John. *Battles of World War I.* (World War I) ABDO, 2003. 32pp. ISBN 978-1-57765-913-6. Grades 5–8.

This account includes eight well-known battles that occurred in World War I before the Americans entered in 1917. Among those discussed are the Marne in 1914 and Ypres in 1917. Photographs and illustrations highlight the text. Maps, Glossary, Chronology, and Index.

1739. Hamilton, John. *Events Leading to World War I.* (World War I) ABDO, 2003. 32pp. ISBN 978-1-57765-914-3. Grades 5–8.

Readers will learn about the events that led to World War I, as the book discusses the conditions and circumstances in the participating countries. Photographs and illustrations highlight the text. Maps, Glossary, Chronology, and Index.

1740. Hansen, Arlen J. *Gentlemen Volunteers: The Story of the American Ambulance Drivers in the Great War: August 1914–September 1918.* Arcade, 1996. 254pp. ISBN 978-1-55970-313-0. Grades YA.

In World War I American volunteers, mainly from Ivy League schools, went to Flanders to drive ambulances. There they took the "Lizzies," or ambulances, through mud and fire while they transported the wounded. Although most of them returned, their experiences gave them a sense of camaraderie that they could not retain at home. Index.

1741. Hatt, Christine. *World War I: 1914–1918.* Watts, 2001. 64pp. ISBN 978-0-531-14611-8. Grades 6–9.

A combination of primary and secondary sources presents background on World War I. Among these are diary entries, government documents, and newspaper accounts. The double-page spreads also contain maps, charts, and photographs about the conflicts of the war and those who fought in it. Illustrations also highlight the text. Index.

1742. Hicks, Brian. *Ghost Ship: The Mysterious True Story of the Mary Celeste and Her Missing Crew.* Ballantine, 2005. 304pp. Paper ISBN 978-0-345-46665-5. Grades YA.

In the spring 1861 the *Mary Celeste* was launched in the Bay of Fundy. Eleven years later, on December 4, 1872, the crew of *Dei Gratia*, a Nova Scotia freighter, found the 100-foot brigantine floating in the Atlantic about 400 miles from Portugal's coast with no one aboard. The last log entry, dated ten days before, placed the ship 300 miles west. In solving this mystery, Hicks traces the known facts about the *Mary Celeste*. The captain died on the maiden voyage to London when the ship hit and sank an English brigantine. Then a storm drove her ashore at Cape Breton, and the crew abandoned her. In the autumn of 1872, Benjamin Spooner Briggs sailed on the refitted ship with his wife and child and seven crewmen, but none were found when Briggs's friend, the captain of the *Dei Gratia*, David Reed Morehouse, boarded the ship. Morehouse claimed the ship for salvage, and a trial began. Finally in 1885, people involved in an insurance scam had the ship deliberately sunk. Photographs and Index.

1743. Howard, Michael. *The First World War.* Oxford, 2003. 154pp. Paper ISBN 978-0-19-280445-7. Grades YA.

These nine chapters cover each year of World War I beginning with the coming of the war and the state of Europe's political liaisons in 1914. Howard notes that generals initially heralded the trench warfare that led to so many casualties as the way to achieve a breakthrough. Their failure is one of the reasons the United States entered the war in 1917. In essence, the narrative concisely covers the material, theory, and argument about the war. Maps and illustrations augment the text. Further Reading and Index.

1744. Jenkins, Martin. *Titanic.* Illustrated by Brian Sanders. Candlewick, 2007. Unpaged. ISBN 978-0-7636-3468-1. Grades 4–6.

This pop-up book includes a 30-inch model of the tragic *Titanic* as it would have been on its voyage in April 1912, with smaller side flaps holding six smaller interior views. It also contains pockets with a ticket, a menu, and other items. Deck plans offer information about the different levels and who could stay on each one, and other pages offer mechanical information and safety features. Chronology.

1745. Kent, Zachary. *World War I: "The War to End Wars".* (American War) Enslow, 2000. Paper ISBN 978-0-7660-1732-0. Grades 6 up.

Starting with the sinking of the *Lusitania* in 1915, Kent relates the progress of World War I from its beginning in Sarajevo in August 1914 until its end in November 1918. This account presents the major battles starting with the Hindenburg Line marked by the Germans, Belleau Wood, the Marne, Saint-Mihiel, and the Meuse-Argonne offensive. Among the leaders on both sides were Captain Baron Manfred von Richthofen, "The Red Baron"; Sergeant York; General Douglas MacArthur; and General John J. (Black Jack) Pershing. During the war, more than 116,000 American soldiers died, as well as 4 million more from other nations. Afterward, President Woodrow Wilson tried to start the League of Nations, but American isolationism defeated his plan. Photographs complement the text. Chronology, Notes, Further Reading, and Index.

1746. Kirchberger, Joe H. *The First World War: An Eyewitness History.* Facts on File, 1992. 402pp. ISBN 978-0-8160-2552-7. Grades YA.

In 1914 Austria-Hungary and Serbia had a disagreement that, fueled by the assassination of Archduke Francis Ferdinand of Austria, escalated into a major war involving Russia, Germany, France, Britain, Japan, and Turkey. By 1917 the United States had joined. This war, also known as the Great War, changed European history. The book includes many firsthand accounts of the war from memoirs, speeches, newspapers, and letters. Some of the commentaries come from T. E. Lawrence (Lawrence of Arabia), Woodrow Wilson, Otto von Bismarck, and Vladimir Lenin. Each chapter includes an essay about the area of the war it presents and a chronology of events. Appendices, Bibliography, and Index.

1747. Leboutillier, Nate. *Eiffel Tower.* (Modern Wonders of the World) Creative, 2006. 32pp. ISBN 978-1-58341-438-5. Grades 3–6.

Gustaf Eiffel constructed the Eiffel Tower in Paris, France, as the center of the 1889 Universal Exposition of the Products of Industry. It became a landmark that symbolizes this city to this day. The author looks at the conception of the Eiffel Tower, its construction, and the public's reaction to it when finished. Photographs highlight the text.

1748. Liberatore, Karen. *Our Century: 1910–1920.* Gareth Stevens, 1993. 64pp. ISBN 978-0-8368-1033-2. Grades 3 up.

Written in the style of a newspaper, this book's short articles give an overview of the decade. Included are statistics, daily life in America, the *Titanic* sinking, Archduke Ferdinand's murder, World War I, the overthrow of Nicholas I of Russia, the Bolsheviks, the flu epidemic, suffragettes, Prohibition, Pancho Villa's border town raids, the first assembly line, progress on the Panama Canal, the Black Sox baseball scandal, Woodrow Wilson, Vladimir Lenin, Louis B. Brandeis, Eugene Debs, Margaret Sanger, D. W. Griffith, Mary Pickford, and Charlie Chaplin. Glossary, Books for Further Reading, Places to Write or Visit, and Index.

1749. Maestro, Betsy. *The Story of the Statue of Liberty.* Illustrated by Giulio Maestro. Mulberry, 1989. 40pp. Paper ISBN 978-0-688-08746-3. Grades K–4.

The building of the Statue of Liberty began in 1871 after Frédérick Auguste Bartholdi visited New York and saw Bedloe's Island in New York Harbor. He saw this place as the perfect setting for a statue that he would create for the French government to present as a gift to the United States on the occasion of its birthday. He completed it in 1884, and money raised by a New York newspaper funded the completion of the base so that it could be mounted when it arrived from France in 1885. Information About the Statue of Liberty.

1750. Malam, John. *You Wouldn't Want to Be a Victorian Mill Worker! A Grueling Job You'd Rather Not Have.* Illustrated by David Antram. (You Woudn't Want To . . .) Franklin Watts, 2007. 32pp. ISBN 978-0-531-18747-0; paper ISBN 978-0-531-13928-8. Grades 3–6.

During the 19th century many children not much older than 11 worked in the cotton mills in England for long hours, low pay, and no education. This book offers a look at this time with humor and cartoon illustrations. Glossary and Index.

1751. Mallon, Bill. *The 1900 Olympic Games: Complete Results for All Competitors in All Events, with Commentary.* (History of the Early Olympics) McFarland, 1997. 351pp. ISBN 978-0-7864-0378-3. Grades YA.

In 1900 the modern Olympics continued as begun in 1896 under Baron Pierre de Coubertin. Among the highlights of these games were the four gold medals won in track and field by Alvin Kraenzlein. The text includes dates, sites, events, competitors, nations, and results of contests. Notes, Bibliography, and Index.

1752. Mallon, Bill. *The 1904 Olympic Games: Results for All Competitors in All Events, With Commentary.* (History of the Early Olympics) McFarland, 1997. 287pp. ISBN 978-0-7864-0550-3. Grades YA.

In 1904 the Olympic Games were held in St. Louis, Missouri, as part of the World's Fair. A part of the games was an unusual activity called "Anthropology Days" in which "primitive" tribes competed against each other. The text records results for archery, track and field, boxing, cycling, diving, fencing, football (soccer), golf, gymnastics, lacrosse, rowing and sculling, swimming, lawn tennis, tug-of-war, weightlifting, and wrestling. The non-Olympic sports played were American football, baseball, basketball, roque, and water polo. Notes, Bibliography, Appendices, and Index.

1753. Mallon, Bill. *The 1906 Olympic Games: Results for All Competitors in All Events, with Commentary.* (History of the Early Olympics) McFarland, 1999. 250pp. ISBN 978-0-7864-0551-0. Grades YA.

The 1906 Olympic Games were the first interim games and were called the Intercalated Athens Olympics. Originally these games were intended to be held every four years in Athens. However, they are not considered official Olympic games. The text records results for track and field, cycling, diving, fencing, football (soccer), gymnastics, rowing and sculling, shooting, swimming, lawn tennis, tug-of-war, weightlifting, and wrestling. Notes, Bibliography, Appendices, and Index.

1754. Mallon, Bill, and Ian Buchanan. *The 1908 Olympic Games: Results for All Competitors in All Events, with Commentary.* (History of the Early Olympics) McFarland, 2000. 536pp. ISBN 978-0-7864-0598-5. Grades YA.

The controversial 1908 Olympic Games were called "The Battle of Shepherds Bush" for their location in London. Not all of the results are available for the competitions in the games, but this volume reports what is still available from 1908 primary sources. All of the sites, dates, events, competitors, and nations are available for boxing, cycling, diving, fencing, field hockey, lacrosse, polo, racquets, swimming, lawn tennis, tug-of-war, weightlifting, wrestling, and yachting, among other sports. Full results are not available for archery, track and field, football (soccer), gymnastics, motor boating, and shooting. Notes, Appendices, Bibliography, and Index.

1755. Mallon, Bill, and Ture Widlund. *The 1896 Olympic Games: Results for All Competitors in All Events, with Commentary.* (History of the Early Olympics) McFarland, 1997. 168pp. ISBN 978-0-7864-0379-0. Grades YA.

In 1896 the modern Olympics began in Athens, Greece, under the impetus of Baron Pierre de Coubertin. The full results of these games, however, do not exist. Based on primary sources from 1896, this book chronicles the dates, sites, events, competitors, nations, and results of various contests. Among the contest events included are track and field, cycling, fencing, gymnastics, shooting, swimming, tennis (lawn), weightlifting, and wrestling. Notes, Bibliography, and Index.

1756. Mallon, Bill, and Ture Widlund. *The 1912 Olympic Games: Results for All Competitors in All Events, with Commentary.* (History of the Early Olympics) McFarland, 2001. 578pp. ISBN 978-0-7864-1047-7. Grades YA.

In 1912 the Stockholm, Sweden, Olympic Games were successful because of the organizational skills of Viktor Balck, "The Father of Swedish Sports." Among the new technologies in use in 1912 were semiautomatic electrical timing and a photo-finish camera. The new events were the decathlon and the modern pentathlon. Among the results included are those for cycling, diving, fencing, rowing and sculling, shooting, tennis, water polo, and yachting. Notes, Appendices, Bibliography, and Index.

1757. Molony, Senan. *Titanic: A Primary Source History.* (In Their Own Words) Gareth Stevens, 2006. 48pp. ISBN 978-0-8368-5980=5. Grades 5–8.

Using primary sources from newspapers, government documents, letters, poems, telegrams, speeches, radio broadcasts, songs, and contemporary interviews, Molony covers the sinking of the *Titanic* in 1912. Photographs, maps, and illustrations enhance the text. Glossary, Chronology, and Index.

1758. Niven, Jennifer. *The Ice Master: The Doomed 1913 Voyage of the Karluk.* Hyperion, 2001. 402pp. Paper ISBN 978-0-7868-8446-9. Grades YA.

In 1913 Vihjalmur Stefansson wanted to explore uncharted land in the Arctic. He had little money so he purchased an inadequate ship, the *Karluk* and brought too few supplies. After a month the ship became trapped and Stefansson left the crew and scientists to get help. These twenty-five eventually had to leave the ship after the ice crushed it and it began sinking. They lived on the ice until spring when they reached Wrangle Island. There they argued with each other and wrote their feelings in their diaries. Eleven of them survived long enough to leave the island when the captain returned from his 700-mile trek to Siberia with another boat. Photographs augment the text. Maps and Notes.

1759. Parks, Peggy J. *Impressionism.* (Eye on Art) Lucent, 2006. 104pp. ISBN 978-1-59018-958-0. Grades 6–9.

Six chapters explore the initial response to impressionism (critics called it "shocking" and "complete craziness"), its roots as a revolution, its difficult growth, its acceptance, and the movement of post-impressionism that followed. Also included are brief biographies of the artists in the movement. Reproductions highlight the text. Notes, Further Reading, and Index.

1760. Pezzi, Bryan. *Eiffel Tower.* Weigl, 2007. 32pp. ISBN 978-1-59036-719-3; paper ISBN 978-1-59036-720-9. Grades 5–9.

At the time of its construction for the World's Fair in Paris in 1889, the Eiffel Tower was an architectural triumph. The author examines the technology behind the structure that made building it possible as well as its significance at the time. Photographs highlight the text. Glossary, Further Reading, Web Sites, and Index.

1761. Pollard, Michael. *The Nineteenth Century.* Facts on File, 1993. 78pp. ISBN 978-0-8160-2791-0. Grades 4–7.

See entry 1476.

1762. Robinson, Shannon. *Cubism.* (Movements in Art) Creative, 2005. 48pp. ISBN 978-1-58341-347-0. Grades 6 up.

Readers learn about the cultural and social influences that fostered this artistic movement from Picasso and Braque onward. Robinson shows cubism in relation to history and the scientific inventions of the time. Large reproductions highlight the text. Chronology, Glossary, Further Reading, and Index.

1763. Ross, Stewart. *The Battle of the Somme.* (World Wars) Raintree, 2004. 64pp. ISBN 978-0-7398-5479-2. Grades 5–8.

Information from primary source documents including firsthand accounts and archival photographs is presented about the Battle of the Somme of World War I. The book includes reasons for the battle and its planning process as well as the strategy involved for the huge British and French offensive against entrenched Germans in 1916 that cost the Allies 58,000 lives on the first day of fighting. The Second Battle of the Somme occurred in 1918. Illustrations augment the text. Maps, Glossary, Further Reading, Chronology, Bibliography, and Index.

1764. Ross, Stewart. *The Russian Revolution.* Heinemann/Raintree, 2002. 78pp. ISBN 978-0-7398-5801-1. Grades 7 up.

This book examines the causes, events, aftermath, and historical significance of the 1917 revolution in Russia, led by Lenin, Trotsky, and Kerensky. Index.

1765. Ross, Stuart. *The Technology of World War I.* (World Wars) Raintree, 2003. 64pp. ISBN 978-0-7398-5482-2. Grades 5–9.

During World War I, new military technology evolved on all fronts—land, sea, and air. New weaponry included torpedoes, airplanes, and poison gas, which antiquated previous ways of fighting. Other new technologies included barbed wire, telephone, telegraph, radio, machine gun advancements, rifles, the super dreadnought, the submarine, and aircraft carriers. Dropping bombs was also new. Photographs highlight the text. Chronology, Glossary, Sources, Further Reading, Web Sites, and Index.

1766. Ruddick, James H. *Death at the Priory: Love, Sex, and Murder in Victorian England.* Grove/Atlantic, 2002. 236pp. Paper ISBN 978-0-8021-3974-0. Grades YA.

After widow Florence Ricardo married Charles Bravo in 1875, they lived in her mansion, the Priory, outside London. Bravo abused her and the servants and dismissed her longtime companion, Mrs. Cox. One night while preparing for bed a few months after the marriage, Bravo collapsed. Physicians who attended him could do nothing, and three days later he died. They decided he had been poisoned, and the details of the case mesmerized Victorian England. Among the suspects were Florence, her secret lover, Dr. James Gully, Mrs. Cox, and a dismissed stable man, George Griffiths. No one was convicted of the crime. After consulting unpublished letters and family papers, Ruddick surmises that Florence Bravo poisoned her husband and was able to hide the crime with the help of her housekeeper. Notes, Reference Sources, and Index. *Edgar Awards* nomination.

1767. Saunders, Nicholas. *World War I: A Primary Source History.* (In Their Own Words) Gareth Stevens, 2005. 48pp. ISBN 978-0-8368-5982-9. Grades 5–8.

Among the topics covered in this overview of World War I using primary sources are the circumstances that led to the war, international leaders of the time, how it affected the rest of the century, memorials to the dead, depiction of the war in art, and artifacts from the war being discovered today. Maps, photographs and illustrations complement the text. Glossary, Chronology, and Index.

1768. Schneider, Dorothy, and Carl J. Schneider. *Into the Breach: American Women Overseas in World War I.* Iuniverse, 2000. 368pp. Paper ISBN 978-0-595-00201-6. Grades YA.

Twenty-five thousand middle-class, educated American women served in Europe during World War I. They were peace activists, journalists, nurses and Red Cross workers, physicians, Salvation Army and YMCA workers, and canteen workers. This account uses primary sources such as written memoirs, diaries, letters, and interviews, with secondary sources such as novels, to tell the story of these women serving in Europe, Asia, and the Middle East, where more than 340 died. An appendix lists the occupations and organizations in which the women served and the number for each. Bibliography and Index.

1769. Strachan, Hew. *The First World War.* Penguin, 2005. 384pp. Paper ISBN 978-0-14-303518-3. Grades YA.

For his thesis that the effects of World War I are continuing to impact history, Strachan offers a number of observations. He also includes sidebars about often-disregarded topics such as the French treatment of deserters. In addition to Western Europe the struggle encompassed Africa, the Middle East, the Pacific, and Eastern Europe and included many participants who are often forgotten—diplomats, sailors, politicians, laborers, women, and children. Strachan notes that England had more loss of life in the First World War than in the Second, and that the Germans lost more than 800,000 soldiers just in the spring of 1918. Many others died from the arrival of Spanish influenza in the summer of 1918. A thorough and readable account of World War I that offers much to ponder. Maps, Photographs, Notes, and Index.

1770. Temple, Bob. *The Titanic: An Interactive History Adventure.* (You Choose) Capstone, 2007. 2007pp. ISBN 978-1-4296-0163-4; paper ISBN 978-1-4296-1182-4. Grades 3–6.

In this story, readers can choose what role they would like to play during the sinking of the *Titanic*, including whether they are saved or die. After that decision they make other choices that are historically plausible, allowing readers to see the situation from different points of view. Color reproductions and maps enhance the text. Bibliography.

1771. Welton, Jude. *Impressionism.* DK, 2000. 64pp. ISBN 978-0-7894-5583-3. Grades YA.

Two-page topics, complemented with reproductions of impressionist paintings and other relevant images, give an overview of this important late 19th-century art movement. Discussions include Manet's painting of modern life, painting outdoors, student life, Monet, the Batignolles group, rebellion against the Salon, color, café life, Renoir, Caillebotte, trains, Sisley's landscapes, gardens, Pissarro's workers, Morisot, Degas, Japanese influence, and Cassatt. Glossary and Index.

1772. Whiting, Jim. *An Overview of World War I.* (Monumental Milestones) Mitchell Lane, 2006. 48pp. ISBN 978-1-58415-471-6. Grades 6–9.

This is a historical overview of World War I in five chapters that covers its causes, battles, the principal figures involved, the end of the war, and the consequences that followed. It concludes with a commentary about the Battle of Jutland. Photographs, sidebars, and illustrations highlight the text. Glossary, Chronology, and Index.

1773. Whiting, Jim. *The Sinking of the Titanic.* (Monumental Milestones) Mitchell Lane, 2006. 48pp. ISBN 978-1-58415-472-3. Grades 5–8.

This volume offers a history of the *Titanic*, from its design and construction to its destruction in 1912. It includes new findings that question whether the sinking of the ship was due to the ship's design or to human misjudgment. It names some of the passengers and their fates as well. Photographs, sidebars, and illustrations highlight the text. Glossary, Chronology, and Index.

1774. Woodworth, Bradley D., and Constance E. Richards. *St. Petersburg.* Chelsea House, 2005. 137pp. ISBN 978-0-7910-7837-2. Grades 11 up.

See entry 1478.

Biography and Collective Biography

1775. Ackerman, Jane. *Louis Pasteur and the Founding of Microbiology.* (Renaissance Scientists) Morgan Reynolds, 2004. ISBN 978-1-931798-13-6. Grades 9 up.

Louis Pasteur (1822–1895) used his microscope and thorough research to prove that germs cause diseases, a discovery that made him the greatest scientist of his age. He saved France's silk industry, started the fields of immunology and microbiology, established the method and the importance of pasteurizing milk, emphasized the anthrax virus, created vaccines, and helped people understand the importance of sanitation in helping to contain contagious diseases. On the other hand, Pasteur's arrogance alienated colleagues when he refused to acknowledge their contributions to his work. Reproductions and illustrations highlight the text. Chronology, Bibliography, Web Sites, and Index.

1776. Adler, Jeremy. *Franz Kafka.* Overlook, 2002. 164pp. ISBN 978-1-58567-267-7; 2004. paper ISBN 978-1-58567-518-0. Grades YA.

This biography of Franz Kafka (1883–1924) uses rarely seen drawings, photographs, letters, and manuscript reproductions to present information about Kafka's life and work. Born in Prague and eventually employed by an insurance company, Kafka wrote on the side. A photograph of the house in which Kafka wrote *The Trial* and *The Metamorphosis* personalizes those works, and a brief discussion presents their themes and Kafka's style. Bibliography, Chronology, and Further Reading.

1777. Aller, Susan Bivin. *J. M. Barrie: The Magic Behind Peter Pan.* (Lerner Biographies) Lerner, 1994. 128pp. ISBN 978-0-8225-4918-5. Grades 6–12.

The author of *Peter Pan*, James Matthew Barrie (1860–1937), was a journalist before his story about a boy who refused to grow up made him famous. Black-and-white photographs enhance the text. Bibliography and Index.

1778. Anderson, M. T. *Strange Mr. Satie.* Illustrated by Petra Mathers. Viking, 2003. 48pp. ISBN 978-0-670-03637-0. Grades 3–6.

Erik Satie (1866–1925), a French composer, spent his career challenging established music conventions. Among the anecdotes are his cleaning habits of using stones instead of water, throwing his girlfriend Suzanne Valadon out the window (she was an acrobat), and collaborations with Picasso and Picabia. Surrealistic illustrations complement the text. Note. *Horn Book Fanfare* and *Bulletin Blue Ribbon*.

1779. Anholt, Laurence. *Matisse: The King of Color.* Illustrated by author. (Anholt's Artists Books for Children) Barron's, 2007. Unpaged. ISBN 978-0-7641-6047-9. Grades 2–5.

While Henri Matisse (1869–1954) recovers from a serious illness, he draws several pictures of his nurse Monique. Later she becomes a religious. Matisse moves to a home near her nunnery and offers Sister Jacques-Marie a gift. He builds a small chapel for her order; but when she sees the white building, she is disappointed for such blandness from the "King of Color." When she walks inside and sees the light streaming through the stained-glass window, however, she realizes what he has done and feels like she is floating in a sea of color.

1780. Bankston, John. *Sigmund Freud: Exploring the Mysteries of the Mind.* (Great Minds of Science) Enslow, 2006. 128pp. ISBN 978-0-7660-2336-9. Grades 6–9.

This biography offers an overview of the life of the father of modern psychology. It relates information about Freud's childhood, his personality and family, and his work as the developer of psychoanalysis. Photographs augment the text. Glossary, Chronology, Further Reading, Web Sites, and Index.

1781. Bardoe, Cheryl. *Gregor Mendel: The Friar Who Grew Peas.* Illustrated by Joseph A. Smith. Abrams, 2006. Unpaged. ISBN 978-0-8109-5475-5. Grades 2–4.

This picture book biography presents the life of Gregor Mendel (1822–1884), the father of genetics. It discusses his studious youth and his decision to become a friar because in that profession he could feed his "body, mind, and soul." He enjoyed gardening as well as helping the poor and the sick, and he wanted to find the law that governed all living things. His discovery of how genes are mutated with dominant and recessive traits has since become one of the bases of genetics. Illustrations complement the text. Bibliography and Note.

1782. Bargalló, Eva. *My Name Is . . . Picasso.* Illustrated by Violeta Monreal. (My Name Is . . .) Barron's, 2006. 63pp. Paper ISBN 978-0-7641-3393-0. Grades 4–6.

Pablo Picasso (1881–1973), one of the greatest artists of the 20th century, spent most of his life in France where he and Georges Braque began the style of cubism. But Picasso did not limit himself; he painted and sculpted in many styles, and his most famous work was *Guernica*, a depiction of the Spanish Civil War in 1937. Illustrations complement the text. Chronology.

1783. Batten, Jack. *Silent in an Evil Time: The Brave War of Edith Cavell.* Tundra, 2007. 135pp. Paper ISBN 978-0-88776-737-1. Grades 7 up.

Twelve chapters relate the life of Edith Cavell (1865–1915). She began training as a nurse in London in 1895 and started a clinic in Brussels in 1907. After World War I began, she worked with the Resistance helping Allied soldiers escape. When a firing squad executed her, anti-German sentiment permeated Great Britain and the United States. Photographs enhance the text. Bibliography and Index.

1784. Berger, Melvin, and Gilda Berger. *Did It Take Creativity to Find Relativity, Albert Einstein?* (Science SuperGiants) Scholastic, 2007. 48pp. Paper ISBN 978-0-439-83384-4. Grades 3–4.

This brief biography looks at the life of Albert Einstein (1879–1955) and his discovery of the theory of relativity and attempts to explain this complex theory so that anyone might understand it. This account also addresses Einstein's disinterest in school, his work as an adult, and some of the other theories he established. An activity involves watching light bend. Photographs and illustrations enhance the text. Chronology and Index.

1785. Bernard, Bruce. *Van Gogh.* DK, 1999. 64pp. ISBN 978-0-7894-4878-1. Grades 6 up.

Vincent van Gogh (1853–1890) never made money from his art. He did not plan to be an artist until he was in his late 20s. This book uses reproductions to give a sense of his life and his art and the influences that shaped both.

1786. Bernstein, Harry. *The Invisible Wall: A Love Story That Broke Barriers.* Ballantine, 2007. 297pp. ISBN 978-0-345-49580-8; 2008. paper ISBN 978-0-345-49610-2. Grades YA.

Four-year-old Harry Bernstein lives with his family near Manchester, England, on a street with an invisible divide down the middle. On one side live the Jews and on the other, the Christians. Their only commonality is poverty. Harry's alcoholic father spends the family's money while his mother tries to sell slightly damaged fruit from their front room. Harry's bright sister, Lily, meets the intelligent Arthur, and the two fall in love. When they are older, they elope and take Harry, now 11, with them. He returns home to tell the family. Their baby unites the two groups of people, and they have a block party to celebrate.

1787. Birch, Beverly. *Marie Curie: Courageous Pioneer in the Study of Radioactivity.* (Giants of Science) Blackbirch, 2000. 64pp. ISBN 978-1-56711-333-4. Grades 4–7.

Marie Curie (1867–1934) had to leave Poland to finish her education. In Paris, at the Sorbonne, she met and married Pierre Curie, and their research led to the discovery of two new elements: polonium and radium. Marie won two Nobel Prizes for her work, created a portable X-ray machine to take to the battle front during World War I to quickly locate shrapnel in soldiers' bodies, and died from an unknown disease eventually identified as radiation poisoning. For More Information, Glossary, Chronology, and Index.

1788. Birch, Beverly. *Marie Curie's Search for Radium.* Barron's Educational, 1996. 48pp. Paper ISBN 978-0-8120-9791-7. Grades 4–7.

With her husband Pierre, Polish-born Marie Curie did important research in Paris that led to the discovery of polonium and radium. Among her other accomplishments was the creation of a portable X-ray machine. For More Information, Glossary, Chronology, and Index.

1789. Brackett, Virginia. *Restless Genius: The Story of Virginia Woolf.* (Writers of Imagination) Morgan Reynolds, 2004. 144pp. ISBN 978-1-931798-37-2. Grades 8 up.

Virginia Woolf (1882–1941), daughter of Julia and Leslie Stephen, lived with her parents in London, and became involved with the Bloomsbury Group during her adult life. She adopted the bohemian lifestyle of those in the group as she practiced her writing while married to her husband, Leonard. She had several mental breakdowns, corresponded romantically with Vita Sackville-West, and took fiction in a different direction at a time when few women were writing and even fewer were publishing. Photographs and illustrations accompany the text. Bibliography, Chronology, Notes, and Index.

1790. Bradley, Michael J. *The Foundations of Mathematics: 1800 to 1900.* (Pioneers in Mathematics) Chelsea House, 2006. 148pp. ISBN 978-0-8160-5425-1. Grades 6 up.

See entry 1490.

1791. Bradley, Michael J. *Modern Mathematics: 1900–1950.* (Pioneers in Mathematics) Chelsea House, 2006. 148pp. ISBN 978-0-8160-5425-1. Grades 6 up.

Ten men and women helped establish the structure of mathematics in the first half of the 20th century. Their discoveries, pertinent information, and a conclusion about their contributions are all included here. David Hilbert (1862–1943) worked with invariant theory and algebraic number theory along with other early problems. Grace Chisholm Young (1868–1944) worked independently with infinite derivatives. Wactaw Sierpinski (1882–1969) investigated number theory at the Polish School of Mathematics. Amalie Emmy Noether (1882–1935) was an abstract algebraist. Srinivasa Iyengar Ramanujan (1887–1920) was an Indian number theorist. Norbert Wiener (1894–1964) was a child prodigy and the father of cybernetics. John von Neumann (1903–1957) worked with mathematics for science and technology with quantum, game, operator, and automata theories. Grace Murray Hopper (1906–1992) was a computer software innovator. Alan Turing (1912–1954) is known as the father of modern computing. Paul Erdös (1913–1996) made diverse mathematical contributions and was known as an eccentric genius. Glossary, Further Reading, and Index.

1792. Brombert, Beth Archer. *Edouard Manet: Rebel in a Frock Coat.* University of Chicago, 1997. 505pp. Paper ISBN 978-0-226-07544-0. Grades YA.

See entry 1492.

1793. Brown, Don. *Odd Boy Out: Young Albert Einstein.* Illustrated by author. Houghton, 2004. Unpaged. ISBN 978-0-618-49298-5. Grades 2–5.

When he was a young boy, Albert Einstein (1879–1955) baffled his teachers because he seemed slow. Only his mathematics, music, and science teachers saw his intelligence. Temper tantrums discouraged his tutors, and he spent hours at home building houses of cards "fourteen stories high." His parents were confused by his behavior, but they supported him and allowed him to roam around Munich alone when he was no more than four. Illustrations depict him separate from other young boys as he was in reality. Bibliography and Notes. *Capitol Choices Noteworthy Titles* (Washington, D.C.).

1794. Burleigh, Robert. *Paul Cézanne.* Abrams, 2006. 32pp. ISBN 978-0-8109-5784-8. Grades 4–8.

This biography offers a brief overview of the life and work of Paul Cézanne (1839–1906). It suggests how readers can think about an artist's decisions when deciding what to include in their pictures and the colors they use in a discussion of some of Cézanne's paintings. The text clarifies Cézanne's initial connection to the impressionists and his adaptations of a freer style, especially after he left for Tahiti. Photographs highlight the text. Bibliography and Glossary.

1795. Burleigh, Robert. *Seurat and La Grande Jatte: Connecting the Dots.* Abrams, 2004. 31pp. ISBN 978-0-8109-4811-2. Grades 3–6.

This biography offers a brief overview of the life and work of Georges Seurat (1859–1891). It suggests how readers can think about an artist's decisions when deciding what to include in their pictures and the colors they use in a discussion of some of Seurat's paintings. The text clarifies Seurat's initial connection to the impressionists and his unique use of dots to create his paintings, developing the style of pointillism. Among his paintings is *Sunday Afternoon on the Island of la Grande Jatte.* Photographs highlight the text. Bibliography and Glossary. *Orbis Pictus Honor Book.*

1796. Caws, Mary Ann. *Virginia Woolf.* Overlook, 2002. 136pp. ISBN 978-1-58567-264-6; 2004. paper ISBN 978-1-58567-520-3. Grades YA.

This biography of Virginia Woolf (1882–1941) includes rarely seen drawings, photographs, letters, and manuscript reproductions that present information about Woolf's life and work. Born and raised in London, she circulated in a group of writers and artists, and some of their works appear in the book. A brief discussion presents her themes and style. Bibliography, Chronology, and Further Reading.

1797. Cocca-Leffler, Maryann. *Edgar Degas: Paintings that Dance.* Illustrated by author. (Smart About Art) Grosset & Dunlap, 2001. 32pp. Paper ISBN 978-0-448-42520-7. Grades 2–4.

Kristin Cole has to make a school report on Edgar Degas (1834–1917). She tells about Degas and his work while adding some interesting facts about her own life. Art reproductions and cartoons augment the text.

1798. Collins, David R. *Tales for Hard Times: A Story About Charles Dickens.* Illustrated by David Mataya. Carolrhoda, 1990. 64pp. ISBN 978-0-8761-4433-6. Grades 4–8.

See entry 1494.

oil paintings, terra cotta sculptures, and children's book illustration. Reproductions highlight the text. Chronology.

1810. Heims, Neil. *Tortured Noble: The Story of Leo Tolstoy.* (World Writers) Morgan Reynolds, 2007. 144pp. ISBN 978-1-59935-066-0. Grades 9 up.

Leo Tolstoy (1828–1910) lived a life of dichotomies. He wanted to be a peasant on a religious pilgrimage, and he left home as a middle-aged man, dressed like a peasant, but with two servants to carry his money and clean clothes. He lived his youth of privilege while compulsively gambling and having sexual adventures that led to self-loathing. As an adult, he examined the opposite sides of relationships, ideology, and his self-image. This portrait includes background information about Russia in his time. Period photographs and illustrations augment the text. Chronology, Notes, Further Reading, Web Sites, and Index.

1811. Jacobs, Francine R. *A Passion for Danger.* Backinprint.Com, 2004. 160pp. Paper ISBN 978-0-595-32850-5. Grades 5–9.

Fridtjof Nansen (1861–1930) of Norway was an explorer, statesman, scientist, and humanitarian. In 1882 he took a sealer into the seas of Greenland and began explorations in the area. In 1893 he spent seventeen months attempting to cross the Arctic Ocean to find the North Pole. Jacobs looks at Nansen's journeys as he related them in his memoirs and presents the numerous dangers he encountered. He was unsuccessful in reaching the Pole, but his information on oceanography, meteorology, and diet helped those who came after him. In 1906 he became Norway's first minister to England. Nansen's receipt of the Nobel Prize in 1922 for his work with World War I refugees shows his interest in helping others. Photographs, Bibliography, Notes, and Index.

1812. Jago, Lucy. *The Northern Lights.* (Vintage) Vintage, 2002. 2002pp. Paper ISBN 978-0-375-70882-4. Grades YA.

Kristian Birkeland (1867–1917) spent his career as a Norwegian scientist researching the mystery of the Aurora Borealis. Although his work was unrecognized at his death, he helped clarify how the Aurora Borealis, electromagnetism, comets, and the sun work together. The three parts of his biography are entitled "Aurora Borealis," "The Terrella," and "Zodiacal Light." In 1899 he took a dangerous expedition to the Norwegian Arctic for the first scientific observation of the northern lights. Ignored in Norway for his discoveries and his research interrupted by World War I and a nefarious business partner, he went to work in Egypt and Japan. Illustrations augment the text. Bibliography and Index.

1813. Kelley, True. *Claude Monet: Sunshine and Waterlilies.* Illustrated by author. (Smart About Art) Grosset & Dunlap, 2001. 32pp. Paper ISBN 978-0-448-42522-1. Grades 2–4.

Steven Packard creates a report about the life and paintings of Claude Monet (1840–1926) for a school assignment. He explains in his report that he has chosen Monet because he likes the way Monet paints sunshine in his pictures. He likes all of the water lily variations that Monet painted while he lived in Giverny, France.

1814. Kerley, Barbara. *The Dinosaurs of Waterhouse Hawkins: An Illuminating History of Mr. Waterhouse Hawkins, Artist and Lecturer.* Illustrated by Brian Selznick. Scholastic, 2001. Unpaged. ISBN 978-0-439-11494-3. Grades 3–5.

Victorian Benjamin Waterhouse Hawkins (1807–1889) wanted people to know about dinosaurs. He had been drawing and sculpting animals all his life, and when he became an adult, he began sculpting dinosaurs by looking at fossil remains. His works still exist in Sydenham, England, as do those that he built for Queen Victoria and Prince Albert at Crystal Palace Park; but the ones he constructed in New York City were destroyed by Boss Tweed. Illustrations enhance the text. *Garden State Book Award* (New Jersey) nomination, *Battle of the Books* (New Mexico) nomination, *Young Readers Choice Awards* (Louisiana), *Children's Book Award* (Rhode Island) nomination, *Children's Book Award* (Colorado) nomination, *Bluebonnet Award* (Texas) nomination, *Beehive Award* (Utah) nomination, and *Caldecott Honor Book*.

1815. Kherdian, David. *The Road from Home.* Beech Tree, 1995. 238pp. Paper ISBN 978-0-688-14425-8. Grades 7 up.

In a first-person point-of-view biography, Kherdian tells the story of his mother, an Armenian girl who endured the wrath of the Turkish government to survive. The historical background shows that modern Turkey continued the persecution of the Armenians begun by "Red" Sultan Abdul Hamid in the 1895–1896 massacres. Although the modern constitution said that the government was founded on liberty, equality, justice, and fraternity, the government decided to settle the "Armenian Question" in 1915. Veron Dumehjian, born to a wealthy Armenian family, enjoyed the material comforts gleaned from her father's poppy gum exporting business. But the Turkish soldiers arrived one day and made the family leave, except for the grandmother whose two sons were serving in the Turkish army. Almost every member of the family died of cholera in a camp, and Veron's mother died of despair soon after. Veron eventually reunited with her father and then her grandmother, but the Turks then ran her and the other Armenians out of yet another town. After she arrived in Athens with a favorite aunt, a family succeeded in persuading her to come to America with them to marry their son, the father of the author. *Newbery Honor Book*.

1816. Klein, Adam G. *Paul Gauguin.* (Great Artists) Checkerboard, 2006. 32pp. ISBN 978-1-59679-729-1. Grades 2–5.

This biography introduces Paul Gauguin (1848–1903) and the various periods in his work. Some of his most famous depict life in Tahiti. The account balances his life story with the discussion of his artworks, and contains a few reproductions. Chronology, Glossary, and Index.

1817. Klein, Adam G. *Vincent van Gogh.* (Great Artists) Checkerboard, 2006. 32pp. ISBN 978-1-59679-730-7. Grades 2–5.

This biography introduces Vincent van Gogh (1853–1890) and the various periods in his work. Some of his most famous works are *Starry Night* and *The Red Vineyard*. The discussion of his life balances that of his artworks, although the book contains few reproductions. Chronology, Glossary, and Index.

1818. Koja, Stephan. *Gustav Klimt: A Painted Fairy Tale.* Translated by Christopher Wynne. (Adventures in Art) Prestel, 2007. 28pp. ISBN 978-3-7913-3704-3. Grades 6–8.

This biography presents the important aspects in the life, times, and work of Austrian painter Gustav Klimt (1862–1918). He painted frescoes, canvases, and theaters with colorful, ornate designs, some accented with gold, as was the practice of the secession movement that he joined. Reproductions of his work include *The Kiss* and *A Farmhouse on Lake Atter*.

1819. Krull, Kathleen. *Marie Curie.* Illustrated by Boris Kulikov. (Giants of Science) Viking, 2007. 142pp. ISBN 978-0-670-05894-5. Grades 5–9.

Marie Curie (1867–1934), daughter of two educated Polish parents, wanted to excel for them and for her country, so she worked as a governess to earn money to study in Paris. This biography follows her childhood, education, and devotion to work as she discovers two new elements, polonium and radium, and joined her husband, Pierre, in laboratory research. She won Nobel Prizes in both physics and chemistry, and had two daughters who were also superb scientists. Although people described her as distant and detached, she spent time during World War I creating a mobile X-ray machine for use in the field, and after the war, opened her Radium Institute for further research. Photographs and illustrations highlight the text. Bibliography, Web Sites, and Index. *American Library Association Notable Children's Books.*

1820. Krull, Kathleen. *Sigmund Freud.* (Giants of Science) Viking, 2006. 64pp. ISBN 978-0-670-05892-1. Grades 6–9.

Sigmund Freud, the creator of psychoanalysis, a new branch of medicine, grew up in Austria. His mother catered to him and demanded that the family do likewise, as demonstrated by the fact that he had a bedroom to himself while the rest of the large family filled three other rooms. The favoritism continued from his wife and colleagues, but Freud was determined to fulfill his mother's dream for him and to become famous. The author explains Freud's theories about unconscious motives; the Oedipus complex; the id, ego, and superego; and Freudian slips. After Hitler came to power, Freud had to escape to London. In the later 20th century other psychoanalysts questioned some of his ideas and methods. Illustrations enhance the text. Appendix, Further Reading, Bibliography, Web Sites, and Index. *American Library Association Notable Children's Books.*

1821. Laidlaw, Jill A. *Paul Klee.* Franklin Watts, 2002. 46pp. ISBN 978-0-531-12230-3. Grades 5–8.

The Swiss artist Paul Klee (1879–1940) was inspired by reverse glass painting in Bavaria. He developed his own style and eventually went to teach at the Bauhaus. The book relies on photographs, reproductions, and news clippings that place Klee within his time. Glossary, Chronology, and Index.

1822. Landmann, Bimba. *I Am Marc Chagall.* Illustrated by author. Eerdmans, 2006. 40pp. ISBN 978-0-8028-5305-9. Grades 2–5.

This biography of Marc Chagall (1887–1985) offers a first-person point of view. He grows up in a shtetl, and he says that all the people of Vitebsk live in his paintings. He paints the things he loves and about which he has dreamed. He has trouble getting viewers to accept his work, but eventually finds fame, and migrates to the United States in 1941. Three-dimensional mixed-media collages enhance the text.

1823. Loumaye, Jacqueline. *Degas: The Painted Gesture.* Illustrated by Nadine Massart. Translated by John Goodman. Chelsea House, 1994. 57pp. ISBN 978-0-7910-2809-4. Grades 4–8.

See entry 1513.

1824. McClafferty, Carla Killough. *Something Out of Nothing: Marie Curie and Radium.* Farrar, 2006. 134pp. ISBN 978-0-374-38036-6. Grades 5–10.

This biography of Marie Curie (1867–1934) shows her as an independent woman who made extraordinarily important scientific discoveries. She struggled to reach Paris from Poland and to attend college, then met Pierre Curie and became happily married. But she could also let her work consume her and was sometimes indifferent to her family. Her work earned her Nobel prizes in both physics and chemistry. Photographs highlight the text. Bibliography, Notes, Web Sites, and Index.

1825. McCormick, Lisa Wade. *Marie Curie.* (Rookie) Children's, 2006. 31pp. ISBN 978-0-51625-040-3; paper ISBN 978-0-51621-445-0. Grades 1–2.

Marie Curie (1867–1934) overcame poverty by going to Paris to attend school and work in laboratories. Her dedication helped her discover the element of radium. She also won two Nobel Prizes, one in physics and one in chemistry. Her daughter joined her for one of the award presentations. Without her contributions to science, X-rays might not yet be a common tool in modern medicine.

1826. MacLeod, Elizabeth. *Marie Curie: A Brilliant Life.* (Snapshots: Images of People and Places in History) Kids Can, 2004. 32pp. ISBN 978-1-55337-570-8; paper ISBN 978-1-55337-571-5. Grades 3–7.

Marie Curie (1867–1934) struggled to study in Poland and moved to Paris where she was able to achieve the greatness for which she is known. The scrapbook aspect of this biography offers parts of her life as she became fascinated by radiation and made important discoveries about it. Double-page spreads with text and photographs include her with other scientists such as Albert Einstein. Her work earned her two Nobel Prizes and changed science. Chronology, Web Sites, and Index.

1827. McNeese, Tim. *Pablo Picasso.* (Great Hispanic Heritage) Chelsea House, 2006. 122pp. ISBN 978-0-7910-8843-2. Grades 8 up.

This biography of Pablo Picasso (1881–1973) focuses on his accomplishments and how he created a positive Hispanic image. He worked in sculpture, ceramics, and the graphic arts his entire life. As an artist he was both a product of the past and a denizen of the future. Reproductions from each phase of Picasso's career illuminate the text. Bibliography, Chronology, Further Reading, Web Sites, and Index.

1828. McPherson, Stephanie Sammartino. *Albert Einstein.* (History Makers Bios) Lerner, 2004. 48pp. ISBN 978-0-8225-0350-7. Grades 3–5.

Albert Einstein (1879–1955) was expelled from school as a youngster but loved his high school. In college he thought his professors were not teaching the most important aspects of science. He wanted to become a professor, but educational politics prohibited his appointment. While working elsewhere, he wrote theories on space, gravity, matter, time, and energy. Eventually he won the Nobel Prize for his work that became known as the theory of relativity. Illustrations highlight the text. Bibliography, Further Reading, Glossary, Maps, Chronology, Web Sites, and Index.

1829. Mason, Antony. *Monet: An Introduction to the Artist's Life and Work.* Barrons, 1995. 32pp. Paper ISBN 978-0-8120-9174-8. Grades 5 up.

As a young man, Claude Monet (1840–1926), one of the most famous French artists, refused to use traditional methods of painting. He captured in his pictures the mood of his surroundings by showing the reflection of the light. He and other artists who thought as he did became the Impressionists. Monet lived by the sea as a young boy, moved to

Paris, almost starved while trying to paint, enjoyed Giverny outside Paris, and developed series of paintings on various subjects, such as Rouen Cathedral and water lilies. Clear reproductions highlight the text, which includes helpful comments about composition. Chronology, Art History, Museums, Glossary, and Indexes.

1830. Matthews, Elizabeth. *Different Like Coco.* Illustrated by author. Candlewick, 2007. 40pp. ISBN 978-0-7636-2548-1. Grades K–3.

As a poor and skinny girl, Gabrielle "Coco" Chanel preferred different things from others who knew her. She determined that she could, and would, be better than the wealthier girls in Paris. When Coco was 12 her mother died, and she had to move to an orphanage. There she learned to sew and make rag dolls. She began designing unusual dresses without corsets while working in a tailor shop, and then sold them in a boutique financed by a man in love with her. At the beginning of World War I, her practical designs delighted buyers, and she began changing both physical and social constraints. Pen-and-ink with watercolor illustrations highlight the text. Chronology and Bibliography.

1831. Mikkelsen, Ejnar. *Two Against the Ice.* Translated by Maurice Michael. Steerforth, 2003. 206pp. Paper ISBN 978-1-58642-057-4. Grades YA.

Ejnar Mikkelsen and his mechanic, Iver Iversen, crossed Greenland to the Arctic in 1910 to search for diaries that three Danish explorers had left behind on a previous expedition. Mikkelsen, more interested in the final goal than details, led the pair into the worst obstacles that could befall them during their three years, including a lack of food (which made it necessary to eat their dogs), scurvy, and enduring slush without sleeping bags. However, their discovery of the diaries that disproved Peary made the journey worth the discomfort for Mikkelsen.

1832. Mis, Melody S. *Edgar Degas.* (Meet the Artists) PowerKids, 2007. 24pp. ISBN 978-1-4042-3839-8. Grades 2–4.

This biography of Edgar Degas (1834–1917) contains many reproductions of his work. It covers his childhood and further developments of his life and his art. Glossary, Further Reading, Web Sites, and Index.

1833. Mis, Melody S. *Paul Cézanne.* (Meet the Artists) PowerKids, 2007. 24pp. ISBN 978-1-4042-3842-8. Grades 2–4.

This biography of Paul Cézanne (1839–1906) contains many reproductions of his work. It describes his life beginning with his childhood, and the development of his art. Glossary, Further Reading, Web Sites, and Index.

1834. Muhlberger, Richard. *What Makes a Degas a Degas?* Viking, 2002. 48pp. ISBN 978-0-670-03571-7. Grades 5–9.

See entry 1521.

1835. Nardo, Don. *Charles Darwin.* Lucent, 2004. 112pp. ISBN 978-1-59018-339-7. Grades 7 up.

See entry 1522.

1836. Olson, Tod. *Leopold II: Butcher of the Congo.* (Wicked History) Watts, 2008. 128pp. ISBN 978-0-531-18552-0; paper ISBN 978-0-531-20501-3. Grades 6–9.

Leopold II (1835–1909), King of the Belgians from 1865 to 1909, has been called greedy. He was the founder and sole owner of the Congo Free State and ran it as his own business venture. He used Henry Morton Stanley to help him claim the area, and in 1904, white officials who had murdered natives during a rubber-collecting expedition in 1903, presumably with Leopold's approval, were arrested and punished. Maps and reproductions augment the text. Bibliography, Glossary, Chronology, Further Reading, Web Sites, and Index.

1837. Otfinoski, Steven. *Bram Stoker: The Man Who Wrote Dracula.* Franklin Watts, 2005. 111pp. ISBN 978-0-53116-750-2. Grades 5–8.

A theatrical manager and author, Bram Stoker (1847–1912) gave life to the character of Dracula (1897). The author looks at Stoker's childhood when he was chronically ill and his mother told him stories, as well as his college education when other writers influenced him, and his career. One chapter relates the many presentations of Dracula both on stage and screen. Archival photographs and illustrations highlight the text. Chronology, Further Reading, Web Sites, and Index.

1838. Parker, Steve. *Louis Pasteur and Germs.* Chelsea House, 1995. 32pp. ISBN 978-0-7910-3002-8. Grades 3–7.

See entry 1525.

1839. Parker, Steve. *Marie Curie and Radium.* Chelsea House, 1995. 32pp. ISBN 978-0-7910-3011-0. Grades 3–7.

Marie Curie (1867–1934) helped to start the atomic age with her work on radioactive elements. She discovered radium while struggling against a lack of money and recognition, illness, and those who believed that women could not be real scientists. The winner of two Nobel Prizes, she is one of the pioneers of science. Photographs and reproductions complement the text. The World in Marie Curie's Time, Glossary, and Index.

1840. Pierre, Michel. *Good Day, Mister Gauguin.* Chelsea House, 1995. 60pp. ISBN 978-0-7910-2811-7. Grades 3–6.

Pierre combines a straightforward account of Paul Gauguin's (1848–1903) life with a fictional story of a child pursuing information about this man at various museums in Paris where Gauguin's paintings hang. Also included are reproductions of the paintings. Glossary and Chronology.

1841. Poynter, Margaret. *Marie Curie: Discoverer of Radium.* Enslow, 2007. 112pp. ISBN 978-0-7660-2795-4. Grades 4–6.

Marie Curie (1867–1934) grew up in Poland, saved money to send her sister to school in Paris, and then followed her there. In Paris she learned a new language and managed to graduate at the top of her class. Her excellence in scientific research led to a Nobel Prize for chemistry and another one for physics. Photographs, Chronology, Notes, Glossary, Further Reading, and Index.

1842. Provensen, Alice, and Martin Provensen. *The Glorious Flight: Across the Channel with Louis Blériot, July 25, 1909.* Illustrated by Alice and Martin Provensen. (Picture Puffins) Puffin, 1987. Unpaged. Paper ISBN 978-0-14-050729-4. Grades K–3.

After many attempts to fly across the English Channel, Louis Blériot (1872–1936) finally succeeded on July 25, 1909. The authors look at his trials and the support of his large family from the point of view of one of his children, who describes the various injuries he sustained on each of his attempts. *Caldecott Medal.*

1843. Reef, Catherine. *Sigmund Freud: Pioneer of the Mind.* Clarion, 2001. 152pp. ISBN 978-0-618-01762-1. Grades 7 up.

Sigmund Freud (1856–1939) discovered groundbreaking methods of treating the mentally ill that led to the birth of psychoanalysis. He developed theories of connecting dreams, desires, and behaviors that have greatly influenced modern society and that remain controversial. This biography shows Freud's intense interest in various subjects while he was growing up and how he tried a number of different ideas before refining his ideas. His theories mattered, but, more importantly, he got humans to think differently about themselves. Archival photographs enhance the text. Bibliography, Glossary, Notes, and Index. *Capitol Choices Noteworthy Titles* (Washington, D.C.).

1844. Resnick, Abraham. *Lenin: Founder of the Soviet Union.* Authors Choice, 2004. 131pp. Paper ISBN 978-0-595-30701-2. Grades 4–8.

Vladimir Lenin (1870–1924) grew up in tsarist Russia and was shocked when he discovered that his older brother had been arrested for being involved in a plot to assassinate tsar Alexander III. His brother was hanged, and Lenin seemed to think that he must take his brother's place in ridding the country of a rotten system of government. He and his colleagues overthrew the government of Nicholas II in 1917 to begin the Russian Revolution. As Lenin took power and oversaw the beginning of the Communist state, people observed that he could be either ruthless or kind, depending on his mood. Time Line and Index.

1845. Rubin, Susan Goldman. *Degas and the Dance: The Painter and the* Petits Rats, *Perfecting Their Art.* Abrams, 2002. 32pp. ISBN 978-0-8109-0567-2. Grades K–4.

When Edgar Degas (1834–1917) lived in Paris, the young ballet students were called "*petits rats.*" But when he watched them, he realized that ballet resembles art because it takes much hard work and practice. His paintings capture the development of ballerinas, and this book includes reproductions from thirty of the more than one thousand of his career works that show the process. The sketches show ballerinas rehearsing, warming up, stretching, and waiting to take their exams. Anecdotes from Degas add to the information in the pictures. *National Council of Teachers of English Orbis Pictus Award Honor Book.*

1846. Rubin, Susan Goldman. *The Yellow House: Vincent van Gogh and Paul Gauguin Side by Side.* Illustrated by Joseph A. Smith. Abrams, 2001. 40pp. ISBN 978-0-8109-4588-3. Grades K–4.

In the fall of 1888 Vincent van Gogh invited Paul Gauguin to visit him in Arles, France, and for two months the men painted together in van Gogh's yellow house. Although their styles were different, as van Gogh painted what he saw around him while Gauguin painted from memory, they influenced each other in new ways. Reproductions of their paintings augment the text. *National Council of Teachers of English Orbis Pictus Award Honor.*

1847. Sabbeth, Carol. *Monet and the Impressionists for Kids: Their Lives and Ideas, 21 Activities.* Chicago Review, 2002. 140pp. Paper ISBN 978-1-55652-297-7. Grades 6–9.

Sabbeth focuses on impressionism, the 19th-century French art movement that came to the fore when artists Claude Monet, Auguste Renoir, Edgar Degas, Mary Cassatt, Paul Cézanne, Paul Gauguin, and Georges Seurat started exhibiting their work in 1874. The text includes twenty-one activities for children such as decorating cookies in Seurat's pointillist style, drawing a face, making a *galette des rois* (Twelfth Night cake), constructing a paper water lily, and playing bingo Monet. Further Reading, Glossary, Web Sites, and Index.

1848. Salvi, Francesco. *The Impressionists.* Illustrated by L. R. Galante and Andrea Ricciardi. (Art Masters) Oliver, 2008. 64pp. ISBN 978-1-934545-03-4. Grades 5–8.

This volume defines impressionism by including what it was, where it happened, those who participated, and its results. Some topics are open air painting, nature, the influence of Japanese art, the 1874 exhibition, and light. Among the artists presented are Edouard Manet, Claude Monet, Pierre-Auguste Renoir, Edgar Degas, Paul Cézanne, Camille Pissarro, Alfred Sisley, Berthe Morisot, Mary Cassatt, Armand Guillaumin, and Gustave Caillebotte. Sources and Index.

1849. Saunders, Barbara R. *Ivan Pavlov: Exploring the Mysteries of Behavior.* (Great Minds of Science) Enslow, 2007. 112pp. ISBN 978-0-7660-2506-6. Grades 5–9.

Ivan Petrovich Pavlov (1849–1936), a Russian scientist, studied the physiology of the central nervous system. His experiments with dogs are well-known and provide the basis for conditioned-reflex and the Pavlov response. His work helped scientists in other fields including psychology and behaviorism. Photographs of places where he lived and worked illustrate the text, which includes much about him and his scientific explorations. Chronology, Further Reading, Glossary, and Index.

1850. Schlitz, Laura Amy. *The Hero Schliemann: The Dreamer Who Dug Up Troy.* Illustrated by Robert Byrd. Candlewick, 2006. 80pp. ISBN 978-0-7636-2283-1. Grades 4–7.

This biography of Heinrich Schliemann (1822–1890) covers his life as a romantic, convinced that the lost city of Troy was an actual place. Schliemann had an unhappy childhood but became a successful merchant who developed a passion for archaeology and antiquities in his middle age. If Schliemann did not like the reality, he wrote whatever he liked in his diary. But he thought that Troy existed so he took a group of people to dig. They found Troy, and Shliemann's Greek wife enjoyed modeling the beautiful gold they discovered. Illustrations complement the text. *Bulletin Blue Ribbon.*

1851. Schoell, William. *Giuseppe Verdi and Italian Opera.* (Classical Composers) Morgan Reynolds, 2007. 128pp. ISBN 978-1-59935-041-7. Grades 9 up.

See entry 1531.

1852. Schoell, William. *Remarkable Journeys: The Story of Jules Verne.* (World Writers) Morgan Reynolds, 2002. 112pp. ISBN 978-1-883846-92-3. Grades 9 up.

Jules Verne (1828–1905) loved science, literature, and adventure when he was a child. He used his vivid imagination to create stories that contained notions which eventually came into reality such as prehistoric animals, diving suits, and rocket boosters. He invented the disaster novel as well. The nine chapters give an overview of his life, and include that his favorite author was Edgar Allan Poe and that his good friend was Victor Hugo. Bibliography, Glossary, and Index.

1853. Severance, John. ***Winston Churchill: Soldier, Statesman, Artist.*** Clarion, 1996. 144pp. ISBN 978-0-395-69853-2. Grades 7–10.

Winston Churchill (1874–1965) saw three wars during his lifetime and was a significant force in one of them, as well as in important peacetime efforts. The author looks at his life from his boyhood through his Boer War participation, his professional achievements, his political career, and his military decisions during World War II. Quotes from his family and from his writings personalize the text. Photographs, Bibliography, and Index.

1854. Slade, Suzanne. ***Albert Einstein: Scientist and Genius.*** Illustrated by Robert McGuire. (Biographies) Picture Window, 2008. 24pp. ISBN 978-1-4048-3730-2. Grades K–3.

Albert Einstein (1879–1955), born in Ulm, Germany, was shy and quiet. When he was 5, the compass his father gave him intrigued him because he wanted to know what made it point north. At 12, he received a geometry book which he studied on his own. He attended college and worked in a patent office before marrying Mileva Maric in 1903. In 1905 he wrote four important papers that changed the concept of human space and time. His new discovery involved a formula, $E=mc^2$. In 1914 he began teaching at a Berlin university, and in 1919, divorced and remarried. In 1921 he received the Nobel Prize for physics, and in 1933 he moved to the United States to continue his research. During World War II he worked on the atomic bomb but never thought anyone would use it. That the United States bombed Japan greatly upset him, but it stopped the war. Chronology, Further Reading, Bibliography, Glossary, Web Sites, and Index.

1855. Smiley, Jane. ***Charles Dickens.*** Viking, 2002. 212pp. ISBN 978-0-670-03077-4. Grades YA.

See entry 1536.

1856. Smith, Denis Mark. ***Garibaldi: A Great Life in Brief.*** Greenwood, 1982. 215pp. ISBN 978-0-313-23618-1. Grades YA.

See entry 1537.

1857. Somervill, Barbara A. ***Pierre-Auguste Renoir.*** (Art Profiles for Kids) Mitchell Lane, 2007. 48pp. ISBN 978-1-58415-566-9. Grades 4–7.

This biography of Renoir (1841–1919) offers a concise examination of his life and work within the context of his times. It details how history may have influenced his subjects, his production, and the critical response to his work. Sidebars enhance the text along with reproductions of his work. Bibliography, Glossary, Chronology, Notes, Further Reading, and Index.

1858. Taylor, Ina. ***The Art of Kate Greenaway: A Nostalgic Portrait of Childhood.*** Pelican, 1991. 128pp. ISBN 978-0-8828-9867-4. Grades YA.

Kate Greenaway (1846–1901) became an important illustrator in late 19th-century England using children and idyllic country scenes as subjects. Her abilities and a complementary relationship with a publisher gained her fame and wealth while she was in her thirties. She supported her family as they moved to more stylish homes with gardens like those she used in so many of her drawings. This account, with accompanying reproductions, looks at her life and some of her triumphs and disappointments, including a perceived relationship with the Victorian critic, John Ruskin. Additionally it is an interesting view of life in Victorian England for the unmarried woman capable of earning her own income. Bibliography and Index.

1859. Thompson, Gare. ***Roald Amundsen and Robert Scott Race to the South Pole.*** (National Geographic History Chapters) National Geographic, 2007. 40pp. ISBN 978-1-4263-0187-2. Grades 2–4.

This brief overview of the lives of Norwegian Roald Amundsen (1872–1928) and the British explorer Robert Falcon Scott (1868–1912), shows how they were linked in their quest to be the first to reach the South Pole. Amundsen earned the prize in 1911, with Scott arriving the following month. Archival photographs and illustrations highlight the text. Glossary, Further Reading, Web Sites, and Index.

1860. Tracy, Kathleen. ***Henry Bessemer: Making Steel from Iron.*** (Uncharted, Unexplored, and Unexplained) Mitchell Lane, 2005. 48pp. ISBN 978-1-58415-366-5. Grades 4–7.

Henry Bessemer (1813–1898) discovered how to make steel cheaply. He also perfected making it quickly and in large quantities, an achievement that changed industry. The text contains some of the science behind this discovery and some information about Bessemer's life. Reproductions accompany the text. Glossary, Chronology, Further Reading, Web Sites, and Index.

1861. Tracy, Kathleen. ***Paul Cézanne.*** (Art Profiles for Kids) Mitchell Lane, 2007. 48pp. ISBN 978-1-58415-565-2. Grades 4–7.

This biography of Paul Cézanne (1839–1906) offers a concise examination of his life and work within the context of his times. It details how history may have influenced his choice of subjects, his production, and the critical response to his work. Sidebars enhance the text along with reproductions of his work. Bibliography, Glossary, Chronology, Notes, Further Reading, and Index.

1862. Venezia, Mike. ***Camille Pissarro.*** Illustrated by author. (Getting to Know the World's Greatest Artists) Children's Press, 2003. 32pp. ISBN 978-0-516-22577-7; 2004 paper ISBN 978-0-516-26977-1. Grades K–5.

See entry 1542.

1863. Venezia, Mike. ***Edgar Degas.*** Illustrated by author. (Getting to Know the World's Greatest Artists) Children's Press, 2000. 32pp. ISBN 978-0-516-21593-8; 2001 paper ISBN 978-0-516-27172-9. Grades K–5.

Edgar Degas (1834–1917) tried to be a lawyer but he loved to paint, especially scenes of Paris and its people. Although he was painting at the same time as the impressionists, he did not share their love of landscape and color and wanted to be able to do different kinds of paintings. He painted many different subjects, but after 1870 he primarily painted ballet figures because he liked them, and people wanted to buy them. When his eyesight began to fail, he painted pastels and made wax models of ballerinas. Among his paintings are *The Bellelli Family, The Orchestra at the Opera House, Orchestra Musicians, Dance Class*, and *Dancing Examination*. Illustrations augment the text.

1864. Venezia, Mike. *Georges Seurat.* Illustrated by author. (Getting to Know the World's Greatest Artists) Children's Press, 2002. 32pp. ISBN 978-0-516-22496-1; 2003 paper ISBN 978-0-516-27813-1. Grades K–5.

The artist Georges Seurat (1859–1891) was interested in the scientific relationship between color and light. His style of pointillism developed as he made shapes with many small spots of color in his work. Among his well-known works are *Sunday Afternoon on the Island of La Grande Jatte, Circus,* and *Bathers at Asnieres.* Illustrations accompany the text.

1865. Venezia, Mike. *Henri de Toulouse-Lautrec.* Illustrated by author. (Getting to Know the World's Greatest Artists) Children's Press, 1995. 32pp. ISBN 978-0-516-02283-3; 2003 paper ISBN 978-0-516-42283-1. Grades K–5.

Henri de Toulouse-Lautrec (1864–1901) was a French painter known for the scenes he painted of Parisian theaters and dance halls in the late 19th century. His growth was stunted because of a childhood accident, but his paintings do not reflect his personal life. Illustrations supplement the text.

1866. Venezia, Mike. *Henri Matisse.* Illustrated by author. (Getting to Know the World's Greatest Artists) Children's Press, 1997. 32pp. ISBN 978-0-516-20311-9; paper ISBN 978-0-516-26146-1. Grades K–5.

Henri Matisse (1869–1954) expected to study law but became ill as a young man and started to paint. He was a leader of the Fauve movement with his interest in light, color, and short strokes. He saw painting as decorative, and he created book illustrations, line drawings, paintings, and murals. Among his famous works are *La Danse* and the inside of the Dominican Chapel in Vence, France. Illustrations and reproductions highlight the text.

1867. Venezia, Mike. *Henri Rousseau.* Illustrated by author. (Getting to Know the World's Greatest Artists) Children's Press, 2002. 32pp. ISBN 978-0-516-22495-4; paper ISBN 978-0-516-26998-6. Grades K–5.

Henri Rousseau (1844–1910) taught himself to paint because he had no money to study. He loved jungles and wild animals in his paintings and tried to picture dreams. He painted colors one at a time in his imaginative works. Illustrations enhance the text.

1868. Venezia, Mike. *Igor Stravinsky.* Illustrated by author. (Getting to Know the World's Greatest Composers) Children's Press, 1996. 32pp. ISBN 978-0-516-20054-5; 1997 paper ISBN 978-0-516-26076-1. Grades K–5.

Igor Stravinsky (1882–1971), a Russian composer, became known for his creation of new rhythmic sounds in music. He tried to recreate in his music sounds that he remembered from his childhood in St. Petersburg, Russia—the beat of horses' hooves, wagon wheels on cobblestones, and church bells. His musical contributions had a great influence on the musicians who came after him. Illustrations enhance the text.

1869. Venezia, Mike. *Johannes Brahms.* Illustrated by author. (Getting to Know the World's Greatest Composers) Children's Press, 1999. 32pp. ISBN 978-0-516-21056-8; paper ISBN 978-0-516-26467-7. Grades K–5.

Johannes Brahms (1833–1897), born in Hamburg, Germany, composed in a variety of musical styles from songs to symphonies. Parents have sung his famous lullaby, originally called "Wiegenlied," to many children since he wrote it. In his best work he combined the ages of romantic music with that of classical. Illustrations highlight the text.

1870. Venezia, Mike. *Marc Chagall.* Illustrated by author. (Getting to Know the World's Greatest Artists) Children's Press, 2000. 32pp. ISBN 978-0-516-21055-1; paper ISBN 978-0-516-27041-8. Grades K–5.

Marc Chagall (1889–1985) used the tiny village in which he was born, Vitebsk, Russia, as the subject in many of his paintings. His pictures, full of color and line, seem like dreams in which all things can happen and combine. Illustrations highlight the text.

1871. Venezia, Mike. *Monet.* Illustrated by author. (Getting to Know the World's Greatest Artists) Children's Press, 1990. 32pp. ISBN 978-0-516-02276-5; paper ISBN 978-0-516-42276-3. Grades K–5.

Claude Monet (1840–1926) especially liked the way colors reflect in water and the way water makes the clouds and sky look. He applied these preferences to his work, and he even set up a studio on a boat so that he could sail on a river and stop and paint wherever he pleased. The text tells his story with reproductions of his work in the impressionist style that he helped to create.

1872. Venezia, Mike. *Paul Cézanne.* Illustrated by author. (Getting to Know the World's Greatest Artists) Children's Press, 1998. 32pp. ISBN 978-0-516-20762-9; paper ISBN 978-0-516-26351-9. Grades K–5.

Paul Cézanne (1839–1906) became known as a father of modern art because all of it can be traced to his work—symbolism, fauvism, cubism, expressionism, and abstract expressionism. He liked to paint the landscape around him, such as Mont Sainte-Victoire, as well as still-life. Illustrations highlight the text.

1873. Venezia, Mike. *Paul Gauguin.* Illustrated by author. (Getting to Know the World's Greatest Artists) Children's Press, 1992. 32pp. ISBN 978-0-516-02295-6; paper ISBN 978-0-516-42295-4. Grades K–5.

Paul Gauguin (1848–1903) spent his youth in Peru and France before becoming a merchant seaman and a stockbroker. He eventually moved to Tahiti. During this time he used flat color in a style that showed an Oriental influence. One of his best known works is *The Yellow Christ*. Illustrations highlight the text.

1874. Venezia, Mike. *Peter Tchaikovsky.* Illustrated by author. (Getting to Know the World's Greatest Composers) Children's Press, 1994. 32pp. ISBN 978-0-516-04537-5; 1995 paper ISBN 978-0-516-44537-5. Grades K–5.

Peter Tchaikovsky (1840–1893) was a great Russian composer who lived in St. Petersburg just as Russians were beginning to want to listen to Russian music. Cartoons complement and comment about the text on alternate pages. The author mentions Tchaikovsky's patron, and also notes that he was unhappy much of the time because he never found someone with whom he could fall in love. (Tchaikovsky's sexual preference is mentioned.) Because Tchaikovsky wrote *The Nutcracker*, he is a composer of whom many children may have heard. More advanced listeners may also have heard the *1812 Overture*.

1875. Venezia, Mike. *Picasso.* Illustrated by author. (Getting to Know the World's Greatest Artists) Children's Press, 1988. 32pp. ISBN 978-0-516-02271-0; paper ISBN 978-0-516-42271-8. Grades K–5.

Pablo Picasso (1881–1973), a renowned 20th-century artist, created a new art style called Cubism. He evolved from it into other styles. His *Guernica* shows his response to the horrors of the Spanish Civil War in 1937, and his other periods also sometimes reflect his emotions. Illustrations enhance the text.

1876. Venezia, Mike. *Pierre Auguste Renoir.* Illustrated by author. (Getting to Know the World's Greatest Artists) Children's Press, 1996. 32pp. ISBN 978-0-516-02225-3; paper ISBN 978-0-516-20068-2. Grades K–5.

Renoir (1841–1919), a renowned impressionist artist, was an important painter of people during the latter half of the 19th century, although he sometimes chose to paint landscapes or still-lifes. His paintings include *Luncheon at the Boating Party* and *Au Moulin de la Galette*. Illustrations enhance the text.

1877. Venezia, Mike. *Van Gogh.* Illustrated by author. (Getting to Know the World's Greatest Artists) Children's Press, 1988. 32pp. ISBN 978-0-516-02274-1; 1989 paper ISBN 978-0-516-42274-9. Grades K–5.

Using a combination of cartoons and reproductions, the text gives an overview of the life of Vincent van Gogh (1853–1890). Although van Gogh lived a rather unhappy life, Venezia gives a positive view of what he accomplished by using the bright colors that van Gogh adapted from Japanese painting. A mix of humor, information, and reproductions of van Gogh's paintings makes this a good introduction to his life and work.

1878. Waxman, Laura Hamilton. *Marie Curie.* (History Makers Bios) Lerner, 2004. 48pp. ISBN 978-0-8225-0300-2. Grades 3–5.

Marie Curie (1867–1934) left her home in Poland to study in Paris. There she began working with X-rays and made certain that X-ray machines were available during World War I, which helped save the lives of many soldiers. She also won two Nobel Prizes, one for her radiology work and another for her chemistry achievements. Illustrations highlight the text. Bibliography, Further Reading, Glossary, Maps, Chronology, Web Sites, and Index.

1879. Welton, Jude. *Monet.* DK, 2000. 64pp. ISBN 978-0-7894-4880-4. Grades YA.

With excellent narrative and graphics, this volume looks at the tools Monet (1840–1926) used as he created his canvases. Twenty-seven mini-chapters follow Monet's development. Chronology, Glossary, and Index.

1880. Whiting, Jim. *Auguste and Louis Lumière and the Rise of Motion Pictures.* (Uncharted, Unexplored, and Unexplained) Mitchell Lane, 2005. 48pp. ISBN 978-1-58415-365-8. Grades 5–8.

The brothers Auguste and Louis Lumière created the cinematographe, one of the first motion pictures. From this invention, they began showing movies. Their discovery changed the world dramatically, and the text includes background of the science on which their work rested. Reproductions accompany the text. Glossary, Chronology, Further Reading, Web Sites, and Index.

1881. Whiting, Jim. *Claude Monet.* (Art Profiles for Kids) Mitchell Lane, 2007. 48pp. ISBN 978-1-58415-563-8. Grades 4–7.

This biography of Claude Monet (1840–1926) offers a concise examination of his life and work within the context of his times. It details how history may have influenced his choice of subjects, his production, and the critical response to his work. Sidebars enhance the text along with reproductions of his work. Bibliography, Glossary, Chronology, Notes, Further Reading, and Index.

1882. Whiting, Jim. *Vincent van Gogh.* (Art Profiles for Kids) Mitchell Lane, 2007. 48pp. ISBN 978-1-58415-564-5. Grades 7 up.

This biography of Vincent van Gogh (1853–1890) covers his childhood, artistic training, travel, influences in his life, and his place in history. It shows his styles and the subjects that he chose to paint as well as the critical reaction to his work. As an impressionist, he was shunned and sold little during his lifetime. A sidebar notes that one of his paintings sold for $82.5 million in 1990 and then disappeared. Reproductions enhance the text. Glossary, Chronology, Notes, Further Reading, Web Sites, and Index.

1883. Yannuzzi, Della. *New Elements: The Story of Marie Curie.* Morgan Reynolds, 2006. 144pp. ISBN 978-1-59935-023-3. Grades 4–8.

Marya Salomee Sklodowska, Marie Curie (1867–1934), faced the death of her mother and older sister when she was 10. She was determined, however, to get an education even though she was female and had no money. After her teen years studying at a "Floating University" which the government would not approve, she left her birthplace of Warsaw, Poland, to study in Paris. There she met her husband, Pierre Curie, and before his early, accidental death, the two of them researched together. Her discovery of radioactive elements earned her two Nobel Prizes, but also killed her because the radiation destroyed her body. Insights found in Curie's own journals and records along with photographs and diagrams enhance the text. Bibliography, Chronology, Notes, Web Sites, and Index.

1884. Yolen, Jane. *The Perfect Wizard: Hans Christian Andersen.* Illustrated by Dennis Nolan. Dutton, 2005. 40pp. ISBN 978-0-525-46955-1. Grades 1–4.

See entry 1553.

1885. Young, Serinity. *Richard Francis Burton: Explorer, Scholar, Spy.* (Great Explorations) Benchmark, 2006. 80pp. ISBN 978-0-7614-2222-8. Grades 5–9.

Sir Richard Francis Burton (1821–1890), a British explorer, was also a soldier, translator, writer, poet, hypnotist, and diplomat. He knew nearly thirty languages and strove to learn about the cultures and religions of the places he explored in the Middle East, South Asia, South America, and Africa. His interest led him on the dangerous journey of entering Mecca disguised as a Muslim pilgrim. The Royal Geographical Society asked him to explore the east coast of Africa, an expedition during which he found Lake Tanganyika. Additionally, he translated *The Book of One Thousand Nights and A Night* and *The Kama Sutra.* Illustrations highlight the text. Maps, Bibliography, Chronology, Further Reading, Notes, Web Sites, and Index.

Graphic Novels, Biographies, and Histories

1886. Doeden, Matt. *The Sinking of the Titanic.* Illustrated by Charles Barnett, III. Graphic Library, 2005. 32pp. ISBN 978-0-7368-3834-4; paper ISBN 978-0-7368-5247-0. Grades 3–5.

When the *Titanic* sank on April 14, 1912, the vessel, *The Californian* was ten miles away. The sinking caused 1,517 deaths, more of men than the women and children who entered the life boats first. Illustrations help readers visualize the story. Bibliography, Glossary, Further Reading, and Index.

1887. Sfar, Joanne, and Emmanuel Guibert. *The Professor's Daughter.* First Second, 2007. 64pp. Paper ISBN 978-1-59643-130-0. Grades 9–12.

Imhotep IV, a mummy awake for the first time in 3,000 years, falls in love with Lillian, the daughter of the renowned Egyptologist Professor Bowell, after she opens his case when her father is away. A number of deaths and mishaps occur when they go out together (Imhotep still in mummy rappings), even the kidnapping of Queen Victoria, after Imhotep's father appears.

DVDs

1888. *Ambient Art: Impression.* Jumby Bay, 2004. 68 min. ISBN 978-0-9744350-5-3. Grades 7 up.

More than 340 works by eleven artists from the impressionist, the neo-impressionist (pointillist), and post-impressionist periods—Van Gogh, Monet, Degas, Cezanne, Renoir, Gauguin, Manet, Seurat, Morisot, Sisley, and Pissarro—appear in the video. Photographs of their major works and commentary on their lives and styles help define the art of the time.

1889. *Blood and Oil: The Middle East in World War I.* Inecom, 2006. 1:52 hrs. ISBN 978-1-59218-042-4. Grades 9 up.

This DVD covers World War I and its aftermath in the Middle East. The boundaries after World War I were redrawn and created conflicts that remain unresolved. The British and French tried to fulfill their own political and economic aims. In chronological order, the program presents the military and diplomatic action and explains the relationship between the European and Middle Eastern theaters. Still photographs, live-action footage, film clips, and maps show the importance of the war in the area with its destruction of the Ottoman Empire.

1890. *Degas and the Dancer.* (Artists' Specials) Devine, 1999. 53 min. ISBN 978-1-894449-47-2. Grades 5–9.

Edgar Degas (1834–1917) is saddled with debt and struggling after his father dies, but he meets a young ballerina named Marie. He helps her develop her talent, and simultaneously she encourages him to persevere with his own style regardless of the hostile Paris establishment. She becomes his model. *Writers Guild of Canada Top Ten Award,*

Golden Sheaf Awards at the Yorkton Short Film and Video Festival, American Library Association Notable Children's Video, The Humanitas Prize, and *Parents' Choice Award* Winner.

1891. *Dropping in on Matisse.* (Art Is . . .) Crystal, 2005. 23 min. ISBN 978-1-56290-342-8. Grades 3–6.

This animated program about Henri Matisse (1869–1954) shows how his style evolved from paintings filled with color to paper cutouts. Puffer the bird asks Matisse, who is sitting in a wheelchair by the window, questions about his life and work, about the art world—including the Fauves and his rivalries with Picasso and Derain—and about his techniques. Six of Matisse's artworks show his different styles in portrait, landscape, and collage.

1892. *Mary Cassatt: American Impressionist.* (Artists' Specials) Devine, 1999. 55 min. Grades 5–9.

Mary Cassatt (1844–1926) lives an orderly life in Paris as an impressionist painter and is a close friend of Edgar Degas. When her brother and his wife arrive with their three unruly children, they disturb her until she realizes she can used them as models. Her niece, Katherine, only wants to marry, but after being exposed to Cassatt's way of living and ideas, she changes her mind. *American Library Association Notable Children's Video, Platinum Award, Oppenheim Toy Portfolio, KIDS FIRST! Coalition of Quality Children's Media, Emmy Award,* and *Parents' Choice Gold Award.*

1893. *Monet: Light and Shadow.* (Artists' Specials) Devine, 2000. 55 min. ISBN 978-1-894449-61-8. Grades 5–9.

While Claude Monet (1840–1926) experiments with his new painting style in 1869, he and his friend Pierre-Auguste Renoir spend days painting the local landscapes outside Paris. Monet has problems selling his work, but he remains optimistic that he will succeed. However, he is so committed to his art that his father stops sending him an allowance. Monet meets a young artist, Daniel, whose father has abandoned him and the two begin to give each other support and confidence. *Top 5 Video of the Year, KidsFirst!*

1894. *Mountain of Ice.* (Final Frontier) WGBH Boston, 2003. 1 hr. ISBN 978-1-59375-632-1. Grades 7 up.

Jon Krakauer, author of *Into Thin Air,* and mountaineer Conrad Anker discuss their trip to the highest peak in Antarctica, the Vinson Massif. They compare their experience with Robert Falcon Scott and Roald Amundsen's 1911 race to be the first to reach the South Pole. Anker shows the importance of proper gear, a specific amount of food, and team training. The video includes discussions of the preparation by Scott and Amundsen and offer reasons why Amundsen's group returned and Scott's did not. The program reveals the importance of the scientific data gathered during the climb for understanding global temperatures and warming.

1895. Venezia, Mike. *Monet.* (Getting to Know the World's Greatest Artists) Getting to Know, 2006. 24 min. Grades K–8.

See entry 1871.

1896. Venezia, Mike. *Vincent van Gogh.* (Getting to Know the World's Greatest Artists) Getting to Know, 2006. 24 min. Grades K–8.

See entry 1877.

1897. *Who Is the Artist? Artists of Line and Color—Dufy, Gauguin, Matisse.* Crystal Productions, 2004. 26 min. ISBN 978-1-56290-319-0. Grades 4 up.

Placing them in historical context, this DVD looks at the characteristics and styles of artists Raoul Dufy, Paul Gauguin, and Henri Matisse. Examples of their works reveal the differences in their themes and their approaches to their subjects.

1898. *Who Killed the Red Baron?* WGBH Boston, 2004. 60 min. ISBN 978-1-59375-108-1. Grades 7 up.

Vintage news footage, animation, and reenactments of dogfights along with comments from historians, war museum experts, pilots, the Baron's great-nephew, and the son of the pilot pursuing the Red Baron recreate the circumstances surrounding the death of Baron Manfred von Richthofen on April 21, 1918, when he was aiming for his 81st kill. New documents indicate that a gunner on the ground fired the shot. Additional coverage of the Baron's life, military training, and the flying skills needed as these airplanes became faster gives a sense of World War I from the air.

1899. *The Windsors: A Royal Family.* WGBH, 2002. 2 DVDS; 4 hrs. ISBN 978-1-59375-157-9. Grades 8 up.

This look at the British royal family, the Windsors, begins with George V in the early 1900s and continues through Elizabeth II's reign. Interviews with government officials, relatives, and staff, along with archival footage and palace-produced film, reveal the history of the family and its relationship with the British public.

1900. *Wings of Madness: The Daring Flights of Alberto Santos-Dumont.* (NOVA) WGBH, 2007. 60 min. ISBN 978-1-59375-656-7. Grades 7 up.

Brazilian-born Alberto Santos-Dupont (1873–1932) manned a gas-powered balloon for a half-hour flight over Paris on October 19, 1901. Later he piloted Europe's first airplane flight. But the fame of the Wright brothers took away his renown as an aviator and inventor, and he became ill and depressed. During World War I, he thought that the plane was his invention, and because it destroyed lives, he felt the blame.

1901. *World War I.* (America in the 20th Century) Media Rich Learning, . 70 min. Grades 7 up.

In an overview of World War I, five segments investigate different aspects of the conflict—"The Roots of War," "European Military Alliances," "The Toll of War," "U.S. Involvement Overseas," and "Supporting the War Effort." Included in the topics discussed are the Zimmerman telegram and the attempt to bring Mexico into the war on the German side, chemical weapons, machine guns and tanks, aerial combat, submarines, the treatment of African Americans, the roles of women, the Espionage and Sedition Act, the Treaty of Versailles, the rise of Imperialism and Nationalism, and trench warfare.

1902. *World War I and Its Aftermath.* Discovery, 2004. 54 min. ISBN 978-1-58738-493-6. Grades 6 up.

In four segments using graphics, interviews, archival film footage, re-creations, and narration, this DVD looks at World War I and other events of that era. "The Rise of Nationalism" in the 1900s focuses on Czarist Russia. "World War I" discusses causes and what a soldier's life in the trenches was like. In "Death from Above: The Red Baron," forensic evidence and detective work suggest who shot down this German flying ace. "Communism and the Soviet Union" examines the fall of Czarist Russia in 1918 and the beginning of communism.

Compact Discs

1903. Bajoria, Paul. *The Printer's Devil.* Illustrated by Bret Bertholf. Narrated by Katherine Kellgren. Recorded Books, 2006. 8 CDs; 9.25 hrs. ISBN 978-1-4193-6623-9. Grades 6–9.

See entry 1594.

1904. Barnes, Julian. *Arthur and George.* Narrated by Nigel Anthony. BBC Audiobooks, 2006. 14 CDs; ca.17 hrs. ISBN 978-0-7927-3862-6. Grades YA.

See entry 1596.

1905. Bernstein, Harry. *The Invisible Wall: A Love Story That Broke Barriers.* Narrated by John Lee. Blackstone Audio, 2007. 8 CDs. ISBN 978-0-7861-5756-3. Grades YA.

See entry 1786.

1906. Bray, Libba. *A Great and Terrible Beauty.* Narrated by Josephine Bailey. (Gemma Doyle Trilogy) Listening Library, 2007. 11 CDs. ISBN 978-0-8072-2376-5. Grades 9 up.

See entry 1600.

1907. Bray, Libba. *Rebel Angels.* Narrated by Josephine Bailey. (Gemma Doyle Trilogy) Listening Library, 2005. 12 CDs; 14 hr. ISBN 978-0-307-28067-1. Grades 8 up.

See entry 1601.

1908. Burnett, Frances Hodgson. *Little Lord Fauntleroy.* Narrated by Donada Peters. Tantor Media, 2008. 5 CDs; 5.5 hrs. ISBN 978-1-4001-3912-5. Grades 5–7.

See entry 1608.

1909. Hartnett, Sonya. *The Silver Donkey.* Illustrated by Don Powers. Narrated by Richard Aspel. Bolinda, 2005. 4 CDs; 4 hrs. 15 min. ISBN 978-1-7409-3586-9. Grades 4–6.

See entry 1623.

1910. Ibbotson, Eva. *A Countess Below Stairs.* Narrated by Davina Porter. Recorded Books, 2007. 8 CDs; 9.5 hrs. ISBN 978-1-4281-6461-1. Grades 8 up.

See entry 1628.

1911. Ibbotson, Eva. *The Star of Kazan.* Narrated by Patricia Conolly. Recorded Books, 2005. 9 CDs; 10.25 hrs. ISBN 978-1-4193-5565-3. Grades 4–8.

See entry 1629.

1912. Lawrence, Iain. *Lord of the Nutcracker Men.* Narrated by Steven Crossley. Recorded Books, 2002. 6 CDs. 6.5 hrs. ISBN 978-0-7887-9788-0. Grades 5–8.

See entry 1639.

1913. Mary Jo, Maichack. *Missing the Muffin Man.* Narrated by Mary Jo Maichack. CDBaby.com, 2006. 1 CD; 37 min. Grades 3–7.

In 19th-century London, Ginny waits for the door-to-door muffin vendor to return so that she can share muffins and tea with her mother. She goes into the street to look for him, is kidnapped and kept in a basement, but a young orphan street thief hiding there helps her escape. During her adventure, she hears that the muffin man has been arrested for his loud bell but that he will soon return to the streets.

1914. Meyer, Carolyn. *Marie, Dancing.* Narrated by Carine Montbertrand. Recorded Books, 2007. 255pp. 6 CDs; 7.25 hrs. ISBN 978-1-4281-3512-3. Grades 6–9.

See entry 1650.

1915. Morpurgo, Michael. *Private Peaceful.* Narrated by Jeff Woodman. Recorded Books, 2005. 5 Cds; 5.25 hrs. ISBN 978-1-4193-5614-8. Grades 7 up.

See entry 1651.

1916. Peters, Elizabeth. *Crocodile on the Sandbank.* Narrated by Susan O'Malley. (Amelia Peabody Mystery) Blackstone Audio, 2007. 8 CDs; 9 hrs. ISBN 978-1-4332-0485-2. Grades YA.

See entry 1660.

1917. Peters, Elizabeth. *The Last Camel Died at Noon.* Narrated by Susan O'Malley. (Amelia Peabody Mystery) Blackstone Audio, 2003. 11 CDs. ISBN 978-0-7861-9734-7. Grades YA.

See entry 1668.

1918. Peters, Elizabeth. *Lion in the Valley.* Narrated by Susan O'Malley. (Amelia Peabody Mystery) Blackstone Audio, 2001. 10 CDs. ISBN 978-0-7861-9643-2. Grades YA.

When Amelia Peabody and her husband Radcliffe return to Egypt with their 8-year-old son Ramses, a criminal kidnaps Amelia, and her family has to discover her location. The fourth volume in the series.

1919. Peters, Elizabeth. *The Mummy Case.* Narrated by Susan O'Malley. (Amelia Peabody Mystery) Blackstone Audio, 2000. 9 CDs. ISBN 978-0-7861-9873-3. Grades YA.

See entry 1670.

1920. Pullman, Philip. *The Ruby in the Smoke.* Narrated by Anton Lesser. (Sally Lockhart Mystery) Listening Library, 2008. 6 CDs; 6 hrs. 26 min. ISBN 978-0-7393-6781-0. Grades 8 up.

See entry 1673.

1921. Pullman, Philip. *The Shadow in the North.* Narrated by Anton Lesser. (Sally Lockhart Mystery) Listening Library, 2008. 8 CDs; 9.5 hrs. ISBN 978-0-7393-7152-7. Grades 8 up.

See entry 1674.

1922. Pullman, Philip. *The Tiger in the Well.* Narrated by Anton Lesser. (Sally Lockhart Mystery) Listening Library, 2008. 11 CDs; 13 hrs. 9 min. ISBN 978-0-7393-7153-4. Grades 8 up.

See entry 1675.

1923. Raphael, Marie. *Streets of Gold.* Narrated by Ruth Anne Phimister. Recorded Books, 2003. 6 CDs; 7 hrs. ISBN 978-1-4025-6523-6. Grades 6–10.

See entry 1678.

1924. Richards, Justin. *The Death Collector.* Narrated by Steven Pacey. Listening Library, 2006. 7 CDs. ISBN 978-0-7393-3539-0. Grades 7 up.

See entry 1680.

1925. Springer, Nancy. *The Case of the Bizarre Bouquets: An Enola Holmes Mystery.* Narrated by Katherine Kellgren. (Enola Holmes Mystery) Recorded Books. 3 CDs; 3.75 hrs. ISBN 978-1-4281-8257-8. Grades 5–8.

See entry 1690.

1926. Springer, Nancy. *The Case of the Left-Handed Lady.* Narrated by Katherine Kellgren. (Enola Holmes Mystery) Recorded Books, 2007. 5 CDs; 5 hrs. ISBN 978-1-4281-4749-2. Grades 5–9.

See entry 1691.

1927. Whelan, Gloria. *Angel on the Square.* Narrated by Julie Dretzin. Recorded Books, 2003. 5 CDs; 5.5 hrs. ISBN 978-1-4025-6594-6. Grades 5–9.

See entry 1709.

1928. Woodruff, Elvira. *The Orphan of Ellis Island: A Time-Travel Adventure.* Narrated by Lloyd James. Blackstone Audio, 2007. 3 CDs; 3.5 hrs. ISBN 978-1-4332-0716-7. Grades 4–6.

In this historical fantasy, Dominic is a fifth-grader who is embarrassed on a class trip to Ellis Island because, as an orphan and foster child, he has no family of his own. He hides in a closet at the site and goes to sleep. He awakens in Italy of 1908, meets three orphaned brothers, and goes with two of them to the United States after the untimely death of the third. He discovers a sense of family and returns to the present where he wakes with more confidence.

EUROPE AND THE BRITISH ISLES, 1919–1945

Historical Fiction and Fantasy

1929. Ackerman, Karen. *The Night Crossing.* Illustrated by Elizabeth Sayles. Yearling, 1995. 64pp. Paper ISBN 978-0-679-87040-1. Grades 2–6.

In 1938 Clara and her family escape over the mountains into Switzerland from Germany as Nazi hostility rises. The family takes with them two silver candlesticks, which become symbols of their freedom after many other family members die in the ensuing Holocaust, and Clara's two dolls, which had belonged to her grandmother. To get the candlesticks across the border, Clara inserts them inside her dolls. *Young Hoosier Book Award* (Indiana) nomination, *SCASL Book Award* (South Carolina) nomination.

1930. Adler, David A. *The Number on My Grandfather's Arm.* Photographs by Rose Eichenbaum. Uri, 1987. 28pp. ISBN 978-0-8074-0328-0. Grades 2–4.

A young girl asks her grandfather about the number tattooed across his forearm. He tells her his story of World War II, not in graphic detail, but so that she can understand that he had a terrible time and almost lost his life during his imprisonment in Auschwitz, a concentration camp. *Sydney Taylor Award.*

1931. Adler, David A. *One Yellow Daffodil: A Hanukkah Story.* Illustrated by Lloyd Bloom. Voyager, 1999. 32pp. Paper ISBN 978-0-15-202094-1. Grades 1–5.

Children who buy flowers from Mr. Kaplan's shop invite him to dinner on the first night of Hanukkah. At first he does not want to come, but when he arrives he begins to remember his childhood in Poland. He lost almost everything during World War II and he remembers seeing a yellow daffodil outside the concentration camp and thinking that if the flower could live, so could he. What he did not lose was a box with his menorah in it, and he gives the menorah to the children. *Notable Children's Trade Books in the Field of Social Studies.*

1932. Alma, Ann. *Brave Deeds: How One Family Saved Many People from the Nazis.* Groundwood, 2008. 96pp. ISBN 978-0-8889-9791-3. Grades 3–7.

A Dutch family creates a hideout at their home on the island of Voorne where they rescue Jews from the Nazis. The author draws on interviews with the family to create a realistic picture of the hardships and fears that these brave people endured. Because a young fictional narrator tells the story by overhearing adults talking, the story becomes historical fiction.

1933. Barnett, Jill. *Sentimental Journey.* Pocket Star, 2002. 512pp. Paper ISBN 978-0-671-03534-1. Grades YA.

During World War II, United States Army Major J. R. Cassidy goes to North Africa to save nuclear scientist Kitty Kincaid from the Nazis. Red Walker falls for a flygirl, Charlotte "Charley" Morrison, who in turn falls for a Royal Air Force pilot, George "Skip" Inskip, a man whose wife and child died in a London bombing. Their stories intersect through love and trying to find safety during war.

1934. Barth-Grozinger, Inge. *Something Remains.* Translated by Anthea Bell. Hyperion, 2006. 390pp. ISBN 978-0-7868-3880-6; 2008. paper ISBN 978-0-7868-3881-3. Grades 5–8.

Erich Levi, 12, and his Jewish family have to make changes in their lives in 1933 as Hitler comes to power and anti-Jewish sentiment spreads in Germany. Erich, his brother Max, and his cousin Erwin face hostility at school and in the community. Only one Gentile friend remains loyal, but only in secret. Soon Erich's father's business fails, and the family realizes that they must try to escape to the United States.

1935. Bartoletti, Susan Campbell. *The Boy Who Dared.* Scholastic, 2008. 202pp. ISBN 978-0-439-68013-4. Grades 6–9.

In October 1942 Helmuth Hübener, 17, imprisoned and awaiting execution for distributing anti-Nazi information, remembers his awakening to Hitler's evils as a Hamburg youth and why he decided to spread the truth about Hitler. This fictionalized biography sees him first as a Nazi supporter who later began listening to BBC radio broadcasts and came to believe that Hitler was wrong. Photographs highlight the text. Chronology and Bibliography. *Capitol Choices Noteworthy Titles* (Washington, D.C.), *Notable Trade Books in the Field of Social Studies.*

1936. Bauer, Jutta. *Grandpa's Angel.* Illustrated by author. Candlewick, 2005. 48pp. ISBN 978-0-7636-2743-0. Grades 1–4.

A grandfather in his hospital bed tells his grandson what a wonderful life he has had. He notes that he was spared—unlike his Jewish friend—in World War II, was nearly hit by a bus, had difficulty surviving after the war, and overcame other challenges. The illustrations depict a guardian angel watching over him in each of the scenes, and when the little boy leaves the room, he is protected by the same angel. Ink and gouache illustrations enhance the text.

1937. Bell, Ted. *Nick of Time.* Griffin, 2008. 432pp. ISBN 978-0-312-38068-7. Grades 6–9.

See entry 1375.

1938. Benn, James R. *The First Wave: A Billy Boyle World War II Mystery.* Soho, 2007. 294pp. ISBN 978-1-56947-471-6. Grades YA.

Lieutenant Billy Boyle, in this sequel to *Billy Boyle* (2006), works as Major Samuel Harding's aide as the American forces prepare to liberate Algeria in 1942. He has fallen in love with Diana Seaton, a British spy. When French lieutenant Georges Dupree's brother Jerome is murdered, Boyle must help solve the case. The prime suspect is Vichy

Captain Villard in a case that becomes more complex when an American supply officer is killed and a drug smuggling operation becomes apparent.

1939. Bennett, Cherie, and Jeff Gottesfeld. *Anne Frank and Me.*   Penguin, 2002. 291pp. Paper ISBN 978-0-698-11973-4. Grades 7–9.

Bored with studying the Holocaust, irritated with her younger sister Little Bit, and focused on her boyfriend Jack, 16-year-old Nicole Burns visits an Anne Frank exhibit with her class, and a gunshot whirls her into Nazi-occupied Paris. She assumes the life of Nicole Bernhardt, daughter of a Jewish doctor and his wife, who enjoys her friends and the privileges of wealth. Soon she has to go into hiding, and on the way to a Nazi concentration camp she meets Anne Frank. Just as she enters the gas chamber, she returns to her home in the 21st century.

1940. Berger, Zdena. *Tell Me Another Morning: An Autobiographical Novel.*   Pars, 2007. 272pp. ISBN 978-1-930464-10-0. Grades YA.

In a series of Nazi concentration camps, Tania faces her brother's death and her mother's decision to die in the gas chamber with her husband. When she returns to Prague after the war, she finds it hard to believe that people have been living normal lives there during this time.

1941. Bergman, Tamar. *Along the Tracks.*   Translated by Michael Swirsky. Houghton Mifflin, 1995. 256pp. Paper ISBN 978-0-395-74513-7. Grades 6–10.

Yankele is 7 when World War II begins, and his family journeys from Lodz, Poland, toward the Urals in Russia. His father joins the Russian army. As Yankele and his mother travel by train, Yankele gets off during a bombing raid but does not get back on before the train leaves. Yankele begins four years of wandering through Uzbekistan, surviving starvation and incarceration by petty theft and careful hiding. He eventually finds his mother and, miraculously, his father, who had been missing in action, alive in Poland. *Bulletin Blue Ribbon.*

1942. Bishop, Claire Huchet. *Twenty and Ten.*   Peter Smith, 1984. 76pp. ISBN 978-0-8446-6168-1; Puffin, 1991. paper ISBN 978-0-14-031076-4. Grades 5–9.

During World War II in France, Janet and twenty of her classmates are evacuated to the countryside with the Catholic sister who teaches them. When ten Jewish children arrive and hide in a nearby cave, all risk their lives by denying any knowledge of the children to the Nazis who come questioning. They continue to feed the children as long as needed. *Child Study Children's Book Committee at Bank Street College Award.*

1943. Bloor, Edward. *London Calling.*   Knopf, 2006. 289pp. ISBN 978-0-375-83635-0; 2008. paper ISBN 978-0-375-84363-1. Grades 6–9.

Martin Conway, a seventh grader who hates his Catholic school, receives an old radio on the death of his grandmother. It becomes a time-travel device that takes him to World War II London where he meets Jimmy, who needs his help. Jimmy wants to know what his answer will be when, before his death, someone asks "What did you do to help?" Through him, Martin begins to answer some of the questions in his own contemporary life.

1944. Borden, Louise. *The Greatest Skating Race: A World War II Story from the Netherlands.*   Margaret K. McElderry, 2004. 44pp. ISBN 978-0-689-84502-4. Grades 3–6.

Piet, 10, dreams of competing in Holland's "Elfstedentocht," a 200-kilometer race held when the canal ice is strong enough and which Pim Muller first won in 1890. He finds out that his skating talent also has a practical value in 1942 when his father asks him to help two neighbor children flee to Belgium. Nazis have arrested their father for radioing messages so he skates them to his aunt's house in Brugge. Note. *Great Lakes Children's Book Award* (Michigan) nomination, *The Land of Enchantments Children's Book Award* (New Mexico) nomination, *Children's Book Award* (South Carolina) nomination, *Bluebonnet Book Award* (Texas) nomination, and *Capitol Choices Noteworthy Titles* (Washington, D.C.).

1945. Borden, Louise. *The Little Ships: The Heroic Rescue at Dunkirk in World War II.* Illustrated by Michael Foreman. Aladdin, 2003. 32pp. Paper ISBN 978-0-689-85396-8. Grades 4 up.

A young English girl who sails on her father's fishing boat, one of 861 small ships that help rescue soldiers from Dunkirk in May 1940, tells the story in verse. The vision of her brother John waiting on shore to be rescued stays in her mind as her father navigates their boat through the harbor amid German planes bombing from overhead. *Capitol Choices Noteworthy Titles* (Washington, D.C.).

1946. Boyne, John. *The Boy in the Striped Pajamas: A Fable.* David Fickling, 2006. 215pp. ISBN 978-0-385-75106-3; 2007. paper ISBN 978-0-385-75153-7. Grades 7–10.

In 1942, Bruno, the 9-year-old son of a Nazi officer, is bored with life after his family moves from Berlin to a place called "Out-With" (Auschwitz). He makes friends with Shmuel, a boy from Cracow who wears striped pajamas and lives behind a fence. Bruno never understands why the boy is there or why everyone else with him wears the same clothes.

1947. Bradley, Kimberly Brubaker. *For Freedom: The Story of a French Spy.* Random House, 2003. 192pp. ISBN 978-0-385-90087-4; Laurel Leaf, 2005. paper ISBN 978-0-440-41831-3. Grades 5–9.

When a bomb drops on the town of Cherbourg, France, in 1940 and kills a pregnant neighbor in front of 13-year-old Suzanne David, Suzanne's life changes. However, she is determined to become an opera singer, so she continues to take voice lessons and participate in rehearsals. As she travels, she sees and hears about the Nazis. By the time she is 16, the French Resistance asks her for information, and she becomes a secret courier and spy known as "number twenty-two." Suzanne cannot even tell her parents of her participation for fear of jeopardizing their lives as well as others. Arrested on June 5, 1944, after her hairdresser betrays her to the Germans, she is freed the next day when the Germans reorganize to fight the Allies during the D-Day invasion. Based on a true story, the novel gives insight into the young adults who worked for the Resistance. *Beehive Young Adults' Book Award* (Utah) nomination, *Dorothy Canfield Fisher Children's Book Award* (Vermont) nomination, *Charlie May Simon Children's Book Award* (Arkansas) nomination, *SCASL Book Award* (South Carolina) nomination, *Mark Twain Award* (Missouri), *Sequoyah Book Award* (Oklahoma) nomination, *Nutmeg Children's Book Award* (Connecticut) nomination, *Student Book Award* (Maine) nomination, *Beehive Award* (Utah) nomination, *Junior Book Award* (South Carolina) nomination, and *Young Hoosier Award* (Indiana) nomination.

1948. Bunting, Eve. *Spying on Miss Müller.* Illustrated by Ellen Thompson. Houghton, 1995. 160pp. ISBN 978-0-395-69172-4; Fawcett, 1996. paper ISBN 978-0-449-70455-4. Grades 4–6.

Jessie and her friends at their Belfast, Northern Ireland, school think their German teacher, Miss Müller, is wonderful. After World War II begins, they change their minds, and start rumors. When they see her climb the stairs to the roof one night, they wonder if she is a spy. Jessie wants to prove her teacher's innocence, so she begins watching her. What she discovers is a tryst between Miss Müller and Mr. Bolton, the Latin teacher. But another friend, Greta, is angry that her father has been killed, and she exposes the lovers. Because teachers cannot be married, Miss Müller is fired, and Mr. Bolton joins the army. Jessie hopes they will be happy, but doubts that they will see each other again. *Young Reader's Choice Award* (Pennsylvania) and *Edgar Awards* nomination.

1949. Carcaterra, Lorenzo. *Street Boys.* Ballantine, 2003. 336pp. Paper ISBN 978-0-345-41099-3. Grades YA.

In Italy in 1943 Corporal Steve Connors stays in Naples to rescue remaining civilians. He meets orphans who have banded together and refuse to leave. They hide in the hills and start their own army to battle the Nazis. Their resistance thwarts the Nazis.

1950. Casanova, Mary. *The Klipfish Code.* Houghton, 2007. 227pp. ISBN 978-0-618-88393-6. Grades 4–7.

In 1940 the Germans invade Norway, and Marit, 10, and her younger brother Lars have to go to Godoy Island to live with their grandfather Bestefar and their Aunt Ingeborg while their parents join the Resistance. On the island, Bestefar commands them to cooperate with the Germans, but Marit becomes especially upset when her teacher is deported for refusing to teach what the Nazis command. Marit finds an injured Resistance worker and risks her life to help him. She completes his task of trading a compass for a bucket of klipfish (codfish). Bestefar eventually takes them to the safety of the Shetland Islands.

1951. Chambers, Aidan. *Postcards from No Man's Land.* Dutton, 2002. 320pp. ISBN 978-0-525-46863-9; Speak, 2004. paper ISBN 978-0-14-240145-3. Grades 9 up.

Jacob Todd, 17, takes his backpack on a trip to Amsterdam at the request of his English grandmother, whose husband died in a nearby town in World War II. Meanwhile, a frail Dutch woman, Geertrui, remembers falling in love at age 19 with a British soldier named Jacob Todd who had come to liberate Holland from German occupation. Jacob plans to visit his grandfather's grave, and he meets and falls in love with a young woman even as a young gay man attracts him. He comes to realize his relationship to the now terminally ill Geertrui, and that nothing is really as it seems. *Carnegie Medal, Horn Book Fanfare, Booklist Editors' Choice,* and *Capitol Choices Noteworthy Titles* (Washington, D.C.).

1952. Charlesworth, Monique. *The Children's War.* Anchor, 2005. 367pp. Paper ISBN 978-1-4000-3207-5. Grades YA.

Ilse Blumenthal, 13, has a Jewish father, Otto, and a Protestant mother, Lore, in Germany at the beginning of World War II. Lore sends Ilse to her Uncle Willy's home in Morocco, but she is returned to Otto in Paris when Willy joins the Foreign Legion to fight Hitler. Ilse expects Lore to be in Paris, but she is not. Ilse has to decide if she will return to Germany and her attentive mother or stay in Paris with Otto who has often been distant toward her. She stays in Paris, and when the Germans arrive, the two escape to

Marseilles. There a "Madam" protects them until the Nazis capture Otto. In Germany, Lore worries about her decision to help her daughter and husband while serving in a privileged household as a nursemaid to Nicolai, a member of the Hitler Youth. Because he often shows anti-Fascist views, she risks her life to save him during a Hamburg bombing and dies in the attempt. Nicolai must cope with the air raids and starvation while Ilse joins the French Resistance. *School Library Journal Best Adult Books for Young Adults.*

1953. Cheng, Andrea. *Lace Dowry.* Front Street, 2005. 120pp. ISBN 978-1-9324252-0-8. Grades 3–7.

Juli, 12, befriends a family of lace makers in Halas, Hungary, in 1936. She especially likes Roza, the daughter hired to stitch her dowry, and their relationship blossoms. Juli loves books, but Roza has no time to study as she must work the family's farm and stitch lace. Juli tries to teach her, and Roza, in turn, shows Juli the stitches. When Roza's mother loses her sight, Juli tries to help her.

1954. Cheng, Andrea. *Marika.* Front Street, 2002. 163pp. ISBN 978-1-8869-1078-2. Grades 7 up.

Marika Schnurmacher, 12, has been raised a Catholic in Hungary. Her main concern is the apartment wall that divides her father and his mistress from herself, her mother, and her brother during 1939. But when the Nazis arrive in Budapest in 1944, they take away her papers, and she must go to a Jewish school. Her father buys her freedom, but her Jewish mother remains imprisoned. They live in anguish until the Nazis leave and they can reunite.

1955. Cooper, Susan. *Dawn of Fear.* Illustrated by Margery Gill. Harcourt, 2007. Paper ISBN 978-0-15-206106-7. Grades 5 up.

Derek lives with his family outside London during World War II, and they have to go to the local shelters almost every night during air raids. When a bomb hits his friend's house one night and kills his friend, the war takes on a different meaning. Derek has to adjust to the huge hole in his life.

1956. Dunmore, Helen. *The Siege.* Grove, 2002. 304pp. Paper ISBN 978-0-8021-3958-0. Grades YA.

In 1941 Leningrad Anna Levin, 22, has to care for her 5-year-old brother, Kilya in a freezing apartment, and look after her sick father, Mikhail, who has deteriorated since his wife's death. Also in the apartment is Mikhail's former mistress, Marina. Then Anna falls in love with a doctor, and Andrei moves in. They struggle to survive during the German assault on Russia and the siege of Leningrad. They vie with others for a last crust of bread.

1957. Durbin, William. *The Winter War.* Wendy Lamb, 2008. 231pp. ISBN 978-0-385-74652-6. Grades 5–9.

Marko, 14, serves as a sky watcher and junior member of the Civil Guard in Finland in 1939 after Russian bombers attack his village on November 30 and kill his best friend. Two family members have to evacuate to Sweden after his father is conscripted. Marko, although limping from polio, serves on the front lines near Savolahti where he becomes a skiing messenger during the little known Winter War of 1939–1940. During this test of manhood, Marko finds a new resilience that he had not expected.

fighting a friend to near death, knowing that a refusal to fight meant that the Nazis would kill him. He does not want his son to think of him as a murderer, so he solves the problem.

1968. Harris, Robert. *Enigma: A Novel.*   Ivy, 1996. 320pp. Paper ISBN 978-0-8041-1548-3. Grades YA.

In 1943 mathematicians and cryptologists gather in England's Bletchley Park to try to decode a German cipher that has stymied both British and American intelligence. Tom Jericho, after a nervous breakdown and a wrecked romance, is still the best code-breaker, and the group needs his mastery if they are to have any possibility of succeeding. Jericho still hopes to patch up his romance, but the woman he loves may have passed classified information to the enemy. Jericho must work to meet his professional and personal challenges. *School Library Journal Best Books for Young Adults.*

1969. Hesse, Karen. *The Cats in Krasinski Square.*   Illustrated by Wendy Watson. Scholastic, 2004. Unpaged. ISBN 978-0-439-43540-6. Grades 3–5.

Two Jewish sisters "pass" for Polish in this series of free verse poems telling their story. As escapees of the ghetto in Warsaw, they try to get food for those still trapped. When sympathizers bring in contraband food on the train, the girls smuggle it inside the ghetto through holes that stray cats use. When the Gestapo hear of the plan, they meet the train with dogs ready to sniff out food and smugglers. But the girls have their cats in baskets, and they let them loose. The cats distract the dogs, and the girls succeed in their mission. Illustrations complement the text. *Young Reader Medal* (California), *Prairie Pasque Award* (South Dakota) nomination, *Children's Book Award* (Georgia) nomination, *American Library Association Notable Children's Books, Capitol Choices Noteworthy Titles* (Washington, D.C.), *Kirkus Reviews Editor's Choice, Parents' Choice Gold Award*, and *Publishers Weekly Best Children's Books.*

1970. Hesse, Karen. *Letters from Rifka.*   Holt, 1992. 148pp. ISBN 978-0-8050-1964-3; Square Fish, 2009. paper ISBN 978-0-312-53561-2. Grades 5–9.

Rifka, age 12 in 1919, flees Russia with her family to escape the Jewish pogroms. She carries with her a beloved volume of poetry by Alexander Pushkin. In the book she writes letters to her cousin, Tovah, telling about her experiences on the journey. Rifka has to endure the humiliation of doctors' examinations, typhus, ringworm treatment in Belgium (during which she loses her hair), and being detained at Ellis Island because of her baldness. Her ability to speak other languages allows her to help a young Russian peasant (her enemy) and an orphaned Polish baby at Ellis Island.

1971. Higson, Charlie. *Blood Fever: A James Bond Adventure.*   (Young Bond) Mixamax, 2006. 335pp. ISBN 978-0-7868-3662-8. Grades 6–9.

When James Bond, 13, returns to England and Eton, he joins the Danger Society. Soon after, he begins a vacation in Sardinia to see his cousin Victor and study the archaeological ruins in the area. What he discovers is that an underground group of criminals, the presumed extinct Millennaria, have kidnapped a young girl. James notices that one of the teachers along on his trip acts strangely, and he must decide if he is involved in the kidnapping and the theft of art treasures on the island.

1972. Higson, Charlie. *Silverfin: A James Bond Adventure.*   (Young Bond) Miramax, 2006. 335pp. Paper ISBN 978-0-7868-3866-0. Grades 6–9.

In 1930 14-year-old orphan James Bond attends Eton and lives with his Aunt Charmain when school is not in session. He goes to Scotland to see his ill Uncle Max and meets Red Kelly on the train. In Scotland, he discovers that the person he dislikes most at Eton, George Hellebore, is visiting his father, Lord Randolph, in the same town. James and Red discover that Red's cousin, Alfie Kelly, has disappeared near Loch Silverfin, on the Hellebore estate. They team up with Meatpacker and Wilder Lawless—and her horse, Martini—to rescue Alfie, but must first overcome a crazy arms dealer who wants domination of the globe.

1973. Hoestlandt, Jo. *Star of Fear, Star of Hope.* Illustrated by Johanna Kang. Translated by Mark Polizzotti. Walker, 1995. Unpaged. ISBN 978-0-8027-8373-8; 2000. paper ISBN 978-0-8027-7588-7. Grades 2–5.

An old woman tells the story of her friend, Lydia, who came to spend the night on her ninth birthday in 1942. Lydia had to wear a star on her sleeve, and when a frightened woman who also wears a star knocks on the door while Lydia is at the narrator's apartment, Lydia wants to go home. The narrator is angry, but Lydia leaves her a present. The narrator never sees her again. She does not know what happened to her; she only knows that no one in Lydia's family was at home the next day or ever again. *Mildred L. Batchelder Honor Award, Sydney Taylor Book Award, IRA Teachers' Choice,* and *American Library Association Notable Books for Children.*

1974. Hull, Nancy L. *On Rough Seas.* Clarion, 2008. 272pp. ISBN 978-0-618-89743-8. Grades 5–7.

Alec Curtis, 14, wants to go to sea as a penance for his cousin Georgie's earlier drowning even though his father wants him to stay in Dover and help with the family's inn. He sneaks on board the skiff *Britannica,* where he works as a part-time galley boy before it begins its mission across the English Channel to Dunkirk in 1940. His experiences trying to help rescue the thousands of stranded soldiers change him.

1975. Ibbotson, Eva. *The Dragonfly Pool.* Dutton, 2008. 377pp. ISBN 978-0-525-42064-4. Grades 5–8.

In 1939 as Hitler threatens, Tally, 12, has to leave London for boarding school at Delderton. She sees a newsreel about Bergania, a small country whose king has refused Hitler the right to cross it. The country invites the school to an international dance festival, and Tally wants to attend. While there, the children see the king being assassinated and they quickly help his son, Karil, by smuggling him out of the country. Karil goes to their school where he is able to hide from Hitler until the war ends six years later. *School Library Journal Best Books for Children.*

1976. Isaacs, Anne. *Torn Thread.* Scholastic, 2002. 188pp. Paper ISBN 978-0-590-60364-5. Grades 6–10.

When she is 12, Eva's father sends her from the Polish ghetto in Bezdin to be with her older sister, Rachel, in a Nazi labor camp in Parschnitz, Czechoslovakia, in hopes that they might survive there. Everyday she struggles with hunger, cold, disease, and hard labor, and the fact that some of the Poles and even some Jews cooperate with the Nazis. But there is one German officer who secretly tries to help the prisoners. Eva and Rachel survive, but they must live from hour to hour until the Allies liberate them. They eventually reach Canada and a new life. *Children's Book Award* (Georgia) nomination, *Student Book Award* (Maine) nomination, *Mark Twain Award* (Missouri) nomination, *Battle of the Books* (North Carolina) nomination, *Young Reader's Choice Award* (Pennsylvania) nomination, *Junior Book Award* (South Carolina) nomination, *Tayshas Reading List* (Texas) nomination, and *Capitol Choices Noteworthy Titles* (Washington, D.C.).

1977. Jackson, Mick G. *Five Boys: A Novel.*   HarperCollins, 2002. 288pp. ISBN 978-0-06-001394-3. Grades YA.

Bobby is evacuated to a village in Devon from London in World War II. Since most of the men are fighting, the village contains women, old men, and five boys born the same autumn who accuse the homesick Bobby of being a Nazi spy and terrorize him. The spinster Lillian Minister allows Bobby to live in her house while another villager, the Captain, makes models of ships wrecked off the nearby coast, and secretly loves Miss Pye, the overweight postmistress. Eventually one of the boys tells Bobby of his fascination with London, and they all become friends. The Bee King arrives, a mysterious figure with an apiary, and he gains a hypnotic control over the boys; eventually his secrets come to light.

1978. Johnston, Tony R. *The Harmonica.*   Illustrated by Ron Mazellan. Charlesbridge, 2004. ISBN 978-1-57091-547-5. Grades 3–6.

Tom reads, sings, and listens to Schubert's music played on a neighbor's gramophone in Poland. Then Tom's father brings him a harmonica, and Tom practices until he can play the Schubert melody that he loves. Nazis disrupt his happy life by sending him to a concentration camp where a commandant demands that Tom play Schubert for him each night before bed. Although he dislikes playing for such an evil man, Tom knows that his fellow prisoners can also hear the music and be momentarily removed from their misery. Illustrations enlighten the first-person text based on a true story. *Young Hoosier Book Award* (Indiana) nomination, *Charlotte Award* (New York) nomination, *Sydney Taylor Book Award Honor*, and *Independent Publisher Book Awards Finalist*.

1979. Kacer, Kathy. *Hiding Edith: A True Story.*   Second Story, 2006. 151pp. Paper ISBN 978-1-89718-706-7. Grades 4–8.

A young Jewish girl, Edith Schwalb, is separated from her family during their Holocaust escape from Austria. In France, Jewish Scouts get Edith to a safe house in the village of Moissac, and the entire village helps conceal one hundred Jewish children there. During Nazi raids, the children hide in the woods. Photographs and maps highlight the text based on the story of a real Edith Schwalb. *Sydney Taylor Book Award* nomination and *Voice of Youth Advocates Nonfiction Honor List*.

1980. Kandel, Charlotte. *The Scarlet Stockings: The Enchanted Riddle.*   Illustrated by Roland Sarkany. Dutton, 2008. 384pp. ISBN 978-0-525-47824-9. Grades 4–8.

In 1923 in London, Daphne, 13, wants to be adopted and become a ballerina. She receives a package at the Orphanage of St. Jude containing a ballet instruction book with a handwritten riddle and a pair of scarlet stockings. A loving greengrocer's family soon adopts her, but Daphne wants to be a ballet star and mistreats the family. She becomes a maid for a musical stage star who helps her and then a Paris ballet company accepts her although the Russian prima ballerina, Ova Andova, tries to kill her. Eventually Daphne suffers for her hard-hearted treatment of her benefactors, but she recovers.

1981. Kerr, Judith. *When Hitler Stole Pink Rabbit.*   Puffin, 2009. 192pp. Paper ISBN 978-0-14-241408-8. Grades 4–7.

Anna's Jewish family leaves Berlin for Switzerland in 1933 after her father disappears. At the border, she has to leave her pink rabbit, her favorite stuffed animal. The family joins her father and goes to France, and later travel on to England. Anna, age 9 when she leaves Berlin, must learn new languages and attend new schools while her family runs from the war.

1982. King, Laurie R. *The Game: A Mary Russell Novel.* (Mary Russell) Bantam, 2005. 439pp. Paper ISBN 978-0-553-58338-0. Grades YA.

In 1924 Mary Russell and her husband, Sherlock Holmes, are summoned to Holmes's brother's house and discover from an oilskin-wrapped packet that a British spy named Kimball O'Hara (the man who inspired Rudyard Kipling to write *Kim*) is missing. They leave for India in search of him, and Russell learns that Holmes knew Kimball when he was younger. They have a number of escapades including a daring rescue of Holmes before they can return to England. *School Library Journal Best Adult Books for Young Adults.*

1983. King, Laurie R. *Justice Hall.* (Mary Russell) Bantam, 2003. 464pp. Paper ISBN 978-0-553-58111-9. Grades YA.

In the fall of 1923 Mary Russell and Sherlock Holmes are shocked to find two men they knew as Bedouin spies at their door. They discover that the men are not Arabs but British aristocrats. Ali Hazr is actually Alistair Hughenfort, and his cousin Mahmoud, Maurice (called Marsh), is the seventh Duke of Beauville. Marsh's older brother and his nephew Gabriel have died and he is an unhappy heir who longs to return to Palestine rather than be imprisoned in the beautiful English estate called Justice Hall. The heir apparent is 9-year-old Thomas Hughenfort of Paris, whose father Lionel died of pneumonia soon after his son's birth in 1914. Eventually, they uncover a mystery surrounding the death of young Gabriel, who was executed during World War I after being wrongly charged with cowardice.

1984. King, Laurie R. *A Letter of Mary: A Mary Russell Novel.* (Mary Russell) Picador, 2007. 288pp. Paper ISBN 978-0-312-42738-2. Grades YA.

Mary Russell, an Oxford theologian, lives with her husband, Sherlock Holmes, in Sussex. Her friend Dorothy Ruskin brings her a document from a Palestinian dig that seems to be a letter from Mariam of Magdala, a woman who calls herself an apostle of Jesus. After Ruskin gives Russell the letter, she dies in a traffic accident that proves to be a murder. Russell and Holmes investigate in this third episode in the series.

1985. King, Laurie R. *A Monstrous Regiment of Women: A Mary Russell Novel.* (Mary Russell) Picador, 2007. 288pp. Paper ISBN 978-0-312-42737-5. Grades YA.

Mary Russell, the assistant to Sherlock Holmes in this sequel to *The Beekeeper's Apprentice*, is living in Oxford, England, after World War I. She still likes Holmes, but her interest in women's rights and her concern for furthering her studies keeps her in Oxford. When she meets Margery Childe, a spiritual adviser to several young women, she wonders why so many of Childe's protégés die and leave their estates to Childe. Her investigation takes her to the back streets of London and various encounters with Holmes.

1986. Knauss, Sibylle. *Eva's Cousin.* Translated by Anthea Bell. Ballantine, 2003. 329pp. Paper ISBN 978-0-345-44906-1. Grades YA.

In the summer of 1944 Marlene, 20, joins her older cousin, Eva Braun, at her mountain retreat, Hitler's villa, the Berghof, where Eva waits to hear from him each day. Marlene is at first impressed by the enormous wealth surrounding Eva and all of her clothes, but she quickly becomes bored. Then Marlene listens to the BBC and has to digest the very different information she is hearing. She also runs into a young Ukrainian boy who has escaped from a nearby work camp and decides to hide him. Eventually Marlene has to question the horrors surrounding her outside the illusion on top of the mountain.

1987. Kositsky, Lynne Willard. *The Thought of High Windows.* Kids Can, 2004. 176pp. ISBN 978-1-55337-621-7; 2005 paper ISBN 978-1-55337-622-4. Grades 7 up.

Esther escapes Germany and the Nazis with other Jewish children at the beginning of World War II. The only way she can escape her fears is by imagining windows and flying out of them. As the war continues, and she becomes even more horrified about life around her, her windows go higher and higher in her imagination. *ForeWord Book of the Year Award Honoree.*

1988. Kushner, Tony. *Brundibar.* Illustrated by Maurice Sendak. Hyperion, 2003. 56pp. ISBN 978-0-7868-0904-2. Grades 14.

When Aninku and Pepicek realize their mother is sick, they rush to town to buy her milk. They need money for this and they plan to earn it by singing. However they are thwarted by a bullying hurdy-gurdy grinder, Brundibar. Eventually, three hundred children arrive and help them triumph over Brundibar. Children at Terezin who were awaiting transport to death camps performed the original opera recounting this story, written in 1938. Illustrations enhance the text. *Capitol Choices Noteworthy Titles* (Washington, D.C.).

1989. Levitin, Sonia. *Journey to America.* Illustrated by Charles Robinson. Aladdin, 1987. 160pp. Paper ISBN 978-0-689-71130-5. Grades 3–7.

In 1938 Lisa's father leaves their Berlin home for a "vacation" in Switzerland. He then goes on to America, and Lisa, her two sisters, and her mother wait for him to send for them. Because the Nazis will not allow them to take any of their belongings when they hear from Lisa's father, they leave for Switzerland carrying nothing. They must remain in Zurich for almost a year before they can arrange passage to America and reunite. *National Jewish Awards.*

1990. Lezotte, Ann Clare. *T4: A Novel in Verse.* Houghton, 2008. 112pp. ISBN 978-0-547-04684-6. Grades 6 up.

In this first-person verse novel, Paula Becker, 13, is deaf in Nazi Germany. The Nazis pass a law called Tiergartenstrasse 4 (T4) that declares that all persons with disabilities should be killed. A priest takes Paula to a woman who teaches her to sign, and then she hides in a church shelter. When T4 officially ends, Paula returns home, bringing a young man named Kurt with her. *Notable Trade Books in the Field of Social Studies.*

1991. Little, Jean. *From Anna.* Illustrated by Joan Sandin. HarperCollins, 1991. 208pp. Paper ISBN 978-0-06-440044-2. Grades 4–6.

Anna, age 9, must leave Germany with her family in 1933, and is concerned about her awkwardness. A doctor in Canada examines her and finds that she has poor eyesight. When she gets glasses, Anna blossoms into a happy young girl.

1992. Littlesugar, Amy. *Willy and Max: A Holocaust Story.* Illustrated by William Low. Putnam, 2006. 224pp. ISBN 978-0-399-23483-5. Grades 2–5.

In Belgium before World War II, Willy and Max become friends when Max's father buys a painting from Willy's father. But when the Nazis come, Max and his Jewish family have to leave. They give their painting to Willy's family to keep from the Nazis, but the Nazis take it anyway. Sixty years later, the painting is found with a note about the two boys and a photograph on the back. Willy finds Max's son and delivers the painting to him, symbolizing their unending friendship.

1993. Livesey, Margot. *Eva Moves the Furniture.* Picador, 2002. 234pp. Paper ISBN 978-0-312-42103-8. Grades YA.

In 1920s Troon, Scotland, Eva McEwen is living with her aunt and her father, who is still grieving for his lost wife. But Eva has two otherworldly companions, a woman and a girl, who help her grow up. The two save her life, help her become a nurse in Glasgow, and stop her chances of marrying the plastic surgeon whom she loves. When she returns to her mother's native village of Glenaird, she marries and has a daughter and eventually discovers the reasons for her companions' presence in her life.

1994. Llywelyn, Morgan. *1921.* Tor, 2002. 445pp. Paper ISBN 978-0-8125-7079-3. Grades YA.

Journalist Henry Mooney wants to be objective about his passive role in the Easter Rebellion, but he has to reevaluate his convictions and decides that he supports a free Ireland. Although he is strongly attracted to Sile, the wife of his friend Ned Halloran, he falls in love with Ella, an Anglo-Irish woman. Ella tries to convince him not to follow Michael Collins and the rebels. Notes.

1995. Lowry, Lois. *Number the Stars.* Houghton Mifflin, 1989. 169pp. ISBN 978-0-395-51060-5; 1998. paper ISBN 978-0-440-22753-3. Grades 4–8.

Annemarie and her friend Ellen pretend to be sisters one night when the Nazis come to Ellen's Copenhagen home to arrest her parents, who have already gone into hiding. Ellen's family and others get to Annemarie's uncle's fishing boat. Annemarie saves them all from the Nazis by using a handkerchief covered with blood and cocaine to deaden the Nazis' search dogs' sense of smell, keeping the Jews from being discovered under a vat of fish. *Newbery Medal, National Jewish Awards, Association of Jewish Libraries Award, Sydney Taylor Book Award, American Library Association Notable Books for Children*, and *School Library Journal Best Book*.

1996. McAlpine, Gordon. *Mystery Box.* Cricket, 2003. 208pp. ISBN 978-0-8126-2680-3. Grades YA.

In 1920 Paris, society magazine writer Carolyn Keene joins Frank Dixon, a private detective, to solve mysteries involving expatriates living there. Carolyn wants to write the "truth," and she thinks this will help her. Frank is trying to track his brother Joe, a missing army pilot from World War I. Among those with whom he communicates are Ernest Hemingway, Gertrude Stein, and Alice B. Toklas. Carolyn meets John Dos Passos and F. Scott Fitzgerald while working on another mystery. Then they begin writing the Nancy Drew and Hardy Boys mysteries.

1997. McBride, James. *Miracle at St. Anna.* Riverhead, 2008. 274pp. Paper ISBN 978-1-59448-360-8. Grades YA.

During World War II in St. Anna di Stazzema, a small Tuscan town in Italy, four African American soldiers from the 92nd Division meet a young Italian boy who has lost his speech. The illiterate Sam Train refuses to leave the boy, and when they take him to safety, they discover that he is the only survivor of a horrible massacre.

1998. McDonough, Yona Zeldis. *The Doll with the Yellow Star.* Illustrated by Kimberly Bulcken Root. Holt, 2005. 96pp. ISBN 978-0-8050-6337-0. Grades 3–5.

A young Jewish girl living in France, Claudine, 9, sees her friends with yellow stars during World War II and decides to sew a star on the inside of her favorite doll's cape. Then she can decide if she wants Violette's star to show. Claudine goes to live with relatives in America, and in a shipboard fire, Violette disappears. After the war ends, her father joins her in New York and they return to France. Since Claudine's mother has died, they no longer want to live there. Back in New York, Claudine grows up, and Violette amazingly reappears. *Children's Choice Book Award* (Iowa) nomination.

1999. McEwan, Ian. *Atonement.* Anchor, 2007. 480pp. Paper ISBN 978-0-307-38884-1. Grades YA.

In 1935 England, 13-year-old Briony Tallis, watches her sister Cecilia and her childhood friend and cleaning lady's son, Robbie Turner, and imagines that she sees something sinister occur between the two. Later that night she mistakenly thinks that Robbie has attacked her cousin Lola and tells the other adults. Robbie goes to prison but is released early to enter the army in World War II. Realizing later what she has done to him, Briony seeks atonement, first as a nurse and then as a writer.

2000. McSwigan, Marie. *Snow Treasure.* Illustrated by Andre LeBlanc. Dutton, 2005. 156pp. ISBN 978-0-525-47626-9; Puffin, 2006. paper ISBN 978-0-14-240224-5. Grades 3–7.

In 1940 Peter Lundstrom and the other children of the neighborhood fool the Nazis who parachute into their Norwegian village and hold it hostage. Peter's uncle tells him that the children can save the country's gold, hidden in the town, by riding their sleds and smuggling the gold bullion attached underneath, to the shore of the fjord. There they can bury the gold under snowmen until his uncle's co-workers can retrieve it for loading onto a camouflaged boat nearby.

2001. Magorian, Michelle. *Good Night, Mr. Tom.* Trophy, 1986. 318pp. Paper ISBN 978-0-06-440174-6. Grades 7 up.

Willie Beech, age 8, evacuates from London in 1939 to a small village, where he stays with Mr. Tom, an old man still mourning the deaths of his wife and son many years before. Willie is fearful of almost everything, but Mr. Tom helps him, and Willie even learns to read. When Willie makes friends with Zach, he discovers laughter. He has to return to his mother in London, but when Mr. Tom does not hear from Willie for several weeks, Mr. Tom goes to London to search for him. Mr. Tom finds Willie locked in the closet where his mentally unbalanced mother has left him. Mr. Tom takes Willie home to adopt him as his son. *International Reading Association Children's Book Award, American Library Association Notable Children's Book, American Library Association Best Books for Young Adults, Horn Book Fanfare Honor List, Booklist Young Adult Editors' Choices, National Council of Teachers of English Teachers' Choices, Notable Children's Trade Books in the Field of Social Studies, Guardian Award, American Library Association Notable Children's Book,* and *Association of Booksellers for Children's Choices.*

2002. Maguire, Gregory. *The Good Liar.* Clarion, 1999. 129pp. ISBN 978-0-395-90697-2. Grades 4–6.

Young Florida girls wanting a good grade on a World War II project, write Marcel De-larue, an old man living in the United States, about his youth. He responds in a long let-ter during which he remembers his childhood in France when the Germans occupied it, and he and his brother always tried to outdo each other with their lies. When the war begins, Marcel has no sense of danger, and friends who are trying to leave France arrive to stay with them. He begins to suspect something when a local rabbi and his followers are arrested. Later his mother makes a huge scene at the market about the Nazis tak-ing her guests away when in reality she is hiding them. Meanwhile, he and his older brother, Rene, befriend a young German soldier; they lie about the relationship, un-wittingly endangering their family. When they discover their mother's concealment of her friends for more than a year, they realize she is the best liar of all.

2003. Matas, Carol. *After the War.* Simon & Schuster, 1997. 128pp. Paper ISBN 978-0-689-80722-0. Grades 6–9.

Unlike eighty members of her family, 15-year-old Ruth survives anti-Semitic pogroms in Poland after the end of World War I, the Ostroviec ghetto, Auschwitz, and Buchen-wald. Ruth joins a Zionist group preparing to travel via ship to illegally enter Israel. The British attack the ship and take her and the others to Cyprus. In the refugee camp there, she finds her brother and eventually escapes with her boyfriend to Israel. *Voice of Youth Advocates Perfect Ten List.*

2004. Matas, Carol. *Code Name Kris.* Aladdin, 2007. 152pp. Paper ISBN 978-1-4169-6162-8. Grades 7–10.

Jesper, whose code name is "Kris," narrates this sequel to *Lisa's War*. He continues to work as a member of the Resistance in Denmark to save the Danish Jews from the Gestapo while Lisa and her brother Stefan, Jesper's best friend, survive in Sweden. Told as a flashback while Jesper is imprisoned, he reveals the German treatment of the Danes. He finally gains his own freedom on liberation day, May 4, which the Danes celebrate by lighting candles in their windows. *Canadian Lester and Orpen Dennys Award.*

2005. Matas, Carol. *Daniel's Story.* Scholastic, 1993. 136pp. Paper ISBN 978-0-590-46588-5. Grades 4–7.

In 1941 Daniel, age 14, takes a train with his family from Frankfurt, Germany, to the Jewish ghetto in Lodz, Poland. Although his family has lived in Frankfurt for more than six hundred years, they have to leave. At Auschwitz and Buchenwald, he recalls photo-graphs from his younger life and contrasts what they meant to him then with his current situation. He and his father survive; other family members do not. *Notable Children's Trade Books in the Field of Social Studies.*

2006. Melnikoff, Pamela. *Prisoner in Time: A Child of the Holocaust.* Jewish Publication Society, 2001. 144pp. ISBN 978-0-8276-0735-4. Grades 6–10.

See entry 1115.

2007. Moeyaert, Bart. *Dani Bennoni: Long May He Live.* Front Street, 2008. 93pp. ISBN 978-1-932425-97-0. Grades 9 up.

In 1939 Mone, the brother of 10-year-old Bing, is drafted into the Belgian army, and Bing fears he will not return. Bing wears Mone's soccer clothes, although they are too large, and begs Dani, a soccer star, to teach him how to play. As Bing listens to the older boys and girls talk, he hears them use words that he knows but in ways that he does not understand. Then, when Dani refuses to teach him soccer, Bing tells the older girls that Dani pays him to pull down his pants.

2008. Morpurgo, Michael. *The Amazing Story of Adolphus Tips.* Scholastic, 2006. 140pp. ISBN 978-0-439-79661-3. Grades 4–7.

In England in 1943, 12-year-old Lily Tregenza has been angrily enduring the absence of her father who is abroad on duty. Then everyone in Lily's village must evacuate for the Allies to practice D-Day landings. Her cat Tips, however, escapes into a restricted area to give birth. An African American soldier, Adolphus (Adie), helps her retrieve it, and they become good friends. As Lily tells this story from her childhood to her grandson, she shares with him the news that she has seen Adie through the years in England and in his Atlanta, Georgia, home and plans to marry him. *Parents Choice Award.*

2009. Morpurgo, Michael. *Toro! Toro!* Illustrated by Michael Foreman. HarperCollins, 2004. 127pp. Paper ISBN 978-0-00-710718-6. Grades 3–7.

This is the story a man tells his grandson about the Spanish Civil War. Antonito lives on a farm near Sauceda, Spain, where his father raises bulls for the bullring (*corrida*). Antonito cares for Paco, a newborn calf, after its mother dies, and leads it into the hills to save it from the bullring. When Antonito returns, he sees the farm burning: Franco's soldiers have ignited it and the village. Antonito returns to the countryside but cannot find Paco. Several weeks later, his Uncle Juan, a Republican soldier, finds him tired and hungry. When Antonito hears of a large black bull chasing Nationalist soldiers, he hopes it is Paco. Illustrations augment the text.

2010. Napoli, Donna Jo. *Fire in the Hills.* Dutton, 2006. 215pp. ISBN 978-0-525-47751-8. Grades 5–9.

In this sequel to *Stones in the Water*, Roberto, 15, eventually gets to Italy after having to translate for a German officer during World War II. Then he meets Volpe Rossa, a lovely resistance worker, who convinces him to join her group. He discovers that his homeland has split into a republic aligned with the Allies and a Fascist dictatorship aligned with Mussolini. He observes the horrors of war as more and more people begin to join the *partigiani*.

2011. Napoli, Donna Jo. *Stones in the Water.* Puffin, 1999. Paper ISBN 978-0-14-130600-1. Grades 5–9.

After sneaking into a movie theater to see an American western in Venice during World War II, Roberto, 13, and his Jewish friend Samuele find themselves rounded up by Nazis and transported to a work camp. They keep each other alive by letting no one see that Samuele is circumcised, and try to help starving Polish Jews. After Samuele dies, Roberto escapes from the camp but has to avoid Germans, wolves, cold, and starvation while trying to reach Italian partisans. *Blue Spruce Young Adult Book Awards* (Colorado), *Young Hoosier Book Awards* (Indiana) nomination, *Golden Sower Awards* (Nebraska), *Notable Children's Books, Battle of the Books* (New Mexico), *Notable Social Studies Trade Books for Young People*, and *Children's Book Awards* (Rhode Island).

2012. Newbery, Linda. *Sisterland.* David Fickling, 2004. 384pp. ISBN 978-0-385-75026-4; Laurel-Leaf, 2006. paper ISBN 978-0-55349-450-1. Grades YA.

Hilly's gay friend Reuben has a Palestinian boyfriend, Saeed, and her sister, Zoë, dates a neo-Nazi punk group follower. When boys severely beat Saeed, Hilly becomes concerned that her sister's boyfriend is involved. Then Hilly falls in love with Saeed's brother, Rashid. At the same time, their grandmother Heidigran, who has Alzheimer's, begins talking about someone named Rachel and her connection to Sarah, a Jewish child who came to England on the *Kindertransport*. What Hilly discovers is that her grandmother Heidi (Sarah) arrived in England in 1939 after she and her older sister, Rachel, were separated. Sarah never saw her sister again. Hilly wonders if this discovery about her Jewish heritage will ruin her relationship with Rashid.

2013. Newton, William. *The Two-Pound Tram.* Bloomsbury, 2003. 208pp. ISBN 978-1-58234-374-7; 2006. paper ISBN 978-1-58234-444-7. Grades YA.

In 1937 Wilfred and his mute brother, Duncan, have only met their parents for lunch on Wednesdays, but they have to decide what to do after their mother leaves with her lover and their father starts entertaining all the young women he meets. They read about a horse-drawn tram for sale in London costing two pounds, and they decide to buy it. Once they purchase the tram they also have to buy a horse to pull it. People want to ride the tram because it reminds them of the past, before Hitler overran Austria and was threatening other parts of Europe. After the Germans start bombing England in 1940, Duncan moves the tram to the Channel and converts it to a signaling station. When he devises a way to shoot down a Stuka with a catapult off the tram's roof, the king and queen come to call and he and Wilfred become famous. *Sagittarius Prize.*

2014. Nolan, Han. *If I Should Die Before I Wake.* Harcourt, 2003. 288pp. Paper ISBN 978-0-15-204679-8. Grades 9 up.

Hilary, a neo-Nazi, has a motorcycle accident and ends up in a "Jew" hospital, where she is blown back in time to the Holocaust and inhabits the body of someone named Chana. Chana (Hilary) faces the hopelessness and terror of the concentration camps and sees Jews betray other Jews when they think themselves better. After Hilary experiences the Holocaust, she has a different perspective when she returns to the present.

2015. Oppenheim, Shulamith Levey. *The Lily Cupboard.* Illustrated by Ronald Himler. Trophy, 1995. 32pp. Paper ISBN 978-0-06-443393-8. Grades K–3.

In 1940 Miriam has to stay with a Dutch farm family because she is Jewish. The family gives her a rabbit, which she names after her father, and she hides with the rabbit in the secret lily cupboard when the Nazis come to search the farmhouse. *Notable Trade Books in the Field of Social Studies.*

2016. Orgel, Doris. *The Devil in Vienna.* Peter Smith, 1995. 243pp. ISBN 978-0-8446-6797-3. Grades 6–8.

When Inge is 13 in 1938, she misses her best friend Liselotte, who has recently moved to Munich with her Nazi storm trooper father. When Inge's letters are returned, she does not understand why. But when Liselotte returns to Vienna after Hitler gains power over the Austrian leader, Schuschnigg, she tells Inge how serious the situation is for the Jews. Inge begins to see other signs while her mother furtively plans for them to leave the country. *Child Study Children's Book Committee at Bank Street College Award, Association of Jewish Libraries Award, Golden Kite Honor Book,* and *Sydney Taylor Book Award.*

2017. Orlev, Uri. *The Island on Bird Street.* Translated by Hillel Halkin. Walter Lorraine, 1984. 162pp. ISBN 978-0-395-33887-2; 1992. paper ISBN 978-0-395-61623-9. Grades 5 up.

Alex, age 11, hides in the ruins of the Warsaw Ghetto after police take his father away during World War II. He uses his ingenuity to stay alive—searching for food and supplies in empty apartments—until his father returns almost a year later. *Sydney Taylor Book Award, American Library Association Notable Books for Children*, and *Association of Jewish Libraries Award*.

2018. Orlev, Uri. *The Man from the Other Side.*   Walter Lorraine, 1991. 186pp. ISBN 978-0-395-53808-1; Puffin, 1995. paper ISBN 978-0-14-037088-1. Grades 7 up.

Marek, age 14, participates in the anti-Semitism rampant in Poland during World War II until he finds out that his own father was Jewish. When he hears this, he starts helping Jews instead, and begins to understand that his anti-Semitic stepfather, a sewer worker, has been covering up his real beliefs so that he can help the Jews. After Marek hides the Jew Jozek in the city, Jozek wants to return to the Warsaw Ghetto at the beginning of the uprising. When Marek guides him through the sewers, he finds himself in the fighting. *Bulletin Blue Ribbon, Mildred L. Batchelder Award, National Jewish Awards, American Library Association Notable Children's Book*, and *School Library Journal Best Book*.

2019. Orlev, Uri. ***Run, Boy Run: A Novel.***   Translated by Hillel Halkin. Walter Lorraine, 2003. 192pp. ISBN 978-0-618-16465-3; 2007. paper ISBN 978-0-618-95706-4. Grades 5 up.

Eight-year-old Srulik escapes from the Warsaw Ghetto after his mother disappears. He acts as his father instructed him: not admitting that he is Jewish when asked, and changing his name to Jure and his identity to a Polish Catholic orphan. He wanders through the Nazi-occupied Polish countryside and works on farms and hides in the forest. He is wounded and loses an arm, but teaches himself how to do tasks that might require two arms and thereby survives throughout World War II. A boy like Srulik did survive the Holocaust.

2020. O'Sullivan, Mark. ***Melody for Nora: One Girl's Story in the Civil War.***   Interlink, 1998. 217pp. ISBN 978-0-8632-7425-1. Grades 7–10.

In 1922, after Nora's mother dies, her father divides the children among relatives in Ireland. Nora, 14, is already a gifted pianist and resents having to live in Tipperary instead of Dublin. She becomes involved in the hostilities in the area through her uncle, who supports the government forces, and his brother on the opposite side, who prefers the Irregulars. Her story and situation show the civil war in Ireland that came about after Ireland's independence from England.

2021. Parkinson, Curtis. ***Domenic's War: A Story of the Battle of Monte Cassino.***   Tundra, 2006. Paper ISBN 978-0-88776-751-7. Grades 5–9.

Domenic and his farm family get caught in the war during 1944, and must fend for their lives when troops threaten all of them sheltering in a Benedictine monastery on Monte Cassino. He and Antonio, 15, who has lost his entire family, risk their lives helping people survive. Before the battle ends, the Allies destroy the monastery, killing some of the Italian refugees. *Manitoba Young Readers Choice Award* nomination.

2022. Pausewang, Gudrun. ***Dark Hours.***   Translated by John Brownjohn. Annick, 2006. 208pp. ISBN 978-1-55451-042-9. Grades 5–8.

German Christian Gisel tells her granddaughter this story in a letter: When she was almost 16, her family fled from advancing Allied forces. Gisel was in charge of her three younger brothers and, after a scary period when they were separated, they found refuge in a shelter while bombs fell. They were trapped in rubble for two days.

2023. Pausewang, Gudrun. *Traitor.* Translated by Rachel Ward. Carolrhoda, 2006. 220pp. ISBN 978-0-8225-6195-8. Grades 7–10.

In 1944 in Stiegnitz, Germany, Anna finds a Russian soldier hiding in her family's barn. She decides to help him by hiding him in a countryside bunker even though she could be shot for sheltering the enemy. In her own family are conflicting loyalties—many refusing to support the Nazis, while her older brother is a soldier on the front. Anna's younger brother Felix is a fanatical supporter of the Hitler Youth and would betray her immediately if he knew her secret. Glossary.

2024. Peet, Mal. *Tamar: A Novel of Espionage, Passion, and Betrayal.* Candlewick, 2007. 424pp. ISBN 978-0-7636-3488-9; 2008. paper ISBN 978-0-7636-4063-7. Grades 8 up.

In 1995 when she is 15, Tamar's beloved grandfather, known as Dart during World War II, commits suicide. He leaves her a box of items that give clues to his experiences during World War II. He and another Dutchman, with the code names Dart and Tamar, parachuted into rural Holland to work as resistance fighters. They stayed on a farm with the beautiful Marijke, with whom Tamar is in love. Dart operates the wireless, receiving and sending encrypted messages. He also falls in love with Marijke, misreading her interest in him. The events that ensue make his life difficult to bear. *Carnegie Medal, Booklist Editors' Choice, Bulletin Blue Ribbon, Kirkus Reviews Editor's Choice,* and *School Library Journal Best Books for Children.*

2025. Peters, Elizabeth. *The Serpent and the Crown.* (Amelia Peabody Mystery) Grand Central, 2006. 496pp. Paper ISBN 978-0-06-059179-3. Grades YA.

In 1921 Amelia Peabody and her family hear of a strange death supposedly caused by a curse. They must go back to the Valley of the Kings to return a stolen statue and solve the mystery.

2026. Pressler, Mirjam. *Let Sleeping Dogs Lie.* Translated by Erik J. Macki. Front Street, 2007. 207pp. ISBN 978-1-932425-84-0. Grades 10 up.

In 1995 Johanna, 18, granddaughter of wealthy former Nazi Party member Gerhard Riemenschneider, owner of a department store, discovers that her grandfather robbed a Jewish family of its business. Meta Levin, an old woman, describes her family's loss during World War II. Shocked, Johanna has to decide whether to remain loyal to her family and her boyfriend, Daniel, or to do what she thinks is right. When her grandfather commits suicide, she decides to act.

2027. Pressler, Mirjam. *Malka.* Translated by Brian Murdoch. Philomel, 2003. 246pp. ISBN 978-0-399-23984-7. Grades 6–10.

In 1943 Dr. Hannah Mai tries to flee from Lawoczne, Poland, across the border to Hungary with her two daughters, Minna, 16, and Malka, 7. Malka becomes ill in the mountains, and Hannah leaves her behind with a family. The family, however, leaves Malka alone. After German soldiers take Malka back across the border, a Polish policeman rescues her, and Malka bonds with his Down syndrome child. Then the policeman takes her to another town and leaves her. She lives alone in a coal cellar looking for food and trying to drink liquids as a lady doctor she barely remembers once told her to do.

In Hungary, her mother searches for her and decides that Malka must have returned to Poland.

2028. Propp, Vera W. *When the Soldiers Were Gone.* Puffin, 2001. 99pp. Paper ISBN 978-0-698-11881-2. Grades 4–8.

In 1945 Henk, 8, leaves the Dutch Christian family with which he has been hiding—and calling "Mama" and "Papa"—to reunite with his real parents who he does not know and who insist on calling him "Benjamin." He enjoys going to school in the city, although he misses the farm and still experiences anti-Semitism. Finally he adjusts to being with his parents again. *Young Reader's Award* (Arizona) nomination, *Sunshine State Young Reader Award* (Florida) nomination, *Children's Choice Book Award* (Iowa) nomination, *Black-Eyed Susan Book Award* (Maryland), *Great Lakes Great Books Award* (Michigan), *Golden Sower Award* (Nebraska), *The Land of Enchantments Children's Book Award* (New Mexico), and *Children's Book Award* (Utah).

2029. Raymond, Patrick. *Daniel and Esther.* Aladdin, 2007. 165pp. Paper ISBN 978-1-4169-6798-9. Grades 9 up.

In 1936 Daniel and Esther meet at a British boarding school where Daniel begins to compose orchestral music. When World War II is declared, Daniel's father wants him to return to America. Esther's Jewish parents expect her to return to her home in Austria, because they have had their passports taken. Daniel hears that his mentor, the man who encouraged his music, has been killed in the Spanish Civil War, as he tells the story in 1939. One never knows what happens to Esther. *Bulletin Blue Ribbon.*

2030. Redmond, Shirley Raye. *Pigeon Hero!* Illustrated by Doris Ettlinger. Aladdin, 2003. 32pp. Paper ISBN 978-0-689-85486-6. Grades K–3.

A carrier pigeon named G.I. Joe braves enemy fire and other hazards of war to deliver a message that prevents the bombing of an Italian town during World War II. The British send the pigeon from Italy to an American air base when all radio and telegraph communication has stopped to let the Americans know that the Germans have withdrawn from the town and they do not need to destroy it. The Lord Mayor of London then awards the bird with a medal, and it lives the rest of its life in the Detroit Zoo. Watercolor illustrations enhance the text.

2031. Reiss, Johanna. *The Upstairs Room.* Crowell, 1972. 196pp. ISBN 978-0-690-85127-4; Trophy, 1990. paper ISBN 978-0-06-440370-2. Grades 5 up.

In 1942 Annie, age 10, and her sister leave their parents and older sister to hide in the upstairs room of a farmhouse in Holland. They expect to be free to leave any day, but the war lasts two more years during which they, as Jews, cannot be seen by anyone without endangering their lives as well as the lives of the generous couple who hides them. The story tells of their two years in the room, including the day when Annie goes outside and hides in the tall wheat, only to be marooned in the hot sun while Nazi soldiers examine the house. *Newbery Honor Book, American Library Association Notable Children's Books, New York Times Outstanding Children's Books, Jane Addams Honor Book, Buxtehude Bulla Prize of Germany*, and *Jewish Book Council Children's Book Award.*

2032. Richter, Hans. *Friedrich.* Peter Smith, 1992. 149pp. ISBN 978-0-8446-6573-3; Puffin, 1987. paper ISBN 978-0-14-032205-7. Grades 5–9.

In 1925 Friedrich's prosperous German Jewish family begins to lose its money while the narrator's poor family rises in society and the narrator's father becomes a Nazi supporter. Friedrich eventually dies from shrapnel, which hits him outside a bomb shelter. His only "crime" is that he is Jewish. *Mildred L. Batchelder Award.*

2033. Roy, Jennifer. *Yellow Star.* Marshall Cavendish, 2006. 227pp. ISBN 978-0-7614-5277-5. Grades 5–7.

In February 1940, when Syvia Perlmutter is barely 5, the Nazis force her and her family into the Lodz, Poland, ghetto. They struggle to survive, and on January 19, 1945, one day before Syvia is 10, they are among the 800 survivors—of the original 250,000 occupants—liberated by the Russians. The rich prose gives the reader insight into a child's incomprehension and sensibility about what is happening around her when she enters the ghetto and sees all the yellow stars worn there. Syvia was one of only twelve children to survive the ghetto, and her niece, Roy, did not hear her story until fifty years later. Syvia remembers the cold, the hunger, blood puddles, and brutality. Her father hides her in the cemetery so that soldiers can not rip her from her home as they do with other children around them. She can never go outside; she is hidden in the cellar, and only hears of the horrors of what happened outside the ghetto after the war ends. *Boston Globe/Horn Book Award Honor* and *School Library Journal Best Books for Children.*

2034. Russo, Marisabina. *Always Remember Me: How One Family Survived World War II.* Illustrated by author. Anne Schwartz, 2005. 48pp. ISBN 978-0-689-86920-4. Grades 2–5.

Rachel goes to visit her Oma and leafs through the family albums. When she looks at one, she knows the people in the pictures. In another, she does not. That one contains her Oma's life in Poland and then in Germany where she lost so much. Thus Rachel learns about the Holocaust and how her grandmother, mother, and aunts suffered. The illustrations themselves are framed like photographs.

2035. Rylant, Cynthia. *I Had Seen Castles.* Harcourt, 2004. 97pp. Paper ISBN 978-0-15-205312-3. Grades 7 up.

John, aged 17 in 1941, wants to enlist immediately when the Japanese bomb Pearl Harbor. He meets Ginny, who is against all war, and when he enlists, he sacrifices their relationship. As he reflects fifty years later while he lives alone in Canada, he thinks of his losses, including Ginny and his country. Although he had wanted to see castles since he was 9, and did get to see them during the war, he wonders if the sacrifices were worth it. No one in the United States understood his suffering, and he had to move to Canada. *New York Public Library Books for the Teen Age.*

2036. Selznick, Brian. *The Invention of Hugo Cabret.* Illustrated by author. Scholastic, 2007. 531pp. ISBN 978-0-439-81378-5. Grades 4–9.

In 1931 orphan Hugo Cabret, 12, repairs clocks inside the walls of a Paris train station and tries to avoid being caught by the police. When a mysterious toy seller and his goddaughter, Isabelle, find him, he becomes concerned that they will discover his automaton, his only remaining link to his father. Hugo and Isabelle discover that her grandfather actually built the automaton that Hugo is trying to restore, and the two of them resurrect the grandfather's films and his reputation, guaranteeing a successful future for Hugo. Complementing the text are movie stills and archival photographs. *Caldecott Award, American Library Association Notable Children's Books, Horn Book Fanfare, Kirkus Reviews Critics Choice,* and *Publishers Weekly Best Books.*

2037. Shemin, Margaretha. *The Little Riders.* Illustrated by Peter Spier. Beech Tree, 1993. 76pp. Paper ISBN 978-0-688-12499-1. Grades 4–6.

Johanna's father takes her to Holland to stay with her grandparents while he and her mother go on a trip. After they leave, the Germans invade Holland, and Johanna cannot return to America. During the last year of the war, a German officer is billeted in Johanna's room, an imposition that infuriates and frightens the family, except that he plays his flute at night. Of most concern to them is protecting the "little riders," the mechanical lead figures that circle the church tower clock at noon each day, which Johanna's grandfather maintains. When the Germans start taking lead for ammunition, he disassembles the riders, planning to hide them. The Germans arrive before he finishes his task, but Johanna and the German officer living in the house carry out his wishes.

2038. Shulevitz, Uri. *How I Learned Geography.* Illustrated by author. Farrar, 2008. Unpaged. ISBN 978-0-374-33499-4. Grades 2–5.

The protagonist, based on Uri Shulevitz's own experiences, escapes the misery of his Polish refugee life in Kazakhstan during World War II. He begins by studying for hours the world map his father brings home. His imagination takes him to exotic places. Watercolor, collage, and ink enhance the text. *Publishers Weekly Best Books, Capitol Choices Noteworthy Titles* (Washington, D.C.), and *School Library Journal Best Books for Children, Notable Trade Books in the Field of Social Studies.*

2039. Skrypuch, Marsha Forchuk. *Aram's Choice.* Illustrated by Muriel Wood. Fitzhenry & Whiteside, 2006. 81pp. ISBN 978-1-55005-352-6; paper ISBN 978-1-55041-354-0. Grades 3–5.

In 1915 Aram, 12, must live in a Greek orphanage. His grandmother is too poor to keep him after bringing him out of Turkey during the Armenian genocide. Other members of their family have died. In 1923 he has the opportunity to emigrate to Canada and travels by cargo ship, ocean liner, and train to a farm in rural Ontario. He tries to keep the younger boys with him safe and has several new experiences such as eating a banana for the first time. Illustrations and a map enhance the text. Glossary, Notes, Further Resources, and Index.

2040. Spinelli, Jerry. *Milkweed.* Knopf, 2003. 224pp. ISBN 978-0-375-81374-0; Laurel-Leaf, 2005. paper ISBN 978-0-440-42005-7. Grades 5–9.

In 1939 an orphan wanders around in Warsaw trying to steal any food he can find, thinking his name is "Stopthief." He does not know his background and understands nothing of what is happening around him. When Nazi "Jackboots" arrive, he greets them with pleasure. He eventually gets the name of Misha and a family with his friend, Janina Milgrom, whom he meets when stealing food. Her family has to move to the ghetto, and he goes with them. There he slips out through the small holes to steal food for them. *Booklist Editors' Choice.*

2041. Spring, Debbie. *The Righteous Smuggler.* (Holocaust Remembrance Book for Young Readers) Second Story, 2005. 149pp. Paper ISBN 978-1-8967-6497-9. Grades 4–7.

In 1940 Amsterdam 12-year-old Hendrik decides to stand by his Jewish friends when they are barred from attending school and other classmates exclude them. He soon recognizes Hitler's intent to rid the country of these people, and starts planning to smuggle them away on boats with his fisherman father, a route attempted much less often than the overland journey to Spain or Switzerland. Maps and archival photographs add interest.

2042. Stuchner, Joan Betty. *Honey Cake.* Illustrated by Cynthia Nugent. (Stepping Stones) Random House, 2008. 101pp. ISBN 978-0-375-85189-6. Grades 1–4.

David, 10, lives in Copenhagen with his family while the Nazis occupy it in World War II. When the Nazis declare that the Jews have to go to concentration camps, the Danes help many Jews escape. David's sister Rachel is in the Resistance, and David's baker father involves him by having David deliver an order of eclairs. David suspects that he is delivering more than food and later discovers that he has delivered a hidden message that helps the Resistance derail a German supply train. Illustrations illuminate the text.

2043. Stuchner, Joan Betty. *Josephine's Dream.* Illustrated by Chantelle Walther. Silver Leaf, 2008. Unpaged. ISBN 978-1-934393-04-8. Grades K–2.

Josephine Baker (1906–1975) could not achieve her dreams in America before civil rights improved, so she went to France after spending an impoverished childhood in St. Louis. She was a dancer who wanted to see her name in lights. The French appreciated her talents, and she remained there, working in the Resistance during World War II. Afterward, she adopted twelve children who lived with her on a country estate in France. Illustrations embellish the text.

2044. Todd, Charles. *A Long Shadow.* (Inspector Ian Rutledge) HarperTorch, 2007. 341pp. Paper ISBN 978-0-06-078672-4. Grades YA.

In 1919 Scotland Yard Inspector Rutledge, a victim of shell shock in World War I, takes his eighth case when someone drops machine-gun shell casings carved with poppies and skulls in front of him. Then Hensley, the town constable of Dudlington, is found in Firth Wood with an arrow in his back near the site of a Saxon massacre. Rutledge goes there and takes his imaginary sidekick, Hamish, but his stalker follows. After Hensley recovers, Rutledge thinks the site where he was placed might be connected to the disappearance of Emma Mason five years earlier, and psychic Meredith Channing offers additional insight.

2045. Toksvig, Sandi Durland. *Hitler's Canary.* Roaring Brook, 2007. ISBN 978-1-59643-247-5. Grades 6 up.

Bamse Skovlund, 10, and his Jewish friend Anton help in the Danish Resistance during World War II. His family refuses to participate because they are actors and do not involve themselves in politics, but when his older brother, Orlando, says that the British are calling the Danes "Hitler's Canary," Bamse thinks the family should change. After Anton's family is forced into hiding, Bamse's mother begins sheltering Jews, and his uncle helps them escape to Sweden in 1943. Their work helps more than eight thousand find safety. The story is based on Toksvig's own family's experience.

2046. Trevor, William. *The Story of Lucy Gault.* Penguin, 2003. 227pp. Paper ISBN 978-0-14-200331-2. Grades YA.

Irish Protestant Lucy Gault, 9 years old, refuses to leave her Irish home with her parents in the 1920s after someone tries to burn down their house. She runs away the night before they plan to depart, and her parents think she is dead. Household staff discover her alive, but her parents have disappeared. She grows up alone on their estate of Lahardane with the help of a caretaker couple. One of the men who tried to torch the house before the Gaults left feels guilty, and when Captain Gault returns to Ireland years later, they seek to arrange a reconciliation.

2047. U'Ren, Andrea. *Mary Smith.* Illustrated by author. Farrar, Straus & Giroux, 2003. Unpaged. ISBN 978-0-374-34842-7. Grades K–2.

In the early 20th century in England, people hired "knocker-ups" for a few pence a week to wake them up. In London's East End in the 1920s, Mary Smith uses a pocket watch during the early morning hours to wake people at their requested time by shooting at their windows with her peashooter. Among her clients are the baker, the train conductor, and laundry maids. Illustrations of color wash and black outlines augment the text. *Beehive Children's Picture Book Award* (Utah) nomination, *Emphasis on Reading Award* (Alabama) nomination, *Children's Choice Picture Book* (Washington) nomination, *Red Clover Award* (Vermont) nomination, and *International Reading Association Children's Book Awards.*

2048. Vander Zee, Ruth, and Marian Sneider. *Eli Remembers.* Illustrated by Bill Farnsworth. Eerdmans, 2007. Unpaged. ISBN 978-0-8028-5309-7. Grades 3–6.

Eli goes to Lithuania with his family and discovers why his grandmother cries each time she lights seven candles for Rosh Hashanah, the Jewish New Year. In the Lithuanian Ponar Forest near Vilnius where she lived, her father and siblings—a total of seven people—died along with 80,000 other Jews when the Nazis shot them in the back, pushed them into a pit, and burned their bodies. Eli immediately understands that he must continue to pass down the family history when he becomes a parent. Oil paintings show the contrast between the warmth of home and the stark reality of the forest.

2049. Waldman, Neil. *The Never-Ending Greenness.* Illustrated by author. Boyds Mills, 2003. Unpaged. ISBN 978-1-59078-064-0. Grades 2–6.

An old man remembers his family's escape from the ghetto in Vilna, Poland, during World War II and their subsequent hiding in the forests around the town. After he migrates to Israel, he helps to plant trees so that his new country can resemble the "never-ending greenness" of his childhood. His attempts correlate with celebrations of Tu b'Shvat, the Jewish New Year of the Trees.

2050. Watts, Irene N. *Finding Sophie.* Tundra, 2002. 136pp. Paper ISBN 978-0-8877-6613-8. Grades 5–8.

After coming to England at age 7 as part of the Kindertransport in 1938, Sophie Mandel, at 14, wonders what will happen when she is reunited with her German Jewish parents. She may prefer to stay with her foster mother, Aunt Em, in London, where she no longer thinks of being Jewish, speaks English, and loves the family. Sophie discovers, however, that her mother was killed in an air raid but that her father is still alive. She must remember her own childhood in Germany to help her make the decision as to whether to stay with Aunt Em or go with her father.

2051. Whelan, Gerard. *A Winter of Spies.* O'Brien/Independent, 2002. 191pp. Paper ISBN 978-0-8627-8566-6. Grades 6–10.

In Dublin during 1920, Sarah Conway, 11, discovers that Ireland's struggle for freedom led by Michael Collins employs not only guns but also spies, lies, and secrets. She smuggles guns, but when she sees the actions of two men who move into the house next door, she notices odd activities and begins to wonder about them.

2052. Whelan, Gloria. *Burying the Sun.* HarperTrophy, 2007. 205pp. Paper ISBN 978-0-06-054114-9. Grades 5–8.

After the Germans declare war on the Russians in 1941, Georgi, 14, wants to enlist in the Red Army but is too young. During the 880-day siege of his city, Leningrad, he does what he can to help while his mother is a nurse on the front and his sister packs up artwork at the Hermitage to save it from destruction or looting. He helps with transporting food across frozen lakes, and he and his neighbors must revel in the little joys of life that might include a chocolate bar, a Shostakovich symphony, or listening to poet Anna Akhmatova read verse over the radio. At one point, he takes a farmer turned solider for a tour of the Hermitage. Since only the empty frames hang on the walls, Georgi describes in detail each painting as if it were in front of them. Bibliography and Glossary.

2053. Whelan, Gloria. *The Impossible Journey.* Harper Trophy, 2004. 256pp. Paper ISBN 978-0-06-441083-0. Grades 5–8.

In this sequel to *Angel on the Square*, Marya, 13, searches for her parents, Katya and Misha, taken by Stalinist Russia's NKVD (Soviet secret police) from their Leningrad home in the middle of the night in 1934. Stalin considers them political dissidents because they are aristocrats. Marya discovers that her father has been sent to a labor camp and that her mother is exiled for three years in Dudinka, Siberia. Marya sells her paintings on the street to earn train fare for herself and her younger brother, Georgi, to travel as far as Yenisey River in Siberia. They will then have to walk a thousand miles to find their mother's town near the Arctic Circle. They travel without passports or official papers, encountering wild animals and an evil fisherman. But many people also help them, including a nomadic Samoyed tribe that provides reindeer transport and food. Later they meet a prison doctor who gives them information about their father. They eventually reach their mother, and their father arrives from a coal-mining camp, only to die in the spring. *Mark Twain Award* (Missouri) nomination and *Children's Book Award* (Rhode Island) nomination.

2054. Wilson, John. *Four Steps to Death.* Kids Can, 2005. 208pp. ISBN 978-1-55337-704-7; paper ISBN 978-1-55337-705-4. Grades 5–8.

In 1942 the Battle of Stalingrad cost one million lives of both German soldiers and Russians. Sergei, at 8, scrounges around for food for his mother in the ravaged city. Also there are Conrad, 18, a German tank officer who wants the city for his homeland; Vasily, 17, a Russian who wants to make his father proud of him; and Yelena, an expert sniper. They all come together in an odd twist at Christmas.

2055. Winspear, Jacqueline. *Birds of a Feather.* (Maisie Dobbs) Soho, 2004. 311pp. ISBN 978-1-56947-368-9; Penguin, 2005. paper ISBN 978-0-14-303530-5. Grades YA.

In 1930 grocery magnate Joseph Wait hires former servant girl and Cambridge graduate Maisie Dobbs to find his daughter Charlotte. Now in her 30s, Charlotte has run away before. Maisie identifies three of Charlotte's friends, including Lydia Fisher, who knew each other during World War I and have ties to the Coulsdon case. Someone murders first with poison and then a bayonet, both times leaving a white feather on the scene. Maisie thinks Charlotte may be the next victim. With her cockney sidekick Billy Beale, she searches for Charlotte. Billy, however, has begun taking pain drugs and his erratic behavior worries both Maisie and Billy's wife, Doreen. Then Maisie's father dies, testing her endurance. The second volume in the series. *School Library Journal Best Adult Books for Young Adults*.

2056. Winspear, Jacqueline. *Maisie Dobbs.* (Maisie Dobbs) Penguin, 2004. 294pp. Paper ISBN 978-0-14-200433-3. Grades YA.

Fourteen-year-old Maisie Dobbs, who after her mother's death has to become a maid for Lady Rowan, often sneaks into the manor library at night to read Hume and Jung. Lady Rowan gets a tutor for Maisie, and Maisie eventually qualifies to attend Cambridge. After a year, World War I begins, and she leaves school to serve on the war front as a nurse. At war's end she returns to London to become a private investigator, and starts her own business in 1929. Her first case seems like simple infidelity, but it takes her to a convalescent home in Kent called "The Retreat" where some highly disfigured surviving soldiers seem to emerge. The owner, a former officer, requires the patients to sign over all of their assets when they arrive. Maisie also falls in love with a military surgeon somewhat disfigured by a war bomb. What else she discovers reveals that when one searches for a person, one may also be searching for a soul. The first volume in the series. *New York Times Notable Books of the Year*, *Edgar Awards* nomination, *Dilys Award* nomination, *Agatha Award*, *Alex Award*, *Macavity Award*, *School Library Journal Best Adult Books*, and *Anthony Award* nomination.

2057. Winspear, Jacqueline. *Pardonable Lies: A Maisie Dobbs Novel.* (Maisie Dobbs) Holt, 2005. 342pp. ISBN 978-0-8050-7897-8; Picador, 2006. paper ISBN 978-0-312-42621-7. Grades YA.

In 1930 Sir Cecil Lawton hires Maisie Dobbs, former servant girl and Cambridge graduate, to find out how his son died during World War I. While dying, Lawton's wife expressed a belief that her son was not dead. Maisie also must deal with Avril Jarvis, who at 13, is accused of murder. Additionally, her friend Priscilla desperately wants to know how her brother died during the Great War. Maisie must return to France, where she was a nurse during the war thirteen years before, to find information. During the process, she risks alienation from her detective mentor, Maurice Blanche. *School Library Journal Best Adult Books for Young Adults*.

2058. Wiseman, Eva. *My Canary Yellow Star.* Tundra, 2001. Paper ISBN 978-0-8877-6533-9. Grades 8 up.

Marta Weiss and her family try to survive after the Germans arrive in Budapest, Hungary, in March of 1944. Even though Marta must wear a "canary" yellow star, she continues her relationship with a Gentile boy, Peter. After Peter disappears and food becomes scarce, her family is evicted. Marta has heard about a man named Raoul Wallenberg who might help the family. She endeavors to find him and ask.

2059. Wolf, Joan M. *Someone Named Eva.* Clarion, 2007. 200pp. ISBN 978-0-618-53579-8. Grades 5–8.

In 1942 soldiers take Milada, 11, from her home in Lidice, Czechoslovia, with nine other children having blond hair and blue eyes to a training center at Lebensborn for "Germanization," where they learn to speak only German and become "proper German" for a German family to adopt. Hitler has chosen to annihilate this town in retaliation for resistance fighters murdering the highest ranking Nazi officer in Czechoslovakia. After Milada leaves, Nazis kill all 173 men and teenage boys in the town and send the women to Ravensbruck concentration camp. The rest of Lidice's children are gassed. Milada remembers her grandmother's last statement to her to always remember who she is, and after she begins her schooling, she understands why she must.

2060. Wulf, Linda Press. *The Night of the Burning: Devorah's Story.* Farrar, 2006. 224pp. ISBN 978-0-374-36419-9. Grades 5–8.

After the First World War, or the Great War, in Europe, gas poisoning, famine, typhoid, and influenza infiltrate Devorah's world and kill some of her relatives. In 1920, after the Cossacks encourage Polish Christians to attack their Jewish neighbors during the "Night of the Burning," 11-year-old Devorah and her younger sister Nechama become the only survivors in their community. A South African philanthropist named Isaac Ochberg asks the two to join the two hundred other orphans he has gathered to take to a new life in Cape Town. A wealthy family there adopts Nechama, and Devorah, distressed that they are separated, determines that she will be happy with her own new family while vowing never to forget her biological parents. *Sidney Taylor Honor.*

2061. Wulffson, Don. *Soldier X.* Viking, 2001. 244pp. ISBN 978-0-670-88863-4; Speak, 2003. paper ISBN 978-0-14-250073-6. Grades 8 up.

In 1944 Eric Brandt, 16, finds himself drafted into the German army and fighting on the Russian front since he speaks Russian. Seriously wounded, he switches uniforms with a dead Russian, pretends amnesia when taken to a Russian hospital, and becomes "X." Tamara, a young Russian nurse's aide discovers his disguise. As their relationship develops, they escape during an attack on the hospital, reach a safe house in Czechoslovakia, and reach Berlin. They run from the horrors of war itself rather than to or from any side. *Teen Book Awards* (Iowa), *Maud Hart Lovelace Book Award* (Minnesota) nomination, *Golden Sower Book Award* (Nebraska), *Battle of the Books* (New Jersey) nomination, *Young Adult Book Award* (South Carolina) nomination, *Tayshas High School Reading List* (Texas), and *Battle of the Books* (Wisconsin) nomination.

2062. Yolen, Jane. *Briar Rose.* (Fairy Tales) Tor, 2002. 190pp. Paper ISBN 978-0-7653-4230-0. Grades 8 up.

Becca's dying grandmother has adamantly declared herself to be Briar Rose, the princess in the Sleeping Beauty tale that she often told to Becca, so Becca promises her Gemma before she dies that she'll find the prince and the castle from her past. In the nursing home room are photographs, newspaper clippings, a ring, and a passport that her grandmother has kept in a box. Becca's investigation leads her to Fort Oswego, New York, a former World War II refugee camp, and to Chelmno, Poland, site of Nazi exterminations. She finds out that a partisan fighter found her grandmother alive in a mass grave and revived her. They married, but after she became pregnant, Nazis murdered her husband. *Mythopoeic Fantasy Award, American Library Association Best Books for Young Adults*, and *American Library Association 100 Best Books for Teens.*

2063. Yolen, Jane. *The Devil's Arithmetic.* Puffin, 2004. 170pp. Paper ISBN 978-0-14-240109-5. Grades YA.

In this historical fantasy, Hannah becomes bored every year at the family Passover Seder. But when she is 13, she opens the door to symbolically welcome Elijah to the feast and finds herself in a Polish village (shtetl) during the 1940s, where everyone calls her "Chaya." She immediately forgets her past as she becomes involved in village life and its fear of the Nazis. When the Nazis take her and her family to a death camp, she only wants to survive. After she returns to her former life, she understands the significance of the Seder and her history, and knows that she will never forget. *National Jewish Awards, Sydney Taylor Book Award*, and *Association of Jewish Libraries Award*.

2064. Zusak, Markus. *The Book Thief.* Knopf, 2006. 553pp. ISBN 978-0-375-83100-3. Grades YA.

In Nazi Germany, Death is tired out by his heavy duties and is intrigued by a young girl named Liesl—living with foster parents and a hidden Jewish fugitive—whose appetite for books sustains her even as it leads her into danger.

History

2065. Abella, Alex, and Scott Gordon. *Shadow Enemies: Hitler's Secret Terrorist Plot Against the United States.* Lyons, 2003. 320pp. Paper ISBN 978-1-59228-142-8. Grades YA.

In 1942 a team of eight Nazi agents with fake documents and explosives left a submarine in Amagansett, New York, bound for New York City. They spoke English well and knew American customs, so they were designated as destroyers of factories and public landmarks. Another team landed in Florida several days later. Both might have succeeded if the leader, George Dasch, had not defected and informed the FBI. Secret military tribunals tried them, convicted them, and sentenced them to electrocution. Bibliography, Notes, and Index.

2066. Adler, David A. *We Remember the Holocaust.* Henry Holt, 1995. 147pp. Paper ISBN 978-0-8050-3715-9. Grades 4 up.

Interviews with Holocaust survivors recount the horrors of Hitler from the time he came to power; through *Kristallnacht* on November 9, 1938; to the Polish killing of Jews in 1947 after the war ended. Millions of people were exterminated for no reason other than their Jewish blood. The guilt of those who survived, and their desire to keep alive the traditions of their forebears, permeate this book. Photographs of people and places enhance the impact of these accounts of the heinous crimes. Bibliography, Chronology, Glossary, Index, and Suggested Reading.

2067. Bachrach, Susan D. *Tell Them We Remember: The Story of the Holocaust.* Little, Brown, 1994. 128pp. Paper ISBN 978-0-316-07484-1. Grades 5 up.

Bachrach uses the same format that the United States Holocaust Museum uses for visitors. She starts with a series of photographs of children and traces their experiences throughout the Holocaust—where they went and, in some cases, where they died. The other photographs also come from the museum's collection. The book follows the chronology of the Holocaust, beginning with life before the Holocaust and Hitler's rise to power in 1933, and follows the survivors through the Nuremberg Trials in 1945 and 1946. Chronology, Further Reading, Glossary, and Index. *Charlotte Award* (New York).

2068. Bartoletti, Susan Campbell. *Hitler Youth: Growing Up in Hitler's Shadow.* Scholastic, 2005. 176pp. ISBN 978-0-439-35379-3. Grades YA.

The author examines the factors that led young people to pledge loyalty to Adolf Hitler during his rise to power. The Hitler Youth was formed in 1926. When Hitler became chancellor of Germany in 1933, more than 3.5 million children were already members. Bartoletti's interviews with former Hitler Youth are revealing. Photographs augment the text. Bibliography, Further Reading, and Index. *Robert F. Sibert Honor Book, Horn Book Fanfare, Booklist Editors' Choice, School Library Journal Best Children's Books, Bulletin Blue Ribbon, Kirkus Reviews Editor's Choice,* and *Capitol Choices Noteworthy Titles* (Washington, D.C.).

2069. Bodden, Valerie. *The Holocaust.* (Days of Change) Creative Education, 2007. 48pp. ISBN 978-1-58341-547-4. Grades 6–9.

The book begins with a description of the terrible conditions in Germany and the rest of the world during the 1930s. The Germans resented their government's surrender in World War I, and nationalism took over other problems so that Hitler, with his message of white supremacy, could capture the country's imagination. Additional information about anti-Semitism in other countries reveals that the Germans were not alone. Other details including full-paged photographs about the Holocaust show its impact. Other information trying to present a balanced view between the two factions is also included. Bibliography and Index.

2070. Burgess, Alan. *The Longest Tunnel: The True Story of World War II's Great Escape.* Naval Institute, 2004. 288pp. Paper ISBN 978-1-59114-097-9. Grades YA.

In March of 1944, 76 Allied prisoners of war crawled through a tunnel nicknamed "Harry" that they had dug underneath the prison at Sagan, Stalag Luft III. Only three survived. The Gestapo caught the others and murdered them without trial—contravening the Geneva Convention. By interviewing the three who survived and checking documents, Burgess reveals a stark saga of World War II. Index.

2071. Chamovitz, Sheila, and Anita Brostoff. *Flares of Memory: Stories of Childhood During the Holocaust.* Oxford, 2002. 384pp. Paper ISBN 978-0-19-515627-0. Grades YA.

This volume shares memories of the 1930s and 1940s from forty Holocaust survivors and includes an examination of Jewish life before World War II and after the liberation. Ninety-two vignettes written as poetry, short prose, or short stories offer a view of their hunger, thirst, coldness, despair, exhaustion, and fear. Also included are memories of American soldiers who participated in the liberation.

2072. Childers, Thomas. *Wings of Morning: The Story of the Last American Bomber Shot Down Over Germany in World War II.* Da Capo, 1996. 276pp. Paper ISBN 978-0-201-40722-8. Grades YA.

In World War II Childers's uncle was one of the ten (two survived) who never returned from the last American bomber shot down over Germany. Through letters and interviews, including some from German villagers who lived near the crash, Childers discovered that ground flak may have led the bomber off course on what turned out to be an unnecessary mission. The two who survived may or may not have been tortured. One may have died because a parachute opened too close to the ground; another may have been trapped inside the plane. In addition to the story of the crash, information about the tension and interminable waiting between flights is presented. Index.*American Library Association Best Books for Young Adults.*

2073. Chorlton, Windsor. *Weapons and Technology of World War II.* (20th Century Perspectives) Heinemann, 2002. 48pp. ISBN 978-1-58810-663-6; paper ISBN 978-1-58810-923-1. Grades 5–8.

In World War II technological improvements enabled the development of radically new weapons such as the long-range rocket and the atomic bomb. Otherwise, the military used the same weapons from World War I, but with major improvements in aircraft and tanks. The author discusses these weapons, their uses, and the effects of their use. Illustrations highlight the text. Bibliography, Further Reading, Glossary, Index.

2074. Connelly, Mark. *Reaching for the Stars: A New History of Bomber Command in World War II.* I. B. Tauris/St. Martin's, 2001. 256pp. ISBN 978-1-860645-91-4; 2002. paper ISBN 978-1-860648-05-2. Grades YA.

In seven chapters, Connelly relates the history of the British bombing of Germany in World War II. He suggests that the British accepted this detestable task because they had to defeat Hitler even though their pilots were inadequately trained and equipped. Before the end of the war, the Bomber Command lost 55,000 men, but had killed more than 500,000 Germans and destroyed 3.37 million houses. Chronology, Notes, Bibliography, and Index.

2075. Corona, Laurel. *The Russian Federation.* Lucent, 2001. 110pp. ISBN 978-1-56006-675-0. Grades 8 up.

Since the collapse of the Soviet Union, the former Soviet republics have faced unexpected economic, political, and social challenges. This text examines the history of the Soviet Union before it was formed, its life from 1922 to 1991, the necessity of restructuring the economy, the politics and nationhoods of each component country, and the arts and entertainment in each. Illustrations enhance the text. Bibliography, Glossary, Chronology, Notes, Further Reading, and Index.

2076. Crew, David F. *Hitler and the Nazis: A History in Documents.* (Pages from History) Oxford, 2002. 171pp. ISBN 978-0-19-515285-2. Grades 7 up.

This history of Adolf Hitler and his rise to power contains information from primary sources such as government papers, Nazi propaganda, letters, diaries, trial and hearings testimony, and reminiscences. The Nazis created a mythical Hitler who represented the German nation, thereby allowing him to develop the racist state, its war machine, and the Holocaust. Photographs complement the text. Bibliography, Web Sites, and Index.

2077. DeSaix, Deborah Durland, and Karen Gray Ruelle. *Hidden on the Mountain: Stories of Children Sheltered from the Nazis in Le Chambon.* Holiday House, 2007. ISBN 978-0-8234-1928-9. Grades YA.

In south-central France, in the village of Le Chambon, the community worked together to save several thousand Jewish children during the Holocaust. The authors interviewed thirty survivors and rescuers and relate their answers in an epistolary style. The photographs that complement the text give an immediacy to the story. Chronology, Maps, Bibliography, Further Reading, Notes, and Index.

2078. Downing, David. *Aftermath and Remembrance.* (World Almanac Library of the Holocaust) World Almanac, 2005. 48pp. ISBN 978-0-8368-5948-5. Grades 5–8.

Downing presents primary documents, maps, and period photographs that give a realistic and thorough account of the Holocaust. The book includes the challenges Jews faced after World War II, an overview of Jewish history, the formation of Israel, the

Nuremberg trial, the Eichmann trial, hunting war criminals, war memorials, and the legacy of the Holocaust. Chronology, Glossary, Further Reading, Web Sites, and Index.

2079. Downing, David. *Fighting Back.* (World Almanac Library of the Holocaust) World Almanac, 2005. 48pp. ISBN 978-0-8368-5946-1. Grades 4–7.

Primary source documents and archival photographs help to explain the reaction of people to the Nazis during the Holocaust of World War II. Although resistance was extremely difficult, people hid Jews or Jews hid in forests or other places. Righteous Gentiles helped as did partisans. Sometimes the resistance movements were openly hostile, jeopardizing their safety as well as that of those they were trying to help. Maps, photographs, and illustrations augment the text. Chronology, Glossary, Further Reading, Web Sites, and Index.

2080. Downing, David. *Origins of the Holocaust.* (World Almanac Library of the Holocaust) Gareth Stevens, 2006. 48pp. ISBN 978-0-8368-5943-0. Grades 6–9.

Primary source documents, maps, and period photographs help to clarify the origins of the Holocaust. The chronicling begins in 922 B.C.E. with an overview of Jewish history and that of anti-Semitism. It continues with the birth of Christianity, the European Enlightenment, the Industrial Revolution, World War I, the creation of the Nazi Party, and the rise of Hitler to power in Germany. Photographs, maps, and illustrations augment the text. Chronology, Glossary, Further Reading, Web Sites, and Index.

2081. Downing, David. *Toward Genocide.* (World Almanac Library of the Holocaust) Gareth Stevens, 2005. 48pp. ISBN 978-0-8368-5945-4. Grades 7–10.

Downing presents primary documents, maps, and period photographs that give a realistic and thorough account of what led to genocide in the Holocaust. The story begins with the outbreak of World War II in Europe and continues to 1942, listing German invasions and occupations. It includes the creation of the ghettos, work camps, and gas chambers and offers information on the Wannsee Conference. Maps, photographs, and illustrations augment the text. Chronology, Glossary, Further Reading, Web Sites, and Index.

2082. Dowswell, Paul. *The Causes of World War II.* (20th Century Perspectives) Heinemann, 2003. 48pp. ISBN 978-1-4034-0149-6; paper ISBN 978-1-4034-4621-3. Grades 5–8.

Dowswell covers the causes of World War II and the reasons for each country's entrance into the war. Adolf Hitler's aggressive acts in countries bordering Germany were the initial impetus for this world war. Illustrations highlight the text. Bibliography, Further Reading, Glossary, and Index.

2083. Drez, Ronald J. *Remember D-Day: The Plan, the Invasion, Survivor Stories.* National Geographic, 2004. ISBN 978-0-7922-6666-2. Grades 5–8.

The text recounts the months leading to the Allied invasion of Normandy on June 6, 1944. It includes the strategy and deception practiced during those days based on the intelligence garnered from the Nazi enemy. Survivors recount the experience. Additional primary sources also describe different aspects of the time. Photographs and illustrations highlight the text. Maps, Notes, Bibliography, Chronology, and Index. *School Library Journal Best Children's Books* and *Beehive Award* (Utah) nomination.

2084. Dwork, Deborah. *Children with a Star: Jewish Youth in Nazi Europe.* Yale University, 1993. 354pp. Paper ISBN 978-0-300-05447-7. Grades YA.

This oral history presents the lives of Jewish children in the Holocaust of World War II as they lived at home, in transit camps, in hiding, in ghettos, and in death and labor camps. Dwork relies on primary sources of diaries, letters, and interviews, and reiterates that only 10 percent of the Jewish children survived. Some of those who shared their stories for this book had never before told anyone of their almost unspeakable experiences. Glossary, Bibliography, and Index.

2085. Dwork, Deborah, and Robert Jan Van Pelt. *Holocaust: A History.* Norton, 2003. 444pp. Paper ISBN 978-0-393-32524-9. Grades YA.

In looking at events since the beginning of the Middle Ages, the authors examine those that led to the rise of Nazism and its inherent evil in the Holocaust. They study the historical relationship among the Jews, Gentiles, and Germans; World War I; National Socialism in the Weimar Republic; the Third Reich and its anti-Semitism; worldwide refugee policies; Jewish and Gentile life under German occupation; the role of the Allied nations in attempting rescues; and the world of the concentration camp. In essence, the Holocaust is seen as an event unto itself that coincidentally occurred during World War II. Maps, Notes, and Index.

2086. Fogelman, Eva. *Conscience and Courage: Rescuers of Jews During the Holocaust.* Anchor, 1995. 393pp. Paper ISBN 978-0-385-42028-0. Grades YA.

Fogelman discusses those people who rescued Jews during the Holocaust of World War II. The book, divided into three parts, looks at "The Rescuers," "The Motivation," and "Postwar." She separates the rescuers into five categories: those who helped because of moral or ethical reasons, those who had a special relationship with the Jewish people, those who opposed the Third Reich and its policies, those in medicine or social work, and children who became involved because of their families. Among well-known helpers were Oskar Schindler, Raoul Wallenberg, and Miep Gies. The list also includes many who were unknown outside their personal circle of friends. Photographs and Index.

2087. Friedman, Ina R. *Escape or Die: True Stories of Young People Who Survived the Holocaust.* Yellow Moon, 1991. 146pp. Paper ISBN 978-0-938756-34-7. Grades 6 up.

Thirty-five million people died in World War II. Six million Jews died in the death camps, but 5 million non-Jews also met death there. Friedman looks at survivors, twelve men and women from Africa, Asia, Europe, and North and South America who, under the age of 20, had both courage and luck. Some of them had never before told their stories of escaping form Germany, Austria, Czechoslovakia, Poland, Holland, Belgium, Ukraine, France, and Hungary. Glossary and Index.

2088. Friedman, Ina R. *The Other Victims: First-Person Stories of Non-Jews Persecuted by the Nazis.* Houghton, 1995. 180pp. Paper ISBN 978-0-395-74515-1. Grades 5–9.

In addition to the millions of Jews persecuted in World War II's Holocaust, 5 million non-Jews were also deliberately murdered. They included gypsies, blacks, Slavs, the disabled, homosexuals, ministers, and Jehovah's Witnesses. This book is a collection of personal interviews with survivors, detailing what they and their families and friends experienced. Other Books of Interest to the Reader and Index.

2089. Gilbert, Martin. *Kristallnacht: Prelude to Destruction.* HarperCollins, 2006. 314pp. ISBN 978-0-06-057083-5; Perennial, 2007. paper ISBN 978-0-06-112135-7. Grades YA.

On November 10, 1938, *Kristallnacht*, "night of the broken glass," Nazi troops and Hitler Youth destroyed Jewish neighborhoods throughout Germany. They burned synagogues, Jewish homes, and Jewish shops. Then they vandalized unburned property. At least a quarter of the Jewish men were arrested, and thousands of Jews were beaten and killed. Readers will learn about this night and the world's reaction to its horror, resulting in the Indian and Chinese governments offering asylum to the victims. From that time on, the Nazis kept their intentions quiet while they continued their annihilation of the Jews. Illustrations augment the text. Bibliography and Index.

2090. Grayling, A. C. *Among the Dead Cities: The History and Moral Legacy of the WWII Bombing of Civilians in Germany and Japan.* Walker, 2006. 362pp. ISBN 978-0-8027-1471-8; 2007. paper ISBN 978-0-8027-1565-4. Grades YA.

The author investigates the bombing of Dresden, Tokyo, and Hiroshima during World War II. This book looks at Britain's "area bombing" of entire German cities because hitting smaller targets was very difficult at that time. Grayling concludes that the bombing did little to help the war effort and unnecessarily sacrificed civilian lives. The Americans, on the other hand, pinpointed their targets and paralyzed the German economy with fewer German lives lost, although they did rely on area bombing in Japan. Photographs enhance the text. Bibliography.

2091. Greenfeld, Howard. *The Hidden Children.* Houghton, 1997. 118pp. Paper ISBN 978-0-395-86138-7. Grades 4 up.

Many children in the Holocaust lived with strangers who risked their lives to protect the them. All Jewish children learned to lie and conceal their true identities. They learned when they could laugh or cry and when they must be silent. Among the places they hid were attics, basements, haylofts, underground passages, orphanages, and convents. All lost their childhood years. For Further Reading and Index.

2092. Haas, Gerda. *Tracking the Holocaust.* Runestone, 1995. 175pp. ISBN 978-0-8225-3157-9. Grades 5 up.

When Gerda Haas's American-born children did not understand why some past happenings were important to her, Haas decided that she must recount her own youth so that her children would know what she had experienced by the age of 23. She traces the stories of eight persons caught in the Holocaust, six of whom survived. She gives a history starting with the beginning of Nazi rule in 1930s Germany. Haas covers Germany, Poland, Denmark, Norway, Holland, Belgium, Luxembourg, France, Italy, Hungary, and the Balkan countries. In most of these countries she places one of the story subjects and describes that person's experiences. Sentencing, Sources, Documentary Material, Map Citation, The Testimonies of Survivors and Victims, and Index.

2093. Hakim, Joy. *The Story of Science: Einstein Adds a New Dimension.* Smithsonian, 2007. 468pp. ISBN 978-1-58834-162-4. Grades 9 up.

Although formatted like a textbook, this look at science in the 20th century presents profiles of key individuals and offers explanations that make their theories accessible to the untrained reader. Among the topics are quantum theory, probability, subatomic particles, inflation, and string theory. Photographs, charts, and diagrams reinforce the text. Further Reading and Index.

2094. Hay, Jeff. *The Treaty of Versailles.* (At Issue) Greenhaven, 2001. Paper ISBN 978-0-7377-0826-4. Grades 9 up.

Twelve primary and secondary sources relate the events that led to the 28 June 1919 signing of the Treaty of Versailles at the end of World War I by exploring the debates and issues surrounding it. Among the issues were the blame of Germany for World War I and the Allies differing on how to treat Germany. The Germans believed they had been betrayed, and their reactions that led to World War II are analyzed here. Photographs and maps augment the text. Chronology, Further Reading, and Index.

2095. Hill, Jeff. *The Holocaust.* (Primary Sourcebook) Omnigraphics, 2006. 400pp. ISBN 978-0-7808-0935-2. Grades 7 up.

Hill covers all aspects of the Holocaust, from its roots to its culmination, through more than one hundred primary source documents such as academic articles, leaflet texts, political position papers, field reports, and personal testimonies from survivors and organization workers. Among the topics are the roots of anti-Semitism, the experiences of those caught in the Holocaust and who had their lives destroyed, Hitler's "Final Solution" actions and policies, the liberation, displaced person camps, and life after the Holocaust ended. Chronology, Glossary, Bibliography, and Index.

2096. Hoare, Stephen. *The Modern World.* Facts on File, 1993. 78pp. ISBN 978-0-8160-2792-7. Grades 4–7.

Any history of the 20th century must discuss the decline of European colonial empires and provide background to World War I, which in turn led to World War II. The post-World War II condition, including the cold war between East and West, stayed in the forefront until the end of the 1980s. Human rights, religious struggles, and space travel continued to be important to societies. Illustrations highlight the text. Glossary, Further Reading, and Index.

2097. Hynson, Colin. *World War II: A Primary Source History.* (In Their Own Words) Gareth Stevens, 2005. 48pp. ISBN 978-0-8368-5983-6. Grades 5–8.

Among the topics covered in this overview of World War II using primary sources are the circumstances that led to the war, international leaders at the time, how it affected the rest of the century, the memorials to the dead that resulted, the depiction of the war in art, and artifacts from that war being discovered today. Maps, photographs and illustrations complement the text. Glossary, Chronology, and Index.

2098. Isserman, Maurice. *World War II.* Facts on File, 2003. 226pp. ISBN 978-0-8160-4938-7. Grades 7 up.

This volume gives an overview of World War II, beginning with Leo Szilard's concern in 1939 that the best people working on nuclear fission were in Hitler's Germany. Szilard was a Hungarian scientist who had recently come to America. His advice led to the Manhattan Project and the development of the atomic bomb later used in Japan. Isserman presents the major events of the war, the major objectives and strategies of the war's leaders, and significant innovations in weapons and tactics. Biographical references to many of the leaders also appear. Recommended Reading and Index.

2099. Kacer, Kathy. *The Underground Reporters.* Second Story, 2006. 156pp. Paper ISBN 978-1-89676-485-6. Grades 5–9.

A group of Jewish teenagers in Budejovice, Czechoslovakia, start a newspaper in which to report their concerns and more pleasant items as conditions worsen between April 1942 and April 1945. Since they are barred from ordinary jobs, they use their creativity to write humorous stories and jokes, poems, gossip, and draw pictures, with additional subtly subversive commentary. They distribute this throughout the community in twenty editions that grow from three to almost twenty-five pages. After they are deported, a Christian woman keeps the copies in her home until one of the survivors returns and retrieves them in 1989. Black-and-white photographs augment the text.

2100. Kaplan, Alice Yaeger. *The Interpreter.* University of Chicago, 2007. 240pp. ISBN 978-0-226-42425-5. Grades YA.

Two American soldiers were accused of murdering French citizens during the final days of World War II. One of the men, an African American named James Hendricks, was sentenced to death, and the other, a white man named George Whittington, who killed a French underground soldier, was acquitted as a war hero. The French political novelist, Louis Guilloux, was the interpreter at the trial, and he kept diaries and wrote a novel after the trial ended. In her study on racial discrimination, Kaplan notes that of seventy American soldiers executed for war crimes in France, fifty-five were African American. Based on interviews with Hendricks's family and the family of the farmer he was accused of killing, she concludes that African Americans often did not receive fair or competent legal counsel. Photographs enhance the text. Notes and Index.

2101. Laqueur, Walter. *Generation Exodus: The Fate of Young Jewish Refugees from Nazi Germany.* Brandeis University, 2001. 332pp. ISBN 978-1-58465-106-2. Grades YA.

Primary documents help to chronicle the lives of young German and Austrian Jews who left their countries as Hitler's rise to power began in 1933. Of the nearly 80,000 in this age group, around 60,000 escaped. These people were from different social and economic strata and moved to locations throughout the world. Many went to Palestine, others to Great Britain, the United States (such as Henry Kissinger), and even India, where Ruth Prawer-Jhabvala relocated. Bibliography, Glossary, and Index.

2102. Lee, Carol Ann. *Anne Frank and the Children of the Holocaust.* Viking, 2006. 242pp. ISBN 978-0-670-06107-5; Puffin, 2008. paper ISBN 978-0-14-241069-1. Grades 4–7.

Many children faced extinction during the Holocaust. The author focuses on Anne Frank and others using personal accounts from survivors, information from extant journals, articles, interviews, and photographs. The chapter headings include quotes from Anne Frank's diary as she tells the story of others who had the same fate as her own. Additionally the book offers background about Hitler's rise to power and the loss of freedom for the Jews. Bibliography.

2103. Levine, Ellen. *Darkness Over Denmark: The Danish Resistance and the Rescue of the Jews.* Holiday House, 2000. 164pp. ISBN 978-0-8234-1447-5; 2002. paper ISBN 978-0-8234-1755-1. Grades 5–8.

Many of Denmark's citizens risked their lives during World War II to protect or rescue their Jewish neighbors and friends from the Nazis. Relying on interviews with more than twenty survivors, rescuers, and resistance fighters, along with careful research to uncover stories about the Danish Resistance, this account is presented in thirteen chapters. Photographs and maps augment the text. Bibliography, Chronology, Notes, and Index. *Student Book Award* (Maine) nomination and *Dorothy Canfield Fisher Children's Book Awards* (Vermont).

2104. Levy, Adrian, and Catherine Scott-Clark. *The Amber Room: The Fate of the World's Greatest Lost Treasure.* Berkley, 2005. 416pp. Paper ISBN 978-0-425-20378-1. Grades YA.

In 1717 Frederick William, King of Prussia, gave Tsar Peter the Great wall panels made of the fossilized resin of prehistoric plants 12 feet high and filled with Baroque carvings. The Amber Room was installed in the Catherine Palace in Pushkin, outside Leningrad (St. Petersburg). The Soviet curator in charge of the room tried to conceal it when the Germans seized Leningrad in 1941, but the Germans found it within three days, dismantled it, and shipped it to Königsberg, Prussia, the site of much of the world's amber. It stayed there until 1945 when the Red Army came looking for looted treasures. However, it has never been found. Scott-Clark and Levy have investigated declassified files of the East German Stasi and the KGB, witnesses and experts, items in Russian research libraries, and information from a number of people willing to share it for money. They suggest that the Red Army destroyed it in April 1945 and spread the propaganda that the West destroyed it. Illustrations, Maps, Notes, Bibliography, and Index. *Original Voices Award* nomination.

2105. Levy, Pat. *The Home Front in World War II.* (World Wars) Raintree Steck-Vaughn, 2003. 64pp. ISBN 978-0-7398-6065-6. Grades 5–8.

Primary source documents and firsthand accounts detail life during World War II for the citizens at home in both Axis and Allied countries—the people who helped in domestic factories and other places. Many became displaced during the bombing of civilian areas, and many were called upon to help when those who fought returned home needing unexpected care. The war changed each country in some way. Illustrations and photographs enhance the text. Maps, Chronology, Bibliography, and Glossary.

2106. Lewin, Rhoda G. *Witnesses to the Holocaust: An Oral History.* Twayne, 1991. 240pp. Paper ISBN 978-0-8057-9126-6. Grades YA.

Lewin presents accounts of Holocaust survivors now living in Minnesota. She also includes accounts of those who liberated the Jews from the concentration camps. The words of the liberators tend to be more vivid because they use emotions to tell their experiences; the victims seem to be almost clinically detached from their ordeals. How they tell the story may be as important as what they say. Index.

2107. Liberatore, Karen. *Our Century: 1910–1920.* Gareth Stevens, 1993. 64pp. ISBN 978-0-8368-1033-2. Grades 3 up.

See entry 1748.

2108. McClafferty, Carla Killough. *In Defiance of Hitler: The Secret Mission of Varian Fry.* Farrar, 2008. 196pp. ISBN 978-0-374-38204-9. Grades 6 up.

As a young American journalist in Germany prior to World War II, Varian Fry saw the beginnings of Nazi anti-Semitism. After returning to New York, he realized he needed to act on behalf of Jews. He went to Marseilles for two weeks using his newly formed Emergency Rescue Committee to help as many refugees escape as possible. His two weeks turned into a year. During that time he helped more than two thousand people escape. He knew the United States would not welcome everyone, so he focused on artists and writers including Heinrich Mann and Marc Chagall. He had to get travel documents for them—sometimes even forged. He sacrificed his marriage and his job in his effort to help these people find new lives. Maps, photographs, and reproductions accompany the text. Bibliography, Notes, Further Reading, Web Sites, and Index.

2109. Mallon, Bill, and Anthony Th. Bijkerk. *The 1920 Olympic Games: Results for All Competitors in All Events, with Commentary.* (History of the Early Olympics) McFarland, 2003. 456pp. ISBN 978-0-7864-1280-8. Grades YA.

The Antwerp, Belgium, Olympics were held in 1920 after the 1916 Olympics were canceled when World War I started. Although the Antwerp organizing committee issued a few typed copies of the results in French, the report was incomplete because of the financial problems resulting from the games. Therefore, the report listed only the medalists for some competitions. The information in this account, however, is based on sources available in 1920 that record all of the results except those for shooting. Other sports included are archery, track and field, boxing, cycling, diving, equestrian, fencing, figure skating, football (soccer), gymnastics, field hockey, ice hockey, modern pentathlon, polo, rowing and sculling, rugby, swimming, lawn tennis, tug-of-war, water polo, weightlifting, wrestling, and yachting. Appendices, Notes, Bibliography, and Index.

2110. Meltzer, Milton. *Never to Forget: The Jews of the Holocaust.* HarperCollins, 1991. 217pp. Paper ISBN 978-0-06-446118-4. Grades 7 up.

By referring to private letters, diaries, memoirs, poems, and songs, Meltzer shows that the 6 million Jews that Hitler destroyed in the Holocaust were real people who struggled day to day just to survive. Meltzer recounts all of the legal changes that Hitler instigated as he rose to power and began his systematic anti-Semitic campaign, which eventually led to the ghettos and the death camps. Chronology, Bibliography, and Index. *American Library Association Best of the Best Books for Young Adults, American Library Association Notable Children's Book, Boston Globe-Horn Book Award for Nonfiction, School Library Journal Best Books, New York Times Outstanding Children's Books, Notable Children's Trade Books in the Field of Social Studies, Jane Addams Award, National Book Award for Children's Literature Nominee, IBBY Hans Christian Andersen Honors List,* and *Sidney Taylor Book Award.*

2111. Meltzer, Milton. *The Rescue: The Story of How Gentiles Saved Jews in the Holocaust.* HarperCollins, 1991. 168pp. Paper ISBN 978-0-06-446117-7. Grades 7 up.

Meltzer includes many stories of Gentiles who defied the Nazis' plan to exterminate the Jews. Among these individuals who showed they would not be cowed by immoral acts, were a peasant, a policeman, a housemaid, a countess, a bricklayer, a priest, an industrialist, a librarian, a washerwoman, a pastor, a clerk, and a priest. Two of the chapters cover Oskar Schindler and the Countess Marushka. Bibliography and Index.

2112. Myers, Nathan. *Paris.* (Cities at War) Simon & Schuster, 1992. 96pp. ISBN 978-0-02-700010-8. Grades 6 UP.

In World War II German troops occupied Paris from 1940 to 1944. Although no fighting occurred in the city, Nazi soldiers abused people, persecuted the city's Jews, and enforced curfews. The French had mixed feelings about their own conduct—collaborating with the Germans could mean saving themselves. Photographs, Notes, Further Reading, and Index.

2113. Patz, Nancy. *Who Was the Woman Who Wore the Hat?* Dutton, 2003. 48pp. ISBN 978-0-525-46999-5. Grades 5 up.

After seeing the hat of a woman on display in Amsterdam's Jewish Historical Museum, Patz reflects about the woman's life. She wonders who she might have been, what her life would have been, and if she ended up a victim during the Holocaust of World War II. By asking particular questions such as wondering if she used cream in her coffee and if she tipped the brim of the hat, Patz moves to the larger questions about the horror of the Holocaust. Photographs augment the text. Chronology.

2114. Reynoldson, Fiona. *Key Battles of World War II.* (20th Century Perspectives) Heinemann, 2001. 48pp. ISBN 978-1-57572-438-6; paper ISBN 978-1-58810-377-2. Grades 5–8.

World War II was fought in four different areas of the world. In the European, Asian and Pacific, Middle Eastern, and African and Mediterranean theaters a number of battles were fought each year from 1939 until 1945. The author looks at the causes of these battles, the battles themselves, and the results of the battles. Illustrations highlight the text. Bibliography, Further Reading, Glossary, Index.

2115. Rhodes, Richard. *Masters of Death: The SS-Einsatzgruppen and the Invention of the Holocaust.* Vintage, 2003. 335pp. Paper ISBN 978-0-375-70822-0. Grades YA.

By the end of 1941 Hitler had deployed a task force called the Einsatzgruppen to Poland and the Soviet Union with the purpose of slaughtering Eastern European Jews. They gunned down thousands of people and buried them in mass graves that prisoners of war had to dig. This difficult account shows both inhumanity and agony. Index.

2116. Rogasky, Barbara. *Smoke and Ashes: The Story of the Holocaust.* Holiday House, 2002. 256pp. ISBN 978-0-8234-1612-7; paper ISBN 978-0-8234-1677-6. Grades 5 up.

Readers will learn a brief history of the roots of Nazi anti-Semitism and some of the reasons for Hitler's rise to power. The book then follows the development of the plan to exterminate the Jews. Quotations from both major and minor Nazi leaders show how they built the ghettos and concentration camps, why they built them, and who built them. Other chapters look at life in the camps for the Jews, their armed resistance in Warsaw, what the United States and Britain did and failed to do about their situation, the Nazi "helpers" of German policeman and bystanders, and the persecution of gay men. Another chapter lists the Nazis tried at Nuremberg and what happened to them. Also presented are contemporary hate groups and those who deny that the Holocaust ever occurred. Photographs, Bibliography, Web Sites, and Index. *Voice of Youth Advocates Perfect Ten List*.

2117. Ross, Stewart. *The Russian Revolution.* Heinemann/Raintree, 2002. 78pp. ISBN 978-0-7398-5801-1. Grades 7 up.

See entry 1764.

2118. Rubin, Susan Goldman. *The Flag with Fifty-Six Stars: A Gift from the Survivors of Mauthausen.* Illustrated by Bill Farnsworth. Holiday House, 2005. 40pp. ISBN 978-0-8234-1653-0; 2006. paper ISBN 978-0-8234-2019-3. Grades 5–8.

In May 1945 as the United States Army and Colonel Richard Siebel made their way to liberate the inmates at Mauthausen, the survivors secretly made a flag, presenting it to their liberators when they arrived. The survivors inadvertently added a row of stars and the flag had fifty-six. The Americans flew it above the camp in gratitude for their welcome. The flag is now displayed at the Simon Wiesenthal Center in Los Angeles.

Wiesenthal was one of those liberated from that camp. Illustrations enhance the text. Bibliography and Index.

2119. Shapiro, Stephen, and Tina Forrester. *Hoodwinked: Deception and Resistance.* Illustrated by David Craig. (Outwitting the Enemy: Stories from World War II) Annick, 2004. 96pp. ISBN 978-1-55037-833-7; paper ISBN 978-1-55037-832-0. Grades 5–9.

Eighteen true stories of two to three pages each describe ways in which the Allies tried to deceive the enemy in World War II. Phony military divisions would make the enemy expect an attack so that a real attack could take place against a less well-defended target. Nonaggression treaties forged through diplomacy could hide major invasions. In Operation Mincemeat, the British used a dead body to mislead the Axis troops. The British even constructed fake towns to confuse the air raiders and broadcast false news on the radio. Illustrations and sidebars augment the text. Bibliography, Maps, and Index. *ForeWord Book of the Year* Honorable Mention.

2120. Shapiro, Stephen, and Tina Forrester. *Ultra Hush-Hush: Espionage and Special Missions.* Illustrated by David Craig. (Outwitting the Enemy: Stories from World War II) Annick, 2003. 96pp. ISBN 978-1-55037-779-8; paper ISBN 978-1-55037-778-1. Grades 9–12.

Nineteen true stories of two to three pages each describe ways in which the Allies tried to deceive the enemy in World War II. Among their activities were covert operations, missions, and raids. The British had a Double Cross System with double agents spreading false information. Italy had "human torpedoes" in the Mediterranean. The Navajo Code Talkers allowed the Allies to succeed in the Pacific. An SS officer named "Scarface" Skorzeny rescued Benito Mussolini from a ski resort. The Brandenburg Regiment of Germany knew foreign languages and customs that allowed them to blend into the enemy troops. Illustrations and sidebars augment the text. Bibliography, Maps, and Index.

2121. Sheehan, Sean. *The Technology of World War II.* (World Wars) Raintree, 2003. 64pp. ISBN 978-0-7398-6064-9. Grades 5–9.

During World War II, warfare developed even more than it had for World War I. Bigger and stronger weapons along with intellectual warfare plagued each side. Among the aspects of this war were medical experiments, chemical and biological weapons, codes, and gas chambers. Each side used such tools as microwave transmissions, the V–1, V-2, radar, and the jet. When the Allies developed the atom bomb, the war ended. Photographs highlight the text. Chronology, Glossary, Sources, Further Readings, Web Sites, and Index.

2122. Steidl, Franz. *Lost Battalions: Going for Broke in the Vosges, Autumn 1944.* Presidio, 2001. 226pp. Paper ISBN 978-0-8914-1727-9. Grades YA.

Although not mainly about the Nisei (Japanese Americans) who volunteered and fought for the United States in World War II, this account shows that their behavior in the Vosges Mountains against the Germans led to their regiment becoming the most decorated unit in American military history. Bibliography and Index.

2123. Stein, R. Conrad. *World War II in Europe: "America Goes to War".* Myreportlinks.com, 2002. 48pp. ISBN 978-0-7660-5094-5; Enslow, 2000. paper ISBN 978-0-7660-1733-7. Grades 7 up.

Stein begins this account of World War II with the story of "Canned Goods." The Germans dressed convicts in Polish army uniforms, then killed them and announced that they were Polish invaders whom they had caught before they infiltrated Germany. Adolf Hitler used this farce to justify his invasion of Poland in 1939. Even though the German people were against war, Hitler declared it anyway. Many Germans were shocked that France and Great Britain supported Poland because they had refused to do anything when Hitler had previously broken the Treaty of Versailles. The other chapters follow the war across Europe. Chronology, Notes, Further Reading, and Index.

2124. Stoff, Laurie. *The Rise and Fall of the Soviet Union.*   Greenhaven, 2005. 192pp. ISBN 978-0-7377-2027-3. Grades 10 up.

Primary and secondary documents offer a variety of opinions about the rise and fall of the Soviet Union. Among those whose writings are included are Lenin, Trotsky, Stalin, Churchill, Hedrick Smith, and Gorbachev. They discuss the overthrow of the czar, early foreign policy, the treatment of women and dissidents, and the fall of the Soviet Union. Photographs and reproductions enhance the text. Glossary, Chronology, Further Reading, Web Sites, and Index.

2125. Tanaka, Shelley. *D-Day: They Fought to Free Europe from Hitler's Tyranny.*   Illustrated by David Craig. (A Day That Changed America) Hyperion, 2004. 48pp. ISBN 978-0-7868-1881-5. Grades 4–7.

Four soldiers who survived the Allied landing on the beaches of Normandy in France on June 6, 1944, give their accounts of the battle. A paratrooper, a P-47 pilot, a combat medic, and a landing craft crew member each give a different point of view on D-Day, a day that may have changed America's destiny. Other information about the battle also appears. Maps, Photos, Further Reading, Glossary, Web Sites, and Index.

2126. Taylor, Peter Lane, and Christos Nicola. *The Secret of Priest's Grotto: A Holocaust Survival Story.*   Kar-Ben, 2007. 64pp. ISBN 978-1-58013-260-2; paper ISBN 978-1-58013-261-9. Grades 6 up.

In 1993 a cave explorer in the Ukraine discovered signs of human habitation, and for ten years he searched for people. He recorded the experiences of those he met who lived in the Priest's Grotto during World War II for 344 days while hiding from the Nazis. He discovered that thirty-eight people—from toddlers to a grandmother of 75—hid in four underground rooms, sealed off from others. A Ukrainian peasant helped the families. They all needed great strength and courage to survive the sensory deprivation of the dark and each other.

2127. Whiting, Jim. *The Story of the Holocaust.*   (Monumental Milestones) Mitchell Lane, 2005. 48pp. ISBN 978-1-58415-400-6. Grades 5–8.

The author chronicles the Holocaust as a part of World War II beginning with the point of view an American soldier who sees it at the end of the war when he helps liberate the prisoners at Dachau, near Munich, Germany. This brief history covers the reasons behind the Holocaust and what factors led to Hitler's rise to power. Photographs intensify the text. Bibliography, Glossary, Chronology, Notes, Further Reading, Web Sites, and Index.

2128. Wiesel, Elie. *From the Kingdom of Memory: Reminiscences.*   Schocken, 1995. 250pp. Paper ISBN 978-0-8052-1020-0. Grades YA.

In a series of essays, Elie Wiesel (1928–) asserts his belief that one must remember the past if one is to have the best life in the present. He discusses the Holocaust, religious faith, war crimes, peace, and freedom. Among the collected speeches are his response to President Ronald Reagan during Reagan's Bitburg visit and his Nobel acceptance address for the Peace Prize in 1986. He asserts that all Jews are concerned with humanity, not merely with "getting even."

2129. Wieviorka, Annette. *Auschwitz Explained to My Child.* Translated by Leah Brumer. Da Capo, 2003. 64pp. Paper ISBN 978-1-56924-552-1. Grades YA.

When the author's daughter of 13 wants to know about the Holocaust and why her grandparents died in it, the French Wieviorka tries to explain it to her. She tells her about Hitler's rise to power, the establishment of ghettos and concentration camps, and the Jewish genocide. In total she bluntly answers the eighty questions that her daughter asks, questions that have bothered historians and philosophers since the horror occurred. *Booklist Editors' Choice.*

2130. Willoughby, Susan. *The Holocaust.* (20th Century Perspectives) Heinemann, 2001. 48pp. ISBN 978-1-57572-436-2; paper ISBN 978-1-58810-375-8. Grades 5–8.

Hitler aimed to exterminate groups of people he felt were not worthy of living— Jews, homosexuals, gypsies, and the disabled. This volume looks at the causes and effects of this policy as well as those who fought against it. In 1943 Jews in the Warsaw Ghetto rose against the Nazis to declare their humanity. They did not fully succeed, but they were heard. Illustrations highlight the text. Bibliography, Further Reading, Glossary, and Index.

2131. Wood, Angela Gluck. *Holocaust: The Events and Their Impact on Real People.* DK, 2007. ISBN 978-0-75662-535-1. Grades 7 up.

The author briefly relates the history of Jewish life in Europe with the exile from Jerusalem in 70, before focusing on the Holocaust and Nazi rule. The narrative includes information about the people living in the ghettos, the Kindertransport, trains to Auschwitz, and other events that occurred during the horror. Holocaust survivors appear in an accompanying DVD. Documentary photographs, Nazi propaganda, and illustrations augment the text. Chronology, Glossary, and Index. *Sydney Taylor Honor Book.*

Biography and Collective Biography

2132. Abeles, Pepter, and Tom Hicks. *Otto, the Boy at the Window: Peter Otto Abele's True Story of Escape from the Holocaust and New Life in America.* Authorhouse, 2004. 176pp. Paper ISBN 978-1-4184-2128-1. Grades YA.

Peter Otto Abeles remembers his Viennese childhood during the 1930s with a strict mother and an unyielding, successful father. After the Anschluss of March 12, 1938, when the Nazis took over Austria, Nazi sympathizers destroyed everything. His family sailed to New York in November 1939 with only ten dollars left of their fortune. In Chicago, two families sponsored them and helped them find a new life. Abeles himself then served in the military and became successful.

as Hitler's power increased. They finally realized that no one would save them and that they had to flee. Fortunately, they safely reached Shanghai, China.

2143. Bankston, John. *Sigmund Freud: Exploring the Mysteries of the Mind.* (Great Minds of Science) Enslow, 2006. 128pp. ISBN 978-0-7660-2336-9. Grades 6–9.

See entry 1780.

2144. Bargalló, Eva. *My Name Is . . . Picasso.* Illustrated by Violeta Monreal. (My Name Is . . .) Barron's, 2006. 63pp. Paper ISBN 978-0-7641-3393-0. Grades 4–6.

See entry 1782.

2145. Birch, Beverly, and Christian Birmingham. *Marie Curie's Search for Radium.* (Science Stories) Barron's Educational, 1996. 48pp. Paper ISBN 978-0-8120-9791-7. Grades 4–7.

See entry 1788.

2146. Borden, Louise. *The Journey That Saved Curious George: The True Wartime Escape of Margret and H. A. Rey.* Illustrated by Allan Drummond. Houghton, 2005. 80pp. ISBN 978-0-618-33924-2. Grades 3–7.

This biography of Margaret and H. A. Rey, creators of *Curious George*, presents their lives in two parts. The first covers their childhood in Germany. Then they married and lived in Rio de Janeiro, Brazil, and Paris, France, before World War II began. In 1940, as German Jews, they were almost unable to escape from France, but a complicated route finally got them to Rio. Then they went to New York. They traveled with several illustrated manuscripts, and after they reached New York they published their first book featuring the protagonist, Curious George. Photographs highlight the text. Bibliography. *William Allen White Children's Book Award* (Kansas) nomination, *Student Book Award* (Maine) nomination, and *Children's Book Award* (North Carolina) nomination.

2147. Bradley, Michael J. *Modern Mathematics: 1900–1950.* Narrated by Kirby Heybourne. (Pioneers in Mathematics) Chelsea House, 2006. 148pp. ISBN 978-0-8160-5426-8. Grades 6 up.

See entry 1791.

2148. Brown, Alan. *The Story Behind George Orwell's Animal Farm.* (History in Literature) Heinemann, 2006. 56pp. ISBN 978-1-4034-8203-7. Grades 6–9.

This biography of George Orwell (1903–1950) includes an overview of his life in the context of his time and culture. When Orwell wrote *Animal Farm*, he was concerned about the political environment, and he explores the results of anarchy in the novel. Photographs and reproductions highlight the text. Glossary, Chronology, Further Reading, Web Sites, and Index.

2149. Bryant, Jen. *Music for the End of Time.* Illustrated by Beth Peck. Eerdmans, 2005. 32pp. ISBN 978-0-8028-5229-8. Grades 4–7.

A French soldier during World War II, Oliver Messiaen (1908–1992) was captured and imprisoned in Stalag 8A. There, a young officer allowed him to compose music in a small room in the toilets. The result was "Quartet for the End of Time." Then the officer found a junky piano for him, a cello for another prisoner, and two more prisoners had their own instruments. The four played this music in a concert for 5,000 prisoners. Charcoal and pastel double-spread illustrations enhance the text.

2150. Caws, Mary Ann. *Virginia Woolf.* Overlook, 2002. 136pp. ISBN 978-1-58567-264-6; 2004. paper ISBN 978-1-58567-520-3. Grades YA.

See entry 1796.

2151. Cohn, Marthe, and Wendy Holden. *Behind Enemy Lines: The True Story of a French Jewish Spy in Nazi Germany.* Three Rivers, 2006. 282pp. Paper ISBN 978-0-307-33590-6. Grades YA.

Marthe Cohn Hoffnung (1920–), daughter in a Jewish family of seven children living in the French town of Metz, 33 miles from the German border, had her life change when Hitler came. She and her family participated in the Resistance, hiding other Jews. Since she spoke perfect German and looked Aryan, she joined the French army and went into Germany, posing as a nurse looking for her fiancé. She was able to obtain valuable information about German plans. In 1990 when she was 80, France awarded her its highest honor of Medaille Militare. Bibliography.

2152. Dabba Smith, Frank. *Elsie's War: A Story of Courage in Nazi Germany.* Frances Lincoln, 2006. 32pp. Paper ISBN 978-1-8450-7006-9. Grades 2–6.

Elsie Kuhn-Leitz (1903–1985), a young German woman, risked her life to help Jewish people flee from the Nazis during World War II. Her father owned the Leitz camera factory near Frankfurt and gave many Jews work in addition to helping them escape Germany. The Gestapo eventually imprisoned Elsie when it caught her helping a man cross into Switzerland, but her father paid a large ransom to keep her from being deported to the camps. Large black-and-white photographs enhance the text.

2153. Dahl, Roald. *Boy: Tales of Childhood.* Farrar, 1984. 160pp. ISBN 978-0-374-37374-0; Puffin, 2001. paper ISBN 978-0-14-130305-5. Grades 3 up.

Dahl lived his early childhood in Wales and England, son of a Norwegian mother and a father who had gone to Wales to start a business supplying ships. His father's early death, soon after the death of Dahl's sister at age 7, did not seem to cause economic distress, because Dahl's mother was able to give the family whatever it needed, including private school (public, in England) education. Dahl's stories of childhood during the 1920s in England show children fascinated with the local store's candy, hiding a dead mouse in one of the candy jars, and admiring the stunning ride of an older boy on his bicycle. Dahl spent summers in Norway and vividly remembers the summer when a doctor removed his adenoids without using anesthesia. His nose was almost severed in a motor car accident, with his mother driving. While he was in school, the Cadbury candy factory sent bars of unmarked candy for the boys to test. Dahl's mother offered him education at Oxford or Cambridge, but with his application for and receipt of a coveted position with Shell Oil, he ends this book.

2154. Dahl, Roald. *Going Solo.* Puffin, 2009. 208pp. Paper ISBN 978-0-14-241383-8. Grades 7 up.

In 1938 Roald Dahl found himself traveling by ship to Dar es Salaam for a job with Shell Oil. He noticed that the British subjects who chose to live and work in this part of the world, and who were accompanying him on the ship, were slightly "dotty." He learned a lot about them and himself during the voyage. After his arrival, he learned to be aware of things around him, such as snakes that might be crawling by. Inspired by an incident in which a lion grabbed a cook's wife, took her toward the jungle, and then dropped her unharmed at the sound of a gunshot, Dahl wrote his first article. When the war with Germany began, he joined the Royal Air Force. His recollection of the severe wounds he received in a crash, his long recovery, and his reentry into the Greek theater of the war—flying a plane in combat although he barely knew how the plane worked—gives a clear picture of the universal uncertainty and confusion of wartime as well as the warmth of humans who help each other.

2155. Delano, Marfe Ferguson. *Genius: A Photobiography of Albert Einstein.* (Photobiographies) National Geographic, 2005. 64pp. ISBN 978-0-7922-9544-0; 2008. paper ISBN 978-1-426-30294-7. Grades 5–9.

This biography of Albert Einstein (1879–1955) recounts his life from a childhood of privilege in Austria to his role in World War II as the originator of the theory of relativity necessary to create the atomic bomb. Ironically, Einstein was a pacifist. He also believed in justice and personal freedom, causing him to speak out against both Hitler and Joseph McCarthy. The book also includes summaries of some of his scientific theories. Illustrations augment the text. Bibliography, Chronology, Notes, Web Sites, and Index.*Capitol Choices Noteworthy Titles* (Washington, D.C.).

2156. Denenberg, Barry. *Shadow Life: A Portrait of Anne Frank and Her Family.* Scholastic, 2005. 240pp. ISBN 978-0-439-41678-8. Grades 5–10.

The four parts of this fictional diary about Anne Frank's family cover living, hiding, dying, and surviving. The first looks at the Frank family in Amsterdam before Hitler's rise to power. In the second, the diary of Anne's older sister Margot describes the family's time in hiding. Then in the third and fourth nonfiction sections, the reality of their lives is clear through stories about them from survivors of Westerbork, Auschwitz, and Bergen-Belsen. Bibliography, Chronology, Notes, and Index.

2157. Eichengreen, Lucille. *From Ashes to Life: My Memories of the Holocaust.* Mercury House, 1994. 217pp. Paper ISBN 978-1-56279-052-3. Grades YA.

In 1933 Cecilia Landau, age 8, had to move from her Hamburg neighborhood because people began jeering at her family. Her father was deported and the Nazis returned his ashes to the family in 1941. Cecilia, her mother, and her sister were deported to Lodz, Poland, where her mother died of starvation and her sister disappeared. Cecilia survived in Lodz for three years before being sent to Auschwitz. At the Sasel work camp she worked in an office where she memorized the names and addresses of forty-two Germans who ran the camp. She became the chief witness against them when the British came to arrest the Nazis. After death threats, she came to the United States with a new name, married a man who had also lost parents in Lodz, and had children. When she returned as Hamburg's official guest in 1991, she found that disdain toward Jews still lingered.

2158. Farr, Michael. *The Adventures of Hergé: Creator of Tintin.* Last Gasp, 2008. 128pp. ISBN 978-0-8671-9679-5. Grades YA.

Georges Remi created the comic book hero Tintin, and this is an account of his life and of his creation, first introduced in 1929. Farr offers seven sketches that include information from the archives and from various interviews with Hergé. Hergé disliked publicity, preferring to express himself in books and to examine all of the topics that interested him—science, world affairs, the avant garde scene, art, Zen Buddhism, and philosophy. His work helped develop contemporary movies. Photographs and illustrations highlight the text. Chronology, Notes, and Index.

2159. Filar, Marian, and Charles Patterson. *From Buchenwald to Carnegie Hall.* University Press of Mississippi, 2002. 225pp. ISBN 978-1-57806-419-9. Grades YA.

This biography of Marian Filar (1917–), renowned pianist and Holocaust survivor, is in five parts and covers his youth and early days of training in a Polish conservatory; his experience in Warsaw and as a refugee and inhabitant of the Warsaw Ghetto; in the Nazi camp at Buchenwald where a German saved his hand after he cut it; freedom and Sol Hurok's discovery of his talent; and coming to America to start his career. At 12, he was a soloist with the Warsaw Philharmonic Orchestra. In 1939 his parents, a brother, and a sister fled with him to Lvov, but the others were killed in the Holocaust. In 1950 he immigrated to the United States, and played at Carnegie Hall in 1952. He retired as a professor of music at Temple University while continuing to play concerts. Index.

2160. Frálon, Jose Alain. *A Good Man in Evil Times: The Story of Aristides de Sousa Mendes.* Basic, 2001. 177pp. ISBN 978-0-7867-0848-2. Grades YA.

Aristides de Sousa Mendes (1885–1954), the Portuguese consul to France living in Bordeaux during World War II, saved many refugees from the fascist bureaucracy in the country. In 1940 he wrote visas for over 10,000 European Jews. The Portuguese dictator, Salazar, never forgave Mendes for his work and he lost both his job and salary, eventually dying destitute. Finally he was honored in Israel, and not until 1988 did Portugal recognize his contribution to the world. Maps and illustrations augment the text. Notes and Index.

2161. Frank, Anne. *The Diary of a Young Girl.* Bantam, 1993. 308pp. Paper ISBN 978-0-553-29698-3. Grades 6 UP.

Anne Frank (1929–1945) and her family lived a normal life in Holland during the 1930s until Hitler came to power in Germany. Her businessman father looked after the family, but when the Nazis entered Holland and occupied it, the Franks had to hide in the abandoned half of an old office; Anne was then 13. Others came to join them, and soon eight people shared two tiny rooms. No one could leave nor be seen from the outside. The few people who knew where they were had to get food to them without being detected. The diary reveals Anne Frank's thoughts and feelings as she coped with this inhumane constraint on her life. *American Library Association Notable Books for Young Adults.*

2162. Friedman, Ina R. *Flying Against the Wind: The Story of a Young Woman Who Defied the Nazis.* Lodgepole, 1995. 202pp. Paper ISBN 978-1-886721-00-5. Grades YA.

Cato Bonjes van Beek (1920–1943) grew up in Nazi Germany. Though not a Jew, she defied Hitler's plans and worked actively for the restoration of individual rights and human dignity. Because she refused to follow the Nazis, she paid the ultimate price. Glossary, Chronology, Further Reading, and Index. *Notable Children's Trade Books in the Field of Social Studies.*

2163. Friedman, Laurie. *Angel Girl.* Illustrated by Ofra Amit. Carolrhoda, 2008. Unpaged. ISBN 978-0-8225-8739-2. Grades 5–8.

During the Holocaust, Herman, 11, becomes separated from his mother in a death camp and never sees her again. He keeps dreaming about her and asking when she will return. One night in a dream, his mother tells him that an angel will save him. And while he stands at a barbed wire fence, a girl brings him an apple each day. At liberation they part, but several years later on a blind date in New York City, they meet again. They marry and live for many years afterward. Illustrations complement the text.

2164. Fuchs, Thomas. *The Hitler Fact Book.* Fountain, 1990. 255pp. Paper ISBN 978-0-9623202-9-3. Grades YA.

Fuchs attempts to dispel myths about Hitler by looking at his decisions and habits on a variety of subjects including appearance, choice of symbols, views, personal choices, and attitudes. Sample chapter headings contain such phrases as "Hitler's Mustache," "Hitler Laughs," "Backstage Hitler," "I Was Hitler's Dentist," and "Games the Fuhrer Played." They assemble an unsettling view of a demented man. Bibliography, Chronology, and Index.

2165. Gauch, Sigfrid. *Traces of My Father.* Translated by William Radice. Hydra, 2003. 133pp. Paper ISBN 978-0-8101-1890-4. Grades YA.

In short vignettes, Sigfrid Gauch recalls his relationship with his Nazi father, a man who served as Himmler's personal physician and helped him slaughter Jews with his eugenics theories. As Gauch prepares for his father's funeral, he remembers him as caring but frail as an old man and refuses to confront his actions during World War II. However, his father never admitted the Holocaust and was anti-Semitic until his death. Gauch wonders if he himself is guilty by association with his own father.

2166. Gelissen, Rena Kornreich, and Heather Dune MacAdam. *Rena's Promise.* Beacon, 1996. 288pp. Paper ISBN 978-0-8070-7071-0. Grades YA.

Rena Kornreich, 17, went to Auschwitz on the first Jewish transport, and she and her sister Danka survived the Nazi death camps for three more years. The narrative tells her story of trying to stay alive while keeping her sister with her during that time in World War II.

2167. Giblin, James Cross. *The Life and Death of Adolf Hitler.* Clarion, 2002. 246pp. ISBN 978-0-395-90371-1. Grades 7–9.

Adolf Hitler (1889–1945) grew up in Austria, wanting to be an artist. He loved dogs and had odd relationships with women. He was also a vegetarian. He then became a brilliant politician whose cruelty led to humiliation and defeat. In a balanced account, Giblin also notes the American institutions that also had anti-Semitic policies at the same time that Hitler was planning to eradicate Jews. Archival photographs and illustrations highlight the text. Bibliography, Glossary, Notes, and Index. *Student Book Award* (Maine) nomination, *Garden State Nonfiction Book Award* (New Jersey) nomination, *Capitol Choices Noteworthy Titles* (Washington, D.C.), and *Robert F. Sibert Medal.*

2168. Goble, Paul. *Hau Kola: Hello Friend.* Illustrated by Gerry Perrin. (Meet the Author) Richard C. Owen, 1994. 32pp. ISBN 978-1-8784-5044-9. Grades 2–5.

As a child in England, Goble liked the outdoors. During World War II, he collected bullet shells and pieces of German bombs that fell close to his house. Because he was intrigued by Indians, he moved to the United States and has been painting about Indian legends and history throughout his adult life.

2169. Goldenstern, Joyce. *Albert Einstein: Physicist and Genius.* Enslow, 2007. 128pp. ISBN 978-0-7660-2838-8. Grades 6–9.

Albert Einstein (1879–1955) formulated one of the most important ideas of the 20th century, the general theory of relativity. He won the 1921 Nobel Prize in physics, and his genius became famous. It saved his life when Hitler began killing Jews in World War II. From his Princeton, New Jersey, home, Einstein helped others to flee Europe, but he refused to become president of Israel. He wanted to continue work on scientific questions, many of which remained unanswered at his death. Photographs, Chronology, Further Reading, Glossary, and Index.

2170. Grabowski, John F. *Josef Mengele.* (Heroes and Villains) Thomson Gale, 2003. 112pp. ISBN 978-1-59018-425-7. Grades 8 up.

Josef Mengele was the man responsible for deciding who, among those Jews entering the gates at Auschwitz concentration camp, would work or would die. He sent thousands to death in the gas chambers and conducted horrible genetic experiments on others, gaining him a reputation as one of the 20th century's most despicable villains. He escaped to South America at the end of the war. Photographs and reproductions augment the text. Notes, Bibliography, Maps, and Index.

2171. Gray, Bettyanne. *Manya's Story: Faith and Survival in Revolutionary Russia.* Runestone, 1995. 128pp. ISBN 978-0-8225-3156-2. Grades 7 up.

See entry 1804.

2172. Grynberg, Micha. *Words to Outlive Us: Voices from the Warsaw Ghetto.* Picador, 2003. 493pp. Paper ISBN 978-0-312-42268-4. Grades YA.

This memoir relies on twenty-nine diaries, journals, and first-hand accounts to detail life fighting starvation and disease while rebelling against the Nazis in the Warsaw Ghetto during World War II. It is divided into the establishment of the ghetto in 1940, the deportations of 1942, the uprising of 1943, and the liberation in 1945. The depravity of the time and how some did survive it shines throughout. It includes maps and rosters of the laborers.

2173. Hager, Thomas. *The Demon Under the Microscope: From Battlefield Hospitals to Nazi Labs, One Doctor's Heroic Search for the World's First Miracle Drug.* Three Rivers, 2007. 340pp. Paper ISBN 978-1-4000-8214-8. Grades YA.

During World War I most of the soldiers who died were victims of infection rather than wounds. After the war Gerhard Domagk, a military medical assistant, focused on this problem and came up with the antibiotic sulfa in 1932. In 1939 he received the Nobel Prize for medicine, but the Nazis prevented him from accepting it. Hager suggests that this drug—not penicillin—should be considered the first miracle drug. Sulfa has helped to eliminate diseases including pneumonia, childbed fever, and gonorrhea. During the early days of sulfa use, the challenge was finding a correct dose—it was prescribed for every kind of malady, with humans functioning as guinea pigs—but without this drug, many victims of the Pearl Harbor bombing would have died. Bibliography, Notes, and Index. *School Library Journal Best Adult Books for Young Adults.*

2174. Hall, Becky. *Morris and Buddy: The Story of the First Seeing Eye Dog.* Illustrated by Doris Ettlinger. Albert Whitman, 2007. 40pp. ISBN 978-0-8075-5284-1. Grades 2–4.

When Morris Frank lost his eyesight in 1924, he heard about Dorothy Harris Eustis, a woman training dogs for police and army work in Switzerland. He goes to Switzerland to see if she can train a dog to help him "see." She helps him learn to trust his German shepherd, Buddy, with his life. Adjusting to the dog takes time, but he is pleased enough to want to start a guide dog program in the United States when he returns home. Illustrations and archival photographs complement the text. An afterword describes Frank's Seeing Eye Dog school. Further Reading and Web Sites.

2175. Haugen, Brenda. *Winston Churchill: British Soldier, Writer, Statesman.* (Signature Lives) Compass Point, 2006. 112pp. ISBN 978-0-7565-1582-9; paper ISBN 978-0-7565-1804-2. Grades 6–9.

See entry 1807.

2176. Hautzig, Esther Rudomin. *The Endless Steppe: Growing Up in Siberia.* Trophy, 1995. 243pp. Paper ISBN 978-0-06-440577-5. Grades 7 up.

In 1941, when she was 10, Esther's family was deported from Vilna, Poland, to Siberia. The Russians accused the family of being capitalists. In Siberia her parents and her grandmother worked in either the field or the mine. Esther went to school, worked at home, and did small jobs for a crust of bread to eat. They survived in Siberia for five years before they could find a way out of their predicament. *American Library Association Notable Children's Books, Boston Globe-Horn Book Honor Book, Jane Addams Award, Sydney Taylor Book Award, New York Times Outstanding Children's Books, Horn Book Fanfare, Lewis Carroll Shelf Award, National Book Award for Children's Literature* nomination, and *Deutsche Jugendliteraturpreis Honorable List.*

2177. Hecht, Thomas T. *Life Death Memories.* Leopolis, 2002. 209pp. Paper ISBN 978-0-967996-01-1. Grades YA.

Thomas T. Hecht (1929–) came from a loving family that was decimated when the Germans arrived in his Polish *shtetl.* Now, as an attorney in New York, he cannot forget. Nazis shot his older brother and his father and threw them into a common grave; the brother he never liked was tortured and blinded before he was shot. Hecht and his mother escaped by hiding in the forest.

2178. Hillesum, Etty. *An Interrupted Life: The Diaries, 1941–1943 and Letters from Westerbork.* Translated by Arnold J. Pomerans. Holt, 1996. 376pp. Paper ISBN 978-0-8050-5087-5. Grades YA.

Etty Hillesum was over 20 when she was taken to Westerbork, the transit camp before Auschwitz. The first half of the book contains the diaries in which she wonders about the situation and shows her continued faith in God. In the second half are letters recounting details of camp horrors. Throughout, she manages to rise above the situation and keep her courage.

2179. Hillman, Laura. *I Will Plant You a Lilac Tree: A Memoir of a Schindler's List Survivor.* Atheneum, 2005. 256pp. ISBN 978-0-689-86980-8; Simon Pulse, 2008. paper ISBN 978-1-4169-5366-1. Grades 8–11.

In Berlin in 1942 Laura Hellman, or Hannelore, 16, volunteered to be deported with her mother and two younger brothers to Poland. The family was separated, and she lived in eight concentration camps during the next three years. She recalls some of the horrors of her experience including the cattle cars, the hard work in stone quarries and salt mines, being raped, and the smell of children's bodies coming from the crematoriums. She made friends, but one was beaten to death because a German soldier befriended her. Hannelore fell in love with Dick, another young prisoner, and they reunited after surviving because of Oskar Schindler's "list," and married after the war ended. No one else in their family photographs survived.

2180. Holliday, Laurel. *Children in the Holocaust and World War II: Their Secret Diaries.* Washington Square, 1996. 409pp. Paper ISBN 978-0-671-52055-7. Grades YA.

This book is a compilation of diaries that 23 young people, ages 10 through 18, kept during the Holocaust in World War II. Holliday comments that Anne Frank and her diary are atypical of the diaries and children in the Holocaust because she stayed in hiding and did not experience the Gestapo harassment or the constant daily search for food and supplies. These children realized that one way to keep their sanity was by writing about their situations. They could say what they thought about the Germans in writing, but never aloud. The writing also gave them a friend in their time of loneliness. Some of these children died after carefully hiding their private thoughts. The children quoted lived in Poland, Holland, Germany, Czechoslovakia, Austria, Hungary, Lithuania, Russia, Belgium, England, and Denmark. Bibliography and Sources.

2181. Hughes, Libby. *Madam Prime Minister: A Biography of Margaret Thatcher.* Iuniverse.Com, 2000. 144pp. Paper ISBN 978-0-595-14638-3. Grades 6–9.

Although she pursued chemistry at Oxford University, Margaret Thatcher (b. 1925) decided to study law after graduation because of her interest in politics. As a child of 11 she showed that she was willing to work. She won a speech contest, asserting to someone that she was not "lucky" to win because she had carefully prepared the speech and deserved the credit. She first ran to become a member of Parliament and then became the head of her Conservative Party. Several years later, the people elected her to be the first woman prime minister. During the ten years she served, Britons nicknamed her the "Iron Lady." Selected Bibliography and Index.

2182. Humes, James C. *Eisenhower and Churchill: The Partnership That Saved the World.* Three Rivers, 2004. 268pp. Paper ISBN 978-0-307-33588-3. Grades YA.

Dwight David Eisenhower (1890–1969) and Sir Winston Churchill (1874–1965), although of different class, had very similar early situations in their lives, education, and military training before World War II began. Both had irresponsible fathers and strong mothers. Their service academies of choice initially rejected them. Churchill at first disliked Eisenhower when they met after the attack on Pearl Harbor, but they became good friends. The sources are undisclosed. Bibliography and Index.

2183. Hurwitz, Johanna. *Anne Frank: Life in Hiding.* Illustrated by Vera Rosenberry. Jewish Publication, 1989. 62pp. ISBN 978-0-8276-0311-0; Camelot, 1999. paper ISBN 978-0-380-73254-8. Grades 2–5.

Anne Frank (1929–1945) was born in Germany, but her family moved to Amsterdam in 1933, because her father had business ties there and hoped to raise his family in a more tolerant political environment. The family was Jewish, and Hitler and the German government were passing laws that denied Jews certain freedoms. Anne's 16-year-old sister received a summons to report to the Nazi government just after Anne's 13th birthday, and the family went into hiding, hoping to survive the war. They did not, and the narrative follows Anne to Auschwitz and to Bergen-Belsen, where first her sister and then Anne died of typhus three months before Anne's 16th birthday. Important Dates, Author's Note, and Index. *Bluebonnet Award* (Texas) and *Notable Children's Trade Book in the Field of Social Studies.*

2184. Irwin, John P. *Another River, Another Town: A Teenage Tank Gunner Comes of Age in Combat—1945.* Random House, 2003. 176pp. Paper ISBN 978-0-375-75963-5. Grades YA.

John Irwin served as a gunner inside a Sherman tank during World War II while he was a teenager. He was delighted to help the army after the Battle of the Bulge because he would not have to finish high school. He recalls how he drove his tank through the last bastions of German resistance during the end of the war and how it killed children when they approached the tank with bombs in hand. But he also recalls complimenting a German tank gunner who was particularly adept against his own tank. He entered slave labor camps after battles and faced those horrors, especially Nordhausen, where the Nazis assembled the V-3 rockets amid piled corpses and skeleton-like survivors. He never doubts the cause in his dispassionate recollection. *Booklist Editors' Choice.*

2185. Isenberg, Sheila. *A Hero of Our Own: The Story of Varian Fry.* Iuniverse, 2005. 349pp. Paper ISBN 978-0-59534-882-4. Grades YA.

During the early years of World War II, a refugee-rescue group sent Varian Fry (1907–1967) to France to help more than one thousand refugees who had become trapped in southern France after escaping Germany. This group included Hannah Arendt, Marc Chagall, Heinrich Mann, and Max Ernst. Fry is the only American honored at Yad Vashem, Israel's Holocaust memorial. The information comes from primary sources including letters, interviews, personal papers, and government reports. Index.

2186. Jackson, Livia Bitton. *I Have Lived a Thousand Years: Growing Up in the Holocaust.* Simon Pulse, 1999. 224pp. Paper ISBN 978-0-689-82395-4. Grades 7–10.

Livia Bitton, 13, went with her Hungarian Jewish family to the Nazi death camp of Auschwitz in 1944. During that year she saw roundups, transports, torture, forced labor, and shootings. She was one of the few adolescents in the camp, and she helped her mother survive as they saved each other from the gas chamber. After the war, she found her brother and heard how their father died.

2187. Jacobsen, Ruth. *Rescued Images: Memories of Childhood in Hiding.* Mikaya, 2001. 96pp. ISBN 978-1-931414-00-5. Grades 6 up.

The childhood of Ruth Jacobson (1932–) was destroyed by the Holocaust. At the age of 8, she was separated from her parents and for the next six years, the Resistance hid her and gave her new identities. Although her family survived, both parents committed suicide within a few years after the war ended. Ruth came to America, and forty years later she mustered the courage to open a box of family photographs. Through them she began to put together her past. Some of these images complement her memoir—collages she made while trying to understand her past and her present. *Bulletin Blue Ribbon.*

2188. Kaiser, Reinhard. *Paper Kisses: A True Love Story.* Translated by Anthea Bell. Other, 2006. 112pp. Paper ISBN 978-1-59051-181-7. Grades YA.

From letters, Kaiser reconstructs the lives of Jewish paleontologist Rudolf Kaufmann and Swede Ingeborg Magnusson during the beginning days of World War II. When the Nazis began their rise to power, Kaufmann lost his job at Greifswald University and went to Italy where, in the summer of 1935, he met Ingeborg on her holiday. Their relationship lasted five years, although they spent only thirteen days together. Additional information from relatives helped Kaiser construct the remainder of their love story.

2189. Kerner, John. *Combat Medic: World War II.* Ibooks, 2006. 265pp. Paper ISBN 978-1-59687-316-2. Grades YA.

John Kerner became a medic during World War II after being called to active duty in 1943. He landed in Normandy after D-Day and was in combat for 264 days in France, the Low Countries, and Germany. Kerner relies on letters saved by recipients written by soldiers on the front, and they give his story an immediacy that memory might not. He was accorded the Combat Medic Award for riding a tank blasting through the siege at Bastogne.

2190. Klein, Adam G. *Pablo Picasso.* (Great Artists) Checkerboard, 2006. 32pp. ISBN 978-1-59679-733-8. Grades 2–5.

This biography introduces Pablo Picasso (1881–1973) and the various periods in his work. The story of his life is balanced with discussion of his artworks; but the text does not contain many reproductions. Chronology, Glossary, and Index.

2191. Klein, Adam G. *Salvador Dalí.* (Great Artists) Checkerboard, 2006. 32pp. ISBN 978-1-59679-728-4. Grades 2–5.

This biography introduces Salvador Dalí (1904–1989) and the various periods in his work. His most famous works include *The Persistence of Memory, Swans Reflecting Elephants*, and *Burning Giraffe.* The chronology of his life balances with the discussion of his artwork, but the volume does not contain many reproductions. Chronology, Glossary, and Index.

2192. Koestler-Grack, Rachel A. *The Story of Anne Frank.* (Breakthrough Biographies) Facts on File, 2003. 32pp. ISBN 978-0-7910-7311-7. Grades 2–4.

The simple text discusses the life of Anne Frank and her family, immortalized by her diary discovered after her family was arrested during World War II. They hid in an attic to escape concentration camps in Nazi-occupied Holland for two years. Her own words describe her life and her hopes during those two years and are supported with additional facts about her. Photographs augment the text. Chronology, Further Reading, Glossary, Web Sites, and Index.

2193. Korobkin, Frieda Stolzberg. *Throw Your Feet Over Your Shoulders: Beyond the Kindertransport.* Devlora, 2008. 182pp. ISBN 978-1-934440-26-1. Grades YA.

As one of the children who got out of Germany on the Kindertransport during World War II, Frieda Korobkin tells her story in detail. She was a child in Nazi-occupied Vienna who was separated from her parents and taken to England. There she wanted to keep her religion and identity as an Orthodox Jew. She includes all that she remembers in hopes that nothing will be forgotten about that evil time in history. Photographs accompany the text. Glossary.

2194. Kramer, Ann. *Anne Frank: The Young Writer Who Told the World Her Story.* (World History Biography) National Geographic, 2007. 64pp. ISBN 978-1-4263-0004-2; 2009. paper ISBN 978-1-4263-0414-9. Grades 4–7.

This biography of Anne Frank (1929–1945) uses a scrapbook layout of diaries, school reports, family photographs, and quotes to emphasize her childhood. She lived in Amsterdam until her family went into hiding in the attic where she wrote her diary. Then when the Nazis found them, she was taken to a camp where she died. Photographs enhance the text. Bibliography, Glossary, Web Sites, Maps, and Index.

2195. Krinitz, Nisenthal Esther, and Bernice Steinhardt. *Memories of Survival.* Hyperion, 2005. 64pp. ISBN 978-0-7868-5126-3. Grades 5 up.

Before she died, Esther Nisenthal Krinitz embroidered thirty-six fabric collages with hand-stitched narrative captions in which she described her Holocaust survival. The first shows her at 10 with her family in a Polish village before the Nazis arrive. In 1942, when she is 15, the Nazis take her family, and she never sees them again. She and her sister survive in the woods before a kind Polish farmer takes them and disguises them as Polish Catholic farm girls. After the Russians arrive, Esther sees the death camps. *Student Book Award* (Maine) nomination, *Sydney Taylor Book Award*, and *Bulletin Blue Ribbon*.

2196. Kristy, Davida. *George Balanchine: American Ballet Master.* Lerner, 1996. 128pp. ISBN 978-0-8225-4951-2. Grades 5 up.

Gyorgy Balanchivadze (1904–1983) never wanted to be a dancer, and after his mother enrolled him in ballet school, he ran away. Yet he returned and discovered that the rigorous training gave him ideas for new movements and new stories to tell through dance. Later he traveled throughout Europe, where he met an American who thought that this art form would be enjoyed in the United States. He changed his Russian name to George Balanchine and created popular dances for Broadway, film, and the circus before forming his own ballet company. The author chronicles his life and his accomplishments. Sources, Bibliography, and Index.

2197. Krull, Kathleen. *Marie Curie.* Illustrated by Boris Kulikov. (Giants of Science) Viking, 2007. 142pp. ISBN 978-0-670-05894-5. Grades 5–9.

See entry 1819.

2198. Laidlaw, Jill A. *Paul Klee.* Franklin Watts, 2002. 46pp. ISBN 978-0-531-12230-3. Grades 5–8.

See entry 1821.

2199. Landmann, Bimba. *I Am Marc Chagall.* Illustrated by author. Eerdmans, 2006. 40pp. ISBN 978-0-8028-5305-9. Grades 2–5.

See entry 1822.

2200. Lebert, Norbert, and Stephan Lebert. *My Father's Keeper: Children of Nazi Leaders: An Intimate History of Damage and Denial.* Translated by Julian Evans. Back Bay, 2002. 288pp. Paper ISBN 978-0-316-08975-3. Grades YA.

In two sets of interviews done forty years apart, the first in 1959, this study shows how children of Nazi leaders have come to deal with their fathers' participation in the genocide of the Holocaust. Among them are children of Hess, Bormann, Gœring, Himmler, and Frank. In the second set are additional interviews with Klaus von Schirach, son of the Hitler Youth leader. Most of the interviewees defended their fathers' actions and only one held the father responsible for all of these deaths. Photographs.

2201. Leslie, Roger. *Isak Dinesen: Gothic Storyteller.* Morgan Reynolds, 2003. 128pp. ISBN 978-1-931798-17-4. Grades 5–12.

Karen Blixen-Finecke (1885–1962) took the pseudonym of Isak Dinesen for her publications. She grew up in Denmark where her father committed suicide shortly before she turned 10. She then met and married Bror Blixen-Finecke and moved with him to

Kenya where they attempted to run a coffee plantation. Their marriage faltered, and she had an affair with Denys Finch Hatton who died in an airplane crash. Dinesen returned to Denmark in 1931 and began writing. The nine chapters cover these different times in her life with the last two focused on her writing career. Photographs augment the text. Chronology, Sources, Bibliography, Web Sites, and Index.

2202. Levine, Karen. *Hana's Suitcase: A True Story.* Albert Whitman, 2003. 112pp. ISBN 978-0-8075-3148-8. Grades 4–9.

In 1998 Fumiko Ishioka, director of the Holocaust education center in Tokyo, received a suitcase for her collection that belonged to a young girl named Hana Brady. She found out that Hana was deported with her older brother from their home in Czechoslovakia to Terezin, and then to Auschwitz, where Hana died. Nazi records reveal Hana's fate and include pictures that she drew in secret art classes at Terezin. But Ishioka also discovered that Hana's brother, George, had survived and emigrated to Toronto, Canada. He sent the photographs of Hana and her family that highlight the text, and he personally visited a group of young students in Tokyo who were trying to spread understanding about the Holocaust. *Sydney Taylor Award.*

2203. Ligocka, Roma, and Iris Von Finckenstein. *The Girl in the Red Coat: A Memoir.* Translated by Margot Bettauer Dembo. Delta, 2003. 292pp. Paper ISBN 978-0-385-33740-3. Grades YA.

Roma Ligocka (1938–) was the inspiration for the character of the red-clad child in the film *Schindler's List.* She recounts her harrowing childhood under the Nazis, her escape with her mother from the Krakow ghetto of dilapidated housing in March of 1943, and hiding with a cousin. She and her parents survived, although her grandmother did not. After World War II she lived in Communist Poland as an acclaimed set and costume designer, actress in theater and in films, and cousin of Roman Polanski. Her difficult past carried over into her seemingly easier postwar life.

2204. Lindwer, Willy. *The Last Seven Months of Anne Frank.* Anchor, 1992. 204pp. Paper ISBN 978-0-385-42360-1. Grades YA.

Lindwer interviewed and filmed six Dutch Holocaust survivors who told about their backgrounds, their captures by the Nazis, their experiences in the camps, and what happened to them when they were liberated. Each knew Anne Frank, and each tells about her final days. In this book, Lindwer gives the complete texts of the interviews, including information omitted from his film documentary of 1988.

2205. Linnéa, Sharon. *Raoul Wallenberg: The Man Who Stopped Death.* Jewish Publication Society, 1993. 151pp. Paper ISBN 978-0-8276-0448-3. Grades 6 up.

Raoul Wallenberg was a Swedish diplomat who went to Budapest, Hungary, during World War II to try to help free the Jews there. He issued passports which he said the Swedish government had authorized for Jews so that they could leave. He also offered diplomatic immunity under the Swedish flag and dared the Nazis to defy him. He disappeared soon after the Soviets came into the city, and stories about his last days are contradictory and uncertain. He was in a prison, but it is uncertain whether he died when the Russians said he did. Index.

2206. Lobel, Anita. *No Pretty Pictures: A Child of War.* HarperCollins, 2008. 193pp. Paper ISBN 978-0-06-156589-2. Grades 6 up.

Anita Lobel grew up as a Polish Jew and survived World War II to live in Sweden for years after. She was 5 when the Nazis arrived, and spent the next five years hiding and running until they captured her and put her in the Ravensbruck concentration camp. Her brother was always with her, disguised as a girl to hide his circumcision. Once she was safe, she luxuriated in being free of lice, and having hair, flushing toilets, clean sheets, and butter. She did not start school until she was 12, and she felt inadequate until she discovered that she could draw. Photographs and illustrations enhance the text. *Children's Book Award* (Massachusetts), *Garden State Teen Book Award* (New Jersey), *Capitol Choices Noteworthy Titles* (Washington, D.C.), *Voice of Youth Advocates Perfect Ten List*, *Bulletin Blue Ribbon*, and *Young Adult Reading Program* (South Dakota).

2207. Lucas, Eric. *The Sovereigns: A Jewish Family in the German Countryside.* Northwestern University, 2001. ISBN 978-0-8101-1182-0; paper ISBN 978-0-8101-1167-7. Grades YA.

The author, who died in 1996, tells of his family living in Germany and trying to deal with ostracism by neighbors. As a young man he left Germany soon after Kristallnacht in 1938 and went to Palestine (to become contemporary Israel ten years later) where he was an active member of the Zionist movement. He recalls his family and the wonderful German village where his father and grandparents lived. He never heard from his parents again after they were deported to a Polish ghetto in 1941.

2208. Lugovskaya, Nina. *I Want to Live: The Diary of a Young Girl in Stalin's Russia.* Translated by Andrew Bromfield. Houghton, 2007. 280pp. ISBN 978-0-618-60575-0. Grades 8 up.

Lugovskaya grew up in Russia during Stalin's Great Terror as a rather wealthy young woman with a room of her own in a large apartment in Moscow when other people endured communal living. The diary covers the years from 1932 to 1937 when she turned 18. Her father was arrested in 1935 for his participation in the Socialist Revolutionary Party. She felt ugly because she was two years older than her classmates and cross-eyed, and boys refused to pay attention to her. The diary reveals her disgust with herself and her inability to cope with her shortcomings. The diary also covers the Stalinist treatment of the citizens, who were made to march in the streets and suffered constant raids. In January 1937 she, her mother, and her twin sisters were arrested and sentenced to five years of hard labor in Kolyma prison camp, most likely for continued anti-Bolshevik ideas and her own attempted suicide. Her diary ended up in NKVD (Stalin's secret police) files. The family survived, and Lugovskaya lived as an artist until she was 74. Photographs complement the text. Bibliography and Notes.

2209. Lynch, Doris. *J.R.R. Tolkien: Creator of Languages and Legends.* (Great Life Stories: People in the Arts) Franklin Watts, 2003. 128pp. ISBN 978-0-531-12253-2. Grades YA.

The stories of J. R. R. Tolkien (1892–1973) came from his love of the English countryside and his difficulties in World War I. He was a professor, a soldier, a father, a writer, and a Catholic, and all this influenced his work. Dead languages fascinated Tolkien, and in *The Hobbit* and *The Lord of the Rings* he created people who needed a language and placed them in a land similar to the country he loved. Photographs highlight the text. Notes, Chronology, Further Reading, Web Sites, and Index.

2210. McCann, Michelle Roehm, and Luba Tryszynska-Frederick. *Luba: The Angel of Bergen-Belsen.* Illustrated by Ann Marshall. Translated by Michelle Roehm McCann. Tricycle, 2004. 40pp. ISBN 978-1-5824-6098-7. Grades 2–6.

Luba Tryszynska, a young Polish Jewish nurse, saved fifty-four Dutch Jewish children who had been abandoned behind her barracks at Bergen-Belsen in the winter of 1944. She sheltered them, scavenged for food, and found clothing to keep them alive. This biography, based on interviews with McCann, reveals that Luba was honored for the achievement fifty years later. Collage illustrations highlight the text. Bibliography and Web Sites. *Spirit Award (Oregon)*, *National Jewish Book Award*, *Jane Addams Honor Book*, and *Eloise Jarvis McGraw Award*.

2211. McClafferty, Carla Killough. ***Something Out of Nothing: Marie Curie and Radium.*** Farrar, 2006. 134pp. ISBN 978-0-374-38036-6. Grades 5–10.

See entry 1824.

2212. McCormick, Lisa Wade. ***Marie Curie.*** (Rookie) Children's, 2006. 31pp. ISBN 978-0-51625-040-3; paper ISBN 978-0-51621-445-0. Grades 1–2.

See entry 1825.

2213. McDonough, Yona Zeldis. ***Anne Frank.*** Illustrated by Malcah Zeldis. Holt, 1997. Unpaged. ISBN 978-0-8050-4924-4. Grades K–3.

This narrative opens with Anne Frank (1929–1945) and her family fleeing their annex home where they lived for two years in Amsterdam during World War II. Then it flashes back to Anne's life before the war and her happiness. In essence, this volume, with accompanying illustrations, shows that Anne's life was not limited to the annex, but that it encompassed a "before" and a not so happy "after."

2214. MacLeod, Elizabeth. ***Albert Einstein: A Life of Genius.*** (Snapshots) Kids Can Press, 2003. 32pp. ISBN 978-1-55337-396-4; paper ISBN 978-1-55337-397-1. Grades 4–7.

Albert Einstein (1879–1955), a poor student, became a brilliant scientist who formed theories of light, gravity, and time that changed humanity's concepts of the Universe. MacLeod gives an overview of Einstein's early thinking, his view of success, physics before his discoveries, his best year for creating, his role as a professor, his concept of the theory of relativity, his fame, his departure from Germany, his role in the creation of the atom bomb that ended World War II, and physics since his death. Photographs highlight the text. Maps, Chronology, and Index.

2215. McNeese, Tim. ***Pablo Picasso.*** (Great Hispanic Heritage) Chelsea House, 2006. 122pp. ISBN 978-0-7910-8843-2. Grades 8 up.

See entry 1827.

2216. McNeese, Tim. ***Salvador Dalí.*** (Great Hispanic Heritage) Chelsea House, 2006. 122pp. ISBN 978-0-7910-8837-1. Grades 8 up.

This biography of Salvador Dalí focuses on his individual accomplishments and how he created a positive Hispanic image. He showed a dream state in his paintings with his precise lines and figures. In essence, he applied psychoanalysis to the art of painting. As an artist he was both a product of the past and a denizen of the future. Reproductions from his paintings enhance the text. Bibliography, Chronology, Further Reading, Web Sites, and Index.

2217. McPherson, Stephanie Sammartino. ***Albert Einstein.*** (History Makers Bios) Lerner, 2004. 48pp. ISBN 978-0-8225-0350-7. Grades 3–5.

See entry 1828.

2218. Markel, Michelle. *Dreamer from the Village: The Story of Marc Chagall.* Illustrated by Emily Lisker. Holt, 2005. 40pp. ISBN 978-0-8050-6373-8. Grades K–4.

This biography presents the life of Marc Chagall (1887–1985), from his childhood to a showing of his work at the Louvre in Paris when he was 90. After living in a Russian shtetl, he attended art school in Paris. He saw things that other boys did not see, and he incorporated these "visions" in his paintings. Illustrations in acrylic complement the text. Glossary. *Picture Book Award* (Georgia) nomination.

2219. Marx, Trish. *Echoes of World War II.* Lerner, 1994. 96pp. ISBN 978-0-8225-4898-0. Grades 5–8.

In pictures of war, one often sees soldiers. The children are less visible, but what happens to the children during a war has a huge impact on the future. Marx follows the paths of six children, four in Europe and two in Asia, through World War II. Some left their parents and others had parents leave them. These six survived, which is why their stories can be told. Photographs augment the text. Index.

2220. Megellas, James. *All the Way to Berlin: A Paratrooper at War in Europe.* Presidio, 2003. 309pp. ISBN 978-0-8914-1784-2; 2004. paper ISBN 978-0-8914-1836-8. Grades YA.

James Megellas served as a platoon leader in the 82nd Airborne Division during World War II. Only a few of his H Company survived to walk in a victory parade at the end of the war because half of his men died as a result of the September 1944 assault across the Waal River. He also lost men on the beaches at Anzio, Italy, and at the Battle of the Bulge. Megellas recalls these two years in his life.

2221. Meltzer, Milton. *Albert Einstein: A Biography.* Holiday House, 2008. 48pp. ISBN 978-0-8234-1966-1. Grades 3–6.

Meltzer covers not only Albert Einstein's (1879–1955) background and achievements but also his beliefs and his personality. He includes that Einstein attended only the college classes in which he had interest and that as an older man, he espoused peace. Additionally, Meltzer states Einstein's theory of relativity in a way that readers can understand it. Photographs augment the text. Chronology and Bibliography.

2222. Meyers, Odette. *Doors to Madame Marie.* University of Washington, 1997. 400pp. ISBN 978-0-295-97576-4. Grades YA.

Odette Meyers moves with her family from Poland to Paris when she is a young girl, but while she is growing up, the Germans occupy Paris. The concierge of the family's apartment is Madame Marie, a woman who helps the Jewish Odette find refuge in the French countryside by pretending to be Catholic. Meyers later visits those villages and interacts with the people who saved her life.

2223. Millman, Isaac. *Hidden Child.* Illustrated by author. Frances Foster, 2005. 80pp. ISBN 978-0-374-33071-2. Grades 4–8.

Isaac Millman (Isaac Sztrymfman), a children's illustrator, survived World War II after his parents died. He last saw his father when he waved to Isaac from behind barbed wire; and his mother bribed a Nazi guard to take her boy out of the camp. In Paris, Hena, also Jewish, found him sitting on a Paris street when he was 9, hid him, and had others look after him in the small French village of Vichy until the war ended. Then an American family adopted him. He later discovered that his parents died at Auschwitz. Photographs and illustrations augment the text. *Great Lakes Children's Book Award* (Michigan) nomination, *Children's Book Award* (South Carolina) nomination, *Booklist Editors' Choice*, *Capitol Choices Noteworthy Titles* (Washington, D.C.), and *Dorothy Canfield Fisher Children's Book Award* (Vermont) nomination.

2224. Mochizuki, Ken. *Passage to Freedom: The Sugihara Story.*   Lee & Low, 1997. 32pp. ISBN 978-1-8800-0049-6. Grades 3–6.

Hiroki Sugihara is 5 years old in 1940, living at the Japanese Consulate in Lithuania. When hundreds of Jewish refugees arrive at the gate wanting visas to Japan, his father decides to disobey the Japanese government and help these people flee the Nazis. Sugihara tells his story as an adult reflecting on his family's involvement in history. *Bulletin Blue Ribbon.*

2225. Myrick, Inge. *The Other Side! The Life Journey of a Young Girl Through Nazi Germany.* Acacia, 2007. 203pp. Paper ISBN 978-0-9792531-3-3. Grades 6–10.

Inge Myrick lived with her non-Jewish family in Chemnitz and Rabenstein, Germany, north of the Czechoslovakian border. Although she participated in the Hitler Youth Movement, she did not understand its tenets. She also does not seem to be aware of any difference growing up in Nazi Germany than at other times.

2226. Nir, Yehuda. *The Lost Childhood: A Memoir.*   Schaffner, 2007. 288pp. Paper ISBN 978-0-971059-86-3. Grades 8 up.

When Yehuda Nir was 9 years old, German soldiers executed his father along with other Jewish men in their Polish town. He, his mother, and teenage sister were able to escape with false documents in 1941. They became Catholic and lived in disguise for the four remaining years of the war. Often Nir had to separate from the others, eating dogs and mice, and hiding in sewers. In the final year of the war, he and his family became prisoners in a German camp. He does not understand how one can forgive the Germans for their inhumane treatment of others.

2227. Noiville, Florence, and Catherine Temerson. *Isaac B. Singer: A Life.*   Farrar, 2006. 192pp. ISBN 978-0-374-17800-0; Northwestern University, 2008. paper ISBN 978-0-8101-2482-0. Grades YA.

This biography of Isaac Bashevis Singer (1904–1991), based on personal recollections; letters; and interviews with friends, family, and associates reveals the dichotomy between his written works and his life. As the son of a rabbi and a rabbi's daughter in Poland, Singer seemed to believe in orthodoxy while attacking it in his work. He loved his wife but carried on extramarital relationships, and wanted to know his son although he abandoned him. He wrote books for children while seeming to dislike them intensely. He was a private tyrant who charmed those he knew in public. Explaining the man remains impossible; the biographer can only show what he did and contrast it with what he said in his fiction. Photographs highlight the text. Bibliography, Notes, and Index.

2228. Opdyke, Irene Gut, and Jennifer Armstrong. *In My Hands: Memories of a Holocaust Rescuer.*   Knopf, 1999. 276pp. ISBN 978-0-679-89181-9; Laurel-Leaf, 2004. paper ISBN 978-0-553-4941-12. Grades 9 up.

The German army made Irene Gut Opdyke (1921–), a young Polish girl of 17, work for them as a waitress because she had blond hair and blue eyes. At the same time, she waged a personal war against the Nazis by assisting the Jews. She passed information to them as well as smuggled them from the work camp into the forest. Then she hid ten Jews in the basement of the Nazi major for whom she worked. He discovered her ploy and would keep them if she agreed to become his mistress. She did. From being raped by Russians to spying on them later, Opdyke had a range of horrible experiences during World War II. *Black Eyed Susan Book Awards* (Maryland), *Tayshas High School Reading List* (Texas), and *Volunteer State Book Awards* (Tennessee).

2229. Palgi, Yoel. *Into the Inferno: The Memoir of a Jewish Paratrooper Behind Nazi Lines.* Rutgers University, 2003. 279pp. ISBN 978-0-8135-3149-6. Grades YA.

Yoel Palgi was the only survivor of a May 1944 mission to encourage Jewish resistance in Hungary and to try to stop deportations to Auschwitz. He parachuted into Nazi-held Yugoslavia with two others, and they were betrayed as soon as they entered Hungary. Palgi escaped after torture and met a small underground Zionist resistance cell. He did have a small part in helping some of the Jews in Budapest stay alive. Notes.

2230. Parker, Steve. *Marie Curie and Radium.* Chelsea House, 1995. 32pp. ISBN 978-0-7910-3011-0. Grades 3–7.

See entry 1839.

2231. Perl, Lila. *Four Perfect Pebbles: A Holocaust Story.* Morrow, 1996. 130pp. ISBN 978-0-688-14294-0; Trophy, 1999. paper ISBN 978-0-380-73188-6. Grades 5–8.

Before experiencing the Holocaust in Bergen-Belsen, Marion Blumenthal Lazan had a happy, secure family life in prewar Germany. Her grandparents had run a business since 1894, but Hitler's decrees gradually decreased their rights until they were forced to move from Hoya to Hanover and then to Holland. Before they could leave for America, the Nazis invaded and deported them to Westerbork, then to Bergen-Belsen, and onto a death train to Auschwitz before the Russians liberated them. Marion's father died of typhus after liberation, however, and she, her mother, and her brother had to spend three years as displaced persons before they eventually arrived in the United States. Photographs and Bibliography. *American Library Association Notable Books for Children.*

2232. Polcovar, Jane. *Rosalind Franklin and the Structure of Life.* Morgan Reynolds, 2006. 144pp. ISBN 978-1-59935-022-6. Grades 8 up.

This biography of Rosalind Franklin (1920–1958) shows that without her research, DNA would not have been discovered as early as it was. Crick and Watson saw her unpublished research, an X-ray diffraction image, on DNA structure and used it without her knowledge. As she died of cancer at the age of 37, she never knew that they used it and without crediting her with the germ of information that led to their success. Photographs highlight the text. Bibliography, Chronology, Notes, Web Sites, and Index.

2233. Poole, Josephine. *Anne Frank.* Illustrated by Angela Barrett. Knopf, 2005. 40pp. ISBN 978-0-375-83242-0. Grades 4–7.

This biography of Anne Frank (1929–1945) looks at Anne's life in the context of Hitler's promotion to power and the ensuing persecution of the Jews. The realistic illustrations show the terror in the streets that Anne would have seen and the anguish of leaving society to hide in an attic. At the end, Nazi boots climb the stairs to the attic, and its inhabitants go to their doom. Chronology. *School Library Journal Best Children's Books*.

2234. Poynter, Margaret. *Marie Curie: Discoverer of Radium.* Enslow, 2007. 112pp. ISBN 978-0-7660-2795-4. Grades 4–6.

See entry 1841.

2235. Radzinsky, Edvard. *Stalin: The First In-Depth Biography Based on Explosive New Documents from Russia's Secret Archives.* Anchor, 1997. 607pp. Paper ISBN 978-0-385-47954-7. Grades YA.

The institutions that Joseph Stalin (1879–1953) created while he ruled the Soviet Union stayed in place until 1991, even though Khrushchev ordered Stalin's body to be removed from its place next to Lenin and buried underground in 1961. Stalin carefully purged all those who knew him before he came to power, and his legacy is a history of mass arrests, deportations, collectivization of Soviet agriculture, and the cold war. Stalin built his system on the secret police and fear, a fear that trickled down to his subordinates because he could and did destroy them as necessary. This text looks at the man and his influence. Bibliography and Index.

2236. Ransom, Candice F. *Maria von Trapp: Beyond the Sound of Music.* (Trailblazers Biography) Carolrhoda, 2002. 112pp. ISBN 978-1-57505-444-5. Grades 4–6.

This biography of Maria Augusta von Trapp, the Austrian singer who escaped during World War II, comes from her own writings. It details her life in Austria singing with her family, on which the movie, *The Sound of Music* is based. It also covers her immigration to America where she initially toured and then settled in Vermont to run a music camp and later manage a ski lodge. Photographs highlight the text. Bibliography, Chronology, Notes, and Index.

2237. Redsand, Anna. *Viktor Frankl: A Life Worth Living.* Clarion, 2006. 150pp. ISBN 978-0-618-72343-0. Grades 8 up.

Victor Frankl always wanted to be a doctor when he was a young boy in Vienna, and he admired the work of Sigmund Freud when he started studying. He developed his own theory of logotherapy, where patients look to the possibilities of the future rather than the pain of the past. During the Holocaust he was arrested and imprisoned in four different concentration camps, including Theresienstadt and Auschwitz. When he applied his technique to many who were incarcerated with him, he helped their survival. From his experiences, including the loss of his wife and parents, and his subsequent remarriage, he wrote *Man's Search for Meaning*. Photographs enhance the text. Bibliography, Notes, Further Reading, and Index.

2238. Reef, Catherine. *Sigmund Freud: Pioneer of the Mind.* Clarion, 2001. 152pp. ISBN 978-0-618-01762-1. Grades 7 up.

See entry 1843.

2239. Rice, Earle, Jr. *Adolf Hitler and Nazi Germany.* Morgan Reynolds, 2005. 176pp. ISBN 978-1-931798-78-5. Grades 7–10.

This biography of Adolf Hitler (1889–1945) details his childhood, his early years as an artist, and his service as a soldier in World War I. Then it traces Hitler's rise as a dictator and leader of the Nazi party along with his excessive zeal to eradicate Jews and others. Photographs enlighten the text. Bibliography, Chronology, Notes, Further Reading, Web Sites, and Index.

2240. Rosenberg, Maxine B. *Hiding to Survive: Stories of Jewish Children Rescued from the Holocaust.* Clarion, 1998. 166pp. Paper ISBN 978-0-395-90020-8. Grades 6 up.

Fourteen people who remember hiding as children during the Holocaust tell their stories. They come from Greece, Belgium, Poland, Holland, Hungary, Lithuania, and France. A farm dog protected one from a German shepherd that was searching a hayloft. Another lay in a tiny hole waiting for her uncle to return and lift the trap door. Some of the survivors have kept up with those who saved them, though others have never seen their rescuers again. They found that those who helped them had a variety of reasons, some perhaps political, but others humane. Glossary and Further Reading. *Bulletin Blue Ribbon.*

2241. Ross, Michael Elsohn. *Salvador Dalí and the Surrealists: Their Lives and Ideas, 21 Activities.* (For Kids) Chicago Review, 2003. 132pp. Paper ISBN 978-1-55652-479-0. Grades 6 up.

Spaniard Salvadore Dali (1904–1989) was a painter, filmmaker, designer, and performance artist. He began as an impressionist painter but expanded to cubism before becoming a surrealist. In his personal life, he was an opportunist and created publicity for himself by disagreeing with contemporary artists including Andre Breton (the "father" of surrealism) and Pablo Picasso. Reproductions of Dali's works enhance the text. Sidebars give information about other artists of the time, various styles, and history. Among the twenty-one activities for children are "Free Association Fun," "Splotch Art," "Host a Dream Ball," "Daliesque Fashion Collage," and "Hair Art." Further Reading, Glossary, Web Sites, and Index.

2242. Rotem, Simhah. *Memoirs of a Warsaw Ghetto Fighter: The Past Within Me.* Translated by Barbara Harshav. Yale University, 1994. 1995pp. ISBN 978-0-300-05797-3; 2001. paper ISBN 978-0-300-09376-6. Grades YA.

In 1943 the Nazis decided to liquidate the Warsaw ghetto in Poland. They did not expect 500 Jewish fighters inside to defy them. After realizing they could not penetrate the ghetto, the Nazis used cannons and aerial bombings from outside it. When the Jews had lost, the author (known as Kazik) at the age of 19 led the survivors out of the ruins through the sewers. Kazik then spent the rest of the war helping the Jews who remained in Warsaw. The narrative tells Kazik's story. References and Index.

2243. Rubin, Susan Goldman, and Ela Weissberger. *The Cat with the Yellow Star: Coming of Age in Terezin.* Holiday House, 2006. 40pp. ISBN 978-0-8234-1831-2; 2008. paper ISBN 978-0-8234-2154-1. Grades 4–7.

Ela Weissberger, 11, goes with her Czech family in 1942 to the Nazi concentration camp, Terezin. As a survivor, she remembers how the children in the camp rehearsed and performed the opera *Brundibar.* Transports were leaving for the death camps but the children helped their friends and teachers find hope for survival with the power of their music. Bibliography and Notes.

2244. Samuel, Wolfgang W. E. *The War of Our Childhood: Memories of World War II.* University of Mississippi, 2002. 356pp. ISBN 978-1-57806-462-3. Grades YA.

Twenty-seven German survivors share their childhood experiences of air raids, soldiers invading their homes, deprivation, and hunger during World War II. They come from Saxony, Bavaria, Berlin, Saxony-Anhalt, Rhineland-Palatinate, Westfalia, Poland, and the Czech Republic. Most of them think their mothers protected them the most, and still the sights, sounds, and smells that remind them of war remain overwhelming. Additionally, most of them have not detailed the situation for their own children. Index.

2245. Schneider, Helga. *Let Me Go.* Walker, 2004. 166pp. ISBN 978-0-8027-1435-0; Penguin, 2005. paper ISBN 978-0-14-303517-6. Grades YA.

Schneider describes her relationship—and her final meeting—with her mother, a former Nazi guard at Auschwitz-Birkenau. She went to her mother's side in 1998, twenty-seven years after she had last seen her. At the time her mother had asked her to try on her SS uniform and offered her jewelry from Holocaust victims, but Schneider refused. Her mother abandoned the family for her career, and Schneider learned later that she had been closely involved with the Nazis and their crimes and still believed their choices were legitimate.

2246. Schomaker, Annemarie Reuter. *Out of the Ashes: Berlin 1930 to 1950.* Authorhouse, 2003. 248pp. Paper ISBN 978-1-4140-1733-4. Grades YA.

The memoir recalls family, life, and experiences in Berlin before and during World War II. Schomaker traveled with her father and his troop of singers and dancers around Germany and Austria before World War II. Her father died in 1940, and everything changed. She attended state schools and lived in foster homes before reuniting with her family in Berlin in 1944 when she was 14. They had to endure air raids and food shortages along with the cold winters. Then her mother was impressed as a Rubble Woman who cleared the streets. The Berlin Airlift helped them survive, and in 1950, the author immigrated alone to the United States. Maps and photographs augment the text.

2247. Sender, Ruth Minsky. *The Cage.* Simon Pulse, 1997. 252pp. Paper ISBN 978-0-689-81321-4. Grades 7 up.

After the war, Nancy's mother tells her about her experiences in the Lodz, Poland ghetto and several concentration camps from 1939 to 1945. She barely escaped execution, and many in her family died. After seven years, a displaced persons bureau helped her find some of her brothers. The horror of the war becomes more immediate to Nancy through her mother's story.

2248. Sendyk, Helen. *The End of Days: A Memoir of the Holocaust.* Syracuse University, 1999. 232pp. Paper ISBN 978-0-8156-0616-1. Grades YA.

During the Holocaust Helen Sendyk lived in the ghetto of Chrzanow, Poland, and saw her brothers trying to join the Polish army or trying to get to Russia or Palestine. Her sisters tried to help the rest of the family. Of her family of twelve, only three survived the Holocaust, and she details how the others died. The reasonably well-off family had to hide from the Nazis at first, but Polish Gentile neighbors would report them. One sibling, bedridden with polio, just had to stay in bed for the Nazis to murder her. Sendyk and her sister survived the labor camps to be freed by Russian troops, but experienced more rejection when they returned home to neighbors who wanted all Jews dead.

2249. Sereny, Gitta. *The Healing Wound: Experiences and Reflections on Germany, 1938–2001.* Norton, 2002. 320pp. Paper ISBN 978-0-393-32382-5. Grades YA.

Sereny watched a Nazi rally in Nuremberg during 1934, and the lockstep movements of the soldiers intrigued her. Not until Hitler and his men came to Austria did she see how horrible they actually were. Since she was Hungarian, she was not sent to the camps, but she decided that she would always talk about the terror and evil in Hitler's plans. She examines the effects of the past on contemporary German youth and their belief in their country. She interviewed an SS guard, and children of the Third Reich trying to understand their fathers' crimes, and comes to the conclusions that the youth are curious and the old are doing their duty.

2250. Siegal, Aranka. *Memories of Babi.* Farrar, 2008. 128pp. ISBN 978-0-374-39978-8. Grades 4–6.

Aranka Siegal recalls her days with her loving grandmother, Babi, on her farm in a Ukrainian Carpathian mountain village. Siegal lived in Hungary but would go across the boarder to see her during the summers before Hitler came. Even though anti-Semitism was an undercurrent, Siegal remembers the loving times of spinning thread, plucking chicken feathers, hunting for mushrooms, cooking, and making Lekvar, the traditional prune spread. In her mind she still hears her grandmother's advice for an honorable life.

2251. Soros, Tivadar. *Masquerade: Dancing Around Death in Nazi-Occupied Hungary.* Arcade, 2001. 288pp. ISBN 978-1-55970-581-3; 2003. paper ISBN 978-1-55970-692-6. Grades YA.

Tivadar Soros (1894–1968) was a lawyer in Budapest, Hungary, when the Germans invaded in 1944. He and his family found new identities and managed to escape by hiding, first in a building that Soros had architects renovate to conceal them. They survived there for ten months while half of the Jews living in Hungary died. The text gives background history and tells of his family's search for new identities, including Soros' experiences with forgers to get needed papers—military papers, labor permits, identification cards with photographs, and ration cards—not only for himself and family but for many of his friends. Soros was the father of the philanthropist George Soros, who fled with him. Notes, Bibliography, and Index.

2252. Soumerai, Eve Nussbaum, and Carol D. Schulz. *A Voice from the Holocaust.* (Voices of the Twentieth Century Conflict) Greenwood, 2003. 160pp. ISBN 978-0-313-32358-4. Grades 6–9.

The author, lecturer, and teacher Eve Nussbaum Soumerai tells of her experience as a child in Nazi Germany while English and history teacher Schulz provides readers with historical background on the Holocaust. Soumerai, a Jew, lived as a child in Nazi Berlin before escaping to the United Kingdom as a refugee. Soumerai witnessed Crystal Night—when Nazis smashed windows in Jewish businesses and started riots—and taking the "Kindertransport." When she was a young adult after the war, she returned to Germany to find out why her family and friends died. Photographs of her family and personal anecdotes give a reality to the times. Bibliography, Chronology, Glossary, Illustrations, and Index.

2253. Spellman, Gloria. *Janusz Korczak's Children.* Illustrated by Matthew Archambault. Kar-Ben, 2007. 40pp. ISBN 978-1-58013-255-8; paper ISBN 978-0-8225-7050-9. Grades 2–5.

Janusz Korczak (1878–1942), born Henryk Goldszmidt, was a wealthy inhabitant of Warsaw, Poland, whose father treated him like an idiot. He became a doctor who worried about those whom others abused. He established an orphanage, and when the Nazis prepared to send the children to the Warsaw ghetto, Janusz went with them. Later, although he was a famous writer and radio show personality, Nazis sent him with the children to Treblinka where he presumably died. Illustrations complement the text. Bibliography and Chronology.

2254. Toll, Nelly S. *Behind the Secret Window: A Memoir of a Hidden Childhood During World War II.* Puffin, 2003. 161pp. Paper ISBN 978-0-14-230241-5. Grades 6 up.

The Nazis began to occupy the town where Nelly Toll lived in 1941. When she was 8 years old in 1943, Nelly Toll and her mother went into hiding in a Gentile family's home in Lwów, Poland. Nelly kept a journal and made vividly colored paintings to forget her world. Her art and the captions she gave the pictures give a sense of the experience. Other members of the family did not return, but Nelly and her mother survived this difficult experience. Color plates of the drawings give insight to the times.

2255. Van Der Rol, Ruud. *Anne Frank: Beyond the Diary: A Photographic Remembrance.* Illustrated by Rian Verhoeven. Puffin, 1995. 113pp. Paper ISBN 978-0-14-036926-7. Grades 5 up.

Photographs and illustrations help to enhance the description of Anne Frank's (1929–1945) life before her family went into hiding when the Nazis arrived in Amsterdam, Holland. Her father, an amateur photographer, reveals her happy childhood while the political life around her continued to deteriorate without her knowledge. The narrative includes excerpts from the diary she wrote while confined in the back rooms during the Nazi occupation, and it continues with explanations of what happened to the family after the Nazis took them to the concentration camps. (This information is available at the Anne Frank House in Amsterdam.) Maps, Chronology, Notes, Sources, and Index of People and Places. *Christopher Award, American Library Association Notable Books for Children, Publishers Weekly Nonfiction Book of the Year, Booklist Editors' Choice, Mildred L. Batchelder Honor, and Bulletin Blue Ribbon.*

2256. Vander Zee, Ruth. *Erika's Story.* Illustrated by Roberto Innocenti. Creative, 2003. 32pp. ISBN 978-1-56846-176-2. Grades YA.

As her family was headed for Dachau, a Nazi death camp, in 1944, Erika's mother threw the infant Erika from the train. A village woman risked her life to save Erika and raise her. Erika imagines what her parents endured in the ghetto and on transports. Erika never knew her real parents, and she can only ask questions about their relationship before they made the decision to try to save her. In a German village in 1995 the author met a woman who related this story. The illustrations show scenes of the indignities that Jews had to face during this bleak time. *Emphasis on Reading Award* nomination and *Flicker Tale Children's Book Award.*

2257. Van Maarsen, Jacqueline. *My Name Is Anne, She Said, Anne Frank.* Translated by Hester Velmans. Arcadia, 2007. 216pp. ISBN 978-1-905147-10-6; 2008. paper ISBN 978-1-905147-42-7. Grades YA.

In this memoir Jacqueline Van Maarsen reveals that she is Anne Frank's friend Jopie, mentioned in Anne's diary. She says that she did not want to be special because her friend had died in the camps. She describes Anne as jealous, demanding, idealistic, ebullient, curious, and secular when they met at a Jewish school in Amsterdam. Although they felt the menace of the Nazis, they never realized what could happen. Van Maarsen herself came from a Jewish father and a French Catholic mother, and when the Nazis arrived, she undid a conversion to Judaism that allowed her to survive. After the war, Otto Frank shared the diary with her, and they discussed its contents. Photographs enhance the text.

2258. Van Maarsen, Jacqueline, and Carol Ann Lee. *A Friend Called Anne: One Girl's Story of War, Peace and a Unique Friendship with Anne Frank.* Penguin, 2005. 176pp. ISBN 978-0-670-05958-4; Puffin, 2007. paper ISBN 978-0-14-240719-6. Grades 4–8.

Jopie van Maarsen, one of Anne Frank's close friends from 1941 to 1942, recalls life in Amsterdam and her luck to be deported and not sent to a concentration camp. She remembers when friends and neighbors, one by one, were rounded up and sent away. She thought that Anne's family had fled to Switzerland when Anne disappeared one day. Not until Otto Frank gave her the letter that Anne had written in hiding did she know that the family had stayed. Her account confirms that Anne was a real teenager who had the same interests and worries as other teenagers, but a very different end. Photographs complement the text. Bibliography and Chronology.

2259. Velmans, Edith. *Edith's Story: The True Story of a Young Girl's Courage and Survival During World War II.* Bantam, 2001. 239pp. Paper ISBN 978-0-553-38110-8. Grades YA.

Edith Velmans-Van Hessen (1925–) survived the Holocaust by pretending to be a daughter in a Protestant household where a German officer was also billeted. She uses her journals and letters to recount her life during this awful time. She remembers pretending that the war was not happening by attending parties and going to a bomb shelter, refusing to be perturbed even when she has to wear a yellow star and is excluded from public places. Eventually she has to hide and leave her life of privilege that included such niceties as receiving a baby grand piano for her 16th birthday. The letters between her and her parents reveal the anguish of their separation, and in the end she tries not to imagine her mother, grandmother, and brother as Auschwitz corpses. Photographs augment the text.

2260. Venezia, Mike. *Henri Matisse.* Illustrated by author. (Getting to Know the World's Greatest Artists) Children's Press, 1997. 32pp. ISBN 978-0-516-20311-9; paper ISBN 978-0-516-26146-1. Grades K–5.

See entry 1866.

2261. Venezia, Mike. *Igor Stravinsky.* Illustrated by author. (Getting to Know the World's Greatest Composers) Children's Press, 1996. 32pp. ISBN 978-0-516-20054-5; 1997 paper ISBN 978-0-516-26076-1. Grades K–5.

See entry 1868.

2262. Venezia, Mike. *Marc Chagall.* Illustrated by author. (Getting to Know the World's Greatest Artists) Children's Press, 2000. 32pp. ISBN 978-0-516-21055-1; paper ISBN 978-0-516-27041-8. Grades K–5.

See entry 1870.

2263. Venezia, Mike. *Monet.* Illustrated by author. (Getting to Know the World's Greatest Artists) Children's Press, 1990. 32pp. ISBN 978-0-516-02276-5; paper ISBN 978-0-516-42276-3. Grades K–5.

See entry 1871.

2264. Venezia, Mike. *Paul Klee.* Illustrated by author. (Getting to Know the World's Greatest Artists) Children's Press, 1991. 32pp. ISBN 978-0-516-02294-9; 1992 paper ISBN 978-0-516-42294-7. Grades K–5.

Paul Klee (1879–1940) became a painter instead of a musician and studied in Switzerland. The titles of his works seem to be as important as his subjects. He liked nature and the world of buildings and machines. Illustrations augment the text.

2265. Venezia, Mike. *Picasso.* Illustrated by author. (Getting to Know the World's Greatest Artists) Children's Press, 1988. 32pp. ISBN 978-0-516-02271-0; paper ISBN 978-0-516-42271-8. Grades K–5.

See entry 1875.

2266. Venezia, Mike. *René Magritte.* Illustrated by author. (Getting to Know the World's Greatest Artists) Children's Press, 2002. 32pp. ISBN 978-0-516-22029-1; 2003 paper ISBN 978-0-516-27814-8. Grades K–5.

Rene Magritte (1898–1967) first worked as a commercial artist in Belgium. When he moved to Paris, he met the surrealists and started to make works that he considered riddles about everyday life. Two of his works are *The Lovers* and *The Man with the Bowler Hat.* Illustrations and reproductions augment the text.

2267. Venezia, Mike. *Salvador Dalí.* Illustrated by author. (Getting to Know the World's Greatest Artists) Children's Press, 1993. 32pp. ISBN 978-0-516-02296-3; paper ISBN 978-0-516-42296-1. Grades K–5.

Salvador Dali (1904–1989) was a Spanish surrealist painter who combined unexpected objects and figures in his paintings. His flamboyant personality is well documented. Illustrations and reproductions augment the text.

2268. Vikram, Seth. *Two Lives.* Perennial, 2006. 503pp. Paper ISBN 978-0-06-059967-6. Grades YA.

Seth (1952–) did not get to know his great-uncle, an Indian dentist, and great-aunt, a German-born Jew, until he left Calcutta at the age of 17 for London and preparation to study at Oxford. His dual biography of these relatives reveals much of Seth's life during the time he got to know them and includes the larger view of the world's 20th-century discords between Hindus and Muslims, Jews and anti-Semites. He wonders, after all of his interpretation, how people ever get married. Photographs highlight the story.

2269. Vogel, Ilse-Margaret. *Bad Times, Good Friends: A Personal Memoir.* Sheep Meadow, 2001. 239pp. Paper ISBN 978-1-878818-98-0. Grades 9 up.

Ilse-Margaret Vogel and her five friends lived in Berlin during World War II. They risked their lives by printing false identification papers and fake food coupons, trading on the black market, and sheltering people hunted by the Nazis. When asked why she stayed in Germany, Vogel said that she had believed the war would soon be over; after it had been going on for a while, she and her friends became used to deprivation. They stayed in Berlin rather than in small towns because in the city, they could hide and could avoid supporting Hitler, whom they hated. The narrative reveals a different view of the war—of Germans who helped to defeat the maniac who had taken over their government. *New York Public Library's Books for the Teen Age.*

2270. Warren, Andrea. *Surviving Hitler: A Boy in the Nazi Death Camps.* HarperCollins, 2001. 160pp. ISBN 978-0-688-17497-2; HarperTrophy, 2002. paper ISBN 978-0-06-000767-6. Grades 5 up.

In 1939 in Poland, Jack Mandelbaum is 12, living contentedly with his family, barely aware that he is Jewish. When he hears about Hitler's war, he thinks it is exciting. Then when Hitler gains power and attempts to annihilate all of the Jews and other undesirables under his control, Jack, now 15, becomes separated from his family and is taken to Blechhammer, a Nazi concentration camp. His hair is shaved off and he gets an identity number (16013). He decides, however, that he will not hate his captors and that he will make friends with others caught in the same struggle. An older prisoner suggests that he "think of it as a game" that if played properly might help him outlast the Nazis. Jack survives three years in the death camps. By May 7, 1945, when the guards abandon the camp, he weighs only 80 pounds. But he is free to walk out of the gate with no one controlling him. Warren constructs dialogue from Jack's memories. Photographs, Bibliography, Further Reading, Web Sites, and Index. *Robert F. Sibert Honor Book, American Library Association Notable Books for Children, Rebecca Caudill Young Readers' Book Award* (Illinois) nomination, *William Allen White Children's Book Award* (Kansas), *SCASL Book Award* (South Carolina) nomination, and *Capitol Choices Noteworthy Titles* (Washington, D.C.).

2271. Waxman, Laura Hamilton. *Marie Curie.* (History Makers Bios) Lerner, 2004. 48pp. ISBN 978-0-8225-0300-2. Grades 3–5.

See entry 1878.

2272. Welton, Jude. *Monet.* DK, 2000. 64pp. ISBN 978-0-7894-4880-4. Grades YA.

See entry 1879.

2273. Wenzel, Angela. *The Mad, Mad, Mad World of Salvador Dali.* Translated by Rosie Jackson. Prestel, 2003. 28pp. ISBN 978-3-791329-44-4. Grades 5–8.

Salvador Dalí (1904–1989) tried to make dreams into concrete pictures. He painted landscapes and objects juxtaposed in irrational ways. This biography describes some of Dalí's best-known paintings including *The Burning Giraffe* and *The Persistence of Memory* and discusses how theories of the day influenced their content. Reproductions augment the text.

2274. Whiteman, Dorit Bader. *Lonek's Journey: The True Story of a Boy's Escape to Freedom.* Star Bright, 2006. 141pp. ISBN 978-1-59572-021-4. Grades 5–8.

Lonek, 11, hides when the Nazis invade his Polish town in 1939, first in a hole under a neighbor's stable. Then he and his family escape to Russian-occupied Poland and are deported to Siberian slave-labor camps. After a deal with the British, Stalin releases them, and for two years Lonek travels on a number of conveyances through the countries of Iran, India, and the Middle East until he reaches Palestine with 1,000 other orphans. He faces anti-Semitism from both the Nazis and other Polish refugees in his attempt to escape the horrors of World War II. Eventually he gets an education and moves to America, never to see his family again. *Young Hoosier Award* (Indiana) nomination.

2275. Whiting, Jim. *Anne Frank.* (What's So Great About . . . ?) Mitchell Lane, 2008. 32pp. ISBN 978-1-58415-581-2. Grades 2–4.

Anne Frank (1929–1945) lived with her family in Amsterdam and enjoyed a life like all other children her age until Hitler came to power. In World War II, her Jewish family had to hide in an attic. She wrote in her diary about this time, being cooped up so that no one would either see or hear them. The text gives an overview of her short life. Illustrations and maps augment the text. Bibliography, Glossary, and Index.

2276. Wiernicki, John. *War in the Shadow of Auschwitz: Memoirs of a Polish Resistance Fighter and Survivor of the Death Camps.* Syracuse University, 2001. 272pp. ISBN 978-0-8156-0722-9. Grades YA.

John Wiernicki, a Gentile, served in the Polish Home Army during World War II. But he fought against the Nazis, and they arrested him in 1943 and imprisoned him in the Auschwitz-Birkenau, Buchenwald, and Sonder concentration camps. Among the men he met were Josef Mengele and Heinz Hilo, the doctors who medically experimented with the prisoners. Eventually he escaped from Ohrdruf during a death march just before the Allied troops arrived. Photographs augment the text. Bibliography, Glossary, and Index.

2277. Wiesel, Elie. *Night.* Translated by Marion Wiesel. Hill & Wang, 2006. ISBN 978-0-374-39997-9; paper ISBN 978-0-374-50001-6. Grades YA.

Elie Wiesel, born in Hungary in 1928, was deported first to Auschwitz and then to Buchenwald, where his parents and younger sister died. This book tells of his experiences through the death of his father in the camp and then liberation by the Americans in 1945. All he and the others could think of was getting food. They had not eaten for more than six days because the Germans had been systematically eliminating as many inmates as they could and had stopped feeding the others. Wiesel says that revenge was not on their minds at the end, only food. This book is a powerful statement on inhumanity.

2278. Worth, Richard. *Heinrich Himmler: Murderous Architect of the Holocaust.* (Holocaust Heroes and Nazi Criminals) Enslow, 2005. 160pp. ISBN 978-0-7660-2532-5. Grades 8 up.

Heinrich Himmler (1900–1945), head of the Reichsfuhrer-SS under Hitler, had charge of the mass destruction that killed more than 11 million people. This biography focuses on his role as the "architect of genocide." It includes statistics, facts, quotes from Nazis about their plans to exterminate Jews, and Himmler's supervision of the Final Solution. Himmler personally hated hunting or the sight of death. Photographs and maps highlight the text. Bibliography, Glossary, Chronology, Notes, Further Reading, Web Sites, and Index.

2279. Zapruder, Alexandra. *Salvaged Pages: Young Writers' Diaries of the Holocaust.* Yale University, 2004. 472pp. Paper ISBN 978-0-300-10307-6. Grades YA.

Fourteen diaries detail the lives of children and their families during the Holocaust. Among them are diaries from Essen, Germany; Paris, France; Brussels, Belgium; Olomouc, Czechoslovakia; the ghettos of Terezin, Vilna, Kovno, and Lodz; Transnistira; Krajno, Poland; and Stanislawow, Poland. Their narratives offer the complexity of ordinary people filled with loneliness, hunger, separation, and other awful experiences during World War II. Bibliography, Notes, and Index. *National Jewish Book Award.*

2280. Zargani, Aldo. *For Solo Violin: A Jewish Childhood in Fascist Italy.* Translated by Marina Harss. Paul Dry, 2002. 330pp. Paper ISBN 978-0-9679675-3-0. Grades YA.

Aldo Zargani (1933–), born in Turin, remembers the years between 1938 and 1945 when the Fascists were persecuting Italian Jews. The Fascists forced his father to end his career as a violinist, and his brother survived. Many relatives and friends, however, died in the Holocaust. The family fled to Asti in northwest Italy where two brothers hid in a Catholic boarding school, with only the monsignor knowing their identity. In the last months, the family hid in the Piedmont Valley with Partisans. He does remember fondly an encounter with an American soldier. His memoir is one of the few about Italian Jews during World War II.

Graphic Novels, Biographies, and Histories

2281. Cain, Bill. *The Battle of the Bulge: Turning Back Hitler's Final Push.* Illustrated by Dheeraj Verma. (Graphic Battles of World War II) Rosen, 2007. 48pp. ISBN 978-1-4042-0782-0. Grades 4–9.

This account presents the details of the World War II battle that took place in Ardennes, France, from December 16, 1944, to January 25, 1945. It includes background on the war as well as commentary on the key commanders involved. Photographs and illustrations highlight the text.

2282. Croci, Pascal. *Auschwitz.* Illustrated by author. Abrams, 2004. 87pp. ISBN 978-0-8109-4831-0. Grades YA.

A Polish couple, Kazik and Cessia, lose a daughter at Auschwitz-Birkenau during World War II and barely survive themselves. The story reveals the brutality and horror of the Holocaust. Croci based his graphic novel content on interviews with concentration camp survivors. The story is presented in black-and-white artwork. Bibliography and Glossary.

2283. Ennis, Garth. *War Stories I.* Illustrated by Chris Weston, et al. Vertigo, 2004. 234pp. Paper ISBN 978-1-4012-0328-3. Grades YA.

This graphic novel recalls four incidents from World War II. A crew of a single German tank tries to escape death by having the Americans capture them rather than the Russians. In a second, a British campaign to drive the Germans from Italy costs many lives. Another shows the platoon of an Airborne infantry enjoying an unexpected and wonderful weekend pass when they find a horde of Nazi plunder. The last story recalls the final days of an escort destroyer battling to protect the vital supply convoys for the Allies.

2284. Ennis, Garth. *War Stories II.* Illustrated by David Lloyd, Carlos Ezquerra, and Cam Kennedy. Vertigo, 2006. 240pp. Paper ISBN 978-1-4012-1039-7. Grades YA.

This graphic novel recalls four incidents during the 1930s and 1940s. The RAF bombing of German industrial cities takes a huge civilian toll. The British special forces attack the desert Afrika Corps and cause destruction. Soldiers from opposing sides share a trench during the Spanish Civil War. The final story presents the pilot of an experimental camship—a small fighter aircraft launched from a merchant ship deck with a catapult—who is expected to ditch in the North Atlantic because no provision exists for him to return to the deck.

2285. Hudson-Goff, Elizabeth, and Jonatha A. Brown. *Anne Frank.* Illustrated by Guus Floor and Jonathan Timmons. (Graphic Biographies) World Almanac Library, 2006. 32pp. Grades 3–5.

This short graphic biography of Anne Frank (1929–1945) depicts her life in the annex based on the diary she wrote during World War II before she was captured and placed in a work camp. A yellow background sets direct quotes from Frank apart from the fictional aspect of the narration. Web Sites.

2286. Kubert, Joe. *Yossel: April 19, 1943.* Illustrated by author. IBooks, 2005. 128pp. Paper ISBN 978-1-5968-7826-6. Grades YA.

Yossel, 15, a Jew in Nazi Poland during World War II, has no rights. The Nazis confiscate Yossel's family's goods and place the family in a crowded Warsaw ghetto. Yossel continues to draw comic book heroes, and the Nazis are impressed and keep him around to draw while the rest of his family is sent to a concentration camp. He joins the Resistance and, instead of being downtrodden and docile, Yossel helps to instigate the Warshaw Ghetto Uprising of 1943 on April 19. The rough pencil art underscores the horrors of the story.

2287. Murray, Doug. *D-Day: The Liberation of Europe Begins.* Illustrated by Anthony Williams. (Graphic Battles of World War II) Rosen, 2007. 48pp. ISBN 978-1-4042-0786-8. Grades 4–9.

This account of D-Day, on June 6, 1944, presents details of the event. It offers background on the war as well as commentary on the major commanders involved. Photographs and illustrations highlight the text. Bibliography, Glossary, Web Sites, and Index.

2288. Spiegelman, Art. *Maus II: A Survivor's Tale and Here My Troubles Began.* Knopf, 1992. 160pp. Paper ISBN 978-0-679-72977-8. Grades 6 up.

In this second half of *Maus*, Vladek Speigelman survives the Auschwitz death camp in Poland and is reunited with his wife. They come to America, but neither can overcome the psychological horrors of losing a child and betrayal by people they trusted. The illustrations depict the Nazis as cats stalking their prey, the Jewish mice. *Pulitzer Prize.*

DVDs

2289. *Allies at War.* Narrated by Brian Dennehy. M P I, 2002. 2 hrs. ISBN 978-0-7886-0443-0. Grades 9 up.

During World War II Charles de Gaulle of France, Sir Winston Churchill of Britain, and Franklin Roosevelt of the United States became allies against the Nazis. In private, their exchanges were less than friendly. At first passionate about his country as the Undersecretary of Defense for France, de Gaulle impressed Churchill, but de Gaulle soon showed his arrogance and independence by not cooperating with the United States, starting operations that clashed with allied plans, and openly criticizing allies that were working to liberate France. Consequently, Churchill tapped de Gaulle's telephone and once kept him in London against his will. Roosevelt and Churchill became close friends and held many secret meetings during the war. Brian Dennehy narrates the video with its documentary footage, reenactments, and still photography. The DVD also contains bonus footage including newsreels of the liberation of Paris.

2290. *Auschwitz: Inside the Nazi State.* Films Media, 2007. 60 min. ISBN 978-1-4213-6085-0. Grades 10 up.

The DVD offers six episodes up to 11 minutes each that cover the events leading to the establishment of Auschwitz and its operation until its demise in 1945. Included are recreations, computer-generated reconstructions, archival film footage, and interviews with former survivors and Nazi soldiers.

2291. *The Boys of Buchenwald.* National Film Board of Canada, 2002. 46 min. Grades 8 up.

Nearly sixty years after they were liberated from Buchenwald, 426 of the thousand boys who survived met in France to revisit the places where they often learned that they were the only survivors of their families, and to discover how to love and to care again. Three of them, Robbie Waisman, Elie Wiesel, and Joe Szwarcberg, remained friends after they learned they no longer had to hoard food, burn mattresses, or fight. Interviews with some of the women who helped them show how much they had to relearn after they left the camps.*Gold Remi Award, WorldFest Film Festival* (Houston), *Bronze World Medal,* and *The New York Festivals.*

2292. *The Churchills.* WGBH, 2003. 2.5 hrs. ISBN 978-1-59375-117-3. Grades 7 up.

This three-volume examination of Britain's powerful Churchill family includes "Aristocratic Adventures," "Moment of Destiny," and "Born a Churchill." Interviews with a wide variety of professionals including historians, journalists, biographers, personal assistants, and Members of Parliament reveal the family's story. Relatives including Winston Churchill's daughter Sarah (Lady Soames), his nephew Peregrine Churchill, his grandson Winston, and his daughter-in-law Pamela Harriman Churchill add more detail. The documentary begins with the meeting and marriage of Winston Churchill's parents, Randolph and Jennie Jerome Churchill. It then covers details of Winston Churchill's entire life, including his role in World War II. Churchill's letters, memoirs, and writings aid the information presented. Video, Photographs, Cartoons, and Reenactments complement the naration.

2293. *Dropping in on Matisse.* (Art Is . . .) Crystal, 2005. 19 min. ISBN 978-1-56290-342-8. Grades 3–6.

See entry 1891.

2294. *Eternal Memory: Voices from the Great Terror.* Narrated by Meryl Streep. National Film Network, 2006. 81 min. ISBN 978-0-8026-0321-0. Grades YA.

During the 1930s and 1940s Joseph Stalin sent millions of Russians to internment camps and had 20 million slaughtered as he took power. This DVD focuses on Ukrainian residents. Survivors and eyewitnesses reveal the horror of his regime.

2295. *Fate Did Not Let Me Go.* Narrated by Liv Ullmann and Martin Sheen. Terra, 2003. 30 min. ISBN 978-1-932321-14-2. Grades 10 up.

In 1985 Ulrich Ollendorf received a letter from his mother that she wrote from the Thereseinstadt concentration camp on August 24, 1942, just before her death. Ulrich had escaped Nazi Germany in the late 1930s, but his parents had been unable to get a visa in time to emigrate. Martin Sheen narrates the story of this letter, finally made public when read at Ulrich's funeral, and Liv Ullman reads it on film. She wanted him to be successful, and his family of doctors shows that he fulfilled her wishes even though he had not received the letter. Family photographs, interviews, archival footage, and the history of Berlin during World War II complete the presentation.

2296. *Gaudi: Life and Works.* Landmark Media, 2007. 57 min. Grades 9 up.

Anton Gaudi (1852–1926), a Spanish architect, is best known for his design of the Sagrada Familia, a cathedral that he began at age 31, and remained uncompleted at his death. The DVD highlights Gaudi's unusual perceptions and his visions. When he graduated, a professor said that he was either a genius or a madman. By the time he died, his works were controversial enough to leave him in poverty. But photographs of his funeral indicate that the populace appreciated what he was trying to accomplish.

2297. Grant, R. G. *World War II: The Events and Their Impact on Real People.* DK, 2008. 192pp. ISBN 978-0-7566-3830-6. Grades 7 up.

This overview of World War II discusses the factors that led to its beginning, and key events from Hitler's invasion of Poland to the final dropping of atomic bombs on Hiroshima and Nagasaki. It also addresses the aftermath of the war. It includes material from primary sources about soldiers, Japanese POWs, witnesses to various events, and ordinary citizens coping with the war. Photographs and maps reinforce the text. Glossary, Chronology, and Index.

2298. *Henry D. Remple: Finding Hope in Troubled Times.* Narrated by Meryl Streep. National Film Network, 2007. 35 min. ISBN 978-0-8026-0720-1. Grades 9 up.

In the late 19th century, the Russian government invited Mennonites from Germany to move there and establish farming communities. When World War I began, the pacifist Mennonites refused to fight. They were ostracized and began seeking asylum in other countries. The DVD presents the experiences of Henry Remple, whose family finally settled in Kansas. The first section presents Dr. Remple, a retired psychologist, talking to students, and the second section offers an interview.

2299. *Hidden Heroes.* Vision Video, 2004. 50 min. ISBN 978-1-56364-771-0. Grades 9 up.

Anne Frank was only one of thousands of people the Dutch Resistance hid from the Nazis during World War II. Interviews with former Resistance fighters, families who hid Jews, and survivors, along with photographs from the 1940s and film clips show the sacrifice and the horror of this situation. Foster families, women in the Resistance, and the 28,000 Resistance fighters who died during the war are those who are the "hidden heroes."

2300. *Hitler's Sunken Secret.* (NOVA) WGBH, 2006. 56 min. ISBN 978-1-59375-319-1. Grades YA.

The Norwegian ferry *Hydro* sank in 1944 when it was carrying atomic bomb ingredients for the Germans. Norwegians had discovered that it was carrying "heavy water" and reported it to the Americans. The Americans asked that the ferry be destroyed regardless of the sacrifice. The Norwegian Resistance sank it. An expedition investigated it sixty years later below Lake Tinn and concluded that the ship might have been a decoy. The DVD presents new findings.

asks what caused it. The second and longest segment presents the ending days of World War II including Hitler's suicide and the search for his bunker. In the third segment aspects of the Allied invasion of France and what the Allies confronted when they arrived show how they were able to succeed. A final short segment comments on the dust bowl, the difficulties of migrants to California in surviving, and the accurate fictional account in John Steinbeck's *The Grapes of Wrath*.

Compact Discs

2314. Bartoletti, Susan Campbell. *Hitler Youth: Growing Up in Hitler's Shadow.*   Narrated by Kathrin Kana. Listening Library, 2006. 4 CDs; 4 hrs. 24 min. ISBN 978-0-7393-3662-5. Grades YA.

> See entry 2068.

2315. Bell, Ted. *Nick of Time.*   Narrated by John Shea. MacMillan Audio, 2008. 10 CDs; 11.5 hrs. ISBN 978-1-4272-0466-0. Grades 6–9.

> See entry 1375.

2316. Bloor, Edward. *London Calling.*   Narrated by Robertson Dean. Listening Library, 2006. 6 CDs; 7 hrs. 30 min. ISBN 978-0-7393-3666-3. Grades 6–9.

> See entry 1943.

2317. Boyne, John. *The Boy in the Striped Pajamas: A Fable.*   Narrated by Robert Trupp. Listening Library, 2006. 4 CDs; 58 min. ISBN 978-0-7393-3705-9. Grades 7–10.

> See entry 1946.

2318. Hager, Thomas. *The Demon Under the Microscope: From Battlefield Hospitals to Nazi Labs, One Doctor's Heroic Search for the World's First Miracle Drug.*   Narrated by Stephen Hoye. Tantor Media, 2006. 10 CDs; 12.5 hrs. ISBN 978-1-4001-3306-2. Grades YA.

> See entry 2173.

2319. Higson, Charlie. *Blood Fever: A James Bond Adventure.*   Narrated by Nathaniel Parker. (Young Bond) Listening Library, 2006. 7 CDs; 8 hrs. 43 min. ISBN 978-0-7393-3893-3; Miramax, 2007. paper ISBN 978-1-4231-0029-4. Grades 6–9.

> See entry 1971.

2320. Higson, Charlie. *Silverfin: A James Bond Adventure.*   Narrated by Nathaniel Parker. (Young Bond) Listening Library, 2005. 7 CDs; 8 hrs. 30 min. ISBN 978-0-307-28437-2. Grades 6–9.

> See entry 1972.

2321. Lowry, Lois. *Number the Stars.*   Narrated by Blair Brown. Random House, 2004. 3 CDs; 2 hrs. 46 min. ISBN 978-1-4000-8556-9. Grades 4–8.

> See entry 1995.

2322. McEwan, Ian. *Atonement.* Narrated by Josephine Bayley. Phoenix, 2006. 5 CDs; ca. 5 hrs. ISBN 978-1-59777-100-9. Grades YA.

See entry 1999.

2323. Peet, Mal. *Tamar.* Narrated by Various. Candlewick, 2007. 10 CDs; 12 hrs. 9 mi. ISBN 978-0-7636-4121-4. Grades 8 up.

See entry 2024.

2324. Peters, Elizabeth. *The Serpent and the Crown.* Narrated by Barbara Rosenblat. (Amelia Peabody Mystery) Harper Audio, 2005. 5 CDs; 6 hrs. ISBN 978-0-06-076013-7. Grades YA.

See entry 2025.

2325. Roy, Jennifer. *Yellow Star.* Narrated by Christina Moore. Recorded Books, 2007. 3 CDs; 3 hrs. ISBN 978-1-4281-3407-2. Grades 5–7.

See entry 2033.

2326. Schneider, Helga. *Let Me Go.* Narrated by Anne Dover. Blackstone Audio, 2004. 4 CDs. ISBN 978-0-7861-8578-8. Grades YA.

See entry 2245.

2327. Vikram, Seth. *Two Lives.* Narrated by Seth Vikram. HarperAudio, 2005. 6 CDs; 8 hrs. ISBN 978-0-06-087894-8. Grades YA.

See entry 2268.

2328. Whelan, Gloria. *The Impossible Journey.* Narrated by Julie Dretzin. Recorded Books, 2003. 4 cass.; 4 hrs. 45 min. ISBN 978-1-4025-7406-1. Grades 5–8.

See entry 2053.

2329. Winspear, Jacqueline. *Birds of a Feather.* Narrated by Kim Hicks. (Maisie Dobbs) Chivers, 2005. 10 CDs; 10.5 hrs. ISBN 978-0-7927-3665-3. Grades YA.

See entry 2055.

2330. Winspear, Jacqueline. *Pardonable Lies: A Maisie Dobbs Novel.* Narrated by Orlagh Cassidy. (Maisie Dobbs) Macmillan Audio, 2005. 10 CDs; 11 hrs. ISBN 978-0-7927-3749-0. Grades YA.

See entry 2057.

EUROPE AND THE BRITISH ISLES, 1946–PRESENT

Historical Fiction and Fantasy

2331. Aboulela, Leila. *Minaret.* Grove, 2005. 276pp. Paper ISBN 978-0-8021-7014-9. Grades YA.

Najwa, daughter of wealthy Sudanese parents, begins a journey at Khartoum University that ends in London where she works as a maid, having lost everything. When a student revolution leads to a coup in Sudan in 1985, Najwa's family is exiled to London. But her father is detained and then hung. Najwa slowly uses her money, gives up her education, and finds out how poorly she is qualified for many jobs. During this distress, she gradually finds Islam.

2332. Almond, David. *The Fire-Eaters.* Random House, 2004. 224pp. ISBN 978-0-385-73170-6; 2005. paper ISBN 978-0-440-42012-5. Grades 7 up.

When Bobby Burns is 12 in 1962, his world turns upside down. There is the Cuban missile crisis, his father becomes seriously ill, and Bobby goes to a new elite school where his classmates scorn him and a masochistic teacher wields unwelcome influence. Bobby's relationships with his friends Joseph and Ailsa Spink, a girl who can heal injured animals in her sleep, are also evolving. On a day trip he and his mother meet Mr. Mc-Nulty, a strongman who eats fire, then return home to find that Bobby's father served with the fire-eater in Burma during World War II. McNulty suffers from war fatigue while Bobby anguishes about his father's illness and the possible end of the world in nuclear disaster. *Guardian Children's Fiction Prize* nomination, *Costa Book Awards, Nestlé Children's Book Prize, Carnegie Medal* nomination, *Boston Globe/Horn Book Awards, Garden State Teen Book Award* (New Jersey) nomination, *Bulletin Blue Ribbon, American Library Association Best Books for Young Adults, Horn Book Fanfare, Kirkus Reviews Editor's Choice,* and *American Library Association Notable Children's Books.*

2333. Baccalario, Pierdomenico. *The Long-Lost Map.* (Ulysses Moore) Scholastic, 2006. 272pp. ISBN 978-0-439-77439-0. Grades 4–6.

See entry 317.

2334. Bauer, Jutta. *Grandpa's Angel.* Illustrated by author. Candlewick, 2005. 48pp. ISBN 978-0-7636-2743-0. Grades 1–4.

See entry 1936.

2335. Baulenas, Lluís-Anton. *For a Sack of Bones.* Translated by Cheryl Morgan. Harcourt, 2008. 368pp. ISBN 978-0-15-101255-8. Grades YA.

In 1949 as Niso tries to fulfill his father's dying wish of finding the bag of bones belonging to Bartomeu Camús, the man who helped his father during Franco's Spanish war, and whom Franco's henchman murdered for his anti-Franco views, he remembers his childhood. In alternating chapters, he recalls having to go to an orphanage after his anti-Fascist father had to join Franco's forces because his mother could not support them. His father tells him to join Franco's forces and work to expose their evil from the inside. He proceeds to act as his father requested.

2336. Beauman, Sally. *Rebecca's Tale.* HarperCollins, 2007. 448pp. Paper ISBN 978-0-06-117467-4. Grades YA.

In this continuation of *Rebecca* by Daphne du Maurier, Colonel Julian, along with his daughter Ellie and the young scholar Terence Gray, investigate the death of Rebecca de Winter, and find Rebecca's diary, a document that complicates their search. Although an orphan, Terence believes that he is somehow connected to Rebecca, but will not talk about his own past. The colonel and Ellie are semi-reclusive, but feeling that he did not do all he could have at Rebecca's inquest makes the colonel want to know more. A serious question remains as to Rebecca's real identity.

2337. Binchy, Maeve. *The Glass Lake.* Dell, 2007. 584pp. Paper ISBN 978-0-385-34176-9. Grades YA.

In the 1950s in Ireland, Kit McMahon and her friend continue to have differences in their values and emotions. A parallel plot involves Kit's mother, who supposedly drowned when Kit was younger, but who really went to London with a lover. Successful in business, Kit's mother pretends to be the mother's friend and begins communicating with Kit, wanting to be near her as Kit passes through her teen years.

2338. Broadbent, Tony. *The Smoke.* Felony & Mayhem, 2005. 302pp. Paper ISBN 978-1-933397-15-3. Grades YA.

In London ("the Smoke" in London underworld slang) just after World War II, everyone is trying to live with rationing and deal with the chaos in the city. Jethro breaks into the Soviet embassy to steal jewels, but when the British Secret Service spots him, it blackmails him to go back into the building to heist a secret code book. At the same time, the Soviets are watching him and planning to retrieve the code book.

2339. Buckley, William F. *Nuremberg: The Reckoning.* Harvest, 2003. 384pp. Paper ISBN 978-0-15-602747-2. Grades YA.

When Sebastian Reinhard is 13, he is sent to his grandmother in Arizona to attend high school while his MIT-educated civil engineer father, Alex, stays in Hamburg with the Nazis. Although German, Sebastian's father does not support the Nazis, but Sebastian never hears from his father again. Later Sebastian serves in the United States military where he goes to Germany to fight his countrymen. In 1945 Sebastian is asked to be a German-American interpreter and interrogator at Nuremberg's Palace of Justice during the War Crimes Tribunal. As he asks questions and hears answers, he comes to understand that his own father was the superintendent for constructing an extermination camp.

2340. Bunting, Eve. *Walking to School.* Illustrated by Michael Dooling. Clarion, 2008. 32pp. ISBN 978-0-618-26144-4. Grades K–3.

Eight-year-old Allison, a Catholic, tries to walk through a gauntlet of Protestant hecklers to her new school in Northern Ireland during The Troubles. She begins to think that her uncle, who is walking with her, may be enjoying the violence, making sure the children cannot be friends. All the fracas causes a button to pop off of Allison's coat. To her surprise, a young Protestant girl retrieves it and hands it to her. Double-page oil-on-canvas paintings enhance the text.

2341. Capouya, Emile. *The Rising of the Moon: A Novel.* Lyons, 2003. 119pp. ISBN 978-1-58574-664-4. Grades YA.

After World War II, Mike, an American merchant marine stranded in France, finds a berth on a ship smuggling between France and Tangier. His first run is to transport ex-Nazi officers to Egypt, during which he gets along with his crew and a fellow captain, MacNamara. Later his bosses ask him to deliver a parcel on the side, offering him a hefty bonus. He refuses, pitching it in the sewer and flying to Paris. Back in the States, Mike agrees to crew for a ship taking guns to British-blockaded Palestine. The British intercept the vessel at sea and place the crew under guard in Cyprus. Mike meets an American-educated Turk who offers him a chance to escape. In Tel Aviv he meets Jewish resistance leaders who want guns, but decides to return home where he learns the fate of his friend MacNamara.

2342. Cheng, Andrea. *The Bear Makers.* Front street, 2008. 170pp. ISBN 978-1-59078-518-8. Grades 6–10.

Kata, 11, and her Jewish family try to survive in Budapest without rebelling against the regimented Hungarian Workers Party after World War II. Her older brother, Bela, escapes to America while the Party takes over her father's factory. Her mother then sews teddy bears and handbags to sell on the black market. Throughout, Kata remembers the times during the war when her aunt hid her and Bela on her farm. Bela tries to rescue the family before they have to give everything to the Party.

2343. Cooper, Patrick. *I Is Someone Else.* Delacorte, 2006. 295pp. ISBN 978-0-385-73269-7; Laurel-Leaf, 2007. paper ISBN 978-0-440-23919-2. Grades 9 up.

Stephen, 15, goes from Britain to France for a summer program in 1966. He meets Jerry and Astrid, two friends of his older brother who has been missing for eighteen months. With the two friends Stephen travels to Istanbul, the last place they saw Rob, and is introduced to sex, drugs, and different cultures. He ventures to Iran, Pakistan, and India, and during this time must come to terms with his own past sexual experience with his teacher, Mr. Wortle.

2344. Cooper, Patrick. *Tell Me Lies.* Delacorte, 2007. 294pp. ISBN 978-0-385-73270-3. Grades 10 up.

Stephen Wiston, 18, finishes his A-level exams and journeys to London to visit his brother in 1969. There he reunites with a former girlfriend, Astrid, who introduces him to the scene of drugs, sex, music, and anti-Vietnam War politics. He becomes engulfed in this new lifestyle, a squatter in a Brixton commune, and a realistic representative of the hippie/flower child era. After someone persuades him to move to the country to The Hollies, Astrid's tragic accident makes him reassess his lack of direction.

2345. Cornwell, Nikki. *Christophe's Story.* Illustrated by Karin Littlewood. Frances Lincoln, 2007. 96pp. ISBN 978-1-84507-765-5; paper ISBN 978-1-84507-521-7. Grades 5–8.

In 1994 hundreds of Rwandans were murdered in mass genocide. Eight-year-old Christophe and his family escape to England, and he tries to adjust to his new life. His teacher writes his story, but instead of being pleased, he is furious. His grandfather had told him that stories have lives and should never be written down. She decides to have a storytelling unit so that Christophe can tell his story to his classmates. They then hear the horrible account of soldiers coming to his home and killing his baby brother before the family could escape.

2346. Dahlberg, Maurine F. *Escape to West Berlin.* Farrar, 2004. 179pp. ISBN 978-0-374-30959-6. Grades 4–7.

Heidi Klenk, 13, does not want to leave East Berlin in 1961, but people have begun to accuse her father of being a "border crosser" when he goes to his comfortable job in West Berlin during the day. Her parents cross the border first. Then the East Germans suddenly close the border as Heidi and her grandmother prepare to leave. Her Oma escapes through an unguarded gap, but Heidi is caught on the barbed wire. The only way she can escape is to swim the Teltow Canal. And even though she has an intense fear of water, she succeeds. *Young Hoosier Award* (Indiana) nomination, *Children's Book Award* (South Carolina) nomination, *Volunteer State Book Award* (Tennessee) nomination, and *Mark Twain Award* (Missouri) nomination.

2347. De Moor, Margriet. *Duke of Egypt.* Arcade, 2002. 256pp. ISBN 978-1-55970-546-2; 2003. paper ISBN 978-1-55970-661-2. Grades YA.

Lucie, owner of a horse farm with her father, meets a handsome stranger, Joseph Plato, in her hometown of Benckelo, in the Twente countryside of eastern Holland in 1963. They fall in love and marry. Sharing a passion for each other, a delight in horses, and the desire to have a successful stable, the two have three children. Joseph, however, leaves every summer and returns in the fall. His gypsy heritage and his family draw him to be with them, and Lucie understands.

2348. Dowd, Siobhan Ann. *Bog Child.* David Fickling, 2008. 336pp. ISBN 978-0-385-75170-4. Grades 7 up.

In 1981 Fergus, 18, needs to study for his A-level exams, but his imprisoned brother decides to stage a hunger strike. Fergus discovers a murdered body in a bog. And finally, his brother's friend blackmails him to smuggle packages for the IRA. When archaeologists identify the murdered girl as from the Iron Age and over 2000 years old, Fergus starts dreaming about what might have happened to her. Throughout, Fergus starts falling in love with the researcher, begins chatting with the enemy guard that he passes on his morning runs to the IRA drop site, and admires his uncle's detachment from politics. But in the end, he discovers that what he thought was the truth is not. *Publishers Weekly Best Books, Capitol Choices Noteworthy Titles* (Washington, D.C.), and *Kirkus Best Young Adult Books.*

2349. Dowd, Siobhan Ann. *A Swift Pure Cry.*   David Fickling, 2007. 310pp. ISBN 978-0-385-75108-7. Grades 7 up.

In southern Ireland during 1984, Shell, 15, looks after her younger brother and sister after their mother Moira Talent dies and their father Joe disappears regularly, almost drowning himself in alcohol, but taking money from the church collection plate to support them. Shell falls in love with the new priest, Father Rose, but realizes the futility of her emotion and becomes pregnant by a classmate, Declan, who leaves for America before finding out that he will be a father. When the baby, a stillborn, arrives, the town first accuses her of murder, then they think that either the priest or Joe are the father of the dead child. *Publishers Weekly Best Books* and *Kirkus Reviews Editor's Choice.*

2350. Doyle, Roddy. *Paddy Clarke Ha Ha Ha.*   Penguin, 1995. 282pp. Paper ISBN 978-0-14-023390-2. Grades YA.

Ten-year-old Paddy Clarke lives with his family in the Dublin neighborhood of Barrytown in the late 1950s. He wants to be tough like his friends and spends his time engaging in malicious but harmless acts such as writing in hardening cement and torturing his little brother. He also has to listen to his parents fight at night. Paddy tries to understand the adult world and to figure out his place in it. *Booker Prize.*

2351. Durrell, Lawrence. *White Eagles Over Serbia.*   Arcade, 1995. 200pp. ISBN 978-1-55970-312-3. Grades YA.

British spy Meuthen works in a mountainous area of Serbia when the Communists and Tito take over Serbia and Croatia. He looks for clues to the murder of another spy. As a Serbian speaker who has survival skills, he finds out about the White Eagles, a Royalist group trying to overthrow the new government. The plot fails, but Meuthen escapes before the group can kill him.

2352. Fleischman, Sid. *The Entertainer and the Dybbuk.*   Greenwillow, 2007. 154pp. ISBN 978-0-06-134445-9. Grades 6–9.

In Europe in 1948 Freddie Birch, a former American bomber pilot, attempts to support himself as a ventriloquist. He meets his departed friend, Avrom Amos, now a dybbuk. The Nazis murdered Avrom, a resistance fighter, after he helped Freddie escape from a POW camp. Avrom needs a living person to help him finish his "business" with the SS colonel who killed him. Avrom's entrance into Freddie's body improves his act, and Freddie gets better bookings. But Avrom refuses to work on the sabbath and demands that Freddie be him at his bar mitzvah. Since Avrom's personality can only be revealed through Freddie's comments, they become filled with information about the awfulness of the Holocaust. During their partnership, Freddie must deal with his own anti-Semitism and other prejudices.

2353. Frei, Pierre. *Berlin.*   Translated by Anthea Bell. Grove, 2006. 425pp. ISBN 978-0-8021-1832-5. Grades YA.

In Berlin during 1945 after the end of World War II, Ben finds the body of a blond, blue-eyed woman in a subway station. Since she is initially misidentified as an American, the Military Police Captain John Ashburner becomes involved with the case along with Inspector Klaus Dietrich. As more women with the same characteristics are found dead, they realize that a serial killer needs to be found before claiming another victim. Among those he targets to sexually assault and strangle with a chain are a movie star, a nurse, a titled diplomat, and a prostitute to the wealthy. After each victim, a story about her past during the war helps them create a profile of the killer.

2354. Friedman, Carl. *Nightfather.* Translated by Arnold Pomerans and Erica Pomerans. Persea, 1995. 130pp. Paper ISBN 978-0-8925-5210-8. Grades YA.

The narrator and her brother Simon know two worlds—theirs and their father's. Their father associates everything with the concentration camp from which he was liberated at the end of World War II and his return to their Dutch town. The children feel guilty for all they have, but they also fear that something similarly irrational could happen to them. *Bulletin Blue Ribbon Book.*

2355. Friedman, Carl. *The Shovel and the Loom.* Translated by Jeanette Ringold. Persea, 1998. 130pp. Paper ISBN 978-0-8925-5231-3. Grades YA.

Chayah, a college student and atheist daughter of Holocaust survivors, becomes a nanny for a 3-year-old Orthodox Jewish boy in Antwerp, Belgium, in the 1970s. She becomes fond of the child and begins to investigate her own heritage. She classifies the three types of responses to her Jewishness by thinking of her father's continual references to being a Holocaust survivor, her mother's refusal to remember, and a family friend's belief that religion is the only thing that brings sense to a chaotic world.

2356. Gabbay, Tom. *The Berlin Conspiracy.* HarperCollins, 2007. 320pp. Paper ISBN 978-0-06-078788-2. Grades YA.

In June of 1963 Jack Teller finds himself in Berlin rather than sitting on the beach at his Florida home. Even though Jack has retired from the CIA, he has answered the request of a Stasi agent to hear about a cold war conspiracy just before President John F. Kennedy is scheduled to arrive in the city. Jack has to filter through what he hears and decide what is a lie and what is the truth in this suspenseful novel.

2357. Gardam, Jane. *The Flight of the Maidens.* Caroll & Graf, 2001. 288pp. ISBN 978-0-7867-0879-6. Grades YA.

Yorkshire women Hetty Fallowes and Una Vane, and Jewish refugee Liselotte Klein prepare to enter Cambridge and London University in 1946. Hetty wants to escape her overbearing mother; Una loves a man with even less money than she; and Liselotte has been sorrowful since leaving Germany in 1939 via the Kindertransport. Their final summer before university offers unexpected changes in social mores and conventions.

2358. Geras, Adele. *The Tower Room.* Harcourt, 2005. 150pp. Paper ISBN 978-0-15-205537-0. Grades 7–10.

Megan's parents die after she starts boarding school. When she is a senior in 1962, she falls in love with the new laboratory instructor. After she runs away with him to London, she realizes that the bloom of love is much more appealing without the responsibility of work and the need for shelter.

2359. Greenlaw, Lavinia. *Mary George of Allnorthover.* Houghton, 2001. 288pp. ISBN 978-0-618-09523-0. Grades YA.

In the 1970s Mary George, 17, lives with her mother Stella in Allnorthover, a small English village, after her father leaves. When the village lunatic sees her one night, he thinks she is an angel who will help retrieve his home from beneath the water reservoir by which she walks. The village discovers his obsession, and Mary tries to escape from him while trying to find her own identity by trying out new styles and smoking pot with her friend, Billy.

2360. Hadley, Tessa. *Everything Will Be All Right.* Holt, 2004. 352pp. ISBN 978-0-224-07174-1; Picador paper ISBN 978-0-312-42364-3. Grades YA.

When Joyce Stevenson is 11, she and her mother Lil, widowed in World War II, and sister and brother move in with Joyce's Aunt Vera, Uncle Dick, and cousins near Falmouth, England. When Vera's youngest child dies of meningitis, Dick leaves Vera for a young woman in town. Years later, from a beauty parlor window, Joyce sees her own husband, an art professor named Ray who had left his wife for her, meet his young art student lover. Then their daughter Zoe goes to Cambridge and falls in love at 19 with Simon. Zoe has their child against Simon's wishes, but then she leaves him. Joyce helps Zoe with Pearl so that Zoe can become an academic expert on Third World problems. Then Pearl, at 17, asks her forgotten father for his help, and the traumas of the family women come into focus.

2361. Helms, Beth. *Dervishes: A Novel.* Picador, 2008. 320pp. Paper ISBN 978-0-312-42619-4. Grades YA.

Grace, her husband Rand, and her 12-year-old daughter Canada, arrive in Turkey in 1975. Grace loves the Ankara embassy posting where Rand does undisclosed work. But after six months of friendships with the other wives, affairs and disagreements disrupt the quiet. Canada falls for another family's houseboy, and Grace begins an affair with Canada's riding instructor while Rand is gone for months. Eventually they become involved in terrible situations from which they have difficulty extricating themselves, and Rand goes missing.

2362. Heuston, Kimberley. *The Book of Jude.* (Front Street) Honesdale, Pa., 2008. 216pp. ISBN 978-1-932425-26-0. Grades YA.

In 1989 Jude, 15, goes with her devout Mormon family to Czechoslovakia where her mother plans to study art on a Fulbright fellowship. While there, the political unrest with its mass demonstrations, and the uprooting from New York are too much for her, and she faces guilt, fear, disassociation, and nightmares, which lead her to destructive acts. At a hospital she is diagnosed with a borderline personality disorder and given medication, but continues to self-destruct. Her father finally brings a Mormon bishop to bless her.

2363. Hinton, Nigel. *Time Bomb.* Tricycle, 2006. ISBN 978-1-58246-186-1. Grades 5–8.

In a flashback, Andy remembers the summer of 1949 when he was 12, riding around London with his friends and exploring a bombed-out manor: Eddie's stepfather abuses him, Manny faces anti-Semitism, Bob tries not to stutter so his father will approve of him, and Andy discovers that his father is unfaithful to his mother. A beloved teacher then punishes the boys unjustly at the end of the school year. At the manor they discover a bomb, and they think that its power will restore their own self-respect. When the bomb explodes, one of them dies, and the rest must live with the consequences.

2364. Koponen, Libby. *Blow Out the Moon.* Little, Brown, 1006. 209pp. Paper ISBN 978-0-316-01480-9. Grades 3–6.

In the 1950s the Koponen family moves from the United States to London, England, where Libby hates her school. Then she gets the chance to attend boarding school at Sibton House in the countryside, and slowly warms to the new setting. She learns to ride a horse, makes friends, and begins to write. Although she leaves after a year, she remembers her experiences with pictures and illustrations.

2365. Kuijer, Guus. *The Book of Everything.* Translated by John Nieuwenhuizen. Arthur A. Levine, 2006. 112pp. ISBN 978-0-439-74918-3. Grades 4–7.

In Amsterdam during 1951, Thomas, 9, tries to escape from the reality of his abusive and deeply religious father by writing down his visions from a magical, imaginary world into a special book. When asked what he wants to be when he grows up, Thomas answers, "Happy," a state that his father does not admit exists. But Thomas's neighbor introduces him to Beethoven and poetry, while a girl with a leather leg helps him gain perspective about his home life. And Jesus talks to him periodically. Finally the family stands up to his father and changes.

2366. Kyuchukov, Hristo. *My Name Was Hussein.* Illustrated by Allan Eitzen. Boyds Mills, 2004. 32pp. Paper ISBN 978-1-56397-964-4. Grades K–3.

Hussein, whose name has been handed down through generations in his family and means "handsome" in Arabic, lives with his Roma family in a small Bulgarian village. When soldiers come with guns in the 1980s and shut down the mosque where Hussein worships, he can no longer pray with his people or leave home at night. A policeman destroys the family's identity cards and forces them to take Christian names. Hussein has to take the name Harry. The people do not like the Roma, often misnamed "gypsies," who migrated to Europe many years ago from India. The widespread prejudice against Hussein and his family causes him to miss his Muslim faith and religious holidays. Illustrations augment the text. The author bases the story on his own life as a Roma child in Bulgaria.

2367. Llywelyn, Morgan. *1949: A Novel of the Irish Free State.* Forge, 2004. 414pp. Paper ISBN 978-0-8125-7080-9. Grades YA.

Ursula, adopted daughter of rebel Ned Halloran, returns from school in Switzerland and gets a job as Ireland's first woman broadcaster at Radio Eireann. As the 1930s pass, Ursula discovers she is pregnant after affairs with two men, neither of whom she wants to marry. In order to escape the infamy of having a child out of wedlock in the Catholic state of Ireland, she moves to Geneva to work for the League of Nations. There she sees World War II erupt but returns home by the end to raise Barry on her father's farm. Then, in 1949, Ireland forms the Republic and the goals of her father, his friend Henry Mooney, and Ursula herself are finally realized.

2368. Mackall, Dandi Daley. *Eva Underground.* Harcourt, 2006. 239pp. ISBN 978-0-15-205462-5. Grades 7 up.

Eva Lott, 14, unwillingly leaves Chicago for Poland in 1978 after her mother's death, with her professor father so he can work with the underground freedom movement. Bored with her new home, having no amenities or extras, she tries to escape but fails. Then she meets Tomek, a young political activist, and through helping his family harvest plums before an intense cold streak and carrying an illegal printing press, she becomes aware of the needs of many who have not always or ever had freedom.

2369. MacLaverty, Bernard. *The Anatomy School.* Norton, 2003. 368pp. Paper ISBN 978-0-393-32457-0. Grades YA.

Martin Brennan has many burdens in his final semester of Catholic high school in Belfast, Northern Ireland, during the 1970s. His mother wants him to enter the priesthood, he has already failed his exams once, he is shy, and he lacks confidence. As the photographer for his school newspaper, he carefully observes those around him and he realizes that the world is not as it has been presented to him.

2370. Mankell, Henning. *A Bridge to the Stars.* Translated by Laurie Thompson. Delacorte, 2007. 164pp. ISBN 978-0-385-73495-0. Grades 6–9.

In 1956 Joel Gustafson, 11, lives with his lumberman father in the bleakness of northern Sweden. Joel wonders why his father always tells him stories of his days as a seaman and why his mother left when he was a young child. To fill some of his time, Joel imagines many things and sometimes wanders at night. He sees a dog outside his window and imagines that it will lead him to the stars. On his outings he meets a woman, an outcast due to her deformed face; a schizophrenic insomniac who drives his car in circles; and Ture, a boy his own age, who tries to convince him to commit vandalism. When one of these adventures almost kills him, his father begins to offer Joel answers to his many questions.

2371. Mead, Alice. *Girl of Kosovo.* Farrar, 2001. 128pp. ISBN 978-0-374-32620-3; Yearling, 2003. paper ISBN 978-0-440-41853-5. Grades 5–8.

An Albanian Kosovar in 1998, Zana Dugolli, 11, faces the ire of Serbs who want to expel any with her background from their homes and the area. Her friend Lena, a Serb, even becomes afraid to play with her. The family, however, seems to lead a semi-normal life. Her family watches ESPN, and her brothers like Nintendo. Simultaneously, they bury guns and sleep in their clothes, ready to leave immediately. Zana is injured in an attack by Serb militiamen who murder her father and two of her brothers. Her father has taught her not to hate the Serb military, and she must combat her feelings. While Zana is in a Belgrade hospital, Lena sneaks in even though it is behind enemy lines. Later, when neighbors threaten Lena, Zana defends her. *Student Book* (Maine) nomination and *Land of Enchantment Book Award* (New Mexico) nomination.

2372. Michaels, Anne. *Fugitive Pieces: A Novel.* Vintage, 1998. 304pp. Paper ISBN 978-0-679-77659-8. Grades YA.

Jakob Beer survives the Holocaust after his entire Polish family dies. Anthanasios Roussos, "Athos," a Greek scholar, rescues him and raises him on a Greek island. Jakob learns from him about Nazi attempts to change archaeological discovery results so that they prove Aryan supremacy, and other denials of the past. Jakob sees Athens and its suffering during the war and goes with Athos to Toronto, where Athos teaches. Athos dies in Toronto, and Jakob continues his work under the influence of the past and the demand of the present. He also becomes a poet, somewhat surprised at the healing power of words after being so hurt by their destruction.

2373. Mitchell, David. *Black Swan Green.* Random House, 2007. 294pp. Paper ISBN 978-0-8129-7401-0. Grades YA.

Jason Taylor, who has a stammer, lives in the boring village of Black Swan Green in Worcestershire, England, in 1982 during the cold war. He feels that he must compete with his intelligent sister and referee his parents' disagreements. Jason worries about Margaret Thatcher's war in the Falkland Islands and his own growing and uncontrollable sexuality, until he meets a reclusive "old witch" who helps him like himself a little better. *Booklist Editors' Choice.*

2374. Moeyaert, Bart. *Brothers: The Oldest, the Quietest, the Realest, the Farthest, the Nicest . . .* Illustrated by Gerda Dendooven. Translated by Wanda Boeke. Front Street, 2005. 163pp. ISBN 978-1-932425-18-5. Grades 6 up.

As the youngest of seven brothers, Bart Moeyaert, has a series of different experiences while growing up in Belgium during the 1960s and 1970s. He collects them into forty-two stories. Among the various vignettes: He is unable to find space on a boat with his brothers, but watches it sink under their weight. He gets the news of their grandmother's death before the others, but they are not impressed when they hear it from him. The brothers try to throw a toad on a hot tin roof or steal a pie from a bakery van. His father is impressed when Bart finds a shell on the beach; and he tends a tiny garden patch while his brothers leave. In other stories, he is either victim or hero.

2375. Morpurgo, Michael. *The Mozart Question.* Candlewick, 2008. 70pp. ISBN 978-0-7636-3552-7. Grades 4–6.

In the 1960s Paolo Levi, 9, secretly takes his father's violin to a street player who repairs it for him and gives him lessons. When his parents discover this, they tell him why his father, a superb musician, decided never to play his violin again. Paolo's father, in the beautiful city of Venice, remembers nearly dying in a death camp and being forced, with Paolo's mother, to play Mozart for the Nazis and calm the prisoners as they marched to the gas chambers. When his parents meet his teacher, Benjamin, they realize that the three of them knew each other in the camps. Paolo acquiesces to his father's request that he never play Mozart, the German's favorite composer, in public.

2376. Orlev, Uri. *The Lady with the Hat.* Translated by Hillel Halkin. Walter Lorraine, 1995. 183pp. ISBN 978-0-395-69957-7. Grades 5 up.

Yulek, aged 17 in 1947, survives in an Italian Zionist training camp although the rest of his family died in concentration camps during World War II. Yulek decides to return to his home in Poland, but when he arrives he discovers that anti-Semitism still pervades the town. He also hears that an English woman has inquired about his family. He thinks that his Aunt Malka, who left years before to marry a Christian, must be searching for him. He knows neither her married name nor her location, only what people have told him about her appearance. After trying to find her, he ends up in Palestine running the British blockade. Among the characters who flesh out the novel are residents of the kibbutz where Yulek ends up and a Jewish girl who, after hiding in a convent during the war, decides she wants to become a nun in Jerusalem. *American Library Association Notable Books for Children, American Library Association Notable Books for Young Adults,* and *Mildred L. Batchelder Award.*

2377. Potok, Chaim. *Old Men at Midnight.* Knopf, 2001. 304pp. ISBN 978-0-375-41071-0; Ballantine, 2002. paper ISBN 978-0-345-43998-7. Grades YA.

In these three short stories, "The Ark Builder," "The War Doctor," and "The Trope Teacher," a "listener," Ilana Davita Dinn, records the lives of the protagonists. Noah, a young Holocaust survivor, and his brother helped an old man build an ark in a synagogue. Another man, Leon Shertov, a Russian Jew, experiences compassion when a doctor helps save his arm from amputation during World War II and whom Stalin later imprisons in his tirade against physicians. In the last, Benjamin Walter, a professor of warfare, adds the story of his father in World War I and himself in World War II.

2378. Pressler, Mirjam. *Let Sleeping Dogs Lie.* Translated by Erik J. Macki. Front Street, 2007. 207pp. ISBN 978-1-9324258-4 0. Grades 10 up.

See entry 2026.

2379. Rees, Celia. *The Wish House.* Candlewick, 2006. ISBN 978-0-7636-2951-9. Grades 9 up.

Richard, 15, meets the Dalton family living in the Wish House while on vacation with his family in the Welsh countryside in 1976. Jay Dalton, the father and an artist, has many quirks, while his daughter, Clio, enjoys a freedom that Richard has not experienced. He falls in love with her, and Jay paints his portrait. What Richard does not understand is what happens when he is not around, and his lack of comprehension creates a tragic situation. In 1982 he reflects back on that summer as he visits an art gallery displaying Clio's and her father's paintings.

2380. Rice, Eva. *The Lost Art of Keeping Secrets.* Plume, 2007. 352pp. Paper ISBN 978-0-452-28809-6. Grades YA.

In the 1950s Penelope Wallace, 18, lives in her family's countryside home that is slowly falling into ruin since her father's death in World War II and her mother's inability to cope. Penelope can think only of clothes and singer Johnnie Ray. In London she shares a taxi with Charlotte Ferris, and Charlotte introduces her to cousin Harry, training in magic, and kind Aunt Clare. Harry asks Penelope to pretend to be his girlfriend so he can make Marina, engaged to George, jealous. Penelope reluctantly agrees but soon realizes that she is no longer pretending affection. Penelope's mother attracts an American who solves the family's money problem, and Harry returns after running away, in love with Penelope.

2381. Schlink, Bernard. *The Reader.* Translated by Carol Brown Janeway. Vintage, 2008. 218pp. Paper ISBN 978-0-307-45489-8. Grades YA.

In post–World War II Germany Michael Berg becomes ill on the way home from school, and a woman of 40 takes him home and nurses him through hepatitis. Knowing nothing about her, he becomes her lover, and she encourages his schooling. One day she disappears inexplicably, and not until he is a law student several years later does he discover her darker side. She is tried as a Nazi criminal and he realizes that she is also illiterate.

2382. Szablya, Helen M., and Peggy King Anderson. *The Fall of the Red Star.* Boyds Mills, 2001. 166pp. Paper ISBN 978-1-56397-977-4. Grades 5–8.

Stephen, age 14, becomes a freedom fighter in Budapest, Hungary, during the revolution in 1956, after the Soviet Union tries to invade and occupy the country. Eight years before, the Communists had taken his father, but Stephen still hopes that his father is alive. Stephen fights in street battles, makes and throws Molotov cocktails, kills someone, and helps his sister deliver her baby. When the Communists win, he, his sister, and his mother flee, but their journey becomes especially perilous when they try to save other people in the swamp they are crossing by boat to the Austrian border.

2383. Ziefert, Harriet. *A New Coat for Anna.* Illustrated by Anita Lobel. Knopf, 1988. 30pp. Paper ISBN 978-0-394-89861-2. Grades K–2.

After World War II, when Anna's coat becomes too small, her mother has no money to buy her a new one. Her mother begins to trade her heirlooms, including a necklace, a gold watch, and a lamp. One item buys wool; another item gets it spun into yarn. Then the yarn becomes cloth, and finally it is a lovely red coat. *American Library Association Notable Books for Children.*

History

2384. Ballard, Robert D. *Finding the Titanic.* Illustrated by Ken Marschall. Scholastic, 1993. 64pp. Paper ISBN 978-0-590-47230-2. Grades 1–4.

Dr. Robert Ballard became fascinated with the story of the *Titanic.* When the tether of the tiny submarine *Alvin* was extended to 13,000 feet, Ballard realized he could reach the wreck two and one-half miles under the sea. In July 1986 he saw the ship that had last been above the water on April 14, 1912. On that night, only 705 of the 1,500 people on board the magnificent ship reached the safety of a rescue vessel, the *Carpathia,* after an iceberg tore through the hull. Ballard returned to the *Titanic* eight times, going inside and reliving the scene based on what he had read or heard from survivors of that doomed voyage. Further Reading, Glossary, and *Titanic* Time Line. *American Library Association Best Books for Young Adults, School Library Journal Best Books of the Year,* and *Horn Book Fanfare.*

2385. Bard, Mitchell. *The Nuremberg Trial.* (History Firsthand) Greenhaven, 2002. 144pp. ISBN 978-0-7377-1076-2; paper ISBN 978-0-7377-1075-5. Grades 7 up.

This presentation of the Nuremberg war crime trials after World War II contains court transcripts, personal remembrances, and newspaper reportage to reveal the military barbarism and heinous crimes that the Nazis committed against humanity. The five chapters begin with a preface and offer two to four essays with introductions.

2386. Bjornlund, Britta. *The Cold War.* (People at the Center of) Blackbirch, 2003. 48pp. ISBN 978-1-56711-765-3. Grades 6–8.

This is a look at the history of the cold war, showing its effects on Europe, Asia, and the United States, with its nuclear threats, hope of détente, and the future relationship between the United States and Russia. The spreads examine some of the military and civilian leaders who had roles in the cold war. Photographs illuminate the text.

2387. Bodden, Valerie. *The Cold War.* (Days of Change) Creative Education, 2007. 48pp. ISBN 978-1-58341-546-7. Grades 6–9.

Bodden begins with a description of the cold war to explain its significance. The volume includes full-page photographs that reveal the difficulties of this escalation of bad will between the United States and the Soviet Union and its effects on others. Other attempts to present a balanced view between the two factions are also included. Bibliography and Index.

2388. Brager, Bruce L. *The Iron Curtain: The Cold War in Europe.* (Arbitrary Borders) Chelsea House, 2004. ISBN 978-0-7910-7832-7. Grades 10 up.

Brager discusses the countries involved in the cold war by giving both perspectives—first of the Soviets and then of the Americans—after the division of Berlin at the end of World War II. He comments that America's containment policy was most likely the best way to keep communism from spreading to other continents. Certain revolts within the Soviet confines were quelled, including those in Hungary and Prague. Finally in 1989, the cold war ended when the Berlin Wall fell. Photographs augment the text. Chronology, Notes, Bibliography, Further Reading, and Index.

2389. Burgan, Michael. *The Berlin Airlift.* (We the People) Compass Point, 2006. 48pp. ISBN 978-0-7565-2024-3. Grades 4–7.

Eight chapters detail the Berlin airlift to save the city's population three years after the end of World War II. The Soviets blocked all traffic into the divided city so that its more than 2 million citizens had no fuel, food, or necessities. Allied planes flew over the city around the clock and dropped their cargo for the people. Eventually the blockade ended when the Soviets realized they could not control the flow of supplies. Photographs highlight the text. Chronology, Glossary, Further Reading, Web Sites, and Index.

2390. Carnegy, Vicky. *Fashions of a Decade: The 1980s.* Chelsea House, 2007. 64pp. ISBN 978-0-8160-6724-4. Grades 5 up.

In the 1980s fashions ranged from designer suits to ripped jeans. Interest in crinolines also returned. Princess Diana's sense of fashion alerted women to elegance and understated clothing. Photographs and illustrations enhance the text. Glossary, Further Reading, Chronology, and Index.

2391. Carter, E. J. *The Cuban Missile Crisis.* (20th Century Perspectives) Heinemann, 2003. 48pp. ISBN 978-1-4034-3806-5; paper ISBN 978-1-4034-4180-5. Grades 4–8.

The causes of the Cuban Missile Crisis, its issues, aftermath, and consequences are covered in this volume. This cold war event took the world to the brink of nuclear war before some people worked to bring a peaceful resolution to the standoff. Among the events discussed are the Bay of Pigs disaster and John F. Kennedy's secret missile-swapping agreement with Khrushchev. Illustrations highlight the text. Bibliography, Further Reading, Glossary, and Index.

2392. Corona, Laurel. *The Russian Federation.* Lucent, 2001. 110pp. ISBN 978-1-56006-675-0. Grades 8 up.

See entry 2075.

2393. Cullen, David B. *The First Man in Space.* (Days That Changed the World) World Almanac Library, 2004. 48pp. ISBN 978-0-8368-5570-8; paper ISBN 978-0-8368-5577-7. Grades 5–8.

In six chapters this volume examines the race between the Soviet Union and the United States to send a human into space. It discusses the situation before the race actually began on April 12, 1961 when Kennedy challenged the United States to succeed; the resulting Space Age; the moon landing in 1969; and space missions following that event. Further discussion concerns the future of space missions and their importance for science. Photographs enhance the text. Maps, Chronology, Glossary, Further Reading, Web Sites, and Index.

2394. De La Bedoyere, Guy. *The First Computers.* (Milestones in Modern Science) World Almanac, 2005. 48pp. ISBN 978-0-8368-5854-9. Grades 6–9.

Readers will learn about the development of computers by examining the early days of analogue computers and what occurred to allow the breakthrough into microcomputers and the technological advancements today. Photographs and illustrations highlight the text. Index.

2395. Fulbrook, Mary. *The Divided Nation: A History of Germany, 1918–1990.* Blackwell, 2003. 416pp. ISBN 978-0-631-23207-0; 2008. paper ISBN 978-1-4051-8814-2. Grades YA.

The smaller section of this text presents the Weimar Republic and the Third Reich, while more than half of the book discusses the two Germanys since 1945. Fulbrook shows the importance of the elite groups from 1918 to 1990, the roles and interaction of various classes, the economy, the place of dissenting groups in the societies, and the international connections. She also reviews the events that led to the end of the divided Germany. Bibliography and Index.

2396. Gottfried, Ted. *The Cold War.* Illustrated by Melanie Reim. (Rise and Fall of the Soviet Union) Lerner, 2003. 160pp. ISBN 978-0-7613-2560-4. Grades 9 up.

Stalin controlled Soviet politics at the end of World War II after losing 11 million soldiers. Then the cold war occurred and several additional leaders followed Stalin before the Union of Soviet Socialist Republics (USSR) collapsed. The narrative covers the leaders who trailed after Stalin including Beria, Malenkov, Khrushchev, Bulganin, Brezhnev, and Gorbachev. They led the USSR to the brink of war, through a nuclear disaster at Chernobyl, and into a democracy. Illustrations and photographs enhance the text. Notes, Further Reading, Chronology, Glossary, and Index.

2397. Gottfried, Ted. *Displaced Persons: The Liberation and Abuse of Holocaust Survivors.* (Holocaust) Twenty First Century, 2001. 127pp. ISBN 978-0-7613-1924-5. Grades 6–12.

The thousands of refugees who immigrated during World War II had to find new homes and new lives, but often they had to adjust to continued anti-Semitism and unforgiving laws. Among the topics covered are the rise of Zionism, the birth of Israel, the displacement of Palestinians, and others who have been unhelpful and hurtful. Chronology, Notes, Glossary, Further Reading, and Index.

2398. Hoare, Stephen. *The Modern World.* Facts on File, 1993. 78pp. ISBN 978-0-8160-2792-7. Grades 4–7.

See entry 2096.

2399. Howard, Amanda. *Robbery File: The Museum Heist.* (Crime Solvers) Bearport, 2007. 32pp. ISBN 978-1-59716-550-1. Grades 3–6.

This volume presents a case for the reader with information about the police procedures, the witness interviews, the forensic evidence gathered, and information about the accused. In Amsterdam a robbery of two van Gogh paintings baffled police. Sidebars add facts. Photographs and illustrations augment the text. Glossary, Further Reading, Web Sites, and Index.

2400. Judge, Lita. *One Thousand Tracings: Healing the Wounds of World War II.* Illustrated by author. Hyperion, 2007. Unpaged. ISBN 978-1-4231-0008-9. Grades 2–5.

A young girl of 6 in the Hamerstrom family is delighted when her father returns from World War II to their farm in the Midwest. Soon after, her mother receives a letter from a German friend, Dr. Kramer, who tells them that the war has left them with nothing. The family mails him food and clothing. He mails back that others now need their help. Many of the Germans send tracings of their feet so that the Hamerstroms can find shoes among their friends that can be sent for children that have nothing. The relief effort helps more than three thousand people. When the girl receives a letter from Eliza, a German girl whose father is missing, she sends Eliza a rag doll. Eliza responds with the gift of a painting of a swallow. Collage and watercolor illustrations enhance the text. *American Library Association Notable Children's Books.*

2401. Kinzer, Stephen. *Crescent and Star: Turkey Between Two Worlds.* Farrar, 2008. 272pp. Paper ISBN 978-0-374-53140-9. Grades YA.

As a nation between Europe and Asia, Turkey could return to some of its previous power in the 21st century if a true democracy were established. This view of Turkey, in ten chapters with "meze" in between, looks at the customs (including water pipe smoking), social life, political paradoxes, and religions in the country. Index.

2402. Langley, Andrew. *The Collapse of the Soviet Union: The End of an Empire.* (Snapshots in History) Compass Point, 2006. 96pp. ISBN 978-0-7565-2009-0. Grades 7 up.

The Soviet Union began with the revolution in 1917, and it continued until 1989 when it fell. At that time, global politics changed forever. The author presents the leaders, plans, downfalls, and problems for all of those involved in this area of the world. Photographs highlight the text. Bibliography, Glossary, Notes, Further Reading, Web Sites, and Index.

2403. Levy, Adrian, and Catherine Scott-Clark. *The Amber Room: The Fate of the World's Greatest Lost Treasure.* Berkley, 2005. 416pp. Paper ISBN 978-0-425-20378-1. Grades YA.

See entry 2104.

2404. Levy, Pat, and Sean Sheehan. *From Compact Discs to the Gulf War: The Mid 1980s to the Early 1990s.* (Modern Eras Uncovered) Raintree, 2005. 56pp. ISBN 978-1-4109-1790-4. Grades 5–9.

The decade from the mid-1980s to the mid-1990s is covered on many topics. Among the subjects included are international politics, fashion, and pop culture. Photographs and illustrations highlight the text. Glossary, Chronology, and Index.

2405. Levy, Pat, and Sean Sheehan. *From Punk Rock to Perestroika: The Mid 1970s to the Early 1980s.* (Modern Eras Uncovered) Raintree, 2005. 56pp. ISBN 978-1-4109-1789-8. Grades 5–9.

This volume covers many topics in the decade between the mid-1970s and the mid-1980s. Among those included are international politics, fashion, and pop culture. It links economic recession and unemployment to the rebellious punk rock that attracted young people. Photographs and illustrations highlight the text. Glossary, Chronology, and Index.

2406. Maass, Peter. *Love Thy Neighbor: A Story of War.* Vintage, 1997. 305pp. Paper ISBN 978-0-679-76389-5. Grades YA.

What Maass saw as a correspondent in Bosnia was fascist Serbian thugs with well-equipped armies slaughtering a group of unarmed civilians who were trying to create a nation based on tolerance. In the rural areas, genocidal attacks destroyed huge groups of non-Serbs. Serbs captured and detained thousands of Muslims in concentration camps. Inmates begged Maass not to ask questions, because answering would cause their deaths after he left. The narrative tells what happened in Bosnia factually as it asks philosophically how humans can let such things happen. Index.

2407. MacDonald, Fiona. *The First "Test-Tube Baby".* (Days That Changed the World) Gareth Stevens, 2004. 48pp. ISBN 978-0-8368-5567-8; 2003. paper ISBN 978-0-8368-5574-6. Grades 5–8.

The six chapters of this book introduce the search for a way to overcome human infertility and the results of this search both ethically and scientifically. The topics discussed include DNA, egg collecting, fertilization, implants, and the morality of such decisions as well as the danger of genetic engineering. References throughout the text to Lesley Brown's treatment and pregnancy support aspects of the procedure. Photographs enhance the text. Chronology, Further Reading, Glossary, Web Sites, and Index.

2408. Mattern, Joanne. *The Chunnel.* (Building World Landmarks) Blackbirch, 2003. 48pp. ISBN 978-1-56711-301-3. Grades 5–8.

At first Great Britain did not want a direct connection to France, but once the country decided to pursue the idea, a number of attempts at a tunnel failed. When the technology was invented that would allow the passage, the Chunnel was built. Today it is an important link between the two countries. Photos,Chronology, Further Reading, Glossary, Web Sites, and Index.

2409. Raven, Margot Theis. *Mercedes and the Chocolate Pilot: A True Story of the Berlin Airlift and the Candy That Dropped from the Sky.* Illustrated by Gijsbert van Frankenhuyzen. Sleeping Bear, 2002. 48pp. ISBN 978-1-58536-069-7. Grades 3–5.

In 1948, at the age of 7, Mercedes Simon lived in West Berlin. Josef Stalin blocked all ground routes into the city so that the 2.2 million West Berliners had neither food nor supplies. The Berlin Airlift began with American and British airplanes flying over and into the city and delivering needed items. One pilot, Lt. Gail Halvorsen, earned the name "Chocolate Pilot" because he and his squadron dropped more than 250,000 candy-loaded parachutes and 20 tons of chocolate and gum to the 100,000 children, an operation he called "Little Vittles." Many years later Mercedes met the pilot who gave her hope. Illustrations augment the text. Note and Epilogue. *Bluebonnet Award* (Texas) nomination, *Beehive Children's Informational Book Award* (Utah) nomination, and *Show Me Readers Award* nomination.

2410. Schmemann, Serge. *When the Wall Came Down: The Berlin Wall and the Fall of Communisim.* Kingfisher, 2006. 127pp. ISBN 978-0-7534-5994-2; 2007. paper ISBN 978-0-7534-6153-2. Grades 6 up.

On November 9, 1989, one of the most surprising events of the 20th century occurred. The Berlin Wall "fell" both physically and psychologically. The wall was constructed in 1961 and destroyed twenty-eight years later. Holders of American passports could cross at Checkpoint Charlie while East Germans could pass neither legally nor physically into West Berlin. The Yalta agreement after World War II led to the Soviets deciding to build the wall and Gorbachev's reforms led the East Germans to tear down the wall. Maps and archival photographs illuminate the text. Bibliography, Glossary, and Index.

2411. Smith, Jeremy. *The Fall of the Berlin Wall.* (Days That Changed the World) Gareth Stevens, 2004. 48pp. ISBN 978-0-8368-5569-2. Grades 5–8.

In six chapters readers will learn about the reasons behind the erection of the Berlin Wall, the changes that had to occur before it could come down, and its subsequent fall. Additionally, the book includes information about the reunification of the two Germanys, the progress of this union, and prospects for the future. Photographs highlight the text. Chronology, Further Reading, Glossary, Web Sites, and Index.

2412. Taylor, David. *The Cold War.* (20th Century Perspectives) Heinemann, 2001. 48pp. ISBN 978-1-57572-434-8; paper ISBN 978-1-58810-373-4. Grades 5–8.

The cold war developed after World War II between the East and West when the two factions began to distrust each other. The author explains some of the major tensions that existed until 1989 when the Berlin Wall fell in Germany. The rivalry concerned military coalitions, ideology, espionage, and psychology. Both groups spent huge amounts of money on a space race and updating their defenses. Illustrations highlight the text. Bibliography, Further Reading, Glossary, Index.

2413. Whiting, Jim. *The Cuban Missile Crisis: The Cold War Goes Hot.* (Monumental Milestones) Mitchell Lane, 2005. 48pp. ISBN 978-1-58415-404-4. Grades 5–8.

The author examines the conflict that led to the Cuban Missile Crisis in 1962 between the Soviet Union's Khrushchev and the United States under John F. Kennedy. Khrushchev evidently did not believe that Kennedy would be a tough opponent, but he proved otherwise, and they had tense negotiations before the situation was defused. Photographs, sidebars, and illustrations highlight the text. Glossary, Chronology, and Index.

Biography and Collective Biography

2414. Acker, Kerry. *Gerhard Schroeder.* (Major World Leaders) Chelsea House, 2003. 116pp. ISBN 978-0-7910-7652-1. Grades 7–10.

Chancellor Gerhard Schroeder (1944–) served Germany as its leader from 1998 to 2005. Acker offers background on Schroeder's life with information about the history of Germany. Then the book assesses how and why he came to power. Photographs highlight the text. Chronology, Further Reading, Web Sites, and Index.

2415. Anderson, Robert. *Salvador Dalí.* Franklin Watts, 2002. 46pp. ISBN 978-0-531-12231-0; paper ISBN 978-0-531-16624-6. Grades 5–8.

See entry 2140.

2416. Armstrong, Karen. *The Spiral Staircase: My Climb Out of Darkness.* Knopf, 2004. 336pp. ISBN 978-0-375-41318-6; Anchor, 2005. paper ISBN 978-0-385-72127-1. Grades YA.

In 1969, when Karen Armstrong could no longer accept the tenets of those who had been training her in the convent for seven years, she decided to leave. She knew nothing about the world outside, and she faced seizures and panic attacks. She studied English literature at Oxford and saw doctors who failed to diagnose her epilepsy. Eventually, in 1976, she discovered what was causing her problems and began a writing career. She found her own spirituality as she interpreted the sacred texts of many of the world's religions. The story of her anguish and discovery is both disconcerting and reassuring.

2417. Bardhan-Quallen, Sudipta. *Jane Goodall.* (Up Close) Viking, 2008. 208pp. ISBN 978-0-670-06263-8. Grades 7 up.

Jane Goodall was interested in animals from childhood. She went to Africa after graduating from high school and became a secretary to anthropologist Louis Leakey. He helped her get a position researching at Gombe. Then she began studying the social relationships of chimpanzees. Photographs enhance the text. Bibliography, Notes, and Index.

2418. Bargalló, Eva. *My Name Is . . . Picasso.* Illustrated by Violeta Monreal. (My Name Is . . .) Barron's, 2006. 63pp. Paper ISBN 978-0-7641-3393-0. Grades 4–6.

See entry 1782.

2419. Berne, Jennifer. *Manfish: The Story of Jacques Cousteau.* Illustrated by Erick Puybaret. Chronicle, 2008. 40pp. ISBN 978-0-8118-6063-5. Grades 3–6.

Jacques-Yves Cousteau (1910–1997) loved flying and cameras, but was especially interested in the sea. He invented the aqualung so that he could go deeper into the ocean to view its treasures. Illustrations complement the text. Note.

2420. Cunningham, Kevin. *Joseph Stalin and the Soviet Union.* (World Leaders) Morgan Reynolds, 2006. 208pp. ISBN 978-1-931798-94-5. Grades 8 up.

Joseph Stalin arrived in Vienna from Georgia in 1913 to do research requested by Lenin. He continued as a revolutionary in 1917 in the Russian Revolution. He later ordered the death of his colleagues Bukharin and Trotsky and rose to power through his decisions to industrialize Russia and place peasants on collective farms. In the 1930s his terrors killed millions of people. Photographs, maps, and other illustrations augment the text.

2421. Dahl, Roald. *Going Solo.* Puffin, 2009. 208pp. Paper ISBN 978-0-14-241383-8. Grades 7 up.

See entry 2154.

2422. di Pasquale, Emanuel. *Cartwheel to the Moon: My Sicilian Childhood.* Illustrated by K. Dyble Thompson. Cricket, 2003. 64pp. ISBN 978-0-8126-2679-7. Grades 2–7.

The poet Emanuel di Pasquale grew up in Sicily in the 1940s and 1950s where he enjoyed the beauty of the mountains and the sea, took special excursions, followed religious and family rituals, and missed his dead father. The poems, arranged by season, evoke the beauty of the country. Illustrations enhance the text.

2423. Duberstein, John. *A Velvet Revolution: Vaclav Havel and the Fall of Communism.* (World Leaders) Morgan Reynolds, 2006. 208pp. ISBN 978-1-931798-85-3. Grades 8 up.

Vaclav Havel, a dissident writer of satirical plays, became the president of the Czech Republic from 1992 to 2002 after the end of the Communist regime. His ability to speak eloquently and his good looks propelled him into the position of leading his country in its first democratic government in many years. His childhood under the Nazis and then his adulthood under the Soviet Union led to his political activism against totalitarianism. Photographs and illustrations highlight the text. Bibliography and Web Sites.

2424. Elish, Dan. *Edmund Hillary: First to the Top.* (Great Explorations) Marshall Cavendish, 2006. 80pp. ISBN 978-0-7614-2224-2. Grades 5–9.

Sir Edmund Hillary (1919–2008) grew up in New Zealand where he decided he would climb Mount Everest. The author chronicles Hillary's preparations for the climb and his success in reaching the summit with the help of Sherpa Tenzing Norgay in 1953. Once at the top, they only stayed about fifteen minutes while Hillary took Norgay's photograph. Then Norgay left chocolates in the snow as an offering while Hillary left a cross. When they began their descent, they found that drifting snow had already covered their tracks, so they had to be as careful on the way down as they had on the way up. Maps, Photographs, Reproductions, Bibliography, Chronology, Further Reading, Notes, Web Sites, and Index.

2425. Ernaux, Annie. *Happening.* Translated by Tanya Leslie. Seven Stories, 2001. 95pp. ISBN 978-1-58322-256-0. Grades YA.

The daughter of working-class parents, Annie Ernaux accidentally became pregnant when she was 23 in 1963. She had to have an illegal abortion, and her hemorrhaging in a Paris dormitory almost killed her. She did not love her partner, and she wanted to stay in graduate school, so she felt she had no choice. She includes diary entries recorded during the experience as she reflects on it. She believes that any experience has the right to be recorded and remembered.

2426. Gelletly, Leeanne. *Gift of Imagination: The Story of Roald Dahl.* (World Writers) Morgan Reynolds, 2006. 160pp. ISBN 978-1-59935-026-4. Grades 9 up.

Roald Dahl (1916–1990) wrote children's books, but there is much more to tell of his life. He served in World War II, wrote adult novels, and was married to actress Patricia Neal. He grew up attending English boarding schools and spending his summers in Norway. Among his well-known books are *Charlie and the Chocolate Factory*. Photographs of friends and family enhance the text. Bibliography, Chronology, Notes, Web Sites, and Index.

2427. Greene, Meg. *Jane Goodall.* Greenwood, 2005. 146pp. ISBN 978-0-313-33139-8. Grades 9 up.

This biography of Jane Goodall (1934–) details her career as a primatologist researching chimpanzees in Gombe although she began her career working for the Leakey family. Her mother was a great influence while Jane was growing up in England and before she left to work in Africa. She has received numerous awards for her research and for her efforts for conservation. Photographs highlight the text. Bibliography, Chronology, and Index.

2428. Grimberg, Tina. *Out of Line: Growing Up Soviet.* Tundra, 2007. 117pp. ISBN 978-0-88776-803-3. Grades 7 up.

During the cold war in Kiev, Tina Grimberg lived with her close-knit family. They stood in long lines, lived in a cramped apartment, had little privacy, and relied on "connections" to avoid the endless bureaucracy. When she was 15, her "undesirable" family (she was Jewish) had the opportunity to leave the Soviet Union, but as they prepared to emigrate, other Russians call them traitors. She offers a view of world so important in the lives of older adults that no longer exists.

2429. Halilbegovich, Nadia. *My Childhood Under Fire: A Sarajevo Diary.* Kids Can, 2006. 120pp. ISBN 978-1-55337-797-9; 2008. paper ISBN 978-1-55453-267-4.

Nadja Halilbegovich, 12, endured the constant bombings and lack of supplies during the siege of Sarajevo during the Yugoslav war. She writes about it in her journal beginning on May 31, 1992. She laments the loss of her normal life before the war, her lack of contact with friends, her anger at the bombings, the deaths, scarcity of food and water, and the seeming indifference of other nations. When an explosion hits her building, she is injured just as she steps outside. Her family eventually escapes through a tunnel and goes to live with an American family in 1995. Photographs enhance the text.

2430. Haugen, Brenda. *Winston Churchill: British Soldier, Writer, Statesman.* (Signature Lives) Compass Point, 2006. 112pp. ISBN 978-0-7565-1582-9; paper ISBN 978-0-7565-1804-2. Grades 6–9.

See entry 1807.

2431. Hendra, Tony. *Father Joe: The Man Who Saved My Soul.* Random House, 2005. 304pp. Paper ISBN 978-0-8129-7234-4. Grades YA.

In 1955 Tony Hendra was 14 when he began a liaison with a married Catholic woman. Her husband discovered them and took Hendra to meet Father Joseph Warrillow, a Benedictine. Surprised that Father Joe thought the only sin to be selfishness, Hendra realized that Father Joe could be both a friend and a confessor, and his life changed. Throughout Hendra's career, he asked Father Joe for his advice. At first, Hendra wanted to join the order, but the priest convinced him to attend Cambridge, where he would perform with his friends John Cleese and Graham Chapman who became part of Monty Python. Hendra became a writer and the editor of *Spy* and *National Lampoon*, thinking that comedy was the best way to help others. He eventually married twice and had children, but he credits Father Joe's wisdom as the guiding force in his life. *New York Times Notable Books of the Year.*

2432. Henke, James. *Lennon Legend: An Illustrated Life of John Lennon.* Chronicle, 2003. 64pp. ISBN 978-0-8118-3517-6. Grades YA.

John Lennon (1940–1980) was a member of "The Beatles," the famous music group that became known during the 1960s. Henke presents Lennon's lyrics and other documents, along with photographs and memorabilia from his wife, Yoko Ono. Accompanying this commemorative work that has the support of the Lennon estate is a one-hour compact disc of Lennon interviews. Additionally, forty facsimiles of documents, such as a report card from his youth, can be removed and handled from pockets in the volume.

2433. Kalman, Bobbie. *Refugee Child: My Memories of the 1956 Hungarian Revolution.* Illustrated by Barbara Bedell. Crabtree, 2006. 223pp. ISBN 978-0-7787-2760-6. Grades 3–6.

At the age of 9 Kalman had to escape with her family from Hungary during the Revolution of 1956. They went to Austria. They hated to leave her grandparents but had no choice. The narrative covers Hungary's history from 1848 to 1956 and its life under Communist rule. Kalman also includes background about her own life as a children's book author. Photographs and illustrations highlight the text. Bibliography and Index.

2434. Kennedy, Pagan. *The First Man-Made Man: The Story of Two Sex Changes, One Love Affair, and a Twentieth-Century Medical Revolution.* Bloomsbury, 2007. 224pp. ISBN 978-1-59691-015-7; paper ISBN 978-1-59691-016-4. Grades YA.

While a woman, Michael Dillon felt like a man trapped in a woman's body. And Roberta Crowell felt like a woman trapped in a man's body. Therefore, they risked everything to change gender. They both had to practice deception, keep secrets, be endlessly humiliated, and face unimaginable problems in their daily lives while they were making the transition. Laura Dillon attended Oxford and became a published author before becoming Michael Dillon. She began to experiment with testosterone and then met Dr. Gillies, a plastic surgeon who was able to change Dillon's anatomy after several surgeries. When Michael met Roberta Crowell in 1949, he felt comfortable because she had been changing from a man into a woman. Dillon traveled to India to study Buddhism and died a pauper after finding happiness with Tibetan monks. His notebooks and memoirs reveal thoughtful insights on the nature of sex and gender.

2435. Kingsland, Rosemary. *The Secret Life of a Schoolgirl: A Memoir.* Three Rivers, 2004. 343pp. Paper ISBN 978-1-4000-5304-9. Grades YA.

Born in Jutogh, in the Indian Himalayas, as the Raj was dying in 1941, Rosemary Kingsland visited England once when she was 5 years old and moved there permanently when she was 7. Her family, including her mother, father, and two siblings, lived with her grandmother in Brighton, but after an argument between her father and her uncle, they moved to Wimbledon. After Kingsland found a dead baby on the local common, they moved to a small village in Surrey, where her father had an affair with the vicar's wife. Kingsland was most upset about the situation when her father gave her favorite doll to the vicar's wife's daughter. Another move found them in Guildford, close to London, before her sister Gracie was born. Distressed by her father's alcoholism and continued infidelity, she left a party and went to a cafe nearby. There she met Richard Burton, 29, an actor she had seen in *Under Milkwood* several months before. She immediately fell in love with him, and her memoir describes the wonder of a first love, especially with someone so intense.

2436. Kittinger, Jo S. *Jane Goodall.* Children's, 2005. 24pp. ISBN 978-0-516249-40-7. Grades 1–2.

Jane Goodall (1934–) has worked extensively with chimpanzees in Africa. This simple text describes her work there. Photographs enhance the text. Glossary, Further Reading, Web Sites, and Index.

2437. Klein, Adam G. *Pablo Picasso.* (Great Artists) Checkerboard, 2006. 32pp. ISBN 978-1-59679-733-8. Grades 2–5.

See entry 2190.

2438. Klein, Adam G. *Salvador Dalí.* (Great Artists) Checkerboard, 2006. 32pp. ISBN 978-1-59679-728-4. Grades 2–5.

See entry 2191.

2439. Landmann, Bimba. *I Am Marc Chagall.* Illustrated by author. Eerdmans, 2006. 40pp. ISBN 978-0-8028-5305-9. Grades 2–5.

See entry 1822.

2440. McNeese, Tim. *Pablo Picasso.* (Great Hispanic Heritage) Chelsea House, 2006. 122pp. ISBN 978-0-7910-8843-2. Grades 8 up.

See entry 1827.

2441. O'Halloran, Maura. *Pure Heart: Enlightened Mind.* Illustrated by Elizabeth O'Halloran. Wisdom, 2007. 311pp. Paper ISBN 978-0-8617-1283-0. Grades YA.

Maura O'Halloran took a degree in mathematical economics and sociology at Trinity College, Dublin, Ireland, and then left for America where she decided to follow the demanding monastic life of Buddhism. In her journal and letters, she does not answer or even question why she made these decisions. Instead, she describes this new life.

2442. Partridge, Elizabeth. *John Lennon: All I Want Is the Truth.* Viking, 2005. 240pp. ISBN 978-0-670-05954-6. Grades 9 up.

This biography of John Lennon (1940–1980) covers his life and includes many anecdotes that reveal his character. His aunt Mini disapproved of him playing the guitar because one could not make a living at it. Lennon did try to find comfort away from the public's eye through "booze, pills, and joints." Partridge places Lennon in the context of his times, which include the music of Elvis Presley, Chuck Berry, and Little Richard, along with the Vietnam War, Watergate, and the civil rights movement. Photographs highlight the text. Bibliography and Index. *Great Lakes Children's Book Award* (Michigan) nomination, *Booklist Editors' Choice, Michael L. Printz Award, School Library Journal Best Children's Books, Bulletin Blue Ribbon, Kirkus Reviews Editor's Choice,* and Capitol Choices Noteworthy Titles *(Washington, D.C.).*

2443. Polcovar, Jane. *Rosalind Franklin and the Structure of Life.* Morgan Reynolds, 2006. 144pp. ISBN 978-1-59935-022-6. Grades 8 up.

See entry 2232.

2444. Radzinsky, Edvard. *Stalin: The First In-Depth Biography Based on Explosive New Documents from Russia's Secret Archives.* Anchor, 1997. 607pp. Paper ISBN 978-0-385-47954-7. Grades YA.

See entry 2235.

2445. Rosner, Bernat, Frederic C. Tubach, and Sally Patterson Tubach. *An Uncommon Friendship: From Opposite Sides of the Holocaust.* University of California, 2001. 209pp. ISBN 978-0-52022-531-2; 2002. paper ISBN 978-0-52023-689-9. Grades YA.

Bernat Rosner (1932–) and Frederic Tubach (1930–) met in California in 1983. Rosner was born a Hungarian Jew and was sent to Auschwitz-Birkenau concentration camp when he was 12. Tubach joined the Jungvolk and grew up the son of a German army officer, suffering hunger and air raids during the war. As they discussed their respective childhoods, they realized that Rosner needed to come to terms with his past while Tubach needed redemption.

2446. Sacks, Oliver. *Uncle Tungsten: Memories of a Chemical Boyhood.* Vintage, 2002. 352pp. Paper ISBN 978-0-375-70404-8. Grades YA.

Oliver Sacks had many fascinations as a child, before he became a distinguished neurologist and bestselling writer. He especially liked loud and smelly chemical reactions, squids, cuttlefish, photography, the periodic table, and H. G. Wells. His mother was a surgeon who showed him how to dissect a human when he was 14. His father was a family doctor who took him on house calls, and his Uncle Dave, nicknamed "Uncle Tungsten," owned a factory that produced tungsten-filament light bulbs. During the London Blitz of World War II he had to attend a sadistic boarding school, but he was able to return home to the excitement he found there.

2447. Sage, Lorna. *Bad Blood.* Perennial, 2003. 288pp. Paper ISBN 978-0-06-093808-6. Grades YA.

Lorna Sage describes her quarrelsome maternal grandparents in this biography about growing up in post-World War II Wales that carefully destroys any perceived myths about idyllic British life in the country. The anti-intellectual rural populace in her tiny town of Hanmer frowned on education because, among other things, it taught proper manners. Her father was a soldier and her mother had grown up in a home with a philandering vicar father; Sage recounts the family's horrible fights and the time she fell down the steps and knocked out her front teeth as a result of trying to intervene. She won a scholarship to study at Durham University and became a literary critic, a distance that allowed her to see her life with a biting humor and reality. *Whitbread Biography Award* and *Editors' Choice New York Times Book Review.*

2448. Samuel, Wolfgang W. E. *German Boy: A Refugee's Story.* University of Mississippi, 2000. 357pp. ISBN 978-1-57806-274-4; Broadway, 2001. paper ISBN 978-0-7679-0824-5. Grades YA.

When Samuel was 10, he, his sister, and his mother were post-World War II German refugees fleeing from their home in Sagan and the advancing Russian army. They lived in refugee camps filled with disease and squalor and were offered no food. Under the Communists at his grandparents' home in Strasburg, they had to face totalitarianism, a situation they avoided under the Nazis. His mother had to exchange sex for food to feed them. Their father, a former Luftwaffe officer, found them and got them transported to a barracks in the American zone. His parents divorced, his mother married a U.S. Army sergeant, and Samuel moved with them to the United States before becoming a career Air Force officer. Index. *School Library Journal Best Adult Books for Young Adults.*

2449. Say, Allen. *El Chino.* Illustrated by author. Walter Lorraine, 1990. 32pp. ISBN 978-0-395-52023-9; 1996. paper ISBN 978-0-395-77875-3. Grades 2–5.

Bill Wong, a Chinese American, became a famous bullfighter in Spain. Say tells his story using the first-person to give a sense of immediacy to Wong's experiences as he won over the Spanish crowd through his exploits with the bull. Say's watercolors give impact to the text. *Bulletin Blue Ribbon.*

2450. Shtern, Ludmila. *Leaving Leningrad.* (Brandeis Series on Jewish Women) Brandeis University, 2001. 176pp. ISBN 978-1-58465-100-0. Grades YA.

Ludmila Shtern grew up in Leningrad, was educated as a geologist, and emigrated to the United States in 1975 with her husband and daughter. She entertains with her stories about both her intellectual family in the Soviet Union and her experiences in the United States trying to get a job. She eventually became a writer and radio host in the United States. She found many similarities in communist and capitalist life as well as the expected differences.

2451. Sís, Peter. *The Wall: Growing Up Behind the Iron Curtain.* Illustrated by author. Frances Foster, 2007. 56pp. ISBN 978-0-374-34701-7. Grades 4 up.

This account of Sís's youth in the Communist city of Prague, Czechoslovakia, from 1954 to 1973 contains the things that influenced his life, from music to art. He learned early that the government refused to offer the facts about some things when snippets of information about music groups, poets, and athletes penetrated the Iron Curtain. He relished getting to the other side of the "wall" because he had to practice his art in secret. His black-and-white illustrations accented with red to represent the Communist regime complement his text. He ends with his feelings for the arts expressed in full color. *Caldecott Honor, Booklist Editors' Choice, Parents Choice Award, Publishers Weekly Best Books, Horn Book Fanfare, Boston Globe/Horn Book Award Honor, American Library Association Notable Children's Books, School Library Journal Best Books for Children, Voice of Youth Advocates Nonfiction Honor, Bulletin Blue Ribbon,* and *Robert F. Sibert Award.*

2452. Spitz, Bob. *Yeah! Yeah! Yeah! The Beatles, Beatlemania, and the Music That Changed the World.* Little, Brown, 2007. 234pp. ISBN 978-0-316-11555-1. Grades 5–8.

This collective biography of the individuals in "The Beatles" begins when John Lennon and Paul McCartney met at a church festival as teenagers in 1957. It ends when Paul decided to leave the group in 1970. It offers background information about each member of the group, their families, and their talent. It discusses their songs with anecdotes discussing the inception of some of them. The group fit into an important musical period during which they made their own indelible mark. Discography, Bibliography, and Index. *Voice of Youth Advocates Nonfiction Honor List.*

2453. Squires, Claire. *Philip Pullman, Master Storyteller: A Guide to the Worlds of His Dark Materials.* Continuum, 2006. 207pp. ISBN 978-0-8264-2764-9; paper ISBN 978-0-8264-1716-9. Grades 8 up.

The British author Philip Pullman has published a trilogy known as His Dark Materials, which has become renowned in the United States. The three books are *The Subtle Knife, The Amber Spyglass*, and *The Golden Compass*. Squires examines all aspects of the three novels including plot, character, and intertextual criticism, and includes a chapter on Pullman's other writings. Bibliography and Index.

2454. Stefoff, Rebecca. *Lech Walesa: The Road to Democracy.* (Great Lives) Fawcett, 1992. 131pp. Paper ISBN 978-0-449-90625-5. Grades YA.

Stefoff focuses on the events in Lech Walesa's (b. 1943) life since 1980, after the Gdansk, Poland, strike that he started. The book includes chapters on his early years and a brief history of Poland, as well as an explanation of the importance of Walesa's contributions to thwarting communist rule in his country.

2455. Stuchner, Joan Betty. *Josephine's Dream.* Illustrated by Chantelle Walther. Silver Leaf, 2008. Unpaged. ISBN 978-1-934393-04-8. Grades K–2.

See entry 2043.

2456. Venezia, Mike. *The Beatles.* Illustrated by author. (Getting to Know the World's Greatest Composers) Children's Press, 1997. 32pp. ISBN 978-0-516-20310-2; paper ISBN 978-0-516-26147-8. Grades K–5.

From around 1964 to 1970, the world's most popular musical group was from Liverpool, England, and called itself "The Beatles." The four men who made up the group had never formally studied music; they taught themselves music as they played the songs they wrote. The four men were John Lennon, Paul McCartney, George Harrison, and Ringo Starr (whose real name is Richard Starkey). People still listen to their music. Illustrations and photographs highlight the text.

2457. Venezia, Mike. *Marc Chagall.* Illustrated by author. (Getting to Know the World's Greatest Artists) Children's Press, 2000. 32pp. ISBN 978-0-516-21055-1; paper ISBN 978-0-516-27041-8. Grades K–5.

See entry 1870.

2458. Venezia, Mike. *Picasso.* Illustrated by author. (Getting to Know the World's Greatest Artists) Children's Press, 1988. 32pp. ISBN 978-0-516-02271-0; paper ISBN 978-0-516-42271-8. Grades K–5.

See entry 1875.

2459. Venezia, Mike. *Salvador Dalí.* Illustrated by author. (Getting to Know the World's Greatest Artists) Children's Press, 1993. 32pp. ISBN 978-0-516-02296-3; paper ISBN 978-0-516-42296-1. Grades K–5.

See entry 2267.

2460. Waxman, Laura Hamilton. *Jane Goodall.* (History Makers Bios) Lerner, 2007. 48pp. ISBN 978-0-8225-7610-5. Grades 3–5.

Jane Goodall (1934–), an animal lover, left her home in England to live in Africa. There she studied chimpanzees and became an expert, contributing much to our understanding of these animals. Illustrations highlight the text. Bibliography, Further Reading, Glossary, Maps, Time line, Web Sites, and Index.

2461. Wenzel, Angela. *The Mad, Mad, Mad World of Salvador Dalí.* Translated by Rosie Jackson. Prestel, 2003. 28pp. ISBN 978-3-791329-44-4. Grades 5–8.

See entry 2273.

Graphic Novels, Biographies, and Histories

2462. Abadzis, Nick. *Laika.* First Second, 2007. 208pp. Paper ISBN 978-1-59643-101-0. Grades 7 up.

Laika was the dog that flew in *Sputnik II* during the cold war conflicts between the United States and the Soviet Union around 1957. The Gulag prisoner Korelev becomes the Chief Designer of the satellite and has to send up an animal within one month. She is a stray who is sent to the Institute of Aviation Medicine where researchers notice her ability to withstand g-forces and lack of gravity; therefore, she is the obvious choice to go to space. Plans do not include her survival, and researchers regret this decision. *Kirkus Reviews Editor's Choice.*

2463. Krohn, Katherine. *Jane Goodall: Animal Scientist.* Illustrated by Cynthia Martin and Anne Timmons. (Graphic Biographies) Graphic Library, 2006. 32pp. ISBN 978-0-7368-5485-6; paper ISBN 978-0-7368-6885-3. Grades 3–5.

This short graphic biography of Jane Goodall (1934–) relates the story of her life as a researcher of chimpanzees in Tanzania and her respect for the wild. A yellow background sets direct quotes from Goodall apart from the fictional aspect of the narration. Web Sites.

2464. Mainardi, Alessandro. *The Life of John Paul II . . . in Comics.* Illustrated by Werner Maresta. Papercutz, 2006. 96pp. ISBN 978-1-59707-039-3; paper ISBN 978-1-59707-057-7. Grades 6–10.

John Paul II (1920–2005), or Karol Wojtyla, became one of Catholicism's most beloved popes. Excerpts from John Paul's writings and other sources reveal his earlier life before he became the pope as well as after. He had a difficult life in Poland but encourages young people to do all that they can and be all that they can. The full color graphic art augments the text.

2465. Maslov, Nikolai. *Siberia.* Illustrated by author. Translated by Blake Ferris and Lisa Barocas Anderson. Soft Skull, 2006. 98pp. Paper ISBN 978-1-933368-03-0. Grades 9 up.

This graphic biography presents the life story of its author, Nikolai Maslov. Maslov worked as a night watchman in Moscow, and when a French editor came by, Maslov handed him pages from his work. The editor gave Maslov an advance, and he was able to tell the story of his youth in Siberia in the 1950s, his army service in Mongolia in the 1970s, and his subsequent fall into despair and alcoholism. In 1971 when Maslov was 17, he left home to work and was drafted. After being rejected by the graphic arts institute, he barely survived the death of his brother. But with pencil-rendered panels he reveals life in the Soviet Union in the years before the fall of the Berlin Wall.

2466. Sacco, Joe. *Safe Area Gorazde: The War in Eastern Bosnia, 1992–1995.* Fantagraphics, 2002. 240pp. Paper ISBN 978-1-56097-470-3. Grades 9 up.

During the war in the former Yugoslavia, Orthodox Christian Bosnian Serbs besieged the Muslim enclave of Gorazde. Sacco went into Gorazde for four months while the Muslims were still inside without electricity or running water. With Muslim school teacher Edin, who served as his translator, Sacco interviewed the townspeople to hear how they coped with the shelling and hunger when their neighbors had betrayed them. Edin admits to Sacco that he can not guess why his former friends would burn down his house. The only way one could ever know why the Serbs acted so viciously would be to ask them directly.

2467. Satrapi, Marjane. *Persepolis 2: The Story of a Return.* Translated by Anjali Singh. Pantheon, 2004. 187pp. ISBN 978-0-375-42288-1; 2005. paper ISBN 978-0-375-71466-5. Grades 7 up.

This graphic biography begins after Satrapi, 14, has left Iran to attend school in Vienna. Differences in her life in the West are exciting as she makes new friends, deals drugs for a boyfriend, and eventually lives in the streets for three months. She returns home, a liberated 18-year-old, marries, and finishes art school. The marriage does not give her the freedom she expects, and her homeland is no longer familiar. She decides to divorce and move to France, with her parents' blessings. The second volume in this autobiography. *Booklist Editors' Choice* and *School Library Journal Best Adult Books for Young Adults.*

DVDs

2468. *The Communist Challenge.* Hawkhill, 2006. 27 min. ISBN 978-1-55979-201-1. Grades 9 up.

This DVD describes the rise and fall of communism during the 20th century while democracy survived. It looks at the history of communism from its beginnings in the Russian Revolution of 1917 and the differing attitudes communism has spawned—from totalitarian states and brutal rulers to Socialist and Social Democratic political parties in western Europe. Communism has also influenced respected figures who have accomplished much for humanity, including Martin Luther King, Nelson Mandela, and Franklin Delano Roosevelt. The emphasis, however, is on the Soviet Union and how the Communist Manifesto of 1848 by Karl Marx and Friedrich Engels was distorted and changed. It concludes with the fall of the Soviet Union under Mikhail Gorbachev in 1989.

2469. *Eternal Memory: Voices from the Great Terror.* Narrated by Meryl Streep. National Film Network, 2006. 81 min. ISBN 978-0-8026-0321-0. Grades YA.

See entry 2294.

2470. *Germany: Facing the Past.* (Global Connections) Chip Taylor Communications, 2001. 20 min. Grades 7 up.

Since East and West Germany have united, a number of changes have occurred: Jews have returned with special immigrant privileges such as resident permits, food/work permits, free schooling for their children, housing, and lessons in German language. Even so, organizations of a neo-nazi culture still exist. Some anti-Semitic Germans who feel they are losing jobs to Jews have joined nationalistic political groups such as the NPD and committed racial violence.

2471. *John Paul the Great: The Pope Who Made History.* Janson Media, 2007. 1 hr. ISBN 978-1-56839-292-3. Grades 9 up.

The Polish Karol Jósef Wojty?a (1920–2005) became Pope John Paul II in 1986 and served Catholics from the Vatican for twenty-seven years. He had admirers from different faiths for his compassion and kindness, and influenced world events, including the fall of Soviet totalitarianism.

2472. *Mother Teresa: Woman of Compassion.* (Great Souls) Vision Video, 2005. 56 min. Grades 9 up.

Mother Teresa of Calcutta, Agnes Gonxha Bojaxhiu (1910–1997), grew up in Skopje, Macedonia, raised by her mother after her father died. She left home on September 26, 1928, and never saw her mother or sister again. She became fascinated by mission work in India, even though she had never seen a nun, and joined the Sisters of Loreto, going first to Ireland before teaching school in India. After she served the poor, Pope Pius XII allowed her to leave her order, and she established the Missionaries of Charity in 1950, a mission that circled the globe. In 1979 she received the Nobel Peace Prize and when she died in 1997 the nation of India gave her a state funeral. Anecdotes from several public figures and filming in France, Macedonia, and England enhance the production.

2473. *The Windsors: A Royal Family.* WGBH, 2002. 2 DVDs; 4 hrs. ISBN 978-1-59375-157-9. Grades 8 up.

    See entry 1899.

Compact Discs

2474. Almond, David. *The Fire-Eaters.* Narrated by Daniel Gerroll. Listening Library, 2004. 4 CDs; 72 min. ea. ISBN 978-1-4000-8563-7. Grades 7 up.

    See entry 2332.

2475. Armstrong, Karen. *The Spiral Staircase: My Climb Out of Darkness.* Narrated by Karen Armstrong. HarperAudio, 2004. 5 CDs. ISBN 978-0-06-059438-1. Grades YA.

    See entry 2416.

2476. Baccalario, Pierdomenico. *The Long-Lost Map.* Narrated by Michael Page. (Ulysses Moore) Brillance Audio, 2006. 4 CDs; 5 hrs. ISBN 978-1-4233-1327-4. Grades 4–6.

    See entry 317.

2477. Mitchell, David. *Black Swan Green.* Narrated by Kirby Heybourne. Random House Audio, 2006. 7 CDs. ISBN 978-0-7393-3248-1. Grades YA.

    See entry 2373.

2478. Rees, Celia. *The Wish House.* Narrated by Christopher Cazenove. Listening Library, 2007. 4 CDs; 4:59 hrs. ISBN 978-0-7393-4863-5. Grades 9 up.

    See entry 2379.

2479. Schlink, Bernard. *The Reader.* Narrated by Campbell Scott. Translated by Carol Brown Janeway. Random House, 2008. 4 CDs; 4.5 hrs. ISBN 978-0-7393-7595-2. Grades YA.

    See entry 2381.

AFGHANISTAN AND THE INDIAN SUBCONTINENT

Historical Fiction and Fantasy

2480. Ali, Thalassa. *Companions of Paradise.* Bantam, 2007. 332pp. Paper ISBN 978-0-533-38178-8. Grades YA.

After the first two novels of the Paradise Trilogy, *A Singular Hostage* and *A Beggar at the Gate*, Englishwoman Mariana Givens lives within the British cantonment in Kabul during 1841. Her Muslim husband, Hassan Ali Khan, thwarts an assassination attempt, and Mariana has had to leave Lahore, her adopted home. The English society where she lives does not recognize her marriage and forces suitors and societal obligations on her. She does not know if her Indian husband still loves her, or if he considers their marriage valid. The surrounding tensions between the British and the Afghans highlight Mariana's interior struggle.

2481. Ali, Thalassa. *A Singular Hostage.* Bantam, 2002. 353pp. Paper ISBN 978-0-553-38176-4. Grades YA.

In 1838 Mariana Givens has come to find a husband among the British officers in India, but learns Urdu from a Muslim munshi and becomes the translator for Governor-General Lord Auckland's sisters. She travels with them for 1,200 miles to Punjab for a meeting with the ailing Maharajah Ranjit Singh, a man whose signature the British need on a treaty. Singh makes hostages of his courtiers' children so they will remain loyal to him, and thinks that one of the children, Saboor, has inherited the Sufi mystical powers of his grandfather and will heal him. After Singh's other wives poison Saboor's mother out of jealously, Saboor is kidnapped from the palace. His rescuers bring him to Mariana, and after becoming attached to the child, she works to return him to his father, Hassan Sahib.

2482. Bosse, Malcolm. *Tusk and Stone.* Front Street, 1991. 256pp. ISBN 978-1-886910-01-0; 2004 paper ISBN 978-1-886910-74-4. Grades 6 up.

As Arjun travels across India in the 7th century, bandits attack the caravan, kill people, kidnap his sister, and drug him before selling him into the army. Arjun begins to rebuild his life, saying that he will serve those well who purchased him. He rises in the military to become an elephant handler and then a mounted soldier. His Brahmin pride wins over his concept of karma when he is a warrior and faces a rival who almost destroys him. Then he must again rebuild his life, this time as a stonecutter and carver. In that profession he becomes introspective about his spiritual beliefs. *State Book Award* (Washington).

2483. Davidar, David. *The House of Blue Mangoes.* Perennial, 2003. 512pp. Paper ISBN 978-0-06-093678-5. Grades YA.

In 1899 Solomon Dorai, head of the Indian village of Chevathar, tries to save his people but uses ways damaging to his family. When Solomon's son becomes involved with a radical terrorist group, his second son, Daniel, makes a cosmetic fortune and takes over the family. When British rule ends, Daniel's son, Kannan, breaks with tradition to marry, and becomes a tea planter. Throughout, the story and customs of India through the first half of the 20th century are thoughtful and informative.

2484. Ellis, Deborah. *Parvana's Journey.* Groundwood, 2003. 199pp. Paper ISBN 978-0-8889-9519-3. Grades YA.

Parvana, 13, must fend for herself after her father's death. She dresses as a boy and goes with other children to locate her family inside the war zone of Afghanistan, in this sequel to *The Breadwinner*. During her search, she takes a baby, the only survivor in a destroyed town; meets Asif, who has lost a leg; and befriends Leila, 8, who believes her magical powers will protect her from land mines. The four join a long line of refugees and finally reach a camp. The family she finds is not the one she was looking for, but she must scavenge with the new one as they try to survive. *Garden State Teen Book Award* (New Jersey) nomination, *Teen Book Award* (Rhode Island) nomination, and *Indian Paintbrush* (Wyoming) nomination.

2485. Farooki, Roopa. *Bitter Sweets.* St. Martin's, 2007. 352pp. ISBN 978-0-312-36052-8; Griffin, 2008. paper ISBN 978-0-312-38206-3. Grades YA.

When Ricky-Rashid Karim, a westernized scholar, marries Henna in India, he immediately discovers that she is not an intelligent 17-year-old, but a lazy, boring 14-year-old. He refuses to consummate the union for several years, but then Shona is born and grows up. She elopes with Parvez, a Pakistani, and moves to London. Her father travels there on business, and he meets Verity, a shy English woman with whom he thinks he could be happy. The family of Rashid, Henna, and Shona continue to deceive each other in myriad ways until Shona, in mid-life, has to decide whether to continue the deceptions or to face the truth.

2486. Gavin, Jamila. *The Blood Stone.* Farrar, 2005. 352pp. ISBN 978-0-374-30846-9. Grades 7 up.

See entry 1079.

2487. Hosseini, Khaled. *The Kite Runner.* Riverhead, 2003. ISBN 978-1-57322-245-7; 2007 paper ISBN 978-1-59448-177-2. Grades YA.

During the 1970s in Kabul, Afghanistan, the Pashtun Amir and the son of his father's Hazara servant, Hassan, grow up as close friends. Amir wants his father's approval, and the one way to earn it would be to win the annual kite-fighting tournament. On the day he wins the contest, he betrays Hassan by doing nothing when he sees him assaulted by a gang. Amir suffers much guilt for his inaction. When the Russians invade the country, Hassan and his father escape to the United States. Eventually Amir returns to Afghanistan where he rescues Hassan's son Sohrab from the Taliban. What he discovers in this return trip and how he responds help redeem him. *Alex Awards, Peach Award* (Georgia) nomination, *School Library Journal Best Adult Books for High School Students, Young Reader's Choice Award* (Pennsylvania) nomination, *Eliot Rosewater Award* (Indiana) nomination, *High School Book Award* (Iowa) nomination, *American Library Association Notable Books Award*, and *Original Voices Award*.

2488. Hosseini, Khaled. *A Thousand Splendid Suns.* Riverhead, 2005. 372pp. ISBN 978-1-59448-950-1; 2008. paper ISBN 978-1-59448-385-1. Grades YA.

Miriam, the illegitimate daughter of a maid and a businessman becomes the wife of Rasheed, a man of 45, in an arranged marriage when she is 15. Another young woman, Leila, is born to educated Kabul parents the night the Communists invade Afghanistan. She meets Tariq, a boy who has lost a leg in an explosion before Tariq and his family flee to Pakistan when the Communists and mujahideen make Kabul unsafe. Leila ends up at the house of Rasheed and Miriam where she must make a terrible choice for her future. She becomes the second wife of Miriam's husband, who bitterly resents her until the two can form a bond.

2489. Lasky, Kathryn. *Jahanara: Princess of Princesses, India, 1627.* (Royal Diaries) Scholastic, 2002. 186pp. ISBN 978-0-439-22350-8. Grades 4–8.

In 1627 Princess Jahanara, 14, the first daughter of the favorite wife of Shah Jahan in India's Moghul Dynasty, writes in her diary. She mentions all of the happenings that she observes from the *purdah*, the secluded world within her father's harem. She notes that they have birthday weigh-ins and that her family moves from one estate to another. She also mentions the weddings, the battles, and the political intrigues swirling around her. Shah Jahan built the Taj Mahal for his wife. Photographs enhance the text. Glossary and Note.

2490. Noyes, Deborah. *When I Met the Wolf Girls.* Illustrated by August Hall. Houghton Mifflin Harcourt, 2007. 40pp. ISBN 978-0-618-60567-5. Grades K–3.

In 1920 Bulu becomes annoyed with the attention that two new girls, Amala and Kamala, are getting from Rev. Singh, the man who runs her orphanage. Wolves had raised the two girls, and they know only to eat on their knees, lick their plates like dogs, move around on all fours, and snarl when Bulu attempts to be friendly. Then Amala dies, and Bulu tries to comfort the lonely girl by teaching her to talk. Illustrations augment the text. Note.

2491. Scott, Paul. *The Day of the Scorpion.* (Raj Quartet) University of Chicago, 1998. 512pp. Paper ISBN 978-0-226-74341-7. Grades YA.

While their father is a prisoner-of-war in World War II, Susan and Sarah Layton live in Pankot, India. Susan marries, has a child, and becomes a widow, a situation with which she is unable to cope. As Sarah watches Susan and those around her, she meets Merrick, a man who imprisoned a British woman's Indian lover on false premises. She accepts him even with his faults. This is the second volume in the Raj Quartet.

2492. Scott, Paul. *A Division of the Spoils.* (Raj Quartet) University of Chicago, 1998. 640pp. Paper ISBN 978-0-226-74344-8. Grades YA.

After World War II ends, Sikhs, Muslims, and Hindus in India begin murdering each other as the British vote to leave. Soldiers who have spent their careers in India have to readjust to a different situation, as do their wives, whose social positions will change when they return to Britain. Sarah and Susan Layton's friends and father are some of those with unexpected upheavals in their lives. Susan's second husband has spent his life destroying the potential for personal success and self-esteem in many Indian lives, and he has difficulty with his loss of power and control. This is the final volume in the Raj Quartet.

2493. Scott, Paul. *The Jewel in the Crown.* (Raj Quartet) University of Chicago, 1998. 480pp. Paper ISBN 978-0-226-74340-0. Grades YA.

In August 1942 the liberal and conservative forces among the British and Indian residents in Mayapore, India, battle when the British police accuse Indians of raping a young woman. As various stories come to light, the reader sees that the society cannot tolerate a sexual relationship between an Indian and a British subject. This is the first of four volumes in the Raj Quartet.

2494. Scott, Paul. *The Towers of Silence.* (Raj Quartet) University of Chicago, 1998. 400pp. Paper ISBN 978-0-226-74343-1. Grades YA.

In 1939 Barbie retires from the Protestant children's mission in Rampur, India, and goes to live with Susan and Sarah Layton's grandmother in Pankot. She becomes distressed enough with the situations that she observes after Mabel's death that she herself dies at the end of the war in 1945. She cannot tolerate what has happened to the people in the country. This is volume 3 in the Raj Quartet.

2495. Selvadurai, Shyam. *Swimming in the Monsoon Sea.* Tundra, 2007. 224pp. Paper ISBN 978-0-8877-6834-7. Grades YA.

In Colombo, Sri Lanka, during 1980, Amrith De Alwis, 14, expects to learn typing and to prepare for the upcoming drama contest. He has been living with Aunty Bundle, his mother's best friend; her husband, Uncle Lucky; and their family since his mother's death eight years before. The circumstances surrounding his mother's marriage to his alcoholic father, never explained to him, have kept the extended family away from them. When Amrith's cousin Niresh, 16, arrives with his father from Canada to sell some property, Amrith falls in love with him and becomes jealous when Niresh pays more attention to Aunty Bundle's daughters. Thus he must also deal with his sexuality during this same summer.

2496. Sheth, Kashmira. *Keeping Corner.* Hyperion, 2007. 281pp. ISBN 978-0-7868-3859-2. Grades 6–9.

In 1918, after being married for 3 years, Leela, 12, looks forward to moving to her *anu*, the time when she will move into her Indian husband's home. She wears bright clothes and jewels and expects a happy life. But he is suddenly killed, and she must shave her head, wear plain clothes, and "keep corner," not go outside for a year. She can never marry and will be shunned by her neighbors as a widow. Only her brother, influenced by the recent teachings of the man speaking about self-determination, Mohandas Gandhi, has the nerve to buck the tradition of the area, and he persuades the family to get a tutor for Leela so that she might go away and become educated. Leela's assignment, as she learns to write, is to record all that happens around her during her year of keeping corner.

2497. Sundaresan, Indu. *The Twentieth Wife.* Washington Square, 2003. 320pp. Paper ISBN 978-0-7434-2818-7. Grades YA.

Mehrunnisa, daughter of a Persian refugee to India, becomes the twentieth wife of the Mughal Emperor Jahangir. When one of his wives, the Empress Ruqayya, saw her at age 8, she had Mehrunnisa become her attendant at court. Mehrunnisa saw Salim— later to become Jahangir—marry another, and she fell in love with him. Some years later, he chose her and adored her. Although she never had a son, she became a powerful woman who ruled the empire in his name for fifteen years.

2498. Venkatraman, Padma. *Climbing the Stairs.* Putnam, 2008. 256pp. ISBN 978-0-399-24746-0. Grades 7–9.

When Vidya is 15 in 1941, her physician father becomes brain damaged in a nonviolent protest march into which she inadvertently took him. She, her older brother, and her mother have to move from Bombay to their grandfather's household in Madras where men and women traditionally separate. The women, only interested in marriage and serving their husbands, treat Vidya disdainfully, and Vidya misses her school and friends. Soon she finds her grandfather's library and sneaks into it to read. Her grandfather discovers her, and he approves. Then he agrees to her college education after her brother, Kitta, runs off to fight in World War II. At the same time, a young man in the household, Raman, and Vidya become attracted to each other. *Notable Trade Books in the Field of Social Studies.*

History

2499. Arnold, Caroline, and Madeleine Comora. *Taj Mahal.* Illustrated by Rahul Bhushan. Carolrhoda, 2007. 32pp. ISBN 978-0-7613-2609-0. Grades 4–8.

This picture book focuses on the love that built the Taj Mahal in India rather than the architecture of the structure. While teenagers, Prince Khurram and the daughter of a court official, Arjumand, meet. They have a secret romance and are married. They rule as Shah Jahan and Mumtaz Mahal until she dies in childbirth in 1631. To honor his love for her and her memory, Shah Jahan has the Taj Mahal built as her mausoleum. Further Reading.

2500. Emadi, Hafizullah. *Culture and Customs of Afghanistan.* Greenwood, 2005. 252pp. ISBN 978-0-313-33089-6. Grades 9 up.

This history of social customs in Afghanistan offers background on a country that fills today's news. Among the topics covered are customs in the various regions of the country, the Soviet occupation, the civil war, the occupation by the Taliban, and the changes since they took over, were quelled, and then came back to the fore in the country. The seven chapters cover the Land, People, and History; Religion and Religious Thought; Literature and the Arts; Architecture, Housing, and Settlements; Social Customs, Cuisine, and Traditional Dress; Family, Women, and Gender Issues; and Lifestyles, Media, and Education. Photographs highlight the text. Bibliography, Glossary, Chronology, Notes, and Index.

2501. Ewans, Martin R. *Afghanistan: A Short History of Its People and Politics.* HarperCollins, 2002. 256pp. Paper ISBN 978-0-06-050508-0. Grades YA.

Afghanistan became Muslim when Arab armies brought Islam in 7th century. Since that time through the 18th century, many invasions, including Genghis Khan and Timur, and tribal conflicts led to the creation of the Afghan empire. In the 19th and early 20th centuries, Britain and Russia battled to gain the country and establish supremacy in Central Asia. In 1919 Afghanistan declared independence and leaders from Daoud to Mullah Omar weakly led. However, a Communist coup overthrew the government in the 1970s, and the Soviets invaded in 1979. When opponents forced the Soviets out in the late 1980s, Afghanistan's resulting civil war destroyed the remaining remnants of religious unity. The Taliban came to power as a result. Photographs, Maps, Notes, Bibliography, and Index.

2502. Ganeri, Anita. *Exploration into India.* Chelsea House, 2000. 48pp. ISBN 978-0-7910-6022-3. Grades 4–6.

This is a look at India from the time of the Indus Valley civilization, before the Aryans and the Greeks arrived. Other chapters cover India to 1001, with its new religions and the guptas; India under the Muslims and the Mogul Empire; the European presence in India; the British Raj, from 1756 to 1947; and modern India. Time Chart, Glossary, and Index.

2503. MacMillan, Dianne M. *Diwali: Hindu Festival of Lights.* (Best Holiday Books) Enslow, 2008. 48pp. ISBN 978-0-7660-3060-2. Grades 2–5.

Hindu beliefs become apparent in this description of an important festival as well as a presentation of the important books, legends, and other traditions associated with the religion. Glossary and Index.

2504. Otfinoski, Steven. *Afghanistan.* (Nations in Transition) Facts on File, 2003. 144pp. ISBN 978-0-8160-5056-7. Grades 7 up.

The author examines the traditions, religions, government, economy, daily life, and cultural heritage of Afghanistan's tribes and ethnic groups from prehistory. The text includes facts and anecdotes that reveal the tensions surrounding the recent Taliban factions, the peacekeeping troops, and the government. Opium remains important for Afghanistan's economic sustenance, but the nation needs support as its people try to overcome the years of warfare and poor crops. Many of its citizens become refugees. The illustrated chapters include information on Afghanistan from prehistory to 1919, from 1919 to 1979 as it becomes a nation, and the invasions beginning in 1979—by the Soviets, the Taliban, and al-Qaeda. Chronology, Maps, Further Reading, and Index.

2505. Wahab, Shaista, and Barry Youngerman. *A Brief History of Afghanistan.* Facts on File, 2007. 308pp. ISBN 978-0-8160-5761-0. Grades YA.

The author examines the history of Afghanistan and its division into two major religious groups, the Sunnis and the Shiites. No ethnic or linguistic unification exists in this country, nor does it have natural borders. Although poor and undeveloped, it contains many mineral and energy resources. The book covers the founding of modern Afghanistan in 1747 under Ahmad Shah through the present. Included are such topics as the "Great Game" between the British and the Russians, the Soviet occupation in the 1980s, the rise of the mujahideen, the Taliban era, and the ensuing civil war. Maps and photographs augment the text. Bibliography, Chronology, and Index.

2506. Webster, Christine. *Taj Mahal.* Weigl, 2007. 32pp. ISBN 978-1-59036-729-2; paper ISBN 978-1-59036-730-8. Grades 5–9.

Considered the finest example of Mughal architecture, the Taj Mahal was completed in 1648 as a gift from Shah Jahan to his favorite wife. It is actually a series of structures carefully integrated into one carefully designed structure. The author examines the technology behind the structure that made it possible to build it and its significance at the time. Photographs highlight the text. Glossary, Further Reading, Web Sites, and Index.

Biography and Collective Biography

2507. Adams, Simon. *Mahatma Gandhi.* (Twentieth Century History Makers) Raintree, 2003. 112pp. ISBN 978-0-7398-5255-2. Grades 7–10.

Mahatma Gandhi (1869–1948) used nonviolent resistance to help India gain freedom from British rule. The author reveals Gandhi's personal history including his education in England and his twenty-one years in South Africa as a lawyer for India's legal rights. He then returned to India to help his people. Photographs and illustrations enhance the text. Bibliography, Glossary, Maps, and Index.

2508. Ansary, Tamim. *West of Kabul, East of New York: An Afghan American Story.* Picador, 2003. 304pp. Paper ISBN 978-0-312-42151-9. Grades YA.

As an Afghan young adult who escaped—with his Pashtun Afghan father and Finnish American mother—to the United States at the beginning of civil strife and war with Russia, Ansary gives insight into himself and the world situation. He divides his memoir into three parts: "The Lost World," "Looking for Islam," and "Forgetting Afghanistan." In the first, he describes his life in his family's clan in Afghanistan, where the family was more important than the individual, and living with parents who met while studying abroad. After he moved to the United States, he attended college and forgot his childhood. But in 1980 he visited the Muslim world in North Africa and Turkey, meeting Muslim extremists, and he describes their logic, unfamiliar and strange to westerners. There he met his own wife, a Jewish woman. In the second part, Ansary relates his siblings' rejection or acceptance of their past and his own personal journey. Ansary gained fame for explanatory e-mails that he sent following the World Trade Center destruction in 2001. *School Library Journal Best Books of the Year* and *Tashas Reading List (Texas).*

2509. Brown, Don. *Far Beyond the Garden Gate: Alexandra David-Neel's Journey to Lhasa.* Illustrated by author. Houghton, 2002. Unpaged. ISBN 978-0-618-08364-0. Grades K–2.

Alexandra David-Neel (1868–1969), after becoming a scholar of Buddhism and Tibet, decided to visit the country. She had to walk thousands of miles to reach Lhasa, the capital, in the early 20th century, and in 1924 became the first western woman to enter the city. Brown uses quotes from David-Neel's writings to tell about her life from childhood through her life as an opera singer who settled finally in marriage in Tunis. Then in 1911, with her husband's approval, she began her journey to Lhasa, a trip that lasted fourteen years. She died at 101. Illustrations and maps enhance the text. Bibliography, and Notes.

2510. Burleigh, Robert. *Tiger of the Snows: Tenzing Norgay: The Boy Whose Dream Was Everest.* Atheneum, 2006. 40pp. ISBN 978-0-689-83042-6. Grades 3–6.

On May 20, 1953, the Sherpa, Tenzing Norgay, accompanied Edmund Hillary to the top of Mount Everest. This formal poem salutes that achievement, noting that as a boy tending yaks on the mountain's side, he dreamt of climbing the five-mile high mountain. The numinous illustrations complement the text.

2511. Demi. *Buddha.* Illustrated by author. Holt, 1996. 42pp. ISBN 978-0-8050-4203-0. Grades 3–5.

Demi presents the 80-year life of Buddha Siddhartha, along with abstract tenets such as the Eightfold Path and Four Noble Truths in the Buddhist faith. As a youth, Siddhartha was sheltered, but when he learned about suffering, he wanted to end it. The illustrations help clarify the text.

2512. Demi. *The Dalai Lama: A Biography of the Tibetan Spiritual and Political Leader.* Holt, 1998. Unpaged. ISBN 978-0-8050-5443-9. Grades 3–6.

This biography of the fourteenth Dalai Lama (1935–) begins with a letter from him in which he worries about the current political situation in Tibet. Following is a description of the country and of the Buddhist religion with information about the search for the fourteenth Dalai Lama after the death of the thirteenth. He was a 2-year old boy who passed the monks' tests and moved to Lhasa where he was educated. The monks called him a "holy terror," and he loved to take things apart and put them back together. The book concludes with China's invasion of Tibet and the Dalai Lama's exile. Exquisite illustrations enhance the text.

2513. Demi. *Gandhi.* Illustrated by author. Margaret K. McElderry, 2001. 32pp. ISBN 978-0-689-84149-1. Grades 3–6.

Mahatma Gandhi (1869–1948) helped bring political and social change to his country of India after studying abroad in England and working in South Africa. Gandhi rid India of British rule and helped the people understand the importance of nonviolence. By the time he died, he only owned fourteen items because he had cleared himself of the trappings of the world. The illustrations contain numerous details to complement the text.

2514. Demi. *Mother Teresa.* Illustrated by author. Margaret K. McElderry, 2005. 32pp. ISBN 978-0-689-86407-0. Grades 4–7.

Agnes Gonxha Bojaxhiu, better known as Mother Teresa (1910–1997) left her mother and her sister at the age of 12 when she felt a calling to be a religious. She spent most of her life in India looking after the poor and trying to raise money to help them survive. Illustrations with designs of India and of the church highlight the text.

2515. Englar, Mary. *Benazir Bhutto: Pakistani Prime Minister and Activist.* (Signature Lives) Compass Point, 2005. 112pp. ISBN 978-0-7565-1578-2; 2007. paper ISBN 978-0-7565-1798-4. Grades 6–9.

Benazir Bhutto (1953–2007) became Pakistan's first female prime minister. Englar presents information about her childhood, education, family's political commitment to Pakistan, prison sentence, and her exile. Illustrations highlight the text. Chronology, Maps, Glossary, Further Reading, Web Sites, and Index.

2516. Halder, Baby. *A Life Less Ordinary: A Memoir.* Translated by Urvashi Butalia. HarperCollins, 2007. 175pp. ISBN 978-0-06-125581-6. Grades YA.

Baby Halder grew up in India as a poor and neglected Bengali woman with an abusive father after her mother left when Baby was four. Married off at 12 to a much older man, she eventually managed to escape her abusive husband with her 3 children and become a maid in Delhi when she was 29. She met Prabodh Kumar, a retired professor, and while working for him, he encouraged her to read everything and to write about her experiences.

2517. Kerr, Jim. *Hillary and Norgay's Mount Everest Adventure.* (Great Journeys Across Earth) Raintree, 2007. 48pp. ISBN 978-1-4034-9755-0; paper ISBN 978-1-4034-9763-5. Grades 4–6.

The biography recounts the achievement of Edmund Hillary (1919–2008) and Tenzing Norkey (1914–1986), who became the first humans to reach the top of Mount Everest. They needed enormous stamina and a lot of good luck to reach the highest point of the earth. Illustrations augment the text. Chronology, Glossary, Further Reading, and Index.

2518. Koul, Sudha. *The Tiger Ladies: A Memoir of Kashmir.* Beacon, 2003. 218pp. Paper ISBN 978-0-8070-5919-7. Grades YA.

Born a Kashmiri Brahmin in 1947, the year that Pakistan and India were partitioned with Kashmiri the disputed land between them, Sudra Koul recalls her grandmother's and mother's stories of their young lives. The three divisions of the narrative are grandmothers, mothers, and daughters. The family was part of a group that revered women and worshipped Durga, the mother-goddess who rode on a magnificent tiger. But soon, the struggle in her homeland began as the two border countries tried to take control. Eventually, she meets a Kashmiri after she is 30, and they move to New Jersey and try to coalesce their Hindu traditions and a secular America.

2519. Lamb, Christina. *The Sewing Circles of Herat: A Personal Voyage Through Afghanistan.* Perennial, 2004. 338pp. Paper ISBN 978-0-06-050527-1. Grades YA.

Christina Lamb, a British foreign correspondent, lived in Pakistan for ten years. There she watched the Taliban rise during the last part of the Russian war and brutalize the people, especially the women. She left in 1989, and in 2001, she returned to hear stories of what happened. Women reported being confined like cows in sheds, a boy watched over one hundred executions because he was entertained, and Lamb heard claims that nowhere does the Koran damn education and say that men should wear beards. She has hope for the people, based on new construction, at least when she wrote this book. Photographs and maps enhance the text. Bibliography.

2520. Mantell, Paul. *The Buddha.* (Childhood of World Figures) Aladdin, 2007. 203pp. Paper ISBN 978-1-416-91543-0. Grades 3–6.

Siddhartha (ca. 563 B.C.E.) rejected his family's comfortable life to take a different path. He became a beggar, and he removed all of the material aspects of his life to become the man known as Gautama Buddha, the founder of Buddhism. A seer declared that he would be a holy man. The fifteen chapters in the text cover his life from his miraculous birth in Nepal to the king and queen of Shakya and his childhood, but also address the contemporary influence of Buddhism. Glossary and Further Reading.

2521. Miro, Asha. *Daughter of the Ganges: A Memoir.* Atria, 2006. 274pp. ISBN 978-0-7432-8672-5; 2007. paper ISBN 978-0-7432-8673-2. Grades YA.

Asha Miro returned to India in 1995 to search for her roots after having spent her life as the adopted daughter in a Catalan family since age 6. She visited the orphanages where she stayed in the hope of learning more about her biological parents. She discovers they are dead, and seven years later, she takes a film crew with her to research the phenomenon of international adoptions. At the village where she was born she meets a sister that she never knew existed. She realizes that their lives could have been reversed had circumstances been different.

2522. Nasrin, Taslima. *Meyebela: My Bengali Girlhood.* Translated by Gopa Majumdar. Steerforth, 2004. 300pp. ISBN 978-1-58642-051-2. Grades YA.

Taslima Nasrin notes that no word exists in Bengali for the concept of a girl's "childhood" so she coins the word "meyebela." In the early 1960s Nasrin lives with her mother's strict Islamic family in East Pakistan before it became Bangladesh in its struggle for independence. She uses a stream of consciousness style to remember aspects of her life; they are disjointed and rambling but always memorable. Her handsome father's infidelity, the uncles who rape her, her suffering mother's belief that doubting and questioning are sinful, her discovery of the arts, and her first notice of her own sexual feelings. Because she listened to her inner voice, she was able to eventually escape and become a writer, a doctor, and an international human rights activist. Nasrin's story may seem extreme, but the fatwa on her life and mass demonstrations against her indicate that she has endured all.

2523. Pastan, Amy. *Gandhi.* (DK Biographies) DK, 2006. 128pp. ISBN 978-0-7566-2112-4; paper ISBN 978-0-7566-2111-7. Grades 3–7.

Mahatma Gandhi (1869–1948) faced discrimination from the British colonists in India while endeavoring to free India through nonviolence and civil disobedience. Educated in Britain as a lawyer, he went to South Africa and practiced civil disobedience and non-violence for Indian communities before he took his battle into India. Today Indians recognize him as "Father of the Nation." Photographs and illustrations augment the text. Web Sites and Index.

2524. Roper, Robert. *Fatal Mountaineer: The High-Altitude Life and Death of Willi Unsoeld, American Himalayan Legend.* Griffin, 2003. 320pp. Paper ISBN 978-0-312-30266-5. Grades YA.

William Francis Unsoeld (1926–1979), a mountaineer, named his daughter after Nandi Devi, India's tallest peak. Then in 1976, his daughter died on the mountain from intestinal problems when Unsoeld took her up to fulfill a dream of communing with her namesake. He was the most influential high-altitude mountain climber of the 1960s and 1970s after ascending Mount Everest's West Ridge in 1963. He was also a spellbinding public speaker and fascinating teacher at Evergreen College. Photographs enhance the text. Index.

2525. Severance, John. *Gandhi, Great Soul.* Clarion, 1997. 144pp. ISBN 978-0-395-77179-2. Grades 6–9.

Mohandas (Sanskrit for "Great Soul") K. Gandhi (1869–1947) helped to free India from British colonialism. Severance gives a balanced account of Gandhi's life from his privileged upbringing and attendance at British schools, his unhappy arranged marriage when he was 13, his experiences in South Africa that influenced his concerns for the rights of individuals, through his contributions to the concept of *satyagraha*, or peaceful resistance. Severance also gives the context of Indian politics that became the focus of Gandhi's protest. Photographs, Bibliography, and Index.

2526. Slavicek, Louise Chipley. *Mother Teresa: Caring for the World's Poor.* (Modern Peacemakers) Chelsea House, 2007. 113pp. ISBN 978-0-7910-9433-4. Grades 8 up.

Surprisingly, not everyone supported Mother Teresa's selection as winner of the Nobel Peace Prize because she believed in neither abortion nor contraception. However, her amazing contribution to the lives of the destitute in India and around the world made her a prime choice for this honor. Bibliography, Chronology, Further Reading, Notes, Web Sites, and Index.

2527. Stewart, Whitney. *Becoming Buddha: The Story of Siddhartha.* Illustrated by Sally Rippin. Heian International, 2005. 32pp. ISBN 978-0-89346-946-7; 2008. paper ISBN 978-0-89346-956-6. Grades 1–4.

This biography of Buddha follows him from the prophecies preceding his birth as Prince Siddhartha through his childhood as the son of wealthy parents. It shows his break with his past and his quest for enlightenment. It also covers his practice of meditation and offers a guide for the reader about trying a simple meditation. Illustrations complement the text.

2528. Tenberken, Sabriye. *My Path Leads to Tibet: The Inspiring Story of How One Young Woman Brought Hope to the Blind Children of Tibet.* Arcade, 2003. 284pp. ISBN 978-1-55970-658-2; 2004 paper ISBN 978-1-55970-694-0. Grades YA.

Sabriye Tenberken became blind at the age of 13 from retinal disease. In college at the University of Bonn, she studied Tibetan culture but had problems reading the materials with character-recognition machinery. She created a Tibetan braille alphabet so that the works would be accessible to the blind. She decided to go to Tibet to teach her braille to blind Tibetan children. After traversing the wilds of the country on horseback for several years, she succeeded in establishing the school, "Braille Without Borders." She found children whose families, embarrassed by their blindness and thinking that God had punished them, kept them out of sight from the community. Tenberken had to bargain for supplies and sleep in flea-infested huts while fighting the Chinese bureaucracy involving foreigners. Because additional bungling tied up funds, she was evicted and had to leave the country immediately. After a journey overland to Nepal and back to Germany, she was able to find ways to continue her work and hopes to expand to other countries. She says that since she has been sighted, she is a visual person who appreciates the beauty around her even though she can no longer see it. *Christopher Book Award*.

2529. Vasishta, Madan. *Deaf in Delhi: A Memoir.* (Deaf Lives) Gallaudet University, 2006. 220pp. ISBN 978-1-56368-284-1. Grades YA.

When Madan Vasishta lost his hearing at age 11 from mumps and typhoid in India, he had to cope with being deaf in a culture that considered such an affliction to make him less than human. His intelligence, however, secured him a scholarship for photography in a Delhi school for the deaf. There he learned Indian Sign Language and met a deaf American woman who told him about Gallaudet College. He applied, got money, and attended, an opportunity that prepared him to become an American professor. The text reveals cultural aspects of India, and photographs highlight it.

2530. Weiss, Ellen. *Mother Teresa: A Life of Kindness.* Illustrated by Tina Walski. (Blastoff! Readers: People of Character) Children's, 2007. 24pp. ISBN 978-0-53114-714-6. Grades 1–3.

The distinguishing character trait of Mother Teresa (1910–1997) has been her kindness. Weiss looks at her kindness to people everywhere, but especially to the homeless and orphaned in India. Illustrations highlight the text. Glossary, Chronology, Further Reading, and Web Sites.

2531. Wolpert, Stanley A. *Gandhi's Passion: The Life and Legacy of Mahatma Gandhi.* Oxford University, 2002. 480pp. Paper ISBN 978-0-19-515634-8. Grades YA.

Mahatma Gandhi (1869–1948), a wealthy Indian child, studied law in England before going to South Africa and facing racism. He then returned to his home and used nonviolence as his method to struggle for independence from Great Britain. He wanted to purify himself so that he would be worthy of trying to influence the public. Gandhi, however, had his shortcomings: he was a poor father, a partisan, and was frustrated with his inability to bring his vision to fruition. Wolpert also examines India's rejection of Gandhi's ideologies, the "Great Soul," and India's role in the nuclear arms race. Bibliography, Notes, and Index.

Graphic Novels, Biographies, and Histories

2532. Tezuka, Osamu. *Kapilavastu: Buddha, Vol. 1.* Vertical, 2003. 400pp. ISBN 978-1-932234-43-5. Grades 6 up.

This first of eight graphic volumes about Siddhartha becoming the Buddha begins with Chapra, a slave, who attempts to escape his life by pretending to be the son of a general while his mother supports his intentions. Naradatta, a monk, tries to understand the foretellings of the birth of the Buddha, and at the same time, Tatta, a child pariah, communes with animals. Tatta sacrifices himself to a snake to save Naradatta and Chapra's mother, while a bandit arrives and wants to know why he does not merely kill the snake. The characters stay together, and with the help of a Brahmin monk, cope with and survive challenges. Eventually, Siddhartha comes into the story, but not until near the end.

DVDs

2533. *Afghanistan: 12 Years of Violence.* Discovery, 2002. 26 min. Grades 9 up.

In October 2001 Afghanistan waited to hear the response from the United States to the September 11 attacks, and BBC correspondent John Simpson wrote a piece about its attitude. His documentary contains his previous stories about Afghanistan from 1989 to 2001 while the Taliban's violence and repression had control of the country. He adds information about the Taliban's treatment of women, the influence of bin Laden and Al Qaeda in Afghanistan, and the role of the country as a base for international terrorism. Footage of people and events complement Simpson's reporting.

2534. *The Clay Bird.* New Yorker Films, 2006. 1:36 hrs. ISBN 978-1-933920-02-3. Grades 7 up.

In the 1960s just before Bangladesh became independent from Pakistan, Anu's (Nurul Islam Bablu) orthodox Muslim father, Kazi, sends him to a *madrasah* (learning center) far from his home. Anu tries to adjust to the difficult conditions at the school and the two factions of moderate and extremist Muslims fighting each other there. At home, his mother begins to rebel against Kazi, especially when their daughter becomes ill and he refuses to allow her to see a doctor since he has decided that homeopathic healing is best. Simultaneously, students, intellectuals, and activists are marching in East Pakistan's streets demanding independence.

2535. *Drowned Out.* Bullfrog Films, 2003. 75 min. ISBN 978-1-56458-047-2. Grades 10 up.

Jalsindhi villagers in central India fought with hunger strikes and rallies against police and endured a six-year Supreme Court case completed in 2000 after 16 million people were threatened with being flooded out by the Narmada Dam. Developers declared that it would aid the wealthy industrialists rather than give water to poor farmers. Choices for those displaced included either moving to city slums, going to a resettlement site, or drowning. One tribal farming family decided to stay because their skills would not support them in another place. *Audience Award Runnerup, San Francisco International Film Festival; Bronze Plaque, Columbus International Film and Video Festival; Honorable Mention, Society for Visual Anthropology Film Festival; Honorable Mention, EarthVision Environmental Film Festival; Full Frame Documentary Film Festival; Bermuda International Film Festival; Wild Spaces Film Festival* (Sydney); *ImagineAsia Festival* (Edinburgh); *Commonwealth Film Festival* (Manchester); *Tiburon International Film Festival; Ashland Independent Film Festival; Documentary Festival* (Istanbul); *Silverdocs, American Film Institute; Robert Flaherty Seminar* (Vassar); *Hot Springs Documentary Film Festival; Amnesty International Film Festival* (University of Wyoming); *Vermont International Film Festival; Global Visions Film Festival; Finger Lakes Environmental Film Festival; Vermont International Film & Video Festival; Annapolis Film Festival; Hazel Wolf Environmental Film Festival; Environmental Film Festival in the Nation's Capital; Chicago International Documentary Film Festival; United Nations Association Film Festival* (Stanford University); *The Environmental Film Festival of Accra; Asian Film Festival* (Turku); *Green Film Festival* (Seoul); *One World Film Festival* (Bratislava); *Alternative Film Festival* (Venice); *Eco Cinema Film Festival* (Rhodes); *Festive dei Popoli* (Florence); *The Norrkoping Film Festival* (Sweden); *Jihlava International Film Festival* (Czech Republic); *1001 Documentary Film Festival* (Istanbul); and *7 Islands International Film Festival* (Mumbai).

2536. *Lost Treasures of Tibet.* Narrated by Liev Schreiber. (Nova) WGBH Boston, 2003. 60 min. ISBN 978-1-59375-743-4. Grades 7 up.

Actor Liev Schreiber describes the politics of Tibet while revealing the lost treasures of Mustang, a remaining center of Tibetan culture. China invaded Tibet in 1950 and outlawed its religion in name but not in spirit. John Sanday, the leader of the American Himalayan Foundation, has worked at restoring the 500-year-old art with members of his group and monks, locals, artisans, and volunteers. Additional interviews with experts and spiritual leaders augment the lovely photography.

2537. *Mother Teresa: Woman of Compassion.* (Great Souls) Vision Video, 2005. 56 min. Grades 9 up.

See entry 2472.

2538. *No More Tears Sister: Anatomy of Hope and Betrayal.* National Film Board of Canada, 2005. 78 min. Grades YA.

In the 1960s after the Sinhalese imprisoned her sister, Nirmala, in Sri Lanka, Dr. Rajani Thiranagama, a mother, author, and anatomy professor, began campaigning against the injustice directed toward the Tamil people. She later broke ranks with the rebel Tamil Tigers and advocated human rights. She was assassinated at the age of 35. In the film Nirmala returns to Sri Lanka with Rajani's husband and grown daughters to tell the story of her passionate sister. *Cine Golden Eagle Award, Gemini Awards, Wim Van Leer in the Spirit of Freedom Award, International Film Festival* (Jerusalem), *India Tri Continental Film Festival,* and *International Film and Video Festival* (Columbus, Ohio).

Compact Discs

2539. Ansary, Tamim. *West of Kabul, East of New York: An Afghan American Story.* Narrated by Tamim Ansary. Blackstone Audio, 2007. 7 CDs; 8 hrs. ISBN 978-0-7861-6077-8. Grades YA.

See entry 2508.

2540. Hosseini, Khaled. *The Kite Runner.* Narrated by Khaled Hosseini. Simon & Schuster, 2003. 5 CDs; 6 hrs. ISBN 978-0-7435-3024-8. Grades YA.

See entry 2487.

2541. Morpurgo, Michael. *King of the Cloud Forests.* Narrated by Michael Morpurgo. BBC Audiobooks, 2007. 4 CDs; 4:07 hrs. ISBN 978-1-4056-5574-3. Grades 4–7.

During the Japanese invasion in 1941, Ashley has to leave his missionary father in China to return to England. Uncle Sung, an old Tibetan doctor, takes him through Tibet, Nepal, and India on their journey, but Ashley must be disguised as a Tibetan boy since whites are suspect in all of these countries. After someone discovers Ashley's disguise, the two hide in the mountains and become trapped in the Himalayas during a blizzard. Uncle Sung leaves Ashley to search for help, but Yetis rescue him and take him to their forest cave. Their gentleness and kindness surprise Ashley.

AFRICA AND SOUTH AFRICA

Historical Fiction and Fantasy

2542. Aboulela, Leila. *Minaret.* Grove, 2005. 276pp. Paper ISBN 978-0-8021-7014-9. Grades YA.

See entry 2331.

2543. Achebe, Chinua. *Things Fall Apart.* Knopf, 1995. 181pp. ISBN 978-0-679-44623-1; Norton, 1008. paper ISBN 978-0-393-93219-5. Grades YA.

When Okonkwo's family starts listening to the Christian missionaries who have come to convert the Ibo tribe of Nigeria in the late 19th century, Okonkwo becomes disturbed. When he tries to assert his superiority, the tribe exiles him. While he is gone, the Christians work to ban certain tribal customs and they open schools in which to teach their own beliefs. When Okonkwo returns, he discovers that his own son has turned away from the tribe's traditions.

2544. Berry, James. *Ajeemah and His Son.* Trophy, 1994. 84pp. Paper ISBN 978-0-06-440523-2. Grades 7 up.

Atu, age 18, and his father are captured in 1807 in Africa while walking to visit Atu's intended bride. They are sold into slavery and transported to Jamaica. There they become separated, and each spends the rest of his life trying to regain his freedom and reunite with the other. Atu survives until the Jamaican slaves are freed on August 1, 1838, but his father does not. *American Library Association Notable Children's Book, American Library Association Best Books for Young Adults, Horn Book Fanfare Honor List, Booklist Books for Youth Editors' Choices, Notable Children's Trade Books in the Field of Social Studies, Bulletin Blue Ribbon Book, Boston Globe-Horn Book Fiction Award*, and *New York Public Library Books for the Teen Age.*

2545. Cornwell, Nikki. *Christophe's Story.* Illustrated by Karin Littlewood. Frances Lincoln, 2007. 96pp. ISBN 978-1-84507-765-5; paper ISBN 978-1-84507-521-7. Grades 5–8.

See entry 2345.

2546. Farmer, Nancy. *A Girl Named Disaster.* Orchard, 1996. 309pp. ISBN 978-0-531-09539-3; Puffin, 1998. paper ISBN 978-0-14-038635-6. Grades 6–9.

With her grandmother's blessing, Nhamo, 11, escapes from a horrible marriage in Mozambique during 1981 to her father's family in Zimbabwe. A two-day journey extends to a year when the boat goes astray. Baboons look after her on an island for a while, and when she finally reaches Zimbabwe, she lives with scientists and learns to survive in civilization before she finds her father's family. The background gives information on the Shona and on South Africa in this unusual novel. *American Library Association Notable Books for Children, American Library Association Best Books for Young Adults, School Library Journal Best Book*, and *Newbery Honor Book*.

2547. Gien, Pamela. *The Syringa Tree: A Novel.* Random House, 2006. 262pp. ISBN 978-0-375-50755-7; paper ISBN 978-0-375-75910-9. Grades YA.

Six-year-old Lizzie Grace sits in her South African backyard syringa tree when she feels troubled, and from there she can see her Afrikaner neighbors and their black workers. Her physician father and her depressed mother try to keep their staff and Lizzie Grace away from the racism outside their home. But Lizzie Grace knows that Salamena, her nanny, has to carry work papers and hide from police. Salamena has a baby girl, Moliseng, born illegally at their home in a white suburb in 1963 and hidden from the brutal police that would banish her. Finally, Moliseng must leave for the Soweto black township, and Lizzie Grace misses her sister-friend terribly. When Moliseng is 14, she leads other children against the police and dies for her efforts.

2548. Glass, Linzi Alex. *The Year the Gypsies Came.* Holt, 2006. 260pp. ISBN 978-0-8050-7999-9. Grades 9 up.

Emily Iris, 12, lives in Johannesburg, South Africa, in the late 1960s with parents who bicker constantly. Their Zulu servant, Buza, offers Emily the comfort she needs as well as a young Australian "gypsy" boy, Streak Mallory, who also has a difficult family. Authorities arrest Buza, however, for not having correct papers, and Emily becomes aware that whites with all their privilege do not suffer the police brutality of apartheid. Additionally, Streak's older brother, Otis, brain-damaged from their father's intense beatings, rapes Emily's older sister, Sarah, leading to Sarah's breakdown and eventual suicide. *American Library Association Best Books for Young Adults*.

2549. Habila, Helon. *Waiting for an Angel.* Norton, 2004. 229pp. Paper ISBN 978-0-393-32511-9. Grades YA.

Lomba, a young journalist in Lagos, Nigeria, is imprisoned in 1997 on false charges. Among the things he experiences in this multilayered story are the death of his friend, Bola, who recklessly condemns the government; the loss of the woman he loves to another man who pays her mother's medical bills; and the burning of the office of the magazine where he works. He also meets with a teenaged delinquent who has recently arrived in the country. The angel for whom Lomba waits is death.

2550. Haley, Alex. *Roots.* Vanguard, 2009. ISBN 978-1-59315-457-8; 2007. paper ISBN 978-1-59315-449-3. Grades YA.

In this book, Alex Haley traces the background of an African American whose ancestor was transported to America as a slave. Through research he finds the African home of his ancestor and his heritage as tribal royalty. Index.

2551. Hill, Lawrence. *Someone Knows My Name: A Novel.* Norton, 2007. 512pp. ISBN 978-0-393-06578-7. Grades YA.

In 1745 slavers take Aminata Diallo, 11, from her West African home through the Middle Passage to slavery in South Carolina. She quickly learns to read and speak English. Her master takes her to New York City where she escapes during an anti-British demonstration. She helps the British compile a book listing black loyalists, "The Book of Negroes." Then they transport Aminata and the other slaves to Nova Scotia and freedom. She plans to reach Sierra Leone with the other slaves but ends up in London in 1802, where the novel begins, as an abolitionist.

2552. Jansen, Hanna. *Over a Thousand Hills I Walk with You.* Translated by Elizabeth D. Crawford. Carolrhoda, 2006. 342pp. ISBN 978-1-57505-927-3. Grades 8 up.

Jeanne d'Arc Umubyeyi, 8, is the only member of her family to survive the 1994 Rwandan genocide. After a German family adopts her, she has to start a new life alone while remembering the horrible things she has seen. Her adoptive mother writes her fictional biography, and in it, Jeanne is jealous of her sister, never close to her teacher father, and content as a Catholic in her upper class Tutsi family in Kibungo. After the Hutu president Habyarimana is assassinated, the Hutus massacre almost a million of her people, including her mother and her brother, and completely change her world. Glossary. *Booklist Editors' Choice, Tayshas Reading List* (Texas), *ForeWord Book of the Year Award, Independent Publisher Book Awards, Multicultural Fiction Award, Benjamin Franklin Award, American Library Association Best Books for Young Adults,* and *Flume Award* (New Hampshire) nomination.

2553. Karr, Kathleen. *Born for Adventure.* Marshall Cavendish, 2007. 208pp. ISBN 978-0-7614-5348-2. Grades 6–9.

Tom Ormsby, 15, is delighted when Henry Morton Stanley (1841–1904) agrees to take him on an 1887 trek to rescue the kidnapped Emin Pasha in the Sudan, Africa. For the years that Tom is on the expedition as it moves from Zanzibar to the Congo's Ituri Forest, he faces attacks from wild animals, barely overcomes jungle diseases, meets Pygmies, and watches untold cruelty toward the native peoples. He overcomes heat, lack of food and water, and tribal attacks. But he thinks quickly and acts properly so that he has an amazing trip before he safely returns home.

2554. Kingsolver, Barbara. *The Poisonwood Bible.* HarperCollins, 1998. 546pp. ISBN 978-0-06-017540-5; Perennial, 2008. paper ISBN 978-0-06-157707-9. Grades YA.

Nathan Price, a stern evangelical Baptist missionary, takes his wife and four daughters to the Belgian Congo in 1949. During the next few years the family's experiences transform them all. In alternating chapters, the daughters describes their experiences as their father remains isolated from the real needs of the people and of his family and as their mother copes as best she can until she is able to return to the United States.

2555. Mankell, Henning. *Secrets in the Fire.* Annick, 2003. 176pp. ISBN 978-1-55037-801-6; paper ISBN 978-1-55037-800-9. Grades 6–10.

Sofia Alface loses her legs in a land mine explosion while running across the Mozambique fields in southern Africa during the civil war of 1975 to 1992. Her sister dies. A doctor, priest, and hospital personnel help Sofia recover, and she is eventually fitted with two artificial legs and taught to walk again. Sofia's stepfather will not allow her to return to the house, and the poverty of the country takes its toll on the citizens. Students have neither books nor supplies, but Sofia learns to sew and support herself.

2556. Mussi, Sarah. *The Door of No Return.* Margaret K. McElderry, 2008. 392pp. ISBN 978-1-4169-1550-8. Grades 8 up.

Zac Baxter, 16, has trouble believing his grandfather Sam's stories that Zac is the last descendant of King Baktu of the Gold Coast, now Ghana. But when Sam Baxter is brutally murdered, Zac realizes that he should investigate. He discovers that after slavers stole King Baktu's son in 1701, King Baktu promised the British government gold and land in return for immunity for his people against slavery. The British agreed, but afterward became leaders in the slave trade and reneged on their recorded bond. Now the bond will embarrass the British, and they are determined to get both it and the gold. Zac's life is threatened, but he knows that he must find the treasure and the bond before the government does, and he travels from England to Ghana.

2557. Naidoo, Beverly. *Out of Bounds: Seven Stories of Conflict and Hope.* HarperCollins, 2003. 175pp. ISBN 978-0-06-050799-2; HarperTrophy, 2008. paper ISBN 978-0-06-050801-2. Grades 6–10.

Naidoo's stories chronicle experiences of young people from various races and ethnic groups during different decades beginning in 1948 as they cope with South Africa's apartheid laws. Children classified as "Colored" or mixed-race could be separated from parents who were reclassified as black. White children in school could be shunned because "Commie" parents had "native" friends. Mothers could be called "girl" and fathers called "boy" by their white employers. The stories show racism, suffering, and the difficulties of people dealing with the color of their skin during these awful years until 2000.

2558. Nanji, Shenaaz. *Child of Dandelions.* Front Street, 2008. 214pp. ISBN 978-1-932425-93-2. Grades 6–9.

Sabine, 15, a Ugandan citizen during 1972, lives with her wealthy parents of Indian descent. They try to have a normal life during the ninety-day period that President Idi Amin gives them to leave the country, but soldiers and citizens terrorize them. Additionally, Sabine's dear uncle disappears, and Zena, a good friend, will no longer speak to her. Her parents have to flee, and Sabine and her brother are able to obtain transit papers for immigration to Canada. When Sabine meets Zena before she departs, she discovers that Zena is engaged to marry Amin.

2559. Rupert, Janet E. *The African Mask.* Backinprint.Com, 2005. 125pp. Paper ISBN 978-0-595-35161-9. Grades 6–9.

In 11th-century Africa, Layo, age 12, goes to the city of Ife to meet her Yoruban husband and learn what job she will have as his wife. Instead of making the pottery for which her grandmother is famous, she finds that she will have to help with bronzes, a medium she does not yet appreciate. She tries to break the agreement, but realizes almost too late that her grandmother knows (better than she) what is best.

2560. St. John, Lauren. *Dolphin Song.* Dial, 2007. 256pp. ISBN 978-0-8037-3214-8. Grades 4–7.

Martine, 11, is sad to leave her white giraffe, Jemmy, when she goes on a two-week school trip with her South African classmates to study marine life off the coast of Mozambique. A storm hits, and she and her classmates go overboard into water filled with sharks. A pod of dolphins rescues them but they end up on a deserted island where they must learn to survive and help the endangered dolphins around them.

2561. St. John, Lauren. *The White Giraffe.* Illustrated by David Dean. Dial, 2007. 180pp. ISBN 978-0-8037-3211-7; Puffin, 2008. paper ISBN 978-0-14-241152-0. Grades 4–7.

Martine, 11, leaves England after her parents die in a house fire, to live with a grand-mother she does not know—the owner of Sawubona, a game preserve in South Africa. Martine, left to grieve on her own, meets members of the local culture through Sendai, a Zulu tribesman, and Grace, the healer. She tells Martine that she has a special gift she must take care of. A rumor of an elusive white giraffe living on the reserve at Sawubona intrigues Martine, but her grandmother says that the animal does not exist. Martine, however, sees the animal and must defend it from poachers.

2562. Slovo, Gillian. *Red Dust.* Norton, 2003. 352pp. Paper ISBN 978-0-393-32399-3. Grades YA.

Sarah Barcant, a New York lawyer, returns to her home in South Africa after fourteen years to help her now dying mentor, Ben Hoffman, in his last Truth and Reconciliation Commission (TRC) case against an apartheid torturer named Dirk Hendricks. Although witness Alex Mpondo has become a member of Parliament and wants to forget the hor-ror of apartheid, the parents of his best friend, Steve Sizela, want to know where they can find their son's body and bury him properly. Barcant and Hoffman suspect that Hen-dricks caused Sizela's death by breaking under torture and pointing to Sizela as having weapons. What they all discover, however, is a truth is more complicated than they had imagined.

2563. Wein, Elizabeth E. *The Empty Kingdom: Mark of Solomon, Book 2.* (Mark of Solomon) Viking, 2007. 223pp. ISBN 978-0-670-06273-7. Grades 7 up.

Abreha, the ruler of Himyar, imprisons Telemakos on the twelfth story of his palace, separated from his sister Athena so he cannot communicate with his family in Aksum. Abreha has punished Telemakos for what he says is treachery by forcing him to work on maps that will be used to destroy Aksum, and has made him wear a bracelet of bells so he cannot explore the palace. Telemakos must use his wits to figure out how to com-municate with his distant parents.

2564. Wein, Elizabeth E. *The Lion Hunter: Mark of Solomon, Book 1.* (Mark of Solomon) Viking, 2007. 223pp. ISBN 978-0-670-06163-1. Grades 7 up.

When Telemakos, King Arthur's half-Ethiopian grandson, is 12 in 6th-century Africa, he is playing with the emperor's pet lions when one mangles his arm. At the same time, his sister Athena is born. His parents become so upset about his arm that they ignore Athena, and he and Athena forge a huge bond. Unrest is escalating in his homeland of Aksum (ancient Ethiopia), and his parents send Telemakos and Athena to live with Abreha, the rule of Himyar, once Aksum's enemy as well. Telemakos enjoys the relative peace of his temporary home until he realizes, as a former government spy, that perhaps they are not as safe there as they thought. *School Library Journal Best Books for Children*.

2565. Wein, Elizabeth E. *The Sunbird.* Viking, 2004. 184pp. ISBN 978-0-670-03691-2; Puffin, 2006. paper ISBN 978-0-14-240171-2. Grades 7–12.

In the sequel to *The Winter Prince* (2003) and *A Coalition of Lions* (2003), Telemakos, the grandson of a British noble and an Aksumite, has to discover who is defying the em-peror's order to stop trading with a country infected with the plague during the 6th cen-tury. Telemakos goes to the salt mines in Afar at the request of his aunt, the British ambassador to Aksum, traveling as a deaf-mute slave. He is captured, however, and treated horribly, but he fulfills his duty to find the culprit.

2566. Whelan, Gloria. *Listening for Lions.* HarperCollins, 2005. 194pp. ISBN 978-0-06-058174-9; Trophy, 2006. paper ISBN 978-0-06-058176-3. Grades 6–9.

In 1919 orphaned Rachel, 13, has lost her missionary parents during the influenza epidemic in British East Africa. When she asks her neighbors, the Pritchards, for help, they engineer a plan for her to take the identity of their daughter, who also died in the epidemic, and return to England to be with her "grandfather." There she can claim the old man's estate for them. Fearing an orphanage, Rachel reluctantly agrees. But in England, she becomes attached to Grandfather Pritchard, sharing enjoyment of the birds outside his window and other interests. Throughout, she wants to return to Africa. Eventually she contrives a satisfactory way to accomplish what she wants. *Sequoyah Award* (Oklahoma) nomination, *Pacific Northwest Young Reader's Award* nomination, *Rebecca Caudill Award* (Illinois) nomination, *Charlie May Simon Children's Book Award* (Arkansas) nomination, *Sunshine State Young Reader Award* (Florida) nomination, and *Volunteer State Book Award* (Tennessee) nomination.

2567. Williams, Mary. *Brothers in Hope: The Story of the Lost Boys of Sudan.* Illustrated by R. Gregory Christie. Lee & Low, 2005. 40pp. ISBN 978-1-58430-232-2. Grades 5 up.

The civil war in Sudan in the 1980s orphans 8-year-old Garang, but he finds strength to help lead other boys hundreds of miles into Ethiopia. They suffer hunger, thirst, exhaustion, and illness on their journey. Then they have to leave this temporary camp and continue to Kenya. As he matures, Garang seeks ways to improve conditions for all of them. Eventually, he and some of the others have a chance to come to the United States. Acrylic paintings illustrate the text. Notes.

2568. Wulf, Linda Press. *The Night of the Burning: Devorah's Story.* Farrar, 2006. 224pp. ISBN 978-0-374-36419-9. Grades 5–8.

See entry 2060.

History

2569. Adinoyi-Ojo, Onukaba. *Mbuti.* (Heritage Library of African Peoples) Rosen, 1996. 64pp. ISBN 978-0-8239-1998-7. Grades 6 up.

Readers will learn about the land, history, social and political life, and religious beliefs of the pygmy Mbuti, and their relationships with other people who live in the same region of central Africa near the Ituri Forest of northeast Zaire. Further Reading, Glossary, and Index.

2570. Archibald, Erika F. *A Sudanese Family.* Photos by Greg Nelson. (Journey Between Two Worlds) Lerner, 1996. 64pp. ISBN 978-0-8225-3403-7; 1997. paper ISBN 978-0-8225-9753-7. Grades 5–7.

This volume includes the history of the Sudanese people as a background for understanding why families from the Sudan have had to leave their homes. Photographs and personal experiences explain the social and religious traditions of Sudan and how the people have had to adapt to a new culture to survive as refugees. Further Reading.

2571. Banqura, Abdul Karim. *Kipsigis.* (Heritage Library of African Peoples) Rosen, 1994. 64pp. ISBN 978-0-8239-1765-5. Grades 6 up.

The Kipsigis, now in the western portion of Kenya, migrated from Egypt through the Sudan. Their proud history shows that they were able to govern themselves with equality. Topics discussed in addition to general history are the organization of their society, initiation, marriage and family, European contact and rule, and a view of their future. Photographs, boxed information, and maps enhance the text. Glossary, Further Reading, and Index.

2572. Barr, Gary E. *History and Activities of the West African Kingdoms.* (Hands-On Ancient History) Raintree, 2007. 32pp. ISBN 978-1-4034-7925-9. Grades 3–6.

In three short chapters, Barr focuses on the structure of the ancient West African kingdoms by looking at the everyday life of the people, arts, culture, games, holidays, and celebrations. The fourth chapter includes instructions for making a mask, a mancala game, and a kente cloth; recipes; and an activity. Photographs and illustrations enhance the text. Glossary, Further Reading, and Index.

2573. Berg, Lois Anne. *An Eritrean Family.* Illustrated by Peter Ford. (Journey Between Two Worlds) Lerner, 1997. 56pp. Paper ISBN 978-0-8225-9755-1. Grades Fam.

Although not a history book, the history of the people of Eritrea is touched on as a background for understanding why families from that nation have had to leave Ethiopia. Photographs and personal experiences explain Eritrean social and religious traditions and how the people have had to adapt to a new culture to survive as refugees from a home they loved. Further Reading.

2574. Boateng, Faustine Ama. *Asante.* Rosen, 1996. 64pp. ISBN 978-0-8239-1975-8. Grades 7 up.

This text examines the history of the Asante in Ghana along with their social life and customs, religion, education, and arts. Further Reading, Glossary, and Index.

2575. Chicoine, Stephen. *A Liberian Family.* (Journey Between Two Worlds) Lerner, 1997. 56pp. Paper ISBN 978-0-8225-9758-2. Grades 3–6.

Although not a history book, this volume includes the history of Liberia as a background for understanding why families from there have had to leave their homes. Photographs and personal experiences explain Liberian social and religious traditions and how the people have had to adapt to a new culture in order to survive as refugees from a land they loved. Further Reading.

2576. Davenport, John. *A Brief Political and Geographic History of Africa: Where Are Belgian Congo, Rhodesia, and Kush?* (Places in Time) Mitchell Lane, 2008. 111pp. ISBN 978-1-58415-624-6. Grades 5–9.

Davenport looks at places on the African continent that no longer exist by placing them on a map and discussing why they have disappeared from present-day geography. Photographs, maps, and reproductions embellish the text. Bibliography, Glossary, Chronology, Notes, Further Reading, Web Sites, and Index.

2577. Edgerton, Robert B. *Africa's Armies: From Honor to Infamy: A History from 1791 to the Present.* Basic, 2004. 328pp. Paper ISBN 978-0-8133-4277-1. Grades YA.

Edgerton notes that Africa's future may be positive since the continent is reviving traditions that the West has disregarded. He traces the difficulties of postcolonial sub-Saharan Africa with its autocratic rulers, famine, diseases including AIDS, and economic collapse. He looks at Africa before the colonial period, its resistance to colonialism, civil wars, military coups and government corruption, and genocide in Rwanda and Burundi, and includes comments about Africa today and in the future. Bibliography, Notes, and Index.

2578. Feelings, Tom. *The Middle Passage: White Ships, Black Cargo.* Illustrated by author. Dial, 1995. 80pp. ISBN 978-0-8037-1804-3. Grades 7 up.

Feelings describes his search for his African past, and John Henrik Clarke's overview of the slave trade follows it. A series of illustrations depicts the events that people forced into slavery had to endure. The strong, truthful scenes include capture, transport on land and sea, rape, murder, life on shipboard, and rats gnawing on a dead body. *Bulletin Blue Ribbon Book, American Library Association Notable Books for Children, American Library Association Best Books for Young Adults,* and *Coretta Scott King Illustrator Award.*

2579. Hall, Linley Erin. *Starvation in Africa.* (In the News) Rosen, 2007. 64pp. ISBN 978-1-4042-0976-3. Grades 6–9.

Using photographs to illustrate the reality of starvation on the huge continent of Africa, the author describes the weather patterns and pests that have contributed to this state. Additionally, conflicts among nations and warring areas of the continent have also kept food from reaching various populations in need. A final chapter suggests ways for those outside of Africa to help those inside. Additional illustrations complement the text. Bibliography, Further Reading, Glossary, Web Sites, and Index.

2580. Hall, Martin, and Rebecca Stefoff. *Great Zimbabwe.* (Digging for the Past) 47pp. ISBN 978-0-19-515773-4. Grades 7–10.

In 1871 the German geologist Karl Mauch found the site of the 14th-century African city, Great Zimbabwe, in what is now known as Mozambique. Readers will learn about the competing theories about the civilization that evolved there, based on racism and the desire to deny that Africans could have created an advanced city so early in history. It offers background on radiocarbon dating of artifacts and other aspects of archaeology necessary to research the people and the place. Photographs and illustrations intensify the text. Glossary, Further Reading, Web Sites, and Index.

2581. Harrison, Peter, Ed. *African Nations and Leaders.* (History of Africa) Facts on File, 2003. 112pp. ISBN 978-0-8160-5066-6. Grades 7–12.

A look at fifty-three independent African countries through photographs. The text tells how they gained independence, looks at their important leaders, and includes a timeline of their progress. Among the leaders presented are Abdelaziz Bouteflika (Algeria), Pierre Buyoya (Burundi), Muammar al-Qaddafi (Libya), and Muhammad Hosni Mubarak (Egypt). Countries include Namibia, Senegal, South Africa, and Zimbabwe. Illustrations and photographs highlight the text. Bibliography, Maps, and Index.

2582. Haskins, James, and Kathleen Benson. *Africa: A Look Back.* (Drama of African-American History) Benchmark, 2006. 68pp. ISBN 978-0-7614-2148-1. Grades 5–8.

In a history of African American roots, the reader returns to 8th-century African slavery and continues to the Middle Passage in six chapters. The authors use narratives for the core of their information. Four chapters cover slave narratives by Olaudah Equiano, Ayuba ben Suleiman Diallo, Mahommah Gardo Baquaqua, and Venture Smith. Chapters contain complementary photographs, illustrations, documents, and maps. Glossary, Bibliography, Further Reading, and Index.

2583. Hetfield, Jamie. *The Asante of West Africa.* (Celebrating the Peoples and Civilizations of Africa) PowerKids, 1997. 24pp. ISBN 978-0-8239-2329-8. Grades K–2.

This simple introduction to a people from West Africa includes ten one-page chapters describing where and how the Asante live, their customs, government, food, and religion.

2584. Hetfield, Jamie. *The Maasai of East Africa.* (Celebrating the Peoples and Civilizations of Africa) PowerKids, 1997. 24pp. ISBN 978-0-8239-2330-4; Rosen, 2005. paper ISBN 978-1-4042-5551-7. Grades K–2.

The Maasai have lived mainly as East African nomads. The text includes ten one-page chapters describing where and how they live, their customs, government, food, and religion.

2585. Hetfield, Jamie. *The Yoruba of West Africa.* (Celebrating the Peoples and Civilizations of Africa) PowerKids, 1997. 24pp. ISBN 978-0-8239-2332-8. Grades K–2.

This simple introduction to a people from West Africa includes ten one-page chapters describing where and how the Yoruba live, their customs, government, food, and religion.

2586. *History of Central Africa.* (History of Africa) Facts on File, 2003. 112pp. ISBN 978-0-8160-5064-2. Grades 7 up.

Central Africa is observed including information on the early civilizations, languages, coastal kingdoms, explorers, missionaries, wars, dictatorships, coups, and society post-independence. The book also studies the Luba-Lunda states, economics, and 21st-century issues. Illustrations highlight the text. Bibliography, Maps, and Index.

2587. *History of East Africa.* (History of Africa) Facts on File, 2003. 112pp. ISBN 978-0-8160-5063-5. Grades 7 up.

Events in East Africa are examined, from prehistory to the 21st century. The narrative includes information about the climate, religions, topography, and languages. It also covers the development of trade, the influence of European colonists, and independence struggles. Illustrations enhance the text. Bibliography, Maps, and Index.

2588. *History of North Africa.* (History of Africa) Facts on File, 2003. 112pp. ISBN 978-0-8160-5061-1. Grades 7 up.

A look at the climate, the religions, the topography of the land, and the languages of the peoples in North Africa. The book examines the Egyptian culture from its beginnings, the Berbers, the Phoenicians, the Arab conquest with the Moors and Ottomans, the colonial era, and the struggles for independence in the area. Illustrations highlight the text. Bibliography, Maps, and Index.

2589. *History of Southern Africa.* (History of Africa) Facts on File, 2003. 112pp. ISBN 978-0-8160-5065-9. Grades 7 up.

Readers will learn about the climate, religions, topography, and languages of the peoples of southern Africa. The narrative also covers the emerging states, European settlement and domination, the uprisings led by the Zulu warriors, apartheid, and liberation. Illustrations augment the text. Bibliography, Maps, and Index.

2590. *History of West Africa.* (History of Africa) Facts on File, 2003. 112pp. ISBN 978-0-8160-5062-8. Grades 7 up.

A look at the climate, religions, topography, and the languages of the peoples of West Africa from prehistory to the present. Illustrations highlight the text. Bibliography, Maps, and Index.

2591. Holland, Heidi. *The Struggle: A History of the African National Congress.* George Braziller, 1990. 256pp. Paper ISBN 978-0-8076-1255-2. Grades YA.

Using interviews with major participants in the fight against apartheid in South Africa and other sources, Holland presents the history of the African National Congress and Nelson Mandela's importance as its ideological head. She divides the history into three sections. The first section covers the founding of the organization in 1912 to the National Party victory in 1948 when apartheid was established. The second covers 1948 to 1960 when the Sharkeville massacre occurred; leaders not imprisoned had to go into exile, and the organization reluctantly changed its policy to include violence if necessary. The third part accounts for 1960 to 1989, when blacks and Afrikaners had many confrontations. Blacks in South Africa merely wanted their rights, but whites were outwardly hostile and repressed them more instead. Index.

2592. Ibazebo, Isimeme. *Exploration into Africa.* Chelsea House, 2000. 48pp. ISBN 978-0-7910-6019-3. Grades 4–6.

Chapters illustrated with photographs and drawings give an overview of African settlement and discovery. They cover Africa to the 1400s and Great Zimbabwe; the traders and visitors from Islamic countries and Europe; the 1500s to the 1800s and the kingdoms of the Guinea Coast and Rozvi; the slave trade to European expeditions searching for the Nile, the Niger, Timbuktu, and routes to the coast; colonization; and Africa today. Time Chart, Glossary, and Index.

2593. Murray, Jocelyn. *Africa.* Facts on File, 2003. 96pp. ISBN 978-0-8160-5151-9. Grades 6–9.

The author examines as many facets of Africa as possible in two sections, history and region, using full-color illustrations and maps. Chronology, Glossary, Gazetteer, and Index.

2594. Ndukwe, Pat I. *Fulani.* Rosen, 1996. ISBN 978-0-8239-1982-6. Grades 7 up.

Readers will learn about the history of the Fulani people and their social and political life, religious beliefs, and relationship with other peoples in their region of West Africa. The Fulani are mainly Muslim, and the area they inhabit stretches from northern Nigeria to Mali and the Atlantic coast. Further Reading, Glossary, and Index.

2595. Ofosu-Appiah, L. H. *People in Bondage: African Slavery in the Modern Era.* Runestone, 1993. 112pp. ISBN 978-0-8225-3150-0. Grades 7 up.

Beginning with ancient civilizations, this volume takes an historical look at slavery and the position of people who do not have power in a society. It focuses on the African slave trade and its relationship to the New World in the 15th century. Churches, governments, and rulers must take the blame for this unsavory practice, because all of them are implicated at one time or another in its advancement. Photographs and drawings augment the text. Index.

2596. Postma, Johannes. *The Atlantic Slave Trade.* (Guides to Historic Events) Greenwood, 2003. 208pp. ISBN 978-0-313-31862-7; University Press of Florida, 2005. paper ISBN 978-0-8130-2906-1. Grades 9 up.

Among the topics covered in these essays discussing forced migration—known as slavery—are the capture and transportation of slaves through the Middle Passage, the identities of those captured, the economics of slavery, the attempt to end slavery, and the legacy of slavery. Biographies of important figures connected to slavery and thirteen primary documents add to the historical authenticity of the period from the 1400s to the final abolition of New World slavery in 1888. Reproductions of illustrations augment the text. Chronology, Bibliography, Glossary, Notes, Further Reading, Web Sites, and Index.

2597. Pouwels, Randall L. *The African and Middle Eastern World, 600–1500.* (Medieval and Early Modern World) Oxford, 2005. 175pp. ISBN 978-0-19-517673-5. Grades 7 up.

Readers will learn about Islam and how it gained millions of followers after the Prophet Muhammad proclaimed it in the 7th century. The book includes information about trade, religion, conquest, and diplomacy among Muslims, Jews, and Christians in all areas of life. The reader can experience being in a caravan during 600 and visualize what might have happened there. The text also includes brief biographies of important Muslim leaders throughout history. Photographs and reproductions enhance the text. Bibliography, Glossary, Chronology, Further Reading, Web Sites, and Index.

2598. Reece, Katherine. *West African Kingdoms: Empires of Gold and Trade.* (Ancient Civilizations) Rourke, 2005. 48pp. ISBN 978-1-59515-508-5. Grades 4–6.

Reece gives an overview of the West African kingdoms of Ghana, Mali, and Songhai, with a history of the first people, the geography of the area, art, architecture, trade, and beliefs covering the years from 300 to 1600. The Berbers ruled Ghana in the 4th century, and by 1493 Mohammed Aski controlled Songhai when it became Muslim. Photographs and illustrations highlight the text. Glossary, Chronology, Further Reading, Web Sites, and Index.

2599. Reef, Catherine. *This Our Dark Country: The American Settlers of Liberia.* Clarion, 2002. 136pp. ISBN 978-0-618-14785-4. Grades 7 up.

Liberia, on the west coast of Africa, was originally established in 1822 as a haven for free African Americans. The book contains information from letters and speeches to show that whites, including Abraham Lincoln, agreed that relocation of this group could solve racial problems in the United States, but few African American leaders supported this approach. Those who settled saw the land as uncivilized and a way to deny them civil rights. In this country, a class system established itself with the Americo-Liberians at the top, but it does indicate that modern Liberia suffers from the conflicts that developed during colonization. Photographs highlight the text. Bibliography, Notes, and Index.

2600. Sallah, Tijan M. *Wolof.* (The Heritage Library of African Peoples) Rosen, 1996. 64pp. ISBN 978-0-8239-1987-1. Grades 7 up.

Readers learn about the land, history, politics, and religious beliefs of the Wolof people. The book also discusses their relationship with the other peoples who live in their region of West Africa on the coast of Senegal and Gambia. Further Reading, Glossary, and Index.

2601. Sharp, S. Pearl, and Virginia Schomp. *The Slave Trade and the Middle Passage.* (Drama of African-American History) Benchmark, 2006. 70pp. ISBN 978-0-7614-2176-4. Grades 5–8.

See entry 1303.

2602. Sparks, Allister Haddon. *Tomorrow Is Another Country: The Inside Story of South Africa's Road to Change.* University of Chicago, 1996. 254pp. Paper ISBN 978-0-226-76855-7. Grades YA.

From the mid-1980s through April of 1994 South Africa underwent a political transformation. Sparks presents the secret discussions among intelligent and patient leaders that transpired during the five years before Nelson Mandela's 1990 release from prison. This book (a sequel to *The Mind of South Africa*, which tells the history of apartheid) presents the events leading to the election of Mandela as the first president of democratic South Africa in 1994. Additionally, Sparks, a newspaper reporter in South Africa, lists ten reasons why he thinks the South African government will survive. Index.

2603. Swinimer, Ciarunji Chesaina. *Pokot.* Rosen, 1994. 64pp. ISBN 978-0-8239-1756-3. Grades 5–8.

Tracing their origin to the Nile River valley, the Pokots have been cattle herders or farmers throughout their history. They have lived in the Upper Rift Valley of western Kenya in thirty different clans, each identified by a totem animal. The author looks at politics and history, European contact and colonial rule, culture, daily life, and the future, with photographs and reproductions. Glossary, Further Reading, and Index.

2604. Thompson, Leonard. *A History of South Africa.* Yale University, 1995. 288pp. ISBN 978-0-300-06542-8; 2001. paper ISBN 978-0-300-08776-5. Grades YA.

This overview of South African history brings the political aspects of the area in terms of race relations to the fore. Thompson begins with the early black settlements and their chiefs who governed by consensus, followed by the arrival of the Dutch East India Company and its establishment of a slave society at the Cape. When Afrikaner, British colonists, and Europeans arrived, they continued the conquest of the African societies. Other subjects include the gold and diamond industries, the South African War, the Union of South Africa under white minority control, the founding and development of the African National Congress, the apartheid era, and the changes with the election of de Klerk in 1989. Chronology and Index.

2605. Udechukwu, Ada Obi. *Herero.* Rosen, 1996. 64pp. ISBN 978-0-8239-2003-7. Grades 7–10.

The Herero are three distinct subgroups sharing a similar language and culture in the contemporary countries of Botswana, Angola, and Namibia. The narrative covers their religion and culture while emphasizing the difficult political life under German and then South African colonists. Further Reading, Glossary, and Index.

2606. Van Wyk, Gary. *Basotho.* Rosen, 1996. 64pp. ISBN 978-0-8239-2005-1. Grades 7 up.

The author examines the history of the Basotho in Lesotho along with the social life and customs, religion, education, and arts. Further Reading, Glossary, and Index.

2607. Wangari, Esther. *Ameru.* Rosen, 1995. 64pp. ISBN 978-0-8239-1766-2. Grades 5–8.

Various traditions disagree on the origin of the Ameru, but in one story they had to escape Egypt, in a tradition paralleling the Israelites' flight from Egypt. The Ameru eventually reached Kenya. In Kenya, the Ameru district lies on the equator around the slopes of Mount Kenya. History about this group, along with information about its social structure, its customs and rituals, colonialism, and its future, appear in the text. Photographs, boxed information, and maps enhance the text. Glossary, Further Reading, and Index.

Biography and Collective Biography

2608. Allen, John. *Idi Amin.* (History's Villains) Blackbirch, 2003. 112pp. ISBN 978-1-56711-759-2. Grades 5–9.

Idi Amin (1925?–2003) rose to power as the brutal president of Uganda. He used ruthless tactics to rule his people, killing thousands of his countrymen to support his life of luxury. Amin was also reckless and inept, and kept his position for only eight years. Allen also discusses what happened to Uganda after Amin's regime was toppled. Photographs augment the text. Bibliography, Maps, and Index.

2609. Arnold, James R., and Roberta Wiener. *Robert Mugabe's Zimbabwe.* (Dictatorships) Twenty First Century, 2007. 160pp. ISBN 978-0-8225-7283-1. Grades 7 up.

Robert Gabriel Mugabe (1924–) at first appeared a good example when he came to power in Zimbabwe's first free election in 1980. But with his greed and brutality, he changed Zimbabwe into a poor, corrupt nation. Sidebars and photographs enhance the text. Maps, Bibliography, Glossary, Chronology, Notes, Further Reading, and Index.

2610. Barnes, Virginia Lee. *Aman: The Story of a Somali Girl.* Vintage, 1995. 349pp. Paper ISBN 978-0-679-76209-6. Grades YA.

The authors retell the story of Aman, the daughter of a Somali woman in the late 1950s who lived apart from her husband and earned her own living. Aman spends her youth needing money and trying to stay a virgin for marriage, undergoing ceremonial genital surgery at age nine. She falls in love with a forbidden male, and she breaks the taboo when she is 13, a decision that ruins her reputation and her ability to make money. By the time she is 19, at the end of the book, she has faced a difficult marriage, war, risk, and poverty in her determination to survive.

2611. Beah, Ishmael. *A Long Way Gone: Memoirs of a Boy Soldier.* Sarah Crichton, 2007. 229pp. ISBN 978-0-374-10523-5; 2008. paper ISBN 978-0-374-53126-3. Grades YA.

At 13 in 1993, Ishmael Beah, lover of hip-hop videos and mischief, had to leave his home in Sierra Leone when rebel forces attacked his village. After he had run for several months, the national army recruited him and made him a full soldier with possession of an AK-47. He reveals how easily a normal boy can be transformed by killing and by readily available cocaine. A few years later, United Nations agents placed him in a rehabilitation center. He came to the United States and graduated from college, a stark change from his teen years. *Booklist Editors' Choice, Alex Awards, Capitol Choices Noteworthy Titles* (Washington, D.C.), and *School Library Journal Best Adult Books for High School Students*.

2612. Beecroft, Simon G. *The Release of Nelson Mandela.* (Days That Changed the World) Gareth Stevens, 2004. 48pp. ISBN 978-0-8368-5571-5; paper ISBN 978-0-8368-5578-4. Grades 5–8.

On February 11, 1990, Nelson Mandela (1918–) was freed from prison where he had been incarcerated, mainly at Robben Island, for twenty-seven years. Mandela had fought against apartheid, a position that the South African government disapproved. He became a national hero and a symbol of freedom. Eventually he was elected president of the country and received the Nobel Peace Prize for his efforts. Photographs augment the text. Time line, Glossary, Further Reading, and Index.

2613. Bowman-Kruhm, Mary. *The Leakeys: A Biography.* Greenwood, 2005. 150pp. ISBN 978-0-313-32985-2. Grades 9 up.

The Leakey family, of Louis Seymour Bazett (1903–1972), Mary D. (1913–), and Richard E., have led the anthropological world for three generations as they have dug in East Africa for fossil evidence of human origins. Their passion for their work reflects their strong personalities and personal interests through the years. This biography of ten chapters offers information about their lives, discoveries, publications, controversies, and legacy. Bibliography, Glossary, and Index.

2614. Brown, Don. *Uncommon Traveler: Mary Kingsley in Africa.* Illustrated by author. Houghton, 2003. Unpaged. Paper ISBN 978-0-618-36916-4. Grades K–3.

Mary Henrietta Kingsley (1862–1900), self-educated during a secluded English rural childhood, decided to explore West Africa alone. After her parents' deaths in 1892, she left her home where she had been housemaid to a bedridden mother, and took two trips, in 1893 and 1894. In Africa she used her knowledge as an ethnologist to learn about the geography and the people. When she returned she wrote about her wondrous experiences. Bibliography. *Horn Book Fanfare, Bulletin Blue Ribbon*, and *Boston Globe/Horn Book Award Honor*.

2615. Coddon, Karin S. *Black Women Activists.* (Profiles In History) Greenhaven, 2004. 220pp. ISBN 978-0-7377-2313-7. Grades 9 up.

This collective biography presents eleven women who have helped fight for African American freedom in the United States and abroad. They are Ida B. Wells-Barnett, Winnie Mandela, Maria Stewart, Mary Ann Shadd Cary, Sojourner Truth, Mary Church Terrell, Mary McLeod Bethune, Fannie Lou Hamer, Maxine Waters, Rosa Parks, and Marian Wright Edelman. Excerpts from biographies, interviews, and essays emphasize their contributions to society. Further Reading and Index.

2616. Cooper, Floyd. *Mandela: From the Life of the South African Statesman.* Illustrated by author. Puffin, 1999. Paper ISBN 978-0-698-11816-4. Grades 1–4.

In this biography of Mandela, Cooper uses "wind" to symbolize the strength that Mandela found from various lessons in his life including the timelessness of African traditions, which helped him become a leader for South Africa. It recalls his youth in his royal family, his school life, he and his partner being the first blacks to open a law office in Johannesburg, his family, his two marriages, and his time in prison. Bibliography.

2617. Denenberg, Barry. *Nelson Mandela: "No Easy Walk to Freedom".* Scholastic, 1991. 164pp. Paper ISBN 978-0-590-44154-4. Grades 5–8.

Denenberg divides this biography of Mandela into three parts: "Roots," "Afrikaners and Apartheid," and "The Struggle." Within these parts, he includes information about Africa, about the Boers and the British, and about the various groups and events that led to Mandela's imprisonment. In 1980 after the Soweto uprising, the white citizens realized that they must either "adapt or die." When they finally seemed to understand that they could not continue with the old government, they freed Mandela and others who had fought for freedom. Photographs highlight the text. Chronology, Bibliography, Maps, and Index.

2618. Dugard, Martin. *Into Africa: The Epic Adventures of Stanley and Livingstone.* Broadway, 2004. 368pp. Paper ISBN 978-0-7679-1074-3. Grades YA.

Dr. David Livingstone spent years in Africa as a missionary, and in March 1866, at the request of the Royal Geographic Society, he left Zanzibar for Mikindary to began an expedition to find the source of the Nile river. He vanished in a few weeks, and no one heard from him for several years. Finally in 1870, an American newspaper tycoon, James Gordon Bennett, Jr., decided to send the young journalist, Henry Morton Stanley, to search for Livingstone. When Stanley found him, his words, "Doctor Livingstone, I presume?" have become immortal. In alternating chapters between the voices of the two men, the reader sees the rise of the drifter Stanley, as Livingstone seems to become more alone. Among the dangers the men encountered were evidence of the Arab slave trade, sleeping sickness, snakes, carnivorous animals, malaria, war, dehydration, and hunger. Eventually, Livingstone was honored with burial in Westminster Abbey. Maps, Illustrations, Prologue, Epilogue, Notes, Bibliography, and Index.

2619. Duke, Lynne. *Mandela, Mobutu, and Me: A Newswoman's African Journey.* Doubleday, 2003. 294pp. ISBN 978-0-385-50398-3. Grades YA.

During the 1990s, African American Duke traveled through Africa, and after her journey, reported her discussions with Africa's heads of state. Two of them who she presents here are Nelson Mandela (1918–) and Mobutu Sese Seko (1930–1997). Among her topics are Mobutu's corruption and Mandela's push for peace. In between, she reports her conversations with citizens who want clean water and other decencies, and to escape from AIDS. Index.

2620. Equiano, Olaudah, and Ann Cameron. *The Kidnapped Prince: The Life of Olaudah Equiano.* Random House, 2000. 133pp. Paper ISBN 978-0-375-80346-8. Grades 7–10.

When prince Olaudah Equiano was a young boy, slavers captured him and took him from his home. He realized that knowledge might save him, and he learned to box, to cut hair, navigate a ship, ride a horse, to load a gun, to do accounts, to trade in order to buy his freedom, and, most important, to read and write. He survived to write his story. He wanted to show that those who said that the lives of slaves were happy were wrong; these people were only interested in protecting their economic welfare. His book became a bestseller soon after its publication in 1789. Eight editions were published within three years in England and America.

2621. Forna, Aminatta. *The Devil That Danced on the Water: A Daughter's Quest.* Grove, 2004. 403pp. Paper ISBN 978-0-8021-4048-7. Grades YA.

As a child of 10 in Sierra Leone during 1974, Aminatta Forna saw police take her physician father to jail because he was supposedly involved in an assassination attempt. He had married her mother in Scotland where he studied, against the wishes of her family, and later brought his wife and three children to Sierra Leone. He joined the All People's Congress, hoping to break the Sierra Leone's People's Party. He became the minister of finance, but his party also became corrupt. After he became involved in politics, his marriage began to disintegrate. His arrest was for treason, and Forna had to struggle to find out his fate—execution.

2622. Fuller, Alexandra R. *Don't Let's Go to the Dogs Tonight: An African Childhood.* Random House, 2003. 336pp. Paper ISBN 978-0-375-75899-7. Grades YA.

From 1972 to 1990 Alexandra Fuller (Bobo) lived in Central Africa. Her parents moved to Rhodesia (now Zimbabwe) when she was 2, and while there, she endured the death of three siblings, one a beloved sister; her mother's fight with alcoholism and then severe depression; the loss of a farm; and a subsequent move to Malawi. They resettled next in Zambia after the Malawi government became overbearing. Her father fought on the British side in the Rhodesian civil war, and her mother taught them to be independent and careful. Bobo learned not to rush into her parents' room at night because they slept with loaded guns beside the bed. Snakes lurked around their home, but they were allowed to live because they killed rats. In this memoir, Fuller writes from the point of view of the child she was at the different stages of her life. The chapter titles often name wars and events that moved the family from place to place.

2623. Gaines, Ann. *Nelson Mandela and Apartheid in World History.* (In World History) Enslow, 2001. 128pp. ISBN 978-0-7660-1463-3. Grades 5–9.

The nine chapters of the text presenting Nelson Mandela's (1918–) life begin with his acceptance of the Nobel Peace Prize. Then Gaines details the apartheid in South Africa and Mandela's role as a freedom fighter before he was arrested and imprisoned. The struggle continued, and eventually, with support throughout the world, apartheid ended, and Mandela was freed. He became the president of the country that imprisoned him, and the world recognized his role in gaining peace and equality for his people. Chronology, Notes, Further Reading, Web Sites, and Index.

2624. Gourley, Catherine. *Beryl Markham: Never Turn Back.* Conari, 1997. 224pp. Paper ISBN 978-1-57324-073-4. Grades 6–10.

Beryl Markham (1903–1986) spent most of her life in Kenya although born in England. She became a pilot in the early days of aviation, setting a record with her trans-Atlantic flight; was a horse trainer; and spent time in Hollywood after publishing a book. Gourley examines Markham's life and the risks that she took without regard to being female. Bibliography and Index.

2625. Holland, Gini. *Nelson Mandela.* Illustrated by Mike White. (First Biographies) Steck-Vaughn, 1997. 32pp. Paper ISBN 978-0-8172-6886-2. Grades K–3.

Nelson Mandela (1918–), the son of a Thembu chief, advocated civil rights for his people in South Africa. After obtaining a law degree and serving twenty-seven years in prison when he challenged the government's laws, he emerged and was elected president of South Africa. This biography is a good introduction to the problems of apartheid. Key Dates.

2626. Hughes, Libby. *Nelson Mandela: Voice of Freedom.* Iuniverse.com, 2000. 144pp. Paper ISBN 978-0-595-00733-2. Grades 6–9.

Nelson Mandela (1918–) has had a major impact on race relations in South Africa, partly by suffering personal deprivation. He helped to establish the African National Congress and the anti-apartheid movements that struggled to give blacks their rights, but he was incarcerated as a political prisoner for twenty-seven years. He became president of South Africa after the period covered in this book ends. Bibliography and Index.

2627. Kamara, Mariatu, and Susan McClelland. *The Bite of the Mango.* Annick, 2008. 216pp. ISBN 978-1-55451-159-4; paper ISBN 978-1-55451-158-7. Grades 9 up.

After a contented childhood in her rural Sierra Leone village, Mariatu Kamara, 12, was first raped by a man that her elders trusted and then faced rebels who wanted to destroy everything they saw. One chopped off both her hands and left her for dead. She made her way to a nearby hospital where she reunited with her remaining family members. She discovered then that she was pregnant, and to keep herself and her son alive, she had to beg in the streets. When journalists wanted to report about her situation, she was skeptical, but Canadians wanted to help her and, after bringing her to their home, offered her an education. Today, she attends college in Toronto and says that tasting a mango gave her the will to live.

2628. Keller, Bill. *Tree Shaker: The Story of Nelson Mandela.* Kingfisher, 2008. 128pp. ISBN 978-0-7534-5992-8. Grades 8 up.

Keller, the author, spent years in South Africa reporting on apartheid and was there in the 1990s when Nelson Mandela (1918–) was freed from prison and the country had its first democratic elections. He also interviewed Mandela. The book offers a short history of the country, an overview of apartheid, Mandela's role in the resistance, his trial, his imprisonment on Robben Island, and life in post-apartheid South Africa. Mandela's parents named him Rolihlahla, a Xhosa word for "tree shaker." Additional resources include photographs, quotations, and other primary sources along with a DVD. Chronology, Notes, and Index.

2629. Kittinger, Jo S. *Jane Goodall.* Children's, 2005. 24pp. ISBN 978-0-516249-40-7. Grades 1–2.

See entry 2436.

2630. Markham, Beryl, and Don Brown. *The Good Lion.* Illustrated by Don Brown. Houghton, 2005. 32pp. ISBN 978-0-618-56306-7. Grades 2–4.

One day in 1906, Beryl Markham and her father visit a neighbor in Kenya with a pet lion. Beryl watches Paddy the lion come closer and closer to her, but she knows that the family trusts the animal. She passes him, and he roars and bites her leg. She feels sorry for Paddy because after that incident, he is kept locked up in a cage. Illustrations enhance the text.

2631. Mathabane, Mark. *Kaffir Boy: The True Story of a Black Youth's Coming of Age in Apartheid South Africa.* Free, 1998. 303pp. Paper ISBN 978-0-684-84828-0. Grades 7 up.

Mark Mathabane (1960–) grows up in South Africa during the time of apartheid. As a child in a black family of Alexandra, his mother and grandmother help him attend school while his father wants to know why it is necessary. He watches black police burst into his home in the middle of the night and treat his parents with disdain because they do not have a pass book for living there. American tennis star Steve Smith discovers his ability to play tennis, and Mathabane is able to get a tennis scholarship to a South Carolina college in 1978.

2632. Myers, Walter Dean. *At Her Majesty's Request: An African Princess in Victorian England.* Scholastic, 1999. 146pp. ISBN 978-0-590-48669-9. Grades 5–8.

Seven-year-old Sarah Forbes Bonetta (b. 1843?), an African (Egbado) princess, was scheduled for ritual sacrifice by the Dahomans, a rival tribe. But an English naval officer saved her. He convinced King Gezo to produce palm oil instead of slaves, and the king offered the child to Queen Victoria. The officer brought the child to England where she lived with Queen Victoria until her arranged marriage to an African missionary. Then Sarah returned to Africa to teach in missionary schools and raise her own family. Among the primary sources are pieces of Sarah's letters, Queen Victoria's diary, and news reports. Photographs enhance the text. *Lonestar Reading List* (Texas), *Young Reader Book Awards* (Virginia), and *Bulletin Blue Ribbon.*

2633. Nivola, Claire A. *Planting the Trees of Kenya: The Story of Wangari Maathai.* Illustrated by author. Frances Foster, 2008. Unpaged. ISBN 978-0-374-39918-4. Grades 2–4.

Wangari Maathai of Kenya won the Nobel Peace Prize in 2004, the first African woman to win this award. She founded the Green Belt Movement that encourages people to repair the environment with simple actions such as planting trees. She studied biology in the United States during the early 1960s and learned the importance of keeping the environment healthy. In Kenya large commercial ventures began to overtake small farms, and women had to walk further to find firewood. Thus began her movement. Watercolor illustrations enhance the text. *Notable Trade Books in the Field of Social Studies.*

2634. Otfinoski, Steven. *David Livingstone: Deep in the Heart of Africa.* (Great Explorations) Marshall Cavendish, 2006. 79pp. ISBN 978-0-7614-2226-6. Grades 5–9.

David Livingstone (1813–1873) explored Africa for three decades. He went as a missionary in 1841, and when drought came to his station at the Kolobeng mission, he went to the north and became the first European to see Victoria Falls. He quickly felt that his religious calling was for exploration rather than as a missionary, and he continued exploring other places, including Zambezi, and participated in a search for the source of the Nile. He observed the slave trade and wanted it eradicated, but he also needed the help of those men. After he lost contact with persons outside of Africa for six years, Henry Morton Stanley came to Africa to find him. Livingstone made contributions toward abolitionism and toward the opening of Central Africa so that missionaries could educate and heal the people. Maps, Photographs, Reproductions, Bibliography, Chronology, Further Reading, Notes, Web Sites, and Index.

2635. Oufkir, Malika, and Michele Fitoussi. *Stolen Lives: Twenty Years in a Desert Jail.* Miramax, 2002. 304pp. Paper ISBN 978-0-7868-8630-2. Grades YA.

For twenty years after her father, an aide to Moroccan King Hassan II, failed to assassinate the king during an attempted coup, Malika Oufkir, her mother, and her five siblings lived in a desert penal colony. When they were repeatedly moved to worse and worse environments, they realized they had been left to die. They dug a tunnel and escaped but were recaptured and held for another five years before they were finally released in 1991.

2636. Rumford, James. *Traveling Man: The Journey of Ibn Battuta, 1325–1354.* Houghton, 2001. Unpaged. ISBN 978-0-618-08366-4; Sandpiper, 2004. paper ISBN 978-0-618-43233-2. Grades 3–6.

Ibn Battuta (1304–1377), born in Morocco and trained as a scholar, began his travels in 1325. He spent twenty-nine years away from home on a journey that started as a trip to Mecca. He traversed Egypt, Jerusalem, Tanzania, Asia, India, and China by foot, ship, and camel. When he returned to Morocco, he told his story to the court secretary, Ibn Juzayy, who recorded it in Arabic. The text comes from this transcription. Maps and Glossary. *School Library Journal Best Books of the Year* and *Capitol Choices Noteworthy Titles* (Washington, D.C.).

2637. Schwarz-Bart, Simone, and Andre Schwarz-Bart. *Ancient African Queens.* Translated by Rose-Myriam Rejouis. (In Praise of Black Women) University of Wisconsin, 2001. 272pp. ISBN 978-0-299-17250-3. Grades YA.

Oral traditions, historical accounts, and folklore form the basis for information about ancient African heroines who ruled from prehistory to the 19th century, from Egypt to South Africa. Beginning with Black Eve and black women ten thousand years ago, they are Ahmose Nefretari, Hatshepsut, and Tiye of Egypt; The Candaces; Daurama (mother of seven Hausa kingdoms); Yennenga (mother of the Mossi people near moden Ghana); Sogolon Konté; Amina of Zaria (the Kush queen who defeated Roman armies); Makeda, Heleni, and Mentowah of Ethiopia; Ana de Sousa Nzinga (challenger of the Portuguese conquest of Angola); Beatrice Kimpa Vita (Congolese prophet whom Christian missionaries burned at the stake); Queen Poku; Sogané Touré; Nandi (mother of Shaka Zulu); Tata Ajeché; Modjadjil I; Ranavalona I; Amina Kulibali and N'Daté Yalla of Senegal; Nongqawuse; Sarraounia; Naga; Manta Tisi; Taitu Bethel; Ranavalona III; and Mamochisane. Enhanced with archival illustrations. Bibliography.

2638. Schwarz-Bart, Simone, and Andre Schwarz-Bart. *Heroines of the Slavery Era.* Translated by Rose-Myriam Rejouis. (In Praise of Black Women) University of Wisconsin, 2002. 272pp. ISBN 978-0-299-17260-2. Grades YA.

Using personal writings from North and South America and the Caribbean from the 15th to the 19th centuries, oral tradition, songs and poems, historical accounts, folk legends, and stories and tales from Egypt to southern Africa, this volume offers a tribute to women in Africa and the African diaspora. Others used these women for work and for sex, but they overcame their personal suffering to rebel and to help others become liberated. Among the heroines included are Aqualtune, a Congolese princess enslaved in Brazil and the Caribbean after leading an army of ten thousand warriors in the Battle of Mbwila; Anastasia, an African (perhaps Angolan) slave in Brazil, considered as the contemporary patron saint of Brazil's blacks; Solitude, a slave in the French West Indies who led the survivors of La Goyave and is revered in contemporary Guadeloupe; and Zabeth, a Haitian slave. From America are Phillis Weatley, the child prodigy slave from Boston whose masters published her poetry; Harriet Tubman, the runaway slave who helped hundreds of other slaves escape to freedom in the United States and Canada; Ellen Craft, a slave who successfully escaped to Philadelphia with her husband; and Sojourner Truth, a former slave who became a famous orator espousing the abolition of slavery and the rights of women. Illustrations and Index.

2639. Schwarz-Bart, Simone, and Andre Schwarz-Bart. *Modern African Women.* Translated by Rose-Myriam Rejouis. (In Praise of Black Women) Modus Vivendi, 2003. 272pp. ISBN 978-0-299-17270-1. Grades YA.

Among the fourteen female African rulers and leaders from the 19th century to the present are queens Madam Yoko of the Kpaa Mende and Sierra Leone's national heroine, Yaa Asantewa of Ghana, and Zauditu of Ethiopia. Government leaders are Ellen Zuawayo of the African National Congress who went to prison fighting for women's and civil rights, and Dulcie September, an ANC member who died supporting freedom. Alice Lensina of Zambia fought British colonial rule and was a Lumpa Church prophet. Well known literary figures include Bessie Head of South Africa, Mariama Ba of Senegal, and Buchi Emecheta who left her Nigerian husband to write. Princess Kesso, a Fulani Muslim princess from Guinea, became one of the world's first black models. Miriam Makeba, an internationally known South African singer banned for speaking against apartheid, and Winnie Mandela, once considered the "mother of the nation" who was jailed for fraud and theft, are also featured. Illustrations and Bibliography.

2640. Slaughter, Carolyn. *Before the Knife: Memories of an African Childhood.* Vintage, 2003. 240pp. Paper ISBN 978-0-375-71346-0. Grades YA.

Carolyn Slaughter grew up in colonial Africa in the country of Botswana during the 1950s after her family moved there when she was 3 years old. Her mother suffered from depression and was withdrawn. Her sadistic father raped her when she was 6. Her sisters, Andrea and Susan, could not comfort her. Finally, Slaughter found a friend in an older girl at school and enjoyed the river view from a nearby tree. Throughout, Slaughter retains an intense hatred for her father while loving the beauty of the continent of Africa.

2641. Swiller, Josh. *The Unheard: A Memoir of Deafness and Africa.* Holt, 2007. 288pp. Paper ISBN 978-0-8050-8210-4. Grades YA.

Josh Swiller became a Peace Corps volunteer in Zambia during the mid-1990s. He had to battle deafness during his efforts to dig wells and work in a health clinic in the rural village of Mununga. During his stint he was accused of deflowering a young girl, learned the language, and survived local bullies who wanted to kill him. He survived to tell his story.

2642. Wa Wamwere, Koigi. *I Refuse to Die: My Journey for Freedom.* Seven Stories, 2002. 368pp. ISBN 978-1-58322-521-9; 2003. paper ISBN 978-1-58322-615-5. Grades YA.

Koigi wa Wamwere (1949–) details his life in Kenya beginning with his childhood, the rise of the Mau Mau during British colonial repression, his years in the seminary, being detained by Jomo Kenyatta, the Daniel Arap Moi years, his exile, and the second trial in his life before freedom in 1997. He was imprisoned for thirteen years and thought he would be executed; however, he refused to stop talking. Eventually, members of the international human rights community saved him. Then he served as the director of Africa's National Democratic and Human Rights Organization. He does not forget that America supported African dictators, and he defends "female circumcision" and Qadaffi. Notes.

2643. Waxman, Laura Hamilton. *Jane Goodall.* (History Makers Bios) Lerner, 2007. 48pp. ISBN 978-0-8225-7610-5. Grades 3–5.

See entry 2460.

2644. Wisniewski, David. *Sundiata: Lion King of Mali.* Illustrated by author. Clarion, 1992. Unpaged. ISBN 978-0-395-61302-3. Grades 2–4.

Sundiata (ca. 1200), son of the second wife of the king of Mali, could neither speak nor walk when he was a boy. His father nevertheless chose Sundiata as his heir, and his griot (the man who told him the history of his people) helped him to both talk and walk. When he seemed powerful enough to take the throne, he left Mali so that he could stay alive. When he was 18, he returned to his homeland to defeat the evil usurper king and claim the throne. His rule returned peace to the people.

2645. Zeldis, Yona. *Peaceful Protest: The Life of Nelson Mandela.* Illustrated by Malcah Zeldis. Walker, 2002. Unpaged. ISBN 978-0-8027-8948-8. Grades 2–5.

Nelson Mandela (1918–), initially named Rolihlahla, was one of the most important political leaders of the 20th century. He was arrested for his protests against South Africa's policy of apartheid and imprisoned for twenty-seven years. He was awarded the Nobel Peace Prize in 1993. In 1994, in the first democratic elections in which all registered South African citizens could vote, Mandela became the first black president. Illustrations highlight the text. Bibliography.

Graphic Novels, Biographies, and Histories

2646. Abouet, Marguerite. *Aya.* Illustrated by Clément Oubrerie. Drawn & Quarterly, 2007. 132pp. ISBN 978-1-8949-3790-0. Grades 10 up.

In 1978 on Africa's Ivory Coast, Aya, 19, becomes disenchanted with her shallow friends, Adjoua and Binton. They show interest in only romance and sex, while she wants to become a doctor. Her father, however, would like to see her marry someone wealthy and likes his boss's son, Moussa. Aya knows that Moussa likes to party more than her friends. Her friend Adjuoua becomes pregnant by Moussa, and the country's class distinctions between the multi-living room mansions and the working class "Yop City" residents come to the fore. Glossary. *Booklist Editors' Choice* and *School Library Journal Best Books for Young Adults*.

2647. Lewis, Trondheim. *Bourbon Island 1730.* First Second, 2008. ISBN 978-1-59643-258-1. Grades YA.

Raphael, who has always been fascinated by pirates, travels as an apprentice to ornithologist Chevalier Despentes to Bourbon Island (known as Réunion, near Mauritius in the Indian Ocean) to look for the last dodo. On the island, the pirate leader Buzzard has been captured, and his men are trying to free him. Raphael unexpectedly finds himself in the middle of a pirate fight involving slavery and colonialism. In the French tradition of graphic novels the figures all appear as animals.

2648. O'Hern, Kerri, and Lucia Raatma. *Nelson Mandela.* Illustrated by D. McHargue. (Graphic Biographies) World Almanac, 2006. 32pp. ISBN 978-0-8368-7881-3; 2007. paper ISBN 978-0-8368-7888-2. Grades 3–5.

This graphic biography presents Nelson Mandela (1918–), an important figure in South African history because he fought against apartheid, for which he went to prison for twenty-seven years. When freed at the end of apartheid, he was elected president of his country and has served as an important spokesperson for equality. The book includes background information important to Mandela's life both in text and pictures.

2649. Stassen, Jean-Philippe. *Deogratias, a Tale of Rwanda.* Illustrated by author. Narrated by Alexis Siegel. First Second, 2006. 79pp. Paper ISBN 978-1-59643-103-4. Grades 9 up.

This graphic novel introduces Deogratias, a Hutu boy in love with Benina, a Tutsi, and he, in turn, describes the Tutsi genocide in Rwanda during 1994. He himself has to become involved and suffers a mental breakdown. He remembers the story through flashbacks as he moves from insane to sane periods and back. The strong story and artwork will remain with its readers.

DVDs

2650. *Africa: Shaped by the Past.* Discovery, 2004. 42 min. ISBN 978-1-58738-954-2. Grades 6 up.

The five segments of this DVD cover the history of Africa from its beginnings to the present. "Life on the River: Egypt's Nile" looks at the source of ancient civilization along with the contemporary fellaheen living on the Nile. "Fabric of African Society: Cloth and Clothing Styles" examines the history of weaving and its importance as a tribal custom. "Sunken City: Alexandria" reveals the submerged city of ancient Alexandria in an underwater expedition. "Slave Trade" shows that Africa ruled the slave trade for thousands of years. "Apartheid's Legacy" discusses the oppressive policy of apartheid and how it still affects its citizens even after it has ended. Live action and animation aid the discussion.

2651. *Refugees in Africa: Another Quiet Emergency.* Films for the Humanities, 2006. 22 min. ISBN 978-1-4213-4110-1. Grades 9 up.

From a segment of *Nightline*, this DVD reveals the plight of the night commuters—African children who travel at night from their small villages to safer cities in order to escape from the Ugandan rebel militia, the Lord's Resistance Army. Since 1994 the militia has kidnapped over 30,000 children and made them commit brutality. Interview with shelter workers and refugees show the horror of this practice and the hope for overcoming this awful fate for these children.

2652. *South Africa, A Case Study.* (Global Human Rights) Disney Educational, 2006. 18 min. ISBN 978-1-59753-083-5. Grades 6 up.

The video looks at human rights abuses in South Africa using archival news footage. It gives an overview of the history of South Africa and the horrible practice of apartheid before it was outlawed.

Compact Discs

2653. Beah, Ishmael. *A Long Way Gone: Memoirs of a Boy Soldier.* Narrated by Ishmael Beah. McMillan Audio, 2007. 7 CDs; 8.5 hrs. ISBN 978-1-4272-0230-7. Grades YA.

See entry 2611.

2654. Fuller, Alexandra R. *Don't Let's Go to the Dogs Tonight: An African Childhood.* Narrated by Lisette Lecat. Recorded Books, 2004. 9 CDs; 10.25 hrs. ISBN 978-1-4025-9040-5. Grades YA.

See entry 2622.

2655. Haley, Alex. *Roots.* Narrated by Avery Brooks. BBC Audiobooks, 2008. 12 CDs; 15 hrs. ISBN 978-1-6028-3386-9. Grades YA.

See entry 2550.

2656. Kingsolver, Barbara. *The Poisonwood Bible.* Narrated by Dean Robertson. Brilliance Audio, 2004. 10 CDs; 16 hrs. ISBN 978-1-59355-951-9. Grades YA.

See entry 2554.

2657. Oufkir, Malika, and Michèle Fitoussi. *Stolen Lives: Twenty Years in a Desert Jail.* Narrated by Edita Brychta. Hyperion Audio, 2006. 5 CDs; 6 hrs. ISBN 978-1-4013-8493-7. Grades YA.

See entry 2635.

2658. St. John, Lauren. *Dolphin Song.* Narrated by Adjoa Andoh. Listening Library, 2008. 5 CDs. ISBN 978-0-7393-6329-4. Grades 4–7.

See entry 2560.

2659. St. John, Lauren. *The White Giraffe.* Narrated by Adjoa Andoh. Listening Library, 2007. 4 CDs; 4 hrs. 47 min. ISBN 978-0-7393-5052-2. Grades 4–7.

See entry 2561.

2660. Whelan, Gloria. *Listening for Lions.* Narrated by Bianca Amato. Recorded Books, 2005. 5 CDs; 4.75 hrs. ISBN 978-1-4193-9410-2. Grades 6–9.

See entry 2566.

AUSTRALASIA AND ANTARCTICA

Historical Fiction and Fantasy

2661. Bainbridge, Beryl. *The Birthday Boys.* Carroll & Graf, 1995. 189pp. Paper ISBN 978-0-7867-0207-7. Grades YA.

In this fictionalized account of the trek to the Antarctic by British explorer Robert Falcon Scott, the story comes from the diaries of five men on the journey: Evans, Wilson, Bowers, Oates, and Scott himself. Oates tells of the final segment, walking to the Pole when they see Roald Amundsen's black flag announcing that he has already arrived and that they are not first. He notes that Scott had disregarded the strength, superiority, and terrain of the hostile Antarctic, and ignored the fact that dogs were the only feasible transport. Then Oates welcomes the disorientation before his death.

2662. Barron, T. A. *The Day the Stones Walked: A Tale of Easter Island.* Illustrated by William Low. Melanie Kroupa, 2007. 32pp. ISBN 978-0-399-24263-2. Grades K–3.

Pico's mother asks him to run and warn his father that a storm is coming to their Easter Island home. Pico's father is carving on the *moai*, the giant stones that legend says protect the island in time of trouble. When the storm hits—a tsunami—Pico is tossed in the water, but he grabs a stone (or it grabs him) and by holding on to it, he survives. And his father is also saved. Illustrations augment the text. Note.

2663. Dubosarsky, Ursula. *The Red Shoe.* (Neal Porter) Roaring Brook, 2007. 179pp. ISBN 978-1-59643-265-9. Grades 7 up.

In 1954 Matilda, 6, and her two sisters, Frances, 11, and Elizabeth, 15, live in Sydney, Australia, after World War II. They must deal with their mentally unstable father, their mother who is unfaithful to him, and the defecting Russian spy next door. Since Matilda does not understand the implications of her situation, she can only observe the men in big black cars who show up next door carrying guns. When the family goes on a picnic, her father attempts to hang himself in front of his brother, who is probably having an affair with their mother. And Elizabeth does not want to return to school, the victim of a mental breakdown. Thus the family's life becomes a backdrop to the international spy story next door.

2664. Farr, Richard. *Emperors of the Ice: A True Story of Disaster and Survival in Antarctica, 1910–13.* Farrar, 2008. 215pp. ISBN 978-0-374-31975-5. Grades YA.

Apsley G. B. Cherry-Gerrard (1886–1959) accompanied Captain Robert Falcon Scott's Antarctic expedition in 1910 as an assistant zoologist who was looking for emperor penguin eggs. This fictional, first-person account based on Cherry-Gerrard's autobiography, tells of the threat of death with almost every movement, and some of the expedition's desire to beat the Norwegian Roald Amundson to the South Pole. When Cherry-Gerrard left the compound with two other men just to find the eggs, he found that like all the other ventures, he became focused on survival. Photographs and maps highlight the text. Bibliography, Chronology, and Further Reading. *Notable Trade Books in the Field of Social Studies.*

2665. Gee, Maurice. *The Fire-Raiser.* Houghton, 2007. 172pp. Paper ISBN 978-0-618-75041-2. Grades 6 up.

In 1915 someone sets a fire in Kitty's New Zealand town. No one knows the culprit, but the children suspect one man of the deed. Although the adults disagree, the children also find benzene cans and rags near his home. When he repeats the arson, the children prove to be correct.

2666. Grenville, Kate. *The Secret River.* Canongate, 2006. 334pp. ISBN 978-1-8419-5797-5; 2007. paper ISBN 978-1-8419-5914-6. Grades YA.

In 1806 bargeman William Thornhill chooses transport to New South Wales, Australia, over a death sentence, for stealing a shipload of expensive woods. His loving family accompanies him. When they arrive in Sydney, no more than a collection of huts, he follows what the others have done before him, staking out some land, which he calls "Thornhill's Point." The aborigines do not recognize land ownership, and eventually a massacre occurs in which Thornhill unwillingly participates. The lone aborigine survivor, Jack, continues to reject Thornhill's claim to ownership and maintains his connection to the land. *School Library Journal Best Adult Books for Young Adults.*

2667. Hartnett, Sonya. *Thursday's Child.* Candlewick, 2003. 272pp. Paper ISBN 978-0-7636-2203-9. Grades 7 up.

Seven-year-old Harper Flute lives in the Australian Outback during the Great Depression. Her brother Tin, 5, the middle child, is buried in a mudslide and is shaken by this accident. He starts to dig tunnels beneath the family's shanty home and makes few appearances above ground over the next years, each time looking more feral than before. Because he has intense hearing, he can tell what is happening at home and wants to take revenge against the family's enemies. As Harper grows older over the next fifteen years, she becomes aware of the duality in the world and that only age will help one move ahead.

2668. Herrick, Steven. *By the River.* Front Street, 2006. 250pp. ISBN 978-1-932425-72-7. Grades YA.

In prose poems, Harry, 14, describes his life in the small Australian town in 1962 where he has lived generally on his own with his brother, Keith, since their mother's death. Their father tends to go through the motions of living, although Harry, Keith, and his dad visit her grave each month. Harry also visits the grave of his friend, Linda, who died in a flood. He gets a crush on the school secretary, Miss Spencer, and when she gets pregnant, she has to leave town in disgrace. He realizes that some people who leave town cannot come back, while those who stay, like his dad, have "half memory" lives.

2669. Hesse, Karen. *Stowaway.* Illustrated by Robert Andrew Parker. Simon & Schuster, 2000. 328pp. ISBN 978-0-689-83987-0; Alladin, 2002. paper ISBN 978-0-689-83989-4. Grades 5–9.

In 1767 when Captain James Cook's ship, the *H.M.S. Endeavour* leaves Plymouth, England, Nicholas Young, 11, stows away to escape his apprenticeship with an abusive butcher. He has to stay on the ship for three years while Cook secretly searches for a lost continent for the British Navy, thought to be between the southern tip of South America and New Zealand. During the voyage, Nick keeps a journal to chart the voyage and to relate the adventures at each port of call. In 1769 when the ship reaches Tahiti, he becomes a crew member as a surgeon's assistant because he can read and write. Nick teaches the man who helped him stow away to read; befriends a Tahitian boy; enjoys the discoveries of the naturalist Joseph Banks; observes floggings and sickness; and witnesses cannibalism. *School Library Journal Best Books of the Year* and *Children's Book Award* (Massachusetts) nomination.

2670. Jeans, Peter Christopher. *Bodger.* UWA, 2001. 279pp. Paper ISBN 978-1-876268-65-7. Grades 9 up.

While Angus McCrea's mother remarries after his father dies in 1945, he and his sister Rebecca must move to the Australian bush with them. Angus helps his stepfather fix pipes for his job at the Water Board, slides in mud, and rides his old bicycle. But getting a puppy—Bodger—for his birthday helps him most in his recovery from losing his father. With new friends, he meets Anna Rosenthal, a Greek widow living nearby. When fires break out near her house, Angus and Bodger run to help her. They discover that a farmer wants to kill her and claim her land, rich with minerals. Angus's growth during the year adds depth to his story.

2671. Jones, Lloyd. *Mister Pip.* Dial, 2007. 224pp. ISBN 978-0-385-34106-6; 2008. paper ISBN 978-0-385-34107-3. Grades YA.

Matilda, 13, does not understand the violence in her village on a tropical island off the coast of Papua New Guinea in the 1990s. Government troops and local armed rebels have been fighting, and the teachers have left. The only remaining white man, Mr. Watts, is married to a local woman thought to be mad. He takes over the class and reads from his favorite novel, Charles Dickens's *Great Expectations*. Although they at first do not understand many of the words, the entire class soon becomes completely engrossed in the novel, Pip and Victorian England seeming more real to them than their own surroundings. Matilda begins to understand that the imagination may be the only way to survive a civil war. *Man Booker Prize* finalist and *Alex Award*.

2672. McKernan, Victoria. *Shackleton's Stowaway.* Random House, 2005. ISBN 978-0-375-82691-7; Laurel-Leaf, 2006. paper ISBN 978-0-440-41984-6. Grades 5–9.

Perce Blackborow (1894–1949), 18, stows away on the *Endurance* in 1914 as Ernest Shackleton leaves for his Antarctic expedition. He has more adventures than he anticipated, including losing the feeling in the toes of his left foot to frostbite. He finally returns home, having survived two years in the cold after ice crushed the ship. In this fictional recounting of his experience, he also has found more boredom, exhaustion, terror, and excitement than he could ever have imagined. Further Resources.

2673. Morgan, Clay. *The Boy Who Spoke Dog.* Dutton, 2003. 144pp. ISBN 978-0-525-47159-2; Puffin, 2005. paper ISBN 978-0-14-240343-3. Grades 4–7.

During the early 1800s orphaned cabin boy Jack, from San Francisco, washes up on an uninhabited island near New Zealand after the ship's crew puts him adrift to save him from drowning on the sinking ship. A group of dogs protecting the local sheep from wild dogs look after him, especially Moxie, a border collie. Jack begins to communicate telepathically with Moxie, and he rescues them from the fangos.

2674. Newton, Robert. *Runner.* Knopf, 2007. 209pp. ISBN 978-0-375-83744-9. Grades 7 up.

Charlie Feehan, 16, lives in Richmond, Australia, in 1919. Since his father is dead, Charlie wants to quit school and go to work so that he can support his baby brother and his mother. Without his mother's permission he becomes an errand boy for a mobster, Squizzy Taylor, who has seen him running each night. Charlie misses school to deliver illegal liquor for Taylor, but soon he discovers his dangerous mistake. When a gang attack cripples Charlie's fellow runner, Norman Nostrils Heath, Charlie is too afraid to help him. Charlie then accepts his neighbor's offer to help him train for the big Bellarat Mile Race. Charlie wins and uses his money to help his disabled friend, Nostrils.

2675. Rees, Douglas. *Smoking Mirror: An Encounter with Paul Gauguin.* Watson-Guptill, 2005. 176pp. ISBN 978-0-8230-4863-2. Grades 8 up.

In 1891 Mexican American Joe Sloan arrives in Papeete, Tahiti, with his French friend Robert, to search for Robert's Tahitian fiancée, Tehane. Someone murders Robert, and Joe is determined to find him while haunted by Smoking Mirror, the Aztec god of loss and change. Joe meets artist Gauguin (1848–1903) who helps him overcome his hostility. Joe falls in love with Tehane and begins to support Gauguin as he tries to find "savage" beauty. Eventually, Gauguin helps Joe confront Smoking Mirror and overcome his suicidal thoughts. Chronology, Notes, and Further Reading.

2676. Scieszka, Jon. *South Pole or Bust (An Egg).* (I Can Read) HarperCollins, 2007. 48pp. Paper ISBN 978-0-06-111640-7. Grades 1–3.

Joe, Fred, and Sam time-travel to 1911 Antarctica and meet Captain Robert F. Scott and his expedition. They help the group find the emperor penguin's eggs. Adapted from the Time Warp Trio series and based on the television series for beginning readers.

2677. Sparrow, Rebecca. *The Year Nick McGowan Came to Stay.* Borzoi, 2008. 208pp. ISBN 978-0-375-84570-3. Grades 8–10.

In Australia during 1989, Rachel Hill is shocked when Nick McGowan, the most popular boy she knows, comes to live with her family. He has been expelled from boarding school for setting off fire alarms. She knows no way to make him think she is worthy of his attentions, and she and her friend, Zoë , snoop around to find out about him. She discovers that Nick is depressed and has contemplated suicide, an unexpected side. They soon see each other's virtues and begin a deep and lasting friendship.

2678. Sperry, Armstrong. *Call It Courage.* Simon & Schuster, 1968. 95pp. ISBN 978-0-02-786030-6; Simon Pulse, 2008. paper ISBN 978-1-4169-5368-5. Grades 5–7.

Matufu knows that facing the thing he fears most, the sea, is the only way to escape the derision of his Polynesian island people, who call him "Boy Who Was Afraid." Almost drowned as a child with his mother, who saved him as she died, he has not recovered from the fear. He takes his dog into a canoe, and they leave. An albatross guides them through a storm toward land, and Matufu saves himself and the dog by killing a tiger shark, octopus, and wild boar. When they see savages on the island, he and the dog sail away in the canoe he built. As he arrives home and his father declares his pride in his son, he dies. His new name, however, is the tribal name by which he is remembered, "Stout Heart." *Newbery Medal.*

2679. Taylor, Theodore. *The Bomb.* Harcourt, 2007. 200pp. Paper ISBN 978-0-15-206165-4. Grades 7 up.

Each chapter in this novel about a 16-year-old boy's concern about U.S. atomic bomb tests on his Pacific island, Bikini Atoll, is introduced with a single statement about an aspect of the bomb. Sorry Rinamu does not believe the government when it tells the islanders, before displacing them, that they will be able to return to the island in two years. Sorry, Grandfather Jonjen, and Tara are the last to leave, thinking that they can be six miles away before the actual drop of Operation Crossroads occurs. They are wrong. The government was also wrong. Almost fifty years after the test, Bikini Atoll will poison anyone who tries to survive on its land. *American Library Association Best Books for Young Adults*, *New York Public Library's Books for the Teen Age*, *Notable Children's Trade Books in the Field of Social Studies*, and *Scott O'Dell Award*.

History

2680. Armstrong, Jennifer. *Shipwreck at the Bottom of the World: Shackleton's Amazing Voyage.* Random House, 2000. 134pp. Paper ISBN 978-0-375-81049-7. Grades 6 up.

In 1914 Ernest Henry Shackleton (1874–1922) and his Imperial Trans-Antarctic Expedition were trapped in their ship, the *Endurance* for nine months. When the ice finally crushed the ship, the group had to cross ice and sea to reach inhabited land. They spent the winter on ice floe camps where they battled diarrhea, insomnia, dehydration, boredom, and despair. Then they drifted on the floes to reach open water. After the dangers of melting ice and the open-boat, they reached a semblance of civilization. The nineteen chapters offer details about their lives, their comments about the experience, the different types of ice, the awful cold, the 800-mile open-boat journey, and the survival of all twenty-seven men. Archival photographs enhance the text. Bibliography and Index. *Horn Book Fanfare, Capitol Choices Noteworthy Titles* (Washington, D.C.), *American Library Association Best Books for Young Adults*, *Horn Book/Boston Globe Book Awards*, *Rebecca Caudill Young Readers' Book Awards* (Illinois), *Battle of the Books* (New Mexico), *Publishers Weekly's Best Books*, *Children's Informational Book Awards* (Utah), *State Reading Association for Young Readers* (Virginia), *Bulletin Blue Ribbon*, and *VOYA: Nonfiction Honor List*.

2681. Arnold, Caroline. *Uluru: Australia's Aboriginal Heart.* Illustrated by Arthur Arnold. Clarion, 2003. 64pp. ISBN 978-0-618-18181-0. Grades 5–8.

Readers will learn about Uluru, formerly Ayers Rock, and Kata Tjuta, tourist attractions within an Australian national park. The lands here have been returned to the aboriginal people, the Anangu, to whom the place has been sacred for at least 10,000 years. Uluru, the largest rock on the earth, towers one thousand feet above ground and extends three miles below. Arnold discusses the geology and the origins of the rock formation along with the landscape and wildlife in the area. Photographs augment the text. Glossary and Index.

2682. Bredeson, Carmen. *After the Last Dog Died: The True-Life, Hair-Raising Adventure of Douglas Mawson and His 1911–1914 Antarctic Expedition.* National Geographic, 2003. 64pp. ISBN 978-0-7922-6140-7. Grades 5 up.

As a youngster, Douglas Mawson loved geology. He later accompanied Ernest Shackleton to Antarctica in 1908 to study glaciers, going as far as the magnetic South Pole and back. He decided not to accompany Robert Scott, but needing more research, he led his own expedition in 1912, the Australian Antarctic Expedition, to study unknown areas of the continent. He, his two companions, Lt. Belgrave Ninnis and Dr. Xavier Mertz, and their sled dogs set out from his base camp to explore the ice shelf. After five weeks, Ninnis perished when he fell into a crevasse with most of the food. During the next few days, Mertz and Mawson had to eat the dogs to survive. They returned to camp alive, but Mertz soon died, evidently poisoned from Vitamin A in the dogs' livers. Mawson recovered and returned home. Photographs, Reading List, Time Line, Web Sites, and Index. *Golden Kite Award* nomination.

2683. Druett, Joan. *Island of the Lost.* Algonquin, 2007. 304pp. ISBN 978-1-56512-408-0. Grades YA.

In 1864 the *Grafton* shipwrecked on one end of uninhabited Auckland Island, and on the other end, the *Invercauld* wrecked. The *Grafton*'s sailors, captained by French gold miner François Raynal and Thomas Musgrave, were headed to Campbell Island for silver-laden tin. They built a cabin and a forge and survived for two years while building another ship to leave the island. Of the nineteen sailors that survived the *Invercauld* wreck, only three remained alive to be rescued. They had been bound for South America from Scotland. The story relies on the survivors' journals to describe their struggles for food, and their furniture, friendship, and use of leisure time. They also had to wash clothes, hunt for sea lions, and make plans for being saved.

2684. Howard, Amanda. *Kidnapping File: The Graeme Thorne Case.* (Crime Solvers) Bearport, 2007. 32pp. ISBN 978-1-59716-548-8. Grades 3–6.

Howard presents a case for the reader with information about the police procedures, the witness interviews, the forensic evidence gathered, and information about the accused. Sidebars add facts. Photographs and illustrations augment the text. Glossary, Further Reading, Web Sites, and Index.

2685. Landis, Marilyn J. *Antarctica: Exploring the Extreme: 400 Years of Adventure.* Chicago Review, 2001. 512pp. ISBN 978-1-55652-428-8. Grades YA.

Readers will learn about four centuries of exploration to Antarctica and the forty expeditions, some successful and others not, made between Magellan's in 1520 to those of 20th-century scientists. Sources include the diaries and narratives of men including Magellan, Cook, Drake, Ross, Scott, Weddell, Shackleton, and Amundsen. The four parts of the text begin with the search for the land mass itself, the islands around it, and its wildlife. Photographs enhance the text. Bibliography, Chronology, Glossary, and Index.

2686. Stevens, Peter F. *The Voyage of the Catalpa: A Perilous Journey and Six Irish Rebels' Flight to Freedom.* Basic, 2002. 400pp. ISBN 978-0-7867-0974-8; 2003. paper ISBN 978-0-7867-1130-7. Grades YA.

In 1876 Captain George Anthony took an American whaling ship, the *Catalpa*, into Fremantle, Australia, and helped rescue six Irish political prisoners from a British prison. These men had been in the British Army in Dublin but had taken a secret Fenian oath to fight for an independent Ireland. The book, in five parts, covers the rebels, their feelings in prison, the decision to rescue them, the situation that allowed the rescue to happen when the men were assigned to duties outside the prison, and the return home. Index.

2687. Torres, John A. *The Ancient Mystery of Easter Island.* (Natural Disasters) Mitchell Lane, 2007. 32pp. ISBN 978-1-58415-495-2. Grades 4–6.

On Easter Sunday in 1722, a Dutch ship discovered a remote Pacific island with huge statues. The author examines these signs of a former culture and discusses how they were constructed and then transported. Presumably a natural disaster led to their erection. Photographs and illustrations augment the text. Chronology, Glossary, Further Reading, Web Sites, and Index.

Biography and Collective Biography

2688. Alexander, Caroline. *The Endurance: Shackleton's Legendary Antarctic Expedition.* Knopf, 1998. 211pp. ISBN 978-0-375-40403-0. Grades YA.

In 1914 Sir Ernest Shackleton took a crew to Antarctica and became stranded in the frozen Weddell Sea. He and the others faced a twenty-month ordeal for survival. Shackleton had almost reached the South Pole in 1909, but failed, and this expedition was meant to change that luck. On May 20, 1916, Shackleton and two companions finally arrived at the Stromness Whaling Company office where station foreman Thoralf Sorlle was working on South Georgia Island. He announced his identity, and Sorlle wept. Photographs highlight the text. *Alex Award.*

2689. Burleigh, Robert. *Black Whiteness: Admiral Byrd Alone in the Antarctic.* Illustrated by Walter Krudop. Atheneum, 1998. 36pp. ISBN 978-0-689-81299-6. Grades 4 up.

Richard Evelyn Byrd (1888–1957) lived alone for months in a small underground structure collecting information on Antarctica's weather and testing his own endurance. The narrative includes entries from Byrd's diary, and the ordeal soon becomes a struggle for life after Byrd becomes ill from carbon monoxide poisoning and needs to be rescued. Oil illustrations enhance the text. *Bulletin Blue Ribbon.*

2690. Gogerly, Liz. *Amundsen and Scott's Race to the South Pole.* (Great Journeys Across Earth) Raintree, 2008. 48pp. ISBN 978-0-4311-9123-2; 2007. paper ISBN 978-1-4034-9761-1. Grades 4–6.

The biography recounts the achievement of Norwegian Roald Amundsen (1872–1928) to reach the South Pole. His race with English explorer, Robert Scott, required much preparation and the journey was grueling and vigorous. Illustrations augment the text. Chronology, Glossary, Further Reading, and Index.

2691. Lawlor, Laurie. *Magnificent Voyage: An American Adventurer on Captain James Cook's Final Expedition.* Holiday House, 2002. 236pp. ISBN 978-0-8234-1575-5. Grades 7 up.

John Ledyard (1751–1789), an American employed as a cook, accompanied Captain James Cook on his third and final voyage on the ship *Resolution*, trying to locate the Northwest Passage. The book includes information from Cook's journals and the writings of others, especially Ledyard. Ledyard wanted to make a name for himself on this voyage, and he recorded the dangers of the Alaskan coast and reaching the Hawaiian islands. He was also aboard ship after Cook was murdered. Archival illustrations augment the text. Bibliography, Glossary, Notes, and Index.

2692. McCurdy, Michael. *Trapped by the Ice! Shackleton's Amazing Antarctic Adventure.* Walker, 2002. 41pp. Paper ISBN 978-0-8027-7633-4. Grades 4–7.

In 1915 Sir Ernest Shackleton tried to cross the Antarctic, but ice stopped and soon sank his ship. Since rescue planes were nonexistent, the crew had to survive without the ship until the ice broke. Their journals tell how they did it without losing a man. Bibliography and Index.

2693. Markle, Sandra. *Animals Robert Scott Saw: An Adventure in the Antarctic.* Illustrated by Phil. Chronicle, 2008. 45pp. ISBN 978-0-8118-4918-0. Grades 2–4.

British explorer Robert Falcon Scott (1868–1912) took two Antarctic expeditions, finally reaching the South Pole in 1912, thirty-five days after Amundsen. The author reveals the animals that were part of his experience. They include his pet Aberdeen terrier, the penguins and petrels on the ice, Manchurian ponies, a dog team, and reindeer hide pajamas and sleeping bags. Archival photographs and acrylic paintings illustrate the text. Glossary, Further Reading, and Web Sites.

2694. Penner, Lucille Recht. *Ice Wreck.* Illustrated by David La Fleur. (Road to Reading) Golden, 2001. Paper ISBN 978-0-307-26408-4. Grades 2–4.

In 1914 Sir Ernest Henry Shackleton (1874–1922) took twenty-seven men and sixty-nine sled dogs aboard a ship, the *Endurance*, on an expedition to the South Pole. They became trapped in the ice and had to survive in the fierce cold of Antarctica for seven months on the ship, five months on the ice floes, and in small lifeboats rowing to a distant island. Shackleton and four others continued to another island to get help for the rest of the crew. All survived in these conditions for eighteen months. Photographs and illustrations highlight the text.

2695. Solomon, Susan. *The Coldest March: Scott's Fatal Antarctic Expedition.* Yale University, 2001. 375pp. ISBN 978-0-300-08967-7; 2003. paper ISBN 978-0-300-09921-8. Grades YA.

In 1912 Robert Falcon Scott (1868–1912) took a British team to the South Pole. The fourteen chapters chronicle their journey, and when they reached the pole in January, they discovered that Roald Amundsen with four other Norwegians had preceded them by a month. Scott and four of his men died on the return, and history has not decided whether he was foolish or a hero. Solomon concludes from her research that the combination of erroneous choices, unpredictable weather in the coldest of winters, and bad luck all contributed to his failure. Maps, sketches, and graphs enhance the text. Index.

2696. Vincent, Erin. *Grief Girl: My True Story.* Delacorte, 2007. 320pp. ISBN 978-0-385-73353-3; 2008. paper ISBN 978-0-385-73386-1. Grades YA.

Australian Erin Vincent's parents are killed in a car accident when she is 14. Her older sister Tracy, 18, resents having to take responsibility for Erin and their toddler brother, Trent, and does not treat them well. Erin herself grieves silently and goes through a number of phases, some rebellious, before finding acceptance.

Graphic Novels, Biographies, and Histories

2697. Hama, Larry. *The Battle of Guadalcanal: Land and Sea Warfare in the South Pacific.* Illustrated by Anthony Williams. (Graphic Battles of World War II) Rosen, 2007. 48pp. ISBN 978-1-4042-0784-4. Grades 4–9.

Many consider the Battle of Guadalcanal, which lasted six months on land and at sea, to be the turning point of World War II. Background about the Japanese and why the war began is followed by information on the war's leaders, the battle itself, and its results. The drawings complement the text in this graphic history. Maps, Bibliography, Glossary, Further Reading, Web Sites, and Index.

DVDs

2698. *Mountain of Ice.* Narrated by Liev Schreiber. (Final Frontier) WGBH Boston, 2003. 1 hr. ISBN 978-1-59375-632-1. Grades 7 up.

See entry 1894.

Compact Discs

2699. Franck, Libby. *Women of the Sea.* Narrated by Libby Franck. Libby Franck, 2003. 1 CD; 1 hr. Grades 7 up.

Three British women used their skills as sailors. Mary Bryant, a Cornwall convict exiled to the penal colony of Australia in 1789 led the only successful escape from the horrible conditions at Botany Bay. She, her husband, and her two children along with other convicts were able to get to Timor. Two other women became pirates on the same ship. Anne Bonny, the spoiled daughter of a plantation owner, and Mary Read, disguised as a man in the English army, were convicted of plunder and murder and were tried in Jamaica in 1721.

2700. Grenville, Kate. *The Secret River.* Narrated by Simon Vance. Blackstone Audio, 2006. 9 CDs; 11 hrs. ISBN 978-0-7861-6792-0. Grades YA.

See entry 2666.

2701. Hartnett, Sonya. *Thursday's Child.* Narrated by Melissa Eccleston. Bolinda Audio, 2004. 4 CDs; 6 hrs. ISBN 978-1-7403-0621-8. Grades 7 up.

See entry 2667.

2702. *Outback: A Journey to the Interior.* Narrated by Dal Burns. Outback Stories, 2002. 2 CDs; 1.5 hrs. ISBN 978-0-9709865-0-4. Grades 6 up.

Dal Burns, storyteller and musician, moved to Australia in the 1960s when he was 17. He encountered homelessness and poverty, and after three years left Sydney for the Outback. There he discovered aborigines and felt at home in their harsh environment and their belief in Dream Time. His entertaining songs pepper this powerful account of a disinherited people.

SOUTHEAST ASIA

Historical Fiction and Fantasy

2703. Cotterill, Colin. *Disco for the Departed.* Soho, 2006. 247pp. ISBN 978-1-56947-428-0; 2007. paper ISBN 978-1-56947-464-8. Grades YA.

In 1977 Dr. Siri Paiboun, the old national coroner, and his assistant, Nurse Dtui, are asked to go to a remote mountain location in the new communist Laos. Dr. Paiboun thinks that he will be able to train Nurse Dtui, who likes the communist regime, but instead, they have to enter a cave where the current president hid before the coup. They see an arm sticking out of concrete, and they have to supervise the disinterment of a body and try to identify it. Dr. Paiboun, who is also a spirit host, experiences strange dreams that help him identify the victim.

2704. Garland, Sherry. *Song of the Buffalo Boy.* Harcourt, 1994. 249pp. Paper ISBN 978-0-15-200098-1. Grades 8 up.

At age 17, Loi remembers an American man from her childhood in 1973, who gave Loi's mother a picture of the three of them before disappearing from her life. Loi, a con-lai (half-breed), and her mother suffer the insults of the neighbors until Loi decides to leave for America with a boy who loves her but whose parents have forbidden him to marry her. Before she leaves, her mother tells her that the man she remembers is not her father. Her mother had to prostitute herself to find food for her own mother during the Vietnam War, and Loi is the result of her decision. *American Library Association Best Books for Young Adults, Notable Children's Trade Books in the Field of Social Studies,* and *New York Public Library's Books for the Teen Age.*

2705. Ho, Minfong. *The Clay Marble.* Sunburst, 1993. 163pp. Paper ISBN 978-0-374-41229-6. Grades 6–9.

Dara, age 12, and her family have to leave their Cambodian farm in 1980 after Communists kill her father in the war. Dara's brother, Sarun, becomes militaristic and shoots her friend by mistake. They finally reach a Thai border refugee camp where they find food and shelter; there they also get rice plants to start over at the war's end, to reform their "clay marble."

2706. Ho, Minfong. *Rice Without Rain.* Lothrop Lee & Shepard, 1990. 236pp. ISBN 978-0-688-06355-9. Grades 7 up.

In Thailand, Jinda, age 17, and her family wonder about the university students who come to their village in 1973 saying that they want to learn about farming. Because the villagers are having a poor rice harvest, they hope for help, and they agree when Ned, the student leader, suggests that they give one-third instead of one-half of their rice to the landlord. Because of this decision, Jinda's father is arrested and sent to prison. When Jinda goes to Bangkok, having fallen in love with Ned, she discovers that he makes speeches supporting Communist ideals. Ned uses her father as an example of governmental oppression. Their story ends realistically.

2707. Kadohata, Cynthia. *Cracker! The Best Dog in Vietnam.* Atheneum, 2007. 260pp. ISBN 978-1-416-90637-7; Aladdin, 2008. paper ISBN 978-1-416-90638-4. Grades 6 up.

Rick Hanski, 17, enrolls in the army and goes to Vietnam, expecting to see the world and avoid a routine job. He becomes a member of the scout-dog team with his partner, Cracker. Cracker, Magnificent Dawn of Venus von Braun, had been trained as a show dog until she broke a leg. Then Willie, her owner, volunteered her to the cause in Vietnam. Cracker and Rick become extremely close as they train to track the enemy, detect booby traps and mines, and rescue POWs. At the war's end, Willie realizes that he can never mean the same to Cracker as Rick does, and gives her to Rick.

2708. Marsden, Carolyn, and Thay Phap Niem. *The Buddha's Diamonds.* Candlewick, 2008. 112pp. ISBN 978-0-7636-3380-6. Grades 4–7.

In Vietnam, Tinh, 10, likes to fish with his father in their new boat, but he has also taken on the adult responsibilities of supporting the family and worshipping. A storm breaks, and although Tinh and his family survive, Tinh feels guilty because he could have saved his little sister from injury, and he could have rescued the family's boat. Instead, he saves his toy car. The water destroys almost everything in the village, and while they struggle to rebuild, Tinh realizes that the important things—the Buddha's "diamonds"—include the intangibles of love, family, and friendship.

2709. Myers, Walter Dean. *Fallen Angels.* Scholastic, 2008. 369pp. Paper ISBN 978-0-545-05576-5. Grades 8 up.

Richie, a 17-year-old African American, enlists in the army and leaves for Vietnam in 1967. He plans to use the money he earns to pay for his brother's school clothes. When he arrives at the front, he realizes that war is quite different from what he expected. After hours of doing nothing, he and his squad have to battle the sly Viet Cong, who often kill before the squad knows they are present. Richie has the "good" fortune of being wounded so that he can return home, but what he has seen continues to disturb his thoughts. *Coretta Scott King Award, American Library Association Best Books for Young Adults, American Library Association Quick Picks for Reluctant Young Adult Readers, Booklist Editors' Choice, Horn Book Fanfare Honor List*, and *School Library Journal Best Book*.

2710. Myers, Walter Dean. *Patrol: An American Soldier in Vietnam.* Illustrated by Ann Grifalconi. Trophy, 2005. 40pp. Paper ISBN 978-0-06-073159-5. Grades 4–8.

While awaiting combat in Vietnam's forests, a young soldier feels terribly afraid and wonders who the enemy might be. When the soldier finally encounters his enemy, he sees that the enemy is his same age. Neither fires. Collage illustrations enlighten the text. *Young Reader Medal* (California) nomination, *Student Book Award* (Maine) nomination, *Great Lakes Great Books Award* (Michigan) nomination, *Dorothy Canfield Fisher Children's Book Award* (Vermont) nomination, *Capitol Choices Noteworthy Titles* (Washington,

D.C.), *Booklist Editors' Choice, American Library Association Best Books for Young Adults, Bulletin Blue Ribbon, Peach Award* (Georgia) nomination, and *Children's Book Award* (West Virginia) nomination.

2711. O'Neill, Susan. *Don't Mean Nothing: Short Stories of Vietnam.* University of Massachusetts, 2004. 272pp. Paper ISBN 978-1-55849-442-8. Grades YA.

During the Vietnam War, the lives of the women who went there changed along with those of the men. They arrived in nurses' uniforms and as USO aides. They had different but difficult problems—an out-of-wedlock child, accidents that maimed, and being among men from all economic and social classes who could rape as easily as revere. Susan O'Neill, the author of these short stories, served in three hospitals "in country," and writes about her experiences as a way of dealing with them.

2712. Shea, Pegi Deitz. *The Whispering Cloth: A Refugee's Story.* Illustrated by Anita Riggio and You Yang. Boyds Mills, 1996. Paper ISBN 978-1-56397-623-0. Grades K–3.

When Mai learns to embroider, her grandmother sells the *pa'ndau* (story cloths) on which she works to traders who come to their Thai refugee camp in the early 1970s. Mai wants to make her own story cloth, but her grandmother tells her that she must first have a story. Mai tells the story of her parents' deaths and escaping with her grandmother to the camp. Her grandmother tells her she cannot sell the cloth until she finishes her story. When Mai decides on an ending, she chooses to keep the cloth. *Notable Trade Books in the Field of Social Studies.*

2713. Smith, Roland. *Elephant Run.* Hyperion, 2007. 318pp. ISBN 978-1-4231-0402-5. Grades 5–7.

In 1941 during the London blitz, the mother of Nick Freestone, 14, sends him to be with his father on his Burmese teak plantation. After his arrival, the Japanese invade, put his father in a prisoner-of-war camp, and take the plantation. Nick has to live with Japanese overseers until he can escape. He meets Mya, a Buddhist monk, a Burmese Robin Hood, a bull elephant, and others who are resisting the Japanese, and they help him rescue his father. Among the things he learns are the use of elephants as draft animals, Japanese gardening, haiku, and Burmese politics, daily life, and spirituality.

2714. Toer, Pramoedya Ananta. *The Girl from the Coast.* Translated by Willem Samuels. Hyperion, 2003. 280pp. Paper ISBN 978-0-7868-8708-8. Grades YA.

A Muslim aristocrat, the Bendoro, spots a beautiful young woman in feudal Java and marries her. He has himself represented at the ceremony as a dagger, and she is sent to his residence as a lowly concubine. In her seeming prison, she despairs for her former life of freedom and pleasure and wonders how someone as horrible as her husband can have so much power when her own kind father has none. In essence, she is more property that he has purchased. The Bendoro eventually takes her child and divorces and banishes her.

2715. Vander Zee, Ruth. *Always With You.* Illustrated by Ronald Himler. Eerdman's, 2008. Unpaged. ISBN 978-0-8028-5295-3. Grades 2–5.

Kim's mother's last words are "I will always be with you," before bombs over their Vietnamese village kill her and damage Kim's eyes. Soldiers take Kim, only 4 years old, to a nearby orphanage where a couple help her feel love. Kim never sees color, but she finally makes a new friend, learns to write, and starts to play with other children. Even though she has little to eat and bombs keep exploding in the distance, she feels secure because of her mother's words. Watercolors enhance the text.

2716. White, Ellen Emerson. *The Journal of Patrick Seamus Flaherty: United States Marine Corps: Khe Sanh, Vietnam, 1968.* Scholastic, 2002. 188pp. ISBN 978-0-439-14890-0. Grades 7–10.

In 1968 Patrick, 18, turns down a college scholarship to join the Marines, and he is sent to Vietnam. He becomes involved in the siege of Khe Sanh and begins to write about it in the diary his father gave him before he left home. He records his loneliness and confusion and his suffering during the four-month North Korean assault. Combat changes him, and he no longer wants friends because they die. Photographs and maps enhance the text. Notes.

2717. Wiggins, Marianne. *John Dollar: A Novel.* Washington Square, 1999. 214pp. Paper ISBN 978-0-671-03955-4. Grades YA.

After her husband dies in World War I, Charlotte goes to Rangoon, Burma, to become a schoolteacher. She finds another life there and enjoys being with a man she meets, John Dollar. They visit an island with other British subjects, but the trip turns into a disaster that only Charlotte survives.

History

2718. Bozonelis, Helen Koutas. *Primary Source Accounts of the Vietnam War.* (America's Wars Through Primary Sources) Myreportlinks, 2006. 128pp. ISBN 978-1-59845-001-9. Grades 8 up.

The book draws from primary sources including letters, diaries, newspaper accounts, songs, speeches, and other documents to access the Vietnam War. It examines the causes of the Vietnam War, military life, and life on the home front to offer insight about those who fought and those who stayed at home during the time. Maps, photographs, and reproductions reinforce the text. Glossary, Chronology, Notes, Further Reading, Web Sites, and Index.

2719. Burrows, Larry. *Vietnam.* Knopf, 2002. 243pp. ISBN 978-0-375-41102-1. Grades YA.

Larry Burrows created these photo essays before he died in action in Laos during 1971. Originally published in *Life* magazine, they reveal much of the tragedy and suffering of courageous soldiers during the Vietnam War. The military allowed him to remove the door from a fighter-bomber so that he could lean out to get unusual shots. Supposedly his request, and not those of other photographers, was granted because the military considered him an artist, not merely a photographer.

2720. Caputo, Philip. *Ten Thousand Days of Thunder: A History of the Vietnam War.* Atheneum, 2005. 128pp. ISBN 978-0-689-86231-1. Grades 7 up.

Caputo examines the significant events and the battles of the Vietnam War in forty-eight topics, referencing the social unrest that evolved in the United States. The background presents the role of communism in the country and profiles various groups including tunnel rats, nurses, villagers, and journalists. It also looks at the war through the viewpoints of Americans, the Viet Cong, North Vietnamese guerrillas, the citizens of other countries, and the American army. A description of each of the battles and the importance of the Ho Chi Minh Trail, the Gulf of Tonkin, the Fall of Saigon, and the DMZ offer further insight. Bibliography, Glossary, Maps, Web Sites, and Index. *Voice of Youth Advocates Nonfiction Honor List.*

2721. Cha, Dia. *Dia's Story Cloth: The Hmong People's Journey of Freedom.* Illustrated by Chue and Nhia Thao Cha. Lee & Low, 1998. 24pp. ISBN 978-1-880000-63-2; paper ISBN 978-1-880000-34-2. Grades 2–4.

While the author's aunt and uncle stayed in a Thai refugee camp, they created a *pa'n-dau* embroidered cloth, which illustrates this text about the Hmong migration from ancient China. The migration continued through Laos, which Cha's people had to leave in the 1960s because of the war; Cha's father joined the loyalists before disappearing. Then they went to Cambodia and over the Mekong River into Thailand as a way to escape the Communist invasions. Cha's family made this journey, and her experiences highlight the history created in the pa'ndau. Bibliography. *New York State Charlotte Award* nomination.

2722. Cottrell, Robert C. *Vietnam: The 17th Parallel.* (Arbitrary Borders) Chelsea House, 2004. 112pp. ISBN 978-0-7910-7834-1. Grades 6–8.

French colonialism and American cold war policies led to the country of Vietnam being arbitrarily partitioned along the 17th parallel into the State of Vietnam and the Republic of Vietnam in 1954 at the Geneva Conference. This division led to much disagreement and the war in Vietnam to reunite the two parts of the original country. The author examines these damaging and improper policies, the American policy based on George Kennan's "Long Telegram," a 1946 report forming the basis of containment. Additionally, Winston Churchill's 1946 "Iron Curtain" speech was a major contribution. Not until 1975 was it reunified. Illustrations and photographs augment the text. Bibliography, Chronology, Further Reading, Notes, and Index.

2723. De Benedetti, Charles, and Charles Chatfield. *An American Ordeal: The Antiwar Movement of the Vietnam War.* Syracuse University, 1990. 495pp. Paper ISBN 978-0-8156-0245-3. Grades YA.

De Benedetti divides the period of the Vietnam War into four parts: 1955–1963, 1963–1965, 1966–1970, and 1970–1975. After the war in Indochina began, it spread to America, and with the war grew a massive antiwar sentiment that challenged cultural norms such as scientific objectivity, religious beliefs, white male dominance, adult standards, acceptance of poverty, the cold war mission, and consensus. This scholarly book discusses the reevaluation of these norms and asserts that the antiwar movement was more about America than Vietnam. Notes, Bibliography, and Index.

2724. Englemann, Larry. *Tears Before the Rain: An Oral History of the Fall of South Vietnam.* Da Capo, 1997. 375pp. Paper ISBN 978-0-306-80789-3. Grades YA.

Engelmann gathered this collection of powerful first-hand stories from people in 1985 about the ending of the Vietnam War, ten years after North Vietnam took over South Vietnam and Saigon was renamed Ho Chi Ming City. The topics discussed with Americans are the last flight from Danang, orphans, congressional delegations, the American Embassy, the CIA, the Defense Attaché Office, the joint military team, the Military Sealift Command, marines, POWs, the media, civilians, and the presidency. Those topics that Engelmann covers with the Vietnamese he interviewed are the military, civilians, children, and victors. A final part looks at the Bui Doi (dust of the earth) and the Vietnamese as a whole. Glossary of Abbreviations and Acronyms and Index.

2725. Gavin, Philip. *The Fall of Vietnam.* (World History) Lucent, 2003. 112pp. ISBN 978-1-59018-182-9. Grades 8 up.

Readers will learn about the fall of South Vietnam in 1975 and its effect on the country and the region. The military victory of the North Vietnamese over the south led to repression and economic difficulties. Other results included a mass exodus of boat people, the invasion of Cambodia, and poor conditions for the Vietnamese people resulting from communist takeover. Photographs augment the text. Bibliography, Notes, and Index.

2726. Goldenberg, Linda. *Little People and a Lost World: An Anthropological Mystery.* (Discovery!) Twenty-First Century, 2006. 112pp. ISBN 978-0-8225-5983-2. Grades 4–8.

In 2003 archaeologists on Flores Island, Indonesia, found a hominid skeleton of a 12,000-year-old woman in the Liang Bua cave who was so tiny—only 3 feet tall—that paleontologists had to decide if she was a homo sapien or a new human species. The author presents information about this find and other "little people" in folklore. In fact, the people on Flores Island have stories about little people as part of their history. Goldenberg also presents comparisons of this figure with other early hominids such as Neanderthals and australopithecine. Photographs and illustrations enhance the text. Bibliography, Glossary, Notes, Further Reading, Web Sites, and Index.

2727. McLeod, Mark. *Culture and Customs of Vietnam.* Greenwood, 2005. 198pp. ISBN 978-0-313-30485-9. Grades 9 up.

This history of social and cultural customs in Vietnam offers background on the flux of the traditional and modern, and socialism and capitalism, that permeate the country. The nine chapters cover the Land, People, and Language; History and Institutions; Thought and Religion; Literature; Art and Architecture; Cuisine; Family, Gender, and Youth Culture; Festivals and Leisure Activities; and Performing Arts. Photographs support the text. Chronology, Bibliography, Glossary, Notes, and Index.

2728. Rodell, Paul. *Culture and Customs of the Philippines.* Greenwood, 2001. 247pp. ISBN 978-0-313-30415-6. Grades 9 up.

This history of social and cultural customs in the Philippines offers background on a country with a wide variety of traditions. The chapters cover the Land, People, and History; Thought and Religion; Art and Literature; Architecture and Housing; Cuisine and Fashion; Marriage, Family, and Gender; Festivals, Theater, Film, Media, and Other Entertainment; Music and Dance; and Social Customs and Lifestyle. Photographs support the text. Chronology, Bibliography, Glossary, Notes, and Index.

2729. Willoughby, Douglas. *The Vietnam War.* (20th Century Perspectives) Heinemann, 2001. 48pp. ISBN 978-1-57572-439-3; paper ISBN 978-1-58810-378-9. Grades 5–9.

The Vietnam War began with a conflict in 1959 and ended on April 30, 1975, when the last American troops left the country. After more than fifteen years, the North Vietnamese won a victory, and the Americans suffered a major political defeat when the Republic of Vietnam (South Vietnam) lost. The author examines the causes of the war, the role of the United States in the war, and the aftermath. Illustrations highlight the text. Bibliography, Further Reading, Glossary, Index.

2730. Winchester, Simon. *The Day the World Exploded: The Earthshaking Catastrophe at Krakatoa.* Collins, 2008. 96pp. ISBN 978-0-06-123982-3. Grades YA.

In 1883 a huge volcanic eruption on the island of Krakatoa killed more than 30,000 people and destroyed the island. The text covers such topics as the science of volcanic eruptions, the Dutch population from the East India Company that inhabited the island, the undersea telegraph available at the time to keep the world informed, and the aftermath of the explosion. Photographs, maps, and illustrations highlight the text. Glossary, Further Reading, and Index.

2731. Young, Marilyn B., and A. Tom Grunfeld. *The Vietnam War: A History in Documents.* (Pages from History) Oxford, 2003. 176pp. Paper ISBN 978-0-19-516635-4. Grades 7 up.

Using documents, speeches, transcripts of conversations, newspapers, magazines, television, songs, memoirs, interviews, and other primary sources, the authors reveal the causes and effects of the Vietnam War. The chapters cover the first Indochina War, Vietnam's overtures to America, and America's response. A temporary peace occurred before Eisenhower's Vietnam, and then it became Kennedy's war. The war expanded as American soldiers went abroad to fight. Experiences covered during the war include those from diverse American cultures and communities including the African Americans and those opposed to the war, both civilian and military. Near its end, the war became Nixon's, and during this period the My Lai massacre occurred. After the bombing of Hanoi, the North Vietnamese began to bargain, and the war finally ended. The text also examines the legacies of the war. Photographs enhance the text throughout. Time line, Glossary, Further Reading, Web Sites, and Index.

Biography and Collective Biography

2732. Arruda, Suzanne Middendorf. *Freedom's Martyr: The Story of Jose Rizal, National Hero of the Philippines.* Avisson, 2003. 106pp. Paper ISBN 978-1-888105-55-1. Grades 6–10.

Jose Rizal (1861–1896) wanted his people in the Philippines to have representation in the ruling Spanish government. He was trained as a doctor, but he also wrote three novels and several poems telling of the problems of the people of his land and of other Pacific islands. His writing excited others to become active politically. Although he was not a traitor, the Spanish executed him for treason just before the American Navy sailed into the port at Manila to liberate the islands from Spanish rule. Photographs highlight the text. Bibliography and Index.

2733. Balaban, John. *Remembering Heaven's Face: A Story of Rescue in Wartime Vietnam.* University of Georgia, 2002. 334pp. Paper ISBN 978-0-8203-2415-9. Grades YA.

Balaban, a conscientious objector, traveled to Vietnam during the war to work for the International Voluntary Services. In 1971 he returned to collect traditional songs. He kept notebooks for twenty years but refused to open them because "their contents [were] unbearable." In 1989 he went to North Vietnam; afterward, he returned to open the notebooks and to relate the terrible things that happened.

2734. Bizot, François. *The Gate.* Translated by Euan Cameron. Vintage, 2004. 320pp. Paper ISBN 978-0-375-72723-8. Grades YA.

In 1971, after François Bizot has been in rural Cambodia as a Khmer pottery and Buddhism scholar for five years, the Khmer Rouge arrest him, accusing him of being a CIA agent, as they begin their methodical genocide. He remembers his relationship with them, especially his interrogator, Ta Douch, who is more a butcher than a humanitarian. None, however, really understand the Buddhist concepts that Bizot uses to show that he is not a CIA agent. When they free him, he has to translate and negotiate at the gate of the French embassy where asylum seekers desperately attempt to escape from sure torture and death. However, the Khmer Rouge ignores international law and storms through the gate as well, taking control of the French compound. When Phnom Penh falls, he manages to escape again, this time bringing children with him.

2735. Brantley, Samuel. *Zero Dark Thirty.* Hellgate, 2002. 270pp. Paper ISBN 978-1-55571-624-0. Grades YA.

During the Vietnam War Samuel Brantley (1943–) served as a Marine aviator, flying A-4 Skyhawks over South Vietnam. Then he became a forward observer for tactical missions during which he had to fly early in the morning at "zero dark thirty." After he left the military and returned home, he could not forget the war and he had difficulty communicating with those who had not had his experiences. Glossary.

2736. Hodgins, Michael C. *Reluctant Warrior: A Marine's True Story of Duty and Heroism in Vietnam.* Ivy, 1997. 400pp. Paper ISBN 978-0-8041-1120-1. Grades YA.

Hodgins served as a lieutenant in Vietnam, and he tells of a soldier's experiences in the rice paddies and the jungles of that war. Additionally, he describes the methods of motivating men to do as well as they could under the unpleasant and adverse conditions.

2737. Huynh, Quang Nhuong. *The Land I Lost: Adventures of a Boy in Vietnam.* Illustrated by Vo-Dinh Mai. Trophy, 1986. 115pp. Paper ISBN 978-0-06-440183-8. Grades 4–7.

Huynh Quang Nhuong grew up in Vietnam during the 1960s and was drafted into the army. A gunshot paralyzed him, and he came to the United States for treatment and further schooling in chemistry. In this book he tells the story of his childhood and the things he remembers. On the list are his beautiful grandmother, crocodiles, horse snakes, killer wild hogs, a two-hundred-pound catfish, taming pythons, fishing in flooded rice fields, and his pet water buffalo. *American Library Association Notable Books for Children, Notable Children's Trade Books in the Field of Social Studies, National Council of Teachers of English Teachers' Choices,* and *Booklist Editors' Choice.*

2738. Kelly, Clara Olink. *The Flamboya Tree: Memories of a Mother's Wartime Courage.* Random House, 2003. 208pp. Paper ISBN 978-0-8129-6685-5. Grades YA.

During World War II Clara Olink Kelly (1913–1970) and her family were interned in a Japanese concentration camp on Java for four years. Her mother helped her and her two siblings survive by finding them food and insisting that they show their manners and decency throughout. From a life of leisure as a Dutch colonial with household servants, her mother went to cleaning out camp sewers. When they eventually returned to Holland, her grandmother only wanted to know why they did not escape.

2739. Kuegler, Sabine. *Child of the Jungle: The True Story of a Girl Caught Between Two Worlds.* Grand Central, 2007. 260pp. ISBN 978-0-446-57906-3. Grades YA.

Sabine Kuegler is 8 in 1980 when her missionary family moves from Germany to the "Lost Valley" in Indonesia and home of the Fayu tribe. In difficult living conditions without running water or electricity, she feels at home living with nature's insects, snakes, and spiders. She and her siblings teach the natives how to play soccer, and the natives teach them how to survive in the jungle. When she is sent to boarding school in Switzerland, she suffers an intense culture shock. She has to learn how to become a western teenager; but after graduating, she is pregnant. She has in succession a failed marriage, a suicide attempt, and a spiritual awakening that help her find herself again. *Booklist Editors' Choice.*

2740. Lord, Michelle. *A Song for Cambodia.* Illustrated by Shino Arihara. Lee & Low, 2008. Unpaged. ISBN 978-1-60060-139-2. Grades 4–6.

Arn Chorn had a lovely childhood in 1970s Cambodia, but the Khmer Rouge separated him from his family and sent him to a work camp. He survived by learning to play the *khim*, a traditional Cambodian instrument. He escaped when Vietnam invaded in 1979, and an American rescue worker, Reverend Peter Pond, brought him to the United States and adopted him. He used his music to fit in to his new country; but he wanted to revive traditional Cambodian art and music, so after the defeat of the Khmer Rouge he returned to his country.

2741. McDonald, Cherokee Paul. *Into the Green: A Reconnaissance by Fire.* Diane, 2003. 272pp. Paper ISBN 978-0-7567-5982-7. Grades YA.

For three years in Vietnam, Cherokee Paul McDonald served as an Artillery Forward Observer. He tells of facing combat, the daily military life, and what being a soldier meant to him. Each of the vignettes realistically recount the war. McDonald disapproves of many in the media who did not portray the men as the stalwart citizens they were. He thinks that the participants were normal men who were doing their best to survive and return home.

2742. Myers, Walter Dean. *A Place Called Heartbreak: A Story of Vietnam.* Illustrated by Frederick Porter. Steck-Vaughn, 1993. 71pp. Paper ISBN 978-0-8114-8077-2. Grades 5–9.

In 1965 Major Fred Cherry was shot down on a routine mission over North Vietnam. He was the forty-third American and the first African American to be captured. The Viet Cong beat him for ninety-two days straight even though his arm and ankle were broken. They finally hospitalized him, but afterward he lived in solitary confinement for almost a year before being imprisoned with other Americans. To communicate, the prisoners used a code of tapping on the walls that the guards could not hear. After being a prisoner for seven and a half years, the war ended, and Fred Cherry was freed. Epilogue, Afterword, and Notes.

2743. Stahl, Bob. *Fugitives: Evading and Escaping the Japanese.* University Press of Kentucky, 2001. 192pp. ISBN 978-0-8131-2224-3. Grades YA.

After the Japanese invaded the Philippines in World War II, Jordan A. Hamner, an engineer, was on an island so isolated that invaders did not occupy it permanently for many months. Hamner decided not to become a prisoner, and he evaded the Japanese with four others by escaping on a boat that they either motored, sailed, or rowed, through 1,500 miles of Japanese waters to Northern Australia. He later returned to work with Philippine guerrillas. Stahl reports with balance on the behavior of the Filipinos during this time.

2744. Stewart, Whitney. *Aung San Suu Kyi: Fearless Voice of Burma.* Iuniverse, 2008. 128pp. Paper ISBN 978-0-595-48320-4. Grades 5 up.

Aung San Suu Kyi is a quiet woman who became the leader of Burma's renewed struggle for democracy. In 1989 the government placed her under house arrest, and from her home she led Burma's National League for Democracy in victory at the polls; however, the military government refused to recognize the election. In 1992 she won the Nobel Prize for Peace, still under house arrest. Stewart interviewed her for this biography. Sources, Bibliography, and Index.

2745. Tram, Dang Thuy. *Last Night I Dreamed of Peace: The Diary of Dang Thuy Tram.* Translated by Andrew X. Pham. Harmony, 2007. 256pp. ISBN 978-0-307-34737-4. Grades YA.

On June 22, 1970, an American soldier shot Dang Thuy Tram in the head as she walked through a North Vietnam jungle. She left a diary that an American going through North Vietnamese documents saved after the war ended. He returned it to her family in 2005. She was a physician from a loving family, devoted to Socialism, and to helping those who needed her. Her diary begins in 1968 when she was 25 and lasts for the next two years. During this time, she wanted peace for both North and South Vietnam while she confronted the horrors of war in the manner that she thought would be most beneficial. Photographs highlight the text. Chronology and Notes. *School Library Journal Best Books for Young Adults.*

2746. Ung, Loung. *First They Killed My Father: A Daughter of Cambodia Remembers.* Perennial, 2006. 240pp. Paper ISBN 978-0-06-085626-7. Grades YA.

Loung Ung was forced to evacuate from Phnom Penh in 1975 at the age of 5. She survived the brutal Cambodian Khmer Rouge under Pol Pot and had to become a child soldier, but her parents—her father a high-ranking government official—did not live. She gives an account of the time beginning in April of 1975, through her stay at Lam Sing Refugee Camp in Vietnam ending in February of 1980. During that period over two million Cambodians died from execution, torture, or starvation.

Graphic Novels, Biographies, and Histories

2747. Aaron, Jason. *The Other Side.* Illustrated by Cameron Stewart. Vertigo, 2007. 144pp. Paper ISBN 978-1-4012-1350-3. Grades 10 up.

While Private Bill Everette leaves Alabama and makes his way to Vietnam as a member of a Marine platoon, another soldier, the idealistic Buddhist Vo Binh Dai, marches to the south to join the revolution and kill the enemy. They meet on the battlefield at Khe Sanh base.

2748. Lat. *Kampung Boy.* (Kampung Boy) First Second, 2006. 141pp. Paper ISBN 978-1-59643-121-8. Grades 4 up.

To show his Southeast Asian *kampung* (village) near a rubber plantation, Lat creates chronological sketches of it with notes on its customs and events. He describes his life as a young Muslim boy going through the ritual hair-shaving ceremony on his 45th day, learning the Koran at the age of 6, being circumcised at 10, and going to the movies around 1960. Then he leaves home for boarding school and almost immediately becomes homesick for his kampung. *Capitol Choices Noteworthy Titles, Garden State Teen Book Award* (New Jersey) nomination, *American Library Association Best Books for Young Adults, Booklist Editor's Choice,* and *Bulletin Blue Ribbon.*

2749. Lat. *Town Boy.* (Kampung Boy) First Second, 2007. 192pp. Paper ISBN 978-1-59643-331-1. Grades 5 up.

In 1968 Mat moves from Kampung to Ipoh with his family when he is 10. He begins attending school and meets Frankie, a Chinese boy who shares his love of rock 'n roll music. They cheat in physical education, discuss record players, and ask girls to the movies. Pen-and-ink cartoon illustrations add humor and life.

Compact Discs

2750. Kadohata, Cynthia. *Cracker! The Best Dog in Vietnam.* Narrated by Kimberly Farr. Listening Library, 2007. 6 CDs; 7.32 hrs. ISBN 978-0-7393-3888-9. Grades 6 up.

See entry 2707.

CANADA

Historical Fiction and Fantasy

2751. Aksomitis, Linda. *Adeline's Dream.* Fitzenroy & Whiteside, 2006. 209pp. Paper ISBN 978-1-55050-323-4. Grades 4–6.

Linna (Adeline), 12, wants to become an opera singer, but when her family moves from her grandmother's home in Germany to Saskatchewan, Canada, into a sod house by a railway, she fears her dream will never be realized. She struggles to learn English, and she holds her father responsible for taking them away from a comfortable, happy life. She does discover that she might have what she wants in the new place.

2752. Anderson-Dargatz, Gail. *The Cure for Death by Lightning.* Anchor, 2002. 294pp. Paper ISBN 978-0-385-72047-2. Grades YA.

In 1941 Beth Weeks, 15, lives on a Canadian farm where she and her family struggle with the shortages of World War II. She tries to escape the advances and beatings of her abusive father, mentally deranged from World War I, but she cannot. She visits a Native American friend on a nearby reservation, and the sense that a coyote's evil spirit permeates the area stays with them even though she finds respite away from the farm.

2753. Atwood, Margaret. *Alias Grace.* Anchor, 1997. 468pp. Paper ISBN 978-0-385-49044-3. Grades YA.

Grace Marks, 16, was accused of the murders of her employer and his pregnant mistress and housekeeper in Canada during the 1840s. Her supposed partner was hanged, and she received a life sentence after relating three different versions of the murder. In Atwood's novel, Grace endures the verbal probing of a doctor who tries to determine if she is guilty or innocent after 16 years in prison. His questions and her answers as he tries to hypnotize her into remembering the truth bring more complexities to light about the rights of and injustices to women during the 19th century.

2754. Bates, Judy Fong. *Midnight at the Dragon Café.* Counterpoint, 2005. 317pp. Paper ISBN 978-1-58243-189-5. Grades YA.

In 1957 Su-Jen Chou, 7, and her mother move from China to a small Ontario town to live with her elderly father above the small restaurant he has purchased. She sleeps between her parents as they adjust to their unhappy relationship, and she takes the name "Annie" in school. When her father's son from a previous marriage, Lee-Kung, comes to live with them, her mother and he begin an affair. Annie witnesses their secret glances in disgust before her mother becomes pregnant. At the same time, the bride for Lee-Kung's arranged marriage, at the insistence of his father, arrives. They all must balance their duties with their desires. *Alex Award*.

2755. Brooks, Martha. *Two Moons in August: A Novel.*   Groundwood, 2008. 199pp. Paper ISBN 978-0-8889-9865-1. Grades 8 up.

Sidonie, aged 16 in 1959, has lost her mother, seen her physician father withdraw from society, and had a friend die in an accident. As she wonders what will happen next, she must also deal with a sister who is less interested in helping than in mistreating Sidonie and her own Chinese boyfriend. Sidonie begins the healing process when another physician's son comes to her Canadian town with his own problems. Helping him cope with his parents' abuse of each other and divorce allows her to dwell less on her own grief.

2756. Carter, Anne. *In the Clear.*   Orca, 2001. 133pp. Paper ISBN 978-1-55143-192-5. Grades 4–7.

Pauline contracts polio as a Canadian child in the 1950s, and by the time she is 12, she wants what other children have. She remembers her hospitalization five years before with the iron lung, the children in her ward, and a horrible nurse. But her father decides to help her change her future by building a hockey rink in the backyard. Then her Tante (Aunt) Marie gives her a hockey stick for Christmas. Her father shows her that she can become a wheelchair hockey player, and she begins to practice in her own backyard.

2757. Chan, Gillian. *The Carved Box.*   Kids Can, 2001. 232pp. ISBN 978-1-55074-895-6; 2004. paper ISBN 978-1-55337-016-1. Grades 6–8.

After studying to be a scholar, orphan Callum, 15, emigrates from Scotland to Upper Canada just after the American Revolution to live with his uncle Rory. He does not have the skills to work and spends his only money on a maltreated dog accompanied by a small carved box. The dog, however, gives him solace during his long days of work as he misses his mother and his home, even though the dog will not stray far from the box. During an accident, the box breaks open, and Dog takes a human shape.

2758. Chan, Gillian. *A Foreign Field.*   Kids Can, 2002. 184pp. ISBN 978-1-55337-349-0; 2004. paper ISBN 978-1-55337-350-6. Grades 7–10.

Ellen, 14, lives near a Royal Air Force base in Canada during World War II. She has to look after her young brother who is mad about airplanes and regularly disobedient. Colin introduces her to Stephen, a young trainee from the base, who visits the family regularly, but Ellen has no interest in him. However, for the next year, their relationship changes and the war becomes real to them. Letters and nightmares show Stephen's side of the war as he misses his family in England, sees the horrors even of training, and loves her. He wills his savings to her before his final mission so that she can become a teacher, and she tells her grandchildren their story.

2759. Cowan, Shannon. *Tin Angel.*   Lobster, 2007. 336pp. ISBN 978-1-897073-68-1. Grades 8 up.

After Ronalda (Ronnie) Page's father dies when she is 14, Louis Moss removes them from the dilapidated family home, Raven's Lodge, to the pulp-mill town of Shelter Bay, becoming the family benefactor while her mother sinks into alcoholism. Ronnie suspects Louis of having an affair with her older sister, Marcia, 16, and she finds comfort in a new friendship with Lee, a fugitive from the American draft system. After Louis sets the lodge on fire and dies, Ronnie is arrested for his murder. At the trial Marcia admits that he is her father.

2760. Crook, Connie Brummel. *The Hungry Year.* Stoddart, 2001. 190pp. Paper ISBN 978-0-7737-6206-0. Grades 2–4.

In 1787 Kate, 12, and her family leave their farm near Albany, New York, and settle near Lake Ontario, Canada. After her mother and grandmother die, she has to do many chores and look after her 4-year-old brothers. Her father is often away during the winter hunting for food. When he does not return, she has to protect the other children when they encounter both bears and wolves. *Silverbirch Award* (Ontario) nomination.

2761. Crook, Connie Brummel. *Meyers' Rebellion.* Fitzhenry & Whiteside, 2006. 279pp. ISBN 978-1-55041-943-6. Grades 4–7.

John Meyers, 15, goes to the Toronto farmer's market in late 1837 to sell produce and finds himself joining William Lyon Mackenzie's Upper Canada Rebellion. His brother George is captured, and he refuses to leave without him. They fight to gain more democracy while under the governance of the British. However, the British are brutal in their attempt to stop the rebellion caused by what many see as hooligans. Among their problems are incarceration in the Kingston prison and attempts to capture a steamship. *Word Guild Canadian Christian Writing Award* and *Canadian Children's Book Centre Finalist.*

2762. Curtis, Christopher Paul. *Elijah of Buxton.* Scholastic, 2007. 341pp. ISBN 978-0-439-02344-3. Grades 4–8.

Elijah Freeman, 11, is Buxton, Canada's first-born free black, and as far as he knows, he is the only baby to have thrown up on Frederick Douglass. Although sometimes considered "simple" by people in the community, he shows that he has courage. When his neighbor, Mr. Leroy, has money stolen that he has been saving for years in order to buy freedom for his wife and children, Elijah blames himself and risks being captured by slave catchers when he crosses the border into Detroit to get the money back. He naively recalls the people and horrors he sees and the dangers of the Underground Railroad when he returns to safety. *Horn Book Fanfare, Newbery Honor Book, Coretta Scott King Award, Parents Choice Award, Dorothy Canfield Fisher Children's Book Award* (Vermont) nomination, *Jane Addams Children's Honor Book, Scott O Dell Award for Historical Fiction, Publisher's Weekly Best Books, American Library Association Notable Children's Books, School Library Journal Best Books for Children, Kirkus Reviews Editor's Choice, Capitol Choices Noteworthy Titles (Washington, D.C.), and* Governor General's Literary Awards *Finalist.*

2763. Debon, Nicolas. *A Brave Soldier.* Illustrated by author. Groundwood, 2002. 32pp. ISBN 978-0-88899-481-3. Grades 2–4.

After war breaks out in Europe in 1914, Canadian soldiers go to fight. One of them, Frank, enlists because he does not want his friends to think he is a coward. However, he knows nothing about Germans or about war. Before a battle in France, he hears Germans talking on the other side of "No Man's Land." By the end of the battle, his comrade is dead, and Frank is wounded. At the end of the war in 1918, nearly 10 million soldiers and 13 million civilians from around the world have died, many of them unaware of the reasons why.

2764. Doyle, Brian. *Pure Spring.* Groundwood, 2007. 158pp. ISBN 978-0-88899-774-6; 2008. paper ISBN 978-0-88899-775-3. Grades 9 up.

During the Korean War Martin O'Boy, 15, lives with Grampa Rip in Canada. He lies about his age to get a job with the Pure Spring soft drink company, but finds out that his partner, Randy, is mentally disturbed, steals from customers, and rants against Jews. Randy discovers Martin's age and blackmails him to keep quiet about his stealing. Then Martin falls in love with one of Randy's victims, Gerty McDowell. He decides to tell her so that he can save his relationship with her. Grampa Rip helps Martin in a way that his father could not.

2765. Doyle, Brian. *Uncle Ronald.* Groundwood, 2004. 144pp. Paper ISBN 978-0-8889-9621-3. Grades 6–8.

Mickey McGuire recalls his life in Ottawa in 1895 when he began bed-wetting at age 12. His mother sent him to his uncle's farm, and Uncle Ronald is the opposite of Mickey's abusive father. His mother joins him after his father beats her severely, and the two expect him to follow. The story also involves a conflict between federal troops and the farm over the collection of back taxes. *Canadian Library Association Book of the Year for Children.*

2766. Draper, Penny. *Terror at Turtle Mountain.* Coteau, 2006. 160pp. Paper ISBN 978-1-55050-343-2. Grades 4–7.

In 1903 Natalie Vaughan, 13, is awakened one morning by a rock slide near Turtle Mountain mine in the Northwest Territory of Canada. The day before she had been lamenting her feelings of inadequacy and her grandfather's dismissal of her as just a child. But today more than 90 million tons of limestone fall on part of the town and trap men in the mine. She works up her courage and, with other townspeople, frantically searches for survivors. She locates and rescues a baby, but that achievement cannot help her overcome the despair of seeing her friends' homes crushed under the rock.

2767. Durbin, William. *The Broken Blade.* Yearling, 1998. 160pp. Paper ISBN 978-0-440-41184-0. Grades 5–8.

Pierre, 13, has to go to work for his father's company in 1800 when his father injures himself in a wood-chopping accident in Canada. Pierre becomes a voyageur, a French-Canadian canoeman. On his first canoe trip to Grand Portage, he ages in many ways and becomes a man. While he has to deal with an unsavory character and mourn the drowning of one of the crew, he also sees the natural beauty of his environment.

2768. Frost, Helen. *The Braid.* Frances Foster, 2006. 95pp. ISBN 978-0-374-30962-6. Grades 8 up.

See entry 1394.

2769. Furey, Leo. *The Long Run.* Shambhala, 2006. 376pp. ISBN 978-1-59030-411-2; Trumpeter, 2007. paper ISBN 978-1-59030-528-7. Grades YA.

During the 1960s Aidan Carmichael and his friends at the Mount Kildare Orphanage in St. John's, Newfoundland, known as the Dare Klub, suffer neglect, cold, hunger and brutality from the Christian Brothers. They cope by secretly training for the city's marathon in the middle of the night. And with this activity, they bond and feel less lonely. *Booklist Editors' Choice.*

2770. Godfrey, Rebecca. *The Torn Skirt.* HarperCollins, 2002. 208pp. Paper ISBN 978-0-06-009485-0. Grades YA.

In the mid-1980s at Mt. Douglas ("Mt. Drug") High in British Columbia, Sara Shaw, 16, has school friends on drugs while at home she takes good care of her irresponsible father, her mother having chosen to remain in a commune. But Sara's father abruptly abandons her when he catches her masturbating in the garden, and she ends up in the back alleys of Victoria with all of the derelicts of society. One of the girls she meets, Justine, has a torn skirt, and Sara feels an affinity with her that leads her through dangerous experiences when trying to find her. Some of the events may be occurring in Sara's mind since a fever with which she was born returns to plague her. Although a kind foster family offers her shelter, she feels more comfortable with the people on the street whom she might help. *Ethel Wilson Fiction Prize* nomination and *American Library Association Quick Picks for Reluctant Young Adult Readers.*

2771. Goldring, Ann. *Spitfire.* Raincoast, 2002. 147pp. Paper ISBN 978-1-55192-490-8. Grades 4–6.

When April Flickers, a girl from a poor family, enters the soap box derby in Whitfield, Ontario, in 1943, she inspires Kathryn Lockhart to do the same, even though Kathryn's brother is also competing. While Kathryn struggles to build her car in her sponsor's back room, bullies destroy April's car. The two join to finish Kathryn's car and name it "Spitfire," to honor the British fighter plane. They win.

2772. Goodman, Joan Elizabeth. *Paradise: Based on a True Story of Survival.* Graphia, 2006. 209pp. Paper ISBN 978-0-618-49481-1. Grades 7 up.

Marguerite de la Roque, 16, wants to escape the French Huguenot household of her strict father in 1542 so she joins her stern Uncle Sieur de Roberval on a journey to the New World. Her Catholic lover Pierre, a stowaway on the ship, is discovered and thrown into the sea. Then she and her chaperone, Damienne, are left on the Island of Demons off the coast of Quebec. Pierre swims to them, and the three try to survive alone. They fight mosquitoes and deal with natives as they try to build shelter for the winter, certainly not a paradise. Then she becomes pregnant and has further concerns.

2773. Harlow, Joan Hiatt. *Star in the Storm.* Margaret K. McElderry, 2000. 150pp. ISBN 978-0-689-82905-5; Aladdin, 2001. paper ISBN 978-0-689-84621-2. Grades 4–7.

Maggie, 12, hides her Newfoundland dog, Sirius, in the woods in 1912 when a new island law comes into effect that outlaws any dog that does not herd sheep. Then when a ship wrecks off the Newfoundland coast, she risks her dog's safety by letting him swim to the sinking vessel and rescue those aboard, including the daughter and grandchild of the despicable man who instigated the law. *Charlie May Simon* (Arkansas) nomination, *Young Reader's Award* (Arizona) nomination, *Nutmeg Children's Book Award* (Connecticut) nomination, *Sunshine State Young Reader Award* (Florida) nomination, *Black Eyed Susan Book Award* (Maryland) nomination, *Student Book Award* (Maine) nomination, *Juvenile Fiction State Book Award* (North Dakota), *Battle of the Books* (New Mexico) nomination, *Readers' Choice Award* (Virginia) nomination, *Capitol Choices Noteworthy Titles* (Washington, D.C.), and *Sasquatch Book Awards* (Washington).

2774. Harris, Christie. *Raven's Cry.* Illustrated by Bill Reid. University of Washington, 1992. 193pp. Paper ISBN 978-0-295-97221-3. Grades 5–10.

When the white men find the Haida people in 1775, they decimate the sea otter which is the Haida's livelihood. In addition to greed, the invading hunters bring smallpox, consumption, death, and vile treatment. By 1884 only 600 of the tribe remained, having suffered horribly from the outsiders who destroyed their culture and defiled their religion.

2775. Hawes, Charles Boardman. *The Dark Frigate.*   Kessinger, 2005. 264pp. ISBN 978-1-4326-0971-9; paper ISBN 978-1-4179-3209-2. Grades 7 up.

See entry 1270.

2776. Hebert-Collins, Sheila. *Jean-Paul Hebert Was There/Jean-Paul Hebert Etait La.* Illustrated by John Bergeron. Pelican, 2004. 32pp. ISBN 978-1-56554-928-9. Grades K–3.

In 1759 the English banish the French Canadians of Acadie (now Nova Scotia). Jean-Paul and some of his family are separated. His group spends time in Pennsylvania and as servants in Georgia before finally settling in Louisiana and reuniting with other family members. The Acadians became the Cajuns of Louisiana and other parts of the Gulf Coast. There his family explains why the English wanted to oust them from their homes.

2777. Holeman, Linda. *Promise Song.*   Tundra, 1997. 260pp. Paper ISBN 978-0-8877-6387-8. Grades 6–9.

Rosetta and her sister Flora lose everything when their parents die, including their country, when they are sent to Canada in 1900. They arrive in Nova Scotia, and different families adopt them. Rosetta becomes an indentured servant, and her master steals her money, but she eventually forms a bond with his wife, and they both escape his harshness to find Flora.

2778. Hudson, Jan. *Sweetgrass.*   Puffin, 1999. 160pp. Paper ISBN 978-0-698-11763-1. Grades 6–9.

Sweetgrass, age 15, a Blackfoot in the 19th century, worries about not being married when most of the younger girls have already become wives. She also worries about whether the boy she loves will have enough horses for her father to approve him, and whether her stepmother will decide that Sweetgrass is responsible enough to be a wife. Her people struggle to live on the Canadian prairie, and after she nurses both her brother and her stepmother through smallpox by feeding them fish (a forbidden food), her father decides that she may marry. *Canadian Library Association Book of the Year, Governor General's Literary Awards, International Board of Books for Young People, American Library Association Notable Books for Children, School Library Journal Best Book*, and *Canada Council Children's Literature Prize*.

2779. Jocelyn, Marthe. *Mable Riley: A Reliable Record of Humdrum, Peril, and Romance.* Candlewick, 2004. 288pp. ISBN 978-0-7636-2120-9; 2007. paper ISBN 978-0-7636-3287-8. Grades 5–9.

In 1901 Mable Riley, 14, lives in Canada's Perth County, Ontario, where her sister teaches. She keeps a diary of her boring life and writes a romantic adventure to keep herself entertained. Then she meets Mrs. Rattle and becomes involved in the struggle of the suffragist movement. Against her sister's advice, she becomes involved in a strike at the local cheese factory, an endeavor that gives her confidence and broadens her interests. *American Library Association Best Books For Young Adults, Notable Social Studies Trade Books for Young People*, and *Children's Book Award* (West Virginia) nomination.

2780. Johnston, Julie. *A Very Fine Line.* Tundra, 2006. 198pp. ISBN 978-0-88776-746-3. Grades 5–8.

In Kempton, Ontario, in 1941, Rosalind, 13, remembers specific moments of her past, but she unhappily receives the news from her aunt that she, as the seventh daughter of a seventh daughter, has the ability to see the future. Rosalind does not know that she is the seventh daughter because her mother has kept her mentally ill sister a secret. As these unwanted abilities begin to plague her, Rosalind decides to overcome her fate by pretending to be a boy named Ross, with short hair and boys' clothes. After several difficulties, she realizes that she must accept herself and her ability.

2781. Kogawa, Joy. *Naomi's Road.* Illustrated by Ruth Ohi. Fitzhenry & Whiteside, 2005. 82pp. Paper ISBN 978-1-55005-115-5. Grades 3–6.

In the 1940s, while Canada and Japan are at war, Naomi and her older brother are taken from their Vancouver home to an internment camp in British Columbia. Although she endures much hardship and faces prejudice, Naomi keeps hoping that life will soon be different. To escape, she plays with her dolls while her brother plays his flute.

2782. Lawrence, Iain. *B for Buster.* Delacorte, 2004. 320pp. ISBN 978-0-385-73086-0; Laurel-Leaf, 2006. paper ISBN 978-0-440-23810-2. Grades YA.

In 1943 Kak, 16, wants to escape his abusive parents in Kakabeka, Canada, so he lies about his age and pretends he is an orphan so he can enlist in the Canadian Air Force. He is quickly transferred to England where he becomes a wireless operator on a plane called *B for Buster*, making night bombing raids over Germany. When Kak returns from his first "op," he is distressed, but Bert, a demoted pilot and pigeon caretaker, helps him cope with his fears of flying and of war. *Garden State Teen Book Award* (New Jersey) nomination, *American Library Association Best Books for Young Adults, Bulletin Blue Ribbon, Capitol Choices Noteworthy Titles* (Washington, D.C.), *Tayshas Reading List* (Texas).

2783. Lawson, Julie. *The Klondike Cat.* Illustrated by Paul Mombourquette. Kids Can, 2004. Unpaged. Paper ISBN 978-1-55337-766-5. Grades 1–3.

In 1896 Noah smuggles his cat Shadow on a steamship bound for the Klondike to search for gold even though his father has said she cannot go. To complicate the journey, Shadow has kittens. When they arrive in Dawson, Noah discovers that cats are bringing huge prices because they are needed to kill mice. He sells the kittens and earns enough money for his father to buy one of the expensive claims and start digging. Illustrations complement the text.

2784. Lee, Jen Sookfong. *The End of East.* Thomas Dunne, 2008. 245pp. ISBN 978-0-312-37985-8. Grades YA.

While looking after her mother following her sisters' departure and her father's death, Sammy pieces together the family's Chinese Canadian history. Her grandfather, Seid Quan, came to Canada when his village paid his passage and returned home three times to marry and have his three children. In Vancouver he had to run a barber shop to earn money to send back to his family although he himself would have liked to return home. His son, Pon Man, arrives, and eventually his wife, Shew Lin, joins him. They negotiate a marriage with a woman in Hong Kong, but the two produce only five daughters and no sons. Sammy returns to look after her mother whose insanity and fear grow as she ages, while Sammy herself needs to forge her own identity.

2785. Little, Jean. *From Anna.* Illustrated by Joan Sandin. HarperCollins, 1991. 208pp. Paper ISBN 978-0-06-440044-2. Grades 4–6.

See entry 1991.

2786. Lunn, Janet. *One Hundred Shining Candles.* Illustrated by Lindsay Grater. Tundra, 2008. 32pp. ISBN 978-0-88776-889-7. Grades 2–4.

Lucy, 10, wants to make her family's 1800 Christmas memorable even though they have no money for presents. Her schoolmaster in Upper Canada tells about homes lit with many candles to brighten the season. Lucy and her young brother make five candles. Her parents are as pleased with her gift as she had hoped they would be.

2787. Lunn, John Loran. *The Mariner's Curse.* Tundra, 2004. 205pp. Paper ISBN 978-0-88776-672-5. Grades 4–7.

Rory Dugan, 12, loves to read about sailors and their ocean exploits. When his mother and her new husband offer to take him across the Atlantic Ocean on a luxury cruise ship, he is delighted. However, he soon meets Mr. Morgan, a sinister man who might even have sailed on the *Titanic* and finds himself remembering his own brother who drowned in a swimming pool several years before. Lucy, also a passenger, helps Rory cope with Morgan, but they find themselves caught up in a mystery involving danger.

2788. Manuel, Lynn. *Camels Always Do.* Illustrated by Kasia Charko. Orca, 2004. Unpaged. ISBN 978-1-55143-284-7; 2005. paper ISBN 978-1-55143-470-4. Grades 1–3.

In 1862 during the Canadian Cariboo gold rush, Cameron either pans gold with his father or dreams about crossing the ocean to see a camel. When Mr. Laumeister imports a herd of them, Cameron is shocked. But their owner does not know how to handle the problems that arise. Cameron and his patient father start looking after the Dromedary Express to keep the twenty-one camels healthy and take them on a supply delivery mission. The camels eventually have to go because Canada's climate is not the best for them. Watercolor and pencil illustrations enhance the text.

2789. Matas, Carol. *Sparks Fly Upward.* Clarion, 2002. 192pp. ISBN 978-0-618-15964-2. Grades 4–8.

In 1910 when the Jewish family of Rebecca Bernstein, 12, has to move from Saskatchewan to start anew in Winnipeg, Canada, her father cannot find work. She has to live with the Kostianuks, a Christian Ukrainian family. Some of the family is actually anti-Semitic, but she and Kostianuk daughter Sophie become close friends after they both contract scarlet fever and rescue small children from a fire in the quarantine hospital where they had been sent. After her grandfather removes Rebecca from Sophie's home, he forbids her to see Sophie. The rabbi, however, guides her in the right way to maintain her friendship.

2790. Matas, Carol. *The Whirlwind.* Orca, 2007. 128pp. Paper ISBN 978-1-55143-703-3. Grades 6 up.

Ben, 15, flees Nazi Germany in 1941 with his family, hoping to find a better life in Seattle. He remembers the horrors of Kristallnacht and seeing his grandparents being taken to the camps. After he arrives, he makes friends with a Japanese American, John Ogawa, but almost immediately, John is sent to an internment camp. Angry with his father for not getting his grandparents visas and for leaving Germany so late, and angry that people treat him poorly because he is German, Ben runs to Canada where he finds even more prejudice against him. Ben's father describes the time as always changing, like a whirlwind.

2791. Michener, James A. *Journey.* Fawcett, 1994. 245pp. Paper ISBN 978-0-449-21847-1. Grades YA.

Lord Luton leaves London in 1897 for the Klondike area of Canada after he hears that someone has discovered gold there. Surprised by the huge distance across Canada, Luton becomes separated from his group and stays in the Klondike for only a few hours before starting his return journey.

2792. Miles, Victoria. *Magnifico.* Fitzhenry & Whiteside, 2006. 262pp. ISBN 978-1-55041-960-3; 2007. paper ISBN 978-1-55041-991-7. Grades 3–6.

In British Columbia in 1939, Mariangela, 11, wants to play the piano, but her Italian immigrant parents decide to arrange accordion lessons for her since she can play her grandfather's instrument. She does not play well, but her teacher, Gioseff DeMarco, tells her amazing stories about his life. They help Mariangela understand her own family better, including why her mother keeps a packed suitcase under her bed, and to deal with the bully who throws rocks at her. *Manitoba Young Readers Choice Award* nomination.

2793. Milner, Donna. *After River.* HarperCollins, 2008. 352pp. ISBN 978-0-06146-299-3. Grades YA.

As Natalie Ward returns home to her mother's death bed, she recalls the events in the family that began during her fifteenth year in 1966 with the arrival of the American draft dodger, Richard "River" Jordan, looking for work on their British Columbia Cascade Mountain dairy farm. His good looks appeal to Natalie, and she seduces him, but then she finds him in bed with her older brother, Boyer. River becomes lost in the mountains and dies. The town mayor then rapes her and blackmails her by saying he will arrest her brother for homosexuality (a Canadian crime until 1969) if she tells. After she has a stillborn baby, she leaves town. The huge rift remains in her family until she returns after the long absence before her mother's final days.

2794. Parkinson, Curtis. *Death in Kingsport.* Tundra, 2007. 215pp. Paper ISBN 978-0-88776-827-9. Grades 6–8.

While Neil, 15, is waiting for the cremation of his dead uncle in a small Canadian town in World War II, he hears a thumping noise from the coffin. He tries to alert his parents, but they ignore him. Afterward, a voice keeps asking him what he heard in the coffin, but the voice will not respond to him. It only says that other deaths in the town are suspicious. Neil asks his friend Graham and some relatives of another person who has died to help him with this mystery. Their investigation reveals unexpected results.

2795. Pearson, Kit. *Looking at the Moon.* Penguin, 2008. 212pp. Paper ISBN 978-0-14-305635-5. Grades 5–9.

In the sequel to *The Sky Is Falling*, Norah and her Canadian "family" spend the summer of 1944 at their lake cottage. She becomes moody and difficult in her third Canadian summer, but she does not realize that her feelings relate to the changes in her body. Otherwise, she has adjusted to this different environment.

2796. Pearson, Kit. *The Sky Is Falling.* Penguin, 2008. 249pp. Paper ISBN 978-0-14-305634-8. Grades 5–9.

Because she does not yet know that she is being sent away, Norah, age 10, is enjoying the dangers of the bombing raids in England as World War II begins. But she has to go to Canada with her 5-year-old brother. The voyage, the new school, and the house where the two adults seem to care more about Gavin upset her. She ignores Gavin, but she finally comes to understand that she is jealous of his loving manner and ability to attract both children and adults. *Geoffrey Bilson Award for Historical Fiction for Young People* (Canada), *Mr. Christie's Book Awards* (Canada), and *Canadian Children's Book of the Year Award*.

2797. Pendziwol, Jean E. *Marja's Skis.* Illustrated by Jirinia Marton. Groundwood, 2007. Unpaged. ISBN 978-0-88899-674-9. Grades 1–3.

Finnish immigrant Marja wants to help her father with his horses and attend school in their Canadian logging town. When she turns 7, Father encourages her to do both. But her father dies, and the family faces new challenges. Skiing home from school one day, Marja sees that someone has fallen though the ice, and she remembers her father's belief that courage lets people do things they never imagined possible. Oil pastels enhance the text.

2798. Pendziwol, Jean E. *The Red Sash.* Illustrated by Nicolas Debon. Groundwood, 2005. 40pp. ISBN 978-0-88899-589-6. Grades 1–4.

In the 18th century a young Métis boy waits for his father, a voyageur, to return from his fur trading at Fort William where he lives with his family. A white gentleman trader's canoe is destroyed during a storm on Lake Superior (Gitchee Gumee), and he helps rescue him. For his bravery, he earns the red sash of the voyageur that he has so coveted.

2799. Razzell, Mary. *Snow Apples.* Groundwood, 2006. 209pp. Paper ISBN 978-0-88899-728-9. Grades 9 up.

Sheila Bray, 16, hates her life in a remote British Columbia outpost during World War II. Her unfaithful father and bitter mother do not want her to become a nurse. Instead she starts dating a handsome carpenter and becomes pregnant. When she asks her father for help, he takes her to abort the pregnancy and then leaves for the last time. She survives a terrible miscarriage and goes back to her mother. Then she becomes aware of her mother's sacrifices for the family.

2800. Rougeau, Rémy. *All We Know of Heaven.* Mariner, 2002. 224pp. Paper ISBN 978-0-618-21922-3. Grades YA.

When he is 19 in 1973, Paul Seneschal enters a Cistercian monastery in Canada where he tries to find the divine through silence and seclusion. He takes the name "Antoine," makes cheese from a hundred-year-old recipe, chants, and reads sacred writings. But at the same time, he has to deal with unexpected actions of other monks and learns that he can never fully escape the world outside. Throughout he struggles with himself sexually and personally, wondering if he has made the best decision for his life.

2801. Russell, Nancy L. *So Long, Jackie Robinson.* Key Porter, 2007. Paper ISBN 978-1-55263-863-7. Grades 4–6.

In 1946 Jackie Robinson played with the Montreal Royals, a minor league team, before the Brooklyn Dodgers selected him. Matt, 12, also new to Montreal, feels empathy with Robinson because he neither speaks French nor plays hockey like the other children. When Matt discovers Robinson, he feels better about his move. Then when Matt helps a building maintenance man, a former Negro League player, clear his name as a suspect to a robbery, Robinson sends Matt a ticket to the championship game.

2802. Skrypuch, Marsha Forchuk. *Aram's Choice.* Illustrated by Muriel Wood. Fitzhenry & Whiteside, 2006. 81pp. ISBN 978-1-55005-352-6; paper ISBN 978-1-55041-354-0. Grades 3–5.

See entry 2039.

2803. Slade, Arthur G. *Megiddo's Shadow.* Wendy Lamb, 2006. 290pp. ISBN 978-0-385-74701-1. Grades 7 up.

On his Saskatchewan farm, Edward Bathe, 16, hears about the loss of his beloved brother Hector in World War I and decides to join Hector's Canadian battalion that is planning to fight the Turks in Palestine. Edward ends up in England where he injures his leg and meets the army nurse, Emily Waters. When Edward sees the awful situation of war that includes heat, disease, wounded horses, and dead friends, he has difficulty understanding his former religious beliefs. Additionally, he discovers that one of his tent mates on the plains near Megiddo (the city of King Solomon) actually enjoys killing. Edward returns to Canada to cope with his mental and physical distresses.

2804. Sommerdorf, Norma. *Red River Girl.* Holiday House, 2006. 226pp. ISBN 978-0-8234-1903-6. Grades 4–7.

A 13-year-old Métis girl of the Ojibwe tribe, Josette Dupre, who lives in St. Eustace, Québec, wants to continue her education in Montreal. She keeps a diary of the years 1846 to 1848 with her widowed French Canadian voyageur father and brothers before and during her journey to St. Paul, Minnesota. Disappointed that she must give up her education, she arrives in St. Paul when it is a small town. But after becoming friends with the local teacher who needs Josette's translating skills in three languages, Josette gets a job as a teacher for the younger children, and the town begins to grow. Glossary.

2805. Spaulding, Andrea, and Alfred Scow. *Secret of the Dance.* Illustrated by Darlene Gait. Orca, 2006. Unpaged. ISBN 978-1-55143-396-7. Grades 4 up.

Watl'kina, 8, decides to sneak out during the night in 1935 to watch masked dancers at a secret Potlatch in Kingcome Inlet. What he does not realize is that the Canadian government has, since 1885, forbidden the Aboriginal people from participating in these Potlatches by which they honor such events as marriage or death. He spots his own father dancing as the Hamatsa, and the adults allow him to stay. But he notes that he never saw his father dancing again. Illustrations enhance the text. Notes and Glossary.

2806. Stenhouse, Ted. *A Dirty Deed.* Kids Can, 2005. 192pp. Paper ISBN 978-1-55337-361-2. Grades 6–9.

In 1952 during the Korean War, Will Samson and his best friend, the Blackfoot Indian Arthur, become distressed when the wealthiest man in the Canadian town of Grayson, Alberta, beats Carface, another young Indian, for supposedly stealing a land deed. As Will and Arthur investigate, they find that a piece of Howe's land rightfully belongs to the Indians and that he has used his manipulation of the Mounties and a group of thugs to control the Indians.

2807. Sterling, Shirley. *My Name Is Seepeetza.* Groundwood, 1992. 128pp. Paper ISBN 978-0-88899-165-2. Grades 5–8.

Seepeetza, better known as Martha at the Indian residential school in British Columbia where she has to live, wets the bed and daydreams about her family ranch on the reservation where she lived before the government forced her to attend school. The nuns make her wear the wet bed sheet over her head, and the children taunt her for having green eyes and looking white. The journal format presents Seepeetza in the sixth grade during the 1950s feeling helpless, afraid, and homesick. The nuns, however, are not always bad, nor are Seepeetza's parents always perfect. *Sheila A. Egoff Children's Book Prize.*

2808. Taylor, Joanne. ***Making Room.*** Illustrated by Peter Rankin. Tundra, 2004. Unpaged. ISBN 978-0-8877-6651-0. Grades 1–3.

In Nova Scotia during the 1800s, John Williams, 18, decides that he needs a home. He takes an axe, a saw, two calves, and two chickens to build his house. Then he gets a wife who needs a pantry and a cradle. When John's parents arrive to live with him and Annie, he builds bedrooms upstairs and a new kitchen. Eventually, he and Annie retire to a new but smaller house on the edge of the property where all of their family lives. Oil paintings embellish the text.

2809. Taylor, Joanne. ***There You Are.*** Tundra, 2004. 199pp. Paper ISBN 978-0-8877-6658-9. Grades 4–7.

After World War II ends, Jeannie Shaw, 12, longs for a friend. But in the small Margaree Valley of Cape Breton Island, there are only 13 families. When a new family arrives, she has great hopes until she sees that their child is a male.

2810. Trottier, Maxine. ***Three Songs for Courage.*** Tundra, 2006. 324pp. ISBN 978-0-88776-745-6. Grades 8 up.

Sixteen-year-old Gordon Wesley, during the summer of 1956 in Erie View, Ontario, spends time with his friends; a new girlfriend, Mary; and his beloved 1950 Pontiac called "Chief." However, Lancer Caldwell's gang and its violence follow Gordon everywhere. When he finds his brother dead from a fall down the stairs, he thinks it is an accident. Then he discovers that Lancer was at his house that same night. Gordon wants to avenge his brother's death by killing Lancer, and he loses sight of all that has been important to him. Then he must make a choice as to whether he will add another dead body to the toll of one.

2811. Urquhart, Jane. ***The Stone Carvers.*** Penguin, 2003. 392pp. Paper ISBN 978-0-14-200358-9. Grades YA.

Tilman, a nomad, and his sister, the homebody Klara Becker, cross the Atlantic with Klara disguised as a man so she will be hired to work on France's Vimy Memorial. Klara mourns her love, Eamon, who died in the trenches, and Tilman lost a leg at Vimy and can no longer wander around as a tramp. From a Canadian family of accomplished stone carvers, they want to create this monument in France to the 11,000 Canadians who died in World War I.

2812. Vande Griek, Susan. ***The Art Room.*** Illustrated by Pascal Milelli. Groundwood, 2002. 24pp. ISBN 978-0-8889-9449-3. Grades K–3.

Emily Carr (1871–1945) was a Canadian artist who loved to paint the natural world and supported herself teaching art to children. Oil paintings enhance the text.

2813. Vreeland, Susan. *The Forest Lover.* Penguin, 2004. 420pp. Paper ISBN 978-0-14-303430-8. Grades YA.

Emily Carr (1871–1945) overcame the Victorian rules of her childhood to become a major figure in modern art. As a Canadian, she transferred the beauty of the wilds of British Columbia before industrialization changed it by traveling alone through much of the territory and painting its totem poles and other artifacts in her work. She was able to show the illegal potlatches in tribal communities as well as the studios of Paris artists before World War I.

2814. Watts, Irene N. *When the Bough Breaks.* Tundra, 2007. 145pp. Paper ISBN 978-0-88776-821-7. Grades 5–7.

Millie Carr, 13, has to face the death of her mother after childbirth during the Great Depression in Ontario. Millie looks after the baby, Eddie, tries to control her 10-year-old brother, Hamish, and handles the housekeeping, while her father, a blacksmith, mourns his loss. Even Millie's two friends cannot help her overcome the burdens that seem endless.

2815. Welvaert, Scott R. *The Curse of the Wendigo: An Agate and Buck Adventure.* Illustrated by Brann Garvey. (Vortex) Stone Arch, 2007. 105pp. ISBN 978-1-59889-066-2; 2006. paper ISBN 978-1-59889-282-6. Grades 5 up.

When Buck, 16, and his sister, Agate, 10, search for their missing parents in the Canadian wilderness in 1898, they have to fight the shape-shifting Wendigo that feeds on humans. A group of Majictaw trying to defeat Wendigo and Coyote, the father of evil, help them. Buck and Agate realize that they must be more than they knew because of the intense supernatural pressure to overcome them. Illustrations enhance the text.

2816. Wynne-Jones, Tim. *Rex Zero and the End of the World.* Melanie Kroupa, 2007. 186pp. ISBN 978-0-374-33467-3. Grades 5–8.

In 1962 Rex Norton-Norton, known as Rex Zero, 10, moves to Ottawa from Vancouver with his parents and five siblings. He must discover new friends for himself as he sees others enmeshed in worries about the possibility of nuclear war. Some of his neighbors build bomb shelters, and his sister rants that the Reds have to be stopped. He, however, merely wants some friends. *American Library Association Notable Children's Books.*

2817. Wynne-Jones, Tim. *Rex Zero, King of Nothing.* Melanie Kroupa, 2008. 217pp. ISBN 978-0-374-36259-1. Grades 5–8.

During 1962 in Ottawa, Rex Norton-Norton (Zero to his friends), 11, wants to get rid of his awful substitute teacher, Miss Garr. But mysteries pop up in other places including secrets in the German letters and photographs that his father keeps from World War II. When Rex finds an address book and takes it to a beautiful woman with a black eye, he decides he will rescue her from her abusive husband. Then he sees pictures of women in black underwear in his friend's magazines and wonders why they are important. The humor and the need for Rex to find solutions to these secrets show his complexity.

2818. Yee, Paul. *The Bone Collector's Son.* Marshall Cavendish, 2005. 144pp. ISBN 978-0-7614-5242-3. Grades 6–9.

In 1907 Bing, 14, has to help his gambler father do the worst work in the city of Vancouver, Canada, which is to dig up bones of the dead to be returned to China for burial. Finally Bing gets a job as someone's houseboy, hoping to escape the ghosts, but this house is also haunted by ghosts that do not want the house to be sold. And when his father digs up a body missing a skull, the ghost of Mr. Shum haunts him because he wants his skull. Bing figures out how to appease both sets of ghosts, and includes other stories in his solution.

History

2819. Bannatyne-Cugnet, Jo. *Heartland: A Prairie Sampler.* Illustrated by Yvette Moore. Tundra, 2005. 37pp. Paper ISBN 978-0-8877-6722-7. Grades 3–5.

This book focuses on different aspects of the North American prairie including its land, agriculture, mining, wildlife, climate, and food. Anecdotes from the author and illustrator who both grew up on the Canadian prairies add interest. Realistic paintings complement the text.

2820. Duble, Kathleen Benner. *The Story of the Samson.* Illustrated by Alexander Farquharson. Charlesbridge, 2008. 48pp. ISBN 978-1-58089-183-7. Grades 2–5.

While with his grandfather, Sam wants to hear the story of his grandfather's sailing days on the *Samson*. The ship had roles as a sealing schooner, whaler, exploration ship, and a trade ship before running aground and sinking off Nova Scotia's coast. His grandfather remembers being on the same waters as the *Titanic* but thinking the distress signals were customs ships' tricks. The *Samson* rescued Ernest Shackleton and his crew mates in Antarctica, helped Admiral Byrd reach the same polar region, and then appeared at an exhibit during the 1933 Chicago World's Fair. Oil illustrations highlight the text. Bibliography, Chronology, Notes, and Web Sites.

2821. Gillis, Jennifer Blizin. *Life in New France.* (Picture the Past) Heinemann, 2003. 32pp. ISBN 978-1-4034-3799-0; paper ISBN 978-1-4034-4284-0. Grades 2–4.

Between 1639 and 1760, life in New France (including Canada, Acadia, and Louisiana) for the colonists was very different from life in their home country. Readers will learn about the food they ate, the clothes they wore, their homes, the type of education, their ability to communicate, the way they moved from one place to another, and their choices for amusement. A comparison between life today and life then is explored. Illustrations enhance the text. Maps and Time Lines.

2822. Gorrell, Gena K. *North Star to Freedom: The Story of the Underground Railroad.* Illustrated by author. Fitzhenry & Whiteside, 1996. 168pp. ISBN 978-0-7737-2988-9; 2004. paper ISBN 978-1-55005-068-4. Grades 5–8.

The focus of this book, unlike other texts about the Underground Railroad, is Canada. Many of the slaves who took the railroad ended their journey in Canada with the help of abolitionists and Quakers along the way. Individual accounts from slaves who settled in Canada add new insights about this ordeal in American history. Reproductions, Bibliography, Further Reading, Notes, and Index.

2823. Granfield, Linda. *Where Poppies Grow: A World War I Companion.* Stoddard, 2002. 48pp. ISBN 978-0-7737-3319-0; Fitzhenry & Whiteside, 2005. paper ISBN 978-1-55005-146-9. Grades 6–10.

See entry 1733.

2824. Hancock, Lyn. *Nunavut.* Fitzhenry & Whiteside, 2003. 76pp. Paper ISBN 978-1-55041-760-9. Grades 3–6.

Although not technically a history book, more than half of this volume deals with the history of this Canadian province. Charts, maps, photographs, and prints illustrate the uniqueness of the area, whose first inhabitants were the distant ancestors of the Inuit who made their way across the Bering Strait from Asia to Alaska around 10,000 years ago. Among the famous people associated with Nunavut and briefly described here are Roald Amundsen, an explorer (1872–1928), and James Houston, a writer (b. 1921). Fast Facts, Glossary, Pronunciation Guide, and Index.

2825. Hotchkiss, Ron. *The Matchless Six: The Story of Canada's First Women's Olympic Team.* Tundra, 2006. Paper ISBN 978-0-8877-6738-8. Grades 7 up.

In 1928 an Olympics experiment was carried out: to allow women to compete. Canada sent six women to the track-and-field event. The book highlights Jane Bell, Myrtle Cook, Bobbie Rosenfeld, Ethel Smith, Ethel Catherwood, and Jean Thompson as they competed in the 100 meters, the 800 meters, 4 x 100 meters relay, running high jump, and the discus throw. The author covers the formation of the team, the training, the trip to Amsterdam, the competition, and their homecoming.

2826. Kelly, James C., and Barbara Clark Smith. *Jamestown, Québec, Santa Fe: Three North American Beginnings.* Smithsonian, 2007. 192pp. ISBN 978-1-58834-241-6. Grades YA.

A look at the 400th anniversaries of Jamestown, Québec, and Santa Fe, detailing how each community interacted with the Native Americans; their political, social, economic, and religious systems; and 150 rare artifacts connected to the three. The English settled Jamestown, the Spanish started in Santa Fe, and the French began Québec. Each one survived and became an important part of the spread of European culture and influence in the New World. The book is designed like a catalog for a traveling exhibit about the three sites. Photographs, maps, reproductions, and illustrations enhance the text. Notes and Index.

2827. McKinley, Michael. *Ice Time: The Story of Hockey.* Tundra, 2006. 80pp. ISBN 978-0-88776-762-3. Grades 5–8.

This volume presents the history of hockey from its origins to the present. The sport gained popularity after 1875 when it moved to inside rinks. It includes information about women's hockey, defunct leagues such as the Pacific Coast Hockey Association and the World Hockey Assocation, players including Wayne Gretzky and Mario Lemieux, coaches, and rules. In 1892 the Canadian Governor-General Lord Stanley donated the Dominion Challenge Trophy, and winning the Stanley Cup has become the goal of every professional hockey player. Photographs, Reproductions, and Index.

2828. Prince, Bryan. *I Came As a Stranger: The Underground Railroad.* Tundra, 2004. 160pp. ISBN 978-0-88776-667-1. Grades 5–8.

The author describes some of the slaves who made their way to Ontario, Canada, on the Underground Railroad and what they found after they arrived, including prejudice. It also gives a background of events leading up to slavery in the United States and Canada. Letters and narratives form the stories of the brave runaways who risked much to escape and others who had the help of known leaders like Frederick Douglass, Harriet Tubman, John Brown, and Levi Coffin. Photographs augment the text. Chronology, Notes, Further Reading, and Index.

2829. Weaver, Janice. *Mirror with a Memory: A Nation's Story in Photographs.* Tundra, 2007. 160pp. ISBN 978-0-88776-747-0. Grades 6 up.

Weaver retraces Canada's history from 1864 with the Confederation Conference to the second Quebec referendum in 1995 with photographs and explanations. She starts with profiles of Canada's early photographers and covers the people and beautiful landscapes of the country. The thematic chapters show Canada at war, opening of the Canadian West, transportation, disasters, and the recent past. Maps and Index.

2830. Worth, Richard. *New France 1534–1763.* (Voices from Colonial America) National Geographic, 2007. 64pp. ISBN 978-1-4263-0147-6. Grades 4–8.

The huge French colony known as New France covered a region that included all or parts of Michigan, Minnesota, Wisconsin, Illinois, Indiana, Ohio, Pennsylvania, Vermont, Maine, and Canada. Primary source materials give information about the struggles of individuals and cultural data of this area. Photographs, reproductions, and illustrations highlight the text. Bibliography, Chronology, Further Reading, Web Sites, and Index.

Biography and Collective Biography

2831. Batten, Jack. *The Man Who Ran Faster Than Everyone: The Story of Tom Longboat.* Tundra, 2002. 112pp. Paper ISBN 978-0-8877-6507-0. Grades 7 up.

Onondaga Nation member Tom Longboat (1887–1949) became one of the world's best runners without proper training and without escaping prejudice. He won the Boston Marathon in 1907 and competed in the Olympic Marathon in 1908. The ten chapters of the text present his life and his legacy to become one of the most important Canadians in history. Photographs highlight the text. Index.

2832. Bogart, Jo Ellen. *Capturing Joy: The Story of Maud Lewis.* Tundra, 2002. Unpaged. ISBN 978-0-8877-6568-1. Grades 3–6.

The Canadian artist Maud Lewis (1903–1970) had birth defects and arthritis, which initially hampered her ability to paint. After she married Everett Lewis and lived in a house with neither plumbing nor electricity, she painted on scraps of wood and cardboard with paint that her husband found on his fish-peddling route. Her primitive folk art with bright colors shows her interpretation of life in Nova Scotia. The text contains full-page reproductions of her paintings with a complementary black-and-white pencil drawing.

2833. Goodman, Joan Elizabeth. *Beyond the Sea of Ice: The Voyages of Henry Hudson.* Illustrated by Fernando Rangel and Bette Duke. (Great Explorers Books) Mikaya, 1999. 48pp. ISBN 978-0-9650-4938-2. Grades 3–6.

Henry Hudson (1570–1611), born in London, made four voyages to North America in the early 17th century while looking for a way to the Orient through a possible Northwest Passage. Each chapter focuses on a voyage, describing its plans, its purpose, its sponsors, and its difficulties. When they came into contact with Native Americans, they often did not treat them very well. Content from Hudson's diaries as well as those of some of his shipmates offer background on their experiences. After working his way from cabin boy at 16, to captain, Hudson presumably died in Hudson Bay, Canada, after crewmen set him, his son, and eight others adrift. Illustrations augment the text. Maps and Index.

2834. Loyie, Oskiniko Larry, and Constance Brissenden. *As Long as the Rivers Flow.* Groundwood, 2003. 40pp. Paper ISBN 978-0-8889-9696-1. Grades 3–6.

Larry Loyie relates his story as a Cree Indian before the government removed him and his siblings from their parents to attend a boarding school to learn the way of the Europeans and forget their own culture. At home in Alberta, Canada, before leaving, he learns the ways of nature and enjoys his close family, earning the name Oskiniko, "Young Man," when he shows patience and discipline. He plays in the forest, goes camping with his Grandma, and faces a grizzly bear. But when he is 10, the white men arrive and threaten to place his parents in prison unless they let the children leave home. Photographs intensify the text.

2835. MacKinnon, Christy. *Silent Observer.* Illustrated by author. Gallaudet University, 1993. 42pp. ISBN 978-1-56368-022-9; Harcourt School, 2001. paper ISBN 978-0-15-314376-2. Grades 2–4.

Christy MacKinnon (1889–1981) became deaf when she was two years old as a result of whooping cough. She went to a special school in Halifax, Nova Scotia, and then received a scholarship to study at the Boston Museum of Fine Arts. She continued drawing and painting throughout her life, working both as a teacher and as a commercial artist. The text and complementary illustrations tell about her childhood of horse-drawn sleighs over frozen lakes, farming life, a one-room school, and her family.

2836. MacLeod, Elizabeth. *Alexander Graham Bell: An Inventive Life.* (Snapshots: Images of People and Places in History) Kids Can Press, 1999. 32pp. ISBN 978-1-55074-456-9; paper ISBN 978-1-55074-458-3. Grades 3–6.

Alexander Graham Bell (1847–1922) liked to experiment and, as a child in Edinburgh, Scotland, he began his investigations. The thirteen chapters of the book tell of his move to Canada where he worked with sound until he invented the telephone. He became especially interested in helping deaf people, and worked with the hearing-impaired in Boston, including Helen Keller. Photographs enhance the text. Chronology and Index.

2837. MacLeod, Elizabeth. *Lucy Maud Montgomery: A Writer's Life.* (Snapshots: Images of People and Places in History) Kids Can Press, 2001. 32pp. ISBN 978-1-55074-487-3; paper ISBN 978-1-55074-489-7. Grades 3–7.

Lucy Maud Montgomery (1874–1942) became one of Canada's most famous writers after she published *Anne of Green Gables.* She grew up on Prince Edward Island in the house that became the model for Anne's home, and eventually married a minister. The scrapbook aspect of this biography offers parts of her life trying to make her dreams into reality in double-page spreads with text and photographs. Chronology, Web Sites, and Index.

2838. Moore, Christopher. *Champlain.* Illustrated by Francis Back. Tundra, 2004. 56pp. ISBN 978-0-8877-6657-2. Grades 4–6.

See entry 1195.

2839. Mowat, Farley. *Born Naked.* Mariner, 1995. 256pp. Paper ISBN 978-0-395-73528-2. Grades YA.

A Canadian writer, Farley Mowat, grew up loving nature, and he became a registered ornithologist at the age of 14. His first efforts to become a writer led to his being fired from a newspaper when he graphically described the underwater mating of the ruddy duck. In this book Mowat, the author of *Never Cry Wolf* and other works, describes his life between the world wars.

2840. Roberts, David. *Escape from Lucania: An Epic Story of Survival.* Simon & Schuster, 2007. 206pp. Paper ISBN 978-1-416-56767-7. Grades YA.

In 1937 Bradford Lashburn, 27, and Bob Bates, 26, climbed Mount Lucania in the Canadian Yukon, which was then the highest unclimbed mountain in North America at 17,150 feet. They had to hike more than a hundred miles before they began their climb because weather kept a pilot from landing with supplies and the two other team members. This book, based on interviews with the participants and their diaries, describes the dangers and deprivations of their achievement. Index.

2841. Wallner, Alexandra. *Lucy Maud Montgomery: The Author of "Anne of Green Gables".* Holiday House, 2006. 32pp. ISBN 978-0-8234-1549-6. Grades 4–6.

Canadian Lucy Maud Montgomery lived with her grandparents on Prince Edward Island where she kept a journal and published a poem when she was 16. Although her submissions received many rejections, she finally had *Anne of Green Gables* published. It quickly earned a large readership. She became a minister's wife and the first Canadian female member of the Royal Society of Arts in England. Notes, Bibliography, and Further Reading.

2842. Xydes, Georgia. *Alexander Mackenzie and the Explorers of Canada.* Chelsea House, 1992. 110pp. ISBN 978-0-7910-1314-4. Grades 5 up.

Alexander Mackenzie (1822–1892) was a man of contradictions. He hated the wilderness, but he conquered western Canada. He wanted to be an aristocrat, but he spent many years freezing in wooden structures. Although a loner, he was forced to keep close company with voyagers and Indians. As a fur trader, he sacrificed his health while revolutionizing the Canadian trade system. During his 1789 and 1793 expeditions, he explored Canada to the Pacific and Arctic Oceans. A river, a mountain range, and a place in western Canada bear his name. Photographs, engravings, and reproductions enhance the text. Chronology, Further Reading, and Index.

Graphic Novels, Biographies, and Histories

2843. Blanchet, Pascal. *White Rapids.* Illustrated by author. Translated by Helge Dascher. Drawn & Quarterly, 2007. 156pp. Paper ISBN 978-1-897299-24-1. Grades 10 up.

A private power company needed a site with hydroelectricity in Canada, and it created White Rapids. It was a boom town until the years after World War II, when the company, now owned by the state, no longer needed it. It then decided to abandon the town, a living organism that it had created. The story follows the town's creation, population, and destruction.

2844. Debon, Nicolas. *The Strongest Man in the World.* Illustrated by author. Groundwood, 2007. 36pp. ISBN 978-0-8889-9731-9. Grades 2–4.

This graphic biography sets Louis Cyr (1863–1912) as an old man in Quebec telling his daughter about his days as a weight lifter who astounded his audiences. He lifted draft horses off the ground and platforms holding eighteen audience members, or bent iron poles into pretzels. His grandfather had encouraged him as a child to do his best. Pictures of him at work indicate that his mind was elsewhere and that being strong involved technique in addition to strength. Photographs and Bibliography. *Boston Globe/Horn Book Award* and *Bulletin of the Center for Children's Books Blue Ribbon.*

2845. Rabagliati, Michel. *Paul Has a Summer Job.* Translated by Helge Dascher. Drawn & Quarterly, 2003. 160pp. Paper ISBN 978-1-896597-54-6. Grades YA.

Paul, 18, lives in Montreal, Canada, in 1979 and desires above all to be free from responsibility. Irritated that he has to stop his art training in high school because of his low grades, he decides to quit school and loaf all summer. After getting a boring job printing raffle tickets in a Montreal print shop, he obtains, like many Quebecois teenagers, a job as a counselor at one of the summer camps for underprivileged children in the mountains surrounding the city. By the end of the summer, he falls in love with his co-counselor, Annie; learns to rock climb; and discovers that he enjoys having the children at camp trust and respect him. Glossary.

DVDs

2846. *The Culture of Canada.* (Canada for Children) Library Videos, 2004. 23 min. ISBN 978-1-57225-900-3. Grades K–4.

Through dialogue and pictures this DVD gives a survey of Canada's culture as well as a brainstorming session between students and their teacher about what one should know about the country. It covers Canada's diverse population and traditional Canadian symbols along with their history. Information about holidays, crafts, and food of the various groups including the French highlight the program.

2847. *The Geography of Canada.* (Canada for Children) Library Videos, 2004. 23 min. ISBN 978-1-57225-901-0. Grades K–4.

This DVD explores Canada's geography through dialogue, pictures, and students discussing with their teacher facts that are well-known about Canada. It reveals the vastness of Canada's geography, the diversity of terrain, and aspects of Canada's provinces.

2848. *Historic Sites of Canada.* Schlessinger, 2007. 65 min. ISBN 978-1-4171-0820-6. Grades 3–7.

Episodes of 12 minutes each cover the following topics: Quebec, Lunenburg, Head-Smashed-In on southern Alberta, Anthony Island, and the Canadian Rockies. Cinematography and narration reveal each site's history after a series of questions to consider. The resources include Activities and Web Sites.

2849. *The History of Canada.* (Canada for Children) Library Videos, 2004. 23 min. ISBN 978-1-57225-900-3. Grades K–4.

This DVD gives a survey of Canada's history through dialogue, pictures, and students brainstorming with their teacher about what one should know about Canada. It covers Canada's history by including videos of actual villages, reproductions, and reenactments of events.

2850. *Joe.* National Film Board of Canada, 2002. 8.51 min. Grades 1–7.

Although born in the West Indies, Seraphim "Joe" Fortes became a valued citizen of Vancouver, Canada, because he helped people. Because people needed to learn to swim or to be protected, he watched over thousands trying to swim in English Bay. Eventually the city began paying him for his services. He saved more than 100 lives and taught many to swim. Some people dishonored him because of his color, but others knew and appreciated his worth. *Bronze Plaque Award, Columbus International Film and Video Festival*, and *Leo Award for Best Overall Sound in an Animation.*

2851. *The Spirit of Annie Mae.* National Film Board of Canada, 2002. 1.13 hrs. Grades 10 up.

Buffy St. Marie, Russell Means, Dennis Banks, Wayne Newell, and journalist Minnie Two Shoes relate the story of Annie Mae Pictou Aquash, who was executed in South Dakota on a lonely back road in 1975. Her murder remains unsolved. At 30, she had become a leader in the American Indian Movement (AIM), a First Nations radical group formed—like the Black Panthers—to protect Native American rights. Additional commentary includes her daughters and young women whom she mentored. *Bronze Plaque Award, Columbus International Film and Video Festival—Jury Award, Big Bear Lake International Film Festival Award of Distinction, Indian Summer Deltavision Film & Video Image, Award for Best Documentary Feature Great Plains Film Festival, 2nd Prize Rigoberta Menchu Tum*, and *First Peoples' Festival.*

2852. *When I Meet My Doom.* National Film Board of Canada, 1998. 46 min. Grades 9 up.

This four-part series discusses the War of 1812. The first segment, "When I Meet My Doom," recreates the events leading to the war and the first battles. The United States declared war against Great Britain, planning to gain control of Canada. General Isaac Brock, with the Shawnee chief Tecumseh, captured Fort Mackinac. General Hull was defeated at Detroit, but Brock died during the winning battle at Queenston Heights. In "Or Leave Our Bones Upon Them," Chief Tecumseh becomes important, but General William Henry Harrison wants him away. The British take Prophetstown and massacre Native Americans at Fort Dearborn, Frenchtown, and Raison River. The Americans fail in the attack on Fort Meigs, Ohio, and Tecumseh becomes furious with Procter's retreat. Americans finally win the Battles of Moraviantown and Lake Erie, and when the British retreat to Canada, pursuing Americans kill Tecumseh. In "So Awful a Night," Americans are against the war with New England threatening to secede because trade is outlawed with Britain and Canada. The Americans win nothing in 1813, but in 1814 they win at the Battle of Chippewa and tie at Lundy's Lane. The fourth segment, "The Rocket's Red Glare," finds the Americans regrouping and the British receiving reinforcements at Quebec. After a stalemate at Niagara, the British come to burn

Washington via the Chesapeake Bay. Finally, the British meet defeat at Lake Champlain and New Orleans. The Treaty of Ghent signed on Christmas Eve, 1814, returned all sides to their original positions before the war, with the Americans and British agreeing never to fight again.

Compact Discs

2853. **Curtis, Christopher Paul.** *Elijah of Buxton.*   Narrated by Mirron Willis. Listening Library, 2008. 8 CDs; ca. 9 hrs. ISBN 978-0-7393-6719-3. Grades 4–8.

See entry 2762.

CHINA, JAPAN, AND KOREA

Historical Fiction and Fantasy

2854. Ballard, J. G. *Empire of the Sun: A Novel.* Simon & Schuster, 2005. 2005pp. Paper ISBN 978-0-7432-6523-2. Grades YA.

Jim lives in Shanghai with his parents during World War II. What he sees is not a world war but a battle between the Japanese and the starving Chinese peasants and refugees. He is accidentally separated from his parents after the bombing of Pearl Harbor and he tries to surrender, as he was told to do if captured. Neither the guards nor the British will take him seriously, and he barely survives the ravages of the war. When he sees the excess of the West in comparison with the lack of goods in the East, he worries about the future for all.

2855. Baricco, Alessandro. *Silk.* Translated by Ann Goldstein. Vintage, 2007. 96pp. Paper ISBN 978-0-307-27797-8. Grades YA.

Hervé Joncour meets a woman without oriental-shaped eyes, presumably the concubine of his silk merchant, Hara Kei, while buying silkworms on his journeys from France to Japan in the 1860s. They never speak to each other, but they begin and carry on an affair limited completely to their exchange of longing glances. When, after he ends his trips to Japan he receives a letter from Belgium written in Japanese, his actions indicate an opportunity lost.

2856. Bell, William. *Forbidden City: A Novel of Modern China.* Laurel-Leaf, 1996. 199pp. Paper ISBN 978-0-440-22679-6. Grades 7 up.

Having a news-cameraman father who works in Beijing, Alex, age 17, expects to enjoy his interest in Chinese history, and he makes friends with some Chinese who admire leaders of the People's Liberation Army. When the army turns on the students and massacres them in Tiananmen Square in the spring of 1989, these friends realize that the people they respected have lied to them. Although not definitive historical fiction, this novel tells a story about a situation important in Chinese history.

2857. Bosse, Malcolm. *The Examination.* Sunburst, 1996. 296pp. Paper ISBN 978-0-374-42223-3. Grades 6–10.

Around 1448 in China, Hong Chen decides to sell his prized fighting crickets to finance his brother's trip to Beijing for the government examinations that can earn his brother fame and lifelong wealth. Troubles and tests of varied kinds—rains, famine, locusts, and pirates—occur during the journey to Beijing. They eventually arrive, and Hong delivers a mysterious letter, which he has carried throughout the trip, to a barber. Hong finds that he has his own "exam" in Beijing while his brother exhibits his knowledge of and belief in Confucius. Both succeed; Chen is welcomed inside the Forbidden City and Hong finds his future.

2858. Chen, Da. *Brothers.* Three Rivers, 2007. 429pp. Paper ISBN 978-1-4000-9729-6. Grades YA.

Half-brothers Tan and Shento grow up in different parts of China during the Cultural Revolution without knowing that each other exists. Tan Long, the son of a general, enjoys the privilege of his father's rank. Shento, the general's bastard son, has a bare existence because his mother committed suicide soon after his birth and his father does not acknowledge his existence. After Chairman Mao's death, the Long family loses favor and leave Beijing for their ancestral home. Shento becomes the new president's head of security, wanting to exact revenge on his father. The two brothers meet when they both fall in love with the beautiful orphan, Sumi Wo, but one eventually helps the other because of their blood tie.

2859. Chen, Da. *Sword.* Laura Geringer, 2008. 232pp. ISBN 978-0-06-144758-7. Grades 6 up.

In ancient China Miu Miu, 15, learns the truth behind her father's death. As a master swordsman, he made the Emperor a wonderful sword, and the Emperor had him killed so that he could never craft another one as good. She decides that she will avenge his death so she disguises herself as a male, and since she has been secretly trained in martial arts, she goes on her way. She meets another warrior and challenges him to a kung fu duel, nearly killing him, but the two realize that they are actually betrothed and pledge their love to kill the Emperor together.

2860. Choi, Sook Nyul. *Echoes of the White Giraffe.* Houghton Mifflin, 1993. 144pp. ISBN 978-0-395-64721-9; 2007 paper ISBN 978-0-618-80917-2. Grades 6 up.

Sookan, age 15, her mother, and her brother leave their Korean home in 1952 to seek refuge in Pusan. In this sequel to *The Year of Impossible Goodbyes*, they live in a shack near other refugee huts on a mountain covered with slick mud. Sookan makes friends with a young man, Junho, but cannot pursue the relationship because her culture forbids such liaisons. She passes her exams and wins a scholarship to attend college in America, but she knows that when she leaves she will see Junho no more. Near the end of the story she finally reunites with the older brothers whom she had longed to find. *American Library Association Notable Books for Children.*

2861. Choi, Sook Nyul. *Gathering of Pearls.* Houghton, 2007. 163pp. Paper ISBN 978-0-618-80918-9. Grades 7 up.

Sookan leaves Seoul, Korea, for New York City, very concerned about her first year of school in a foreign country. She must simultaneously learn a new language and a new culture in this conclusion to the stories *Year of Impossible Goodbyes* and *Echoes of the White Giraffe.* Her sister's responses to her letters berate her changes from her old attitudes. Sookan feels guilty about her thoughts, but her college friend suggests that Sookan not let her sister run her life. When Sookan receives news of her mother's death, she grieves and knows that she must continue her own strand of "pearls."

2862. Choi, Sook Nyul. *Year of Impossible Goodbyes.* Houghton Mifflin, 1991. 176pp. ISBN 978-0-395-57419-5; Dell, 1993. paper ISBN 978-0-440-40759-1. Grades 5–9.

Sookan, who is 10 years old in 1945 when World War II ends, faces the Russian invasion after the Japanese leave North Korea. She, her mother, and her brother are separated from her father and three older brothers. The Russians capture people trying to escape across the Thirty-Eighth Parallel and detain her mother, but Sookan and her brother successfully escape to the south. The story tells about the Japanese occupation and what the soldiers did to the people, including the moving of female workers in the knitting factories to the war front to become prostitutes. *Bulletin Blue Ribbon Book* and *School Library Journal Best Book.*

2863. Clavell, James. *Noble House: A Novel of Contemporary Hong Kong.* Dell, 2009. 1200pp. Paper ISBN 978-0-385-34326-8. Grades YA.

In 1841 the first *tai-pan* (corporate head) of Noble House, a Hong Kong trading company, said that he would do anything for the person who could present the other half of a specific coin. When two Americans arrive in 1963, they do not understand the history behind Hong Kong business or the unwritten rules of trade. The Chinese know how to get as much as possible from their deals, and the British control everything. Competition between Noble House and its rival causes intrigue to develop at various levels of the corporation's society.

2864. Clavell, James. *Shōgun.* Dell, 2009. 1200pp. Paper ISBN 978-0-385-34324-4. Grades YA.

In 1600 John Blackthorne shipwrecks in Japanese waters. Jealous Spanish and Portuguese Jesuits in Japan translate for him and misrepresent his intentions. But Toranaga, the man positioning himself to become shōgun of all Japan, realizes that Blackthorne is honest, and he frees Blackthorne from prison. He matches Blackthorne with a trustworthy Japanese instructor, with whom Blackthorne falls in love. After watching Blackthorne's progress, Toranaga sees that the former ship's pilot is the one man in Japan who will not conspire against him.

2865. Coerr, Eleanor. *Mieko and the Fifth Treasure.* Puffin, 2003. 79pp. Paper ISBN 978-0-698-11990-1. Grades 4–7.

Meiko, age 10, has four tangible treasures—a sable brush, an inkstick, an inkstone, and a roll of rice paper. She remembers her art teacher telling her, before the bomb dropped on Nagasaki, Japan, in 1945, that she had a fifth treasure—beauty in her heart. But the bomb hurts her hand, and she can no longer paint as she did before. In her new school near her grandparents' farm, she feels isolated, and the children tease her about her scar. She must search deeply to regain the fifth treasure.

2866. Coerr, Eleanor. *Sadako.* Illustrated by Ed Young. Putnam, 1993. 48pp. ISBN 978-0-399-21771-5; Puffin, 1997. paper ISBN 978-0-698-11588-0. Grades K–3.

When Sadako was 2, the atomic bomb dropped on her home in Hiroshima. At 12, she developed leukemia. When a friend tells her that the gods will cure a sick person who folds 1,000 paper cranes, she starts folding. She never completes the thousand, but her classmates finish them after she dies. The illustrations and text make this version of *Sadako and the Thousand Paper Cranes* (1977) more appropriate for younger readers.

2867. Coerr, Eleanor. *Sadako and the Thousand Paper Cranes.* Illustrated by Ronald Himler. Putnam, 2002. 80pp. ISBN 978-0-399-23799-7; Puffin, 2001. paper ISBN 978-0-698-11900-0. Grades 4–6.

Sadako survived the bombing of Hiroshima in 1945. She loved to run and was a racer in her junior high school before she contracted leukemia ten years later. In the hospital, she began making paper cranes for good luck; she completed 664 before her death. Her classmates made the rest of the 1,000 cranes to be buried with her. They also published her letters.

2868. Cole, Joanna. *Ms. Frizzle's Adventures: Imperial China.* Illustrated by Bruce Degen. Scholastic, 2003. 48pp. ISBN 978-0-590-10822-5; 2008. paper ISBN 978-0-590-10823-2. Grades 1–5.

When Wanda, Arnold, and Ms. Frizzle are whisked back in time to ancient China, they learn about the Grand Canal, the Great Wall, kung fu, silk, and more when they journey to Beijing to get the emperor to help a farm village with failing rice crops in the South.

2869. Compestine, Ying Chang. *Revolution Is Not a Dinner Party.* Holt, 2007. 248pp. ISBN 978-0-8050-8207-4. Grades 4–6.

The daughter of surgeons in Wuhan, China, during the Cultural Revolution that began in 1972, Ling, 9, watches families around her suffer when Comrade Li of the Red Guard moves into their apartment. Soon her own family faces the same treatment. She worries when her father disappears, and she confronts school bullies who taunt her for being "bourgeois," but is determined to keep her long hair. When lice infest it, she has to cut it. After Chairman Mao dies in 1976, she and her mother ecstatically reunite. *Parents Choice Award*, *Publishers Weekly Best Books*, *American Library Association Notable Children's Books*, and *Tayshas Reading List* (Texas) nomination.

2870. DeJong, Meindert. *The House of Sixty Fathers.* Illustrated by Maurice Sendak. Trophy, 1987. 189pp. Paper ISBN 978-0-06-440200-2. Grades 5–8.

The sampan on which Tien Pao is sleeping washes down river from Hengyang where his parents work at the American airfield. When he comes ashore, he and his pig begin the long walk back to the area through the Japanese-occupied territory of China. When an American airman crashes his plane nearby, Tien Pao helps him, and the Americans in turn look after him. All sixty of the airmen in the area want to adopt him, but he wants to find his family. *Newbery Honor Book*, *American Library Association Notable Books for Children*, *International Board of Books for Young People*, and *Child Study Association Children's Book Award*.

2871. Demi. *The Magic Pillow.* Illustrated by author. Margaret K. McElderry, 2008. 40pp. ISBN 978-1-4169-2470-8. Grades 3 up.

At an inn during a snowstorm during China's Tang Dynasty, Ping meets a magician who does such wonderful things that Ping feels dejected about his own chances to ever achieve anything. But Ping sleeps on a pillow that the magician lends him. He dreams that he becomes wealthy, then loses his power, then regains it, and that his descendants do the same repeatedly. He wakes up understanding that money and fame do not last but that a good heart will. Note.

2872. Fritsch, Debra M., and Ruth S. Hunter. *A Part of the Ribbon: A Time Travel Adventure Through the History of Korea.* Illustrated by Ken Cotrona. Turtle, 1997. 216pp. Paper ISBN 978-1-880336-11-3. Grades 4–6.

Although the way into fantasy is awkward, Jeffrey, 13, and his 6-year-old sister go with their tae kwon do instructor back into the Korea of two thousand years ago. They see the periods of history and the development of the sport.

2873. Fritz, Jean. *Homesick: My Own Story.* Illustrated by Margot Tomes. Putnam, 1982. 160pp. ISBN 978-0-399-20933-8; Puffin, 2007. paper ISBN 978-0-14-240761-5. Grades 3–7.

Born in China, Jean Fritz came to America when she was 10. During the last two years she and her parents spent in Hankow, China, the conflict between Chiang Kai-shek (Sun Yat-sen's successor) and Mao Tse-tung was beginning. The autobiographical story is catalogued as fiction because Fritz tells her story as a storyteller rather than as an autobiographer. The reader lives with a child who first meets adult problems, such as the death of another child, the divorce of a friend's parents, and a war in which her servant friends are hurt by enemies and by families turned Communist. Background of Chinese History, 1913–1927.

2874. Goto, Scott. *The Perfect Sword.* Charlesbridge, 2008. Unpaged. ISBN 978-1-57091-697-7. Grades 3–5.

In the Tokugawa period of 16th-century Japan, master sword maker Michio, a sword-smith's apprentice, and his Sensei create a perfect sword. They interview samurai, warriors, and nobles who want it, but not until they find the person who is truly dedicated to a better life for others will they sell it. Glossary and Notes.

2875. Gratz, Alan. *Samurai Shortstop.* Dial, 2006. 280pp. ISBN 978-0-8037-3075-5; Puffin, 2008. paper ISBN 978-0-14-241099-8. Grades 7 up.

In 1890 Toyo, 16, obtains a Western education at Ichiko, a prestigious Japanese boarding school in Tokyo, while simultaneously receiving the traditional samurai training. The previous year he saw his uncle commit "seppuku," or ritual suicide, rather than give up being a samurai as the emperor had commanded. Then Toyo's father had to decapitate his brother, a practice based on the ritual's requirement. His father makes Toyo watch and tells Toyo that he must later do the same for him. But instead, Toyo uses his training to play baseball, the imported game from America, so he can help himself and his team. *American Library Association Best Books for Young Adults* and *Capitol Choices Noteworthy Titles* (Washington, D.C.).

2876. Greenway, Alice. *White Ghost Girls.* Grove, 2006. 168pp. Paper ISBN 978-0-8021-7018-7. Grades YA.

American teenager Frankie and her younger sister Kate live in Hong Kong during the Maoist Cultural Revolution in 1967 with their war-photographer father and artist mother. Their father spends much time in Vietnam, and their mother loses herself in her painting while waiting for his visits. An amah (nanny) looks after them and calls them "white ghost girls." Because Frankie is reckless and desperately trying to get their parents' attention, Kate feels responsible for keeping her safe. When Frankie decides to run away in the marketplace, Red Guards kidnap her and force Kate to take a package to a nearby police station. A bomb inside it kills a woman and burns a child, and Kate has to deal with the dangers that Frankie has brought upon them.

2877. Haseley, Dennis. *Twenty Heartbeats.* Illustrated by Ed Young. Roaring Brook, 2008. 32pp. ISBN 978-1-59643-238-3. Grades 2–4.

When Homan, an artist, takes many years to finish the picture of a prized horse in ancient China, his wealthy client confronts him. Then Homan makes several strokes that take twenty heartbeats. Irritated that he has paid heavily for such a quickly finished picture, the man turns to leave and sees thousands of paintings that Homan has made in preparation for his final work. Cut paper collages complement the text.

2878. Haugaard, Erik Christian. *The Boy and the Samurai.* Houghton, 2005. 221pp. Paper ISBN 978-0-618-61511-7. Grades 6–9.

The orphan Saru, or "monkey," is both homeless and friendless, surviving by begging and living near a temple shrine. Saru becomes friends with a kind samurai and helps him rescue his wife from the warlord's castle in 16th-century Japan. His plan saves the three of them plus a priest who has acted as his mentor. Saru realizes that he must always tell the truth, because it will keep him free. *Parents' Choice.*

2879. Haugaard, Erik Christian. *The Revenge of the Forty-Seven Samurai.* Houghton, 1995. 240pp. ISBN 978-0-395-70809-5; paper ISBN 978-0-618-54896-5. Grades 6–9.

Jiro is a lowly servant in a deceased samurai's household during the fourteenth year of Genroku (1701) under the shogun Tokugawa Tsunayoshi. There he observes the plans for revenge against Lord Kira, the man whose demands on Lord Asano caused him to commit ritual suicide. Jiro assists in preparing for the final fight against Lord Kira, although he wonders why the samurai retainers want to sacrifice themselves. Because he is not a samurai, he can question their values and be glad that he does not have to make a life-and-death decision on such a seemingly insignificant point. *American Library Association Notable Books for Children* and *American Library Association Notable Books for Young Adults.*

2880. Haugaard, Erik Christian. *The Samurai's Tale.* Houghton, 2005. 256pp. Paper ISBN 978-0-618-61512-4. Grades 7–10.

As he reflects on his past, Taro remembers his life in Japan around 1550 when he served his master, Lord Akiyama, as a servant's servant, a stable boy, a secret messenger, and finally, as a samurai. After he had learned to write, he sent a servant to carry his love poems to a nobleman's daughter with whom he had fallen in love. He and the girl had to escape the enemy by disguising themselves. *American Library Association Notable Children's Book.*

2881. Hong, Chen Jiang. *Little Eagle.* Illustrated by author. Enchanted Lion, 2007. 32pp. ISBN 978-1-59270-071-4. Grades 3–6.

In China during the 15th century, the orphan Little Eagle becomes an apprentice to Master Yang, a Kung Fu master, even though Master Yang is disappointed that Little Eagle used force to defeat bullies. He teaches Little Eagle, and the two of them respond to General Zhao and his troop's attack when trying to get the secret of the martial art style, but they mortally wound Master Yang. Little Eagle carries on his tradition without revealing its source. Chinese scroll paintings intensify the text.

2882. Hong, Chen Jiang. *The Magic Horse of Han Gan.* Illustrated by Claudia Zoe Bedrick. Enchanted Lion, 2006. 37pp. ISBN 978-1-59270-063-9. Grades 1–5.

During the Tang Dynasty in the 9th century, Han Gan becomes a famous Chinese painter of horses after growing up as a poor boy. A warrior comes to him and wants one of his magical horses, and Han Gan makes one of his painted horses come alive. Although the horse goes to battle and always wins with the warrior, it never eats nor sleeps. Finally, it disappears one night, distressed at the destruction of war. Illustrations enhance the text.

2883. Hong, Lily Toy. *The Empress and the Silkworm.* Illustrated by author. Albert Whitman, 1995. 32pp. ISBN 978-0-8075-2009-3. Grades 1–4.

When a silkworm falls into the tea of the Empress Si Ling-Chi, she takes it out and notices a long, shiny thread unwinding from its body. Supposedly this event led her husband, the Yellow Emperor Huang-Ti, to begin manufacturing silk fabric. The story includes background on silk science and the silk trade.

2884. Hoobler, Dorothy, and Thomas Hoobler. *The Demon in the Teahouse.* Puffin, 2005. 181pp. Paper ISBN 978-0-14-240540-6. Grades 5–9.

In the 18th century, Seikei, 14, goes to the Yoshiwara district of Edo at Judge Ooka's request to find out what relationship a popular geisha has to arsons and murders in this sequel to *The Ghost in the Tokaido Inn.* He takes a job as an errand boy at the Teahouse of the Falling Cherry Blossoms, learns about the geishas, and has to protect himself and the geisha Umae from the bitter widow of a samurai. In his effort to help Judge Ooka and prove himself worthy of becoming a samurai, Seikei becomes trapped on a roof enveloped in flames, and suffers threats, tricks, being drugged, and being framed in his effort to find the killer. *Sequoyah Award* (Oklahoma) nomination and *Capitol Choices Noteworthy Titles.*

2885. Hoobler, Dorothy, and Thomas Hoobler. *The Ghost in the Tokaido Inn.* (Samurai Mystery) Philomel, 1999. 214pp. ISBN 978-0-399-23330-2. Grades 5–9.

In 1735 during Japan's Tokugawa period, Seikei, 14, longs to be a samurai. But his father is a merchant, and he can do no more in his society than follow his father. When he stops over at Tokaido Inn, he sees a legendary ghost stealing a samurai's jewel. He saves a falsely accused guest and impresses Judge Ooka. He hires Seikei to help him investigate the crime. His assignment is go backstage at Kabuki theaters and often act honorably like a samurai. Judge Ooka encourages him to observe, be logical, and to reason carefully. Seikei succeeds. *Bulletin Blue Ribbon.*

2886. Hoobler, Dorothy, and Thomas Hoobler. *In Darkness, Death.* (Samurai Mystery) Philomel, 2004. 208pp. ISBN 978-0-399-23767-6; Puffin, 2005. paper ISBN 978-0-14-240366-2. Grades 6–10.

In this sequel to *The Demon in the Teahouse,* when someone murders the Samurai Lord Inaba in his sleep, Judge Ooka and Seikei, 14, his young apprentice, have only a bloodstained origami butterfly as a clue. Although they think a ninja did it, the question remains as to who hired the ninja. Judge Ooka sends Seikei to the Etchu Province with the quiet Tatsuno to discover who made the paper used for the butterfly. The two obtain permission to go to Mount Miwa, and there Seikei finds the answer. *Nutmeg Children's Book Award* (Connecticut) nomination, *Edgar Allen Poe Awards, Black Eyed Susan Book Award* (Maryland) nomination, *Children's Book Award* (South Carolina) nomination, *Children's Book Award* (West Virginia) nomination, and *Battle of the Books Award* (Wisconsin) nomination.

2887. Hoobler, Dorothy, and Thomas Hoobler. *A Samurai Never Fears Death.* (Samurai Mystery) Sleuth, 2007. 198pp. ISBN 978-0-399-24609-8. Grades 5–9.

In Japan during 1737 Seikei, 16 and now a samurai after being adopted by Judge Ooka, has to return with him to visit Osaka. Since Seikei's biological family is there, he sees them. To celebrate his arrival, he attends a puppet show with his brother and sister. Since the plays convey messages about the politics and restive class system, they are especially popular. He discovers, however, that his sister's lover, the puppet master's apprentice, has been accused of murdering the master. Seikei knows that has to use the skills that Judge Ooka has taught him to find the real murderer.

2888. Iggulden, Conn. *Genghis: Lords of the Bow.* Delacorte, 2008. 400pp. ISBN 978-0-385-33952-0. Grades YA.

Genghis Khan (1162–1227), once an outcast orphan, begins his quest to conquer the Chin empire in the sequel to *Birth of an Empire.* With the help of his brothers, Kachiun and Chaser, he first strikes the Xi Xia Kingdom south of the Gobi Desert and enters China by circumventing the Great Wall. He then travels to Yenking, capital of the empire, leaving devastation behind him. To gain the city, he starves its people into submission. Genghis has some setbacks, such as a shaman who tries to mislead him and difficulties fathering his first-born son, but he always remains concerned about his family and his tribe as he pursues his goals.

2889. Krebs, Laurie. *We're Riding on a Caravan: An Adventure on the Silk Road.* Illustrated by Helen Cann. Barefoot, 2005. 32pp. ISBN 978-1-84686-108-6; 2007. paper ISBN 978-1-84148-343-6. Grades 1–4.

A family leaves Xi'an, China, to begin their year-long trip down the two-thousand-mile long Silk Road to sell their silks at the Kashgar bazaar. They ride camels and take donkeys, oxen, and wagons with them. Along the way, they cross the the Yellow River at Lanzhou, see the oasis at Dunhuang with the huge sand dunes surrounding it, and the vineyards of Turpan, all while the seasons change. Finally they reach Kashgar to sell at the Sunday market and then prepare to return home.

2890. Li, Pi-Hua. *Farewell My Concubine: A Novel.* HarperCollins, 1994. 255pp. Paper ISBN 978-0-06-097644-6. Grades YA.

As young boys, Duan Xialou and Cheng Dieyi train to sing at the Peking Opera before the Japanese invade China. With much work and punishment, they become stars from their interpretation of the two roles in the opera *Farewell My Concubine.* Cheng, however, becomes the character from the opera who loves Duan, and when Duan marries in real life, Cheng is intensely jealous.

2891. Lord, Bette Bao. *The Middle Heart.* Fawcett, 1997. 372pp. Paper ISBN 978-0-449-91232-4. Grades YA.

In the 1930s a motley group forms a friendship in China. They include Steel Hope, the second son of the fallen House of Li; Mountain Pine, Steel Hope's crippled servant; and Firecrackers, a grave keeper's daughter disguised as a boy. As China enters war, they separate. Firecrackers becomes an opera singer who learns to perform while bombs fall nearby, and Steel Hope becomes an engineer who participates in the underground fighting the Japanese while revering the revolution. Mountain Pine becomes a writer and a hermit. When they meet again, their different paths and different ideologies test their friendship.

2892. McCaughrean, Geraldine. *The Kite Rider.* HarperTrophy, 2003. 320pp. Paper ISBN 978-0-06-441091-5. Grades 5–9.

Haoyou, 12, lives in China in 1281 under the foreign emperor, Kublai Khan, whose Mongol warriors have just conquered the Sung Dynasty. Haoyou must protect his widowed mother from his greedy Uncle Bo and a suitor, Di Chou, who caused his father's death by giving him the dangerous job of a "wind tester" on a huge kite for the *Chabi*, a ship preparing to sail. Haoyou joins the mysterious Miao Je's traveling circus as part of an act with his cousin, Mipeng, in which he masters kite-riding, a skill where he is strapped to its crossbars, and pretends to speak to spirits while flying through the sky. Miao plans to take the circus to Kublai Khan's court. A kamikaze wind almost kills the boy as it destroys Kublai Khan's fleet on its way to invade Japan. *English Smartie Prize, BBC Blue Peter Prize for Best Book to Keep Forever, School Library Journal Best Books of the Year, American Library Association Notable Books for Children and Young Adults, Beehive Young Adults' Book Award* (Utah) nomination, *Horn Book Fanfare*, and *Rebecca Caudill Young Readers' Book Award* (Illinois) nomination.

2893. McCunn, Ruthanne Lum. *God of Luck.* Soho, 2007. 256pp. ISBN 978-1-56947-466-2; 2008. paper ISBN 978-1-56947-518-8. Grades YA.

Slavers capture Ah Lung from China between 1840 and 1875 and force him to become an indentured slave in Peru's guano mines under cruel overseers. His wife, Bo See, continues to work in the family's silk factory while trying to support the family. When she succeeds in making extra money, the family hires men to look for Ah Lung, one of the million men stolen for work in the Americas.

2894. Maruki, Toshi. *Hiroshima, No Pika.* Morrow, 1982. 48pp. ISBN 978-0-688-01297-7. Grades 4–7.

In 1945 Mii is 7 years old. She and her parents experience the chaos following the blast of the atomic bomb dropped by the American airplane, the *Enola Gay*. In shock, Mii carries her chopsticks for several days before she realizes that they are still in her hand. After some time, her father dies, and Mii never gets any larger than she was when the bomb fell. The expressionist illustrations heighten the fury of the scene without overly realistic gore. *Mildred L. Batchelder Award, Jane Addams Children's Book Award*, and *American Library Association Notable Books for Children*.

2895. Matthews, Andrew. *The Way of the Warrior.* Dutton, 2008. 152pp. ISBN 978-0-525-42063-7. Grades 5–9.

In pre-Edo 16th-century Japan Jimmu Shimomura becomes an orphan when Lord Ankan causes his parents to commit ritual suicide to preserve the family's honor. His father's samurai bodyguard, Araki Nichiren, then trains Jimmu as a samurai so that he can take revenge on Lord Ankan for his actions. After Nichiren dies, Jimmu becomes first a castle guard and then a bodyguard for Ankan. However, Ankan seems very different from the man he has been taught to hate. He must decide what his honorable action must be.

2896. Min, Anchee. *Wild Ginger.* Mariner, 2004. 224pp. Paper ISBN 978-0-618-38043-5. Grades YA.

In 1969 during the Cultural Revolution Maple, 14, fears the bully Hot Pepper, a violent Maoist in her class. Wild Ginger, ostracized because her deceased father was half-French, matches Hot Pepper's personality, and fights back since she wants to become the "ultimate" Maoist. She even takes a vow not to marry because love is bourgeois. But Wild Ginger has a problem living up to her ideals when she falls in love with Evergreen. She asks Maple to keep them apart, but Maple begins to fall in love with Evergreen herself.

2897. Mowll, Joshua. *Operation Red Jericho.* Illustrated by Benjamin Mowll, Julek Heller, and Niroot Puttapipat. (The Guild of Specialists) Candlewick, 2005. 288pp. ISBN 978-0-7636-2634-1. Grades 7 up.

Rebecca MacKenzie, 15, keeps a diary of her experiences on the China coast in 1920. She and her brother, Doug, must leave their home in the Sinking region of China after their parents strangely disappear, to live with their uncle, a sea captain. After they board his ship in Shanghai, they learn about a secret society, the Honourable Guild of Specialists, that might have something to do with their parents and with their uncle. This is the opening volume in the series. *New York Public Library Book for the Teen Age, Great Stone Face Award* (New Hampshire) nomination, and *Oppenheim Toy Portfolio Gold Award Winner.*

2898. Mowll, Joshua. *Operation Typhoon Shore.* Illustrated by Julek Heller, Niroot Puttapipat, and Ben Mowll. (The Guild of Specialists) Candlewick, 2005. 288pp. ISBN 978-0-7636-3122-2; 2008. paper ISBN 978-0-7636-3808-5. Grades 5–8.

Doug and his sister, Becca, in this sequel to *Operation Red Jericho*, run aground on a volcanic island with their uncle, Captain MacKenzie, on his ship, *The Expedient.* The siblings are only interested in finding their parents while their uncle worries about a missing gyrolabe. When the two find a 1533 painting, they hope it may contain information about their parents. But first, they must fight Kalaxx warriors who are against their uncle's secret organization.

2899. Namioka, Lensey. *The Coming of the Bear: A Novel.* Tuttle, 2005. 235pp. Paper ISBN 978-0-8048-3613-5. Grades 7 up.

The samurai Matsuzo and Zenta and their boat are dashed onto the island of Ezo (Hokkaido) by an unexpected squall at sea. The Ainus, a strange, round-eyed people, surround them and look after their wounds. They see how hard the life is for this group, and they realize that they are captives. They have to plan an escape to a Japanese compound on another part of the island. The Japanese, however, are planning war against the Ainus to gain more land. The two captives help to stop the war by identifying the Ainu traitors.

2900. Namioka, Lensey. *An Ocean Apart, a World Away: A Novel.* Laurel-Leaf, 2003. 197pp. Paper ISBN 978-0-440-22973-5. Grades 7–10.

Yanyan, 16, decides to become a doctor while at her Nanking, China, home in the 1920s, but she must go to America. She leaves to study at Cornell University, where she faces prejudice, has problems with independence including her inability to cook for herself, and is lonely. However, she has her own mistaken prejudices toward Westerners and disregards a professor who says that women cannot understand physics. She also finds friendship and pleasure in her accomplishments. *Young Adult Book Award* (South Carolina) nomination.

2901. Namioka, Lensey. *Ties That Bind, Ties That Break.* Laurel-Leaf, 2000. 154pp. Paper ISBN 978-0-440-41599-2. Grades 7–10.

In 1911 in Nanjing, China, Tao Ailin, the third daughter in a wealthy family, decides at age 5 that she will not have her feet bound. The mother of the groom in her arranged marriage cancels it, and after her father dies when Ailin is 12, her uncle removes her from the missionary school with the "Big Noses" where she has learned English and other subjects, telling her she can be a nun, a farmer's wife, or a concubine. She becomes the nanny for children of American missionaries, and when she is 16 she leaves China to go with them to San Francisco. There she meets and marries a young Chinese restauranteur. She remembers her own history when her former fiancé comes into her husband's restaurant. *American Library Association Best Books for Young Adults*, *Rebecca Caudill Young Readers' Book Award* (Illinois), *Young Readers Choice Awards* (Pennsylvania), *Tayshas High School Reading List* (Texas), and *Capitol Choices Noteworthy Titles* (Washington, D.C.).

2902. Noyes, Deborah. *Red Butterfly: How a Princess Smuggled the Secret of Silk Out of China.* Illustrated by Sophie Blackall. Candlewick, 2007. 32pp. ISBN 978-0-7636-2400-2. Grades 3–6.

When the princess in China's royal family—the only silk producer in the world—leaves home to marry the king of Khotan in a far-off desert, she decides to take some silkworms inside her elaborate hairstyle. The most guarded secret of the family is that the silkworms feed on mulberry leaves, but she risks death to carry this secret with her in her hair. Ink-and-watercolor illustrations beautifully complement the text.

2903. Park, Frances, and Ginger Park. *The Royal Bee.* Illustrated by Christopher Zhong-Yuan Zhang. Boyds Mills, 2000. Unpaged. Paper ISBN 978-1-56397-867-8. Grades K–3.

When destitute Song-ho hears the school bells in a nearby Korean valley in the late 19th century, he walks to the school and asks if he may attend. The teacher tells him that only wealthy children are allowed. Song-ho realizes that schooling is the only way he might be able to escape working in the fields, so he stands outside the school and listens to the lessons. When the teacher, Master Min, realizes how serious Song-ho is about learning, he allows him inside. Then Song-ho earns the honor of representing the school in the spelling bee at the Governor's palace. He wins and brings acclaim to the school. Illustrations complement the text. *Children's Book Award* (South Carolina) nomination and *Capitol Choices Noteworthy Titles* (Washington, D.C.).

2904. Park, Linda Sue. *Archer's Quest.* Clarion, 2006. 167pp. ISBN 978-0-618-59631-7; Yearling, 2008. paper ISBN 978-0-440-42204-4. Grades 4–7.

Kevin Kim, a sixth-grader in Dorchester, New York, sees an arrow fly through the air and pin his baseball cap to the wall. The arrow was shot by Koh Chu-Mong, the great archer from 1st-century B.C.E. Korea. He claims to have fallen off his tiger and landed in Kevin's bedroom. Cars frighten him, as do other modern trappings such as lights, computers, telephones, and beds. Kevin needs to help the archer return to his home and time, and while they try to find a way, the archer entertains Kevin with stories from Korea's history. He teaches Kevin that he has unexpected self-sufficiency.

2905. Park, Linda Sue. *The Firekeeper's Son.* Illustrated by Julie Downing. Clarion, 2004. ISBN 978-0-618-13337-6. Grades K–3.

Sang-hee's father is injured in Korea during the early 1800s. His job is lighting the evening signal fire on the mountain near their home by the sea to send news to the king, and Sang-hee assumes his father's occupation. If the king does not see a fire, he thinks trouble has occurred, and he sends out his soldiers. However, Sang-hee wants to see the soldiers just one time so he has to decide if he will light the fire. Illustrations highlight the text. *Parents Choice Award, Monarch Award* Nomination, *Volunteer State Book Awards* (Tennessee), *Irma S. & James H. Black Honor, Bluegrass Award* (Kentucky) nomination, *Asian Pacific American Award for Illustration in Children's Literature, Picture Storybook* (Georgia) nomination, and *Young Hoosier Award* (Indiana) nomination.

2906. Park, Linda Sue. *A Single Shard.* Clarion, 2001. 160pp. ISBN 978-0-395-97827-6; Yearling, 2003. paper ISBN 978-0-440-41851-1. Grades 4–8.

In 12th-century Korea, the orphaned Tree Ear, 10, lives under a bridge in the care of Crane-Man, who is lame. The two scrounge for food in garbage because they are not thieves. When Tree Ear sees the potter Min creating beautiful celadon bowls in Ch'ul'po, he becomes fascinated and returns to see the finished product. One breaks in the fracas as Tree Ear is discovered, and Min makes him work for nine days to pay off the debt. The wood chopping for the kiln and cutting clay in preparation for throwing is difficult, but Tree Ear prevails, and Min allows him to stay with food for his pay. Eventually, Min entrusts him with beautiful bowls to take to the royal court in Songdo. On the long, arduous journey, robbers shatter the work, but Tree Ear pushes forth with one "single shard." *Newbery Medal, Rebecca Caudill Young Readers' Book Award* (Illinois), *Dorothy Canfield Fisher Children's Book Award* (Vermont) nomination, *Children's Book Award* (Massachusetts) nomination, *Sequoyah Book Awards* (Oklahoma) nomination, *Charlie May Simon Children's Book Award* (Arkansas), *School Library Journal Best Books for Children*, and *Capitol Choices Noteworthy Titles* (Washington, D.C.).

2907. Park, Linda Sue. *When My Name Was Keoko.* Dell Yearling, 2004. ISBN 978-0-4404-1944-0. Grades 6–10.

When the Japanese occupy Korea from 1940 to 1945, Sun-hee, 10, and her older brother, Tae-yul, can never display the symbols of their country in public and must study Japanese language and culture. Then the Emperor of Japan commands that all Koreans take Japanese names. Sun-hee becomes Keoko, and Tae-yul takes the name of Nobuo. The family tries to keep their culture by hiding a potted Rose of Sharon tree, the symbol of Korea, inside their shed. During the war, Sun-hee admires their introspective father and follows his lead by writing when she feels especially distressed with the reality of their lives. Tae-yul, on the other hand, appreciates their uncle's participation in the underground resistance even when his uncle must go into hiding. When Tae-yul worries about having to reveal his uncle's location, he goes into the Japanese army to show false loyalty; however, he is chosen to be a kamikaze pilot. *Jane Addams Children's Book Award* nomination, *Dorothy Canfield Fisher Children's Book Award* (Vermont) nomination, *School Library Journal Best Books of the Year, American Library Association Notable Books for Children, Charlie May Simon Children's Book Award* (Arkansas) nomination, *Sunshine State Young Reader's Book Award* (Florida) nomination, *Rebecca Caudill Young Readers' Book Award* (Illinois) nomination, *Black-Eyed Susan Book Award* (Maryland) nomination, *Mark Twain Award* (Missouri) nomination, *Land of Enchantment Book Award* (New Mexico) nomination, *Sequoyah Book Award* (Oklahoma) nomination, *Beehive Children's Fictional Book Award* (Utah) nomination, *Publishers Weekly Best Children's Books, Bluegrass Award* (Kentucky) nomination, *Mitten Award, Capitol Choices Noteworthy Titles* (Washington, D.C.), and *Student Book Award* (Maine) nomination.

2908. Paterson, Katherine. *The Master Puppeteer.* Illustrated by Haru Wells. Fitzerald, 2007. 180pp. ISBN 978-1-4242-0841-8; Trophy, 1989. paper ISBN 978-0-06-440281-1. Grades 7 up.

Jiro, apprentice to the harsh master of the puppet theater, Yoshida, wants to find the identity of Saber, the bandit who robs from the rich to feed the poor during the famine in 18th century Japan. Jiro and Acedia's son become friends and share concerns about the starving people outside of the theater. When they see family members among the group, they become especially distressed. *National Book Award for Children's Literature Winner, American Library Association Notable Children's Books*, and *School Library Journal Best Books*.

2909. Paterson, Katherine. *Of Nightingales That Weep.* Illustrated by Haru Wells. Fitzgerald, 2007. 172pp. ISBN 978-1-4242-0842-5; Trophy, 1989. paper ISBN 978-0-06-440282-8. Grades 5 up.

Taiko, age 11, likes to remember her samurai father instead of the ugly potter that her mother married after her father's death. She is happy to serve the child emperor at the Heike imperial court with her beauty and her lovely singing voice. After several years, her talents intrigue Hideo, an enemy Genji spy, and she refuses to come home to help her pregnant mother and stepfather. When she does return, her mother and brother have died, and an accident scars her face. She can no longer expect to return to Hideo, and she begins to see the inner beauty of the potter. *Phoenix Award* and *American Library Association Notable Children's Books*.

2910. Paterson, Katherine. *The Sign of the Chrysanthemum.* Fitzgerald, 2007. 132pp. ISBN 978-1-4242-0838-8; Trophy, 1988. paper ISBN 978-0-06-440232-3. Grades 7 up.

Muna wanders around the city in 1170 to find his father after his mother dies. He meets a man whom he likes, but the man is a disreputable, unemployed samurai—a ronin. The ronin wants Muna to report to him about the movements of two warring factions, the Gengi and Heike, while the youth works for a sword maker who refuses to arm men deemed unworthy of his efforts. When Muna decides to stop informing the ronin, the sword maker appoints him as an apprentice.

2911. Place, Francois. *The Old Man Mad About Drawing: A Tale of Hokusai.* Translated by William Rodarmor. David R. Godine, 2003. 128pp. ISBN 978-1-56792-260-8. Grades 3–7.

During the early 19th century, the orphan Tojiro, 9, delivers rice cakes in Edo (now Tokyo) to an old man, Hokusai, who draws all the time. He gradually becomes Hokusai's friend and then his assistant. Hokusai teaches Tojiro the process of woodblock engraving, and Tojiro studies his earlier art. Tojiro enjoys examining Hokusai's sketchbooks, called manga. Ink and watercolor illustrations enhance the text. Illustrated Glossary.

2912. Preus, Margi. *The Peace Bell.* Illustrated by Hideko Takahashi. Holt, 2008. ISBN 978-0-8050-7800-8. Grades K–3.

During World War II Yoko's grandmother watched soldiers take the village temple bell, and it could no longer ring 108 times to celebrate midnight on New Year's Eve. The villagers assumed the bell had been melted, but they heard that American soldiers had taken it to Minnesota. Years later, the Americans sent it back to her village, and they could once again listen to the lovely tone of its ringing.

2913. Rowland, Laura Joh. *Shinju.* HarperCollins, 1996. 367pp. Paper ISBN 978-0-06-100950-1. Grades YA.

Sano, formerly a tutor and samurai but now a police officer, finds the remains of a young man bound to a beautiful woman dragged from the Sumida River in Edo during January, 1689. He suspects shinju, or ritual double suicide, as the cause. As he follows his routine investigation, he finds deceit that leads to murder instead. His search takes him into the seamy city that will become Tokyo, and shows the privileged class, the townspeople, the pleasure district, and the everyday society of late 17th-century Japan.

2914. Ruby, Lois. *Shanghai Shadows*. Holiday House, 2006. 284pp. ISBN 978-0-8234-1960-9. Grades 6–9.

Ilse Shpann, 12, her older brother, Erich, and their parents escape Austria in 1939 at the beginning of World War II and go to Shanghai where they live poverty-stricken for five years in a tiny apartment. They scrimp and work any job to feed themselves and pay their rent, with their father able to play his beloved violin for money only a few times. Soon Erich joins a resistance movement hostile to the Japanese, and when his mother's hidden American citizenship becomes known, she has to go to a Japanese internment "civil assembly center." Ilse and her depressed father continue their survival struggle.

2915. Rumford, James. *The Cloudmakers*. Houghton, 2006. Unpaged. Paper ISBN 978-0-618-68951-4.

In 751 Arab troops win a battle in Turkestan and capture Young Wu and his grandfather. To keep from being sold into slavery, Young Wu tells the Sultan of Samarkand that his grandfather makes clouds. For seven days, Grandfather makes paper from hemp and lye, as the Chinese did beginning in 105. Although the paper is not a cloud, the Sultan realizes that he has a prize, and keeps the two with him.

2916. Russell, Ching Yeung. *The Lichee Tree*. Illustrated by Christopher Zhong-Yuan Zhang. Boyds Mills, 1997. 128pp. ISBN 978-1-56397-629-2. Grades 4–6.

In the 1940s Ying, 10, looks forward to selling the lichees on her tree when they ripen. She expects to use the proceeds for a trip to Canton where she can buy glass beads and watch the foreigners. When the village thief robs the family, Ying knows that she will have to help them. Although she lives with the backdrop of confusion in the Chinese world, she focuses on getting her profit from the lichees.

2917. Say, Allen. *Grandfather's Journey*. Illustrated by author. Walter Lorraine, 1993. 32pp. ISBN 978-0-395-57035-7; Sandpiper, 2008. paper ISBN 978-0-547-07680-5. Grades K–3.

The narrator's grandfather leaves Japan as a young man to see America in the early 20th century. He travels around the country wearing western clothes. After he returns to Japan, he marries. Then he brings his bride to San Francisco and raises his daughter. They go to Japan to live, with the grandfather planning to return for a visit. But World War II destroys his plans as well as his home and his city. The narrator carries on his grandfather's dream by living in America and raising his own daughter there. *Bulletin Blue Ribbon Book* and *Caldecott Medal*.

2918. Say, Allen. *Kamishibai Man*. Illustrated by author. Walter Lorraine, 2005. 32pp. ISBN 978-0-618-47954-2. Grades 1–3.

In Japan Kamishibai ("paper theater") men were itinerant storytellers who traveled on bicycles mounted with a big, wooden box from which they would present a story, using picture cards to illustrate the major points. The box also held drawers of candy which the storyteller would sell to support himself. Each time the Kamishibai man told the story, he would change the cliffhanger so that children would return to hear a continuation of the story. In Say's version, a Kamishibai man decides to pedal back to his old neighborhood for one last performance, and although the children watch television, their parents return to hear his story, and he ends up on the television news. *Children's Book Award* (North Carolina) nomination.

2919. Scieszka, Jon. *Marco? Polo!* Illustrated by Adam McCauley. (Time Warp Trio) Viking, 2006. 90pp. ISBN 978-0-670-06104-4. Grades 3–6.

Joe and his friends Fred and Sam are transported from the local YMCA pool to find themselves journeying to China with Marco Polo and his father. The trio pretend to be astrologers in order to travel the Silk Road and retrieve the magical book that enables their travels. Along the way, Joe teaches Marco Polo how to play the game that bears his name and rescues him from bandits and a sandstorm.

2920. Scieszka, Jon. *Sam Samurai.* Illustrated by Adam McCauley. (The Time Warp Trio) Viking, 2001. 80pp. ISBN 978-0-670-89915-9; Puffin, 2004. paper ISBN 978-0-14-240088-3. Grades 4–6.

While trying to complete a Haiku assignment, Joe, Fred, and Sam end up in 17th-century Japan where their behavior annoys a Samurai warrior. But they cannot return to the present until they find the Book. They meet Tada Hona and his cruel war leader, Owattabutt, and even the boys' own great-granddaughters who have an advanced understanding of how to get the Book and help them.

2921. Sijie, Dai. *Balzac and the Little Chinese Seamstress.* Knopf, 2001. 208pp. ISBN 978-0-375-41309-4; Anchor, 2002. paper ISBN 978-0-385-72220-9. Grades YA.

When two boys go to the Chinese countryside for re-education during the 1960s Cultural Revolution, they have the task of carrying buckets of excrement, but they entertain the village; the unnamed narrator has the ability to play the violin, and the other, Luo, can recreate films he has seen in town. In this same town they meet a the beautiful daughter of a local tailor, whom Luo romances, and read works of forbidden Western writers. When they discover the writings of Balzac, their world changes because of the power of his words.

2922. Snow, Maya. *Sisters of the Sword.* HarperCollins, 2008. 288pp. ISBN 978-0-06-124387-5. Grades 6 up.

In Japan during 1216 teenagers Kimi and Hana witness their uncle murdering their father, the Jito (Lord Steward) of the Kai province. As they escape, they come across a local dojo (samurai training school), disguise themselves as males, and go inside to get jobs. Even though they are royalty, they happily work as servants while they train. Both know how to fight and have dreamed of being samurai so that they can overturn the wrongs done to their family.

2923. Thompson, Holly. *The Wakame Gatherers.* Illustrated by Kazumi Wilds. Shen's, 2007. Unpaged. ISBN 978-1-885008-33-6. Grades 1–3.

Nanami spends a day in Japan with her maternal grandmother from Maine, and her other grandmother, Baachan, who is Japanese. They walk along the ocean shore to gather wakame, the seaweed harvested in their village. The grandmothers remember their respective responses and experiences during World War II. Illustrations enhance the story.

2924. Tschinag, Galsan. *The Blue Sky.* Translated by Katharina Rout. Milkweed, 2006. 209pp. ISBN 978-1-57131-055-2; 2007. paper ISBN 978-1-57131-064-4. Grades 7 up.

Dshurukuwaa, a young Tuvan sheepherder in the Altai Mountains of Mongolia around 1950, begins to wonder whether the old traditions of his people—especially that the sky is a sheltering force—are appropriate when his siblings leave the yurt for boarding school, his grandmother dies, and his dog, Arsylang, dies from poison set out to kill wolves threatening the herd. This autobiographical novel remembers Irgit Shynykbai-oglu Dshurukuwaa's childhood in the land of throat singers before he went to study in Germany and took the name Galsan Tschinag. Glossary and Notes.

2925. Whelan, Gloria. *Chu Ju's House.* HarperCollins, 2004. 240pp. ISBN 978-0-06-050724-4; Trophy, 2005. paper ISBN 978-0-06-050726-8. Grades 5–9.

Chu Ju, 14, worries about her newly born baby sister in China because she knows that a family can have only two children, and two girls will be unwelcome. She escapes during the night with her sister and supports her by working on a sampan with a fisherman family, tending silk worms in an orphanage, and planting rice seedlings on a farm. After writing letters about the mistreatment of the orphans, she has to escape again and meets Han Na and her son, Quan, in their rice paddy. When Quan leaves for the city, Chu Ju reads his letters to his mother. Throughout, she remains loyal to those she meets and tries to make their lives better. *Read-Aloud Book Award* (Indiana) nomination, *Young Hoosier Book Award* (Indiana) nomination, *William Allen White Children's Book Award* (Kansas) nomination, and *Great Stone Face Book Award* (New Hampshire) nomination.

2926. Williams, Susan. *Wind Rider.* Laura Geringer, 2006. 309pp. ISBN 978-0-06-087236-6; HarperTrophy, 2008. paper ISBN 978-0-06-087238-0. Grades 5–8.

In Central Asia, around 4000 B.C.E., Fern finds a wild foal trapped in a bog but tells no one because her tribe eats horses. She names the foal Thunder and makes time to be with Thunder. Then she decides to sit on the horse, something of which her tribe has never thought. When her secret surfaces, the tribe sees that Thunder can carry loads, and Fern is allowed to keep the horse. Then her work training horses defies the roles of women within her community.

2927. Yan, Mo. *Shifu, You'll Do Anything for a Laugh.* Arcade, 2001. 224pp. ISBN 978-1-55970-565-3; 2003. paper ISBN 978-1-55970-671-1. Grades YA.

Under Mao, Mo Yan, as a child, experienced extraordinary deprivation, and he describes his hunger, relentless enough for him to eat coal and even iron. A man rescues an abandoned newborn girl from a sunflower field even though he knows his society only values male children. Villagers must watch executions of "traitors" and recycle the corpses. But Yan uses humor to remember this time in the eight short stories collected here.

2928. Yep, Laurence. *Mountain Light.* Fitzgerald, 2007. 281pp. ISBN 978-1-4242-0444-1; Trophy, 1997. paper ISBN 978-0-06-440667-3. Grades 8 up.

During the 1850s Squeaky, 19, has to escape the Chinese Manchu soldiers while trying to survive battles with fellow Chinese from different clans. He makes alliances, one of which is with Cassia. After her father's death, he goes to America to see her brother, who has been working in the gold fields.

History

2929. Allan, Tony. *The Rise of Modern China.* (20th Century Perspectives) Heinemann, 2002. 48pp. ISBN 978-1-58810-661-2; paper ISBN 978-1-58810-921-7. Grades 5–8.

China has endured many changes during the last decades. In 1949 Mao Zedong gained control of China after winning the Chinese Civil War. His Communist Party of China established the People's Republic of China. Chiang Kai-shek and his Chinese Nationalist Party went to the island of Taiwan. In the late 1970s the Republic of China began to develop a multi-party democracy. Illustrations highlight the text. Bibliography, Further Reading, Glossary, and Index.

2930. Allen, Thomas B. *Remember Pearl Harbor: American and Japanese Survivors Tell Their Stories.* (Remember) National Geographic, 2001. 57pp. ISBN 978-0-7922-6690-7. Grades 5–9.

Japanese and American men and woman offer their eyewitness testimony to the bombing of Pearl Harbor during World War II. The narrative starts in Kyushu, Japan, where Japanese pilots and submarine crews trained for the attack. It then relates the responses of survivors at Pearl Harbor from the cockpit of a plane, the deck of a ship, and the shore. A final chapter tells how Japanese Americans were unjustly interned in the United States after the bombing. Photographs augment the text. Bibliography and Index. *Prairie Pasque Book Award* (South Dakota) nomination.

2931. Anderson, Jameson. *History and Activities of Ancient China.* (Hands-On Ancient History) Raintree, 2007. 32pp. ISBN 978-1-4034-7922-8. Grades 3–5.

In three short chapters, this text focuses on the structure of ancient China by looking at the everyday life of its people, and its arts, culture, games, holidays, and celebrations. The fourth chapter includes instructions for making an abacus and paper, recipes, and an activity. Photographs and illustrations enhance the text. Glossary, Further Reading, and Index.

2932. Beller, Susan Provost. *Battling in the Pacific: Soldiering in World War II.* (Soldiers on the Battlefront) Lerner, 2003. 96pp. ISBN 978-0-8225-6381-5. Grades 5–8.

Readers will learn about the events leading to the war, the principal battles, and the major leaders involved. The horrors that the Allied troops faced and the ensuing conflicts are also noted. Fact boxes offer extraneous but important information about such topics as Tokyo Rose. Black-and-white photographs highlight the text. Bibliography, Chronology, Further Reading, Web Sites, and Index.

2933. Beshore, George W. *Science in Ancient China.* (Science of the Past) Scholastic, 1998. 64pp. Paper ISBN 978-0-531-15914-9. Grades 5–8.

An introduction to China and its science precedes chapters on different developments from this culture. They include scanning the heavens, basic science and mathematics, healing and herbal medicine, finding food for the people, roads and canals, tools and technology, and modern society's debt to the ancient culture for its discoveries. Photographs and drawings enhance the text. Glossary, Further Reading, and Index.

2934. Bjorklund, Ruth. *Projects About Ancient China.* (Hands-On History) Benchmark, 2006. 48pp. ISBN 978-0-7614-2257-0. Grades 4–6.

Bjorklund offers information about the ancient Chinese and projects to help understand the people. These include a bellows, a farmer's home with a pine-needle or leaf roof, a paper lantern, and a bird of joy kite. Photographs and illustrations augment the text. Glossary, Further Reading, Web Sites, and Index.

2935. Bodden, Valerie. *The Bombing of Hiroshima and Nagasaki.* (Days of Change) Creative Education, 2007. 48pp. ISBN 978-1-58341-545-0. Grades 6–9.

A photo-essay, the narrative begins with a description of the bombings to show their significance. It includes photographs that reveal the horrible experiences of those who suffered the atomic bomb. It includes testimonies from those who survived, along with orphaned children and those burned by the fires. Other information about World War II includes the Pearl Harbor attack, the war in Europe, the views of soldiers, and the Manhattan Project. Bibliography and Index.

2936. Burgan, Michael. *The Korean War.* (20th Century Perspectives) Heinemann, 2003. 48pp. ISBN 978-1-4034-1144-0; paper ISBN 978-1-4034-3857-7. Grades 4–8.

The Korean War began in 1950 and ended in 1953 when a ceasefire agreement was signed. The war between two rival Korean governments, both supported by other countries, began when each tried to take control of the other. When South Korea refused to hold new elections after the North Koreans did not do well in free elections of May 1950, the communist North Korean Army invaded the southern area. Also examined are the issues, the causes, and the effects of this war. Illustrations augment the text. Bibliography, Further Reading, Glossary, Index.

2937. Cotterell, Arthur. *Ancient China.* Photographs by Allen Hills and Geoff Brightling. DK, 2005. 72pp. ISBN 978-0-7566-1382-2. Grades 4–7.

China is the world's oldest civilization and was controlled under one empire from 221 B.C.E. until 1912 C.E. The first great dynasty lasted from 1650 to 1027 B.C.E. The dynasties include the Shang, Zhon, Qin, Han, Sui, Tang, Song, Yuan, Ming, Quing, and then the People's Republic beginning in 1949. The text, with full-color photographic highlights, covers the health, farm life, waterways, cities, homes, food, clothes, and beliefs of the Chinese people. Index.

2938. Deal, William E. *Handbook to Life in Medieval and Early Modern Japan.* (Handbook to Life) Facts on File, 2005. 415pp. ISBN 978-0-8160-5622-4; Oxford, 2007. paper ISBN 978-0-19-533126-4. Grades 10 up.

This is a look at medieval and early modern Japanese culture and history. Its coverage begins in 1185 with the Kamakura period and continues through the Edo period in 1868. The twelve subject areas discussed are history, government, society, economy, religion, art, travel, performing arts, daily life, environment, population, and warriors and warfare. Photographs and illustrations augment the text. Bibliography and Index.

2939. Dean, Arlan. *Terra-Cotta Soldiers: Army of Stone.* (Digging Up the Past) Childrens, 2005. 48pp. ISBN 978-0-51625-124-0; paper ISBN 978-0-51625-093-9. Grades 5–8.

Dean presents the archaeological discovery of 8,000 terra cotta soldiers in China in 1974. They had been buried since the 3rd century with the emperor Qin Shi Huangdi.

The book includes background on what these soldiers tell scholars about the time. Among the anecdotes is that men who installed booby traps to foil grave robbers were themselves executed since they knew how to avoid the deadly arrows that would shoot from a triggered trap. Photographs complement the text. Glossary and Further Reading.

2940. Demi. *The Legend of Lao Tzu and the Tao Te Ching.* Illustrated by author. Margaret K. McElderry, 2007. 48pp. ISBN 978-1-4169-1206-4. Grades 3 up.

The Chinese figure Lao Tzu, supposedly born at the age of 81, may or may not have written the book of wisdom, the *Tao Te Ching.* Demi's beautiful illustrations and designs, along with the text, tell the legend of his life. Twenty verses from the work describe the various ways to live in accordance with the Way of Heaven. She also includes Taoist symbols.

2941. Des Forges, Roger V., and John S. Major. *The Asian World, 600–1500.* (Medieval and Early Modern World) Oxford, 2005. 173pp. ISBN 978-0-19-517843-2. Grades 7 up.

An imaginary dinner party forms the setting for this discussion of nine centuries of culture, conflict, and empire in Korea, China, Japan, and India. The text covers many, many topics using primary source documents and other information. Among them are economy, religion, noble family rivalries, ethnicity, and power. Photographs, reproductions, and illustrations illuminate the text. Glossary, Chronology, Further Reading, Web Sites, and Index.

2942. Dutemple, Lesley A. *The Great Wall of China.* (Great Building Feats) Lerner, 2005. 96pp. ISBN 978-0-8225-0377-4. Grades 9 up.

Through the centuries, the Great Wall of China grew from several short walls into the longest wall in the world, over 4,000 miles along China's northern border. The author examines the building of these shorter walls and how and why they were connected. Among the reasons is China's desire to isolate itself from the rest of the world, but the wall itself has affected Chinese civilization and culture in other ways. Photographs, illustrations, maps, and diagrams highlight the text. Index.

2943. Gay, Kathlyn, and Martin Gay. *Korean War.* (Voices from the Past) Twenty First Century, 1996. 64pp. ISBN 978-0-8050-4100-2. Grades 7–9.

Letters, diaries, and newspaper accounts give an overview of the Korean War, in which America fought for South Korea as part of United Nations troops from 1950 to 1953. Photographs, Maps, Further Reading, Notes, and Index.

2944. Granfield, Linda. *I Remember Korea: Veterans Tell Their Stories of the Korean War, 1950–53.* Houghton Mifflin, 2003. 136pp. ISBN 978-0-618-17740-0. Grades 6 up.

Between 1950 and 1953, the United States and Canada fought in Korea. Granfield presents the personal accounts of thirty-one men and women, many of them teens who served in the "Forgotten War" in Korea. It covers the soldiers' fears and their courage on the battlefield, the recreation available to the troops and the food they ate, the war's impact on their families and those of the Korean soldiers, and the lasting effects of fighting in this war. Photographs, Time line, Glossary, Bibliography, Web Sites, and Index.

2945. Grayling, A. C. *Among the Dead Cities: The History and Moral Legacy of the WWII Bombing of Civilians in Germany and Japan.* Walker, 2006. 362pp. ISBN 978-0-8027-1471-8; 2007. paper ISBN 978-0-8027-1565-4. Grades YA.

See entry 2090.

2946. Hanel, Rachael. *Samurai.* (Fearsome Fighters) Creative Education, 2007. 48pp. ISBN 978-1-58341-538-2. Grades 5–8.

The author looks at the social conditions surrounding the rise of the samurai in Japan and details their weapons, fighting techniques, and armor. The book includes background on the traditional role of the samurai as well as rituals practiced, including the gruesome *seppuku* during which a defeated samurai was expected to disembowel himself. Archival reproductions augment the text. Bibliography, Glossary and Index.

2947. Ingram, Scott. *The Song Dynasty.* (Life During the Great Civilizations) Blackbirch, 2003. 48pp. ISBN 978-1-4103-0056-0. Grades 5–7.

The Song Dynasty ruled in China from 960 to 1279, after the Five Dynasties and Ten Kingdoms era and before the Yuan Dynasty. It was the first government in the world to issue banknotes and paper money and was the first Chinese dynasty to establish a navy. The expansion of rice cultivation allowed such a food surplus that the dynasty had a population of over 100 million people. The middle and lower rungs of government became more important for such a large group of people. The four chapters of the text cover the dynasty's government, the incorporation of Confucianism in everyday life, the largest city in the world, the technology developed, and the industry founded. Black-and-white reproductions and photographs augment the text. Maps, Further Reading, Glossary, Notes, Web Sites, and Index.

2948. Kamachi, Noriko. *Culture and Customs of Japan.* Greenwood, 1999. 187pp. ISBN 978-0-313-30197-1. Grades 9 up.

This history of social customs and culture in Japan offers much background. The segments cover the land, people, history, religions, religious thought, literature, arts, architecture, housing, settlements, social customs, cuisine, traditional dress, family, women, gender issues, lifestyles, media, and education. Photographs augment the text. Bibliography, Glossary, Notes, and Index.

2949. Ko, Dorothy. *Every Step a Lotus: Shoes for Bound Feet.* University Of California, 2001. 162pp. Paper ISBN 978-0-52023-284-6. Grades YA.

This book offers a history of footbinding in China as a cultural phenomenon. It equates a rite of passage into womanhood within the Confucian system that valued domesticity. As a result, shoe-making gained status as integral to the footbinding itself because of the beautifully embroidered shoes that were small or a "lotus" (flower). It reports that footbinding did not break bones but reshaped the foot so that it would fit in a pointed shoe. The motifs embroidered on the shoes such as fish and golden coins were symbolic to the women who wore them. Photographs reinforce the text. Bibliography, Notes, and Index.

2950. Lankov, Andrei. *North of the DMZ: Essays on Daily Life in North Korea.* McFarland, 2007. 346pp. Paper ISBN 978-0-7864-2839-7. Grades YA.

While the Kim dynasty has ruled North Korea for sixty years, some have managed to survive the daily tyranny. They have kept their own values while Kim Jong Il has refused to let them express themselves. The narrative discusses the political system and the requirements of the citizens to wear badges and to accept food as distributed to them. It includes much information about the daily coping that each must do. Photographs enhance the text. Bibliography and Index.

2951. Lawton, Clive A. *Hiroshima: The Story of the First Atom Bomb.* Candlewick, 2004. 48pp. ISBN 978-0-7636-2271-8. Grades 5–8.

This photo-essay presents the history and politics surrounding the atomic bomb and its devastation of Hiroshima at the end of World War II. It covers both sides of the question of whether bombing Hiroshima was the right thing for the United States to do to end the war. It includes Einstein's letter warning Roosevelt, Japanese treatment of American prisoners of war, the aftermath of the explosion, the cold war, and antinuclear protests. Chronology and Notes.

2952. Leckie, Robert. *Okinawa: The Last Battle of World War II.* Penguin, 1996. 220pp. Paper ISBN 978-0-14-017389-5. Grades YA.

The author presents all aspects of the Okinawa landing, from its planning to its execution, as well as the ground fighting and the fierce action of the Japanese at sea using their kamikaze planes and ships. Leckie believes that Japan would have surrendered without either the bomb or the invasion and that Truman dropped the bomb to show Stalin his power. However, Okinawa was decisive because a Japanese victory would have heightened the conviction of the Japanese military inner sanctum that Japan should never accept an Allied surrender offer, even with Hirohito's influence to the contrary. Bibliography and Index.

2953. Littlefield, Holly. *Colors of Japan.* Illustrated by Helen Byers. Carolrhoda, 1997. 24pp. ISBN 978-0-8761-4885-3; paper ISBN 978-1-57505-215-1. Grades K–3.

Colors become the central theme for information about Japan's trains, cities, customs, and history. Index.

2954. Lord, Bette Bao. *Legacies: A Chinese Mosaic.* Fawcett, 1991. 242pp. Paper ISBN 978-0-449-90620-0. Grades YA.

While Lord lived in China from 1985 to 1989, she interviewed many Chinese persecuted by Mao's Cultural Revolution. This book shares those interviews while also describing her experiences and her family's history. Among the accounts included are those of a veteran of Mao's Long March in 1934, an artist, an actress, a teacher, an entrepreneur, a journalist, and a peasant. Chronology.

2955. MacMillan, Dianne M. *Chinese New Year.* (Best Holiday Books) Enslow, 2008. 48pp. ISBN 978-0-7660-3038-1. Grades 2–5.

Although Chinese people live all over the world, they observe their New Year as they have for thousands of years. The text presents the history of the holiday as well as the way it is currently celebrated. Glossary and Index.

2956. Mann, Elizabeth. *The Great Wall: The Wonders of the World Book.* Illustrated by Alan Witschonke. Mikaya, 1997. 48pp. ISBN 978-0-965049-32-0; 2006. paper ISBN 978-1-931414-12-8. Grades 7–8.

The first attempts at building a wall in China occurred as early as 200 B.C.E., although success did not occur until after Kublai Khan began to rule. When the wall was completed, it was a giant attempt at keeping enemies out of the country. Chronology and Index.

2957. Marx, Trish. *Elephants and Golden Thrones: Inside China's Forbidden City.* Illustrated by Ellen B. Senisi. Abrams, 2008. 48pp. ISBN 978-0-8109-9485-0. Grades 6 up.

This overview of Beijing's Forbidden City, built in the early 1400s, presents stories from seven narrators—from elephants and other animals to a princess's ghost—about the Ming and Qing dynasties. The emperors begin with Khengde and end with Puyi, eventually a pawn of the invading Japanese. Photographs and images accompany the text. Bibliography, Chronology, and Glossary.

2958. Morley, Jacqueline. *You Wouldn't Want to Work on the Great Wall of China! Defenses You'd Rather Not Build.* Illustrated by David Antram and David Salariya. (You Wouldn't Want To . . .) Franklin Watts, 2006. 32pp. ISBN 978-0-531-12424-6; 2007. paper ISBN 978-0-531-12449-9. Grades 3–6.

Those who helped build the Great Wall of China suffered hardships of weather and survival. The author shows that those who built it were first imprisoned and then forced to work on the wall for several years. Sidebars and illustrations complement the text.

2959. O'Connor, Jane. *Emperor's Silent Army: Terracotta Warriors of Ancient China.* Viking, 2002. 48pp. ISBN 978-0-670-03512-0. Grades 4–7.

In 1974 Chinese farmers found a hidden tomb that happened to be the burial site of China's first emperor, Qin Shihuang (259–210 B.C.E.). Inside were more than 7,000 life-size terra cotta warriors. Photographs augment the text. Bibliography and Index. *Booklist Editors' Choice, Student Book Award* (Maine) nomination, *Prairie Pasque Book Award* (South Dakota) nomination, *Volunteer State Book Award* (Tennessee) nomination, and *Beehive Children's Book Award* (Utah) nomination.

2960. Santella, Andrew. *The Korean War.* (We the People) Compass Point, 2006. 48pp. ISBN 978-0-7565-2027-4. Grades 4–7.

The seven chapters cover the advent of the Korean War, its progress, and its conclusion. On June 25, 1950, North Korean troops entered South Korea. The United States responded by sending troops to help the South Koreans. Other help came from members of the United Nations in combat units, food, medical teams, and supplies. The war lasted for over three years, with both soldiers and civilians dying as a result of the invasion. Photographs enhance the text. Glossary, Bibliography, Chronology, Further Reading, Web Sites, and Index.

2961. Schomp, Virginia. *Japan in the Days of the Samurai.* Benchmark, 2001. 80pp. ISBN 978-0-7614-0304-3. Grades 5–8.

The author looks at Japan's chronological and cultural history, belief system, society, and legacy through 1868 in five parts. Among the topics covered are its gods and warriors, divine rulers, the beginning of the samurai, invasions, feudal system, artistic treasures, Shinto, Buddhism, Confucianism, Christianity, Zen, and its surviving traditions as a country opened to the West late in its history. Photographs and illustrations highlight the text. Bibliography, Glossary, Chronology, Further Reading, and Index.

2962. Shuter, Jane. *Ancient China.* (Time Travel Guides) Raintree, 2007. 64pp. ISBN 978-1-4109-2719-3; paper ISBN 978-1-4109-3045-3. Grades 5–9.

Written as a travel guide to ancient China, this volume relates cultural and historical details of the time. Using a time-travel framework and the present tense, Shuter shows maps and imparts facts about the culture, locations including the Great Wall, relics and artifacts, and other salient information. Photographs and reproductions enhance the text. Glossary, Chronology, Further Reading, and Index.

2963. Shuter, Jane. *Ancient China.* (Excavating the Past) Heinemann, 2005. 48pp. ISBN 978-1-4034-5995-4. Grades 4–6.

Shuter presents the results of archaeological excavations in ancient China. The book includes background on science, religion, and culture. It includes the first single kingdom dynasty, Xia (2205–1700 B.C.E.), and continues through the Mongol conquest of China in 1279. Maps, photographs and reproductions augment the text. Glossary, Chronology, Further Reading, and Index.

2964. Spence, Jonathan D. *The Search for Modern China.* Norton, 1997. 867pp. Paper ISBN 978-0-393-97351-8. Grades YA.

Spence gives an overview of Chinese history, beginning with the fall of the last Ming emperor in 1644 and ending with the 1989 Tiananmen Square massacre in Beijing. Spence's accounts of the early Qing Dynasty, the Taiping Revolt beginning in 1850, the 1911 Republic, the 1919 May Fourth Movement, the 1949 People's Republic, and the 1989 incident in Tiananmen Square include the views of various groups of people as they grappled with the changes in their lives from the traditional to the modern. He views Mao as a man who knew what he wanted to do and relentlessly pursued his goal. Spence shows all strata of society in all areas of this vast country as they socialized and defended against the enemy within as well as the enemy outside. Illustrations, Maps, Glossary, Chapter Bibliographies, and Index.

2965. Stein, R. Conrad. *The Korean War: "The Forgotten War".* Enslow, 1994. 128pp. ISBN 978-0-8949-0526-1. Grades 6–9.

Although 54,000 Americans died in the Korean War, fought from 1950 to 1953, many Americans at home lost interest because they did not understand the threat of Communist control spreading when the North Koreans invaded South Korea. This war did not have the media coverage common today. With photographs this book looks at the war and its effects on those who fought and on their families. Chronology, Further Reading, and Index.

2966. Stein, R. Conrad. *World War II in the Pacific: Remembering Pearl Harbor.* Myreportlinks.com, 2002. 48pp. ISBN 978-0-7660-5093-8. Grades 7 up.

In chronological order, the author examines World War II in the Pacific from the bombing of Pearl Harbor on December 7, 1941, through the signing of the surrender on the *U.S.S. Missouri* on September 2, 1945. Black-and-white photographs and maps enhance the text. Further Reading, Chronology, and Index.

2967. Tames, Richard. *Hiroshima: The Shadow of the Bomb.* (Point of Impact) Heinemann, 2006. 32pp. ISBN 978-1-4034-9140-4; paper ISBN 978-1-4034-9149-7. Grades 5–8.

The two-page chapters in this discussion of the atomic bomb offer an account of the bombing of Hiroshima, the aftermath of the attack, and the historical impact. It also notes the debates surrounding the attack regarding the impact of nuclear power. Photographs and reproductions intensify the text. Glossary, Chronology, Further Reading, and Index.

2968. Turner, Pamela S. *Hachiko: The True Story of a Loyal Dog.* Illustrated by Yan Nascimbene. Houghton, 2004. 32pp. ISBN 978-0-618-14094-7. Grades K–3.

A dog named Hachiko waited at a Tokyo train station each afternoon for his master, Dr. Ueno, to return home. In 1925 Dr. Ueno died unexpectedly and, unaware of this, of course, Hachiko returned to the station every day to wait for him for the next ten years. During that time, Kentaro, a young observer, befriended the dog. After Hachiko's death, admiring citizens placed a bronze statue at Shibuya Station to honor this dog, and a festival occurs every April in his honor. *Diamond Primary Book Award* (Arkansas) nomination, *Booklist Editors' Choice, Notable Social Studies Trade Books for Young People, Sequoyah Book Award* (Oklahoma) nomination, *Young Reader's Choice Book Award* (Pennsylvania) nomination, and *Picture Book Award* (South Carolina) nomination.

2969. Weatherford, Jack W. *Genghis Khan and the Making of the Modern World.* Crown, 2004. 352pp. ISBN 978-0-609-61062-6; Three Rivers Press, 2005. paper ISBN 978-0-609-80964-8. Grades YA.

Although called a barbarian throughout history, Genghis Khan of Mongolia may have been as progressive a ruler as he was influential. Weatherford, an anthropology professor, traced Genghis Khan's paths into places westerners had never visited, into the "Great Taboo," many miles on horseback, to use what he terms an "archaeology of movement." The Mongols, with no more than 100,000 warriors, captured more land in 25 years during the 13th century than the Romans took in 400 years. The text describes the revolutionary aspects of the Mongol military campaign as it invaded Imperial China, Baghdad, and European castles from Siberia to India, Vietnam to Hungary, and Korea to the Balkans. Weatherford found through a suppressed Mongol text, the "Secret History," that Genghis Khan was a free trader who unified disparate groups of people, a Christian, a parent, and loving husband to several wives. His people had an international paper currency, a postal system, and they spread the technologies of printing, the cannon, the compass, and the abacus. He suggests that the Mongols played a role in beginning the western Renaissance period. Bibliography, Glossary, Notes, Maps, and Index.

2970. Webster, Christine. *Great Wall of China.* (Structural Wonders) Weigl, 2007. 32pp. ISBN 978-1-59036-723-0; paper ISBN 978-1-59036-724-7. Grades 6–9.

Webster examines the Great Wall of China, giving its cultural history and current status along with information about the architecture. She also discusses construction and who the workers were. The narrative includes background about the importance of the wall to each dynasty that helped build it. Photographs, maps, and illustrations highlight the text. Glossary and Web Sites.

2971. Wilkinson, Philip. *Chinese Myth: A Treasury of Legends, Art, and History.* (World of Mythology) Sharpe Focus, 2007. 96pp. ISBN 978-0-7656-8103-4. Grades 5–8.

The book begins with the creation story and adds other stories about the civilization. Among topics covered are the music, culture, religions, gods and their roles, and the afterlife. Photographs of artwork enhance the text. Chronology, Further Reading, Glossary, Web Sites, and Index.

Biography and Collective Biography

2972. Bacon, Ursula. *Eternal Strangers.* M, 2007. 280pp. Paper ISBN 978-1-59582-099-0. Grades YA.

See entry 2142.

2973. Behnke, Alison. *Kim Jong Il's North Korea.* (Dictatorships) Twenty First Century, 2007. 160pp. ISBN 978-0-8225-7282-4. Grades 7 up.

Chæong-il Kim (1942–) came to power in Korea in 1994 on the death of his father, Kim Il Sung, the founder of North Korea in the 1940s. In his country, communism continues to thrive. The book describes the attitudes toward his lifestyle and thoughts about him throughout the international community. Sidebars and photographs enhance the text. Maps, Bibliography, Glossary, Chronology, Notes, Further Reading, and Index.

2974. Blumberg, Rhoda. *Shipwrecked: The True Adventures of a Japanese Boy.* Trophy, 2003. 80pp. Paper ISBN 978-0-688-17485-9. Grades 5–9.

A fatherless Japanese boy, Manjiro Nakahama (1827–1898), a fisherman, became marooned during a storm on an island for six months in 1841. An American whaling ship captain rescued him and took him to Massachusetts where, as John Mung, he learned navigation and English. When he earned some money in the gold rush, he returned to Japan, risking the punishment of death, since it was forbidden to leave Japan. He was imprisoned for several months while he told the government officials about the United States. His testimony earned him the rank of samurai and helped open Japan to the West. *Booklist Editors Choice, School Library Journal Best Books of the Year, Tennessee State Book Award* (Volunteer) nomination, *State Reading Association for Young Readers Program* (Virginia) nomination, and *Sasquatch Book Award* (Washington) nomination.

2975. Brady, James. *The Coldest War: A Memoir of Korea.* Griffin, 2000. 248pp. Paper ISBN 978-0-312-26511-3. Grades YA.

In a highly personal memoir, Brady discusses his participation in the war, which began in 1950 with North Korea's trespass over the 38th Parallel. The war ended in 1953 after 54,000 Americans had been killed. Brady suggests that Korea was the last campaign of World War II and the first battle of Vietnam. He was 23 during his year in Korea, and he carefully details his experience. Index.

2976. Chen, Da. *China's Son: Growing Up in the Cultural Revolution.* Laurel-Leaf, 2004. 212pp. Paper ISBN 978-0-440-22926-1. Grades 6–9.

Da Chen, forced to stop studying during Mao's Cultural Revolution while growing up in rural China during the 1960s, returns to school when Mao dies and earns a seat at Beijing University. Because his family owned property, Mao targeted them and they had much to endure during this time, especially when neighbors, teachers, and other students mistreated them.

2977. Childress, Diana. *Marco Polo's Journey to China.* (Pivotal Moments in History) Twenty First Century, 2007. 160pp. ISBN 978-0-8225-5903-0. Grades 5–8.

Marco Polo (1254–1323) spent twenty-four years in Asia. The author describes the cultural and political aspects of various places that Polo stayed including Venice, China, and with the Mongols Genghis and Kublai Khan. She also attempts to trace the routes that he took, information that he omitted from his own accounts. Photographs and illustrations complement the text. Bibliography, Glossary, Chronology, Notes, Further Reading, Web Sites, and Index.

2978. Chun Yu. *Little Green: Growing Up During the Chinese Cultural Revolution.* Simon & Schuster, 2005. 112pp. ISBN 978-0-689-86943-3. Grades 6–10.

Little Green (Chun Yu) (1966–) was born in China at the beginning of the Cultural Revolution. Her father was removed from the home, and the Red Guard forced her family into re-education and the study of Mao's Little Red Book. She lived either with her grandmother in the country or her mother in the city during this unsettled and difficult time.

2979. Clercq Zubli, Rita la Fontaine de. *Disguised: A Wartime Memoir.* Candlewick, 2007. 366pp. ISBN 978-0-7636-3329-5. Grades 9 up.

When the Japanese entered Sumatra during World War II, Rita la Fontaine de Clercq Zubli's priest suggested that she disguise herself as a male and become "Rick." She took his advice and escaped conscription as a "comfort woman" for the soldiers. Her Dutch-Indonesian family became prisoners of war, but the family was treated well because "Rick" knew Japanese, having studied the language. Prison wardens used her language skills to run the camps, and she, in turn, fought for the prisoners to have food rather than torture. She had to fend off males who tried to seduce her as well as endure other unexpected situations. Glossary.

2980. Cohen, Roger. *Danger in the Desert: True Adventures of a Dinosaur Hunter.* Sterling, 2008. 189pp. ISBN 978-1-4027-5706-8. Grades 6–9.

Roy Chapman Andrews (1884–1960) made many exciting expeditions during his life and accomplished significant finds including the first-discovered fossils of dinosaur eggs and a velociraptor. He traveled through China and Mongolia in the 1920s and 1930s and then had a career at the American Museum of Natural History. Among the places and subjects mentioned in the fifteen chapter titles are the Gobi Desert, Flaming Cliffs, New York City, whales, tropical islands, typhoons, sharks, Yunnan, camels, sandstorms, skeletons, and bandits. Illustrations augment the text. Bibliography and Index.

2981. Demi. *Su Dongpo: Chinese Genius.* Illustrated by author. Lee & Low, 2006. 32pp. ISBN 978-1-58430-256-8. Grades 4–7.

After a jealous rival had the Chinese poet, scholar, and statesman Su Dongpo (1037–1101) exiled, he worked happily on his farm. But the new emperor appointed him as secretary. He was exiled a second time, and when he again returned, he fell ill and died. Other talents that he exhibited were those of philosopher, engineer, architect, and humanitarian, and he remains today the "heart and soul of Chinese culture." Luminous illustrations complement the text.

2982. Freedman, Russell. *Confucius: The Golden Rule.* Illustrated by Frederic Clement. Scholastic, 2002. 48pp. ISBN 978-0-439-13957-1. Grades 4–8.

Although Confucius (551–479 B.C.E.) was born poor, he rose to China's ruling class. However, he eventually quit his job and became an itinerant philosopher. During this time, he examined humans and made assessments that fill *The Analects.* He established his own Golden Rule: "Do not impose on others what you do not wish for yourself." He also included insights about education, government, nobility, equality of humans, and the purpose of living. These ideas spread to the West and influenced the Enlightenment. Since little is actually known about Confucius's life, his teachings remain the most important way of knowing him. Notes and Annotated Bibliography. *Publishers Weekly Best Children's Books, School Library Journal Best Books of the Year, American Library Association Notable Books for Children, National Council of Teachers of English Orbis Pictus Award Honor Book, ABC Children's Booksellers Choices Awards, Capitol Choices Noteworthy Titles* (Washington, D.C.), and *Student Book Award* (Maine) nomination.

2983. Gao, Anhua. *To the Edge of the Sky: A Story of Love, Betrayal, Suffering, and the Strength of Human Courage.* Overlook, 2003. 398pp. ISBN 978-1-58567-362-9. Grades YA.

Gao was orphaned at a young age when her parents, Communist army workers, died. Maoist policies then disarmed her, and someone in her family betrayed her so that she was imprisoned. Eventually she escaped.

2984. Gay, Kathlyn. *Mao Zedong's China.* (Dictatorships) Twenty First Century, 2007. 160pp. ISBN 978-0-8225-7285-5. Grades 7 up.

This biography of Mao Zedong (1893–1976) describes life in pre-revolutionary China and Mao's ascendancy to power. It details events during his leadership and "Post-Mao Turmoil and Judgments." Although the book documents Mao's life thoroughly, some of the sources may either be unclear or outdated. Photographs and illustrations highlight the text. Bibliography, Glossary, Chronology, Notes, Further Reading, Web Sites, and Index.

2985. Geyer, Flora. *Mao Zedong: The Rebel Who Led a Revolution.* (World History Biography) National Geographic, 2007. 64pp. ISBN 978-1-4263-0062-2. Grades 5–8.

Geyer looks at the childhood of Mao Zedong (1893–1976) in China using a scrapbook layout. The four main sections of the text include the historical context of his life and the daily lives of people during his time, and offers side material on related topics. The narrative, however, does not mention his poetry or the deaths of 38 million peasants during his "Great Leap Forward." Photographs enhance the text. Bibliography, Glossary, Web Sites, Maps, and Index.

2986. Goldberg, Enid A., and Norman Itzkowitz. *Genghis Khan: 13th-Century Mongolian Tyrant.* (Wicked History) Watts, 2007. 128pp. ISBN 978-0-531-12596-0. Grades 6–8.

This examination of Genghis Khan (1162–1227) reveals his role as a ruthless ruler who devastated the rebellious city of Tirmiz. He was a well-known figure, known as merciless, intelligent, and organized. He brought a written language to his Mongols and then he added codified laws. He also displayed religious intolerance for all the Mongols under his rule. Photographs and illustrations highlight the text. Bibliography, Glossary, and Web Sites.

2987. Ingram, Scott. *Kim Il Sung.* (History's Villains) Blackbirch, 2003. 112pp. ISBN 978-1-4103-0259-5. Grades 5–9.

Kim Il Sung (1912–1994), the former ruler of North Korea, started a war that killed millions of people and almost caused a nuclear holocaust in the world. He took the resources of his country and used them for a personal luxurious lifestyle for more than forty years. Illustrations augment the text. Bibliography, Maps, and Index.

2988. Jiang, Ji-Li. *Red Scarf Girl: A Memoir of the Cultural Revolution.* HarperCollins, 1997. 285pp. ISBN 978-0-06-027585-3; Collins, 2008. paper ISBN 978-0-06-166771-8. Grades 6 up.

When Ji-Li Jiang was 12 in 1966, she was intelligent and a leader, but the Cultural Revolution changed her life. No longer were intelligence, talent, or wealth respected. She had always believed that the Communist Party was kind and that Chairman Mao was dearer than her parents. When her father is detained, she must decide whether to renounce him or the Party. *Capitol Choices Noteworthy Titles* (Washington, D.C.).

2989. Kent, Zachary. *Genghis Khan: Ruler of the Mongol Empire.* (Rulers of the Ancient World) Enslow, 2007. 160pp. ISBN 978-0-7660-2715-2. Grades 7–9.

This biography of Genghis Khan (1162–1227) places his life in historical perspective including his time as the leader of the Mongols who greatly enlarged their Empire. He developed military techniques that allowed him to overcome tribes and generals and then lead them. Illustrations, maps, and photographs enhance the text. Chronology, Further Reading, Glossary, Notes, Web Sites, and Index.

2990. Koestler-Grack, Rachel A. *Kim Il Sung and Kim Jong Il: A Ruling Dynasty.* (Major World Leaders) Chelsea, 2003. 118pp. ISBN 978-0-7910-7648-4. Grades 6 up.

The father and son duo of Kim Il Sung and Kim Jong Il served as Korean leaders who wanted a united Korea. Their policies of self-reliance and self-defense were the basis of their politics. The author examines the background of their lives with information about the history of Korea. Then she assesses how and why they came to power. Photographs highlight the text. Chronology, Further Reading, Web Sites, and Index.

2991. Kuwahara, Yasuo, and Gordon T. Allred. *Kamikaze: A Japanese Pilot's Own Spectacular Story of the Famous Suicide Squadrons.* American Legacy Media, 2007. Paper ISBN 978-0-976154-75-4. Grades YA.

First published in 1957, this autobiography of Kuwahara opens when he receives a visitor in 1943 who congratulates him for his academic achievements. Then the man recruits him into the Japanese Emperor's air force where he trains as a kamikaze pilot, a flyer who dive-bombs into a target to gain honor for himself and for his Emperor. Beaten and tormented daily, he loses his sense of humanity and individuality. His descriptions of war as terrifying still resonate.

2992. Lee, Gus. *Chasing Hepburn: A Memoir of Shanghai, Hollywood, and a Chinese Family's Fight for Freedom.* Harmony, 2004. 528pp. Paper ISBN 978-1-400-05155-7. Grades YA.

Gus Lee recalls the stories he heard about his parents and their meeting. His mother, Da-tsien, is the daughter of a Chinese man who did not believe in tradition, refusing to subject his 3-year-old girl to having her feet broken in the foot-binding ceremony. Conversely, her mother rejects her and her big feet. Da-tsien meets Zee Zee, a young pilot, who lives across the street from her in Shanghai. They watch American movies together and fall in love. After marrying and having two daughters, the second of whom Da-tsien rejects in the traditional fashion, Zee Zee tries to kill Mao Tse-tung before fleeing from China to search for his idol, Katharine Hepburn. Da-tsien and her two daughters walk miles across China during the Japanese occupation, and finally join him in California, where Gus Lee is born. Although his mother died when he was 5, Lee feels compelled to tell the story.

2993. Li, Cunxin. *Dancing to Freedom: The True Story of Mao's Last Dancer.* Illustrated by Anne Spudvilas. Walker, 2008. 40pp. ISBN 978-0-8027-9777-3. Grades 1–5.

Li Cunxin (1961–), born into poverty in Mao's China, had a chance to study dance at the Beijing Dance Academy when he was 11. He determined that he would be the first in his country to get a cultural change abroad when he was picked to dance for the Houston Ballet. Then he defected to the United States and was able to eventually bring his family to be with him. Illustrations intensify the text. *Notable Trade Books in the Field of Social Studies*

2994. Li, Cunxin. *Mao's Last Dancer.* Walker, 2008. 290pp. ISBN 978-0-8027-9779-7. Grades 6–9.

Li Cunxin (1961–) was born into poverty in Mao's China as a sixth son. He was chosen to audition for Madame Mao's Beijing Ballet Academy when he was 11, and when he passed, he was able to provide food for himself, unlike his family. After two trips to the United States, he defected to join the Houston Ballet. Later his parents were able to join him. Photographs enhance the text. Chronology. *Notable Trade Books in the Field of Social Studies.*

2995. Li, Moying. *Snow Falling in Spring: Coming of Age in China During the Cultural Revolution.* Melanie Kroupa, 2008. 176pp. ISBN 978-0-374-39922-1. Grades 6–9.

In 1958, when Moying is 4, the Great Leap Forward begins in China, and a large brick furnace is installed in her courtyard where neighbors must work and throw in bits of scrap metal to produce an inferior steel. She is sent to Foreign Language School when she is 9, but her life changes in 1968 when the Cultural Revolution begins. Red Guards attack her teachers and the school principal hangs himself. Her mother is sent to the country to teach, and the government denounces her father and sends him to a labor camp. Her father sneaks in a list of books to her that help her survive this horrible time. Eventually, she escapes China to attend Swarthmore College. Photographs illuminate the text. *Notable Trade Books in the Field of Social Studies*

2996. McCully, Emily Arnold. *Manjiro.* Farrar, 2008. Unpaged. ISBN 978-0-374-34792-5. Grades 3–6.

In 1841 when Manjiro, 14, and four other fishermen were swept away from Japan in a storm, they became shipwrecked on an island for six months. Because a Japanese law promised death to anyone who left the country and tried to reenter, they could not return home. An American whaling ship rescued them, and Captain Whitfield took Manjiro home with him to New Bedford, Massachusetts, where he taught him to plant, cultivate, harvest, and ride a horse, illegal in Japan except for samurai. Manjiro attended school and graduated at the top of his class. Then he went to San Francisco during the California gold rush and collected $600 of gold dust in seventy days. After nine years, he returned to Japan with two of his castaways. Imprisoned for seven months, he told the officials that Americans desired to trade and that they had wonderful inventions such as railroads, wristwatches, telegraphs, and drawbridges. His stories led to the opening of Japan to the western world. Watercolors complement the text. Bibliography, Maps, and Note. *Notable Trade Books in the Field of Social Studies.*

2997. Mochizuki, Ken. *Be Water, My Friend: The Early Years of Bruce Lee.* Illustrated by Dom Lee. Lee & Low, 2006. 32pp. ISBN 978-1-58430-265-0. Grades K–2.

Although born in San Francisco while his father toured with the Cantonese Opera Company, Bruce Lee (1940–1973), an international film star, grew up in Hong Kong during the 1940s and 1950s. He disliked school, and having more interest in martial arts, he slowly began to understand the underlying aspects of the discipline. He did not at first understand that the sport had a gentleness to it until he compared it to the gentleness of water that could, through force, break anything in the world. He got into trouble with the police when he was 18, and his parents sent him to San Francisco. Acrylic paintings augment the text.

2998. Ray, Deborah Kogan. *Hokusai: The Man Who Painted a Mountain.* Illustrated by author. Farrar, Straus & Giroux, 2001. 40pp. ISBN 978-0-374-33263-1. Grades 2–5.

Tokitaro (1760–1849), the "First Born," never knew his father, and his mother died when he was 6. He changed his name many times until he decided on "Hokusai," meaning "North Star Studio." He started drawing at 5, and created more than 30,000 works. He painted laborers, kabuki actors, mountains, and markets. His most famous pictures are "Thirty-Six Views of Mount Fuji" and "The Great Wave Off Kanagawa." His work influenced later European artists, especially the Impressionists. The wash, charcoal, and colored-pencil illustrations highlight the text. *Parents Choice Award.*

2999. Senker, Cath. *Marco Polo's Travels on Asia's Silk Road.* (Great Journeys Across Earth) Raintree, 2007. 48pp. ISBN 978-1-4034-9751-2; paper ISBN 978-1-4034-9759-8. Grades 4–6.

The biography recounts the travels of the medieval trader and explorer, Marco Polo (1254–1323?) who wanted to see the world. He befriended Kublai Khan and eventually wrote about his exploits so that others could know some of the wonders he had seen. Illustrations augment the text. Chronology, Glossary, Further Reading, and Index.

3000. Shane, C. J. *Mao Zedong.* (People Who Made History) Greenhaven, 2003. 205pp. ISBN 978-0-7377-1494-4; paper ISBN 978-0-7377-1494-4. Grades 10 up.

Primary and secondary documents offer an overview of the life and career of Mao Zedong (1893–1976). They include background on his rise from a peasant worker to a Communist organizer, the May Fourth Movement and Mao, the Long March, his People's Republic, improving public health, his Great Leap Forward, the Cultural Revolution, his cult, the transition from his dictatorship to Deng Xiaoping, an evaluation of the Communist Revolution in China, his victims, and his memory. Chronology, Further Reading, and Index.

3001. Shen, Fan. *Gang of One: Memoirs of a Red Guard.* University of Nebraska, 2004. 279pp. ISBN 978-0-8032-4308-8; Bison, 2006. paper ISBN 978-0-8032-9336-6. Grades YA.

Fan Shen becomes enamored with Mao's Cultural Revolution in China and joins the Red Guards as a child, while his parents are listed as anti-revolutionaries. But he makes an error in his writing that says Mao should not live, and he must go to a remote peasant village for re-education. He becomes completely disillusioned with Mao, and he uses subterfuge and self-education to survive. Eventually he secures his prizes, a passport and a flight to San Francisco. *Booklist Editors' Choice.*

3002. Shen, Tong, and Marianne Yen. *Almost a Revolution: The Story of a Chinese Student's Journey from Boyhood to Leadership in Tiananmen.* University of Michigan, 1998. 342pp. Paper ISBN 978-0-4720-8557-6. Grades YA.

Shen Tong escaped from China to the United States after the massacre in Tiananmen Square on June 3 and 4, 1989. One of the worst spots in the fighting on June 4 happened to be in front of his own home, but he comments that the students could have instituted a better plan that would have stopped the tragedy. Tong, one of the leaders of the political demonstrations that incited the attack, had previously established the Olympic Institute, a student organization to discuss new ideas about science, philosophy, and politics. He tells the story of his family life in China and his education before he had to leave his country.

3003. Spence, Jonathan D. *God's Chinese Son: The Taiping Heavenly Kingdom of Hong Xiuquan.* Norton, 1997. 352pp. Paper ISBN 978-0-393-31556-1. Grades YA.

After taking his Confucian state exams in China and failing twice, Hong Xiuquan (1814) became ill; in his feverish state, he had a dream in which he saw himself as the savior of his people. He declared that the evils of crime and drugs were vices in the Chinese government, rather than noting that they had been brought in by the British, and people decided that he was a prophet. They organized militia and collected weapons while placing Hong Xiuquan inside a fortress, and they tried to take over the country. What they began was the Taiping Rebellion, and by the time it ended, 20 million people had died. Spence looks at this man who wielded such extraordinary influence in 19th-century China. Bibliography and Index.

3004. Spivak, Dawnine. *Grass Sandals: The Travels of Basho.* Illustrated by Demi. Atheneum, 1997. 40pp. ISBN 978-0-689-80776-3. Grades 1–4.

Basho was one of the greatest Japanese haiku poets. He loved Japan and spent much of his later life walking through the land and writing his haiku to describe its beauty. Each spread includes a Japanese character for a word appearing in both a haiku and the story.

3005. Weston, Mark. *Honda: The Boy Who Dreamed of Cars.* Illustrated by Katie Yamasaki. Lee & Low, 2008. Unpaged. ISBN 978-1-60060-246-7. Grades 3–5.

Soichiro Honda (1906–1991), son of a Japanese blacksmith, fell in love with cars when he first saw one in 1914. He became a mechanic, inventor, race car driver, and car-dynasty owner. After World War II he developed small motorcycles and began designing and manufacturing fuel-efficient automobiles. He was a perfectionist who encouraged his workers to contribute their ideas to the company, listened to them, and looked after them. Acrylic illustrations intensify the text. Notes.

3006. Xie, Bingying. *A Woman Soldier's Own Story: The Autobiography of Xie Bingying.* Translated by Lily Chia Brissman. Columbia University, 2001. 281pp. ISBN 978-0-231-12250-4. Grades YA.

As a young girl in China's Hunan Province with a scholar father and a traditional mother, Xie Bingying (1906–2000) wanted to be educated. Her feet were bound when she was 8, and she had an arranged marriage, but she refused to compromise her desires. She became a soldier in Chiang Kai-shek's Northern Expedition, and then developed into an educator, writer, and feminist. Against Mao, she moved to Taiwan in 1948.

3007. Ye, Ting-Xing. *My Name Is Number 4: A True Story of the Cultural Revolution.* Griffin, 2008. 230pp. Paper ISBN 978-0-312-37987-2. Grades 8 up.

Ting-xing Ye (1952–), called Ah-Si because she was the fourth child in her family, describes the horror of living during the Chinese Cultural Revolution. The government confiscated her father's prosperous Shanghai factory in 1959, and when he demanded the compensation promised him, he was relegated to menial work within the factory. A fall paralyzed him, and he died three years later. Then her mother died soon after. Since the revolutionaries labeled Ah-Si and her siblings as capitalists and landlords, she went to a prison farm at 16 where she stayed for 6 years. As people left the countryside, she took and passed an entrance exam to Beijing University. She was determined to finish her education despite the terrible life she was forced to lead.

Graphic Novels, Biographies, and Histories

3008. Hama, Larry. *The Battle of Iwo Jima: Guerrilla Warfare in the Pacific.* Illustrated by Anthony Williams. (Graphic Battles of World War II) Rosen, 2007. 48pp. ISBN 978-1-4042-0781-3. Grades 4–9.

The narrative begins with background about the Japanese and why World War II began. It then focuses on the arrival of three Japanese botany students as the battle at Iwo Jima is about to begin, and reveals that the Japanese generals had spent some time in the United States. Additional information that humanizes the war augments the drawings and text in this graphic history. Maps, Bibliography, Glossary, Further Reading, Web Sites, and Index.

3009. Ross, Stewart. *Instruments of Death.* Illustrated by Inklink. DK, 2007. 48pp. ISBN 978-0-7566-2566-5; paper ISBN 978-0-7566-2565-8. Grades 3–6.

When a young boy named Shen must become the zither player for the Emperor of China, he becomes involved in an assassination conspiracy. He faces pirates and rescues the Emperor's friends as they face death. As a reward, he must play for important people at a large banquet. After the intrigues, Shen's boss, the first Emperor of the Qin dynasty, becomes the person responsible for uniting the disparate groups in China into one country.

3010. Tome, Kei. *Kurogane 1.* Del Rey, 2006. Unpaged. Paper ISBN 978-0-345-49203-6. Grades 7 up.

In feudal Japan, when Jintetsu, a young assassin, begins to search for his father's murderer, dogs attack him. Genkichi, a scientist/samurai with no master, finds him and reanimates him into a character similar to the Frankenstein monster, half-human and half-steel. He cannot talk and has little memory, but he is a superb swordsman whose only companion is the talking sword that Genkichi gave him. Genkichi uses him for his own revenge battles, and Otsuki, a waitress in his hometown, has to decide if she can love Jintetsu with his new appearance.

3011. Tome, Kei. *Kurogane 5.* Del Rey, 2006. Unpaged. Paper ISBN 978-0-345-49207-4. Grades 7 up.

In feudal Japan, Jintetsu wanders around wondering about the value of his restored life.

3012. White, Steve. *The Battle of Midway: The Destruction of the Japanese Fleet.* Illustrated by Richard Elson. (Graphic Battles of World War II) Rosen, 2007. 48pp. ISBN 978-1-4042-0783-7. Grades 4–9.

The author presents the Battle of Midway from June 4 to 7, 1942. Introductory background precedes a description of the battle, the strategies of both the United States and Japan, the Japanese expectation for victory, and the ultimate American victory that ended the Japanese offensive.

DVDs

3013. *Ancient Chinese Inventions.* Landmark Media, 2002. 4 DVDs; 26 min. ea. Grades 7 up.

Experts review ancient China's contributions to world civilization in four segments titled "Weaponry, Agriculture and Games," "Magnetism, Seismometry, Shipbuilding," "Astronomy and Chronography," and "Printmaking, Armaments, and Rocketry, Government." With computer and television technology, technicians recreate clocks, missiles, seismographs, astronomical instruments, and paddleboat warships that the Chinese introduced. Other important inventions have been navigational methods, the rudder, the compass, gunpowder, and the stirrup.

3014. *China: A Case Study.* (Global Human Rights) Disney Educational, 2006. 18 min. ISBN 978-1-59753-084-2. Grades 6 up.

This video looks at human rights abuses in China using archival news footage. It discusses Mao's Cultural Revolution and the problems in the country leading to the Tiananmen Square protests and the curtailing of the few freedoms that had developed.

3015. *Dynasties of China: 2000 B.C. to 1600 A.D.: Back in Time.* (Hands-On Crafts For Kids Series 6) Chip Taylor Communications, 2003. 30 min. Grades 4–6.

This production begins with a list of materials displayed on the screen and read by the narrator. Teachers construct objects from Chinese culture. They include a terra cotta picture frame, abacus, foam dragon, tetrahedron kite, and symbolic book cover with calligraphy. Each item helps explain an important aspect of Chinese culture.

3016. *The Japanese Empire: 300 A.D. to 1800 A.D.: Back in Time.* (Hands-On Crafts for Kids Series 6) Chip Taylor Communications, 2003. 30 min. Grades 4–6.

This production begins with an audible listing of the materials appearing on the screen. Teachers demonstrate the construction of Japanese objects. They include a bunraku, pagoda frame, bonsai, tea lights, and sand garden. The items help to introduce important aspects of Japanese culture.

3017. *Mujaan.* CustomFlix, 2004. 25 min. Grades 6 up.

This DVD seeks to illustrate how nomads have lived off the land for centuries using natural elements. The entire community joins together to change a standing tree into a felt-covered round house using only primitive tools that can be carried on a cart. A Mujaan (craftsman) shows the ritual and gentle way to butcher a sheep and cook it. The people can support themselves without modern conveniences. *Banff Mountain Film Fes-*

tival, Trento Film Festival, AuTrans Festival International du Film, and *Slamdance Film Festival.*

3018. Park, Linda Sue. *The Firekeeper's Son.*   Illustrated by Julie Downing. Nutmeg Media, 2005. 14 min. ISBN 978-0-9771510-5-9. Grades K–3.

See entry 2905.

3019. *Sinking the Supership.*   (NOVA) WGBH, 2004. 50 min. ISBN 978-1-59375-390-0. Grades 7 up.

The Japanese battleship built during World War II, the *Yamato,* was the largest ever constructed. During a suicide mission, an explosion sank the ship and the three thousand sailors aboard were lost. The DVD describes the ship and reconstructs its design and its fatal mission. Historical footage, reenactments, and photographs enhance the production.

3020. *Soul of the Samurai.*   Cinema Guild, 2005. 46 min. ISBN 978-0-7815-1107-0. Grades 7 up.

This DVD describes the historical significance, the development of, and the continuing role of the samurai in Japan. Sociologists trace the tradition for a thousand years using woodblock prints, 3-D animation, interviews, and narration as sources. The bravest warriors are considered samurai who live by the "way of the warrior" code of honor. Those who have left that path become "ronin." Western culture has infiltrated since the opening of Tokyo in 1854 with Admiral Perry's arrival and other exchanges since the 1900s.

Compact Discs

3021. Coerr, Eleanor. *Sadako and the Thousand Paper Cranes.*   Narrated by Christina Moore. Recorded Books, 2002. 1 hr. ISBN 978-1-4025-2333-5. Grades 2–6.

See entry 2867.

3022. Compestine, Ying Chang. *Revolution Is Not a Dinner Party.*   Narrated by Jodi Long. Listening Library, 2007. 4 CDs; 73 min. ea. ISBN 978-0-7393-6161-0. Grades 4–6.

See entry 2869.

3023. Gratz, Alan. *Samurai Shortstop.*   Narrated by Arthur Morey. Listening Library, 2006. 6 CDs; 74 min. ea. ISBN 978-0-7393-3639-7. Grades 6 up.

See entry 2875.

3024. McCaughrean, Geraldine. *The Kite Rider.*   Narrated by Cynthia Bishop. Full Cast Audio, 2003. 6 CDs; 6 hrs. ISBN 978-1-932076-38-7. Grades 5–9.

See entry 2892.

3025. Park, Linda Sue. *Archer's Quest.*   Narrated by Feodor Chin. Listening Library, 2007. 3 CDs; 3 hrs. 48 min. ISBN 978-0-7393-3866-7. Grades 4–7.

See entry 2904.

3026. Park, Linda Sue. *The Firekeeper's Son.* Illustrated by Julie Downing. Narrated by Norm Lee. Recorded Books, 2004. 15 min. ISBN 978-1-4193-1761-3. Grades K–3.

See entry 2905.

3027. Park, Linda Sue. *A Single Shard.* Narrated by Greame Malcolm. Listening Library, 2004. 3 CDs. ISBN 978-1-4000-8495-1. Grades 4–8.

See entry 2906.

3028. Park, Linda Sue. *When My Name Was Keoko.* Narrated by Jenny Ikeda and Norm Lee. Recorded Books, 2003. 6 CDs; 6.25 hrs. ISBN 978-1-4025-5535-0. Grades 6–10.

See entry 2907.

MIDDLE EAST

Historical Fiction and Fantasy

3029. Amirrezvani, Anita. *The Blood of Flowers: A Novel.* Little, Brown, 2007. 368pp. ISBN 978-0-316-06576-4; Back Bay, 2008. paper ISBN 978-0-316-06577-1. Grades YA.

In Iran during the 17th century, when her father dies without leaving her a dowry, a Persian girl of 14 must go to the house of Gostaham, her wealthy rug designer uncle, and become his servant in Isfahan. He begrudgingly teaches her his trade and soon she is very good. When Fereydoon, the son of a wealthy horse trader, notices her, he wants her to accept a *sigheh*, a temporary marriage contract that he can renew at will. She learns how to satisfy him and herself, but he will not take her for a permanent wife because she has no money. She breaks the contract, and Gostaham throws her out of his house. She decides to become a rug maker on her own and, after having a rug stolen from her, she succeeds, is reunited with Gostaham, and starts her own business in the shah's harem. *School Library Journal Best Books for Young Adults*.

3030. Bellairs, John. *The Trolley to Yesterday.* Illustrated by Edward Gorey. (Johnny Dixon) Penguin, 2004. 192pp. Paper ISBN 978-0-14-240266-5. Grades 4–6.

See entry 940.

3031. Clinton, Cathryn. *A Stone in My Hand.* Candlewick, 2002. 208pp. ISBN 978-0-7636-1388-4; 2004. paper ISBN 978-0-7636-2561-0. Grades 6 up.

In Gaza City during 1988, Malaak, 11, and her Palestinian family live under Israeli military occupation. A Palestinian terrorist bomb blows up a bus when her father is crossing the border to find work in Israel, but she does not know what happened to him and waits for him to come home each day. Her mother finally tells her, and then she begins to worry about her older brother, Hamid, wanting to join the Islamic Jihad. Her friend Tariq sees Israeli soldiers shoot his father. Throughout, Malaak's older sister prefers watching Egyptian soap operas on television. These disparate situations reveal the diversity within families, the terror in which they have to live, and how spiritual communion can offer strength when the physical is no longer possible. *Booklist Editors' Choice, Peach Teen Readers Choice Book Award* (Georgia) nomination, and *Dorothy Canfield Fisher Children's Book Award* (Vermont).

3032. Dietrich, William. *The Rosetta Key.* (Ethan Gage) HarperCollins, 2008. 352pp. ISBN 978-0-06-123955-7; Harperluxe paper ISBN 978-0-06-146881-0. Grades YA.

See entry 1388.

3033. Farmer, Nancy. *Clever Ali.* Illustrated by Gail De Marcken. Orchard, 2006. 32pp. ISBN 978-0-439-37014-1. Grades K–4.

In Egypt during the 12th century, Ali, 7, has a greedy pet that steals cherries from the Sultan of Cairo for whom Ali's father keeps carrier pigeons. Ali has three days to find six hundred cherries, or his father will be thrown in jail. Ali sends pigeons to Syria asking for cherries to be tied to their feet and returned. But the Sultan casts Ali into the oubliette (a dark, bottomless hole) where he meets a good demon who helps him trick the cruel Sultan. Illustrations containing classical Arabic script complement the text. Notes.

3034. Grossman, David A. *Duel.* Translated by Betsy Rosenberg. Bloomsbury, 2004. 112pp. ISBN 978-1-58234-930-5. Grades 5–7.

David, 12, lives in Jerusalem in 1966. His friend, 70-year-old Heinrich Rosenthal, lives in the Beit Hakerem Home for the Aged and is an intelligent photographer. Mr. Rosenthal receives a letter from Rudy Schwartz, an old classmate once known as the "bully of Heidelberg University" who accuses him of stealing a priceless painting. The bully challenges Mr. Rosenthal to a duel if he does not return the artwork; Mr. Rosenthal accepts. Mr. Rosenthal did not steal the painting, and David must find out what happened to it before the two men kill each other. He uncovers a story from thirty years before about two paintings, one of a woman's eyes and the other of her mouth, that the artist gave to the two men. David's work stops the senseless duel to the death. *Sydney Taylor Book Award.*

3035. Henderson, Kathy. *Lugalbanda: The Boy Who Got Caught Up in a War: An Epic Tale from Ancient Iraq.* Illustrated by Jane Ray. Candlewick, 2006. 80pp. ISBN 978-0-7636-2782-9. Grades 3–6.

The king of Uruk tells the prince Lugalbanda of Sumeria (probably the father of Gilgamesh) and his older seven brothers to conquer the walled city of Aratta. Lugalbanda becomes ill on the journey, and his brothers put him in a cave with provisions. He befriends the Anzu, a bird armed with shark's teeth and eagle's talons, before persuading it to give him supernatural power. Lugalbanda rushes to the battle site, discovers the unfinished siege, and asks for more help from the goddess Inana. She says the king should restore Aratta rather than destroy it. The king does as commanded, and Uruk conquers. Watercolors complement the text. (As the oldest-known written story, it comes from clay tablets recovered in the area known as contemporary Iraq and translated in the 1970s.) *Capitol Choices Noteworthy Titles* (Washington, D.C.).

3036. Makiya, Kanan. *The Rock: A Tale of Seventh-Century Jerusalem.* Vintage, 2002. 368pp. Paper ISBN 978-0-375-70078-1. Grades YA.

At one time, during the 7th century, one could be both Muslim and a Jew as K'ab was when he accepted Islam but did not abandon his Jewish heritage. Ishaq, his son, is commissioned to design a mosque on the Rock, the place where Adam fell from Paradise, Abraham attempted to sacrifice Isaac, Jesus overturned the tables, and Muhammad ascended to heaven. This spot where Judaism, Christianity, and Islam converged becomes a place of contention.

3037. Mead, Alice. ***Dawn and Dusk.*** Farrar, 2007. 152pp. ISBN 978-0-374-31708-9. Grades 5–9.

Azad, 13, lives with his distant father half of the year and with his mother the other half. He discovers that his mother left his father seven years before because of his cowardly decision to become an informer to the Iranian secret police. As a Kurd living in Sardasht, Iran, under the repressive government of Ayatollah Khomeini, Azad and his family hear that the Iraqi despot, Saddam Hussein, is trying to eradicate the Kurds and will attack them with chemical weapons. The family has to flee Iran for Turkey. As Azad remembers the situation after he is safely in Maine, he wonders why his pleasant life in the hills was so disrupted.

3038. Moore, Christopher. ***Lamb: The Gospel According to Biff, Christ's Childhood Pal.*** HarperCollins, 2003. 598pp. Paper ISBN 978-0-380-81381-0. Grades YA.

Joshua (Jesus) had a boyhood pal, Biff, who knew him the best of anyone, so the Angel Raziel resurrects Biff (Levi bar Alpheus) and tells him to stay in a St. Louis hotel room until he writes the story of Josh's childhood. Biff recalls traveling with Josh in the East looking for the wise men Balthasar, Gaspar, and Melchior, who gave him gifts at his birth after Mary Magdalene (Maggie) became betrothed to Jakan the jerk. Josh knows that he is the Messiah, but he does not know how to act. In the East, they come in contact with a different religion and unknown cultures. Eventually they return to Israel, and Biff explains the events that led to Josh's crucifixion. *Southern Independent Booksellers Alliance Book Awards* nomination and *Book Sense Book of the Year* nomination.

3039. Moshiri, Farnoosh. ***The Bathhouse: A Novel.*** Beacon, 2003. 183pp. Paper ISBN 978-0-8070-8357-4. Grades YA.

In 1980s Iran, a high school graduate of 17 is imprisoned in an old bathhouse. After her brother becomes involved with revolutionary leftists, police ransack her home and arrest her. In a cell with others, she can leave only to be questioned and tortured, to go to the toilet, or to shower once a week. She gets new cellmates as the others disappear; she is almost executed. She is finally released, and her period starts just as it had when she entered the cell initially.

3040. Oz, Amos. ***Soumchi.*** Translated by Penelope Farmer. Toby, 2003. 71pp. Paper ISBN 978-1-59264-038-6. Grades YA.

Soumchi, age 11 and living in British-occupied Jerusalem just after World War II, is delighted with the bicycle his uncle gives him, even though it is a girl's bicycle. He ignores the jeers of others and dreams that he is riding toward the heart of Africa. He shows the bicycle to his friend, who wants to trade his new train set for it. Soumchi accepts the trade, and then gets involved with a neighborhood bully, a dog, and locks himself out. At the same time he loves Esthie, who knows that he has written a love poem for her. As he says, things change, and they do before the story ends.

3041. Rachlin, Nahid T. ***Jumping Over Fire.*** City Lights, 2006. 261pp. Paper ISBN 978-0-87286-452-8. Grades YA.

Nora Ellahi and her adopted brother, Jahan, have to leave their home in Masjid-e-Suleiman, an oil city in Iran, with their doctor father and American mother when Khomeini comes to power in 1978. The two have had a romantic relationship and hope that they can become independent of each other in America, even with its anti-Iranian sentiments. Jahan hates the American attitude and chooses to return to Iran to fight in the Iran-Iraq war. Nora delights in the freedoms that she cannot have in Iran so their paths diverge as they find their own identities.

3042. Sasson, Jean. *Ester's Child.* Windsor Brooke, 2009. 448pp. Paper ISBN 978-0-967673-77-6. Grades YA.

The lives of three families intersect in Lebanon after World War II. Joseph and Ester Gale determine that they will survive the Warsaw ghetto and the Holocaust to find their daughter stolen by a sadistic Gestapo officer. When they go to Israel after the war, someone kidnaps their infant son. Then George Antoun tries to comfort his barren wife after the Jews force them from Palestine in 1948. Finally Christine Kleist, a young German nurse, becomes a volunteer in a Lebanese refugee camp, trying to make amends for her father's past as an SS officer. Michel, son of the Gales, has become an Israeli officer who hates the Arabs, and Demetrius Antoun is a Palestinian doctor who hates the Israelis. Eventually the lives of the four offspring—Kleist, Demetrius Antoun, and Michel and Jordan Gale—intersect in shocking ways.

3043. Sayres, Meghan Nuttall. *Anahita's Woven Riddle.* Abrams, 2006. 368pp. ISBN 978-0-8109-5481-6. Grades 8 up.

In Iran during the 1880s, Persian nomad Anahita, 16, searches for the perfect husband. She makes riddles and carpets and desires to learn but does not want to marry the khan, the elderly chief of her tribe, who has been chosen for her. She convinces the mullah and her father to let her hold a contest that will help her find a man who will appreciate her interests. She will select the man who can guess the riddle she has woven into her wedding carpet. Alternating chapters between Anahita and her suitors—the khan, a schoolteacher, a prince, and a shepherd (her childhood friend)—offer a look at life in Iran and its prevalent tribes. The khan declares that he will take away the family's migratory and water rights, but her father still allows her to choose her yar, her soul mate. Glossary. *American Library Association Best Books for Young Adults.*

3044. Stolz, Joelle. *The Shadows of Ghadames.* Translated by Catherine Temerson. Random House, 2004. 119pp. ISBN 978-0-385-73104-1; Yearling, 2006. paper ISBN 978-0-440-41949-5. Grades 5–8.

During the late 19th century in Ghadames, Libya, Malika will soon be 12 and be completely confined to a world of women allowed to walk only along the rooftops. She longs to travel like her trader father and to learn to read. She wonders what lies beyond women's veils. While her father is away, two of his wives offer unexpected hospitality to a wounded male. When they talk to him as he heals, he tells them about life outside their walls. His information only makes the outside world more desirable to her. *American Library Association Notable Children's Books, Mildred L. Batchelder Award,* and *Booklist Editors' Choice.*

3045. Temple, Frances. *The Beduins' Gazelle.* Illustrated by David Bowers. HarperCollins, 1998. 160pp. Paper ISBN 978-0-06-440669-7. Grades 6–9.

Halima and Atiyah, betrothed since birth, look forward to a desert wedding in the Middle East in 1302. Uncle Saladeen, however, decides that Atiyah should study the Koran in Fez. Then Halima and her camel become separated from their tribal caravan during a sandstorm as they migrate toward water. An enemy sheikh sees her and decides that she will become one of his wives. In this book, the same Etienne presented in *The Ramsay Scallop* meets Atiyah at the university in Fez and helps him rescue Halima from the greedy sheikh.

3046. Thoene, Bodie, and Brock Thoene. *The Jerusalem Scrolls.* (Zion Legacy) Penguin, 2002. 272pp. Paper ISBN 978-0-14-200151-6. Grades YA.

In the fourth book of the series, Moshe Sachar and Alfie Halder hide in an underground Jewish library where they discover a scroll telling the story of Miryam M. and her occasional lover, centurion Marcus Longinus. Miryam's family gave her in marriage to an old man, but he dies, and she is wealthy. She insists that she will be sexually free, and she must go into exile and then ruin for her beliefs. Marcus fails to protect her, but when he hears the new preacher Yeshua, he becomes aware that life has more than he has noticed.

3047. Thoene, Bodie, and Brock Thoene. *Jerusalem Vigil.* (Zion Legacy) Penguin, 2001. 322pp. Paper ISBN 978-0-14-029856-7. Grades YA.

In 1948 Arab forces try to remove Jews from the Holy City when the British leave and David Ben-Gurion gains power in the new state of Israel. Among the people involved in these developments are Lori and Jacob Kalner, who arrive in Israel and are immediately put to work—Jacob in the army and Lori as a nurse—in this first volume of the Zion Legacy series.

3048. Thoene, Bodie, and Brock Thoene. *Jerusalem's Heart.* (Zion Legacy) Penguin, 2002. 328pp. Paper ISBN 978-0-14-200038-0. Grades YA.

The third volume of the Zion Legacy series recounts the process of Israel becoming a nation in 1948. Jacob Kalner leads a fight to defend Jerusalem from the Arab Legion, but Jordan's King Abdullah reclaims it for the Arabs. Pilot David Meyer flies a Messerschmitt at the Egyptians and defeats them.

3049. Thoene, Bodie, and Brock Thoene. *Jerusalem's Hope.* (Zion Legacy) Penguin, 2003. 264pp. Paper ISBN 978-0-14-200357-2. Grades YA.

In the sixth entry in the Zion Legacy series, during the 1948 war of Independence in Israel, Moshe Sachar hides beneath the Temple Mount and opens another of the ancient scrolls about the miracles of Yeshua of Nazareth, a Roman centurion, and three orphans who serve as messengers to Zadok, a shepherd in Bethlehem.

3050. Thoene, Bodie, and Brock Thoene. *Stones of Jerusalem.* (Zion Legacy) Penguin, 2003. 266pp. Paper ISBN 978-0-14-200188-2. Grades YA.

In a secret tunnel beneath the Temple Mount, Moshe Sachar reads in an ancient scroll about the Roman centurion Marcus Longinus and the woman he loves, Miryam. After Miryam meets Yeshua, she finds a home for poor, especially unwed, mothers. Marcus slowly comes under the influence of Yeshua himself and becomes the Good Samaritan. This is the fifth installment of Zion Legacy.

3051. Thoene, Bodie, and Brock Thoene. *Thunder from Jerusalem.* (Zion Legacy) Penguin, 2001. 311pp. Paper ISBN 978-0-14-100218-7. Grades YA.

In the sequel to *Jerusalem Vigil*, the Arab Legion streetfights with Moshe Sachar's Jewish irregulars in May 1948. When an English-educated Bedouin, Major Tariq Athani, arrives he advises the Arabs against fighting Jews on holy ground, but Jordanian King Abdullah has to bow to politics. Jewish commandos inflict heavy damage on armored Syrians, and others bomb an Egyptian column marching through the Negev Desert. Eventually, the Arab Legion prepares to withdraw, with the Israelis getting the upper hand.

3052. Uris, Leon. *Exodus.* Bantam, 1989. 608pp. Paper ISBN 978-0-553-25847-9. Grades YA.

Ari Ben Canaan becomes a leader for the establishment of the Jewish state after World War II. He and many others battle to save the orphaned children who have gathered in Palestine after escaping concentration camps at the end of the war. Kitty, an American nurse, realizes she must stay in Israel to help those who need her. As people sacrifice their lives for a place to be free, others prepare the state to come into being.

3053. Waldman, Neil. *The Never-Ending Greenness.* Illustrated by author. Boyds Mills, 2003. Unpaged. ISBN 978-1-59078-064-0. Grades 2–6.

See entry 2049.

History

3054. Allon, Hagit, and Lena Zehavi. *The Mystery of the Dead Sea Scrolls.* Illustrated by Yossi Abolafia. Jewish Publication Society, 2004. 60pp. Paper ISBN 978-0-8276-0800-9. Grades 4 up.

Six chapters tell the story of Daniel, 11, who decides to do his school project on the Dead Sea Scrolls, which were discovered in 1945. He finds out that even the scrolls have further mysteries that need to be solved. He goes to the Shrine of the Book at Jerusalem's Israel Museum and meets the curator, who allows him to examine the ancient texts and learn about their discovery. Then he journeys to Qumran in the Judean Desert to meet archaeologist Yigal, who shows him where a shepherd boy found the scrolls. Yigal tells him about the Essenes, the religious sect that probably created the scrolls, enabling Daniel to write a thorough report. Illustrations highlight the text.

3055. Aronson, Marc. *Unsettled: The Problem of Loving Israel.* Ginee Seo, 2008. 184pp. ISBN 978-1-4169-1261-3. Grades YA.

This examination of Israel covers its beginnings until the present day. It discusses its status as a religious and a democratic state, its global obligations, and its political challenges. The five parts of the text ask how Israel came into being, what it is, whether winning the war with Egypt in 1967 ruined Egypt, whether Israelis can occupy conquered lands and remain idealistic, and how it can be a truly strong and democratic state as a Jewish homeland. Within each part are several chapters that cover different aspects of the question. Photographs accompany the text. Bibliography and Notes. *Kirkus Best Young Adult Books.*

3056. Barr, Gary E. *History and Activities of the Islamic Empire.* (Hands-On Ancient History) Raintree, 2007. 32pp. ISBN 978-1-4034-7926-6. Grades 3–6.

In three short chapters, the book focuses on the structure of the ancient Islamic Empire by looking at the everyday life of its people, arts, culture, games, holidays, and celebrations. The fourth chapter includes instructions for making a tughra and a pachisi gameboard, recipes, and an activity. Photographs and illustrations enhance the text. Glossary, Further Reading, and Index.

3057. Beshore, George W. *Science in Early Islamic Culture.* (Science of the Past) Scholastic, 1998. 64pp. Paper ISBN 978-0-531-15917-0. Grades 5–8.

An introduction to early Islamic culture and its science precedes chapters on various developments. They include mathematics, astronomy, the study of optics or light and vision, alchemy, and contemporary debt to the culture for its discoveries. Drawings and reproductions supplement the text. Glossary, Further Reading, and Index.

3058. Bodden, Valerie. *Suez Canal.* Creative, 2006. 32pp. ISBN 978-1-58341-441-5. Grades 3–6.

The author presents the history of the Suez Canal and provides information about the desert surrounding it prior to its construction during the 19th century. She also examines the public's reaction to this decision. The Suez Canal has offered water transport between Europe and Asia without having to circumnavigate Africa, and has revitalized the area in which it was built. Photographs and maps enhance the text. Glossary and Index.

3059. Davenport, John. *A Brief Political and Geographic History of the Middle East: Where Are Persia, Babylon, and the Ottoman Empire?* (Places in Time) Mitchell Lane, 2008. 2008pp. ISBN 978-1-58415-622-2. Grades 5–9.

The author looks at places in the Middle East that no longer exist by placing them on a map and discussing why they have disappeared from present-day geography. Chapters look at the Battle of Gaugamela in 331 B.C.E., Darius after Gaugamela, Mesopotamia and Gilgamish, Assyria, Chaldeans and Achaemenids, the Babylonian Exile, Alexander's Empire, the Ptolemies and their power, the Battle of Carrhae, the Byzantine military, Saladin, the Ottoman Turks, and the Great Arab Revolt. Photographs, maps, and reproductions embellish the text. Bibliography, Glossary, Chronology, Notes, Further Reading, Web Sites, and Index.

3060. Downing, David. *The Making of the Middle East.* (The Middle East) Raintree, 2005. 56pp. ISBN 978-1-4109-1620-4; 2006. paper ISBN 978-1-4109-1626-6. Grades 5–9.

This volume offers a brief history of events that have created the recent political problems in the Middle East. Short biographies of important figures in Iran also aid in understanding the significance of the country. Archival photographs, maps, and text boxes enhance the content. Glossary, Chronology, Further Reading, and Index.

3061. Feiler, Bruce. *Walking the Bible: An Illustrated Journey for Kids Through the Greatest Stories Ever Told.* HarperCollins, 2004. 108pp. ISBN 978-0-06-051117-3. Grades 5–8.

Bruce Feiler describes his journeys to places named in the Bible and describes them as they appear today and how they might have been during the historical time. Among the places included are the intersection of the Tigris and Euphrates Rivers as a possible location for the Garden of Eden, Turkey and Noah's Ark, Ur and Abraham's home, the Egypt of Moses and Joseph, and Mount Sinai where Moses received the Ten Commandments. Photographs and maps embellish the text.

3062. Ford, Nick. *Jerusalem Under Muslim Rule in the Eleventh Century: Christian Pilgrims Under Islamic Government.* (Library of the Middle Ages) Rosen, 2003. 64pp. ISBN 978-0-8239-4216-9. Grades 5–8.

The center of the world during the Middle Ages was Jerusalem. The author examines life for Muslims and non-Muslims in Jerusalem with specific discussion of Jewish and Christian life. Among the persons presented are Abraham ben Isaac Al-Andalusi, Abu Baqr Ibn Al-Arabi, Iftikhar Al-Daulah, Rabbi Jonah the Elder, Abu Mu'in Nasir Ibn Khusrau, Caliph 'Abd Al-Malik, Daniel Al-Qumusi, and Rabbi Solomon Ha-kohen ben Yehosef. Illustrations highlight the text. Glossary, Bibliography, Further Reading, Web Sites, and Index.

3063. Frank, Mitch. *Understanding the Holy Land: Answering Questions About the Israeli-Palestinian Conflict.* Viking, 2005. 160pp. ISBN 978-0-670-06032-0. Grades 7 up.

This guide to the Holy Land contains twelve questions that refer to the conflict in the area. It asks about the Israeli-Palestinian conflict, who the Israelis were before, how it began, how Israel was founded, the Arabs' reaction to Israel, the identity of the PLO, the intifada, the Oslo peace process, life today in this area, and how the rest of the world responds to the conflict. The answers reveal truths as well as misconceptions that each side has against the other. Clearly, each group has valid claims for wanting this land. Photographs and maps highlight the text. Bibliography, Chronology, Glossary, and Index. *Voice of Youth Advocates Nonfiction Honor List* and *Bulletin Blue Ribbon*.

3064. Graham, Amy. *Iran in the News: Past, Present, and Future.* (Middle East Nations in the News) Myreportlinks.com, 2006. 128pp. ISBN 978-1-59845-022-4. Grades 4–8.

This overview of Iran includes background on its history and culture as well as its recent political situation. Chapters also cover religion, geography, and the economy. It also includes links to Web Sites such as newspapers and other international sources. Photographs and illustrations highlight the text. Glossary, Chronology, Notes, Further Reading, Web Sites, and Index.

3065. Gritzner, Jeffrey A., and Charles F. Gritzner. *North Africa and the Middle East.* (Modern World Cultures) Facts on File, 2006. 120pp. ISBN 978-0-7910-8145-7. Grades 9 up.

Geography has greatly influenced the history and culture of North Africa and the Middle East. The author examines the diverse environment of the area, the natural landscape, the existing climate and ecosystems, its role as the cradle of civilization, the influence of the West, the population and settlement of the area, the cultural aspects of geography, how the troubled region looks ahead, and its historical context from the Sumerians, Hittites, Hyksos, Assyrians, and Egyptians. Photographs complement the text. Maps, Bibliography, and Index.

3066. Hancock, Lee. *Saladin and the Kingdom of Jerusalem: The Muslims Recapture the Holy Land in A.D. 1187.* (Library of the Middle Ages) Rosen, 2003. 64pp. ISBN 978-0-8239-4217-6. Grades 5–8.

Ninety years after the Christians captured Jerusalem, Saladin united the Islamic groups to fight. In 1187 he recaptured Jerusalem and destroyed much of the Christian kingdom. This text catalogues Saladin's military campaigns and presents the Crusades as the Muslims saw them. Included is a look at everyday life for Muslims, Jews, and Christians based on primary sources, along with clear information about the tools of battle and the process of the war. Reproductions enhance the text. Bibliography, Maps, Web Sites, and Index.

3067. January, Brendan. *The Iranian Revolution.* (Pivotal Moments In History) Twenty First Century, 2008. 160pp. ISBN 978-0-8225-7521-4. Grades 7–9.

Since the Iranian people despised their leader, Reza Shah, because he catered to foreign business and ruled as a dictator, they were quite willing to overthrow his government. In 1979 Ayatollah Khomeini returned from exile in Paris to lead the revolution against the Shah. He and the people created a new government based on the Islamic religion. During this period, the Iranians took hostages from the American embassy in Tehran and held them for 444 days, from 1979 to 1981. Oddly, the Iranians decided to shed one oppressive regime for another. The book also includes background information about the Shiite and Sunni sects in Islam. Photographs and illustrations highlight the text. Bibliography, Chronology, Notes, Further Reading, Glossary, Web Sites, and Index. *Notable Trade Books in the Field of Social Studies.*

3068. King, John. *Iran and the Islamic Revolution.* (The Middle East) Raintree, 2005. 56pp. ISBN 978-1-4109-1623-5; 2006. paper ISBN 978-1-4109-1629-7. Grades 5–9.

The text examines the background of the rise of an Islamic Republic in Iran, the reasons for Iran's hostility to the United States, and Iran's role in the Middle East and the rest of the world. Short biographies of important figures in Iran also aid understanding of the significance of the country. Archival photographs, maps, and text boxes enhance the narrative. Glossary, Chronology, Further Reading, and Index.

3069. King, John. *Iraq Then and Now.* (The Middle East) Raintree, 2005. 56pp. ISBN 978-1-4109-1622-8; 2006. paper ISBN 978-1-4109-1628-0. Grades 5–9.

The author examines the conflicts in the Middle East such as the changes in Iraq, the Israeli-Palestinian differences, and the role of oil in politics both in the region and throughout the world. This book also contains thoughts about Iraq's conflict with the United States, why the United States invaded Iraq, and how it affects the globe. Archival photographs, maps, and text boxes add interest. Glossary, Chronology, Further Reading, and Index.

3070. King, John. *Israel and Palestine.* (The Middle East) Raintree, 2005. 56pp. ISBN 978-1-4109-1621-1; 2006. paper ISBN 978-1-4109-1627-3. Grades 5–9.

The causes of the Israeli-Palestinian conflict, the possibilities of a settlement in this conflict, and how this conflict affects the rest of the world is this book's focus. Also included is a look at the role of oil in the region and throughout the globe. Archival photographs, maps, and text boxes add to the narrative. Glossary, Chronology, Further Reading, and Index.

3071. King, John. *Oil in the Middle East.* (The Middle East) Raintree, 2005. 56pp. ISBN 978-1-4109-1624-2; paper ISBN 978-1-4109-1630-3. Grades 5–9.

The author looks at the Middle East and the role of oil in the region, both as a positive resource and a source of conflict. He includes much of the history of the region, the significance of the colonial experience, and interaction of Middle Eastern countries with the West. Archival photographs, maps, and text boxes add to the text. Glossary, Chronology, Further Reading, and Index.

3072. Lewis, Bernard. *The Middle East: A Brief History of the Last 2,000 Years.* Scribner, 1997. 448pp. Paper ISBN 978-0-684-83280-7. Grades YA.

In this comprehensive history, beginning with the 7th century in the Middle East, Lewis makes two major points. He believes, first, that everything that happens in the Arab world has parallels in past history, and second, that the West is winning its struggle with Islam, and has been winning since the Ottomans had to sign the Treaty of Car-lowitz in 1699. A major reason for the Western victory is that Muslim indifference to the technology and innovation that began in the West as early as the 16th century has kept Muslims from being able to compete on either sea or land. Among Lewis's proofs of Islam's decline are Napoleon's quick defeat of Egypt in 1798, the Ottoman Empire's dis-solution after World War I, and the survival of Israel. He also asserts that Saddam Hus-sein's attempt to seize Kuwait in 1990 was typical of Middle Eastern behavior. Other information fills this valuable book. Bibliography and Index.

3073. Lewis, Bernard. *Race and Slavery in the Middle East: An Historical Enquiry.* Oxford, 1992. 184pp. Paper ISBN 978-0-19-505326-5. Grades YA.

Lewis shows how slavery spread in the Islamic world even though people denied that the Islamic world had ever been connected to slavery. He says that racial con-sciousness became racial prejudice in the Islamic world, but that slavery was not the demeaning system that existed in the United States. He gives examples from every pe-riod of Islamic history to support his thesis and the idea of the economic function of slavery and of the social function of racism. Bibliography and Index.

3074. Macaulay, David. *Mosque.* Walter Lorraine, 2003. 96pp. ISBN 978-0-618-24034-0; 2008. paper ISBN 978-0-54701-547-7. Grades 6 up.

In Istanbul during 1595, Admiral Suha Mehmet Pasa, a wealthy man, hires an archi-tect to build a mosque. As the architect plans the building, he draws meticulous ren-derings of it plus the religious college, soup kitchen, public baths, and the admiral's tomb, all placed near a busy port. The complex represents both religious and social as-pects of the society, and the planning must incorporate these within its supporting piers and arches while it lies on the *kibla*, a line that both points toward and radiates from Mecca. Glossary. *Publishers Weekly Best Children's Books*, *Voice of Youth Advocates Nonfiction Honor List*, and *School Library Journal Best Books for Children*.

3075. MacMillan, Dianne M. *Ramadan and Id al-Fitr.* (Best Holiday Books) Enslow, 2008. 48pp. ISBN 978-0-7660-3045-9. Grades 2–5.

A brief look at Muhammad's life, the pillars of Islam, and the role of the mosque in the life of Muslims precedes discussion of Ramadan, the holiday during the ninth month of the Islamic lunar calendar. Ramadan ends on the first day of the tenth month with Id al-Fitr, a celebration that lasts for a day. Glossary and Index.

3076. Pouwels, Randall L. *The African and Middle Eastern World, 600–1500.* (Medieval and Early Modern World) Oxford, 2005. 175pp. ISBN 978-0-19-517673-5. Grades 7 up.

See entry 2597.

3077. Price Hossell, Karen. *The Persian Gulf War.* (20th Century Perspectives) Heinemann, 2003. 48pp. ISBN 978-1-4034-1143-3; paper ISBN 978-1-4034-3856-0. Grades 4–8.

This volume covers the Persian Gulf War that began on August 2, 1990, and ended on February 28, 1991. A coalition force of 35 nations fought Iraq after it invaded Kuwait. The fighting was confined to Iraq, Kuwait, and areas of Saudi Arabia. Also examined are the issues, the causes, and the effects of this war. Illustrations augment the text. Bibli-ography, Further Reading, Glossary, Index.

3078. Roaf, Michael. *The Cultural Atlas of Mesopotamia and the Ancient Near East.* Checkmark, 1990. 238pp. ISBN 978-0-8160-2218-2. Grades YA.

Three sections—"Villages," "Cities," and "Empires"—show the history, geography, anthropology, and archaeology of Mesopotamia and the Near East. Topics include Babylon, Ur, warfare, ivory carving, and the origin of writing. Maps and illustrations augment the text. Bibliography, Chronology, Glossary, and Index.

3079. Rouss, Sylvia A. *Reach for the Stars: A Little Torah's Journey.* Illustrated by Rosalie Ofer. Pitspopany, 2005. 40pp. ISBN 978-1-930143-82-1. Grades 3–5.

When Israeli astronaut Ilan Ramon boarded the *Columbia* space shuttle he carried a miniature Torah given to him by its guardian, Joachim Joseph. During World War II a rabbi's wife had told her children that the yellow star they had to wear on their clothes was to remind them that God was near. The rabbi then gave the Torah to Joseph when they were in a concentration camp, and when Joseph was freed, he took it with him to Israel. Unfortunately, the shuttle exploded and, along with it, the Torah.

3080. Schaffer, David. *Saudi Arabia in the News: Past, Present, and Future.* (Middle East Nations in the News) Myreportlinks, 2006. 128pp. ISBN 978-1-59845-026-2. Grades 5–9.

A look at the history and contemporary aspects of Saudi Arabia, including information on its traditions, terrorism, religion, business, and culture. Bibliography, Glossary, Web Sites, Further Reading, Notes, Maps, and Index.

3081. Steele, Philip. *The Middle East.* (Kingfisher Knowledge) Kingfisher, 2006. 64pp. ISBN 978-0-7534-5984-3. Grades 4–7.

This volume offers a history of the Middle East as the birthplace of civilization and continues to the present, introducing the modern nations that make up the area: Egypt, Jordan, Saudi Arabia, Yemen, Oman, the Gulf states, Iraq, Iran, Afghanistan, Turkey, Syria, Lebanon, Israel, and the Palestinian territories. It covers occupations (such as merchants), daily lives, and concerns. Photographs and illustrations highlight the text. Bibliography, Glossary, Web Sites, and Index.

3082. Worth, Richard. *The Arab-Israeli Conflict.* (Open For Debate) Benchmark, 2006. 127pp. ISBN 978-0-7614-2295-2. Grades 7 up.

This book includes an examination of the Arab-Israeli conflict from 1000 B.C.E. to March 2006. Among the topics covered are the Zionist movement, the Palestinians and their right to return, Yasir Arafat and the Palestine Liberation Organization (PLO), and a background on the settlements. Primary sources support the interpretations, and sidebars add more commentary. Photographs, maps, and reproductions reinforce the text. Chronology, Notes, Further Reading, Web Sites, and Index.

3083. Zurlo, Tony. *Syria in the News: Past, Present, and Future.* (Middle East Nations in the News) Myreportlinks, 2006. 128pp. ISBN 978-1-59845-025-5. Grades 5–9.

Readers will learn about the history and contemporary aspects of Syria, including information on its traditions, religion, business, economy, and culture. Bibliography, Glossary, Web Sites, Further Reading, Notes, Maps, and Index.

Biography and Collective Biography

3084. Barakat, Ibtisam. *Tasting the Sky: A Palestinian Childhood.* Melanie Kroupa, 2007. 176pp. ISBN 978-0-374-35733-7. Grades 7 up.

In 1981 Ibtisam Barakat, a teenager, boarded a bus for Ramallah, but Israeli border soldiers checked the bus and detained her. She then recalls her early experience at the start of the 1967 Six-Day War when soldiers raided the Palestinians' homes and bombed them before the family could escape across the border to Jordan. She lived under occupation, but was able to attend the United Nations schools for refugees where she fell in love with chalk, the Arabic alphabet, and a first-grade teacher who saw her intelligence. The memoir informs readers about customs of Palestinians and her early life while showing that although of a different culture, she loved the same opportunities that all children everywhere love. *Booklist Editors' Choice, School Library Journal Best Books for Children, Kirkus Reviews Editor's Choice,* and *American Library Association Notable Children's Books.*

3085. Brezina, Corona. *Al-Khwarizmi: The Inventor of Algebra.* (Great Muslim Philosophers and Scientists of the Middle Ages) Rosen, 2006. 112pp. ISBN 978-1-4042-0513-0. Grades 7 up.

Al-Khwarizmi (813–846) was one of the important scientists and mathematicians of the Muslims. Among the topics covered, in addition to the little that is known about Al-Khwarizmi's life, are an overview of the Middle East and how Islam began and spread around the world. Maps and illustrations enhance the text. Glossary, Bibliography, Chronology, Further Reading, and Index.

3086. Darraj, Susan Muaddi. *Hosni Mubarak.* (Modern World Leaders) Chelsea House, 2007. 128pp. ISBN 978-0-7910-9280-4. Grades 8 up.

As president of Egypt since the assassination of Anwar Sadat on October 6, 1981, Hosni Mubarak (b. 1928) has had both success and failure. In 1997 extremists murdered tourists at Queen Hatshepsut's Temple, and he had to handle that crisis. Readers will learn about Mubarak's childhood, his readiness for power, significant historical events in Egypt, and his political beliefs. Photographs highlight the text. Bibliography, Chronology, Further Reading, and Index.

3087. Demi. *Jesus: Based Upon the King James Version of the Holy Bible.* Margaret K. McElderry, 2005. 48pp. ISBN 978-0-689-86407-0. Grades 4–7.

This "biography" examines the life of Jesus Christ. It covers Gabriel's announcement to Mary that Jesus will be born, his birth in a manger, his miracles, the Last Supper, and the Crucifixion. The text follows the King James version of the Bible, and the illustrations, containing touches of gold, complement the text.

3088. Demi. *Muhammad.* Margaret K. McElderry, 2003. Unpaged. ISBN 978-0-689-85264-0. Grades 3 up.

In the year 570, Muhammad was born in Mecca, and through the years, he believed in worshiping only one God. When Muhammad was 40, he had a revelation from the angel Gabriel that he was the messenger of God. For the next twenty-three years, he received revelations which scribes recorded, and these messages comprised the Qur'an, the sacred scripture of Islam. More than one-quarter of the world follows Islam. Illustrations recreate designs found in the Islamic world, but according to tradition, no faces have been included. Muhammad appears in the book as a gold silhouette. *Middle East Book Awards, Booklist Editors' Choice*, and *Beehive Children's Informational Book Award* (Utah) nomination.

3089. Finkelstein, Norman. *Theodor Herzl: Architect of a Nation.* Lerner, 1991. 128pp. ISBN 978-0-8225-4913-0. Grades 5–9.

Although Theodor Herzl (b. 1860) died in 1904, he was reburied with honors in Israel on August 17, 1949. He had worked on the possibility of a homeland for the Jews during most of his lifetime in Austria, almost fifty years before the state was founded. He was a journalist and playwright who believed that the only way to escape the torment of anti-Semitism was to have a place for Jews to live together in Israel. He worked tirelessly with Jewish leaders to establish a base for a new nation. He helped with the First Zionist Congress which met in 1897. Notes, Glossary, and Index.

3090. Friedman, Thomas. *From Beirut to Jerusalem: Updated with a New Chapter.* Anchor, 1995. 588pp. Paper ISBN 978-0-385-41372-5. Grades YA.

Newspaper correspondent Thomas Friedman describes his experiences with Arab and Israeli friends during his days as a journalist in their countries. In relating anecdotes of people he has met, he gives a clear indication of the turmoil in the country of Lebanon. Why people continue to fight becomes understandable but not acceptable. Index.

3091. Hampton, Wilborn. *War in the Middle East: A Reporter's Story: Black September and the Yom Kippur War.* Candlewick, 2007. 128pp. ISBN 978-0-7636-2493-4. Grades 6 up.

From the 1970 Black September altercation in Jordan to the 1973 Yom Kippur War, the author served as a UPI correspondent in the Middle East. The text contains a history of the region and begins with the story of the Popular Front for the Liberation of Palestine's hijackings of three airliners. Hampton was trapped in an Amman hotel with neither electricity nor water during Black September. After relating briefly the events between the two wars, he describes the Yom Kippur War from Tel Aviv and the inherent dangers in his news gathering inside the war zones of the Golan Heights and the Sinai Desert. To file his stories, Hampton used the advanced technology of the day—telex and telephone. The end covers a few of the subsequent events including the assassinations of Egypt's Anwar Sadat and Israel's Yitzhak Rabin. Photographs enhance the text. Bibliography and Index.

3092. Holliday, Laurel. *Children of Israel, Children of Palestine: Our Own True Stories.* Washington Square, 1999. 358pp. Paper ISBN 978-0-671-00804-8. Grades YA.

Thirty-six men, women, and children describe their lives as they have been and are currently surviving in the turmoil of Israeli and Palestinian conflicts. Some of the accounts start before the 1948 war ends. Even though they often want revenge, they also want peace as much. Photographs augment the text. Bibliography and Chronology.

3093. Khan, Aisha. *Avicenna (Ibn Sina): Muslim Physician and Philosopher of the Eleventh Century.* (Great Muslim Philosophers and Scientists of the Middle Ages) Rosen, 2006. 112pp. ISBN 978-1-4042-0509-3. Grades 7 up.

Avicenna (Ibn Sina) (980–1037), a renowned physician of the court during the 11th century, was considered to be one of the greatest physicians in history. He also traveled and spread his philosophies. Other topics include an overview of the Middle East and how Islam began and spread around the world. Maps and illustrations enhance the text. Glossary, Bibliography, Chronology, Further Reading, and Index.

3094. Raatma, Lucia. *Queen Noor: American-Born Queen of Jordan.* (Signature Lives Modern World) Compass Point, 2005. 112pp. ISBN 978-0-7565-1595-9; 2007. paper ISBN 978-0-7565-1803-5. Grades 6–9.

This biography of Jordan's Queen Noor reveals her American heritage and childhood before she met and married King Hussein of Jordan in 1978. She attended Princeton as Lisa Halaby before she met the king, and she decided to marry this older man in just three months. She had many obstacles to overcome, including the disdain of the Jordanian people because of her background. But she eventually became a Middle Eastern insider. Photographs augment the text. Chronology, Notes, Further Reading, Web Sites, and Index.

3095. Reed, Jennifer. *The Saudi Royal Family.* (Major World Leaders) Chelsea House, 2007. 120pp. ISBN 978-0-7910-9218-7; 2002. paper ISBN 978-0-7910-7187-8. Grades 5–8.

This collective biography covers key members of Saudi Arabia's royal family. They include King Abdul Aziz of the New Kingdom; King Saud, the Black Sheikh (1953–1964); King Faisal, the Hero (1964–1975); King Khalid, the Quiet One (1975–1982); King Fahd, the Businessman (1982–2005); and the contemporary ruler, King Abdullah. Photographs and illustrations augment the text. Bibliography, Chronology, Further Reading, and Index.

3096. Sahebjam, Freidoune. *The Stoning of Soraya M.* Translated by Richard Seaver. Arcade, 1995. 144pp. Paper ISBN 978-1-55970-270-6. Grades YA.

Soraya, born in 1951 in an Iranian village during the reign of the Shah, was married at 13 by her parents to a husband who beat her and her seven children. His somewhat questionable business takes him to the city, where he eventually finds another woman. A holy man who comes into the village after the Ayatollah Khomeini comes to power urges him to ask for a divorce, after which the holy man propositions Soraya. Soraya' s aunt, however, overhears the suggestion and runs him out of the house. Taking revenge on Soraya, the holy man hints that she has been unfaithful and that the townspeople will be purified if they stone her to death, just as they are when they throw stones at the pillars representing the devil outside of Mecca. In 1986, they did just that. Soraya M. and probably more than 1,000 women like her have been unjustly stoned during this regime. Her aunt told this macabre story to the author, a reporter.

3097. Sendyk, Helen. *New Dawn: A Triumph of Life After the Holocaust.* Syracuse University, 2002. 200pp. ISBN 978-0-8156-0735-9. Grades YA.

Sendyk, after her recollection of the Holocaust in *The End of Days*, remembers here the efforts to get British Mandated Palestine to found the state of Israel after she, her sister, and her cousin reached Tel Aviv in Palestine in May of 1946. They reunite with a surviving brother to rebuild their lives there and in America. By the end of 1956, Sendyk is married and an administrator who continues to defend her faith.

3098. Shahak, Bat-Chen. *The Bat-Chen Diaries.* Translated by Diana Rubanenko. Kar-Ben, 2008. 112pp. ISBN 978-0-8225-8807-8; paper ISBN 978-0-8225-7223-7. Grades 5–8.

A suicide bomber killed Israeli teen Bat-Chen Shahak in 1996. Included in this look at her life are letters, doodles, and diary entries. As an idealist, she was discovering the painful realities that can interfere with one's anticipated daily life. But what makes this collection noteworthy is the shortness of Bat-Chen's life. Photographs augment the text.

3099. Shehadeh, Raja. *Strangers in the House: Coming of Age in Occupied Palestine.* Penguin, 2003. 256pp. Paper ISBN 978-0-14-200293-3. Grades YA.

When Israel defeated the Arab armies, it forced Palestinian lawyer, writer, and activist Raja Shehadeh and his family from their home. They had to suffer under decades of military occupation. Born in 1951, he did not know freedom because his movements were limited, his schools were inferior, and his leaders often imprisoned. His father, also a lawyer and a voice for peace, was assassinated, and Shehadeh then became a radical. He helped found Al-Haq, an affiliate of the International Commission of Jurists, in an effort to understand his own life.

3100. Sofer, Barbara. *Ilan Ramon: Israel's Space Hero.* Kar-Ben, 2003. 63pp. ISBN 978-0-8225-2055-9. Grades 3–6.

Ilan Ramon (1954–2003), Israel's first astronaut, died in the space shuttle *Columbia's* explosion during reentry into the atmosphere. The book identifies the special items that he took with him for the Jews of the world. In turn, they have commemorated him. Chronology, Web Sites, and Index.

3101. Stanley, Diane. *Saladin: Noble Prince of Islam.* HarperCollins, 2002. 48pp. ISBN 978-0-688-17135-3. Grades 4–8.

Salah al-Din (Saladin), a Kurd, joined the army of the Turkish Sultan Nur al-Din when he was 14 after hearing stories of how the Christians had conquered Jerusalem and left the dead from all religions lying around. He became the leader of the "barbarian horde" against Richard the Lionheart in the 12th century and was known as the "marvel of his time." His people had been defeated in the First Crusade, and he rose to help them. He was courageous, merciful, humane, and generous, but willing to protect his people at all costs. Glossary, Bibliography, and Notes. *Publishers Weekly Best Children's Books, American Library Association Notable Books for Children, Capitol Choices Noteworthy Titles* (Washington, D.C.), *Booklist Editors' Choice,* and *Student Book Award* (Maine) nomination.

3102. Steffens, Bradley. *Ibn al-Haytham: First Scientist.* Morgan Reynolds, 2007. 128pp. ISBN 978-1-59935-024-0. Grades 5–8.

Ibn al-Haytham (or "Alhazen") (965–1039), born in Basra (Iraq), was a pioneer of scientific deduction. Familiar with Aristotle, Euclid, Archimedes, and Ptolemy, he used experimentation and deduction for his observations. His most influential work for contemporary times was his treatise on light and optics, *The Book of Optics.* His discovery of the *camera obscura* may have been the catalyst that changed western art. Illustrations highlight the text. Bibliography, Chronology, Notes, Web Sites, and Index.

3103. Stewart, Gail B. *Saddam Hussein.* (Heroes And Villains) Lucent, 2003. 96pp. ISBN 978-1-59018-350-2. Grades 8 up.

Saddam Hussein (1937–2006) maintained control over Iraq for more than twenty years through a ruthless dictatorship that used terror tactics. He violated the rights of his subjects in order to contain them and keep power. Some, however, remained devoted to him. Photographs and reproductions augment the text. Bibliography, Maps, and Index.

3104. Viegas, Jennifer. *Al-Kindi: The Father of Arab Philosophy.* (Great Muslim Philosophers and Scientists of the Middle Ages) Rosen, 2006. 112pp. ISBN 978-1-4042-0511-6. Grades 7 up.

Al-Kindi (d. ca. 873) was an important early Muslim scientist, philosopher, and calligrapher. The Greeks greatly influenced his thought, but he examined more thoroughly the underpinnings and intellect and the emotion of sorrow. He also made major accomplishments in music and cryptanalysis (code breaking). Other topics include an overview of the Middle East and how Islam began and spread around the world. Maps and illustrations enhance the text. Glossary, Bibliography, Glossary, Chronology, Further Reading, and Index.

3105. Wagner, Heather Lehr. *Anwar Sadat and Menachem Begin: Negotiating Peace in the Middle East.* (Modern Peacemakers) Chelsea House, 2007. 122pp. ISBN 978-0-7910-9000-8. Grades 8 up.

Both Anwar Sadat and Menachem Begin received the Nobel Peace Prize for their efforts to establish peace in the Middle East. The author examines their contributions to the efforts, beginning with a summary of the 1973 October War and the events at Camp David. Also covered are their Nobel speeches, their assassinations, and other pertinent information. Photographs highlight the text. Bibliography, Chronology, Further Reading, Notes, Web Sites, and Index.

3106. Williams, Colleen Madonna Flood. *Yasir Arafat.* (Major World Leaders) Chelsea House, 2002. 112pp. ISBN 978-0-7910-6941-7; paper ISBN 978-0-7910-7186-1. Grades 5–8.

As president of the Palestinian National Authority, Yasir Arafat (1929–2004) won the Nobel Peace Prize when he and Israel's Prime Minister Begin tried to negotiate peace in the Middle East. He was an able leader who eventually did not complete the peace plan, some critics assuming that he refused to move against his unwilling constituents. He was an Al-Fatah member until 1963. Then he became the leader of the PLO. Black September and the ensuing war lasted from 1969 to 1974. Then on November 13, 1974, a peace negotiation was attempted. However, none of this lasted. Photographs and illustrations highlight the text. Chronology, Further Reading, and Index.

3107. Worth, Richard. *Saladin: Sultan of Egypt and Syria.* (Rulers of the Middle Ages) Enslow, 2007. 160pp. ISBN 978-0-7660-2712-1. Grades 7–9.

Before Saladin conquered Jerusalem in 1187, he had established his reputation as an intelligent ruler and military strategist in the Muslim world. The author discusses the Crusader Kingdoms, the Third Crusade, Saladin's battle against Richard I, and his final years. It includes primary sources such as Muslim historians contemporary to Saladin and recent historians including Amin Maalouf and Karen Armstrong. Illustrations and photographs enhance the text. Chronology, Further Reading, Glossary, Notes, Web Sites, and Index.

3108. Zenatti, Valerie. *When I Was a Soldier: A Memoir.* Bloomsbury, 2007. 240pp. Paper ISBN 978-1-59990-059-9. Grades YA.

In 1988 French emigree Valerie Zenatti looks forward to her two-year Israeli Army service. She enjoys the training, but when she has to face the politics and propaganda, she wonders who the enemy actually is. She is sympathetic to the Palestinians though not to the point of yielding any of Jerusalem, but as a non-religious Jew she has no interest in observant Jews and their non-service from the military. When she finishes, she has a different perspective about people and life.

Graphic Novels, Biographies, and Histories

3109. Satrapi, Marjane. *Persepolis: The Story of a Childhood.* Illustrated by author. Knopf, 2003. 160pp. ISBN 978-0-375-42230-0; 2004. paper ISBN 978-0-375-71457-3. Grades 7 up.

Marjane Satrapi remembers her life in Tehran from ages 6 to 14 during the Islamic Revolution when the Shah was overthrown, and Iran fought Iraq. Having been the daughter of Marxist parents and the great-granddaughter of one of Iran's last emperors, Satrapi had an unusual perspective from which to observe the change in rulers, public citizen whippings, and revered revolutionary heroes. Her parents detested the Shah, but they are equally disturbed by the rapid rise of the fundamentalist mullahs who become even more tyrannical. As a child, she made her games fit the event—becoming a prophet or Fidel Castro or pretending with her friends that the loser of a game would be tormented similarly to those in the Shah's prisons. As a teenager, she is personally distressed with the mullahs curbing of Western fashion, especially when she has to wear the veil. During the war with Iraq, her friends' homes are bombed, her playmates die, and no one can have parties. Concerned about her determined independence, Satrapi's parents send her to Austria. Her black-and-white cartoons highlight the text. The first volume in this autobiography. *New York Times Notable Books of the Year, Booklist Editors' Choice, Library Journal Best Books of the Year, Alex Awards, Great Lakes' Great Books Award* nomination, *School Library Journal Best Adult Books, Garden State Teen Book Award* (New Jersey) nomination, *Capitol Choices Noteworthy Titles* (Washington, D.C.), and *Peach Award* (Georgia) nomination.

3110. Satrapi, Marjane. *Persepolis 2: The Story of a Return.* Translated by Anjali Singh. Pantheon, 2004. 187pp. ISBN 978-0-375-42288-1; 2005. paper ISBN 978-0-375-71466-5. Grades 7 up.

See entry 2467.

DVDs

3111. *Blood and Oil: The Middle East in World War I.* Inecom, 2006. 1:52 hrs. ISBN 978-1-59218-042-4. Grades 9 up.

See entry 1889.

3112. *City Walls—My Own Private Tehran: Three Generations of Women.* Filmakers, 2007. 52 min. Grades YA.

Three generations of Iranian women describe the constraints on their lives. The filmmaker's grandmother had to marry at 13, and her husband spent any money he had on opium and alcohol. She became a maid and a wet nurse to support her six daughters. One of those daughters, the filmmaker's mother, married and divorced. The filmmaker herself, Sonia, was a child of the revolution who was allowed to attend school in Switzerland. Unmarried Iranian women still have major restrictions on their lives in their patriarchal society without any benefits remaining from the 1979 revolution.

3113. *David Malouf: An Imaginary Life.* Chip Taylor, 2003. 55 min. Grades 7 up.

David Malouf (1934–) has written important 20th-century novels including *Remembering Babylon, Johnno, 12 Edmondstone Street, The Great World, The Year of the Foxes, The Gold Coast,* and *An Imaginary Life.* He grew up in Australia as the child of a Lebanese-Christian father and an English-Jewish mother of Portuguese descent. Readings and interviews with scholars and colleagues reveal the importance of his work and his world.

3114. *Iran-Iraq War.* (The World at War) New Dimension Media, 2005. 20 min. ISBN 978-1-59522-631-0. Grades 9 up.

Iraq invaded Iran in 1980, and the Iran-Iraq war lasted until 1988. The war involved chemical weapons, long-range missile attacks, and destruction of oil shipping lanes. News footage with maps and graphics introduce important people and underlying reasons for the conflict.

3115. *Israel and Palestine: A Divided Land.* Knowledge Unlimited, 2004. 42 min. ISBN 978-1-55933-308-5. Grades 5 up.

Both Israel and Palestine have historical claims on the same land, and control over this land has shifted through time. The segments of this DVD cover Jewish persecution in Europe, British control of Palestine, Zionism, modern Jewish migration, the Holocaust, and the creation of Israel after World War II. The DVD also covers the war for Israel's independence in 1948, Nasser's desire to unite the Arab nations, and the Six-Day War of 1967 that gave Israel control of the West Bank and Golan Heights. These two peoples have opposing ideas, goals, and motivations.

3116. *Six Days in June: The War That Redefined the Middle East.* W G B H, 2007. 1:48 hrs. ISBN 978-1-59375-784-7. Grades 9 up.

From June 5 to June 10, 1967, the Israelis fought the Arabs and the United States fought the Soviet Union in a war that changed the American policy toward the Middle East. Interviews, primary source documents of film footage, radio and television broadcasts, and photographs show how the Middle Eastern countries still blame the United States and Britain for supporting Israel.

3117. *A Team for Peace.* Landmark Media, 2004. 45 min. Grades 7 up.

Johann Koss, winner of several Olympic medals at the 1994 Lillehammer games, agreed with Mahatma Gandhi that children who played together could be friends. He formed a soccer team of Palestinian and Israeli students and entered them in the largest international youth tournament, the Norway Cup in Oslo. Their coaches, an Arab and an Israeli, worked together with them, based on Koss's nonprofit, Right to Play. The DVD presents this team and their efforts for peace at the local level.

3118. *Two Islamic Regimes in Cairo.* (Glories of Islamic Art) Landmark Media, 2007. 45 min. Grades 11 up.

Cairo displays the heritage of two Islamic regimes—the Shi'ite Fatimids who came from North Africa and the Mamluks, slave soldiers who seized freedom and established a Sunni dynasty. This video shows the beautiful architecture they created—the Al-Athar Mosque, for example, where Sunnis worship today—and profiles key characters including the governor Ibn Tulun and the caliph Hakim. The DVD points out the reverence that Islam has shown through the centuries for knowledge and learning. When this respect began to disappear, the religion began to weaken, but there are hopes that the new library in Alexandria will begin to strengthen Islam again.

3119. *The Umayyads and Their Capital, Damascus.* (The Glories of Islamic Art) Landmark Media, 2007. 45 min. Grades 11 up.

The Umayyads, the first Islamic dynasty, formed their capital at Damascus. Their power spread through Syria, and they left a heritage of grand buildings including the Great Mosque of Damascus and the Dome of the Rock in Jerusalem. They adapted materials and ideas including columns and capitals from the Byzantines. Their achievements also spread to Spain in Andalusia and the included the influence of Salah-al-Din, Saladin, the warrior who defeated the crusaders. He started his own regime, the Ayyubids, and its legacies include Aleppo, a citadel that Tamerlane finally conquered.

Compact Discs

3120. Amirrezvani, Anita. *The Blood of Flowers: A Novel.* Narrated by Shohreh Aghdashloo. Hachette audio, 2007. 11 CDs; 13 hrs. ISBN 978-1-59483-912-2. Grades YA.

See entry 3029.

3121. Dietrich, William. *The Rosetta Key.* Narrated by Jeff Woodman. (Ethan Gage) HarperAudio, 2008. 11 CDs; 12.5 hrs. ISBN 978-0-06-146885-8. Grades YA.

See entry 1388.

3122. Friedman, Thomas. *From Beirut to Jerusalem.* Narrated by Thomas L. Friedman. HarperAudio, 2006. 3 CDs; 3 hrs. ISBN 978-0-06-128425-0. Grades YA.

See entry 3090.

3123. Hosseini, Khaled. *A Thousand Splendid Suns.* Narrated by Atossa Leoni. Simon & Schuster, 2007. 11 CDs; 12 hrs. ISBN 978-0-7435-5445-9. Grades YA.

See entry 2488.

3124. Moore, Christopher. *Lamb: The Gospel According to Biff, Christ's Childhood Pal.* Narrated by Fisher Stevens. HarperAudio, 2007. 464pp. 12 CDs; 15 hrs. ISBN 978-0-06-123878-9; HarperCollins, 2003. paper ISBN 978-0-380-81381-0. Grades YA.

See entry 3038.

MEXICO, CARIBBEAN, SOUTH AND CENTRAL AMERICA

Historical Fiction and Fantasy

3125. Abelove, Joan. *Go and Come Back.* Puffin, 2000. 176pp. Paper ISBN 978-0-14-130694-0. Grades 8–10.

After anthropologists Joanna and Margarita arrive in Poincushmana, Peru, in the 1970s, they meet Alicia and other members of the tribe who question their purpose. The anthropologists seem stingy because they do not offer them things. During the course of the year, the women observe the tribal customs of farming, child rearing, marriage, sex, and death. Alicia adopts a child whose father is beginning to abuse her, and through the child, the women and Alicia begin to communicate. *Garden State Teen Book Award* (New Jersey).

3126. Alphin, Elaine Marie. *A Bear for Miguel.* Illustrated by Joan Sandin. (I Can Read Books Level 3) HarperTrophy, 1997. 64pp. Paper ISBN 978-0-06-444234-3. Grades K–3.

In the 1980s María's father cannot work because the guerrillas will punish him if he works in El Salvador's government-owned factory, and the government will punish him if he works for the guerrillas. He has to trade family items for food, and María goes with him to the market. After her father goes away, she finds people who want to trade food for her stuffed bear, her favorite thing. They want to give the bear to their wounded son, and she decides to help both her family and the child. Glossary.*Americas Award for Children's and Young Adult Literature* nomination.

3127. Alvarez, Julia. *Before We Were Free.* Knopf, 2002. 192pp. ISBN 978-0-375-81544-7; 2004. paper ISBN 978-0-440-23784-6. Grades 6 up.

In 1960, 12-year-old Anita de la Torre has to adjust to the abrupt departure of her friends and cousins, the Garcia girls, from the Dominican Republic. While pining about her crush, Sam, an American boy, she realizes that adults are whispering around her and that the secret police (SIM) are camping in her driveway. The story reveals her realizations as a naive girl trying to understand her family's changing situation while adults attempt to overthrow the dictatorship of General Trujillo, El Jefe. After the assassination, Anita's father and uncle are arrested, and she and her mother go into hiding in a friends' closet, as reported in her diary. Eventually they survive, but many have been tortured and killed during the terrible last years of the regime. *Pura Belpré Award, Sequoyah Book Award*

(Oklahoma) nomination, *Dorothy Canfield Fisher Children's Book Award* (Vermont) nomination, *Reader's Choice Awards* (Virginia) nomination, *Americas Book Award*, *American Library Association Best Books for Young Adults*, *American Library Association Notable Children's Books*, *Capitol Choices Noteworthy Titles* (Washington, D.C.), *Volunteer State Book Award* (Tennessee) nomination, and *Young Adult Book Award* (South Carolina) nomination.

3128. Alvarez, Julia. *In the Time of the Butterflies.* Algonquin, 1994. 325pp. ISBN 978-1-56512-038-9; Plume, 1995. paper ISBN 978-0-452-27442-6. Grades YA.

The three Mirabel sisters—Minerva, Patria, and Maria Teresa—become martyrs of the movement during the liberation of the Dominican Republic from Trujillo in 1960 when they are murdered while returning from visiting their husbands in prison. Their sister Dede remembers their unique attributes as young girls.

3129. Benitez, Sandra. *Bitter Grounds.* Picador, 1998. Paper ISBN 978-0-312-19541-0. Grades YA.

Between 1933 and 1977, three generations of El Salvadoran women face political upheaval. In their different social classes, they have unequal economic benefits and educational opportunities, but are united in their fear of the future.

3130. Berry, James. *Ajeemah and His Son.* Trophy, 1994. 84pp. Paper ISBN 978-0-06-440523-2. Grades 7 up.

See entry 2544.

3131. Bridal, Tessa. *The Tree of Red Stars.* Milkweed, 1998. 287pp. Paper ISBN 978-1-57131-023-1. Grades YA.

When the privileged Magda is 15 in Montevideo, Uruguay, her life changes direction when she hears Che Guevara address a university rally. She begins to see the poverty of the underclass in her country and to understand how they have been downtrodden. She then spends a year abroad in Michigan before returning to join the Tupamaros guerrilla movement to overcome the government. Eventually the military arrests her, and when a high-ranking friend helps her get a release, he is arrested. She goes to Europe for seven years where she implores human-rights agencies to help free him.

3132. Chupack, Edward. *Silver: My Own Tale as Written by Me with a Goodly Amount of Murder.* Thomas Dunne, 2008. 275pp. ISBN 978-0-312-37365-8. Grades YA.

Long John Silver from *Treasure Island* tells the story of his life from the days of his poverty-stricken childhood through his time as a pirate captain, while en route to London for his execution. When he was a motherless orphan living in the streets, a homeless blind man looked after him until he got a job in a tavern. There Long John met Black John, one of the greatest pirates of the day, and boarded his ship, the *Linda Marie*. This man gave Long John his name. Through his life, Long John has pursued a particular treasure, the location of which is contained in a set of clues hidden in Edward Peach's old Bible. Long John spares only two women from the Carolinas, sisters Mary and Evangelize, from the ships he takes in his life long quest.

3133. Collison, Linda. *Star-Crossed.* Knopf, 2006. 408pp. ISBN 978-0-375-83363-2. Grades 9 up.

After her father's death in 1760, penniless Patricia Kelley, 17, leaves the British boarding school she has attended for ten years and heads for his estate in Barbados. She stows away aboard a merchant ship, and when she is discovered begins to help the overworked ship's doctor, Aeneas MacPherson. At night, she dresses in men's clothing and climbs the rigging. There she meets Brian Dalton, a bosun's mate beneath her social class. In Barbados she discovers she cannot claim the property, and she marries the surgeon. They work against yellow fever and, after he dies, she disguises herself again and signs on as a ship's surgeon. On the same ship is Dalton, and no longer fettered by social status, the two can express their love.

3134. Dorris, Michael. *Morning Girl.* Hyperion, 1999. 74pp. Paper ISBN 978-0-7868-1358-2. Grades 3–7.

In 1492 Morning Girl and Star Boy live with their parents on a Bahamian island. Their world changes when Columbus finds them and imposes new concepts of culture on their society. *Scott O'Dell Award.*

3135. Duranto, Julia. *The Walls of Cartagena.* Illustrated by Tom Pohrt. Simon & Schuster, 2008. 152pp. ISBN 978-1-4169-4102-6. Grades 4–7.

Calepino, 13, arrived in Cartagena as a baby on a slave ship where his captured mother died at his birth. A kind white noblewoman raises him and gives him an education. He learns to read and is gifted enough to learn eleven languages. He then serves as a translator for the Jesuit priest, Father Pedro, who takes water, food, and medicine to the captives on the slave ships in dock, and he works with Dr. López in the leper colony. When Calepino sees a newly arrived captive from Angola with her son, he vows to help them, and his contact with the Jewish Dr. Lopéz, whose family was persecuted in the Inquisition, helps him. Small pencil drawings embellish the text.

3136. Engle, Margarita. *The Surrender Tree: Poems of Cuba's Struggle for Freedom.* Holt, 2008. 176pp. ISBN 978-0-8050-8674-4. Grades 7 up.

During the period 1850 to 1899, Cuba fought for its independence from Spain. Free-verse poetry presents Rosa, a traditional healer, who helps runaway slaves and deserters in caves and other hideaways; her husband, José, a freed slave; and Silvia, a slave camp escapee whom Rosa teaches nursing skills. The man pursuing them all, known as Lieutenant Death, wants to capture and kill them because they have escaped the system that he admires. Included is a reference to the "reconcentration" camps where captured slaves, sometimes minus their ears, which Lieutenant Death displayed, were held prisoner. Chronology and Note. *Newbery Honor Book, Pura Belpré Award, Americas Award for Children and Young Adult Literature, Jane Addams Children's Book Award, Children's Book Committee Award for Poetry,* and *Notable Trade Books in the Field of Social Studies.*

3137. Falconer, Colin. *Feathered Serpent: A Novel of the Mexican Conquest.* Three Rivers, 2003. 374pp. Paper ISBN 978-1-4000-4957-8. Grades YA.

The father of Aztec Malinali (Don Marina) tells her that she will bring the downfall of Motecuhzoma when the Feathered Serpent arrives. Motecuhzoma's men immediately kill him and enslave her. When Spanish conquistador Hernán Cortés appears on the scene, Malinali thinks he is the Feathered Serpent. She speaks seven languages and becomes his translator and consort, telling him the local customs, including the tearing out of hearts, and others give him gold. Her help made it easier for Cortés to conquer them all, and her name is still maligned in Mexico nearly five hundred years later.

3138. Finley, Mary Peace. *Soaring Eagle.* Eakin, 1998. 166pp. Paper ISBN 978-1-57168-281-9. Grades 4–9.

In Mexico in 1845 Julio Montoya wonders who his family is, because he is blond-haired and green-eyed. When Julio's father returns to Taos, the two follow the trail to Bent's Fort. After Apaches kill his father, Julio must survive a snowstorm, a wolf attack, and then snowblindness. Cheyenne Indians find him, nurse him back to health, and claim him as one of their own. While wondering about his childhood, Julio adapts to this new tribe and earns his own name, Soaring Eagle. He never answers his questions, but he finds surrogate family support.

3139. Flores-Galbis, Enrique. *Raining Sardines.* Deborah Brodie, 2007. 160pp. ISBN 978-1-59643-166-9. Grades 4–6.

In pre-revolutionary Cuba, Don Rigol, a wealthy landowner, decides that he wants the mountain near the town he controls. He starts clearing the jungle for his coffee plantation, but Ernestina, his spoiled daughter's classmate, and her friend, Enriquito, decide that they will save the wild horses living on the mountain. Soon, however, they understand that Don Rigol's real purpose is to find the gold that, according to Taino legend, is in the mountain. The two become involved in a series of adventures, some filled with magic realism, as they strive to save both the horses and the gold. They eventually succeed.

3140. Garland, Sherry. *In the Shadow of the Alamo.* Gulliver, 2001. 288pp. ISBN 978-0-15-201744-6. Grades 6–8.

Having never before left his village, Lorenzo Bonifacio, 15, finds himself conscripted in the Mexican Army for ten years. His troop is to retake the Alamo from the North American settlers. He and the wealthy Esteban Esquivel, 17, avoid each other initially, but they become friends as they face hardships such as hunger and poor weapons, and deal with the cruel and egotistical Santa Anna who wants personal glory regardless of the cost.

3141. Greene, Jacqueline Dembar. *Out of Many Waters.* Iuniverse, 2006. 200pp. Paper ISBN 978-0-595-38047-3. Grades 5–8.

After being kidnapped by Portuguese Catholics during the Portuguese Inquisition in 1648, sisters Isobel (age 12) and Maria (age 16) try to escape from Brazil in 1654 by stowing away on different ships. Hoping to reach Amsterdam, where she thinks her parents and Maria might be, Isobel reaches New Amsterdam instead. After enduring storms and pirates, she becomes one of the 23 immigrants to be New Amsterdam's first Jewish refugees. *One Foot Ashore* tells Maria's story. *Sydney Taylor Honor Book* and *New York Public Library Book for the Teen Age.*

3142. Ibbotson, Eva. *Journey to the River Sea.* Penguin, 2002. 304pp. ISBN 978-0-525-46739-7; Puffin, 2003. paper ISBN 978-0-14-250184-9. Grades 4–7.

In 1910 wealthy orphan Maia Fielding leaves London's Mayfair Academy for Young Ladies with her governess, Miss Minton, to live with relatives on the Amazon River near Manaus in Brazil. The Carter family turns out to be more interested in the girl's money than in Maia. Mr. Carter is a thief running a nearly defunct rubber plantation, and Mrs. Carter and her twin daughters, Beatrice and Gwendolyn, stay inside their home, more interested in tea than in their surroundings. Maia and Miss Minton must sneak out to enjoy the area's natural beauty. Among others who appear are a child actor, Clovis King, whom Maia met on the ship to Brazil, and a runaway named Finn, a local Indian boy and son of the recently deceased Mr. Taverner, a naturalist. When British agents arrive to take Mr. Taverner's son back to England, they do not know what he looks like;

therefore, Maia helps to thwart the transfer. *Nene Award* (Hawaii) nomination, *Sasquatch Reading Award* (Washington) nomination, *Children's Book Award* (West Virginia) nomination, *Capitol Choices Noteworthy Titles* (Washington, D.C.), *American Library Association Notable Children's Books; Beehive Award* (Utah) nomination; *Rebecca Caudill Award* (Illinois) nomination, *Children's Book Award* (Massachusetts) nomination, *School Library Journal Best Children's Books*, and *Reader's Choice Award* (Virginia) nomination.

3143. Johnson, Charles. *Pieces of Eight.* Illustrated by Jennie A. Nelson. (Footprints in Time) Discovery, 1989. ISBN 978-0-944770-00-9. Grades 3–6.

David and Mitchell worry about the house they've moved into because a sea captain once owned it. Eventually they meet the ghost of a sailor in the house and ask him to help them meet Blackbeard the pirate. He takes them to 1716 in the Caribbean where Blackbeard's crew captures them and forces them to serve on his ship. They encounter terrible storms, endure naval battles, and meet cannibals with the Brothers of the Coast before the ghost saves them.

3144. Kirwan, Anna Wilson. *Lady of Palenque: Flower of Bacal.* (Royal Diaries) Scholastic, 2004. 204pp. ISBN 978-0-439-40971-1. Grades 4–7.

ShahnaK'in Yaxchel Pacal (Green Jay), 13, leaves her Mayan father, King Hanaab Pacal, of Lakamha City (Palenque) to meet her future husband, King Fire Keeper, in Xukpip during 749. On her journey, she faces both natural disasters and human enemies. She has to become self-reliant, overcome homesickness, and must serve her husband as a "xoc," a reader or an accountant, as her mother had done. Photographs augment the text. Notes and Maps.

3145. Krill, Dareen. *Escape from Treasure Island.* (Uncle Duncle Chronicles) Lobster, 2006. 335pp. Paper ISBN 978-1-897073-31-5. Grades 4–6.

Sixth-grader Sage Smiley looks forward to spending the summer with his Uncle Dunkirk. During their visit, Sage discovers that Uncle Dunkirk has a magic stone that will take him anywhere at any time. The two end up on Treasure Island when their World War II Supermarine Spitfire plane crashes. John Silver's men capture Uncle Dunkirk, but together they save a group of prisoners and claim the abundant treasure. *Manitoba Young Readers' Choice Award.*

3146. Lasky, Kathryn. *Pirate Bob.* Illustrated by David Clark. Charlesbridge, 2006. 32pp. ISBN 978-1-57091-595-6. Grades K–3.

Bob, a pirate, has the job of cutting steering cables to cripple ships that he and his shipmates plan to loot. When the pirates attack, each one has a specific job to complete in order to accomplish their mission. Bob's friend, Yellow Jack, shares with him his hopes and dreams and desire for happiness. Watercolor and ink illustrations complement the text.

3147. McCunn, Ruthanne Lum. *God of Luck.* Soho, 2007. 256pp. ISBN 978-1-56947-466-2; 2008. paper ISBN 978-1-56947-518-8. Grades YA.

See entry 2893.

3148. Machado, Ana Maria. *From Another World.* Illustrated by Lúcia Brandão. Translated by Luisa Baeta. Groundwood, 2005. 136pp. ISBN 978-0-8889-9597-1; 2006. paper ISBN 978-0-8889-9641-1. Grades 4–8.

Mariano and his friends Leo, Elisa, and Teresa, help his parents transform an old Brazilian coffee plantation into an inn, and during the process, Mariano meets the ghost of Rosario, a slave girl from the 1800s. She tells them how their owner locked the family in a burning barn to avoid freeing them when slavery was outlawed. She asks for their help. Only her brother Amaro survived to inherit the plantation. Later Leo and Elisa's grandmother tells them the family's history, and they surmise the rest of the story. Little by little, Mariano records the story although he has never set quietly to even read a book. Machado received the *Hans Christian Andersen Award* for her body of work.

3149. O'Dell, Scott. *The Captive.* Houghton, 1979. 244pp. ISBN 978-0-395-27811-6. Grades 7 up.

In the first of a trilogy, Julian, a seminarian, arrives in the New World from Seville, Spain, in 1506. He realizes that the captain has come for gold rather than to save the heathens, and Julian refuses to keep his share of the loot. The natives, however, think that the blond Julian is the risen Kukulcán, come back to life after 400 years to save them. When Julian sees the power that his disguise gives him over the Mayan priests, the thrill seduces him.

3150. Rosario, Nelly. *Song of the Water Saints.* Vintage, 2003. 256pp. Paper ISBN 978-0-375-72549-4. Grades YA.

Three generations of Dominican women—Graciela, Mercedes, and Leila—span the 20th century. Graciela escapes a life of poverty and marries her lover. He disappears, and she meets an American, works as a maid briefly, and returns to her family and a young daughter, Mercedes. Mercedes marries Andres, a dwarf, and begins a new life with him in New York City during the 1980s. Eventually, she must care for her strong-headed 12-year-old granddaughter Leila in New York, who inherits Graciela's restless traits.

3151. Schmidt, C. A. *Useful Fools.* Dutton, 2007. 262pp. ISBN 978-0-525-47814-0. Grades 8 up.

Alonso, 15, is a *cholos*, an Indian who lives on the edge of Lima, Peru, around 1980. His mother, Magda, organizes the clinic where the father of a white girl, Rosa, is a physician. Alonso meets Rosa at the clinic, and they fall in love. When the Senderistas, Shining Path revolutionary guerrillas, bomb the clinic, Alonso's mother dies and the police show no more compassion than the bombers. The bombers call her a "useful fool" for the government for organizing the clinic. Alonso's drunken father loses his job, and the family must move to a dwelling with neither electricity nor running water. Since he is so desperate, the guerrillas persuade Alonso to join them in the mountains. Alonso and Rosa tell their stories in alternating viewpoints. *Booklist Editors' Choice.*

3152. Scieszka, Jon. *Me Oh Maya.* Illustrated by Adam McCauley. (Time Warp Trio, # 13) Penguin, 2003. 80pp. ISBN 978-0-670-03629-5; Puffin, 2005. paper ISBN 978-0-14-240300-6. Grades 3–5.

This book plops Joe, Fred, and Sam into the ring-ball court in Chichen Itza, Mexico, in 1000 where they must play for their lives against a Mayan High Priest, Kakapupahed, after he sentences them to death as a sacrifice to the harvest gods. Fortunately, their basketball skills enable them to win the battle with a little help from the high priest's nephew, Jun. Before they can get back to Brooklyn, they learn about the Mayan calendar and some differences between Mayan culture and their own. *Garden State Children's Book Awards* (New Jersey) nomination.

3153. Sciuba, Katie. *Oye, Celia! A Song for Celia Cruz.* Illustrated by Edel Rodriguez. Holt, 2007. 32pp. ISBN 978-0-8050-7468-0. Grades K–4.

A young girl carries her favorite salsa superstar Celia Cruz (1925–2003) record, and happens to see a neighborhood dance party. She repeats the lyrics to some of the songs that Cruz sang to her loyal Cuban audience and shows the range of emotions that Cruz created. Illustrations enhance the text.

3154. Strickland, Brad. *The Guns of Tortuga.* Aladdin, 2003. 195pp. Paper ISBN 978-0-689-85297-8. Grades 5–8.

In the 1680s orphan Davy Shea, 12, accompanies his surgeon uncle, Patch, on the frigate *Aurora.* The vessel's secret mission is to rid the seas of pirates, especially the evil Jack Steele. Captain Hunter goes ashore at Tortuga, a notorious pirate den, to ask the men there to help him stop Steele. He discovers that pirates are holding British officers, and he wants to rescue them. He asks Davy to go undercover as a servant boy on the ship to aid the mission.

3155. Torrey, Michele. *Voyage of Plunder: A Chronicle of Courage.* (Chronicles of Courage) Knopf, 2005. 192pp. ISBN 978-0-375-82383-1; Yearling, 2007. paper ISBN 978-0-440-41887-0. Grades 7–12.

In 1696 Daniel Markham, 14, is on his way with his father and new stepmother from Boston to Jamaica when pirates led by Josiah Black board the ship and murder his father. Then they press him into service on their ship, where he learns about the connection between his father and Black. The murder had been carefully planned. Daniel wants to stay alive, and comes to realize he is more like Black than he could have imagined. Bibliography, Further Reading, and Glossary.

3156. Vargas Llosa, Mario. *The Feast of the Goat.* Translated by Edith Grossman. Picador, 2002. 432pp. Paper ISBN 978-0-312-42027-7. Grades YA.

Vargas Llosa interweaves the story of Rafael Trujillo?s brutal dictatorship of the Dominican Republic and of his assassination in 1961 with the experiences of Urania Cabral, who returns to the country three decades later and learns more about the regime and about her father, Trujillo?s secretary of state.

3157. Veciana-Suarez, Ana. *Flight to Freedom.* Orchard, 2002. 215pp. ISBN 978-0-439-38199-4. Grades 6–9.

Yara, 13, records her life in 1967 Havana, Cuba, where she hates the youth work camps, rations, and hostility toward her anti-Castro family. When her father applies to leave Cuba, he is sent to the countryside to harvest coffee while awaiting permission. She continues to record her life after they arrive in Miami, Florida, to unite with other relatives. She has to learn a new language and cultural differences while her father is convinced they will not have to stay too long. Even though family tension continues throughout, Yara enjoys the freedoms that her new home offers. *Sunshine State Young Reader Award* (Florida) nomination.

3158. Wechter, Nell Wise, and Bruce Tucker. *Teach's Light.* University of North Carolina, 1999. 160pp. Paper ISBN 978-0-8078-4793-0. Grades 4–7.

When Corky Calhoun and Toby Davis, two teenagers from North Carolina's Outer Banks, decide to find Teach's Light in the Little Dismal Swamp, they experience a sudden explosion and find themselves in 1681 England. There they safely float above the town and watch the orphaned Edward Teach decide to stow away on a ship crossing the Atlantic. Teach (soon to be known as Blackbeard) begins a career as a pirate in the Caribbean aboard the *Queen Anne's Revenge*. British soldiers finally behead him during a sea battle. When Corky and Toby return to the present, they have not found the light that supposedly guards some of Blackbeard's treasure, but they have learned a lot about the man who might have hidden it.

3159. Whelan, Gloria. *The Disappeared.* Dial, 2008. 144pp. ISBN 978-0-8037-3275-9. Grades 6 up.

In Buenos Aires, Argentina, in 1976, military police arrest Silvia Diaz's 17-year-old brother Eduardo for opposing the government. Silvia decides to save him by making General Lopez's son, Norberto, fall in love with her and free Eduardo. She fears Eduardo will become one of *los Desaparecidos* (the Disappeared), never to be seen again. After she risks her own safety and her reputation, she discovers that her physician father has bargained for Eduardo's life by promising to give General Lopez lifesaving surgery.

3160. Wood, Barbara. *Daughter of the Sun.* St. Martin's, 2007. 480pp. Paper ISBN 978-0-312-36368-0. Grades YA.

When Hoshi'tiwa's farmer father brags about the rain jars she has made, Jakl, the Dark Lord of Center Place—their Toltec capital, enslaves the 17-year-old girl, planning to use her special gift to stop the acute drought around the city. Instead of doing as expected, Hoshi'tiwa starts saying what she thinks about life and suggesting change. Jakl begins to fall in love with her, but Lady White Orchid, an aristocrat who wants Jakl for herself, has other plans. Yet another character, Xikli, hopes to use the drought to stage a coup and remove Jakl from power. Eventually Hoshi'tiwa emerges as a leader herself.

3161. Yolen, Jane. *The Ballad of the Pirate Queens.* Voyager, 1998. Unpaged. Paper ISBN 978-0-15-201885-6. Grades 3–6.

This story, in ballad form, tells about two famous pirate queens, Anne Bonney and Mary Reade, who try to save their ship in 1720 when the governor's men climb aboard in Port Maria Bay; their pirate husbands and other crew members stay below drinking and gambling. The women stand trial along with the men, but they are set free because they are pregnant. The men, however, are convicted and hang on the gallows. Author's Note. *Bulletin Blue Ribbon Book, International Reading Association Children's Choices* and *American Library Association Notable Books for Children.*

History

3162. Ackroyd, Peter. *Cities of Blood.* (Voyages Through Time) DK, 2004. 144pp. ISBN 978-0-7566-0729-6; 2005. paper ISBN 978-0-7566-1367-9. Grades 4–7.

Readers learn about the "mother culture" of the Olmec in Mesoamerica and the ancient cities and life of the Maya, Aztecs, and Incas. The book presents information about religion, politics, warfare, and the path to their destruction. Tenochtitlan, an Aztec city, was the largest city outside Asia in the early 1500s and other important cities were the Mayan Tikal and the Incan Machu Picchu. These societies practiced human sacrifices and cannibalism. Photographs highlight the text. Chronology and Glossary.

3163. Aveni, Anthony. *The First Americans: From the Great Migration to the Splendid Cities of the Maya.* (The First Americans) Scholastic, 2005. 125pp. ISBN 978-0-439-55144-1. Grades 4–6.

Before explorers arrived in the Americas, the natives had accomplished much. Among the first Americans were the Taíno; League of the Iroquois; the Ohio Moundbuilders; the Anasazi; the Kwakiutl, Tlingit, and Haida; the Timucua; and the Mississippian pyramid city of Cahokia. The text covers the religion, food, dress, social organization, and customs of these cultures that arrived in the Americas by boat or land bridge. Photographs, sidebars, and illustrations highlight the text. Maps, Chronology, Web Sites, and Index.

3164. Bingham, Jane. *The Aztec Empire.* (Time Travel Guides) Raintree, 2007. 64pp. ISBN 978-1-4109-2730-9; paper ISBN 978-1-4109-3046-0. Grades 5–9.

Written as a travel guide to the Aztec Empire, this book relates the cultural and historical details of this time period. Using a time-travel framework and the present tense, Bingham shows maps and imparts facts about the culture, locations, relics and artifacts, and other salient information such as the two calendars. Photographs and reproductions enhance the text. Glossary, Chronology, Further Reading, and Index.

3165. Bingham, Jane. *The Inca Empire.* (Time Travel Guides) Raintree, 2007. 64pp. ISBN 978-1-4109-2731-6; paper ISBN 978-1-4109-3047-7. Grades 5–9.

Written as a travel guide to the Inca Empire, this narrative relates cultural and historical details of this time period. Using a time-travel framework and the present tense, Bingham shows maps and imparts facts about the culture, key locations, relics and artifacts, and other salient information. Photographs and reproductions enhance the text. Glossary, Chronology, Further Reading, and Index.

3166. Carey, Charles W. *Castro's Cuba.* (History Firsthand) Greenhaven, 2004. 205pp. ISBN 978-0-7377-1654-2. Grades 7 up.

Primary sources including interviews, articles, and first-person accounts present Fidel Castro's 1959 revolution against the Cuban government. The writings include the words of Castro and Che Guevara, a member of the revolutionary group. The text also offers an assessment of the current situation in Cuba. Photographs and illustrations highlight the text. Bibliography, Chronology, Notes, and Index.

3167. Clifford, Barry. *Real Pirates: The Untold Story of the Whydah, from Slave Ship to Pirate Ship.* Illustrated by Kenneth Garrett. National Geographic, 2007. 175pp. Paper ISBN 978-1-4262-0262-9. Grades YA.

In 1715 the *Whydah*, a sailing vessel, made one trip to Africa and returned to the Caribbean with a cargo of slaves. Then "Black Sam" Bellamy captured her, pirated treasure on the sea, and took her off Cape Cod where she sank two months later. The ship was raised in 1984 and, after looking at the cargo and piecing together some of the evidence about the pirates, researchers theorize that the pirates were multiethnic men who lived in a democratic society and probably were much happier than they would have been serving as slaves or working at hard labor. Only one instance of plank-walking has been recorded, and pirates did not bury their treasure. Photographs, maps, and illustrations enliven the text. Bibliography.

3168. Finkelstein, Norman. *Thirteen Days/Ninety Miles: The Cuban Missile Crisis.* Iuniverse, 2001. 160pp. Paper ISBN 978-0-595-15654-2. Grades YA.

Using information recently declassified, Finkelstein describes the events that led to the discovery that the Soviet Union had placed missiles in Cuba and John F. Kennedy's resulting blockade of the country. Because communication was much less rapid at that time, tension developed that could have led to a nuclear war. Finkelstein recreates that tension. Bibliography and Index.

3169. Freedman, Russell. *Who Was First? Discovering the Americas.* Clarion, 2007. 88pp. ISBN 978-0-618-66391-0. Grades 5–9.

Freedman examines the various theories about who actually discovered the Americas. He includes the voyages of Columbus, the belief that the Chinese explorer Zheng may have come, and the possibility that Vikings settled in Newfoundland around 1000 Native Americans were also here, most likely having crossed from Siberia over an ice bridge according to theories that have recently been questioned. Among the clues about origins are Stone Age migration, DNA links, and carbon-dated artifacts. Photographs and illustrations enhance the text. Bibliography, Notes, and Index. *Horn Book Fanfare, Booklist Editors' Choice, Voice of Youth Advocates Nonfiction Honor List, Kirkus Reviews Editor's Choice,* and *School Library Journal Best Books for Children.*

3170. Galvin, Irene Flum. *The Ancient Maya.* Benchmark, 1996. 80pp. ISBN 978-0-7614-0091-2. Grades 6–8.

Galvin presents the Mayan culture through its art, poetry, religion, language, and way of life. Among the topics are hieroglyphs, the three separate Mayan calendars, and the study of astronomy, which the Mayans pursued. Illustrations aid the text. Bibliography, Chronology, Further Reading, Glossary, and Index.

3171. Ganeri, Anita. *Ancient Maya.* Illustrated by Chris Forsey. (Ancient Civilizations) Compass Point, 2006. 32pp. ISBN 978-0-7565-1677-2; paper ISBN 978-0-7565-1758-8. Grades 3–5.

A look at the Mayan civilization's daily life. Among the topics are how the Maya ruled their cities, their interest in studying the stars, and how they worshiped their gods. Additional information covers their arts, crafts, fashion, food, and agriculture with sidebars offering clarification. Illustrations and maps enrich the text.

3172. Gay, Kathlyn. *Spanish American War.* (Voices from The Past) Twenty First Century, 1995. 64pp. ISBN 978-0-8050-2847-8. Grades 7–9.

Letters, diaries, and newspaper accounts give an overview of the causes, the battles, and the results of the Spanish American War, which the United States fought against Spain in 1898. Photographs, Maps, Further Reading, Notes, and Index.

3173. Gruber, Beth. *Ancient Inca: Archaeology Unlocks the Secrets of the Inca's Past.* (National Geographic Investigates) National Geographic, 2006. 64pp. ISBN 978-0-7922-7827-6. Grades 3–7.

While excavating the Inca, archaeologists have unexpectedly discovered mummies, including one called the "Ice Maiden"; pottery; textiles; and Coricancha, a magnificent temple of worship that allows researchers to understand the Inca's spiritual culture more insightfully. Information about the archaeologists' processes of study helps to clarify the lives of the Inca. Photographs highlight the text. Bibliography, Glossary, Chronology, Further Reading, Web Sites, and Index.

3174. Hamilton, John. *A History of Pirates.* (Pirates!) ABDO, 2007. 32pp. ISBN 978-1-59928-761-4. Grades 3–6.

Readers will learn about the history of pirating, focusing on the Golden Age of Piracy between the late 1600s and the mid-1700s. It includes background about daily life on a pirate ship, the politics of piracy, weapons that pirates preferred, and rules of engagement. Photographs and reproductions enhance the text. Glossary and Index.

3175. Hamilton, John. *A Pirate's Life.* (Pirates!) ABDO, 2007. 32pp. ISBN 978-1-59928-762-1. Grades 3–6.

The author examines a pirate's life aboard ship. The book includes background about what they wore, what their assignments might be, the punishments they received for breaking rules, and the circumstances of female pirates. Photographs and reproductions augment the text. Glossary and Index.

3176. Harris, Nathaniel. *Ancient Maya: Archaeology Unlocks the Secrets of the Maya's Past.* (National Geographic Investigates) National Geographic, 2008. 64pp. ISBN 978-1-4263-0227-5. Grades 4–7.

Readers learn about the Mayan civilization as they read about the archaeological discoveries at places such as Palenque and Uxmal. Information about the methods used by archaeologists and their tools (satellite technology, for example) and techniques add interest.

3177. Hibbert, Clare. *Real Pirates: Over 20 True Stories of Seafaring.* Illustrated by John James. Enchanted Lion, 2003. 48pp. ISBN 978-1-59270-018-9. Grades 5–9.

This book, which is divided into the four geographical areas—the Caribbean, the Atlantic, the Pacific, and the Indian Ocean, presents twenty different pirate stories. Among pirates discussed are William Fly, Captain Crabbe, Black Bart, Blackbeard, William Kidd, Anne Bonny, and Mary Read. Each had special talents and, with the help of pirate tools, collected booty in whatever way they chose. Information about life aboard ship and fighting techniques show a pirate's life. Illustrations enhance the text.

3178. Hinshaw, Kelly Campbell. *Ancient Mexico.* (Art Across the Ages) Chronicle, 2007. 32.pp. ISBN 978-0-8118-5670-6; paper ISBN 978-0-8118-5671-3. Grades 1–3.

The author either asks questions of young readers or points out details in accompanying photographs and reproductions that help readers understand ancient Mexico's art.

3179. Hynson, Colin. *You Wouldn't Want to Be an Inca Mummy! A One-Way Journey You'd Rather Not Make.* (You Wouldn't Want To . . .) Franklin Watts, 2007. 32pp. ISBN 978-0-531-18744-9. Grades 3–6.

The author describes the life of an Inca ruler and how he might have controlled his empire. He also discusses the royal household, religious customs, the feast day of the sun, how mummies dried, and what happened to rulers when they became mummies—deceased rulers were worshiped as if they were gods. Illustrations enhance the text. Glossary and Index.

3180. Jovinelly, Joann, and Jason Netelkos. *The Crafts and Culture of the Ancient Aztecs.* (Crafts of the Ancient World) Rosen, 2006. 48pp. ISBN 978-0-8239-3512-3. Grades 4–8.

The author examines the culture and the crafts in Aztec society. Information about daily life, beliefs, warfare, language, and art appears under culture. Topics discussed as crafts are a warrior helmet (warfare), a mosaic mask (rituals and celebrations), a Chacmool statue (religion and beliefs), the codex writing and literature), the Great Temple (art and architecture), an Aztec bowl (Aztec craftspeople), beaded jewelry (decorative arts), and an Aztec flute (leisure and play). Illustrations enhance the text. Glossary, Chronology, Further Reading, and Index.

3181. Konstam, Angus. *Scourge of the Seas: Buccaneers, Pirates and Privateers.* Osprey, 2007. 240pp. ISBN 978-1-84603-211-0. Grades YA.

Containing background information about pirates, this volume covers the differences between pirates, who attacked any ship regardless of nationality; privateers, who were persons or vessels under government contract; and buccaneers, who were generally French and English raiders of the Spanish Main. The next three sections discuss each group's culture and traditions, including dress, hygiene, organization, weapons, and tactics in battle. Short profiles of famous pirates complete the discussion. Reproductions, charts, and maps enhance the text. Bibliography, Glossary, and Index.

3182. Kops, Deborah. *Palenque.* (Unearthing Ancient Worlds) Twenty First Century, 2008. 80pp. ISBN 978-0-8225-7504-7. Grades 5–9.

This discussion of the excavation of Palenque, in Peru, begins with the visit of John Stephens and Frederick Catherwood to the site in 1840. Excavations in the 20th century, especially that of Mexican archaeologist Alberto Ruz Lhuillier, found the burial site of a Mayan ruler underneath the Temple of the Inscriptions. Much difficulty surrounded the dig, and the Americans and the Mexicans had problems decoding the Mayan hieroglyphics that offered information about the place. Photographs, maps, diagrams, and illustrations highlight the text. Bibliography, Glossary, Chronology, Notes, Further Reading, Web Sites, and Index.

3183. Levy, Janice. *Celebrate! It's Cinco de Mayo! Celebremos! Es el Cinco de Mayo.* Illustrated by Loretta Lopez. Albert Whitman, 2007. 32pp. ISBN 978-0-8075-1176-3. Grades 2–4.

A simple history of the Mexican holiday Cinco de Mayo. On May 5, 1862, the Mexicans won the Battle of Puebla against the French. The current-day celebration usually includes a parade, mariachi music, a family meal, a piñata, and a retelling of the story of freedom. Instructions for making a maraca and a serape also appear.

3184. Lewin, Ted. *Lost City: The Discovery of Machu Picchu.* Illustrated by author. Philomel, 2003. 48pp. ISBN 978-0-399-23302-9. Grades K–4.

Yale professor Hiram Bingham went searching for Vilcapampa in 1911 deep in the forests of Peru. Instead he found the lost ruins of Machu Picchu. The text looks at Bingham's trek through the jungle and uses rhetorical questions to build suspense about the finds along the way, from a grand stone staircase to the view of the ruins from a nearby mountain. Double-page watercolor illustrations complement the text. Bibliography.

3185. Lourie, Peter. *Hidden World of the Aztec.* (Ancient Civilizations of the Americas) Boyds Mills, 2006. 48pp. ISBN 978-1-5907-8069-5. Grades 3–6.

When the Spaniards came to Mexico, they wanted to erase any traces of the Aztec culture. They did not eradicate the ruins, however, and archaeologists have conducted excavations of the Great Temple, now covered with streets in downtown Mexico City, and the Temple of the Moon, north of the city in Teotihuacan. Nine chapters cover the history of the Aztecs and Toltecs and what the excavations have revealed about their society. The text concludes that human sacrifice was not nearly as common as history has suggested. Photographs illuminate the text. Bibliography.

3186. Lourie, Peter. *The Mystery of the Maya: Uncovering the Lost City of Palenque.*　Boyds Mills, 2001. 48pp. ISBN 978-1-56397-839-5; 2004 paper ISBN 978-1-59078-265-1. Grades 5–8.

This book presents findings about the ancient Maya that have come to public attention during the recent location and excavation of Palenque, Mexico, in the middle of the jungle. It recalls various aspects of the dig, the ruins, the people in the area, and the landscape. Photographs and maps augment the text. Bibliography, Glossary, and Index.

3187. Lubber, William. *Pirateology Guidebook and Model Set.*　(Ologies) Candlewick, 2007. 24pp. ISBN 978-0-7636-3582-4. Grades 3–7.

The author describes life on a pirate vessel, covering such subjects as how pirates entertain themselves and how they punish offenders. Also included is a ship model to help readers visualize the descriptions in the text.

3188. Maestro, Betsy. *The Discovery of the Americas.*　Illustrated by Giulio Maestro. Mulberry, 1992. Unpaged. Paper ISBN 978-0-688-11512-8. Grades K–4.

Beginning with the migration of peoples into North and South America more than 20,000 years ago, the author presents theories and facts about the settlements discovered on the two continents. Cultures and explorers before Columbus include the Mayans, possibly Saint Brendan from Ireland in the 6th century, the Vikings Bjarni Herjolfsson in the 10th century and Leif Ericsson in the eleventh, possibly Prince Madoc of Wales in the twelfth, and the Hopewell mound builders. Explorers after Columbus mentioned in the text are Italians John Cabot in 1497 and Amerigo Vespucci in 1499, Vasco Nuñez de Balboa from Spain in 1513, and Ferdinand Magellan from Portugal in 1519. Additional Information, Some People of the Ancient and Early Americas, The Age of Discovery, How the Americas Got Their Name, and Other Interesting Voyages.

3189. Maestro, Betsy. *Exploration and Conquest: The Americas After Columbus: 1500–1620.* Illustrated by Giulio Maestro. Mulberry, 1997. Unpaged. Paper ISBN 978-0-688-15474-5. Grades K–4.

Noting that Spanish discovery of the New World ignored or exploited the people who had lived there for years, the authors describe the feats and effects of explorers after Columbus. Balboa (1513) saw the Pacific. Ponce de León (1513) found Florida. Magellan began his voyage around the world in 1519, while Cortés overpowered the Aztecs. Pizarro and deSoto (1532) conquered the Incas in Peru when Cabez de Vaca was in Texas. DeSoto went to Florida in 1539, and Coronado left Mexico in search of the Seven Cities of Gold in 1540. After Spain lost interest in America, European explorers arrived. John Cabot, Giovanni da Verrazano, Jacques Cartier, and John Hawkins (who began the slave trade) came. Britain's Francis Drake, Martin Frobisher, Humphrey Gilbert, John Davis, Walter Raleigh (at Roanoke), John White, and Virginia Dare added their names to history. After 1600, famous arrivals were John Smith, John Rolfe, Champlain, and Henry Hudson. Where these people arrived on shore, the indigenous cultures disappeared. Additional Information, Table of Dates, Some Other Explorers, North America—1500–1620, Contacts Between Native Americans and European Explorers, Impact of the European Arrival in the Americas, Native American Contributions to the World, and European Colonies and Settlements in the New World.

3190. Mann, Elizabeth. *Tikal: The Center of the Maya World.* Illustrated by Tom McNeely. Mikaya, 2002. 47pp. ISBN 978-1-931414-05-0. Grades 4–8.

Tikal, the largest city in the Mayan world, prospered through trade and military triumphs from around 800 B.C.E. until 900 C.E. Among its people were mathematicians, architects who built pyramids, agriculturalists, and astronomers. They also had a writing system. The author explains that settlers chose the location because it was a passable trade route through Mesoamerica. He looks at customs including bloodletting, sport to the death, and human sacrifice. Illustrations complement the text. Glossary and Chronology.

3191. Mathews, Sally Schofer. *The Sad Night: The Story of an Aztec Victory and a Spanish Loss.* Illustrated by author. Clarion, 2001. Unpaged. Paper ISBN 978-0-618-11745-1. Grades 4–6.

Mathews has based her artwork on the twenty Aztec codes and codex fragments that survived the Spanish destruction of the Aztecs, further explained in the book. The Aztecs had built a strong empire, beginning with Tenochtitlán, in fewer than 200 years, and their King Montezuma was the most powerful man in Mexico. Aztec troubles began in the year of 1 Reed (1519), when they expected the return of their feathered serpent god, Quetzalcoatl, in the guise of a man. Instead, Hernán Cortés arrived, and they mistook him for the god. They bestowed gifts of gold on Cortés, but the Spanish took Montezuma prisoner instead of thanking him. Other events led to Montezuma's death, the defeat of the Spaniards, and the last battle the Aztecs would ever win. Cortés returned with more men the next year to end the Aztec domination. Today the area is Mexico City, where some of the Aztec gold was recently found, having been melted and then lost by the Spaniards when they were trying to escape their first defeat.

3192. Matthews, Rupert. *You Wouldn't Want to Be a Mayan Soothsayer! Fortunes You'd Rather Not Tell.* (You Wouldn't Want To . . .) Franklin Watts, 2007. 32pp. ISBN 978-0-531-18746-3. Grades 3–6.

A Mayan soothsayer would have given advice about culture, religion, and life. A soothsayer's son explains how one becomes a soothsayer, detailing the gods and the days that celebrate them, the Wayeb festival (five days culminating with the New Year), the warriors and their cults, and what a soothsayer would see in the planets. Unpleasant aspects of the job include having to taste disgusting food, pierce holes in the royal family's tongues, and offer human sacrifices to the gods. Illustrations highlight the text. Glossary and Index.

3193. Morris, Neil. *Pirates.* (Amazing History) Smart Apple Media, 2008. 32pp. ISBN 978-1-59920-104-7. Grades 4–6.

This book contains information about pirates, corsairs, privateers that were legally hired to attack ships, vessels, weapons, and gear. Also included are short biographies of famous pirates and an overview of modern piracy. Glossary and Web Sites.

3194. Owen, James A. *Lost Treasures of the Pirates of the Caribbean: Secret Maps, Legends, and Lore Revealed!* Illustrated by Jeremy Owen. Simon & Schuster, 2007. 27pp. ISBN 978-1-416-93960-3. Grades 5–7.

This history of piracy offers thirteen treasure maps supposedly commissioned by a Charleston mapmaker family. They contain actual routes that real pirates took, the location of shipwrecks, and legends of pirate treasure never recovered. A fourteenth map hides somewhere amid the text and photographs of leering pirates like John Rackham and George Lowther.

3195. Rice, Earle, Jr. *A Brief Political and Geographic History of Latin America: Where Are Gran Colombia, La Plata, and Dutch Guiana?* (Places in Time) Mitchell Lane, 2008. 111pp. ISBN 978-1-58415-626-0. Grades 5–9.

Readers will learn about places in Latin America that no longer exist by viewing them on a map and discussing why they have disappeared from present-day maps. It begins with European contact and covers South American history. Photographs, maps, and reproductions embellish the text. Bibliography, Glossary, Chronology, Notes, Further Reading, Web Sites, and Index.

3196. Rosso, Norma. *The Aztec News: Philip Steele.* Candlewick, 2009. 32pp. Paper ISBN 978-0-7636-4200-9. Grades 5 up.

In newspaper form, this approach to the Aztecs highlights fashion, sports, trade, food, and the military. Each page has headlines, sometimes with classifieds advertising a variety of items that the Aztecs used. Highly readable and slightly sensational, the news under a headline such as "Spanish Flee City" seems much more accessible than in a textbook. Maps and Index.

3197. Seaworthy, Oscar. *Port Side Pirates!* Illustrated by Debbie Harter. Barefoot, 2007. Unpaged. ISBN 978-1-84686-062-1; 2008. paper ISBN 978-1-84686-205-2. Grades K–3.

Children make up the crew of a pirate ship under an adult captain in these song lyrics. The book also contains a picture of a labeled pirate's galleon and information about famous pirates.

3198. Sherrow, Victoria. *The Aztec Indians.* Chelsea House, 1993. 79pp. ISBN 978-0-7910-1658-9. Grades 3–6.

The Aztec empire began in 1325 when the wandering Mexica Indians settled near present-day Mexico City. They grew in strength by establishing a trade network. Despite their wealth and daily rituals, the capital fell to the Spanish in 1521. Photographs and reproductions enhance the text. Glossary, Chronology, and Index.

3199. Silate, Jennifer. *The Inca Ruins of Machu Picchu.* (Wonders of the World) KidHaven, 2005. 48pp. ISBN 978-0-7377-3068-5. Grades 4–8.

The author provides an overview of the city of Machu Picchu, in Peru, first discussing how Hiram Bingham discovered the ruins in 1911. Then Silate describes the construction of the buildings and the need for agricultural terraces and stone staircases on the vertical land. Additionally, the book includes information about the importance of protecting and preserving the ruins for the future. Photographs and illustrations highlight the text. Glossary, Further Reading, and Index.

3200. Sonneborn, Liz. *The Mexican-American War: A Primary Source History of the Expansion of the Western Lands of the United States.* Rosen, 2005. 64pp. ISBN 978-1-4042-0180-4. Grades 5–7.

Readers will learn about the Mexican-American War fought between 1846 and 1848. The book offers background on the conflict, the battles, and its conclusion through primary sources. Photographs and illustrations highlight the text. Bibliography, Glossary, Chronology, Further Reading, and Index. *Voice of Youth Advocates Nonfiction Honor List.*

3201. Stein, R. Conrad. *The Aztec Empire.* Benchmark, 1996. 80pp. ISBN 978-0-7614-0072-1. Grades 5–8.

Readers will learn about the artifacts, monuments, domestic scenes, and historical aspects of the Aztecs as they look at the history, beliefs, and lifestyles of the people. The author also notes the influence of the Aztecs on modern Mexico and discusses the discovery of the ruins of Tenochtitlan. Photographs, Drawings, Bibliography, Chronology, Further Reading, Glossary, and Index.

3202. Stein, R. Conrad. *Cortés and the Spanish Conquest.* (Story of Mexico) Morgan Reynolds, 2007. 160pp. ISBN 978-1-59935-053-0. Grades 6 up.

Cortés arrived in the Americas and met the Aztecs. The author examines the rise of the Aztecs to power and how Montezuma ruled them. Cortés, interested in exploration and conquest, carefully annihilated them and claimed victory in 1521. The text thoroughly covers his process with illustrations and photographs to enhance. Bibliography, Chronology, Notes, Further Reading, Web Sites, and Index.

3203. Stein, R. Conrad. *The Mexican Revolution.* (Story of Mexico) Morgan Reynolds, 2007. 144pp. ISBN 978-1-59935-051-6. Grades 7–12.

In 1910 a revolution began that challenged the rule of Mexican soldier-statesman Porfirio Diaz. The author looks at this period of history in ten chapters, each centering on one of the political figures in the revolution, including Zapata, Pancho Villa, Madero, Huerta, and Carranza. Stein discusses the underlying causes of the revolution, such as inequity in land ownership, the racial and regional differences in the country, attitudes toward the Catholic Church, and the involvement of foreign governments. During the conflict, one in eight Mexicans died in battle, from disease, or from hunger; however, these problems were little known outside the country even after the revolution ended in 1920. Chronology, Further Readings, and Index.

3204. Stein, R. Conrad. *The Mexican War of Independence.* (Story of Mexico) Morgan Reynolds, 2007. 144pp. ISBN 978-1-59935-054-7. Grades 7–12.

Eleven chapters cover the road to Mexican independence. The story begins in 1521 with Hernando Cortés's overthrow of the Aztec empire. Finally in 1855, after three centuries of Spanish rule, Agustín Cosme Damián de Iturbide overthrows Antonio Lopez Santa Anna. One of the most important aspects of the desire for independence was the disparity in the racial hierarchy when the Spanish ruled. Illustrations and photographs enhance the text. Bibliography, Chronology, Notes, Further Reading, Web Sites, and Index.

3205. Temple, Bob. *The Golden Age of Pirates: An Interactive History Adventure.* (You Choose) Capstone, 2007. 2007pp. ISBN 978-1-4296-0162-7; paper ISBN 978-1-4296-1181-7. Grades 3–6.

In this story, readers can choose whether to play the role of pirate or a person marooned on a desert island while pirates roamed the oceans. After that decision, they make other decisions that would be historically plausible during that time. Readers have the chance to view events from both points of view. Color reproductions and maps enhance the text. Bibliography.

3206. Thomson, Ruth. *Aztecs.* Creative, 2004. 32pp. ISBN 978-1-932889-09-3. Grades 4–6.

The text and illustrations give facts about social, religious, and political aspects of the Aztec civilization in thirteen two-page spreads. Projects with directions for making items directly related to the Aztecs, from simple to difficult, give further insight. Glossary and Index.

3207. Whitaker, Robert J. *The Mapmaker's Wife: A True Tale of Love, Murder, and Survival in the Amazon.* Basic, 2004. 368pp. ISBN 978-0-7382-0808-4; Delta paper ISBN 978-0-385-33720-5. Grades YA.

See entry 1304.

3208. Whiting, Jim. *The Bermuda Triangle.* (Natural Disasters) Mitchell Lane, 2007. 32pp. ISBN 978-1-58415-497-6. Grades 4–6.

In 1945 five United States Navy torpedo bombers disappeared in a geographic triangle formed by Bermuda, Puerto Rico, and Miami. Other planes and ships have also disappeared in this area, and no one can be certain why. Among the natural causes posited are wormholes, aliens, or storms. One concept is that methane gas bubbles can sink a ship immediately. Photographs and illustrations enhance the text. Chronology, Glossary, Further Reading, Web Sites, and Index.

3209. Wulffson, Don. *Before Columbus: Early Voyages to the Americas.* Twenty First Century, 2007. 128pp. ISBN 978-0-8225-5978-8. Grades 5–9.

The author examines whether other civilizations arrived in the New World before Columbus and suggests that Columbus received credit for arriving in the New World first because of the printing press, good publicity, and backing by royalty. Other groups that might have come before include the Vikings, Chinese, Irish, and Africans. The Phoenicians could have fled their Greek conquerors in 146 B.C.E. and landed in New Hampshire where they built Stonehenge-shaped monuments and etched Phoenician letters. The Irish could have arrived in New England—signs of Irish monks living in the country more than 1,000 years ago do exist. The "white" Mandan tribe in North Dakota could have resulted from Prince Madoc's Welsh expedition in the 12th century. West African gold spearheads have appeared in the Olmec people's treasures. Legends, sagas, oral and written histories along with archaeological discoveries support some of Wulffson's theories. Photographs and reproductions highlight the text. Bibliography, Notes, Further Reading, Web Sites, and Index.

3210. Wyborny, Shelia. *Life During the Aztec Empire.* (Life During the Great Civilizations) Thomson Gale, 2003. 48pp. ISBN 978-1-56711-736-3. Grades 5–7.

Readers get a brief overview of the society, religion, history, and achievements of the Aztecs during the heyday of the empire. Photographs, sidebars, and reproductions enhance the text. Maps, Further Reading, Glossary, Notes, Web Sites, and Index.

Biography and Collective Biography

3211. Appel, Ted. *José Martí: Cuban Revolutionary and Poet.* (Hispanics of Achievement) Chelsea House, 1992. 120pp. ISBN 978-0-7910-1246-8. Grades 5 up.

In Cuba, José Martí (1853–1895) is one of the most revered figures. He was a communicator, an organizer, a political theorist, and a guerrilla fighter. When he was 16, the Spanish imprisoned him for organizing against them and exiled him to Spain, where he studied at Madrid's Central University. He returned to Cuba and led an insurrection in 1878. Again he was exiled, this time to the United States, where he spent fifteen years working for Cuban independence. In 1892 he founded the Cuban Revolutionary Party and went to Cuba to fight the Second War of Independence. He died before his party won. Photographs enhance the text. Chronology, Further Reading, and Index.

3212. Bell-Villada, Gene H. *García Márquez: The Man and His Work.* University of North Carolina, 1990. 247pp. ISBN 978-0-8078-4264-5. Grades YA.

This biography introduces the politics of Colombia, as well as the life and works of García Márquez, by interweaving them in the text. The information on García's *One Hundred Years of Solitude* and *The Autumn of the Patriarch* are invaluable to persons interested in those extraordinary works. The influence of writers such as Faulkner and Joyce on García Márquez becomes clear in the discussions. Bell-Villada sees the works as histories rather than merely magical realism, a term that he sees as a limitation of their magnitude. Bibliography and Index.

3213. Bernier-Grand, Carmen T. *Frida: Viva la Vida/Long Live Life.* Illustrated by Frida Kahlo. Marshall Cavendish, 2007. 64pp. ISBN 978-0-7614-5336-9. Grades 7 up.

Frida Kahlo (1907–1954) had a complicated life. This biography, composed of twenty-six free-verse poems with reproductions of Kahlo's paintings, offers an overview of her life. The themes presented include her bout with polio, her family problems, her two marriages to Diego Rivera, her injury as a teenager that led to thirty-one operations, her miscarriages, and other incidents during which she continued painting and celebrating life. Notes. *Booklist Editors' Choice, American Library Association Notable Children's Books,* and *Pura Belpré Honor.*

3214. Brown, Monica. *My Name Is Gabito/Me Llamo Gabito: The Life of Gabriel García Márquez/La Vida de Gabriel García Márquez.* Illustrated by Raúl Colón. Luna Rising, 2007. 32pp. ISBN 978-0-87358-908-6. Grades 2–4.

Gabriel García Márquez (1928–) remains one of the world's and certainly Colombia's great authors. This picture book reveals his childhood and the influence of his family in encouraging his imagination. It explains his complicated writing style of magic realism so that young readers can grasp its concept. Text appears in both English and Spanish and sometimes in the lovely illustrations accompanying it. *Pura Belpré Honor* and *American Library Association Notable Children's Books.*

3215. Cline-Ransome, Lesa. *Young Pelé: Soccer's First Star.* Illustrated by James E. Ransome. Schwartz & Wade, 2007. 40pp. ISBN 978-0-375-83599-5. Grades K–2.

In Bauru, Brazil, in the 1940s and 1950s, a poor boy named Edson Arantes do Nascimento kicked and dribbled enough soccer balls—including those made from wound rags and tied with string—with his shoeless and ill-dressed team to become the greatest soccer player of all time. People called him Pelé. By the time he was 17, he was playing for Brazil's national team, and in 1958 he led it to its first victory ever in the World Cup. Oil paintings enhance the text.

3216. Condé, Maryse. *Tales from the Heart: True Stories from My Childhood.* Translated by Richard Philcox. Soho, 2004. 147pp. Paper ISBN 978-1-56947-347-4. Grades YA.

Maryse Condé recalls her childhood growing up in Guadeloupe and going to Paris every year with her parents and seven older siblings. She remembers her mother as a person who was seriously concerned about honor and place, especially as the educated but illegitimate child of an illiterate woman. She recounts moments of loss and unfulfilled dreams, and even though she shows little joy, she seems happy to recall these times. *Prix Yourcenar.*

3217. Connolly, Sean. *Castro.* (A Beginner's Guide) Hodder & Stoughton, 2002. 96pp. Paper ISBN 978-0-340-84612-4. Grades 9 up.

Fidel Castro (1927–) took power in Cuba in 1959, and the country remained a Marxist society even after the Soviet communist bloc collapsed. The author examines Castro's life, his role as "commander-in-chief" of the Cuban government, and the people with whom he has agreed and disagreed. He has been called "the last Cold Warrior" as he has outlived Mao, Khrushchev, Kennedy, and Nixon. Chronology, Bibliography, Glossary, Illustrations, Maps, and Index.

3218. Cox, Vicki. *Oscar Arias Sánchez: Bringing Peace to Central America.* (Modern Peacemakers) Chelsea House, 2007. 118pp. ISBN 978-0-7910-8999-6. Grades 8 up.

Because of his work trying to establish a peace accord among several Central American countries, Oscar Arias Sánchez won the Nobel Peace Prize. He helped Costa Rica, Nicaragua, Honduras, El Salvador, and Guatemala find a way to talk with each other. Illustrations augment the text. Bibliography, Chronology, Further Reading, Notes, Web Sites, and Index.

3219. Dale, Shelly. *Juan Quezada.* Illustrated by author. Translated by Teresa Mlawer. Norman, 2003. 40pp. ISBN 978-0-970861-74-0; paper ISBN 978-0-970861-75-7. Grades 1–4.

The potter Juan Quezada of the village of Mata Ortiz, Chihuahua, Mexico, rediscovered pottery methods used by the Casas Grandes Indian tribe of northern Mexico. After finding an ancient pot he spent years trying to recreate the techniques of the vanished Paquimé potters. His findings led to the rejuvenation of his village and rescue from poverty. He describes the method and how he makes his own pottery. Ink, watercolor, and colored-pencil paintings augment the text. Glossary and Further Reading.

3220. Délano, Poli. *When I Was a Boy Neruda Called Me Policarpo.* Illustrated by Manuel Monroy. Translated by Sean Higgins. Groundwood, 2006. 84pp. ISBN 978-0-8889-9726-5. Grades 5 up.

Poli Délano and his diplomat family lived with "Tio Pablo" Neruda (1904–1973) in Mexico, when Poli was eight. In seven chapters he relates some of the unusual aspects of Neruda's interests and personality that he observed as a child. He had a pet badger, El Niño, and Neruda ate grasshoppers, worms, and ants. Neruda gave Poli goggles when they visited Acapulco so he could explore underwater. In a restaurant, Neruda, an anti-fascist, became angry at an insolent German. But Neruda also taught Poli about fate and competition. The book looks at some of Neruda's poems.

3221. Engle, Margarita. *The Poet Slave of Cuba: A Biography of Juan Francisco Manzano.* Illustrated by Sean Qualls. Holt, 2006. 183pp. ISBN 978-0-8050-7706-3. Grades 7 up.

When Juan Francisco Manzano (1797–1854) was a young slave in Cuba, his mistress loved him and had him perform his poetry for guests. She promised him freedom at her death, but instead, he was given to a crazy women who beat him. At the age of 16 he managed to escape and survived through the tiny kind acts of others, making art any way he could. He did escape, and triumphantly. *Bulletin Blue Ribbon, Booklist Editors' Choice, American Library Association Best Books for Young Adults, Americas Book Award, IRA Children's Book Award,* and *Pura Belpré Award.*

3222. Fry, Frieda, and Margaret Frith. *Frida Kahlo: The Artist Who Painted Herself.* Illustrated by Tomie DePaola. Grossett & Dunlap, 2003. 32pp. Paper ISBN 978-0-4484-2677-8. Grades 2–5.

Written as a child's report, this biography of Frida Kahlo gives basic facts about Kahlo's life. She had polio as a child and then was injured in a bus accident at 18 and had to spend much of her time in bed. Later she married muralist Diego Rivera and continued with her painting. Readers will learn about art terms. Illustrations reminiscent of Kahlo's style complement the text.

3223. Guidici, Cynthia. *Adriana Ocampo.* (Hispanic-Americans) Raintree, 2005. 64pp. Paper ISBN 978-1-4109-1305-0. Grades 4–8.

Adriana Ocampo, a planetary geologist, spent her childhood in South America. She immigrated to California where she pursued her interest in science, and this led to work at NASA's Jet Propulsion Laboratory. Photographs illustrate the text. Glossary, Chronology, Further Reading, and Index.

3224. Guzmán, Lila, and Rick Guzmán. *Diego Rivera: Artist of Mexico.* (Famous Latinos) Enslow, 2006. 32pp. ISBN 978-0-7660-2641-4. Grades 3–4.

A child who loved trains, Diego Rivera (1886–1957) became known for his murals painted on the walls of public buildings showing Mexican history and heroes. The author focuses on these works. Photographs augment the text. Glossary, Chronology, Further Reading, Web Sites, and Index.

3225. Guzmán, Lila, and Rick Guzmán. *Frida Kahlo: Painting Her Life.* (Famous Latinos) Enslow, 2006. 32pp. ISBN 978-0-7660-2641-4. Grades 3–4.

Frida Kahlo (1907–1954) overcame medical problems as a child including polio and a terrible accident that resulted in many operations. She accomplished this by painting her own and other women's lives. The author examines the types of art she produced and the media she used. Photographs augment the text. Glossary, Chronology, Further Reading, Web Sites, and Index.

3226. Hamilton, Sue. *Blackbeard.* (Pirates!) ABDO, 2007. 32pp. ISBN 978-1-59928-758-4. Grades 3–6.

This biography presents the life of Edward Teach (d. 1718), known as Blackbeard, who gained notoriety for plundering on the coasts of Virginia and North Carolina. The author examines details of life aboard pirate ships, the weapons used, and the rules of engagement that pirates used while fighting. Maps, photographs, and reproductions embellish the text. Glossary and Index.

3227. Hamilton, Sue. *Captain Kidd.* (Pirates!) ABDO, 2007. 32pp. ISBN 978-1-59928-759-1. Grades 3–6.

This biography gives an overview of the life of William Kidd (d. 1701), a sea captain who was hired to chase pirates. It includes information about his early voyages through his death on the gallows after the rogue and mutineer Robert Culliford helped to expose his deeds. Readers will learn about details of life aboard pirate ships, the weapons they used, and the rules of engagement that pirates followed while fighting. Maps, photographs, and reproductions embellish the text. Glossary and Index.

3228. Hamilton, Sue. *Henry Morgan.* (Pirates!) ABDO, 2007. 32pp. ISBN 978-1-59928-760-7. Grades 3–6.

The Welsh pirate Sir Henry Morgan (1635?–1688) served the English government in the Caribbean. He attacked Spanish merchant ships and eventually his overthrow of Panama ended Spanish domination in the New World. Also included are details of life aboard pirate ships, the weapons used, and the rules of engagement that pirates used while fighting. Maps, photographs, and reproductions embellish the text. Glossary and Index.

3229. Havelin, Kate. *Che Guevara.* (Biography) Twenty-First Century, 2007. 112pp. ISBN 978-0-8225-5951-1. Grades 7 up.

This biography presents Ernesto (Che) Guevara (1928–1967), a man who supported Fidel Castro in his revolution to overthrow the Cuban government. Che placed his beliefs in social and political change above his family and his health. Included is the mention of his famous motorcycle journey as well as other travels in Africa and South America toward the end of his life. *Time* magazine named him as one of the most influential figures of the 20th century. Photographs accompany the text. Bibliography, Chronology, Further Reading, Web Sites, and Index.

3230. Hiltebrand, Ellen Urbani. *When I Was Elena.* Permanent, 2006. 304pp. ISBN 978-1-57962-124-7. Grades YA.

When Ellen Urbani was 22, she went from the University of Alabama to Guatemala to serve in the Peace Corps. She discovered that all her preconceptions were incorrect. She tells the story of this experience and the people that she met, both locals and volunteers. One had been a victim of incest, others had borne one child after another, they had lost loved ones, they had no money, and only one seemed to be happily married. They all become her friends and appear in her memoir.

3231. Holland, Gini. *Diego Rivera.* Illustrated by Gary Rees. Steck-Vaughn, 1998. 32pp. Paper ISBN 978-0-8172-6890-9. Grades K–3.

Diego Rivera (1886–1957) was a Mexican mural painter who refused to compromise his subject matter for anyone. This brief biography gives a balanced view of Rivera and his political beliefs as well as his artistic philosophy that people of all social and economic strata should be able to enjoy art. Key Dates.

3232. Holzhey, Magdalena. *Frida Kahlo: The Artist in the Blue House.* (Adventures In Art) Prestel, 2003. 28pp. ISBN 978-3-7913-2863-8. Grades 3–6.

This biography of Frida Kahlo (1907–1954) contains information about her life and more than forty full-color reproductions of her work. Among the themes in her work are trees, deer, family members, monkeys, friends, flowers, tears, and wheelchairs. Questions encourage readers to wonder about her and her life as a partial invalid while she was creating her art.

3233. Kallen, Stuart A. *Rigoberta Menchú: Indian Rights Activist.* (20th Century's Most Influential Hispanics) Lucent, 2007. 104pp. ISBN 978-1-59018-975-7. Grades 5 up.

Rigoberta Menchú suffered much abuse as a Mayan child in Guatemala. This experience led her to champion the rights of indigenous people in her country. Much controversy has circled her life, but she won the Nobel Prize for her work. Photographs and reproductions enhance the text. Chronology, Notes, Further Reading, Web Sites, and Index.

3234. Kogan, Deborah Ray. *To Go Singing Through the World: The Childhood of Pablo Neruda.* Farrar, 2006. 32pp. ISBN 978-0-374-37627-7. Grades 3–6.

This biography presents the verse of Chilean poet Pablo Neruda (1904–1973) along with facts about his life. He grew up in a pioneer town near the Chilean rain forest where nature inspired his poetry. His stepmother told fascinating stories, and the settlers, commerce, and interesting things that came to town were integrated into his work. When he was a teenager, he met the Nobel Prize-winning writer Gabriela Mistral and, after reading his poems, she recognized his ability and encouraged him to write. Mixed-media illustrations complement his poetry. Note and Chronology.

3235. León, Vicki. *Uppity Women of the New World.* Conari, 2001. 260pp. Paper ISBN 978-1-57324-187-8. Grades YA.

This collective anecdotal biography presents 225 women who lived from the early 1500s to the mid-1800s. The groups, featuring women who helped to launch and establish the colonies in the Americas, New Zealand, and Australia are "First Ladies and Superlative Travelers," "Spies and She-Merchants," "Chain Breakers and Rebellion Makers," "Creative Boatrockers and Career Widows," "Swashbucklers and Gender Benders," "Game Dames and Granite Grannies," "Early Aussies and South Sea Self-Starters," "Headline Makers and Risk-Takers," and "Celebrity Kin and Significantly Overlooked Others." Illustrations augment the text. Bibliography, Notes, and Index.

3236. Lewis, J. Patrick. *Blackbeard the Pirate King.* National Geographic, 2006. 32pp. ISBN 978-0-7922-5585-7. Grades 5–7.

In the 18th century Edward Teach, known as Blackbeard, frightened many during his pirating. However, not until his final fight does evidence exist that he ever killed anyone. In fact, Teach might have shown humanitarian concern when he lifted his blockade of Charleston to allow medical supplies—rather than gold—to pass through. Lewis uses poems for his biography of Teach. Illustrations from masters such as N. C. Wyeth and Howard Pyle augment the text.

3237. Litwin, Laura Baskes. *Diego Rivera: Legendary Mexican Painter.* (Latino Biography Library) Enslow, 2005. 128pp. ISBN 978-0-7660-2486-1. Grades 6–9.

The author examines the life of Mexican artist, Diego Rivera (1886–1957) in nine chapters. The text begins with his childhood in an extraordinary family, the influences on him, and his training. It details his career as well as his private life involving complex

624 — MEXICO, CARIBBEAN, SOUTH AND CENTRAL AMERICA

and difficult relationships with women, including his wife, Frida Kahlo. Additional commentary about the political aspects of Rivera's life shows his interest in the Zapatistas and Trotsky. At one time, he had a dramatic ideological conflict with Nelson Rockefeller when he included a portrait of Vladimir Lenin in his RCA Building mural; Rockefeller had this work destroyed. Photographs and illustrations complement the text. Chronology, Notes, Further Reading, Web Sites, and Index.

3238. Main, Mary. *Isabel Allende: Award-Winning Latin American Author.* (Latino Biography Library) Enslow, 2005. 128pp. ISBN 978-0-7660-2488-5. Grades 6–9.

Isabel Allende, a Latin American author from Chile, has had many experiences that have influenced her writing. This biography includes background on her childhood, her family, and her career. Photographs and illustrations highlight the text. Bibliography, Chronology, Notes, Web Sites, and Index.

3239. Miller, Calvin Craig. *Che Guevara: In Search of Revolution.* (World Leaders) Morgan Reynolds, 2006. 192pp. ISBN 978-1-931798-93-8. Grades 7 up.

This biography of Ernesto Guevara (1928–1967) covers his life as a young rebel, a guerrilla in training, his meeting with Fidel Castro, his failed rebellions, and his death in the jungle. Born into a wealthy but socialist-leaning Argentinean family, he decided to study medicine. In his travels around South America he became dispirited about the difficulty of peasant life under despotic rulers. He determined that a socialist government throughout the continent would be the best, and he dedicated his life to this goal. Photographs highlight the text. Bibliography, Chronology, Notes, Web Sites, and Index.

3240. Miller, Calvin Craig. *Reggae Poet: The Story of Bob Marley.* Morgan Reynolds, 2007. 128pp. ISBN 978-1-59935-071-4. Grades 9 up.

Bob Marley (1945–1981), son of a British father and Jamaican farm girl, grew up in poverty in the tiny town of Nine Miles, Jamaica. Both his poverty and his biracial identity made life difficult for him until he formed a musical group with his friend called the Wailers. They developed the style of music called reggae, a form that made them famous worldwide. Marley was a Rasta who believed that marijuana was important in his religion, and he became embroiled in Jamaican politics. Additionally, his romantic life was complicated with marriage and infidelity. This biography covers all these aspects of his short life. Photographs and reproductions enhance the text. Bibliography, Chronology, Notes, Web Sites, and Index.

3241. Mora, Pat. *A Library for Juana.* Illustrated by Beatriz Vidal. Knopf, 2002. Unpaged. ISBN 978-0-375-80643-8. Grades 1–3.

Juana Inés de la Cruz (1651–1695) wanted to pursue an education after learning to read at the age of 3 but found that women were forbidden entry to the university. She disguised herself and succeeded, becoming one of Mexico's finest scholars of the 17th century. Her escape into a convent allowed her time to think and write freely as a poet, playwright, and song writer. Her library became one of the largest in the Americas. Glossary and Note.

3242. Palacios, Argentina. *¡Viva Mexico! A Story of Benito Juarez and Cinco de Mayo.* Illustrated by Howard Berelson. Steck-Vaughn, 1992. 32pp. Paper ISBN 978-0-8114-8054-3. Grades 2–5.

A Zapotec Indian in Mexico, Juarez (1806–1872) was eleven before an uncle began to teach him to read during breaks from farming and sheep herding. Because his state had no public schools, Juarez soon went to Oaxaca, 40 miles away, to study. By working to pay for his schooling, he eventually became a lawyer in 1831. After he ran for governor of his state and won, he established schools throughout the area and became president of Mexico in 1861. The French, however, soon arrived to conquer Mexico. On Cinco de Mayo in 1862, the Mexicans beat the French at the Battle of Puebla, but the French imported reinforcements and governed for five more years until Juarez and his underground finally defeated them.

3243. **Parrado, Nando, and Vince Rause.** *Miracle in the Andes: 72 Days on the Mountain and My Long Trek Home.* Crown, 2006. 291pp. ISBN 978-1-4000-9767-8. Grades YA.

On October 13, 1972, Nando Parrado and his Uruguayan rugby teammates crashed while flying through the Andes in a snowstorm. He was stranded with a head injury for seventy-two days at 12,000 feet above sea level, and he and a few others survived the ordeal. As one after the other died, those remaining had to eat, so they cannibalized the dead bodies. Parrado's own mother and sister died in the crash. He has given inspirational talks about his ordeal and how he lived from moment to moment, trying to stay alive. His main sustenance was the memory of his father and his desire to reunite with him. He eventually hiked through the mountains with others to find help, and those remaining at the site were finally rescued by helicopters. *Booklist Editors' Choice.*

3244. **Pitluk, Adam.** *Standing Eight: The Inspiring Story of Jesus "El Matador" Chavez, Who Became Lightweight Champion of the World.* Da Capo, 2006. 248pp. ISBN 978-0-306-81454-9; 2007. paper ISBN 978-0-306-81535-5. Grades YA.

At the age of 7, in 1979, Jesus "El Matador" Chavez moved to America illegally and took the name Gabriel Sandoval. He lived in Chicago, did well in school, and went to a gym called "El Matador" to learn how to box. Unfortunately he became involved with a gang, was arrested for a robbery, and received a seven-year sentence. He spent two years in solitary after fighting while in prison. When he was released, he was deported to Mexico. Multiple attempts to return to the United States illegally failed. With the help of a friend, he finally gained legal passage, won most of his matches, and became the multiple world champion in the featherweight, super-feather, and lightweight boxing classes. Bibliography and Index.

3245. **Schwarz-Bart, Simone, and Andre Schwarz-Bart.** *Heroines of the Slavery Era.* Translated by Rose-Myriam Rejouis. (In Praise of Black Women) University of Wisconsin, 2002. 272pp. ISBN 978-0-299-17260-2. Grades YA.

See entry 2638.

3246. **Serrano, Francisco.** *The Poet King of Tezcoco: A Great Leader of Ancient Mexico.* Illustrated by Pablo Serrano. Groundwood, 2007. Unpaged. ISBN 978-0-88899-787-6. Grades 4–6.

The king of Tezcoco, Nezahualcâoyotl (1402–1472) ruled an area that is now where Mexico City stands. When he was 16, he saw a usurper murder his father, and he escaped. After fleeing for a time, he finally was able to reclaim his throne after forming an alliance with neighboring states. As a Toltec ruler, he established a new code of laws, introduced several governing bodies and cultural institutions, founded a university, and created extensive gardens containing myriad plant species (some still extant). At the same time, he wrote poetry. This biography incorporates lines from his poems with information about his life. Folk-art illustrations and maps enhance the text. Glossary, Chronology, and Further Reading.

3247. Stavans, Ilan. *On Borrowed Words: A Memoir of Language.* Penguin, 2002. 263pp. Paper ISBN 978-0-14-200094-6. Grades YA.

Ilan Stavans, born in Mexico City's Jewish ghetto, went first to Israel and then to the United States. He spent time as a student activist and theology student before becoming a professor at Amherst College. In this biography of six chapters, the reader learns that Stavans spoke Yiddish rather than Spanish as a child, and never felt like a Mexican. When he arrived in New York, he began to feel "at home" because of his love of literature. To him, the role of language was paramount to understanding who he was as a multilingual writer such as Joseph Conrad, Vladimir Nabokov, and Joseph Brodsky. Index.

3248. Stein, R. Conrad. *Benito Juárez and the French Intervention.* (Story of Mexico) Morgan Reynolds, 2007. 160pp. ISBN 978-1-59935-052-3. Grades 6 up.

Benito Juárez (1806–1872), a poor Zapotec shepherd boy, rose to power as Mexico's first Indian president. He wanted to lead the nation according to the Mexican Constitution, but the French intervened in 1863 when Napoleon III appointed Maximilian von Hapsburg as the emperor of Mexico. After Juárez drove the French out of the country, he continued his reforms. He has since been noted as the Father of Mexico. Illustrations and photographs enhance the text. Bibliography, Chronology, Notes, Further Reading, Web Sites, and Index.

3249. Stille, Darlene R. *Eva Peron, First Lady of Argentina.* (Signature Lives Modern World) Compass Point, 2005. 111pp. ISBN 978-0-7565-1585-0. Grades 8 up.

Eva Peron (1919–1952) married Juan Peron, the man who became Argentina's president. She had been a poor child who tried acting but failed, and then she became involved in politics. She became a symbol in Argentina for helping the working poor and was remembered as a saint by many. Photographs enhance the text. Bibliography, Chronology, Maps, Notes, Glossary, Further Reading, and Index.

3250. Venezia, Mike. *Diego Rivera.* Illustrated by author. (Getting to Know the World's Greatest Artists) Children's Press, 1994. 32pp. ISBN 978-0-516-02299-4; 1995 paper ISBN 978-0-516-42299-2. Grades K–5.

Diego Rivera (1886–1957), a Mexican painter, wanted his art to be accessible to all the people. He began to paint murals of everyday life in Mexico on walls outside for everyone to enjoy. Illustrations highlight the text.

3251. Venezia, Mike. *Frida Kahlo.* Illustrated by author. (Getting to Know the World's Greatest Artists) Children's Press, 1999. 32pp. ISBN 978-0-516-20975-3; paper ISBN 978-0-516-26466-0. Grades K–5.

Frida Kahlo (1907–1954), daughter of a Mexican mother and German father, was hit by a bus when she was preparing to enter medical school. She began painting while trying to recuperate. The colors and bold lines of her Mexican home attracted her, and she liked the modern surrealistic method of connecting unlike things. Among her works are *The Frame* and *The Velvet Dress*. She was married to Diego Rivera. Illustrations highlight the text.

3252. Winter, Jonah. *Diego.* Illustrated by Jeanette Winter. Translated by Amy Prince. Knopf, 2007. Unpaged. ISBN 978-0-679-81987-5; 1994. paper ISBN 978-0-679-85617-7. Grades 1–4.

In Spanish and English, the text tells the story of Diego Rivera (1886–1957). As a child, he became ill after his twin brother died, and his parents sent him to live with a healer. When he came home, his father gave him some chalk, and thereafter all he wanted to do was draw. His studies took him to Paris; in Italy, he got the idea of painting murals. When he returned to Mexico, he painted murals about everything he saw, because he wanted to share art and his concept of life with the people. *Bulletin Blue Ribbon.*

3253. Winter, Jonah. *Frida.* Illustrated by Ana Juan. Arthur A. Levine, 2002. 32pp. ISBN 978-0-590-20320-3. Grades K–3.

Frida Kahlo dealt with the calamities of her life in Mexico by learning to draw. As a child, she had polio and was bedridden. Then when she was 18, she had an accident while trying to board a bus that left her in perpetual pain. Although she was often alone as a child, her fantasy life with an imaginary friend and influence from her father's art kept her working. Rather than cry herself, she painted tearful self-portraits. The somewhat surrealistic acrylic and wax illustrations incorporate motifs from Kahlo's work.

3254. Wooten, Sara McIntosh. *Frida Kahlo: Her Life in Paintings.* (Latino Biography Library) Enslow, 2005. 128pp. ISBN 978-0-7660-2487-8. Grades 6–9.

The artist Frida Kahlo (1907–1954) was born in Coyoacan, Mexico, and suffered greatly as a young girl from polio and severe injuries from a bus accident. She later gained fame not only for her own work but also as the wife of mural artist Diego Rivera. She was also politically astute and had strong views about the government. Photographs and illustrations complement the text. Chronology, Notes, Further Reading, Web Sites, and Index.

Graphic Novels, Biographies, and Histories

3255. Dixon, Chuck. *El Cazador.* Illustrated by Steve Epting. Hyperion, 2006. 144pp. Paper ISBN 978-1-4231-0927-3. Grades 9 up.

In 1687 the pirates Brethren of the Coast highjack the galleon *La Misericordia* as it makes its way from Mexico to Spain. After the pirates unload the treasure onto the *Devil's Due*, First Mate Billio becomes the new captain. But when he enters the captain's quarters, Donessa Hidalgo murders him and takes over. She christens the ship *El Cazador (The Hunter)* and captains it as Lady Sin, searching for her family, who were kidnapped and held on the *Devil's Due*. They encounter slave traders, natives, and men who cannot decide between loyalty and greed before finding Lady Sin's family.

3256. O'Donnell, Liam. *Blackbeard's Sword: The Pirate King of the Carolinas.* Illustrated by Mike Spoor. (Graphic Flash) Stone Arch, 2007. 48pp. ISBN 978-1-59889-309-0. Grades 3–5.

In six chapters, the reader learns about the demise of the pirate Blackbeard. Lieutenant Maynard and men of the Royal Navy request help in navigating the maze of coves along the Carolina coastline from local fishermen Jacob Webster and his father.

Jacob, however, thinks that Blackbeard is a hero and misleads the men so that they run aground. Illustrations enhance the text.

DVDs

3257. *Ancient Aztec: The Fall of the Empire.* (Ancient Civilizations for Children) Schlessinger, 2007. 19 min. ISBN 978-1-4171-0369-0. Grades 3–7.

Filmed on location in Mexico, this DVD offers information about the fall of the ancient Aztec Empire. It presents life with the arrival of Hernando Cortez and his Spanish troops. It continues with an overview of the clash between the two cultures that led to the death of Montezuma II and the fall of Tenochtitlan. The reenactments give viewers a look into the life of the Aztecs and the ways in which archaeologists have obtained some of the knowledge we now have about this civilization.

3258. *Ancient Aztec Empire.* (Ancient Civilizations for Children) Schlessinger, 2007. 19 min. ISBN 978-1-4171-0368-3. Grades 3–7.

This live-action program filmed on location in Mexico gives information about the ancient Aztec Empire. It covers daily life, agriculture, food, roles of males and females, myths, and religion with a mention of human sacrifice. The reenactments offer viewers a sense of the time during the Aztec period and how archaeologists have discovered some of the facts that we know today.

3259. *Bloqueo: Looking at the U.S. Embargo Against Cuba.* Cinema Guild, 2004. 45 min. Grades 9 up.

In 1962 the United States tried to topple Cuban Premier Fidel Castro by setting up an economic and financial embargo that continues today. The embargo has proved ineffective and private groups have tried to stop it. The Cuban people have had a diminished standard of living, and the Soviet Union's demise reduced availability of goods even further. But the Cuban culture has survived throughout this time of deprivation. Interviews with Cuban citizens define their current state. *International Festival of New Latin American Cinema (Cuba), International Festival of Documentaries, Three Continents (Venezuela), Reel World's Cuban Film Festival, Cine Latino (Germany),* and *World Community Film Festival (Vancouver).*

3260. *Haiti Rising: Celebrating the First Black Republic.* Green Valley Media, 2003. 108 min. ISBN 978-0-9614313-2-7. Grades 9 up.

Two films celebrate the 200th anniversary of the Haitian Revolution: "Black Dawn," an animation of the revolution, and "Haitian Pilgrimage." "Black Dawn" recalls the inhumane treatment of slaves, the migrations forced upon them, the role that voodoo played in the planning and execution of the uprising, and the success in 2004. "Haitian Pilgrimage" follows a family returning to Haiti from their home in New York. The family practices voodoo (vodun) and visits the waterfall sacred to both voodoo and Christian believers. Extra features include an interview with Danny Glover.

3261. *The History of Mexico.* Schlessinger, 2004. 23 min. ISBN 978-1-57225-874-7. Grades K–5.

This video presents the cultural, historical, and geographical backgrounds of Mexico from prehistory to the present. Maps, artwork, computer animation, and contemporary segments filmed in Mexico discuss the famous people, the festivals, and the traditions of the country.

3262. *The Mayans: 300 B.C. to 800 A.D.* (Hands-On Crafts for Kids Series 6: Back in Time) Chip Taylor Communications, 2003. 30 min. Grades 4–6.

Following a list of needed materials, different teachers construct objects from the Mayan culture. The crafts include a headdress, a Mayan pot, a stela, a stepped frame, and an astronomy wall hanging. Each item helps explain an important aspect of Mayan culture.

3263. *Wings of Madness: The Daring Flights of Alberto Santos-Dumont.* (NOVA) WGBH, 2007. 56 min. ISBN 978-1-59375-656-7. Grades 7 up.

See entry 1900.

Compact Discs

3264. Alvarez, Julia. *Before We Were Free.* Narrated by Julia Alvarez. Random House, 2004. 5 CDs; 5 hrs. ISBN 978-1-4000-8995-6. Grades 6 up.

See entry 3127.

3265. Dorris, Michael. *Morning Girl.* Narrated by Eliza Duggan, Riley Duggan, and Terry Bregy. Audio bookshelf, 2005. 2 CDs; 1.5 hr. ISBN 978-0-974171-16-6. Grades 3–7.

See entry 3134.

3266. Franck, Libby. *Women of the Sea.* Narrated by Libby Franck. Libby Franck, 2003. 1 CD; 1 hr. Grades 7 up.

See entry 2699.

3267. Parrado, Nando, and Vince Rause. *Miracle in the Andes: 72 Days on the Mountain and My Long Trek Home.* Narrated by Josh Davis. Random House Audio, 2006. 5 CDs; 6 hrs. ISBN 978-0-7393-3258-0. Grades YA.

See entry 3243.

AUTHOR/ILLUSTRATOR INDEX

Reference is to entry number.

TITLE INDEX

Reference is to entry number.

SUBJECT INDEX

Reference is to entry number.

ABOUT THE AUTHOR

LYNDA G. ADAMSON is Professor Emeritus of Literature, Prince George's Community College, where she has taught American, Children's, and Comparative Literature courses. She has published 12 reference works. Her many books include *Thematic Guide to the American Novel* (2002), *Notable Women in American History* (1999), and *Recreating the Past: A Guide to American and World Historical Fiction for Children and Young Adults* (1994).